The
Windows 3.1
Bible

by

Fred Davis

PEACHPIT PRESS

The Windows 3.1 Bible
Fred Davis

Peachpit Press, Inc.
2414 Sixth St.
Berkeley, CA 94710
(800) 283-9444
(510) 548-4393
(510) 548-5991 (fax)

Cover design by Studio Silicon   Back cover portrait of Fred Davis by Larry Ravitz

Interior design by Olav Martin Kvern

Production by Merrill Peterson, Matrix Productions

NOTICE OF LIABILITY:

TRADEMARKS:

Library of Congress Cataloging-in-Publication Data

Davis, Frederic E. (Frederic Emery)
    The Windows 3.1 bible / Fred Davis.
      p. cm.
    Includes index.
    ISBN 0-56609-015-6
    1. Windows (Computer programs) 2. Microsoft Windows (Computer
file) I. Title.
    QA76.76.W56D37 1992
    005.4′3—dc20   92-38806
                                                       CIP

ISBN: 0-56609-015-6

0 9 8 7 6 5 4 3

Printed and bound in the United States of America

 Printed on recycled paper

Contents

PART 3   Advanced Windows Techniques

Foreword

Philippe Kahn
Founder and CEO,
Borland International

Software is often too difficult to use; it doesn't behave in the ways we would expect. Windows is an important leap forward that attempts to overcome this hurdle of ease of use.

At Borland, an enormous amount of effort has been expended to ensure that our Windows software becomes a natural extension of the way people work and think, whether in corporate America or for personal use. Once you learn how to use Windows 3.1, you'll be able to quickly learn the thousands of applications that run with it.

Despite its advances, though, Windows 3.1 can be challenging just to install, let alone use. Because it's designed to run on a variety of hardware, and because it works on top of many versions of DOS, it can be complicated to set up and use. If you just settle for the program out of the box—or if it comes with your system—you won't be taking full advantage of its power and capabilities. Not unless you read this book: *The Windows 3.1 Bible.*

Fred Davis has witnessed the development of the personal computer from the inside as have few others. At age eleven, he learned to program BASIC on the original system at Dartmouth. An Apple II enthusiast, he became editor-in-chief of *A+* at age 28; later, he served as editor-in-chief of *MacUser.* Fred has coauthored ten computer books, including the first hardware expansion guide to the IBM PC, and then *Desktop Publishing,* an award-winning work that helped to popularize the term. Following his bent for the newest in technology, he went to *PC Magazine,* where, as director of the world's largest independent computer testing laboratory, he set up new guidelines for conducting benchmark tests. More recently, as technology editor for *PC Week,* he founded the *PC Week* product testing labs and helped establish *PC Week*'s position as the leading product information source for corporate computing.

What makes this book different from any other book on Windows is the insider information it provides. Here you'll find hundreds of tips and warnings that can save you endless hours of aggravation, as well as the latest information on compatibility.

What distinguishes Fred in all his work and his books—as well as in his television and radio appearances—is his ability to make the complex obvious. In his friendly and humorous way, Fred brings all the complexities of computing down to the basics. And because he has broad experience with the basics not only of Windows but of the entire universe of graphical interfaces, by the time you finish this book, whether you're a beginner or an old hand, you'll have learned a lot, laughed a little, and gotten a perspective on Windows that Microsoft's documentation would certainly never give you!

Philippe Kahn
Scotts Valley, California

Preface

In the beginning Microsoft created DOS. But the interface was formless and cumbersome, and a darkness was cast over the screens of the users. Then Gates said, "Let there be Windows," and there were brightly lit screens with icons and windows where darkness had been before. Then Gates said, "Let the users spring forth from their offices and homes to buy Windows, and let the third-party software developers and hardware vendors share in the bounty of the interface." And it was so.

Since its genesis in April of 1992, Windows 3.1 has become the fastest-selling software to hit the PC market since DOS. Windows 3.1 solved many problems that plagued Windows 3.0, and has reaped the benefits of an enthusiastic reception in the marketplace, with millions of copies sold each month.

Although Windows promises simplicity, it still presents a complex and sophisticated operating system. With the addition of TrueType, multimedia extensions, and the ability to integrate applications with OLE, Windows 3.1 increases your power—but adds even more complexity. That's why anyone who intends to use the program should buy this book. In fact, if you're browsing this paragraph in the bookstore, I urge you to head for the cash register right now. If you're a Windows user, this book can change your life.

This weighty tome answers everything you always wanted to know about Windows but were afraid to ask. Included with the explanations and examples are healthy doses of advice, insightful tips, and even a few chuckles. Some of my readers claim that this book (read in manuscript form) even improved their sex lives—now they're not staying up all night grappling with software that's supposedly "easy to use."

I conceived the idea for this book when I first saw Windows 3.0, back in 1990. At the time, I was director of the testing laboratories for *PC Magazine*. I was in charge of developing a strategy for testing the zillions of products the magazine evaluates each year. Having worked with computers of all shapes and sizes since the 1960s, I could tell that Windows

3.0, although slightly flawed, was destined to dominate PC operating systems for some time to come.

So, in the summer of 1990, I set out to write the most comprehensive and comprehensible guide to Windows ever written. It was a far bigger job than I had ever dreamed, taking a solid two years to research and write—definitely an epic of biblical proportions. Early on I realized that this book would deal with Windows 3.1 rather than the 3.0 version, which came and left during the time in which the book was written. Fortunately, the folks at Microsoft invited me to hunker down with 3.1 in its earliest development phases, so I was able to track the program for more than a year before its release.

As a computer journalist for the past ten years, I'm trained as a professional cynic. This means that I automatically bring a healthy dose of skepticism to claims made by software and hardware companies. My experience includes running the product testing labs at *PC Magazine, PC Week*, and *MacUser Magazine*—in fact, I started the latter two labs. I've used every GUI known to personal computerdom, and run Windows on hundreds of different computer systems. That makes me a nerd with an attitude. So throughout this book, I've tried to debunk any Windows myths and misrepresentations and help you gain a sense of perspective on Windows as well.

I hope you enjoy and use this book.

Acknowledgments

I'd like to thank the following cast of characters for helping me bring this book to life: Sylvia Paull, for her devotion to editing the beast through numerous drafts and revisions; Ted Nace at Peachpit Press, who embraced this massive project when other publishers got cold feet; Merrill Peterson at Matrix Productions, for his expert job of steering this monster through the production process; Jessie Wood, for her meticulous job of copyediting; Lenny Bailes, who helped me navigate the rough waters of DOS memory management and provided technical feedback on other chapters; Dave Jacobs and Amy Shelton, who provided me with their experience and perspective on Windows multimedia; Charlie Bermant, who shared his tips on Windows printing; Chris Stetson, for his help with screen shots and his moral support; and Gateway 2000, for providing me with a system I could dedicate to torture-testing Windows.

Lots of other people, too numerous to list, have also helped, prodded, and encouraged me along the way, and I'd like to thank every one of them as well. Finally, I'd like to apologize to my friends and family for using this book as an excuse for avoiding almost every kind of social engagement for the past two years, and I hope they don't forget to invite me to all their parties in the future.

Thanks one and all for helping—I couldn't have done it without you.

Introduction: How to Use This Book

Windows encompasses a territory that's both broad and deep. Even this thousand-page book can't cover every aspect of the terrain, from the trial-sized applets Microsoft includes with every Windows package to the thousands of applications now available for Windows users. As a result, I decided to stake certain limits, to focus on the Windows environment itself, rather than detailing the various Windows applets, such as Paintbrush, Terminal, and Write. This comprehensive look at Windows provides you with a much more detailed picture of every aspect of the operating system, regardless of what specific applications you are using. Frequent signposts along the way offer concrete examples, tips, illustrations, and hands-on strategies for making the best possible use of the complex group of programs and files that comprise Windows 3.1.

In addition, this book addresses only the plain vanilla version of Windows 3.1—right out of the box, the way you would buy it in a store. But the good news is that other versions of Windows 3.1, listed below, share the same basic interface, so much of what you learn in this book can also be applied to these versions:

➤ **Windows for Pen Computing 3.1** A group of extensions to Windows 3.1 that provide pen-based input and handwriting recognition capabilities. A promising technology, pen-based computing still isn't quite ripe.

➤ **Windows for Workgroups 3.1** A network-specific version of Windows 3.1 that provides peer-to-peer networking and e-mail capabilities. Although it's too early to tell, initial reports indicate that this version could prove to be a big hit.

➤ **Windows NT 3.1** Not yet available at this writing, this high-end version of Windows provides capabilities similar to those offered by OS/2 and Unix. Windows NT 3.1 abandons DOS to provide its own sophisticated 32-bit operating system. Several years from now, it might be the big winner.

Windows 3.1 presents an interface design that provides consistency and simplicity to the way all Windows applications work. In contrast, the technical guts of the program demonstrate a daunting complexity; they also require an understanding of both DOS and the workarounds developed to hide DOS from the average user. This book spans both sides of this dichotomy by organizing itself into three levels of complexity:

➤ **Part 1: Mastering the Windows Environment** For users new to Windows 3.1, this section provides a detailed guided tour of the program's installation, operation, and use.

➤ **Part 2: Inside Windows** This part of the book introduces some of the main technical issues related to Windows hardware, such as printing, display systems, mice, networking, communications, and multimedia. It also shows you how to take advantage of Dynamic Data Exchange (DDE) and Object Linking and Embedding (OLE) to integrate your applications and data.

➤ **Part 3: Advanced Windows Techniques** For advanced users, here is the nitty-gritty on fine-tuning the performance and compatibility of Windows, optimizing interactions between DOS and Windows, overcoming installation problems, resolving hardware conflicts, and diagnosing system crashes.

The reasoning behind this structure is to start with the easy stuff, then move gradually into the more technical realms. If you're relatively new to Windows, I recommend you start at the beginning, which explains the terms and concepts related to Windows 3.1 in context. If you're already an experienced Windows user, you can scan the familiar stuff, and then jump into the book as needed.

I hope that this book will earn a place next to your system, particularly if you make use of the comprehensive index to quickly target a specific topic. In fact, the index has been constructed as a cross-reference glossary—just turn to the boldfaced page number to locate the definition of that term, explained in context.

For experienced Windows users who are browsing through the book, these four icons indicate items of special interest:

Insider's Tip   A special tip, trick, or technique

Danger Zone

A Windows trouble-spot or pitfall and how to avoid it

Dynamite Product

A third-party product of interest

New in 3.1

A major feature or change that was not present in Windows 3.0

For those of you who delve into the more technical sections, here are some of the conventions I use to designate information. Angle brackets (< >) identify any input you need to supply in a computer statement or command. For example, the line

```
LOADHIGH <file name> <parameters>
```

indicates that the word LOADHIGH should be typed exactly as shown, and that you need to supply the <file name> and <parameters>. If you specify MOUSE.COM as the <file name> and /Y as the <parameters>, you would create this line:

```
LOADHIGH MOUSE.COM /Y
```

To specify a file name, use the name of the file itself if it is located in a directory that is listed in your system's PATH statement. Otherwise, you should specify the directory path as part of the file name, as shown in this example:

```
LOADHIGH C:\WINDOWS\MOUSE.COM /Y
```

Although it's not always technically necessary, I recommend that you always specify the complete path in case your DOS directory path is changed.

Finally, the convention in this book is to use all uppercase letters for statement and command lines, but unless I state otherwise, you can use lowercase letters as well. For example, the previous statement line could also be entered as:

```
loadhigh c:\windows\mouse.com /y
```

I hope you find this book easy to use. If you have any comments or suggestions, write to me in care of Peachpit Press and I'll consider them for the next edition.

PART 1

Mastering the Windows Environment

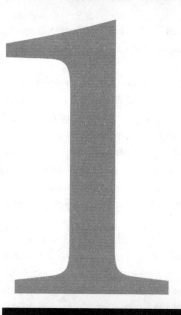

Introducing Windows 3.1

Microsoft Windows advances the state of computing on your PC to a new threshold in three critical areas: features, performance, and ease of use. Besides introducing a significantly new graphical user interface, or "GUI" for DOS, Windows improves the performance of your operating system in such areas as memory management, multitasking, and software links

3

that allow you to exchange information between applications. These various improvements also enrich the entire environment for building application programs.

One way to measure the success of any operating system is by the volume of its followers. By this standard, Windows could win any popularity contest. With tens of thousands of different applications to date, the gamut of Windows programs stretches from spreadsheets and wordprocessors to presentation graphics and desktop publishing. The promise of capturing even a small portion of the multimillion-user installed base has encouraged the development of thousands of new programs. Without a doubt, Windows has firmly established itself as the leading software development platform for the rest of the twentieth century.

The megabuck advertising budget that Microsoft set aside for blitzkrieging the media has paid off handsomely. Month after month, computer journals have devoted an ever-increasing amount of space to reviews of Windows applications. In fact, several new magazines devoted exclusively to Windows have been launched, and Windows products dominate more and more space in PC trade shows.

I'm assuming that you, too, have been swept up in the wave of Windows enthusiasm. Congratulations—I think your faith is well justified. But even if you're someone without the faith, someone who's had Windows foisted on you by your boss, why just tolerate it when you can actually put it to work for you? Either way, without a detailed understanding of the software and hardware resources that the environment offers, and without a command of the utilities that let you control and customize it, you won't be able to take full advantage of Windows. And, as with any software product, it's the extras—the tips, the tricks, the little insights—that give you the incomparable pleasure that comes with truly understanding and mastering your environment. Which is what computing, and Windows, is all about.

If you stop your efforts after installing your Windows environment, along with an application or two, you're bound to miss out on some of the most important advances in personal computing, advances designed to increase your productivity and your creativity. And the more you learn about the Windows environment, the more you'll enhance your enjoyment of computing. For starters, you'll be able to use a new feature called *drag and drop* that allows you to drag a file icon onto a printer icon, for example, and thereby automatically print that file. Or, using multimedia extensions, you can become your own sound or video editor, with the ability to record, edit, and play sounds or run interactive animations directly on your screen.

With Windows, you can make your personal computer more personal. When DOS was the only system around, most PC screens looked pretty much the same. But these days, you can customize your screen by selecting or designing icons, changing the colors of menus and buttons, and splashing your Windows desktop with any pattern, from fleurs-de-lis to flying toasters. Windows brings individuality to the forefront, so that every system reflects the personality and preferences of its user.

Underlying the capabilities and flexibility of Windows is a vast array of features and options. This book is designed to help you learn the inner secrets of Windows so you can optimize your system and your software. These secrets and pointers will help you harness all the power that Windows offers. With Windows 3.1, consider that you've installed a new engine in your computer. This book will show you all the new controls at your command, and how to best use them to rev up your engine.

The Windows Family Tree

Windows is a graphical user interface with a heritage. It belongs to a large family of interfaces that can all be traced to the same source: Xerox's Palo Alto Research Center (PARC). During the 1970s, PARC was home to seminal work by such computer scientists as Alan Kay (now an Apple Fellow) and John Warnock (chairman of Adobe Systems). Products emanating from ideas developed at Xerox PARC revolutionized the computer industry. They include Xerox's own Star Workstation (a commercial failure); Apple Computer's failed Lisa and its highly successful Macintosh (which catalyzed an industry-wide move to GUIs); the Unix-based interfaces, including OpenLook from Sun Microsystems, Open Software Foundation's Motif, and NeXT's NextStep; and IBM's OS/2 Presentation Manager and Workplace Shell.

Of course, Windows 3.1 is part of its own species: Windows. As such, 3.1 represents the latest step in Microsoft's evolution of Windows. Windows 1.0 was first announced in 1983 but didn't ship for two years, until 1985—a year after the first Macintosh (and thus the first successful operating system based on a graphical user interface) had been launched. By the late 1980s, Windows had evolved into a second incarnation that included versions 2.0, 2.1, 2.2, and Windows 386. Not until 1990 did the first commercially successful and widely adopted version of Windows—3.0—appear. Thus, although Windows is often seen as a new product, it's been around almost as long as the Macintosh operating system.

The details of the Windows interface are based loosely on a software design specification called the **SAA CUA,** for **System Application Architecture Common User Access**, developed at IBM several years ago. IBM published SAA CUA—and sought adherence to this standard from developers— partly in response to the success of the consistent graphical environment offered by the Apple Macintosh. SAA CUA attempts to define a standard way of designing user interfaces so that applications on a variety of dissimilar systems can work pretty much alike. IBM has stated that in the long term all of its computers, from micros to mainframes, will sport similar SAA CUA-based interfaces.

When IBM first outlined its SAA CUA specification, the intent was to make all user interfaces look similar, especially OS/2 Presentation Manager and Windows. Indeed, Windows 2.x and Presentation Manager 1.x shared a similar appearance. However, in 1991, IBM and Microsoft severed their long-standing joint development efforts, the very efforts that had led to the creation of DOS and the PC standard. The result was a parting of the look-alike quality of OS/2 and Windows.

Microsoft is now developing Windows into a new 32-bit version called Windows NT that can run on both Intel-based PCs and a new breed of high-powered personal computers based on the MIPS R4000 RISC chip. IBM's OS/2 2.0, on the other hand, now wears a different interface than that of Windows, but it can run existing Windows applications. And taking an even further departure from its former alliance with Microsoft, IBM has decided to align itself with Apple Computer to form a venture called Taligent, which will ultimately merge OS/2, Unix, and the Macintosh interface into a next-generation operating system. This system will be positioned to compete with Windows NT because it will be able to run on both Intel- and RISC-based personal computers.

Clearly, the stakes for the dominant operating system of the nineties are high. But whichever system wins the most supporters (and DOS still seems to claim the lion's share), most major computer vendors now recommend some sort of GUI—Windows, Macintosh, or OS/2—because it's easier for people to use. Although programmers, macro writers, and other power users will continue to work with command-line interfaces, more and more every-day computer work will be done using a GUI. And if early returns count, Windows looks like a sure winner. It has already established itself as the fastest-selling software product of all time, with an installed base that has already surpassed that of the Macintosh. After DOS, Windows is the second most popular operating system in use today, and if the trend continues, Windows systems may soon surpass DOS-only systems.

Comparing Windows 3.1 with 3.0

The original version of Windows 3, version 3.0, was introduced in May 1990. Between that time and April 1992, when version 3.1 was launched, Microsoft issued two maintenance upgrades that fixed some bugs and added drivers but made no real changes to the environment. Windows 3.1, however, represents a major overhaul of 3.0 because it provides better performance throughout the environment and adds major improvements to File Manager, Program Manager, and the Control Panel. Other important additions include TrueType font software, multimedia extensions, drag and drop capabilities, and improved network support.

While I'm on the subject of versions, in this book I use the term *Windows* to refer to Windows 3.1. Otherwise, I'll refer specifically to Windows 2.x, 3.0, or NT. The only exception to this format is when I'm comparing significant differences between Windows 3.0 and 3.1; then, I'll reiterate the version numbers for added clarity.

Fortunately for users who upgrade from Windows 3.0, Windows 3.1 has far more similarities than differences. The one big exception is File Manager, which in 3.1 corrects many of the problems inherent in the design of the earlier version. On the cosmetic side, many of the Program Manager icons have been spiffed up by acquiring a three-dimensional look. The 3D look has also been extended to many of the graphics that appear throughout Windows 3.1 (Figure 1.1).

FIGURE 1.1

Windows 3.0 and 3.1 Icons

Windows 3.0 Icons

File Manager   Control Panel   Recorder   Print Manager   Windows Setup   Terminal   Accessories

Windows 3.1 Icons

File Manager   Control Panel   Recorder   Print Manager   Windows Setup   Terminal   Accessories

The 3D icons in Windows 3.1 only hint at just how far this program has come, but the improvements over 3.0 are more than cosmetic.

The differences between Windows 3.0 and 3.1 fall into two main categories:

➥ Changes to the user interface, which simplify use of the system

➥ Software extensions, such as TrueType and multimedia, that add new functions and capabilities to the Windows environment

. . . .

Improvements to the Windows User Interface

File Manager, Program Manager, and the Control Panel, taken together, constitute the main components of the Windows interface. Of the three, File Manager has undergone the most improvement, including a major increase in speed and usability. The 3.0 version of File Manager made it difficult to copy files and maintain subdirectories because the contents of only one drive or directory could be displayed in a window at once, so you had to choose between displaying the directory tree or the contents of a directory in the window. The new File Manager resolves this problem by using a split window that shows the directory tree with the selected volume on the left side and the contents of the selected directory on the right. With this format, you can browse easily through many directories—simply click on a folder in the directory tree to activate a window that will display its contents instantly. The new File Manager also lets you view the contents of more than one directory or drive at a time, which is like advancing from the washtub to the washing machine when it comes to handling your computer housekeeping chores (Figure 1.2).

. . . .

FIGURE 1.2

Changes to File Manager

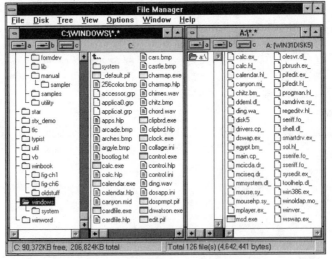

A major overhaul to File Manager eliminates many of its previous shortcomings. You can now view the contents of more than one directory or drive at a time.

The new File Manager does even more than allow you to easily browse through directories. It also displays more information on disk space and usage, adds better network support, and allows other operations to run in the background. And you can now cancel certain functions, so you can abort a long procedure, such as a search through a CD-ROM. File Manager also behaves better when you select a drive that doesn't contain a disk by letting you easily cancel your choice; before, you encountered a seemingly endless cycle of dialog boxes complaining that no disk was in the drive.

Program Manager in Windows 3.1 has also been supercharged to add features and increase its speed. You can now specify a startup group, and all of the items it contains will be launched when you start up Program Manager. Other improvements include strengthened Dynamic Data Exchange (DDE) capabilities for those who want to program Program Manager, and added support for system administrators that allows them to configure a specific level of functionality for each user. Microsoft has also added many new icons and made it easier to browse through icons and assign them to program items. Program Manager now consumes less system memory, which lets you create more groups and makes Program Manager less obtrusive when you are running other applications.

Another small but handy improvement applies to both File Manager and Program Manager: they now remember their last configuration exactly. And in the new version, many more of the dialog boxes, especially those related to the frequently used File menu, are more consistent in appearance and usage. This effort toward conformity benefits almost all Windows applications that use common dialog boxes.

Another pick-up for the Windows interface is increased use of the drag and drop concept. This lets you drag a file icon and drop it on top of an icon that represents a printer or program in order to perform an operation on a file. For example, you can drag a file icon from any File Manager window and drop it onto the Print Manager icon or into the open Print Manager window to print that file. Or you can drag a file icon from File Manager and drop it onto a Program Manager group icon or any open group window to instantly create a new Program Manager icon for the file.

To help you exercise a greater level of control over your Windows environment, the Control Panel now contains a number of improvements and new features, including a status bar at the bottom that provides information about the various controls (Figure 1.3).

FIGURE 1.3
Control Panel

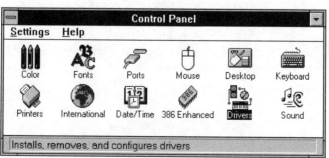

You're more in control of your environment with the new Windows Control Panel.

The Control Panel's Desktop now includes a built-in screen saver, with a password option to protect your system if you leave it running unattended. The screen saver helps protect your screen from prying eyes, and you can select from several different graphic displays.

With the new Color controls in the Control Panel, you can set all the color elements for the interface, such as buttons, disabled text, and highlighting. Windows contains several new predesigned color schemes, including three that increase the legibility of LCD displays on laptop computers.

The Control Panel also features two new controls. **Drivers** allows you to select device drivers for use with Windows, and **Sounds** gives you the ability to assign specific sounds to various events in the Windows environment. For example, you can select a rousing bugle piece to be played every time you start Windows, and the sound of a toilet flushing whenever you quit. The Control Panel also has a new MIDI Mapper control, so you can activate whatever MIDI-capable device is connected to your computer from within Windows. Finally, because the Control Panel is also expandable, third-party vendors can add new controls for additional items, such as CD ROM drives, LaserDiscs, and sound cards.

Accessing special characters that lacked keys on the keyboard, such as accented letters and the copyright symbol, was a real hassle in Windows 3.0. To simplify access to these special symbols, Windows includes a new utility called Character Map, which also lets you browse through all the special characters of the various Windows fonts installed in your system (Figure 1.4).

FIGURE 1.4

Character Map

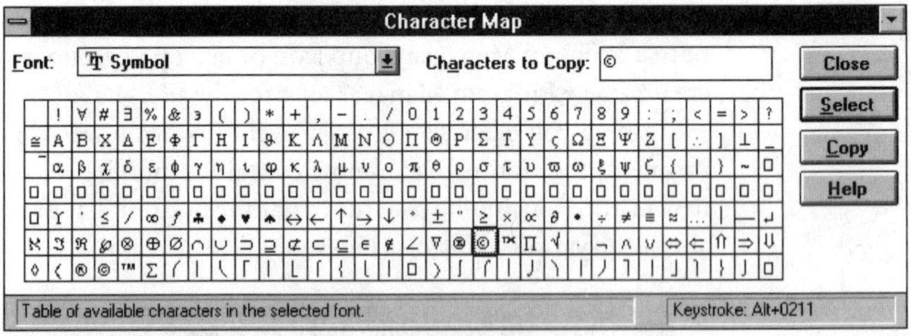

Thanks to the new Character Map utility, you can select any special character easily—or just browse through the menu of special characters that Windows fonts have to offer.

• •

Improvements to the Windows Environment

The new version of Windows represents a considerable amount of effort to improve the functionality, capabilities, and performance of the environment itself. The new extensions apply to setup and installation, TrueType fonts, printing, network operation, application integration, the online help system, and multimedia.

In order to help people get up and running with Windows as effortlessly as possible, Microsoft has made **installing** Windows easier than ever. A new Express Setup option lets you set up and run a generic Windows system within a few minutes on most systems. Once it's running, you can easily tweak the settings or install and deinstall various options using the improved Setup utility program (Figure 1.5).

• • • • • • • • • • • • • •
FIGURE 1.5
Setup Dialog
Box for
Deinstalling
Options

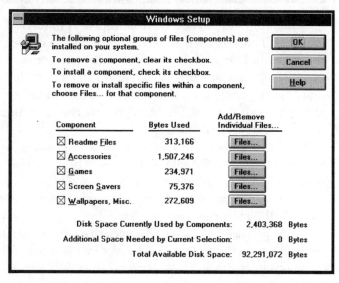

The new Setup utility lets you do a quick install, then add or remove components later on.

Windows typography enters a new era with the addition of **TrueType** fonts, a technology developed in conjunction with Apple as part of an attempt to displace PostScript, a popular font technology developed by Adobe Systems. Although TrueType will never replace PostScript, it adds an excellent scalable font technology to Windows that provides PostScript-like benefits to anyone with an HP Laserjet-compatible printer. PostScript and TrueType are scalable fonts. This means that each font comes as a disk file, which in turn installs a font outline that can be scaled to any point size, as you can see from the font controls in the Control Panel (Figure 1.6).

• • • • • • • • • • • • • •

FIGURE 1.6

*Font Dialog Box
from Control
Panel*

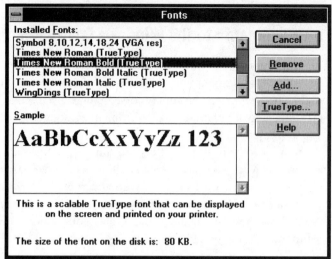

*Windows 3.1
features new
TrueType
fonts that
can be
scaled to
any point
size.*

Scalable fonts eliminate the need for special printer cartridges, soft fonts, and screen fonts. As a way to get TrueType off to a roaring start, Microsoft also sells TrueType versions of the excellent Lucida type family created by digital-typography pioneers Chuck Bigelow and Kris Holmes. True to the digital age, a special Lucida font has been optimized to look attractive when sent as a fax. If the new File Manager isn't enough reason to upgrade to version 3.1, TrueType definitely is.

Another weakness of Windows 3.0 was **printing**, and version 3.1 addresses several of the softest spots. New printer drivers included with Windows speed up operations through the use of special software and the ability to support the faster 19,200 baud speed offered by the HP LaserJet Series II, III, and many compatible printers. As a result, printing is now almost instantaneous. Installing printers, changing printer drivers, and connecting to network printers is also easier in 3.1: you can perform all these operations from either the Printer controls in the Control Panel or directly from the Print Manager while you are working with another job. Finally, the Print Manager itself has undergone a performance tuning—it now spools in your documents much faster—which means that you wait less time to reassume control of your system after you issue the Print command. Taken together, these improvements dramatically boost the performance of Windows printing.

Network support in Windows 3.1 offers several new advantages. Each time you start a Windows session, you are automatically reconnected to the same network drivers and printers from your previous session. Previously, you often had to reestablish all your connections every time you launched a session. For network administrators, 3.1 provides improved installation procedures and better network drivers that should help avoid some of the networking struggles caused by 3.0.

To help you find your way around all these new features, Windows includes an improved **Help** utility that provides context-sensitive help for many Windows programs and utilities. The context-sensitive help facility lets you access onscreen information about all the dialog boxes in Program Manager, File Manager, Control Panel, Windows Setup, Print Manager, and the PIF Editor. Third-party applications can also choose to use the new context-sensitive help.

One of the most ambitious extensions to the Windows environment is the **Object Linking and Embedding** (**OLE**) technology that allows you to integrate off-the-shelf packages to create compound documents or custom applications. OLE uses the Dynamic Data Exchange (DDE) facility to transfer and share information in interesting new ways. OLE, although innovative, is only a first step toward the development of a long-term vision Microsoft calls "Information at Your Fingertips." The idea is that eventually you'll be able to access any kind of data and process information easily, through a new graphical user interface coupled with advanced technology.

OLE is actually two separate but related concepts: object linking and object embedding. The term *object* refers to a piece of information—a chart, a snippet of text, a database record, or even a sound file. Object linking allows you to use the same information object in several different documents. For example, if you have a high-resolution color photo that takes up a megabyte of disk space, you can paste a linked copy of the image into several different documents, thereby saving space on your disk because only the original version is saved—the linked copies are merely pointers to the original image. Any changes you make to the original will appear in the linked documents; thus, when you edit your linked image with a paint program, you're automatically updating any linked copies contained in your wordprocessing or desktop publishing programs as well.

The other half of OLE, object embedding, allows you to create compound documents that contain *live data components,* data that is bonded to other documents and applications that created it. For example, you can create a chart in a spreadsheet or graphics package and embed it in a wordprocessing document, as shown in Figure 1.7.

To edit the chart while you're using Word, simply open the chart. This automatically opens Excel. Make your changes. Then return to Word. With OLE, you can "roll your own" integrated software applications by cleverly linking and embedding information into interactive compound documents.

FIGURE 1.7
OLE Example

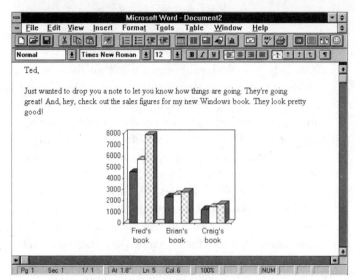

A chart from Microsoft Excel can be embedded in a Word document.

Rounding out the major improvements to the Windows 3.1 environment are new **multimedia extensions** and controls. Windows 3.1 provides many of the Windows Multimedia Extensions (MME) that are part of the Multimedia PC (MPC), which is supported by many hardware manufacturers. These extensions serve as programming hooks for incorporating sound and animation into Windows applications. To whet your appetite for multimedia, Windows includes two utilities to show off its new wares.

Media Player is a simple application that provides controls similar to those on a tape deck, which you can use to play animations, sound files, or MIDI music files (Figure 1.8).

FIGURE 1.8
Media Player

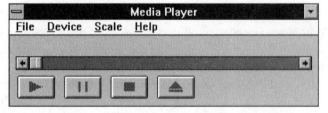

Media Player provides simple, familiar controls for playing multimedia files.

Sound Recorder lets you record, edit, and play back sound files, provided you have a Windows-compatible sound card with an appropriate input for a microphone, tape player, or whatever sound source you plan to use (Figure 1.9).

In addition to providing a better environment for Windows applications, Windows 3.1 also enhances its **support for running DOS** programs. In version 3.1, more PIFs (program information files) are supplied to help

FIGURE 1.9

*Sound
Recorder*

*Sound Recorder is a
simple digital record-
ing system.*

common DOS programs run easily under Windows. The Windows mouse
driver now works with DOS applications that are running in a window, but
you will still need to load a separate DOS mouse driver. Also, you can now
select from among a variety of font sizes for your DOS sessions, which allows
you greater flexibility in setting up your DOS-in-a-window applications.
Figure 1.10 shows how you can view several DOS sessions on a normal-size
screen simultaneously by using a small font size.

FIGURE 1.10

Small Fonts

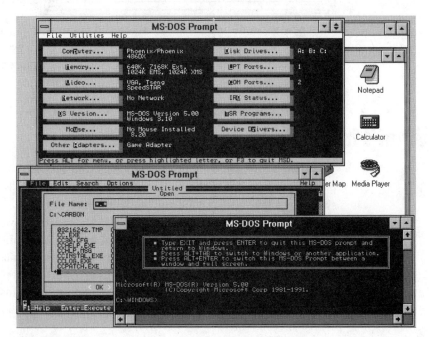

*Using smaller fonts makes room for more DOS sessions on a normal
VGA screen.*

Now, when you run DOS applications in 386 enhanced mode, your
applications perform better when running in the background; it's also faster

to switch between applications. Finally, Windows 3.1 adds better support for third-party memory managers like QEMM and 386MAX.

Although not included as part of the standard retail package, Windows 3.1 heralds another major thrust for Windows: pen-based computing. In conjunction with the announcement of Windows 3.1, Microsoft also introduced Windows for Pen Computing, a set of software extensions to Windows 3.1 that provides a system for using a pen or similar stylus as the primary input device for operating the computer (Figure 1.11).

FIGURE 1.11

Pen Windows

With Windows for Pen Computing, a version of Windows 3.1, you can use a pen or stylus to enter text and to operate the computer.

A new generation of pen-based notepad computers is coming up, and Windows for Pen Computing, which is based on Windows 3.1, looks like a major contender for dominating this exciting new personal computing platform.

What's in the Box

Windows 3.1 is a retail software product, sold either as a specific retail package or bundled with a system. If you buy Windows bundled with a system by a hardware vendor, you'll usually find it's been preinstalled on the hard disk. If the product has been bundled by a dealer, however, it may or may not have been preinstalled. Because of its popularity and added value, Windows is frequently bundled with other products, such as mice, multimedia upgrade kits, and software applications. No matter which way you obtain your copy, however, it almost always contains a set of installation disks and two user's guides, *Getting Started with Microsoft Windows* and *Microsoft Windows User's Guide*.

Many manufacturers, including Dell, Gateway, and Zeos, place their label on the outside of the Windows product when they bundle it with their systems. In these cases, the manuals and software are usually identical despite the change on the cover, but sometimes the software has been modified and this can affect how your system operates, particularly if the setup program has been altered. Ways to address this potential problem are discussed in Chapters 4 and 16.

In addition to the two manuals, the retail package of Windows 3.1 as sold by Microsoft contains the following:

   ➤ **A registration card**. The Setup program makes several attempts to remind you to return this card so that Microsoft can place your name on a list to receive news about Windows updates, seminars, and new Windows applications from, you guessed it, Microsoft.

   ➤ **A list of Microsoft support services**. This includes phone numbers for Microsoft's technical support, technical workshops, and other support information.

   ➤ **The software itself**. Two versions of Windows are sold by Microsoft, one with $5\frac{1}{4}$-inch floppy disks and the other with $3\frac{1}{2}$-inch floppy disks. The $5\frac{1}{4}$-inch version includes seven 1.2MB floppy disks; the $3\frac{1}{2}$-inch version is supplied on six 1.44MB floppy disks. From now on, regardless of size, I'll refer to a complete disk set, whether the six- or seven-disk version, as the *Windows installation disks*. Keep these disks handy even after you've installed Windows. As I'll discuss later in this book, you may need them from time to time.

Insider's Tip

If you're buying Windows, or a Windows upgrade kit, and your machine contains both $3\frac{1}{2}$-inch and $5\frac{1}{4}$-inch drives, I recommend using the $3\frac{1}{2}$-inch format—it uses one less disk, the disks are smaller and more durable, and because it doesn't require a paper sleeve (as do $5\frac{1}{4}$-inch disks), it's easier to use.

What's on the Disks

So you've torn open the box, filled in your registration card (or, as most people do, ignored it), and are ready to move on to the software pay dirt: the Windows 3.1 installation disks. Here's what these disks will load onto your computer:

   ➤ The Windows Setup installation program

   ➤ Device drivers for standard types of hardware

   ➤ The Windows 3.1 environment and system files

➻ Sample programs and utilities

The following list summarizes what you'll find on each floppy disk in the set of six $3\frac{1}{2}$-inch 1.44MB disks, in case you need to retrieve one of the files on those disks later on—and there's a good chance you might.

➻ Disks 1 and 2 contain the Setup program, the Help program, and the files (such as GDI.EXE, KERNEL.EXE, and USER.EXE) that form the heart of the Windows environment, device drivers, some compressed system files, and a utility for expanding compressed files.

➻ Disk 3 contains Windows system utilities and sample applications, such as Write (a wordprocessor), and Paintbrush (a color paint program).

➻ Disk 4 contains additional system utilities, such as Program Manager, File Manager, and the 386 enhanced mode kernel.

➻ Disk 5 contains more system files for the 386 enhanced mode kernel, and more fonts.

➻ Disk 6 contains mainly printer drivers.

Now It's Time for a (De)tour

The rest of this chapter provides a quick trip through Windows 3.1—just long enough to acquaint you with its graphical landscape. Whether you consider this a tour or a detour depends on the level of your experience. If you know your way around Windows, you may want to skip the rest of this chapter, or just scan it, and delve right into the rest of the book. If you're a newcomer, you'll find a crash-course on Windows 3.1, with a complete description of all the components of the interface, such as windows, menus, icons, and dialog boxes. You'll also learn the essentials for installing Windows and for running applications. So if you're new to Windows, get ready for an information-packed race through the Windows countryside.

Windows 3.1 Quick Start

To get Windows 3.1 up and running quickly, you'll need this basic equipment:

➤ An IBM-compatible PC with at least a 286 CPU, with a 386 or higher recommended

➤ At least 1 megabyte of RAM, with 4 megabytes or more recommended

➤ About 10 megabytes of free hard disk space, with 20 or more recommended

➤ A display adapter that works with Windows, with VGA or better recommended

➤ An optional, but highly recommended, mouse or other pointing device

➤ DOS version 3.1 or higher, with version 5.0 or higher recommended

The minimum requirements—a 286 with 1 megabyte of RAM and 10 megabytes of free hard disk space—are hard to take seriously. Such a system would crawl along at a speed that would be unbearably slow at times. A more realistic minimum is a 386SX with 2 to 4 megabytes of RAM and 40 to 80 megabytes of available hard disk space. A serious user should have at least a 25MHz 386 with 8 megabytes of RAM and as much free hard disk space as the pocketbook will allow. Let's face it, Windows eats system resources as fast as you can feed them into your system, so I usually recommend that companies planning to install Windows seriously consider going with a 486.

Also, if you have any memory-resident DOS programs or TSRs (terminate-and-stay-resident) running, make sure you turn them off before trying to install Windows. And if you're logged onto a network, it's a good idea to log off first, unless, of course, you are installing Windows from a network server.

When you're ready to get started, install Windows using the Express Setup option. Simply insert disk 1 of the Windows installation disks into any available floppy disk drive, log onto that drive, and type "setup" at the DOS prompt; the Windows Setup installation program handles everything else, letting you know in a message box what it's doing along the way.

Danger Zone

Some displays, printers, networks, input devices, and other hardware items do not work with the default drivers supplied on the Windows installation disks and therefore Windows does not recognize them. They require special device drivers, which the hardware manufacturer or reseller usually provides. You may also be able to download drivers from a bulletin board. You'll also usually need a special OEMSETUP.INF file that tells Windows how to install the driver. The appendices at the end of this book provide a list of major manufacturers and their products.

The Setup program first attempts to determine your system configuration by using special software-sensing techniques. Then it follows the script contained in the SETUP.INF file on disk 1 and creates the necessary Windows files on your hard disk in a directory of your choice (by default, WINDOWS). Setup automatically creates a subdirectory named SYSTEM (this name should not be changed) within the main Windows directory. The SYSTEM directory contains the most critical system files, such as the Windows graphics kernel and device drivers. To personalize the copy, enter your name and answer a few simple questions, such as what type of printer you have (if you have one); you should be up and running in less time than it takes to watch the evening news.

(Power-user alert! Experienced Windows users upgrading from version 3.0 may wish to use the Custom Setup option instead of Express Setup in order to keep closer tabs on the installation process.)

If you have trouble installing Windows, or if Setup warns you that it has found an incompatible device driver or TSR, try creating a plain vanilla AUTOEXEC.BAT and CONFIG.SYS file. (Remember to first create a bootable floppy disk and back these files up to that floppy disk before replacing them.) Reboot your system, then try installing Windows again. Once Windows is up and running, you can compare the original AUTOEXEC.BAT and CONFIG.SYS files that you backed up with the plain vanilla ones, and add the items in your old startup files to the new ones, one line at a time, rebooting after each modification. This process will help you narrow down the offending line.

If you have trouble with the installation process or the Setup program, you may want to learn about the Custom Setup options, discussed in Chapter 4 and in Chapter 16, which provide the nitty-gritty, step-by-step details of exactly how the setup process is scripted to work. If you still can't get Windows installed on your own, you probably have a serious incompatibility problem with your system hardware. In that case, I advise you to first contact the vendor who sold you the computer; then, try the manufacturers of your key peripherals, such as your disk and display adapter. Give them your model numbers, and ask them if they are aware of any incompatibilities with Windows 3.1. Or, if worse comes to worst, call the Microsoft technical support line at the number listed in Appendix C.

Insider's Tip

If you want to use your mouse with DOS programs that you are running in a Window, you'll need to install a DOS-level mouse driver. If you have a Microsoft-compatible mouse, copy the MOUSE.COM file from the installation disks using the Expand utility, place the file in your Windows (or another) directory, and add the following line to your AUTOEXEC.BAT file:

```
C:\WINDOWS\MOUSE.COM /Y
```

This assumes that the driver is located in a directory named WINDOWS. For further information about mouse drivers, see Chapter 8.

Up and Running

If you are new to Windows, you should warm up slowly; start with the Tutorial utility, which briefly reviews all the parts of a window and provides some practice in using the mouse. Then, to acquire more mouse experience, try your hand at the Solitaire card game simulation that Microsoft bundles with Windows.

When you start Windows, you'll first see Program Manager, a "shell" program designed as a colorful, simple way to start up your programs (both Windows and DOS), but that's all it does. If you need to copy files or manage directories—computer "housekeeping" functions—you'll need to turn to File Manager. Windows lets you change shells, and third-party shell programs such as Norton Desktop and WinTools provide a single-interface approach to shell design.

A time-tested way to explore Windows is to use the hacker-approved method: just poke around! It's fairly safe to click on menus, icons, and windows in Program Manager. You can close document windows within most applications by typing Ctrl+F4. To cycle through document windows, type Ctrl+F6 (or, in some programs, Ctrl+Tab). To browse through the running applications, type Alt+Tab, or review them all by holding down Alt while repeatedly pressing Tab. To close an application window, which will quit you from the application, type Alt+F4.

Of course, whenever you want to get out of a tough situation, there's always the Esc (Escape) option, usually the upper-leftmost key on the keyboard. Windows, like DOS, often lets you bail out midway through an action by hitting Esc—everyone's favorite panic button. If you've cornered yourself into a dialog-box-within-a-dialog-box situation, you may have to press Esc several times to return to the main screen.

While you're mousing your way around, you can tap into Windows' context-sensitive help by clicking on a Help button, if it's available, or by simply pressing the F1 key while highlighting a new selection or performing a similar action. Windows will then do its best to retrieve the appropriate help system information (Figure 1.12).

Windows Help provides handy but limited support. If you need additional information, you can always turn to the index of this book, which

••••••••••••••
FIGURE 1.12
*Help Screen
from Program
Manager*

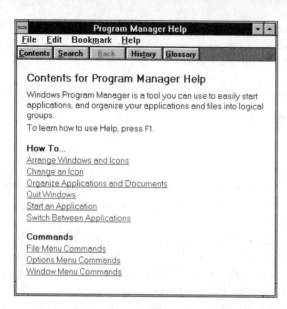

When all else fails, you
can always issue a call
for Help by pressing the
F1 key.

provides a more complete reference to the Windows 3.1 environment than either the manuals or the online help system.

To quit Windows, simply quit whatever application is defined as your shell—Program Manager or any other shell you have selected. Double-click on the shell's control menu box to quit the shell and exit Windows. Or, if you're still getting used to the mouse, type Alt+F4.

To restart Windows from DOS, simply type **WIN** at the DOS prompt; Windows should start right up. If it doesn't, check to make sure that your main Windows directory is listed in the PATH statement in your AUTOEXEC.BAT file, discussed in detail in Chapter 13.

To automatically launch Windows whenever you start your computer, place the line

```
WIN
```

at the end of your AUTOEXEC.BAT file. Just make sure it always remains the very last line in the file. Many installation programs edit this file and sometimes place other lines at the end of the file. If that happens, you'll need to edit the AUTOEXEC.BAT file by hand, cutting out the WIN statement line and pasting it back in at the very end of the file. To abort the automatic Windows startup process, press Ctrl+C; this will halt the execution of the AUTOEXEC.BAT batch file.

The most common way to start Windows along with another application is to place its program item icon in the Program Manager's Startup group. Here's another way to do this if you just want to start up an application with

Windows on a one-shot basis: enter **WIN (application file) (document file)**. For example, to start Windows with the Notepad application, type

```
WIN NOTEPAD
```

Or, to start Windows along with a document called TODO.TXT, type

```
WIN NOTEPAD TODO.TXT
```

Be sure to add the directory path to the file name if you include a document and a program that are in different directories.

Windows a la Mode

Windows 3.1 runs in one of two modes: standard mode or 386 enhanced mode. Microsoft's documentation calls *standard* mode "the basic operating mode for Windows," but I think it should be known as the substandard mode. The other mode, 386 enhanced, should really be the standard way you run Windows. Here's the difference: standard mode is a trimmed-down version of Windows designed to run in less memory on systems with older 286 processors, whereas 386 enhanced mode only runs on 386 systems or higher. (Windows 3.0 offered yet a third mode called real mode, which would run on ancient 8088 processors with just 640K. But system performance in real mode was definitely unreal, so Microsoft wisely dropped it from version 3.1.) Performance of so-called standard mode on a 286 with only one megabyte of RAM leaves much to be desired. As I've said before, you should really have a 386 or higher (the higher the better!) for running Windows, so 386 enhanced mode should be your normal modus operandi.

There is one good use for the so-called standard mode, however, even if you've passed the 386 threshold. Because Windows standard mode takes less memory, and because it places fewer demands on system resources, it can be used to troubleshoot problems in your system. For example, certain hardware incompatibility problems can prevent Windows from running in 386 enhanced mode. You can then run Windows in standard mode while resolving the compatibility problem.

Insider's Tip

To force Windows to start in standard mode, type **WIN /s** at the DOS prompt; to have it start in 386 enhanced mode, type **WIN /3** at the prompt. Windows runs faster in standard mode on 386 systems with less than 3 megabytes of RAM. However, if you have 4 or more megs, you should run in 386 enhanced mode.

Whenever Windows starts up, it takes a peek at your system hardware to determine whether to run in standard or 386 enhanced mode. If you've got a 386 or higher with at least 2 megabytes of memory, Windows automatically runs in 386 enhanced mode. To ascertain what mode you are running in, just summon the About dialog box in either Program Manager or File Manager by typing Alt,H,A (Figure 1.13).

FIGURE 1.13

About Box from Program Manager

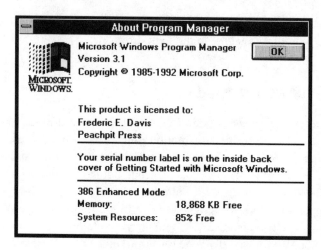

The About box in Program Manager lets you know whether you're running Windows in standard or 386 enhanced mode.

Insider's Tip

Microsoft includes an undocumented utility program named WINVER.EXE; the sole purpose of this program is to report what mode and what version of Windows you're running. Set up a program item icon for this tiny utility if you're insatiably curious about your Windows mode or version status.

Windows 3.1 Readme Files

Experienced PC users who've just installed Windows 3.1 should be familiar with several files that Windows Setup automatically copies to the Windows directory during installation. These files contain last-minute updates and advanced technical material not provided in the two manuals. SETUP.TXT is a plain text file that can be read with any text editor, so you can read it from DOS, if necessary, before installing Windows. The file contains information about hardware and software anomalies that have known incompatibilities with Windows; you'll probably only need to read it if the normal installation fails, or if you're having trouble with an older application written for version 3.0.

The other informational files installed in your Windows directory are supplied as Windows Write documents in a format that can be read onscreen or printed for further reference.

➤ README.WRI. Includes last-minute changes and notes that didn't make it into the printed manuals

➤ PRINTERS.WRI. Contains detailed information about specific fonts and printers

➤ NETWORKS.WRI. Contains technical details for installing certain network drivers, along with other connectivity and communications concerns

➤ SYSINI.WRI. Documents some of the settings and procedures for modifying the SYSTEM.INI file

➤ WININI.WRI. Documents some of the settings in the WIN.INI file

Bundled Starter Applications

Once you've installed Windows, Program Manager greets you with its groups of brightly colored icons, which include these starter applications:

Write

Write, a basic wordprocessor.

Paintbrush

Paintbrush, a simple color paint program.

Terminal

Terminal, a bare-bones telecommunications program.

Cardfile

Cardfile, a miniature database.

Calendar

Calendar, an onscreen personal calendar.

Solitaire

Solitaire, a simulation of the addictive solitaire card game.

Minesweeper

Minesweeper, a new, cute little logic game.

These simple applications give you the chance to familiarize yourself with your new Windows environment. Paintbrush, Write, and Cardfile even support OLE, so you can use them to test this new feature. Microsoft supplies these "applets," as they're nicknamed, in order to demonstrate the computing possibilities of Windows and to whet your appetite for buying full-blown Windows applications (including, no doubt, Microsoft's own excellent assortment). Like a Swiss army knife, the Windows package provides what seems to be a staggering array of useful, though limited, tools. You wouldn't want to try setting up a full-fledged database using Cardfile any more than you would want to cut down a tree using the saw from your Swiss army knife.

This book focuses on the Windows environment itself, and therefore does not cover the Windows applets in depth. However, I do use the applets in some examples and tips, because they are familiar to almost every Windows user. For more information on the applets, refer to their online help and the *Windows User's Guide*.

Bundled Utilities

In addition to these starter applications, Microsoft includes many useful utility programs.

Windows
Setup

Windows Setup, the same program you use to install Windows, can also be used to reinstall device drivers or to set up DOS programs.

Control Panel

Control Panel lets you customize your environment and set a variety of systems options.

Help

Help, the online help system.

Notepad

Notepad, a bare-bones text editor for editing system files.

Calculator

Calculator, an onscreen calculator with both a simple and a scientific mode.

Clock

Clock, an onscreen clock with an analog or digital display.

Clipboard Viewer

Clipboard, a viewer utility that lets you see what's in the Windows clipboard.

Character Map

Character Map,* a utility for accessing special characters and symbols in Windows fonts.

Sysedit

Sysedit, a very Spartan text editor that allows you to simultaneously open and edit WIN.INI, SYSTEM.INI, AUTOEXEC.BAT, and CONFIG.SYS files.

Recorder

Recorder, a simple macro creation and playback utility.

WinVer

Version, a simple utility that displays the version number and current mode of Windows.

EXPAND.EXE

Expand, a utility for decompressing files stored on the Windows installation disks.

Print Manager

Print Manager, a print spooler that lets you queue print jobs and print them in the background.

PIF Editor

PIF Editor, which allows you to edit the Program Information Files (.PIF files) that tell Windows how to run DOS software.

Object Packager

Object Packager,* a utility for creating OLE data objects.

RegEdit

RegEdit,* a utility for editing the OLE registration database.

Dr.Watson

Dr. Watson,* a diagnostic utility for tracking down the cause of Windows' crashes.

MSD.EXE

Microsoft Diagnostics,* a diagnostic utility to help troubleshoot problems in your hardware or system configuration.

Media Player

Media Player,* which allows you to play multimedia files.

Sound Recorder

Sound Recorder,* a utility that lets you record, edit, and play back digitized sound.

*This utility is new in Windows 3.1.

Windows Setup and the Control Panel are explained in detail in Chapter 4. All the relatively simple utilities—Help, Notepad, Calculator, Clock, Clipboard, Character Map, Sysedit, Recorder, Version, and Expand—are discussed in depth in Chapter 5. The Print Manager is covered in Chapter 7; the secrets of the PIF Editor are revealed in Chapter 14; the Object Packager and RegEdit are described in the chapter on OLE, Chapter 9; Chapter 11 discusses the Media Player and Sound Recorder; and Chapter 17 reveals the details of the diagnostic utilities, Microsoft Diagnostics and Dr. Watson.

Getting Familiar with Your Electronic Desktop

Now that I've discussed what you'll find in the box, and how to get Windows up and running, it's time to examine its physiognomy. What kind of interface has Microsoft crafted with these windows, icons, menus, and dialog boxes?

A key concept behind Windows, and indeed most GUIs, is the **desktop metaphor**. With most GUIs, your computer screen is designed to mirror your desk, complete with papers, folders, and tools for working. The full-screen background becomes your desktop, and the various windows and icons represent conceptual objects, such as papers (documents), filing drawers (volumes), file folders (directories and groups), and tools (applications).

Program Manager, using icons to depict various desktop tools, follows the desktop metaphor more closely than does any other part of the Windows program. For example, File Manager acts as your filing cabinet, as its icon within Program Manager suggests. Other icons represent a pen, a paintbrush, a calculator, a card file, and other tools. Program Manager's desktop metaphor gives you a familiar base for approaching myriad features and controls. If you get lost, you can always return and view your computer hardware and software as a desk on which to arrange your office tools and documents. The only disadvantage to the desktop metaphor is the ability you now have to accumulate clutter—just as you can with a real desktop!

Windows uses four main graphical building blocks to construct its interface: windows, menus, icons, and dialog boxes.

As the name suggests, the **window** is the basic building block of the Windows environment. A window is a graphic element used to define a visual workspace on your computer display. A window can always be moved, and (usually) resized; you can either shrink or expand a window. You can also rearrange the windows on your desktop. The screen background upon which the various windows and their contents are displayed is referred to as the **desktop**.

Menus are a system for presenting the commands in an application. By forcing applications to present their commands in a similar fashion, most Windows applications work the same way. You will find the File and Edit menus in the same places in most Windows programs; not only that, these menus are also likely to contain the same or similar commands. Even the keyboard commands are generally consistent; for example, the exit command—Alt,F,X—is the same in almost every Windows program.

Icons can be small pictorial buttons that can represent applications, documents, other files, directories, special controls, or other items—icon designers can exercise quite a bit of freedom as to what icons will represent. The underlying concept of the icon is similar to that of an international road sign: the meaning should be implicit in the graphic.

Dialog boxes are used by Windows to request information from you. Dialog boxes come in three flavors: those that simply present a message; those that ask you to make a yes or no choice—for example, "Save Changes Before Quitting?"; and those that present an almost bewildering array of options, which in turn may include dialog boxes that bring up dialog boxes that bring up even more dialog boxes.

Windows is designed so that all four of these elements can be manipulated best with some sort of pointing device, most commonly a mouse. As the mouse is moved around on the actual desktop, a small pointer, usually shaped like an arrow, appears on the screen. The pointer sometimes changes its shape to let you know that it can be used for a special task while it is in its altered state. The basic mouse actions involve pointing at something on the screen and then either clicking on it, double-clicking on it, or dragging the object somewhere. Clicking is simple: just give the left mouse button a quick push (Mini-tip for lefties: yes, you can change that to the right button, as described in Chapter 4). Double-clicking means just that: two quick clicks of the mouse in rapid succession. To adjust the period of time between the clicks, use the Control Panel. Dragging involves a series of actions: point to something on the screen, press and hold down the left mouse button, and "drag" whatever you have thus grabbed to its new location. Finally, you release the mouse button to drop your repositioned object into place.

You can also manipulate windows, menus, icons, and dialog boxes from the keyboard. In fact, Microsoft has made sure you can operate everything in Windows without having to rely on a pointing device. Experienced DOS users and proficient typists may find it faster to issue many Windows commands from the keyboard rather than take their hands off the keyboard to use the mouse. That's why I include the keyboard equivalents for all the commands in this book.

Together, these four main elements—windows, icons, menus, and dialog boxes—form the core of the Windows graphical user interface. You'll need to thoroughly understand how to use them in order to completely master your Windows interface, so let's take a close look at each.

Windows

In creating the Windows environment, Microsoft defined a standard system for programmers that provided the basic building blocks for the two main types of windows, technically known as the **client** and **child**. The system is based on the Multiple Document Interface (MDI), which provides a Windows application with a standard interface—both programming and visual—for displaying multiple documents within an application window. The client window contains the running application, and the child window (or windows) contains documents or other subcomponents within the application's window. Each child window usually represents and displays a separate document.

An **application window** defines the screen area dominated by a single application, and a **document window** represents a so-called child window within an application window. Although most sources agree on the use of the term "application window," a child window is sometimes referred to as a "secondary window" and document icons as "secondary-window icons." Because it's more descriptive, I'll stick with the term "document window." A document window can contain various elements: in Program Manager, groups; in File Manager, directories; and in other programs, anything from sound wave files to live video images. In addition, both document and application windows can contain a wide variety of interface components, such as those depicted in Figure 1.14.

Moving and Resizing Windows. You can move application windows around on the desktop and position them any way you like, even with portions moved off the screen. Document windows, however, can only be moved

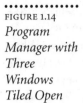

FIGURE 1.14

Program Manager with Three Windows Tiled Open

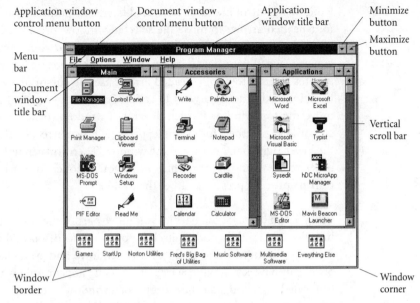

The anatomy of a Windows application: an application window title bar, a menu bar, document window title bar, application window control menu button, document window control menu button, window border, window corner, vertical scroll bar, Maximize button, and Minimize button.

around within the application window to which they belong. To move either type of window with a mouse, simply grab the window's title bar, press down on the mouse, drag the window to a new location (its outline will move correspondingly as you drag it), and release the mouse button when it is positioned at your desired location. If you want to abort the move at any point of the operation, simply press the Esc key before releasing the mouse button.

To adjust the size of a window, position the mouse over any of the four sides of a window (the pointer changes into a two-headed arrow when it's on target), and drag the window border with the mouse to reposition just that edge. Or you can grab the window corner to lengthen or shorten two adjacent sides at the same time. To abort the resizing, press the Esc key before releasing the mouse button. The minimum size for any window is about 2 inches wide by 1 inch tall, but this can vary depending on the resolution and size of your display.

Windows can also be moved and resized using the cursor keys. To select an application window, press Alt+Tab to cycle through the application windows. To select a document window, press Ctrl+F6. When the window you want is selected, issue the appropriate command (Resize or Move) from the window's Control menu, as described later. The pointer then changes into a four-headed arrow. To move the selected window, press the cursor keys; an outline of the window moves in correspondence to your key presses. When you've reached your new position, press Enter. To resize a window, after the pointer turns into a four-headed arrow, use the cursor arrow keys to select the window border you want to resize. For example, press the up arrow to move the top window border. To grab a window corner, press two of the cursor keys together; for example, pressing down arrow+right arrow selects the lower right-hand corner of the window. Then you can use the arrow keys to resize the window; press Enter when you're done. To abort the moving or resizing process, press Esc rather than Enter.

Using Scroll Bars. Scroll bars let you move part of the contents of a window into view when the window itself is too small to display all its contents at once. Application windows, document windows, and even sections of dialog boxes can have scroll bars. Scroll bars usually appear only when they might be needed, so if you alter the contents of a window, allowing everything to be viewed on one screen, your scrolls bars will usually disappear. The reverse happens when you add contents to a window so that it can no longer display all its contents. The vertical scroll bar appears along the right-hand side of the window, and the horizontal scroll bar is located at the bottom of the window. The position of the button in the scroll bar also provides a visual indication of your location in the window.

To scroll the contents of a window, you can

➤ **Grab the scroll button** in the middle of the bar and drag it with the mouse. To move to the top of the window's contents, drag the scroll button to the top of the vertical bar. To get to the bottom of the window, drag the scroll button down the bar.

➤ **Click on the arrow buttons** on either end of the scroll bar to move the contents up or down in small increments.

➤ **Hold the mouse button down** while pointing at one of the arrow buttons on either end of the scroll bar to scroll the contents continuously.

➤ **Click on the scroll bar** itself, in between the scroll button and the appropriate arrow button, to move the window's contents in increments of one window at a time.

Some applications also let you scroll using the keyboard. Table 1.1 shows the commonly supported conventions for keyboard scrolling.

TABLE 1.1

Common Conventions for Keyboard Scrolling

Keystroke	Scrolls
Up arrow	Up one line
Down arrow	Down one line
Page Up	Up one window
Page Down	Down one window
Ctrl+Page Up	One window to the left
Ctrl+Page Down	One window to the right
Home	To the beginning of the line
End	To the end of the line
Ctrl+Home	To the beginning of the document
Ctrl+End	To the end of the document

Application Windows. In Windows, an application window always contains a running program. You can find the name of the program and other information related to it in the title bar, at the top of the application window. If you open more than one window, the title bar of the active window—the window that you currently have selected—appears in a different color or intensity than the title bars of the dormant windows.

The left end of the window's title bar contains the Control menu, also called the System menu; to access this menu, click once on its button, or press Alt, spacebar; or, if the window contains a DOS session, press Alt+spacebar. The Control menu contains commands that allow you to manipulate, resize, or close windows, and it's particularly well suited for keyboard users; mouse handlers can accomplish most of these tasks in other ways. For example, you can shrink an application window all the way down to an icon by either clicking the window's Minimize button at the right end of the title bar, or by typing Alt, spacebar,N. To expand the window to fill the entire screen, press the Maximize button, or type Alt, spacebar,X.

Insider's Tip

Here's an undocumented feature to maximize an application window to full screen: double-click in the title bar. If the window is already maximized, double-clicking in the title bar will restore it to its premaximized size. This trick can also be used to maximize a document window, but because the title bar is then shared with the application, you will need to use the Restore button to shrink it back to its original size.

The Control menus of most application windows include the commands shown in Table 1.2.

Menu Command	Keystroke	Description
Restore	Alt,spacebar,R	Restores application window to previous size
Move	Alt,spacebar,M	Lets you move application window using the keyboard cursor arrow keys
Size	Alt,spacebar,S	Lets you resize window using the keyboard cursors
Minimize	Alt,spacebar,N	Reduces application window to icon
Maximize	Alt,spacebar,X	Enlarges application window to full screen
Close	Alt+F4	Closes the application window, and quits the application
Switch To …	Ctrl+Esc	Switches to the Task Manager's list of running applications

To close an application window, double-click its Control menu button; choose Close from the Control menu (Alt+F4); or select Exit from the File menu (Alt,F,X).

Application windows that contain DOS sessions can also include the Control menu selections shown in Table 1.3.

Menu Command	Keystroke	Description
Edit	Alt+spacebar,E	Displays a cascading menu with Mark, Copy, Paste, and Scroll.
Settings	Alt+spacebar,T	Displays dialog box that lets you adjust settings for DOS multitasking.
Fonts	Alt+spacebar,F	Lets you change the fonts used in the DOS window.

If you're running a full screen DOS session, you can still press Alt+spacebar to bring up the Control menu.

Document Windows. The contents of the document windows can vary from program to program, depending on the preferences of the developer. For example, Program Manager uses document windows to represent groups. Its document windows contain program item icons, which represent either applications or documents. File Manager uses document windows for the contents of volumes and directories, and Microsoft Word for Windows uses the document windows for wordprocessing documents.

Document windows all share the application window's menu bar. If you select a command from a menu, it will usually affect the contents of the active document window. To activate a document window, click anywhere on it, or press Ctrl+Tab repeatedly until the window is selected. When more than one document window is open, the active one will display a different colored title bar, and it will appear in the foreground of any other overlapping document windows.

The Control menu buttons in both the application and the document windows are almost identical except that the horizontal bar in the center of the button is smaller in the document window. To access the document window's Control menu, press its button, or type Alt,Minus. The Control menu may contain special commands specific to particular applications, but almost all such Control menus contain the commands shown in Table 1.4.

TABLE 1.4
Common Windows Control Menu Commands

Menu Command	Keystroke	Description
Restore	Alt,Minus,R	Restores the document window to its previous size.
Move	Alt,Minus,M	Lets you move the document window using the keyboard cursor arrow keys.
Size	Alt,Minus,S	Lets you resize the document window using the arrow keys.
Minimize	Alt,Minus,N	Reduces the document window to an icon.
Maximize	Alt,Minus,X	Enlarges the document window to the full size of the application window.
Close	Ctrl+F4	Closes the document window.
Next	Ctrl,F6 or Ctrl+Tab	Switches to the next document, regardless of whether it is a window or a minimized document icon.

If the document window is a separate window within the application window, the button for its Control menu is positioned at the left end of the document window title bar. If you press the document window's Maximize button or double-click on the window's title bar (or issue the Maximize command from the keyboard by typing Alt,Minus,X), the document window grows to fill the entire application window and a number of changes will occur. Figure 1.15 shows the same Program Manager application shown in Figure 1.14 after the Maximize button for the Applications group was pressed.

FIGURE 1.15

Same Program Manager Application Window in Figure 1.14, Maximized

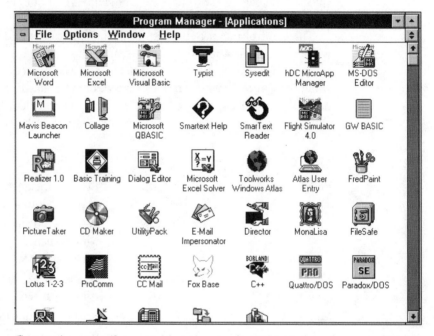

This is the same Program Manager application window shown earlier, with one of the groups maximized so that it fills the entire application window.

When a document window is maximized, it no longer has its own title bar; as a result, the document window title is usually incorporated into the application window title bar. Also, the document window's Control menu now appears at the left end of the menu bar, and the Restore button is at the right end of the menu bar. The Restore button contains two tiny triangles on top of each other, one pointing up, the other pointing down. If you click on the Restore button with a mouse, the document window shrinks back to its previous size.

Danger Zone

Document windows can be displayed only within the boundaries of the application window to which they belong, although they can be larger than the application window. If one or more document windows is too large to be displayed within the application window, the application crops the document windows (Figure 1.16). If this happens, you'll have to engage in some resizing, rearranging, or scrolling around in order to access your scroll bars and other controls.

• • • • • • • • • • • • •
FIGURE 1.16
Cropped Document Windows

In Windows, application windows sometimes crop document windows, thus making their controls inaccessible.

To view the portions of the document windows that are out of sight, you can use the scroll bars, or you can move and resize the document windows themselves. But there's an easier way to get around this problem. Many Windows applications provide special commands that automatically arrange the document windows inside the application window. Both Program Manager and File Manager, for example, offer Cascade and Tile commands (found on the Windows menu). The Cascade command places the windows in an overlapping configuration, in the shape of a slightly spread-out stack (Figure 1.17), whereas the Tile command arranges all the document windows so they fit inside the application window without overlapping (Figure 1.18).

Even if you have only one window open, the Tile command can still prove handy. For example, if the scroll bars of a document window are inaccessible because that window is cropped within an application window, issuing the Tile command resizes the document window so that it fits entirely within the open application window, thus revealing all of its controls.

To close a document window, double-click its Control menu button, choose Close from the Control menu (Ctrl+F4), or choose Close from the File menu (Alt,F,C). At this point, a dialog box may appear to ask if you want to save any changes before closing the window, just in case you have made changes since your last save.

FIGURE 1.17
*Cascaded
Windows*

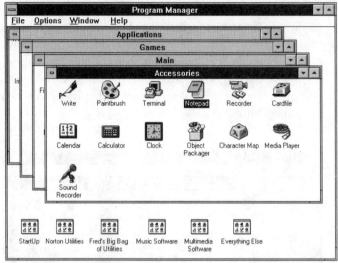

*The Cascade
command
arranges
document
windows in
an overlap-
ping configu-
ration.*

FIGURE 1.18
*Tiled
Windows*

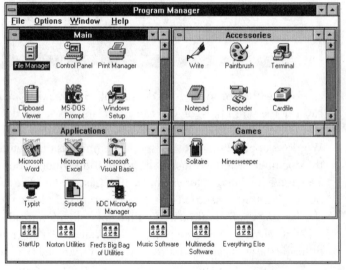

*The Tile
command
partitions
the applica-
tion window
equally
among all
the open
document
windows.*

Menus

Menus contain all the major commands in a program. You can issue a
command by simply making a menu selection, whereas in a command-based
environment like DOS, you have to recall the exact spelling or syntax of the
command in order to issue it. Menus also contain other items, such as lists of
open files or windows, styles for depicting text (such as bold), or the names
of cascading menus, which in turn reveal further choices.

To make this moveable feast possible, Windows uses two different types of menus: control menus and application menus. **Control menus** are fairly generic and thus change little from application to application. **Application menus**, however, are the command center of any Windows program and contain all the basic operation commands specific to an application. Because Microsoft has rigorously encouraged developers to standardize on the layout of the command structure, you'll find that you can use the same command— such as Alt,F,X to exit an application—for almost any Windows application.

Application menus are found on the menu bar of virtually all application windows, and although they can vary widely from program to program, the first two menus are usually a File menu and an Edit menu (Figure 1.19).

FIGURE 1.19
Application Window with File Menu Pulled Down

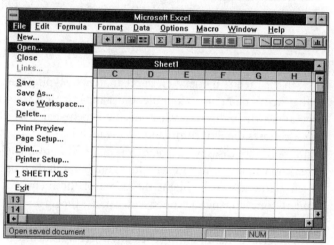

Menus contain the main commands for an application, and almost every program includes a File menu.

The menu bar shows the names of the menus you can use to select commands. Note that menus can be pulled up or down, depending on their length and the available space on the display (Figure 1.20).

Selecting a menu with a mouse is easy; you can either pop it up or pull it down. To pop it up, just point to the name on the menu bar and click once to display the menu. Point to the item on the menu you want to choose, and click once again to choose it. Alternatively, you can use the pull-down method familiar to Macintosh users: point to the menu, hold the mouse button down, drag the mouse to the item you want to choose (it will then be highlighted), and release the button to choose it. Pulling a menu up works the same way: just point and drag up instead of down.

The mouse is not always the fastest way to work in Windows, and you can use the Alt key in combination with other keys to choose frequently issued commands without having to take your fingers off the keyboard while typing. To access a menu, press the Alt key (or F10), followed by the underlined

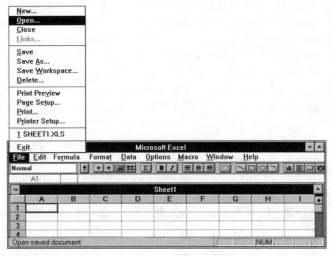

•••••••••••••
FIGURE 1.20

*Application
Window with
Menu Pulled
Up*

*Menus are
bidirectional;
you can pull
them up or
down, depend-
ing on how
much room
you have.*

letter in the menu's name; then select an item by typing the underlined letter in that item's name. For example, the standard Alt,F,X command to quit a program works in this way: Alt accesses the menu bar, F selects the File menu, and X chooses the Exit command on the menu.

In those rare cases when the menu names do not include an underlined letter, you can press Alt to select the menu bar and then use the right arrow or left arrow key to highlight the name of the menu you wish to select. Similarly, once the menu is open, you can use the up and down arrow keys to highlight a menu item and then press the Enter key to select the menu item.

To deselect a menu, simply click anywhere outside the menu, or press Alt (or F10) to return to the application; or press Esc to close the menu but remain on the menu bar ready to select a different menu.

Sometimes a command is placed directly on the menu bar. In these cases, the name is usually followed by an exclamation point, as shown in Figure 1.21. Such a command behaves like a button; just click on it with the mouse (or press the Alt key plus the underlined letter) to issue it.

•••••••••••••
FIGURE 1.21

*Menu Bar
with
Command*

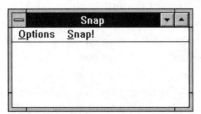

*Here's a menu bar with a command
placed directly on it.*

Menus also follow certain other conventions:

➣ Items appear dim on a menu to indicate that a command or option is not available at the time—often because something, such as text for formatting, must be selected before the command can be applied to it.

➣ Menu items are often followed by keyboard combinations as a quick reference to the keyboard shortcuts for the program.

➣ A check mark before a menu item indicates that that command or option is currently in effect. To turn the item off and remove the check mark, simply choose the command again. To toggle the item on and off, just keep choosing it.

➣ If a menu item is followed by an ellipsis (...), it's a tip-off that choosing that item will bring up a dialog box that requires your input.

➣ If a menu item contains a small triangle at the end, it is a cascading menu. If you choose this item, a submenu appears with additional choices that can be chosen just like regular menu items (Figure 1.22).

FIGURE 1.22

Cascading Menu

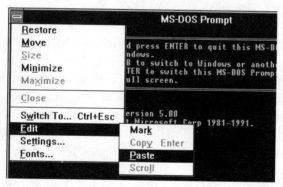

A cascading menu item marked with by a small triangle after its name reveals a menu-within-a-menu when you select it.

Icons

Icons defy any one definition because they are used to represent a hodge-podge of materials and functions, such as applications, documents, disk files, directories, and special controls. Every Windows program contains at least one unique icon, and developers seem to strive for individuality in their icon designs. Although icons should give you a visual clue as to what they represent, sometimes creativity gets out of hand.

Icons often represent some type of program or data file. Sometimes icons act like buttons. Clicking, or often double-clicking, on an icon is like pushing its button and usually activates the icon. For example, to open an application in Program Manager, double-click on a selected program item icon.

Microsoft has created six primary types of Windows icons:

 Application icon

Program
Manager

 Document icon

StartUp

 Program item icon

Read Me

 Volume icon

Directory icon

File icon

You'll also encounter many other types of icons in specific applications.

Application Icons. When you minimize an application, either by clicking on the window's Minimize button or by selecting Minimize from the window's Control menu (Alt,spacebar,N), the program's application window shrinks into a single icon on the Windows desktop and swallows, so to speak, any document windows that are open (Figure 1.23).

• • • • • • • • • • • • • •
FIGURE 1.23
*Windows
Desktop with
Minimized
Application
Icons*

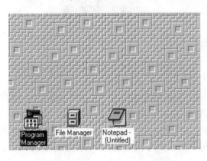

Program Manager, File Manager, and Notepad look like this when they're minimized into application icons.

An **application icon** represents a program that is still running, but in its iconic form the program consumes less system memory and other resources as well. Double-clicking on it, or selecting it and typing Alt,spacebar,R, enlarges it to its former size.

When you minimize an application into an icon, it drops to the bottom of your screen and queues after any other application icons, from left to right.

With one exception, you can move an application icon anywhere on the desktop, either with the mouse or with the keyboard-oriented Move command on the icon's Control menu (Alt,spacebar,M). The only restriction is that you can't place an application icon into an open window, because an application cannot run inside another application. If you attempt to place an application icon in an open window, it is placed on top of the window instead.

Danger Zone

Application icons can often be confused with Program Manager's program item icons. Because the application icon is always on the desktop—even though you can position it on top of a group window in Program Manager— you will notice that if you move the window the icon doesn't move with it. The application icon usually absorbs some of the desktop pattern on your screen, but sometimes even this telltale sign is absent. If you're not sure, close the window; an application icon will remain in the same place on the desktop once the window is closed.

Document Icons. A **document icon** is simply a document window that you have minimized. Document icons, like the document windows they represent, are found only within the bounds of the application windows (Figures 1.24a and 1.24b).

FIGURE 1.24 (a)
Document Icons in Program Manager

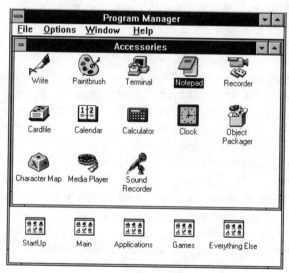

(a) Document windows and icons in Program Manager and (b) in File Manager (see next page) appear only inside application windows.

Document icons and windows are used only in applications, like Program Manager and File Manager, that let you simultaneously open two or more documents, directories, or groups. Although document icons (and their corresponding document windows) often do represent traditional documents, such as wordprocessors and paint programs, they can designate anything the program designers wish. Despite variations in the use of document

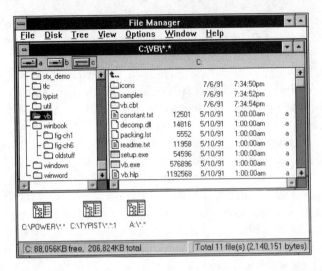

FIGURE 1.24 (b)
Document Icons in File Manager

windows and icons, Microsoft encourages Windows developers to adhere to certain guidelines.

Active document windows can be minimized into document icons by pressing their Minimize buttons, or by typing Alt,Minus,N. The window then implodes into an icon that takes its place at the bottom of the appropriate application window. You can move document icons freely within that window by dragging them with a mouse (or by typing Alt,Minus,M and using the arrow keys), but you can't move them outside the boundary of the application window onto the desktop.

Here are two ways to explode the icon back into a document window:

Double-click on the icon; or click once on the icon to pop up the Control menu, then choose Restore from the menu. From the keyboard, use Ctrl+Tab to cycle through the document icons; when the one you want is selected, issue the Restore command by typing Alt,Minus,R.

To maximize the document icon so that the resultant document window takes up the full size of the application window, click once on the icon to pop up the Control menu, then choose Maximize from the menu. Or double-click on the icon to restore it to a window; then press its Maximize button if needed. From the keyboard, select the document icon (Ctrl+Tab) to cycle through them, then type Alt,Minus,X to issue the Maximize command.

Insider's Tip

Here's a way to skip two steps worth of mousing around if you need to shrink a document window that's been maximized to fill the application window. Just issue the Minimize command from the keyboard (Alt,Minus,N). This avoids having to first restore the window to its smaller size in order to access the Minimize and Maximize buttons, which are replaced by a Restore button when the document window is maximized.

Program Item Icons. Program Manager employs its own class of icons, called **program item icons** (Figure 1.25).

FIGURE 1.25

Program Item Icons

Double-click on these attractive program item icons, or buttons, to launch Windows programs.

A program item icon does not represent an actual file; it is merely a special type of button for launching Windows applications. Because it's just a button, when you delete a program item icon, you are merely removing it from a Program Manager group; you're not actually deleting the file. This makes Program Manager ideal for computer novices because inadvertently zapping a program item icon won't delete a file.

Danger Zone

Because the icons are only aliases for files, people sometimes mistake copying such icons for copying the files they represent. To copy a file, you must use File Manager.

Program item icons usually represent applications, or applications with associated documents, but they can also represent macro files, batch files, and other processes that can be run from a computer. You can create program items for launching either Windows or DOS programs, and you can create a program item icon that launches an application together with a specific file or group of files. Windows creates several groups filled with program item icons during the installation process.

The fastest way to create a new program item icon is to drag a file icon from one of File Manager's open directory windows, then drop it into an open group window (or on top of a group icon) in Program Manager. At this point, Windows automatically places a new program item icon in the destination group. If you corralled an application file (.EXE, .COM, .BAT, or .PIF file), Windows creates an icon that will launch the application when it is activated. If you brought in a file that represents a data file that Windows has associated with a particular application, an icon is created that will start the application and load the file you snagged as well. To create an icon from the keyboard, issue the New Command from the File menu (Alt,F,N) to access the Program Item Properties dialog box. To obtain your icon, complete the information in this box, as described in Chapter 2.

You can move program item icons from one group window to another within Program Manager, but you cannot move them outside of Program Manager's application window. To move an icon with the mouse, simply drag it from an open group window and drop it in any other group window or on top of any group icon. To move a program item icon with the keyboard, first select it by moving from icon to icon within a group window using the cursor arrow keys, then issue the Move command from the File menu by typing Alt,F,M. This brings up a dialog box that lets you select the new destination group for your selected icon.

To view or change the properties of a program item icon, including changing its picture, select the icon and choose Properties from the File menu (Alt+Enter), or just hold down the Alt key and double-click on the icon. A dialog box appears, as shown in Figure 1.26, that provides the key controls for program item icons.

• • • • • • • • • • • • • • •
FIGURE 1.26

Program Item
Properties
Dialog Box

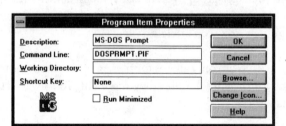

The Program Item Properties dialog box lets you control what a program item icon does and what it looks like.

You can assign any name you like to a program item icon, although sometimes it will have the same name as the file that it will start. If you dragged a program item icon from File Manager, for example, it would have the same name as its file. To identify what file is activated by a program item icon, remember to check the icon's Properties (Alt+Enter). For the complete scoop on how to use program item icons, see the next chapter, which is devoted to Program Manager.

Insider's Tip

Because program item icons are only aliases for actual files, a single file can have several aliases; that is, several icons can represent the same application or file. Overuse of this feature can cause confusion, but you can use this quirk to your advantage. For example, you can place aliases of your main applications in all the groups; then your key programs can be launched easily, no matter which group window you have open.

Volume, Directory, and File Icons. You should also know about three other major types of icons: volume, directory, and file icons. All of these are specific to File Manager (Figure 1.27).

FIGURE 1.27

File Manager Window with Volume, Directory, and File Icons

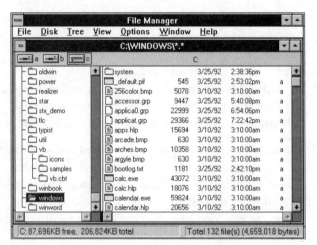

Volume, directory, and file icons reside only in File Manager.

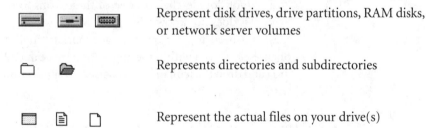

Represent disk drives, drive partitions, RAM disks, or network server volumes

Represents directories and subdirectories

Represent the actual files on your drive(s)

Volume icons represent the various storage volumes that are connected to your system and are recognized by Windows. You may encounter the following varieties of volume icons: floppy disk, hard disk drive (or a hard disk drive volume partition), RAM disk, CD-ROM drive, or network volume. Volume icons appear at the top of the directory window, and usually depict the type of storage device that they represent, either floppy or hard. Volume icons are always followed by a letter that represents the logical drive letter used by DOS (such as A:).

Directory icons represent directories and subdirectories; they are depicted as yellow file folders. They appear in the directory tree window and directory windows. As you can see in Figure 1.27, an open directory is depicted as an open file folder, whereas the rest are shown closed.

Danger Zone

File and directory icons represent the actual items on your storage devices, so if you delete any of these icons, you will actually delete those files or directories from the storage device!

File icons are found only within File Manager's directory windows; they represent the actual files on your storage device. There are three main types of file icons:

Represents a Windows or DOS program file that you can execute; in other words, it contains the extension .EXE, .COM, .PIF, or .BAT. To start the program, double-click on this icon.

Represents a data file that is associated with a particular application. Windows can recognize data files by their file extensions—it knows, for example, that files ending with .WRI can be opened with Write and that files ending in .BMP can be opened with Paintbrush. You can double-click on this type of icon to simultaneously open the document and its application.

You cannot double-click on one of these icons to open it, because Windows does not know what program works with it. To edit these files, you need to first open an appropriate application and then open the file from within the application that can edit it. Or you can drag and drop the icon onto the icon of an application that can work with it.

Dialog Boxes

Dialog boxes constitute the fourth building block of the Windows interface. As its name suggests, a **dialog box** is a mechanism for the exchange of information. Windows uses dialog boxes to request information that it needs to complete an action, or to present you with an important message. Any menu item that's followed by an ellipsis (…) indicates that a dialog box will pop up when you select that item.

Often, a dialog box presents you with a selection of options related to a command or procedure that you initiated by choosing a menu item. The options are pretty standard fare: you usually get to press some buttons, check a box or two, or select options from a list. Then there's a checkpoint step: you're asked to press an "OK" button to carry out the task; or you can bail out with a "Cancel" button (Figure 1.28).

• • • • • • • • • • • • •
FIGURE 1.28
Dialog Box

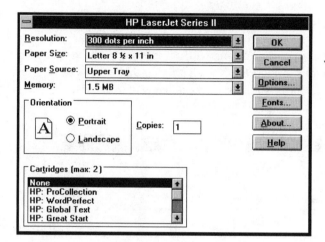

A dialog box provides options for you to press, check, or select.

Some dialog boxes display warnings and cautionary information; these are also called **alert boxes** (Figure 1.29). These dialog boxes either warn you about the dire consequences of an action you're attempting to take, or explain why you can't do what you're trying to do. To make these alert boxes go away, click on the appropriate button.

• • • • • • • • • • • • •
FIGURE 1.29
Alert Box

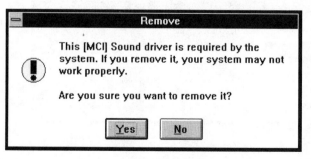

An alert box presents a warning or message explaining why your action is either dangerous or can't be completed.

If a dialog box contains a title bar, you can move it to a different spot on your screen by either grabbing the title bar with the mouse and dragging the dialog box to its new location, or by using the dialog box's Control menu—just type Alt,Spacebar,M and move the box with the cursor arrow keys.

Command Buttons. Almost every dialog box contains a command button labeled "OK," which you press to accept the dialog box. In an alert box, the OK button may be the only button, and you press it to acknowledge that you got the message. Most dialog boxes, however, contain several command buttons, including an OK button, a Cancel button, and a button allowing you to select another option.

One of the command buttons is usually highlighted by a distinctly darker outline. This is your current selection; if you press Enter, the highlighted button is pushed.

Command buttons with an ellipsis in the label (such as some of the buttons in Figure 1.28) call another dialog box requesting further information. Buttons followed by guillemets (») expand the current dialog box to reveal additional options (Figure 1.30).

••••••••••••
FIGURE 1.30
Button
Followed by
Guillemets

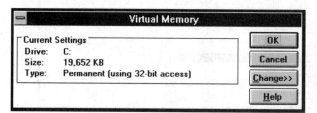

Command buttons followed by guillemets (») expand a dialog box to reveal additional options.

The active command buttons, those that can be selected, use solid colors to display their names; the names of inactive command buttons are dimmed or grayed. Figure 1.31 shows examples of both active and dimmed command buttons.

••••••••••••
FIGURE 1.31
Command
Buttons in
Dialog Box

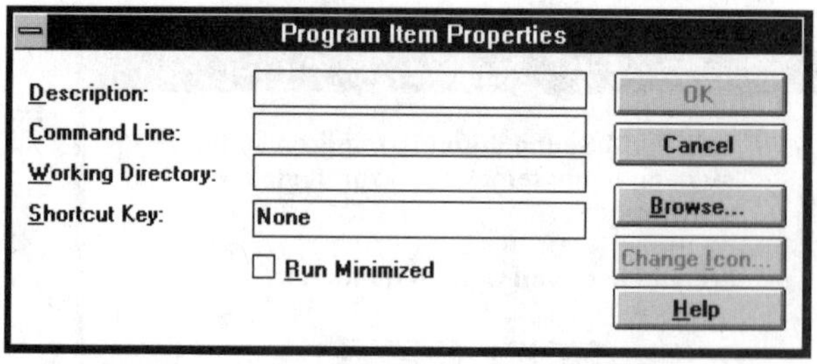

Command buttons in a dialog box may be active or dimmed.

To select an active button, click on it with the mouse; press the Alt key while typing the letter that is underlined in the button; or repeatedly press Tab to cycle through the various items in the dialog box—including the buttons—until the button you want is highlighted (Insider's Mini-tip: to cycle backward through the items, press Shift+Tab.). Then press either Enter or the spacebar to simulate pressing the button.

List Boxes. A **list box** contains a list of options from which you can pick and choose. If all the options won't fit in the box at one time, scroll bars will be available (Figure 1.32.)

Usually you can select only one item from a list box, but in some cases multiple selections are permitted. To select a single item using a mouse, scroll through the list, click on the item to highlight it, and then click the appropriate command button to complete the action. Or, in many list boxes, you can just double-click on the item to select it and to activate the related command button at the same time.

To choose an item in a list box from the keyboard, navigate through a scrolling list with the up and down arrow keys until the item you want is selected. Or, in a long list, just type a letter, such as P, and the list automatically scrolls to the first item that begins with P.

FIGURE 1.32
*List Box with
Scroll Bars*

The list box presents you with a list of options.

If the list box permits, you can also select multiple items in a list box, either sequentially or nonsequentially. To select contiguous items in a list, use a technique called *shift-clicking*: click on your first selected item in the list, then press and hold down the Shift key while clicking on the last item in the sequence; to cancel the selection, release Shift and click any single item. From the keyboard, use the arrow keys to reach the first item, then press and hold down Shift while using the up and down cursor arrow keys to extend your selection. To reduce the selection, use the opposite direction arrow key. To cancel the entire contiguous selection, just release Shift and press either arrow key.

To select nonsequential items in a list box, you have to use a mouse, because Windows lacks a keyboard equivalency. With the mouse, you can use a procedure called *control-clicking*, similar to the shift-clicking process just described. Click once on your first selected item in the list. Then press and hold down Ctrl while clicking on any other items in the list. To deselect an item, hold down Ctrl and click on it; this will not affect the rest of your current selections. To cancel all the selections, simply release Ctrl and click on any individual item in the list.

Drop-down List Boxes. Dialog boxes that are either small or crowded (or both!) often make use of a **drop-down list box**. A variant of the regular list box, the drop-down list box initially appears as a small box with a single line of text that contains the currently selected item in a list of options (Figure 1.33).

A **drop button** appears at the right end of the drop-down list box. When you push the drop button, a standard list box, complete with scroll bars when

••••••••••••••
FIGURE 1.33
*Drop-down
List Box
Collapsed*

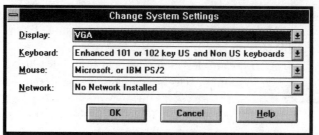

*The drop-down
list box displays
the currently
selected option.*

needed, appears below the original rectangle (Figure 1.34). To push the drop button from the keyboard, press Tab until the list box is selected; then press Alt+down arrow to make the list drop below the box.

••••••••••••••
FIGURE 1.34
*Drop-down
List Box
Expanded*

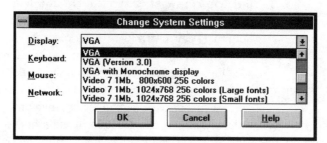

*The drop-down
list box expands
to display a list
box filled with
more options.*

Once the drop-down list is open, you can scroll though the list and click on an item with the mouse to select it. Or, from the keyboard, navigate through the list using the up and down arrow keys; then press Alt+down arrow or Alt+up arrow to select the highlighted item and collapse the list back into a box.

Insider's Tip

You don't have to drop the list down in order to scroll through the choices. When the list box is collapsed, press the up or down arrow keys to step through all the items in the list.

Check Boxes. The nature of a **check box** in computing is similar to its function on polling forms. With only enough space to contain the letter X, check boxes come in one of two states: empty, which signifies that the corresponding option has not been selected, and containing an X, which designates that the corresponding option is currently in effect (Figure 1.35).

As you can see from Figure 1.35, multiple items can be checked at once. To place an X in a check box, click in the box with the mouse. To delete an X from a check box, click again in the box. From the keyboard, press Tab repeatedly until the option you want to change is selected, then press the

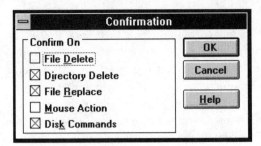

FIGURE 1.35
Check Box

Click to place an X in the box you want to select.

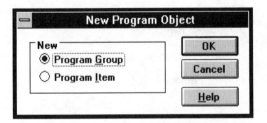

··············
FIGURE 1.36
Radio Buttons

Radio buttons allow you to exercise your options; selecting one deselects the others.

spacebar to place an X in a box or to remove it. Or, if the option contains an underlined letter in its name, you can press Alt+(the underlined letter) to toggle the X in that box on or off. Any item that is dimmed reflects a currently unavailable option.

Radio Buttons. Radio buttons are used to represent a list of mutually exclusive options. Just like the push buttons on a car radio, pushing one selects that option and deselects the others in the group (Figure 1.36).

When you select a radio button, a black dot appears in its center to distinguish it from the other buttons in the group. Sometimes an item will be dimmed, signifying that the option is not currently available. Click on an empty button and the black dot appears, making that the currently selected option. From the keyboard, you can press Tab repeatedly until the group of radio buttons is selected, then use the arrow keys to navigate up and down the list of buttons; or, if the option name contains an underlined letter, you can press Alt+(the underlined letter) to select that button.

Text Boxes. Most dialog boxes provide you with a standard list of options, but sometimes you will need to enter information into a dialog box. In that case, the dialog box contains one or more text boxes—rectangular boxes where you enter your information (Figure 1.37).

··············
FIGURE 1.37
Text Box

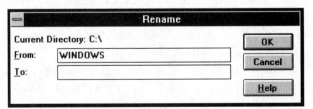

A text box lets you type information, either text or numbers, into a dialog box.

When you select an empty text box, a flashing cursor (also known as the **insertion point**) appears. If the text box already contains text, it will most likely be highlighted. Anything you type replaces the highlighted text entirely.

To delete the highlighted text, press Delete or the backspace key. To edit the highlighted information, first click anywhere in the box; this action deselects the text in the box and places the insertion point wherever you clicked. From the keyboard, press Tab repeatedly until the text box is selected, and then either start typing to replace highlighted text or use the right and left arrow keys to deselect the text and move the insertion point around in the box.

In a large text box, you may need to select some of the text to edit it. To select a single word, double-click on it with the mouse. For a longer selection, point to where you want the selection to start and drag to where you want it to end. From the keyboard, use the right and left arrow keys to move the insertion point cursor to where you want the selection to start. To extend the selection, you have three choices:

➧ Press and hold down Shift while using the arrow keys to extend the selection one character at a time in either direction.

➧ Press Shift+End to extend the selection to the end of the text box.

➧ Press Shift+Home to extend the selection back to the beginning of the text box.

Once the text is selected, you can delete it by pressing either the Delete key or the backspace key.

Using Applications

Windows provides several important advantages for running programs—which is what computing is all about. With Windows' consistent user interface and command structure, it's easier to learn new programs, because they all work alike. And Windows provides a standard operating system environment for accessing hardware; as long as the hardware device, such as a display or printer, contains a driver that works with Windows, all programs can take advantage of it. With most DOS applications, on the other hand, every program requires its own specific device driver.

The benefits of Windows also extend to DOS programs. Several DOS programs can be run at once, either in full-screen mode—that is, with a "normal" DOS appearance—or in individual windows, if you have a 386 or higher processor. You can use Windows to start and run a DOS program, and you can copy and paste information between Windows and DOS programs. In addition, most major Windows programs, such as Word, WordPerfect, and Lotus 1-2-3, can read and write the files of their DOS counterparts.

Many Windows programs can also easily exchange data with their Macintosh counterparts, through a network connection, through modem exchange, or by exploiting the Macintosh's capability to read and write DOS-formatted diskettes directly. For the greatest flexibility, use a dedicated PC-to-Mac-and-back utility, such as MacLink Plus.

Windows also allows you to run several applications at the same time. You can run a wordprocessing program in the foreground, for example, while a telecommunications program in the background simultaneously downloads a large file from a bulletin board or online service. At the same time, you can run a graphics program in another window and have that program extract spreadsheet information, then convert the data into a chart. Of course, you'd need a 386 with more than 2 megabytes of RAM to accomplish such a feat. Given the relatively low cost of investing in such equipment and RAM, the added benefits of Windows multitasking power make it well worth the cost.

Windows 3.1 can run various types of programs designed for either Windows or DOS, including

➺ All programs designed for Windows 3.1

➺ Most programs designed for Windows 3.0

➺ Most programs designed for DOS 3.1 or later

➺ Some DOS memory-resident programs (TSRs)

➺ A very few programs designed for Windows 2.x

Obviously, any program written expressly for 3.1, or labeled as 3.1-compatible on its packaging, should run with Windows 3.1—provided you have the necessary processor, memory, free hard disk space, and other system requirements the program needs to run. Because Windows 3.0 and 3.1 share many more similarities than differences, most programs written for version 3.0 will also work with 3.1.

Certain Windows 3.0 programs, especially those that incorporate networking and communications, or that use special multimedia drivers, may not be compatible with 3.1 and will require updating. Updated versions are available to address most of these compatibility problems—if your software is dated before April 1992 and you're having problems, contact the manufacturer or your dealer to check whether an upgrade is available. (Phone and fax numbers for some of the major manufacturers are listed in Appendix C.) Upgrade fees can range from the reasonable (anywhere from $5 to $25 to cover the cost of disks, documentation, and handling) to the questionable ($75 or more) that make you wonder whether your money is being used to see the company through its financial troubles or to finance a new division.

Danger Zone

I don't recommend using applications that were written for versions of Windows before 3.0, such as 2.x, because many of them crash the system and can mess up your work. Also, some early programs may appear to run, but they can secretly modify system files, such as WIN.INI, thereby corrupting other applications that will normally work with 3.1. It's happened to me, and now I consider pre-3.0 Windows applications akin to viruses!

DOS 3.1 and later programs usually run fairly well with Windows 3.1, but I recommend using at least DOS 3.3, and preferably 5.0 or higher. DOS 5.0 was the first version of DOS that Microsoft expressly designed to run with Windows, and subsequent versions promise to contain even more amenities designed specifically for Windows. The only good reason to use an earlier version of DOS is to run DOS applications that require such a version.

Although many memory-resident DOS programs, also called TSRs (for terminate-and-stay-resident), can be run from within Windows, quite a few are incompatible and will need to be run before you start Windows. TSRs are either utilities, such as hardware drivers, or pop-up programs that display a mini-application when a certain key-combination is pressed.

Starting a Program from Windows

Windows provides several different ways to start a program, depending on the program and what you use as your shell. To start a Windows or DOS program from Program Manager, double-click on its program item icon; from File Manager, double-click on its file icon; or from either shell, issue the Run command.

Windows recognizes four different file types as programs that it can run, which are identified by these three-letter DOS file name extensions:

➤ .EXE—executable program files such as in most Windows application files

➤ .COM—command program files, which usually are DOS programs

➤ .PIF—Program Information File—a special file full of tweaks for a particular DOS program that helps it run better with Windows

➤ .BAT—DOS batch files that are often used to start DOS programs

In certain cases, other file types, which represent Windows-compatible programs, can be used by special programming environments, such as Visual

Basic (.FRM) or Toolbook (.TBK), but they will appear to Windows as document files associated with an application rather than as program files. These files may behave like Windows applications in most other respects.

Running with Program Manager

To start an application from Program Manager, simply double-click on its program item icon. From the keyboard,

1. Press Ctrl+Tab until the group that contains the program item is selected; if the group is an icon, press Enter to open it into a window.

2. Use the cursor arrow keys to move around from icon to icon in the open group window; press the first letter of an icon's name to move to it directly.

3. When the desired program item icon is selected, press Enter to run it.

If Program Manager does not include an icon for the program you want to run, choose the Run command from the File menu (Alt,F,R); the Run dialog box appears (Figure 1.38).

FIGURE 1.38
Run Dialog Box

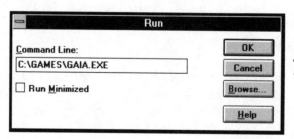

Enter the program's name, click OK, and your application is off and running.

To run a program, select the Command Line text box by clicking in it or by typing Alt+C; then type the DOS path name of the program, with any desired switches or options that would be valid for entry at a DOS prompt. Click OK, or press Enter, to execute your instructions entered in the Command Line box. For example, you would enter the path name

```
C:\GAMES\GAIA.EXE
```

to run the GAIA.EXE program located in the GAMES directory on the C: drive. If your AUTOEXEC.BAT file contains a path statement for the GAMES directory, you'll only need to enter the file name GAIA into the text box, rather than the full path name, which includes the drive and directory.

An easier method of specifying the file—especially if you don't remember the full path name—is to press the Browse button (Alt+B). The Browse dialog box that appears searches through your storage devices for files that you can then easily select with a click. The Browse dialog box is a standard Windows dialog box that allows you to review the various drives, directories, and files available to your system (Figure 1.39).

••••••••••••••
FIGURE 1.39
Browse
Dialog Box

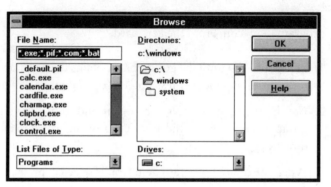

The Browse dialog box lets you easily browse through all of your drives, directories, and files.

New in 3.1

The Browse dialog box has been improved for Windows 3.1, making it easier to find that proverbial needle-in-a-haystack file. This dialog box, which also goes by the names Open and Import, is common to many Windows applications, and frequently includes enhancements specific to the application that is using it.

The Browse dialog box makes itself omnipresent on the Windows interface because it's used so often for the Open command on an application's File menu. To select items in this box, apply the standard dialog box procedures I discussed earlier in this chapter. Start by selecting the drive you want, then pick the directory (double-clicking on a closed file folder icon opens up a directory to reveal subdirectories; double-clicking on an open folder icon closes the directory and moves you up one level in the directory tree), and finally select a file from the scrolling list box in the File Name section.

Here's how you can access the controls of the Browse dialog box from the keyboard (These controls work with most similar dialog boxes.):

1. Type Alt+V, down arrow to reveal the list of drives; use the cursor arrows to highlight the desired drive, and press Enter to select the drive.

2. Type Alt+D to select the list of directories, and then use the up and down arrows to move up and down the list; press Enter to select the directory.

3. To change the criteria defining what files are displayed, reveal the contents in the List Files of Type list box by pressing Alt+T,down arrow; use the cursor arrows to highlight the desired criteria (Hint: *.* will show all the files.); press Enter to select the listed criteria, such as *.*.

4. To select a file, keep pressing Tab until you move to the File Name list box; use the up and down arrows to navigate the list; when the file you want is highlighted, press spacebar to select the file.

5. Press Tab repeatedly until the OK button is selected; then press Enter to leave the Browse dialog box and return to the Run dialog box.

One more choice remains after you've entered the name of the file to run in the Run dialog box's Command Line box. If you want to run the program as a minimized icon at the bottom of your screen rather than as an open window, select the Run Minimized check box by either clicking in it or by typing Alt+M. Just click again, or press Alt+M again, to remove the check from the box.

When the file name has been specified, and the Minimized option has been considered, you're ready to click OK, or press Enter, to run the selected file. The Run command works the same way in Program Manager as it does in File Manager. It's also included in some third-party programs, and this again demonstrates how knowledge of one technique in Windows can be applied to several different programs.

Running with File Manager

Another way to start programs is from File Manager. File Manager includes file icons for all files on your drives, or accessible over a network, which means that any file can be located to run. Program Manager, on the other hand, is limited to those programs that have been set up to work with it.

The easiest mouse method for starting a program from File Manager is to double-click on the program's file icon:

1. First select the drive and directory you want.

2. Then select the file icon of your designated file and double-click on it.

From the keyboard, if you know the file name and directory path of the program you want to run, you can use the Run command mentioned earlier: just type Alt,F,R to get the Run box; type the name or use the Browse button to select the program file; and press Return to run the program.

You can use the following procedures to browse through the various drives, directories, and files accessible to your system and take advantage of File Manager's graphical display of information.

1. Press Ctrl+(the letter of the drive you want to select).

2. Use the up and down arrow keys to navigate through the list of directories; you can press Enter to expand a highlighted directory so that it reveals any of its subdirectories.

3. Press Tab to move to the right half of the directory window; this side contains a list of all the files in the directory that you just selected.

4. Use the up and down arrow keys to select the file name of the program.

5. Press Enter to run the highlighted file.

Most files that can run applications end with the extensions .EXE, .COM, .PIF, or .BAT and contain a special file icon in File Manager that depicts a small rectangle with a blue upper edge (Figure 1.40).

•••••••••••••
FIGURE 1.40
File Manager
Application
Icon

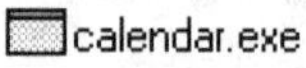

☐ calendar.exe   *You can simply double-click on an application file icon in File Manager to run a program.*

New in 3.1

You can drag a document file and place it into another application window to initiate another action. Using this new feature, I frequently find myself dragging a document icon and dropping it into the Print Manager window—or on top of its minimized icon—to quickly print the file. Or you can drag a data file icon and drop it on an application icon to open the file and application together.

Drag and drop capabilities are also affected by Object Linking and Embedding (OLE) technology, introduced in Windows 3.1. If you drag a file icon and drop it into an OLE-aware application, the file might embed itself as an object inside the document at the place where you dropped it. The biggest drag about drag and drop? It's a mouse-only operation and thus can't be activated from the keyboard.

• •

Running from the DOS Prompt

You can start most DOS applications from either Program Manager or File Manager using the methods I've already discussed, but in some instances it's handier to start certain programs from the DOS prompt. Any program that involves a multistep startup process, such as an interactive batch file, might require special commands you need to type before starting the program. In such cases, it's easy to access the DOS command prompt and use most of the DOS commands you would use without Windows.

There is one drawback, however: when you use the DOS command prompt, your application uses the default DOSPRMPT.PIF (program information file), which may not optimize the performance of your DOS program, and might even prevent it from running.

Danger Zone

If you are running a DOS command line session within Windows, do not use the Undelete command or run disk optimizers and defragmenter utilities. These commands will mess with parts of the DOS filing system, which Windows tries to prevent other programs from accessing. In order to run such programs, first quit Windows. See Chapter 14 for a more complete discussion of potential conflicts between DOS and Windows.

To start a DOS session from Program Manager, double-click on the MS-DOS Prompt icon, which starts a DOS session in full-screen mode.

You can run a DOS session in a window only if you are running in 386 enhanced mode—286 users can only run DOS sessions full screen. To switch any DOS session between a windowed and a full-screen display, press Alt+Enter (Figure 1.41).

FIGURE 1.41

DOS-in-a-Box

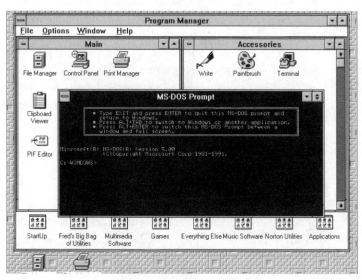

As long as you're operating a 386 or better, you can run DOS sessions in windows alongside your Windows applications.

To switch between your DOS session and Windows, type Alt+Tab—the same combination that cycles you through your other running Windows applications.

Insider's Tip

When you are running a DOS session in a window, you are really running a program called COMMAND.COM, which is technically known as the *DOS command processor*. This program generates the prompt and interprets what you type into the command line, passing it on to the underlying DOS operating system. When you start a DOS program at the DOS prompt, COMMAND.COM unloads itself and turns control of the window over to the application running in it.

To start a DOS session from File Manager, simply double-click on the COMMAND.COM file, or select it from the keyboard as outlined earlier. Then a DOS session starts, using the default PIF information, which, unless you've changed it, will run the DOS session in full-screen mode. However, it's often better to start your DOS session using a .PIF file rather than by starting the COMMAND.COM file, or directly from the DOS program's own file. To start a full-screen DOS session from File Manager, run the file DOSPRMPT.PIF—this uses the PIF settings determined by Windows Setup.

.PIF files provide Windows with a custom profile of how to run a particular application. .PIF files contain details such as whether the program should run in a window or full screen; how it should use memory; and what priority it should receive in Windows' multitasking scheme. If you want to tweak the performance of DOS applications running under Windows, you should become familiar with PIFs, which are discussed in Chapter 14.

Although you can minimize a DOS prompt session window into an application icon, you can't close a DOS window by double-clicking on its Control menu button, the usual procedure to close other Windows programs. To quit a DOS session, you must first quit any applications you are running in that session and return to the DOS prompt. Once at the DOS prompt, type Exit to end the DOS session and return to Windows.

- -

Multitasking with Windows

One of the most powerful features of Windows is its ability to provide your PC with multitasking capabilities. Multitasking lets you run multiple tasks—in other words, several applications—at the same time. However, to benefit from this feature, you'll need a 386 or better system. Windows needs to use 386 enhanced mode in order to employ advanced memory management and disk caching techniques to create virtual RAM, which allows it to run several programs simultaneously.

In addition to processor requirements, multitasking gobbles up RAM voraciously—each time you start another program, Windows needs more RAM to devote to the new program. Although an idle program may not require much RAM, especially if it is being run as a minimized icon, if you intend to run lots of programs simultaneously, each in its own window, you'll need at least 8 megabytes of RAM and tens of megabytes of free space on your hard disk for Windows to use as virtual memory. Just running a few applications simultaneously can require at least 4 megabytes of RAM.

Insider's Tip

If you can't run a program for lack of memory, a dialog box appears to inform you of the problem. To determine how many programs you can run at once, you'll need to survey your applications to see how they consume system resources. To calculate the resources a program will use, check the About dialog box in either Program Manager or File Manager (Alt,H,A) for a display of the amount of free virtual RAM (usually much larger than the amount of actual RAM chips you have installed) and the amount of free system resources, expressed as a percentage of the total. Check these numbers, run a program, then check them again while the program is running to determine how much of your system resources it requires. You can go through this process for each of your programs to determine precisely what you'll be able to run at one time, given your system's RAM and hard disk resources.

If you've got the hardware horsepower, Windows multitasking can provide a dynamic environment for running both Windows and DOS programs simultaneously. Multitasking allows you to cut, copy, and paste information from application to application, or to use advanced features such as OLE, which lets you create integrated documents that combine functions from various programs. All this can yield a synergistic combination of unique services. Later in the book, I'll explore these advanced features. For now, I'll cover the basic skills that you need to run several applications at once with Windows.

Switching from Program to Program. Although your screen can contain numerous open windows at any one time, you can select only one window at a time. To work on a window, of course, you need to select it; your selection is called the **active window**, and it is the only window affected by most menu selections. The active window appears in the foreground, that is, in front of any other open windows, and its title bar usually displays a different color than those used in the other windows.

Programs can run either in full-screen mode, in a window, or as a mini-mized icon. No matter what form it's running in, you can easily switch from program to program either by using the Task List (described a little later) or by repeatedly pressing Alt+Tab.

New in 3.1

If you hold down the Alt key while pressing the Tab key, you can cycle through all the applications that are running, with the title of each applica-tion—neatly framed with a picture of its icon—appearing successively in the center of your visual desktop (Figure 1.42).

. . . .

FIGURE 1.42

Program Switching with Alt+Tab

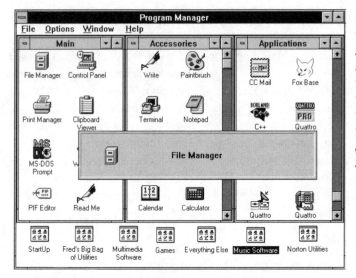

Hold down the Alt key and repeat-edly press the Tab key to cycle through all the pro-grams that are running.

While you are using Alt+Tab to cycle through your applications, you can return directly to your original application by holding down the Alt key while pressing Esc. To cycle forward, hold down Alt while repeatedly pressing Tab; to go backward, hold down Alt+Shift while repeatedly pressing Tab.

To pause when you are cycling through the applications in order to expand one to full screen, simply release the Alt and Tab keys to select the application and click the Maximize button; or type Alt,spacebar,X. To turn the application into an icon, press the Minimize button; or type Alt,space-bar,N.

Insider's Tip

If you use Program Manager to launch your applications from program item icons, you can create your own custom keyboard shortcuts to instantly launch specific applications, and, once running, to quickly switch to an application with a unique keystroke combination. To do the latter, select the application's program item icon and check its Properties (Alt+Enter). Then select the Shortcut Key text box by clicking in it or pressing Alt+S. Press a key on the keyboard; whatever key you press is shown in the text box as Ctrl+Alt+(the key you pressed). For example, you could get the Properties for the Control Panel program item icon, select the Shortcut Key text box, and press the letter C, which would appear as Ctrl+Alt+C in the text box (Figure 1.43). Once assigned, whenever you press Ctrl+Alt+C, the Control Panel starts, or if running, it will leap to the foreground as the active window.

FIGURE 1.43
Properties for Control Panel Icon with Ctrl+Alt+C

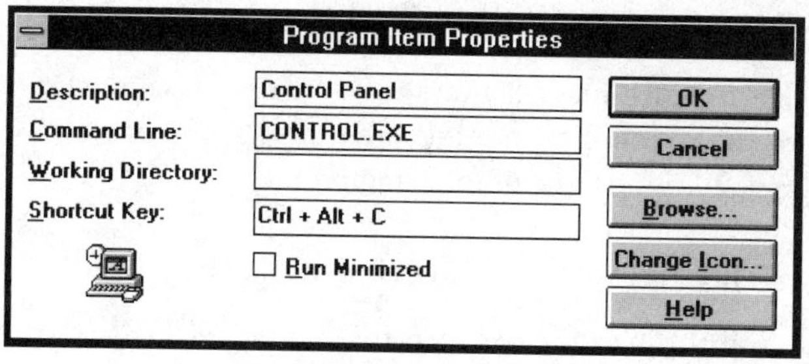

Program Item Properties

Description:	Control Panel
Command Line:	CONTROL.EXE
Working Directory:	
Shortcut Key:	Ctrl + Alt + C
	☐ **R**un Minimized

OK
Cancel
Browse...
Change **I**con...
Help

You can create your own keyboard shortcut for starting and switching to applications by using the Properties feature of Program Manager.

Arranging Windows and Icons on Your Desktop

Now that you've taken a look at how to control windows, it's time to learn how to organize the windows, and their icons, on your screen. The freedom to arrange application windows and icons on your visual desktop in any way you prefer can lead to havoc, just as it can on a real desktop. To prevent a desktop maelstrom, you'll have to clean things up from time to time.

But what if it's already too late? You've got windows piled on top of windows, and you can't find an application window because it's buried under a pile of other open windows. In Windows, if things get too messy on your desk, you can always summon your synthetic secretary. Just double-click on any empty space on the desktop, or press Ctrl+Esc, to summon the Task List. This handy little desktop assistant is available throughout the Windows environment. It can automatically rearrange the windows on your desktop; find any application that is open and bring it instantly to the foreground; or allow you to quit any of your applications in order to free your system resources (Figure 1.44). If you like to do things the hard way, you can also issue the Task List by choosing Switch To from the Control menu of most application windows (Alt,spacebar,W).

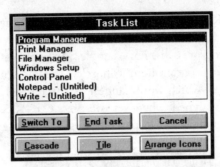

Press Ctrl+Esc to bring up the
Task List, which lets you switch
among applications, rearrange
their windows, or quit them
altogether.

The top portion of the Task List window contains a list box displaying the names of any applications that are running. To switch to one of these applications, apply any one of these methods:

➡ Use the mouse to double-click on its name in the list.

➡ Scroll through the list with the mouse, click once on the program you want, then press the Switch To button.

➡ From the keyboard, use the up and down arrows to scroll through the list box; when the program to which you want to switch is highlighted, press Enter.

In addition to these maneuvers, here's a trick for moving directly to a program in the list box: just press the first letter of its name.

Need some help getting organized? If your minimized application icons have drifted around the desktop and you'd like to corral them, click on the Arrange Icons button, or press Alt+A. The wandering icons regiment themselves into an orderly line across the bottom of your application window.

For some automated assistance in arranging your application windows, the Task List offers two buttons: Cascade (Alt+C) and Tile (Alt+T). These commands operate similarly to the way in which they arrange Program Manager document windows (see Figures 1.17 and 1.18). The Cascade command places the windows in an overlapping stack, whereas the Tile command resizes all the open application windows so that they all fit onto the desktop without overlapping (Figures 1.45 and 1.46).

Insider's Tip

Here's an undocumented feature of the Task List's Tile command: you can control whether your windows will be tiled horizontally or vertically. Normally, Task List tiles the open windows vertically, in a side-by-side arrangement. If you want to tile the windows horizontally, with one stacked on top of the other, hold down the Ctrl key while issuing the Tile command.

• • • • • • • • • • • • • •
FIGURE 1.45
*Application
Windows
Cascaded*

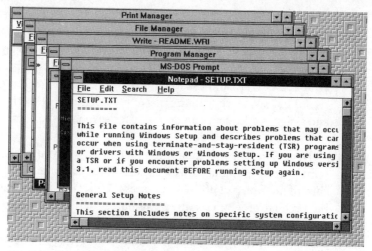

Use the Task List's Cascade command to arrange your application windows into a neat, overlapping stack.

• • • • • • • • • • • • • •
FIGURE 1.46
*Application
Windows
Tiled*

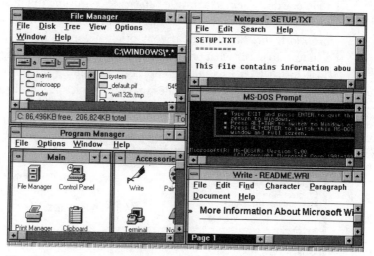

The Task List's Tile command allows you to arrange your application windows so that they don't overlap.

To quit an application, select its name in the list box and press the End Task button (Alt+E). You can quit Windows this way by selecting Program Manager (if it's your primary shell) and pressing the End Task button.

To bail from the Task List at any time, click on the Cancel button or press Esc.

Resort to using Cascade or Tile only if your desktop is in total disarray, or if you don't have a mouse. It's far better to organize your windows yourself, so the final arrangement incorporates your individual priorities and tastes.

Insider's Tip

When arranging your application windows, leave a 1-inch strip at the bottom of your screen. Place your most frequently used icons in this strip, freeing the rest of the screen for your work. To quickly align all the icons at the bottom of the screen, press Ctrl+Esc for the Task List; then, Alt+A to arrange the icons; and Esc to remove the Task List. For further automation, record this sequence with the macro recorder utility described in Chapter 5, and assign the sequence an even shorter keyboard shortcut.

Depending on the application, Windows lets you run multiples of the same program simultaneously. For example, each time you run an additional copy of the Notepad utility, it requires less memory because it shares some of the original program's software resources. Other applications, such as File Manager, let you run only one program at a time—if you try to start another copy of File Manager, Windows simply selects the running program.

Danger Zone

Although running multiples of an application allows you to open up more than one document at a time, it can create confusion. You may forget that you were using a copy of the program, and fear, for a moment, that your work has been lost; this can happen if your original copy is hidden behind another window. To check what programs are running, press Ctrl+Esc to bring up the Task List, which lists all the copies of a running program. The Task List example in Figure 1.47 indicates that four copies of Paintbrush are running simultaneously.

• • • • • • • • • • • • • •
FIGURE 1.47
*Task List with
4 Copies of
Paintbrush*

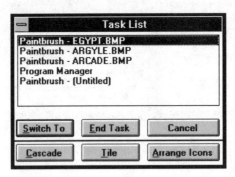

Windows lets you run more than one copy of a program at a time. If you want to see what's running, just check the Task List.

• •

Using the Windows Clipboard

Like the Macintosh, Windows extends the desktop metaphor to include the concept of a virtual clipboard. As with a real clipboard, you can use the Windows clipboard to transfer information from one location in a document to another, or even from one application to another, in a process similar to cutting and pasting. When you "clip" information from one location, Windows stores the selected data in a special area of memory, nicknamed the clipboard. Even after you "paste" something from the clipboard, a copy of it remains, so that it can pasted as many times as you like. To clear the clipboard, you must either replace its contents with new information you cut or copy onto it; or purge it with the Clipboard Viewer utility (see Chapter 5). Otherwise, it will not be emptied until you quit Windows altogether. To view the contents of the clipboard, you can also use the Clipboard Viewer; this multifunctional utility can also be employed to save the contents to a disk file and reload it with another disk file. Again, see the appropriate section in Chapter 5 for all the details.

The cut, copy, and paste process is a matter of déjà vu to anyone who's done it with paper, scissors, and glue:

1. Select some data or other information—text, numbers, or graphics—from an application.

2. Use the Copy command (Ctrl+C), on the Edit menu of most programs, to copy the selected information to the clipboard. The original remains undisturbed. Or use the Cut command (Ctrl+X) to remove the selected information from the original document and place it into the clipboard.

3. Click at your intended insertion point, or use the keyboard to place the insertion point cursor in the proper location.

4. Use the Paste command (Ctrl+V) to transfer a copy of the information from the clipboard to the insertion point in the destination document.

You can paste the data anywhere in the same document, or in any other document, even one in a different application, provided that the destination application can understand the transferred data type. Text, numbers, and certain other types of information can be copied from DOS applications, but nothing can be cut from a DOS window. Some types of data can also be pasted into a DOS window, but if you paste anything more complicated than simple text or numbers, you may run into trouble.

To create a live link to the original data, you can use the Paste Special (Alt,E,S) or the Paste Link (Alt,E,L) command from the Edit menus of programs that support this type of intelligent pasting.

You can also make a copy of the current screen display and place it in the clipboard. Simply press the Print Screen key to place a bitmapped version of the current screen in the clipboard. The screen grab is saved in a format compatible with files containing the .BMP extension. These files can be edited, saved, and printed in the Paintbrush applet included with Windows, or by most other third-party Windows graphics programs. To capture the active window, rather than the entire screen, press Alt+Print Screen; a copy of the active window is placed in the clipboard. From this point, just as with the full-screen grab, you can paste the copy into Paintbrush or any other program that works with .BMP files.

. . . .

Opening, Saving, and Closing Documents

Earlier in this chapter, I discussed how document windows behave, and how you can control them. This section addresses the documents themselves: how to open them, switch between several that may be open within an application window, and then save and close them. The information presented here applies to the vast majority of Windows applications, which goes to prove that the more you know about Windows, the more you know about a new application—even before you've ever seen it!

To open a document from within a Windows application, select the Open command (Alt,F,O) from the File menu. This brings up the Browse dialog box discussed earlier and shown in Figure 1.39. To step into the text box within the dialog box, you can either type the path name of the file or browse through any of the drives, directories, and files available to your system—either locally on floppy or hard disks, or across a network on hard disks or servers.

To save a file, choose the Save command from the File menu (Alt,F,S). Or, if you want to save the file under a different name, choose the Save As command (Alt,F,A). Either way, when you first save a file, a dialog box similar to the Browse dialog box appears. You'll use this dialog box to locate the directory in which you want to save the designated file. (Insider's Mini-tip: To find a file name that's not already in use, you can view the names of existing files with the file browser.)

To switch from document to document within an application window, click anywhere in the desired document with the mouse; this document moves to the foreground and becomes the active window. If no windows are visible, choose Next from the document window's Control menu, or press Ctrl+F6 repeatedly until the document you want is selected.

To close a document, choose Close from the application's File menu (Alt,F,C). Or, to save a keystroke, use the Close command on the document window's Control menu by typing Ctrl+F4. The document will ask if you want to save your changes—if you've made any—as a precaution against losing some of your work before it closes.

. . . .

Quitting Applications

When you're ready to call it quits, Windows offers you several exit lines. You can select Exit from the program File menu (Alt, F, X), or, in many programs, you can just type Alt+F4. If several applications are open, cycle through them with Alt+Tab; then quit them one at a time by typing Alt+F4.

Insider's Tip

Windows that contain a DOS program or a command-line session are tougher to quit. First, you must quit any running DOS programs; if you started from a PIF, quitting the application closes it, but if you started from a DOS prompt, you'll need to type Exit. However, if a DOS program has crashed, you might not be able to return to the DOS prompt. In this case, try to stop the crashed program by pressing Ctrl+C and Ctrl+Break. If that doesn't work, and the program is running in a window, go to the Windows Control menu and choose Settings (Alt,spacebar,T). Then press the Terminate button (Alt+T). If you are running the DOS session full screen, press Alt+Tab to return to Windows; then press Ctrl+Esc to bring up the Task List; select the DOS session; and press the End Task button (Alt+E). Either method will halt the DOS session in a rather unfriendly manner, so I advise you to quit Windows and reboot your system.

. . . .

Of Mice and Keyboards

Eek! A mouse! Many DOS users are less than enthusiastic about the prospects of using a mouse, and their displeasure with having to learn how to use the rodent has deflected many a potential DOS user from Windows. To ease the transition for the keyboard-bound to Windows, Microsoft has ensured that the program can be operated almost entirely from the keyboard. This capability definitely gives Windows an operational edge over the Macintosh, which is totally mouse-dependent.

But, this said, I think it's stupid and inefficient to use Windows entirely from the keyboard. After all, Windows is a graphical user interface, not a command-line based program. Although many commands in Windows can best be issued from the keyboard, it's cumbersome to use Windows without a mouse. The pointing device is a key element of most GUIs, and Windows works best when you combine a mouse and the keyboard to operate the environment.

For most Windows applications, the mouse offers the best solution as a general-purpose pointing device. Other pointing devices, such as styluses and pens, may be well suited for special applications, such as paint programs or pen-based applications. In fact, a special version of Windows, called Windows for Pen Computing, was designed for use with a pen-shaped pointing device instead of a mouse. Because most Windows users purchase mice, however, I use the terms *mouse* and *pointing device* interchangeably in this book.

To show you the current position of the mouse, the *pointer*—a floating graphic that is always visible—represents your mouse movements on the screen. The pointer can assume many shapes, depicting actions in visual terms. Most commonly, the pointer appears as an arrow pointing to the left at a 115-degree angle. But in text fields, for example, the pointer assumes the shape of an I beam, signifying that you can enter or select text at that point. And all too frequently, your pointer assumes the shape of an hourglass, to let you know that your computer is acting on something. This means you cannot initiate any other action until the cursor returns to its pointing or other active form (Figure 1.48).

FIGURE 1.48
*Various
Cursors*

Get the point? The mouse pointer can assume many different shapes, depending on what you are doing.

Kicking Your Keyboard into Overdrive

Many DOS users argue that the graphic environment with its mouse-centric orientation will slow them down. But you can cut through this graphics barrier by learning the keyboard shortcuts for Windows and its applications. This section lists many of the keyboard commands that you can use with Windows.

In Windows, there's often more than one way to issue a command from the keyboard. For example, to issue the Copy command in Program Manager from the keyboard, you can hold down Alt to access the menu bar, type F (the underlined letter in the menu name) to select the File menu, and then press C (the underlined letter in the menu item). But that's not your most direct route. If you look at the File menu (Figure 1.49), you'll notice that the keystroke F8 appears next to the Copy command. This is your tip-off to a keyboard shortcut: just press F8 to issue the Copy command and save yourself a couple of keystrokes.

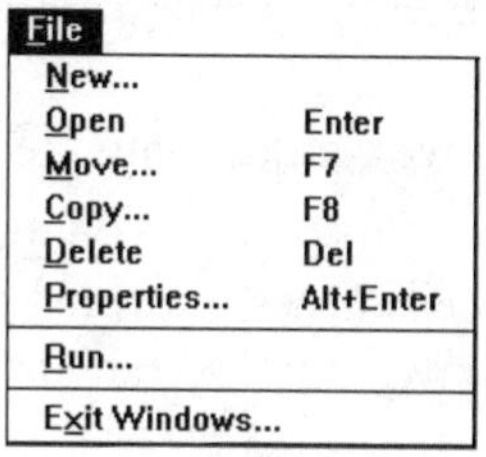

FIGURE 1.49
Keyboard Shortcuts on File Menu

File	
New...	
Open	Enter
Move...	F7
Copy...	F8
Delete	Del
Properties...	Alt+Enter
Run...	
Exit Windows...	

The File menu from Program Manager includes these keyboard shortcuts.

The F8 keyboard shortcut is just one among many offered by the Windows environment and its applications. Of course, a little memorization is required for the frequently issued commands, but because Microsoft encourages developers to apply consistent application designs, many of the keyboard sequences that you learn now should apply to other programs that you will encounter over the next several years. By the way, in this book, whenever I limit my presentation of keyboard shortcuts to one, I'll select the one that requires the fewest number of strokes.

TABLE 1.5
Common Windows Keyboard Shortcuts

Keyboard Shortcut	Description
Enter	Opens selected icon; selects menu item; presses OK button in dialog box
Esc	Cancels current action; abandons dialog box; cancels menu selection
Del	Deletes selected item
F1	Gets Help
F7	Moves selected icon
F8	Copies selected icon
Ctrl+Esc	Gets Task Manager
Ctrl+F6 or Ctrl+Tab	Selects next document window or document icon
Ctrl+F4	Closes document window
Ctrl+Slash (/)	Selects all items in a list box
Ctrl+Backslash (\)	Cancels all items selected in list box, except for the current one
Ctrl+Right Arrow	Moves cursor one word to the right
Ctrl+Left Arrow	Moves cursor one word to the left
Ctrl+Home	Moves cursor to the beginning of the document
Ctrl+End	Moves cursor to the end of the document
Print Screen	Copies the entire screen onto the clipboard

	Keyboard Shortcut	Description
TABLE 1.5 *(cont.)*	Alt+Print Screen	Copies the active window onto the clipboard
Common Windows Keyboard Shortcuts	Alt+Enter	Gets properties for selected icon in Program Manager and File Manager; switches a DOS application between full screen and a window
	Alt+spacebar	Opens Control menu of an application window
	Alt+minus sign (−)	Opens Control menu of a document window
	Alt+Tab	Rotates through running applications
	Alt+Shift+Tab	Rotates through running applications in reverse order
	Alt+F4 or Alt,F,X	Quits an application
	Alt or F10	Selects first menu on the menu bar
	Alt+(a letter)	Selects the option or area in a dialog box that contains the underlined letter
	Alt,F,N	Opens a new file
	Alt,F,O	Opens an existing file
	Alt,F,C	Closes an open file
	Alt,F,S	Saves a file
	Alt,F,A	Saves a file using a different name
	Alt,F,P	Prints a file
	Alt+down arrow	Opens drop-down list box; selects highlighted item in list box
	Tab	Moves clockwise from option to option in a dialog box
	Shift+Tab	Moves counterclockwise from option to option in dialog box
	Shift+F4	Tiles all open windows
	Shift+F5	Cascades all open windows
	Shift+an arrow key	Extends or cancels selection in a text area one character at a time
	Shift+Home	Extends current selection to first character in a text area
	Shift+End	Extends current selection to the last character in a text area

Although Microsoft has done an admirable job of making Windows usable from the keyboard, it hasn't always optimized the keyboard shortcuts so they can be typed with one hand. Often, you'll do better to use the keyboard and mouse simultaneously, thus bringing new meaning to the word multitasking.

Cutting, copying, and pasting are three of the most commonly used keyboard shortcuts best executed by using the mouse and keyboard combination. If, for example, you wanted to place part of one paragraph into another paragraph solely by using the mouse, you'd have to follow all these steps: select the text you want to move; choose Cut from the Edit menu to capture the selected text and transfer it to the Windows clipboard; point to its destination with the mouse; click; and select Paste to transfer the text from the clipboard to its destination. But using both the keyboard and the mouse simplifies the whole process: just select the text with the mouse; type Ctrl+X to cut it; click at its destination; and type Ctrl+V to paste it.

New in 3.1

In Windows 3.0 and in some Windows applications, common keyboard equivalents force you to place your hands in awkward positions: you might have to move your left hand to the right side of the keyboard; you might need two hands to perform an operation; and some operations require the use of your right hand, which means it must be removed from the mouse. Windows 3.1 replaces some of these difficult commands with easier-to-use alternatives. For example, Shift+Del—the keyboard shortcut for the Cut command in 3.0—uses two keys on the right-hand side of the keyboard, thus requiring you to either reach across the keyboard or remove your hand from the mouse. In Windows 3.1, however, Microsoft adopted some conventions used on the Macintosh to free the right hand for placement on the mouse. Table 1.6 lists these differences.

• • • • • • • • • • • • • •

TABLE 1.6

Shortcut Differences Between 3.0 and 3.1

Command	Shortcut in 3.0	Shortcut in 3.1
Cut	Shift+Del	Ctrl+X
Copy	Ctrl+Ins	Ctrl+C
Paste	Shift+Ins	Ctrl+V
Undo	Alt+backspace	Ctrl+Z

This system locates the commands in the lower-left part of the keyboard, where you can execute them easily with your left hand. Because all four of these editing commands are also used by the Macintosh, you won't have to relearn anything if you work on both platforms. However, if you are used to the older 3.0 commands such as Shift+Del, they still work in 3.1.

Here's a system for remembering these four important commands:

➤ Ctrl+Z for Undo—Z for Zap, the last thing you did

➤ Ctrl+X for Cut—X crosses out a written word

➤ Ctrl+C for Copy—C for Copy

➤ Ctrl+V for Paste— looks like an editor's insertion mark

Insider's Tip

Some applications still use the older keyboard shortcuts, but enterprising users can make them consistent with the new commands by using a macro recorder, such as the Recorder utility included with Windows. You can create a macro that lets you single-handedly issue the equivalent of a two-handed keystroke combination. Also, some programs include built-in macro facilities that let you remap these combinations within the program. A good system for keystroke shortcuts employs a mnemonic device for remembering the commands—combine the first letter of the command you wish to execute with the appropriate control key; for instance, Ctrl-S for Save and Ctrl-P for Print. The macro technique can also be used by left-handed mouse manipulators to remap the common controls normally accessed from the right side of the keyboard.

Summary

Windows makes personal computers more personal. With Windows, you can customize your computing style; from the keyboard shortcuts you choose to the way you use the mouse to choose items from the menu. Even when it comes to picking out the color and patterns for your wallpaper, Windows leaves the decisions to you. Windows 3.0 set a new standard for ease of use and functionality in the PC-compatible universe when it was introduced in spring of 1990. Windows 3.1, introduced in spring of 1992, offers even more in these areas. With the greatly improved design of File Manager, it is now easier than ever to gain graphical control over your computer's operating system. Improvements in Program Manager directed at system administration make Windows more suitable for corporate environments, and extensions to Windows in the areas of multimedia and handwriting recognition create an even more powerful platform for application development.

Now that you've taken a look at some of the basic concepts underlying Windows, it's time to move on to the main components of the graphical user interface shell: Program Manager, File Manager, and the Control Panel. Together, these three tools enable you to control and manipulate your Windows system. Program Manager provides a simple interface for launching applications and specific documents. This aspect of Windows also extends the flexibility systems administrators have in controlling user access to the system. File Manager provides a graphical system for working with disk drives, network storage, and other operating system concerns. The Control Panel allows you to quickly perform operations on your programs as you're working with them. By mastering these areas, you'll be well on your way to becoming a Windows power user—and even if you already are one, you may still pick up a trick or two.

Insider's Tech Support: Getting Started

Q: Who should upgrade to Windows 3.1?

A: I hate to sound like an ad for Microsoft, but pretty much everyone who's using 3.0 should upgrade. The Microsoft management, bean-counters, and stockholders must all be smiling about the fine job that its software engineers accomplished with Windows 3.1. Although the differences might appear small at first, the new performance and features will prove a boon to almost every user. Improvements to File Manager alone (which was brain dead in 3.0) make the upgrade worth its relatively low price.

Q: What are the biggest reasons *not* to upgrade to Windows 3.1?

A: There are only two good reasons not to upgrade: First, you have an important application that is not compatible with version 3.1. However, there's a workaround for this situation. You can install both Windows 3.0 and Windows 3.1 in different directories. If you do this, be careful to modify the path statement in your AUTOEXEC.BAT file so that only one of the directories is listed at a time.

The only other reason not to upgrade would be that your system will only run Windows in real mode, and won't work with either standard or 386 enhanced mode. Real mode has been removed from Windows 3.1.

Q: I've heard there's an Easter egg in Windows 3.1. What is an Easter egg and how do I find it?

A: An Easter egg is a hidden feature of a software program created by programmers to commemorate their fame and glory for doing such a wonderful job on the software. In other words, it's a software ego trip. To find the Easter egg in Windows 3.1, hold down Ctrl+Shift and then select the About box—usually the last item on the Help menu—from Program Manager, File Manager, or any of the bundled applets and utilities (even SysEdit!). Then double-click on the icon in the About box located in the upper left-hand corner. Nothing will happen—this is normal. Keep holding down Ctrl+Shift; click the OK button to send the About box away; and then select About to bring up the box again. Double-click on the icon in the upper left-hand corner again. The bottom half of the box is replaced by a waving flag containing the Windows logo and a message thanking all the people who created the program.

But wait, there's more. (It's not just an ego trip—it's an ego voyage.) Keep holding down Ctrl+Shift, click OK to send the About box away, and select it again. This time, the icon of a Microsoft muckymuck, such as Bill Gates or Steve Ballmer (different figures pop up randomly), appears in a framed window in the bottom half of the About box, while a seemingly endless list of credits scrolls by.

Program Manager: Your Windows Launching Pad

Program Manager was designed as your personal Windows launching pad. Simply double-click on one of its brightly colored icons, and the corresponding application will start. But Program Manager can't do much else; if you need to perform serious work operations, you'll have to call on File Manager, the more capable partner in the Windows graphical user interface.

Program Manager and File Manager are **graphical shells**. A shell is a program that introduces a system for running your programs and organizing applications, data, and other files. Unlike the Macintosh, which provides a single graphical shell, called the Finder, Windows includes two graphical shells: Program Manager and File Manager. Together, they offer an easy-to-use and powerful graphical interface for operating your computer. Unfortunately, neither shell alone provides both these features simultaneously: Program Manager contributes to ease of use, and File Manager provides the power.

The two shells differ in function, design, and philosophy. Program Manager is designed to look good and to be simple to use. With an array of attractive multicolored icons, Program Manager offers a straightforward method for running and organizing your Windows applications. Program Manager also provides a layer of protection between you and the computer; because its icons are merely aliases for the real files, accidently deleting them does not delete the actual file.

Program Manager serves as the primary shell: it appears when you first install Windows; it runs during your entire Windows session; and quitting it terminates your session.

File Manager, on the other hand, with its handful of simple, stark icons, is designed to help you organize and maintain your files and to handle other essential housekeeping chores, such as copying and arranging files, creating directories, and formatting new floppy disks. In function, File Manager is the more powerful of the two shells, but it's also more complex, and therefore more difficult to master than Program Manager. Also, because its icons represent the actual files and directories on your drives, File Manager doesn't offer the safety net of Program Manager; novices can wreak havoc on their systems if they're not careful when using File Manager.

. . . .

Program Manager: Computing Sunny Side Up

What a way to start your work day! Besides providing a host of visually attractive icons, Program Manager helps you organize your programs and some of your important documents into conceptual groups that can be arranged any way you like.

After you install Windows and start it, Program Manager's application window pops up. This window contains a document window titled Main, one of Program Manager's groups. Nested within the Main group window are the icons for starting File Manager, Control Panel, Print Manager, Clipboard Viewer, MS-DOS Prompt, Windows Setup, and PIF Editor (Figure 2.1). The Main group also includes a Write document named ReadMe, which contains some last-minute information that didn't get into the manuals.

FIGURE 2.1

Program Manager Startup Screen

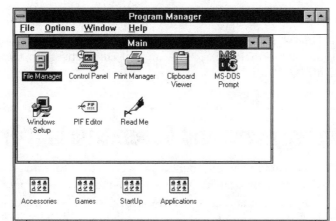

After installing Windows, the first thing you'll see is Program Manager's application window, which contains the open document window for the Main group.

Under the Main window in a new setup, along the bottom of the Program Manager window, you'll see Program Manager group icons, which represent minimized groups, such as Accessories and Games. Setup fills the Accessories group with the icons for Write, Paintbrush, Terminal, Clock, Calendar, Notepad, Cardfile, Character Map, Sound Recorder, and Media Player. In the Games group, Setup places the icons for Solitaire and Minesweeper. Setup also creates a group called Startup; the default for this group is empty—whatever icons you wish to place here will be started whenever you start Windows.

If you instructed the Setup program to install additional applications during the installation process, your shell should also contain an Applications group, which will include whatever Windows and DOS programs Setup found on your system. Of course, experienced Windows users will probably arrange their groups differently, and installation programs for third-party Windows applications often create their own groups and icons. It's easy to rearrange Program Manager's icons and groups; later in this chapter, I present some schemes for organizing your icons and groups so your desktop won't look like a cyclone just hit it.

I mentioned earlier that you begin and end your Windows session with your primary shell. If Program Manager is your primary shell (that is, the shell specified in the SYSTEM.INI initialization file), it is always running during your Windows session, either in the background behind the active application window or minimized as an icon on the desktop. To end your

Windows session, you must first return to Program Manager and exit it, either by selecting the Exit command from the File menu, or by pressing Alt,F,X, or by using the application-closing shortcut, Alt+F4. Any of these commands quits Program Manager and Windows at the same time.

Danger Zone

If you have altered the layout or arrangement of any of your Program Manager groups or icons, Program Manager will not save them unless you choose the Save Settings on Exit command from the Options menu (Alt,O,S).

Organizing Programs and Documents into Groups

A main component of Program Manager is the **program group**. A group is a collection of program item icons that Windows uses to represent collections of applications and, in some cases, specific documents. Although Windows makes some assumptions about how to group your icons during installation, you can group them in any way you please. You can also easily rename the existing groups, create new groups, and move program item icons from one group to another.

Although both Windows groups and DOS subdirectories can be used to organize your files, they differ significantly. First, unlike DOS directories, which can contain many nested levels of subdirectories, groups cannot contain any other groups; in other words, a group can contain program icons, but not icons for other groups (Insider's Mini-tip: Actually, I've discovered a secret way to overcome this limitation, but it's for serious hackers only; see Appendix B, Hacker Tools and Hints). Second, the icons designating various applications and their documents are only aliases for the real files they represent, so you can delete program item icons without deleting the corresponding files. This alias buffer also allows system administrators to prevent users from accessing certain files. The final major distinction between a Windows group and a DOS directory concerns the display of files; with groups, files that are not relevant to running an application are usually hidden from view. This simplifies the visual display of information and reduces screen clutter.

As a preview note to File Manager, which is explored in the next chapter, I should mention that unlike Program Manager, this shell is structured just like DOS directories. That's because File Manager really is a complete DOS shell, which allows you to view and work with icons that actually represent their corresponding files and directories.

Doing It with Groups

Program Manager is a fairly standard Windows application: its group windows are technically Windows document windows, and its group icons are therefore document icons. As such, you can control them as you would control document windows and icons in any other Windows application. As I noted in the last chapter, this consistency among applications will accelerate the time it takes for you to learn other Windows programs.

To view the contents of a group icon (or any document icon, for that matter), simply open it. This will cause the icon to expand into a window (Figure 2.2). Because this action occurs so frequently, Windows gives you three different options for triggering it:

➤ With the mouse, double-click on the group icon you want to open.

➤ From the keyboard, press Ctrl+Tab (or Ctrl+F6) until your targeted group icon is highlighted; then press Enter to open it.

➤ If the icon or window for a group is buried or otherwise obscured, select the group name from a list that appears at the end of the Window menu (Figure 2.2). Do this with a mouse click or by pressing Alt,W,(the number preceding the name of the group).

FIGURE 2.2

Window Menu

You can open a group quickly, even if its icon or window is buried, by selecting its name from a list on the Window menu.

Because the command sequence for using the Window menu is limited to three keys (for example, Alt,W,1), Windows allows only a single digit to precede each of the group names listed on the menu. This limits the menu to listing a maximum of nine groups (1 through 9). If more than nine group windows are open, Program Manager places the item "More Windows ..." at the bottom of the Windows menu. If the group you want isn't one of the nine choices listed on the menu, then you can choose the More Windows command from the Window menu (Alt,W,M) to bring up the Select Windows dialog box. Needless to say, this process is cumbersome because it introduces two extra steps. The Select Windows dialog box contains a list of all your Program Manager groups (Figure 2.3).

••••••••••••••
FIGURE 2.3
*Select
Windows
Dialog Box*

If you have more than nine groups, you may have to select the group from this dialog box rather than from the list on the Window menu.

When several group windows are open simultaneously, your average computer screen can resemble an Escher maze. To clean up the clutter, use any of the techniques described in the last chapter for working with document windows:

➣ To resize all of the group windows automatically, use either the mouse or the keyboard to select the Tile command (Shift+F4) or the Cascade command (Shift+F5) from the Window menu.

➣ Resize the window with the mouse by simply dragging any of the window's borders in the proper direction.

➣ Using the keyboard, select Size from the Control menu (Alt,Minus,S); use the arrow keys to move the pointer to the targeted border; use the arrow keys again to move the border to the desired position; and finally, press the Enter key when the window is the desired size.

➣ To reduce some of the mess, shrink some of the group windows down to icons by selecting them and pressing their Minimize buttons (Alt,Minus,N); then straighten them out with the Arrange Icons command on the Window menu (Alt,W,A).

Insider's Tip

To nip clutter in the bud, you can force an application to start up as a minimized icon rather than in a window. Just hold down Shift while double-clicking on the application's program item icon.

To expand a group window to the full size of the Program Manager application window, press the Maximize button (Alt,Minus,X). To restore the window to its former size, press the double-arrowed Restore button (Alt,Minus,R). Or use this undocumented shortcut: double-click on the window's title bar to either maximize or restore it.

Windows characteristically provides an almost bewildering array of alternatives for accomplishing the same task. Minimizing a group window is a prime example. When you're ready to minimize the active group window (only one can be active at a time), select your favorite shrinker. Note that you can't close a Program Manager's group window and make it go away altogether; you can only minimize it. Here are the choices, in my order of preference:

➼ Click on the Minimize button.

➼ Double-click on the Control menu box.

➼ Press Ctrl+F4.

➼ Choose the Close command from the Control menu.

➼ Press Alt,Minus,N.

➼ Press Alt,Minus,C.

• •

Creating Groups

Creating a new group is easy. Simply choose New from the File menu (Alt,F,N); the New Program Object dialog box appears with options to create a new Program Group or Program Item (Figure 2.4).

FIGURE 2.4
New Program Object Dialog Box

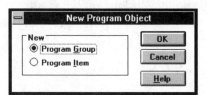

This dialog box lets you create a new Program Group or Program Item.

Select the Program Group radio button (Alt+G); then either click OK or press Enter. When you select the Program Group radio button, the Program Group Properties dialog box appears with an empty Description text box and an empty Group File text box (Figure 2.5).

FIGURE 2.5
Group Properties Dialog Box

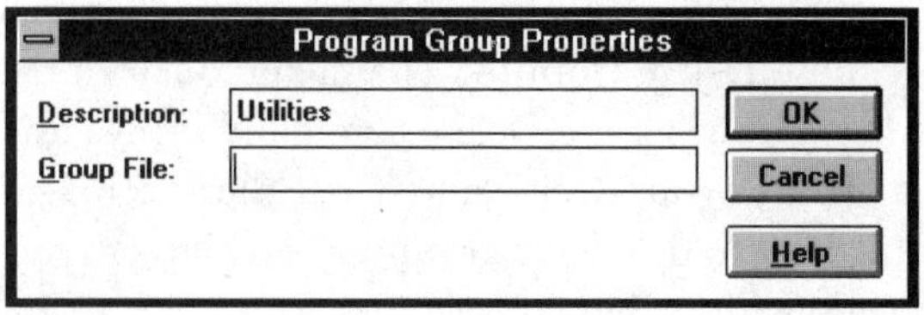

Once you've entered the Group name in the description box (and optionally given the Group File a name), you can tell Program Manager to create a group by clicking OK.

Every group needs a name, so select the Description text box (Alt+D) and type the name of the new Group. Keep it short to save space on your desktop. Then, if you want, select the Group File text box (Alt+G) and type any valid DOS file name up to eight characters long, but not the extension. Do not use an extension in the file name because Program Manager automatically places the extension .GRP at the end of the name.

If you leave this box empty, Program Manager automatically creates a name based on the first eight characters of whatever you entered into the Description box plus the .GRP extension. If this name is already taken, it will try to create new names by using only the first seven letters plus 1, 2, 3, and so forth. Once you've specified your names, click OK or press Enter to create the group.

· ·

Changing a Group's Name

It's easy to change the name of an existing group, but you first need to minimize the group window into a group icon. To complete this shrinking act, just use the mouse to press the minimize button (Alt,Minus,N). The icon should now be highlighted; if not, reselect it. Next, choose Properties from the File menu (Alt+Enter); this will retrieve the same Program Group Properties dialog box you see when you create a Group, except that the text boxes contain the applicable information. Or you can use the shortcut of holding down Alt while double-clicking on the group icon. You can then enter a new name in the Description text box, or edit the name that is already there.

· ·

Deleting a Group

Deleting a group is even easier than creating one. First, select the group you want to zap by either clicking on it with the mouse or by pressing Ctrl+Tab (or Ctrl+F6) until it's highlighted. Then minimize it to an icon, if it isn't already one, by pressing the group's Minimize button or by typing Alt+spacebar+N. Make sure the icon's menu is not showing—if it is, press Esc. Then choose Delete from the File menu; or from the keyboard, press the Delete key. Choosing the Delete command brings up a dialog box that asks you to confirm your decision to delete the selected group (Figure 2.6).

If you still want to delete the group, click on Yes or type Y or Enter. If the dialog box causes you to hesitate, click on No or type N.

FIGURE 2.6
*Delete Dialog
Box*

*When you delete a group, Windows gives you one last chance to change
your mind.*

You can also eliminate a group by first deleting all the icons inside it and
then pressing Delete. If a group window is empty, you don't need to shrink it
down to an icon before you delete it.

Also, remember that because the program item icons in the groups are
merely aliases for the actual files, deleting a group does not delete any of the
files. They're still on your hard disk.

New Group Features in Version 3.1

New in 3.1

The ability to create a Startup group has been added to Program Manager.
Whenever Program Manager is run, all the items in the Startup group are
automatically run as well. If Program Manager is your primary shell, initiat-
ing a Windows session also launches all the items in the Startup group. To
prevent the items in the Startup group from loading, hold down the Shift key
while Windows is starting.

To create a Startup group—if you don't already have one—simply create
a group using the description name Startup. To denote a different name for
the Startup group, add the STARTUP statement to your PROGMAN.INI file. For
example,

```
STARTUP=Open Sesame
```

automatically starts all the program icons contained in the group Open
Sesame. (For full details, see the section on editing PROGMAN.INI in Chapter
15.) Because Windows will run all the program icons in the Startup groups,
you'll probably want to limit this group to a few items, unless you've got
many megabytes of RAM in the double digits. If you want the application to
start up as a minimized icon, issue the Properties dialog box for the icon
(Alt+double-click or Alt+Enter) and check the Run Minimized (Alt+R)
option.

Insider's Tip

What should you place in your Startup group? I recommend including Dr. Watson, the diagnostic utility, so that it will always be on call. Another handy item is the Clock utility, to keep you abreast of the time (and even the seasons!). The Print Manager, if set to run as a minimized icon, allows you to drag a file from File Manager to the Print Manager's icon to quickly print the file. (See the next chapter for more details on drag and drop.) I also recommend you load a utility, such as System Resource Monitor, that monitors Windows' use of memory and other system resources (see Chapter 12).

New in 3.1

Windows 3.1 has improved the way group files are loaded. Program Manager now loads group files in an order determined by the settings contained in the PROGMAN.INI file rather than by their numeric sequence in this file. Thus numeric gaps are irrelevant to the loading process, and you can also specify which group will be the active group when Program Manager first starts. Microsoft even applied a painterly touch to the group icons in 3.1—they are now colorized and depict miniature group windows.

Working with Program Item Icons

Like the first flowers of spring, Program Manager icons immediately capture the eye with their bright colors; they also cleverly depict the contents of your applications and documents. You can activate program item icons by selecting and opening them like buttons. Just double-click with the mouse on the icon, or use the arrow keys to move to any icon and then press the Enter key to open it. If the icon represents an application, that application starts when you open its icon. If the icon represents a document, opening it simultaneously opens the document and its associated application. (I'll tell you how to set up icons for documents in just a bit.)

Insider's Tip

Want to shrink your Program Manager down to size and conserve a little of your system's resources? To reduce it to the stature of an application icon whenever you run an application, simply choose the Minimize on Use command from the Options menu (Alt,O,M). A check mark appears next to the command's name on the Options menu.

Moving Program Item Icons

To move a program item icon from one group to another, it's easiest to use the mouse. Make sure both groups are open, then point to the icon, hold down the mouse button, and drag the icon into its new home. For keyboard masochists, here's the rather cumbersome alternative:

1. Use the arrow keys to select a program item icon.

2. Press Alt,F,M to choose the Move command from the File menu.

3. When the Move Program Item dialog box appears, press Alt+down arrow to open the list box (Figure 2.7) that contains the names of the groups. This dialog box lets you move program icons from group to group without a mouse.

4. Press the up or down arrow key until the name of the destination group is highlighted.

5. Press Enter to complete the command and move the icon to the highlighted group.

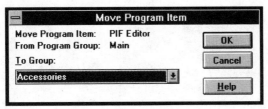

FIGURE 2.7

Move Program Item Dialog Box

The Move Program Item dialog box helps you move program item icons from group to group without a mouse.

Danger Zone

You cannot place more than 40 program item icons in a single group. Actually, stuffing your group with more than 20 will probably obscure some of your icons within a typical window.

Arranging Program Item Icons

After you've added several icons to a group, or resized a group window, it may be spring cleaning time for your desktop. If you're ambitious (or manually oriented!), you can arrange the icons yourself by moving each one with the mouse. Or you can let Windows do the arranging for you. Just move the icons into your desired general positions; then choose Arrange Icons from the Window menu (Alt,W,A) to neatly order all the icons in the current group (Figure 2.8).

You can set the computer on automatic pilot so that your icons will always be arranged after any resizing. Just choose Auto Arrange from the Options

FIGURE 2.8

*Arranging
Icons*

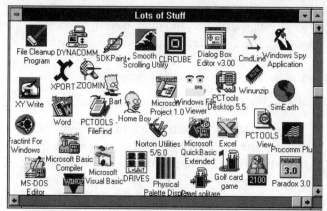

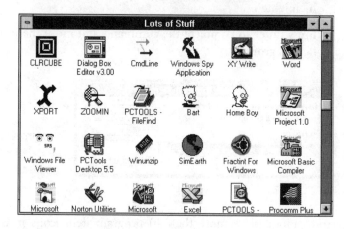

*Before and
after: The top
screen shows
icons before
they were
aligned using
the Arrange
Icons com-
mand. The bot-
tom screen
shows the rear-
ranged icons.*

menu (Alt,O,A); a check mark appears next to its name on the menu when
this feature is active (Figure 2.9).

FIGURE 2.9

*Auto Arrange
from the
Options Menu*

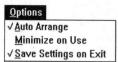

*Keep your icons forever in line: just make sure
Auto Arrange is checked on the Options menu.*

Danger Zone

When you're rearranging icons with a mouse, don't confuse program item
icons with icons representing minimized applications. An application icon
may appear to be inside a group window, but it's actually on top of the
window. Usually, an application icon picks up a small amount of the desktop's background pattern, if there is any, as an indicator that it resides on
your desktop rather than inside Program Manager. If you're not sure, try
minimizing the group window: the program icons will disappear, but the
application icons will remain.

The Life Cycle of Program Item Icons: Creation, Change, and Deletion

These creatures are born, change, and die. The only difference between their lives and ours is that you can control their destinies. Here's how.

In the Beginning, program item icons are created in four basic ways:

➤ By an installation or setup program such as Windows Setup

➤ By using Program Manager's New command

➤ By using Program Manager's Copy command

➤ By dragging in files from File Manager

Table 2.1 reviews these four methods and discusses their advantages and disadvantages.

	Method	Advantages	Disadvantages
TABLE 2.1 *Four Ways of Creating Program Icons*	Windows Setup	Automated; handles many applications at once	Doesn't set up document files; places all icons in one group
	New command	Easy to remember; command-line flexibility	Multistep process; requires typing accuracy; must specify path
	Copy and modify	Command-line flexibility; good way to add new documents; keeps path intact	Multi-step process; requires some typing
	Drag from File Manager	Fast; accurate; adds path automatically	Requires a mouse; must add command-line switches or change icons by hand

Most of the time, I prefer to drag in an item from File Manager and then modify the command line or icon as needed. But Windows lets you have it your way, so feel free to draw from these methods as they suit your needs and tastes.

• •

Windows Setup

It's automated! It's the Windows Setup utility, which originated the program item icons you first saw after Windows installation. If, during installation, you instruct Windows Setup to create program item icons for either Windows or DOS applications, Setup searches through the drives you specify for programs it recognizes.

You can use Windows Setup for adding new program item icons at any time, not just during the Windows installation process. Unless you've subsequently moved it, the Windows Setup program will be in the Main group. Follow these steps:

1. Run Windows Setup by double-clicking its icon or by selecting it from the keyboard and pressing Enter.

2. Choose Setup Applications from Setup's Options menu (Alt,O,S). This brings up the first of the Setup Applications dialog boxes (Figure 2.10).

3. In the first Setup Applications dialog box, select either Search for Applications or Ask You to Specify an Application. Then click OK or press Enter.

4. If you selected Ask You to Specify an Application, another dialog box appears named Setup Applications (Figure 2.11). In the Application Path and Filename box, type in the name of the program file with its complete path, or use the Browse button (Alt+B) to automatically place this information in the box. Next, select the Add to Program Group drop-down list box (Alt+A), and select the destination group (Alt+ down arrow) for the program item. Click OK or press Enter to complete.

5. If you selected Search for Applications, a different Setup Applications dialog box appears (Figure 2.12). Select a path or drive from the Setup Will Search list that appears in this dialog box. Then click on the Search Now button (Alt+S). This causes Setup to search the path or drive you indicated; when it's finished, it lists any program files that it recognized in yet another dialog box called Setup Applications (Figure 2.13). Sometimes Setup is unsure how to match a PIF (Program Information File) with its appropriate DOS application, particularly when two or more DOS programs have the same .PIF file name. If Setup runs into an ambiguity, it presents a dialog box that asks you to identify the DOS program so it can assign it the proper PIF (Figure 2.14).

6. In the Applications Found on Hard Disk(s) list box, highlight the applications you want to add to Program Manager by clicking on them with the

mouse; use the arrow keys to navigate the list and press the spacebar to select each item. Then click on the Add button (or press Alt+A) to move those entries to the Setup for Use with Windows list box. Alternatively, press the Add All button (Alt+D) to move all of the entries. (If you add an item by mistake, select it and press the Remove button (Alt+R).

7. Click OK or press Enter to confirm your selections. Setup then adds program item icons to the group named Applications. If you don't have this group, Setup creates one.

FIGURE 2.10

First Setup Applications Dialog Box

When you choose the Setup Applications command from Setup's Options Menu, this dialog box appears. It lets you choose between two totally different functions: (1) whether you want Setup to search through your disk for applications; or (2) whether you want to create an icon for a specific application.

FIGURE 2.11

Second Setup Applications Dialog Box

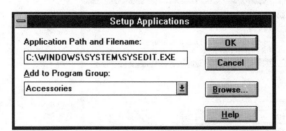

This version of the Setup Applications dialog box lets you name a specific application for which Setup will create a specific icon.

FIGURE 2.12

Third Setup Applications Dialog Box

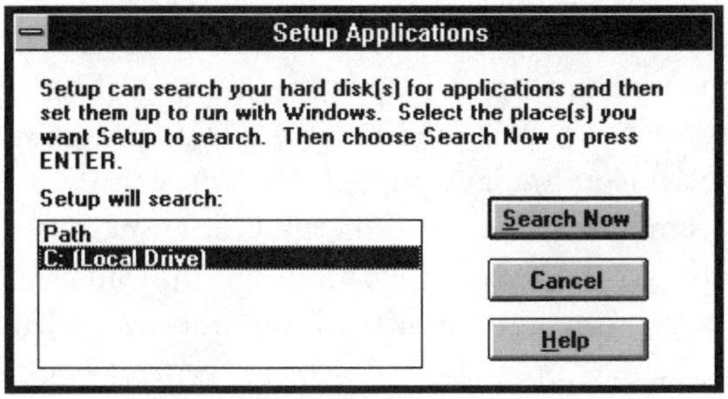

This version of the Setup Applications dialog box lets you specify a path or disk drive for the Setup search.

• • • • • • • • • • • • • •
FIGURE 2.13
*Fourth Setup
Applications
Dialog Box*

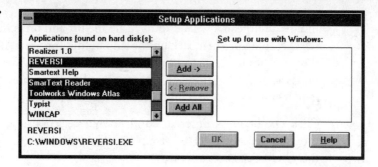

This Setup Applications dialog box lists the programs that Setup
found on your hard disk and lets you select any applications for which
you want Setup to create an icon.

Danger Zone

Windows Setup notifies you of almost all the Windows applications it finds,
even those that are incompatible with Windows 3.1; and it may not make the
necessary modifications to system files, such as WIN.INI. (The installation
program for the application will make those modifications.) As a result, the
icons that Setup creates won't necessarily be able to run all the programs that
are found in the Applications Found on the Hard Disk(s) section of the
Setup Applications dialog box shown in Figure 2.13.

• • • • • • • • • • • • • •
FIGURE 2.14
*Fifth Setup
Applications
Dialog Box*

If Setup finds a DOS
program that it cannot
identify, it presents
this dialog box, which
asks you to make the
identification.

Windows Setup is a good matchmaker, joining your programs with
the most appropriate icon. Windows applications all include original icons.
Setup uses a generic DOS icon for some DOS programs, but it can also
assign a special icon to many popular DOS programs. Windows Setup will
create program item icons for all the applications you've chosen, but it will
only place the icons in the Applications group. Your Windows Setup program will even create a group named Applications (if you don't have one)
for storing the new program item icons it generates. Once the process is
finished, you can move the new icons into other groups.

New in 3.1

In Windows 3.0, Setup placed any Windows programs it found in a group titled Windows Applications; DOS programs were relegated to a group titled Non-Windows Applications. Microsoft seems to have taken DOS programs back into the fold with 3.1; all applications are now embraced in the Applications group. Each group is limited to 40 program item icons; Setup automatically creates new groups—Applications 2, 3, etc.—to store any overflow.

For DOS applications, Windows Setup searches for a PIF related to that application. A PIF includes a variety of parameters that control how a DOS application will interact with Windows, and therefore a proper PIF is essential for running many a DOS program to its best advantage. Windows includes PIF profiles for a large number of applications; these profiles are stored in the APPS.INF file. Windows Setup refers to these profiles to create PIFs for the DOS applications that it finds during its search of your files. (For a detailed discussion of PIFs, see Chapter 14.)

If Windows Setup finds a PIF profile for a DOS application in the APPS.INF file, it introduces that program into the Applications Found on Hard Disk(s) section of the Setup Applications dialog box. Windows Setup uses any special icon that is associated with the program in the APPS.INF file. If there is no special icon, Setup grabs the generic DOS icon that is part of Program Manager's built-in icon collection.

I'll discuss the technical aspects of Windows Setup later on (Chapter 4 explains how to use the Windows Setup utility, and Chapter 16 discusses how to edit the SETUP.INF and APPS.INF files.). For now, you should be aware of what Setup cannot do.

➤➤ Windows Setup doesn't search for documents. If you want to set up program item icons for documents, you'll need to use another creation method.

➤➤ Windows Setup doesn't make modifications that may be necessary to WIN.INI, SYSTEM.INI, or AUTOEXEC.BAT; this can cause Setup to create dysfunctional icons.

➤➤ Windows Setup can't install many applications that contain special installation procedures, such as those that run from batch (.BAT) files, or those that require modifications to startup files.

➤➤ Even if Windows Setup creates an icon for a program, there's no guarantee this application will really work. Be careful with DOS programs that use high memory and with programs created for earlier versions of Windows.

Insider's Tip

You can use Setup to restore your groups in the event they all become damaged. First, use Setup to rebuild your original Main, Accessory, and Games groups. To do this, run Setup by choosing the Run command from the File Menu (Alt,F,R) and typing **SETUP /P** into the Command Line text box; the initial off-the-shelf Windows groups are recreated. Then run Setup from within Windows, and follow the instructions just given to create a new Applications group. This method returns you to square one fairly quickly, although it won't restore everything to its former condition. You may need to run the installation program that came with an application to properly reinstall many Windows programs.

Some older Windows applications won't work at all with Windows 3.1; others seem to run fine for awhile, but then crash. Compatibility concerns apply not just to icons created by Windows Setup but also to those you create using any of the methods for installing program item icons discussed in "The New Command," next.

Insider's Tip

Want to make an educated guess? Here's a visual rule-of-thumb to quickly determine whether a program was designed for Windows 3.0 or 3.1: check the Windows logo on the product's package or documentation.

This is the rectangular Windows trademark, which Microsoft used during the reign of Windows 3.0.

This wavy icon was introduced as Microsoft's new Windows trademark just before the release of Windows 3.1.

The compatibility problem can be resolved by updating your programs as necessary. Enlightened developers will upgrade registered owners for free, or at a nominal charge, but most charge an upgrade fee, which can range from reasonable (a small fraction of the original price) to outrageous (close to what the original program cost). Before you buy a product, I advise you to take into consideration its upgrade policy. I think it's to the benefit of both users and software companies to upgrade products at reasonable rates; doing so keeps users satisfied, enhances the company's reputation, and discourages software piracy.

All in all, Windows Setup is handy for making basic program item icons for many applications at once, particularly when you're first installing Windows. But Setup is limited—you can't install all the various types of program item icons you're likely to need. So, if you want to get the most from Program Manager, it's important to know the other methods for adding program icons.

The New Command

If you want all the flexibility and precision you'd expect to get by creating program item icons from scratch, and you don't mind some extra typing, then New command is for you. Located on the File menu, New (Alt,F,N) allows you to create icons that represent either applications or individual documents; Windows Setup only installs icons for applications. With the New command—and the Copy and Drag methods described later in this chapter—you can create a single icon for opening a specific document together with its corresponding application, even with many DOS programs.

Here's how to create program item icons for Windows programs, DOS programs, and their corresponding data files using the New command.

1. Select a group to contain the new icon (Ctrl+Tab).

2. Choose New from the File menu (Alt,F,N) to display the New Program Object dialog box.

3. If the radio button marked New Program Item is not selected, click on its button (Alt+I). Then click OK, or press Enter.

4. The Program Item Properties dialog box appears (Figure 2.15). This dialog box allows you to set the various options necessary for creating a new program item icon.

5. Enter a short description of the program or document in the Description box (Alt+D); although you're not limited to DOS names, the name should be brief.

6. In the Command Line box (Alt+C), enter the DOS command line to be executed when the icon is opened. This can be as simple as the program file name (for example, WINFILE.EXE), or it can include a complete path with a program, document file, and option switches. If you want, click on the Browse button (Alt+B) to search for the file and to place its full path name in the Command Line box.

7. Use the Working Directory box (Alt+W) to specify a working directory for file storage and retrieval while the application is running.

8. Use the Shortcut Key box (Alt+S) to specify a keyboard shortcut combination that will activate this program or document. Shortcut keys are based on three- or four-key combinations; as a default, if you press a key, Program Manager assigns Ctrl+Alt+(the key you select). Other valid combinations are Ctrl+Shift+(the key you select) and Ctrl+Alt+Shift+(the key you select).

9. To start the application as a minimized application icon rather than as an open window, check the Run Minimized option (Alt+R).

10. The icon that Program Manager proposes to use, if any, is displayed in the lower-left corner of the dialog box. To change it, click on the Change Icon button (Alt+I). Select an icon from the Change Icon dialog box, and return to the Program Item Properties dialog box.

11. When you're ready to create the program item icon and place it in the active group window, click OK or press Enter.

Barring any impediments along the way, you should have your new icon by now. Be sure to test your icon right away, because it will be easier to fix while the details of its creation are still fresh in your mind. If you need to tap into the Windows context-sensitive help during this process, click on the Help button (Alt+H).

• • • • • • • • • • • • • •
FIGURE 2.15
Program Item
Properties
Dialog Box

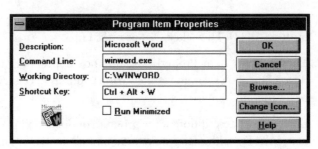

This dialog box allows you to set the various options for creating a new program icon.

If you are upgrading to Windows 3.1 from 3.0, note that the Working Directory, Shortcut Key, and Run Minimized options are new to 3.1.

Insider's Tip

Want to skip some steps to create a new program item icon? Here's how to skip the first three steps listed earlier and zoom to an empty Properties box: select a group window to contain the new item and hold down the Alt key while double-clicking on any empty space in the window.

Command-Line Versatility. The Command Line text box of the Program Item Properties dialog box can include a variety of commands in addition to file names. You can enter any valid DOS command, along with a file name, and you can also add switches and other parameters that control the behavior of an application. For added power, you can even load several documents per application, so when you click on your icon, it automatically starts your application and all the documents related to a particular project.

Here's how to instruct the Command Line text box to start up an application automatically when you click on its associated icon. Simply enter the file name, with or without its extension, in the Command Line box. (Or you can use the Browse box to place its name and its full directory path there automatically.) This procedure works for any file name that contains the extension .EXE, .COM, .BAT, or .PIF.

To create an icon that starts an application together with a specific document, enter the document file name in the Command Line box either by typing it or by using the Browse button. But remember, if your icon only contains a document file name, then you won't be able to open your document file unless its extension, such as .DOC, is associated with a corresponding application, and its extension is properly listed in the extensions section of your WIN.INI file. If you specify a data file in the Command Line box that is not associated with a specific application, Program Manager displays the Invalid Path dialog box as a warning (Figure 2.16), but it will still allow you to create the program item icon.

FIGURE 2.16
*Invalid Path
Dialog Box*

When you try to create an icon for a data file that is not associated with a specific application, Program Manager displays this dialog box.

If your WIN.INI file lacks the proper extensions, you can create an icon that will launch an application and document together by adding the document file name after the name of the application in the Command Line box. For example, to create a document icon that starts a copy of Microsoft Word for Windows installed in a directory called WORD and then loads a document named BIGSTUFF.TXT, enter

```
C:\WORD\WINWORD.EXE BIGSTUFF.TXT
```

in the Command Line box. If the application and data file are in different directories, enter both directory paths. For example,

```
C:\WORD\WINWORD C:\DATA\BIGSTUFF.TXT
```

Whatever application you specify in the Command Line box takes precedence over any application associated with a file name extension (if any) listed in the Extensions section of the WIN.INI file. Thus, in the previous example, the WINWORD.EXE program (Word for Windows) is used to open the text file BIGSTUFF.TXT, which overrides the Extensions statement association of .TXT files with NOTEPAD.EXE (the Windows Notepad utility). Furthermore, you don't need to specify the .EXE extension of an executable file, because Windows will run with it anyway, so save yourself some typing and avoid running up against the 80-character limit of the Command Line box.

Many Windows applications allow you to open several documents simultaneously. You can take advantage of this feature to create a single icon that will open an application and several documents at once. Just type all the file names of your selected documents, using a space after each entry, after the application in the Command Line box. For example, to create an icon that starts Word for Windows and loads two document files named LOADING.DOC and WHATSUP.DOC, located in a directory called DOCS, enter

```
C:\DOCS\LOADING.DOC WHATSUP.DOC
```

To save time and space, the application name can be omitted as long as the file extensions are associated with the WINWORD.EXE application, and Word's directory is listed in your PATH statement. Also, if a different working directory is specified, then you must specify the application file name as well as the document file name.

The Command Line box can also be used to transmit additional parameters, such as switches, that invoke various options when used to run a program. For example, the /N switch tells Word for Windows to start up without a new, empty document; here's how a command line using the /N switch might look:

```
C:\WORD\WINWORD /N
```

Your entries in the Command Line box must be absolutely precise, or else your program icons won't work properly, if at all. Even the slightest error, such as an extra space or the lack of one, can incapacitate an icon.

To save time, use the Browse button (Alt+B) to enter the application file name and its full directory path; after the file name, enter the documents, switches, or other parameters that you wish to pass on to the application at startup.

Danger Zone

Although it's possible to omit the path name of a document or program in the Command line box if the directories are listed in your DOS PATH statement, I don't recommend it, so use the Browse button liberally. Installation programs for both DOS and Windows applications can sometimes modify

your AUTOEXEC.BAT file. This can trigger accidental errors in your DOS PATH statement, or it can cause the PATH statement to exceed the default 127-character limit imposed by DOS. These errors will make it impossible to run the application without specifying its complete path. (See the section on DOS in Chapter 13 for details on how to edit and correct problems in the PATH statement, and how to increase your DOS environment space to accommodate a longer path.)

Insider's Tip

If you have only a few applications and directories, you can rely on the PATH statement. Otherwise, you should use complete path names in the Command Line box, even if the directory path is listed in your PATH statement. It's a little more of a hassle, but this ensures that your system can always find the file (or files) related to the icon, in case your PATH is changed. Use the Browse button liberally. You will have to remember to update the Command Line box to reflect any changes you make to the directories on disk, such as moving files or renaming directories, because these modifications will affect all program item icons already given a precise path.

Creating Icons for DOS Applications. Windows Setup will valiantly attempt to locate DOS applications and install them in the Applications group in Program Manager. Unfortunately, the program doesn't come adequately armed for the task. It lacks a wide enough selection of PIF profiles; an awareness of many DOS programs, which can introduce problems; and any procedure for creating document icons. Consequently, if you need to create icons for DOS applications and documents, you're better off using the New command (or the Copy and Drag commands described later), as well as some of the manual methods described in this section.

The same guidelines used to create icons for Windows applications apply to DOS applications as well, with a few major exceptions. To specify a DOS application in the Command Line box, use one of these three methods:

➻ Enter the name of the .EXE or .COM file that runs the application itself, just as you would with any Windows application.

➻ Enter the name of a DOS batch file (.BAT extension) that contains commands to start the program.

➻ Enter the name of the Program Information File (.PIF extension) that gives detailed information on how to best run the program on your system.

Insider's Tip

Specifying the PIF is your best choice, because a PIF gives Windows vital details for managing a DOS program (such as memory requirements, the use of expanded memory, and the use of text or graphics modes), and any of the other three file types (.EXE, .COM, or .BAT) can be invoked from a PIF. Some PIFs are created by Setup from information contained in settings profiles (included with Windows in the APPS.INF file). Others are provided by the developers of DOS applications. And you can create them yourself, using the Windows PIF Editor and the guidelines I provide later in the book.

Windows cannot run a DOS application without a PIF. If no PIF exists for an application, Windows will instead use the _DEFAULT.PIF to run the program. If you like, take a look at this PIF with the PIF Editor to identify the default settings. Fine-tuning these settings can often improve the performance of DOS sessions running under Windows. If you change the settings, the modified settings will then be used as the default.

To save memory and optimize performance, you should create a .PIF file for the specific application, and enter the .PIF file in the Command Line box when you create a program icon for the application. For example, to create an icon that starts the DOS program EDITOR.EXE from its .PIF, enter

```
C:\EDITOR.PIF
```

in the Command Line box.

If you specify document files along with a .PIF, the .PIF file is treated as if it were the application file name. For example, to create an icon that starts the EDITOR.EXE program from its .PIF, along with the document file named WHATSUP.DOC, enter

```
C:\EDITOR.PIF WHATSUP.DOC
```

in the Command Line box.

You can also use the Command Line box to enter switches and other parameters that the application can use when it's started.

Danger Zone

You can specify shortcut keys and working directories for DOS programs using either the PIF Editor utility or Program Manager. However, when both methods have been used to specify either a keyboard shortcut key or a working directory, the choices specified in Program Manager take priority.

When you're operating Windows in standard mode, you'll have to run DOS applications in a full screen. When you're in 386 enhanced mode, however, you can operate a DOS program in its own window or full screen.

If you run it in a window, the program becomes part of your graphical desktop. If you use smaller fonts in your DOS windows, you can view several programs running simultaneously. You're paying for this multiviewing privilege, however; DOS programs run more quickly and consume less memory in full-screen mode. You can easily toggle between the window and full-screen modes by pressing Alt+Enter. To switch between a full-screen DOS session and your Windows desktop, simply press Alt+Esc or Alt+Tab.

Running Windows in 386 enhanced mode does more than improve your viewing experience. You can also do the following:

➻ Run DOS programs in the background

➻ Regulate the relative amount of processor time devoted to each DOS program

➻ Use the Windows Clipboard to copy and paste less than a full screen of text between Windows and DOS programs

You can run the DOS command processor (COMMAND.COM) from Windows just like any other DOS application. In fact, during installation, Setup creates a program item icon named MS-DOS Prompt in your Main group that lets you activate a DOS command line session. The session continues until you type EXIT at the DOS prompt.

The MS-DOS Prompt icon starts a full-screen DOS session by running COMMAND.COM with the settings contained in the DOSPRMPT.PIF file, which is created by Setup based on instructions in the SETUP.INF file. This PIF is new in Windows 3.1, so if you're upgrading, be sure to use the DOSPRMPT.PIF instead of the old COMMAND.PIF file; otherwise, Windows may confuse this latter file with COMMAND.COM.

The default DOSPRMPT.PIF file runs the DOS session in full-screen mode, so if you are running in 386 enhanced mode and want your sessions to be run in a window, you'll need to use the PIF Editor to change the Display Usage setting from Full Screen to Windowed. You can do this either by editing the DOSPRMPT.PIF file directly or by copying it, modifying the copy, and then renaming the copy to something like WINPRMPT.PIF and creating a separate icon that will start a DOS session in a window.

You can use the DOS prompt session to run a DOS program without setting up a program item icon—simply run it as you would from DOS. However, this will cause the program to be run using the settings in DOSPRMPT.PIF, and these settings may not work well for some programs.

Danger Zone

Stepping in and out of DOS from Windows carries its risks. DOS disk utility programs that alter the DOS File Allocation Table (FAT), such as disk optimizers, file undelete utilities, old backup software, and older backup programs, may also damage your system if you run them in Windows. If you have to use these utilities, quit Windows first. Other DOS commands to avoid running from within Windows include Append, Assign, Format, Fdisk, Join, Recover, Select, and Subst.

New in 3.1

Windows 3.1 helps to shield you from potential conflicts between DOS and Windows. For example, in Windows 3.0, if you typed WIN at the prompt in a DOS session, Windows would try to reload itself, with the result that your system would almost always crash. If you were running your DOS session in full-screen mode, there was no visual clue that Windows was running; this disaster was particularly easy to enact over and over again. With Windows 3.1, however, if you type WIN at the prompt, Windows alerts you that it's already running. In addition, if you type the Ctrl+Alt+Del key combination that reboots your system when issued from DOS, Windows 3.1 issues a message alerting you that you are in Windows and asking whether you really want to reboot.

Picking the Proper Icons. Program Manager features a variety of attractive icons; you should take advantage of this cornucopia, particularly because it's easy to change icons that represent applications and documents.

To select an icon for a program item, use the Change Icon button (Alt+I) in the Program Item Properties dialog box (Figure 2.15). You'll notice that this button is dimmed until you enter something in the Command Line box; in other words, you can't choose an icon until you specify the file name.

When you press the Change Icon button, the Change Icon dialog box appears (Figure 2.17).

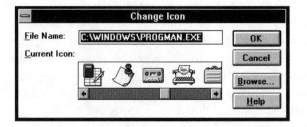

This dialog box allows you to choose an icon to represent an application or document.

Note that the File Name box already contains the name of the file that appeared in the Command Line box. To scroll through the list of icons in the dialog box, mouse with the scroll bars, or use the left and right arrow keys on the keyboard.

New in 3.1

Windows 3.1 vastly improves the selection of icons by redesigning the Change Icon dialog box. In Windows 3.0, the Change Icon dialog box displayed only one icon at a time, and you had to type the complete path of an icon-containing file; in 3.1, you can simply click on the Browse button.

As shown in Figure 2.17, the Change Icon dialog box from Windows 3.1 displays a scrolling list of icons and contains a Help button and a Browse button. Use the Browse button to choose a file that contains whatever icons you want. Program Manager includes the icons shown in Figure 2.18.

FIGURE 2.18

*Program
Manager Icons*

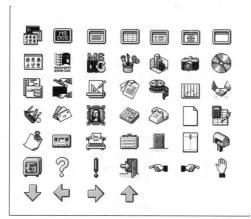

*These icons are included
in Program Manager
(PROGMAN.EXE file).*

Version 3.1 also introduces a collection of icons especially designed for use with DOS programs. These DOS-related icons are contained in a Dynamic Link Library (DLL) file called MOREICONS.DLL, which Setup copies into your main Windows directory during installation (Figure 2.19).

FIGURE 2.19

*DLL File
Provides
DOS-Related
Icons*

*Windows 3.1
includes DOS-
related icons,
which are con-
tained in a
Dynamic Link
Library file called
MOREICONS.DLL.*

To obtain additional choices for icons, enter the name of any Windows application file (or other file that contains Windows icons) in the File Name box. Icons usually fall into one of these three file types, as denoted by the extension:

➤ Windows program files with the .EXE extension contain the icons associated with the corresponding applications.

➤ Icon files, usually designated by the extension .ICO, contain a single icon.

➤ Dynamic Link Libraries, which bear the extension .DLL, can contain many things, including other icons.

Once you've targeted an icon-containing file, click on the OK button to return to the Program Item Properties dialog box.

If you want to add some visual pizzaz to Program Manager, check out these icons, which I plan to issue in a separate *Windows 3.1 Bible* disk pack (Figure 2.20).

FIGURE 2.20

*Sample
Snazzy Icons*

To increase the variety of your icon stash, here's a peek at just a few of the more than 100 icons that will be issued in a separate Windows 3.1 Bible disk pack.

If you want to edit icons or create your own, you can use one of the many icon editor utilities, such as the IconWorks utility program (Figure 2.21).

FIGURE 2.21

IconWorks

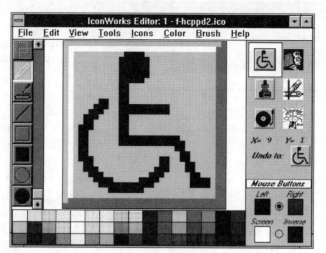

The IconWorks utility lets you edit existing icons or create your own.

The Copy Command

Sometimes, instead of starting from scratch with the New command, you can use the Copy command (F8) to create an icon by copying and then modifying an existing one. This technique works well when you want to create a number of icons that share similar properties.

For example, suppose you want to create separate icons for six form letters written with your wordprocessor. Assuming that all the icons share similar attributes (path, application, icon, etc.), you could just create a single new icon with all the shared information and then replicate it five times. To alter the document file name in the Command Line box of the Program Item Properties dialog box for each of the five replicated icons, use the modification process described in the next section. In this way, each of the new file names would correspond to the replicated five documents with their associated icons.

To copy a program item icon, just select it, hold down the Ctrl key, drag the copy of the icon wherever you wish (within the same group or into another group), and then release Ctrl and the mouse button.

Even if you don't have a mouse for copying icons, you can still squeak by from the keyboard. Just select an icon by pressing the Tab or arrow keys. Then choose the Copy command from Program Manager's File menu by pressing F8. The Copy Program Item dialog box appears and already contains two entries: the name of the program item that is being copied (that is, whatever you typed into the Description field in the Program Item Properties dialog box), and the name of the group from which you are copying that item (Figure 2.22).

FIGURE 2.22

*Copy
Program Item
Dialog Box*

This dialog box allows you to specify the destination group for program item icons that you duplicate from the keyboard.

In the Copy Program Item dialog box, use the To Group text box to select the destination group for the new icon. Press Alt+down arrow to reveal the list, and press the up and down arrow keys to navigate. Once the destination group is selected, press Enter to complete the copy operation.

The To Group text box lists all the valid groups, including the group that contains the original item. This means you can copy an icon to its present group, thus creating an exact twin—which you can then modify as needed. Because program item icons are only aliases for the real files, Program Manager permits you to keep duplicate items in the same group with the identical name; in File Manager, on the other hand, only one icon can exist for each file, because these icons actually represent the files they designate.

Modifying Program Icons

When might you need to modify an icon? Take the situation I just discussed, where you copied an existing icon so you could modify its information. Or you might need to change an icon introduced by an installation program or dragged in from File Manager. Perhaps you need to modify the path of an icon. Whatever the reason, modifying an existing program item closely resembles the process for creating a new one, except for these first few steps.

1. Select the icon you want to modify.

2. Choose the Properties command from the File menu (Alt+Enter).

3. The Program Item Properties dialog box appears, with the current description, command line values, working directory, and icon.

4. Change the values as desired, and add any additional parameters you need. Use the Browse button as described previously to replace the current contents of the Command Line box, and press the Change Icon button to select another icon if you want.

5. Click OK to complete the operation.

Insider's Tip

Mouse users can skip the first two steps just listed—simply hold down the Alt key while double-clicking on a program item icon to immediately call up that icon's Program Item Properties dialog box.

Dragging In Files from File Manager

I always save the best for last, so I'm ending with my favorite, the "dragging in the file from File Manager" method. You may need to modify the icon after it's created, but dragging it in from File Manager gives you a head start. Unfortunately, there's no keyboard equivalent, so if you lack a mouse, you're trapped with one of the methods previously described.

First, make sure that both Program Manager and File Manager application windows are open on the Windows desktop. Arrange Program Manager and File Manager windows on the screen so that you can see both the file you want to add (in File Manager file list) and its eventual destination in Program Manager (either a group window or a group icon). If those are your only open applications, you can arrange them quickly by summoning the Task Manager (Ctrl+Esc) and pressing the Tile button (Alt+T).

In File Manager, select a file, drag it from a File Manager window across the desktop into a Program Manager window, and drop it either into the targeted group window or on top of the group icon. As you drag it, the mouse pointer turns into the shape of a file icon; if you drag several files simultaneously, the pointer changes into a special multiple-file icon. Whenever and wherever you release the mouse button, a new program item icon emerges for each of the files you have dragged. This process works for both application and data files.

If necessary, you can edit an icon by selecting it and choosing Properties from the File menu; or hold down Alt while double-clicking on the icon. But you may not need to; Program Manager does an admirable job of assigning the various properties to new icons created this way. It completes the path of the document in the Command Line box, and tries to determine the appropriate icon: the main icon of the application for a Windows program, for example. For a document, Program Manager searches the Extensions statement list in the WIN.INI file and selects the main icon for that file type's associated application. For example, if you drag a .TXT file from File Manager into Program Manager, the Notepad icon is assigned to it. Don't worry about adding any application names to the Command Line box, unless a document file has an extension that lacks a corresponding application.

Running Programs Without Icons

Yes, Virginia, you can run a program without an icon. Just issue the Run command from the File menu (Alt,F,R) and enter the name of the program in the Run dialog box (Figure 2.23).

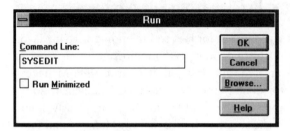

Issuing the Run command (Alt,F,R) brings up this dialog box, which allows you to run a program that lacks a program item icon.

Remember, the program must be in the current directory or in a directory listed in your DOS PATH statement; otherwise, you must enter the full path name for the program. If the program is in the path, just enter its file name—skip the .EXE extension to save a few keystrokes. You can add any switches or other optional parameters after the application file name, if you like.

To start the program as a minimized icon (the equivalent of holding down Shift while double-clicking on it), select the Run Minimized option in the box by pressing Alt+M.

The Browse button (Alt+B) brings up the standard Browse dialog box that lets you specify a path and file name for placement in the Command Line box.

Insider's Tip

Nimble keyboarders can get a document and its corresponding application off to a running start with the Run command, provided that the document's file extension is associated with an application. Simply press Alt,F,R; type the document file name; then press Enter.

Quitting Program Manager

If Program Manager is set as your primary shell, it will always be running, even when you are using a different application. When you quit Program Manager, you will also quit your Windows session. To have Program Manager reconstruct the arrangement of your group windows and the icons they contain the next time you start Windows, make sure that Save Settings on Exit is checked on the Options menu. You can peek at the Options menu to check the status of this item by clicking on it or by typing Alt,O. If the Save Settings on Exit item is unchecked, choose it from the menu to activate it.

Insider's Tip

To save the arrangement of your Program Manager groups and icons without exiting Program Manager (and therefore Windows), hold down the Shift key while you select Exit from the File menu (Alt,F,X).

When you're ready to quit, choose Exit from the File Menu (Alt,F,X); or, as a shortcut, double-click on the Control Menu box. If any other applications are still running, Windows automatically closes them unless an unsaved document is open in one of the applications. In that case, you'll have a chance to save any changes you've made. Then one last dialog box will appear to tell you that your Windows session is about to end, giving you one last chance to change your mind.

New in 3.1

You can assign a special sound to play whenever you exit Windows, thanks to one of the new features added to 3.1's multimedia extensions. For example, I've set up my system so that Arnold Schwarzenegger can be heard saying "I'll be back," whenever I quit a session. See Chapter 4 for details.

. . . .

Organizing Your Work with Program Manager

Program Manager provides you with ways to create icons and group them together, but it doesn't dictate how things should be grouped. In fact, the program could be said to apply an anarchistic approach to organization: each according to his (or her) own needs. You can be creative, or you can just let Windows do the grouping for you with the Tile and Cascade commands discussed earlier. But installation programs tend to create groups that contain only one or two icons, whereas generally it's better to have fewer groups, each containing a greater number of icons. So you should really take advantage of the flexibility and capabilities Program Manager provides for creating your icon groups. To give you some idea of what's possible, I'll present some different approaches for organizing things with Program Manager, but feel free to modify or combine them to suit your own particular work habits.

The Faulty Default Arrangement

Some groups just emerge like primeval life forms when you first install Windows. The Setup program creates the Main, Accessories, Games, and Startup groups; and if you used Setup to search through your drives for specific programs, expect to see an Applications group as well. Groups and icons are initially arranged as shown in Figure 2.1. If you have installed any third-party Windows programs, separate groups for those programs may be taking up territory on your desktop as well.

The original arrangement created by Windows Setup must have signified something to someone at Microsoft, but it's never made much sense to me. The Main group contains File Manager and a mess of minor utilities and Windows accessories. Sure, File Manager's important, but where are the bundled Windows applets, such as Write, Paintbrush, and Terminal? They are in the Accessories group, along with the rest of the utilities and real accessories.

An unwelcome change in Windows 3.1 is the merging of Windows and DOS programs into a single Applications group, which Windows Setup can create at your request. In Windows 3.0, Setup created a separate group for DOS programs called Non-Windows Applications. Because Windows and DOS programs operate and are manipulated in distinctly different ways, it makes sense to keep the two groups segregated.

Of course, if you've been running Windows for a while and are using several different applications, you can create a complex, perhaps even chaotic, Program Manager setup, such as the one depicted in Figure 2.24.

To relieve this chaotic scene, use the Tile command (Shift+F4), which will provide some semblance of order to the various open group windows. Figure 2.25 depicts the screen in Figure 2.24 after you've applied the Tile command.

Although the Tile command provides a quick fix to a messy screen, it doesn't really help you organize your icons in a sensible way. Tile reduces your group windows to approximately the same size, no matter how many icons they contain, so many of your important icons are hidden from view. In order to find these icons, you may have to scroll through many tiny windows for a considerable amount of time. Fortunately, there are some better ways to attain a meaningful arrangement.

FIGURE 2.24

Program Manager Screen with Lots of Windows and Icons

Windows' veterans should be on guard for symptoms of information overload: too many different groups and icons will clutter your Program Manager and make it difficult to locate items when you need them.

FIGURE 2.25

After the Tile Command

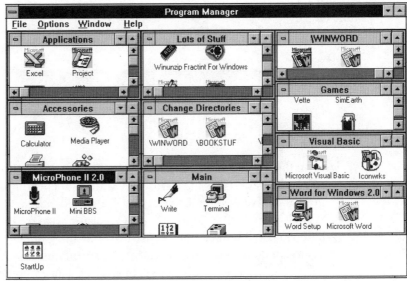

This is how the cluttered screen in Figure 2.24 looks after the Tile command has been used.

• •

A More Sensible Arrangement

Beginners and light Windows users could create three groups: one for programs, another for utilities and accessories, and a third to store icons that represent data files rather than applications. To illustrate this kind of setup, I've created the Program Manager screen shown in Figure 2.26.

• • • • • • • • • • • • • •
FIGURE 2.26
*Program
Manager with
Groups for
Programs,
Utilities, and
Data*

*Some people may find this a more practical way to arrange their
Program Manager groups than the default arrangement created by
Windows Setup.*

In this arrangement, I've placed File Manager, Write, Paintbrush, Terminal, Calendar, Notepad, Cardfile, Word, and Excel in a group named Programs. I've put the Control Panel, Print Manager, MS-DOS Prompt, Windows Setup, PIF Editor, Clock, Calculator, Macro Recorder, Character Map, Sound Recorder, and Media Player in the Utilities group. The Data group contains icons that represent documents used by the various programs. You can extend this concept by creating data groups that represent the data files for specific applications. Also, if you use DOS applications, you can create a separate DOS Applications group for those programs, because Windows 3.1 no longer does this for you.

· ·

Group 'em Like Directories

Another scheme for program management is to assign program item icons to all or some of your files. In this way you can create a group that is reminiscent of a DOS subdirectory, which contains both the program and its associated data files (Figure 2.27). To do this operation quickly, just create a new group to represent the directory, open File Manager in a window, select the files en masse from a directory window, and drop them into the new group window to create the program item icons.

· · · · · · · · · · · · ·
FIGURE 2.27
Group with
Word
Application
Icon and
Document
Icons

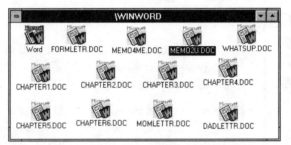

By assigning pro-
gram item icons to
both an application
and its documents,
you can create a
group similar to a
DOS subdirectory.

Program Manager normally assigns the same icon to files that represent both applications and their associated documents. Using unique icons for special purposes can help you differentiate between files, especially when you're working with many programs and documents. For example, when a data file is dragged into Program Manager from File Manager, Program Manager assigns an application's icon to all the data files with extensions that are associated with that particular application. Suppose, however, that you wanted to distinguish an icon for an application from an icon for one of its documents. In fact, if you look carefully at Figure 2.27, you'll notice that the Word for Windows application icon looks different from its document icons. Here's how to achieve this effect:

1. Combine a 3D button template with the normal Word icon, or modify it in some other way using the IconWorks utility or another icon editor.

2. Use the new icon as the program item icon for the application itself by selecting it in the application's Program Item Properties dialog box.

3. Now drag a Word document file icon into Program Manager from File Manager, and voila!

Notice that since I switched icons, the Word program icon now looks different from its application icon.

You can use this procedure to make all your application icons look different from their document icons. In this way, you'll know at a glance whether an icon represents a document or an application.

Make Your Own Iconic Stationery Pads

Another way to arrange program items is to set them up as **stationery pads**, which can be used to generate form letters, spreadsheet grids, page-layout templates, or whatever other master form you want to generate. Figure 2.28 shows how I've set up a few icons as stationery pads for some commonly reusable document templates.

FIGURE 2.28

Word Stationery Pads

These program item icons were set up as reusable stationery pads.

To create a stationery pad icon, follow these steps:

1. Use the procedures described earlier in this chapter to create a program item icon for the document file you intend to use as a template.

2. Set the original file that you will use as a template to Read Only by accessing the file's properties in File Manager (see the next chapter for details on how to set the properties for a file).

3. After you open a document, use Save As on the application's File menu to save the file. Because its file attributes are set to Read Only, you won't be able to accidently save over, and thereby delete, the original document.

If you use several items as stationery pads, you can separate them from icons representing regular data files by creating a special group for just these items.

Switch Directories with the Press of a Button

Attention power users: here's another way, involving directories, to make your Program Manager work harder for you. Whether you have a very large hard disk—which you really need in order to run Windows effectively—or whether all your files are located in a couple of large directories, you should consider a scheme for creating directories and subdirectories on your drives to help organize your programs and data files. The trouble with such a system is that if you always start an application from its main program item icon, the program will always be logged into the same working directory;

thus, each time you want to work with the data files in a different directory, you'll have to navigate through the Browse dialog box. Don't worry, though, there's an easy fix: you can create special program item icons that will automatically start an application using a specific directory. Then just click that special icon to start up the application in a specific working directory.

The example group in Figure 2.29 shows how I set up several program item icons to start the Word program from various data directories.

FIGURE 2.29

Icons as
Directories

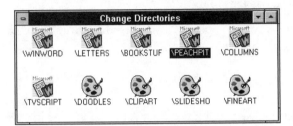

These program item icons are set up as buttons that will start a program in a particular directory.

Earlier in this chapter, I told you about the Working Directory section of the Program Item Properties dialog box, which is a new feature in Windows 3.1. (Alt+double-click on an icon to get to this box.) You can use this feature to quickly set up icons that will start a program in the directory of your choice. For example, the two Properties dialog boxes (Figure 2.30) show how I set up Word to start in different directories.

FIGURE 2.30

Two
Properties
Dialog Boxes

Program Item Properties	
Description:	Word
Command Line:	C:\WINWORD\WINWORD.EX
Working Directory:	C:\WINWORD
Shortcut Key:	None
	☐ Run Minimized

OK
Cancel
Browse...
Change Icon...
Help

Program Item Properties	
Description:	Word \BIBLE
Command Line:	C:\WINWORD\WINWORD.EX
Working Directory:	C:\BIBLE
Shortcut Key:	None
	☐ Run Minimized

OK
Cancel
Browse...
Change Icon...
Help

These two Properties dialog boxes will create icons that each start the same program, but in a different directory.

You'll notice that the only differences between the two dialog boxes are the name in the Description box and the path information in the Working Directory box.

Here's how to quickly create several icons that start the same program in different directories:

1. Create a new program item icon (Alt,F,N; Alt+I; Enter).

2. Set up the Command Line (Alt+C) for the program; use Browse (Alt+B) if necessary.

3. Choose an icon (Alt+I) for the program if you don't like what Program Manager assigns to it.

4. Make as many copies as you have directories in which you want the program to start.

Now, for each of the copied icons,

1. Select the Description text box (Alt+D) and type in a new name; use the name of the directory or any other description.

2. Select the Working Directory text box (Alt+W) and enter the full path name of the directory in which you want the program to start; note that you cannot use the Browse button for the Working Directory box.

Insider's Tip

Attention, power users! If you are working with lots of icons in each of your groups, or if, for other reasons, you want to conserve screen real estate in Program Manager, here's a hot tip. You can create a more compact icon arrangement by tweaking some settings in the [Desktop] section of your WIN.INI file. By adjusting these four statement lines—IconSpacing, IconVerticalSpacing, IconTitleFaceName, and IconTitleSize—you can pack your icons in like sardines, and thus view more of them at once while reducing the space they consume on your Windows desktop. To find out how to adjust these values, see the section of Chapter 15 that deals with editing WIN.INI.

· ·

How to Regroup Without Having to Rebuild

So you've taken some of the tips in this section to heart—or devised an even better system of your own. Now it's time to think about backing up your work. One way to preserve your arrangement of groups and icons is to make the group files themselves read-only, by setting the file's attributes with File Manager—you can identify the group files by the .GRP extension in their names. The .GRP files contain encoded information about the contents of a Program Manager group. Another approach is to make a backup of the .GRP files, along with a backup of your PROGMAN.INI file, which contains the information about where each group should be placed. Here's how to do this:

1. Create a directory called OLDGRP (or whatever name works for you).

2. Copy all your .GRP files from the main Windows directory into the OLDGRP directory and rename the extension on all the group files from .GRP to something like .GR1. Hint: Do it in one step from the DOS prompt by typing:

```
COPY *.GRP C:\WINDOWS\OLDGRP\*.GR1
```

3. Copy the PROGMAN.INI file into the OLDGRP directory and rename it something like PROGMAN.IN1 so that you can tell it's related to the .GR1 files.

After you've made your backup copies of the .GRP files and the PROGMAN.INI file, you can return to your original setup by simply replacing the existing files with the old ones. However, you should probably back up your current setup before returning to the old one, just in case you change your mind, or find an unexpected problem with your old arrangement. If you used the file names that I suggested for the backups, you could then rename your current group files using the .GR2 extension, and rename your corresponding PROGMAN.INI to PROGMAN.IN2.

You can also use this technique to create more than one custom Program Manager setup, which is especially useful if another person shares your computer. For example, let's say Lucille and Lenny both use the same computer at home. Lucy's a power user who works with lots of programs and files, but Lenny only uses the system to write letters and play games. Lucy wants to make sure that Lenny doesn't muck up all her stuff, and Lenny thinks Lucy's setup makes it too hard to find the stuff he wants. The solution to this potential strife? Lucy (who's probably read this book!) simply backs up all of her files with the .GR1 and .IN1 extensions; then she creates a trimmed-down desktop for Lenny, which only includes groups for writing, games, and utilities. She saves this Lenny-specific configuration with the .GR2 and .IN2 suffixes. Then she creates two batch files to start Windows, one named LUCY.BAT, the other LENNY.BAT. The LUCY.BAT file looks like this:

```
COPY C:\WINDOWS\*.GR1 C:\WINDOWS\*.GRP
COPY C:\WINDOWS\PROGMAN.IN1 C:\WINDOWS\PROGMAN.INI
WIN
COPY C:\WINDOWS\*.GRP C:\WINDOWS\*.GR1
COPY C:\WINDOWS\PROGMAN.INI C:\WINDOWS\PROGMAN.IN1
```

And here's what the LENNY.BAT file looks like:

```
COPY C:\WINDOWS\*.GR2 C:\WINDOWS\*.GRP
COPY C:\WINDOWS\PROGMAN.IN2 C:\WINDOWS\PROGMAN.INI
WIN
COPY C:\WINDOWS\*.GRP C:\WINDOWS\*.GR2
COPY C:\WINDOWS\PROGMAN.INI C:\WINDOWS\PROGMAN.IN2
```

When Lucy types **LUCY** at the DOS prompt to start Windows, the batch file replaces the existing groups with her preset arrangement before running Windows, and then backs up her groups after quitting Windows. Likewise for Lenny when he types **LENNY** at the prompt. If you start Windows in the middle of a batch file—as in the above examples—the rest of the batch file will run after you quit Windows.

Playing the Shell Game

You can play the shell game any way you want. If you make regular use of different applications and data files, you might want to set up File Manager as your primary shell. Or you might want to use a third-party shell such as Norton Desktop (see Chapter 6).

To change the primary shell program, just edit the SHELL=statement in the SYSTEM.INI file. Use either the Notepad or the Sysedit utility to open the SYSTEM.INI file. A few lines down, you should see the SHELL=statement, which will read

```
SHELL=PROGMAN.EXE
```

signifying that PROGMAN.EXE—better known as Program Manager—is the primary Windows shell, which runs on that system during your entire Windows session. If you change the line to read

```
SHELL=WINFILE.EXE
```

then Windows loads the WINFILE.EXE program—better known as File Manager—as the primary shell. (See Chapter 15 for complete details on editing the SYSTEM.INI file.)

Insider's Tip

Want to bypass the standard shells? Here's an undocumented feature of Windows: almost any program can be specified as the shell. So if you want to set up a system dedicated to a single Windows application, such as Excel—which might be handy if you were developing a turnkey accounting system—you just specify SHELL=EXCEL.EXE. Starting Windows then starts Excel immediately, and quitting Excel terminates the Windows session. If the system also contains a command to start Windows in its AUTOEXEC.BAT file, it would be turned into a dedicated accounting system.

Features for Systems Administration

New in 3.1

The new Program Manager in Windows 3.1 includes several useful features for system administrators, consultants, and other advanced users responsible for organizational computing needs. These features include:

➤ The ability to define a startup group

➤ The ability to specify a working directory for an application

➤ The ability to share groups over a network

➤ The ability to configure Program Manager so as to limit its functionality and prevent unauthorized access to a system

➤ Enhancements to the DDE commands that other programs can use to access Program Manager

I've already discussed the first two items in the list—startup groups and working directories—earlier in this chapter. In the next section, I'll cover the remaining items to give you an overview of Program Manager's new capabilities, and I'll also refer you to other sections of this book that provide additional related information.

Sharing Groups

Program Manager groups may now be shared by many users over a network; this represents a significant improvement in Windows 3.1. When used on a network, the groups are available to users as read-only files that cannot be altered. As a network administrator, you only need to set the group files (denoted by .GRP) to read-only, and Program Manager will prevent users from moving or deleting any icons within the group. For further details about working with Windows over a network, see Chapter 10.

• •

Restricting Access to Program Manager Commands

Also new in the Windows 3.1 version of Program Manager is its ability to allow you to limit or restrict the commands that users will be able to access. Thus you can now prevent users from changing their Program Manager groups, quitting Program Manager, or running any other programs.

To set these restrictions, you'll need to edit the PROGMAN.INI file (see Chapter 15). In the PROGMAN.INI file, you will need to create a section called [Restrictions], if one doesn't already exist. The [Restrictions] section can contain up to five statements that limit user actions when running Program Manager on the system with the PROGMAN.INI file.

• • • • • • • • • • • • • •

TABLE 2.2
Statements in
PROGMAN.INI
File and What
They Control

Statement in PROGMAN.INI	What It Controls
NoRun=1	Disables the use of the Run Command on the File Menu
NoClose=1	Prevents the user from exiting Program Manager (Can be used to prevent access to DOS)
NoSaveSettings=1	Prevents the user from saving any changes made to Program Manager's icons or groups
NoFileMenu=1	Removes File menu
EditLevel=<0-4>	Limits what the user can do to groups

The last of these options, the EditLevel statement, allows you to grant a user five different levels of permission for modifying groups, as shown in Table 2.3.

• • • • • • • • • • • • • •

TABLE 2.3
The EditLevel
Statement and
Levels of
Permission

EditLevel Statement	What a User Can Do
EditLevel=0	No restrictions (default)
EditLevel=1	Users cannot create, delete, or rename any groups
EditLevel=2	Users cannot delete any items
EditLevel=3	Users cannot change a Command line for any program icon
EditLevel=4	Users cannot change any properties of any program icon

When combined with the NoRun=1 statement, use of EditLevel=4 prevents users from running any applications other than those used in Program Manager. However, if you want to prevent users from running any other applications, you'll also have to restrict usage to some of the items normally found in Program Manager itself. File Manager, for instance, allows users to run applications, and some applications contain their own Run menus or use macro languages capable of launching other applications.

Dynamic Data Exchange and Program Manager

Program Manager can communicate with other applications through standard Windows DDE (Dynamic Data Exchange) commands. Windows 3.0 provided limited DDE support for Program Manager, but version 3.1 gives other programs almost full control over its capabilities. Details on DDE are provided in Chapter 9, but for now, here's a list of the special DDE commands supported by Program Manager:

➥ CreateGroup. If the group named already exists, activates it; otherwise, creates a new group with the name you specify

➥ AddItem. Creates a new icon in the currently selected group

➥ DeleteGroup. Deletes the group you specify

➥ ExitProgram. Exits Program Manager

➥ ShowGroup. Minimizes, maximizes, or restores a group

➥ ReplaceItem. Deletes an icon that you specify, but remembers the position so that it can be replaced using the AddItem command

➥ DeleteItem. Deletes the program icon you specify from the active group

➥ Reload. Updates the information in a group after modification

Insider's Tip

In addition to these commands, Windows 3.1 allows another program to request information from the DDE topic titled PROGMAN. To identify which groups are present, request the information with the Group item alone. To request information about program items within a particular group, you must specify Groups together with a particular group name. The information is returned to the requesting program in a DDE variable called CF_TEXT. If you request the list of groups, it is returned as a list separated by carriage returns. If you ask for the specifics on a particular group, the response includes the group name, the path to the group file, and the total number of items in the group. It also contains a line for each icon, indicating the command line, default directory, icon path, position in the group, icon index, and hotkey, plus a flag to indicate whether the application should be run minimized.

• •

Summary

Program Manager provides a friendly and straightforward launching pad for your applications. It also offers several options for systems administration and configuration, helping administrators control access and use of the applications for better protection of network resources. Cosmetically, changes to Program Manager between versions 3.0 and 3.1 may seem slight, but much work went on "behind the screens." Both performance and functionality are increased, but Program Manager now consumes less of your system's memory resources, which allows you to create more groups without robbing your system of too much RAM.

Although Program Manager presents an affable interface, it still doesn't allow you to perform most tasks usually associated with a computer operating system. For these jobs, you'll have to turn to Program Manager's homelier but harder-working sibling, File Manager, the subject of the next chapter.

• •

Insider's Tech Support: Program Manager

Q: I tried to start a program with the Run command, but it didn't work properly.

A: First thing to check are problems with your path. Did you specify one at all? If so, did you specify it correctly? If the path looks OK, you should check to see if the program requires other files (such as DLLs or settings files) that are not in the current path or directory. If so, place the required directories in your path statement and try again.

Q: I can't seem to run a DOS session in a window, only full screen.

A: Windows may be running in standard mode rather than in 386 enhanced mode. Obviously, if you're running on a 286, you can't run in 386 enhanced mode, but even if you have a 386 or higher, you may be running in standard mode without knowing it. When Windows first starts, it takes a peek at your hardware configuration to determine whether to run in standard or in 386 enhanced mode. If you have a 286, or if you have a 386 with what Windows considers to be too little memory—say a megabyte—Windows starts in standard mode. Also, if Windows is started from a batch file, check to see if it is being started with the WIN /s switch, which forces it to start in standard mode. You can force Windows to start in 386 enhanced mode by typing WIN /3 at the DOS prompt.

Q: How can I tell what mode I'm running in?

A: Choose About Program Manager from the Help menu (Alt,H,A). The current mode is reported in the About dialog box.

Q: I tried to start a program from its icon, but it didn't work, and I get an "Application Execution Error." Is this dangerous?

A: Sounds dangerous, but usually it's not. This dialog box is most commonly triggered by an incorrect path for the program item icon. If you create an icon in Program Manager and subsequently move the file represented by that icon to a different directory, or rename the file or the directory containing the file, Program Manager will not be able to find the file any more and will generate the ominous dialog box (remember that the icon is only an alias). To correct the problem, hold down Alt and double-click on the offending icon to access its Program Item Properties dialog box; then use the Browse button to reselect the proper file. This will ensure that the correct path is entered for the icon.

Q: Is it possible to shrink the size of a DOS session window so that an entire DOS screen (80 characters wide by 25 lines) takes up less than the full Windows screen on a normal 640x480 VGA display?

A: Yes. You can change the font size used in the DOS window to effectively shrink the size of the window. However, the smaller the font, the more difficult it will be to read the screen. See Chapter 14 for information on how to change the fonts in the DOS session.

Q: My Program Manager groups have become corrupted and do not load properly.

A: You may have too many files in your Windows directory. Or some other application, such as a Setup or installation program, has tried unsuccessfully to modify the files. Or maybe your hard disk is full. For safety's sake, it's a good idea to make backups of the groups. To do this, back up the corresponding .GRP files, along with the PROGMAN.INI file. If the .GRP files have accidentally been moved to another directory, the PROGMAN.INI file will probably not have been updated properly; this will also generate an error message. If worse comes to worst, you can use Setup to rebuild your original Program Manager groups.

Q: When Auto Arrange is active, all the icons snap to a grid that leaves either too much or too little space between the icons. Is it possible to change this?

A: Yes. Open the Control Panel and select the Desktop icon. When the Desktop dialog box appears, select the Icon Spacing controls, which let you adjust the number of pixels between icons. See Chapter 4 for more information on using the Control Panel.

Q: The titles of my icons are so long they overlap, making them hard to read.

A: The Desktop section of the Control Panel contains a check box named Wrap Title. If your titles are not wrapped, it's easy for them to overlap. Make sure there is an X in the Wrap Title check box to alleviate this problem.

Q: Why are some items missing from menus in my Program Manager?

A: Your system administrator (or someone else) has added restriction statements to your PROGMAN.INI file. If you don't have access to this file, ask the person who does to change these statements.

File Manager: A Graphical Way to Work with Files

No serious Windows user can live on Program Manager alone. Although Program Manager provides a straightforward way to run programs, you'll also need to organize and manage your files. To format a disk, copy files, or browse through your hard disk directories, you'll need to call on File Manager, a graphical shell that provides most of the functions you'd find in DOS.

And, if you're willing to take the time to learn how to use it, File Manager can enhance the flexibility and power of your programs by adding sophisticated features, such as drag and drop, and object linking and embedding (OLE).

File Manager was designed to provide a comprehensive graphical operating system; in other words, anything you can do with a traditional operating system like DOS, you can do *graphically* with File Manager. In DOS, you type commands at the prompt to perform system housekeeping and file organization tasks; in Windows, File Manager provides a visual metaphor of your computer's filing system. Using this graphical system, you can manage your system by manipulating file icons that represent the storage devices available to your computer.

Figure 3.1 depicts the various icons in File Manager. These icons provide intuitive images, although the designs are not as elegant as those offered by some of the third-party shells, such as WinTools (Tool Technology Publishing) and New Wave (Hewlett Packard).

FIGURE 3.1

File Manager Icons

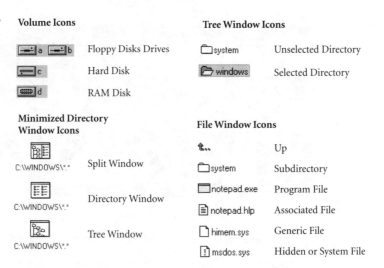

These icons, unlike those in Program Manager, are immovable within their respective windows, although you can drag them into other windows.

The Advantages of File Manager

File Manager doesn't introduce any low-level changes to the basic DOS file system; it simply translates the DOS functions into a graphic format. But File Manager offers far greater ease of use than you'd ever attain in the command-driven universe. When you work with a large number of files, you can select large groups and then perform an operation on all of them simultaneously, whereas in DOS you'd often have to perform a separate operation for each file.

Compared with DOS, Windows' File Manager offers these improvements:

➡ It's **more interactive**. If you use a mouse, you can see your files move from directory to directory as you move the mouse. As you manipulate items with the mouse, the cursor changes status to alert you to special conditions and events; for example, the pointer becomes an hourglass while a task is being processed. This kind of user feedback creates the essential "bonding" necessary between you and your computer.

➡ The use of a **graphical user interface** eliminates the need to memorize the long series of commands required to perform the equivalent functions under DOS.

➡ You can interconnect different events by using **drag and drop**: just drag files from File Manager and drop them in a different place to initiate a particular action. For example, you can create a new program item icon in Program Manager simply by dragging a file icon from File Manager and dropping it into a Program Manager group. Or you can drop a file on top of the Print Manager in order to print the file quickly. This kind of object-oriented file manipulation has no corollary in the command-line oriented DOS world.

Despite all these improvements, sometimes you may still want to issue a DOS command, such as the powerful XCOPY. To use DOS from within Windows, double-click on either a DOS prompt icon in Program Manager or on the corresponding .PIF file in File Manager. You can even issue DOS commands from within File Manager by entering the command in the Run dialog box (Alt,F,R).

· ·

New File Manager Features in 3.1

New in 3.1

Improvements to File Manager in Windows 3.1 are so dramatic, they alone provide enough reason to upgrade. The 3.0 version of File Manager was a dog—it operated at a snail's pace, left you no chance to bail out once you started an operation, and didn't let you view more than one directory tree window at a time.

Version 3.1 resolves all these problems. You can now view more than one directory tree at a time, using a split window that lets you view the directory tree on the left side and the contents of any directory on the right. Because you can browse through all the files on your various drives without having to open a separate window for each directory, it's far easier to copy files and subdirectories from one drive or directory to another. File Manager clearly labels disk drives, windows, and network paths to provide important information about file sizes and disk capacities. Better networking support makes it easier to connect and disconnect from network drives.

Windows 3.1 also provides a host of new amenities. You can now select from a wide variety of fonts. Using a smaller font allows you to display more information in a window, or the same amount of information in a smaller window. Microsoft also put File Manager through a major performance tune-up. The time required to update information on the screen has been vastly reduced, and File Manager is much speedier at scanning information on a drive when you first log on. A new Quick Format option makes it easier to reformat a disk and copy files to it.

For you software archaeologists who might be curious about the MS-DOS Executive shell that appeared in earlier versions of Windows, it's now extinct.

Organizing Files

File Manager, like DOS, allows you to organize the assorted files (programs, data, or whatever) that are stored on the various storage devices connected to the system, either directly or through a network. Such storage devices are usually referred to as **volumes**. A **volume** can be a discrete physical entity, such as a floppy disk or a hard disk drive, or it can be a conceptual entity called a **logical device**, such as a RAM disk, a partition on a larger hard disk, or a section of a remote server that is connected to your system across a network. The actual files reside inside the various volumes; these files contain the programs and raw data that are encoded as bits and bytes on the storage device.

Because a storage device can contain many thousands of files, DOS uses **directories** and **subdirectories** to organize groups of files. In File Manager's desktop metaphor, volumes are analogous to a file drawer, and directories are like file folders. This hierarchy of files, directories, and volumes is common to almost every computer operating system, and Windows users are free to arrange these organizational tools as they please.

Danger Zone

The more files you've created, the more sense it makes to adhere to a uniform structure for arranging them. Otherwise, you'll waste time searching your disk drive whenever you need to locate a particular file. Try grouping directories together and then placing them within another directory. Voila! You've just nested subdirectories within a directory. When you need to access these nested subdirectories later on, use the mouse to burrow down to your target.

Powering Up

To start File Manager, click on its icon in the Program Manager window, or issue the Run command (Alt,F,R) and type **WINFILE**. File Manager, like most Windows applications, includes a main application window that contains document windows. These document windows display the files and directories in a particular volume.

The first time you start File Manager, its main application window opens to reveal a directory window, which in turn displays the contents of the current drive in a split window. The left half of the window contains the directory tree, and the right half includes the icons for the files and subdirectories located within the current directory (Figure 3.2).

FIGURE 3.2

*First Time
File Manager
Screen*

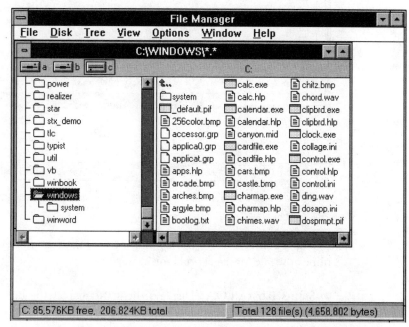

This is how File Manager might look after you first power it up.

You'll notice that File Manager displays much of your system's vita: the number of files in the current directory, available disk space, the size of the currently selected file or directory, and other particulars. The status bar at the bottom of the main File Manager application window tracks your selections.

The information in the status bar varies, depending on the item you've selected in the directory window. For example, click on a directory in the left window to see the volume's drive letter and the amount of free space on it. If you've selected one or more file icons in the right window, the left panel of the status bar shows the number of files you've selected and their aggregate size. This immediate visual feedback is handy when making backups or copying files from disk to disk (Figure 3.3). By adding to or subtracting from your selection, you can easily determine how to fit the files that you wish to copy onto the target disk.

FIGURE 3.3
*File Manager
Screen
Showing
Status Bar
and Number
of Files*

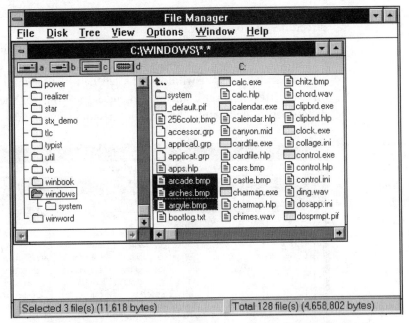

The status bar reveals how many files you have selected and their aggregate size.

Three commands on the Option menu (Figure 3.4) allow you to determine how File Manager will look at startup:

➤ **Status Bar** (Alt,O,A) Displays the status bar at the bottom of the File Manager application window.

➤ **Minimize on Use** (Alt,O,M) Causes File Manager to start up as an icon rather than as a window.

➤ **Save Settings on Exit** (Alt,O,E) Starts up File Manager as you last left it.

FIGURE 3.4
Option Menu

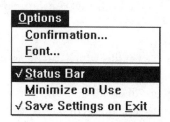

Check the Status Bar on the Option menu so that File Manager can communicate with you.

I strongly suggest that you keep the status bar turned on, because it provides you with important details about directories and files. You'll probably want to leave Minimize on Use off, unless you plan to place File Manager inside Program Manager's Startup group.

Quitting

To quit File Manager, double-click on the control icon at the left end of the File Manager application window title bar, or use one of these generic Windows keyboard methods:

➤ Alt+F4

➤ Alt,spacebar,C

➤ Alt,F,X

If File Manager is your primary shell, quitting it terminates your current Windows session and returns you to the DOS prompt.

When you start File Manager, it re-creates your most recently used configuration—provided, of course, that the same files and directories are still present on your system (volumes that are attached on a network will often disappear) and provided that you checked the Save Settings on Exit option. If this menu item is not checked, any system settings you altered during your current File Manager session will be abandoned.

Insider's Tip

The information related to your File Manager's previous setup and configuration is stored in the [Settings] section of the WINFILE.INI file, discussed in Chapter 15. To save several different File Manager drive setups, here's how to take a "snapshot" of each: Quit File Manager (check Save Settings on Exit) and then back up the WINFILE.INI file from a DOS prompt by typing

```
COPY WINFILE.INI WINFILE.IN1
```

This creates a copy of the WINFILE.INI file, which can be used later to restore File Manager to its previous state. Then restart File Manager and set up your next configuration. When you are finished, quit File Manager and back up the now-modified WINFILE.INI under a different name, such as

```
COPY WINFILE.INI WINFILE.IN2
```

Repeat the process for as many other setups as you want to save. To start File Manager with one of your setups, just type the desired configuration over the WINFILE.INI file before you start File Manager. For example, to replace your WIN.INI file with the WINFILE.IN2, type

```
COPY WINFILE.INI WINFILE.IN2
```

If you don't want to quit File Manager, you can also take a snapshot of a setup and save it by holding down the Shift key while choosing Exit from the File menu (Alt,F,X).

Directory Windows

Windows 3.1 ushered in major improvements to File Manager's **directory windows**, making them speedier, easier to work with, and more informative. It also consolidated what were two windows into a single window, which can be configured in three ways (Figures 3.5, 3.6, and 3.7):

➡ The **default split-window** display, which shows the directory tree on the left and the contents of the selected directory on the right

➡ A **directory-tree-only** display

➡ A **file list** display, which contains only the files and directories in a given directory

FIGURE 3.5
*Default
Split-Window
Display*

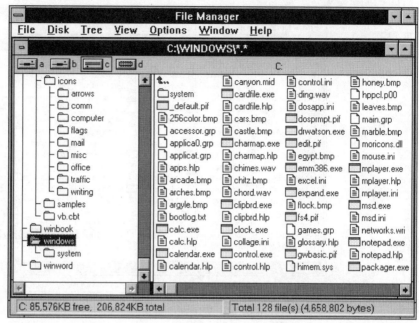

Directory windows in File Manager are usually split screen. The left side shows the directory tree, and the right side displays the contents of a selected directory.

FIGURE 3.6
*Directory-Tree-
Only Display*

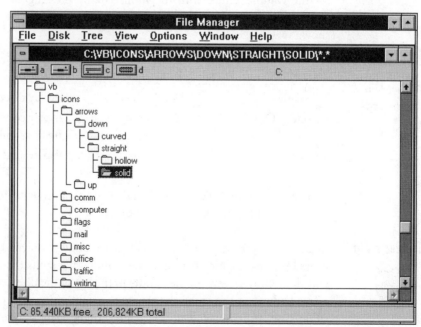

To see nothing but a directory tree, choose Tree Only from the View menu.

FIGURE 3.7
*File List
Display*

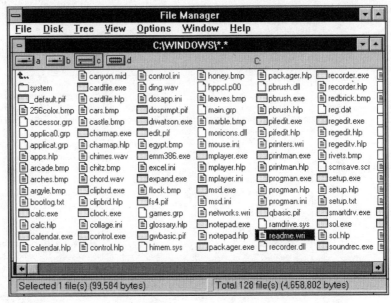

To see a view of the files and directories contained in a given directory, choose Directory Only from the View menu.

To switch between these views, select the appropriate document window for the volume, either with the mouse or by pressing Ctrl+Tab until the window is highlighted. Then choose a command from the View menu, as shown in Table 3.1.

TABLE 3.1
*View Menu
Commands*

View Menu	Keyboard	Action
Tree Only	Alt,V,E	Display directory tree only
Directory Only	Alt,V,O	Display contents of a directory only
Tree and Directory	Alt,V,R	Display split window

The split-window view is the default, because it presents the best overview of how your files and directories are organized.

Insider's Tip

In addition to the keyboard shortcuts listed above, you can obtain different views by using the mouse to grab the handle that splits the windows. For a Directory Only view, grab the handle to the left of the directory window; for a Tree Only view, drag it all the way to the right of the directory window. In either case, you can recreate the split-window view by grabbing the split handle, which is tucked away in the lower left corner of the window.

The title bar at the top of a directory window shows the current directory path, followed by a DOS wildcard representation (for example, *.*) of the file selection criteria. Directory windows in File Manager behave like any other document windows: they can be minimized into an icon (Alt,Minus,N); maximized to occupy the full application window (Alt,Minus,X); restored to their original size (Alt,Minus,R); or closed altogether (Ctrl+F4) (Figure 3.8). File Manager imposes only one restriction: one window must always remain open, even if it is minimized as an icon.

FIGURE 3.8

File Manager with Window Icons

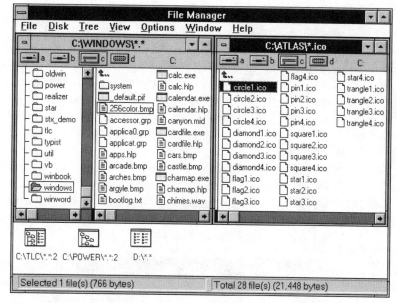

The directory windows in File Manager work like normal document windows. When a window is minimized into an icon, you can see whether the view is Split, Tree, or Directory by the corresponding icon. The drive letter and path of the directory displayed are used as the icon's title.

The top of each directory window contains a row of icons that represent the storage devices, both physical and logical, that are attached to your computer. These are the **volume icons**, identified by a standard DOS drive letter, which appears after the volume icon itself. At the right-hand end of the volume icon bar is the DOS drive letter of the currently selected volume, followed by the label of the volume enclosed by square brackets. The volume label appears only if you have assigned a label to the disk. If you have selected a network drive, the network name is displayed there instead.

File Manager attempts to determine the appropriate volume icon, whether it is a floppy disk, hard disk, CD-ROM, or some other storage device. The following list shows the various volume icons you may encounter:

Floppy disk drive

Hard disk drive or partition

CD-ROM drive

Remote drive connected via a network

RAM drive

You can tell which volume is currently selected because it's highlighted by a small rectangle that surrounds it in the volume icon bar of each directory window (see Figure 3.8). To switch to a different volume, click once on the appropriate volume icon. (A double-click opens an additional directory window.) From the keyboard, press the Tab key to move into the volume icon bar, use the right and left arrow keys to move from icon to icon, and press the spacebar to select the volume. Or, for a shortcut, just press Ctrl+(the letter of the volume you wish to select)—for example, press Ctrl+B to select the B: drive.

To display more volumes than the space on your volume icon bar allows, switch the display of a directory window to a different volume. Either choose the Select Drive command from the Disk menu (Alt,D,S) or double-click anywhere in the volume icon bar—except on a volume icon—to bring up the Select Drive dialog box (Figure 3.9).

FIGURE 3.9
*Select Drive
Dialog Box*

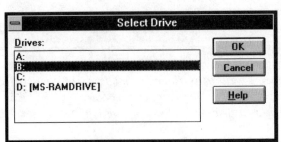

You can use the Select Drive dialog box to choose which volume you want displayed in the directory window.

Danger Zone

Prepare to take a siesta while File Manager conducts a volume search on a CD-ROM or large-capacity hard disk. The extra time is required because as you switch from one volume to another, File Manager searches through the contents of the destination volume so it can create the proper display for the directory window. To halt the search, press Esc. File Manager then displays only part of the directory tree; you'll also be informed of this action in the status bar. Also, if you are switching to a large volume, make sure that Indicate Expandable Branches is not checked on the Tree menu, because this operation further slows down the switch.

. . . .

Opening More Directory Windows

You can open more than one directory window to display the contents of either the current volume or a different volume. It's definitely handy to have two directory windows open at the same time if you are planning to copy or move files from one volume to another. Here are the various methods for opening a new directory window:

➤ Double-click on the volume icon of a directory.

➤ From the keyboard, press Tab to select the volume icon bar, use the cursor arrow keys to select a volume icon, and press Enter.

➤ Choose the New Window command from the Window menu (Alt,W,N); a new directory window opens to display another view of the same directory.

➤ Hold down the Shift key while double-clicking on a file folder icon in a directory tree; from the keyboard, select the file folder icon and press Shift+Enter.

Although several windows can be open simultaneously, only one can be active. Menu selections affect only the active menu. To select an open window, click anywhere in it with the mouse. If a window is buried, you can select it from the list at the bottom of the Window menu (Alt,W,+the number of the window). From the keyboard, cycle through the open directory windows by pressing Ctrl+Tab until the window you want is activated. Like Program Manager, File Manager offers both Cascade (Alt,W,C or Shift+F5) and Tile (Alt,W,T or Shift+F4) options for arranging its document windows.

Insider's Tip

If you choose the Tile command from the Window menu, File Manager tiles the windows horizontally, as shown in Figure 3.10. To see more directories at once, try this undocumented trick for tiling windows vertically, as shown in Figure 3.11: hold down the Shift key while choosing the Tile command from the Window menu. To tile windows horizontally from the keyboard, press Alt,W,T; the keyboard shortcut (Shift+4) tiles them vertically.

FIGURE 3.10
Horizontally Tiled Windows

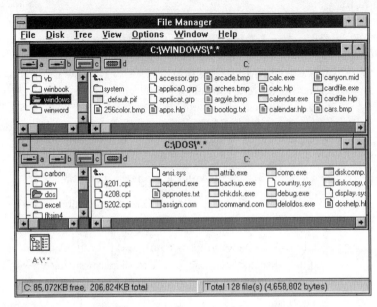

If you choose Tile from the Window menu with the mouse, or use the keyboard combination Alt,W,T, File Manager tiles its open windows horizontally.

FIGURE 3.11
Vertically Tiled Windows

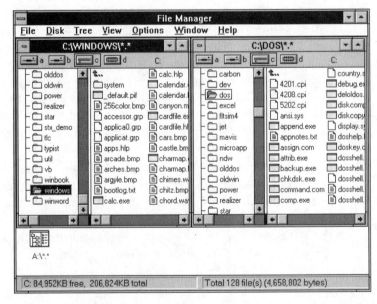

To open windows vertically in File Manager, hold down the Shift key while choosing Tile from the Window menu with the mouse, or use the keyboard shortcut Shift+F4.

· ·

Inside the Directory Windows

In addition to navigating from directory to directory using the tree, you can also wend your way through the directory levels from within a directory window. Double-click on the up icon at the top of the directory window to move up one directory level; or double-click on a file folder icon to delve inside that subdirectory. From the keyboard, press the backspace key to move up one directory level, or select a file folder icon with the cursor keys and press Enter to view the contents of that subdirectory.

Danger Zone

If your media are on the move, the contents of your directory window won't necessarily be accurate. When you change a floppy disk or other type of removable disk, or when you manipulate volumes across a network, be sure to choose Refresh from the Windows menu (F5) to update the information in the window. Refresh closes all but the current branch.

· ·

Splitting Up the Window

By default, the split-window display is divided equally, but you can easily change the space allotment between the directory tree and the contents of the selected folder. Simply move the mouse cursor over the black section below the dividing line that separates the two areas; when the pointer is correctly positioned, it changes shape to signify that a horizontal adjustment can be made (Figure 3.12). Then hold down the mouse button, drag the dividing line (now highlighted) to the desired location, and release the mouse button. (Insider's Mini-tip: If you're viewing a tree-only window, just click on the split handle in the lower left corner of the window to change to a directory-only view.)

· · · · · · · · · · · · · ·
FIGURE 3.12
*Split
Adjustment
Cursor*

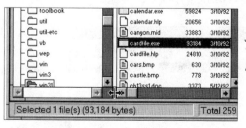

The cursor changes shape as you adjust the location of the split in a directory window.

To change the location of the split from the keyboard:

1. Choose Split from the View menu (Alt,V,L); this causes the dividing line to appear at the current split position.

2. Use the right and left arrow keys to move the dividing line to the desired splitting position.

3. Press Enter to split the window at the new position; or press Esc to revert to the original split.

. . . .

Changing the Font for the Directory Windows

The Font command on the Options menu lets you alter the size of the screen font used in File Manager. For example, because characters on a very high-resolution display can become exceedingly small, you can use the Font option to increase the font size and make them more readable. Or you can use a small font to fit more entries in a directory window.

To make a selection, you can choose any typeface, or style, installed on your Windows system, but your font sizes can only range from 4 to 36 points:

1. Choose Fonts from the Options menu (Alt,O,F), which causes the Font dialog box to appear (Figure 3.13).

2. Select a typeface from the Font list box (Alt+F).

3. Select a Style option (such as Regular, Bold, or Italic) from the Font Style list box (Alt+Y).

4. Specify the Point Size of your selected font in the Size list box (Alt+S).

5. If you want the display to use upper case, remove the X from the Lower Case check box (Alt+L); otherwise, all fonts will be displayed in lower case.

6. The Sample section of the Font dialog box depicts your currently selected font. If you're satisfied, click OK or press Enter.

FIGURE 3.13
Font Dialog Box

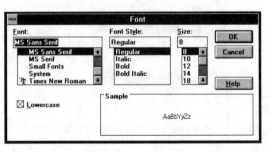

The Font Dialog box lets you choose a font for use in all your directory windows.

If you experiment with font size, you'll notice that anything less than 8 points is illegible, whereas type sizes larger than 18 points would look better on an outdoor billboard. If you want to shrink the font to fit more entries in each window, try using the Small Fonts typeface at 8 points.

Trees and Branches

The **directory tree** represents an expandable schematic outline of all the directories and subdirectories contained in the currently selected volume. The tree starts in the upper left of the window with the root directory of a selected volume. Any directories contained within the root directory branch off below it.

You can select only one directory at a time in the directory tree. You'll recognize the selected directory because it contains an open file folder icon, with its icon and directory name highlighted and surrounded by a dotted rectangle. This dotted rectangle is called the **selection cursor**. You can scroll through the directory tree with a mouse and move the selection cursor to a directory by simply clicking on it. From the keyboard, use any one of the shortcuts shown in Table 3.2 to navigate through the directory tree.

TABLE 3.2
Keyboard Shortcuts for Navigating Through the Directory Tree

Keyboard	Action
Up arrow	Moves selection cursor up one directory
Down arrow	Moves selection cursor down one directory
Right arrow	Moves selection cursor to first subdirectory contained within the current directory
Left arrow or backspace	Moves selection cursor up one directory level
Control+up arrow	Moves selection cursor to the previous directory in the same level if there is one
Control+down arrow	Moves the selection cursor to the next directory in the same level if there is one
Home or backslash	Moves selection cursor to the root directory
End	Moves selection cursor to the last directory in the tree
Page Up	Scrolls directory tree up by one window
Page Down	Scrolls directory tree down by one window
(Any letter)	Selection cursor jumps to the next directory beginning with the letter pressed
Plus sign (+)	Expands the current directory
Minus sign (−)	Collapses the current directory

TABLE 3.2 *(cont.)* *Keyboard Shortcuts for Navigating Through the Directory Tree*	Keyboard	Action
	Tab or F6	Switches between the directory tree, the directory contents window, and the drive icons
	Shift+Enter	Opens a file-list window showing the contents of the selected directory

By default—and to save time—File Manager does not indicate which of the displayed directories are expandable (Figure 3.14).

FIGURE 3.14
Directory Tree Window with Branches Collapsed

In its default mode, File Manager doesn't indicate which directories contain subdirectories.

However, you often need to know where subdirectories are located in order to retrieve a particular file or directory. To indicate which branches are expandable, choose Indicate Expandable Branches from the Tree menu (Alt,T,I). File Manager then places a plus sign inside all the file folder icons that contain other directories and a minus sign in any folders that are expanded to show subdirectories (Figure 3.15).

To speed up File Manager, turn this feature off by choosing Indicate Expandable Branches (Alt,T,I) again.

To expand a directory so that it shows all its subdirectories, highlight a directory tree and double-click on it, or press Enter. You can also select the Expand One Level command from the Tree menu, or press the Plus key.

FIGURE 3.15
*Indicate
Expandable
Branches*

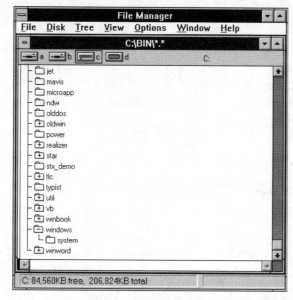

A plus sign inside a file folder identifies any directory that contains one or more subdirectories; a minus sign indicates that the directory is already displaying its subdirectories.

To expand a directory so that it shows all its subdirectories and all the subdirectories within those subdirectories (if any), highlight it and press the Asterisk (*) key, or choose Expand Branch from the Tree menu. Similarly, choosing Expand All from the Tree menu or pressing Ctrl+* expands all the directories and subdirectories in the currently selected volume (Figure 3.16). If you have a large disk, this can take a while.

FIGURE 3.16
*Directory Tree
with All
Branches
Expanded*

Here's how a directory tree looks with all of its branches expanded.

Insider's Tip

Here's an undocumented method for expanding the entire directory tree for a volume: simply hold down the Shift key while clicking on a volume icon.

Once a branch is expanded, the plus sign inside its folder turns into a minus sign. Double-click on the minus sign to collapse it. You can also collapse a branch by choosing Collapse Branch from the Tree menu. To collapse a branch from the keyboard, simply select it and press the minus key.

Creating New Directories

To create a new directory,

1. Select the directory in which you want to place the new directory.

2. Choose Create Directory command from the File menu (Alt,F,E) to bring up the Create Directory dialog box (Figure 3.17).

3. Select the Name box (Alt+N) and enter a valid DOS directory name. You should enter a full path name if you want to situate your new directory somewhere other than in the current directory.

4. Click OK or press Enter.

FIGURE 3.17

Create Directory Dialog Box

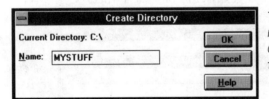

Type a valid directory name in the box and click OK to create a new directory.

Working with Directories and Files

Because directories and files both appear in your directory windows as icons, you can manipulate or search for them using the same techniques. If you use a mouse, you should be familiar with the basic movements described in Table 3.3.

TABLE 3.3	Mouse action	Icon action
Basic Mouse Movements for Manipulating Icons in File Manager	Click	Selects the icon and deselects any icons you previously selected
	Double-click	Opens the icon — for example, starts an application
	Shift+click	Selects a contiguous group of icons. If another icon is selected, this selects the new icon along with all the icons in between, allowing you to select a sequential group of icons
	Ctrl+click	Selects the icon without deselecting any icons you have already selected, allowing you to select a number of nonsequential icons
	Ctrl+Shift+click	Like Shift+click, but selects a contiguous group of icons without deselecting any icons
	Drag	Moves an icon if the destination directory is on the same drive, or copies the icon if the destination is on a different drive
	Ctrl+drag	Forces copying of icons rather than moving
	Alt+drag	Forces moving of icons rather than copying

Selecting Icons

The concept of first selecting an object, then issuing a command or applying another action to it, is fundamental to Windows and most other graphical interfaces. To select an icon in the directory contents list, click on either its icon or its name. Or, from the keyboard,

➤ Use the cursor arrow keys to move the selection bar one item at a time.

➤ Press End to reach the last item in the list.

➤ Press Page Up to return to the first icon in the previous window.

➤ Press Page Down to go to the last icon in the next screen.

➤ Press Home to return to the first item in the list.

➤ Type a letter to jump directly to that place in the alphabetical file list.

To select a group of icons for just a few files, you can use either the mouse or keyboard. For a large group of files, especially if they share a similar file extension, you may find it faster to use either the Select Files command or the Search command, described in the next two sections.

To quickly select all the items in the currently active directory, enter Ctrl+Slash (/). To cancel all the selections in the active window, enter Ctrl+backslash (\).

To select a contiguous group of icons, click on the first icon in the group, hold down the Shift key, and click on the last icon in that group (Figure 3.18).

....

FIGURE 3.18

Selecting Contiguous Files

Press Shift+click to select a group of icons in consecutive order with the mouse.

To select a contiguous group of icons using the keyboard,

1. Use the arrow keys, or one of the selection shortcut keys described in Table 3.3, to highlight your first item.

2. Hold down the Shift key while you press the arrow keys (or other shortcut keys) to move to the last item in your selected group.

To use the mouse to select icons that are not in consecutive order, click on your first selected item, then press and hold down the Ctrl key while you click once on each successive icon. Figure 3.19 shows a window with a number of noncontinguous icons selected.

If you accidentally select the wrong icon, don't panic; just keep holding down the Ctrl key and click on the icon again. This will abort your single selection without deselecting the rest of your icons.

FIGURE 3.19

Selecting Noncontiguous Files

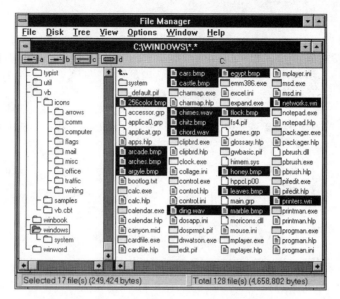

Use Ctrl+click to select icons that are not in consecutive order.

To select a noncontiguous group from the keyboard,

1. Press Shift+F8; this will cause the selection cursor to blink.

2. Use the arrow keys (or other cursor shortcut keys) to move the selection cursor to the next item.

3. Press the spacebar to select the item; to deselect it, press the spacebar again.

4. Repeat steps 2 and 3 until all the items you want have been selected.

5. Press Shift+F8 to finish.

To cancel a selection from the keyboard, press Shift+F8; use the arrow keys to move to an item; then press the spacebar to deselect it. Repeat as necessary, then press Shift+F8 to complete the operation.

The process for selecting groups of groups is similar. With the mouse,

1. Select the first group by clicking on its first item, then hold down the Shift key while clicking on the last item.

2. Hold down Ctrl while clicking on the first item in the next group. Hold down Ctrl+Shift and click on the last item in this group.

3. Repeat step 2 to select additional groups.

From the keyboard,

1. Select the first group by moving the selection cursor to the first item, then hold down the Shift key and move the selection cursor to the last item.

2. Press Shift+F8 to start the blinking selection cursor.

3. Use the arrow or other shortcut keys to move the blinking cursor to the first item in the second group.

4. Press the spacebar.

5. Hold down the Shift key and use the arrow keys to extend the selection to the last item in the second group.

6. Press Shift+F8 to complete the operation.

7. Repeat steps 2 through 6 to select additional groups.

The Select Files Command

New in 3.1

The Select Files command, new in Windows 3.1, presents a powerful method for selecting and deselecting files using the DOS wildcard characters. The Select Files command is often the easiest way to select large groups of similar files. To use this command, choose Select Files from the File menu (Alt,F,S); the Select Files dialog box appears (Figure 3.20).

FIGURE 3.20
Select Files
Dialog Box

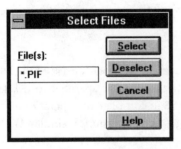

The Select Files dialog box lets you select or deselect files using DOS wildcards.

This box presents the double wildcard *.*, which can be used to select all the files in the active directory. To specify a different criterion, select the File(s) box (Alt+F) and enter any valid DOS wildcard. For example, *.PIF would select all the .PIF files in a directory; and B*.* would select all the files beginning with the letter B. When you've specified the selection criterion, click on the Select button (Alt+S). Repeat this process to enter other selection criteria, then click on the Close button or press Enter to finish the process.

You can also use the Select Files command to deselect a group of files that are specified using a DOS wildcard. To do this, issue the Select Files command, enter a valid selection criterion, and click on the Deselect button (Alt+D). You can repeat the process to deselect other files using DOS wildcards. When you're finished deselecting, click on the Close button or press Enter.

The Search Command

The Search command collects and presents everything that meets your search criterion in a Search Results window. To send out a search party, choose Search from the File menu (Alt,F,H); the Search dialog box appears (Figure 3.21).

FIGURE 3.21

Search Dialog Box

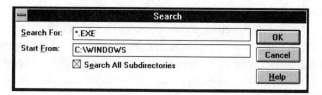

You can look for lost files and directories, or select a group of items that meet a common search criterion, by using the Search dialog box.

To find a specific file or directory, select the Search For box (Alt+S) and enter its full name, including extension. You can use the asterisk and question mark wildcards if you don't know the exact spelling, or if you want to select a group of files in multiple directories that meet the search criterion specified by the wildcards. The Start From box contains the name of the current directory. To start the search in a different directory, select the Start From box (Alt+F) and enter a path name. To search through all the subdirectories located in the branch of the Start From directory, check the Search All Subdirectories check box (Alt+A); otherwise, your search will be limited to files in the Start From directory itself. To search the entire drive or volume, enter the DOS designation for the root directory, for example, c:\. Click OK or press Enter to start the search.

Once Windows has done its detective work, the Search Results window appears, with a list of the files or directories that match your request (Figure 3.22).

FIGURE 3.22

Search Results Window

The Search Results window presents the items that meet your selection criterion.

This window also lists the complete path name of each item it finds, and the status bar of the File Manager window lists the number of items found in the search. If your search yields no match, the File Search Error dialog box appears to let you know that nothing was found.

The Search Results window behaves like a typical directory window. You can move and resize it, minimize it into an icon, and sort, view, and manipulate the items inside it. There is one restrictive difference, though: you can move items from the Search Results window, but you cannot copy or move items into this window.

If you make any changes to a volume that you searched and a Search Results window is open, a dialog box appears to ask if you want to update the window. Choosing Yes performs a new search of the altered volume.

Copying or Moving Icons

File Manager is often used to move icons or to copy them from one directory to another, or to another drive for backing up files.

You can easily copy or move an icon or group of icons, whether they represent files or directories. The original location of the icons—or the **source**—can be a file folder icon in the directory tree or any icon in an open directory window. The target area to which your icons will be moved or copied—the **destination**—can be almost any representation of a directory or volume: an open directory window, a minimized directory window icon, a file folder icon in the directory tree, or a volume icon in the volume icon bar.

As with other Windows operations, you can manipulate icons using either the mouse or the keyboard. From the keyboard, the procedures described next are fairly straightforward: select the icons you want to manipulate and issue the commands directly from the keyboard. However, when you're using a mouse, File Manager applies a different interpretation to your Move and Copy mouse commands. When you drag icons to another directory located inside the same volume, File Manager interprets this as the Move command, so it deletes the original icons after you have released them to their destination. When you drag icons to a directory on a different volume, however, File Manager interprets this as the Copy command, so it leaves the original icons intact on the source volume and transfers copies to the destination directory on the other volume.

Here's how to override these Move and Copy command assumptions. To override the copy assumption, which *copies* your icons as you drag them, hold down the Shift key while dragging the icons to the destination. The original files will now be deleted instead. To override the move assumption, which *deletes* your originals, hold down the Ctrl key while dragging the icons to their destination. The files will now be copied instead.

To move an icon or group of icons using the keyboard,

1. Select the items.

2. Choose the Move command from the File menu (F7). The Move dialog box appears (Figure 3.23).

3. The From box contains the names of any selected items. To move something else, press Alt+F to select the From box, then type the name of the file or directory into the box.

4. Select the To box (Alt+T) and type the name of the destination. When you type a file name in the To box, the selected file or directory is renamed to your new entry.

5. Press the Enter key to complete the operation.

FIGURE 3.23
Move Dialog Box

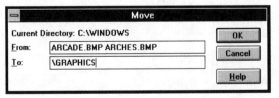

The Move dialog box lets you use the keyboard to move files or directories.

To copy files or directories from the keyboard,

1. Select the items.

2. Choose Copy from the File menu (F8) to bring up the Copy dialog box (Figure 3.24).

3. The names of the selected items appear in the From box (Alt+F). To copy something different, type in the name of a file or directory.

4. Select the To box (Alt+T) and type in the path of the destination directory.

5. Press Enter or click OK.

FIGURE 3.24
*Copy Dialog
Box*

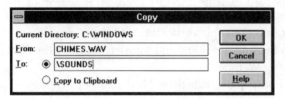

*The Copy dialog box
lets you copy files or
directories from the
keyboard.*

Whenever you copy or move files to another directory, File Manager monitors your actions and presents you with a warning if any of the source files or directories contain the same names as items in the destination directory (Figure 3.25). To suppress the display of these dialog boxes, you can use the Confirmation command described in the next section.

FIGURE 3.25
*Confirm File
Replace
Dialog Box*

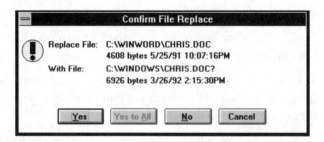

*If you are moving or copying an item into a directory and both have the
same name, Windows presents this dialog box to help protect you from
accidentally replacing the directory.*

New in 3.1

The Confirm File Replace dialog box in Windows 3.1 now provides the path name, file size, and creation date and time for each of the files that shares the same name. This information lets you tell at a glance whether the two files are the same.

When confronted with a confirmation dialog box, you can choose

➤ The Yes button (Alt+Y) to replace the destination item with the original item

➤ The No button (Alt+N) to prevent the replacement of that item

➺ The Yes To All button (Alt+A) if you are copying or moving more than one file and want to replace all the duplicated files without being continually asked for confirmation—but use this option with care

➺ The Cancel button (Esc) to bail from the move or copy without replacing the items

Regulating Confirmation Dialog Boxes

File Manager displays a dialog box whenever you make almost any kind of move. Although dialog boxes often provide critical information, this almost excessive use of these Doubting Thomases is designed to provide novice users an extra layer of protection. Once you feel comfortable with Windows, you can eliminate some levels of confirmation.

To adjust confirmation settings, choose the Confirmation command from the Options menu (Alt,O,C). This calls up the Confirmation dialog box (Figure 3.26).

FIGURE 3.26
Confirmation Dialog Box

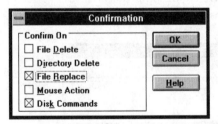

The Confirmation command lets you regulate when you will be interrupted by confirmation dialog boxes.

The Confirmation options dialog box contains five options, which if checked causes Windows to take these actions:

➺ **File Delete** (Alt+D) Warns you twice before it deletes any files.

➺ **Directory Delete** (Alt+I) Displays an additional warning message before it deletes any directories.

➺ **File Replace** (Alt+R) Warns you before it writes over existing files in any move or copy operation.

➺ **Mouse Action** (Alt+M) Warns you every time you're about to make a decisive move with your mouse.

➺ **Disk Commands** (Alt+K) Warns you before it formats or copies any disks or other volumes.

To turn off an option, click in its check box to remove the X, or type the keyboard shortcut just listed.

Insider's Tip

Experienced users should turn off Mouse Action, File Delete, and Directory Delete, but exercise caution when deleting directories. I suggest that you leave File Replace checked because it's all too easy to accidentally replace the newer version of a file with the old one, instead of the other way around. The same applies to the Disk Commands box; it's a drag to try to recover files from an accidentally formatted disk, and if you happen to copy over a disk, its original contents may never be recoverable, even with the help of a utilities recovery program.

Deleting Directories and Files

Here's how to zap an icon or directory that's outlived its usefulness. Select the items you want to delete, then press Del or choose the Delete command from the File menu. The Delete dialog box will always appear, no matter which Confirmation options you have selected (Figure 3.27).

FIGURE 3.27
Delete Dialog Box

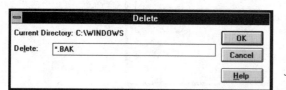

File Manager always checks with you to make sure you didn't just press the Del key by accident.

The Delete dialog box contains the name of your selection. Click OK or press Enter to accept what is listed, or to enter the name of a different directory or file. You can use the DOS wildcard characters * and ? to delete a group of files. Depending on the confirmation level you have set, you may have yet another chance to bail. Usually, however, you are presented with the Confirm File Delete dialog box, depicted in Figure 3.28.

FIGURE 3.28
Confirm File Delete Dialog Box

The Confirm File Delete dialog box gives you a chance to cancel your decision to delete a file.

As the deletion proceeds, File Manager displays its progress in the dialog box. If you chicken out mid-way, press the Cancel button (Esc) to stop the destruction ... if it isn't already too late.

• •

Naming and Renaming Directories and Files

Because Windows uses DOS as its filing system, a file or directory name can only contain eight characters, in addition to an optional file extension of three characters, which is separated from the main name by a period. Although not a strict requirement, both Windows and DOS users have adopted a standard convention for naming files. The first eight characters designate the actual file name, and the extension—that is, the last three characters following the name—denote the file type. For example, the extension .BMP denotes a bitmapped graphics file; the extension .TXT signifies a plain ASCII text file. Although extensions such as .BMP and .TXT are used by convention, certain file extensions—most notably .EXE, .COM, .PIF, and .BAT—should not be used for anything but the specific file types that they represent. This is because Windows will usually attempt to execute any file with one of these extensions; thus, your system might crash if Windows tried to run a nonexecutable data file.

DOS also reserves these other terms for its own use: CON, AUX, COM1, COM2, COM3, COM4, LPT1, LPT2, LPT3, PRN, and NUL. Additionally, a valid name must start with either a letter or a number, and it cannot contain any spaces. However, the name itself can contain other characters except for these symbols:

\ | ? / , < > " ; : [ ] + = .*.

Note that the period can be used only to precede an extension. But feel free to partake of these symbols:

` ~ ! @ # $ % ^ & ( )— _ { } '

The only exception to the DOS name restrictions applies to accessing network servers that support other naming systems. For example, some OS/2-based servers support the use of long file names, which can exceed eight characters, contain spaces, and exhibit other anomalies. If you encounter trouble specifying a long file name on a network server, try enclosing it in quotation marks.

Danger Zone

When renaming a directory, you may also need to update any references to that directory contained in path statements throughout the Windows environment. You may also have to modify your AUTOEXEC.BAT and .INI files and your program item icons.

However, if you want to rename a directory, the process is straightforward. Select its directory icon and choose the Rename command from the File menu (Alt,F,N). This will invoke the Rename dialog box (Figure 3.29).

FIGURE 3.29

Rename Dialog Box

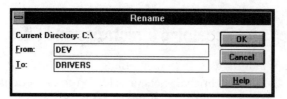

Use the Rename dialog box to change the name of either a directory or a file.

The current name appears in the From box; enter a different name if you want to rename a directory. If the name in the From box is OK, select the To box (Alt+T) and type in the new directory name. When you're satisfied with the new name, click the OK button (or press Enter). Or, you can bail out by clicking Cancel or pressing the Esc key.

The process for renaming a file is similar. Select the file's icon and choose Rename from the File menu (Alt,F,N). Type a valid DOS file name in the To box, then click the OK button to activate the change. To rename a group of files in one fell swoop, use the standard DOS wildcards (* and ?) in both the From and To boxes.

Insider's Tip

Unfortunately, when you rename a file, expect to find a blank To box in the Rename dialog box. Microsoft seems to have lacked the good sense, or courtesy, to ensure that Windows placed the name of the selected file in both the From and To boxes. Most of the time, renaming requires only a slight modification to the existing name. Luckily, there's a good workaround: select the name in the From box and press Control+C, which copies the name; then click in the To box, or press Alt+T, and type Control+V to paste the copied name into the To box. From there, apply standard techniques for editing the name.

If you choose a file name that is already in use—when you're naming or renaming a file or directory—a dialog box appears to ask if you want to replace the existing file.

. . . .

Viewing Files in a Directory Window

File Manager by default displays all the files in the directory by name only and in alphabetical order. However, with the commands on the View menu you can select what files should be shown in the directory window and how they should be viewed. The View commands let you

➥ Select whether the directory window will display the directory tree, the file list, or both

➥ Specify the amount of detail to be included in the file list

➥ Alter the order of the file list

➥ Filter the file list so that only certain types of files are presented

The View menu contains a collection of commands and options for viewing information about files in the directory (Figure 3.30).

FIGURE 3.30
View Menu

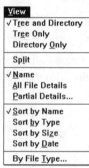

You'll find a variety of commands and options for viewing information about files in the View menu.

Check marks appear in front of the menu options you've selected. The first three items affect how a directory window is displayed: the Tree and Directory option (Alt,V,R), which is the split-window view; Tree Only (Alt,V,E); or Directory Only (Alt,V,O).

Listing the Details. The next trio of commands contains the Name, All File Details, and Partial Details commands. The Name option (Alt,V,N) is the default; it lists the file names in alphabetical order. The All File Details option (Alt,V,A) presents a single alphabetized list of the files, along with a six-column table that lists everything you'd ever want to know about each file: its icon, file name, file size, date and time of the last modification, and file attributes (Figure 3.31).

FIGURE 3.31
*All File
Details Option*

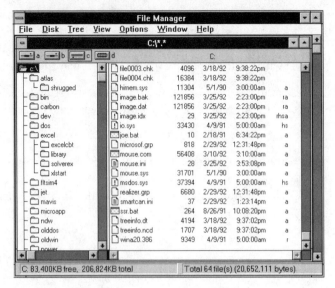

*When the All
File Details
option is
chosen, the
directory win-
dow presents
a complete
list of infor-
mation about
each file.*

The Partial Details option (Alt,V,P) lets you set all the intermediary steps between the Name and the All File Details commands, using the Partial Details dialog box (Figure 3.32).

FIGURE 3.32
*Partial
Details
Dialog Box*

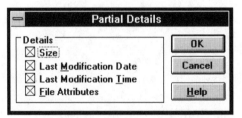

*The Partial Details option
allows you to choose which
pieces of additional file information are shown in a directory window.*

The Partial Details dialog box presents you with four choices:

➤ **Size** (Alt+S) Displays the size of each file in bytes.

➤ **Last Modification Date** (Alt+M) Shows the date the file was last changed according to the calendar in the computer's system clock.

➤ **Last Modification Time** (Alt+T) Shows the time the file was last changed according to the system clock.

➤ **File Attributes** (Alt+F) Shows the attributes—hidden, system, archive, or read-only—that are in effect for each file.

New in 3.1

Ordering the Files. It's often handy to sort the files in a directory window in another order besides alphabetical (the default choice). The file-sorting commands are listed in the View menu, making it easier to issue them and also to check which sorting method is in effect. The View menu contains these sorting options:

➵ **Sort by Name** (Alt,V,S) Lists the files in alphabetical order (the default setting).

➵ **Sort by Type** (Alt,V,B) Sorts the files first by their file name extension, then in alphabetical order by their file name. This is handy if you're working with a directory that contains many files, because it groups similar files together. For example, all the files created with Microsoft Word contain the extension .DOC, and will appear together, alphabetized within that group.

➵ **Sort by Size** (Alt,V,Z) Sorts files from the largest to the smallest. This is most useful when you're moving or copying to a floppy disk with limited space. Knowing the size of the files you want to copy helps you determine whether they'll fit; you can check the cumulative total in File Manager's status bar.

➵ **Sort by Date** (Alt,V,D) Sorts by the date you last modified the file, from the most recent to the earliest date. This setting helps you identify the files you worked on most recently and keeps them in plain sight at the top of the window.

Filtering the Files. The last option on the View menu, By File Type (Alt,V,T), brings up a dialog box that allows you to filter out files from being displayed in the directory window. By default, File Manager displays all of the files and directories in the selected directory except for system files and other hidden files. To indicate that all files will be displayed, the By File Type dialog box initially appears with the DOS double wildcard (*.*) (Figure 3.33).

FIGURE 3.33

*By File Type
Dialog Box*

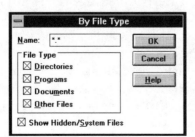

The By File Type dialog box allows you to filter out the files you don't want to view in a directory.

If you want tighter criteria for inclusion, select the Name box (Alt+N) and enter the wildcard specification for a group of files. For example, type *.TXT if you only want to view text files.

The four check boxes that follow the Name box allow you to determine what will be displayed in a directory window:

➤ **Directories** (Alt+D) Displays subdirectories within the selected directory.

➤ **Programs** (Alt+P) Displays files with the extension .EXE, .PIF, .COM, or .BAT.

➤ **Documents** (Alt+M) Displays document files associated with particular applications.

➤ **Other Files** (Alt+O) Displays all nonprogram files not associated with documents.

The Show Hidden/System Files check box (Alt+S) at the bottom of the dialog box lets you display those files for which the System or Hidden file attribute has been set. Windows and DOS do not usually display these files.

Danger Zone

It's fine to display the System or Hidden files, and I usually do. But because they are often crucial to your computer's operation, they are kept out of sight, where you will be less likely to accidentally modify or delete them. The bottom line: it's fine to look at them, but don't mess with them unless you know what you are doing.

File Attributes. File Manager was designed, among other things, to provide easier access to the esoterica of the DOS filing system. In the section above, I covered ways to view the file attributes using the All File Details and Partial Details commands on the View menu. Here's what the file attributes mean and how you can easily change them using File Manager.

A file may contain any, none, or all of four **file attributes** supplied by DOS and identified by the letters A (for Archive), H (for Hidden), R (for Read Only), and S (for System). These file attributes appear in the last column when the All File Details view is displayed in the directory window (see the All File Details View shown in Figure 3.31).

The DOS file attributes (also called **file flags**) are visible only when either the All File Details item is checked on the View menu, or the File Attributes box is checked in the Partial Details dialog box. To alter one or more of these attributes, just select the file that you want to change and choose the Properties command from the File menu (Alt+Enter); or with the mouse, hold down the Alt key and double-click on a file icon. This brings up the Properties dialog box (Figure 3.34).

· · · · · · · · · · · · · ·
FIGURE 3.34
*Properties
Dialog Box*

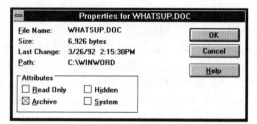

The Properties dialog box displays information about an item and also allows you to change its file attributes.

The top half of the Properties dialog box lists the file name, the size of the file in bytes, the date and time of the last change, and the path where the file is located. Below this information are check boxes for each of the four file attributes, which can be set to do the following:

➤ **Read Only** (Alt+R) Lets you read the information in but prevents the file from being edited or deleted. When applied to network directories, the Read Only privileges usually can't be changed by an individual user.

➤ **Hidden** (Alt+I) Causes the file to be hidden from view in a DOS directory listing.

➤ **System** (Alt+S) Signifies that the file is a DOS system file, preventing it from being displayed in a DOS directory listing. If these files were altered or deleted, your system might not work.

➤ **Archive** (Alt+A) Indicates that a file has been modified since the last time a backup was made. Backup programs use this flag to identify files you've changed since the last backup.

The contents of both the File Name (Alt+F) and Path (Alt+P) items in the Properties dialog box can be selected and copied into the Windows Clipboard by pressing Ctrl+C; however, you cannot change these items in this dialog box. Instead, you must use the Rename command described earlier. If you're connected to a network, the Properties dialog box may contain additional items related to your privileges for accessing or modifying the file.

Insider's Tip

To change the attributes for a group of files, first select the group, then choose Properties from the File menu (Alt+Enter). A check box with an X denotes that all of the files share that particular attribute; if the box is empty, none of the files share that attribute. A gray box indicates that the selected files use different settings for that particular attribute. Check your selections and click OK or press Enter to apply the group attributes.

• •

The Four Different Types of Files

Program Manager isn't the only launching pad for your Windows programs—you can also use File Manager to run a program, either on its own or together with a data file. But first, you need to be familiar with four basic icons. An executable program carries its own special icon, as does a data file that is associated with an application. If a data file has been associated with an application, simply double-click on it and the program runs with that data file already loaded.

Only the program file and document file icons can be used to run a program. Here are the four icons that File Manager uses to classify and visually differentiate the various files in a directory window:

☐notepad.exe	Program files (that is, files that bear the extension .EXE, .COM, .BAT, or .PIF); double-click on this icon to run the program that it represents.
▤ notepad.hlp	A document file associated with a particular application; double-click on this icon to run the application with the document file already loaded.
▢ himem.sys	A generic file not associated with any application; double-click on one of these icons and you'll see a dialog box telling you that no association exists for this file.
▣ msdos.sys	A hidden or system file; you can only see these files if the Show Hidden/System check box is selected in the By File Type dialog box. Don't mess with these files unless you know what you're doing.

Running Program Files. File Manager defines four kinds of program files, as designated by these extensions:

➠ .EXE For most Windows and many DOS programs

➠ .COM Usually DOS programs

➠ .BAT Batch files, often used to start DOS programs

➠ .PIF Keeps track of special settings for DOS programs

To launch a program, whether it's Windows or DOS, from its corresponding program file icon in the directory window, use one of these methods:

➠ Double-click on its icon or file name with the mouse.

➠ Select the icon with the mouse and choose Open from the File menu.

➠ Select an icon using the keyboard and press Enter.

When you run a program that starts in a window, that window appears in front of the File Manager window. If the program starts as a maximized window that requires the full screen, then it replaces the File Manager window. If you want File Manager to shrink down to an application icon whenever you run a program from it, select Minimize On Use from the Options menu (Alt,O,M).

Associations. With just one double-click, you can open a file represented by a document icon along with the application that can edit it, and have Windows load it as well, provided that the file name extension for that document matches, or is associated with, the program that can open it. For example, if you double-click on a document file that ends in .WRI, you open its associated program, Write, and load that document in one step.

The same double-click action won't work on a generic icon, because it lacks an associated application. Instead, the dialog box shown in Figure 3.35 appears.

· · · · · · · · · · · · · · ·
FIGURE 3.35
Cannot Run
Program
Dialog Box

The Cannot Run Program dialog box appears when you try to open a file icon that is not associated with an application.

You can also change associations, or add new ones, by choosing the Associate command from the File Menu. For example, by default .TXT files are associated with the Notepad utility. However, you can change this so that the .TXT files are opened by any wordprocessor you associate it with. To create a new association, follow these steps:

1. Select a data file with the extension that you want to associate with an application.

2. Issue the Associate command (Alt,F,A); this brings up the Associate dialog box (Figure 3.36).

3. The file extension you selected in step 1 is listed in the Files with Extension text box; you can type new data or change old data in this box.

4. Select the desired application for opening the selected data file from the Associate With drop down list box (Alt+A;Tab;down arrow). If it is not listed, either enter the name of the application (include the path) or use the Browse button (Alt+B) to select an application file and place its full path name in the box.

5. Click OK or press Enter.

FIGURE 3.36
Associate
Dialog Box

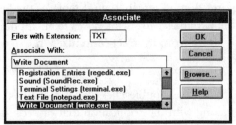

You can use the Associate dialog box to quickly establish an association between a type of data file (denoted by its extension) and an application that can work with that type of file.

When you establish a new association, all the files with that extension will be promoted from generic file icons to document icons.

You can apply the same method to change an existing association. For example, to change the association for .TXT files from the default association with Notepad to Write, select any file with the .TXT extension, issue the Associate command, and then select Write from the Associate With drop-down list box, as just described.

Danger Zone

Remember, under Windows, you can associate a file extension with only one application at a time; otherwise, two applications would compete to open the same file.

What if you install a new Windows graphics program, for example, that associated itself with .BMP files during its installation process? By default, .BMP files are associated with Windows Paintbrush, but the most recent association takes precedence. (Remember, there can be only one associated application per file type.) To change the association of .BMP files back to Paintbrush, use the process just described.

Sometimes you may want to remove an association between an application and a particular file type. This could happen if you have removed the associated application from your system, or if you use two applications for editing that type of file, and you don't want Windows to select one of its own. To remove the association, follow the same procedure as described above except select the "(none)" choice in the Associate With dialog box.

Insider's Tip

You can also match data files to a corresponding application by using the Registration information database (see Chapter 9), which is automatically updated by most Windows applications. The registration information is listed in both the [Extensions] and the [Embedding] sections of WIN.INI, as described in Chapter 15.

Other Ways of Running Programs. In the Windows tradition of providing more than one way to skin a cat, you can also open a file by choosing the Run command from the File menu. Just take these steps:

1. Choose Run from the File menu (Alt,F,R). The Run dialog box appears (Figure 3.37).

2. If a file was selected before you issued the Run command, its name appears in the Command Line box. You can accept this name or type any statement that DOS will accept, such as an application name, one or more document names, and any relevant application switches or other parameters. If you specify both an application and a document, be sure to include their full path names if they're not located in the same directory. To open a document file that is associated with an application in the same directory, simply enter the document file name.

3. To open the application as a minimized icon at the bottom of your screen, rather than in a window, check the Run Minimized check box. This is a handy way to start DOS applications that would otherwise take up the entire screen.

FIGURE 3.37
*Run Dialog
Box*

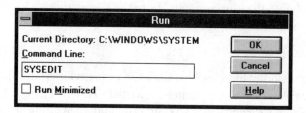

*To summon this box, choose the Run command from the File menu.
Then type in the name of a program, click OK, and you're off and running.*

Insider's Tip

A handy way to open a document file together with an application—even if it's an unassociated application—is to drag the file icon and drop it on top of your targeted application. For example, Windows associates .TXT files with Notepad, but you could drag a .TXT file and drop it onto Write, and edit it with that program as well.

Printing Files and Directory Listings

New in 3.1

File Manager's printing facility has been greatly enhanced with Windows 3.1. You can now print most files using the print facilities of their associated applications.

To print a file directly from File Manager, highlight it and choose Print from the File menu (Alt,F,P). This opens its associated application, and the file prints on the default printer (the one currently selected in the Windows Control Panel).

Danger Zone

Some applications, especially those designed for Windows 3.0, do not support printing through File Manager. You might have to open the application and print the file from within that program, or adjust the settings for that file extension type using the Regedit utility described in Chapter 9.

The drag and drop method also works for printing a file. Drop a file on top of a Print Manager file icon, an open Print Manager window, or Print Manager's minimized application icon. To make the most effective use of this trick, start up Print Manager as a minimized icon at the beginning of your Windows session by including it in the Startup group; then the icon will be easily accessible for printing.

Insider's Tip

File Manager lacks an easy way to print a listing of the directory contents, but here's a trick for printing a simple directory listing. First select a directory; then choose the Run command from the File menu (Alt,F,R). When the Run dialog box emerges, type

```
COMMAND.COM /C DIR > LPT1:
```

into the Command Line box. Click OK or press Enter; the directory listing is sent as plain text to the printer connected to the LPT1 port. This trick works by running a copy of COMMAND.COM and then using it to run the DIR command. The greater-than symbol (>) is a DOS instruction that redirects the output of a command or program that would normally be sent to the display to a specific location, in this case the LPT1 printer port.

Don't be alarmed if your screen suddenly goes black for a moment—that's normal. If nothing prints right away, your printer may require a linefeed at the end of text. If so, first take the printer off line if necessary (this requires pressing the On-Line button on some printers), then press the linefeed button (sometimes labeled "Formfeed") on your printer's front panel. Refer to your printer's documentation to see if there is a way to relieve this problem permanently.

Another variation on this theme is to redirect the output of the DIR command to a text file. For example, to save the contents of the currently selected directory in a file named THISDIR.TXT, you could issue the Run command, then type these directions into the Command Line box:

```
COMMAND.COM /C DIR > THISDIR.TXT
```

This trick lets you open the directory listing in a wordprocessor or other application for formatting, printing, sorting, or any other operation.

Using File Manager for Disk Housekeeping

File Manager handles the important housekeeping chores for keeping your disks and volumes in good order, such as formatting, copying, and creating bootable system disks.

New in 3.1

One major advance is the new Quick Format option, which lets you reformat a disk quickly. Also, File Manager now does a better job of distinguishing the various sizes and formats of floppy disk drives.

For disk maintenance, use these commands on the Disk menu:

➤ **Copy Disk** (Alt,D,C)

➤ **Label Disk** (Alt,D,L)

➤ **Format Disk** (Alt,D,F)

➤ **Make System Disk** (Alt,D,M)

The following sections describe how these commands actually work.

Copy Disk

When you are copying disks, both the source disk and the destination disk must be the same size and format. If you have only one $3\frac{1}{2}$-inch drive and one $5\frac{1}{4}$-inch drive, you'll need to pick one of them as both the source and the destination, then swap disks when Windows prompts you. If the destination disk is not formatted, the Copy command formats it while copying. To copy a disk, follow this procedure:

1. Make sure the disks you want to copy are in the appropriate drives.

2. Choose Copy Disk from the Disk menu (Alt,D,C). The Copy Disk dialog box appears if you have two or more floppy drives (Figure 3.38). If you have only one drive, copying begins immediately, and you can skip the next three steps.

3. Select the drive containing the original (or source) disk from the Source In list box.

4. Select the drive containing the intended duplicate from the Destination In list box.

5. Click OK or press Enter.

FIGURE 3.38
*Copy Disk
Dialog Box*

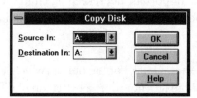

The Copy Disk dialog box appears if you attempt to copy a disk and have two or more floppy drives.

A status box appears asking for one last verification. Click OK, and another status box informs you what percentage of the disk has been copied. Remember, if you copy over an already used disk, all the information on the destination disk will be destroyed.

Label Disk

The Label Disk command allows you to create a volume label for a disk that lacks one, or to change the volume label of an existing disk. In order to label a disk, it must already be formatted. To label a disk, follow these steps:

1. Select the volume icon of a disk (Ctrl+drive letter of the disk).

2. Choose Label Disk from the Disk menu (Alt,D,L). The Label Disk dialog box appears (Figure 3.39).

3. Type the name for your disk into the Label text box.

4. Click OK or press Enter to assign the label to the disk.

FIGURE 3.39
*Label Disk
Dialog Box*

Use this dialog box to name or rename your disks.

You can use any valid, volume label name. By DOS standards, this means the name can contain no more than 11 characters, can include spaces but no tabs, and cannot contain any of the following symbols:

```
*  ?  /  \  !  .  ,  ;  :  +  =  <  >  [  ]  (  )  &  ^
```

Format Disk

Before a new disk can be used, it needs to be formatted. Formatting prepares the disk for use by erasing any information it contains, by marking directory and data areas for information placement, and by blocking off portions made unusable by the manufacturing process or other causes.

To format the disk, follow this procedure:

1. Insert the disk into any available drive.

2. Choose Format Disk from the Disk menu (Alt,D,F). The Format Disk dialog box appears (Figure 3.40).

3. Select the letter of the drive that contains the disk from the Disk In list box (Alt+D).

4. Select the disk capacity in the Capacity list box (Alt+C).

5. Enter any desired options in the Options area. Type a volume label for the disk in the Label box (Alt+L). If you want this to be a system disk, check the Make System Disk check box (Alt+M). For used disks only, you can expedite the formatting process by checking the Quick Format check box (Alt+Q); the Quick Format option merely deletes the file allocation table and root directory of the disk, and doesn't really format the disk or scan for defects.

6. Click OK or press Enter to start formatting.

FIGURE 3.40
*Format Disk
Dialog Box*

Formatting disks with File Manager is a snap. Just select the disk, fill in the specs, and click OK.

A status box keeps you apprised of the formatting progress. When the format is complete, another dialog box will appear asking if you want to format another disk.

Insider's Tip

To format a hard disk, you'll need to exit Windows; then, from DOS, run the FORMAT and FDISK utilities in that order.

Make System Disk

If you've already formatted your disk but forgot to make it a system disk (a disk you can use to boot DOS), here's how to add the system files:

1. Insert a formatted blank disk into a drive.

2. Choose Make System Disk from the Disk menu (Alt,D,M). If your computer has two or more floppy disk drives, the Make System Disk dialog box appears (Figure 3.41). Otherwise, File Manager immediately begins to copy the system files to the floppy drives.

3. Either use the mouse or press Alt+down arrow to reveal the drop-down list of disk drives in the Copy System Files to Disk In box. Then select the letter of the drive that contains a blank formatted floppy disk.

4. Click OK or press Enter to copy the system files to the specified disk.

FIGURE 3.41
Make System Disk Dialog Box

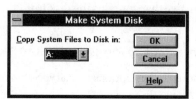

The Make System Disk dialog box allows you to turn a blank, formatted disk into a disk that you can use to boot DOS.

The Make System Disk command merely transfers three files to your disk, one of which—COMMAND.COM—creates the DOS prompt.

Remember that only empty, formatted disks can accept the DOS system files. If you use the Make System Disk command with a disk that is not empty, an alert box appears to prevent you from completing the command.

Insider's Tip

The three files that File Manager transfers to a disk during the Make System Disk process (COMMAND.COM, IO.SYS, and MSDOS.SYS) take up about 100K of disk space—the exact amount depends on what version of DOS you are using. You can free up this space, and use your disk for more data storage, but you won't be able to boot DOS from that floppy disk any more. First make sure that the Show Hidden/System box is checked in the View menu's By File Type dialog box, so that you can view the two hidden .sys files. Then select and delete the three files—COMMAND.COM, IO.SYS, and MSDOS.SYS.

Inserting One File into Another with OLE

Windows programs that feature Object Linking and Embedding capabilities usually allow you to use File Manager to embed one file into another file or to link one file to another. For example, if a .BMP graphics file created with Paintbrush has been embedded into a wordprocessing document created with Write, you can double-click on an icon of the graphic image in Write to launch Paintbrush. When you're finished editing your graphics, close Paintbrush and you're still in Write, with the embedded graphic now modified. (See Chapter 9 for more information.)

With a mouse, the process of embedding is simple. First make sure that the OLE client application is running, and that the document you want to embed is open in a visible File Manager window. Then drag the file icon from File Manager into the open document window of the other application. To link—rather than simply embed—the two files, use the same process, but press Ctrl+Shift while you drag the file icon from File Manager into the other application's document window.

To embed or link files using the keyboard, first use the Copy command to copy a file onto the Windows clipboard. To do this, select a file and choose the Copy command from the File menu (F8). This brings up the Copy dialog box, shown earlier in Figure 3.24. Select the Copy to Clipboard option (Alt+C) and click OK or press Enter. Then open the target document and use the client program's Paste Special or Paste Link command to embed or link the file on the clipboard.

Primary Shell Conversion

It makes more sense to set up File Manager as your primary shell if you plan to run different applications and if data files are situated in a number of directories and storage devices. This lets you start and end your Windows sessions with File Manager instead of Program Manager. To change the primary shell, simply change the SHELL= line in the [boot] section of the SYSTEM.INI file to read SHELL=WINFILE.EXE. (See Chapter 15 for more information on the SYSTEM.INI file.)

You could also keep Program Manager as your primary shell, but set up Windows so that File Manager is loaded automatically at startup. This adds to the initial loading time for Windows, but gives you instant access to File Manager thereafter. This compromise works well when you use File Manager frequently but aren't ready to adopt it exclusively. While in Program Manager, simply place a copy of the File Manager program item icon into the Startup group and select the Minimize on Run option in the icon's Properties dialog box. Then, when you start your Windows session, File Manager appears minimized as an icon at the bottom of your screen.

Insider's Tip   The trick just described also works in reverse. You can specify File Manager as your primary shell in the SYSTEM.INI file as just outlined, then change the LOAD= statement in WIN.INI to read LOAD=PROGMAN.EXE; this loads Program Manager as an icon upon startup. In the same way, you can specify any other programs for automatic loading upon startup.

Network Concerns

New in 3.1   In a major improvement, File Manager now remembers the network connections that were established during your last session and tries to reconstruct your former network volumes, so that you no longer have to reconnect your network drives each time you start up Windows.

If your system is connected to a network, you can work with almost any of the volumes on the network if you know its exact path and whatever password is required to access it. Also, be sure that the network software is loaded before you start Windows. (This is usually done automatically.) Depending on your network, you should look at the Network section of the Control Panel to determine how certain settings can affect your connection.

You'll need to use special procedures, described next, for handling network volumes with File Manager. However, because network drivers vary widely, you may not always see the dialog boxes exactly as they appear in this section. These examples are presented to give you a general feel for using File Manager to work with networks.

Before you can select a network volume for use with File Manager, the volume must be connected to Windows. If you don't see a volume icon for the network drive you are seeking, follow these steps:

1. Choose Network Connections from the Disk menu (Alt,D,N) to summon the Network Drive Connections dialog box (Figure 3.42).

2. The next available volume letter appears in the Data Drives list box (Alt+D). Accept the default choice, choose a drive letter from this list, or type the drive letter you want to assign to the volume into the box.

3. In the Path box (Alt+N), type the network path name that specifies the network volume you want to access. With some networks, a Browse button is available to help you select a path.

4. If a password is necessary to access that volume, type it in the Password box.

5. Some networks provide a Connect button that you need to press to attach the drive to your system. If you only want to make a temporary connection to this network volume, hold down the Shift key while clicking on the Connect button.

6. Click Close, or press Enter.

• • • • • • • • • • • • • •
FIGURE 3.42
*Network
Drive
Connections
Dialog Box*

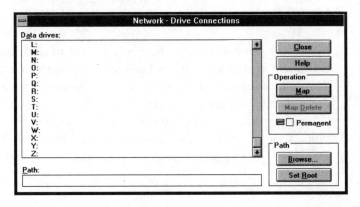

The Network Drive Connections dialog box lets you access servers and other network volumes across a network.

To connect to additional network volumes, repeat steps 2 through 5 until all your connections have been made.

File Manager keeps track of the network drives that you access in order to make it easier for you to log onto them next time. To connect to a network volume at a later date, select Network Connections. When the dialog box appears, click on the Previous button (Alt+P). This brings up the Browse Connections dialog box (sometimes called the Previous Network Connections dialog box), which allows you to choose a network path drawn from a list of previous connections (Figure 3.43).

• • • • • • • • • • • • • •
FIGURE 3.43
*Browse
Connections
Dialog Box*

Browse Connections

	OK
Servers/Volumes:	Directories:
PCW_1/PCW_MAC1:	Cancel
PCW_1/SYS:	
PCW_1/VOL1:	
PCW_2/SYS:	Help
PCW_2/VOL1:	
PCW_3/DB1:	
PCW_3/MAIL:	Attach...
PCW_3/SYS:	
PCW_4/PCW_ART1:	Detach...
PCW_4/SYS:	

*The Browse Connections dialog box lets you select a connection from
the past.*

To disconnect from a network drive, choose Network Connections from
the Disk menu (Alt,D,N). This brings up the familiar Network Drive Connections dialog box (see Figure 3.42). Then select a network volume from the
list in the Data Drives dialog box. When it's highlighted, click the Disconnect
button and then on the Close button.

Insider's Tip

In 386 enhanced mode, you may not be able to disconnect from those
network drives that were attached before you started your Windows session.
You'll have to quit your Windows session, disconnect from your network
drives at the DOS prompt, and then restart Windows.

Some network volumes that run under non-DOS operating systems can
support the use of long file names, which can contain several words and
spaces, but you may need to enclose names that contain spaces in quotation
marks.

Danger Zone

If you are connected to a network volume that supports the use of long file
names, you can view these names in a File Manager directory window, and
move or copy these files to another volume or directory on the network that
supports long file names. If you try to move them to a directory that doesn't
accept long file names, File Manager presents a dialog box that suggests a
shorter name. Also, under most circumstances, you can only copy or move
these files; you can't open them with a double-click, or drag and drop them.

Organizing Your Drives and Directories

When setting up your directory structure, first do some organizing. Start by
clearing out all unnecessary files from your root directory. The root directory
should contain other directories—it should not be a repository for files.

Leave only those files necessary for system startup, such as COMMAND.COM, IO.SYS, MSDOS.SYS, AUTOEXEC.BAT, and CONFIG.SYS. If your DOS program hasn't already done so, you should also collect all DOS files and place them in a separate DOS directory. (Be sure to update your PATH statement in AUTOEXEC.BAT to include the new DOS directory.)

Place every application in a directory of its own, rather than inside the Windows directory. Otherwise, you might have to disentangle applications from the main Windows directory (by default named \WINDOWS) when you install more than one version of Windows, such as a normal and a multimedia version, or 3.1 and 3.0. Many applications create their own directory as a default, and most let you alter the default choices in case the application normally installs into the \WINDOWS directory. Remember, if you do move an application into a new directory, you may have to change any path names that refer to that application and/or place the new directory in the PATH statement of your AUTOEXEC.BAT file.

Attention, multimedia users: here's a real headache-saver for keeping track of which drivers go with which applications. Create a \DRIVERS subdirectory within the directory of any application that uses special drivers. If the install program copies drivers for the application into the \WINDOWS directory or into the \WINDOWS\SYSTEM directory, then you should copy the drivers to the applications directory as well, just in case some other application's installation program overwrites a critical driver.

There is no hard and fast method for organizing your files into directories and subdirectories. Decide on a scheme based on whatever is most intuitive to you. One common system is to create directories for major categories, such as applications, data, utilities, and games. Although you have great flexibility in how to organize things, and in how many branching subdirectory levels you can have, DOS imposes a few limitations on Windows.

The number of files or directories that you can place within the root directory is limited, and depends on the type of disk:

➡ 360K $5\frac{1}{4}$-inch or 720K $3\frac{1}{2}$-inch disk: 112 files.

➡ 1.2MB $5\frac{1}{4}$-inch or 1.44MB $3\frac{1}{2}$-inch disks: 224 files.

➡ Most hard disk drives (depending on what type of DOS or other utilities you are using): 512 files.

You can create subdirectories within the root directory, and subdirectories within those subdirectories, to design a complex branching directory tree that includes many nested subdirectories. The only restriction is that DOS can only allocate 63 characters to the full path name of a directory, so you shouldn't place a subdirectory inside the directory named

`C:\ACAD\PROJECT9\NEWONES\NORTHCAL\BERKELEY\HOUSES\4BEDRM\NEWPLANS`

which provides eight levels of nested subdirectories.

However, if your directory names were shorter, you could create more nested layers. In fact, in the days of DOS, the experienced user kept directory names as short as possible to save work when typing path names. With Windows, it makes more sense to make directory names as descriptive as possible, because you rarely need to enter a path name by hand, and descriptive names provide more information as you browse through the directory tree.

Insider's Tip

For a major reorganization of files and directories, arrange your File Manager windows so that you can easily inspect the contents of two directories and their specifics, such as the file size and creation date, on a standard 640x480 VGA display. Here's how:

1. Maximize File Manager to fill the screen.

2. Open a second File Manager window by double-clicking on the Volume icon for a particular drive.

3. Hold down the Shift key and choose the Tile command from the Window menu to tile the windows vertically.

4. Choose All File Details from the View menu.

5. Set the second window to a Directory Only view.

6. Adjust the size of the windows so the screen appears similar to the one in Figure 3.44.

FIGURE 3.44

*File Manager
Setup for
Housekeeping*

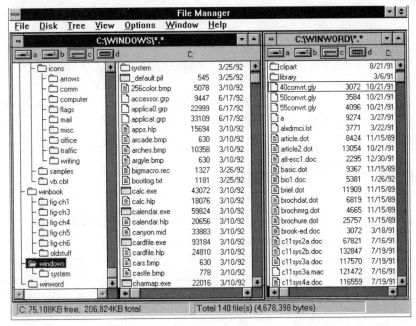

This arrangement of two File Manager windows provides one split window showing the directory tree and directory and another window with only the directory, so that you can view the file name, file size, and creation date for both directories.

If your eyesight is good, you can reduce the size of the window by using the Small Fonts typeface at 8 points. To change fonts, choose Fonts from the Options menu, as described in "Changing the Font for the Directory Windows," earlier in this chapter.

Summary

File Manager is a more comprehensive shell than Program Manager and parallels the actual organization of programs and data on the storage devices within your computer system. File Manager provides most DOS functions from the comfort of a graphical interface.

Other graphical user interfaces, such as the Macintosh, integrate program and file management into a single facility. For this reason, it's odd that Microsoft chose to divide the operation of Windows into two halves. In my more cynical moments, I wonder if this bifurcation of the interface was created by Microsoft's legal department to avoid possible infringement on

Apple's Macintosh copyrights, rather than by the company's interface designers.

Someday, perhaps, Microsoft will combine the right and left brain hemispheres of Windows—Program Manager and File Manager—into one integrated personality. But in the meantime, third-party developers are taking their own approaches by providing alternate shell environments for Windows, some of which are described in Chapter 6.

Insider's Tech Support

Q: File Manager doesn't remember my previous setup.

A: File Manager can lose track of your setup if it can't find the drives you logged onto during your last session. This can happen if you're not logged onto a network drive that was previously available, or if you had an open window for a floppy disk drive and the drive is now empty. Less frequently, this can be caused by a damaged or missing WINFILE.INI file, which is where File Manager keeps track of its previous settings.

Q: When I drag a file and drop it on the Print Manager, it doesn't print.

A: In order for drag and drop to work with the Print Manager, the data file's extension must be associated with an application, and that application must support the Windows 3.1 drag-and-drop capabilities.

Q: When I drag an icon and drop it into another application to use OLE, it doesn't work.

A: For drag and drop to run with OLE, the application must support the new version of OLE found in Windows 3.1.

Q: How do I retrieve a file that I accidentally deleted?

A: If you're using DOS 5 or later, you can quit to DOS and use the Undelete command. If you're using an earlier version of DOS, you can use a utility, such as Norton Utilities or PC Tools. Undelete programs provide only a loose safety net, however, and sometimes it's impossible to recover a file.

Q: How can I create several different File Manager configurations?

A: One method is to use the macro Recorder utility to reconfigure your File Manager and then run the appropriate macro to obtain the desired configuration. Or you can configure File Manager the way you want it, and then make a copy of the WINFILE.INI file using a different name. Repeat this process for as many different configurations as you need, and save each under a different name. Before starting Windows, copy the desired configuration and rename it WINFILE.INI.

Q: I have a command on my File Manager menu that isn't mentioned in this book or in the Windows documentation.

A: File Manager allows additional commands to be added to its menus through the use of dynamic link libraries (DLLs). To check what commands have been added to your File Manager menus, open the WINFILE.INI file and you will see these additions in the [AddOns] section of the file.

4

Controlling the Environment with Setup and Control Panel

Windows provides an ingenious way for allowing all your applications to take advantage of your computer's hardware: it basically translates the controls necessary to operate specific hardware devices into a standard Windows dialect, known as a device driver.

In this way, all PC-compatibles and hardware accessories appear similar to Windows and to your Windows applications as well. This feature marks a major improvement over DOS-only systems.

But it's not entirely that simple. In order to optimize your system's performance, you'll need to (1) install the proper drivers and (2) configure the options related to your drivers, such as choosing a screen resolution or setting up a printer. To perform these operations, you'll need to use **Windows Setup** and the **Control Panel**, which together provide the principal tools for installing and managing your hardware drivers and for customizing your Windows environment. Both these programs work by modifying your Windows initialization files, which instruct Windows in how to work with your hardware.

Windows
Setup

· · · · · · · · · · · · · ·
FIGURE 4.1
*Windows
Setup Icon*

Windows Setup installs and lets you change the various device drivers on your system. When you install Windows and run Setup from the DOS prompt, a special file called SETUP.INF walks your system through this carefully choreographed routine, which takes these actions:

➤ Determines what hardware is in your system

➤ Analyzes how your hardware is configured

➤ Decides what device drivers are necessary to run Windows

➤ Decompresses and copies the device drivers and Windows system files that it thinks you need onto your computer's hard disk

➤ Creates and modifies the Windows initialization files: SYSTEM.INI and WIN.INI

➤ Modifies the DOS startup files, CONFIG.SYS and AUTOEXEC.BAT

➤ Creates your initial Program Manager groups and icons

You can run Setup after installation to change hardware drivers. Setup copies any device driver files it needs either from the original Windows installation disks or from third-party driver disks into your \SYSTEM subdirectory (which should be located in your main Windows directory) and records the drivers that it installs in the SYSTEM.INI file. Most changes you make with Setup don't take effect until you restart Windows. You can also run Setup after installation to create program item icons and to remove or add components to your Windows environment, such as accessories and wallpaper patterns.

A new **Express Setup** feature gets most systems up and running with a minimum of time and effort. For those who want more control over the installation process, 3.1 includes a **Custom Setup** option and the ability to create automated installation procedures using a new setup template file called SETUP.SHH, which complements the SETUP.INF file.

Control Panel

FIGURE 4.2

Control Panel Icon

The Control Panel provides graphical controls for managing and customizing your Windows environment. With the Control Panel, you can do such things as

➣ Configure printers and fonts

➣ Configure virtual memory and set up a permanent swap file

➣ Adjust the responsiveness of the mouse and the keyboard

➣ Set the speed of your computer's communications ports

➣ Create a password to protect your system

➣ Create new color schemes for your Windows desktop

➣ Install and configure multimedia device drivers

The Control Panel almost always contains these controls: **Color, Fonts, Ports, Mouse, Desktop, Printers, International, Keyboard, Date/Time, Drivers, Sound,** and (for a 386 or higher processor) **386 Enhanced**. The Control Panel is expandable, and can also include controls for networks, MIDI, multimedia devices, pen-based computers, and whatever other applications have installed their own Control Panel modules. The Control Panel also includes a screen saver with password protection, and a status line that provides information about the various controls. Unlike changes you make using Setup, most Control Panel changes take effect as soon as you save them.

Windows Setup

It's got a bifold destiny: the Windows Setup program can be used for both installation and post-installation activities. In the latter capacity, you can use Setup to add program items to Program Manager or to change hardware device drivers for your display, mouse, keyboard, and network. Setup runs in two different modes: DOS mode and Windows mode. The first time you run Setup—to install Windows—it runs in DOS mode. Suddenly, halfway through the installation procedure, it metamorphoses into a graphical environment and thereafter runs in Windows mode. After installation, Setup can be run in either DOS or Windows mode; however, in most cases you'll want to run it in its graphical incarnation, from within Windows. In certain situations, described later, you'll be forced to quit Windows and run Setup in DOS mode from the command prompt.

Here's how to use Setup for installing Windows on your system. First, I'd advise you to turn off any DOS TSRs or other memory-resident software, because they are common sources of installation problems. Also, log off from your network—unless, of course, you're installing Windows from a network server (see Chapter 10). Then make a backup of your AUTOEXEC.BAT and CONFIG.SYS files. Although Setup usually backs up these files automatically, if your installation process is tricky, it may be difficult to sort among all the various backups of these two critical system files. Because both DOS and Windows rely on these files, you should also create a bootable floppy disk (format a disk and use the Make System Disk option in File Manager) and copy your backup of AUTOEXEC.BAT and CONFIG.SYS to the floppy disk, so that you can always reboot your system.

You'll also need to know some details about your hardware before you install Windows. At a minimum, you should know the name of your printer and what port (LPT1:, COM1:, a network port, and so forth) it is using. Here's what you need to be able to identify:

➤ The **display system** (such as EGA, VGA, or XGA) you have installed and its available graphics resolution modes (usually related to how much video memory is on the display card—see Chapter 8)

➤ The kind of **mouse** or other pointing device you are using, if any

➤ The details about your **network**, if any, and the network names of any servers, printers, or other devices you want to use

➤ Any other **hardware idiosyncrasies** of your system, such as special keyboards, storage products, or data compression boards (for example, Stacker)

➤ Any special memory management programs or other **system-wide utilities** (for example, QEMM or 386MAX) you want to use with Windows

➤ The **brand** (for example, Microsoft, IBM, or Digital Research) and **version number** of **DOS** you are using

Insider's Tip

You can investigate your system configuration by using the MSD.EXE utility described in Chapter 17. MSD.EXE—commonly called the Microsoft Diagnostics—uses the same techniques as Setup to probe the internals of your system, but it does so in much greater detail. This utility runs from DOS, so you can run it before installing Windows.

Setup will be a breeze if you have a plain vanilla PC—that is, a single, standalone PC, preferably a solid 386 or better clone with a few megabytes of RAM, a standard VGA display, a Microsoft-compatible mouse, and an HP Laserjet-compatible printer. Otherwise, you may encounter some rough sledding during installation, particularly if you're using anything out of the ordinary in the line of displays, printers, networks, input devices, or memory managers.

Although Microsoft provides an admirable number of third-party drivers on the standard Windows installation disks, the enormous universe of so-called "IBM PC compatibles" includes much third-party hardware that will not work properly, if at all, with the default drivers supplied on the Windows installation disks. Microsoft also issues periodic updates to its Windows Driver Library, an ongoing collection of Windows device drivers for third-party hardware that did not make it onto the standard Windows 3.1 installation disks. Otherwise, you may have to get the driver from the manufacturer, or download it from a bulletin board, before you can successfully install Windows.

Upgrading from 3.0 to 3.1

Upgrading to 3.1 from 3.0 turns out to be harder than installing 3.1 from scratch. Although Setup is fairly smart about upgrading—it preserves your Program Manager groups and many other settings, for example—potential conflicts between device drivers used in the two versions, compounded by other incompatibility woes, can make upgrading painful. Systems attached to networks and those with multimedia extensions create the worst compatibility problems.

Usually, I recommend installing 3.1 over 3.0; that way, you avoid potential system conflicts that can arise from having two versions of a program running on your computer simultaneously. However, if you have an application that can only run in a 3.0 environment, you're better off installing separate versions. But note that if you do install a separate version of 3.1, it will not save any Program Manager icons or other custom settings from your 3.0 environment. To preserve these settings, copy your entire Windows directory, with all of its contents (except for applications), to a new directory with a different name (for example, \WIN31), as opposed to the default \WINDOWS. Then you can install Windows 3.1 over the duplicate directory and create a version that preserves your original configuration.

Danger Zone

If you do install 3.1 in a separate directory and retain your version of Windows 3.0, you'll have to carefully juggle the PATH statement in your AUTOEXEC.BAT file. Only one of the directories, for example \WIN31 or \WINDOWS, should be specified in the PATH statement at a time. Otherwise, the software may become confused and try to run components from both versions at once, possibly leading to corruption of your data or to a system crash. One solution is to set the PATH statement temporarily using the TEMP statement in a batch file to start the version of Windows you want to run.

If you do decide to install 3.1 over 3.0, here's what will happen. Setup will strive to preserve your Program Manager groups and their icons, as well as the current hardware configuration settings for your computer, monitor, mouse, keyboard, and network. If Setup detects a standard device driver from Windows 3.0, it replaces it with an updated 3.1 version, if available. Setup checks the dates of all the files in your existing installation and will not replace a file whose creation date is more recent than the ones on the installation disks. (In the initial release of Windows 3.1, all the files were dated 3/10/92 at 3:10 AM—a 3.1 insider's joke?)

Setup will not replace a third-party device driver that runs on 3.0, regardless of its file date. Sometimes you'll want to override this default action to enhance performance. For example, Windows 3.1 now includes a SuperVGA driver, which may provide better performance than the third-party 3.0 driver that remains in your system. To replace this driver with the new 3.1 version, run Setup from within Windows after installation. (Insider's Mini-tip: If you have problems with terminal programs after upgrading to 3.1, you may need to replace the third-party comm driver with the Windows 3.1 comm driver, COMM.DRV. Multimedia drivers can also create problems and often need to be replaced.)

Danger Zone

The Windows 3.1 Setup program is also careful when editing your AUTOEXEC.BAT and CONFIG.SYS files. Normally it preserves the LOADHIGH= statement in AUTOEXEC.BAT and the DEVICEHIGH= statement in CONFIG.SYS. So as not to disturb the order for loading device drivers and other memory-resident software into your computer's upper memory—which is critical to your system's performance—check to see that Setup did not accidentally alter this loading sequence.

• •

Preparing for Installation

Next you need to decide if you want to use **Express Setup** or **Custom Setup**. Express Setup provides a quick and dirty approach; if you're unsure about which method to choose, and this method works for you, skip the rest of this section and head for the Control Panel. With Express, the Setup program attempts to sniff out your hardware and software configuration on its own; takes a quick peek to see if you have enough hard disk space and suggests ways to trim the size of the Windows installation if there's not enough room; and then proceeds to install Windows according to its best guesses, only pausing to ask you for a few details, such as your name and the name of your printer. In Express Setup, Windows is installed in a directory called WINDOWS, unless you already have a directory with that name; in that case, Setup asks you to supply a different name.

The other option, Custom Setup, lets you monitor the setup process. You can regulate these operations:

- Choose and name the directory for installing the Windows files.
- Inspect and verify the specific details of your hardware configuration, such as the monitor, mouse, keyboard, network, and printer.
- Select which Windows components are loaded onto your hard disk, thus allowing you to keep your installation lean and mean if you're low on space.
- Monitor the changes that Setup makes to your CONFIG.SYS and AUTOEXEC.BAT files, which is always a good idea if your files contain special settings.
- Create program item icons for applications on your hard disk during the installation process.
- Adjust your virtual memory settings, which Windows uses when it is running in 386 enhanced mode. If you specify a permanent swap file, a new feature called FastDisk bypasses DOS to allow Windows to directly control many popular hard-disk controller cards. This alone can dramatically improve your system's performance.

To gain further control over Setup's behavior, you can start it in combination with the option switches shown in Table 4.1.

Insider's Tip

Set yourself up! You can create custom Setup scripts by editing the SETUP.SHH and SETUP.INF files, as described in Chapter 16. Custom installation scripts are useful for large sites, VARs, OEMs, consultants, and other users who want to adapt Setup to accommodate specific hardware installations and software configurations.

TABLE 4.1
*Starting
Setup in
Combination
with Option
Switches*

Switch	Description
/A	Starts Setup in Administrative mode. This mode expands and copies all the files on the installation disks to a network server and sets the Read-Only attribute for all of these files (see Chapter 10).
/B	Instructs Setup to install Windows for a system with a monochrome display.
/C	Prevents Setup from searching for TSRs before installation.
/I	Forces Setup to ignore automatic detection of your hardware configuration.
/N	Tells Setup to install a shared copy of Windows onto your system from a network server (see Chapter 10).
/T	Forces Setup to search the drive for software that may be incompatible with either Setup or Windows.
/H :*<filename>*	Runs Setup in batch mode to install Windows using an automated settings file (see Chapter 16).
/O:*<pathname>*	Lets you specify the path where the SETUP.INF file is located.
/S:*<pathname>*	Lets you specify the path for both SETUP.INF and the Windows installation disks.
/P	Rebuilds the original Program Manager groups.

Running Setup

To install Windows for the first time, insert installation disk 1 into any available floppy disk drive, log onto that drive, and type **SETUP**. Setup first checks what type of processor and how much memory you have. If it doesn't find at least 386K of conventional memory available, Setup stops running, and you'll have to free more memory before beginning installation again. Setup then investigates the SETUP.INF file to determine whether it has been corrupted, and also queries DOS to ensure that you are running version 3.1 or higher. If there is a problem with either situation, a dialog box appears asking you to correct the problem.

Setup next checks your current DOS path for any existing versions of Windows. If this search yields nothing, Setup starts looking through all of the hard disks attached to your system (but not network drives). If Setup finds Windows 3.1 already installed on the system, it changes into its maintenance mode, which lets you change system drivers—this is what normally happens when you run Windows from the DOS prompt after installation. If Setup finds an older version of Windows, such as 3.0, or no Windows at all, it issues the initial Welcome to Setup screen. This screen provides you with three choices:

➤ **Press F1** Brings up initial help for Setup

➤ **Press Enter** Initiates the installation process

➤ **Press F3** Quits Setup without installing Windows

Press Enter, and then Setup inspects the software that is currently running in your system to make sure you aren't running something incompatible with Setup or Windows. If you are, Setup warns you and provides another opportunity to quit so that you can disable these programs or utilities. If all is well, you can proceed to the second installation screen, which lets you choose either Express or Custom Setup. To choose Express Setup, press Enter. Setup installs Windows, pausing only to ask you for your name and the name of your printer. Pressing C initiates Custom Setup, which is the method described in the rest of this section.

If you chose Custom Setup, the next screen displays the directory in which Setup proposes to install Windows. If you are upgrading, your current Windows directory is displayed; otherwise, Setup proposes installing Windows on Drive C: in the subdirectory named \WINDOWS. If you wish to override this, enter a different drive and/or directory (Figure 4.3).

Setup next checks to see if the volume you specified contains enough disk space to install Windows. If there's *Lebensraum,* installation proceeds; if there isn't enough space, Setup warns you and suggests some items that can be sacrificed, such as wallpaper and Readme files. If there still isn't room for Windows, the program then asks you to choose a different hard disk drive (or partition). If this is your only drive, you'll have to quit Setup (by pressing F3) and remove some files from your hard disk. If you're setting up Windows from scratch, Windows files consume about 8 to 10 megabytes (the amount can vary, depending on what options you select). And even if you're upgrading, installation can still gobble up as much as 5 more megabytes. Keep in mind that these are bare minimum requirements and don't provide for swap files or special options, such as additional printer fonts, network drivers, or multimedia extensions. A more reasonable minimum is 20 megabytes— more if you're installing lots of applications, fonts, or other items.

FIGURE 4.3
Windows Setup Install Screen

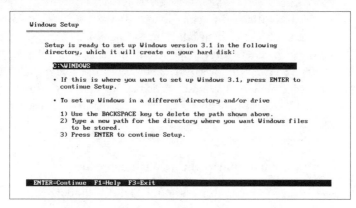

The default drive and directory for Windows is C:\WINDOWS, but you can name it anything you like.

If there is room for installation, Setup creates your designated directory. If you're upgrading, Setup merely adds the Windows environment files to the existing directory. In some cases, Setup may modify some system files already in place.

Soft Guessing Your Hardware

Before adding any files to the directory you've specified, Windows Setup first inspects and then estimates the specifics of your hardware/software configuration. You'll have a chance to verify the estimates presented by the screen, as shown in Figure 4.4.

FIGURE 4.4
Windows Setup Main Hardware Configuration Screen

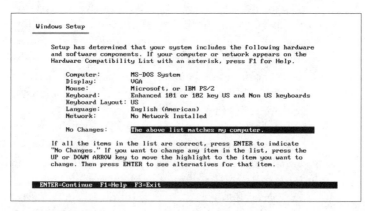

Custom Setup estimates what components are in your computer system and displays an appropriate configuration screen for your approval.

Inspect the list carefully to make sure that the Setup utility correctly guessed your system components. An asterisk after a component indicates an uncertain guess—you'll probably need a special third-party driver for that component. If necessary, manually change any of the items that were incorrectly assumed. When everything looks right, press Enter to proceed. Use this same procedure for selecting or changing any of the Setup options described later.

Danger Zone

In rare cases, your system can bounce you back to the DOS prompt or even stall your system at this point in the process. This can occur because Windows Setup polls your system (to analyze your hardware configuration) by issuing a barrage of specific, low-level signals to your system—processor, memory, ports, and peripherals. All this probing can cause a system crash. If Setup does not make it to the main configuration screen, try this trick: Run Setup from the DOS command prompt by typing

```
setup /i
```

Using the /i switch prevents Setup from attempting any hardware detection, thereby avoiding the polling signals that can potentially stall some systems. In response to your command, Setup displays a default list of hardware options without guessing at your components. You must then manually adjust each setting before proceeding, so you should have all the names of your hardware components and any third-party device drivers you need on hand.

The Eight Hardware Heavies

Windows requires a specific device driver for each component of your system: **Computer, Display, Mouse, Keyboard, Keyboard Layout, Language, Code Page,** and **Network**. You'll need to define each of these items so that Windows can use one of its own device drivers; a driver from the Microsoft Windows Driver Library; or one from a third-party manufacturer.

Although several device drivers may work with a particular device, using exactly the right one can dramatically enhance the features and performance of Windows. For example, a SuperVGA card can display more colors—or a higher resolution—than the standard VGA adapter. The standard VGA driver allows you to use that card in 640x480 resolution with 16 colors, but a custom driver enables your system to achieve the full capabilities of your SuperVGA card.

You can tell Windows Setup that two of the categories—Mouse and Network—are not attached to devices, but you still need entries for these categories, if only to indicate that no device is attached.

To change the device driver, use the arrow keys to highlight the item, then press Enter to see a list of alternative devices (Figure 4.5). Use the arrow keys to navigate through the list of alternative drivers and highlight another one. To designate a third-party driver, select Other at the end of the list.

Setup prompts you for the drive and path of the driver file; the default location is the root directory on Drive A:. When you're finished specifying all the drivers, press Enter to return to Setup's system configuration screen. You can specify and change all eight kinds of drivers by following this same procedure.

Computer. The first item in your Windows Setup screen lets you specify your main hardware asset: your computer. The standard choice is "MS-DOS System." If you're unsure which computer driver to use, start with the "MS-DOS System" selection. Windows provides setup configurations for these IBM-compatible computers:

MS-DOS System

AST Premium 386/25 and 386/33 (CUPID)

AT&T PC

Everex Step 386/25 (or compatible)

Hewlett-Packard: all machines

IBM PS/2 Model P70

IBM PS/2 Model L40sx

NCR: all 386 and 486 based machines

NEC PowerMate SX Plus

NEC ProSpeed 386

Toshiba 1200XE

Toshiba 1600

Toshiba 5200

Zenith: all 386 based machines

AT&T NSX 20: Safari notebook

MS-DOS System with APM

Intel 386SL Based System with APM

To choose the configuration for one of the listed systems, or to install the drivers and configuration information necessary for another system, use the screen shown in Figure 4.5.

If your system isn't on this list and isn't compatible enough for Windows, make sure your hardware vendor provides a special system configuration disk that allows your system to work correctly with Windows. Once you've selected a system configuration or supplied your own, simply press Enter to return to Setup's main hardware configuration screen.

•••••••••••••••
FIGURE 4.5
*Windows
Setup List of
Computers*

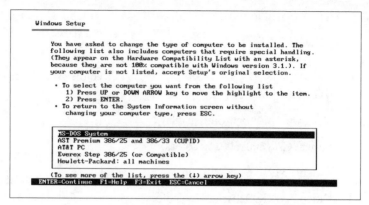

```
Windows Setup

   You have asked to change the type of computer to be installed. The
   following list also includes computers that require special handling.
   (They appear on the Hardware Compatibility List with an asterisk,
   because they are not 100% compatible with Windows version 3.1.). If
   your computer is not listed, accept Setup's original selection.

      • To select the computer you want from the following list
           1) Press UP or DOWN ARROW key to move the highlight to the item.
           2) Press ENTER.
      • To return to the System Information screen without
           changing your computer type, press ESC.

   ┌─────────────────────────────────────────────────────────────┐
   │ MS-DOS System                                                 │
   │ AST Premium 386/25 and 386/33 (CUPID)                         │
   │ AT&T PC                                                        │
   │ Everex Step 386/25 (or Compatible)                            │
   │ Hewlett-Packard: all machines                                 │
   └─────────────────────────────────────────────────────────────┘
      (To see more of the list, press the (↓) arrow key)
   ENTER=Continue  F1=Help  F3=Exit  ESC=Cancel
```

Choose one of the computer system device drivers from this Windows
Setup screen. If it's not on the list, get ready to use your third-party
disk.

Display. After you have reconfigured Windows to suit your computer, you
can do the same for your display hardware. A complete display system—your
"window" on Windows—consists of these elements:

➡ The **video monitor** or other display device

➡ The **display card** that connects the monitor to the computer and produces the graphic images

➡ The **Windows device driver** that translates the Windows GDI (Graphics
Device Interface) information into a form that can be understood by a
particular display adapter

Setup does its best to identify your display adapter. If the guess is incorrect, though, you'll have to specify a particular driver by hand. The Windows
installation disks provide Setup information for these display adapter cards
(other drivers are available from Microsoft or the manufacturer of your
video card):

8514/a

8514/a (small fonts)

Compaq Portable Plasma

EGA

EGA black and white (286 only)

EGA monochrome (286 only)

Hercules monochrome

IBM MCGA (286 only)

Olivetti/AT&T monochrome or
PVC display

QuadVGA, ATI VIP VGA, 82C441
VGAs

TIGA (small fonts)

TIGA (large fonts)

VGA

VGA (version 3.0)

VGA with monochrome display

SuperVGA (800x600, 16 colors)

Video 7 512K, 640x480, 256 colors

Video 7 512K, 720x512, 256 colors

Video 7 1MB, 800x600, 256 colors

Video 7 1MB, 1024x768 256 colors (large fonts)

Video 7 1MB, 1024x768, 256 colors (small fonts)

XGA (640x480, 16 colors)

XGA (small fonts)

XGA (large fonts)

XGA (640x480, 256 colors)

Note that the Video 7, XGA, TIGA, and 8514/a drivers are the only ones in this list that support 256 or more colors.

Insider's Tip

If you don't know what type of display adapter you have, try a VGA first, then an EGA. Many special-purpose display adapters are compatible with one of these standard adapter types. If this doesn't work, cycle through the rest of the choices, but be forewarned: specifying the wrong display type may be able to start Windows but it can also result in dumping some ugly garbage or nothing at all onto your screen. If none of these options works, it's time to call tech support!

In many cases, especially with the SuperVGA, TIGA, or XGA display card, I urge you to get the latest Windows display driver from your video card manufacturer. The driver makes it possible to access advanced features on a card—such as higher resolution and additional colors—and manufacturers are constantly perfecting their Windows display drivers.

A good display adapter card and custom drive can dramatically accelerate graphics processing and thus speed up the entire Windows environment. In Windows, applications pass graphical commands to Windows in a special language known as GDI (Graphics Device Interface). The GDI language describes complex graphics as constructs of graphics primitives, such as rectangles, arcs, circles, and other geometric shapes. The display driver receives these GDI calls from Windows and interprets them into instructions specific to your display adapter card. Therefore the driver is a critical element in determining ways to optimize the processor on the graphics card. Windows graphics accelerators—either as software or as add-in cards—have also been developed to boost performance, as described in Chapter 8.

Insider's Tip

If you are using an old 286 system with EGA, switch to monochrome mode to increase the speed at which a screen is drawn.

Mouse. If Setup did not correctly guess what mouse you are using, you can use the Mouse setup option to select a device driver for your mouse or other pointing device. Windows offers the following mouse device drivers:

HP Mouse (HP-HIL)

Logitech

Microsoft, or IBM PS/2

Genius serial mouse on COM1

Genius serial mouse on COM2

Mouse Systems serial or bus mouse

Mouse Systems serial mouse on COM2

No mouse or other pointing device

Olivetti/AT&T keyboard mouse

If you disconnect your mouse, change the mouse device driver setting to the "No Mouse or Other Pointing Device" option; otherwise, some keyboard actions may not work properly.

Insider's Tip

If you're unsure about what driver to select in the Mouse option screen, try "Microsoft or IBM PS/2"—many mice and trackballs can use this driver.

Keyboard. To change the Windows device driver that Setup suggests using for the keyboard, select the Keyboard item in the main screen of Setup and then use the process described earlier. Windows supports the use of the following keyboards:

All AT-type keyboards (84 to 86 keys)

AT&T '301' keyboard

AT&T '302' keyboard

Enhanced 101 or 102-key US and non-US

Hewlett-Packard Vectra keyboard

Olivetti 101/102 A keyboard

Olivetti 83-key keyboard

Olivetti 86-key keyboard

Olivetti M24 102-key keyboard

PC/XT 83-key keyboard

PC/XT-type keyboard (84 keys)

If your keyboard is not on this list, you may need a third-party device driver. Most keyboards conform to the Enhanced 101 or 102 standards, but some require special keyboard drivers, such as the DataDesk SwitchBoard, which can be configured for options, such as an add-in trackball.

Keyboard Layout. Windows Setup lets you alter your keyboard so that it can provide the special characters and keyboard layouts required by different languages. As opposed to the Keyboard option, which designates the actual keyboard device driver, the Keyboard Layout option lets you choose a dynamic link library (DLL) that works together with the keyboard device driver to fool Windows into thinking that the keys conform to a different layout standard, such as the Dvorak layout or a foreign language layout.

The Windows installation disks provide support for the following keyboard layouts:

Belgian	Finnish	Spanish
British	German	Swedish
Canadian multilingual	Icelandic	Swiss French
Danish	Italian	Swiss German
Dutch	Latin American	U.S.
French	Norwegian	U.S.—Dvorak
French Canadian	Portuguese	U.S.—International

To install a third-party driver, scroll to the end of the list, select Other, press Enter, and place the disk with the driver into the appropriate drive.

Language. Windows supports the use of special language device drivers, which provide foreign translations of the system messages displayed in dialog boxes, alert boxes, and other Windows screen elements. The default choice, if you bought your package in the United States, is English (American). The Windows installation disks provide the following language drivers:

Danish	French	Norwegian
Dutch	French Canadian	Portuguese
English (American)	German	Spanish
English (International)	Icelandic	Swedish
Finnish	Italian	

Code Page. The Code Page setting is used by DOS to determine a character set for the language (French, German, and so forth) installed in your system.

When Setup probes your computer system during the beginning of installation, it identifies the Code Page that DOS is using and selects the same one to run with Windows. If you change the Code Page, you'll need to update your Windows driver as well. Microsoft provides these Code Page drivers on the Windows installation disks:

French-Canadian (863)	Multilingual (850)
English (437)	Nordic (865)
Icelandic (861)	Portuguese (860)

If you need another language, you have to provide your own Code Page driver.

Network. Although Windows 3.1 works better with local area network (LAN) software than 3.0 did, Windows' networking is still in a state of evolution. Thus, be warned: before altering any of the network settings in Windows, review your network manual and know how to contact your network administrator. After installing Windows, your network shell may have to be rebuilt even if you are upgrading from 3.0 to 3.1. For tips on network installation and administration, see Chapter 10.

To allow your networked computer to access hard disks, printers, modems, and other peripherals, you will have to install DOS-specific device drivers by specifying them in either your CONFIG.SYS or AUTOEXEC.BAT file.

Danger Zone

If you're connected to a local area network, you may need to disconnect from the network to successfully install Windows. Otherwise, network pop-up or e-mail messages sent to your computer can disrupt Setup and even cause your system to crash. If you need to access files on your network during the installation process, then follow your network's procedures for suppressing the reception of messages while you're installing Windows.

To select a network driver for Windows, follow the procedure described earlier for all the other components of your Windows environment. Before you can select a Windows network device driver, you must first install the network hardware and its software into the DOS layer of your system. The DOS-level network drivers are usually loaded by one of your DOS startup files (AUTOEXEC.BAT and CONFIG.SYS), depending on what type of network you are using.

The Windows installation disks include support for these networks:

3Com 3+ OPEN	Microsoft LAN Manager
3Com 3+Share	Microsoft Network (or 100% compatible)
Artisoft LANtastic	Novell Netware
Banyan Vines	DEC PATHWORKS
IBM OS/2 LAN Server	TCS 10Net
IBM PC LAN Program	

· ·

After the Hardware Configuration Is Over

After you've specified all the device drivers, you're ready to begin the installation of your Windows environment. When you see the line "The above list matches my computer" highlighted in the No Changes section of the Setup configuration screen, press Enter. This signals Windows that you accept the configuration as displayed. At this point, Windows begins to select and decompress the files that are necessary to start Windows in standard mode, and creates a special scaled-down version of the SYSTEM.INI file so that Setup can restart itself in Windows Mode. Setup uses the file SYSTEM.SRC as the source file for creating SYSTEM.INI. Setup then copies itself (SETUP.EXE) to your main Windows directory and copies SETUP.INF to your Windows \SYSTEM subdirectory.

At this stage, Windows asks you to insert the second and then the third of the installation disks into the floppy disk drive. After transferring some more files, Setup changes from a character-based to a graphical program. When it's complete, you will see the initial graphical Windows Setup screen, which contains a dialog box requesting your name and company (Figure 4.6).

Danger Zone

If you never make it to Setup's graphical mode, you can safely assume your Windows Setup program has aborted. In this case, you'll probably be returned to the DOS prompt; or you'll be in a state of no return, meaning your system may have crashed. Usually, a Setup failure occurs because Windows has incorrectly guessed your hardware configuration or because you've specified an improper driver. If this happens, double-check the components you've specified and reconfirm your driver selections.

FIGURE 4.6
*Name and
Company
Dialog Box*

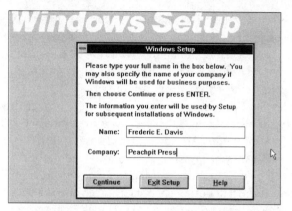

Setup requires that you enter your name in this
dialog box before proceeding with installation.

Windows requires that you enter something in the Name box in order to
proceed; company information is optional. Setup records the information
and displays it in the About dialog boxes for all your bundled Windows
programs. Setup then displays the name and company information you've
entered in a second dialog box and asks for a confirmation.

Next, you'll have to determine how your installation will proceed (Figure 4.7).

FIGURE 4.7
*Setup Dialog
Box with
Three Choices*

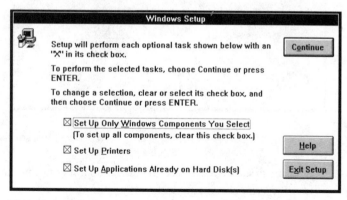

This dialog box lets you choose what will be installed.

The dialog box presents you with these three choices:

➡ Set Up Only Windows Components You Select

➡ Set Up Printers

➡ Set Up Applications Already on Hard Disk(s)

If this is a first-time installation, a check box with an X precedes each of these items; if it's a reinstallation, only the first item is checked. The first item lets you choose what optional files Windows should install, so you can trim the amount of hard disk space needed for installation. To install all of the components, remove the X from this option.

The Set Up Printers option helps you install printer drivers for printers connected to your system, either locally or over your network.

Set Up Applications Already on Hard Disk(s) instructs Setup to look on any hard disks attached to your system for Windows and DOS applications. Windows then creates Program Manager icons for these applications.

If you left the first option checked, a screen appears with a dialog box that lets you choose what components to exclude (Figure 4.8).

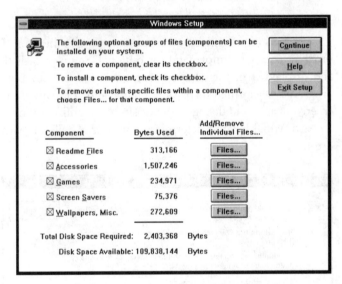

Custom Setup provides this dialog box so you can remove files from the Windows installation to save space on your disk.

You can remove any of these five optional Windows components:

➡ **Readme Files** A collection of technical documentation that didn't make it into the Windows manuals

➡ **Accessories** The Windows applets and bundled utility programs, along with their help files

➡ **Games** The Solitaire and Minesweeper games and their help files

➡ **Screen Savers** The screen saver modules available in the Desktop section of the Control Panel

➡ **Wallpapers, Misc.** The bitmapped graphics files used to wallpaper your desktop, as well as the sound and MIDI files

To remove an entire component, clear the X from its check box. To remove specific files within a component, click on the file's button to the right of that component; this brings up a list of the files. As you deselect components or files, the status lines at the bottom of the dialog box are updated to show you how much space the remaining components will take and how much free space is available on your hard disk. Don't worry about making all the choices at this point, because after you install Windows you can run Setup again to access this dialog box. At that time, you can either remove or add components that were not installed or removed during installation.

After you choose the components you want Windows to install, Setup presents you with the Virtual Memory dialog box, which allows you to view or change your swap file settings if you are using a 386 or higher system (Figure 4.9).

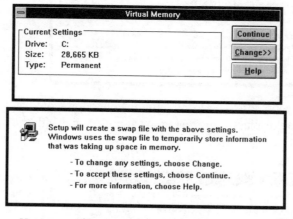

When performing a Custom Setup, you'll see this dialog box, which displays Setup's suggestion for creating a swap file.

You can adjust your settings now or wait until the Setup process is complete. To use FastDisk, press the Change button to expand the dialog box and access the swap file settings (see "Setting Up a Swap File," later in this chapter). As you continue the installation process, Windows Setup prompts you for the other installation disks as it needs them. At each prompt, you can alter the path name for the location of the installation files, in case you need to specify a different drive or directory. Setup also presents an onscreen gauge showing what percentage of the installation process has been completed, and Microsoft sends messages pitching you on various features of Windows and reminding you to send in your registration card.

· ·

Adjustments to the DOS Startup Files

Next, Windows Setup determines whether the AUTOEXEC.BAT and CON-FIG.SYS files exist on the particular root directory you've selected for installing Windows. Windows needs to add certain lines to both of these DOS startup files. If the files already exist, Windows Setup modifies them; if one or both are missing, Setup creates them and adds the required statements. Setup also searches your AUTOEXEC.BAT and CONFIG.SYS files and compares them against a list of incompatible drivers in SETUP.INF. If it finds any, you will see a dialog box identifying the offending drivers or commands.

Before Setup modifies either of your startup files, the dialog box shown in Figure 4.10 appears. You can have Windows automatically make all the modifications (the default); you can review and edit Windows changes before they are installed (the recommended option); or you can make all the necessary modifications at a later time.

FIGURE 4.10

Setup Dialog Box with Modify Startup File Options

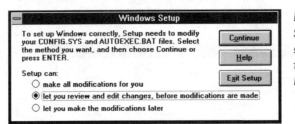

During a Custom Setup, Setup presents this dialog box for dealing with your DOS Startup files.

If you chose the second option, you are presented with a special dialog box that displays your original startup file along with the new version (Figure 4.11).

FIGURE 4.11

Dialog Box for Setup System Startup

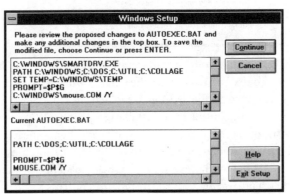

Windows Setup lets you control the modifications to your AUTOEXEC.BAT and CONFIG.SYS files.

The top part of the dialog box shows the modified version of your startup file with the changes that Setup proposes to make, and the box underneath it shows the original file. The scroll bar synchronizes the scrolling of both windows, so that you can inspect the files in tandem. Remember to make any additions or changes to the file in the top box.

Setup saves your old startup files with the extension .OLD; for example, your original CONFIG.SYS is renamed and saved as CONFIG.OLD. If a file with that name already exists, Setup uses a consecutive numbering system in the extension to save the file—for example, CONFIG.001.

Setting Up Your Printer

To assist you in your printer configuration, Windows Setup temporarily presents a section of the Control Panel utility known as the **Printers dialog box** (Figure 4.12). If you click on the Add button in this screen, Windows provides a list of available printers and printer drivers. Each printer driver can be configured with a variety of options. You can configure your chosen printers now, or run this Printers setup box later, from within Windows. For details about setting up printers, see Chapter 7.

FIGURE 4.12

*Printers
Dialog Box*

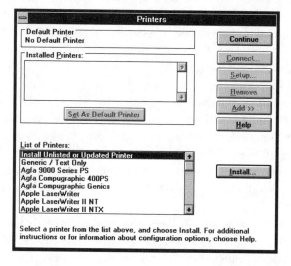

Windows Setup displays the Printers dialog box from the Control Panel so that you can designate printers and printer drivers during installation.

If you are upgrading your copy of Windows, Setup uses the printer that was previously installed and skips this step, unless you have selected the Setup option to set up additional printers.

Setting Up Applications

Windows Setup now builds the default Program Manager groups (described in detail in Chapter 2). These program groups contain the icons for the Windows accessories and Windows sample programs.

Custom Setup lets you instruct Setup to search through your hard drives for Windows and DOS applications and then create program item icons for them in Program Manager. The programs it finds are listed in the Setup Applications dialog box (Figure 4.13).

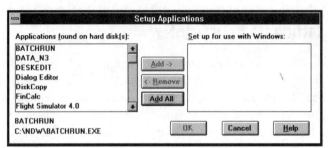

FIGURE 4.13

Setup Applications Dialog Box

You can tell Setup to create program item icons for the Windows and DOS applications it finds on your hard disk.

When creating icons for DOS applications, Setup searches for a PIF, or Program Information File, related to that application from a list of PIF profiles stored in the APPS.INF file. Setup then places the names of any DOS programs it finds into the "Applications found on hard disk(s)" section of the Setup Applications dialog box.

Windows Setup creates program item icons for all the applications—both Windows and DOS—that you choose in the Setup Applications dialog box, but it will only place the icons in the Applications group within Program Manager. Setup creates a group named Applications (if you don't have one) for storing the new icons, and, because Program Manager groups are limited to 40 program item icons each, Setup automatically creates new groups—named Applications 2, 3, etc.—to store any icons over that number.

Danger Zone

The program item icons for Windows applications created by Setup may not work. Dysfunctional icons can result because Setup can't modify system files, such as WIN.INI, which might be needed to run the program. For this reason, use the installation program supplied with the Windows application, rather than the Windows Setup program.

Completing the Installation

After you've selected the various installation options, Windows Setup brings up the Exit Windows Setup dialog box. If this is a first-time installation, the dialog box offers you two choices: Reboot or Return to DOS (Figure 4.14).

FIGURE 4.14

*Exit Windows
Setup Dialog
Box for
Rebooting*

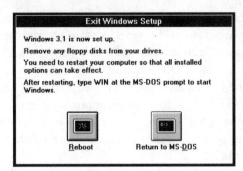

*Exeunt Setup! The Exit Win-
dows Setup dialog box tells you
that Setup's installation process is complete and lets you
choose whether to reboot or
return to DOS.*

To start using Windows, select the Reboot option. To exit to DOS, choose
that option, but be aware that Windows may not run properly without
rebooting your system. Note that if you are installing Windows from a
network, Setup always returns you to DOS.

If you are reinstalling Windows and your DOS startup files did not
require major modifications, Setup presents you with a different dialog box,
which lets you choose between restarting Windows and returning to DOS. In
such cases, rebooting your system isn't necessary (Figure 4.15).

FIGURE 4.15

*Exit Windows
Setup Dialog
Box for
Restarting
Windows*

*If you're reinstalling Windows,
Setup lets you restart
Windows without having to
reboot your system.*

If you abort your installation before it's completed, remove all the files
and subdirectories that Windows Setup placed on your hard disk before you
restart the installation process. In that case it's best to do a complete installation from scratch.

Setting Up a Swap File

New in 3.1

If you're installing Windows on a 386 or higher system with at least 10 mega-
bytes of free (post-Windows installation) hard disk space, you may want to
create a permanent swap file on your hard disk, and thus enable FastDisk.
This is one of the best ways to increase the performance of Windows.
Whether you ran Custom or Express Setup, you have to explicitly instruct
Windows to use FastDisk—it is not installed by default.

Swap files were around in Windows 3.0, and they have been used by many other operating systems for years. A **swap file** is an area of your hard disk that Windows uses to literally swap data between RAM and the hard disk, thus creating what is rather nebulously referred to as "virtual memory." By extending the capacity of RAM with hard disk space, a swap file can make it appear to Windows applications as if much more RAM is present. That's why the About boxes (Alt,H,A) in Program Manager and File Manager usually report a greater availability of RAM than your computer actually contains.

A swap file can also complement the functions of the SMARTDrive disk-caching software to speed up disk access. SMARTDrive's cache makes your hard disk seem to run faster by caching parts of programs and data files in RAM, so that frequently used information doesn't have to be retrieved from the hard disk over and over again. Thus SMARTDrive uses RAM to speed up the hard disk, whereas a swap file uses hard disk space to augment RAM.

Windows uses two types of swap files: permanent and temporary. Temporary swap files—which use random sectors of the hard disk for swapping—are automatically created by Windows on the fly, as needed. Permanent swap files use a contiguous area of the hard disk that is reserved specially for their use and thus work faster because Windows always knows the exact locations of the information to be swapped. Temporary swap files, on the other hand, retard Windows operations because the program has to ascertain where the swapped information has been temporarily stored, or needs to be stored.

Express Setup does not create a permanent swap file unless you have a large, contiguous block of free disk space. Custom Setup, on the other hand, presents the Virtual Memory dialog box (see Figure 4.9), which lets you create a swap file on your own. In deciding how to set up your swap file, you'll have to choose the amount of hard disk space you're willing to sacrifice for a higher performance level. You'll also have to consider whether you want to run FastDisk, which is activated only by a permanent swap file. When used with certain hard disk controller cards (containing controller chips made by Western Digital), FastDisk can result in an impressive performance boost; but because FastDisk is also incompatible with certain hard disk controller cards, it can potentially damage your hard disk and thus should be avoided if you are not absolutely sure of compatibility issues. Now you know why Setup does not install it by default.

You can view the status of your swap file, change the swap file from a temporary to a permanent one, turn FastDisk on and off, or change the drive location or size of the swap file by using the 386 enhanced controls in the Control Panel, as described later in this chapter.

- -

Running Setup After Setup

Depending on your tasks, you can run Setup from within Windows or from DOS after Windows has already been installed. From Windows, Setup is able to change only four of the eight device drivers (Display, Keyboard, Mouse, and Network).

In order to change one of the other four categories (Computer, Keyboard Layout, Language, or Code Page), you have to run Setup from the DOS prompt. The Language option can also be changed using the International section of the Control Panel, as discussed later in this chapter. To change the four device drivers using Setup from DOS, follow the same instructions outlined earlier for the DOS part of installation. This time, however, if you select a driver different from the existing configuration, Setup often prompts you to place an original Windows installation disk in the floppy disk drive. Therefore, before you run Setup, make sure those installation disks are available, as well as any necessary disks for third-party device drivers.

To run Setup from DOS after Windows has been installed, type **SETUP**, as you did for the initial installation. [If the Windows directory isn't in your current PATH statement (which it normally is) you'll need to specify the appropriate path before running Setup, or run Setup from within that directory. Otherwise, Setup may become confused and start a new Windows installation rather than change device drivers.] Next, you'll see the slightly different version of Setup's main configuration screen shown in Figure 4.16.

. . . .
FIGURE 4.16

*Windows
Setup Main
Hardware
Configuration
Screen with
Changes
Complete*

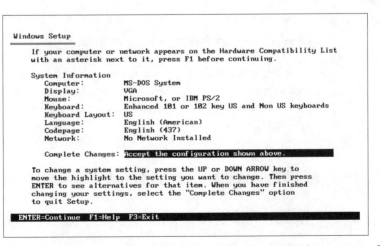

```
Windows Setup

    If your computer or network appears on the Hardware Compatibility List
    with an asterisk next to it, press F1 before continuing.

    System Information
        Computer:           MS-DOS System
        Display:            VGA
        Mouse:              Microsoft, or IBM PS/2
        Keyboard:           Enhanced 101 or 102 key US and Non US keyboards
        Keyboard Layout:    US
        Language:           English (American)
        Codepage:           English (437)
        Network:            No Network Installed

    Complete Changes:  Accept the configuration shown above.

    To change a system setting, press the UP or DOWN ARROW key to
    move the highlight to the setting you want to change. Then press
    ENTER to see alternatives for that item. When you have finished
    changing your settings, select the "Complete Changes" option
    to quit Setup.

    ENTER=Continue  F1=Help  F3=Exit
```

The character-based configuration screen appears when you run Setup from DOS after the initial Windows installation process.

Select your new drivers. Your SYSTEM.INI file records your configuration changes (Figure 4.17).

• • • • • • • • • • • • •
FIGURE 4.17
SYSTEM.INI
*File Showing
Section with
Device Drivers*

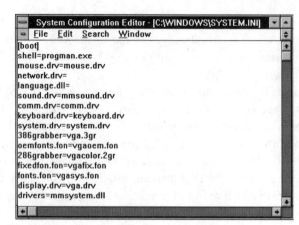

*You can always
check your SYSTEM.INI
file to see what driv-
ers are installed.*

During installation, Windows records your designated device drivers in the SYSTEM.INI file, which it reads each time you start your Windows session. To see a list of the currently installed drivers, inspect the SYSTEM.INI file with either the Notepad or the SYSEDIT utility.

Insider's Tip

To change a device driver without using Setup, edit the SYSTEM.INI file by hand, and manually copy the necessary driver into the Windows directory. (You may need to first decompress it with the Expand utility.)

• •

Running Setup from Inside Windows

You can run Setup from within Windows to easily change four common device drivers: Display, Keyboard, Mouse, and Network. To change any of these device drivers, open the Windows Setup icon in Program Manager, or double-click on the SETUP.EXE file icon in File Manager. You'll see the Windows Setup main window (Figure 4.18).

• • • • • • • • • • • • •
FIGURE 4.18
*Windows
Setup Main
Window*

Windows Setup	
Options **Help**	
Display:	VGA
Keyboard:	Enhanced 101 or 102 key US and Non US
Mouse:	Microsoft, or IBM PS/2
Network:	No Network Installed

*This screen
appears when you
run Setup from
within Windows
after installation.*

This screen only allows you to change the display, keyboard, mouse, and network drivers. To change any of these device driver settings, choose the Change System Settings command from the Options menu (Alt,O, C). The dialog box shown in Figure 4.19 appears.

FIGURE 4.19

Change System Settings Dialog Box

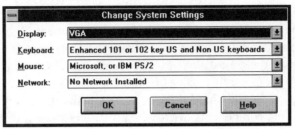

The Change System Settings dialog box allows you to change some of the device drivers supplied with Windows.

To change a device driver, highlight your new selection on the drop-down list. Remember to keep your Windows installation disks handy, because you may be prompted for one. If Setup discovers that your selected driver is already on your hard disk, you can use the existing driver or install a new one from a floppy.

Be careful when installing device drivers that are not supplied on the Windows installation disks. Third-party drivers often require special installation procedures, and some even supply their own setup information files, with special details about the particular driver. Microsoft tells third-party developers to name their setup files OEMSETUP.INF, and most do so. Some installation procedures for third-party display drivers either provide their own SETUP.INF file or try to replace or modify this file in your \SYSTEM subdirectory. It's unwise to alter your SETUP.INF file; instead, rename the third-party SETUP.INF file to OEMSETUP.INF and place it on the same disk and directory housing the third-party display drivers. Remember that disk 1 of your installation disks contains a fresh copy of your SETUP.INF file, in case you need it.

Danger Zone

Installing a new device driver sometimes creates an incompatibility that can prevent Windows from running properly. This can even occur with the drivers supplied with Windows. One of the most common problems is choosing the wrong display driver; Windows will start, but you may not be able to see anything on your screen. To recover, press Alt+F4,Enter to quit your shell. To replace an incompatible driver, run Setup from DOS; from this point, you can reinstate your previous driver or reinstall a different one.

When running Setup from Windows, you can have Setup **search through your hard disk to set up program items** in Program Manager for any

Windows and DOS applications it finds. To use this feature, select Options from the Setup screen and choose the Set Up Applications option (Alt,O,S). This causes the Set Up Applications dialog box to appear (see Figure 4.13). This method works fine for setting up DOS applications, but there are better ways to create these icons for Windows applications.

When running Setup from Windows, you can also **add or remove various optional components of the Windows environment**. To do so, choose Add/Remove Windows Components from the Options menu (Alt,O,A). This brings up the same dialog box that you see during Custom Setup (see Figure 4.8). You can use this dialog box to remove unnecessary items and thus free up space on your hard disk, or to add items that Setup did not install. Removing components deletes the actual files from your hard disk. When adding items, be sure to have your Windows installation disks on hand.

Insider's Tip

If you upgraded to 3.1 from 3.0, and suspect you're having trouble with a device driver, use File Manager to inspect the file creation dates of the drivers inside the \SYSTEM subdirectory. Setup sometimes fails to update a driver that needs to be updated; thus the easiest way to spot a problem driver is often by a date on the driver file that is older than the Windows files on your installation disks. Replace the old driver with the new one by copying it over from the installation disk (you will need to use the Expand utility described in the next chapter), or delete the old driver and rerun Setup.

Hands On the Environment: The Control Panel

Once Windows and its device drivers have been installed by Setup, the Control Panel lets you modify the options related to some of the device driver functions. The Control Panel presents the graphical controls for the various options and features that Windows offers and allows you to establish your own settings to customize many aspects of your Windows environment. With the Control Panel, you can change the color scheme of your windows and desktop, assign sounds to certain system events, set the time and date of your computer's internal clock and calendar, adjust the tracking speed of your mouse, change keyboard options, install and remove fonts, configure serial ports, install printer drivers, configure multimedia options, and more.

The Control Panel contains a group of icons for these categories: **Color, Fonts, Ports, Mouse, Desktop, Keyboard, Printers, International, Date/Time, Drivers, Sound,** and—if you have a 386 or higher processor—**386 Enhanced** (Figure 4.20).

FIGURE 4.20
Control Panel on a 386

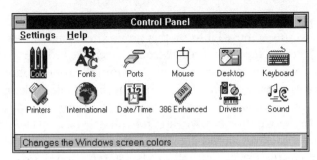

The Windows Control Panel for a 386 non-networked system presents these options.

The Control Panel is expandable, so your system can also include a Network icon and a MIDI Mapper icon if you have the appropriate connections and/or driver. Your Control Panel might also provide controls for multimedia devices, pen-based computers, and other hardware devices and software applications, depending on what you have installed in your system.

Each of the controls correlates to a section in a Windows initialization file (WIN.INI, SYSTEM.INI, or other file ending in .INI), which is modified each time you change and save any of the Control Panel settings (see Chapter 15). Most Control Panel changes are activated immediately, unlike changes you institute with Setup, which usually require that you restart Windows.

New in 3.1

The Control Panel in 3.1 includes 3D icons and more: the Desktop section has a built-in screen saver with a password option that protects your system when it's unattended. Screen savers were originally designed to prevent phosphor burn-in on your video monitor by displaying a constantly moving pattern; these days, they're mostly used to keep your screen private, or to provide some fun. The new built-in screen saver lets you select from several different graphic animations, but it's no match for commercial screen-saver packages.

The Color controls enable you to set all the color elements for the interface, including buttons and disabled text. Several new predesigned color schemes have been added, including three specifically created to increase the legibility of LCD displays used in laptop computers.

The Control Panel also features three new controls related to multimedia: Drivers, Sound, and MIDI Mapper. Drivers allows you to select device drivers for use with Windows, and Sound gives you the ability to assign specific sounds to various events in the Windows environment. The MIDI Mapper control lets you configure whatever MIDI-capable device is connected to your computer from within Windows. And a new status line at the bottom of the Control Panel provides brief descriptions of the various controls.

The Control Panel usually resides in Program Manager's Main group, unless you've moved it to another group after Windows was installed. Double-click on the Control Panel icon to open the program's application window, which contains the control icons for the various options. Or, from File Manager, you can run the Control Panel by double-clicking on its file icon, CONTROL.EXE, which is normally located in your main Windows directory. Once the Control Panel is up and running (as depicted in Figure 4.20), double-click on any icon to select it and bring up its dialog box, which contains the specific controls for the item the icon represents. For example, double-click on the Color icon to reveal the dialog box that contains the color-coordinating controls.

From the keyboard, you can select the control icons in one of two ways:

➺ Move from icon to icon with the arrow keys and press Enter to open the Control icon.

➺ Access the individual control icons from the Settings menu, which contains a list of the icon names, by typing Alt,S, and the underlined letter in the Settings menu for the option you want. For example, to open the Desktop icon, type Alt,S,D (Figure 4.21).

FIGURE 4.21

Settings Menu

If you're using the keyboard, the Settings menu provides a quick way to access a Control Panel icon from the keyboard.

Here's what these Control Panel icons offer you:

Color Specify an existing color scheme for your visual desktop and its related elements, or create an altogether new scheme of your own design.

Fonts Add or delete screen fonts, TrueType fonts, and plotter fonts. (HP LaserJet cartridges/soft fonts are managed with the Printer icon. For other fonts, such as PostScript or Bitstream, refer to the documentation.) The Fonts icon in the Control Panel is discussed in Chapter 7.

Ports Designate the default serial port (COM port) settings for your modem or for other serial communications links.

Mouse Configure your mouse or other pointing device and set the tracking speed, which determines how fast the pointer moves across the screen in relation to movement of the mouse. You can also set the length of the interval that designates a double-click. In addition the mouse controls let you swap the functions of the left and right buttons.

Desktop Choose decorative background patterns and wallpaper for your Windows desktop; adjust the rate at which the cursor blinks; control an invisible grid that keeps items in line on your desktop; select a screen saver and set a password to protect your system; set the spacing between Program Manager icons; and decide whether to wrap titles of icons.

Keyboard Adjust the amount of time that your computer waits after you hold down a key before it starts automatically repeating that key, and how fast a key repeats itself once it starts doing so.

Printers Install, configure, change, and remove printers. You can set printer options, such as output ports and network connections; determine paper size and page orientation; select font cartridges and soft fonts; control the graphics resolution of the printer; and access the Print Manager utility. Details about the Printer icon are covered in Chapter 7.

International Set values for country, language, date, time, number, and currency formats. Changing this setting doesn't convert Windows into another language, it only affects how numbers in these formats are handled by Windows applications for displaying, sorting, and other uses.

Date/Time Set the system date and time using scrollable controls.

386 Enhanced Set options that are available only if you are running Windows in 386 enhanced mode. You can specify swap file settings for configuring the use of virtual memory and turning on FastDisk; control the amount of processor time allotted to foreground and background applications in multitasking operations; and resolve any contentions that can arise when more than one application tries to access a communications port at the same time.

Drivers

Drivers Install, change, configure, and remove drivers for hardware, such as sound boards, pen input systems, and other optional hardware devices.

Sound

Sound Assign special sounds—from beeps to music to any noise—to different Windows events, such as startup and shutdown. Works only if you have installed a sound card or speaker driver.

Network

Network Connect with Windows-compatible networks, usually to log on and off, change your password and network ID, or connect to special network services. This icon appears only if your network is properly installed. Chapter 10 reviews the controls for this icon.

MIDI Mapper

MIDI Mapper Control the connection of a MIDI synthesizer and configure it to work with Windows. This option is available only if your system contains a Windows-compatible MIDI driver. This driver needs to be connected to an appropriate MIDI synthesizer, either on a board inside your system or through an external MIDI cable. Chapter 11 reviews the controls for this icon.

Color

Color

It's easy to go hog wild when you personalize your system with the Control Panel's Color feature. You can concoct color combinations to draw attention to certain items, or to please (or shock) the eye. Windows uses colors to highlight and differentiate 21 components of its graphical user interface, including menus, title bars, buttons, scroll bars, and window borders. You can now use the Control Panel to set all 21 colors. Table 4.2 shows the names of the 21 elements and what they affect.

TABLE 4.2
Components of the GUI and the Areas They Affect

Element name	Area affected
Active Border	The border of the currently selected window
Active Title Bar	The title bar of the currently selected window
Application Workspace	The workspace within an application window
Background	The screen background; your Windows desktop
Button Face	The surface of a button
Button Hilight	The highlights on the top and left side of a button

Element name	Area affected
Button Shadow	The shadow of a button
Button Text	The text used in a button's name
Disabled Text	Text that is dimmed because it is part of an item that is currently unavailable
Hilight	The background area behind highlighted text
Hilighted Text	The highlighted text itself
Inactive Border	The border of any inactive windows
Inactive Title	The title bar of any inactive windows
Inactive Title Bar Text	The title-bar text of any inactive windows
Menu	The background color of all your menus
Menu Bar Text	The text of all of your menus
Scrollbar	The color of the empty area in a scroll bar
Active Title Bar Text	The text of a window's title bar
Window Background	The workspace within a window
Window Frame	The color of the lines that frame your windows
Window Text	The text in your windows

With a color monitor, you can paint your interface areas with any color that your display adapter and driver can produce in Windows. With a standard 16-color VGA card and monitor, your screen can display up to 16 colors simultaneously. With a standard 256-color SuperVGA card, you gain only four extra colors, but these 20 can be selected from any of the 256 colors on your card. To exceed the 20-color limit, you'll need either a 16-bit color card (more than 32,000 colors) or a 24-bit color card (millions of colors). (Insider's Mini-tip: SuperVGA cards that feature advanced DAC chips can sometimes display more than 20 solid colors, provided your card contains enough video memory; check the documentation.)

You can extend your color palette beyond its 16- or 20-color limit for solid colors by using **dithered colors**. Even on a 16-color display, you can create hundreds of different dithered colors by mixing two existing colors to create an intermediate shade. Dithered colors can vary from a good approximation of a solid color to a mottled mess, depending on what colors are available and what you're trying to create. Dithered colors will work to paint some of the bigger components, such as title bars or scroll bars, but you must use solid colors for these items:

➤ Window Frame

➤ Window Background

➤ Menu Bar

➤ Button Face

➤ Highlight

➤ All text items (Window Text, Menu Text, Active Title Bar Text, Inactive Title Bar Text, Button Text, Disabled Text, Highlighted Text)

If you select a dithered color for one of the interface components listed above, Windows automatically selects the closest solid color in the palette. Although you can use dithered colors for the other items, I recommend against it for two good (and solid!) reasons. First, some dithered colors look speckled, because they contain little marks—traces of the dithering attempt. Dithered colors also drain performance power from your display system, because it takes Windows longer to redraw the screen. For these reasons, I recommend that you use all solid colors in your color scheme, and also set the Active and Inactive Border elements to the same color. Because Windows can suck up system resources so fast, you should take advantage of every little tune-up tip—such as forsaking the use of dithered colors—to help tweak your performance.

Danger Zone

Use the color palettes carefully, and pay attention to the legibility of the sample screen. It's all too easy to set the Menu Text and Menu Bar elements to the same color, which causes the menus to disappear into the bar!

If your monochrome display can display varying shades of gray, then you'll be able to assign different grayscale values, as well as either solid or dithered shades of gray, to the various graphical components. The actual data that defines all your available color schemes is contained in the [color schemes] section of the CONTROL.INI file. The [colors] section of WIN.INI, on the other hand, contains information about what color is currently assigned to each screen element.

Windows calls each color combination a "color scheme" and comes with these predefined color schemes:

Windows Default	Cinnamon	Hotdog Stand
Arizona	Designer	LCD Default Screen Settings
Black Leather Jacket	Emerald City	
Bordeaux	Fluorescent	LCD Reversed— Dark

LCD Reversed—Light	Pastel	The Blues
Mahogany	Patchwork	Tweed
Monochrome	Plasma Power Saver	Valentine
Ocean	Rugby	Wingtips

Changing the default color scheme—which uses only white, gray, and dark blue for coloring all 21 interface components—is one of the easiest ways to spiff up and personalize your Windows environment. The only advantage to the default scheme is that it uses only solid colors.

Insider's Tip

Attention, portable computer users! Some LCD displays present graphics and text in "reverse video" mode: white is swapped for black and vice versa. The default Windows color scheme looks awfully ugly on such a display, so you should change it to one of the color schemes that starts with "LCD." Or turn off the reverse video mode—with either a switch, a key combination, or a software utility—and use one of the monochrome or grayscale schemes, depending on your type of display. If you have a plasma display, use the Plasma Power Saver scheme (or make your own variation on it), because it uses darker colors that drain less power than do bright colors.

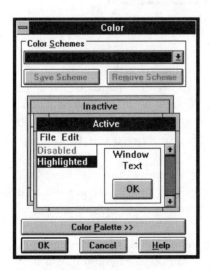

To select a predefined color scheme or to create a new one, double-click on the Color icon (Alt,S,C). This causes the Color dialog box to appear (Figure 4.22).

To choose a preconfigured color scheme, ranging from the modest Windows Default to the flashy Fluorescent, select your choice from the Color Schemes drop-down list box. To see the choices, click on the down-arrow button at the right end of the Color Schemes box, or use the up and down arrows to scroll through the list of color schemes; the sample screen in the dialog box changes to reflect the colors in each of the schemes as you scroll through them.

To select a color scheme, click on it; or, from the keyboard, highlight it with the arrow keys and press Alt+down arrow. If the list was dropped down, either action causes the list box to shrink back into a single-line text box that displays the name of the new color scheme. Click OK to implement your new scheme, or click Cancel (Esc) to return to the Control Panel window.

To create your own color scheme, you must start with an existing one. Once you've selected a starting scheme, click the Color Palette button near the bottom of the Color dialog box, or press Alt+P to access your painter's palette. This causes the Color window to double and reveals these features: the Screen Element drop-down list box; the Basic Colors and Custom Colors palettes; and a large button labeled "Define Custom Colors" at the bottom. On a color monitor, the expanded Color window resembles the one shown in Figure 4.23, which offers 48 different colors in the Basic Colors palette.

• • • • • • • • • • • • • •
FIGURE 4.23
*Expanded
Color Window*

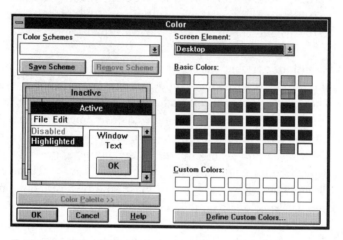

Press the Color Palette button in the Color dialog box to display additional color controls.

If your system contains a 16-color VGA display card, your palette will include 48 colors: 16 solid and 32 dithered. With a standard 256-color SuperVGA display card, you can access 20 solid and 28 dithered colors. With a 16-bit (or greater) display card, on the other hand, all 48 colors in the Basic Colors palette are solid; there is no dithered selection, unless you've created one.

A monochrome—rather than a grayscale—display limits the Basic Colors palette to 16 dithered black-and-white patterns. These are dithered grayscale patterns that let you modestly customize your desktop on a one-color monitor.

Any color, whether dithered, grayscale, or solid, is easy to apply to the 21 interface components. First, select a screen component by pointing at it in the sample screen displayed in the left half of the expanded Color window. The diagram in Figure 4.24 labels each of the 21 interface components included in the sample screen.

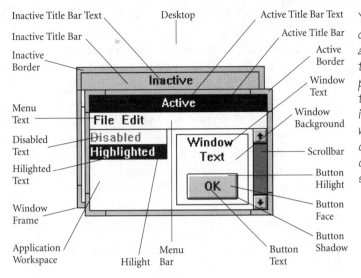

•••••••••••••
FIGURE 4.24
Sample Window in Color Window

Inactive Title Bar Text

Inactive Title Bar

Inactive Border

Menu Text

Disabled Text

Hilighted Text

Window Frame

Application Workspace

Desktop

Inactive

Active

File Edit

Disabled
Highlighted

Window
Text

OK

Hilight   Bar

Active Title Bar Text

Active Title Bar

Active Border

Window Text

Window Background

Scrollbar

Button Hilight

Button Face

Button Shadow

Menu   Button
        Text

You can customize any of these parts of the screen interface with your choice of color schemes.

Insider's Tip

Because the sample screen encompasses only a limited space, two of your choices—the Highlight feature and the OK button—operate a little differently. The first time you click on the Highlighted area of the sample menu, it selects the Highlight element; clicking again will select the Highlighted Text element. The sample OK button can be used to select more than one element; repeated clicking cycles you through the Button Face, Button Shadow, Button Highlight, and Button Text.

The name of the interface element you have selected for a color change appears in the Screen Element section on the right side of the expanded Color dialog box. You can also use the Screen Element drop-down list box to select any of the interface components. To access the Screen Element list box, just click on its down-arrow button and scroll through the drop-down list; click on the screen element to collapse the Screen Element drop-down list, and the name of the element you selected for coloring appears in the shrunken box.

From the keyboard, select the Screen Element box by pressing Alt+E; then use the up and down arrows to scroll through the choices in the list without actually dropping down the list. If you do want to reveal the drop-down list from the keyboard, follow these steps:

1. Type Alt+down arrow to drop the list.

2. Use the up and down arrow keys to traverse the list.

3. When your desired element is highlighted, press Alt+down arrow to select it.

Whenever you select a screen element, the corresponding box of color you selected in the Basic Colors palette is outlined with a thick black line. To change the color of the selected component, just click on any other color square in the Basic Colors palette. Remember, because the Control Panel selects a proximate solid color instead of a dithered color for certain elements, sometimes you'll end up with white text on a white background— which is fine if you don't want to be able to read the text (or have your competitors read it). Be sure to monitor your color choices carefully by viewing the sample screen in the left side of the expanded Color dialog box; this screen instantly reflects the new color you've chosen for that element.

Here's how to select a color from the keyboard:

1. Press the Tab key until the Basic Colors palette is selected.

2. Use the arrow keys to navigate from color box to color box within the palette.

3. Press the spacebar to choose the highlighted color for the selected screen element.

Over the Blue, Green, Shocking Pink Horizon. If the standard 48 colors don't fulfill your creative needs, never fear. With the Custom Color Selector controls, you can mix up 16 colors of your own creation and apply them to the various interface components. To concoct a new color, click the large Define Custom Colors button at the bottom right of the Color window, or press Alt+D to press this onscreen button. You'll see the Custom Color Selector window (Figure 4.25), which you can use to define the Custom Colors squares in the Color window.

You can either modify the Basic Colors or mix entirely new ones. To mix a custom color, try one of these three techniques:

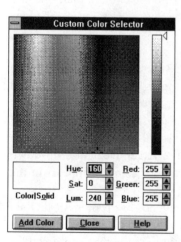

FIGURE 4.25
*Custom
Color
Selector
Window*

*With the
Custom Color
Selector
screen, you
can pick your
own colors.*

➡ Mix a color by sight in the Custom Color Selector's color refiner box, using the mouse.

➡ Specify numbers for the hue, saturation, and luminosity values of a color, using the HSL color model employed by many Windows graphic programs.

➡ Adjust the numbers for the red, green, and blue elements of a color, using the RGB color model popularized by the video industry.

Mixing Colors by Sight. Picking a new color by sight is a snap. To select a palette, use the **color refiner map**—the large, colored, square box that dominates the Custom Color Selector window. This box provides a visual map of all the available colors in the color spectrum. To select a specific color, move the mouse into the color refiner map, position the pointer so that it points to a color, and then click. A small cross-hair cursor marks your selected color. The Color/Solid box presents a larger section of your selected color. If you chose a solid color, the entire box contains only that color. If you chose a dithered color, the left side of the box displays the dithered color and the right side contains what Windows determines to be the nearest solid color. If you decide to select the nearest solid color, double-click on it, or press Alt+O.

Once you choose your color, you can fine-tune it by altering its luminosity, using the vertical luminosity bar to the right of the color refiner box. The luminosity bar depicts a range of brightness, from black through all the intensities of the selected color to white. To adjust luminosity, slide the triangular pointer up and down along the right side of the bar. As you move the pointer, note that the luminosity value (in the Lum box) and the values in the Red, Green, and Blue (or RGB) boxes all change accordingly. RGB and HSL values, the color refiner map, and the Color/Solid box are all interactive; only one color can be selected at a time, and whenever you modify a color, all the other items are correspondingly updated.

When you're pleased with the color you have picked, click in any box in the Custom Colors palette, empty or not, that you want to hold the new color, and then click the Add Color button to place the new color in the box.

The HSL Method. To use the HSL method for defining a color, you'll work with the hue, saturation, and luminosity values in their respective boxes in the Custom Color Selector box. You can change the values of these qualities by clicking on the small arrows (up to increase the value and down to decrease the value) on the right side of each box. Or highlight the number in the increment box with the mouse and type in a new value from the keyboard. If you don't have a mouse, press Tab until the appropriate increment box is highlighted; or type the Alt key in combination with the letter representing the aspect you want to change:

➤ Alt+H to select the Hue text box.

➤ Alt+S to select the Sat text box.

➤ Alt+L to select the Lum text box.

To place your new color in one of the 16 boxes of the Color window's Custom Colors palette, press the Add Color button in the Custom Color Selector window. Windows places your new color in the first available box of the palette, working from left to right.

Once you've selected the appropriate text box, typing a new value replaces the one that is highlighted. The colors in the Color/Solid box change to reflect your new values, as do the RGB values.

The RGB Method. The RGB method for specifying color is similar to the HSL procedure. In this case, you'll adjust the red, green, and blue color values listed in the Custom Color Selector box using the same techniques you applied for the Hue, Sat, and Lum boxes, except you'll substitute the R, G, and B keys in the Alt key combinations just described. As you change the RGB values, note that the colors in the Color/Solid box also change along with the HSL values.

To place your new color in one of the 16 boxes of the Custom Colors palette of the Color window, press the Add Color button in the Custom Color Selector window.

Saving New Color Schemes. Your customized colors and color schemes only apply to the current Windows session, unless you name and save them. To save a new color scheme for future Windows sessions, first close the Custom Color Selector window, if it is open. Then click on the Save Scheme button on the left side of the Color window (Alt+A). The Save Scheme dialog box appears (Figure 4.26). Enter a name for your new color scheme and press OK.

FIGURE 4.26
*Save Scheme
Dialog Box*

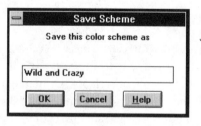

Save the Scheme: be sure to save your color scheme if you want to use it in future work sessions.

From now on, your new scheme will appear in the drop-down list of color schemes on the Color screen. The data for the color scheme is saved in the CONTROL.INI file. To remove a scheme that's become an eyesore, highlight it and press the Remove Scheme button (Alt+M). (You can't, however, remove the Windows Default color scheme.)

Whether or not you saved your color scheme, to activate it, press the OK button in the lower left corner of the Color window (or press Enter). Press Cancel (Esc) to retain the previous color scheme.

Ports

Your computer probably contains at least two serial ports, and perhaps as many as four, numbered sequentially: COM1, COM2, COM3, COM4. Sometimes these ports are attached to actual sockets that let you connect cables from your system to such peripherals as a modem, mouse, or scanner. Other ports are used by special add-in hardware, such as fax boards; although these ports do not provide a typical serial connector, your system still needs to reserve them for whatever hardware you decide to add.

Serial port sockets on your system come in two main formats: a 25-pin DB25 cable connector, and a smaller 9-pin DB9 connector. If your system contains only two serial ports, COM1 and COM2, you will typically use them to plug in a mouse and a modem. With only two serial ports, you'll probably leave the port controls alone, but you may need to change the communications settings, such as baud rate, parity, data bits, stop bits, and flow control. However, if you are using COM3 or COM4, you should be familiar with all the controls provided in the Ports section of the Control Panel, including the Advanced Setting section, which lets you adjust the IRQ (interrupt-request) and base port address for each port.

To access the controls available through the Ports icon of the Control Panel, double-click on the icon, or type Alt,S,P. The Ports dialog box appears (Figure 4.27).

FIGURE 4.27
Ports Dialog Box

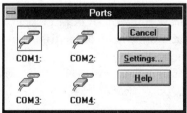

You can use the Ports controls to change settings for any of the four serial communications ports displayed in this preliminary dialog box.

The Ports dialog box simply lets you pick the port. Double-click on the icon of the port you want, to access its Settings dialog box. From the keyboard, press Alt+(the COM port number) to select a port. For example, Alt+3 selects COM3. Then type Alt+S to press the Settings button. Either method brings up the Settings dialog box (Figure 4.28).

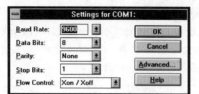

FIGURE 4.28
Settings Dialog Box

Five parameters in every port: the Settings dialog box allows you to set these five parameters: baud rate, data bits, parity, stop bits, and flow control.

With the Settings dialog box, you can set five different parameters for each port:

➤ **Baud Rate** (Alt+B) Sets the speed of your port: 110, 300, 600, 1200, 2400, 4800, 9600, or 19200; the default setting is 9600

➤ **Data Bits** (Alt+D) Sets the number of bits in each data character: 4, 5, 6, 7, or 8; most common settings are 7 and 8; default setting is 8

➤ **Parity** (Alt+P) Helps you select an error-checking scheme for ensuring transmission accuracy: Even, Odd, None, Mark, or Space; choice should match device connected to port; default setting is None

➤ **Stop Bits** (Alt+S) Allows you to select the number of timing units between transmission of data characters: 1, 1.5, or 2; the default setting is 1

➤ **Flow Control** (Alt+F) Allows you to choose a type of communications handshaking: Xon/Xoff, Hardware, or None; needs to match the device connected to the port; default is Xon/Xoff software handshaking

Click on the drop-down arrow to reveal the list of choices for any of these settings and select the one you want. Or, from the keyboard, press the Alt key combination just listed and use the up and down arrows to scroll through the choices without having to drop the list down. If you need to access the Advanced settings for the port, see the next section.

After adjusting your port settings, click OK or press Enter to accept your choices. This brings you back to the main Ports dialog box. Select any other ports and change their settings if you need to; then close the Ports dialog box to return to the Control Panel and automatically record the data related to any changed settings in the [ports] section of the WIN.INI file.

Insider's Tip

For most mice and modems, the data settings should be 8, N, 1, and Xon/Xoff (8 data bits, no parity, 1 stop bit, software handshaking). To set a port for a modem, adjust it to the modem's highest speed. To lower the speed for a particular communications service or file transfer, alter the speed of your communications software, not the port setting. If your high-speed modem is operating at a lower baud rate than it should, check its port to see if it's been adjusted to a lower setting.

If you are using only COM1 and COM2, and these ports came pre-installed in your system, you probably won't have to worry about the Advanced Settings controls: Windows can detect up to two serial ports during installation and sets the values for the Advanced Settings accordingly. You may have to fuss with Advanced Settings, however, if you want to use COM3 or COM4, or if your serial ports are nonstandard. To access the Advanced Settings, open the Ports icon in the Control Panel to reveal the Ports dialog box; then select a port, as just described. When the Settings dialog box appears (see Figure 4.28), click on the Advanced button (Alt+A). The Advanced Settings dialog box appears (Figure 4.29).

· · · · · · · · · · · · · ·
FIGURE 4.29
Advanced Settings Dialog Box

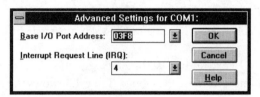

You can set the base port address and the interrupt request line (IRQ) for the selected port in the Advanced Settings dialog box.

The Advanced Settings dialog box contains two choices:

➤ **Base I/O Port Address** Sets the hexadecimal memory address that Windows will use to access the computer's base I/O (Input/Output) port, corresponding to the selected COM port. You can select these addresses: 03F8, 02F8, 03E8, 02E8, or 02E0. If you select Default, Windows will try to guess the appropriate DOS or system Base I/O port.

➤ **Interrupt Request Line** (IRQ) Lets you specify which interrupt Windows will use for accessing the selected COM port. You can select any number from 2 to 15, or you can select Default, which has Windows make its best guess at an appropriate IRQ.

Danger Zone

Whenever you simultaneously use either COM 1 and COM3 or COM2 and COM4, Windows will usually try to access the same interrupt for these pairs. To do this, it applies a technical scheme known as **interrupt-sharing**. A common interrupt-sharing scheme lets COM1 and COM3 share the interrupt number 4, and COM2 and COM4 share IRQ number 3. Some computers, however, don't support interrupt-sharing, so you'll need to assign a different IRQ value to each port. Check your system's documentation (or the documentation for the serial interface card if it was added separately) if you are unsure about interrupt-sharing.

Another problem can be created because certain add-in cards use interrupts as well. In this case, you'll need to identify what IRQ numbers are already in use. The Microsoft Diagnostics utility, described in Chapter 17, can provide you with details about your interrupts. In order to change interrupts, some add-in cards may also require you to flip switches or change jumpers on the board, so keep that hardware documentation handy!

If you've figured out which devices are using what interrupts, and you're lucky enough to still have four left, you can assign them to the various COM ports. If you only have three interrupts left, you can assign different IRQs to COM1, COM2, and COM3, and let COM4 share the same interrupt as COM2. With such a troika configuration, you will be able to use COM1, COM2, and COM3 simultaneously, or COM1, COM3, and COM4—but you won't ever be able to use COM2 and COM4 at the same time.

The Base I/O Port Address setting lets you choose from the various I/O addresses common to most PC clones. Table 4.3 shows the most frequently used port addresses.

TABLE 4.3

*Most Common
Port Addresses*

Port	Address
COM1	03F8
COM2	02F8
COM3	03E8
COM4	02E8

Any changes you make to the base I/O port address settings do not take effect until you restart Windows, which is why the Control Panel brings up a dialog box asking if you want to restart Windows when you've made any I/O address changes. The Microsoft Diagnostic utility can help you determine what base I/O addresses are in use.

Mouse

Mouse

The Mouse icon on the Control Panel lets you adjust the tracking and double-click speeds of your pointing device. You can also use this icon to swap the functions of the left and right buttons. A new feature, Mouse Trails, helps to keep the mouse from disappearing on LCD displays. For the complete rundown on pointing devices, see Chapter 8.

To access the controls, double-click on the Mouse icon. The exact nature and configuration of the controls depends on your Mouse driver. The Mouse dialog box shown here represents the device driver for the standard Microsoft mouse (Figure 4.30).

FIGURE 4.30

Mouse Settings Dialog Box

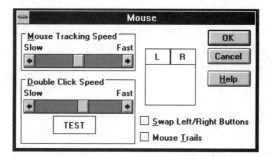

The Mouse settings dialog box controls the speeds of mouse tracking and double-clicking; lets you swap the left and right buttons; and lets your mouse leave trails on LCD displays.

To adjust the Mouse Tracking Speed, move the button on the vertical bar toward either end, fast or slow. For finer tuning, click on the right arrow to accelerate tracking, or on the left arrow to decrease the tracking speed. Click again on either of the arrows to make further adjustments.

Insider's Tip

If your mouse movements are consuming too much desk space, increase the tracking speed. On the other hand, if small movements of your mouse turn your pointer into a long-distance jumper, slow down the tracking speed. When you make these changes, exercise restraint! A slight adjustment can cause a great difference in the operation of your mouse. Any adjustments made to the tracking speed take effect immediately, so you'll be able to see the results and compensate if you've over-adjusted.

The double-click speed is the maximum amount of time that can elapse between two consecutive clicks and still constitute one double-click. To set up this parameter, move the button along the horizontal bar or click on the arrow at each end, as you did to adjust the mouse tracking speed. This adjustment also takes effect immediately. Try it with the Test button located in the Mouse dialog box; a valid double-click darkens the button.

For the lefthanded, the ambidextrous, or those with a cramp in their right index finger from too much mouse clicking, Windows lets you swap the functions of the left and right mouse buttons. Under the standard arrangement, if you press the left mouse button, the box on the Mouse settings screen containing the L darkens. Pressing the right mouse button darkens the area in the R box. If you click on the check box titled Swap Left/Right Buttons, the L and R box positions are reversed, and so is the operation of your mouse buttons. Use this feature with care, however. Because role reversal takes place instantly, you may panic for a split-second when you try to change the setting by clicking with the wrong button.

New in 3.1

The Mouse Trails option benefits users of laptops with LCD displays, especially passive LCD displays, which often tend to make the pointer disappear unless you move it at a snail's pace. When checked, the Mouse Trails option leaves a trail of pointer icons across the screen. This feature only works, however, if your machine contains a display driver supporting it; otherwise, the option is dimmed in the dialog box.

Desktop

Desktop

The Desktop section of the Control Panel lets you manipulate the appearance and behavior of your graphical desktop, as well as the look of the background area for displaying your icons, windows, and other onscreen items. The other controls that affect the appearance of your interface are located under the Color icon, described earlier in the chapter. The Desktop icon provides these controls:

➡ **Screen Saver** Select a screen saver for Windows to display when you are not using the computer; also, set a password to discourage anyone from accessing your system when it's left unattended

➡ **Pattern** Select and edit a repeating bitmap pattern that Windows will use as your desktop background

➡ **Wallpaper** Display any .BMP or .RLE graphics file, ranging from a simple, repeating tiled pattern to a dramatic, full-screen photograph or work of art

➡ **Applications** Turn fast Alt+Tab switching on and off

➡ **Icons** Control the spacing of an icon along an imaginary alignment grid used by Windows, and activate or deactivate the switch for the text-wrapping of titles under icons

➡ **Sizing Grid** Activate and adjust an imaginary grid used to automatically align Windows elements with the Granularity option; and with the Border Width option, alter the thickness of the borders around your windows

➡ **Cursor Blink Rate** Adjust the speed at which the cursor blinks

To change any of these settings, open the Desktop icon in the Control Panel. This activates the Desktop dialog box (Figure 4.31).

● ● ● ● ● ● ● ● ● ● ● ● ●

FIGURE 4.31

Desktop Dialog Box

Do it with your desktop! The Desktop dialog box contains settings for changing the appearance and behavior of your graphical desktop.

Pattern. With the Pattern settings, you can select and design a small repeating bitmap pattern (8x8 pixels) for your Windows graphical desktop. When first installing Windows, Setup creates a solid background pattern, but you can easily change it with the controls in the Pattern section at the top of the Desktop dialog box. The Pattern section contains a drop-down list box, labeled Name, and the Edit Pattern button. The Name box displays the name of the current bitmap pattern. The default solid color desktop setting is indicated by the selection "(None)" in the Name box.

To access an existing pattern, select it from the Name drop-down list box. From the keyboard, press Alt+N to select the Name box. If you don't want to open the drop-down list box, simply cycle through your pattern choices with the arrow keys. To drop the list, press Alt+down arrow and use the up and down arrow keys to highlight your choice. To select your choice, press Alt+(up or down arrow). Windows offers these patterns in the list box: None, 50% Gray, Boxes, Critters, Diamonds, Paisley, Quilt, Scottie, Spinner, Thatches, Tulip, Waffle, and Weave.

Using a mouse or other pointing device, you can create your own patterns. (Windows doesn't provide a way to edit desktop bitmap patterns from the keyboard.) To start your bitmapped masterpiece on a blank canvas, select (None) in the Name list box, then click on the Edit Pattern button. The Desktop-Edit Pattern dialog box appears, containing a large, magnified square with no pattern in its center (Figure 4.32).

• • • • • • • • • • • • • •
FIGURE 4.32
Desktop-Edit Pattern Dialog Box

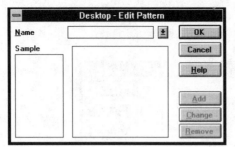

To start with a blank canvas for a new desktop pattern, select (None) in the Name box; then click on the Edit Pattern button.

To edit an existing pattern, select it in the Name box and then press the Edit Pattern button. The Desktop-Edit Pattern dialog box now contains your designated pattern, ready to edit (Figure 4.33).

• • • • • • • • • • • • • •
FIGURE 4.33
Thatches Pattern in the Desktop-Edit Pattern Dialog Box

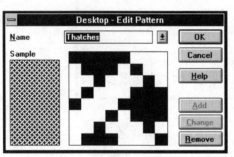

Ready, set, edit! To edit an existing bitmap pattern, simply select it in the Name box and press the Edit Pattern button.

To inspect bitmap patterns in detail, use the close-up view provided by the bit editor in the center of the Desktop-Edit Pattern dialog box. When this box is open, you can view all the available patterns by navigating through them with the up and down arrow keys.

The procedure for editing a pattern is the same whether you start from a blank or an existing pattern. Use the mouse to toggle pixels in the bit editor on and off, thus creating your pattern—it's crude, but it works. The bit editor in the Desktop-Edit Pattern dialog box contains an 8x8 pixel grid that uses only two colors: the Desktop color and the Window Text color. (To set these colors, use the Control Panel's Color icon, described earlier.) To change the color of any grid pixel, just click on it. To return to the original color, click again. While you're creating a pattern in the bit editor, you can view the results in the Sample screen to the left of your bit editor grid.

Your pattern is repeated over and over on the desktop to create a grid that contains many replicas of itself. Creative mouse artists, perhaps inspired by Escher, can create interlinking patterns, like the Thatches pattern shown in Figure 4.33.

To save a new pattern and overwrite a previous one, select the Change button (Alt+C). To save both the new and the old versions, or one created from scratch, you'll need to enter a name for your new creation in the Name box; click on the Add button (Alt+A) and then the OK button (Enter) to return to the main Desktop dialog box. Pressing Cancel (Esc) on the Edit Pattern screen returns you to the Desktop box without saving any of your changes or new patterns, even if you pressed the Change or Add buttons.

Once you're back at the Desktop dialog box, you can select your new pattern from the Name drop-down list box. With your pattern highlighted, simply click OK (Enter) to activate the pattern and return to the Control Panel.

To remove a pattern from the list, press the Edit Pattern button on the Desktop screen. Scroll down the Name list box to the soon-to-be-extinct pattern and click on the Remove button (Alt+R) to delete the pattern. If you change your mind, press Cancel (Esc) at any time to retain your pattern. When you're finished, press OK (Enter).

New in 3.1

Applications. The Applications section of the Desktop dialog box contains a check box labeled Fast "Alt+Tab" Switching, which, if turned on (the Setup default is on), speeds up switching from one application to another, especially if several applications are open at once. This feature allows you to hold down the Alt key while repeatedly pressing Tab to cycle through the running applications. Provided that this feature is checked, a special dialog box appears that sequentially displays the name and icon for each application that is running when you press successfully both the Alt and Tab keys (Figure 4.34).

FIGURE 4.34
*Fast Alt+Tab
Switching
Dialog Box*

Switching from program to program is shamelessly easy when you use the new Fast "Alt+Tab" Switching feature, which cycles through your running applications.

Keep holding down Alt and press Tab again to switch to your next running application, and continue pressing Tab until you reach the program you want. Then release the Alt and Tab keys, and—voila!—the selected program's open window jumps to the foreground of your screen. If it was minimized as an icon, the icon is restored to the preminimized window. You can reverse the direction at any time by holding down Alt+Shift and pressing Tab. Or press Esc at any time to bail from the switch and return to your original application.

If the Fast "Alt+Tab" Switching box is not checked, the running program's window pops up at the forefront with each successive Alt+Tab. Although this option gives you a full view of your programs as you cycle through them—as opposed to the name-and-icon-only view provided by the fast switching option—it does slow down your operations.

New in 3.1

Screen Saver. The Screen Saver section of the Desktop dialog box lets you select a moving pattern that will be displayed on the screen when the Windows system is left unattended for whatever amount of time you specify. When you return to the system, the slightest move of the mouse, or the press of any key on the keyboard, causes the screen saver to vanish, and your work to reappear, just where you left it. In addition, the Screen Saver controls let you set a password that must be entered in order for the screen saver to disappear. Although it's not as foolproof as a commercial computer security product, this feature does keep idle passersby from reading what's on your screen, and discourages well-intentioned bumblers from "helping you out" (screwing up your system) if you step away for a while.

A screen saver theoretically helps prevent the phosphor burn-in that can be caused when a bright image is displayed in the same place on the screen for too long. Many longtime DOS users have noticed a DOS prompt burned into the upper left corner of their computer display; this is the telltale ghost of phosphor burn-in. However, this is a problem only on older monochrome displays, and doesn't affect most color screens. Instead these screen savers provide privacy and fun.

You'll need to turn on the screen-saver function manually—Windows Setup does not activate it. To choose a screen saver, select the Name drop-down list and pick a name. From the keyboard, type Alt+A to select the Name box and then use the up and down arrows to scroll through the choices. Then select the Delay box and use the small up and down scroll arrows at the right end of the box to change the value in the box; this represents how many minutes of inactivity must elapse before the screen saver takes effect. From the keyboard, press Alt+D to select the Delay box; then, type the number of minutes that should elapse before the screen saver appears.

To audition your screen saver, press the Test button (Alt+E); to end the tryout, move the mouse or press any key.

A screen saver can't be activated if your currently selected application is a DOS program, even if it's minimized as an icon. So make sure your currently active program is a Windows one—that way you'll get the benefit of a screen saver and its password protection.

Danger Zone

Screen savers can sometimes disrupt programs that are running in the background, such as a communications program that is doing a lengthy download. If your system is burdened with I/O-intensive tasks, it's a good precaution to turn off your screen saver.

Most screen savers include customization options; these let you set the colors, patterns, speed of motion, and other elements, such as a password feature, that affect the behavior of your screen saver. To access the screen-saver customization controls, press the Setup button (Alt+U) in the Screen Saver section of the Desktop dialog box. This brings up the dialog box that contains the setup controls for your selected screen saver. Each dialog box is different, depending on the options provided by the screen saver. For example, Figure 4.35 shows the setup controls for the Mystify screen saver, and Figure 4.36 illustrates the controls for the Starfield Simulation.

FIGURE 4.35
Mystify Screen Saver Controls

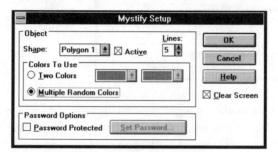

The custom setup controls for the Mystify screen saver let you select the colors, number of lines, and available shapes.

FIGURE 4.36
Starfield Simulation Screen Saver Controls

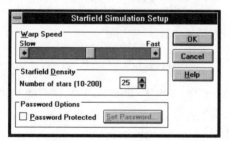

The Starfield Simulation screen saver includes a Warp Speed setting to control how fast the stars fly by and a Starfield Density to determine how many are flying.

The screen saver setup dialog boxes in Figures 4.35 and 4.36 both contain a Password Options section. A password works in conjunction with the screen saver. Once the screen saver is activated, anyone who touches the mouse or the keyboard is confronted with a dialog box that requires them to enter the proper password (Figure 4.37).

FIGURE 4.37
Password Intervention Dialog Box

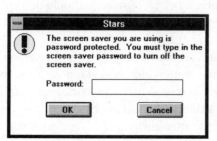

This could be a pain in the pass: if you set a password, once your screen saver comes on it won't go away until you enter the proper password.

To set a password, place an X in the Password Protected check box, shown in Figures 4.35 and 4.36. Toggle the check box on and off by clicking in the box. From the keyboard, press Alt+P to select the Password Protected box and press the spacebar to toggle the X on and off. The Set Password button goes from dim to dark once you place the X in the check box. Click on the button to select it, or press Alt+S. The Change Password dialog box appears (Figure 4.38).

• • • • • • • • • • • • • •
FIGURE 4.38
*Change
Password Dialog
Box*

You can use the Change Password dialog box to set a new password or to change an existing one (if you know it).

The first line in the Change Password dialog box is Old Password (Alt+O). Ignore this box if you are setting your first password. Otherwise, you must type in the current password before you can proceed; all other choices in this dialog box stay dim until you supply the right password. To finish changing the password, proceed as if you were creating a new one.

To create a new password:

1. Click in the New Password text box (Alt+N selects it from the keyboard).

2. Type in your password—you're allowed up to 20 characters.

3. Click in the Retype New Password box (Alt+R) and type in the password again so that Windows can verify it.

4. Click OK (Enter) to return to the custom setup dialog box for the selected screen saver.

To turn off the password feature, simply remove the X from the Password Protected check box. If you've forgotten your password, read Appendix B, Hacker Tools and Hints, for a fix. (Tamperers should note, however, that this fix can disrupt the system and may leave its traces.)

Wallpaper. Does that 8x8 two-color pattern grid give you the prison-cell blues? Try wallpapering your Windows desktop with the images from any .BMP file to lend your screen a dramatic backdrop. The .BMP file name extension designates a standard Windows bitmap file, so you can use many Windows graphics programs, such as the bundled Paintbrush applet, to create or edit .BMP files to use as Windows wallpaper.

Take another look at the main Desktop controls dialog box shown in Figure 4.31; you'll see that the Wallpaper section of the Desktop dialog box contains these elements: a drop-down list box named File and a pair of radio buttons, Center and Tile. The File list box displays all the .BMP files that are in the main Windows directory. If you want your self-designed .BMP files to show up automatically, be sure they are located in this directory. Use the standard method for accessing a drop-down list with the mouse to select a file for your wallpaper. Or, from the keyboard, type Alt+F to select the File list box, then use the arrow keys to scroll through the list without dropping it down. Or you can just type the name of the file (with its full path, if it's not in the current directory) directly into the list box without bothering to drop it down.

Windows provides these bitmap files to use as wallpaper:

256 Color	Castle	Leaves	Tartan
Arcade	Chitz	Marble	Thatch
Arches	Egypt	Redbrick	Winlogo
Argyle	Flock	Rivets	Zigzag
Cars	Honey	Squares	

A further variation of your wallpaper design depends on the placement of bitmap files. You can either center a single bitmap image on your screen or use a file image in a repeating tile pattern to fill your entire screen. Some bitmap images already fill the whole screen, or beyond—if the image won't fit in the screen, Windows won't display it, and you'll need to crop the image using a paint program before you can use it as wallpaper. For example, if you have an 800x600 pixel image, you will need to trim it down to 640x480 pixels to fit on a standard VGA display.

The wallpaper appears on top of the desktop pattern. If the wallpaper covers your entire screen—as it does when you select the Tile option—your desktop bitmap pattern will be completely hidden from view. To achieve a "picture frame" effect, select a centered bitmap file smaller than the size of your screen. Your desktop pattern will show around the edges and "frame" your wallpaper.

Whether you tile or center, first select your .BMP file in the Wallpaper list box. Then, to center a single image, select the radio button labeled Center with the mouse, or type Alt+C. To tile the maximum number of copies of the image onto your screen, click on the Tile radio button, or type Alt+T. As with all radio buttons, only one choice can be activated at a time. Click OK in the Desktop dialog box (or press Enter) to approve the new wallpaper and return to the Control Panel. Under most circumstances, the new wallpaper selection takes effect immediately.

Danger Zone

Beware the memory requirements of big bitmaps: a 1024x768 pixel wallpaper image with 256 colors that is scanned from a photograph may look spectacular, but it consumes an equally spectacular amount of RAM. If the image is too big to store in memory, Windows boycotts the art show, and no wallpaper is displayed.

If you're receiving out-of-memory alerts when there's a large bitmap file on your desktop, try turning off the wallpaper feature by selecting None in the Wallpaper File drop-down list box. Instead, use one of the Desktop patterns discussed earlier in this section; these 8x8 pixel patterns require minimum amounts of RAM.

Insider's Tip

Here's a way to cut down your memory requirement by 75 percent: reduce an image to 25 percent of its original size, then select Tile to arrange four smaller images on your screen instead of one large one. Another way to reduce the memory requirement of an image, aside from cropping it, is to reduce the number of colors it uses. But there's a trade-off: if you convert a 640x480 pixel, 256-color image into a 16-color image, you'll also lose some of the color resolution and probably gain some graininess as well. A better technique is to use a utility or graphics program to convert the image into an .RLE file (run-length encoded), which compresses the image file without loss of resolution.

If you are creating your own .BMP files for use as tiled wallpaper patterns and want to make sure they fit exactly without cropping, Table 4.4 gives dimensions that will work:

TABLE 4.4

Dimensions of single tile (pixels)	How it tiles on the screen
160x160	4 tiles across and 3 rows down at 640x480
160x96	4 tiles across and 5 rows down at 640x480
80x 80	8 tiles across and 6 rows down at 640x480
64x 60	10 tiles across and 8 rows down at 640x480
200x200	4 tiles across and 3 rows down at 800x600
200x120	4 tiles across and 5 rows down at 800x600
80x75	10 tiles across and 8 rows down at 800x600
256x256	4 tiles across and 3 rows down at 1024x768
256x128	4 tiles across and 6 rows down at 1024x768

Of course, other resolutions will work as long as they divide equally into the screen resolutions you select.

To specify an offset, in pixels, for starting your tiled wallpaper, add these two statement lines to the [Desktop] section of your WIN.INI file:

➤ **WallpaperOriginX** This line indicates how many pixels from the left of the screen to start tiling.

➤ **WallpaperOriginY** This line indicates how many pixels from the top of the screen to start tiling.

This example,

```
WallpaperOriginX=10
WallpaperOriginY=20
```

would offset the first tile 10 pixels from the left of the screen and 20 pixels from the top. You can tweak these settings to reposition odd-sized tiles and make them fit better together on the screen. Refer to Chapter 15 for further details on working with the WIN.INI file.

Icons. Windows does its best to space icons so that they will not overlap on the screen; the size of the widest icon is used as a guide to determine the distance between neighboring icons. To adjust icons yourself, look at the Icons section of the Desktop dialog box, which contains two items: a control for setting the spacing between icons and a check box to activate word wrap for your icon titles. If the titles of your icons overlap, you can increase the spacing between them, or wrap their titles, or do both.

To select the Icon Spacing controls, click on them with the mouse, or type Alt+I. The controls include a simple text box, followed by two small arrow keys. The number in the box represents the distance in pixels—from the center of one icon to the center of its neighbor—that Windows will use to position its icons on the screen.

To set a spacing value, type a number directly into this box, or use the mouse to alter the value by clicking on the small up or down arrows. The upper limit for icon spacing is 512; on a typical VGA monitor, this spacing positions the icons at a considerable distance from one another. The lower limit for icon spacing depends on the resolution of your display; on a 640x480 pixel VGA display, the minimum value is 32 pixels.

Insider's Tip

The default icon spacing is 75 pixels; anything less than 55 pixels will probably make your icons appear cramped unless you reduce or eliminate the icon titles. If too many of the labels on your icons overlap, try increasing the distance between icons in 10-pixel increments, starting with 85 pixels. If you exceed 100 on a standard 640x480 pixel VGA display, however, the icons will be so far apart that it won't be as easy to navigate around your screen.

The other control in the Icons section is a check box labeled Wrap Title. You can toggle this option on and off either by clicking in the box or by pressing Alt+W. If a check appears in the box, your icon titles will be neatly wrapped, as shown in Figure 4.39. Figure 4.40 illustrates unwrapped icon titles.

• • • • • • • • • • • • •
FIGURE 4.39
Icons with Wrapped Titles

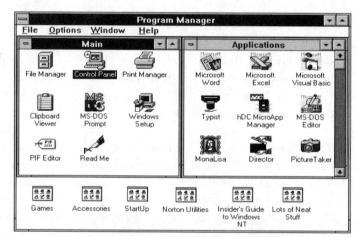

This is how icons look with their titles wrapped.

• • • • • • • • • • • • •
FIGURE 4.40
Icons with Unwrapped Titles

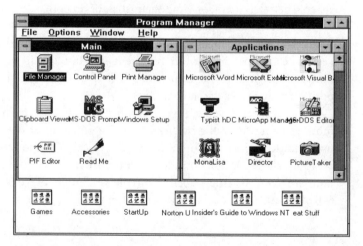

Here's how those same icons look with their titles unwrapped; as you can see, this doesn't work too well if your icons have long titles.

New in 3.1

Windows 3.1 includes four special statement lines—IconVerticalSpacing, IconTitleFaceName, IconTitleSize, and IconTitleStyle. These statement lines influence the positioning of icons and the fonts used in their titles, but they can only be used if you're willing to edit WIN.INI by hand, as described in Chapter 15.

Sizing Grid. The Sizing Grid section of the Desktop dialog box contains two settings: Granularity and Border Width. The Granularity setting is used to activate and deactivate an imaginary grid—and to set the spacing of the grid lines—which Windows uses to align application windows and minimized application icons. It does not exert its magnetic influence on anything other than applications; document windows, icons, and so on are not affected. When you turn on this alignment grid, application windows and minimized application icons snap in place along the imaginary grid, as the intersections on the grid force these screen objects into alignment.

To change the Granularity setting, select its box in the Sizing Grid section by clicking on it, or type Alt+G. The Granularity value can range from 0 (off) through 49. Windows Setup sets this value to 0 during installation, which means the grid is turned off. To activate the grid, set the Granularity to 1 or more. Each increment of 1 in granularity increases distances between grid lines by an additional 8 pixels. Desktop anarchists can set the Granularity value back to 0 to escape Window's control and place items wherever they please.

Keep the Granularity setting low unless your display has a high resolution. A setting of 2, for instance, places the grid lines 16 pixels apart; a setting of 49 positions grid lines at intervals of 392 pixels. On a 640x480 pixel VGA display, a setting of 49 yields only two grid intersections for your entire screen. In fact, any setting of more than five should be reserved for a high-resolution monitor, where pixel distances are not as great.

You can adjust the width of the usually thin borders surrounding any resizable window on your desktop. To slim these lines even more or to add substance to them, alter the value in the Border Width increment box of the Sizing Grid section of the Desktop dialog box. To select this box, click on it with the mouse, or type Alt+B. To change the value, type a new value between 1 and 50 into the box or click on the small up and down arrows on the right.

The default value of 3 works fairly well. If you do adjust the border, you might want to stay within the range of 2 to 5, for a comfortable border that's within reach. For laughs, try a setting of 20, or even 50—the maximum—which produces a border larger than its window!

Cursor Blink Rate. To alter the rate at which the cursor blinks, select the Cursor Blink Rate scroll bar and drag it to either the Fast or Slow end, depending on your preference. From the keyboard, press Alt+R to select the scroll bar, then use the right and left arrow keys to move the scroll button toward either the Slow or Fast end. A sample cursor to the right of the controls blinks at the selected rate, to give you immediate feedback as you adjust the speed. If you want to specify an actual time interval between blinks, you can do so with millisecond accuracy by editing the Cursor-BlinkRate statement in the [Windows] section of WIN.INI, as described in Chapter 15.

Keyboard **Keyboard**

The Keyboard icon in the Control Panel allows you to set the amount of time before a key starts to repeat itself and also to adjust the rate at which it automatically repeats once it gets started. To access the Keyboard controls, double-click on its icon or type Alt,S,K; the Keyboard dialog box appears (Figure 4.41).

FIGURE 4.41
*Keyboard
Dialog Box*

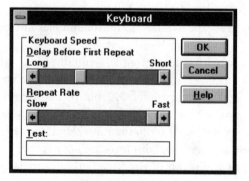

The Keyboard dialog box lets you decide how much time will elapse before a key starts to repeat itself and how rapidly it repeats.

To adjust the amount of time before a key starts to repeat itself, select the Delay scroll box and drag the scroll button toward the Long end to increase the delay, or toward the Short end to decrease it. To make fine adjustments, click on the scroll arrows on either end of the scroll bar. From the keyboard, type Alt+D and use the right and left arrow keys to move the scroll button toward either the Long or Short end of the scroll bar.

To adjust the rate at which the key repeats once it starts going, select the Repeat Rate scroll box and drag the scroll button toward the right, to the Fast end, to increase the repeat rate; reverse this to slow down the repeat rate. Again, you can click the small scroll arrows to adjust a small amount with each click. From the keyboard, type Alt+R, then use the right or left keyboard arrow to move the scroll button toward the Fast or Slow end.

To test your settings, move to the Test box by clicking in it, or press Alt+T, then hold down any alphanumeric key. Now you can test the speed and tweak the settings until you're satisfied.

International

International

Was fur ein Nerd sind Sie? Need to express yourself in another tongue? The International icon in the Control Panel allows you to specify settings for basic foreign format concerns, such as currency, time and date, and numbers. However, changing these settings doesn't actually change the language of your entire interface: it just changes your keyboard layout and the way that numbers for the respective languages are sorted, manipulated, and displayed by Windows. To switch your entire Windows system to another language, you'll need to order a special foreign-language version of Windows through Microsoft's international sales division. Polyglots will be pleased to discover that Windows is available in many foreign languages.

The U.S. version of Windows comes installed with the U.S. standards for all its numeric formatting options. Similarly, a Windows version for another language includes that country's settings. If you travel to other countries or conduct international correspondence, you may want to change some of your default U.S. settings so that you can use the date, time, currency, and other formats of that country, without having to actually switch to a foreign language version of Windows. To do so, open the International icon to activate the International dialog box (Figure 4.42).

FIGURE 4.42

International Dialog Box

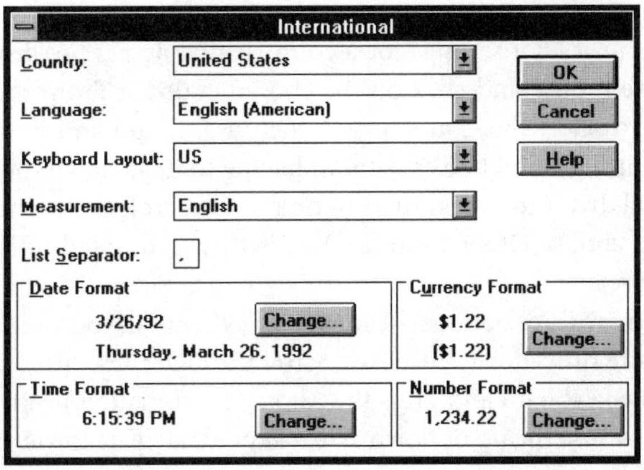

International		
Country:	United States	OK
Language:	English (American)	Cancel
Keyboard Layout:	US	Help
Measurement:	English	
List **S**eparator:	,	

Date Format
3/26/92   Change...
Thursday, March 26, 1992

Currency Format
$1.22   Change...
($1.22)

Time Format
6:15:39 PM   Change...

Number Format
1,234.22   Change...

The International dialog box lets you change the keyboard layouts, number formats, and other settings to turn your PC into a polyglot.

You can set these nine International controls:

➤ **Country** (Alt+C) Choose from a list of Country profiles with preset values for eight other settings: Language, Keyboard Layout, Measurement, List Separator, Date Format, Time Format, Currency Format, and Number Format. You can also change the other settings or create new ones.

➤ **Language** (Alt+L) Select what language to use when sorting information, including the use of accented and other special characters.

➤ **Keyboard Layout** (Alt+K) Choose special keyboard layouts that conform to conventions used in the countries listed in this box. This list also contains the Dvorak layout (no relation to my friend John C.) and lets you substitute your U.S. keyboard for this ultraefficient layout system.

➤ **Measurement** (Alt+M) Choose between the sensible metric system and that crazy English system that we're saddled with.

➤ **List Separator** (Alt+S) Specify a symbol or special character for separating items in a list—the U.S. convention is a comma.

➤ **Date Format** (Alt+D) Control how the date is displayed.

➤ **Time Format** (Alt+T) Control how the time is displayed.

➤ **Currency Format** (Alt+U) Format currency values.

➤ **Number Format** (Alt+N) Adjust how numbers are displayed.

The first International setting, Country, contains a drop-down list box with choices of preset profiles for 28 countries. Your choice of Country determines the contents of the other eight items, such as Language, Keyboard Layout, and so on. (You can also change these other items individually.) To select a profile of settings for a country, first access the drop-down list box with the mouse and click on the chosen country. From the keyboard, type Alt+C to select the Country box, then use the up and down arrow keys to scroll through the choices without having to drop down the box. If you have a special driver for a country not on the list, scroll to the end of the Country list and choose Other Country. You're then prompted to insert a disk with that driver.

The next three options—Language, Keyboard Layout, and Measurement—all feature drop-down list boxes. Scroll through these lists with the mouse or from the keyboard and press the Alt key combination just listed to select the option; or use the up or down arrow keys to navigate through the list without dropping it down.

The Language setting offers a drop-down list box with 14 different language settings; these determine how Windows applications sort information. The Language setting lets Windows know how to deal with special characters, such as diacritical marks, when sorting lists of text. The Language choices listed here are identical to those found in the Language section of Windows Setup. Refer to the "Language" section under "Setup" earlier in this chapter for the list.

The Keyboard Layout drop-down list box gives the 20 different keyboard arrangements that were discussed earlier. The Measurement drop-down list box contains only two settings: English (the default) and metric.

The List Separator box contains a single character. In English, the comma is used to separate the items in a list. In certain other countries, the semicolon separates the items. Type any other character to replace this separator if appropriate.

Date Formats—Short and Long. The first boxed section at the bottom of the International dialog box allows you to set the Date Format. This section displays the current format for dates in both the short and long date formats. To customize these settings, click on the Change button or type Alt+D to activate the International–Date Format dialog box (Figure 4.43).

FIGURE 4.43
*International–
Date Format
Dialog Box*

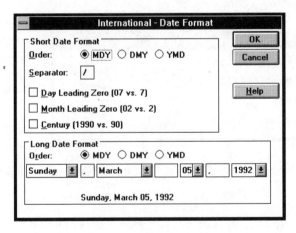

*Set the date format
you prefer using
the controls in the
International–Date
Format dialog box.*

Use the first section of the Date Format dialog box to select the short date format options. The Order setting determines the sequence of month, day, and year. To change this setting, click on one of the three radio buttons, or type Alt+O and use the arrow keys to select a button. In the Separator text boxes, use a single character to separate the month, day, and year. The U.S. default is a slash. To change it, highlight the box with the mouse or type Alt+S and type any one character.

When you select Day Leading Zero or Month Leading Zero, a zero precedes any day or any single-digit date. Toggle these check-box options on and off by clicking with the mouse, or press Alt+D for day. Toggle the second check box with the mouse or press Alt+M for month. The third check box instructs Windows to insert the century when formatting the year date, using 1992, not 92. Toggle this check box with the mouse or use Alt+C.

You can also control the long date format in your Windows system. Use the Order option in this section of the International–Date Format dialog box to set the sequence of month, day, and year. Select and adjust this option with the usual mouse or keyboard methods and you'll see a drop-down list box for specifying either a long or short format for day of the week. This is followed by a text box for an optional separator and then three list boxes for the month, day, and year options. The sequence in which these boxes appear depends on what you chose for the Long Date Format setting, and your entries are reflected at the bottom of the screen. When you're satisfied with your date format, click OK or press Enter to return to the main International dialog box.

Time Format. The Time Format section in the International dialog box (Figure 4.44) shows the current settings and the Change button, which operates in the same fashion as does the one for Date Format, described in the previous section.

FIGURE 4.44

*International–
Time Format
Dialog Box*

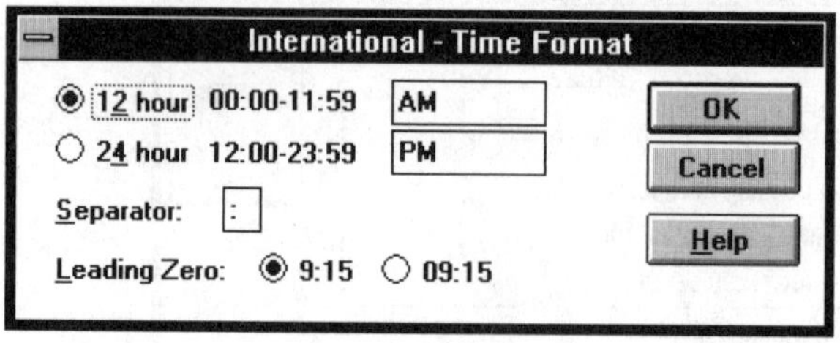

*Control the way
your system time is
displayed with the
settings in this dia-
log box.*

In the International–Time Format dialog box, you can control these time format elements:

➤ **A 12- or 24-hour time** display. Select with a radio button, or type Alt+2 for 12-hour time, or Alt+4 for 24-hour time.

➤ **AM or PM**, after the time. AM is the U.S. default. You can edit or overwrite this entry, or leave it blank. (For example, a military time format could be followed with the word *hours*. Or you might enter EST or PDT.)

➤ **A separator character for the hours, minutes, and seconds** in the time display. To change the default setting, highlight it with the mouse or type Alt+S; then enter any single character.

➡ **A leading zero**, in front of single-digit hour entries. Click a radio button, or select it from the keyboard by typing Alt+L and using arrow keys.

When you finish setting up your time format, click OK or press Enter.

Currency Format. The International Currency Format dialog box, which appears when you click the mouse or type Alt+U, contains the settings for the currency number (Figure 4.45).

FIGURE 4.45
International–
Currency
Format
Dialog Box

International - Currency Format		
Symbol Placement:	$1 ⬍	OK
Negative:	($123.22) ⬍	Cancel
Symbol:	$	Help
Decimal Digits:	2	

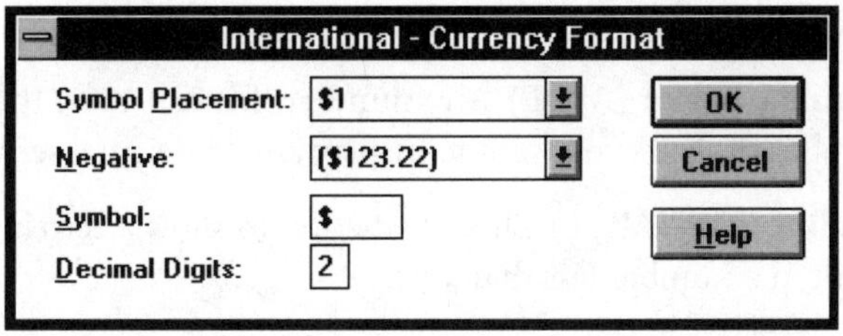

Use this dialog box
to format your
money.

You can select the items in this window, as usual, by clicking on them with the mouse or by typing Alt plus the underlined letter in the option name, then accessing the drop-down list boxes.

Here's a list of the options you can set in the Currency Format dialog box:

➡ **Symbol Placement** (Alt+P) Lets you select one of these arrangements for placing the money symbol: $1, 1$, $ 1, 1 $.

➡ **Negative** (Alt+N) Lets you control the display of negative money amounts. Several formats are available, including ($123.22), –$123.22, $–12.22, $123.22–, (123.22$), –123.22$, 123.22–$, and 123.22$–.

➡ **Symbol** (Alt+S) In a U.S. version of Windows, a dollar sign ($). For the Symbol setting, you can type up to four characters in the text box.

➡ **Decimal Digits** (Alt+D) Lets you specify how many digits are displayed after the decimal point. The U.S. default is two.

Number Format. Number Format is the last option in the International dialog box. To bring up the Number Format dialog box, click on the Change button or type Alt+N (Figure 4.46).

Using the standard mouse and keyboard scrolling and selection techniques, you can control these elements:

➡ **1000 Separator** (Alt+S) Uses a comma as the default setting, but you can replace it with any other character you wish to use as the thousands separator in numbers.

FIGURE 4.46
*International–
Number
Format
Dialog Box*

*Use this dialog box
to display numbers
in the format you
prefer.*

➥ **Decimal Separator** (Alt+D) Normally contains the default period in the
U.S. version. A comma is a typical alternative for this setting.

➥ **Decimal Digits** (Alt+E) Any number, from 0 to 9, that designates the
number of digits you want to display after a decimal separator.

➥ **Leading Zero** (Alt+L) Choose whether to show a zero before the decimal
point in a number less than one.

Click OK or press Enter to return to the main International dialog box.

Date/Time **Date/Time**

The Date/Time icon in the Control Panel provides an easy way to set the date
and time of your system clock. Changing this setting affects DOS and the rest
of your system, not just the Windows environment. These settings are stored
directly by your computer's system clock, and not in an .INI file, as are the
other items in the Control Panel.

To change the setting, open the Date/Time icon by double-clicking on it
or by typing Alt,S,T; the Date & Time dialog box appears (Figure 4.47).

FIGURE 4.47
*Date & Time
Dialog Box*

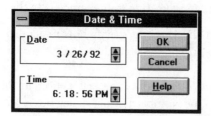

*This box allows you to set the time
and the date of your system clock.*

To change the day, month, or year, select the date controls (Alt+D); then
highlight the specific element by clicking on it, or press Tab to move to it.
Next, type in a new number or use the arrows at the right to scroll to the
value you want. To change the hour, minute, second, and AM/PM elements,
select the Time box (Alt+T), which works in the same way as the day control.

When you've set the date and time to your liking, click OK, or press Enter to return to the Control Panel.

• •

386 Enhanced

386 Enhanced

You'll see this icon only if you're running in 386 enhanced mode.

The 386 enhanced settings allow you to control the way in which multiple applications compete for system resources, such as peripheral devices, and also how resources are allocated to both the Windows and DOS applications running during your Windows session. These controls also include the Virtual Memory settings that let you take advantage of the FastDisk feature.

When you are running more than one application in 386 enhanced mode, several different applications may periodically request the use of available peripheral devices, such as printers or a modem. If both of the contenders are Windows programs, there's no problem—Windows automatically manages the situation. But if one of the applications vying for use of a port is a DOS program, then watch out—Windows can't make DOS programs behave. As a result, contention for the port or device may occur, with the potential for causing transmission errors or, in rare cases, even a complete system crash.

The 386 Enhanced section of the Control Panel lets you arbitrate how Windows will handle these discordant situations. To access its settings, open the 386 enhanced icon by double-clicking on it in the Control Panel, or type Alt,S,3. The 386 enhanced dialog box appears (Figure 4.48).

• • • • • • • • • • • • • •
FIGURE 4.48
*386 Enhanced
Dialog Bog*

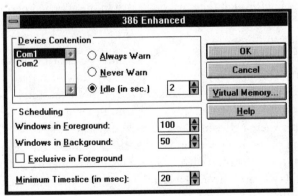

With 386 enhanced settings, you can control how DOS applications use peripheral devices and other system resources, and you can turn on FastDisk's 32-bit access.

The Device Contention section contains a list box designating the active peripheral ports in your system. Select the desired port by clicking on it with the mouse, or type Alt+D and use the arrow keys to navigate the list. Immediately to the right of the list box are three radio buttons; you can select only one of these, either by clicking on it or by typing one of the following Alt key combinations:

➡ **Always Warn** (Alt+A)

➡ **Never Warn** (Alt+N)

➡ **Idle** (Alt+I)

Selecting Always Warn causes Windows to display a warning message when a DOS application tries to use a port already in use by another application (Figure 4.49).

FIGURE 4.49
Device Conflict Alert Box

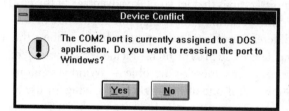

When Always Warn is selected, Windows displays this warning to let you choose which application can use a contested port.

This warning box lets you choose which of the contesting applications will use the port. You should use the Always Warn setting most of the time, because it lets you resolve any conflicts before they happen.

The Never Warn option can be dangerous, because you're giving Windows permission to let any application use this port at any time, with no warning. When two applications try to use the same port, the result is garbled data going through the port, or a crash in the attached peripheral, or even in your computer system itself. Select this option only when you're positive that no such conflicts can occur.

If you want it both ways—a warning, but not in advance—try the Idle option. This option provides a special window of opportunity for another application to grab a particular device without causing Windows to display the warning. You can set this value from 1 to 999 seconds. Generally, a setting of somewhere between 1 and 30 seconds works best.

The Scheduling section in the 386 enhanced dialog box controls the amount of CPU time each DOS application demands when it's in the foreground (you are currently using the program) or in the background (you are currently working in another program). This processing time is measured in units 1 millisecond. The Foreground and Background numbers determine how much time each application uses proportionately. The Windows defaults of 100 and 50 allow an application to use twice as much time in the foreground as in the background.

The Windows in Foreground option (Alt+F) allows you to adjust the processing time normally shared by all Windows applications. When a DOS application runs in the foreground, Windows uses the value that you set in the Windows in Background box (Alt+B) to determine the share of processing time to give Windows applications. The value of each entry can range from 1 to 10,000, but the significance of the setting depends on the ratio between the setting and the combined value of the .pif file settings of any other working DOS applications. The Windows in Background value represents the processing time shared by all the Windows applications in the background when a DOS application is running in the foreground (see Chapter 14 for a complete explanation of this complex topic).

Here's what to do if you want Windows programs to always take complete priority. Place an X in the Exclusive in Foreground check box (Alt+E toggles this setting) to tell Windows to allocate 100 percent of the computer's processing time to a Windows application when it is active, and to suspend any DOS applications that may be running in the background.

The Minimum Timeslice (Alt+M) scrolling box lets you set the number of consecutive milliseconds Windows gives to an application before processor control switches to another application. All Windows applications automatically share one time slice. The setting in this box is used for the benefit of DOS applications, which each receive an individual time slice of the specific size you designate.

Virtual Memory. The Virtual Memory button in the 386 Enhanced dialog box is your ticket to faster Windows performance. You can use this option to install a permanent swap file and thus create some virtual memory that fools Windows into thinking you have more RAM than is actually installed in your system. And better yet, you can use these controls to turn on FastDisk and give your Windows system a big performance pick-me-up—as long as you can sacrifice a large, contiguous hard disk space and your hard disk controller is compatible with controller chips made by Western Digital (most are).

To access these controls, click on the Virtual Memory button, or press Alt+V. The Virtual Memory dialog box appears (Figure 4.50).

FIGURE 4.50

Initial Virtual Memory Dialog Box

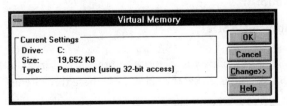

The first incarnation of the Virtual Memory dialog box only lets you survey the current settings.

The Virtual Memory dialog box first appears in a contracted form that displays only the current settings; it provides no controls for changing them. The shrunken box reports this information:

➤ **Drive** The hard disk drive being used for your swap file

➤ **Size** The size in kilobytes of your current swap file

➤ **Type** Your type of swap file (temporary or permanent), and whether you are using a normal DOS BIOS or the new FastDisk 32-bit access to work with the hard disk

To alter any of these settings, click on the Change button (Alt+C). The Virtual Memory dialog box expands, revealing the swap file controls (Figure 4.51).

FIGURE 4.51
*Expanded
Virtual
Memory
Dialog Box*

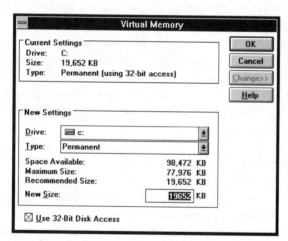

The expanded version of the Virtual Memory dialog box contains the controls for using swap files.

When the Virtual Memory dialog box is expanded, a New Settings section is added at the bottom of the box, which reports this information:

➤ **Space Available**

➤ **Maximum Size**

➤ **Recommended Size**

This information helps you determine how large (or small!) to make your permanent swap file. To set the values, use these three items:

➤ **Drive** (Alt+D) A standard drop-down list box that lets you select a drive for placing your swap file (use your fastest drive).

➤ **Type** (Alt+T) A drop-down list that lets you select one of these options: Temporary, Permanent, or None. Temporary is the default setting; Permanent allows you to activate FastDisk; and None is the choice of last resort—it lets you turn off the use of swap files altogether (and bog your system down accordingly!).

➤ **New Size** (Alt+S) A small text box in which you can enter a number that represents how much hard disk space, in kilobytes, you want to devote to your permanent swap file. By default, the New Size box contains the amount of space suggested in the Recommended Size box; if you want to use a different size, select the box and type in your new choice.

Insider' Tip

To activate FastDisk, set up a permanent swap file, then place a check in the box labeled Use 32-bit Disk Access, located at the bottom of the expanded Virtual Memory dialog box. If you don't see this check box, your controller card probably doesn't work with the standard Windows FastDisk driver. You may still be able to use FastDisk, however, if you can obtain a third-party driver that supports your controller card. FastDisk will be activated automatically the next time you start your permanent swap file, which requires that you quit and then restart Windows. If FastDisk is operating properly, the Type section of the Virtual Memory dialog box presents this message: "using 32-bit access." See Chapter 12 for a more detailed discussion of FastDisk and virtual memory.

Drivers

· ·

Drivers

In addition to the main device drivers installed during Setup, Windows uses a variety of supplementary device drivers, which allow you to install third-party devices, particularly multimedia devices, such as sound cards, input devices, laser disc players, and whatever else engineers can concoct.

The Drivers icon in the Control Panel allows you to install and remove these various device drivers. Usually, the device driver is provided by a third party on its own disk. If you're going to install a new driver, therefore, make sure you have any such disk handy.

To access the control, activate the Drivers icon by double-clicking on it or by typing Alt,R; the Drivers dialog box appears (Figure 4.52).

The Drivers dialog box lists all the drivers installed in your system. To install a new driver, click on the Add button, or press Alt+A. This brings up the Add dialog box, which lists all the drivers that Windows detects in its directory. You can install one of these drivers, or add one that's not listed, by

FIGURE 4.52
Drivers
Dialog Box

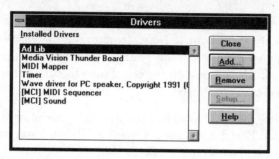

The Drivers dialog box
allows you to install
device drivers that
can't be installed from
Setup.

choosing "Unlisted or Updated Driver." When the Install dialog box appears, get ready to insert the disk containing your third-party driver. If the driver is located on your hard disk or on a network server, type the drive and directory into the dialog box, or use the Browse button to select a directory graphically. If a driver requires that you specify other options, the driver presents its own Setup dialog box (Figure 4.53). In some cases, you will need to restart Windows in order for the driver to take effect; if this occurs, you'll see the appropriate dialog box.

FIGURE 4.53
Speaker
Driver Dialog
Box

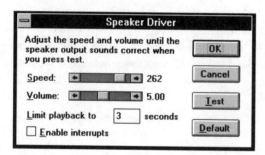

Drivers often include a
setup dialog box, such as
the one shown here for
the speaker driver.

Danger Zone

If a third-party driver requests that you set a port address or interrupt (IRQ), make sure you select an unused one. Use the IRQ Status option of the Microsoft Diagnostics utility described in Chapter 17 to identify which interrupts are already in use. Also, note that the Control Panel will generate an Error message if you attempt to install an updated version of a driver that is already installed in your system. You'll have to remove the old driver first.

Once it's installed, a driver can be readjusted at any time. Just activate the Driver icon and open its dialog box, select the driver, and click on the Setup button (Alt+S). If the button is dimmed, the driver has no options. For particulars about how to adjust any of its settings, check your driver's accompanying documentation.

To remove a driver, open the Drivers dialog box from its icon, highlight an installed driver, and click on the Remove button (Alt+R). A confirmation dialog box gives you one last chance to reconsider. Click Yes or press Enter to proceed with the removal. Another dialog box asks if you want to restart Windows—and thereby zap the driver immediately—or return to your current Windows session, which means your driver won't be removed until you restart Windows.

Sound

Sound

Dynamite Product

To use the new audio capabilities of Windows 3.1, you'll need a sound driver or sound board. The best way to add audio to your computer is to buy a sound output add-in board. I recommend either the Sound Blaster Pro from Creative Labs or Pro Audio Spectrum from MediaVision. Both provide an earful of features, yield excellent voice and music quality, and are supported by many DOS games to produce great arcade-style sound effects.

Sound boards range from less than $100 to $1,000, and some PCs are now bundled with a sound card. The less expensive boards only play back sound files, whereas the more expensive models record and play back sounds (digital recordings). Some boards even include music-synthesis chips, which produce sounds rivaling those created by professional synthesizers. In fact, if you've got MIDI software and some other tools, you can transform your Windows system into a desktop music and recording studio that will blow away what the pros were doing just a few years back. Chapter 11 covers multimedia hardware and software that takes advantage of Windows 3.1's new built-in sound capabilities.

Once you have installed a Windows-compatible sound driver (using the Drivers icon discussed earlier) you'll be able to assign sounds to these system events:

➠ Asterisk

➠ Critical Stop

➠ Default Beep

➠ Exclamation

➠ Question

➦ Windows Exit

➦ Windows Start

For example, my PC starts up with Bullwinkle the Moose saying "Presto!"; my Default Beep is the roadrunner going "meep-meep"; and when I quit, I hear Schwarzennegger's famous refrain from *Terminator:* "I'll be back!"

To access the controls, double-click on the Sound icon in the Control Panel. The Sound dialog box appears (Figure 4.54).

FIGURE 4.54
Sound Dialog Box

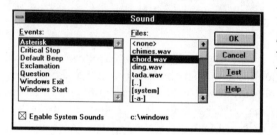

The Sound dialog box lets you assign sounds to various Windows system events.

In the Sound dialog box, highlight a system event from the Events list (Alt+E). If a sound is already assigned to that event, it is highlighted in the Files list (Windows sound files end with the .WAV extension); otherwise None is selected. Next, go to the Files list (Alt+F) and highlight a sound file. To hear the contents of this sound file, click the Test button (Alt+T).

A check box named Enable System Sounds at the bottom of the box contains an X when the sounds are turned on. To toggle this option on and off, click in the checkbox or press Alt+N.

Summary

Windows Setup and the Control Panel work together as a team to install and maintain your Windows environment. Setup, which can run from either DOS or Windows, lets you create a new Windows installation or update your existing one, and controls the device drivers and hardware configuration settings needed to run Windows. Windows 3.1 introduces an Express Setup option that streamlines the installation process. Another Setup enhancement allows you to install third-party device drivers and configurations for your computer display adapter, mouse, and network from within Windows. Setup also now offers custom setup options, including the ability to create automated installation scripts using a special file called SETUP.SHH.

The Control Panel provides an array of graphical controls that let you manage and customize your Windows environment as well as install device drivers for multimedia devices and other hardware accessories. In Windows 3.1, the Control Panel has gained a number of improvements, including a Drivers section that lets you install and configure device drivers; a Sound section for assigning sounds to specific Windows events; and a MIDI Mapper section for configuring a MIDI synthesizer to work with Windows. Windows 3.1 also adds improvements to some of the existing controls: the Desktop section now provides a screen saver with password protection, and the 386 Enhanced section lets you control your virtual memory settings and configure your swap file, including the important ability to turn on the FastDisk 32-bit disk access.

Insider's Tech Support

Q: Why am I unable to install Windows?

A: Most of the problems with installing Windows result from an incompatible system configuration. Some of these problems can be resolved simply, but others require nothing less than a major upgrade. Windows installation is the hardest part of learning Windows. Once you are over this hurdle, things usually get much better. Because of the complexities in answering this question, I'll break it down into groups of major symptoms and problems.

First, you need to make sure your system can run Windows 3.1. The bare minimum requirements are a 286 or higher processor with at least 1 megabyte of RAM, configured with 640K as conventional memory and 256 kilobytes as extended memory. However, this minimalist configuration will not let you use all of Windows' features. You'll also need to have at least 7 megabytes of free hard disk space and an EGA or better display adapter. Windows 3.0 ran on 8088 and 8086 systems and also worked with CGA adapters. Windows 3.1 will not run with these older systems or with CGA.

In order to run Windows in 386 enhanced mode, you'll need to have at least a 386 or higher processor with 2 megabytes of RAM, with 1 megabyte of this configured as extended memory. You'll also need to have at least 8 megabytes of space available on your hard disk. Keep in mind that these are the minimum requirements for running Windows; to take full advantage of the Windows environment, you'll really need additional resources. If you are unclear as to how your memory is configured, and about the difference between expanded and extended memory, see Chapter 12. Also, Chapter 17 describes the use of the Microsoft Diagnostics utility, which can be run from DOS before installing Windows to generate a detailed report about how your system is configured.

* * * * *

If Setup crashes during installation, it usually happens at one of three stages. Moments after you run it, Setup analyzes the TSRs and other memory-resident software in your system. If it finds an incompatibility, it alerts you, but sometimes the probing itself causes the system to crash. If Setup crashes during these initial few seconds, type

SETUP /T

at the DOS prompt. This instructs Setup to check for TSRs and other software that could cause potential problems. In general, it's a good idea to turn off all your TSRs before installing Setup. Sometimes Setup cannot detect an incompatible TSR; be sure to check the SETUP.TXT file on installation disk 1, which includes the latest information about TSRs that are known to be incompatible with Windows.

To prevent TSRs from being loaded into your system, back up your existing CONFIG.SYS and AUTOEXEC.BAT files, and create a new barebones version of each file.

The next point at which Setup can crash is while it is performing its automatic detection of your hardware configuration. This can cause Setup to return you to the command prompt or even hang your system completely, so that you have to reboot. If Setup crashes and no TSRs are running, this auto-detection feature is a likely culprit. To work around this, type

SETUP/I

at the DOS prompt, which instructs Setup not to perform its auto-detection routines. You'll then need to specify the computer system, display adapter, and other hardware components by hand, as described in the beginning of this chapter.

The third point at which Setup can crash is when it switches from DOS to Windows mode. This is usually caused by an incorrect hardware selection, most commonly the display adapter driver. To overcome this problem, try using one of the two generic adapter drivers, EGA or VGA. If neither works, contact the manufacturer of your display adapter to make sure it's compatible with Windows 3.1. For more information about display problems, refer to Chapter 8.

* * * * *

If you upgraded to 3.1 over your existing Windows 3.0 installation, the likely cause of failure to install is an incompatible device driver. Setup does not replace device drivers it doesn't recognize, so if you installed a third-party device driver in Windows 3.0, it may require upgrading. In some cases, you can upgrade to one of the drivers provided on the installation disks by running Setup and selecting the new driver. In other cases, you'll need to obtain a third-party driver from the manufacturer. Third-party drivers are also available on the Windows Drivers Library disks, available from Microsoft; or you can download them from Microsoft's technical support Bulletin Board System (BBS); see Appendix C for the phone number.

When upgrading to 3.1 over an existing 3.0 installation, your .INI files can become corrupted. To overcome this, you'll need to install 3.1 in a new directory and then reinstall all your applications by hand. This tedious procedure is necessary to ensure that your .INI files are rebuilt from scratch.

Q: Setup asks for a disk that I place in the drive but doesn't recognize it.

A: This problem can be caused by three things. Your disk may be defective or damaged. Quit Setup and type **DIR** to see a directory listing. If all the files are in the directory, the disk is probably OK. Another cause could be that your disk-caching software is caching the floppy disk drive. To prevent this, turn off the disk-caching software by removing the line that installs it in either your CONFIG.SYS or AUTOEXEC.BAT file; then reboot your computer and run Setup again. If you are not using disk-caching software, it could be that your computer is unable to determine that you've changed disks. This can usually be solved by adding a DRIVPARM statement to your CONFIG.SYS file and then rebooting your system. For full details on how to use the DRIVPARM statement, refer to your DOS manual. If you are using 5¼-inch. 1.2 megabyte drive configured as drive A:, try this DRIVPARM statement:

```
DRIVPARM=/D:0 /F:1
```

Q: I use Setup to create program item icons, but the programs won't run.

A: If you are trying to run a DOS program, it could be that Setup misinterpreted what PIF to use when setting up the application; or your DOS program may not have its own PIF and may not work with the default PIF. Refer to Chapter 14 for information on how to adjust the PIF. If you are having problems trying to run a Windows program, it's likely that the program requires modifications to your .INI files in order to run. Setup merely creates an icon for the application file and does not make the necessary file modifications. To correct this problem, you'll need to reinstall the applications using the installation programs that were included with them.

Q: I'm using a 386 (or 486) system, but I don't see the 386 Enhanced icon in the Control Panel.

A: The 386 Enhanced icon is present in the Control Panel only when you are running in 386 enhanced mode. If your system has less than 2MB of memory, Windows starts in standard mode by default even if you have a 386 or higher processor. Even with 2MBs of memory, if less than 1MB is configured as extended memory, Windows cannot run in 386 enhanced mode. You can try to force Windows to run in 386 enhanced mode by starting it with the /3 switch; to do this, type

```
WIN /3
```

Conversely, if you start Windows using the /S switch, this forces it to start in standard mode, even on a 386 or higher processor. You won't see the 386 Enhanced icon when Windows is running in standard mode.

Mastering the Bundled Windows Utilities

Programs, programs, everywhere! That's what you'll see when you peruse your Windows directory and the \SYSTEM subdirectory within it. Almost everyone wants to know what programs are installed on their system, so it's time to explore all the other goodies Microsoft crammed onto your installation disks. Although this chapter—unlike the preceding chapters—doesn't cover anything that's critical to your operation of Windows, you'll derive far more benefit from this multifaceted software package if you learn how to use its utilities.

Windows is not a single program; rather, it incorporates many programs, assembled in a single package. These programs can be broken down into five categories: operational, core, DOS, applets, and utilities.

Operational programs deal with installing and running your Windows environment: Program Manager (PROGRAM.EXE), File Manager (WINFILE.EXE), Setup (SETUP.EXE), and the Control Panel (CONTROL.EXE).

Core programs, which are tucked out of the way in the \SYSTEM subdirectory, are used to actually run Windows. The core programs provide the graphics, memory management, and other software components that together let you run a Windows session. Activated by the WIN.COM program in your main Windows directory, these programs include

➤ **DOSX.EXE** Standard mode DOS extender

➤ **DSWAP.EXE** Task swapper used by DOS sessions when running standard mode

➤ **GDI.EXE** The Graphics Device Interface; this program actually creates the graphics for Windows and all its applications

➤ **KRNL286.EXE** The Windows kernel program for standard mode

➤ **KRNL386.EXE** The Windows kernel program for 386 enhanced mode

➤ **USER.EXE** Core components of the Windows graphical interface

➤ **WIN386.EXE** Core components for Windows 386 enhanced mode

➤ **WSWAP.EXE** Windows task swapper for standard mode

A third category of Windows programs contains **DOS disk and memory management software** that Setup installs and configures through the AUTOEXEC.BAT and CONFIG.SYS files. These utilities for DOS include

➤ **SMARTDRV.EXE** The SmartDrive disk cache program

➤ **HIMEM.SYS** The DOS XMS memory manager

➤ **EMM386.EXE** The DOS EMS memory manager for the 386

The rest of the programs on your Windows installation disks fall into two main categories: **applets** and **utilities**. This chapter deals with utilities— those little gems that can help you obtain online help, view and edit your system files, and access special characters. Some of these utilities remain completely undocumented in the Windows retail package. Although they're not as powerful as the full-fledged software they represent (you can't do integrations on the Calculator, for example), taken together they let you expand the functions of your Windows program and iron out any problems that prevent its smooth operation.

As for the applets included on your disks, they remind me of those tidbits offered as product samples at supermarket end-aisles: they whet your appetite without satisfying your hunger. If you're new to Windows and feel like salivating, read the following summary of the applets. Otherwise, skip to the utilities for more nutritious fare.

The Bundled Applets: A Lightweight Software Sampler

The applets are scaled-down versions of commercial application software (hence the nickname *applets*). Microsoft includes them to provide new users with instant gratification when they first get Windows up and running. I'm sure Microsoft dishes these applets out to immediately impress new users and to entice them to purchase real applications, particularly the kind of software that Microsoft itself develops and markets.

Windows includes six applets, some of which can be handy for quick-and-dirty jobs—but if you're trying to do some real work, forget it. For example, Terminal is only good for one-way communications: it lets you make calls, but you can't receive them. So you can dial CompuServe, but you can't receive files from another user. But then again, this applet and the others are free.

For the curious, here's a description of the bundled applets, with a somewhat cynical explanation for their inclusion.

Write

Write The best of the applets, built by Microsoft to tempt you into buying Word.

Paintbrush

Paintbrush Could have been great, but suffers from serious flaws; written by ZSoft as a promo for its other paint programs.

Terminal

Terminal A one-way communications link; provided by FutureSoft, the purveyors of Dynacomm, which provides two-way communications.

Cardfile A cute little graphical rolodex; from Microsoft.

Cardfile

Calendar A miniature appointment book; from Microsoft.

Calendar

Solitaire and **Minesweeper** The fun stuff! Microsoft added these to promote its Entertainment Packs for Windows.

Solitaire   Minesweeper

Part fun, part advertising, and part program, the applets that could have been useful were deliberately crippled so that they wouldn't encroach on the sales territory of their developers. I suppose you shouldn't look a gift program in the menu, but I personally ignore the applets in favor of real applications that haven't been lobotomized.

The Bundled Utilities

The Windows retail package is a grab bag stuffed with lots and lots of handy utilities. Of the 10 utilities covered in this chapter, Expand is the only one that is a DOS, rather than a Windows, utility. Table 5.1 introduces the utilities described in this chapter.

TABLE 5.1
Windows 3.1
Utilities

Icon	Utility Name	File Name	Description
Help	**Help**	WINHELP.EXE	Revamped for Windows 3.1, Help is a rudimentary hypertext help system. Help files can be accessed by running this utility or through an application's Help menu.
Notepad	**Notepad**	NOTEPAD.EXE	The Notepad utility allows simple, nondisruptive editing of text files.
SysEdit	**System Config- uration Editor**	SYSEDIT.EXE	The System Configuration Editor is a handy bare-bones text editor that allows you to simultaneously open the four most important system files: WIN.INI, SYSTEM.INI, AUTOEXEC.BAT, and CONFIG.SYS.

Icon	Utility Name	File Name	Description
Recorder	**Recorder**	RECORDER.EXE	A simple macro-creation and playback utility, Recorder helps you to automate routine tasks.
Character Map	**Character Map**	CHARMAP.EXE	A utility new in 3.1, the Character Map lets you use special characters without having to remember arcane Alt+(ANSI) key combinations.
Clipboard Viewer	**Clipboard Viewer**	CLIPBRD.EXE	A simple but important utility, the Clipboard Viewer lets you manage the contents of the Windows Clipboard.
Calculator	**Calculator**	CALC.EXE	In its standard mode, the Calculator offers the same basic math functions you'd expect in the no-frills dimestore variety. Switch into its scientific mode, however, and you have a full-function scientific calculator.
Clock	**Clock**	CLOCK.EXE	This is the planet's simplest computer utility. Its function is to display the system time. Someone at Microsoft probably wrote this on a coffee break!
Version	**Version**	WINVER.EXE	Another simple utility, this merely identifies the version number and current mode of Windows.
Expand	**Expand**	EXPAND.EXE	This DOS program allows you to decompress files stored on the Windows installation disk.

In addition to the 10 utilities discussed here, other chapters in the book describe several other utilities (I told you there were lots of them!).

Print Manager Controls the printing process (see Chapter 7)

PIF Editor Lets you edit Program Information Files that help DOS programs run better from Windows (see Chapter 14)

PIF Editor

Registration Info Editor Lets you update and edit the application registration database used by OLE (see Chapter 9)

RegEdit

Object Packager A new feature that lets you package a document so that it will work with OLE (see Chapter 9)

Object
Packager

Microsoft Diagnostics A DOS diagnostic utility, new to 3.1, that reveals many of the details concerning your computer's hardware and system configuration (see Chapter 17)

Microsoft
Diagnostics

Dr. Watson A new Windows 3.1 diagnostic utility that helps track down the cause of system crashes (see Chapter 17)

Dr. Watson

Sound Recorder A digital sound recording and playback utility (see Chapter 11)

Sound
Recorder

Media Player A simple control panel modeled after a VCR that lets you play back multimedia files, such as sounds and animations (see Chapter 11)

Media Player

Help

Help

If you need assistance while you're in Windows, a couple of mouse clicks or the quick press of the F1 key summmmons the Windows online help facility (Figure 5.1).

• • • • • • • • • • • •
FIGURE 5.1
*Opening
Windows Help
Screen*

*The Windows Help facility
provides an easy-to-use
quick reference system
for Windows and many of
its applications.*

Windows has an online Help system that lets you browse through or search for information in an onscreen window. The same facility is used for getting context-sensitive help about applications and for providing online documentation for them. The Windows Help facility gives you several different ways to access information. You can scan the index, browse through the various Help files, or search for a particular keyword or phrase.

New in 3.1

Windows 3.1 provides a context-sensitive help system: for example, many dialog boxes contain Help buttons that take you directly to the appropriate page in the online help file.

The name of the Help program is WINHELP.EXE, and its default location is the main Windows directory. You can use Help in one of two ways:

➤ Start it on its own by running the WINHELP.EXE file directly and then choosing a particular help file.

➤ Summon Help from within an application that provides a Windows Help-compatible file, designated by the .HLP file extension. This method lets you get context-sensitive help, if it is provided by the application.

For quick assistance, follow the path of least resistance: press the F1 key—your Windows panic button. In some applications, you can press F1 while a menu item or dialog box option is selected to get help about that item. No matter which method you select, summoning help launches the Windows Help utility (WINHELP.EXE) along with the specific Help file for your application. This utility identifies your location, then places you directly at the appropriate site in the Help file.

If more than one application is running, F1 elicits help only for the foreground application. For example, if you ask for Help while running Program Manager in the foreground and Write in the background, you'll get PROGMAN.HLP—the Help file for Program Manager. To get help for Write, you'll need to select its window and then press F1.

Danger Zone

If you have trouble running Help for an application, make sure the proper .HLP file is located either in your main Windows directory or in another directory listed in your current PATH statement.

Choose Help from the menu to search for a specific Help topic, or launch the Help program (WINHELP.EXE) and then open any Help file; an associated application does not need to be running. Help files, denoted by the .HLP extension, are included for most of the Windows utilities and applets, as well as for the Help program itself. You can double-click on any of these file names in File Manager to launch Help together with a particular help file. If you start Help on its own, by running WINHELP.EXE, it starts without loading any associated Help file. This is a good way to browse through the various Help files, or to look at a particular Help file without launching its associated application. In your browsings, you'll notice that help is not available for Clock, System Configuration Editor, Version, and Dr. Watson.

A typical Help menu—opened from an application—offers this choice of help topics:

➤ **Contents** (Alt,H,C) Displays the Contents page of the application's help file

➤ **Search for Help On** (Alt,H,S) Searches the index of topics in the application's help file

➤ **How to Use Help** (Alt,H,H) Loads the file WINHELP.HLP, which provides the Help information on the Windows Help utility itself

Most Help menus conclude with the About item (Alt,H,A). Choosing this item yields a dialog box that describes the particulars of the application: its version number, copyright information, memory usage, and other details the developer wanted you to know (Figures 5.2 through 5.5).

FIGURE 5.2

Collage About Box

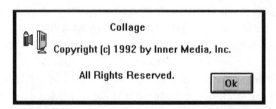

FIGURE 5.3

Microsoft Word About Box

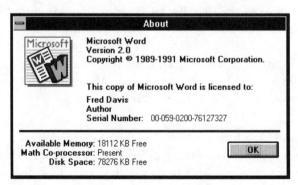

FIGURE 5.4
Realizer
About Box

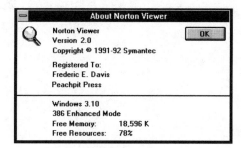

FIGURE 5.5
Norton Viewer
About Box

You'll probably call up Help most frequently in conjunction with a particular application, which may use the Windows Help utility, its own help facility, or a combination of the two. For example, Program Manager's Help menu features the normal Help utility choices and a unique choice called Windows Tutorial (Figure 5.6).

FIGURE 5.6
Program
Manager's Help
Menu

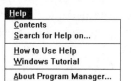

The Windows Tutorial choice on the Help menu starts a separate program called WINTUTOR.EXE.

The Windows Tutorial augments the standard Help facility by providing a basic onscreen course in mouse manipulation. Choosing the Windows Tutorial (Alt,H,W) activates the WINTUTOR.EXE program, which Setup normally copies into your main Windows directory during installation.

Insider's Tip

You can run any program you like from the Windows Tutorial item on the Help menu by renaming your other program WINTUTOR.EXE. (Of course, be sure you have either renamed or removed the original tutorial file.) I use this technique to quickly bring up the System Configuration Editor from Program Manager—I just renamed SYSEDIT.EXE to WINTUTOR.EXE. Or you might want to replace the file with a custom tutorial developed by your company. If you want to get fancy and actually change the menu name to match your new program choice, you'll need to use the Windows Resource Toolkit, described in Appendix B.

The Help Contents Page. The F1 button often leads you directly to the Contents page, unless your application provides context-sensitive help. In any case, you can always see an outline of the information in your help file by accessing the Contents page (Figure 5.7).

••••••••••••••
FIGURE 5.7
Contents Page of Program Manager Help File

The Contents page of this Program Manager Help file presents an outline of the Help topics.

To go directly to the Contents page of a Help file, choose Contents from the Help menu of that application, or start the Help utility from scratch and then open a help file. If you have already leaped into the middle of a help file, you can always return to the Contents page by pressing the Contents button (Alt+C) at the top of the Help window.

Like a typical table of contents, the Contents page provides an alphabetical outline of the topics contained in that file. You can scroll to view the entire list if it extends beyond a single window. If an item is linked to additional information, the mouse pointer turns into the shape of a small hand as you pass over the item. Just click the mouse to activate an onscreen button that will direct you to more information. For example, each underlined topic on the index page represents a hot button—click on it to zoom to the corresponding page in the Help file.

Keyboard users can navigate through the underlined topic items in the Help Index page by using the Tab key to move from topic to topic. To read a selected topic, just press Enter. Here's a list of the special shortcut keys you can use while running Help:

Tab   Moves the selection clockwise through a list of topics and buttons

Shift+Tab   Moves the selection counter-clockwise

Ctrl+Tab	Highlights all the topics and buttons in a Help window
Ctrl+Ins	Copies the current page of Help, or the currently selected annotation, onto the Clipboard without using the Copy dialog box
Shift+Ins	Pastes the Clipboard contents into the Annotation dialog box

Insider's Tip

When you are using some Windows applications—notably those from Microsoft such as Word and Excel—pressing Shift+F1 changes the cursor into a question mark. You can then click on a command, menu item, button, or other on-screen item to obtain help about that item.

Send Out a Search Party. Although you can poke your way around the Contents page to explore the contents of the Help file, that's not always the fastest way to access specific information. The best way to extract a quick answer from Help is to use the Search function. To initiate a search, click on the Search button (Alt+S) to bring up the Search dialog box (Figure 5.8).

FIGURE 5.8

Search Dialog Box

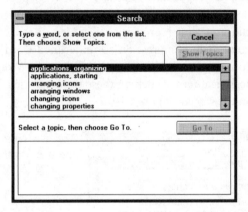

If you know what you want, summoning the Search dialog box is the fastest way to get information.

Type a word in the text box of the Topics section (Alt+W); you'll see a scrollable list of all the matching keywords in the Go To section. Figure 5.9 shows the Search dialog box when it first appears: the first entries in the list of topic keywords are visible, but the Topic text box and the Go To section are blank.

As soon as you type a word in the Topic box, Help searches through the list of keywords until it finds a match. If no match is available, you'll need to scroll through the list of keywords and pick the topic that most closely matches the subject for which you need help. When you select a topic by its keyword (type in the word and press Enter; or double-click on it in the list), the Go To section at the bottom of the dialog box displays a list of the actual topic pages relating to the keyword (Figure 5.9).

• • • • • • • • • • • • •

FIGURE 5.9

*Search Dialog
Box with
Topic Selected*

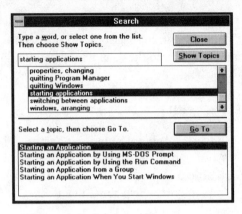

*Pick the specific help page
from the list in the Go To box,
and you're instantly trans-
ported to the proper place in
the Help file.*

Each entry in the Go To box represents a specific page in the Help file. Sometimes several pages are listed, so you'll need to narrow your search further. Once you select a page in the Go To box, double-click on it or press the Go To button (Alt+G) to jump right to it.

Underlined Words Are Especially Helpful. On any Help page, words may appear underlined with either a solid or a dotted line. As mentioned before, words with a solid underline represent subject areas that are linked to other areas of the current Help file; press on an underlined word to jump to the page in the Help file that contains related information. Words with dotted underlines are technical terms; click on these to reveal their definitions in a small window on the screen (Figure 5.10).

• • • • • • • • • • • • •

FIGURE 5.10

*Underlined
Term with
Pop-Up
Window*

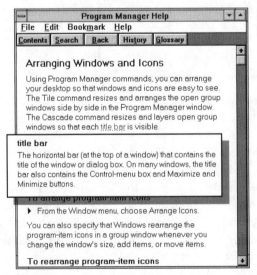

*Words with a dotted under-
line are vocabulary terms.*

The pop-up window with the definition remains on the screen until you click again. From the keyboard, use Tab to move among the items in the Help window; when the selected term is highlighted, press Enter to reveal the pop-up window and Esc to send it back into hiding.

Finding Your Way Back. Just like Hansel and Gretel wandering about the woods, you might easily lose your way without some method for retracing your steps. Help provides two buttons at the top of its window to do just that: Back and History.

The simplest technique for retracing your recent steps, one step at a time, through the current Help session is to press the Back button (Alt+B).

History, on the other hand, lets you view your entire trail of bread crumbs and return to any page you have already visited. Press the History button (Alt+H) and up pops the History dialog box, which contains a scrolling list of all the Help topics you have viewed during your current session (Figure 5.11).

FIGURE 5.11

*Windows
Help History
Dialog Box*

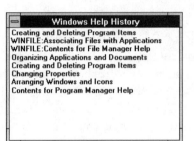

The History button brings up this dialog box, which lets you retrace your steps through all the Help pages that you have viewed during your current session.

The list of topic page names in the History box is presented in reverse chronological order (most recent first), and even includes the pages you've viewed in any other Help file (its name is displayed in all capitals). For example, in Figure 5.11, the entry

`WINFILE: Contents for File Manager Help`

lets you know that the "Contents for File Manager Help" entry is located in the WINFILE.HLP file. If the History box truncates most of the topic page names when it first appears, just grab the lower right corner of the box with the mouse and drag it open to accommodate the full names.

Bookmarks. If you'd like to return to a particular page in the Help file, insert a bookmark there by choosing Define from the Bookmark menu (Alt,M,D). If you haven't defined a Bookmark in your current session, the Define command is the only item on the menu (Figure 5.12).

Bookmark
Define...

FIGURE 5.12
Bookmark Menu with No Bookmarks Defined

Choose Define from the Bookmark menu to place a bookmark on the current page of the Help file.

When you choose Define from the Bookmark menu, the Bookmark Define dialog box appears. This dialog box contains a text box labeled Bookmark Name—a list box that contains any bookmarks you've previously set in the current Help file—and three buttons: OK, Cancel, and Delete (Figure 5.13).

Bookmark Define
Bookmark Name:
Changing Properties
Arranging Windows and Icons
Creating and Deleting Program Items
Organizing Applications and Documents
Starting an Application by Using MS-DOS Pror
The odd-ball commands
This is where I always mess up
OK
Cancel
Delete

FIGURE 5.13
Bookmark Define Dialog Box

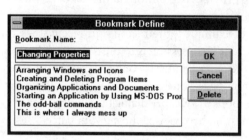

To add or remove a bookmark, use the Bookmark Define dialog box.

To define a bookmark that will return you to the current page in the Help file, first name it, then click OK (Enter). When the dialog box appears, the Bookmark Name text box contains the name of the topic covered on the page. To change the name, simply edit the name in the text box.

You can also use this dialog box to delete an existing bookmark. First select its name in the list box, then click on the Delete button or press Alt+D. Bookmarks are automatically saved along with their corresponding Help file until you manually delete them.

Any bookmarks you've named and defined for a Help file are assigned sequential numbers and listed on the Bookmark menu whenever that Help file is open (Figure 5.14).

Bookmark
Define...
1 Creating and Deleting Program Items
2 Organizing Applications and Documents
3 Arranging Windows and Icons
4 This is where I always mess up
5 Starting an Application by Using MS-DOS Prompt
6 The Odd-Ball commands
7 Changing Properties

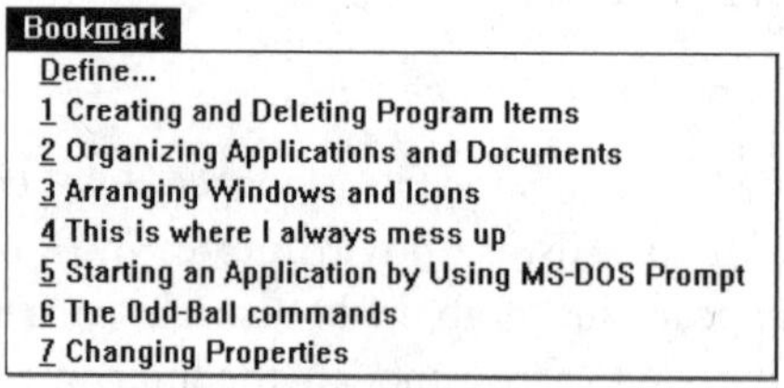

FIGURE 5.14
Bookmark Menu Listing Several Bookmarks

The Bookmark menu lists any bookmarks that you've defined for that particular Help file.

To select a bookmark, click on its name in the menu with the mouse, or type Alt,M, (the menu number on the bookmark). Each Help file saves its own list of bookmarks, which are specific to it and thus cannot be transferred to another Help file.

Writing Notes to Yourself. Help lets you attach notes to a specific page in a Help file. To add a note, go to the current page and choose Annotate from the Edit menu (Alt,E,A). This calls up the Annotate dialog box (Figure 5.15).

FIGURE 5.15
Annotate Dialog Box

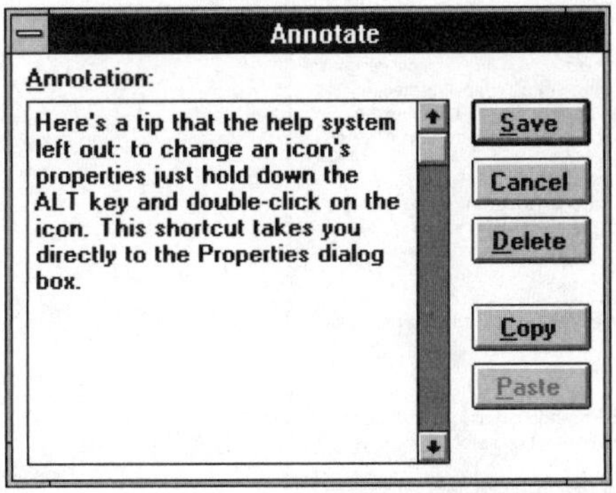

Use the Help Annotation dialog box to enter your own notes.

This dialog box contains a large scrolling text box—Annotation (Alt+A)—and a row of five buttons:

- **Save** (Alt+S) Save whatever you have typed in the Annotation text box
- **Cancel** (Esc) "Never mind!"
- **Delete** (Alt+D) Remove your annotation from the Help page
- **Copy** (Alt+C) Copy whatever is selected in the Annotation text box
- **Paste** (Alt+P) Paste whatever is on the clipboard into the Annotation text box

Enter any notes you want to associate with the current page of the Help file, then click OK to save the annotation. Once you've made an annotation to a topic, a paper clip icon appears to the left of the topic name in the Help file (Figure 5.16). To see the annotation, simply click on the paper clip icon. Or, from the keyboard, press the Tab key until the paper clip is highlighted; then press Enter to reveal the annotation.

Insider's Tip

The Annotate feature allows you to add bits of information specific to your Windows installation, such as notes about your software, hardware, or networking components. You may also want to assign a bookmark to the pages you annotate so that you can access them quickly. However, if you need to add extensive information, you should consider building your own help system, as described later in this section.

FIGURE 5.16
*Help Window
Showing
Paper Clip
Icon*

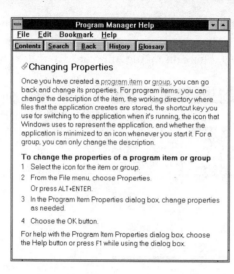

*The paper clip icon indicates
that a note is attached to
this topic page.*

You can also use the Help Annotation dialog box to edit or delete an existing note. Editing is simple: the annotation can be edited directly in the text box. (Select the list box by pressing Alt+A.) To delete the annotation, simply click on the Delete button and press Alt+D.

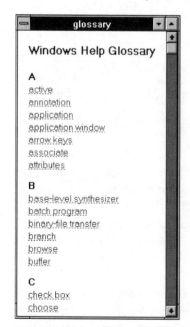

FIGURE 5.17
*Help Glossary
Dialog Box*

Press the Glossary button (Alt+G) to get instant relief from Windows technobabble.

Other Help Features. The top of the Help utility's application window contains a button bar with the various Help options, which almost always include buttons for Contents, Search, Back, History, and Glossary. The first four of these standard buttons were just discussed; the last one, Glossary, provides a limited technical dictionary (Figure 5.17).

The Glossary dialog box contains a list of the terms it defines. The terms are all underlined with a dotted line; this is your tip-off that a click on a word will issue a box with its definition (from the keyboard, press Tab, then Enter). Other programs can also install new buttons in the button bar.

The Help utility includes four menus—File, Edit, Bookmark, and Help. Except for Bookmark, these operate pretty much as they would in any other Windows or Macintosh program. Here's a quick survey of these other Help features.

The **File** menu—which comes first, as with most programs—offers four choices:

➤ **Open** (Alt,F,O) Lets you open a particular Help file without having to start that application first

➤ **Print Topic** (Alt,F,P) Lets you print the text of the current topic page

➤ **Print Setup** (Alt,F,R) Takes you to the standard Printer Setup dialog box (see Chapter 7)

➤ **Exit** (Alt,F,X) The universal command for quitting a Windows program

As is traditional, the **Edit** menu follows next. Edit restricts itself to two entrees: Copy and Annotate (which was just discussed). There's a special procedure for copying information in the Help utility—you can't just select the text with the mouse, as you would ordinarily do in a Windows document. Instead, you must first choose the Copy command from the Edit menu (Alt,E,C); this brings up a special Copy dialog box unique to Help (Figure 5.18).

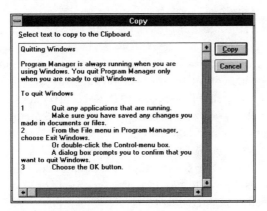

FIGURE 5.18
*Help's Copy
Dialog Box*

To copy anything in Help onto the Windows clipboard, you must first activate this dialog box, which translates the Help topic page into plain text.

Select text from the Copy dialog box, then press the Copy button (Alt+C); the selected text is transferred to the Windows clipboard for pasting into another application. The extra step of using the Copy dialog box is required to translate the topic page—where text is often a button—into a standard text format that will work with your other programs.

The Help utility's last menu is its own **Help** menu, one of the sparsest in its genre. Here are its three choices:

➤ **How To Use Help** (Alt,H,H) Opens the WINHELP.HLP file.

➤ **Always on Top** (Alt,H,T) Forces the Help window to remain on top of any other window. A check mark next to the item indicates that this feature is active.

➥ **About Help** (Alt,H,A) Brings up Help's About box.

Helping Yourself. If you want to add extensive information to a Help file, the Annotate command isn't enough: you can only attach one note per page. Paper clips are handy reminders, but they don't relate to anything else. You want more. You want to be able to display the added information on its own page and link it to any related topics using the standard Help features, such as underlining words to identify them as hot buttons.

To create your own Help file, you'll need to use the Windows Help Compiler, included with the Windows Software Development Kit (SDK). First, create two documents—a topic and a project file—in the Microsoft RTF (Rich Text Format) file format. To do this, you'll need a wordprocessor that supports RTF, such as—you guessed it!—Microsoft Word. The topic file contains all the information on the actual topic pages, and the project file is a program control file that guides the Help Compiler in creating the final .HLP file.

Dynamite Product

Creating the RTF topic and project files can be a pain, but the clever folks at Blue Sky Software have devised an easier way with a product called RoboHELP. This program is a collection of DLLs (dynamic link libraries) that work together with Word for Windows and the Help Compiler to make creating your own help file a snap. The RoboHELP system adds a special set of controls that lets you easily create new topics, link items to one another, and create pop-up windows with definitions of terms and other information.

RoboHELP automatically creates the project file, leaving you the task of defining the information for the topic pages and determining ways to link pages. If you can't find RoboHELP at your usual software source, contact Blue Sky directly (see Appendix C).

Insider's Tip

Custom Help files shouldn't be the sole domain of software developers. These files can help authors document procedures for using network devices or other special kinds of hardware or software. Creative Help authors can also use custom Help files to write simple hypertext booklets on any subject, from employee handbooks to restaurant guides or even joke books.

You can use a Help file even if it isn't linked to an application. For example, APPS.HLP is a standalone Help file that contains information about Windows 3.0 applications that have compatibility problems with 3.1. To access a standalone Help file, create an icon for it in Program Manager by dragging in the .HLP file from File Manager. Your standalone file will run with Help automatically because .HLP files are already associated with the Help utility.

Notepad

The Notepad

The Windows Notepad can be used to read, edit, and write generic ASCII text files. Although you can only open files smaller than 50K with Notepad, its paucity of features actually adds to its value. Because it doesn't insert any formatting information into a file, as do most wordprocessors, Notepad is critical for editing system files, such as WIN.INI, where formatting commands could crash the system. Most wordprocessors insert invisible formatting codes for elements such as font changes or special characters, which can wreak havoc on your system initialization files and prevent Windows or an application from functioning properly.

To start Notepad, click on its application icon in Program Manager, or run NOTEPAD.EXE from File Manager. If you start Notepad by running the application alone, you'll be presented with an empty, untitled document window (Figure 5.19).

FIGURE 5.19

*An Empty
Notepad File*

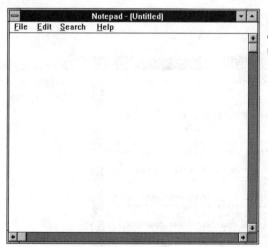

*Notepad starts with an
empty, untitled document
window.*

Notepad can also be launched simultaneously with a single associated text file (you can open only one file at a time). To do this in Program Manager, create a program icon that specifies both NOTEPAD.EXE and the name of a text file. Or, from File Manager, simply double-click on any file whose file name extension is associated with the NOTEPAD.EXE application; by default, Notepad is associated with files containing the .TXT or .INI extension. Use the Extensions statement of your WIN.INI file or File Manager's Associate command (see Chapter 3) to specify the file extensions of the ASCII text file types you wish to edit with Notepad.

These file name extensions are commonly used to identify plain ASCII text files that you may want to associate with the Notepad:

⌠ **.1ST** For read-me files; for example, README.1ST

⌠ **.ASC** For ASCII text files

⌠ **.BAK** For backup files, such as AUTOEXEC.BAK

⌠ **.CFG** For configuration and settings files

⌠ **.ME** For read-me files; for example, READ.ME

⌠ **.SYS** For configuration files; for example, CONFIG.SYS

⌠ **.TOO** For read-me files; for example, README.TOO

Wrap Session. Unlike a wordprocessor, Notepad does not automatically wrap text to the next line when it reaches the right-hand edge of your window. This allows you to create lines that are longer than the width of the window (Figure 5.20). To view the entire length of your lines, use the horizontal scroll bar.

• • • • • • • • • • • • • •
FIGURE 5.20
*Notepad with
Lines Longer
than Width of
Window*

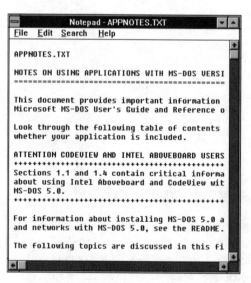

Notepad doesn't automatically wrap lines to fit into the window.

To end a line of text and start a new one, press Enter to insert a carriage return. This ensures that the line will actually end at the carriage return. Notepad also offers a Word Wrap feature that automatically wraps lines to fit in its window, but the actual length of the line remains unaffected (Figure 5.21).

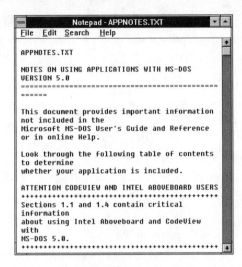

FIGURE 5.21
Notepad with Word Wrap On

With Word Wrap turned on, Notepad wraps text in the display.

To turn Word Wrap on, choose it from the Edit menu (or press Alt,E,W). To disable wrapping, and see where your lines really end, as defined by carriage returns, reissue the Word Wrap command.

Editing Your Notes. Notepad uses editing techniques that are similar to other Windows wordprocessors. To navigate within a document, try one of the keyboard shortcuts shown in Table 5.2; they allow you to skip around a document with awesome agility.

TABLE 5.2
Keyboard Shortcuts for Navigating in a Document

Press	To Move
Right arrow	One character to the right
Left arrow	One character to the left
Ctrl-right arrow	One word to the right
Ctrl-left arrow	One word to the left
Up arrow	Up one line
Down arrow	Down one line
PgUp	Up one screen
PgDn	Down one screen
Home	To the beginning of the current line
End	To the end of the current line
Ctrl+Home	To the beginning of the text file
Ctrl+End	To the end of the text file
Ctrl+PgDn	The window display to the right
Ctrl+PgUp	The window display to the left

You can select text using standard mouse techniques; or Notepad provides the shortcut combinations shown in Table 5.3 to let you select text from the keyboard. Most of these shortcuts use the navigation keys in combination with the Shift key.

TABLE 5.3
Keyboard Shortcuts for Selecting Text

Press	To Select or Deselect
Shift+right arrow	One character to the right
Shift+left arrow	One character to the left
Ctrl+Shift+right arrow	One word to the right
Ctrl+Shift+left arrow	One word to the left
Shift+down arrow	From the insertion point to the end of line and moves down one line
Shift+up arrow	From the insertion point to the beginning of line and moves up one line
Shift+PgUp	The insertion point and moves it up by one window; then selects the text in between
Shift+PgDn	The insertion point and moves it down by one window; then selects the text in between
Shift+Home	The text from the insertion point to the beginning of the line
Shift+End	The text from the insertion point to the end of the line
Ctrl+Shift+Home	The text from the insertion point to the beginning of the document
Ctrl+Shift+End	The text from the insertion point to the end of the document

To select all of the text in a file, Notepad provides a shortcut command, Select All, which appears on the Edit menu (or type Alt,E,S). Notepad highlights all the text to show that it is selected. To deselect it, click anywhere in the text section of the window.

Finders, Keepers. The Notepad's Search menu contains two commands, Find and Find Next, which help locate occurrences of text within a document. Unlike most wordprocessors, the Notepad Search command cannot automatically change what it finds; that is, it does not perform search and replace operations.

To search for text within a Notepad document, choose Find from the Search menu, or press Alt,S,F. The Find dialog box appears (Figure 5.22).

FIGURE 5.22

Find Dialog Box

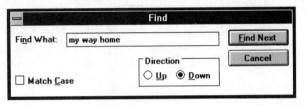

Search and Ye Shall Find: the Find dialog box lets you enter a text string to search for a specific text within a Notepad document.

Select the Find What text box (Alt+F) and enter the text string that you wish to locate. Keep in mind that the Notepad Find command does not work with the DOS wildcard characters asterisk (*) and question mark (?). Normally, the Match Upper/Lowercase check box is empty; click on it (or press Alt+C) if you want the search to be case sensitive, matching upper- and lowercase letters exactly.

Two radio buttons, labeled Up and Down, appear at the bottom of the Find dialog box. By default, the Find command searches from the insertion point to the end of the document. If you select the Up option (Alt+U), the Find command searches from the insertion point back to the beginning of the document.

After entering a text string and setting any other options, click OK. Notepad then searches in the specified direction and selects the first occurrence of that text. (If Notepad doesn't find the string you've specified, a dialog box appears to inform you.) You can edit the selected text, or select the Find Next command (F3) to locate the next occurrence of that text. With the Find Next command, all your previous settings are applied as Notepad searches for the next occurrence of the string.

It's a Date. Notepad also gives you a shortcut command for inserting the time and date into a document. Choose the Time/Date command from the Edit menu (F5). Notepad places the current system time and date at the insertion point, in the format specified in the Control Panel.

To automatically place the time and date in a document each time you open it, simply type .LOG at the left margin on the very first line in the file; then—because the command has to occupy a line on its own—press Return. Each time Notepad opens the file, it automatically adds the current time and date to the end of the file, according to whatever format you specified in the Control Panel (Figure 5.23). Make sure the .LOG statement is the first line of the file; otherwise, it won't be time stamped.

FIGURE 5.23

A Time-Log File

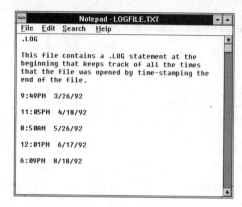

Type .LOG at the beginning of a text file to have Notepad automatically place the time and date at the end of the file each time it is opened.

Undo. Notepad, like many Windows applications, lets you undo only your last action. Simply choose the Undo command from the Edit menu (Ctrl+Z).

Size Limits. This feature limits your work so much, you're forced to go out and buy a different text editor. Perhaps that was the intention. Because Notepad can only open files of about 52K in size, and can only edit files of 45K at the largest—regardless of your available RAM or system resources— you'll have to use a different program in order to edit a longer file, such as the SETUP.INF and APPS.INF files used by Setup. If you edit such files with a wordprocessing program, be careful to save the file as a text-only document; do not try to format it.

Notepad Printing. Notepad's minimalist printing facility consists of three File menu commands: Print Setup, Page Setup, and Print. Of course, before you can print, you need to set up a printer for use with Windows. If you haven't done this, or if you want to change to a new printer, choose the Print Setup command from the File menu, or press Alt,F,R, which calls up the standard Printer Setup dialog box.

To change the default margin settings, or to add a simple header or footer to your printout, choose Page Setup from the File menu (Alt,F,T). This calls up the Page Setup dialog box (Figure 5.24).

FIGURE 5.24

Page Setup Dialog Box

The Page Setup dialog box allows you to alter the margin settings and to specify simple headers and footers.

To specify a header, click in the Header box (Alt+H) and then enter your preferred header. Do the same to enter a footer, but click in the Footer box (Alt+F). By default, Notepad centers headers and footers on the page, but you can alter their position by typing one of three special codes into the text box:

&l	Places the header or footer flush with the left margin
&r	Places the header or footer flush with the right margin
&c	Centers the header or footer between the left and right margins

Notepad also recognizes these four additional codes:

&f	Adds the current file name in a header or footer
&d	Adds the current system date
&t	Adds the current system time
&p	Adds sequential page numbers, starting with 1

These four codes can be used alone, in combination with text, or with other codes, including the three formatting codes. For example, to create a header with the name of the file flush left and the page number flush right, type this into the Header text box:

```
&l&f&r Page &p
```

To set a margin value, click on the appropriate text box: Left (Alt+L), Right (Alt+R), Top (Alt+T), or Bottom (Alt+B). Then enter a margin setting in inches. When you've completed the Page Setup box, click OK to return to your document. Now you can print the file by choosing Print from the File menu (Alt,F,P).

Saving Your Notes. To save a Notepad file, choose Save from the File menu (Alt,F,S). If the file has not yet been saved, the File Save As dialog box appears. Otherwise, the new version is automatically saved on the disk.

To save your existing file under a new name, choose Save As from the File menu (Alt,F,A). This brings up the File Save As dialog box, but with one difference: the Filename text box now contains the name of the current file. Either edit that name or enter a new name; then click OK (Enter) to save the current file under the new name.

Opening Notepad Files. To edit an existing file, choose Open from the File menu (Alt,F,O); the File Open dialog box appears. The top of the File Open dialog box contains a text box, entitled Filename. Here you'll see the DOS wildcard character (*) followed by the extension .TXT. This signifies that Notepad will open, by default, all files ending with the .TXT extension. The scrolling Files list box in the lower left corner of the Files Open dialog box displays only files from the selected directory that have the .TXT extension.

To view all the files in the directory in the Files list box, select All Files (*.*) from the List Files of Type drop-down list box.

SysEdit

The System Configuration Editor

The System Configuration Editor—which I call SysEdit for short—is a utility program that allows you to simultaneously edit the four most critical system startup files: SYSTEM.INI, WIN.INI, CONFIG.SYS, and AUTOEXEC.BAT. SysEdit's text-editing capabilities are even more primitive than those found in Notepad, but unlike Notepad, which can open only a single file at any given time, SysEdit allows you to open these four (and only these four) files at the same time.

Danger Zone

Because SysEdit allows you to open all four system files at once, your mistakes can be multiplied by four, with the greater likelihood that an inadvertent change could cause a system crash. If you exercise a little caution, however, this utility can offer you a panoramic view of your most important system files.

As if to prevent widespread public knowledge of SysEdit, Microsoft makes scant reference to it and practically hides the program file, SYSEDIT.EXE, inside the \SYSTEM subdirectory of your main Windows directory. To bury its presence even more, Windows doesn't install SysEdit in Program Manager on startup. But SysEdit is a utility that every power user will want to have on hand. To create a Program Manager icon for it, drag it in from File Manager (or use any of the other methods described in Chapter 2).

Start SysEdit as you would any other application. Because SysEdit works only with the four system files, you don't have to specify them; they'll appear automatically. The four windows will overlap in a cascading arrangement, displaying the title bars of each file (Figure 5.25).

To select any of these files, simply click on the title bar to bring that window to the top of the stack. Keyboard users can choose the name of the file from the Window menu, using the keystrokes shown in Table 5.4.

TABLE 5.4

This Keystroke	Selects the Document Window of This File
Alt,W,1	SYSTEM.INI
Alt,W,2	WIN.INI
Alt,W,3	CONFIG.SYS
Alt,W,4	AUTOEXEC.BAT

FIGURE 5.25

*SysEdit
Window*

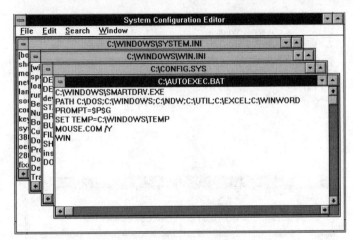

*With Sys-
Edit, you
can edit the
four most
important
system files
simulta-
neously.*

In some cases, more than one copy of these files may be contained somewhere on your drives; SysEdit displays only the ones that are actually in use. In order to discover which files were opened by SysEdit, scan the path names of the open files by inspecting the list on the bottom half of the Window menu. Click on the name Window on the menu bar, or type Alt,W to reveal the Window menu (Figure 5.26). Inspecting this menu is a handy way to determine exactly which system files are active in case different directories contain duplicate startup files.

FIGURE 5.26

*Window
Menu*

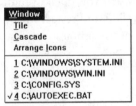

*SysEdit's Window menu lets you quickly check
the path names of the startup files that
your system is currently using.*

You can also shrink any of the four document windows into icons within the SysEdit window (Figure 5.27).

Laziness is good enough justification to have SysEdit automatically arrange the documents or their icons. You can apply the standard techniques by using these commands on SysEdit's Window menu:

➤ **Arrange Icons** (Alt,W,I) Lines up the document icons at the bottom of the application window

➤ **Tile command** (Alt,W,T) and **Cascade command** (Alt,W,C) Both operate much as they do in Program Manager

FIGURE 5.27

*Minimized
Document
Icons*

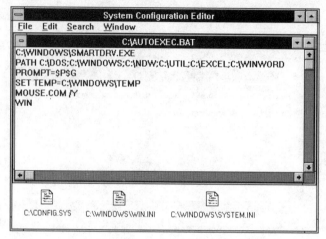

You can minimize the four file windows into document icons. But these icons sure are ugly!

To close any of the four files or document windows individually, double-click on its Control icon or choose Close from the Control menu (Alt,Minus,C). However, if you close a window in SysEdit, remember that you cannot reopen it during your current SysEdit session because the utility only works with four files, with four constant names, and therefore does not have an Open command on its File menu. These four files are launched automatically and simultaneously when you open SysEdit. So to reopen a file you've closed, you must quit SysEdit and restart the program.

The File menu in SysEdit is one of the simplest you'll see in Windows. It contains these five selections:

➣➣ **Save** (Alt,F,S) Save a file

➣➣ **Print** (Alt,F,P) Print a file

➣➣ **Print Setup** (Alt,F,T) Designates a printer other than your currently selected one

➣➣ **Exit** (Alt,F,X) Quit SysEdit

➣➣ **About** (Alt,F,B) Because SysEdit has no Help menu, the About box can be selected here

SysEdit's Edit menu is as sparsely populated as the File menu. It offers the commands shown in Table 5.5.

TABLE 5.5
SysEdit Edit Menu

Command	Shortcut	Action
Undo	Ctrl+Z	Undo last edit action
Cut	Ctrl+X	Cut selected text to clipboard
Copy	Ctrl+C	Copy selected text to clipboard
Paste	Ctrl+V	Place contents of clipboard at insertion point
Clear	Del	Delete current selection
Select All	Alt,E,S	Select entire contents of active document window

You can also apply most of the Notepad keyboard shortcuts listed in the previous section.

SysEdit's third menu, Search, contains three commands:

➡ **Find** (Alt,S,F) Lets you search for a text string in the active document window

➡ **Next** (F3) Searches for the next instance of the text string, from the current insertion point, to the end of the file

➡ **Previous** (F4) Searches for the specified text string backward through the file to the beginning

Recorder

The Recorder

Recorder provides a simple way to record and play back macros that contain keystroke and mouse actions. Compared with a full-fledged macro utility, such as CE Software's ProKey for Windows or the batch utility included with Norton Desktop for Windows, Recorder is a bit brain dead; nonetheless, it can be very handy for doing simple things—and after all, it's free.

A few straightforward tasks do match Recorder's limited capabilities. You can trim a long menu selection and dialog box sequence down to a single key combination; create automated demonstrations; and develop a self-running continuous demo that won't quit until the computer is turned off. I also use Recorder to save text strings, such as my name and address, for quick placement in a wordprocessor. You can even use Recorder to re-create a picture or format a document.

Recorder can work in a specific application or globally within all applications, but it only works with Windows applications. You can pass information to a DOS application with Recorder by taking control of the Clipboard, but you can't use Recorder as a DOS macro facility.

Danger Zone

Exercise extreme caution when using Recorder to track commands issued with the mouse. Because Recorder interprets all your mouse actions literally, any slight difference in the arrangement of your Windows desktop can trigger a major variance in the way your macro is replayed. I suggest you use the keyboard equivalents whenever possible to select items from menus and other tasks, which is why I've given keyboard equivalents for the major commands throughout this book.

Running Recorder. Run Recorder either from its Program Manager icon or directly from the RECORDER.EXE file in File Manager. Remember, you must run Recorder when creating macros and when you replay them. If you frequently use macros created with Recorder, you can save time by placing the program item icon for a macro file into the Startup group in Program Manager, and set it to start along with Recorder as a minimized icon.

To record a macro, double-click on the Recorder icon and select Record from the Macro menu (Alt,M,R). The resulting Record Macro dialog box allows you to assign a macro name and a shortcut key, and to set some other options (Figure 5.28).

••••••••••••••
FIGURE 5.28
*Record Macro
Dialog Box*

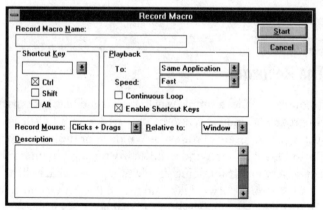

Using the Record Macro dialog box, you can name a macro, assign it a shortcut key, and set several options.

The Record Macro dialog box contains these sections:

➡ **Record Macro Name** (Alt+N) Name your macro

➡ **Shortcut Key** (Alt+K) Assign a shortcut key to your macro

➡ **Playback** (Alt+P) Control how your macro is replayed after recording

➻ **Record Mouse** (Alt+M) Control how the mouse is recorded: everything; only clicks and drags; or nothing

➻ **Relative To** (Alt+R) Specify whether mouse movements will be recorded relative to the selected window or to the entire screen

➻ **Description** (Alt+D) Enter a lengthy description of your macro; a good place for mini-documentation, if you plan to distribute your macro

Type the name of your macro (maximum 40 characters) in the Record Macro Name text box; if that's not enough, use the Description text box at the bottom of the Record Macro dialog box. You must specify either a name or a shortcut key for all macros; or you can use both. I usually specify a shortcut key and a short name; if you deplete all the available shortcut key combinations during a session of macro mania, you can create more macros and assign them names only. (You can invoke name-only macros by name as described later in this section.)

The Shortcut Key—used to issue the macro from the keyboard—can be selected from a large number of key combinations. Shortcut key combinations usually use two keys. In a two-key combination, one key must be either Ctrl, Shift, or Alt (place an X in the appropriate check box, or, from the keyboard, move to a choice with Tab, then use the spacebar to toggle the boxes on or off); the other can be almost any key on the keyboard (type it into the Shortcut Key box, or pull down the names of nonalphabetic keys from the scroll box below the text box). In a three-key combination, the first two keys must be either Ctrl+Shift, Ctrl+Alt, or Alt+Shift, and the third can be any other key. For four-letter macros, the first three keys must be Ctrl+Shift+Alt, and the fourth can be any other key.

Danger Zone

Recorder offers you almost too many choices for shortcut keys. For example, Recorder will let you assign many Alt key combinations that are already used by Windows or other applications. You can check this book for key combinations used by Windows and check your other manuals for potential conflicts with your Windows applications. As a general rule, avoid Alt-only key combinations; Ctrl+Shift is a good choice if you're unsure, because it's seldom used by Windows or third-party applications.

If you're creating one of your first macros, type the second letter of a two-key combination into the Shortcut Key text box, and your key combination will use the default of the Ctrl key as the first key in the combination. For example, to write a macro to type your password for access to an online service, you could choose the combination Ctrl+P; this would prevent anyone from discovering your password by watching you type.

The defaults for the other settings in the dialog box—Playback, Record Mouse, and Relative To—will usually be adequate for creating simple macros that generate text strings, such as a password or address. The Record Mouse and Relative To options need to be set before you record your macro, but the Playback options can be changed later if necessary.

To select the Playback section of the Record Macro dialog box, click on one of its options or press Alt+P and use Tab to move from setting to setting. As usual, the up and down arrow keys scroll through the choices in the drop-down lists, and the spacebar toggles check marks in the check boxes. These are your options for macro playback:

➤ **To** A drop-down list box that allows you to specify whether the macro will be used only in the application in which it was recorded, or globally throughout Windows. For example, you might want to restrict the use of one password macro to your e-mail program and another to your terminal program.

➤ **Speed** A drop-down list box that allows you to vary the playback speed of the macro, between the recorded speed (useful for demonstrations) and a fast speed (useful for command shortcuts).

➤ **Continuous Loop** When checked, this option causes the macro to repeat itself indefinitely in a continuous loop (another useful feature when creating demos).

➤ **Enable Shortcut Keys** When checked, this option lets you disable or enable the use of other Shortcut Keys during playback. Remove the X to block any other macros from playing while you are recording a new macro.

Below the Shortcut Key and Playback sections is the Record Mouse drop-down list box (Alt+R), which lets you choose which types of mouse movements, if any, will be recorded in your macro:

➤ **Clicks+Drags** The general-purpose default setting records all your clicks, double-clicks, and drags. Mouse movement is recorded only while the button is held down.

➤ **Everything** Records every darned thing the mouse does; watch out when using this option!

➤ **Ignore Mouse** Because recording mouse actions is so unpredictable, this is the setting I use most often. This also lets you use the mouse for setting things up without having those mouse actions become part of the macro.

Danger Zone

If you choose Everything, absolutely everything will be recorded. This means you will not be able to gracefully cease recording your macro—even your selection of the Recorder icon to stop recording the macro will be recorded. You'll have to use the Ctrl+Break macro terminator to stop recording. For this reason, make sure you place a check mark next to Control+Break Checking on the Options menu, as described in the next section, if you ever use the Everything option.

The box labeled Relative To, next to the Record Mouse list box, allows you to specify whether your macro will be recorded relative to the currently selected window (which is the default setting) or relative to the entire screen. The default setting works well if you want to run the macro later, when the window is in a different position on the screen. However, if you're working with several applications, it's sometimes best to maximize each window, record the macro relative to the entire screen, and then restore the window after recording. Remember to always maximize and restore with keyboard commands, not with the mouse, in case the program windows are in a different place the next time the macro is run.

The Recorder permits you to embed up to five levels of macros within one another; in fact, that's the default setting (which you can turn off by removing the X from the Enable Shortcut Keys check box in the Record Macro dialog box). To nest the macros, invoke one macro while you are recording another by pressing its shortcut keys. Note that only the key combination you press is recorded, not the actual macro sequence it generates, which you may see being played out on your screen. This means you can make changes to a macro sequence without affecting its host macro. But before you alter a macro that is invoked by another macro, make sure you aren't setting up a chain of reactions you did not intend.

Other Recorder Options. You can also combine two macro files by choosing the Merge command from Recorder's File menu (Alt,F,M). The File Merge dialog box appears (Figure 5.29).

FIGURE 5.29

*File Merge
Dialog Box*

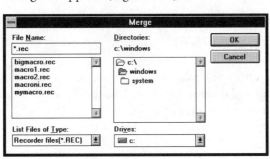

This dialog box lets you merge two macro files into one.

If you are merging two macro files that contain some identical macros, you should delete the duplicates. If Recorder discovers any duplicate shortcut key assignments (either for the same or different macros), it deletes the duplicate shortcut keys from the second of the two merged files—that's one reason you should assign a name, even a short one, to all your macros—and it presents an alert box warning about the duplicates. If you see this alert box, or if you suspect some other conflict (such as key commands used by a particular application), choose the Properties command from the Macro menu (Alt, M, P). The Macro Properties dialog box appears, allowing you to assign new keyboard shortcut keys to the duplicates (Figure 5.30).

• • • • • • • • • • • • • •

FIGURE 5.30

Macro Properties Dialog Box

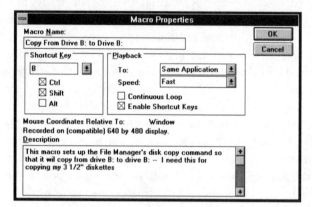

Play it again, Sam! The Macro Properties dialog box bears a striking resemblance to the Record Macro dialog box shown in Figure 5.28.

The Macro Properties dialog box contains many of the same commands as the Record Macro dialog box described earlier in this section, and lets you modify the way an individual macro works. Use the Macro Properties dialog box to change these designations:

➺ The macro's name or description

➺ The assignment of shortcut key combinations

➺ The Playback To option from "Same Application to "Any Application"

➺ Whether the macro plays back once or in a continuous loop

➺ Whether the macro will recognize other shortcut keys

For example, you could use this dialog box to temporarily disable a key combination and thereby free those keys for use in another macro.

The Options menu provides other options for using the Recorder (Figure 5.31).

FIGURE 5.31
Options Menu

Options
√ Control+Break Checking
√ Shortcut Keys
√ Minimize On Use
Preferences...

The Options menu displays check marks in front of selected options.

The first three options—Control+Break Checking, Shortcut Keys, and Minimize On Use—are active if preceded by a check mark.

➡ **Control+Break Checking** (Alt,O,C) If this option is checked, pressing Ctrl+Break terminates a macro; if it's not checked, Recorder ignores the Ctrl+Break key combination.

➡ **Shortcut Keys** (Alt,O,S) If checked, macros run normally; if not checked, this option disables the detection of shortcut keys and puts Recorder to sleep for a while. Use this option to temporarily suppress the use of macros whenever you are running an application with conflicting key combinations.

➡ **Minimize on Use** (Alt,O,M) Checking this option causes Recorder to start as a minimized icon.

➡ **Preferences** (Alt,O,P) This option lets you specify your preferred Default settings in the Record Macro dialog box.

The default setting for Control+Break Checking is to leave it checked so that you can bail from a continuously running macro. Otherwise, you'll have to terminate the Recorder program or restart your computer to stop the macro from looping continuously. There are some instances when you'll want to deactivate Control+Break Checking: for playing a self-running demo, so that no one can stop it; or if you want to nest the Ctrl+Break key combination inside another macro. To reactivate the option, choose it from the menu.

The last item on the Options menu, Preferences, brings up the Default Preferences dialog box, for choosing default settings when you record a new macro (Figure 5.32).

FIGURE 5.32
Default Preferences Dialog Box

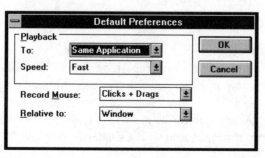

The Default Preferences dialog box lets you tell Recorder what default settings you prefer.

The Default Preferences dialog box contains these settings:

➤ **Playback To** (Alt+P) Lets you choose whether the macro will work with any application as a default, or is limited to run in the one in which it was recorded

➤ **Playback Speed** (Alt+P,Tab) Lets you choose normal or fast playback as the default

➤ **Record Mouse** (Alt+M) Lets you set the default for how mouse movements are recorded

➤ **Relative To** (Alt+R) Lets you choose whether the default recording for mouse movements is relative to a window or to the entire screen

Insider's Tip

An undocumented feature of Recorder allows you to view—but not edit—the actual recorded script. You'll see a numbered list of every event in the macro, including the time that each step took when you recorded it. The time values are used when you play back a macro at the recorded speed. At fast playback, however, Recorder ignores these time values and cranks through the macro as fast as it can. The ability to view the script is useful for debugging it. To view the script, hold down Shift while choosing Properties from the Macro menu (Alt,M,P). Figure 5.33 shows the secret Macro Events dialog box.

• • • • • • • • • • • • •

FIGURE 5.33

Macro Events Dialog Box

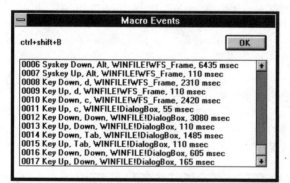

Hold down Shift while choosing Properties from the Macro menu to see this secret Macro Events dialog box, which contains the actual script of your macro.

A Sample Macro. Although the Recorder utility has its limitations, it's useful for automating some repetitive tasks. The following example demonstrates how to use Recorder to create a command macro that activates and deactivates the password feature of your screen saver (discussed in the last chapter). A simple Recorder macro can replace the several steps normally required to do this operation with a single-step key combination, provided your Windows screen saver supports the use of a password (most do). Here's what you do:

1. Start Recorder and choose Record from the Macro menu (Alt,M,C).

2. Type the name "Password On/Off Switch" into the Record Macro Name text box.

3. Type the letter P into the Shortcut Key box.

4. Make sure that the default Ctrl check box contains an X, and place another X in the Shift box; this, along with step 3, specifies Ctrl+Shift+P as the shortcut key.

5. Select Ignore Mouse in the Record Mouse drop-down list.

6. Optional: type a description, such as "toggles the screen-saver's password option on and off."

The settings for this macro are depicted in the Record Macro dialog box shown in Figure 5.34.

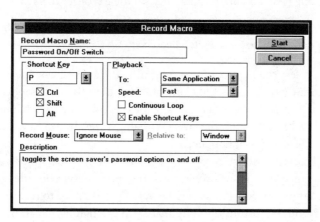

FIGURE 5.34
*Record Macro
Dialog Box
Settings for
Password
On/Off Switch*

*Your settings
for the example
Password On/Off
Switch macro
should look this.*

Once you've set up the Record Macro dialog box, click on the Start button (Alt+S) to begin recording your macro. Recorder shrinks to an icon, which flashes to indicate that a macro is being recorded. To create the actual macro, follow these steps:

1. Press Alt,F,R to bring up the Run dialog box.

2. Type **control** into the Command Line box. (It's better to run the Control Panel this way, rather than select its icon, because the icon position can change.)

3. Press Enter to remove the Run dialog box and actually run the Control Panel.

4. Press Alt,S,D to bring up the Desktop Controls dialog box.

5. Press Alt+U to push the Setup button in the Screen Saver section of the Desktop Controls and issue the setup dialog box for the current screen saver.

6. Press Alt+P to select the Password Options section of the screen saver's Setup dialog box.

7. Press the spacebar to toggle the X in the Password Protected check box.

8. Press Enter to return to the Desktop Controls dialog box.

9. Press Enter again to close the Desktop Controls and return to the Control Panel.

10. Press Alt+F4 to close the Control Panel.

11. Terminate the macro by pressing Ctrl+Break. If Control+Break Checking is turned off, double-click on the Recorder icon to end the macro.

12. Recorder displays a box asking if you want to save the macro, continue recording, or cancel it. Select Save.

To test the macro, press Ctrl+Shift+P, then sit back and watch the show: Windows first opens the Control Panel, then the Desktop icon, then brings up the screen saver's Setup dialog box, toggles the switch, and finally winds its way back through the layers of dialog boxes. In a fast system, you'll hardly be able to see it all happen.

I advise against recording macros that include mouse actions; if you rearrange your icons or windows, the mouse won't be able to find them the next time you run a macro. However, if you do need to record mouse actions, and you are confining your macro to a single application, you'll need to decide whether the application window or the screen should be used as the reference point for your mouse movements. Then adjust the corresponding settings in the Relative To box, which allow you to define whether your movements are relative to the active window or to the entire screen.

Running Macros. To issue a macro, Recorder must be running and the file containing your macro must be loaded. Then press the appropriate shortcut keys; or double-click on the macro's name in the Recorder window; or select it with the cursor arrow keys. Then choose Run from the Macro menu (Alt,M,R). To stop a continuously looping macro, press Ctrl+Break if that option is activated; otherwise, you may have to reboot your computer.

Only one macro file can be loaded at a time. To use two macros at once, apply the Merge command to join the two files into one. However, Recorder limits your urge to merge by restricting the macro file to 64K, no matter how much free memory is available. Also, because Recorder is sensitive to the screen resolution of your monitor, any macros that use mouse actions may not work properly if you change your display resolution—another good reason to stick to explicit keyboard equivalents for all mouse actions, if possible.

The easiest method to speed access to a macro is to create a program item icon for your macro file. Macro files end with the .REC file extension. Just drag the file icon for the macro from File Manager into Program Manager to quickly create a program item icon. Then hold down Alt and double-click on your new program item icon to access its Properties dialog box. Place an X in the Run Minimized check box so that Recorder will run as an icon. When you double-click the icon, you'll both start up Recorder and load the macro file. Then you can use the macros in that file.

To make your macros available anytime during your Windows session, you can load them automatically. First use the Merge command (Alt,F,M) to join any individual macro files that contain your intended macros. Then create a program item icon for the macro file as described earlier. (Remember to set the Run Minimized option.) Place the new icon in the Startup group, and the macro file will be automatically loaded when you start Windows.

Insider's Tip

Here's an undocumented way to create a program item icon that will not only run Recorder together with a macro file but will also start a particular macro by simulating the pressing of a key combination. You can place this icon in the Startup group to initiate the macro every time you start Windows, thus replicating the concept of the AUTOEXEC.BAT file for Windows.

To do this, you'll need to specify certain options in the Command Line section of the icon's Properties dialog box. To get started, hold down Ctrl while dragging the Recorder icon in Program Manager; this creates an exact duplicate of the icon. Then hold down Alt while double-clicking on the icon to open the Properties box. In the Command Line box, enter RECORDER, followed by the -H switch, the macro shortcut key, and the name of its parent macro file. This is the syntax of the entries in the Command Line box:

```
RECORDER -H <special code for the shortcut key><name of the
          macro file>
```

For example, suppose you have a macro triggered by Ctrl+Shift+A that opens several programs and arranges them in a convenient way for working on a special project. This macro is contained in a file named ARRANGE.REC, which is stored in the \MACROS directory of your C: drive. To create a program item icon for this macro, here's what you would enter into the Command Line box of the icon's Properties dialog box:

```
recorder -H ^+A c:\macros\arrange
```

Note that Recorder assumes the .REC extension on the ARRANGE.REC macro file name (specifying the PATH is always smart), and that the -H switch should be upper case. The up-carat (^) and plus sign (+) represent special codes for the Ctrl and Shift keys in the Command Line options. (% represents the Alt key.)

· ·

Character Map

The Character Map

The Character Map utility provides a simple way to view the character sets for all the various fonts installed in your system. It also lets you access the characters for cutting and pasting into your document, which allows you to use special characters that aren't on the keyboard without having to search for and type in arcane ANSI codes. The Character Map utility, CHARMAP.EXE, is installed by Setup as an icon in Program Manager's Accessories group. Running Character Map brings up the window shown in Figure 5.35.

· · · · · · · · · · · · · ·
FIGURE 5.35
Character Map Window, Times Roman Typeface

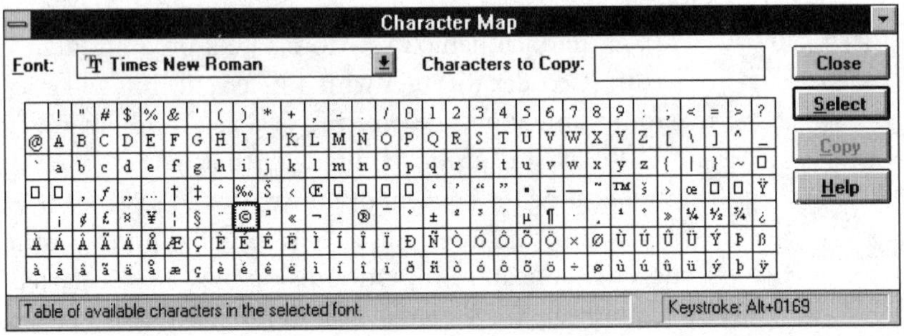

![Character Map window showing the Font drop-down list with Times New Roman selected, a grid of available characters, Characters to Copy field, and buttons for Close, Select, Copy, and Help. Keystroke: Alt+0169]

The Character Map utility, new in 3.1, provides a handy way to view and access special character sets.

The Character Map window contains a large grid with a graphical display of all the characters in the currently selected typeface. Above the grid is a drop-down list box labeled Font (Alt+F), that lets you select the typeface for your desired character set. Figure 5.36 shows one of the TrueType typefaces Windows provides, Wingdings, which consists of nothing but symbols, icons, and dingbats.

•••••••••••••
FIGURE 5.36

Character Map Window, Wingdings Typeface

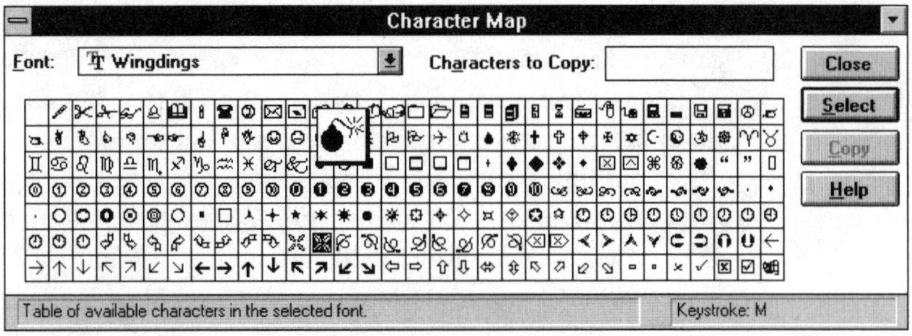

Also new in 3.1 is the Wingdings TrueType typeface, composed entirely of symbols, icons, and dingbats. Press and hold on a character to see an enlarged view.

The characters as displayed in the grid are often shrunk to a less-than-optimum resolution. To get an enlarged view of an individual character, hold down the mouse button while pointing at it.

To copy the character for pasting into another application, double-click on it. From the keyboard, press Tab to move the cursor into the character grid, then use the cursor arrow keys to navigate through the grid. Then click on the Select button (Alt+S). Whatever your method, your selected character is placed in the Characters to Copy box at the top of the Character Map window. When your actions are finished, push the Copy button (Alt+C) to transfer anything in the Characters to Copy box onto the Clipboard. Once the characters are on the Clipboard, switch to any document and choose the Paste command (Ctrl+V). Sometimes the character will be transformed when pasted; this occurs when your document is in a different font. To reset the character, highlight it and select the correct font from within the application.

Here's a shortcut for quitting Character Map: press Esc, and the window vanishes.

Clipboard
Viewer

The Clipboard Viewer

The Clipboard, with its cut, copy, and paste capabilities, is an integral part of the Windows environment. Just cut or copy an area of text, numbers, or graphics from one application, switch to another application, issue the Paste command (usually Ctrl+V), and you'll transport the data to its new terrain, faster than the Orient Express could carry double agents from Paris to Istanbul. The ability to integrate information among documents from different applications distinguishes Windows from DOS, and although the Clipboard is just a metaphor for an area of memory in Windows, as a concept it can be taken literally.

Some Windows applications make even better use of the Clipboard facility by offering the ability to paste live data into a document using DDE or OLE, thus linking data to another application. The Clipboard also provides a bridge between your Windows and DOS programs—you can paste text and sometimes graphics from DOS programs to Windows applications, and, under certain conditions, even paste Windows text into a DOS application.

The basic Clipboard commands—Cut (Ctrl+X), Copy (Ctrl+C), and Paste (Ctrl+V)—are described in Chapter 1. To use them, follow these steps:

1. Select the targeted information.

2. To cut the information, choose Cut. Or, to leave a copy behind, choose Copy.

3. Click in or otherwise move the insertion point to the targeted spot.

4. Issue the Paste command to insert the information contained on the Clipboard.

Your targeted application may not always understand the information you attempt to paste into it. For example, the Notepad won't let you paste in a bitmap image that is cut or copied from Paintbrush. In this case, the application's Paste command is dimmed on the Edit menu to prevent you from pasting in alien data. Sometimes the program will try to accept the information on the Clipboard but be unable to interpret it—with unpredictable consequences for your system. Also, the Clipboard does not accept all data types.

Insider's Tip

Version 3.1 improved the reliability of the Windows screen capture facility. To copy an image of the entire screen to the Clipboard, press the Printscreen key; to copy the active window only, use Alt+Printscreen. (Some older keyboards may not work with this combination; try Shift+Printscreen instead.) Screen images are copied to the Clipboard in the .BMP file format used for generic Windows bitmaps.

If you're afflicted with short-term memory loss, use the Clipboard Viewer utility to view the contents of the Clipboard before you paste it into your document. You can also use the Clipboard Viewer to save a disk image of the Clipboard's contents for later use (the contents of the Clipboard are lost when anything new is placed in it). To perform these operations, turn to the program CLIPBRD.EXE, the Clipboard Viewer (Figure 5.37).

FIGURE 5.37
*Clipboard
Viewer
Window*

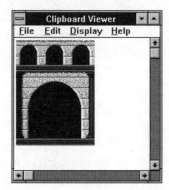

The Clipboard Viewer utility lets you view
the contents of the Windows clipboard.

The Clipboard Viewer contains four menus: File, Edit, Display, and Help.
The Clipboard Viewer's File menu contains only three commands:

➤ **Open** (Alt,F,O) Lets you open a previously saved Clipboard file

➤ **Save As** (Alt,F,A) Lets you preserve the contents of the Clipboard in a disk
file for future use

➤ **Exit** (Alt,F,X) Quits the Clipboard Viewer

Use the Save As command to save a Clipboard file to disk; later, you can
issue the Open command to open that disk file and paste the saved Clipboard
contents into another file. If you want to access frequently used bits of
data—like logos and contract clauses—create program item icons for them
using the extension .CLP (used by the Clipboard Viewer for its disk files).
Then activate the icon to load your data into the Clipboard. If the Clipboard
already contains data, a dialog box pops up to ask whether you want to
replace the current contents.

The Clipboard's Edit menu sports but a single command: Delete (Del).
Use it to delete the current contents of the clipboard.

Insider's Tip

Data on the Clipboard is held in Windows memory, so if the Out of Memory
dialog box appears when you try to run an application, try clearing the
Clipboard with the Delete command to free some system resources.

On the Display menu, specify the format in which you want the Clipboard to display its contents. The items listed on the Display menu change to
reflect the type of information currently contained in the Clipboard (Figure
5.38).

The first section of the Display menu contains the Auto selection, which
is the default setting. Beneath this are the specific types of data formats

FIGURE 5.38
*Clipboard
Display Menu*

The specific items listed in the Display menu vary
according to the data formats compatible with the
Clipboard's contents.

compatible with the current contents of the Clipboard. Choose any of these
to preview the results in any of the available formats. Dimmed data formats
cannot be viewed. Often, the items on the Display menu will provide details
that are good to know when you are linking or embedding data using DDE
or OLE (see Chapter 9 for further details).

The Calculator

Calculator

The Windows Calculator is handy for making quick calculations that don't
justify starting up Excel or another mathematical application. Calculator is
really a two-in-one utility: a standard calculator that resembles its dimestore
counterpart in looks and operation; and a scientific calculator, with statistical
functions, that can operate in binary, octal, and hexadecimal modes. Both the
scientific and standard modes operate in numbers ranging from -10^{307} to
$+10^{307}$.

To start Calculator, click on its icon in Program Manager, or run the file
CALC.EXE in File Manager. When you first use Calculator, it opens in its
standard mode (Figure 5.39).

FIGURE 5.39
*Standard
Calculator*

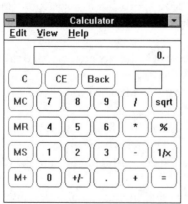

The standard calculator resembles its
handheld, dimestore counterpart.

To operate Calculator, click on its buttons with the mouse or type a keyboard equivalent, as defined in Table 5.6.

Button	Keyboard	Action
+	+	Add
-	-	Subtract
*	*	Multiply
/	/	Divide
+/-	F9	Change sign
%	%	Percentage
1/x	r	Reciprocal
sqrt	@	Square root
Back	Backspace or left arrow	Delete last (rightmost) digit
C	Esc	Clear current calculation
CE	Del	Clear current number
=	= or Enter	Perform function on displayed number and previous number (press again to repeat function)
MS	Ctrl+M	Save displayed value in memory
M+	Ctrl+P	Add displayed value to contents of memory
MR	Ctrl+R	Place memory contents in display
MC	Ctrl+C	Clear memory

The numbers that you type from the keyboard—or paste from the Clipboard—appear in the display at the top of the calculator. Click on the equal button (press Enter) when you want to perform a specific calculator function on the last two numbers; the result is placed in the display.

Calculator's memory is a simple, single-value register. When you save a number to memory, a small M appears in the box below the Calculator's display. When you clear the memory, or whenever the memory value becomes zero, the M disappears. If you use the MS button (Ctrl+M) to save a new number to memory, it will replace the current number held in memory.

Calculator is convenient to use with the Windows Clipboard for performing quick calculations and pasting them into other applications, such as your wordprocessor. To transfer the data, use the standard Copy and Paste commands on Calculator's Edit menu and on the menu of the other application.

Be aware, however, that Calculator interprets characters literally, exactly as if they were typed on the keyboard.

Calculator assigns special meaning to eight characters when it receives them from the Clipboard, as shown in Table 5.7.

Character	Meaning
:	Before a letter, the : indicates Ctrl (for example, :C is equivalent to Ctrl+C). Before a number, : indicates a function key (for example, :1 is equivalent to F1).
c	Equivalent to Ctrl+C (clear).
e	Signifies that the following number is in scientific notation when calculator is in decimal mode.
m	Equivalent to Ctrl+M (save to memory).
p	Equivalent to Ctrl+P (add to memory).
q	Equivalent to Esc (clear current calculation).
r	Equivalent to Ctrl+R (display memory contents).
\	Equivalent to the Dat key (in scientific mode).

The Scientific Calculator. You can use Calculator's View menu to switch between the scientific and standard modes; just select a mode from the menu, or press Alt,V,S for the scientific mode, or Alt,V,T for the standard mode. The scientific mode includes numerous additional calculator buttons, two sets of radio buttons, and a pair of check boxes (Figure 5.40).

FIGURE 5.40
*Scientific
Calculator*

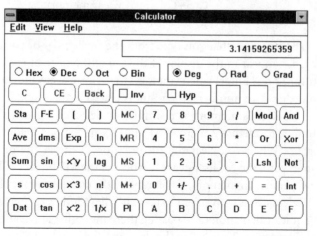

The scientific calculator gives you access to advanced scientific and statistical functions.

The first group of radio buttons lets you select from among the four available number systems: hexadecimal, decimal, octal, or binary. You can convert numbers between any of these four systems. To convert from binary to decimal, for example, click on the Binary radio button, type the binary number, and then click on the Decimal radio button. When converting numbers to hexadecimal, octal, or binary, the three radio buttons under the Calculator's display offer Dword, Word, or Byte options.

Otherwise, these same three radio buttons control the way you express angles. The default is degrees (Deg), but you can change it to either radians (Rad) or gradients (Grad).

Beneath the radio buttons are the three buttons C, CE, and Back, which operate as they do in the standard mode. Next to these buttons are two check boxes, Inv and Hyp. A check in the Inv box lets you do the inverse trigonometric or other functions. For example, if the Inv box is checked, the sine function returns an arc-sine instead. Similarly, a check in the Hyp box lets you do hyperbolic functions.

Table 5.8 below provides a command reference for the scientific calculator.

TABLE 5.8
Scientific Calculator Commands

Button	Keyboard	Description
1/x	R	Calculates reciprocal.
(	(	Opens new parentheses level (up to 25 levels).
)	)	Closes parentheses.
And	&	Bitwise AND.
Ave	Ctrl+A	Mean of values in statistics box. With Inv, the mean of the squares.
Bin	F8	Uses binary number system.
Byte	F4	Returns lower 8 bits of current number.
cos	0	Cosine. With Inv, arc-cosine. With Hyp, hyperbolic cosine. With Inv and Hyp, arc hyperbolic cosine.
Dat	Ins	Places a number from the statistics box into the display.
Dec	F6	Uses decimal number system.
Deg	F2	Inputs angles in degrees (decimal only).
dms	M	Converts degrees to degree-minute-second format. With Inv, converts displayed number to degrees.
Dword	F2	Returns full 32-bit number.

Button	Keyboard	Description
Exp	X	Exponent; maximum value +307 (decimal only).
F-E	V	Toggles between scientific notation and standard display (decimal only).
Grad	F4	Inputs angles in gradients (decimal only).
Hex	F5	Uses hexidecimal number system.
Hyp	H	Hyperbolic trigonometric function for sine, cosine, and tangent.
Int	;	Integer.
Inv	I	Inverse of function.
ln	N	Natural logarithm (base E). With Inv, calculates E raised to the power of the number in current display.
log	L	Common logarithm (base 10). With Inv, 10 raised to the power of the number in display.
Lsh	<	Binary left shift. With Inv, binary right shift.
Mod	%	Modulus (remainder of x divided by y).
n!	!	Factorial.
Not	~	Bitwise NOT.
Oct	F7	Uses the octal number system.
Or			Bitwise OR.
PI	P	Pi. With Inv, displays two times pi.
Rad	F3	Inputs angles in radians (decimal only).
s	Ctrl+D	Standard deviation with population parameter set to n−1. With Inv, standard deviation with population parameter n.
sin	S	Sine.
Sta	Ctrl+S	Brings up statistics box.
Sum	Ctrl+T	Sum of the numbers in the statistics box. With Inv, the sum of the squares.
tan	T	Tangent.
Word	F3	Returns lower 16 bits.
x^y	Y	x to the y power. With Inv, y root of x.
x^2	@	Square. With Inv, square root.
x^3	#	Cube. With Inv, cube root.
Xor	^	Bitwise Exclusive OR.

Performing Statistical Calculations. Click on the Sta button or press Ctrl+S to bring up the statistics box (Figure 5.41).

FIGURE 5.41
Statistics Box

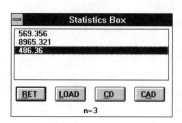

The Statistics Box lets you perform statistical calculations, such as averages and standard deviations.

You can enter a series of values in the top part of the Statistics Box. Beneath this area are four buttons: Ret, Load, CD, and CAD. The Ret button (Alt+R) switches to the calculator while retaining the statistics box entries. The Load button (Alt+L) loads the currently selected number from the statistics box into the calculator display. The CD button (Alt+C) clears the selected number. And the CAD button (Alt+A) clears all numbers.

To use the statistics box, position it so that you can easily work with the buttons on the calculator. After you enter each value, click on the Dat button (press the Ins key). Then click on the button for a statistical function: Ave (Ctrl+A) for average, Sum (Ctrl+T) for total, or S (Ctrl+D) for standard deviation. The result appears in the main display. To close the statistics box, double-click on the window control icon, or press Alt,Minus,C.

The Clock

Clock, or CLOCK.EXE, provides your onscreen desktop with a resizable clock. It displays the system time, either analog or digital, in a single, resizable window, as obtained from your computer's clock. Because it's quite limited, you can't even use the Clock utility to set the clock; to do this, you must use the Time/Date controls in the Control Panel.

The Clock sports a single Settings menu that contains the following commands:

➤ **Analog** (Alt,S,A) Selects a round clock face, complete with hour, minute, and second hands

➤ **Digital** (Alt,S,D) Selects a digital clock, with the date, if you like

➤ **Set Font** (Alt,S,F) Lets you choose the font used by the digital clock

➤ **No Title** (Esc) Makes the title bar and menu bar disappear or reappear

➠ **Seconds** (Alt,S,S) If checked, the Clock displays the seconds

➠ **Date** (Alt,S,T) If checked, the Clock displays the date

➠ **About Clock** (Alt,S,B) Brings up a dialog box with version information

The menu commands for the Clock utility provide two basic modes: Analog and Digital. Choose Analog for a traditional, round clock face, with an hour and a minute hand, and—if the Seconds option is checked—a sweeping second hand (Figure 5.42).

FIGURE 5.42
Analog Clock

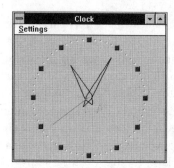

Check the time in old-fashioned analog fashion: round face, with hour, minute, and second hands.

Choose the Digital command and you switch to one of those newfangled digital clocks, with your selection of typefaces. The basic digital clock displays the hour and minute, as well as seconds and the date, if either option is checked on the Settings menu (Figure 5.43).

FIGURE 5.43
Digital Clock

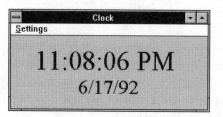

The Clock can assume a digital look if watching the second hand swirl around makes you dizzy.

The Set Font command on the Settings menu brings up the Font dialog box, which lets you choose a font for the display in the digital clock (Figure 5.44)

When selecting a font, keep in mind that some fonts look best at certain sizes, so when you resize your clock window, do it gradually to check on the appearance of your font. TrueType and other scalable fonts make good choices if you plan to resize your digital clock window often.

•••••••••••••
FIGURE 5.44
*Font Dialog
Box*

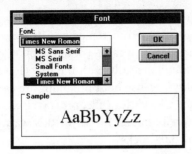

You can select any installed font for
use with the digital clock.

The No Title command (Esc) removes the title and menu bars from the clock window (in analog or digital mode), which causes the clock to fill up its entire window; double-click anywhere on the clock face to issue the command. If the title and menu bars are already gone, press Esc or double-click on the clock face to return them so that you can access the menu.

The Seconds command toggles the display of seconds on and off in both the analog and digital clock modes. The Date command displays the date below the time in the digital clock, and adds the date to the title bar of both the analog and digital clocks. Adding the date to the title bar enables you to refer to it when the clock is minimized as an icon. If you want to keep the time handy without taking up much desktop space, minimize Clock into an icon that continues to display the current time—and the date—in either analog or digital mode (Figure 5.45).

•••••••••••••
FIGURE 5.45
*Minimized
Clock Icons*

You can display the current time and date
when the Clock utility, either analog or digital,
is minimized to an icon.

When the Clock starts up, it assumes its former settings, size, and position. This feature makes it handy for placing in your Startup group.

Insider's Tip

Here's a timeless tip for using the Clock as an alternative screen saver. Maximize the Clock's window to fill your entire screen; then press Esc to remove the title and menu bars. Presto! You have a giant clock screen saver. To erase it, hit Esc or double-click anywhere on the clock to bring back the title bar. Or double-click on the title bar to restore the window to its previous size, or minimize it to an icon. You'll notice that when the digital clock is enlarged, the time is displayed in 3D relief. For a timesaving way to access this screen saver, create a macro that runs the clock (if the clock is already running, this selects the clock's window) and maximizes it to full screen.

Another tip: In Windows 3.0, you could run as many instances of the clock as your memory would allow. This was handy if you used a large, virtual desktop and wanted clocks in various areas. You can't do this in Windows 3.1 because it is designed to remember its last position on the screen and its other settings. But you can retrieve the old Clock utility from Windows 3.0 and use it simultaneously with the 3.1. However, be sure to rename the old Clock utility because both programs are called CLOCK.EXE. You'll also need to copy the Clock's font file, DIGITAL.FON, which the Windows 3.0 clock requires for its digital mode. In this way, you'll have the benefits of both the 3.1 and 3.0 Clocks.

Version

Version

The Version utility, WINVER.EXE, is the simplest one included with Windows. Analogous to the DOS command VER, it simply reports the version number of Windows that you are currently running. This utility enables other programs to configure themselves properly. You can also use it as a quick way to identify your version of Windows and to determine whether you are running Windows in standard or 386 enhanced mode.

Setup copies the WINVER.EXE file to your main Windows directory, and you can set up a program item icon for it by simply dragging its file icon from File Manager into Program Manager. When you run the utility, you are presented with the dialog box shown in Figure 5.46.

FIGURE 5.46
WINVER
Dialog Box

The Windows Version utility simply reports what version of Windows you are running, and whether it is running in standard or 386 enhanced mode.

To send the dialog box away, click OK or press Esc. The version utility can also be run from DOS if you type **WINVER** at the prompt.

Expand

Expand

Expand is a simple DOS utility program that decompresses files while copying them from one location to another. In order to save money, Microsoft applied a compression process to shrink most of the Windows files, thus reducing the number of installation disks by almost half. Consequently, most files on your original installation disks (such as device drivers) must first be decompressed using Expand before Windows can use them. Setup decompresses these files on its own as part of the installation process. To transfer any files from the installation disks onto your system after the installation, you'll need to decompress them by hand using the Expand utility, EXPAND.EXE, which Setup copies to your Windows directory during installation.

Running Expand is like using many DOS commands. Its command syntax takes the form

```
EXPAND <-R> <source> <destination>
```

where <source> is the name of one or more compressed files and <destination> is either the name you designate for the decompressed file(s) or the directory to which you want to copy the file(s). The <-R> switch is a special option that automatically renames the expanded file; however, this only works if the file was compressed using the -R switch. (Luckily, all the files on the Windows 3.1 installation disks fall into this category.)

For example, to decompress the HP LaserJet printer driver from an installation disk in drive A: and copy it to your \SYSTEM subdirectory, place the installation disk with the driver into the floppy disk drive and type

```
EXPAND A:HPPCL.DR_ C:\WINDOWS\SYSTEM\HPPCL.DRV
```

Here's another example that uses the special -R switch. Assume that you have already copied the compressed MOUSE.CO_ file from your installation disks to your Windows directory. You now want to expand it into the MOUSE.COM mouse driver so that you can use your mouse with DOS programs running in a window. You type

```
EXPAND -R MOUSE.CO_
```

This causes the Expand utility to automatically rename the file as it decompresses it. You can also use the Expand command with valid DOS wildcards (such as * and ?), but only for specifying the <source>. For example, to copy all the device driver files from an installation disk in drive A: to a directory named \DRIVERS, you could type

```
EXPAND -R A:*.DR_ C:\DRIVERS
```

which would automatically rename the drivers as it copied them onto your hard disk. If all this sounds a bit complicated, Expand can also prompt you for input as you go along. However, if you want to use the prompting method, you should also use the -R switch to fully automate the expansion process.

The following lines illustrate an interactive session (what you enter is indicated in boldface type):

```
EXPAND -R

Microsoft (R) File Expansion Utility Version 2.00
Copyright (C) Microsoft Corp 1990-1991. All rights reserved.

Enter the location and name of the compressed file to expand.
(Example: A:\HIMEM.SY_)

Compressed file: A:\MOUSE.CO_

Enter the location and/or name for the expanded file.
(Example: C:\WINDOWS\HIMEM.SYS)

Expanded file: C:\WINDOWS

Expanding a:\mouse.co_ to c:\windows\mouse.com.
a:\mouse.co_: 31328 bytes expanded to 56408 bytes, 80%
increase.
```

Note that you need only enter the directory location when you are prompted for the "Expanded file:". Because you used the -R switch to run Expand, the file is automatically renamed as it is decompressed and copied.

. . . .

Summary

Getting to know the 10 utilities described in this chapter can expedite and enrich your work with Windows and Windows applications. With Help, a simple on-line help facility, temporary salvation is but a keystroke away. Notepad lets you edit system files without fear of introducing shady, possibly corrupting characters. You can use SysEdit to open and edit the four most important system files simultaneously. With Recorder, you can capture simple keyboard and mouse actions in macros to replay. Character Map provides a way to view and select special symbols for any of your installed fonts or typefaces. Calculator gives you a simple mode as well as an advanced scientific calculator. Clock tells you the time, and the Version utility informs you of the Windows version number you are running. Clipboard lets you manage the contents of the Windows Clipboard. Expand lets you decompress files from the Windows installation disk.

Most of these utilities are pretty much the same as they were in Windows 3.0, with Help and Clock reflecting the most extensive upgrades. Character Map is new to 3.1. All of these utilities are worth knowing, yet SysEdit and Version are completely undocumented in the Windows manuals.

Insider's Tech Support: Bundled Utilities

Q: What should I do if the Help file for an application is missing?

A: Windows Setup provides a feature that lets you remove components from a complete Windows installation, including the Help files, in order to save space on your disk. You can use Setup to reinstall these files, as discussed in Chapter 4. You can also retrieve these files individually from the installation disks by copying them to your system using the Expand utility.

Q: I can't open a file with Notepad.

A: The file is probably larger than 50K. Notepad only works on fairly small files, so try opening the file with Write or another text editor.

Q: I closed a file in SysEdit and want to open it again, but there's no Open command on the File menu.

A: You'll need to quit SysEdit and start it again, because there is no way to reopen a file once you close it.

Q: I can't stop my macro from recording.

A: You probably haven't checked the "Control+Break Checking" feature on the Recorder's Options menu. You may have to quit Recorder, restart, and check this item before recording.

Q: I used Character Map to select a special character, but when I paste it into my application, it changes into something different.

A: Some applications convert the typeface of whatever data you paste into the current typeface of the application. Select the text you pasted in—even if the characters are now wrong—and then choose the typeface you had selected in Character Map.

Q: Graphics looks distorted in the Clipboard Viewer.

A: On the Clipboard Viewer's Display menu, the Auto selection is the default. Try choosing one of the other options—this should clear up the distortion.

6

Enhancing the Environment with Third-Party Shells

One of the watchwords for Windows is flexibility. Although the software comes bundled with two shells—Program Manager and File Manager—Microsoft designed Windows so that it is relatively easy to replace these shells with alternatives created by third-party developers. Developers have risen to the occasion: more than a dozen commercial and shareware shells now offer you excellent alternatives. Some of these programs, like Norton Desktop, aim to fatten up your environment with copious quantities of new features and attractions, whereas other alternatives, such as WinTools, create a trimmed-down shell with only the essentials for running programs and your system. After sifting through the various offerings, I've culled a short list of what I consider the best third-party shells available for Windows 3.1.

➠ **Norton Desktop for Windows** From the makers of Norton Utilities for DOS (Symantec), this is far and away the most popular utility offered for Windows.

➠ **WinTools** With a more straightforward interface, newcomer WinTools (from Tool Technology Publishing) is gaining a strong following.

➠ **Power Launcher** This is a minimalist shell that hides much power. Appearing in a simple button bar across the top of your screen, so-called Power buttons can be programmed with complex macros and custom commands.

➠ **Rooms for Windows** From XSoft, a subsidiary of Xerox PARC—originators of the graphical user interface and the mouse—this program provides an innovative way to organize files and applications according to tasks or other criteria.

➠ **Pub Tech File Organizer** This old timer goes the furthest toward making your Windows desktop work like a Macintosh.

➠ **NewWave** The original third-party Windows shell, now in its fourth version, Hewlett-Packard's NewWave offers the most technical sophistication.

Deciding which shell will best suit you depends on your computing needs, level of expertise, and, as always, your personal preference. This chapter reviews the salient features of the six shell programs just introduced, points out any disadvantages to their use, and demonstrates how they can be applied in typical work examples.

Norton Desktop for Windows

The latest version (2.0) of Norton Desktop for Windows actually contains several bundled products. The main components are these:

➠ **Norton Desktop** Combines the functions of Program Manager and File Manager into a single shell

➤ **Norton Utilities** A Windows grab bag akin to Norton's DOS utilities

➤ **Norton Antivirus** Protects and repairs your facilities

➤ **Norton Backup** Provides automated backup capabilities

As if this quartet weren't enough, Symantec includes a host of other utilities, such as a macro language, several calculators, a file viewer, and a system diagnostic utility.

Version 2.0 of Norton Desktop makes several major improvements to its previous version, including dramatically better performance, better drag and drop capabilities, support for TrueType fonts, the antivirus module, better support for networks, and an uninstall program, which lets you completely remove Norton Desktop or individual components of the program.

Norton Desktop converts any of your existing Program Manager groups into Norton **Quick Access groups** and preserves your existing configuration, including the Startup group. This means that any items you've set to launch when Windows is started will do so when you start Norton Desktop. You can add more items into the Norton Quick Access groups after you've switched over. The Quick Access groups look and operate just like the Program Manager groups they replace, so your investment in learning is also preserved (Figure 6.1).

FIGURE 6.1

*Norton Quick
Access Groups*

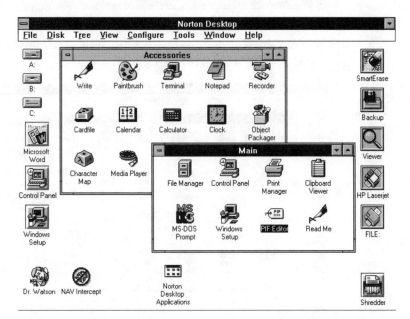

Program Manager groups are carried over into Norton Desktop and converted into Quick Access groups.

FIGURE 6.2
List View

You can re-configure your Quick Access groups as a list of icons with their titles.

The Quick Access groups can be viewed in three different ways. In the Icon view, they appear identical to Program Manager groups. In the List view, the groups appear as a vertical list of all the icons in the group (Figure 6.2).

The List view is especially handy for icons with long titles, ensuring that the titles won't overlap or become too crowded. However, this view consumes more space on your screen, so it's best to use it only if you have a few icons in a group. You can also view a Quick Access group in the Toolbox view (Figure 6.3).

With the Toolbox view, your group is turned into a floating palette of icons that abandon their titles altogether to provide fast access to the icons in the group while using the least amount of space. This view works best when you want to keep a bunch of programs or utilities instantly available onscreen.

FIGURE 6.3
Toolbox View

The Toolbox view lets you access your icons while taking up the least space on your screen.

You can also launch programs and manage files within the unified interface that Norton Desktop presents (Figure 6.4).

FIGURE 6.4
Norton Desktop

Norton Desktop for Windows provides program-launching and file-management capabilities in a unified interface.

Icons down the left side of the Norton Desktop represent the various disk drives attached to your system. Different types of icons represent a $5\frac{1}{4}$-inch disk, a $3\frac{1}{2}$-inch disk, a hard disk, or a network drive. To view the contents of a drive, simply double-click on its icon; a directory browser, similar to the Windows 3.1 File Manager, is displayed (Figure 6.5).

FIGURE 6.5
Desktop File Browser

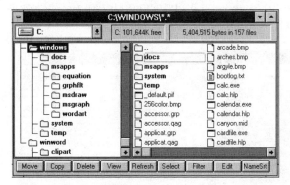

The Norton Desktop file browser is similar to Windows File Manager, but includes several additional features.

As in File Manager, a directory tree is displayed in the left half of the window and the contents of the currently selected directory in the right half. The row of buttons at the bottom of the file browser offers fast access to your most frequently used commands; you can customize this bar by using the Button Bar command on Norton Desktop's Configure menu. One of the handiest features of the Norton Desktop file browser is the file-selection capability of the right mouse button: just hold down the right button and drag to select a group of files. Click the button marked View to invoke the **Viewer** utility, which opens up a viewing window attached to the bottom of your directory browser (Figure 6.6).

FIGURE 6.6
Desktop Viewer

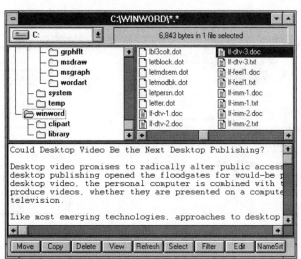

The Norton Desktop Viewer provides 70 different file-viewing filters to let you view the contents of wordprocessing, database, spreadsheet, graphics, and other files.

When you click on a file icon, a portion of its contents is displayed in the Viewer window.

The Viewer utility can also be used as a standalone program to view the complete contents of one or more files. As you can see in Figure 6.1, the Viewer icon appears on the desktop as the magnifying glass. Simply drag a file or group of files and drop them on top of the Viewer icon to open each file in its own window, displaying its contents (Figure 6.7).

FIGURE 6.7
*Viewer with
Text and
Graphics
Windows
Open*

You can drag several files and drop them on the Viewer together to inspect their contents.

If you need to find a document on your drive and don't want to take the time to manually view each one, you can use the **SuperFind** utility to search through the files on your drive; to find a file that contains a specific text string; or to match other search criteria, such as the date the file was created (Figure 6.8).

FIGURE 6.8
*SuperFind
Dialog Box*

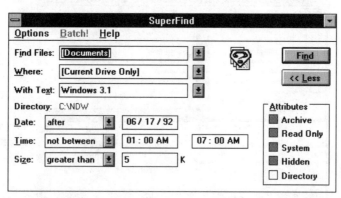

The SuperFind utility lets you search your disk drive to find a file that contains a text string or that meets other search criteria.

If you want to eliminate a file, Norton Desktop provides two utilities, **SmartErase** and **Shredder**. Both of these can be set up as icons on the desktop; just drag the file you want to discard and drop it onto the icon to dispose of it. SmartErase also allows you to recover a file you have erased. Just double-click the SmartErase icon and a special file browser appears (Figure 6.9).

FIGURE 6.9

SmartErase File Browser

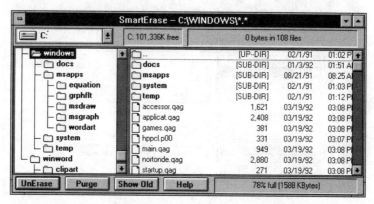

SmartErase provides a graphical way to undelete files after you've already marked them for extinction.

SmartErase is the graphical equivalent of the undelete function that made Norton Utilities for DOS a requisite utility. Any files that have not been overwritten appear in the SmartErase file browser. Simply click on a file and press the Unerase button at the bottom of the SmartErase window to resuscitate your file. If you really do want to discard the file, click the Purge button to permanently delete your file and free up your hard disk space. In effect, SmartErase conceals the files you've marked for deletion and retains them for a period that you can specify, or until that disk space is required for a new file. However, don't become reliant on SmartErase, because a file you need may have been overwritten and thus irreparably damaged. SmartErase only provides a safety net for haphazard deletions.

Insider's Tip

For files that contain private or sensitive information, Norton Desktop provides a Shredder utility. As with SmartErase, you can simply drag files and drop them onto the Shredder to delete them; but unlike SmartErase, files dropped on the Shredder are gone forever. The Shredder actually erases the information on your disk so that not even the most talented hacker could ever retrieve the data.

Another major component of Norton Desktop for Windows is the **Norton Backup** program, originally sold as a separate utility. Norton Backup provides a full complement of backup features, such as the ability to back up an entire device or only certain files (Figure 6.10).

FIGURE 6.10

*Backup
Dialog Box*

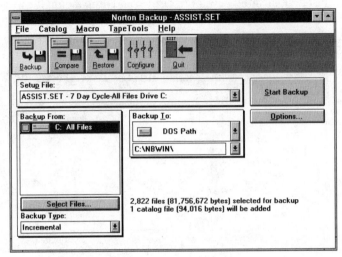

Norton Backup provides a comprehensive backup and restore capability, with a variety of automation and scheduling features.

Norton Backup also offers many customization options. You can create sets of files for backup, such as wordprocessing files, database files, spreadsheet files, and so on. The program also lets you initiate backups automatically at a certain time, or to back up files on an ad hoc basis by dragging them and dropping them on the Backup icon, which can be placed anywhere on your desktop. The initial shipments of Norton Desktop version 2.0 lacked the ability to back up files onto a tape drive—a big limitation. If you have one of these early versions, contact Symantec for an updated version.

If your disk is acting strangely, the **Disk Doctor** utility performs a comprehensive diagnostic of all the drives connected to your system. The Disk Doctor inspects your partition table, boot record, file allocation table, directory structure, file structure, and lost clusters (Figure 6.11).

Danger Zone

However, because you cannot repair disk problems while Windows is running, you'll have to quit Windows and run the Disk Doctor's repair facilities directly from DOS.

The Scheduler is a sophisticated utility that can display a message at any predetermined time and date. Its most powerful feature is the ability to run a program at a predetermined time, so you could initiate any kind of automated action, from a backup of your data to a telecommunications script to almost any sequence of tasks you can concoct by combining the macro and batch capabilities of Norton Desktop (Figure 6.12).

FIGURE 6.11

Disk Doctor

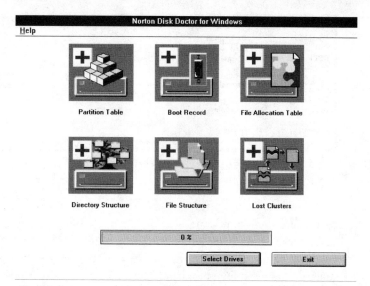

The Disk Doctor utility does a complete diagnostic checkup of your disk drives.

FIGURE 6.12

*Scheduler
Add Event
Dialog Box*

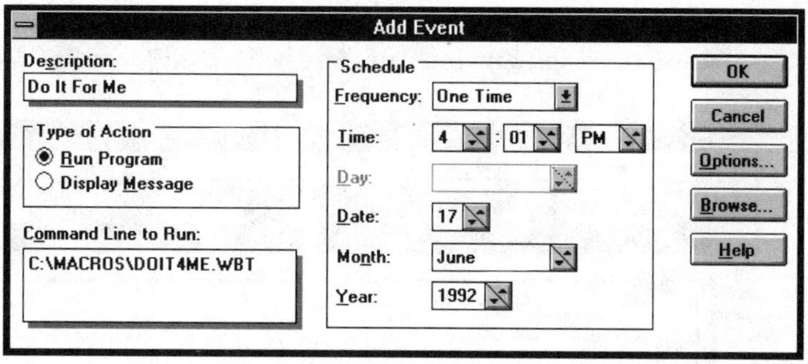

The Scheduler utility can display a reminder message or trigger the execution of a program or macro file.

Although Windows provides a very simple macro recorder (see Chapter 5), it doesn't support the use of a batch language for automating complex tasks. The lack of a good batch language is one of the major drawbacks in Windows; even DOS has a reasonable batch language. Norton Desktop provides **Batch Builder**, a fairly sophisticated batch language, with DDE support and an online quick reference (Figure 6.13).

The batch language supports the use of passwords and most disk and DOS commands, as well as the ability to modify your .INI files. In addition, Batch Builder is network savvy; it supports a number of commands that allow you to log on and off the network. Multimedia commands for playing

FIGURE 6.13

*Reference
Window for
Batch Builder*

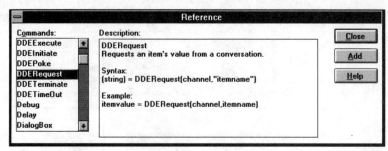

The Batch Builder utility is a powerful batch language that includes an
online quick reference to help you create powerful batch files.

MIDI files and sounds are also included, enabling you to create a macro
complete with its own song-and-dance routine. The Batch Builder utility
works in conjunction with the Macro Builder utility, so that you can build
macros that contain both batch commands and recordings of onscreen
mouse actions.

Another handy utility included with Norton Desktop is the **SysInfo** program, which provides detailed information about your system configuration,
disk drives, and memory usage, as well as details about what TSRs, soft device
drivers, and software interrupts are being used (Figure 6.14).

● ● ● ● ● ● ● ● ● ● ● ● ●
FIGURE 6.14

*System
Information
Window*

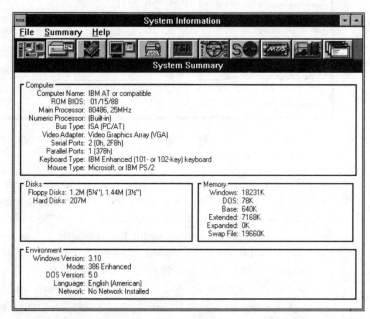

The SysInfo utility provides detailed reports about your system configuration and memory usage.

Compared with the Microsoft Diagnostics utility included with Windows, the SysInfo utility is easier to use, provides more information, and displays the information in a more organized fashion. Like the Microsoft Diagnostics utility, SysInfo can prepare a printed report of the 11 different system features for which it provides details.

Norton Desktop includes three onscreen **calculators**: a financial calculator, a scientific calculator, and a tape calculator. The financial and scientific calculators provide an onscreen version of their dimestore counterparts, with buttons appropriate to their respective disciplines (Figure 6.15).

FIGURE 6.15
Financial and Scientific Calculators

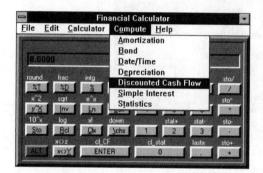

The financial and scientific calculators provide custom buttons appropriate to their respective disciplines.

The tape calculator deserves special mention because it provides an onscreen simulation of a paper-tape printout for your onscreen calculator. This solves one of the biggest complaints with similar calculator utilities, which lack a calculator tape for verification or as a printed record. The numbers you enter are displayed in a scrolling window above the calculator (Figure 6.16).

In addition to viewing the tape in the onscreen window, you can also print it out, or save the tape to a file that can be opened later and reworked—a real advantage over its desktop counterpart because it gives you a calculator with an unlimited number of memories. As another convenience, text labels can be added to the numbers, so you can identify the nature of each calculation.

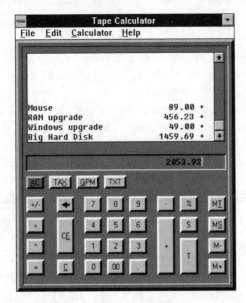

FIGURE 6.16

*Tape
Calculator*

*The tape calculator provides
an onscreen simulation of the
paper tape from your
onscreen calculator.*

Beyond this smorgasbord of utilities, Norton Desktop bundles several
lesser, although useful, utilities:

➺ **Desktop Editor** A souped-up version of the Windows Notepad, this utility lets you safely edit system files, without the annoying file-size limitation of Notepad. Desktop Editor provides several other niceties, such as
the ability to compare two files, insert a file into another file, and assign
your own custom shortcut keys.

➺ **Disk Copy** This simple utility does just what it says: it lets you copy a
floppy disk from one drive to another.

➺ **Format Disk** This little utility brings up a simple dialog box that lets you
format a floppy disk. It generally provides the same options you'd find in
File Manager, but also lets you save special Unformat information, so that
you can recover data in case you accidentally format a disk.

➺ **Key Finder** Similar to the Character Map utility in Windows, Key Finder
has a slight edge in features.

➺ **Sleeper** A screensaver utility with password protection, Sleeper (unlike
the built-in screensaver Windows includes) can play screensaver modules from a variety of programs, including After Dark, Intermission, and
Screenery.

Last but not least, Norton Desktop includes the complete **Norton Antivirus** utilities, formerly sold as a separate package that cost almost as much as Norton Desktop. The antivirus tools include an antivirus TSR that loads from DOS to provide ongoing monitoring and protection from viruses; an intercept module that runs as a minimized icon during your entire Windows session to help protect from infection while Windows is running; and a scanning module that runs as an application within Windows to scan any floppy or hard disks for more than a thousand different viruses. In most cases, the virus scanner can also remove the virus and repair some of the damage it might have caused.

In addition to the various utilities, Norton Desktop includes a variety of features for customizing many other operations, such as password protection. For example, each icon can be assigned a password, and you can assign a separate password to access any menu items. In addition, Sleeper provides a password for the screensaver. Keep in mind, however, that these passwords are meant only to deter tampering, and don't really provide high-level security.

Norton Desktop also lets you configure and create menus in almost endless variations. For starters, you can change the order of items listed in menus. The program comes with two default configurations: Short menu, designed for the casual user who wants protection from most of the options; and Full menu, for the power user who wants all the features listed on the menus. You can configure the Control menu for your various Windows applications and add commands to it that let you run or switch to specific applications. You can also add a Launch Manager command to the Control menu that lets you build a Launch List, a hierarchical menu that lets you quickly access your most commonly used applications. You can even add custom items to a menu that will issue a command line to take you directly to a specific document. You can assign your own shortcut keys to existing menu items or to new menu items. You can also add your own menus and load them with commands, or—in combination with Batch Builder—initiate macros or batch commands.

The desktop itself makes full use of the drag and drop metaphor; you can drag files onto applications to launch them, whether you're viewing them in a directory window or as icons on the desktop. This is an advantage over the more limited drag and drop capabilities of Windows File Manager. With the ability to launch applications from a menu item, from an icon in a Quick Access window or a Quick Access toolbox, or from an icon located on the desktop itself, Norton Desktop provides a comprehensive and flexible system for running your Windows programs and managing your files.

WinTools

The WinTools shell replaces Program Manager, File Manager, and Task Manager, and is distinguished from all other Windows shells by making the heaviest use of drag and drop. WinTools consumes less of your system's memory and proves more elegant in operation and aesthetic in design than Program Manager. It replaces File Manager with its own dual-window filing system; and for Task Manager, it substitutes a virtual screen utility, which lets you quickly switch to any application in its expanded virtual desktop. Its understated interface minimizes complexity while offering a surprising amount of power. In fact, WinTools requires only half the amount of system resources needed by Windows Program Manager, although it provides more features and functionality than the three Windows shells it replaces.

One of the most noticeable features of WinTools is the total absence of menus (Figure 6.17).

FIGURE 6.17

WinTools Shell

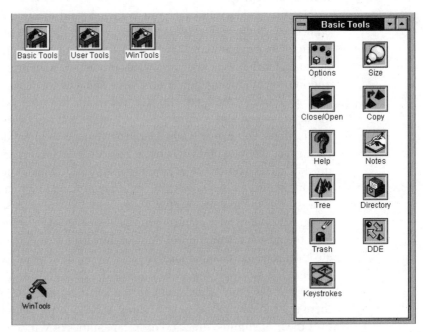

The WinTools shell doesn't have any menus; to issue commands, you must access its icons.

The icons in WinTools are called **tools**; they can represent programs, files, commands, macros, or special utilities. Most actions in WinTools are accomplished by dragging a tool and dropping it onto another. For example, to copy an item, drag it and drop it onto the Copy tool; to delete it, drop it onto the Trash tool. Once an item is placed in the trash, you still have an opportunity to retrieve it if the trash has not yet been emptied. Just open the Trash tool and use its Restore feature (Figure 6.18).

FIGURE 6.18

Trash Tool

WinTools provides trash management: If you want to recover an item you've thrown away—before the trash has been emptied—just search through the trash to retrieve the discarded item.

With both Windows Program Manager and Norton Desktop, it's easy to clutter your screen with windows and icons. WinTools uses two techniques to reduce the amount of desktop clutter: a **hierarchical grouping structure** and **virtual screens** for storing information. In the grouping arrangement, there is a hierarchy consisting of desk sets, desks, and tools. A **desk set** is a group of desks, and a **desk** is a group of tools, which are icons that can represent programs, files, utilities, macros, and so forth. A virtual desktop manager, called Big Sky, lets you create up to 16 **virtual screens** for storing tools and running programs. Big Sky is similar to other third-party utilities that provide a virtual desktop, such as More Windows from Artisoft, WideAngle from Attitash, and the Big Desk utility. Because Big Sky is integrated into the WinTools environment, however, you can use it to configure desk sets, desks, and tools to open in a specific area of the virtual desktop.

When you first install WinTools, you are provided with three **desk sets**:

➡ The **Basic Tools** desk set contains 11 predefined tools that can be used to customize or create your other tools. The Basic Tools are Options, Size, Close/Open, Copy, Help, Notes, Tree, Directory, Trash, DDE, and Keystrokes.

➡ The **WinTools** desk set contains WinTools itself; the Image Librarian utility; and the Big Sky virtual desktop utility.

➡ The **User Tools** desk set contains a collection of desks. These desks are analogous to groups in Windows Program Manager; in fact, the desks that you begin with include any Program Manager groups that were set up when you installed WinTools. These groups are converted into desks, and thus retain much of your former Windows configuration.

To access your familiar Windows accessories and other programs, simply open the User Tools desk set and click on the desk that corresponds to the Program Manager group containing the items you want. For example, to access Windows Setup, open the Main desk; you'll see a window reminiscent of the Main group in Program Manager (Figure 6.19).

FIGURE 6.19
Main Desk

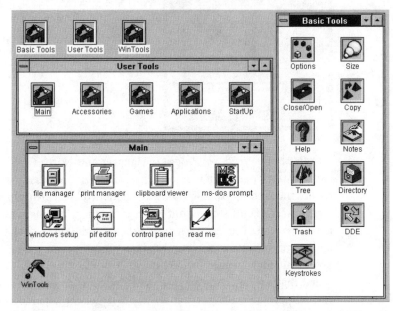

WinTools preserves your Program Manager groups by converting them into desks that are contained in the User Tools desk set.

Although all your original Windows programs, accessories, and utilities remain, you can use the Basic Tools desk set to reconfigure and enhance them as well. In fact, using the 11 Basic Tools, you can create more tools that can be added to other desks or desk sets, or configured into a special icon bar, which you can access in conjunction with your other programs. The Basic Tools are the primary building blocks of WinTools; the following paragraphs take a quick look at each one.

The **Tree tool** and **Directory tool** are the file management components of WinTools and are comparable to Windows File Manager. When you click on the Tree tool, you're presented with a hierarchical view of the directory tree of your currently selected disk drive (Figure 6.20).

To view the contents of a directory, open the Directory tool; the directory window opens adjacent to the tree window. Once both the tree and directory windows are open, they are synchronized: as you click on a directory in the tree window, the contents of that directory are displayed in the directory window, providing a system much like Windows File Manager (Figure 6.21).

FIGURE 6.20

Tree Tool

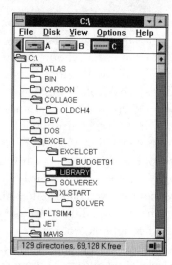

The Tree tool presents a graphical outline of the directory structure of your
storage volumes.

FIGURE 6.21

Directory Tool

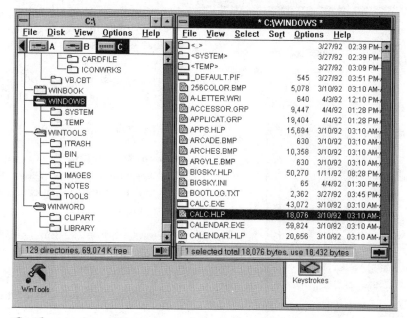

The Tree tool and Directory tool windows can be synchronized to
provide a dual-window view similar to the split-window system
used in Windows File Manager.

Insider's Tip

Because the Tree tool is separate from the Directory tool, you can detach the
directory from the tree and thus open several such windows. In this way, you
can independently view trees and directories from several different volumes.

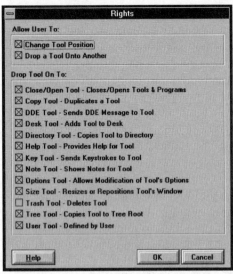

•••••••••••••
FIGURE 6.22
Rights
Dialog Box

WinTools lets you set a wide variety of rights for each tool. For example, the Rights dialog box lets you prevent a user from deleting a tool.

•••••••••••••
FIGURE 6.23
Global Options
Tool Palette

The Global Options function of the Options tool lets you control settings that pertain to the entire WinTools environment.

The **Options tool** lets you control how a tool appears on the screen and how it can be used. As for appearance, you can determine such things as how the tool is positioned on the screen, what icon it uses, what special notes or help information you want associated with it, and what trash management features you want associated with it. Options related to the use of a tool allow you to do such things as assign a password to it, schedule it to be activated at a certain time and date, and set the rights a user will have for modifying the tool (Figure 6.22).

The Options tool can be used either to set global options that apply to the entire WinTools environment or to set Options specific to a particular tool. To access the global options, open the Options tool by double-clicking it: the **Global Options tool palette** appears (Figure 6.23).

The Global Options tool palette contains icons for these nine Global settings:

➤ **Align** Set options for the alignment grid.

➤ **Confirm** Control the display of confirmation dialog boxes for actions such as deleting a tool, adding a tool, or exceeding your rights for a tool.

➤ **Fonts** Choose the fonts used by the WinTools environment.

➤ **Help** Customize the Help system for the WinTools environment or for a particular tool.

➤ **Misc.** Customize the environment by changing the color of the tool borders or by displaying the time or free system resources under the WinTools icon.

➤ **Notes** Attach notes to a tool.

➥ **Rights** Control what rights users have to particular tools.

➥ **Screen** Configure a simple screen saver and set the screen saver's password.

➥ **Trash** Set trash options; as with Norton Desktop, you can prevent trashed files from being immediately deleted.

To set the options for an individual tool, drag its icon and drop it on top of the Options tool, which causes the Tool Options dialog box to appear (Figure 6.24).

FIGURE 6.24

Tool Options Dialog Box

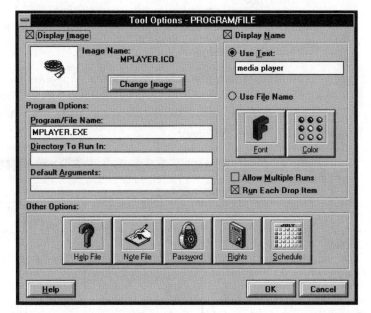

Drag a tool and drop it on the Options tool to bring up this dialog box, which lets you set the options for that tool.

Using this method, you can access the controls to change the tool's icon, assign it a working directory, protect it with a password, customize its help, add special notes for display when the tool is used, and schedule the tool that automates its activation.

Here's a rundown of the other tools included in the Basic Tools desk set:

➥ **Size tool** Control the size and location of a program's window when it is run.

➥ **Help tool** Quickly access WinTools Help and create custom Help files for your tools.

➺ **Notes tool** Create notes for specific tools.

➺ **Trash tool** Drag an item and drop it on this tool to delete it. Drag a desk set and drop it on this tool to close it. Or double-click the tool to restore deleted files and set the options for trash management.

➺ **Copy tool** Drag any tool or desk and drop it on this tool to duplicate it.

➺ **Close/Open tool** Hide tools outside the view of an open desk window and close programs that are running.

➺ **DDE tool** Send DDE messages to applications and create DDE scripts to automate tasks.

➺ **Keystrokes tool** Create simple macros by sending keystrokes to an application.

In addition to Basic Tools and Big Sky, the WinTools desk set provides an **Image Librarian** utility that lets you view bitmap files and icons, capture an area of the screen to turn into a bitmap or an icon, and change the size of a bitmap graphic (Figure 6.25).

FIGURE 6.25

Image Librarian

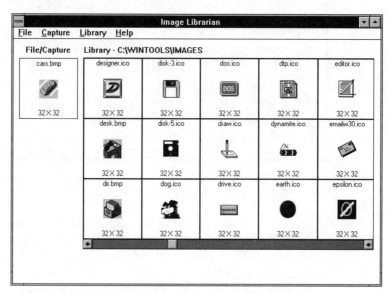

The WinTools Image Librarian helps you catalog the various icons and other graphic bitmaps; it also enables you to grab a part of any image for use as an icon.

WinTools takes the drag and drop metaphor to new heights, offers a straightforward interface for new users, and also includes advanced features, such as DDE capabilities and network administration options. However, Norton Desktop provides far more utilities, and some of the WinTools functions are still a little rough around the edges. For example, the Keystrokes tool requires you to write what amounts to a small program that indicates the keystrokes codes for the various keys you want recorded. And although the Image Librarian provides a handy way to manage your icons and bitmap files, it falls far short of Norton's Desktop Viewer utility. In fact, WinTools provides nothing comparable to Norton's Viewer, which seems like a big deficiency in the WinTools drag and drop environment. Because WinTools lacks keyboard equivalents for many of its functions, using a mouse is mandatory. Despite these few shortcomings, however, WinTools provides an accessible and powerful shell that is by far the most visually appealing of those on the market.

Power Launcher

Power Launcher, from hDC, enhances the Control menu on all your application windows, so you can directly launch a program, initiate a macro, and add other custom options (Figure 6.26).

FIGURE 6.26

*Power
Launcher
Menu*

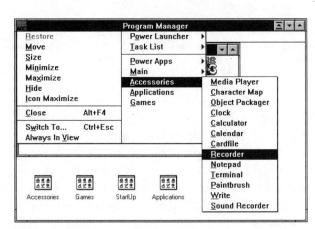

Power Launcher enhances the Control menu of application windows with items that let you launch a program, run a macro, and run other built-in utilities.

With Power Launcher, you can customize the Control menu to suit your needs by placing frequently used programs and commands within easy reach. Adding new commands, macros, and submenus is fairly easy because of Power Launcher's **Menu Configuration** utility, which you access—naturally—from the Power Launcher menu (Figure 6.27).

••••••••••••
FIGURE 6.27
*Configure
Menu Dialog
Box*

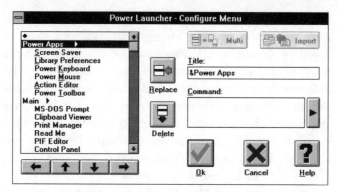

The Menu Configuration utility lets you add new items, change the names of items, rearrange the menu, and import Program Manager groups to use as submenus.

Power Launcher 2.0 adds support for OLE and the ability to play both sound files and MIDI files from buttons or scripts. Another new capability lets you create scripts so that buttons can be drag-and-drop targets.

The most noticeable new feature of Power Launcher 2.0 is its toolbar. The toolbar provides a convenient command center because it organizes a variety of functions into a thin strip, which uses only a small area along the top of your screen (Figure 6.28).

••••••••••••
FIGURE 6.28
*Power
Launcher
Toolbar*

The Power Launcher toolbar provides onscreen access to programs, commands, and Power Launcher's other features.

The Power Launcher toolbar lets you launch applications, access File Manager, view system information, and create special onscreen buttons that can be used to initiate macros, run applications, or perform other tasks. The first item at the left side of the toolbar is a command line area that lets you type in and execute any hDC Enhanced Command. These include any DOS command that you can issue without running a separate DOS session, as well as commands that are Windows specific, which form the core of Power Launcher's macro language. To execute a short macro, simply type it in—or just type in the first few characters of a command—and Power Launcher automatically completes the command. You can also type the name of a program or the names of several applications together with their documents and macro scripts by separating each item with a semicolon.

The next entry on the toolbar is the **File Manager button**, which displays the name of your currently selected directory. When you click on this button, it opens Windows File Manager or any other file management utility that you have set up to work with Power Launcher. In this way, Power Launcher is compatible with third-party shells such as Norton Desktop.

The **System Information button** displays three tiny status indicators, which serve as meters indicating the availability of system resources, memory, and disk space. These meters are updated on an ongoing basis as you use your system; they change from green to yellow to red, to let you know when you are running out of any of these three components. Click on the System Information button to call up the System Information window, which provides more detail about the use of your system resources (Figure 6.29).

FIGURE 6.29

*System
Information
Window*

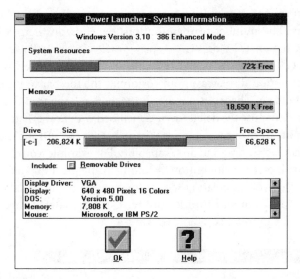

*The System Infor-
mation window pro-
vides details about
available system
resources, memory,
disk space, and
other elements of
your hardware and
software configura-
tion.*

The next item on the toolbar is the **Virtual Desktop Map button**. Click on this button to bring up the Virtual Desktop Map window (Figure 6.30). Power Launcher, like WinTools, includes its own virtual desktop utility, which can provide you with a maximum of 64 virtual screens of information. The default setting, shown in Figure 6.30, is a 3x3 screen grid, providing a total of nine times the space of your actual display. You can configure this virtual desktop to any size, up to 8x8 screens, for a maximum of 64 screens. The Virtual Desktop Map displays the location of the various windows and icons open in any of the virtual screens, and allows you to quickly switch to another screen or move an application from one screen to another. The status bar at the bottom of the Virtual Desktop Map shows the full title of whatever your cursor is pointing at.

FIGURE 6.30
*Virtual
Desktop Map
Window*

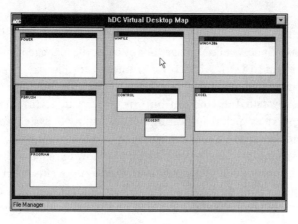

With a press of your
Virtual Desktop
Map button, you
can view and navi-
gate your virtual
desktop.

Next on the Power Launcher toolbar is a group of configurable **Power buttons**. The number of these buttons depends on the resolution of your display: for an EGA or VGA display, you'll see seven Power buttons; for a SuperVGA display (800x600 resolution), you'll see fifteen buttons. With a high-resolution display, you can customize the toolbar to include more than fifteen buttons. These buttons are all attached to Enhanced Command scripts. You can either use the default scripts included with Power Launcher or you can program your own to customize the toolbar. These buttons take advantage of the Windows 3.1 drag and drop capability. For example, you can drag a file icon and drop it on the Print button to automatically print that file.

To assist you in creating scripts for the Power buttons, Power Launcher includes a **Command Builder** utility that automates your construction of Enhanced Commands (Figure 6.31).

FIGURE 6.31
*Command
Builder Utility*

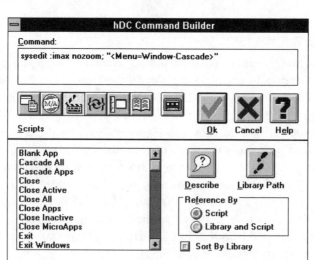

Command
Builder is an
onscreen pro-
grammer's
assistant
that helps
you create
Enhanced
Commands for
use with Power
Launcher.

hDC also provides a group of what it calls **PowerApps**—utilities that augment the capabilities of Power Launcher. The most significant of these are the Power Tool Box, Action Editor, Power Keyboard, and Power Mouse. The **Power Tool Box** utility lets you create a floating onscreen tool box filled with buttons (Figure 6.32).

FIGURE 6.32

Power Tool Box Utility

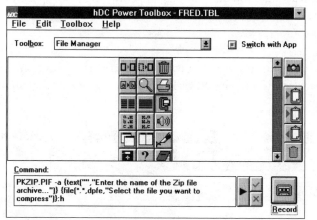

Create a floating palette of onscreen command buttons with the Power Tool Box utility.

The buttons in the Power Tool Box represent Enhanced Commands, and are therefore akin to the Power Buttons on the toolbar. To get you started, Power Launcher supplies the following preconstructed buttons:

➡ **Trash** Click this button, and a dialog box appears requesting the name of a file to delete. Drag a file and drop it on the button to delete it without a dialog box.

➡ **Compress** Click on the button to display a dialog box asking for the name of a PKZIP archive and another dialog box that asks for a file to add to this archive. Or just drag a file and drop it on the button to save a step.

➡ **Sound** Drop a .wav sound file or .mid MIDI file on the Sound button to play the sound. You can also click on the button to get a dialog box prompting you for the file name.

➡ **Write** Click the button to get a dialog box requesting the name of a Write file to open; or drag files and drop them on the button to open them automatically. A separate instance of Write is opened for each file.

➡ **Notepad** Works like the Write button: either click for a dialog box, or drag the files and drop them on the button to open all the files automatically.

➡ **Print** Click to open Print Manager or drag a file and drop it on the button to print it.

➡ **Terminal** Click on the button and a dialog box asks you for a file to upload. Drag a file and drop it on the button to launch Terminal and upload the file automatically.

Insider's Tip

The tool box buttons you create can also be targets for a variety of drag and drop actions. You can create separate tool boxes for specific applications, and you can save sets of tool boxes as files to maximize your flexibility in creating custom setups.

The **Action Editor** utility lets you create objects that contain Enhanced Commands and embed them into any document that supports OLE (Figure 6.33).

• • • • • • • • • • • • •

FIGURE 6.33

Action Editor Utility

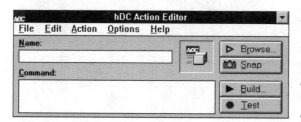

Action Editor is an OLE-server application and therefore lets you work with any documents that work as OLE client applications.

When you embed an action in a document, it looks and works similarly to a Program Manager icon. To execute the Enhanced Command represented by the icon, simply double-click on it.

The **Power Keyboard** utility lets you assign Enhanced Commands to single keys or key combinations on your keyboard (Figure 6.34).

• • • • • • • • • • • • •

FIGURE 6.34

Power Keyboard Utility

The Power Keyboard utility lets you create different keyboard assignments, to work with specific applications, or global assignments for your entire Windows environment.

The keyboard map can be rearranged to suit the particular layout of your keyboard, and it colors whatever keys have already been assigned to specific macros.

The **Power Mouse** utility does for your mouse what Power Keyboard does for your keyboard—it lets you assign Enhanced Commands to clicks or double-clicks of any mouse button (with two- or three-button mice), or to combinations of key presses and mouse clicks. Similarly, Power Mouse lets you assign mouse macros to specific applications or use them globally. For example, you could set up a special group of mouse commands for use with Excel, as I've done in Figure 6.35, so that clicking on the right mouse button issues the Recalculate Now command.

FIGURE 6.35

Power Mouse Utility

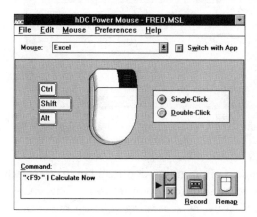

The Power Mouse utility lets you assign Enhanced Commands to mouse clicks or keyboard and mouse click combinations.

hDC Power Launcher is a utility that can be used either as an adjunct to your existing shell or as a replacement for Program Manager. When used as your shell, Power Launcher conserves system resources while providing more functions and greater flexibility than Program Manager. Power Launcher is best suited for the sophisticated user who feels comfortable with DOS commands and Enhanced Command macro language; in that case, quite a number of shortcuts can be devised. The Enhanced Command language addresses the lack of a macro language for Windows, and the ability to attach Enhanced Commands to onscreen buttons multiplies the power of your macros. Although not recommended for the faint of heart, Power Launcher—as its name implies—should find a warm reception among Windows power users.

Rooms for Windows

This program was developed by Xerox PARC, the research think tank that developed the graphical user interface. Rooms for Windows lets you create any number of virtual desktops, called **rooms**. Each room can contain applications, either running in a window or as a minimized icon; special buttons, which you can press to run programs or open specific documents; and doors, which let you move from room to room. Figure 6.36 depicts a single room.

• • • • • • • • • • • • • •

FIGURE 6.36

A Single Room

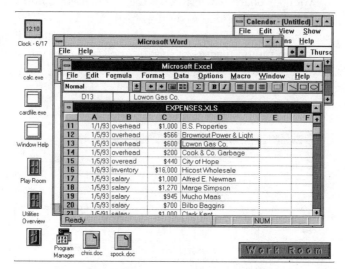

Each room represents a virtual desktop that contains a group of programs, buttons, and doors.

The arrangement of programs, doors, and buttons in each room remains undisturbed as you move from room to room. This enables you to switch between projects easily. By separating your various projects into different rooms, you can trim the amount of clutter that often occurs when all of your projects are open on a single desktop.

Rooms for Windows also lets you create buttons that represent programs or specific files; clicking on a button gives you quick access to the tools and information related to a project, without your having to detour to Program Manager or File Manager. The buttons also save memory by providing fast access to programs without the need to keep them running.

Rooms for Windows lets you organize several rooms into a group called a **suite** (Figure 6.37).

The **Overview** screen displays all the rooms in a particular suite. To go to a room, just click on it from the Overview screen, and voila! You're there. To go to another room, either return to the Overview Screen or use a **door**. A door is a special type of icon that you can set up to link one room to another. For example, you can create a door icon for a room full of utilities that you want to be able to access quickly, and then place that door in all of your other rooms. Each room also contains a back door, which returns you to the room you just left.

FIGURE 6.37

A Suite of Rooms

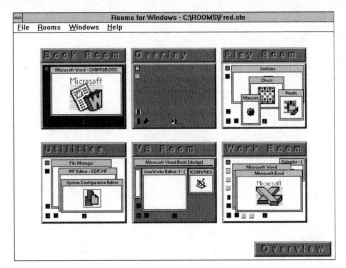

A suite is a group of rooms, each containing its own desktop layout.

From the Overview screen, you can double-click on a miniaturized window or icon in any room to get a close-up look at that item. The Overview screen only lets you view a program or application; to actually work with an item, you need to go to its room.

A group of rooms can be saved together as a suite, thus providing yet another level of organization on the virtual desktop. For example, you could create a suite for each of your projects; each suite could contain several rooms, with each room containing an associated group of programs and documents. In this way, if you use a wordprocessor, a spreadsheet, and a project management program for a single project, you could create a suite that contained the wordprocessor in one room, the spreadsheet in another room, and the project management software in a third room. Each room would contain files relevant to your particular subject, and all three rooms could be saved as a suite specific to that project. To start up your project next time and load all the various documents, files, and programs automatically, you'd just open that suite.

Insider's Tip

The concept of suites allows your system to store a large number of completely different configurations, which you can easily reload. Suites are also handy when several people share a computer. Users can each have an individual collection of suites and quickly return to their work exactly as they left it.

Each suite contains a special room, called the **Overlay** room (Figure 6.38). Anything you place in the Overlay room—an application, a button, or a door—is simultaneously placed in all the rooms in that suite. For example, to quickly gain access to your Utilities room from any other room, create a door for the Utilities room in the Overlay room. The door for the Utilities room

•••••••••••••
FIGURE 6.38
Overlay Room

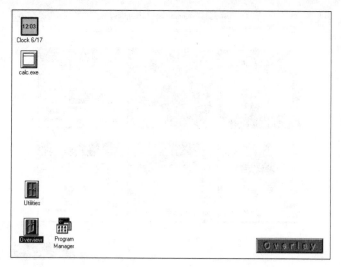

The Overlay room is a special room that serves as a template for items shared by all the rooms.

now shows up in all your other rooms. You can also place an application such as the Clock and a button that runs File Manager in the Overlay room, so that they will be available in all your other rooms.

To create a new room, just choose its command from the Rooms menu. You can name the room anything you want. The new room automatically contains the items in the Overlay room. You can then fill it with other items that you create or bring in from other rooms. You can also copy an object from one room into another room, in order to access that same object. When you copy a program, you don't actually run a separate instance of the program—you are only making it available in the new room. One of the convenient features of Rooms for Windows is that a copy of a program can be independently resized and repositioned in each room.

To move an object from one room to another, simply go to the Overview screen and grab its icon from one window and place it in another. You can also copy or move objects from one room to another by simply carrying them through one of the doors. For example, you can carry data from a wordprocessor document from one room into another room. When you carry an object and move it, you are carrying the single instance of that object with you. When you carry an object and copy it, the copy is placed in the new room and the original is left in the prior position.

In addition to moving and copying, which both use a single instance of an application, you can also start a second instance of an application in another room. However, this feature is available only if the application program itself lets you run more than one instance of it. The Windows Paintbrush applet, for example, lets you run several instances of it, so that you could have several applets open in different rooms. File Manager, on the other hand, lets you run only one instance of the program at a time.

Rooms for Windows also provides access to DOS programs either as buttons or as full-screen DOS rooms. A full-screen DOS room is a special room dedicated to a specific DOS program; it appears in the Overview screen as a room containing a large black DOS screen (Figure 6.39).

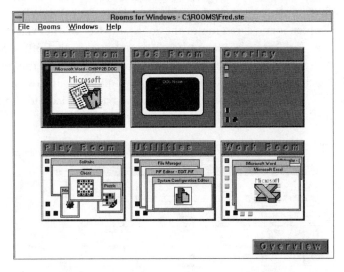

FIGURE 6.39
*Overview
Screen
Containing
DOS Screen*

You can create a full-screen DOS screen that runs a specific DOS application along with a particular file.

Insider's Tip

You can also create special DOS buttons, which you can place in any room to open a DOS window within that room or start up a specific DOS command. Pressing the DOS command button issues the command contained in that button. For example, a DOS button that contains the DOS command to copy files with a particular extension to a specific backup disk would allow you to perform regular backups of whatever files you specified.

Rooms for Windows provides a flexible and innovative system for arranging your applications and documents. This program is especially useful if you work on a large number of different projects or if more than one person is sharing a computer. Although virtual desktop utilities (either those included with other shells or standalone utilities) provide some similar capabilities in terms of letting you configure a larger desktop space, Rooms for Windows goes beyond the concept of a simple, expanded virtual desktop. It provides the ability to create onscreen buttons to start applications or open documents and offers ways to save groups of desktops as suites. The suite concept is especially powerful, because it lets you save elaborate and complex setups that would otherwise prove daunting to reconstruct manually. In some ways, Rooms for Windows is limited as a shell, however, and it's best to use it in conjunction with another shell, such as Program Manager, included as part of Windows. And finally, the program runs a bit sluggishly at times, especially when you're running low on system memory or resources.

Pub Tech File Organizer

The Pub Tech File Organizer from Publishing Technologies was one of the first third-party shells for Windows; and of all the shells discussed in this chapter it most resembles the look and feel of the Macintosh. However, Pub Tech's interface is not nearly as polished as that of the Macintosh, and indeed it is the homeliest of all the shells reviewed in this chapter. Like the Macintosh, Pub Tech consolidates the functions of Program Manager and File Manager into a single shell, and provides an icon for every file on your disk and a file folder for every directory (Figure 6.40).

FIGURE 6.40
*Pub Tech
Desktop*

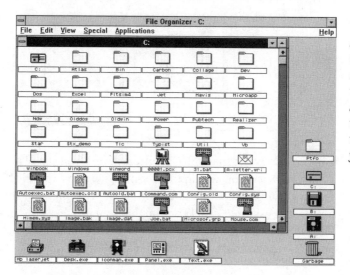

The Pub Tech desktop provides iconic representations of disk drives, directories, and all the files on your disk.

In Pub Tech, the desktop presents all your files, directories, and peripheral devices in a clearly marked fashion. The menu bar is always visible across the top of the screen, and the contents of each drive on your system are displayed in a window. Each drive window contains a group of file folders representing directories on the drive, and icons that represent each of your files. Pub Tech automatically assigns different icons to different file types; you can further customize the look of your desktop by assigning icons based on a file's extension. For example, in Figure 6.40, executable files are depicted by a small keyboard with a hand on top. The various types of disk drives are identified by unique icons, with $3\frac{1}{2}$- and $5\frac{1}{4}$-inch drives each designated by a different drive icon. Pub Tech was the first shell to provide drag and drop printing capabilities, and any installed printer appears on the desktop with its own icon.

The Pub Tech desktop also makes clever use of visual cues. For example, if a disk is not in a drive, you see an outline of the disk, and the drive label informs you that no disk is present. The garbage can swells to indicate that it contains trash; when you double-click on it, a window opens to display the files that have been targeted for deletion. Figure 6.41 depicts a desktop with a diskless drive and an engorged garbage can.

FIGURE 6.41

Floppy Disk Drive Icons Without Disks; a Full Garbage Can

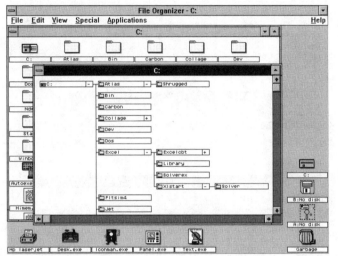

Pub Tech gives you visual clues about the status of the items on your desktop.

This figure also illustrates Pub Tech's Tree directory view, which provides a hierarchical directory tree that displays the structure of your disk drive. The Tree view is handy for pruning and grafting your directory tree, but working in Pub Tech's normal File Folder view is the easiest way to organize your desktop. In the normal File Folder view, simply double-click on a File Folder to open a window that displays the folder's contents (Figure 6.42). Notice that Excel contains several subdirectories, also represented by file folders. The Excel program uses its normal application icon, but Pub Tech designates the Excel spreadsheets by icons that represent miniature worksheets.

Moving files from directory to directory is a simple matter: just drag a file's icon and drop it on top of the file folder that represents the destination directory. Similarly, to delete a file or directory, just drag it and drop it onto the garbage can. If you select several files or directories, the cursor changes into the shape of a butterfly net to inform you that your action will apply to all the currently selected icons. To select a group of icons, you can either click on them individually or hold down the mouse button and drag a selection marquee around them (Figure 6.43).

•••••••••••••
FIGURE 6.42
*Open Excel
Folder*

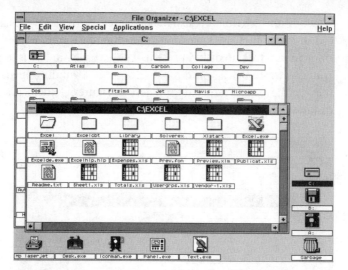

*Double-click
on a folder to
open a window
that displays
its contents.*

•••••••••••••
FIGURE 6.43
*Selection
Marquee*

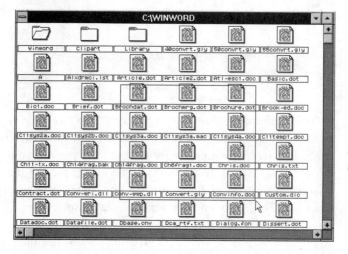

*To select a
group of
icons, hold
down the
mouse button
and drag a
selection
marquee
around the
group.*

With Windows Program Manager, you can only select a group of icons one by one.

Another Pub Tech feature missing from the Windows shell is the ability to directly edit the name of a file. In File Manager and Program Manager, you have to select an icon, call up a dialog box, and enter the new name into the dialog box. In Pub Tech, file and directory icons can be edited by simply clicking on the name and then using standard Windows editing techniques for changing all or a portion of the name (Figure 6.44).

FIGURE 6.44

*Changing
the Name
of an Icon*

*To change the name of an icon, simply click on its
name and edit it.*

Because the icons in Pub Tech actually represent real DOS files and
directories, editing their names changes the names of the actual files or
directories.

Pub Tech allows you to create a variety of **preconfigured desktop setups**,
which can contain any desktop components, such as icons, open directory
windows, or open applications. This gives you a convenient way to create and
access a customized setup for your different projects. For example, you could
set up a spreadsheet desktop for your accounting; a graphics desktop that
opens a paint program; and a general working desktop that places your most
frequently used application icons on the screen (Figure 6.45).

FIGURE 6.45

*Custom Desk
Setups*

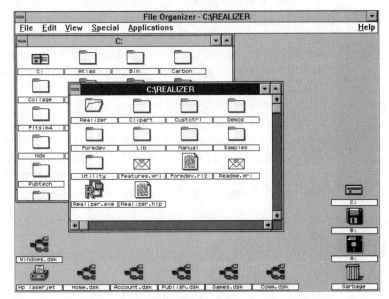

*The files ending with the .DSK extension represent custom desktops, set
up for particular tasks.*

Another handy feature of Pub Tech is the ability to print a directory
listing of the contents of a disk directly from the File menu—another
feature noticeably absent from the Windows File Manager. To run a program, as with most of the other Windows shells, double-click on its icon; or
for frequently used applications, place them on the Applications menu
(Figure 6.46).

FIGURE 6.46
Applications Menu

Applications
<u>A</u>ssign application to key...
<u>R</u>emove application...
R<u>u</u>n options...
CONTROL.EXE
DESK.EXE
ICONMAN.EXE
PANEL.EXE
PBRUSH.EXE
PRINTMAN.EXE
PROGMAN.EXE
TEXT.EXE

You can add your most frequently used programs to the Applications menu.

Pub Tech File Organizer provides a simple, straightforward shell for Windows. By consolidating the functions of Program Manager and File Manager into a single interface, it reduces the complexity of working with your system. For people who switch between Windows and a Macintosh, Pub Tech also provides the closest analog of the Macintosh interface on a PC, albeit with less visual appeal. On the down side, your desktop can become fairly cluttered with windows and icons, and the program is slow at some operations. Also, although the program includes a variety of its own utilities, it's not as robust a selection as what Norton Desktop provides. Pub Tech does not include its own built-in macro language or batch facility, but you can purchase separately a companion product called BatchWorks, from the same vendor. The 3.1 version reviewed in this chapter provides little in the way of specific enhancements for Windows 3.1; Publishing Technologies is working on a major overhaul with version 4.0, which promises to significantly upgrade both the functions and the interface of this shell.

NewWave

Hewlett-Packard's NewWave 4.0 is the latest incarnation of an ambitious reworking of the Windows interface. The other Windows shells discussed in this chapter are merely that: shells designed to let you use regular Windows programs. NewWave, on the other hand, is a technically sophisticated replacement for the entire Windows environment, which even supports its own NewWave-specific applications, in addition to standard Windows programs. One way in which NewWave extends beyond Windows is its ability to completely shield the user from DOS and the DOS filing system. NewWave introduces its own file system that supports the use of long file names—up to 32 characters each. At the same time, NewWave keeps the file's real DOS name, but protects you from having to know anything about it.

NewWave also takes object orientation further than Windows itself or any of the other shells. In fact, the object-oriented metaphor of NewWave is centered around **compound documents**, which can contain text objects, graphics objects, database objects, and so on. Rather than open a document inside an application, as with Windows or DOS, with NewWave you open the application from within the document. For example, if your document contains both text and graphics, you click on the text to bring up the text editing program; similarly, you click on the graphics object embedded in the document to summon the graphics program. HP actually pioneered the concept of compound documents in Windows several years ago with earlier versions of NewWave, and Microsoft has recently jumped on the bandwagon with its object linking and embedding (OLE). OLE-capable applications are now directly compatible with NewWave 4.0, thus solving incompatibility problems that plagued earlier versions.

NewWave's sophistication makes it both more simple and more complex than Windows itself. It's simpler because users don't need to deal with DOS; in addition, the NewWave shell is easy to use and integrates the Program Manager/File Manager dichotomy inherent in Windows 3.1. The object-oriented software model helps you focus on the work you are performing, rather than on the operational complexities of the computer's software. If you're on a network, NewWave lets you share documents and software tools related to a project without having to know the server drive or path of the various files and programs related to the project.

Danger Zone

However, this ease of use comes at a steep price in setting up the environment. NewWave features a sophisticated and inherently complex internal programming mechanism, which the system administrator needs to master in order to properly configure and set up the program. A novice user would have a tough time getting the maximum benefit from NewWave without the help of an expert.

NewWave consists of three main components:

➤ **Desktop Organizer** This is the shell that lets you access DOS, Windows, and NewWave applications and associated data files as icons with descriptive titles unrelated to their actual DOS file names. You can easily organize your work with the use of the familiar desktop metaphor, complete with file folders, a file drawer, and a waste basket.

➤ **WorkGroup Library** Designed to make it simpler for a group of people to work on a project, the WorkGroup Library simplifies the use of local area networks; users can easily access documents and tools related to work in progress.

➼ **Work Automation** The NewWave Agent provides a sophisticated macro facility that can automate many routine tasks. The Agent facility is the most comprehensive and sophisticated macro facility found in the Windows universe, with a full-fledged programming language that encompasses DOS, Windows, and NewWave applications.

When you're working with NewWave, the center for all your operations is your NewWave **Desktop Organizer**. The Desktop contains your various projects, tools, information sources, and utilities in a simple and straightforward interface (Figure 6.47).

FIGURE 6.47
*NewWave
Desktop
Organizer*

The NewWave Desktop Organizer provides a simple and straightforward interface for organizing the data and applications in your computer.

The icons on the NewWave Desktop represent the various **Objects** and **Tools** available for your use. NewWave makes an important distinction between Objects, which represent data linked to applications, and Tools, which are usually utility programs. When you install an application in NewWave, you can install it as an Object type or as a Tool. The premise of NewWave is that the focus of computing resources is data, rather than computing applications. The metaphor for an application in NewWave is a stationery pad composed of various objects. Rather than open an application and then start a data file from within that application, you in effect tear off a blank data object from the inexhaustible supply provided by the application.

To start a new task in NewWave, you create a new Object with the Create a New command, which brings up the Create a New dialog box (Figure 6.48).

••••••••••••••
FIGURE 6.48
*Create a New
Dialog Box*

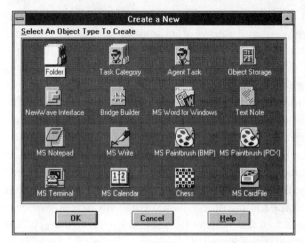

The Create a New
dialog box contains
icons that repre-
sent the stationery
pads (that is, appli-
cations) from which
you can create a
new document.

To create a new Object, you must choose a type of Object by selecting an icon from the Create a New dialog box, much as you would tear off a blank sheet from a stationery pad. In this way, you don't have to be concerned—as you would in DOS or Windows—about finding an application on your disk or even how to start it. Once you've created a new Object, opening it starts the application you need for editing it. Furthermore, you can name the objects with long descriptions, without worrying about the DOS file-name limitation (Figure 6.49).

••••••••••••••
FIGURE 6.49
*Group of
Objects with
Long File
Names*

Each Object you create inherits the icon of the application used to create it and can be given a descriptive title unrelated to its DOS file name.

If you install an application as an Object type, you can use it to create many individual Objects. It's best to set up an application as an Object type, rather than as a Tool, if it generates data. Tools, in contrast, appear only once in NewWave and represent an application not associated with a data file. NewWave includes several built-in Tools, including the File Drawer, used for filing the Objects you create; the Waste Basket, which contains deleted Objects; the Printers tool, for printing your objects; and the NewWave Agent, for automating tasks and creating macros. You can also install your own tools into NewWave by simply dragging the application files from Windows File Manager and dropping them onto the NewWave Desktop.

Installing applications as Object types is a bit more complicated. Any applications that you bring into NewWave must be configured with the **Bridge Builder** tool, which extends the capabilities of applications to make them compatible with the NewWave environment. For example, NewWave keeps track of the name of the person who created every Object as well as the last person to work on it. This is especially helpful for workgroup setups, and is not available in either DOS or Windows.

NewWave 4.0 provides an **Auto-Bridging** function that greatly simplifies the creation of bridges to DOS and Windows applications. In earlier versions of NewWave, this process was manual and required an in-depth knowledge of NewWave as well as of the application being bridged. With the new Bridge Builder and its Auto-Bridging feature, NewWave users have a much easier time using DOS and Windows applications as NewWave Object types.

Another new feature NewWave 4.0 is the **Object Finder**, which helps you quickly locate and open Objects available to your system, either locally or across a network (Figure 6.50).

FIGURE 6.50
*Find Object
Dialog Box*

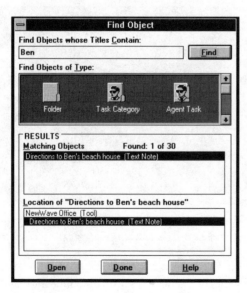

You can use the Object Finder to locate objects of a given type, or those with a specific title, or even all the objects that contain a certain word in the title.

The Object Finder lets you locate various objects according to your search criteria, and lets you open the Object directly without first having to return to the Desktop.

Perhaps the most powerful component of NewWave is its sophisticated **Agent**. The Agent includes a BASIC-like procedural language that can be used to automate complex tasks that span DOS, Windows, and NewWave applications. The Agent can perform multiple tasks at a time, and one task can call upon the services of another task, so that tasks and macros can be used as building blocks to simplify the creation of complex, automated procedures. Opening the Agent (the secretive-looking guy with the shades) brings up the Agent Window (Figure 6.51).

FIGURE 6.51

Agent Window

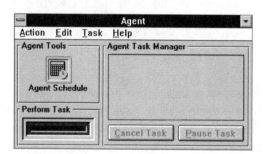

The Agent Window is a new feature of NewWave 4.0 that provides a central command post for managing and scheduling all the Agent tasks.

The Agent Window displays all the tasks currently being performed by the Agent and allows you to pause or cancel any of the current tasks. You can also use the Agent Window to open the Agent Schedule, for tests that need to be performed at a given time or on a repetitive basis. Agent tasks can also be triggered by specific events in NewWave and DOS (Figure 6.52).

FIGURE 6.52

*Agent
Schedule
Dialog Box*

Sun	Mon	Tue	Wed	Thu	Fri	Sat
Repetitive Schedule						
			1	2	3	
4	5	6	7	8	9	10
11	12	13	14	15	16	17
18	19	20	21	22	23	24
25	26	27	28	29	30	31

Action Edit Objects Days Dates Task Help
October 1992

The NewWave Agent can perform tasks when triggered by certain events, such as a change to a NewWave Object or DOS file.

For example, you can trigger the execution of a task when a NewWave Object or even a DOS file is modified. This feature allows you to monitor shared projects on a network; you can have the Agent notify you when a user modifies a document on the server or completes a job you were expecting. An Agent task can make direct use of both DDE (Dynamic Data Exchange) for accessing other applications and DLLs (dynamic link libraries) for tapping advanced Windows programming functions. For example, Borland's Paradox engine is a powerful database server that is implemented as a Windows DLL. A NewWave Agent can access this DLL directly and have it perform a database query without your first opening the front-end software typically used to access the database. By combining the Agent Task Language with the ability to directly access DDE and DLLs, the NewWave Agent has complete command of almost all resources available to Windows applications and the NewWave environment. However, learning how to make full use of the Agent's capabilities requires a considerable amount of computer expertise.

Summary

The five shells discussed in this chapter present only a sampling of the many commercial and shareware shells available for Windows. No one shell is right for everyone, and your choice will depend mostly on your level of technical expertise and personal preferences.

Norton Desktop for Windows is by far the most popular third-party shell; even if you don't use the desktop itself as your shell, its grab bag of utilities is worthwhile for almost any Windows user.

WinTools provides Windows with the most attractive interface, and although it offers much power in some areas, its features are a bit skimpy in others.

Power Launcher is a minimalist shell that works by enhancing your Control menu to provide you with an onscreen toolbar. Power Launcher will make DOS users happy because it provides them with a powerful command line facility for saving steps and otherwise accelerating their operations.

Rooms for Windows offers an innovative twist on the concept of an expanded virtual desktop; the program allows you to organize your applications and data files into a collection of virtual desktops, which you can easily save and retrieve without having to reconfigure your former setup.

Pub Tech File Organizer is one of the oldest Windows shells, and it's beginning to show its age. Good for novices, Pub Tech is the Windows shell that looks and works most like the Macintosh.

NewWave is the most technically ambitious third-party shell, but its technical prowess comes at the expense of ease of use. Although NewWave provides unique capabilities for networked computer environments—it's the only one to protect you completely from DOS—it can be daunting for new Windows users. Although easy to use once it's set up, NewWave requires much system engineering for proper configuration.

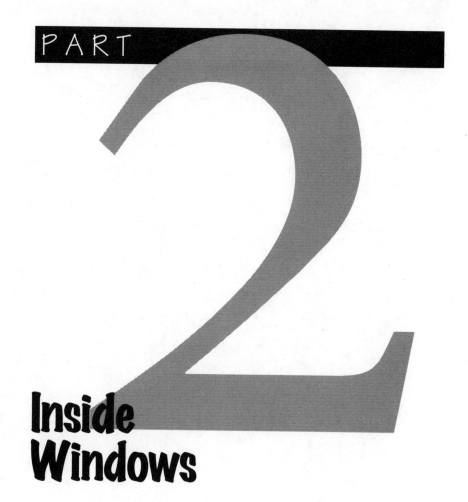

PART

2

Inside
Windows

7

Windows Fonts and Printing

The graphical user interface—designed at Xerox PARC in the seventies—made possible the first great leap forward into the field of desktop publishing: with a GUI, you were able to match the results on your screen with those on your printer. This well-known WYSIWYG capability (for What You See Is What You Get) first took hold on the Macintosh, which popularized the graphical user interface and spawned a second breakthrough: the **PostScript** system for computer typography, which spurred desktop publishing in a way that can be compared with the impact of the Gutenberg press on the medieval printing trade.

PostScript was jointly developed in 1985 by Apple and Adobe Systems to create a standard computer language that could be used to describe how a page looked. This page description could then be sent to any output device, from a printer to a typesetting machine. PostScript also added the benefit of removing the "jaggies"—those ragged edges—from printed characters by providing computer typefaces that could be scaled to any size. As a result, characters on screen and off the printer looked as if they had been typeset and printed professionally, thanks to a Macintosh computer and its companion Apple LaserWriter printer, both relatively inexpensive printing tools. Today, most serious desktop publishers have standardized on PostScript.

New in 3.1

It didn't take long for Microsoft to see the WYSIWYG light. First it adopted the graphical user interface, with the launch of Windows in 1985. But the corresponding revolution of a PostScriptlike typography didn't come about until the introduction of Windows 3.1. Built into every Windows 3.1 program is **TrueType**, a computer typography system jointly developed by Apple and Microsoft that is akin to PostScript (but just different enough to evade lawsuits!). TrueType provides both WYSIWYG capabilities and scalable typefaces, and it irons out your jagged fonts to create a professional look on screen and on paper.

TrueType enhances Windows printing as well by providing typefaces that appear the same on the screen as on the printed page, with almost any kind of printer, from HP LaserJet to PostScript Typesetter. Unlike Windows 3.0 and DOS applications, TrueType provides fully scalable typefaces, so that the type on your computer display is seamlessly matched to the type on the printed page.

Luckily, the addition of TrueType does not slow down printing; in fact, it accelerates the process. In Windows 3.1, when you issue the Print command your document is spooled to disk much faster than in 3.0, so you can return to your application before the process is completed. In addition, the printing process itself is dramatically faster.

Windows 3.1 also allows you to control your typography totally from your computer, because you can load typefaces into your system from a standard computer disk, thereby making most printer font cartridges obsolete. Instead of having to spend hundreds of dollars on different printer cartridges—which provide only a limited number of fonts and point sizes, often require separate installation of screen font software, and are incompatible among different printers—you can simply load any TrueType font onto your hard disk and gain access to that typeface in all its font sizes. TrueType provides a universal page description language that works on any printer with a Windows driver, from dot matrix to laser to professional typesetting machines.

Another advantage of TrueType is that it offers a unified system of computer typography for both the Macintosh and Windows. If you use TrueType fonts in a Windows document, you can transfer the document to a Macintosh, or vice versa, and it will look the same.

Dynamite Product

Although TrueType offers many of the capabilities of PostScript, if you plan to do serious desktop publishing you will need to get the Windows version of PostScript: **Adobe Type Manager** (ATM). Adobe Type Manager provides the same benefits to Windows as does TrueType and includes the industry-standard PostScript language. Most importantly, Adobe Type Manager provides access to the enormous library of professional PostScript typefaces. Luckily, with Windows you can have it both ways.

Indeed, the universe of Windows fonts and typography is both large and expanding. TrueType, PostScript, and other third-party typography solutions abound, and all enjoy a surprising breadth of support from typeface and printer vendors. Special font-conversion utilities, such as **Alltype** and **FontMonger**, can translate between TrueType, PostScript, and other kinds of typefaces and fonts to help solve the compatibility problems that can arise from such a fertile profusion of products.

In this chapter, I'll first discuss Windows typography; then the Windows printing process, including the use of Print Manager; and finish with a discussion of individual printers.

. . . .

Typography

Confusion pervades the terminology of typography. Print shops—using the traditional elements of lead type and printing presses—developed definitions for the terms typeface, typestyle, and font. Then came computers and turned everything topsy turvy. For traditional printers, **typeface** means something different from **font;** but for computer users, a typeface is a font, and both designate a general design for a group of characters. For example, Arial, Courier, and Palatino are all typefaces—or fonts. Adding a new twist to the typography name-game, Microsoft has coined another term, **font family**, which refers to a group of typefaces or fonts with similar characteristics.

All typefaces have been grouped into five font families, which Windows uses for font installation and mapping to the display and printer.

➤ **Roman** Serif typefaces, such as Times New Roman (TrueType) and Times Roman (screen)

➤ **Swiss** Sans serif typefaces, such as Arial, Small Fonts, MS Sans Serif, and Helvetica

➤ **Modern** Stylized fonts and typefaces

➤ **Script** Handwritinglike fonts

➤ **Decorative** Highly embellished display fonts and symbol fonts

In addition, Microsoft uses the term **font style** as a synonym for **typestyle**, which describes characteristics such as bold, italic, and regular (also called roman). The term **font effects** refers to special type attributes, such as underline, strike through, and the assignment of a particular color.

Windows also uses some other font terminology to describe spacing between fonts, which can be either fixed or proportional. In **fixed fonts**, each character takes an equal amount of space, whereas in **proportional fonts**, characters retain their own intrinsic widths. Don't confuse this with the term **width**, which describes whether a typeface has been **condensed** (space has been removed from between the characters) or **expanded** (space has been added between characters).

In addition, Windows classifies fonts into three categories, based on how they are created for display on the screen or for printing. **TrueType fonts** use a special system of drawing the font outline and then filling it in; this allows fonts to be scaled to any size, or to be rotated on the screen or printer and then filled in to the optimum resolution of your display device. The other two types of fonts—raster and vector—were carried over from Windows 3.0.

Raster fonts are stored as bitmap images at specific point sizes; they only look good when presented in the specific sizes in which they are stored. Most of the Windows 3.0 fonts are rasters—they cannot be scaled or rotated.

Vector fonts are drawn on the screen or printer using a mathematical description of the typeface design. Originally employed by pen plotters, these fonts have been used by other Windows applications (before 3.1) requiring fonts that could be resized and rotated.

Here's a rundown of the various different fonts and typefaces that work with Windows:

➵ **TrueType** Scalable typefaces for both your screen and printer. One of the best new features included in Windows 3.1, TrueType prints fast on most laser printers.

➵ **PostScript** Scalable typefaces for both screen and printer. Requires the additional purchase of Adobe Type Manager, but is the standard in professional desktop publishing operations.

➵ **Screen fonts** Raster fonts used by Windows to display text on the screen.

➵ **Vector fonts** Also called plotter fonts, these scalable fonts are intended mainly for use with pen plotters.

➵ **Printer fonts** Fonts built in or loaded into the printer. You need a matching screen font to view these properly in Windows. Examples of printer fonts are device fonts, printable screen fonts, and soft fonts.

➵ **Device fonts** Built into your printer or plugged into it in the form of a cartridge.

➵ **Cartridge fonts** A form of device font that includes products such as the cartridges that plug into HP LaserJets.

➵ **Soft fonts** Software-based fonts for your printer. These fonts are installed on your hard disk and downloaded to the printer as needed. Soft fonts usually need to be loaded into your system with their own installation program.

Not every printer can use all these different types of fonts; this chapter covers the font types specific to the different brands of printers. When you are using printer, device, cartridge, or soft fonts, you should try to obtain the matching screen fonts for each typeface. The **printer font** is essential for quality output; a **screen font** only triggers the appearance of an attractive font on your screen.

What happens when your screen and printer fonts don't match? If you have the screen font but not the printer font, your laser printer may react by producing your screen font in what resembles a crude dot-matrix style. But if you're still using an old dot matrix printer, then screen fonts, or even plotter fonts, may be acceptable. In some cases, your printer may substitute one of its built-in fonts for the screen font.

If, on the other hand, you have the printer font but not the screen font, then Windows will substitute a screen font, plotter font, or TrueType font that most closely matches your printer font. Although what you see on the screen may not exactly equal what you get on your page, Windows will still try its best to use the printer font dimensions to determine line and page breaks and any other onscreen formatting decisions.

. . . .

TrueType Fonts

If you're using TrueType, all the hassles of matching screen fonts and printer fonts disappear. TrueType is one of the most accommodating programs of its kind, with the ability to convert its fonts to PostScript for printing, and to other fonts as well, such as HP LaserJet's PCL 4. Along with Windows, Setup installs an all-purpose collection of 14 basic TrueType typefaces, so you have access instantly to these new faces:

➡ **Arial** A sans serif face that is a clone of the popular Helvetica typeface

➡ **Arial Italic** The italic version of Arial

➡ **Arial Bold** The bold version of Arial

➡ **Arial Bold Italic** An Ariallike design that incorporates both bold and italic styles

➡ **Courier New** The monospaced typewriter look lives! A nice low-tech look

➡ **Courier New Italic** The italic version of Courier New

➡ **Courier New Bold** The bold version of Courier New

➡ **Courier Bold Italic** A Courierlike design that incorporates both bold and italic styles

➡ **Symbol** Lots of interesting symbols for math, charts, games, or whatever

➡ **Times New Roman** A respectable serif face that is a clone of the popular Times typeface

➡ **Times New Roman Italic** The italic version of Times New Roman

➡ **Times New Roman Bold** The bold version of Times New Roman

➡ **Times New Roman Bold Italic** A Timeslike design that incorporates both bold and italic styles

➡ **Wingdings** A cool collection of icons, dingbats, and special symbols, which contains everything from telephones to computer parts to a bomb with a lit fuse

Figure 7.1 shows a sample of each of the 14 TrueType typefaces included with Windows 3.1.

FIGURE 7.1

TrueType Typefaces

Arial
AaBbCcDdEeFfGgHhIiJjKkLlMmNnOoPpQqRrSsTtUuVvWwXxYyZz
1234567890!@#$%^&*()[]{}\|"':;<>,.?/~`

Arial Italic
AaBbCcDdEeFfGgHhIiJjKkLlMmNnOoPpQqRrSsTtUuVvWwXxYyZz
1234567890!@#$%^&()[]{}\|"':;<>,.?/~`*

Arial Bold
AaBbCcDdEeFfGgHhIiJjKkLlMmNnOoPpQqRrSsTtUuVvWwXxYyZz
1234567890!@#$%^&*()[]{}\|"':;<>,.?/~`

Arial Bold Italic
AaBbCcDdEeFfGgHhIiJjKkLlMmNnOoPpQqRrSsTtUuVvWwXxYyZz
1234567890!@#$%^&*()[]{}\|"':;<>,.?/~`

Courier New
AaBbCcDdEeFfGgHhIiJjKkLlMmNnOoPpQqRrSsTtUuVvWwXxYyZz
1234567890!@#$%^&*() [] {}\|"':;<>,.?/~`

Courier New Italic
AaBbCcDdEeFfGgHhIiJjKkLlMmNnOoPpQqRrSsTtUuVvWwXxYyZz
1234567890!@#$%^&() [] {}\|"':;<>,.?/~`*

Courier New Bold
AaBbCcDdEeFfGgHhIiJjKkLlMmNnOoPpQqRrSsTtUuVvWwXxYyZz
1234567890!@#$%^&*() [] {}\|"':;<>,.?/~`

Courier New Bold Italic
AaBbCcDdEeFfGgHhIiJjKkLlMmNnOoPpQqRrSsTtUuVvWwXxYyZz
1234567890!@#$%^&*() [] {}\|"':;<>,.?/~`

Symbol
ΑαΒβΧχΔδΕεΦφΓγΗηΙιϑφΚκΛλΜμΝνΟοΠπΘΘΡρΣσΤτΥυςϖΩωΞξΨψΖζ
1234567890!≅#∃%⊥&*()[]{}∴|∀∍:;<>,.?/~

Times New Roman
AaBbCcDdEeFfGgHhIiJjKkLlMmNnOoPpQqRrSsTtUuVvWwXxYyZz
1234567890!@#$%^&*()[]{ }\|"':;<>,.?/~`

Times New Roman Italic
AaBbCcDdEeFfGgHhIiJjKkLlMmNnOoPpQqRrSsTtUuVvWwXxYyZz
1234567890!@#$%^&()[]{}\|"':;<>,.?/~`*

Times New Roman Bold
AaBbCcDdEeFfGgHhIiJjKkLlMmNnOoPpQqRrSsTtUuVvWwXxYyZz
1234567890!@#$%^&*()[]{}\|"':;<>,.?/~`

Times New Roman Bold Italic
AaBbCcDdEeFfGgHhIiJjKkLlMmNnOoPpQqRrSsTtUuVvWwXxYyZz
1234567890!@#$%^&*()[]{}\|"':;<>,.?/~`

Windings
🖎✂✃✄✆✈✉☜☞♌︎♍︎♎︎♏︎✎✐✑✒✓✔✕✖✗✘☺☻☹♥♦♣♠•◆
○□■▯▱▭▮►□→□□◆◇◆◇✢✣✤✥✦✧✩✪✫☒☓☐☑☒

Put a face on your documents with one of these 14 TrueType fonts.

Each TrueType typeface consists of two files, which both reside in the \SYSTEM subdirectory of your main Windows directory. These two font files use the same name but different extensions: one ends in .FOT and the other in .TTF.

Arial, Courier New, and Times New Roman are available as separate fonts in regular, bold, italic, and bold italic styles. Primitive computer typography software merely fattened a character to make it bold, or slanted it to make it italic; this resulted in irregular and often unaesthetic type. The TrueType typefaces adhere to the classic standard, which calls for the creation of a special typeface for each typestyle; Arial, for example, includes the files shown in Table 7.1 for each of its special fonts.

· · · · · · · · · · · · ·

TABLE 7.1
TrueType Fonts and Their Files

File Name	Font Name
ARIAL.FOT, ARIAL.TTF	Arial Regular
ARIALBD.FOT, ARIALBD.TTF	Arial Bold
ARIALI.FOT, ARIALI.TTF	Arial Italic
ARIALBI.FOT, ARIALBI.TTF	Arial Bold Italic

Each application handles the implementation of bold, italic, and other styles slightly differently. Some applications list each style of font separately. Most applications just list the regular font, and then provide a separate style command for bold, italic, and bold italic. When you access the style command, the program first checks to see whether the stylized font is available. If it is not, some applications can mutate the normal font, but this results in a less attractive alternative. The outline and shadow styles, for example, are almost always created through mutation, rather than through the use of a separate font file.

Dynamite Product

Hundreds of third-party TrueType typefaces are available for use with Windows. In addition, Microsoft has commissioned a set of 44 typefaces, called the Microsoft TrueType Font Pack for Windows, which includes 22 typefaces designed by Monotype Typography, Inc. Together with the 13 of the 14 TrueType typefaces included in Windows 3.1, these **Monotype fonts** closely match the 35 standard fonts included with most PostScript printers.

Table 7.2 lists the TrueType font families and their equivalent PostScript font families. Each font family includes a separate regular, italic, bold, and bold italic typeface.

The design of typefaces cannot be copyrighted—this is one area where look-and-feel does not apply. Only the name of the typeface can be protected

TABLE 7.2
*Postcript
Equivalents of
TrueType
Fonts*

TrueType Font Family	PostScript Font Family
Arial	Helvetica
Arial Narrow	Helvetica Narrow
Bookman Antiqua	Palatino
Bookman Old Style	Bookman
Century Gothic	Avant Garde
Corsiva	Zapf Chancery
Courier New	Courier
Sorts	Zapf Dingbats
Symbol	Symbol
Times New Roman	Times Roman

by copyright law; therefore the general Helvetica design is called Arial in Windows, and some type vendors call it Swiss or Dutch. Although these TrueType typefaces are roughly equivalent to their PostScript counterparts, there are some significant differences. First, there are some subtle design variations between the two types of characters. The spacing, furthermore, can vary so much that line length and therefore page lengths are not equivalent between the two typefaces.

In addition to these Monotype fonts, the TrueType Font Pack includes 22 Lucida typefaces developed by digital typography pioneer Chuck Bigelow and calligrapher Kris Holmes. The TrueType Font Pack includes the following Lucida typefaces:

➻ **Lucida Blackletter** The olde English look

➻ **Lucida Bright** A distinctive, easy-to-read serif typeface

➻ **Lucida Bright Demibold** A bold version of Lucida Bright that is not too heavy

➻ **Lucida Bright Italic** The italic version of Lucida Bright

➻ **Lucida Bright Demibold Italic** A somewhat bold, italicized version of Lucida Bright

➻ **Lucida Bright Math Symbols** Special symbols for mathematicians

➻ **Lucida Bright Math Italic** An italic math font; not an italic version of Lucida Bright Math Symbols

➻ **Lucida Calligraphy** Resembles the calligraphic lettering on a diploma

➻ **Lucida Fax** A special typeface optimized for legibility for fax machine transmission

➤ **Lucida Fax Demibold** A heavier version of Lucida Fax

➤ **Lucida Fax Italic** An italic version of Lucida Fax

➤ **Lucida Fax Demibold Italic** A heavier version of Lucida Fax Italic

➤ **Lucida Handwriting** A simulation of human handwriting, based on the handwriting of Kris Holmes

➤ **Lucida Math Extension** Even more math symbols for those mathematicians who aren't satisfied with Lucida Bright Math Symbols and Lucida Bright Math Italic

➤ **Lucida Sans** An especially readable sans serif typeface for those who think Arial is ugly

➤ **Lucida Sans Demibold** A heavier version of Lucida Sans

➤ **Lucida Sans Italic** An italic version of Lucida Sans

➤ **Lucida Sans Demibold Italic** A heavier version of Lucida Sans Italic

➤ **Lucida Sans Typewriter** A sans serif alternative to Courier reminiscent of the IBM Selectric

➤ **Lucida Sans Typewriter Bold** A bold version of Lucida Sans Typewriter

➤ **Lucida Sans Typewriter Oblique** A slightly italicized version of Lucida Sans Typewriter

➤ **Lucida Sans Typewriter Bold Oblique** A bold version of Lucida Sans Typewriter Oblique

The TrueType Font Pack fleshes out the basic selection of TrueType typefaces included with Windows 3.1 and is highly recommended for anyone using a laser printer.

To identify inclusion of TrueType, many applications—including the applets bundled with Windows, such as Write and Paintbrush—are preceded by a special TT symbol (Figure 7.2).

FIGURE 7.2
*Font Menu
with TT
Symbols*

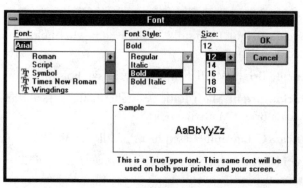

The TT symbol tips you off that this is a TrueType typeface. Use these whenever you can: they look good and print quickly.

In order to speed up the display or printing of a TrueType font, Windows creates a special font cache to store the rendered bitmaps. Each time you select a TrueType font at a specific size, Windows creates a bitmap of all the characters in that font; this process can cause a slight lag on slower systems. However, because these bitmaps are stored in the font cache, you won't experience a delay when you reuse these fonts.

Danger Zone

On the other hand, if you use a plethora of fonts and a multitude of different sizes within a single document, you will probably notice a slowdown in your system performance and your printing speed. This is because the font cache has become overloaded with all the rendered bitmaps, and the cache has to be swapped out to the hard disk more often.

This problem occurs with all Windows fonts, not just TrueType. Although a fat font cache can induce a state of lethargy in your system, Windows allows up to 1170 TrueType fonts to be active simultaneously. Because one True-Type typeface provides fonts of all sizes, it requires far less space than would an equivalent raster font, which with a few exceptions requires a separate font file for each point size.

TrueType typefaces can be printed on any printer that supports the Windows universal printer driver. This means that the font will look the same, whether it's printed on a dot-matrix printer, a laser printer, or a typesetting machine.

If you're upgrading to 3.1 from 3.0, you'll want to keep these TrueType considerations in mind. Windows 3.1 does not alter any of the fonts that you specified in your various Windows documents. To upgrade your old documents to take advantage of TrueType, open them, select the type, and then reselect the TrueType font you wish to use. Some vendors offer utilities that automatically upgrade documents for TrueType; refer to your user documentation to see if this feature is offered.

TrueType uses a different method for spacing characters than the procedure employed in Windows 3.0. The new method, called **ABC widths**, allows applications that were designed for 3.1 to position characters more accurately on both the screen and the printer, especially if you use a different style, such as bold or italic. With some applications that predate Windows 3.1, your TrueType fonts may look very strange on the screen; not to worry, they'll print just fine.

Insider's Tip

You can use the [FontSubstitutes] section of WIN.INI to reassign old Windows fonts to new TrueType fonts. In fact, if you've upgraded from 3.0 to 3.1, Windows Setup substitutes Arial for the old Helvetica, Times New Roman for the old Times, and Courier New for the old Courier. See Chapter 15 for more information about editing the WIN.INI file.

Danger Zone

TrueType Font Embedding. Because each computer system tends to be installed with a different set of fonts, there's no guarantee that you can print a document on one computer so that it resembles the way it was created on another computer. Although WYSIWYG provides a visual correlation between what you see on your screen and the output from your printer, this principle doesn't always apply across different computers. This discrepancy most typically occurs in an office, where the carefully formatted document you prepared on your own system looks as if it's been through a mangler when printed on your colleague's system, which has been installed with different fonts.

Typeface troubles also emerge when you send a disk to a service bureau for output, unless you include the typefaces on the disk. Although this is a common practice, it's an added hassle and a potential copyright violation, because most commercial typefaces are licensed for only one machine.

To help solve some of these problems with document portability, Microsoft has devised three different levels of TrueType font embedding, ranging from highly restrictive to open. Embedding solves the problem by including the actual fonts along with the document.

The decision as to which level of embedding to select is left up to the developer. At the most restrictive level, developers can prevent their fonts from being embedded into a document. If **no embedding** is allowed, applications that support font embedding won't let you embed the restricted typeface into a document; as a result, the recipient will be compelled to purchase the typeface or make a font substitution. Most PostScript fonts have this level of restriction; but because it's a hassle, this restrictive choice is seldom exercised by most developers. If you find you can't embed a font, complain to its developer about the use of this heavy-handed restriction.

At the middle level of restrictions, the TrueType typeface can be developed as **read-only** for the purpose of embedding. This allows the document to be viewed and printed with the proper typeface when it's transferred to another computer system. However, that typeface is only temporarily installed on the machine, and the recipient is not able to modify the document or use the typeface in any other document or application. Many large-font vendors sell TrueType fonts with the embedding status set to read-only. This choice allows documents to be freely exchanged while protecting the developer's ability to sell more copies of the typeface.

As a third alternative, font developers can set their font embedding status to **read-write**. With read-write embedding, a document that embeds a True-Type font actually contains a fully installable copy of the font itself. When a document containing a read-write TrueType font is sent to another user, the recipient can freely edit the document and view or print it. In addition, the read-write fonts can be used by other applications on the recipient system and can usually be installed permanently on the other computer, as if that user had purchased the font.

Insider's Tip

The read-write font can then be used in any other Windows application that works with TrueType and is designed to support font embedding. If these two conditions are met, the font can even be embedded again and sent to another user. All 14 TrueType fonts included with Windows 3.1, as well as the 44 fonts included in the TrueType Font Pack, are set to read-write embedding status. The read-write capability of the 44 read-write fonts in the pack makes it a particularly desirable package, as compared with most commercially available font packs, which are set to read-only.

TrueType Versus PostScript. Which is better, TrueType or PostScript? There's no easy answer, because each system has its intrinsic strengths and weaknesses. For Windows 3.1 users, Truetype is included free—which certainly makes it attractive. For professional desktop publishers and typesetters, PostScript is much more entrenched, so it has the clear advantage in this arena. Although TrueType works with PostScript printers by converting TrueType fonts to PostScript fonts on the fly, some applications require the real PostScript. To get PostScript for Windows, you'll need to purchase Adobe Type Manager, which provides a scalable type for your screen and printer and thereby offers roughly the same functionality as TrueType.

As for performance, TrueType prints faster to HP LaserJets, whereas ATM works better with PostScript printers, because the printer and system fonts are similar. Both products do a slow but admirable job printing on dot-matrix and inkjet printers.

Insider's Tip

Because of the predominance of PostScript in desktop publishing, many such products for Windows come bundled with Adobe Type Manager. If you're already buying one of the other software packages, the additional cost of ATM is usually minimal; sometimes the software vendor bundles ATM as a "free" sales incentive.

An important difference between the two typefaces has to do with **hinting**, a technique used to include information in an outline typeface. This process helps to compensate for the discrepancies that occur when gently flowing outlines are converted to gridlike bitmaps, and enables fonts to be displayed as characters on screens and printers. Both TrueType and PostScript are based on outline fonts, and both use some form of hinting.

Hinting provides the computer with information that adjusts the outline so that the strokes that make up each character are better aligned with bitmapped output devices, such as the dots on a printer or the pixels on a monitor. This process greatly increases legibility of the text, especially when small type is displayed on your computer monitor or on a 300 dpi laser printer; but hinting becomes irrelevant on a 1200 dpi typesetting machine, because more pixels are available for displaying each character.

Whereas TrueType incorporates the hints into the typeface file, PostScript places hinting in the font rasterizer, which draws the characters on the screen. With TrueType, each character in the typeface can contain its own hints. As a result, software that displays TrueType on your screen can be more efficient, because it doesn't need to calculate hinting on the fly; it just reads the hinting information contained in the typeface. The drawback with TrueType is that once the typeface is created, hinting cannot be improved. For example, the Wingdings typeface in Windows 3.1 contains no hinting, so small point sizes look bad on the screen. To make them look decent, you'd need to get a new version of Wingdings that contained hinting information.

With PostScript, the hinting information is contained in the PostScript rasterizer—the software that converts the outline of the font into a bitmap for screen display or printer output. PostScript fonts come in two flavors: the older, Type 3 fonts do not contain hinting; the newer Type 1 fonts contain hints that tell the rasterizer how much to distort the outlines for all the characters in a typeface (rather than for each character, as with Truetype) in order to adjust them for low-resolution output devices.

Insider's Tip

The bottom line in the TrueType versus PostScript debate is this: for professional typesetters, print shops, and desktop publishing services, hinting is irrelevant, and PostScript is the standard typeface for professional publishing. If you just need a straightforward and inexpensive (often free) way to make your laser printer produce attractive documents, I recommend True-Type. Because of its approach to hinting, TrueType looks best at comparatively low resolutions, such as with 300 dpi laser printers and 640x480 VGA monitors, which are the staple of the PC market.

Screen Fonts Used by the Windows System

Windows includes a selection of raster fonts for displaying the text of menus, dialog boxes, window titles, and other system components. The default screen font used by Windows 3.1 is named System and comes in a variety of resolutions to support different display modes. Table 7.3 shows which files contain the **System font**:

	Font File Name	Display Mode	Resolution
TABLE 7.3 *System Fonts for Standard Displays*	EGASYS.FON	EGA and AT&T	640x350 (640x400 for AT&T displays)
	VGASYS.FON	VGA	640x480
	8514SYS.FON	8514/a	1024x768

The System font is assigned by Windows Setup based on your choice of display, and its setting is stored in the [boot] section of the SYSTEM.INI file. For example, this line specifies the VGA System font:

```
FONTS.FON=VGASYS.FON
```

Insider's Tip

You can change this font if you like; for example, if you kick your SuperVGA display into a high-resolution mode, such as 800x600, you may want to substitute the 8514SYS.FON file.

Windows also uses two other types of raster fonts for displaying items on the screen: the **Fixed font** and the **OEM font** (formerly called the Terminal font). The Fixed font is nonproportional and was used as the primary system font by the ancient Windows 2.0; it's provided for compatibility with older applications. The OEM font, also nonproportional, is used to display OEM text visible in the Clipboard Viewer utility. In addition, it's used by Windows applications, such as Terminal, that require a font with a fixed width. Telecommunications displays often assume fixed spacing, so that rows, columns, tables, and online menu choices will be displayed properly on the screen.

In any case, Windows Setup installs the Fixed and OEM fonts that match your computer's display. The Fixed and OEM font files are shown in Table 7.4.

	Display	Resolution	Fixed Font	OEM Font
TABLE 7.4 *Fixed and OEM Fonts for Standard Displays*	EGA	640x350 (AT&T 640x400)	EGAFIX.FON	EGAOEM.FON
	VGA	640x480	VGAFIX.FON	VGAOEM.FON
	8514/a	1024x768	8514FIX.FON	8514OEM.FON

Like the System font, the Fixed font and OEM font assignments are listed in the [boot] section of the SYSTEM.INI file. The following two lines are an example based on a VGA display:

```
OEMFONTS.FON=VGAOEM.FON
FIXEDFON.FON=VGAFIX.FON
```

• •

Other Windows Screen Fonts

Microsoft provides five other **raster font sets** that are used primarily for screen displays, although some can be applied to dot-matrix printers as well. These are the five fonts:

➠ **Courier** A fixed-width serif font reminiscent of a typewriter, supplied in 10, 12, and 15-point sizes

➠ **MS Sans Serif** A proportional font in the style of Helvetica, supplied in 8, 10, 12, 14, 18, and 24-point sizes

➠ **MS Serif** A proportional font in the Times tradition, supplied in 8, 10, 12, 14, 18, and 24-point sizes

➠ **Small** A proportional font designed to look good when size is under 8 points, supplied in 2, 4, and 6-point sizes

➠ **Symbol** A proportional font composed of math symbols, supplied in 8, 10, 12, 14, 18, and 24-point sizes. Note that this font has the same name as the very different Symbol TrueType font.

These five raster fonts are used to label icons in Program Manager and to label trees, directories, and files in File Manager. The default font is MS Sans Serif at 8 points. You can change both the typeface and the font size used by either Program Manager or File Manager.

To change the fonts used in File Manager, simply choose the Fonts command from File Manager's Options menu and select a new font from the Font dialog box. Selecting a smaller font (such as the tiny Small Fonts) lets you see more items in the Tree and Directory windows; selecting a larger font makes it easier to read text at a high screen resolution, which shrinks everything on your display.

File Manager font selections are stored in the WINFILE.INI file. Here's what the settings would look like with the fonts changed to Small Fonts:

```
Face=Small Fonts
Size=7
LowerCase=1
FaceWeight=400
```

To change the font for Program Manager icons, you'll need to open the WIN.INI file and add two statement lines to the [desktop] section. The **IconTitleFaceName=** statement specifies the typeface you want to use, and the **IconTitleSize=** statement specifies the point size of the font. For example, to change the typeface for icons in Program Manager to Arial Narrow at 8 points you would add the lines

```
IconTitleFaceName=ARIAL NARROW
IconTitleSize=8
```

The five raster fonts are provided in six different resolutions: four that match specific displays and two for use with printers. The files for these fonts are COUR(X).FON, where the X varies from B to F; SSERIF(X).FON; SERIF(X).FON; SMALL(X); and SYMBOL(X).

For example, the various MS San Serif font files supplied with Windows are SSERIFA.FON; SSERIFB.FON; SSERIFC.FON; SSERIFD.FON; SSERIFE.FON; and SSERIFF.FON. The set of five fonts installed for a VGA display are COURF.FON, SSERIFF.FON, SERIFF.FON, SMALLF.FON, and SYMBOLF.FON.

The B through F designation identifies the resolution of the font according to the values shown in Table 7.5.

. . . .

TABLE 7.5

Resolution and Aspect Ratios of Raster Fonts

Letter	Device	Horizontal by Vertical Resolution	Aspect Ratio
B	EGA display	96dpi by 72dpi	1.33:1
C	Printer	60dpi by 72dpi	1:1.2
D	Printer	120dpi by 72dpi	1.67:1
E	VGA display	96dpi by 96dpi	1:1
F	8514/a display	120dpi by 120dpi	1:1

These raster fonts are supplied in a variety of specific point sizes; for example, MS Sans Serif includes 8, 10, 12, 14, 18, and 24-point font sizes. Windows can scale these fonts to any even multiples of those sizes. However, at very large sizes, these fonts will appear jaggy around the edges. You can use these fonts for printing if their resolution and aspect ratios closely match those of your printer. You may need to refer to your printer manual to determine what horizontal and vertical ratios it's capable of producing in order to find the raster font that makes the best match.

Windows Setup installs the fonts needed for your display, but you can use the Fonts icon in the Control Panel, as described later in this chapter, to add any of these fonts if you wish to use them for printing, or if you change your display resolution. Some printers, such as a pen plotters, cannot print raster fonts, regardless of resolution or aspect ratio; for such printers, you'll need to use vector or TrueType fonts.

Insider's Tip

The raster fonts installed in your system are listed in the [fonts] section of your WIN.INI file. You can look at this to see what point sizes are available for each font. Also, if you're upgrading to 3.1, Setup replaces the Tms Rmn and Helv fonts with the MS Serif and MS Sans Serif fonts, respectively, by remapping them in the [fontSubstitutes] section of the WIN.INI file.

In addition to the raster fonts, Windows includes three **vector font files**: ROMAN.FON, MODERN.FON, and SCRIPT.FON. These vector font files contain mathematical instructions for drawing the lines necessary to create these typefaces; they were originally used by pen plotters, where the pen actually followed the instructions to draw the character on paper.

Before TrueType, vector fonts were the only scalable fonts, and some developers used them to create large characters or special type effects, such as rotated text. The inclusion of these vector fonts provides compatibility with such applications and can also be used with pen plotters. However, I recommend using TrueType if you want scalable type on anything other than a plotter.

Table 7.6 identifies which kinds of fonts work with different printers.

TABLE 7.6
Printer and Font Compatibilities

Printer	TrueType Fonts	Raster Fonts	Vector Fonts
HP LaserJet-compatible	Yes	No	Yes
PostScript	Yes	No	Yes
Dot matrix	Yes	Yes	Yes
Pen plotter	No	No	Yes

Fonts Used by DOS Applications

Insider's Tip

Windows 3.1 introduces the ability to easily select from among a variety of fonts for displaying character-based DOS applications when they are run from within Windows. However, this feature is available only in 386 enhanced mode. The advantage of being able to select a different font size for your DOS application goes beyond aesthetic considerations. By being able to select smaller-size type, you can now present a full screen of a DOS display in a window that is much smaller than a standard VGA display. This allows you to have several DOS applications running at once in full view. Or you can keep a single window open without obscuring the rest of your Windows screen.

To change the font for your DOS application, first open a windowed DOS session, then choose the Font command from the DOS Windows Control menu. This brings up the Font Selection dialog box (Figure 7.3).

FIGURE 7.3

Font Selection Dialog Box

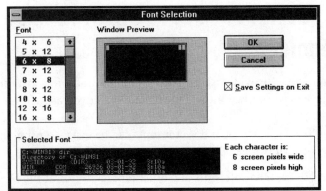

Windows 3.1 lets you select a variety of font sizes for displaying character-based DOS applications in a window.

The following font files contain the fonts you can select for your DOS applications:

➡ **DOSAPP.FON** Standard VGA font sets

➡ **CGA40WOA.FON** Fonts for CGA 40-column display

➡ **CGA80WOA.FON** Fonts for CGA 80-column display

➡ **EGA40WOA.FON** Fonts for EGA 40-column display

➡ **EGA80WOA.FON** Fonts for EGA 80-column display

➡ **HERCWOA.FON** Fonts for Hercules display

These fonts are based on the U.S. standard DOS character set, which in turn is based on your computer's Code Page 437. (Code Pages can be changed using DOS mode Setup, as explained in Chapter 4.) If you'd rather use the multilingual character set, specified by Code Page 850, you'll have to use these font files (except for APP850.FON) in conjunction with the XLAT850.BIN translation table:

➡ **APP850.FON** or **VGA850.FON** Standard VGA font sets

➡ **CGA40850.FON** Fonts for CGA 40-column display

➡ **CGA80850.FON** Fonts for CGA 80-column display

➡ **EGA40850.FON** Fonts for EGA 40-column display

➡ **EGA80850.FON** Fonts for EGA 80-column display

➡ **HERC850.FON** Fonts for Hercules display

Your choice of fonts depends on which video grabber file you are using. Note that the CGA fonts used with DOS applications are employed to simulate the CGA display within a DOS session that is running in a window, regardless of what type of display you are actually using.

Installing Fonts

Windows provides several different methods for installing new fonts, depending on the font and the printer driver you are using:

➡ TrueType, raster, and vector fonts can be installed using the Fonts icon in the Control Panel.

➡ **HP LaserJet soft fonts** and other types of fonts for the HP LaserJet can be installed on your hard disk by using the printer driver's font installer. In some cases, you may also need to add the fonts to Windows by using the Fonts icon in the Control Panel.

➡ **Device fonts**, such as font cartridges, can be added to Windows by accessing the Printer icon in the Control Panel.

➡ **PostScript fonts** are installed with the utilities included with Adobe Type Manager.

Some third-party soft fonts can be installed first on your hard disk using the utility supplied with the soft fonts, and then installed in Windows using the Fonts icon in the Control Panel.

Using the Font Controls in the Control Panel

To view, install, or remove a TrueType, raster, or vector font, start the Control Panel and open the Fonts icon (Alt,S,F); the Fonts dialog box appears (Figure 7.4).

This dialog box contains a scrollable list called Installed Fonts (Alt+F). A large box beneath the list, called Sample (Alt+S), lets you view a sample group of characters in whatever font is selected. This provides a convenient way to browse through all the fonts installed in your system. To view an installed font, simply scroll the box using the scroll arrows and point to a font in order to display it in the Sample box.

The names shown in the Fonts dialog box are followed by information identifying the font. For example, a list of numbers indicates these are raster

FIGURE 7.4
Fonts Dialog Box

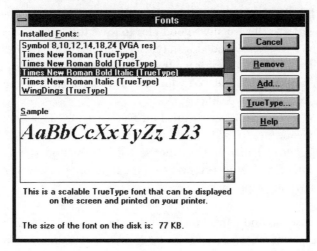

The Kingdom of Fontal Delights: view, install, or remove fonts using the Fonts dialog box.

fonts, and therefore nonscalable. Unless you use the given font sizes, or multiples of them, your fonts will probably look bad. Information in parentheses also identifies the font: screen fonts are followed by information such as (VGA res), (EGA res), or (8514 res); plotter fonts are identified by (Plotter); and TrueType typefaces by (TrueType).

To install a new screen, printer, plotter, or TrueType font, click on the Add button in the Fonts window, or press Alt+A. The Add Fonts dialog box appears (Figure 7.5).

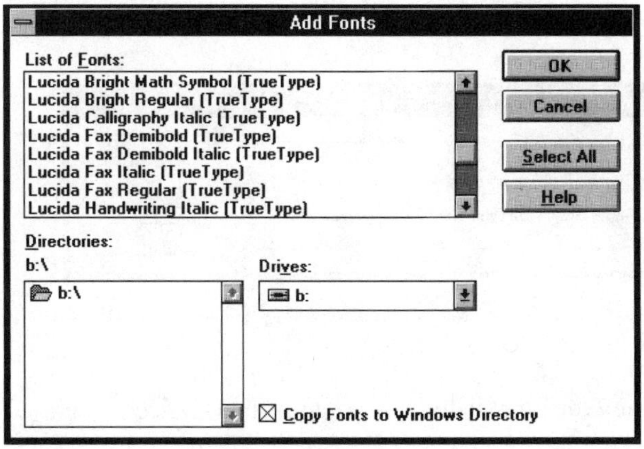

FIGURE 7.5
Add Fonts Dialog Box

The Add Fonts dialog box lets you add TrueType typefaces, screen fonts, printer fonts, and plotter fonts to Windows.

Use the Browse button to search the drive and directory in order to locate the font files that you want to install. The box named List of Fonts (press Alt+L to select) contains a list of font files that Windows sees in whatever directory you just selected. Select the fonts you want to install. To add all the listed fonts, press Select All (Alt+S).

Use the check box Copy Fonts to Windows Directory (Alt+C) and do just what it says. It's usually a good idea to leave this box checked, unless you're using a CD-ROM loaded with typefaces. In this case, remove the check mark to install the fonts but leave them on the source CD-ROM drive. This can save considerable space on your hard disk, particularly if you are accessing a large CD-ROM type library.

When you've selected your font files, click OK. This signals Windows to copy your files to the \SYSTEM subdirectory of your Windows directory, and the Control Panel updates the related information stored in the [fonts] section of your WINI.INI file. TrueType fonts are pairs of files ending in .TTF or .FOT; other fonts use the extension .FON.

Insider's Tip

Because the Add Fonts box lists the contents of only one directory at a time, if you want to install a large group of fonts at one time, first place them all in the same directory. You can then select the entire group at one time.

Some applications, such as CorelDraw, automatically install fonts into your system and update the WIN.INI file. Because these fonts and others you've installed into Windows gobble up memory and space on your hard disk, I recommend you install only those fonts you are actually using. Sure, it's tempting to have a long list of fonts available just a few clicks away, but it's better to keep your system mean and lean; anyway, installing fonts as you need them is fairly straightforward.

If you are installing TrueType fonts, click the button labeled TrueType (Alt+T) to reveal a dialog box that contains two other options (Figure 7.6).

• • • • • • • • • • • • •
FIGURE 7.6
*TrueType
Dialog Box*

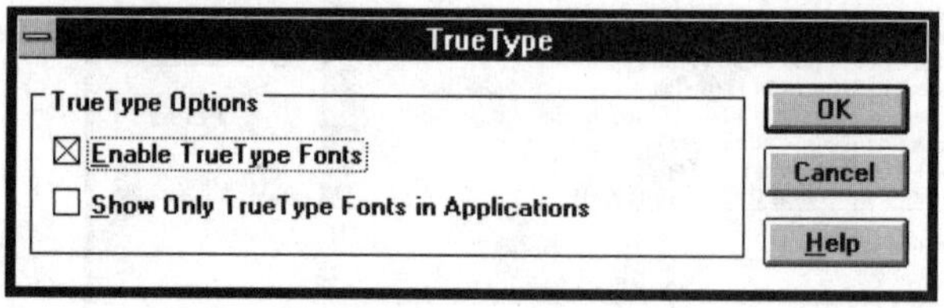

TrueType
┌─ TrueType Options ─────────────┐   OK
☒ Enable TrueType Fonts   Cancel
☐ Show Only TrueType Fonts in Applications   Help

You can use the TrueType dialog box to decide whether to use only True-Type, or to not use it at all.

The TrueType dialog box contains two choices:

➤ **Enable TrueType Fonts** (Alt+E) Disable this option to save yourself some system resources.

➤ **Show Only TrueType Fonts in Applications** (Alt+S) Restrict yourself to using only these great new scalable typefaces in your Windows applications.

Remove the check from the first option to disable TrueType if you want to free the memory the fonts would consume for other applications. Disabling TrueType is temporary and does not remove the actual font files from your system. You should be careful with the other option, Show Only TrueType Fonts in Applications: some applications are incompatible with this feature, which can prevent any fonts from being listed in that application. If this happens to you, turn this option off.

To remove a typeface, simply highlight it in the Installed Fonts area of the Fonts dialog box and then click on the Remove button (Alt+R) to cause the Remove Font dialog box to appear (Figure 7.7). If you need to free up some space on your disk, select the Delete Font File From Disk check box, and the files will be zapped—but remember, it will be tougher to reinstall them if you zap the original files. Repeat as necessary to remove all unwanted fonts and typefaces.

• • • • • • • • • • • • • •

FIGURE 7.7

Remove Font Dialog Box

The Remove Font dialog box lets you remove a font from Windows and option-ally delete the file from the disk.

Danger Zone

Prevent this fontal lobotomy! Don't remove the MS Sans Serif font set, because Windows uses this for system purposes. (Windows 3.0 used the Helv font, which Setup replaces when you upgrade.) If MS Sans Serif isn't available, Windows substitutes a different font, which could make some onscreen items more difficult to read, depending on the font that is selected.

Sometimes when you print a document it may contain fonts that are not installed in your system. This could happen if you receive a document from someone else or if you removed a font that was previously installed. In such cases, Windows does its best to substitute a font that approximates the missing one. With TrueType fonts, Windows can make a better substitution, because it can call on TrueType to render the character. And if TrueType fonts are embedded in a document, you can print them properly without the need for substitution.

• •

Windows Printing

To capitalize on the Windows graphical environment, you need more than a good display system for getting top performance on screen; you should also have a good graphics-capable printer. Because Windows handles everything on a page, including typefaces, as graphics, a graphics-capable printer is crucial. Sure, you can use an "old fashioned" daisy-wheel printer that can only print characters, but you'll forego the graphical enrichment that Windows can provide for your printed output.

Insider's Tip

I recommend a laser printer, especially with today's bargain street prices for Windows-capable laser printers from Hewlett-Packard, Okidata, and other manufacturers, which run at well below $1,000. In the under $500 price range, several good 24-pin dot-matrix and inkjet printers also work well with Windows.

During the standard setup process, you are asked to enter the name of the printer or printers connected to the system. At that point, Windows installs the appropriate drivers—software routines that address the printer's specific capabilities with regard to Windows—for each device. Windows includes **printer drivers** that support most printers available for PCs and compatibles; these are listed at the end of this chapter.

The proper driver is what allows the concept of WYSIWYG to succeed. In theory, this means that the images appearing on the monitor are identical to what emerges from the printer. This can't be taken literally, however. For instance, many more people use color monitors than use color printers. To achieve "true WYSIWYG," in this case, you would need to get an expensive color printer. In the second place, the shape, size, and lower resolution of most monitors, in comparison to the printed page, assures something closer to WYSCPBWYG (What You See Can't Possibly Be What You Get).

Two utilities control printing within Windows. **Print Manager**, a separate application that is placed into the Main application group at installation, acts as traffic cop and coordinates all printing activities. In addition, the Control Panel features a **Printers icon** that provides the controls necessary for the installation and setup of printers.

. . . .

The Printers Icon in the Control Panel

To set up a printer, if you didn't already do so during Windows installation, or to change some options on the printer you've already installed, you need to access the **Printers dialog box**. You can reach this dialog box by opening Print Manager and choosing Printer Setup from the Options menu, or by opening the Printers icon in the Control Panel (Figure 7.8).

When you first open the Printers icon, the Printers dialog box appears in a scaled-down form. (If you haven't installed a printer driver yet, the dialog

FIGURE 7.8
*Printers
Dialog Box*

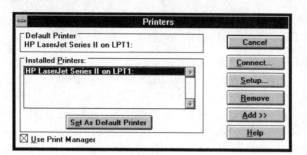

The main Printers dialog box lets you install, configure, enable, or remove printers from the Windows environment.

box is presented in its expanded form.) The scrolling list titled Installed Printers includes the printers you added when you installed Windows, plus any you've installed subsequently.

The Default Printer box (immediately above the Printers list) shows which printer Windows is using as your default. Most Windows applications use this default printer automatically, unless you specifically select another from within the application. Only one printer can be designated the default printer. The default printer should be the output device that you use the most.

To change the default printer selection, simply double-click on another printer in the Installed Printer list. From the keyboard, select the Installed Printers list by typing Alt+P; navigate through the printer list with the arrow keys; highlight a selected printer; and press Alt+E to push the Set As Default Printer button. The change takes effect immediately, and the printer name appears in the Default Printer box. The next time you start Windows, the driver for the new printer will be loaded automatically.

These buttons on the right side of the dialog box provide other functions:

➤ **Close** Closes the Printers dialog box. (If you access this dialog box through Print Manager 's Option menu, this button is labeled Cancel.)

➤ **Connect** Brings up the Connect dialog box, which lets you select the output ports for printing data. You can select from all I/O ports installed in the system; other devices, such as a fax modem; or even redirect output to a file for printing later or on another system. As a matter of course, Windows assumes that the printer will be using the LPT1 port. If you are using a different LPT port, or a serial printer, the IBM Personal Page Printer (the EPT option supports this, but requires an internal expansion card), or a file, make a selection in this box.

➤ **Setup** Brings up the printer setup dialog box, which contains information specific to the driver, such as resolution, portrait/landscape orientation, and other specifics. Different printer drivers present different dialog boxes, discussed later in this chapter.

➥ **Remove** Deletes the highlighted printer driver from the system, after a confirmation from the dialog box.

➥ **Add** Brings up the Add dialog box, which lets you install a new printer driver. Select a printer name from the long list of models shown in the list box. If the driver files are not already installed, Windows then prompts you to insert the appropriate driver disk in a floppy drive. If the machine you have is on the list, Windows requests one of the original installation disks. To install a third-party driver or one that is not on the list, select the first entry, Install Unlisted or Updated Printer; you'll be prompted to insert a third-party disk with the new driver.

Below the Set As Default Printer button is the Use Print Manager check box. (This check box will be missing if you access the dialog box through Print Manager's Options menu.) If this box is checked, Windows will control your printing jobs. Under most circumstances, you'll want to keep this box checked; to change this setting, click on the box or press Alt+U.

Installing a Printer. Even if you have only one physical printer, you may want to install more than one printer driver. Additional drivers can be used for the same printer when you're applying different applications, such as when your printer offers more than one emulation mode (Hewlett-Packard and PostScript, for example). You can also use an additional driver with a single printer to redirect a printout to a disk file rather than to a printer.

To install a printer, click on the Add button (Alt+A). The Printers dialog box expands downward, introducing a new section: the List of Printers (Figure 7.9).

FIGURE 7.9

Expanded Printers Dialog Box

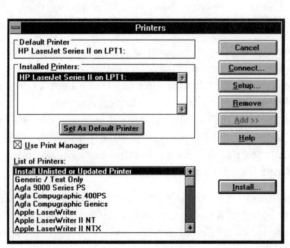

Grow your own! When you press the Add button, the Printers dialog box grows a List of Printers.

Use the mouse or type Alt+L to activate this list. Highlight the designated printer, click on the Install button (or type Alt+I), and the Control Panel prompts you for the disk containing the printer driver.

If the \SYSTEM subdirectory in your Windows directory already contains a printer driver for the printer you selected, a dialog box appears asking whether you want to use your current driver or install a new one. Select the Current button to use your existing driver; select the New button to use a new driver. Specifying a new driver replaces your old one and causes all the printers that use it to switch to the new driver as well.

To install an unlisted printer, or to update a driver for a printer on the list, you'll need a disk containing that printer driver. Select the first item in the list, Install Unlisted or Updated Printer and click on Install button. A dialog box appears asking for the disk with the new printer driver. When you insert the disks requested by the Control Panel, the driver will be copied onto your hard disk. If the printer driver is already on your hard disk or network server, type the drive letter and the path name of the directory that contains the printer driver file.

If you're unsure of the driver file's location, use the Browse button to peruse the various drives and directories connected to your system. Depending on the printer driver you select, you may be presented with yet another dialog box prompting you for the disk or directory path, where font files or other files required by the printer driver are located.

The model name of the printer (not the file name of the driver) then appears in the Installed Printers list. If this is the first printer driver you've installed, it is automatically listed as the default printer and is assigned the LPT1 printer port. If your printer is not connected to this port, use the Connect button to specify another port.

Choosing a Printer Port. If you're using a standalone PC—that is, it's not connected to a network—your printer is probably connected to one of the **LPT parallel ports**. But some printers are connected to a **serial COM port**, and others, such as the IBM Personal Page Printer, to the EPT port (which requires a special add-in card). If you're using a network, your method of connecting to a printer depends on the network (see Chapter 10).

Most PC systems can have up to three parallel ports—LPT1, LPT2, and LPT3—and up to four serial ports—COM1, COM2, COM3, and COM4. However, PCs are commonly equipped with only one parallel port and two serial ports. If you need more, the solution is to use add-in cards to supply extra ports; these cards are both inexpensive and easy to obtain. If you're unsure what ports you have available in your system, quit Windows and run the Microsoft Diagnostics utility, described in Chapter 17.

To specify an output destination for your printer, highlight the name of the printer and click on the Connect button; the Connect dialog box appears (Figure 7.10).

• • • • • • • • • • • • • •
FIGURE 7.10
*Connect
Dialog Box*

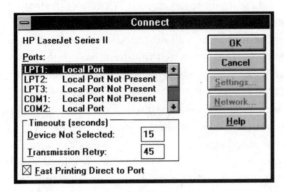

The Connect dialog box lets you tell Windows which port your printer is connected to.

The Ports section of the Connect dialog box offers these options for a printer destination:

➤ LPT1, LPT2, and LPT3 for specifying one of the parallel ports.

➤ COM1, COM2, COM3, COM4 for serial port designations.

➤ EPT for a special port mounted on an add-in card for the IBM Personal Page Printer.

➤ FILE tells Windows not to use a port at all, but to send the output to a disk file. If you select this choice, Windows prompts you for a file name for your output each time you print.

➤ LPT1.DOS and LPT2.DOS are reserved for special network printing options. These two ports redirect Windows printing through DOS. This option also works with some DOS-based printer-sharing devices that have trouble recognizing standard LPT parallel ports when you are running Windows.

Insider's Tip

If you're having compatibility problems printing to an LPT port, you can change the entry in the Ports section of the Connect dialog box from LPT1 to LPT1.DOS, for example. Usually, Windows bypasses DOS to access the LPT ports directly, which is faster than going through DOS. Changing this entry redirects the output through DOS, which alleviates most compatibility problems with parallel port hardware or network software.

You can also prevent Windows from accessing an LPT port directly by removing the X from the Fast Printing Direct to Port check box. Either method can slow down printing, but both can improve compatibility of the printing process.

As you scroll through the Ports list, Windows lets you know if it doesn't detect a port by placing the words "Not Present" after the port name. A hardware conflict is evident when you're sure that a port is actually connected but Windows reports it is not.

Most PC systems use standard default settings for the base I/O port, and hardware interrupts for the serial and parallel ports. The default settings for the parallel ports are as shown in Table 7.7.

TABLE 7.7
Default Settings for Parallel Ports

Port Name	Default Interrupt	PC Default Address	PS/2 Default Address
LPT1	7	0378h	03BCh
LPT2	5	0278h	0378h
LPT3	7	03BCh	0278h

Use the Microsoft Diagnostics utility to see if you can sniff out the configuration of your ports, and if there's a conflict, or if it doesn't match the defaults in the table above, refer to your hardware documentation to learn how to change the I/O port addresses or interrupts accordingly.

If your printer is connected to a serial port, the port should also be configured so that it adheres to the default I/O port and interrupt settings used by Windows. Although it's possible to change these settings, do so only if it's absolutely necessary. It's a far, far better idea to change the hardware configuration of your port to match the default settings than to change your settings to match an aberrant hardware configuration. Table 7.8 shows the default settings for the serial ports for both PCs and PS/2 systems:

TABLE 7.8
Default Settings for COM Ports

Port Name	Default Interrupt	Default I/O Address
COM1	4	03F8h
COM2	3	02F8h
COM3	4	02E8h
COM4	3	02E0h

To view and change the COM port settings, press the Settings button in the Connect dialog box. This brings up the same COM port settings controls that you can also access through the Ports icon in the Control Panel, discussed in Chapter 4. If your printer is connected to a COM port, check the documentation to see what settings it requires; the most common printer settings are 9600 baud, no parity, 8 data bits, and 1 stop bit, with hardware handshaking. **Handshaking** controls the flow of data to the printer and thus prevents the computer's print buffer from overflowing. Some printers use XON/XOFF software handshaking. Because print buffers can fill up quickly when printing from Windows, if you have a serial printer you shouldn't disable the handshaking option. Note that printing through a serial port is considerably slower than printing through a parallel port.

Insider's Tip

The available ports and their settings are listed in the [Ports] section of the WIN.INI file. You can add any DOS device name or file name directly to the [Ports] section, and that item will appear in the Ports list of the Connect dialog box. For example, you could add the statement

```
OUTPUT.PRN=
```

to the section, and the file OUTPUT.PRN will appear as a port to Windows. Select the new entry, and the output of your printer is redirected to that DOS file. To print the file, copy it to the printer port.

Beneath the Ports list in the Connect dialog box is a "Timeout (seconds)" section. This section lets you specify the amount of time that will elapse before you are notified of a printer problem. The first item—Device Not Selected—specifies the number of seconds that Print Manager will wait for the printer to respond that it is ready to print.

After the specified number of seconds has elapsed, a dialog box appears to tell you that the printer is offline. The default setting of 15 seconds allows plenty of time for the printer to wake up and respond. If you get this dialog box, it may indicate that your printer is improperly connected, turned off, or suffering from some technical malady.

The second item in the Timeout section—Transmission Retry—specifies the number of seconds that the printer can remain engaged in its own work without notifying Windows that it's finished processing the data that has been sent to it.

After this amount of time elapses, you'll see a dialog box declaring that your printer cannot accept any more data. The default settings are 90 seconds for PostScript printers and 45 seconds for all others. These defaults are usually sufficient, unless you're printing a complex document that contains many graphics and different typefaces. In this case, the printer can take significantly longer to process each chunk of information; this is particularly true for PostScript printers, which may require a setting of several minutes in order to prevent an unnecessary warning message from appearing on your screen.

Installing a Printer Twice. Windows lets you install the same printer more than once by assigning the output to different ports. You can exploit this technique to install your printer twice: once to create real printed output and then again to redirect the output to a disk file. By printing to a disk file, you can easily defer the print job until later or transfer the file to a different system for printing.

For example, you could add your HP LaserJet twice to the Installed Printer list and configure the first LaserJet to send output to LPT1, and the second LaserJet to send output to a disk file. To install the same printer twice, select it in the List of Printers box and press the Install button.

You can use this trick to create a disk file that can be printed on a printer attached to another computer system—for example, one in a service bureau, where your copy can be printed on a laser printer for better quality and, if you prefer, in color. In such a case, you might install a printer that isn't even connected to your system by redirecting its output exclusively to disk rather than to one of your system ports.

. . . .

Using Print Manager

The other main controls for printing are located in the Print Manager utility, which is automatically installed as part of Program Manager's Main program group. While some people may ignore Print Manager completely, it's essential for those who must control a variety of different output needs. Print Manager controls and coordinates different printer jobs originating from within Windows; it can also direct output to different printers connected to your system.

For example, if you were to order Windows Write to print a draft document on a 24-pin printer, Paintbrush to send a drawing to a LaserJet, and Excel to print a graph on a plotter, Print Manager could choreograph the whole operation. In theory, you could execute all of these operations simultaneously, and write a memo to your boss as you wait for completion. In practice, the efficiency of such an operation depends directly on your PC's system resources and available memory to complete the job.

Note that Print Manager is not involved if your printing is redirected to a disk file. Also, network printing is usually handled by a special network printing utility; you can, however, use Print Manager to view a network printing queue (see Chapter 10.)

In most cases you don't have to start Print Manager; it starts automatically when you issue the Print command from an application and appears as a minimized icon at the bottom of your screen. When the document is finished printing, the Print Manager icon disappears.

Insider's Tip

A special drag-and-drop feature lets you drag a file icon from File Manager and drop it onto the Print Manager icon (or into the Print Manager window, if open) to automatically print that document. Note that some applications do not support this drag-and-drop feature. To take advantage of drag and drop, you may want to keep the Print Manager icon handy during your entire Windows session. Just make a copy of the Print Manager icon in Print Manager and place it in the Startup group.

Although Print Manager usually appears as an icon, you can open it into a window as you would any other minimized application icon. Figure 7.11 depicts an open Print Manager window.

· · · · · · · · · · · · ·
FIGURE 7.11

Open Print Manager Window

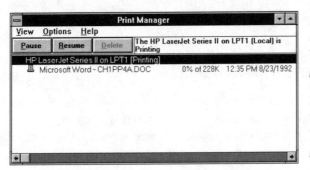

Print Manager lets you keep track of what print jobs are underway and lets you reassign the priority given to the various printing tasks.

Print Manager presents a simple and straightforward interface. All of the installed printers are displayed in the main window, in large type. The active printer is highlighted in the main window, and its name is shown again in a text line to the right of the three button controls: Pause, Resume, and Delete. Print Manager contains only three menu items: View, Options, and Help (and the last one doesn't really count because it's not specific to Print Manager).

Print Manager is one of the few Windows applications that does not include Printer Setup as part of the File menu. (As a matter of fact, Print Manager is one of the few Windows programs that lacks a File menu entirely.) Instead, Printer Setup is the last item on the Options menu. Providing access to the printer setup dialog box from within Print Manager saves you time, in case you want to make a quick switch without having to return to the application.

The printer list in the main window shows the items in the print queue. Each file is listed in the order in which it will be printed, and is depicted beneath whatever printer it is assigned. In addition, the queue indicates the current status of these files as a percentage of the job completed, and whether the printer in question is printing or idle. Figure 7.12 shows a printer status list in a Print Manager window, which contains two installed printers.

FIGURE 7.12

Print Manager Window with Two Installed Printers

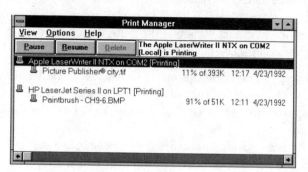

Both of the installed printers and the jobs they are processing in their queues are shown in the Print Manager window.

The name of each installed printer is followed by information about each of the files in the print queue. This information includes the title of the print job (usually the name of the application and the document being printed), the size of the file in kilobytes, the percentage of the file that has printed (if it's the current print job), and the time and date you sent the file to Print Manager. Note that Print Manager can only handle 20 print jobs at a time. The current print job—that is, the file in the queue that is currently being printed—is identified by an icon of a printer, which precedes the title of the print job.

The files in each print queue are listed in the order in which their print commands were issued. However, you can change the order of the files in the queue as long as you don't affect the first file listed (unless the printing job has not yet commenced). To make a change, select the item, drag it to the new position in the list, and release the mouse button; or select the file with the Enter key, hold down Ctrl, and move the file to the desired location in the queue with the up or down arrow keys.

The ability to rearrange your print jobs provides a definite advantage when you suddenly decide you need to immediately print a document that is at the end of the list. However, this feature only goes so far. You cannot move a print job from one printer to another in the queue, as from a 24-pin dot matrix to the laser. To do this, you would need to delete the job from Print Manager, then return to the application, and reroute the task to a different printer.

The three dialog buttons at the top of the Print Manager window help to control printing tasks:

➤ **Pause** (Alt+P) To interrupt the printing on a local print queue, first select the individual file, then click the Pause button. Printing stops, and the file's notation on the queue reflects that the job has been temporarily halted. You'll find yourself using this control when you discover a mistake, or when you need to cut the noise of a dot-matrix printer as you answer the phone.

➤➤ **Resume** (Alt+R) Unsurprisingly, this button provides the antidote to Pause. When a paused item, such as a printer or file, is highlighted, click Resume to restart the job at the point it was interrupted. Like Pause, the change is immediately reflected in the status list.

➤➤ **Delete** (Alt+D) This button removes a task from the local print queue at any time, and halts the task if it is in progress. In either case, a dialog box appears and asks for confirmation of the Delete command.

The Pause command can sometimes be generated by your system, as when you run out of paper. At that point, you are prompted to refill the paper tray; afterwards, return to Print Manager and click Resume. The print job picks up where it left off.

The ability to pause a print job on a network print queue depends on the network software and the control it offers to the individual workstation. These limits often reflect the need to prevent a user from messing with another person's files as much as they do with smooth network operation.

To delete a single item from a print queue, simply highlight it and press the Delete button. A dialog box appears to confirm your action. If you want to delete all files from the local print queue, choose the Exit command from the View menu.

Danger Zone

If you delete a print job that is printing a file containing graphics, you may need to either reset your printer, or, in some cases, toggle it off and on. Otherwise, the printer can hang in the middle of printing a graphic because it is waiting for an End of File command—which never arrives.

Insider's Tip

Print Manager creates temporary spool files in the directory specified by your system's TEMP variable—usually your \TEMP subdirectory. The temporary spool files created by Print Manager start with ~SPL and end with the extension .TMP. Normally Print Manager deletes these files after they have been printed. If your system crashes or is shut down in the middle of a print job, however, you may wind up with some leftover .TMP files; if this happens, check for the leftover files and delete them. If you want to print them out first, just copy them to your printer port. For example, if your printer is connected to LPT1, you could open a DOS session and type

```
COPY C:\WINDOWS\TEMP\~SPL????.TMP LPT1:
```

This assumes that your TEMP variable specified the C:\WINDOWS\TEMP directory.

Print Speed Modification. The designation of Windows as a "multitasking" system irks some purists. The system does appear to do several things at once, but looks are deceiving. In fact, DOS is a single-tasking operating system that can do only one thing at a time. Windows actually simulates multitasking through a process called **time slicing**, which allocates alternating microseconds to different functions, making it appear as if the system is performing several simultaneous tasks.

When "multitasking" a print job, the intent is to execute the Print command and continue to the next task. In this situation, it's usually more important to allocate your system's processor power to a new application or task rather than to print a particular document immediately.

Because printing places a big burden on a computer's processor, Print Manager lets you set the priority that printing should receive when running in the background, as opposed to the other tasks that you are running in the foreground. You can actually designate Print Manager's entitlement to the processor pie, with a choice of High Priority, Medium Priority, or Low Priority on the Options menu.

These choices control time slicing between Print Manager and your other applications. The check mark on the menu next to a priority command indicates it as the active option. The option stays active until it is turned off, or until you select a different priority from the Options menu.

➤ **High Priority** Selecting this option places an emphasis on printing tasks and allocates a majority of processing power to output. This prints documents quickly, but can cause other applications to bog down considerably. Even on a fast 386, scrolling through a dialog box can be tedious if Print Manager is processing a hefty print job.

➤ **Medium Priority** To distribute processing power evenly between Print Manager and other applications, choose Medium Priority. This is the default setting.

➤ **Low Priority** To place the emphasis on applications other than Print Manager, choose this option, which slows down printing tasks while allowing other applications to run at a faster rate.

View Options. Print Manager's View menu contains various options pertaining to the print queue:

➤ **Time/Date Sent** When checked (the default), the print queue displays the time and date (according to your system clock) at which you initiated the Print command for a particular document.

➥ **Print File Size** When this item is checked (the default), the print queue displays the size of each file that is being printed.

➥ **Refresh** When you're printing to a network, the network software periodically informs Print Manager about the status of your print jobs. To query the network about the status of print jobs between updates, select this option.

➥ **Selected Net Queue** When you print to a network printer, Print Manager usually displays only files that you are printing. Choose this option to view the entire queue for the network printer to which you are currently connected.

➥ **Other Net Queue** Use this option to view the print queues for network printers to which you are not connected. This is handy if there are several printers on the network and you want to print your document on the printer with the shortest queue.

➥ **Exit** Quits Print Manager. If Print Manager is processing any print jobs, a dialog box appears asking if you want to cancel printing those files.

Print Manager Messages. You can receive two types of messages related to printing a document, one generated from Windows and the other from Print Manager. A Windows system message will always be displayed, regardless of your settings in Print Manager. Such a message may alert you with a dialog box, stating, for example, that your printer is offline or not connected.

Messages generated by Print Manager itself, on the other hand, can be controlled. Such a message might appear, for example, if you selected manual paper feed on your printer; Print Manager would alert you when to insert paper.

You can control how these Print Manager messages are displayed through these choices on the Options menu:

➥ **Alert Always** Print Manager will interrupt whatever you are doing to display a message, even if Print Manager is running in the background.

➥ **Flash If Inactive** The Print Manager icon or the title bar of the inactive Print Manager window flashes until you enlarge the icon or make the window active and respond to the message. This is the default.

➥ **Ignore If Inactive** If the Print Manager window is inactive or running as a minimized icon, all Print Manager messages will be ignored. You can then address the problem at your convenience by selecting the Print Manager window or restoring the minimized icon to a window.

Printing from Windows Applications. Most Windows programs provide the ability to print a document directly from the File menu. Some programs include a separate Print menu, but most install the Print command on the File menu as the leftmost choice on the menu bar. Consequently, the keyboard sequence Alt,F,P is one of the standard ways to begin the print job.

Another way to print a file—provided your application supports this method—is to drag the file's icon from File Manager and drop it onto the minimized Print Manager icon or into the open Print Manager window.

The appearance of a printed document is affected by

➨ The fonts and formatting options you choose from within an application (as the application permits)

➨ The ability of your printer to print the fonts and formats you've chosen

TrueType fonts, combined with a TrueType-compatible printer driver, provide the best match between typeface and printer. If you're not using True-Type, it may take some tweaking to print documents the way you want them to look.

Most Windows applications also provide a Printer Setup command on the File menu, which lets you choose different printers and configure the options related to the driver of your selected printer. Changing the printer is meant to be as easy as changing a TV channel. When you choose Printer Setup, you'll see a dialog box with a list of all the installed printers. Select a printer from the list and Windows designates it as your active printer for that application and any others, until you select a different printer.

In addition, some applications produce output through the use of special drivers. For example, many presentation graphics packages use a special printer driver to redirect graphics to a modem for transmission to a service bureau, which produces slides. Fax modem software often works the same way; instead of sending a document to a printer, it redirects the output—fonts, graphics, and all—to a fax modem.

Printing from DOS Applications. DOS applications bypass Windows when it comes to printing—even if you are running the DOS application from within Windows. Were you to print from WordPerfect for DOS, for example, the job would be sent directly to the printer port that is selected from within that DOS application.

In 386 enhanced mode, Windows controls the use of printer ports for both Windows and DOS applications, even though DOS applications bypass the rest of Windows' printing facilities. This ensures that two applications don't try to use the printer port simultaneously.

If you have trouble printing a DOS application, make sure that it works with the type of printer you are using. You will need to select the printer from within the DOS application, because the choices made in Windows do not directly affect the DOS program.

If you want to reformat a DOS document to take advantage of Windows fonts, you must first transfer it to a Windows application. Once there, the application can be reformatted in one of these three ways:

➽ Many Windows applications, such as Word for Windows, WordPerfect for Windows, and Ami, read the file formats of DOS wordprocessing applications, complete with formatting commands, such as bold, page margins, and so forth. If you cannot open a document created with a DOS program directly, you may be able to **save the document from the DOS program in a format that your Windows wordprocessor can understand**, such as RTF (Microsoft's Rich Text Format).

➽ The next rung down the latter of compatibility would be to **save your DOS document as a text only file** and then open it in your Windows application. For example, even the bundled Write applet can open plain text files and allow you to perform a considerable amount of fancy formatting.

➽ If all else fails, you can always resort to **cutting and pasting information from a DOS window into a Windows application**. This option requires the most fussing and reformatting, but is often your only choice if your DOS application doesn't let you save text only or save text at all. With this method, you can bring virtually anything from your DOS application into a Windows application for formatting and printing.

For more information about how DOS applications behave in Windows, see Chapter 14.

. . . .

Individual Printers

Using special hardware drivers that translate instructions to the printer, Windows achieves the versatility to work with the vast majority of printers. This enables Windows to print information generated by any Windows-compatible application onto any printer, because the driver handles the translation. With DOS applications, on the other hand, the applications themselves had to be compatible with the printer—unless you were satisfied with the looks of plain, unformatted text.

All this accessibility demands a price, however: each printer driver provides its own idiosyncratic set of controls, which show up in the printer setup dialog box. Some drivers are specific to only one model of printer, and other drivers work with a family of printers.

Although the controls are often laid out differently in each driver's **printer setup dialog box**, they share many of the same options. Most printer controls let you print your pages in either a portrait (vertical, which is the default) or landscape (horizontal) orientation. You'll usually see buttons with labels such as Info, Help, or About; click on these buttons to see how your driver works with Windows and how to adjust its settings.

Most printer settings dialog boxes also offer the following selections:

➟ **Paper Source** Specifies single sheet or continuous feed.

➟ **Paper Size** Specifies letter, legal, or other size.

➟ **Page Orientation** Selects Portrait (vertical) or Landscape (horizontal).

➟ **Copies** Specifies the number of copies of each page that you want to print.

➟ **Resolution** Specifies graphical resolution, either in grades (such as high, medium, low) or pixel numbers (such as 200x200). Higher resolution yields a better graphical quality but decreases print speed.

➟ **Cartridges** Selects font cartridges that are compatible with a specific printer.

➟ **Fonts** Installs or deletes soft fonts specific to the printer.

➟ **Memory** Specifies the amount of printer memory.

Important differences exist among printer drivers, and adjustments may have to be made for different printers.

Insider's Tip

Just as Windows itself benefits from the added RAM in your computer, Windows printers can work faster with extra memory installed in your printer. If you have several megabytes of RAM installed in your printer, the Windows print drivers will be able to store many TrueType fonts and other graphics to speed up printing.

The drivers can also monitor the amount of free memory in the printer, in order to try to retain the fonts that are stored in the memory. In this way, your next print job will be accelerated, because the fonts don't need to be retransmitted to the printer.

To take advantage of additional memory installed in your printer, you need to inform your printer driver of the amount of memory contained in your printer by adjusting the Memory setting in the printer setup dialog box. Don't overestimate the amount of memory contained in your printer; you could cause the print driver to overload your printer with information and generate an Out of Memory error.

. . . .

Printer Drivers

Windows provides 40 different printer drivers that directly support more than 260 models of printers and allow you to work with hundreds of other compatible models. Some printers only require a Windows printer driver, identified by the file extension .DRV; but other printers—such as many PostScript printers—will run only if you combine the Windows driver with one or more other files that provide additional support features. The various support files fall into these categories:

➡ **UNIDRV.DLL** The universal dynamic link library that supports many laser and most dot-matrix printers. The UNIDRV.HLP file is the Windows Help file for the universal printer library and should be copied to your hard disk along with any printer drivers that require this DLL.

➡ **GENDRV.DLL** A dynamic link library with generic printer information.

➡ **PostScript printer description files** All PostScript printers use the same printer driver (PSCRIPT.DRV), but many require a special printer description file, which ends with the extension .WPD and supplements the Post-Script driver with specific details about particular printer models. The Help file for the PostScript driver is PSCRIPT.HLP.

➡ **DMCOLOR.DLL** The dynamic link library used in conjunction with UNI-DRV.DLL to support color printing on dot-matrix printers.

➡ **Soft font installation utilities** Four files—FINSTALL.DLL, CAN_ADF.EXE, SF4019.EXE, and SFINST.EXE—provide soft font installation utilities for printers that allow downloading of fonts from a disk. The file FINSTALL.HLP is the Help file for the FINSTALL.DLL font installer.

By combining the 40 printer drivers with one of these other support files, Windows is able to work with almost any printer you'll ever encounter.

If you're somewhere out in the printer hinterlands, however, with a printer that's not on this list, you can try one of these workarounds, which all basically involve setting up your printer to mimic a more common variety:

➥ **Laser printers** If your printer has an HP LaserJet-compatibility mode—sometimes called HP PCL compatible—you can set it up as a HP LaserJet Plus or HP LaserJet Series II. For example, I set up my OkiLaser 400 (which is not one of the 260 printers listed later in this chapter) as a LaserJet Series II, and it operates flawlessly. If you have a PostScript laser printer, you can often set it up as an Apple LaserWriter Plus. And you can usually set up your color PostScript printer as a QMS ColorScript printer.

➥ **Dot-matrix printers** Most dot-matrix printers can emulate either an Epson or an IBM-Proprinter. If it's a 24-pin printer compatible with an Epson, you can set it up as an Epson LQ-1500. If it's a 24-pin IBM-compatible printer, try it as an IBM Proprinter X24. For a 9-pin printer that's IBM compatible, try it as a regular IBM Proprinter. For a 9-pin Epson compatible with a narrow carriage, try an Epson FX-80; for a wide carriage, an Epson FX-100.

➥ **Pen plotters** Most pen plotters are compatible with those made by Hewlett-Packard, and they can often be used when set up as an HP7475A plotter.

➥ **None of the above** If you can't get anything to work, or if you have an old daisy-wheel or text-only printer, you can set it up using the Generic Text Only printer. This setup uses the TTY.DRV printer driver (the Help file for this driver is TTY.HLP), and simply spits out the text of your document from the printer port. Graphics, obviously, are ignored.

The printer drivers included on the installation disks of the Windows 3.1 retail package fall into six main categories:

➥ **HP LaserJet and compatibles**

➥ **PostScript**

➥ **Dot-matrix**

➥ **Other laser and dot-matrix**

➥ **Inkjet**

➥ **Pen plotter**

Danger Zone

Windows 3.0 versions of laser printer drivers don't support TrueType, so be sure to upgrade your printer driver with the appropriate Windows 3.1 driver. Occasionally Setup does not replace an existing driver; about the only way to check this is to look at the file creation date in File Manager. If it's older than 3/10/92, you probably have a 3.0 driver.

The listings for specific printer drivers later in this chapter identify the specific files that you'll need to copy from the installation disks (remember to use Expand). If you have a third-party printer with an old 3.0 driver, get a new driver from the printer manufacturer or from the Windows Driver Library disks.

HP LaserJet-Compatible Printers. By far the most commonly used printer with Windows, the HP LaserJet family includes those made by Hewlett-Packard as well as dozens of compatibles made by other manufacturers. Also included in the HP dynasty are printers that use LED displays instead of lasers to create the images imprinted on the paper. The HP LaserJet family employs a page description language called HP PCL, for Hewlett-Packard Printer Control Language. These printers can use TrueType fonts, font cartridges, downloadable soft fonts, or vector screen fonts. However, they cannot print raster screen fonts.

If you're using an HP PCL-compatible printer, TrueType should be your first choice. The Windows printer drivers were optimized for printing TrueType on these printers, and 3.1 has made major strides in boosting the printing speed for the HP PCL compatibles. The HP LaserJet printers fall into one of these five categories, which HP compatibles usually emulate as well:

➡ **HP LaserJet** The original HP laser printer, it used only a single font cartridge but didn't work with downloadable soft fonts. You won't find many HP LaserJets still in use, because most of them were upgraded.

➡ **HP LaserJet Plus** An upgrade to the original LaserJet, still limited to one font cartridge, but works with downloadable soft fonts. Most LaserJet-compatible printers sold by third parties are compatible with the LaserJet Plus.

➡ **HP LaserJet II** Improves on the LaserJet Plus design by allowing the use of two font cartridges simultaneously. Also uses slightly different escape codes for functions such as selecting the paper tray.

➡ **HP LaserJet IID** and **IIP** Improves on the LaserJet II design by allowing bitmapped fonts to be rotated. In addition, the IID provides two-sided printing.

➡ **HP LaserJet III series** Improves on the previous models by adding its own (non-TrueType) technology for scaling fonts—called Intellifont—and a special image-enhancement mode for printing more realistic grayscale images, such as photographs. Although you can obtain cartridges and soft fonts with the special scalable Intellifonts, I recommend going with True-Type because of its document compatibility among many different printers.

Before the advent of TrueType, the most popular way to add fonts to an HP LaserJet-compatible printer was by using a font cartridge. You can select font cartridges using the printer setup dialog box for HP compatible printers, shown below in Figure 7.13.

. . . .
FIGURE 7.13
*HP Laserjet
Dialog Box*

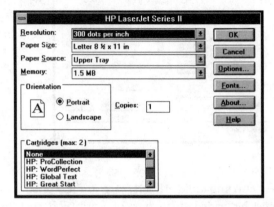

An HP LaserJet or compatible printer usually displays this standard printer setup dialog box.

The printer driver supplied with Windows 3.1 supports all the standard HP font cartridges available as of April 1992. If you have a third-party font cartridge, a custom font cartridge, or a post-Windows 3.1 HP font cartridge, you may need to obtain a special printer cartridge metrics file—identified by the file extension .PCM—which contains information about positioning the fonts on your screen and on the page. To install it, use the HP Font Installer, described later in this section.

Insider's Tip

If you have a custom font cartridge, you can create your own .PCM files using the Windows Printer Font Metric Editor. To get the PFM Editor Kit, contact your Microsoft dealer or call Microsoft.

Downloadable soft fonts are also provided for laser jets and compatibles by Hewlett-Packard and a number of third-party font vendors. Downloadable fonts from HP can be installed using the Font Installer utility, but most third-party downloadable fonts require their own installation program. Sometimes, a soft font installation utility creates an appropriate screen font; if not, Windows substitutes one of its own screen fonts. To install a soft font (or a .PCM file for a cartridge), access the Font Installer by clicking the Fonts button in the printer setup dialog box. The HP Font Installer dialog box appears (Figure 7.14).

LaserJet-compatible soft fonts can be downloaded to the printer on either a temporary or a permanent basis. Permanent fonts reside in the printer's memory until you turn it off. Temporary fonts, on the other hand, are only downloaded when the printer driver encounters that specific font in a document that you are printing. Once you print the document, the soft font is deleted from the printer's memory.

•••••••••••••
FIGURE 7.14
*Font Installer
Dialog Box*

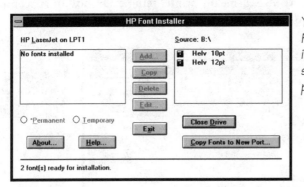

You can use the Font Installer to install downloadable soft fonts for your printer.

Danger Zone

In some LaserJet-compatible printers, such as the Apricot Laser, temporary soft fonts must be loaded at the start of a print job; such fonts cannot be accessed if they are encountered in a document that is printing. In such cases, you're better off using TrueType.

To download the soft fonts on a permanent basis, select the Permanent option during the installation process. You'll be presented with a dialog box asking if you want to download the fonts now or at Startup. If you select Now, the fonts will be installed right after you exit; this will delete any other downloaded fonts in the printer.

If you select the Startup option, Windows copies a special file, PCLSFOYN.EXE, to your hard disk and creates a special batch file called SFLPT1.BAT (assuming there is an LPT1 printer port), which asks you at system startup whether you want to download the permanent soft fonts at that time. This process also adds a line to your AUTOEXEC.BAT file, which causes the SFLPT1.BAT file to run during your system startup.

Danger Zone

The SFLPT1.BAT file makes use of the TEMP= statement in AUTOEXEC.BAT. If the TEMP= statement is not set up properly, the SLFPT1.BAT file won't work, and your fonts won't be downloaded. See Chapter 13 for further details on how to use the TEMP= statement in AUTOEXEC.BAT.

By default, the Font Installer creates a directory on your hard disk called \PCLFONTS, to store the soft font files and related files, such as SFLPT1.BAT and PCLSFOYN.EXE, and the soft fonts themselves, which are stored in files that bear the .USP file extension. In addition, Windows requires a special printer fonts metrics file, denoted by the extension .PFM, which provides such information, as the proper size and spacing for printing the soft font.

Insider's Tip

The soft fonts installed in the Windows system are listed in the [HPPCL, LPTx] section of the WIN.INI file, where x is the number of the LPT port to which the printer is connected. Each soft font is specified on its line in this section, and usually includes the name of both the .PFM and .USP files. However, if you download soft fonts at Startup, the .USP file reference is removed temporarily from WIN.INI; Windows downloads the fonts by checking WIN.INI while it's running.

If you install a third-party font that uses the same name as a font already installed in your system, you'll need to change the name of either the newcomer or your existing font. (Keep in mind that you can't change the name of a cartridge font.) To change a font name, select a font from the list of installed fonts and click on the Edit button, which brings up the Edit dialog box (Figure 7.15).

••••••••••••••
FIGURE 7.15
Edit Dialog Box

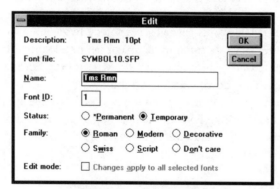

Every font needs a different name; use this dialog box to rename any duplicates.

Type a new name in the Name box for the font you've selected and click OK.

Danger Zone

When you change the name of a font, try not to change any of the other items in the Edit dialog box, such as Font ID or Family. Such changes can confuse Windows about the font's characteristics and may prevent it from being able to use the font at all.

Whenever you reinstall Windows, you lose the soft font entries in the WIN.INI file. Normally, you'd have to use the Font Installer to reinstall them and regenerate their associated .PFM files. However, an undocumented feature of Windows allows you to create a special file called FINSTALL.DIR, which contains the soft font information used by WIN.INI and thereby allows you to recreate your soft font entries without the hassle of going through the Font Installer process.

To create a FINSTALL.DIR file, click the Fonts button in the printer setup dialog box to access the Font Installer; then hold down Ctrl+Shift, while clicking on the Exit` button. The Create Installer Directory File dialog box appears (Figure 7.16)

FIGURE 7.16
Create Installer Directory File Dialog Box

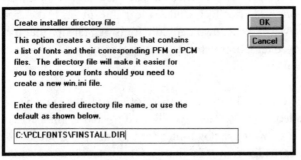

This dialog box lets you create a special file with information about your downloadable soft fonts.

The Create Installer Directory File dialog box contains a text box with the suggested directory and file name for saving your soft font information. You should leave the file name FINSTALL.DIR and specify the directory for storing your downloadable fonts (usually \PCLFONTS, by default). To make sure the Installer Directory File contains a current list of all your soft fonts, use this undocumented procedure to create a new FINSTALL.DIR file whenever you add or remove any downloadable soft fonts.

To reinstall your soft fonts from the FINSTALL.DIR file after you've started Windows, bring up the Font Installer dialog box and hold down Ctrl+Shift while clicking on the Add Fonts button. A special version of the Add Fonts dialog box appears (Figure 7.17).

FIGURE 7.17
Add Fonts Dialog Box

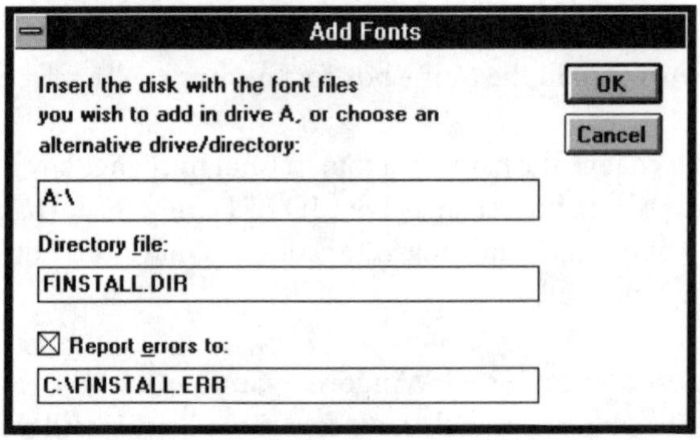

Add Fonts

Insert the disk with the font files you wish to add in drive A, or choose an alternative drive/directory:

`A:\`

Directory file:

`FINSTALL.DIR`

☒ Report errors to:

`C:\FINSTALL.ERR`

OK

Cancel

This special dialog box lets you quickly reinstall soft fonts from the FINSTALL.DIR file.

In this special Add Fonts dialog box, enter the drive, directory path, and file name of the FINSTALL.DIR file, then click OK. You are returned to the Font Installer dialog box, and the soft fonts are listed on the right side of the box. Select the fonts and click on the Move button; when prompted for a directory, enter the directory path where the soft fonts are installed. Windows doesn't actually take the time to copy the fonts; it just updates WIN.INI so that you can use the fonts.

Danger Zone

Downloadable soft fonts are installed for a printer connected to a specific port. Therefore, if you change the printer's port assignment, none of your soft fonts will be available. To access them, use the Copy Fonts to New Port button, located in the Font Installer dialog box. You will also need to use the Copy Fonts to New Port button if you are using more than one HP LaserJet-compatible printer, because the fonts are specific to the port.

LaserJet-compatible printers are limited to 16 downloadable soft fonts per page. If you try to print a page with more than 16 soft fonts, a dialog box pops up with this message:

```
PCL PRINTING WARNING: SOFT FONT PAGE LIMIT:
SOME FONTS WILL BE SUBSTITUTED
```

If you see this dialog box, click the OK button to continue with your print job; however, keep in mind that only the first 16 fonts will be printed correctly.

An Error 20 message on the front panel of your printer also represents an alert from your printer that you've exceeded the printer's memory limit on how many fonts can be downloaded. If this happens, press the Continue button on the front panel of the printer. If this error occurs when you think it shouldn't, you may have downloaded some permanent soft fonts into the printer that are taking up most of the printer's memory. You can clear the memory by downloading the temporary soft fonts again, or, if worse comes to worst, by turning the printer off and on.

The following list shows the various models of HP LaserJet-compatible printers that use the HPPCL.DRV driver, which in turn uses the UNIDRV.DLL and associated Help file. All these printers also use the FINSTAL.DLL soft font installer.

Agfa Compugraphic Genics	HP LaserJet 2000
Apricot Laser	HP LaserJet Series II
Epson EPL-6000	HP LaserJet IID
Epson EPL-7000	HP LaserJet IIP
Epson GQ-3500	HP LaserJet IIP Plus
HP LaserJet	Kyocera F-Series (USA)
HP LaserJet Plus	Kyocera F-5000 (USA)
HP LaserJet 500+	NEC Silentwriter LC 860 Plus

Okidata LaserLine 6	Panasonic KX-P4420
Okidata OL-400	QuadLaser I
Okidata OL-800	Tandy LP-1000
Olivetti ETV 5000	Tegra Genesis
Olivetti PG 108	Toshiba PageLaser12
Olivetti PG 208 M2	Unisys AP9210
Olivetti PG 308 HS	Wang LDP8

The following list of LaserJet III series printers use the HPPCL5A.DRV driver and require two different help files: HPPCL5A.HLP, and HPPCL50.HLP.

HP LaserJet III

HP LaserJet IIID

HP LaserJet IIIP

HP LaserJet IIISi

Danger Zone

The Windows 3.0 LaserJet III driver used the incorrect resolution setting of 75dpi when printing from certain applications, so if you're printing a document created in Windows 3.0 and it looks weird, you may need to access the Resolution controls in the printer setup dialog box and reset the resolution to 75dpi; this way, the document will print as it appeared in 3.0.

Another glitch concerns the Intellifont for Windows, version 1.0, Font Installer, which installs an old LaserJet III printer driver that is incompatible with Windows 3.1. To work around this problem, complete the Intellifont installation and then reinstall the LaserJet III printer driver.

PostScript Printers. The PostScript font and printing technology, like TrueType, provides scalable outline fonts that can be printed at any size (although some applications only go up to 127 points), rotated to any angle, and printed on a wide variety of output devices. The first PostScript laser printer, the Apple LaserWriter, included 17 fonts; the next version, the Apple LaserWriter Plus, came with 35 fonts. You can set up many PostScript printers as an Apple LaserWriter Plus because they usually include the same 35 fonts.

If your PostScript printer isn't on the list below and doesn't work with the Apple LaserWriter Plus, you'll need to get a .WPD file that provides a printer description for that specific model from the printer manufacturer. A Windows 3.0 version of the .WPD file will still work for 3.1; however, if you do obtain a new 3.1 version of a .WPD file, you'll need an OEMSETUP.INF file to install it. If you're using a laser printer that's been converted to PostScript capabilities by the addition of a PostScript plug-in cartridge, try installing it as an Apple LaserWriter Plus.

The initial printer setup dialog box for a typical PostScript printer resembles a Russian peasant doll; once opened, it leads to several other dialog boxes that reveal many additional controls for PostScript printers (Figure 7.18).

FIGURE 7.18

Typical PostScript Printer Setup Dialog Box

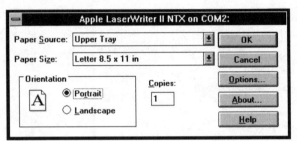

A typical setup dialog box for a PostScript printer presents a deceptively barren scape.

To access the next dialog box, which contains further options, click on the Options button. The Options dialog box for a PostScript printer contains controls that allow you to scale your page image, from 0 to 100 percent, or that instruct Windows to divert your printing to special Encapsulated PostScript files, which can be used by a service bureau in disk form to print on a typesetting machine or PostScript-compatible color printer (Figure 7.19).

FIGURE 7.19

Options Dialog Box

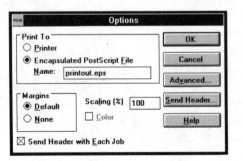

The Options dialog box contains additional controls for PostScript printers.

Most PostScript printers allow you to download additional PostScript fonts to the printer. Downloadable PostScript fonts are available from companies such as Adobe and Bitstream, but because they include their own utilities for installing these fonts, you can't use the Windows PostScript driver to install them. If you install additional PostScript fonts, you won't be able to scale them onscreen unless you purchase Adobe Type Manager, but you can install specific sizes of screen fonts. (Remember to limit yourself to the sizes you plan to use, unless you've got memory to spare.)

TrueType fonts usually work well with PostScript printers. However, the printer treats them as downloaded PostScript fonts, which often means that they print more slowly than the PostScript fonts that are built into the printer. When you're printing TrueType fonts to a PostScript printer, Windows handles the scaling of the outline and converts the font into either a bitmap or an Adobe Type 1 font format. To control how they are sent to the printer, click on the Advanced button in the Options dialog box (Figure 7.20).

• • • • • • • • • • • • • •
FIGURE 7.20
Advanced
Options
Dialog Box

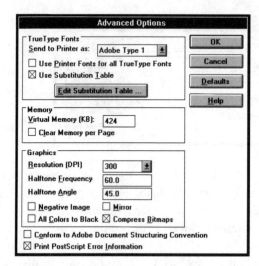

The Advanced Options dialog box lets you specify a variety of settings to control PostScript printing.

In the Send to Printer as list box, you can choose either Adobe Type 1 or bitmap as your method of sending TrueType fonts to the printer.

Even if your PostScript printer does support downloadable fonts, you may want to substitute the built-in printer fonts for your TrueType fonts, because this requires less printer memory and can speed the printing process. Place an X in the Use Printer Fonts for All TrueType Fonts check box. Specify the PostScript font that will replace the TrueType font by editing the information in the [FontSubstitutes] section of the WIN.INI file, as described in Chapter 15. Although print speed will be accelerated, your screen fonts may not exactly match your printed output.

Some PostScript printers don't let you download fonts; thus you won't be able to print TrueType fonts. The Windows PostScript printer driver will do its best to substitute the most closely matched PostScript fonts; or you can edit the Substitution Table to make the choices yourself. Click on the Edit Substitution Table button in the Advanced Options dialog box to bring up the Substitution dialog box (Figure 7.21).

• • • • • • • • • • • • • •
FIGURE 7.21

Substitution Dialog Box

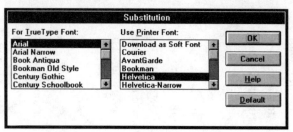

Use the Substitution dialog box to do your own matching of TrueType to PostScript fonts.

To match fonts, click on the TrueType font you want to replace in the For TrueType Font list on the left side of this dialog box; then click on the PostScript printer font in the right-hand list, titled Use Printer Font.

Insider's Tip

Try this workaround to take full advantage of your printer and still use different types of fonts. Get a utility, such as AllType or Font Monger, which lets you convert between many different font formats. With either utility, you can convert your PostScript fonts into TrueType, and then use the TrueType font for displaying on screen. Then fake out your printer by using the Substitution dialog box to substitute the PostScript-to-TrueType converted font for the real PostScript font contained in your printer.

Virtual memory is another option you can control in the Advanced Options dialog box. Adjusting the amount of virtual memory in your printer can speed printing, help free some memory for use by other Windows applications, and alleviate a few printer problems you may encounter.

To determine the amount of virtual memory in your printer, print the TESTPS.TXT file, which should be located in your main Windows directory. This file contains a PostScript program that will print a page listing how much virtual memory you have. Some PostScript printers, such as the Apple LaserWriter NTX, allow you to attach a hard disk drive directly to the printer, providing many megabytes of virtual memory.

The Windows PostScript driver can detect certain errors that Print Manager cannot. The only way to view these errors is to print them out after the printing process. To obtain these error messages, place an X in the Print PostScript Error Information check box at the bottom of the Advanced Options dialog box.

All PostScript printers use the PSCRIPT.DRV printer driver; for some printers, this driver is all that's required. For others, a .WPD file is also needed. Table 7.9 lists the most common brands of PostScript printers, along with the .WPD files supplied on the Windows 3.1 installation disks. If no .WPD file is indicated under the PostScript description, the printer requires only the regular PSCRIPT.DRV printer driver.

TABLE 7.9
PostScript Printers and Their Description Files

Supported Printer	PostScript Description File	Supported Printer	PostScript Description File
Agfa 9000 Series PS		HP LaserJet IID PostScript	HPIID522.WPD
Agfa Compugraphic 400PS		HP LaserJet IIP PostScript	HPIIP522.WPD
Apple LaserWriter		HP LaserJet III PostScript	HPIII522.WPD
Apple LaserWriter II NT		HP LaserJet IIID PostScript	HP_3D522.WPD
Apple LaserWriter II NTX		HP LaserJet IIIP PostScript	HP_3P522.WPD
Apple LaserWriter Plus		HP LaserJet IIISi PostScript	HPELI523.WPD
AST TurboLaser/PS		IBM LaserPrinter 4019 PS17	IBM17521.WPD
Dataproducts LZR-2665		IBM LaserPrinter 4019 PS39	IBM39521.WPD
Digital Colormate PS	DECCOLOR.WPD	IBM LaserPrinter 4029 PS17	4029173O.WPD
Digital DEClaser 1150	DEC1150.WPD	IBM LaserPrinter 4029 PS39	4029393O.WPD
Digital DEClaser 2150	DEC2150.WPD	IBM Personal Page Printer	
Digital DEClaser 2250	DEC2250.WPD	IBM Personal Page Printer II-30	
Digital DEClaser 3250	DEC3250.WPD	IBM Personal Page Printer II-31	
Digital LN03R ScriptPrinter		Linotronic 200/230	L200230&.WPD
Digital PrintServer 20/turbo	DECLPS20.WPD	Linotronic 330	L330_52&.WPD
Digital PrintServer 40		Linotronic 530	L530_52&.WPD
Epson EPL-7500	EPL75523.WPD	Linotronic 630	L630_52&.WPD
Hermes H 606 PS (13 Fonts)	HERMES_1.WPD	Microtek TrueLaser	MT_TI101.WPD
Hermes H 606 PS (35 Fonts)	HERMES_2.WPD	NEC Colormate PS/40	NCM40519.WPD

TABLE 7.9 (cont.)
PostScript Printers and Their Description Files

Supported Printer	PostScript Description File
NEC Colormate PS/80	NCM80519.WPD
NEC Silentwriter LC890	N890_470.WPD
NEC Silentwriter LC890XL	N890X505.WPD
NEC Silentwriter2 90	N2090522.WPD
NEC Silentwriter2 290	N2290520.WPD
NEC Silentwriter2 990	N2990523.WPD
OceColor G5241 PS	O5241503.WPD
OceColor G5242 PS	O5242503.WPD
Oki OL840/PS	OL840518.WPD
Olivetti PG 303	
Olivetti PG 306 PS (13 Fonts)	OLIVETI1.WPD
Olivetti PG 306 PS (35 Fonts)	OLIVETI2.WPD
Olivetti PG 308 HS Postscript	
Panasonic KX-P4455 v51.4	P4455514.WPD
PostScript Printer	
QMS ColorScript 100	
QMS-PS 800	

Supported Printer	PostScript Description File
QMS-PS 800 Plus	
QMS-PS 810	
QMS-PS 820	Q820_517.WPD
QMS-PS 2200	Q2200510.WPD
Seiko ColorPoint PS Model 04	SEIKO_04.WPD
Seiko ColorPoint PS Model 14	SEIKO_14.WPD
Tektronix Phaser II PX	PHIIPX.WPD
Tektronix Phaser II PXi	TKPHZR21.WPD
Tektronix Phaser III PXi	TKPHZR31.WPD
TI microLaser PS17	TIM7521.WPD
TI microLaser PS35	TIM35521.WPD
Triumph Adler SDR 7706 PS13	TRIUMPH1.WPD
Triumph Adler SDR 7706 PS35	TRIUMPH2.WPD
Unisys AP9415	U9415470.WPD
Varityper VT-600	
Wang LCS15	
Wang LCS15 FontPlus	

Dot-Matrix Printers. Dot-matrix printers once dominated the world of personal computers. However, over the past few years they've been replaced by low-priced laser printers, especially for use with Windows. Because millions of dot-matrix printers are still around, however, Microsoft has strived to ensure that Windows can print both text and graphics on them.

On dot-matrix printers, each character is composed of a collection of small dots. Early dot-matrix printers used a group of 9 pins in the print head to create the matrix of dots; modern models use 24-pin print heads to achieve much greater graphics resolutions. Both types of printers support TrueType—it looks pretty ragged on 9-pin printers, but the output from 24-pin printers can almost rival that of a laser printer.

My biggest complaint about dot-matrix printers is the incredible amount of noise they generate. As the print head moves across the pages, the pins are literally hammered through a ribbon onto your paper, and if several printers are running at once in your office, you might have grounds for seeking a noise-violation inspection from OSHA. The hammering process does have one advantage, though: it's useful for printing through multipart forms, commonly used in accounting software.

Dot-matrix printers work with their own built-in device fonts (usually a limited selection of ugly fonts), with TrueType, and with raster and vector screen fonts. By virtue of the new Windows 3.1 universal printer library (UNIDRV.DLL), most dot-matrix printers can now work with TrueType. Windows creates the bitmapped image for TrueType fonts and sends it in graphics format to the printer. Because graphics prints so slowly on some of these printers, you might try using the less pleasing but speedier built-in fonts whenever looks don't count and you've got a long document to print.

The printer setup dialog box for dot-matrix printers usually lets you specify your graphics resolution in dots per inch (Figure 7.22).

FIGURE 7.22

Dot-Matrix Printer Setup Dialog Box

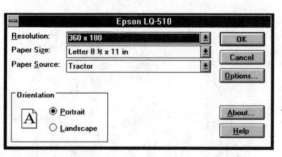

A typical dot-matrix printer setup dialog box lets you specify the physical characteristics of your print job.

As resolution increases, so does the print quality and the time to produce a page. For printing drafts, set the resolution low; use the maximum resolution only for final copy. Many 9-pin dot-matrix printers support a high-resolution graphics mode, which can be as much as double the normal graphics resolution. Because Windows sends TrueType to dot-matrix printers as graphics, enabling the high-resolution mode improves the appearance of your TrueType and graphics. The gain in resolution, however, comes at the expense of speed.

The printer setup dialog box for a dot-matrix printer may also contain options for setting the paper size and paper feed (either tractor or single sheet). Automatic paper feed is available only for Fujitsu dot-matrix printers. If your printer supports font cartridges or soft fonts, click on the Fonts button to bring up a dialog box that lets you install the fonts. Examples of such printers are some 24-pin printers manufactured by Epson and NEC.

Some dot-matrix printers can also print in color through the use of a multicolored ribbon. Windows supports these printers with the universal color support library, DMCOLOR.DLL. As supplied with Windows, this color library is installed only if you specify a Citizen color printer, although some other brands are compatible with the Citizen.

Danger Zone

Windows Print Manager sometimes pauses while printing, which can interrupt the flow of data to a dot-matrix printer. Some printers will just wait for the flow of information to resume. Others—especially those set up as an IBM Proprinter X24, Epson MX-80, or some varieties of the Okidata 24-pin printer—can "hiccup" and thereby halt the printing process or spew out garbage.

If this happens, turn off Print Manager through the Printers icon in the Control Panel. If this doesn't work, access the Connections dialog box through the Printers icon and redirect your printer output to the FILE port, as described earlier in the chapter. To print the file, copy it to your printer port from the DOS command prompt using the standard DOS Copy command.

24-Pin Dot-Matrix Printers. If you're going to use a dot-matrix printer with Windows, a 24-pin printer provides far more attractive text and graphics than do the older 9-pin models. However, 24-pin printers vary considerably; they print at different resolutions and with different **aspect ratios**. (The aspect ratio is the ratio between the vertical and horizontal dots that constitute an image.)

For example, the Epson 24-pin and IBM Proprinter 24 series can print in 120x180 resolution (1:1.5 aspect ratio), 180x180 (1:1), and 360x180 (2:1). Others, like the NEC 24-pin, provide a 360x360 resolution. The printer's 180x180 resolution is usually best for printing raster screen fonts because they use a 1:1 aspect ratio. A 180x180 dpi screen font is available from Epson if you really need one.

Table 7.10 lists all the drivers and related files necessary to support the corresponding 24-pin printers. If your printer isn't on the list, it can often be set up using an Epson printer or an IBM Proprinter, provided that the printer emulates one of these two models. (This may require flipping some DIP switches on your printer to change its emulation mode, so check the manual.)

TABLE 7.10

24-Pin Printer Drivers and Supported Printers

Printer Driver	Supported Printer	Printer Driver	Supported Printer
CIT24US.DRV*	Citizen GSX-130	PROPRN24.DRV	IBM Proprinter X24
	Citizen GSX-140		IBM Proprinter X24e
	Citizen GSX-140+		IBM Proprinter XL24
	Citizen GSX-145		IBM Proprinter XL24e
	Citizen PN48	NEC24PIN.DRV	NEC Pinwriter CP6
EPSON24.DRV	Epson L-750		NEC Pinwriter CP7
	Epson L-1000		NEC Pinwriter P5XL
	Epson LQ-500		NEC Pinwriter P6
	Epson LQ-510		NEC Pinwriter P7
	Epson LQ-800		NEC Pinwriter P9XL
	Epson LQ-850		NEC Pinwriter P2200
	Epson LQ-950		NEC Pinwriter P5200
	Epson LQ-1000		NEC Pinwriter P5300
	Epson LQ-1050	OKI24.DRV	Okidata ML 380
	Epson LQ-1500		Okidata ML 390
	Epson LQ-2500		Okidata ML 390 Plus
	Epson LQ-2550		Okidata ML 391
	Epson SQ-2000		Okidata ML 391 Plus
	Epson SQ-2500		Okidata ML 393
FUJI24.DRV	Fujitsu DL 2400		Okidata ML 393 Plus
	Fujitsu DL 2600		Okidata ML 393C
	Fujitsu DL 3300		Okidata ML 393C Plus
	Fujitsu DL 3400	PANSON24.DRV	Panasonic KX-P1123
	Fujitsu DL 5600		Panasonic KX-P1124
			Panasonic KX-P1624

*You'll also need to use a DMCOLOR.DLL driver file from the color library for all these Citizen printers.

9-Pin Dot-Matrix Printers. The 9-pin dot-matrix printers are the dinosaurs of the printer world. But just as Windows reaches down the evolutionary path to work with 286 computers, it also does its best to maintain compatibility with these older dot-matrix printer models.

Again, these printers print at different resolutions and with different aspect ratios. The Epson 9-pin and IBM Proprinter typically print at an aspect ratio of 1.67:1. The Epson 9-pin driver supports these resolutions: 120x72 (aspect ratio of 1.67:1), 120x144 (1:1.2), and 240x144 (1.67:1). You can print raster screen fonts using the D font set (120x72 dpi) with the 120x72 and 240x144 printer resolutions; the D font set can also be used at half-point sizes with the 240x144 printer resolution.

Table 7.11 describes the drivers and printer models of 9-pin dot-matrix printers supported by the files on the Windows 3.1 installation disks. All these printers use the UNIDRV.DLL driver library, and the Citizen printers also require a DMCOLOR.DLL driver file from the color library.

	Printer Driver	Supported Printer	Printer Driver	Supported Printer
TABLE 7.11 *9-Pin Printer Drivers and Supported Printers*	CIT9US.DRV	Citizen 120D	EPSON9.DRV	Epson JX-80
		Citizen 180D		Epson LX-80
		Citizen 200GX		Epson LX-86
		Citizen 200GX/15		Epson LX-800
		Citizen HSP-500		Epson LX-810
		Citizen HSP-550		Epson MX-80
	EPSON9.DRV	Epson DFX-5000		Epson MX-80 F/T
		Epson EX-800		Epson MX-100
		Epson EX-1000		Epson RX-80
		Epson FX-80		Epson RX-80 F/T
		Epson FX-80+		Epson RX-80 F/T+
		Epson FX-85		Epson RX-100
		Epson FX-86e		Epson RX-100+
		Epson FX-100		Epson T-750
		Epson FX-100+		Epson T-1000
		Epson FX-185	FUJI9.DRV	Fujitsu DX 2100
		Epson FX-286		Fujitsu DX 2200
		Epson FX-286e		Fujitsu DX 2300
		Epson FX-850	FUJI9.DRV	Fujitsu DX 2400
		Epson FX-1050	PROPRINT.DRV	IBM Proprinter

• • • • • • • • • • • • • •
TABLE 7.11 *(cont.)*
*9-Pin Printer
Drivers and
Supported
Printers*

Printer Driver	Supported Printer	Printer Driver	Supported Printer
PROPRINT.DRV	IBM Proprinter II	OKI9IBM.DRV	AT&T 473/478
	IBM Proprinter III		IBM Graphics
	IBM Proprinter XL		Okidata ML 92-IBM
	IBM Proprinter XL II		Okidata ML 93-IBM
	IBM Proprinter XL III		Okidata ML 192-IBM
OKI9.DRV	Okidata ML 192		Okidata ML 193-IBM
	Okidata ML 192 Plus		Okidata ML 320-IBM
	Okidata ML 193		Okidata ML 321-IBM
	Okidata ML 193 Plus	PANSON9.DRV	Panasonic KX-P1180
	Okidata ML 320		Panasonic KX-P1695
	Okidata ML 321		

Inkjet Printers. Much like dot-matrix printers, inkjets attack the paper with ink; but because they spray rather than hammer dots of ink onto the paper, they produce far less noise and a much higher resolution, approaching that of a laser printer. In addition, some inkjet printers—such as the HP DeskJet 500C and the HP PaintJet series—support color printing by mixing the primary colors of ink as they're sprayed onto the page. Inkjet printers provide an economical alternative to laser printers, with black-and-white models selling for a couple of hundred dollars and good-quality color models available for less than $1,000.

The world of inkjet printing with Windows, however, has more than its fair share of anomalies. It seems as if many printer drivers require some kind of adjustment to work well with an inkjet.

For starters, take the printer drivers for the HP DeskJet and DeskJet Plus, which work with a wide variety of fonts, including TrueType fonts, vector fonts, and even many downloadable soft fonts designed for HP LaserJets. Both of these printers can print at resolutions of 75, 150, or 300 dpi, and you can install downloadable soft fonts using the Font Installer utility described earlier in the section on HP LaserJets. But to use downloadable fonts on a DeskJet, you must upgrade its memory with a special RAM cartridge provided by HP. Be sure to specify the amount of printer memory in the printer setup dialog box when using this cartridge.

Here's another case where you need to tweak things to make the inkjet work properly. If you're using the HP DeskJet 500 with the 500C printer driver supplied by HP, adjust the resolution to 300 dpi in the printer setup dialog box. Also, add this line to the [DJ500] section of your WIN.INI file:

```
PRTRESFAC=0
```

If you're using the DeskJet 500 with the printer driver provided by Windows, and you're trying to print an envelope using Word for Windows 2.0, you may run into problems. You'll need to add this line to the [Microsoft Word 2.0] section of WIN.INI:

```
HPDSKJET=+1
```

With the HP PaintJet series color printer, the Windows printer driver creates a full page of graphics in Windows at 180x180 dpi resolution, and then sends the completed page to the PaintJet as a bitmap graphics file. This process produces great-looking graphics but sends a huge print spool file to Print Manager, which can considerably bog down your printing.

To pick up the pace, open the printer setup dialog box and place an X in the Fast Printing Direct to Port check box to bypass Print Manager for this particular driver. You can install PaintJet soft fonts, identified by the extension .PJF, with the Font Installer described in the HP LaserJet section. However, these soft fonts are not downloaded to the printer; instead, the printer driver uses them to compose the page before sending it to the PaintJet.

If you're using a Canon Bubble-Jet printer, make sure that the printer's DIP switches are set to the factory-default position of Off. Also, if you're using this printer at its highest resolution mode of 360x360 dpi and part of the graphics is missing or disfigured, set the printer's DIP switch for controlling the Graphic Density option to the High position. Refer to the printer's documentation for the location and operation of these switches.

Table 7.12 lists the printer driver files and printer models supported by the Windows 3.1 installation disks. All these printers use the DRV.DLL driver library file.

TABLE 7.12
Inkjet Printer Drivers and Supported Printers

Printer Driver	Supported Printer	Printer Driver	Supported Printer
CANON10E.DRV	Canon Bubble-Jet BJ-10e	DJ500C.DRV	HP DeskJet 500C
		EXECJET.DRV	IBM ExecJet
CANON130.DRV	Canon Bubble-Jet BJ-130e	HPDSKJET.DRV	HP DeskJet
			HP DeskJet Plus
CANON330.DRV	Canon Bubble-Jet BJ-300		HP DeskJet 500
	Canon Bubble-Jet BJ-330	PAINTJET.DRV	HP PaintJet
			HP PaintJet XL
DICONIX.DRV	Diconix 150 Plus	THINKJET.DRV	HP ThinkJet (2225 C-D)

Other Printers. Although most laser and dot-matrix printers fall into one of the categories just discussed, Windows 3.1 also supports a host of other printers. Tables 7.13 and 7.14 list the printer drivers, soft font installers, and printers supported by the Windows 3.1 installation disks. All these printers require the use of the UNIDRV.DLL driver library file as well.

The TTY.DRV driver is provided as a way to simply send plain text to the printer port, and can be used as a driver of last resort.

TABLE 7.13
Miscellaneous Printer Drivers and Supported Printers

Printer Driver	Supported Printer	Printer Driver	Supported Printer
CITOH.DRV	AT&T 470/475	IBMCOLOR.DRV	IBM Color Printer
	C-Itoh 8510	IBM5204.DRV	IBM QuickWriter 5204
DM309.DRV	Olivetti DM 109	PS1.DRV	IBM PS/1
	Olivetti DM 309	QWIII.DRV	IBM QuietWriter III
ESCP2.DRV	Epson LQ-570 ESC/P 2	TI850.DRV	TI 850/855
	Epson LQ-870 ESC/P 2	TOSHIBA.DRV	Toshiba P351
	Epson LQ-1070 ESC/P 2		Toshiba P1351
	Epson LQ-1170 ESC/P 2	TTY.DRV	Generic/Text Only

TABLE 7.14
Printer Drivers Requiring Special Soft Font Installers

Printer Driver	Soft Font Installer	Supported Printer
IBM4019.DRV	SF4019.EXE	IBM Laser Printer 4019
LBPII.DRV	CAN_ADF.EXE	Canon LBP-8 II
LPBIII.DRV	CAN_ADF.EXE	Canon LBP-4
	CAN_ADF.EXE	Canon LBP-8 III
PG306.DRV	SFINST.EXE	Hermes H 606
	SFINST.EXE	Olivetti PG 306
	SFINST.EXE	Triumph Adler SDR 7706

The Canon LBP-8 Mark III and Mark IV printers use their own outline font technology. These two printers work with their own internal fonts or Windows vector screen fonts. The Canon series II and III laser printers do not directly support TrueType fonts. To print TrueType fonts on these printers, you can treat them as graphics, but this will slow down your printing. To make this work, an X must be present in the Enable TrueType check box in the printer setup dialog box. Normally, this check box contains an X when the printer is first installed; however, if it's not there, you won't be able to print TrueType fonts because they won't be available on the Fonts menu within your Windows application.

IBM's Laser Printer 4019 can print TrueType fonts, its own internal device fonts, vector fonts, and special IBM downloadable fonts and font cards. To install these IBM fonts, use a special IBM version of the Font Installer utility SF4019.EXE.

Pen Plotters. Pen plotters are often used with CAD programs for creating schematic diagrams, architectural drawings, and other documents where it's desirable to have an actual pen draw the image. A plotter is also handy for creating overhead transparencies for presentations. Plotters work with Windows vector fonts and the plotter's built-in device fonts, but not with True-Type or raster fonts.

Sometimes, when printing documents on a pen plotter, you may have to experiment with different margin settings from within your application. You can also try flipping on the plotter's Expand switch, which increases the plotting area but can sometimes decrease the quality of the output. Refer to your plotter's documentation for more information on adjusting the margins through hardware settings.

The plotters on the following list all use the HPPLOT.DRV pen-plotter driver supplied with Windows 3.1. Many other plotters can emulate one of these HP plotters; refer to your hardware documentation to see if you need to flip a DIP switch to access the plotter's HP emulation mode.

AT&T 435	HP 7585A	HP DraftPro DXL
HP 7470A	HP 7585B	HP DraftPro EXL
HP 7475A	HP 7586B	HP DraftMaster I
HP 7550A	HP ColorPro	HP DraftMaster II
HP 7580A	HP ColorPro with GEC	
HP 7580B	HP DraftPro	

· ·

What To Buy

Windows works with hundreds of printers, because Microsoft wants to eliminate every excuse for not getting Windows. Offering widespread printer support works toward that end—at least on a perception level.

Early versions of OS/2, in fact, were plagued by printer drivers that didn't work properly. This delayed delivery of the system, and also angered users who couldn't get it to print properly. Microsoft is motivated not to repeat this mistake, for both marketing and functional reasons: You don't want to make the customer mad, and it's important for a visually based system to have proper output.

Adapting an older printer for use with Windows is a fairly simple—although inexact—process. A printer driver for the IBM Proprinter, to use the popular example, uses screen and printer fonts that are really close look-alikes rather than identical twins. For Proprinter owners who don't want to buy a new printer just because they bought Windows, the pairing will be close enough.

Most likely, if you're just buying into Windows, you won't welcome the extra expense of a new printer. But if you are in the market for a new printer and know that a good percentage of your computing time will be spent under Windows, the next section lists a few fiats in ascending order of importance, depending on your commitment to WYSIWYG:

Get a Printer with a Windows Driver. Before you buy a printer from any source, make sure that it is supported by a Windows driver. At installation, Windows lists several hundred printers supported by drivers included in the Windows package; you can also look at this list from the Add button in the Control Panel's printer module. If you are purchasing a printer for use with Windows, make sure it's listed here, or exact a promise from the manufacturer that a current driver is supplied in the package.

In fact, a printer that isn't included on this list is probably either very new or very old. As for the latter, you are taking your chances, anyway. You could argue that anyone who buys a printer at a garage sale is most likely aware of the inherent risks. As for new-model printers, one that does not supply either a Windows driver or compatibility with an existing Windows driver is probably not such a good deal.

Go Laser. In the computer marketplace, a component becomes affordable to most users when it dips below the $1,000 level. The modern laser printer slipped beneath that price barrier a few years back, and, as I mentioned earlier, it drove the market for dot-matrix printers down. Although improvements have been made to both laser and 24-pin dot-matrix printers, if you ever plan to print graphics, you should definitely purchase a laser printer. Several Windows software vendors consider even the "best" dot matrix printer to be obsolete.

When shopping for a laser printer, you may need to go past the $1,000 "threshold of pain" to get the features that really enhance its performance under Windows. In any event, you should look for these features:

➤ Make sure the printer has at least **1.5 MB of memory**, or the ability to expand to that point. With any less, graphical printing is hopelessly slow.

➤ Make sure that the printer has **download capabilities**, so that it can load fonts from an external source, such as your PC.

➤ Seek a speed of at least **8 PPM** (pages-per-minute), unless you really don't mind waiting. In reality, 4 PPM might be enough for a single user who doesn't print high volumes of pages. Everybody wants faster and cheaper, but you can't always get both in the same place.

➤ **Shop around**. Laser printers don't quite qualify as commodity items, but they still share more of the same features than differences. For instance, a printer with a particular laser engine—the system's most important component—may cost several hundred dollars less than a different machine with the same engine. So before you buy a laser printer through mail order or at one of the computer superstores, research the components that go into that particular brand—you may be getting a good deal, or no deal at all.

Go Color. Using Windows with a standard black-and-white printer can be a prescription for frustration if you're graphically inclined. You develop magnificent multicolored, multisourced documents, which become monochromatic at output. The solution is to invest in a color printer or plotter. The entry point to color isn't quite as high as you may expect—the HP DeskJet 500C costs less than $1,000. However, the leap between a cheap color printer and the next level, a thermal transfer unit, requires an extra $3,000.

Choosing a color printer, like other equipment decisions, is application driven, based on the WYGDOWYWTDWI (What You Get Depends on What You Want to Do with It) principle. The two major application choices for color printer are graphics design and desktop presentation. For design, you will want to get a printer that can handle larger pages, so you can print full-sized drawings with room around the edges to indicate instructional markings. For presentations, size is of secondary importance, but you will want a printer that can create high-quality overhead transparencies.

Summary

With the incorporation of TrueType fonts, Windows 3.1 ups the ante for enhancing your printing quality. Of course, you'll need to match the quality of your screen fonts with a printer capable of producing high-level output. You can either upgrade whatever you've got now—and Microsoft has made it easy to do this by providing hundreds of drivers that act as a translator between an application and your printer—or choose from hundreds of laser printers now available on the market.

Insider's Tech Support: Fonts and Printing

Q: My TrueType fonts don't work.

A: A number of things can cause problems with TrueType fonts. TrueType does not work well on computers with less than 2 megabytes of RAM. If TrueType fonts are not being displayed on your screen properly, you may be using a third-party video driver that is not fully compatible with TrueType. If the driver is older than 3/10/92, you probably need an updated version. Similarly, if TrueType fonts are not printing properly, you may have an incompatible third-party printer driver. You should replace a driver older than 3/10/92 with one on the Windows installation disks or a 3.1-compatible third-party printer driver.

Less common problems with TrueType crop up with font conversion utilities, which can sometimes corrupt the converted fonts, or with the use of an old version of Bitstream FaceLift, which is incompatible with some Windows 3.1 display drivers.

Q: A different font than the one I selected is being printed.

A: No, it's not divine intervention. There may be a problem in the [Fonts] section or the [FontSubstitutes] section of your WIN.INI file. The [Fonts] section lists the fonts that are loaded into your computer section at Startup, and the [FontSubstitutes] section tells Windows to substitute one font for another. Application programs sometimes modify these sections without informing you. See Chapter 15 for details on how to interpret and edit these sections of WIN.INI to correct any problems.

Q: I installed TrueType fonts, but none of them show up in my applications.

A: Some applications that were written before the introduction of 3.1 don't support the use of TrueType. Do this test: see whether the True-Type fonts appear in the Windows Write applet. If they do, the problem is with your application. If not, check the Fonts icon in the Control Panel. Click on the TrueType button and make sure that there is an X in the Enable TrueType Fonts check box. If an X is already there, the TrueType fonts may have become corrupted. Remove them using the Control Panel's Fonts icon and then reinstall them.

Q: I'm having trouble with my printer.

A: The printing process is one of the most common trouble spots, because anything can fail—the printer itself, the cable, the driver, or the port. In addition, Windows itself can induce conflicts. The best way to handle printer problems is to examine the elements of your system one at a time, starting with the hardware and moving to the software. Here are some of the first things to check:

➤ **Make sure the printer is turned on and online**. This oversight happens more often than many people would care to admit, and is a prime cause of printer problems.

➤ **Check your cable**. Windows applications require that all pins on all printer cables work, whereas some DOS applications can run with less. Also, make sure that the cable is securely plugged into both the printer and your system.

➤ **Maintain a full paper tray and toner cartridge.** If the paper tray is empty, the printer may or may not inform Windows of the problem. Toner sometimes runs out without warning, and is a leading cause of image inconsistency.

➤ **Test your printer.** Try printing a test page from the printer; most printers have a self-test feature that lets you print a test page (check the printer manual). If the self-test doesn't produce a page, then your printer is probably broken.

➤ **Print a test file**. Print a short text file from the Windows Notepad utility. If this works, you can track down the problem to a specific application. Otherwise, try running a similar test from DOS (the Editor included with DOS 5 works well for this). If you can print from DOS, the problem is with your Windows installation, driver, or configuration.

➤ **Make sure that your AUTOEXEC.BAT file includes a SET TEMP statement** that references a valid directory. See Chapter 13 for more information on the SET TEMP statement. Also, make sure that your hard disk has enough room to hold its spool of temporary files.

➤ **Delete any leftover, temporary spool files** (these start with ~SPL and end with .TMP) from the TEMP directory.

➤ **Check the printer driver.** Make sure you are using the proper driver, and that it is Windows 3.1 compatible (it should be dated 3/10/92 or later).

➤ **Check the port assignment.** Make sure the printer is actually connected to its assigned port—it could have been accidently redirected to another port or location through a MODE command in DOS, or by some other utility.

➤ **Check your network connections.** If you are printing to a network printer, make sure it is properly configured within Printer Setup (Chapter 10).

➤ **Print through DOS.** Try the Fast Printing to Port command in the Printers/Connect portion of the Control Panel. This may isolate the problem in cases where a switchbox is used to control several different printers from one source.

Q: My graphics are printing too small.

A: Choose Print from the applications File menu and check the scaling factor in the Printers dialog box; you may need to adjust it upwards. You may also need to remove the X from the Use Printer Resolution check box.

Q: I'm getting an error message saying that Windows cannot print.

A: If you're using a network, this could be a problem with the network driver. Or, if you're using a print-sharing device, you may need to force Windows to print through DOS by editing the [Ports] section of your WIN.INI file and changing the LPT1:= statement to LPT1.DOS= to redirect printing.

If you're printing to a local printer on an LPT1 port, and not using a network or print-sharing device, the printer itself may be sending an error message to Windows (perhaps the printer is offline or has a paper jam), or the printer may be connected to a defective cable. You can change cables to see if that's the problem.

You could also be exceeding the time-out limits set by Windows for the printer. Two time-outs that can generate error messages are the Device Not Selected setting, which is the period Windows waits for a printer to go online, and the Transmission Retry setting, the amount of time Windows waits while the printer is busy processing. Try increasing these values to eliminate the error message.

Q: Bitmapped graphics files are taking a long time to print.

A: Unfortunately, this is normal. To speed up printing of graphics, try printing at a lower resolution. The printer setup dialog box for many printers allows you to select a lower than normal resolution. The HP LaserJet II, for example, normally prints at 300 dpi, but you can select 150 dpi as a way to accelerate printing. There's a trade-off, though: you lose resolution and therefore quality in the printed output.

Interacting with the Interface: Displays, Mice, and Keyboards

For interacting with your computer, punch cards are out. For Windows users, a display system, a mouse, and a keyboard are in. Windows, like any good graphical interface, requires a display system that shows off the graphical components to their best advantage, as well as a mouse or other device for pointing to and selecting those components. Windows uses the display system to

429

present itself to you, and the mouse allows you to control the Windows environment. Although the mouse is a crucial component of a graphical interface, the keyboard is imperative for data entry, and often provides an easier way of issuing commands.

Here, then, is an overview of your display system, which in turn includes a video add-in card, a monitor, and Windows-compatible display driver software; of pointing devices, predominantly mice but also trackballs, styluses, and pens; and the venerable keyboard, which has survived relatively unchanged from the mechanical typewriters of the last century to the new age of computers.

Display Systems

A good display system exploits the Windows environment—and its applications—to their best advantage. Your display system actually encompasses three components: the **monitor**, the **adapter card**, and the **display driver** that allows Windows to take advantage of the capabilities of the adapter card. The adapter card affects the visual quality of your display more than the monitor itself, because the adapter controls the resolution, number of colors, and amount of visible flicker. In turn, the monitor needs to match the output signal of the adapter card, so these two items must be compatible with each other.

New in 3.1

Windows 3.1 has increased the speed of graphics display and performance. To accomplish this, Microsoft improved the drivers supplied on the Windows installation disks and fine-tuned the internal graphics capabilities of Windows. Windows 3.1 also includes several important new drivers:

➤ **SuperVGA** Provides 800x600 resolution at 16 colors and works with the vast majority of SuperVGA adapter cards

➤ **Video Seven** Provides drivers for the FastWrite, 1024i VRAM, and VRAM II adapter cards that can yield 256 colors at resolutions as high as 1024x768

➤ **XGA** For interlaced XGA displays on PS/2s at resolutions as high as 1024x768 with 256 colors

➤ **TIGA** For TIGA-compatible adapter cards that work at all the resolutions in monochrome 16-color and 256-color modes

All Windows drivers that provide resolutions higher than 640x480 now feature the ability to use either small or large fonts to accommodate monitors of varying sizes. Using larger fonts improves the legibility of text at high resolutions, whereas smaller fonts minimize the amount of room required by windows and menus on your desktop.

The new Windows 3.1 display drivers have also improved their ability to work with DOS applications running in a window. The drivers now work faster, allow you to run DOS graphics programs in a window, portray colors more accurately, and select a variety of different-sized fonts for use within DOS windows. Also, the new EGA, VGA, and SuperVGA drivers provided with Windows 3.1 offer a mouse trails feature that makes the mouse pointer easier to locate on LCD displays.

Different Display Standards

Microsoft has done its best to accommodate all the major display standards in the IBM PC universe. The Windows installation disks provide a wide variety of display drivers that support most of the display adapter standards except for the old **CGA** (Color/Graphics Adapter) display, which crops up on older systems, especially laptops and portables. However, you can still use your CGA display with Windows 3.1 if you obtain a CGA display driver from the Windows Driver Library, available from Microsoft on disk or through the company's online support system (see Appendix C).

In the early 1980s, Hercules developed its own monochrome display adapter to challenge IBM's display boards. The original **Hercules monochrome adapter** displayed high-quality text, as well as high-resolution monochrome graphics, so it garnered the support of most leading developers as well as users of desktop publishing and CAD applications. Windows also supports this older display.

By the mid-1980s, the IBM Enhanced Graphics Adapter (**EGA**), emerged as the most popular display adapter for the IBM PC. EGA systems came with a puny 64K of display memory (in the standard configuration), which allowed for only a 4-color display. It could accept up to 256K, which allowed for a 16-color display, at a resolution of 640x350 pixels. Because EGA uses rectangular pixels, and Windows was designed for the square pixels of VGA (described next), Windows distorts its images on EGA displays. Although most people now buy the higher-resolution VGA display, EGA displays are still common on older 286 systems.

The now-standard Video Graphics Array (**VGA**) display adapter emerged with the introduction of the IBM PS/2 in 1987. Unlike the earlier CGA and

EGA displays, which use digital signaling techniques to control the number of colors on your monitor, VGA monitors employ analog signaling, so they can potentially display millions of colors. Most VGA adapter cards, because of data-bit limitations, can manage only a small fraction of this potential, and usually display either 16 or 256 colors.

VGA's **standard resolution** is 640x480 pixels—about 30 percent higher than the resolution of a standard television set. However, a TV image often looks more realistic than the graphics on a VGA computer display, because it has better color-depth resolution.

Pixel resolution measures the number of spots of light on the monitor. A 640x480 pixel resolution of the VGA display indicates that there are 640 pixels—or picture elements—for each line, and 480 lines of pixels on the monitor.

Color-depth resolution measures the number of bits of color information that each pixel is capable of displaying. In a 4-bit-per-pixel system, you're limited to 16 colors that can be simultaneously displayed on the screen. The reason is that each bit is actually a binary number, containing two choices (0 or 1), so with 4 bits, you have 16 possible combinations. Similarly, with 8 bits per pixel, you can get 256 colors; with 16 bits per pixel, more than 32,000 colors; and with 24 bits, more than 16 million.

Insider's Tip

To achieve a photorealistic color image, you need to use a 24-bit display, which devotes 8 bits to each of the three primary colors of light—red, green, and blue. However, by optimizing the computer's color palette, you can display photorealistic images on a 16-bit display with only a slight loss of color quality. Some images can even be squeezed onto a 256-color palette; however, the loss in color resolution results in a fair quality but less-than-realistic looking image.

The **amount of memory on your video board** affects both the pixel resolution and the number of colors that can be displayed; the video board must contain enough memory to address all the pixels on the display multiplied by the number of bits of color resolution per pixel. Thus, an 8-bit-per-pixel VGA card capable of displaying 256 simultaneous colors requires twice as much memory as does a 4-bit per pixel VGA card that can display only 16 colors at a time.

You can often install **additional video RAM chips** on your adapter card to produce higher resolutions or more colors. SuperVGA cards enhance standard VGA by allowing you to add memory to increase colors and resolutions. Most display cards require special video RAM chips, which is not the same kind of RAM you use to expand the memory in your computer systems. These special RAM chips run at higher speeds and are considerably more expensive than standard computer RAM. Some boards allow you to expand memory using the more standard RAM chips; however, performance is sometimes impaired by this trade-off.

To use resolutions higher than 640x480 pixels, your monitor must be able to accommodate the required **horizontal scan frequencies**. For a SuperVGA card at 800x600, for example, your monitor must be capable of supporting at least a 35 kHz horizontal scan rate; at a 1024x768 resolution, you need to support at least a 49 kHz horizontal scan rate. Some display systems feature a range of scanning rates; for example, SuperVGA is offered in horizontal scan rates ranging from 35 to 48 kHz. As a rule of thumb, the higher the frequency of the horizontal scanning rate, the better the quality and greater the stability of the image.

As a general guideline, the following resolutions work best with these scanning rates:

➡ **640x480** 31.5 kHz

➡ **800x600** 35 to 48 kHz

➡ **1024x768** 48 to 72 kHz

Don't confuse the horizontal scan rate with the **vertical scanning frequency**, which is the rate at which a monitor redraws the screen image. This measure affects the amount of flicker on your monitor. The standard vertical scanning frequency is 60 Hz, which redraws the screen 60 times per second. Newer adapter cards support higher vertical scan rates—typically 72 Hz, the standard in Europe—to reduce flicker and create a more stable image.

Table 8.1 summarizes the characteristics of the major PC display standards that are supported by drivers shipped with Windows.

• • • • • • • • • • • • • •
TABLE 8.1
Technical Specifications for PC Display Standards

Display Standard	Pixel Resolution	Color Resolution	Number of Colors	Video RAM Required	Horizontal Scan Frequency in kHz
EGA	640x350	4-bit	16	256K	21.8
Hercules	720x348	1-bit	1	64K	21.5
MCGA	640x480	2-bit	4	128K	21.5
VGA	640x480	4-bit	16	256K	31.5
Video7 VGA	640x480	8-bit	256	512K	31.5
Video7 VGA	720x512	8-bit	256	512K	35 to 48
Video7 VGA	1024x768	8-bit	256	1 MB	48 to 69
SuperVGA	800x600	4-bit	16	256K	35 to 48
SuperVGA	800x600	8-bit	256	512K	35 to 48
8514/a	1024x768	4-bit	16	512K	48 to 69

Display Standard	Pixel Resolution	Color Resolution	Number of Colors	Video RAM Required	Horizontal Scan Frequency in kHz
8514/a	1024x768	8-bit	256	1 MB	48 to 69
XGA	640x480	4-bit	16	512K	31.5 to 35.5
XGA	640x480	8-bit	256	512K	31.5 to 35.5
XGA	1024x768	8-bit	256	1 MB	48 to 69
TIGA	1024x768	4-bit	16	512K	48 to 69
TIGA	1024x768	8-bit	256	1 MB	48 to 69

Many of the display standards run at resolutions other than the ones listed in Table 8.1. For example, a standard VGA card can run in more than a dozen different video modes. Some of these resolutions, such as VGA's 320x200 256-color mode, do not work with Windows, whereas others, such as SuperVGA cards that offer 1024x768 resolution, require special drivers not supplied on the Windows installation disks.

Windows 3.1 provides drivers for Video Seven VGA cards that can display 256 colors, provided the card contains at least 512K of video RAM. The drivers included with 3.1 have been performance-tuned to speed up the display and provide better compatibility with the mouse. However, these drivers do not work in all modes with all Video Seven cards. Table 8.2 lists which Video Seven cards provide 256-color capability using the Windows 3.1 drivers.

Video Seven Card	640x480	720x512	800x600	1024x768
FastWrite 512K	Yes			
1024i 512K	Yes			
VRAM 512K	Yes	Yes		
VRAM II 512K	Yes	Yes		
VRAM II 1MB	Yes	Yes	Yes	Yes

Expanding Your Desktop

Running Windows at a higher resolution lets you work with a larger onscreen desktop. A resolution of 800x600—the standard for SuperVGA—increases the area of your desktop by more than 50 percent (Figure 8.1).

Increasing your screen resolution to 800x600 pixels provides additional room to display windows, icons, and other onscreen paraphernalia. Most

FIGURE 8.1

*Comparison
of SuperVGA
and VGA*

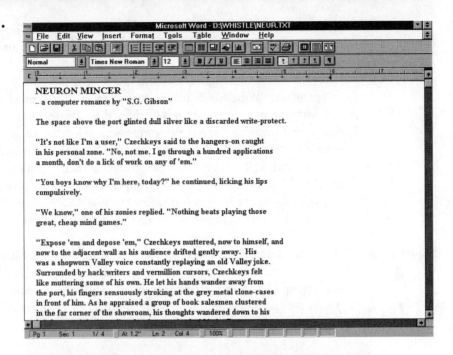

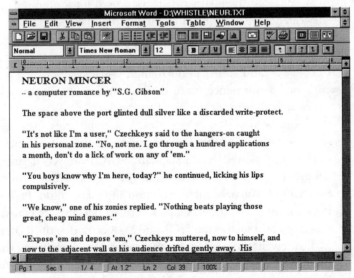

*A SuperVGA display of 800x600 pixels lets you see considerably
more on your screen than does a standard VGA resolution of
640x480 pixels.*

importantly, on such a screen you can display the full width of a standard
$8\frac{1}{2}$x11-inch page. With either a VGA or SuperVGA display, Windows uses 96

pixels to display each inch of your actual document. Thus, on a SuperVGA display of 800x600, you can view almost the entire width of an 8½x11-inch page (800 divided by 96).

As you move to a higher resolution, and keep the same screen size, the images in your Windows display appear to shrink. On a small monitor, this shrinking can make menus, window titles, dialog boxes, and other interface components difficult to read. To compensate, select the Large Fonts option when installing your display driver. A better alternative is to increase the size of your monitor. If you go to resolutions higher than 640x480, I recommend using a 15- or 16-inch display for a SuperVGA at 800x600 resolution; this keeps the size of the images equivalent to those on a normal VGA monitor. For a 1024x768 resolution, a 17- to 19-inch display is appropriate.

Insider's Tip

Monitors are measured diagonally, so increasing the size by just a couple of inches can add a significant amount of area to your display. For example, stepping up to a 16-inch monitor from a 14-inch one increases your display area by around 30 percent; going from 14 to 17 inches gives you 50 percent more space.

Admittedly, these larger displays do sell for a premium price. However, they can be well worth the investment, especially for desktop publishing and graphics applications. Keep in mind, though, that increasing the resolution of your display—whether by changing the number of pixels or the number of colors—can hamper performance. Usually, supporting additional colors cuts into performance more than increasing the pixel resolution, but this varies according to the design of the card.

Going beyond 256 colors most noticeably cuts into performance. For example, a 1024x768 display card capable of a 16-color display normally runs only slightly slower than a standard VGA. However, if you go beyond 256 colors, even at 640x480 resolution, you can slow down your display system noticeably. If you need high resolution and many colors, I recommend investing in a more advanced adapter card, either an accelerated card or a co-processed card such as the TIGA and XGA cards described later in this section.

If you want more colors for the least outlay of cash, you should try one of the newer VGA cards that incorporate the Sierra RAM DAC, such as the Diamond Speedstar or Orchid Fahrenheit card. These cards can produce more than 32,000 colors and provide almost photorealistic images, although you'll need to get special drivers for them. Some of these cards also provide a special 1280x960 high-resolution mode when used on monitors with a minimum scan frequency of 72 KHz; the drawback is that this high-resolution mode usually employs an interlaced display.

Danger Zone

When using resolutions higher than 640x480, be on the lookout for **interlaced displays**. In an interlaced display, the video gun of the monitor's video tube creates the image by writing every other line on the screen, and then returns to the top of the screen to fill the empty lines—that is, it interlaces the empty and the written lines. Thus, an interlaced 1024x768 display system is really a 1024x384 display that scans the face of the video tube twice. This double-passage causes a noticeable flicker, which varies depending on how quickly your eyes react to images, your distance from the screen, and whether fluorescent lighting is present (such lighting produces its own flicker that can accentuate the screen flicker).

This flicker can sometimes be so pronounced that it causes eyestrain or headaches. IBM and other companies that sell interlaced displays also recommend using longer-persistence phosphor for these monitors, but such phosphors—which is what cause the screen image to appear—introduce yet another problem: They make the screen appear dimmer, and can even leave ghostlike trails of former images when you move the mouse, a window, an icon, or another object.

If you prefer a higher screen resolution, you should obtain a **noninterlaced display**, which is much easier on the eyes. For a noninterlaced display, you'll need these three components:

➡ A display adapter card that supports noninterlaced video modes

➡ A video monitor that supports noninterlaced video, and that has a high enough vertical scan frequency to work with the display card

➡ A software configuration for the display card that works with noninterlaced video

Even if both your display card and monitor support noninterlaced video, you may need to run a configuration utility from DOS, adjust jumpers or DIP switches on the card, or even set a switch on the monitor to obtain noninterlaced video. If your card and monitor are mismatched, you may experience flicker, distortion of images on your monitor, or a short, fat display that takes up only part of the screen.

Insider's Tip

You can use a special software trick to create a virtual display several times larger than your actual display. The technique works by letting you scroll around the virtual display area, which could be several times the size of your actual display, by using your screen as a window on this larger desktop area.

Many utility packages include this type of virtual display driver, including More Windows from Artisoft and WideAngle from Attitash. Several of the third-party shell programs described in Chapter 6 also provide virtual display capabilities.

Figure 8.2 shows an example of how BigDesk—a shareware utility—creates an expanded virtual desktop for your Windows display.

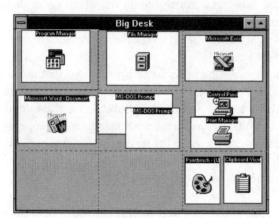

FIGURE 8.2

Expanded Virtual Desktop

BigDesk demonstrates a virtual display utility that expands your Windows desktop without the need for additional hardware.

Monochrome VGA

Monochrome VGA provides a lower-cost version of VGA that comes in two basic varieties: **monochrome** and **grayscale**. The monochrome VGA systems are most often found in laptop computers and display only 1-bit color. The grayscale type of monochrome VGA usually offers 4-bit color with 16 shades of gray. These grayscale systems actually use a 16-color VGA adapter card, which displays varying brightnesses of a single color on the monochrome monitor. For a strictly monochrome display, install Windows using the "VGA with Monochrome Display" driver; for a grayscale monochrome display, use the standard VGA driver.

Monochrome monitors cost considerably less than color monitors, but color adds information: Windows running in color is worth the price of an upgrade to a VGA color monitor. Besides, a monochrome VGA system often includes a color VGA adapter card, so you'd only need to upgrade the monitor. If you do upgrade, use Windows Setup to change the display driver from monochrome to color as well. If you're not sure whether your monitor is strictly monochrome or grayscale, switch between the monochrome display driver and the standard VGA driver using Windows Setup.

When the standard VGA color palette is displayed in monochrome, many of the resulting brightnesses appear similar, making it difficult to discern individual colors. You'll need to change your Windows color scheme to "Monochrome," using the Color icon in the Control Panel; or create your own grayscale color scheme. Don't confuse this with the "VGA with Monochrome Display" driver supplied with Windows. This driver provides 1-bit color for strictly monochrome displays, such as the kind found in laptops. Laptop users with LCD displays can also select from among several color schemes created expressly for LCD screens—these choices begin with the letters LCD. (See Chapter 4 for more details.)

Insider's Tip

If you're using a monochrome LCD laptop display, try to set the video mode so that it displays white text on a black background instead of the normal Windows video mode, which places black text on a white background—this configuration can wear out certain LCD displays. Check the documentation included with your laptop for specific instructions on how to reverse the video mode.

VGA on the Motherboard

In most personal computers, the display hardware consists of a monitor and a display adapter card that's plugged into one of the bus slots inside the computer system. Some models, including certain ones produced by IBM, place VGA circuitry onto the motherboard. If your system's motherboard contains the VGA circuitry, you can just plug a monitor into the display connector at the back of your system unit.

Unfortunately, if you want to upgrade your video display and you have VGA built onto the motherboard, you'll have to insert the new card and bypass the built-in VGA circuitry. Usually, you can disable VGA circuitry on the motherboard by changing the position of some on-board jumper connectors or DIP switches. In rare cases, the system can have difficulty recognizing the new card, and you'll need to contact the manufacturer of your computer system to learn the workaround.

TIGA Display Adapters

In the late 1980s, Texas Instruments introduced a video adapter technology called **TIGA** (Texas Instruments Graphics Architecture) as a high-performance alternative to VGA. A number of manufacturers use TIGA to produce screen resolutions of 1024x768 pixels and above. These TIGA-based boards include the Hercules Graphics Station card and the NEC Graphics Engine card.

Most TIGA adapter cards contain special TIGA system software that must be installed by DOS before use with Windows. This driver is usually contained in the TIGACD.EXE file. Windows 3.1 specifically requires use of TIGA version 2.05 or later. If you're having trouble operating your TIGA-based adapter with Windows, run the TIGACD.EXE file, which came with your display card; it should identify the version of TIGA software your system is using.

If a Windows-compatible version of your TIGA software is properly installed in DOS, the Windows Setup program usually detects your TIGA adapter and automatically installs the TIGA display driver. Windows Setup provides two TIGA drivers, one for small fonts and one for large.

The small-fonts TIGA driver provides the same size screen fonts as does the standard VGA card, but these fonts are too small for resolutions of 1024x768 and higher, unless you are using a large monitor. On monitors less than 16 inches, use the large-fonts TIGA driver instead. Be sure to use the TIGA display driver included with Windows 3.1, unless your display card includes a special driver that is specifically marked as 3.1 compatible.

Danger Zone

If you are upgrading from Windows 3.0 to 3.1 and were using an older, third-party TIGA driver, Setup may not have installed the new Windows 3.1 TIGA driver. In that case, your display may not work. If this happens, run Setup again and specifically identify your display as a TIGA; this will cause Setup to install the new 3.1 driver.

If you are using a DGIS display adapter designed by Graphics Software Systems, you may run into incompatibilities when you upgrade to Windows 3.1. These adapters include the NEC MultiSynch Graphics Engine, the GSS 1000 series, the HP IGC10 and IGC20, and the Zenith A-649. If you have one of these boards, you should obtain a new driver from the manufacturer. As a temporary workaround, many of the DGIS boards are TIGA compatible; if so, you can use the TIGACD.EXE DOS-level driver supplied with the board, and then select the TIGA driver included with Windows 3.1.

You can't use Windows Setup to change the screen resolution of a TIGA adapter. Instead, you need to run the DOS TIGAMODE.EXE utility (or a similar one) supplied with your adapter card. Be sure to quit Windows before changing the TIGA resolution. However, you should still use Setup to install the Windows TIGA driver with either small or large fonts, depending on the size of the monitor and the pixel resolution you are using with the card.

8514/a Display Adapters

In its attempt to outperform VGA, in the late 1980s IBM introduced the **8514/a adapter** card as an accessory for its PS/2 series. This display adapter provides 256 simultaneous colors from a palette of 262,400, at 1024x768 resolution—which is no more than is provided by some SuperVGA displays.

IBM's 8514/a implementation has three serious drawbacks: its displays are interlaced; it only works with the MCA bus (whereas similar cards by ATI and Paradise work with AT and EISA busses); and it is not backward compatible with VGA. Thus, if you want to produce a VGA image, you'll need separate VGA circuitry—on either a board, a separate add-in card, or the motherboard—to pass the image onto the 8514/a adapter and through to your monitor.

Danger Zone

If you're using an 8514/a adapter and a VGA adapter to pass a VGA signal through to the 8514/a, Windows may be unable to detect the memory used by the VGA adapter. You'll need to exclude the memory address areas used by that adapter from use by Windows. To do this, use the EMMExclude= statement in the [386Enh] section of your SYSTEM.INI file. For example, the statement line

```
EMMExclude=C400-C7FF
```

excludes the area that usually causes the memory conflict.

Another problem can be caused when older VGA cards require an updated RAM DAC chip. If your RAM DAC is too old, you may have problems switching between full-screen DOS sessions run from within Windows. In some cases, you'll be presented with a blank screen after making a switch. If this happens, update the RAM DAC or the video card.

If your screen blanks while running a DOS session with an 8514/a adapter, you can sometimes retrieve the display by typing "**MODE CO80**" at the now-invisible DOS prompt. This forces the display into the color 80-column mode, which sometimes makes the display reappear.

- -

XGA Display Adapters

In 1990, IBM introduced its XGA display adapter, which provides 256 colors at 1024x768 resolution, as well as a high-performance 640x480 256-color mode. Another special mode of the XGA adapter can display 65,536 simultaneous colors at a 640x480 resolution.

Like IBM's 8514/a card, its XGA card is interlaced and available only for the MCA bus. Third-party developers are just starting to offer noninterlaced, XGA-compatible cards for the ISA and EISA busses, but these are not nearly as prevalent as either the VGA or TIGA cards. Owners of ISA and EISA systems should note that certain TIGA adapter cards (see previous section) offer noninterlaced resolutions and performance that can rival and even exceed those of XGA.

XGA was designed with bitmapped graphics in mind, so it provides better Windows performance than does the 8514/a adapter, which was developed for CAD packages and therefore optimized to draw lines rather than bit-maps. IBM's XGA card works only with a 386 or better, and it is limited to two resolutions: 640x480 and 1024x768. Excluded is the useful mid-range resolution of 800x600, which is standard with SuperVGA cards.

When you install Windows on a system with an IBM XGA adapter, Setup installs it using 640x480 resolution at 16 colors, even if your XGA is capable of more colors or a higher resolution. This default is used to maintain compatibility with the plasma screen found on the PS/2 Model 75 portable. If you're using a normal video monitor, and want to use 640x480 with 256 colors, or 1024x768 at 256 colors, you'll need to run Setup again and select one of the following three choices:

➧ **XGA (640x480, 256 colors)** Use this with monitors that have horizontal scan frequencies less than 35 KHz

➧ **XGA (small fonts)** Configures your card to display 1024x768 with 256 colors; use this on large monitors (at least 15 inches)

➧ **XGA (large fonts)** Configures the card to display 1024x768 with 256 colors, but installs larger screen fonts, which makes the text more readable on a small display

Danger Zone

If your display adapter does not support whatever XGA configuration you select in Setup (for example, you don't have enough memory on your card), Windows will not load properly, and you'll be returned to the DOS prompt next time you attempt to start a Windows session. If this happens, run Setup from DOS and reselect the 640x480, 16-color XGA driver.

If you're using an XGA display system, you'll need to watch for potential incompatibilities with the EMM386 expanded memory manager, because it competes for the same upper memory area. You'll need to manually exclude the area of upper memory used by the XGA card.

To identify the range in upper memory used by your XGA adapter, you should run the System Configuration Program on your PS/2 reference disk (or another diagnostic utility) to select the Display Memory Map option. The most common address range is C600 through C7FF. To prevent EMM386 from using this address range, use the X= switch on the DEVICE= line that installs EMM386 in your CONFIG.SYS file (as described in the Chapter 13). For example, the statement line:

```
DEVICE=EMM386.EXE X=C600-C7FF
```

would exclude the upper memory area C600 through C7FF.

Furthermore, you can't use the memory area B000-BE00 for EMM386 because the XGA adapter uses this area when Windows is running in 386 enhanced mode. If you have a PS/2 Model 75 portable with the plasma screen or you are using your XGA adapter in 640x480, 16-color mode, you must also include either the NOEMS switch or the RAM switch when installing EMM386 (see Chapter 13).

Display Drivers

Using the correct and most recent display driver available is one of the most important aspects of configuring your Windows system, because it opens up a vast world of hardware possibilities. Unlike DOS, Windows doesn't require applications to directly address each different type of adapter.

Instead, all programs address a Windows graphics kernel, called the **GDI (Graphics Device Interface)**, which remains the same regardless of what physical adapter card is actually installed. To make its adapter compatible with Windows, the manufacturer must provide a device driver that translates GDI instructions to the physical specification of the particular adapter card. Thus, the field of future video products is wide open—as long as you have a Windows display driver, you'll be able to use any future type of display.

Changing Display Drivers

With its generous list of supplied display drivers, Windows can work with most of the existing display products on the market. For example, the SuperVGA driver new to Windows 3.1 supports 800x600, 16-color resolution on most SuperVGA cards, such as those produced by ATI, Cirrus Logic, Everex, Genoa, Orchid, Paradise, STB, Trident, and other cards compatible with the Super VGA standard set by VESA (Video Electronics Standards Association). Table 8.3 lists the display drivers included with Windows 3.1.

Danger Zone

The 800x600 SuperVGA driver supplied with Windows adheres to the VESA standard. Many SuperVGA cards work with this standard, and therefore work with the driver supplied with Windows. For those few cards that don't incorporate this standard, you'll need to obtain a special driver from the manufacturer to use them with Windows at 800x600 resolution.

• • • • • • • • • • • • •
TABLE 8.3

Display Driver	Supported Display
8514.DRV	8514/a
CPQAVGA.DRV	Compaq Advanced VGA
EGA.DRV	EGA
EGAHIBW.DRV	EGA with 128K RAM
EGAMONO.DRV	EGA monochrome
HERCULES.DRV	Hercules monochrome
OLIBW.DRV	Olivetti / AT&T monochrome or PVC display
PLASMA.DRV	Compaq Portable plasma
SUPERVGA.DRV	Super VGA (800x600—16 colors)
TIGA.DRV	TIGA
VGA.DRV	VGA
VGAMONO.DRV	VGA monochrome, MCGA
V7VGA.DRV	Video Seven VGA with minimum of 512K (FastWrite, VRAM, 1024i, and compatibles)
XGA.DRV	XGA

When you select a display to install, Setup searches the SETUP.INF file to identify what driver, fonts, and other tweaks (such as special lines added to SYSTEM.INI) are necessary to complete the configuration. To change a display configuration,

1. Run the Windows Setup.

2. Choose Change System Settings from the Setup Options menu (Alt,O,C). The Change System Settings dialog box shown in Figure 8.3 appears.

3. To change to one of these display drivers, click on Display to drop down the list. Use the scroll arrow to move down the list, and click on the name of the display driver that most closely matches your adapter.

4. Click OK to change the display driver setting.

If the driver you select is not yet installed on your system, Windows asks you to insert one of the Windows installation disks. Windows then reads the device driver from the disk, and the new display driver will be recognized when you restart your system.

If your monitor and display adapter type aren't listed in the Display drop-down list box, select the last choice in that list box, "Other display (Requires disk from OEM)"; Windows Setup will instruct you to insert the

• • • • • • • • • • • • •

FIGURE 8.3

*Change
System
Settings
Dialog Box*

Select your display type from the drop-down list of supported displays, or choose "Other display (Requires disk from OEM)" to install a third-party display driver.

disk provided by the driver manufacturer into drive A. Or (if the driver is stored elsewhere), use the backspace key to delete the A:\. Then type in the path for the new display driver's program. Once you've inserted the driver disk into Drive A, or adjusted the path if necessary, Windows Setup reads the necessary driver files and copies them onto your hard disk.

If your video adapter isn't supported by the drivers included on the Windows installation disks, contact the manufacturer to get an updated driver, if it's available. Most manufacturers of display adapters now provide Windows drivers. Such a driver may let you access special features of the board, such as support for higher resolutions or more colors.

Some display adapter boards, such as the TIGA cards discussed earlier, require special installation procedures, because they load custom device drivers into DOS. To determine this, be sure to consult the instructions for your adapter board.

• •

Updating Your Drivers

To prevent most hardware compatibility difficulties, select display systems that are specifically designed to work with Windows. If a driver is needed for the display adapter card you want to use, be sure the card comes with a fully optimized Windows device driver.

Display technology is constantly being improved to keep pace with the new Windows environment. Keep abreast of technical changes in these ways:

➥ Contact the appropriate manufacturer and upgrade your hardware.

➥ Visit and join your local Windows or PC user group.

➥ Read platform-specific computer publications.

➠ Hook up to online information services and explore their special Windows forums. (See Appendix C for a list of Windows-related publications, user groups, and product information telephone numbers.)

Dynamite Product

In some cases, you'll discover third-party hardware drivers, such as video drivers, that can dramatically improve the capabilities of your existing drivers. Most hardware manufacturers lack the technical expertise to create a truly optimized video driver. Panacea, which has made a specialty of fine-tuning Windows video drivers, has developed the WinSpeed video drivers to boost performance.

Driver problems may emerge when Setup initially attempts to identify your system's hardware configuration and peripherals and then suggests which device drivers should be used after installation. Because the Windows Setup program cannot identify each vendor's specific product model—there are thousands on the market—it employs a generic description of the product. Thus there is much opportunity for underutilization or misuse of drivers.

For example, suppose Windows Setup identifies normal VGA as your adapter type, instead of detecting the specific SuperVGA card manufacturer. The default driver that Setup selects will not let you take advantage of the additional resolution or colors available on your card. Your 256-color Super-VGA card is thus reduced to 16 colors!

Another problem can occur if you haven't updated your display driver for Windows 3 or 3.1; you'll be missing out on whatever improvements the manufacturer of your display might have made in the interim. You should check with the manufacturer of each of your hardware components to see if you have the most recent hardware driver.

You should also be alert to another potential problem: when you upgrade to 3.1 from 3.0, Setup will not update third-party display drivers or even some Microsoft drivers that it does not recognize. For example, if you were using a TIGA, XGA, SuperVGA, or third-party VGA driver, Setup may not upgrade you to the new Windows 3.1 drivers. If any of your driver files are dated prior to 3/10/92, you'll need to upgrade them.

Finally, if your standard VGA display worked properly with Windows 3.0, but you experience problems when running DOS applications from within Windows 3.1, you may need to run Setup and select the "VGA (Version 3.0)" entry, which provides better compatibility with older VGA display adapter cards.

Danger Zone

Windows 3.1 requires that your third-party device drivers must provide their own setup files, which must be named OEMSETUP.INF. If your display driver disk still relies on replacing the SETUP.INF (as was the case with Windows 3.0), you'll need to manually rename the third-party SETUP.INF file to OEMSETUP.INF and place it in the directory with the third-party driver files. If a third-party installation program overwrites your original SETUP.INF file (located in the \SYSTEM subdirectory of your main Windows directory), you can transfer a fresh copy from installation disk 1.

Also, don't follow the directions supplied with some third-party drivers (usually those that shipped prior to the introduction of Windows 3.1) to overwrite the SETUP.INF file in the \SYSTEM subdirectory. After renaming your driver to OEMSETUP.INF, you should not copy it or the OEM drivers directly to the \SYSTEM subdirectory, because Setup may be unable to recognize them. Instead, place the OEMSETUP.INF file and the driver files in some other directory or on a floppy disk.

Once Setup has recognized your third-party drivers and OEMSETUP.INF file, Setup copies the OEMSETUP.INF file to the \WINDOWS\SYSTEM directory and renames it OEM0.INF. (If you install additional third-party drivers, the next OEMSETUP.INF file is renamed OEM1.INF, then OEM2.INF, and so on.)

After the initial upgrade installation, you can use Setup to switch back and forth between video modes by telling it to look for drivers in the \SYSTEM subdirectory. You will probably get a message displaying the date of the driver currently in the directory and asking whether you want to replace it.

Insider's Tip

Be on the lookout for files with .DLL, .FON, and .DRV extensions dated earlier than 3/10/92—this is your tip-off that these files were probably created for Windows 3.0 and may cause problems with version 3.1. If you were using a third-party display driver with 3.0, Setup may not have replaced it when you installed Windows 3.1. The best way to avoid this hassle is to select standard VGA when you install 3.1, and rerun Setup after the installation is completed.

Video Grabber Files

When you run DOS applications from within Windows, two special system software components—**WinOldAp** and the **grabber**—translate the DOS display into a graphics format that Windows can display. WinOldAp comes in two versions:

➡ **WINOA286.MOD** Used when running standard mode

➡ **WINOA386.MOD** Used when running 386 enhanced mode

The WinOldAp file works in conjunction with one of several grabbers. Windows provides different grabber files, specific to whatever display driver you are using and the mode in which you are running Windows. In standard mode, you can only run DOS applications full screen; the 286 grabbers, in turn, only support the PrintScreen function and the copying and pasting of a full screen of text between Windows and DOS applications.

In 386 enhanced mode, because you can run DOS applications in a window—enabling the DOS applications to be run inside virtual DOS machines—the display of the DOS machines is handled by a special virtual display device. The 386 grabbers offer added capabilities, such as the ability to cut and paste portions of a screen, including graphics.

Windows provides the virtual display devices and grabbers listed in Table 8.4, which are mixed and matched to provide support for the various types of displays.

TABLE 8.4

Virtual Display Device Drivers and Associated Grabbers for Standard PC Displays

Display	Virtual Display Device	286 Grabber	386 Grabber
8514/a	VDD8514.386	VGACOLOR.2GR	VGADIB.3GR
CGA	VDDCGA.386	CGA.2R	
Compaq Portable plasma	VDDCGA.386	CGA.2GR	PLASMA.3GR
Compaq Advanced VGA	VDDAVGA.386	CPQAVGA.2GR	
EGA	VDDEGA.386	EGACOLOR.2GR	EGA.3GR
EGA monochrome	VDDEGA.386	EGAMONO.2GR	
Hercules monochrome	VDDHERC.386	HERCULES.2GR	HERC.3GR
Olivetti/AT&T mono-chrome or PVC	VDDCGA.386	OLIGRAB.2GR	PLASMA.3GR
QuadVGA, ATI VIP VGA, 82C441 VGAs	VDDCT441.386	VGACOLOR.2GR	VGA30.3GR
SuperVGA (800x600 - 16 colors)	*VDDVGA	VGACOLOR.2GR	VGA.3GR
TIGA	VDDTIGA.386	VGACOLOR.2GR	VGADIB.3GR
VGA	*VDDVGA	VGACOLOR.2GR	VGA.3GR
VGA (Windows 3.0 version)	VDDVGA30.386	VGACOLOR.2GR	VGA30.3GR
VGA monochrome	*VDDVGA	VGAMONO.2GR	VGADIB.3GR
Video Seven VGA with minimum of 512K	V7VDD.386	VGACOLOR.2GR	V7VGA.3GR
XGA	VDDXGA.386	VGACOLOR.2GR	V7VGA.3GR

In addition, in 386 enhanced mode, your grabber file needs special Windows screen font files containing the character sets that enable the grabber to simulate DOS screen fonts. Table 8.5 shows which font files and grabbers can work together.

TABLE 8.5
Grabber Files and Associated DOS Screen Fonts

Grabber	Standard Characters	International Characters
EGA.3GR, TIGA.3GR,	CGA40WOA.FON	CGA40850.FON
VGA.3GR, VGA30.3GR,	CGA80WOA.FON	CGA80850.FON
VGADIB.3GR, V7VGA.3GR	EGA40WOA.FON	EGA40850.FON
	EGA80WOA.FON	EGA80850.FON
HERC.3GR	HERCWOA.FON	HERC850.FON
PLASMA.3GR	EGA40WOA.FON	EGA40850.FON
	EGA80WOA.FON	EGA80850.FON

The Display Drivers in SYSTEM.INI

A number of different statements in your SYSTEM.INI file affect your display. The display driver and grabber files are listed in the [boot] section, which is usually the first section of the SYSTEM.INI file. The following three lines demonstrate how these items are identified for a standard VGA display:

```
display.drv=vga.drv
386grabber=vga.3gr
286grabber=vgacolor.2gr
```

The [386Enh] section of SYSTEM.INI identifies the virtual display driver used in 386 enhanced mode and the special font files that the 386 grabber uses to simulate DOS screen fonts. The following statement lines are examples of the items that would be in effect for a standard VGA display:

```
display=*vddvga
EGA80WOA.FON=EGA80WOA.FON
EGA40WOA.FON=EGA40WOA.FON
CGA80WOA.FON=CGA80WOA.FON
CGA40WOA.FON=CGA40WOA.FON
```

The first line specifies ***vddvga**, the standard VGA virtual device driver; the asterisk (*) signifies that this driver is incorporated in the WIN386.EXE file, so you don't need a separate file.

If your video card manufacturer doesn't offer 3.1 drivers yet, or if you're still waiting for them to be sent to you, you may be able to use your old 3.0 drivers in conjunction with Windows' VGA30.3GR file. To do so, run Setup and install the 3.0 drivers. Then check the listing in SYSTEM.INI after installation. Look for the line

```
386grabber=VGA.GR3
```

This is the standard 3.1 grabber. You should change it to read

```
386grabber=VGA30.3GR
```

This tells Windows to use a special 3.1 grabber, which is compatible with older 3.0 video drivers. If the file hasn't already been copied into your \SYSTEM subdirectory, you'll need to copy the VGA30.3GR file from the installation disks using the EXPAND.EXE utility described in Chapter 5.

Other drivers may also add their own sections to the file. The following lines demonstrate what the SuperVGA driver adds to identify its mode of operation:

```
[display]
svgamode=41
```

A number of SuperVGA adapter cards work with higher monitor-refresh rates when run in 800x600 resolution. The higher refresh rate is desirable because it reduces the amount of flicker on your screen. If both your Super-VGA card and video monitor can operate at a higher refresh rate, you can add the line

```
svgamode=106
```

to the Display section of your SYSTEM.INI file. Note that this special mode works only with the SuperVGA driver included with Windows 3.1 and third-party drivers that specifically support this mode. On some systems, the addition of this statement line can cause problems, so you should delete this setting from SYSTEM.INI or revert it to its prior setting value.

The Video 7 driver can also add a section and statement similar to the following one to identify its modus operandi:

```
[v7vga.drv]
WidthXHeight=640x480
FontSize=small
```

For details about how to edit and interpret the information in your SYSTEM.INI file, refer to Chapter 15.

• •

Using Two Displays with Windows

Dynamite Product

Innovative hardware developers are beginning to design special video cards for Windows that allow you to use more than one monitor simultaneously. One example is the Dual VGA Plus adapter card from ColorGraphics Communications Corp., which allows you to connect two monitors to a special SuperVGA card. Each monitor can display 800x600 resolution, providing a combined screen area of 1600x600. The two monitors can be mapped to a unified display area so that a window can simply be dragged from one monitor to another.

Another method of using two displays is to connect a second monochrome display adapter—either an MDA or a Hercules card—and compatible monitor, in addition to a standard VGA card. This technique is only for the technically astute, and doesn't provide as polished a solution as the Dual VGA Plus adapter, mentioned above. Also, this technique works only if you install your VGA card as an 8-bit rather than as a 16-bit card. Some VGA cards require that you flip some DIP switches, change jumpers, or even place them in an 8-bit slot in order to provide 8-bit operation.

Because both the MDA and Hercules standards are now outdated, you should probably be able to pick up an MDA adapter and monitor at a swap meet or used-computer exchange for a song. An MDA display works with a VGA display because the two systems normally do not use the same memory areas, as would two regular VGA cards. Whereas the VGA display can be used for displaying Windows, the MDA display will be available only to DOS applications that support the use of such a display.

If you decide to use this method, you'll need to add this line to the [386Enh] section of your SYSTEM.INI file:

```
DualDisplay=TRUE
```

This forces Windows to reserve the MDA memory area for use by your second display adapter. If you open a DOS window in a small window on the VGA screen, you can transfer it to a full-sized display on the monochrome monitor by typing **MODE MONO**. This allows you to view simultaneously both the Windows display on the VGA monitor and the DOS application on the monochrome monitor. The small-screen representation of the DOS application remains on the VGA monitor; to switch back and forth between it and Windows, simply click the mouse in the small-screen window on the VGA display.

If you use a Hercules card, you may also be able to run DOS applications that support Hercules monochrome graphics on the second monitor.

Display Ergonomics

Two factors affect how easy your monitor is to use and how safe it is: the quality of the video monitor itself and the way you set it up. When selecting a monitor, go for a **noninterlaced display**, if at all possible. Note that some display cards that are noninterlaced at lower resolutions, such as 640x480, switch into an interlaced mode when used in the higher resolutions, such as 1024x768. Check the specifications and documentation of your adapter card to determine if this is the case.

Also pay attention to the scanning rates. Your monitor should work together with your display adapter at a **high scanning rate** to minimize flicker. Because Windows displays text as graphics, the quality of your display system affects both text and graphics applications. A good-quality display minimizes flicker and distortion, which can lead to eyestrain and headaches.

When buying a monitor, you should also consider its **dot-pitch** — the size of the spots on the monitor that are used to create the pixels. Generally, the smaller the dot pitch, the clearer and sharper the images on the display. I recommend avoiding monitors with a dot pitch that exceeds .31mm.

Insider's Tip

If you're stuck with an interlaced display or a display with a low refresh rate, you can do several things to minimize the flicker. First, keep away from fluorescent lighting. Fluorescent lights emit a flicker of their own that can exaggerate the monitor's flicker. If your office is lit largely by fluorescent lights, get an incandescent desk lamp; the light from this lamp will over-whelm the fluorescent light.

Sometimes your adapter and monitor can be reconfigured to work with a higher refresh rate or a noninterlaced mode, so check your manual. Another trick is to select a color scheme in the Control Panel that uses all solid colors, rather than dithered colors or patterns. The solid colors appear more stable on the display.

The configuration of your display also affects the ergonomics and safety of your system. The most troublesome problem is glare, so set up your monitor to avoid incoming light from a window or artificial light source. If you can't reposition your monitor, the so-called antiglare accessories that fit over your monitor screen can be helpful, but quality varies widely, so test the screen first to be sure that it allows a clear view of the monitor.

Some monitors are treated to minimize glare; one method etches a tiny grid into the monitor's surface, which gives it the appearance of frosted glass. I personally dislike this technique because it seems to reduce the overall sharpness of images on your screen. A better glare-reduction method treats the screen with a special coating called **OCLI**. This coating is usually available only on higher-priced monitors.

Insider's Tip

You should place your monitor slightly below eye level, but not too far down. Your eyes should naturally rest on the monitor's surface, so that you don't need to crane your neck up or down. Many computer desks are designed so that the monitor is high enough only when placed on top of your system unit. If you have a tower-shaped case, or if you prefer not to place your system unit underneath your monitor, you may need a monitor stand to boost the height of your monitor. (I use old phone books.) A swivel-base is a good accessory for a monitor because it allows you to fine-tune the viewing angle. However, don't use it as a substitute for placing the monitor at the proper height.

The most controversial ergonomic issue related to display systems concerns **VDT emissions**. Video monitors and television sets produce a certain amount of energy emissions, ranging from electromagnetic radiation to high-pitched audio waves. The scientific jury is still out as to whether these emissions pose significant health hazards, but emotions run high on this issue. Some people feel that these emissions are dangerous because they can potentially cause cancer and birth defects; others say that less radiation is emitted than one would expect from a bedside electric alarm clock.

Some of the better-quality monitors from big companies such as NEC and Sony offer low-emission versions, which contain more shielding inside the monitor case. This increased shielding is usually associated with a higher price tag, though.

Personally, I think the danger from these monitors is minimal, especially in monitors of recent manufacture. The only ones that I consider to be potentially dangerous are monitors produced in the early 1980s and some of the large-screen color monitors built before 1986. Significant public awareness of the potential health threat of VDT emissions and the potential onslaught of product liability lawsuits has prompted most monitor manufacturers to provide increased shielding on all their monitors. And cathode-ray tube video monitors will soon be replaced with entirely different screen materials, such as color LCD, which does not produce these emissions.

. . . .

Windows Graphics Accelerators

One of the hottest topics in the world of Windows is **graphics acceleration**. Because Windows is a graphical user interface, much of your system's performance depends on its ability to execute Windows graphics instructions.

The Windows graphics kernel, called the GDI (Graphics Device Interface), is responsible for drawing all the images on your screen, both text and graphics, while you're running Windows. A standard VGA card has no inherent intelligence of its own—it merely serves as a frame buffer for your video display. This means that your computer's CPU chip must perform all the GDI instructions; that is, the chip must render graphics to send to the VGA card, which in turn stores the information in its buffer before sending it to the display. The higher the resolution of your display and the more colors in the image, the greater the workload on your CPU.

Insider's Tip

That's why a graphics accelerator can sometimes boost your performance more than an upgrade in processor speed. However, boosting your processor speed does contribute to graphics performance, and graphics accelerators often perform best when used with a high-speed CPU.

If you decide to add a graphics accelerator here are some of your choices:

➥ **Faster drivers** Products such as WinSpeed from Panacea offer the lowest-cost solution—speed is boosted by using a new driver with the VGA card you already own. WinSpeed and similar products provide fine-tuned Windows drivers that support popular display cards. Although these don't help to offload graphics functions from the CPU, they can still provide noticeably improved graphics performance.

➥ **Accelerated graphics cards** A more modern breed of VGA card, these cards include additional circuitry that performs some of the most common graphics operations used in Windows, thereby offloading these tasks from the CPU chip to improve overall system performance. Examples include boards that use the 86C911 and 928 chips from S3, the Mach 8 chip from ATI, and the W5086 chip from Weitek.

➥ **Coprocessor cards** These cards contain a programmable, onboard processor chip that offloads many of the graphics operations normally performed by the CPU chip. Coprocessor cards are typified by the 8514/a, TIGA, and XGA standards discussed earlier.

➥ **Bus-cycle acceleration** These cards decrease the number of bus cycles that the CPU must complete in order to perform graphics operations. The Chips & Technologies 82C453 chip uses this approach.

»+ **Bus mastering cards** Available only for systems with an EISA or MCA bus, bus mastering video cards take advantage of the advanced bus capabilities these systems provide.

»+ **Local bus video** This strategy integrates the display adapter into the local bus of the CPU chip, which bypasses the normal expansion bus to achieve the highest possible data transfer speeds.

Some video cards with substantially the same hardware design provide varying levels of performance, depending on the quality of the driver supplied with the card. This applies to standard cards, accelerated cards, and coprocessor cards. Windows video drivers can be difficult to write; hence developers seem to be continuously tweaking and fine-tuning their drivers. Be sure to contact the manufacturer of your video card to get the latest Windows 3.1-compatible driver.

Insider's Tip

If your display card is a plain vanilla, unaccelerated VGA card, you can give it a performance boost by switching to the WinSpeed video drivers from Panacea. WinSpeed works with the ATI, Paradise, Trident, Tseng, and Video 7/Headland VGA cards at resolutions of up to 1024x768. Note that the WinSpeed 1.0 installation program (INSTALL.EXE) does not work properly with Windows 3.1 and corrupts your SETUP.INF file. Contact Panacea for an updated installation program.

No matter how good your Windows video driver is, it can only perform as well as the hardware on your adapter card. The accelerated graphics cards are a newer breed of VGA cards, which assume many of the graphics operations normally performed by the computer's CPU chip. This frees the CPU for performing other tasks and also speeds up the transfer of graphics information from your system to your display adapter card. Rather than transferring the entire image to the card, you only need to send the graphics instructions. This type of video accelerator is typified by the Diamond Stealth VRAM card.

The ATI Graphics Ultra and Portacom Eclipse II cards are fixed-function cards that assume specific graphics functions, such as line drawing and bitblt (bit-block transfers). These fixed-function cards use special chips, such as the S3 chips, Weitek chips, and ATI chips. The S3 chips are by far the most common and also offers the best overall performance. Although these fixed-function chips are not programmable, they take over the toughest graphics processing tasks and are fairly inexpensive, compared with fully programmable coprocessors.

Another relatively low-cost acceleration technique adds a special chip to your card; this can halve the number of bus cycles the CPU needs to perform for each graphics operation. This tactic is employed by Chips & Technologies in its 82C453 chip, which is included in the Artist Graphics WinSprint 100 adapter, for example.

Graphics coprocessor cards, such as TIGA, XGA, and 8514/a cards, feature programmable chips that can execute most of the graphics operations used in Windows. These take a greater load off the CPU chip than do fixed-function cards, but you pay a price—several cost more than $1000. These coprocessor-style cards often offer advanced features, such as the ability to work with video signals, because they essentially provide a graphics computer on a card.

Danger Zone

Although accelerator coprocessor chips on your display adapter card can speed up system performance significantly, they are still limited by the bottlenecks imposed by the computer's expansion bus. The ISA bus presents the worst barrier; upgrading to an EISA or MCA bus can improve the flow, but either bus still cuts into the performance capabilities of your display adapter.

The ultimate solution is to bypass the bus altogether and tap the CPU chip's **local bus**; this approach allows extremely high-speed transfer of information between your CPU chip and the display adapter. To implement this technique, however, you'll need to have the display adapter's circuitry built directly onto the computer's motherboard or into a special direct-access slot called a **local bus slot**. If you're a Windows speed demon, you should definitely consider local bus video.

Although this local bus strategy offers the best potential for speeding up your system's graphic capabilities, it also carries the highest price: you'll have to buy a new system. Also, be forewarned—many systems with display adapters built into the motherboard run at the same speeds as the system's expansion bus, because they don't use the local bus strategy. Therefore, buying a system with a display adapter built into the motherboard is no guarantee that you'll be achieving higher speeds and better performance. Get a system with a local bus slot instead.

Because local bus video is a fairly young technology, the industry standards for its implementation are still evolving. Currently, three approaches are available:

➻ A proprietary system developed by a manufacturer—watch out for these

➻ A VESA local bus standard called **VL-BUS**—I recommend this choice

➻ An Intel local bus standard

The VESA local bus has taken the early lead, but this standards battle is far from over.

What the Future Will Bring

Because custom device drivers can extend the breadth and power of Windows—independent of VGA or any other standard—Windows encourages the development of new graphics products for the IBM-compatible family of PCs. Advanced displays that can attain resolutions as high as 2048x2048 were previously unavailable to the majority of PC users. The advent of Windows changed this situation, because with the proper software driver, all Windows applications can now access this resolution. As a result, more graphics display systems are being introduced now than at any other time in the history of the PC.

New display systems include boards capable of displaying millions of colors and presenting realistic images of photographic quality on your screen. With Windows 3.1, PC owners can achieve the same level of video quality that Macintosh users have enjoyed for years. To underscore this point, leading Macintosh manufacturers, such as Radius and RasterOps, have introduced high-quality graphics boards for the PC family that far surpass the capabilities of VGA.

Another trend is the incorporation of television signals as part of the display system. The most common of these boards are called "video in a window" cards; they are popular for multimedia applications because they allow input from a video disk player or VCR to be displayed in a moveable window (see Chapter 11). Other vendors are experimenting with the addition of TV circuitry directly onto these cards; soon couch potatoes can turn into desk potatoes as they view their favorite television shows in a window on their computer screens.

Insider's Tip

As mentioned earlier, some hardware manufacturers are providing one or more local bus slots on the computer's motherboard to directly access the processor's bus and increase video speed. Although local bus is primarily used for video, high performance disk controllers and network adapters are also being developed for local bus slots.

As for monitors, it seems to me that video monitors will ultimately be replaced by flat-screen color monitors, such as the active-matrix LCD displays now appearing on high-end laptops. These color, flat-panel displays provide exceptionally sharp images and virtually no flicker, because they are based on liquid crystal rather than on the cathode-ray tube technology found in standard video monitors. LCD monitors produce a better-quality display; they are also lighter and easier to set up, and eliminate the potential risk of VDT emissions.

Mice and Other Pointing Devices

Pointing devices can include many different types of handheld objects, from the well-known mice to trackballs, graphics tablets, pens, touch screens, and joysticks. About half of all PCs are connected to a mouse or other pointing device; a few years ago, fewer than 10 percent were pointer driven. Windows has increased the demand for mice, and Microsoft itself has benefitted in mouse sales, having sold almost 10 of the more than 30 million on the market. Logitech leads in mouse sales, having racked up sales of 15 million units.

Of all the pointing devices, the mouse is the most commonly used. For some applications, especially graphic arts and CAD, the graphics tablet and stylus provide a natural way to work with Windows. In Windows for Pen Computing—a set of extensions to Windows 3.1—a pen-shaped stylus is used as the main input device and operating instrument.

Pointing Device Ergonomics

Your choice of a mouse or other pointing device should be based on ergonomic concerns as well as on the functionality and features of the hardware itself. Your first decision will be whether to use a mouse or another pointing device. Personally, after years of hands-on experience, I find the mouse the easiest to operate, with trackballs placing second. Pens, like their real counterparts, can cause writer's cramp; if you choose a pen, the thicker the stylus, the easier it is to hold for long periods.

Light pens and touch screens are intended for special-purpose applications, such as information kiosks and other dedicated systems. Although these pointers will work with Windows, I don't recommend them for the average user. Holding a light pen to your screen for long periods of time can tire your arm. Touch screens require the use of your finger, which also is tiring, and these screens smudge easily.

Insider's Tip

If you do settle on a mouse, try handling several different types to determine what fits in your hand most comfortably. When you grab a well-designed mouse, your hand rests on the mouse in a relaxed position, with your thumb and pinky grasping the sides to control its movement, leaving your three middle fingers free for pushing the buttons directly under them. Everybody's hands are proportioned differently, so you may find one brand of mouse easier to operate. The mouse button should be easy to press without having to arch your finger, because this can cause it to cramp after repeated clicking. If your finger tires from clicking too much, try learning some of the keyboard equivalents for mouse commands given in this book.

The placement of your mouse is also important. You shouldn't have to reach too far forward for the mouse, because this can strain your shoulder. The mouse should be level with the height of your elbow or slightly lower; reaching up for it can tire your arm. If your finger or wrist tires from using the mouse, switch it to your other hand and select the Swap Left/Right Buttons feature of the Control Panel to readjust the mouse buttons.

If your wrist tires, you may want to invest in some type of wrist cushioning product, which helps prevent carpal tunnel syndrome as well. Two of these products are the WristPad, a rectangular bar of foam covered with a soft fabric that elevates your wrist to the height of the mouse, and the WristSaver Mousepad, which integrates wrist support with a mousepad, but is slightly less comfortable.

Mice, Trackballs, and Graphics Tablets

This most common pointer was invented more than 20 years ago by Doug Englebart, a researcher at Tymenet. Englebart's first mouse was made of wood, supported by wheels, and topped by a tiny red button. The mouse didn't roar, however, until 1984, when Apple introduced the mouse-operated Macintosh and focused both industry and user attention on the benefits of this little device.

What makes a mouse? Whatever the variations, all mice are held in the hand and are moved to control the corresponding movements of a pointer on the computer screen. Most, but not all, have either two or three buttons. And they usually have tails—a cord connecting them to the computer— although cordless mice are roaming on more desktops than ever.

Although mice differ widely in physical design, they all contain an internal tracking mechanism to transmit their movements to the computer. All mice track movement by recording horizontal and vertical motions, and do so by using a mechanical, optomechanical, or optical mechanism.

Mechanical mice, such as the ones from Microsoft, contain a rolling ball that tracks the mouse motions. The ball turns two rollers that are positioned at right angles to each other. One roller records vertical motion; the other tracks horizontal motion; and both drive mechanical encoders that send the horizontal and vertical signals to the computer. The mouse driver software translates those signals into X and Y coordinates, and then applies those coordinates to control the pointer movement on your screen.

Optomechanical mice, such as those built by Logitech (and Apple as well), contain the same type of ball as do mechanical mice, but the rollers are connected to optical encoders, which use light to send signals to the computer and subsequently to the pointer on the screen. According to Logitech, the optomechanical design is more durable than the strictly mechanical one and offers a lifespan of 300 miles of mouse movement, as opposed to the 50 to 100 miles of movement provided by the Microsoft mouse.

Optical mice operate only with a special marked mouse pad. Coated with a reflective surface, this pad is printed with a lined grid. As you move the mouse over the special pad, photosensors inside the mouse decode the reflections of the grid into horizontal and vertical movements. The Mouse System's PC Mouse is an example of this species. Because optical mice don't contain moving parts, they are reputed to be more reliable and accurate; on the other hand, if you lose the special mouse pad, you're incapacitated!

Insider's Tip

Before you buy a mechanical or optomechanical mouse, make sure the ball is easy to remove. Because these devices gather dust, you'll eventually need to do a little mousecleaning. To clean your mouse, turn it on its back and twist or push down the ring surrounding the mouse ball. (The bottom of the mouse often contains iconic instructions for how to remove the ring.) The ring will come off, allowing you to remove the ball. If the ball itself is dirty, clean it with mild soap and water; make sure you dry it thoroughly.

Now look inside the ball's cavity and inspect the roller that comes in contact with the ball. If these rollers are encrusted with crud—as often happens after the mouse has been used for a while—clean them off carefully with a cotton swab dipped in isopropyl alcohol. Never use water to clean the innards of your mouse! Once the rollers are clean, replace the ball and then line up the tabs on the ring so the ring inserts easily. Finally, twist or push the ring back into place.

Resolution of the Mouse

The sensitivity of the mouse tracking mechanism determines the quality of its resolution. Resolution depends on the level of movement your mouse mechanism can detect and transmit to the computer; it's measured in **points per inch** (ppi). If the resolution of a particular mouse is rated at 200 ppi, for example, its tracking mechanism can detect movements as small as 1/200th of an inch. This is usually the resolution ratio for your bargain-basement variety of mouse. Microsoft's and Logitech's offerings claim resolutions of 400 ppi.

In general, the greater the points per inch of mouse resolution, the more control you'll have over the behavior of your mouse. If you're planning to do much detailed work, such as drawing, the higher resolution mouse will provide the ability to draw fine details that might be difficult with a low-resolution mouse.

Danger Zone

Beware of bargain-basement mice with inflated resolution claims. Some mail-order ads boast inexpensive mice with resolutions as high as 2500 ppi. The resolution of these mice is really much lower—the higher resolution is actually provided by software, not the mouse. When resolutions are listed as a range, such as from 200 to 1000, or, in general, if they exceed 400 ppi, be suspicious.

In most early mice, there was a direct one-to-one ratio between the resolution in ppi of mouse movements to the pixels on the screen. If your mouse device driver uses such a ratio, each time you move your mouse an inch, the pointer moves 200 pixels on the screen.

Contemporary mouse drivers, such as the one Microsoft includes with Windows, offer a range of options for determining resolution. By selecting an option from a variable setting driver, you can change the ratio of ppi to pixels from the regular one-to-one standard in order to either increase or decrease your mouse's **tracking speed** on the screen. Beginning mouse users usually prefer the slower tracking speeds, because the mouse is less sensitive to unpracticed movements. Experienced users usually prefer the higher tracking speeds, because they don't have to move the mouse as much to accomplish most tasks.

To alter the tracking speed, adjust the Tracking Speed option in the Mouse dialog box of the Windows Control Panel utility (Figure 8.4.).

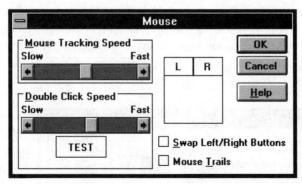

The Mouse Tracking Speed option in the Control Panel's Mouse dialog box lets you adjust the ratio of mouse movement (ppi) to onscreen pointer movement (pixels).

Why would you want to alter the one-to-one ppi-to-pixel ratio? Let's say you've barely got any desk space for moving your mouse around. To reduce the amount of space you need, just increase the tracking speed. Speeding up the tracking mechanism lets you move the mouse only a little in order to cover large distances on the screen, for such actions as menu selection and dialog box navigation. Slowing down the tracking speed gives you more precise control over your mouse, for performing fine detail work.

Some mouse drivers also provide **ballistic tracking** (or ballistic gain). With this speed-sensitive feature, the faster you move the mouse, the farther the cursor travels on the screen. With a ballistic mouse, for example, you can direct the screen pointer as quickly as you can move your mouse. Some users find such fast tracking an impediment; they prefer an undistorted, direct correlation between mouse and pointer movements.

Buttons

Windows recognizes only two mouse buttons, although many mice include a third button. One button is considered the primary button; you use this button for your main clicking, double-clicking, and dragging actions. Windows itself does not make direct use of the secondary button; the action of this button depends on whatever application has implemented it. In Microsoft Word, for example, you can use the second button to make text selections not available with the main button.

Utility programs, such as the Power Mouse utility included with Power Launcher (described in Chapter 6), let you assign special commands to the second and third mouse buttons. For example, assigning your second button the function of the Enter key lets you quickly click OK in a dialog box; assigning the third button as the Alt key lets you easily Alt+ click on a Program Manager icon to view its properties.

The Windows Control Panel lets you choose your primary button; the left button is the Windows default. If you're left-handed, it's easy to change the default by adjusting the Swap Left/Right Buttons setting in the Control Panel's Mouse dialog box. When you click on this option, the Left and Right buttons in the schematic diagram of the mouse (just above the option button) switch (Figure 8.5).

FIGURE 8.5

Swap Left/Right Buttons Checked in Mouse Dialog Box

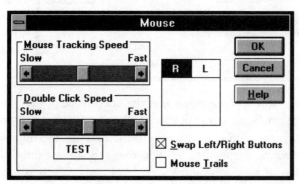

The Swap Left/Right Buttons setting in the Mouse dialog box changes the button labels in the schematic diagram of the mouse.

Another option in this box allows you to change the interval between the two clicks in the double-click command. If you're a slow clicker, your computer might interpret a double-click as two separate clicks. You can use the sliding elevator bar and the Test box in the Double Click Speed section of this dialog box to change the double-click speed. Just slide the elevator box toward Slow or Fast; then click on the Test box to readjust the interval after you try it out. The box turns black when a valid double-click is recognized by Windows.

Scurrying for mouse supremacy, some vendors have produced mice with three buttons, particularly in the Unix world, where three-button mice abound. Very few Windows programs support more than two buttons; however, some mice include drivers that allow you to assign the third button to act as a function key for a frequently issued keystroke sequence or macro.

If you're using a three-button mouse with a standard Windows mouse driver, you'll need to determine which buttons correspond to the two recognized by the standard driver. To do this, click a mouse button on the Mouse icon of the Control Panel. This highlights either the L or the R button in the schematic diagram of the mouse in the Mouse dialog box, so you can tell at a glance which buttons are being interpreted by Windows.

. . . .

Mouse Drivers

Mice—as with most hardware peripherals that are connected to a computer—require special device drivers that instruct the computer how to interpret incoming signals. Mice can contain a customized driver, or they can emulate a Microsoft, Mouse Systems, Logitech, or other standard driver.

Windows includes drivers for these mice:

Mouse	Mouse Driver	Virtual Mouse Driver
Genius serial mouse on COM1	MSCMOUSE.DRV	MSCVMD.386
Genius serial mouse on COM2	MSC3VC2.DRV	MSCVMD.386
HP Mouse (HP-HIL)	HPMOUSE.DRV	*VMD
Logitech mouse	LMOUSE.DRV	LVMD.386
Microsoft, or IBM PS/2	MOUSE.DRV	*VMD
Mouse Systems serial or bus mouse	MSCMOUSE.DRV	MSCVMD.386
Mouse Systems serial mouse on COM2	MSC3BC2.DRV	MSCVMD.386
No mouse or other pointing device	NOMOUSE.DRV	*VMD
Olivetti/AT&T Keyboard Mouse	KBDMOUSE.DRV	*VMD

If your mouse is on this list, or emulates one of these, you can use the appropriate driver right away. Otherwise, you'll need to insert a disk with the driver for your mouse, or you'll have to identify which type of mouse yours emulates. Note that the choice labeled "Mouse Systems serial mouse on COM2" applies only to three-buttoned mice. If you're using a Mouse System's two-button serial mouse on COM2, you should use the regular "Mouse Systems serial or bus mouse" choice.

If your mouse was already connected to the system when you installed Windows, the Windows Setup program (in text mode) will ask to confirm or change its guess (Figure 8.6).

· · · · · · · · · · · · · · ·
FIGURE 8.6

*Windows
Setup
Identifies
Your Mouse*

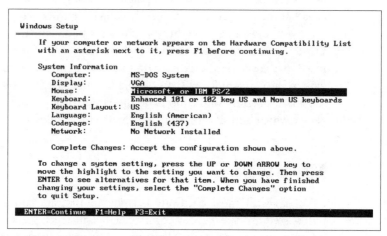

Windows Setup does its best to guess what mouse you are using.

If the selection is incorrect, scroll down the driver list to the correct choice and press Enter. Sometimes Setup incorrectly identifies a Logitech as "Microsoft, or IBM PS/2." In that case, you'll need to manually change the selection to Logitech. If your mouse isn't on the list, and the manufacturer supplied you with a Windows 3.1-compatible driver, select "other mouse (requires disk from OEM)." When prompted, insert the disk with the mouse driver into the drive of your choice (the default is the root directory of drive A). After reading in the driver, Setup continues with the installation process.

Suppose you want to add or change to another type of pointing device after you've already installed Windows? You can do this using Setup from within Windows. If your mouse isn't on the list, get the driver disk ready. Then, following the instructions outlined above, choose "Other mouse," insert the disk, and you're ready to use your mouse.

Insider's Tip

On some laptops with LCD displays (mostly passive, rather than active-matrix), the pointer can easily disappear if you move it more quickly than the LCD screen can update its graphics. To combat this problem, called submarining, the Control Panel's Mouse icon provides a special **Mouse Trails**

option that leaves a trail of pointer icons across the screen. This feature only works, however, if your machine contains a display driver supporting it, such as the EGA, VGA, and SuperVGA drivers included with Windows 3.1.

• •

DOS Mouse Drivers

New in 3.1

In addition to a Windows driver, most mice include DOS-compatible driver software. In Windows 3.1, you can now use your mouse in a DOS program that is running in a window in 386 enhanced mode. However, to take advantage of this feature, you'll need to load a Windows 3.1-compatible DOS driver before Windows is started. If you are not using any DOS programs, don't install the DOS driver—it will consume some of your conventional RAM.

DOS mouse drivers are supplied either as a TSR, identified by the .COM file extension, or as a device driver, identified by the .SYS file extension. The .COM files should be loaded using your AUTOEXEC.BAT file, and the .SYS drivers should be loaded using a DEVICE= statement in your CONFIG.SYS file.

Microsoft includes the following mouse drivers with Windows 3.1:

➥ **LMOUSE.COM** Logitech DOS mouse TSR

➥ **MOUSE.COM** Microsoft DOS mouse TSR

➥ **MOUSE.SYS** Microsoft DOS mouse driver

➥ **MOUSEHP.COM** Hewlett-Packard DOS mouse TSR

➥ **MOUSEHP.SYS** Hewlett-Packard DOS mouse driver

If Setup identifies a Microsoft or IBM PS/2 mouse, it usually copies either the MOUSE.COM or the MOUSE.SYS driver to your Windows directory and adds the appropriate statement line to either your AUTOEXEC.BAT or CONFIG.SYS file. Similarly, if Setup detects a Logitech mouse, it copies the LMOUSE.COM file to the Windows directory and install it in AUTOEXEC.BAT.

Danger Zone

Setup will not install the DOS mouse driver unless you are using a genuine Microsoft mouse or an IBM PS/2 or Logitech mouse that Setup can specifically identify as such. Also, the DOS mouse driver must already be installed in your AUTOEXEC.BAT or CONFIG.SYS file. If all of these conditions are not met, Setup will probably fail to install the DOS mouse driver for you. It's a good idea to inspect your AUTOEXEC.BAT and CONFIG.SYS files to check what mouse driver has been installed, if any.

If you need to install your DOS mouse driver manually, use the EXPAND.EXE utility to copy the mouse drivers from the Windows Setup disk. I recommend using the MOUSE.COM version of the driver, rather than the MOUSE.SYS driver, because it provides more features. However, MOUSE.COM can cause compatibility problems with some systems, so you may need to switch to the MOUSE.SYS driver. You should have only one mouse DOS driver loaded into your system, so if you change from one driver to another, be sure to delete the previous driver statement.

To install the MOUSE.COM driver in AUTOEXEC.BAT, add the following line to the file:

```
MOUSE.COM/Y
```

The /Y switch disables the use of a "sprite" cursor—a special hardware cursor available with some video adapter cards that can cause serious compatibility problems with Windows video drivers. This /Y switch also works with the MOUSE.SYS driver and should be included if you install this driver in your CONFIG.SYS file. For example, the line in CONFIG.SYS would read

```
DEVICE=MOUSE.SYS/Y
```

Insider's Tip

Earlier versions of the DOS mouse driver provided a /U switch that loaded the driver into the high memory area. The /U switch can cause compatibility problems with some systems, so this switch has been removed from the mouse drivers included with Windows 3.1. If you want to load your mouse driver into high memory, use the "loadhigh" feature of DOS 5 and later.

If you're using a third-party mouse driver, check with the manufacturer to see if the driver is compatible with Windows 3.1. If it isn't, you can still use your existing mouse DOS driver, but you'll probably be limited to using the mouse in DOS applications only when they are running in full-screen mode.

Danger Zone

I strongly recommend that you install the DOS mouse driver in one of your startup files rather than load it from within Windows. Remember, the DOS mouse driver must be loaded before Windows is run in order for you to use the mouse with DOS sessions that are running in a window. Although it's possible to load the MOUSE.COM driver from a DOS session running in Windows, this can lead to error messages—or it can crash your mouse driver.

- -

Connecting Your Mouse

Mice and other pointing devices are attached to your system in one of three ways, depending on the type of mouse:

➤ A **serial mouse** is connected to a COM port.

➤ A **bus mouse** is connected to an add-in card that plugs into a slot inside the system.

➤ A **Pointing Device Port (PDP) mouse** is connected to a special mouse port on your system unit.

The serial mouse-to-COM port connection is the most common arrangement. Serial mice are usually less expensive than bus mice because they don't require an add-in card. The disadvantage of the serial mouse is that it uses one of your COM ports. Some systems have only one COM port, which may already be used by a modem, printer, or other serial device; if that's the case, you'll have to get either a serial card with more COM ports or a bus mouse.

Also, because both mice and COM ports can be configured for either 9-pin or 25-pin connectors, you'll have to match your COM port with your mouse connector pins. Most serial mice include adapters that work with either 9- or 25-pin adapters. If yours doesn't, you'll need to get the appropriate serial port converter, available in most computer stores.

Danger Zone

If you're using a serial mouse, connect it to the COM1 port, if at all possible. This will prevent erratic behavior of the mouse and certain compatibility problems with communications software. Modems and other serial peripheral devices can be connected to COM2 and higher. If COM1 is not available for your mouse, you can connect it to COM2; the COM3 and COM4 ports do *not* support the use of serial mice with Windows.

The bus mouse does not require a COM port because it attaches directly to its own connector on a special add-in card. This add-in card takes up a slot inside your system. Even if you have an available slot, if you have other peripherals you may not have a free hardware interrupt request line (IRQ), which lets your system communicate with hardware devices. If you run out of serial ports, add-in slots, or IRQs, you may have to disconnect something in order to attach your mouse. You can use the Microsoft Diagnostics utility described in Chapter 17 to investigate the status of your system's IRQs.

The InPort mouse interface card comes with the Microsoft bus mouse and is the most common bus mouse in use. Other companies, such as MicroSpeed, also offer InPort interfaces designed for InPort-compatible devices. The InPort card is a small card with one chip. It contains three jumper blocks: one to configure the card for a normal slot or for the special Slot 8 found in XT-style systems; another to tell your system whether this is the primary or a secondary InPort card (you can attach a maximum of two); and a third to set the hardware interrupt used by the InPort card at either 2, 3, 4, or 5.

The Pointing Device Port (PDP) provides the best alternative: a built-in mouse connection. The PDP is built into the motherboard of IBM PS/2s, some Compaqs, and certain other systems. If you have a PDP, simply plug your mouse into it. It's usually located next to the keyboard connector on the back of the system unit. The PDP is gaining popularity among systems manufacturers; all PS/2s use it, and PDP input devices are manufactured by such companies as IBM, Microsoft, Mouse Systems, Logitech, Calcomp, Kensington, and MicroSpeed.

Some mice, such as the newer Logitech models, can be used with more than one of these connection methods. Check your documentation to see if an adapter is available that allows it to be used with a different connector.

. . . .

Mouse Ratings

It's time to review the mice themselves. From the hundred or so available on the market, I've selected a few to describe because they offer the widest assortment of performance and features within a reasonable price range.

Dynamite Product

Microsoft Mouse. The standard against which all other mice are measured, this competent product grabs almost half of all mice sales each year. Because this is Microsoft's own product, compatibility with present and future Windows versions is assured.

The Microsoft Mouse is available in serial, PS/2-style PDP, InPort, and bus versions. It sports a clean, ergonomic design and fits comfortably into your palm. Because its two buttons are mounted flush against its surface, they're easy to push. The ball is positioned slightly forward of center, can be easily removed for cleaning, and grips most flat surfaces with a good amount of traction. The Microsoft mouse should be good for 50 to 100 miles of mouse travel, which is equivalent to 10 years of everyday use.

This mechanical mouse boasts a resolution of 400 dpi and ballistic tracking that provides a wide range of tracking speeds, from exceedingly fast to excruciatingly slow. With the ballistic control turned up high, you can cover an entire VGA screen using only one square inch of desk space. But don't set the ballistic control too high, or you'll have trouble controlling the cursor.

Microsoft also supplies a special mouse control utility that provides more features than the standard Control Panel settings for the mouse (Figure 8.7).

FIGURE 8.7

Mouse
Control
Utility

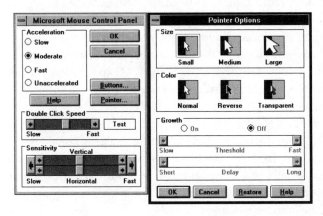

Microsoft ships
this special
mouse control
utility with its
mice.

This special mouse utility, POINT.EXE, lets you change the color of the mouse pointer so that it stands out more clearly on LCD displays and also lets you control the size of the pointer. A larger pointer is easier to see when you're running Windows in a high-resolution mode that shrinks everything on the screen. A special "growth" setting enlarges the pointer while it's moving quickly and returns it to its normal size for doing detailed work.

Logitech Mice. Logitech is the overall leader in mouse sales and offers many models of mice, unlike the mono-mousical Microsoft. The centerpiece of Logitech's mouse line is the MouseMan, a 400 ppi ballistic mouse that is unique in the industry because it is offered in both righthanded and left-handed versions.

The MouseMan is about 30 percent larger in size than the Microsoft mouse, and offers the most advanced ergonomic design—the larger size makes it easier to simply rest your hand on it, and the mouse ball is situated closer to the rear, making it easier on your wrist to position the cursor. The MouseMan is also offered in a serial version that includes both 9- and 25-pin connectors as well as a special adapter that plugs into PDP mouse ports. The MouseMan has three buttons, and includes a special Windows software utility that lets you assign the buttons to macros or keystrokes.

In addition to the MouseMan line, Logitech offers the Kidz mouse, a small-sized mouse designed especially for children—it even looks like a mouse. Although the Kidz mouse is cute, it's definitely for kids only, because the earlike buttons are spaced too closely for an adult to use comfortably. For families in which adults and children use the same computer, Logitech provides a special extension cable that allows you to connect both the Kidz mouse and a normal mouse at the same time.

On the cutting edge of mouse design, Logitech provides a three-button cordless radio mouse. Most other cordless mice employ an infrared beam, which can be inadvertently broken by real objects on your desk. The radio design ensures continuous transmission to the receiver.

At the high end of the mouse spectrum, Logitech features the 3-D mouse. This mouse, designed for high-end CAD applications, is the only mouse that provides full three-dimensional positioning.

IBM PS/2 Mouse. IBM introduced its only mouse in 1987 to compete with the hegemony of the Macintosh mouse. The original PS/2 Mouse, manufactured for IBM by Alps, has a basic two-button mechanical design. This mouse pales in comparison with Microsoft's offering, but because of IBM's name and marketing muscle, it has managed to win a significant percentage of the mouse market.

Danger Zone

The original PS/2 Mouse provides only 200 dpi resolution, is designed with sharp edges that make it uncomfortable to hold, and works only with IBM's PDP found on PS/2s, Compaqs, and a few other systems. You can use the PS/2 mouse with either the Windows PS/2 or the Microsoft mouse driver.

The paucity of features offered by this PS/2 Mouse is matched by the quality of its documentation. In fact, the PS/2 manual includes some information on operating this mouse that's absent from the actual PS/2 Mouse documentation. Here are two good things I can say about this mouse: It comes with a comparatively long cord (nine feet), and the ball is easy to remove for cleaning.

Mouse Systems: PC Mouse, White Mouse, and OmniMouse. In 1982, Mouse Systems was the first company to make mice for the PC, two years before Apple introduced its mouse-centric Macintosh. Mouse Systems, now a subsidiary of KYE, is still a big cheese in the mouse market with its PC Mouse, White Mouse, and OmniMouse. The PC Mouse is the company's flagship line. Though touted by the manufacturer as "the industry's most accurate mouse," there's actually little performance difference between it and the Microsoft product.

The steeply priced PC Mouse is a three-button optical mouse available in serial, PS/2, and bus versions. Because it's optical, you must use it with the reflective grid-lined mouse pad, included in the package. This pad is on the small side, but Mouse Systems will replace it with a larger one. The PC Mouse can be made to emulate a two-button mouse in Windows by sliding a small switch on the back of the mouse.

In addition to the high-end PC mouse, Mouse Systems offers two less expensive models: the White Mouse and the OmniMouse. The White Mouse, a three-button mechanical mouse, and the optomechanical Omni-Mouse, are offered in both serial and bus versions. Neither requires a special reflective pad.

Appoint MousePen. The MousePen from Appoint, Inc. is a mouse substitute with a distinctive design. Instead of the standard mouse design, the MousePen is shaped somewhat like a pen and ends in a small block that contains a pea-sized ball. The block has two small buttons that replicate the mouse buttons.

The MousePen is a ballistic mouse supplied in three versions: a desktop edition, which is the standard model; a professional model, which includes a third button for controlling the cursor speed; and a portable model, which has a shorter cord.

The MousePen resembles a political candidate: you either love it or you hate it. Its main following is among laptop users, who claim you can easily use the MousePen on your leg when you are cramped into an airline seat without enough room to maneuver a traditional mouse. Some desktop users like it becomes it feels more like a pen—something I have a hard time appreciating as a benefit. Its detractors say that using it is like trying to write with a ballpoint pen on waxed paper because the small ball doesn't always make firm contact with the surface and tends to skip.

The manufacturer supplies two different balls to correct the skipping problem that occurs with the regular ball. These other balls use a rougher, more textured surface that solves the skipping problem but creates a cleaning problem: they both pick up dirt and dust almost as well as a small vacuum cleaner.

Tandy Serial Mouse and Tandy 2-Button Mouse. Yes, you can get a cheap mouse at your local Radio Shack or Tandy computer store. Tandy's Serial Mouse is a two-button mechanical mouse with 200 dpi resolution, but it contains only a 25-pin serial connector. This mouse emulates Microsoft's, so it works fairly well with the Microsoft Mouse driver supplied with Windows.

Tandy's 2-Button Mouse is optomechanical, with a 200 dpi resolution. It is designed to connect to the mouse port of IBM PS/2s and other machines with built-in mouse ports, such as Compaqs and Tandys. The 2-Button is shaped like a crescent, which feels slightly awkward in the palm, but it performs reasonably well. If your mouse dies on a Sunday, it's reassuring to know you're only a shopping mall away from a cheap replacement. Except for emergencies, however, I'd favor any other mouse in this roster.

ProHance PowerMouse 100 and ProMouse. In yet another attempt at building a better mouse, ProHance has designed the 40-button, 200 dpi PowerMouse 100. Two large buttons correspond to those on simpler mice, but the 38 other buttons are tiny and provide a variety of functions. Here is a list of the PowerMouse 100's added features:

➥ Ten small, labeled buttons suggesting operations such as copy, move, and adjust width (functions used with its 1-2-3 macro package)

➥ A group of buttons labeled as a numeric keypad, with calculator functions

➥ Some keyboard equivalents, such as Enter, Esc, and backspace

➥ A powerful macro program that can use mouse-button combinations to connect 240 of its maximum 255-character macros to its 40 buttons

The PowerMouse can connect to either a 9- or a 25-pin serial port. ProHance supplies its own Windows driver and a special Windows template that defines many of the PowerMouse keys with macros to accomplish common Windows tasks. This is one of the most expensive mice available and users either love it or hate it. If you want to singlehandedly roll around a miniature keyboard, this may be the mouse for you.

ProHance also offers the ProMouse, which is a scaled-down version of the PowerMouse. Shaped more like the Microsoft mouse, the ProMouse features only 10 buttons, which you can assign to initiate macros or to replace frequently used keys. Although the ProMouse is more comfortable to use than the PowerMouse, the 10 buttons are quite small and therefore difficult to access.

Bargain Mice. With Windows, you are going to use your mouse frequently, so I suggest investing in a good-quality mouse that fits your hand well. If you are budget conscious, however, bargain mice abound—some are offered for as little as $10. It might be worth keeping a couple of these mice around as spares in case your main mouse goes down for repairs.

Two serviceable bargain mice are the Pet Mouse from IMSI and the Merit Mouse from National Computer Accessories. The Merit Mouse lists for only $17.99 and is one of the best of the low-cost mice. A small switch on the bottom of the Merit Mouse lets you switch it between Microsoft's and Mouse System's compatibility modes, either of which can be used with Windows.

Trackballs

Imagine turning your mouse on its back and adding a drop of growth hormone to its roller ball. Presto! You've got a trackball. The unit housing the trackball is stationary; to move the pointer on the screen, just roll the protruding ball with your fingers. Trackballs require much less desk space than do mice, and they allow you to perform coarse operations, like menu selection, with greater speed and less hand movement. (Trackballs are used in video games for speed of movement and quick control over the cursor.) On the other hand, you get more precise control with a mouse, especially with drawing programs and CAD.

Although trackballs conserve space on your desk, they're not as comfortable as mice to use for long periods of time. When you're moving the ball with your fingers, you can't use your fingers to press buttons. If you move the ball with your palm, you have to lift your palm to access buttons.

Despite their ergonomic limitations as compared to mice, I recommend the following trackballs as the best of the bunch.

Logitech TrackMan. This is one of the most ergonomically designed trackballs for righthanded users, but the placement of the buttons makes it awkward for lefthanders. The rolling ball is placed on the left side, with three buttons to the right of it, so you can keep your hand fully opened; the thumb manipulates the ball, and the fingers are free to click buttons. The TrackMan is available in both serial and bus versions, and is compatible with the Logitech Mouse driver included with Windows.

MicroSpeed PC-Trac. The PC-Trac is on the ergonomics designer track as well. Taking a cue from a competitor, MicroSpeed borrowed Microsoft's Dove soap-bar style of design. This shape allows your hand to rest more naturally than it does on most other trackballs. Two large semicircular buttons on either side of the ball accommodate different hand sizes. A third button, in the center above the ball, locks the pointer for dragging a selection.

The PC-Trac is available for all the methods of mouse attachment. This trackball works with the Microsoft Mouse driver included with Windows.

Kensington Expert Mouse. Despite its name, this is actually an oversized trackball. It resembles a billiard ball, with half of the 2-inch ball protruding from the unit. The Expert Mouse is at the high end of the price spectrum, for either the serial, PS/2, or bus version. The stability of the large ball and solid feel of the unit have earned it popularity among Macintosh users.

Mouse Systems PC Trackball. In addition to its various mice, Mouse Systems also offers a three-button trackball. The PC Trackball has an innovative, dome-shaped design, which places the three buttons at the base of the dome, just below the ball. This makes it more comfortable to move the ball with two fingers while resting your thumb on the left or right button. It's also one of the more economical trackballs, and is available in serial and bus versions.

Keyboard and Trackball Combo. If you've got a cluttered desk or a small computer stand that doesn't have enough room for either a mouse or a trackball, then try this quick and cheap fix: Chicony's Keyboard KB-5581. This keyboard comes with 101 keys and an integrated trackball; it requires the same amount of space as a standard 101 keyboard. The no-frills trackball has only 200 dpi resolution, but the complete package, which includes keyboard plus a trackball, costs less than either purchased separately. The trackball works with the Microsoft Mouse Windows driver.

This product's only drawback lies with the design of the keyboard, which contains two horizontal rows of keys at the top. As a result, it's easy to accidentally press a function key instead of a number, and vice versa.

Microsoft Ballpoint and Logitech TrackMan Portable. Most laptops were not designed with mice in mind. The best laptop design that incorporates a mouse alternative is the Apple PowerBook, with its small trackball located below the keyboard. Until PC vendors pick up on Apple's design principle, you'll need to choose your own pointing device for your PC portable.

The three leading alternatives are the Appoint MousePen, mentioned earlier, and two miniature trackballs, the Microsoft Ballpoint and the Logitech TrackMan Portable, which look surprisingly similar. These semicircular devices contain a small trackball on one side; to use them, you grasp the device between thumb and palm. You move the small trackball with your thumb and press buttons along the sides of the device with your fingers.

Danger Zone

Both the Ballpoint and the TrackMan Portable can be clamped onto the side of a portable computer. However, the Ballpoint can be more easily adjusted to different angles of attachment. Each system uses slightly different brackets, which can be a factor in determining your purchase. Some laptop designs don't work well with one or the other kind of bracket, so you should test them out first.

Graphics Tablets

Graphics tablets, or **digitizing tablets**, are the most precise and most expensive pointing devices. A standard graphics tablet measures $8\frac{1}{2}$x11 inches, but both larger and smaller models are also available. An electromagnetic sensor is embedded in the surface of the tablet. To move your computer pointer, you need either a stylus or a puck.

Artists find that a pen-shaped stylus provides the most natural drawing tool. Some sophisticated drawing programs support graphics tablets with a pressure-sensitive stylus that thickens your brush stroke, to resemble an actual painting technique, when you press harder against the tablet. The puck, most often used in CAD applications, is shaped somewhat like a mouse and contains a cross-hair sight for precise cursor placement.

Graphics tablets can be expensive; the cost depends on size, resolution, and options. If you're a serious graphic artist or CAD user, you should consider one of the Windows-compatible graphics tablets manufactured by Wacom, Kurta, GTCO, and CalComp.

Mouse Settings in the Windows Initialization Files

The two Windows initialization files, SYSTEM.INI and WIN.INI, contain information about the mouse driver that Windows is using. From the SYSTEM.INI file, you can learn which mouse driver Windows will use; from WIN.INI, you can acquire information about the settings for the active driver.

Table 8.6 gives the statement lines in SYSTEM.INI that relate to the mouse.

TABLE 8.6 *Summary of Mouse Settings in SYSTEM.INI*	Statement Line	Description
	Mouse.drv=	When located in the [boot] section, tells Windows what mouse driver to use.
	Mouse.drv=	When located in the [boot.description] section, tells Windows how to display the name of the driver.
	Mouse=	Located in the [386Enh] section, tells Windows what virtual mouse driver to use.
	MouseInDosBox=	Located in the [NonWindowsApp] section, specifies whether the mouse should be supported when running a DOS program in a window.
	MouseSyncTime=	Located in the [Standard] section, specifies how many milliseconds can elapse between mouse data bytes before Windows determines that a mouse data packet is complete. This statement only affects computers that use an IBM PS/2-style mouse interface and only when Windows is running in standard mode.

Table 8.7 shows the statement lines in WIN.INI that are used by the standard Microsoft mouse driver.

Statement Line	Description
DoubleClickSpeed=	This is the number of milliseconds that can elapse between two clicks to constitute a double-click.
SwapMouseButtons=	When set to NO, the left button is the primary button; when set to YES, the right button is the primary button.
MouseSpeed=	This switch can only be set to 0 (no acceleration), 1, or 2; when set to 1 or 2, the exact speed will be determined by the statements MouseThreshold1 and MouseThreshold2.
MouseThreshold1=	This is used in conjunction with MouseSpeed= and MouseThreshold2= to determine the tracking speed of the mouse.
MouseThreshold2=	This is used in conjunction with MouseSpeed= and MouseThreshold1= to determine the tracking speed of the mouse.
MouseTrails=	This value can be set to any number from 1 to 7 to designate how many cursor images should trail behind the mouse pointer on an LCD display.
DoubleClickWidth=	This can be used in conjunction with DoubleClickHeight= to define an area on the screen equal to a single double-click.
DoubleClickHeight=	This can be used in conjunction with DoubleClickWidth= to define an area on the screen equal to a single double-click.

For details on editing the statement lines in WIN.INI and SYSTEM.INI refer to Chapter 15.

Danger Zone

If you are using a Logitech or Genius mouse in a DOS window—a capability that is new in Windows 3.1—you should make sure that the following line appears in your SYSTEM.INI file:

```
local=pc$mouse
```

Note that this line is case sensitive and must be entered in lowercase letters.

Keyboards

The keyboard still plays a major role in what is partially a mouse-controlled environment. You need a keyboard for data entry, and many commands are more easily and quickly issued from the keyboard, because you don't have to remove your hands from the keyboard to reach for and use the mouse.

In fact, you don't even need a mouse to run Windows—almost every command can be issued from the keyboard. This keyboard capability gives Windows an operational edge over the Macintosh, which is totally mouse-dependent. With Windows you can have the best of both worlds, the keyboard and the mouse, each according to its most efficient use and your preference.

Keyboard Ergonomics

The keyboard may pose the single biggest health hazard associated with your computer. The link between VDT emissions from the monitor and specific health hazards is still under debate, but use of the keyboard has been proven to cause a variety of hand and wrist injuries, known collectively as **repetitive stress injuries**.

The two most common of these injuries, **tendonitis** and **carpal tunnel syndrome**, are caused by poor typing habits and an improper work setup. If you pound on the keyboard while typing, or type for a long time in an awkward position, you can place too much stress on your muscles and connective tissues. You can also hurt yourself by repeating the same motion over and over again without providing enough rest for the tendons in your wrist and hands. These repetitive motions can lead to chronic swelling of the tendons, or tendonitis, with symptoms ranging from numbness to severe pain.

Prolonged, repetitive motion places an undue amount of stress on the tendons that pass through a small area of the wrist known as the carpal tunnel. Carpal tunnel syndrome occurs when the tendons become so swollen that they press on the nerves going to the hand and cause a condition that can make it impossible to type or use your hands for almost anything. An operation to alleviate the pain or pressure caused by repetitive hand motion has become one of the most common surgical procedures in the United States, but it is often ineffective at eradicating the problem. That's why prevention is your best recourse.

The best prevention methods are to take frequent short breaks from typing and to position your keyboard and body properly. During your breaks, stretch your fingers gently or squeeze a small ball or hand-gripper.

Also, pay attention to the positioning of your keyboard. The keyboard should be level with your wrists—flexing your wrists too far forward or bending them back can damage them.

Other movements to avoid: don't cradle the phone between your ear and shoulder while you type (get a headset instead); and don't place your palms on the desktop and bend your wrists up so that your fingers can reach the keys.

Dynamite Product

If you tend to bend your wrists, invest a few dollars in a foam wrist-saver pad that is placed along the front of your keyboard. Resting your palms on such a pad elevates it from the desktop and keeps your wrists on a more even plane with the keyboard.

You can also adjust the height of the keyboard itself, and adjust the height of your chair in relation to the keyboard. You should aim for a position that places the keyboard at a slightly lower level than your elbow. Most desks are 29 inches high, which is considered about 3 inches too high for comfortable typing. You can sometimes remedy this height problem by getting a special keyboard drawer that is attached under the desk. (This is considerably easier than sawing 3 inches off the legs of the desk!). You should look for a keyboard drawer that includes a built-in wrist rest, such as the Keyboard and Mouse Support drawer offered by Wholesale Ergonomic Products.

Insider's Tip

A good desk, a wrist support pad, and a fully adjustable office chair may be the most important computer accessories you can buy. If you meet resistance to getting this equipment at the office, complain loudly, and remind your boss that more than half of all job-related disability claims are now being generated by repetitive motion disorders.

· ·

Keyboard Device Drivers

Windows provides four device drivers that accommodate most varieties of PC keyboards:

➥ **KEYBOARD.DRV** The default driver used for most standard keyboards

➥ **KBDHP.DRV** The driver needed by all Hewlett-Packard machines

➥ **KBDMOUSE.DRV** The Olivetti/AT&T keyboard mouse driver for systems such as the AT&T 301 that have a keyboard/mouse combination

➥ **KBDOLI.DRV** For Olivetti machines

These four keyboard drivers support the following varieties of keyboards:

➡ AT-style 84 to 86 keys

➡ AT&T 301 and 302

➡ Enhanced 101-key or 102-key (U.S. and non-U.S.)

➡ Hewlett-Packard Vectra (DIN)

➡ Olivetti 101 and 102 A

➡ Olivetti 83-key, 86-key, and M24 102-key

➡ PC/XT-style 83-key and 84-key

Most PC-compatible keyboards conform to the Enhanced 101 or 102 standards, but if your keyboard is not on this list, you may need a third-party device driver. In that case, contact the manufacturer.

Danger Zone

Some older 286-based systems with 83-entry keyboards don't handle address line 20, as the IBM AT does, which makes them incompatible with the Windows keyboard device drivers. If you have one of these keyboards, try to get an updated keyboard BIOS chip from the manufacturer—otherwise, you'll have to get a new keyboard.

To change the Windows device driver for the keyboard, run Setup from within Windows, choose the Change System Settings command from the Options menu, and select the Keyboard drop down list (Figure 8.8).

FIGURE 8.8

Change System Settings Dialog Box

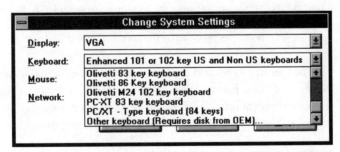

The Change System Settings dialog box in Windows Setup lets you change the device driver for your keyboard.

Select the keyboard driver from the list; or, if you want to install a third-party keyboard driver, select the "Other Keyboard (Requires disk from OEM)" at the end of the list.

Windows Setup lets you alter your keyboard layout to work with various layouts for other countries, which use special characters and symbols. To change the keyboard layout you will need to start Setup from the DOS prompt when Windows is not running.

After running Setup from DOS, use the Keyboard Layout option to select a different layout. The Keyboard Layout option lets you select a dynamic link library (DLL) that works together with the device driver to provide a different layout standard, such as the Dvorak or a foreign language layout.

Windows includes dynamic link libraries that work with the keyboard device drivers to support the keyboard layouts listed in Table 8.8.

TABLE 8.8
Keyboard Layouts and Their Associated Link Libraries

Keyboard Layout	Dynamic Link Library	Keyboard Layout	Dynamic Link Library
Belgian	KBDBE.DLL	Italian	KBDIT.DLL
British	KBDUK.DLL	Latin American	KBDLA.DLL
Canadian multilingual	KBDFC.DLL	Norwegian	KBDNO.DLL
		Portuguese	KBDPO.DLL
Danish	KBDDA.DLL	Spanish	KBDSP.DLL
Dutch	KBDNE.DLL	Swiss-French	KBDSF.DLL
Finnish	KBDFI.DLL	Swiss-German	KBDSG.DLL
French	KBDFR.DLL	Swedish	KBDSW.DLL
French-Canadian	KBDCA.DLL	U.S.*	KBDUS.DLL
German	KBDGR.DLL	US-Dvorak	KBDDV.DLL
Icelandic	KBDIC.DLL	U.S.-International	KBDUSX.DLL

*The KBDUS.DLL file is used only for certain nonstandard U.S. keyboards, such as the Olivetti M24 102-key keyboard. Most U.S. keyboards do not require a DLL file and work with the default settings provided by the keyboard driver file (such as KEYBOARD.DRV).

The Control Panel also contains a Keyboard icon that allows you to set the amount of time before a key starts to repeat itself, as well as to adjust the automatic repeat rate. To access the Keyboard controls, start the Control Panel and open the Keyboard icon to reveal the Keyboard dialog box (Figure 8.9).

FIGURE 8.9
Keyboard Dialog Box

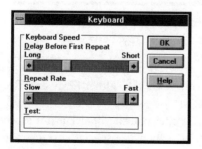

The Keyboard icon in the Control Panel lets you adjust the amount of time before a key starts to repeat itself and the rate at which it automatically repeats.

To change the amount of time that elapses before a key repeats itself, use the scroll button in the Delay scroll box to alter the length of the time elapsed. To adjust the rate at which the key repeats once it gets going, use the scroll button in the Repeat Rate scroll box. To test your settings, move to the Test box, then hold down any alphanumeric key on the keyboard.

. . . .

The Keyboard Settings in SYSTEM.INI

The [boot] section of the SYSTEM.INI file contains the statement line that identifies the file name of the keyboard driver you are using. The following statement line, for example, indicates that you are using the standard Windows keyboard driver:

```
keyboard.drv=keyboard.drv
```

The [keyboard] section of the file contains several statement lines that further define the keyboard currently installed in your system. Table 8.9 summarizes these statements.

TABLE 8.9

Statement Line	Description
keyboard.dll=	Specifies the dynamic link library (DLL) that defines the layout for special keyboard configuration, such as the Dvorak or foreign-language layout. Only needed if you are not using the standard layout for U.S. keyboards.
oemansi.bin=	Specifies the file that contains the OEM/ANSI code-page translation table. Only needed if you are using a code-page translation table other than code-page 437, which specifies the U.S. OEM character set.
type=	Identifies the type of keyboard you are using.
subtype=	In conjunction with the type= statement, further identifies the type of keyboard you are using.

For further details about these statements, and information on how to edit the SYSTEM.INI file, refer to Chapter 15.

. . . .

The Dvorak Keyboard Layout

One of the goals of Windows is to help boost your computing productivity—although given the demands Windows places on your system, it often seems as if the reverse were true. The standard keyboard, similarly, seems to offer productivity, but at quite a cost: the learning curve can be quite steep, and for some, insurmountable—or at least not worth the effort of forgoing the hunt-and-peck method. In addition, the standard keyboard supplied with most computers was intentionally designed to slow you down. In fact, the layout of your keyboard is one of the most antiquated elements of your computer interface.

Standard keyboards use what is called the QWERTY layout (named after the first six keys on the top row of the keyboard), designed in 1872 by Charles Scholes, one of the coinventors of the typewriter. The cockeyed QWERTY layout was designed to prevent keys from jamming. If frequently used keys were placed at opposite ends of the keyboard, keys would be less likely to jam. As a result, keys didn't jam but the fingers of an average typist covered 16 miles on a QWERTY keyboard during a normal workday. Fortunately, there's an alternative to the QWERTY keyboard: the Dvorak keyboard. Named after efficiency expert August Dvorak, this keyboard places the most commonly used letters on the so-called home row, which is the middle row of letters.

According to Dvorak's research, almost 70 percent of commonly used words—about 3,000—could be typed from the home row of his keyboard. By comparison, only 120 commonly used words can be typed from the home row of a QWERTY keyboard. As a result, your fingers would travel only 1 mile during a typical day of typing on a Dvorak layout. Because the fingers do less traveling, accuracy has been shown to improve by almost 15 percent, and typing speed by 20 percent.

Insider's Tip

Despite its many advantages, the Dvorak keyboard, which was patented in 1936, has remained obscure, and its followers, although devoted, are few and far between. Some Dvorak proponents must have influenced Microsoft, however, because Windows provides a built-in capability to remap your keyboard to the Dvorak layout. To do this, you'll need to run Setup from the DOS prompt, then select the U.S. Dvorak option in the Keyboard Layout section (Figure 8.10).

Once you select this option, your keyboard is reconfigured for the Dvorak layout whenever you run Windows. If you want to use this layout with DOS programs as well, you'll need to run them from within Windows. The Dvorak layout rearranges your keys as shown in Figure 8.11.

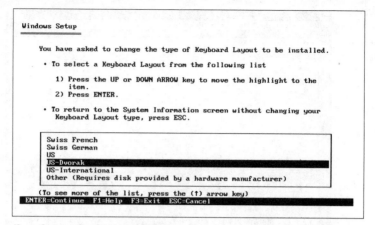

```
Windows Setup

    You have asked to change the type of Keyboard Layout to be installed.

    • To select a Keyboard Layout from the following list

        1) Press the UP or DOWN ARROW key to move the highlight to the
           item.
        2) Press ENTER.

    • To return to the System Information screen without changing your
      Keyboard Layout type, press ESC.

    ┌──────────────────────────────────────────────────────────────────┐
    │ Swiss French                                                       │
    │ Swiss German                                                       │
    │ US                                                                 │
    │ US-Dvorak                                                          │
    │ US-International                                                    │
    │ Other (Requires disk provided by a hardware manufacturer)          │
    └──────────────────────────────────────────────────────────────────┘

        (To see more of the list, press the (↑) arrow key)
   ENTER=Continue   F1=Help   F3=Exit   ESC=Cancel
```

Run Setup from the DOS prompt, then select the U.S. Dvorak option from the Keyboard Layout section.

The Dvorak layout changes the location of most of the letters, numbers, and punctuation keys on your keyboard—the six QWERTY keys are now ',.PYF.

Insider's Tip

If your conversion to the Dvorak layout is permanent, you may want to rearrange the keycaps on your keyboard as well. Most keyboards allow you to pull the keycaps directly off (pull gently, or obtain a special keycap puller tool from your dealer). Then replace them according to the layout depicted in Figure 8.11.

Dynamite Product

If you're just learning to type or want to improve your typing skills, several typing tutor programs support the use of the Dvorak keyboard layout. My recommendation is "Mavis Beacon Teaches Typing," an excellent Windows typing program for both QWERTY and Dvorak layouts from The Software Toolworks. This program is both educational and entertaining, and can be used by adults and kids. A clever feature is the program's ghostlike "guide hands," which show you how to type correctly (Figure 8.12).

FIGURE 8.12

*Ghost Guide
Hands*

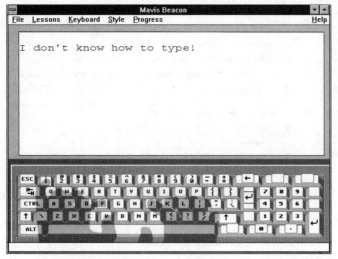

Mavis Beacon
Teaches Typing
and Mavis's
ghost (or her
hands)
accompanies
you at the
keyboard.

For more information about the Dvorak keyboard layout, contact the Dvorak International support group (see Appendix C).

Entering ANSI Characters

One of the toughest keyboard feats in Windows 3.0 was to enter special letters, such as accented letters and foreign currency symbols, which are not represented by actual keys on your keyboard. These are often referred to as the **ANSI characters,** named after the ANSI Character Set—a method for specifying 256 characters and symbols using the numbers 0 through 255.

New in 3.1

Windows 3.1 has improved its support for the ANSI character set. A group of characters (in the ANSI range 0130 through 0159) has been added to Windows 3.1. For example, ANSI value 0153 now yields the trademark sign.

Windows 3.1 has also made it easier to access the complete ANSI character set. In Windows 3.1, the Character Map utility (discussed in Chapter 5) provides easy access to these special characters.

If you need to enter a special character from the keyboard, first determine its ANSI numeric code. Table 8.10 lists the standard ANSI character codes, but because these values can vary by typeface, you may need to refer to the specific documentation included with your font package. You can also use the Character Map, as described in Chapter 5, to identify which key combination to press.

•••••••••••••••
TABLE 8.10
ANSI
Characters

ANSI Value	ANSI Character	ANSI Value	ANSI Character	ANSI Value	ANSI Character	ANSI Value	ANSI Character
32	(space)	66	B	100	d	134	
33	!	67	C	101	e	135	
34	"	68	D	102	f	136	
35	#	69	E	103	g	137	
36	$	70	F	104	h	138	
37	%	71	G	105	i	139	
38	&	72	H	106	j	140	
39	'	73	I	107	k	141	
40	(	74	J	108	l	142	
41	)	75	K	109	m	143	
42	*	76	L	110	n	144	
43	+	77	M	111	o	145	'
44	,	78	N	112	p	146	'
45	-	79	O	113	q	147	"
46	.	80	P	114	r	148	"
47	/	81	Q	115	s	149	•
48	0	82	R	116	t	150	–
49	1	83	S	117	u	151	—
50	2	84	T	118	v	152	
51	3	85	U	119	w	153	
52	4	86	V	120	x	154	
53	5	87	W	121	y	155	
54	6	88	X	122	z	156	
55	7	89	Y	123	{	157	
56	8	90	Z	124			158	
57	9	91	[	125	}	159	
58	:	92	\	126	~	160	
59	;	93	]	127		161	¡
60	<	94	^	128		162	¢
61	=	95	_	129		163	£
62	>	96	`	130		164	¤
63	?	97	a	131		165	¥
64	@	98	b	132		166	¦
65	A	99	c	133		167	§

ANSI Value	ANSI Character	ANSI Value	ANSI Character	ANSI Value	ANSI Character	ANSI Value	ANSI Character
168	¨	190	¾	212	Ô	234	ê
169	©	191	¿	213	Õ	235	ë
170	ª	192	À	214	Ö	236	ì
171	«	193	Á	215	×	237	í
172	¬	194	Â	216	Ø	238	î
173	-	195	Ã	217	Ù	239	ï
174	®	196	Ä	218	Ú	240	ð
175	¯	197	Å	219	Û	241	ñ
176	°	198	Æ	220	Ü	242	ò
177	±	199	Ç	221	Ý	243	ó
178	²	200	È	222	Þ	244	ô
179	³	201	É	223	ß	245	õ
180	´	202	Ê	224	à	246	ö
181	µ	203	Ë	225	á	247	÷
182	¶	204	Ì	226	â	248	ø
183	·	205	Í	227	ã	249	ù
184	¸	206	Î	228	ä	250	ú
185	¹	207	Ï	229	å	251	û
186	º	208	Ð	230	æ	252	ü
187	»	209	Ñ	231	ç	253	ý
188	¼	210	Ò	232	è	254	þ
189	½	211	Ó	233	é	255	ÿ

Once you've determined the ANSI numeric code for the special character you want to type, make sure your computer's numeric keypad is active. (Usually, a light on your keyboard glows to indicate that the keypad is active, and pressing Num Lock toggles it on and off). Hold down Alt while you type the ANSI code from the numeric keypad—you can't use the numbers on the top row of the keyboard. Be sure to include a zero in front of the code number.

For example, to type the copyright symbol, locate its ANSI code, which for most typefaces is 169, and hold down Alt while typing 0169. If you don't use the zero, Windows will interpret the code as the computer's built-in character set, which contains many of the same characters as the ANSI set, but can vary by manufacturer. Sound complicated? Well, now you know why Microsoft created the Character Map utility.

Danger Zone

ANSI characters that are typed into a Windows document (or pasted into a document from Character Map) may not be interpreted properly if you open the document later with a DOS application. Also, remember that not every font uses the same character set.

Summary

The display, mouse, and keyboard provide the hardware interface between you and your computer; in other words, these elements enable you to physically interact with Windows. All directly affect the performance of Windows and of your system as well.

The display system consists of a Windows driver, a display adapter card, and the actual display itself (usually a video monitor). All three components are critical to the performance of your system: the adapter card controls the resolution and number of colors that can be produced; monitors need to match the output signal of the adapter card; and the Windows display driver allows you to take advantage of the adapter card's capabilities.

In addition, Windows graphics accelerators can take some of the load off your system's CPU for graphics operations. These devices range from simple software drivers to fixed-function graphics cards and sophisticated graphics coprocessor cards. One of the most promising areas of graphics acceleration is the local bus systems that bypass the computer's normal expansion bus to provide the display adapter with direct access to the CPU chip.

The mouse or other pointing device allows you to manipulate onscreen objects, issue commands, select text, and perform other functions. Although the mouse is an important part of a graphical interface, Windows is not completely dependent on it, and you can still operate the system from the keyboard alone.

Even with a mouse, you'll also need a keyboard for data entry; and often a keyboard allows you to issue commands more quickly than would be possible with a mouse, because you don't have to remove your hands from the keyboard.

Daring folks and efficiency maniacs can also avail themselves of Windows' built-in capability to convert the standard keyboard layout to the more competent Dvorak layout. However, you'll be breaking from the pack, and other people who unwittingly use your Dvorak-configured computer might think they are on the verge of a nervous breakdown.

. . . .

Insider's Tech Support

Q: My display isn't working properly.

A: Problems with the display card fall into three main categories: conflicts with the upper memory area of your computer; incompatibilities with the third-party display driver; and problems with self-configuring display cards that use nonmaskable interrupts.

Memory conflicts should be eliminated first, because they are the most likely to occur. To check this out, start Windows by typing

```
WIN /D:X
```

Starting Windows in this special diagnostic excludes the memory used by adapters from being accessed by Windows. On most systems, this is the area from A000 to FFFF. If your problem disappears, you can try to force Windows to exclude a smaller area of memory, where most of the trouble occurs, by adding this line to the [386Enh] section of your SYSTEM.INI file:

```
EMMExclude=C400-C7FF
```

Excluding this range resolves problems with VGA adapters that Windows might not be able to recognize; it also resolves any conflicts that might occur if you use both an 8514/a and a VGA adapter. In rare cases, this statement may not exclude enough memory. If this happens, increase the memory range to be excluded to either C000-CFFF or A000-CFFF. Another possibility is that your memory manager has attempted to use one of these regions; refer to Chapter 12 for instructions on how to exclude upper memory areas from the memory manager's control.

Problems with nonmaskable interrupts typically appear after a Windows logo appears briefly on your screen; after the logo scrolls off the bottom, the screen turns blank. This problem occurs with so-called self-configuring adapter cards, also called auto-switch cards. If this happens, Windows is probably still running, although you can't see it on the screen. Press Alt+F4, Enter to exit Windows. (If several programs are running, you may have to press Alt+F4 several times.) You'll then have to check the documentation for your display adapter or contact the vendor to determine how to disable the nonmaskable interrupt feature of the card before you can restart Windows.

Symptoms indicating problems with the display driver vary widely, from a blank screen to a screen filled with distorted video. The easiest solution is to use the drivers included with the Windows 3.1 installation disks or to obtain updated drivers for any unsupported cards.

Stepping down in resolution can sometimes temporarily eliminate a problem, so that you can use your card while you're waiting for an updated driver. For example, if you're having trouble in SuperVGA mode, try using the regular VGA driver. Or, if you're using one of the VGA selections, specify another VGA option in Setup to see if a different configuration will work for your adapter.

Q: I upgraded from Windows 3.0 to 3.1, and my VGA adapter doesn't seem to work when I run DOS programs from within Windows.

A: Run Setup and select the "VGA (version 3.0)" option as your display adapter type.

Q: I upgraded from Windows 3.0 to 3.1, and my SuperVGA adapter doesn't seem to work.

A: Setup may not have updated your SuperVGA driver. Rerun Setup and change your selection to the Windows 3.1 800x600 16-color driver, which provides better compatibility than Windows 3.0 drivers.

Q: I'm using a PS/2 and am having trouble with my display adapter.

A: Some newer PS/2 systems use XGA adapters. With these you should install Windows using the 640x480 16-color mode for your XGA adapter and then rerun Setup, specifying a higher resolution mode from within Windows. If you upgraded from Windows 3.0 to 3.1 and you were previously using an IBM-supplied XGA Windows driver, you'll need to rerun Setup and select the XGA driver supplied with Windows 3.1, because Setup may not have automatically updated this.

If your PS/2 has an 8514/a adapter, see the corresponding section earlier in this chapter.

Q: When I try to run a DOS program in Windows 386 enhanced mode, I get an error message saying that I have an incorrect system version.

A: This is probably caused by a mismatched virtual display driver and 386 grabber file. Refer to the tables earlier in the chapter to make sure that you have properly matched files. For example, for the VGA and Super-VGA drivers included with Windows 3.1, the [Boot] section of your SYSTEM.INI file should contain the line

```
386grabber=VGA.3GR
```

and the [386Enh] section should contain the line

```
display=*VDDVGA
```

If you have a third-party display driver for Windows 3.1, it may use the built-in Windows virtual display device and grabber files, or it may provide one or both of its own replacement files. If you're using an older Windows 3.0 driver, you'll need to make sure that the VGA30.3GR grabber file and the VDDVGA30.386 virtual display device file are specified in the SYSTEM.INI file. Note that some third-party display drivers for Windows 3.1 also use one or both of these Windows 3.0 compatibility files.

Q: TrueType fonts are not displayed properly on my screen.

A: Some Windows 3.0 video drivers, such as the ATI Ultra Crystal font drivers, do not work properly with Windows 3.1. If your display board is compatible with a different adapter standard, try using one of the drivers from the Windows installation disks. For example, several of the ATI boards will work with the 8514/a driver. The best solution, however, is to obtain an updated 3.1-compatible driver from the board manufacturer.

If you're already using an up-to-date driver, the problem may be caused by corruption of your TrueType font files. To fix this, open the Fonts icon in the Control Panel, delete the font (don't check the "Delete file from disk" option), and then reinstall the font.

Q: Windows crashes when I try to run a DOS application that uses my TIGA adapter.

A: The TIGA adapter permits only one application to run at a time, and Windows counts as that one application. You'll need to quit Windows before trying to run another DOS program that uses the TIGA adapter.

Q: When I switch to a high-resolution video mode, my display becomes distorted.

A: If the image on the screen is completely garbled, then either your adapter card or your video monitor does not work with the resolution you have chosen. If it's a problem with the video adapter, you might lack the memory on the card to support that resolution; in this case, add memory to the card. Less frequently, you may need a ROM update to your adapter card to support the high-resolution driver.

In other cases, the monitor may not support the higher scanning frequency output when it switches into a higher-resolution video mode. If the image on your screen bleeds over the edges or appears squashed, then you'll need to adjust the image dimensions on your monitor. Refer to the documentation included with your monitor.

Also, make sure you haven't attempted to use noninterlaced mode on your display adapter with a monitor that doesn't support it. Try configuring your VGA card for "interlaced" video to see whether this corrects the problem.

Q: After I changed my hardware configuration, my display adapter started drawing images much more slowly than before.

A: Check to be sure that your adapter card is running in 16-bit mode. Some cards require different configuration settings that switch the card from 8- to 16-bit mode. To determine whether your card does this, check its documentation.

Another problem can be caused if you have an 8-bit device that is using an area of upper memory near the area used by your display adapter; if so, the adapter will be forced into 8-bit mode. To determine what areas of memory your devices are using, run the Microsoft Diagnostics utility described in Chapter 17, and then try to relocate the memory used by the 8-bit device to a memory address higher than E000.

Q: I get an error message saying "Windows cannot set up an upper memory block at segment B000."

A: Windows is competing with your display driver for the monochrome adapter address range located in the area from B000 to B7FF, which is a problem only in 386 enhanced mode. You can start Windows by typing **WIN /S** to force it to start in standard mode while you're solving the problem.

The Windows installation disks contain a special device driver called MONOUMB2.386 that resolves this conflict in most cases. You'll need to use the Expand utility to copy this from the installation disks and install it in your system by adding a DEVICE=MONOUMB2.386 statement in the [386Enh] section of your SYSTEM.INI file.

Another solution is to exclude the region from B000 to B7FF from the control of your memory manager (see Chapter 12 for details) and then place this statement in your SYSTEM.INI file:

```
EMMExclude=B000-B7FF
```

Q: I get an error message saying that I have an incompatible display adapter.

A: Most display adapters work with Windows, so unless you have an oddball adapter card, this message probably indicates that you don't have a complete set of drivers for the adapter you are using. A complete set of display drivers includes the driver file itself, identified by the .DRV file extension; the 286 and 386 grabber files, identified by the extensions 2GR and 3GR, respectively; and a virtual display driver file, which usually starts with the letters VDD and ends with the extension .386.

If your display adapter is not supported by one of the standard drivers that ships with Windows 3.1, contact the manufacturer to obtain updated driver files. In the meantime, see if your display adapter can be configured as a standard adapter, such as EGA, VGA, or 8514/a; then try to run Setup and specify the standard adapter name as a temporary fix while you await the proper drivers.

Q: When I run DOS programs that use CGA graphics mode in a window, I get snowlike distortion in that window on my screen.

A: Some CGA graphics programs produce this "snow" due to a small incompatibility with Windows. To fix this condition, add the following line to the [386Enh] section of the SYSTEM.INI file:

```
CGANoSnow=ON
```

This setting clears up the problem but can slow Windows down a little bit, so don't add this line unless it's absolutely necessary.

Q: I'm having trouble with my Hercules Graphics Station adapter.

A: This adapter uses the TIGA driver in Windows 3.1. If you're using the Windows 3.1 TIGA driver and still run into trouble using 386 enhanced mode, add the following line to the [386Enh] section of SYSTEM.INI:

```
EMMExclude=C000-CFFF
```

Q: My mouse doesn't work with Windows.

A: The most common problems that prevent a mouse from working with Windows are an incorrect mouse driver or a hardware conflict. If your mouse is not one of the standard types listed by Windows Setup, check your mouse manual to see if it is compatible with one of the choices that is listed by Setup. For example, many mice are compatible with the

Microsoft or Logitech driver. Sometimes the mouse needs to be recon-figured to provide this compatibility, so check your mouse documenta-tion. If you have an oddball pointing device that won't work with any of the drivers, you'll need to contact the manufacturer to obtain a compatible mouse driver.

Hardware problems that can disable the mouse usually develop because the mouse is attached to the wrong serial port or because there is an interrupt conflict with another hardware device. The mouse should only be connected to the COM1 or COM2 serial port, prefera-bly COM1. Double-check to make sure your mouse isn't accidentally connected to COM3 or COM4; although DOS supports this method of connection, Windows does not. To determine if you have an interrupt conflict, run the Microsoft Diagnostics program described in Chap-ter 17 and reassign the interrupt on your mouse card to an unused interrupt.

Q: My mouse doesn't work with a DOS application running in a window.

A: For the mouse to work with DOS applications running in a window, you need to load a DOS mouse driver such as MOUSE.COM that specif-ically supports this feature, which is new to Windows 3.1. Third-party DOS mouse drivers may require upgrading to provide this feature.

Also, the DOS mouse driver should be loaded before you run Win-dows, and the Windows grabber file (usually identified by the file extension .3GR) must also support this mouse-in-a -window feature.

Finally, your DOS application must be able to support the use of a mouse. To test this, see if the mouse works when the DOS application is running in full screen, or when Windows is not running. If it does work in these modes, this usually indicates that the grabber file does not support the new 3.1 feature.

Q: My mouse pointer jumps around the screen even when I'm moving the mouse slowly.

A: Unexpected cursor acrobatics can be caused by three things:

➥ You may have a hardware interrupt conflict with another device. To solve this, run the Microsoft Diagnostics utility and change the interrupt of your mouse or other device.

➥ Your mouse may be too dirty. See the section earlier in this chapter on how to clean your mouse.

➤ You may have an old serial card. Some early serial I/O cards use an incompatible chip, imprinted with the word "WINBOND." If your serial I/O card has this chip on it, you'll need to replace it.

Q: My Microsoft mouse (or Ballpoint) came with a program called POINT.EXE, which lets me change my mouse acceleration and other settings. Should I use this program or the Control Panel?

A: As long as your POINT.EXE program is version 8.0 or higher, you should use it instead of the Control Panel to adjust the settings on your mouse, because it provides more options. If you are using the POINT.EXE program, watch out for problems that can arise from having more than one copy of your MOUSE.INI file. Both the POINT.EXE program and the Microsoft mouse driver controls in the Control Panel create their own MOUSE.INI file. These programs can share the same MOUSE.INI file, so make sure that you either place the POINT.EXE program in your Windows directory or set your MOUSE environment variable to indicate your Mouse directory.

The settings you make with POINT.EXE can be preserved by running a companion program, POINTER.EXE (also included with your Microsoft mouse or Ballpoint) at startup. Note that if you install your Microsoft mouse by using the setup program included with your mouse utility disks, a RUN=POINTER.EXE statement is placed in your WIN.INI file.

Q: My keyboard either malfunctions or slows down when I'm running Windows in 386 enhanced mode.

A: If your keyboard slows down, you may be low on memory, or your foreground application may not be getting enough processing priority. To increase the priority of a foreground application for all its activities, adjust the Foreground Priority setting in the [386Enh] section of the Control Panel, or, for a DOS application, in its .PIF file. A better technique is to edit the KeyBoostTime= statement in the [386Enh] section of SYSTEM.INI; this will grant a foreground application more priority only when it is receiving keystrokes.

Other aberrant keyboard behavior that appears while running Windows in 386 enhanced mode can often be solved by editing one of the other keyboard-related statements in the [386Enh] section of SYSTEM.INI. These statements include KeyBufferDelay=, KeyIdleDelay=, KeyPasteDelay=, KeyPasteSkipcount=, KeyPasteCRSkipCount=, and KeyPasteTimeout=. See Chapter 15 for information on how to edit these values to correct keyboard problems.

Integrating Windows Applications with OLE and DDE

Without becoming a programmer, you can now integrate information created by one program into a document created by another program. To accomplish this legerdemain, Windows 3.1 offers three tools: the Clipboard, DDE, and OLE.

As the primary mechanism for transferring information from one program to another, the **Clipboard** allows you to use the Cut (or Copy) and Paste commands to capture information from one program and then shuttle it to another. Once transferred to another program, the original information abandons all ties to its origin and becomes incorporated in a static form. The Clipboard works with most Windows applications, and even lets you exchange a limited amount of information with DOS programs.

DDE (**dynamic data exchange**) represents a rung up the ladder as a data-sharing technique. DDE not only allows programs to communicate with each other through Windows as the translating medium, it also includes a standard language for Windows applications to send messages directly to each other. For example, you could use DDE to link certain numerical information in a spreadsheet to data in a wordprocessing document; whenever the data in the spreadsheet changed, the corresponding numbers in the wordprocessing document would automatically be updated as well.

OLE (**object linking and embedding**, pronounced "oh-lay") combines the functions of the Clipboard and DDE to provide a more powerful way of sharing information among several applications. Information from one document can be either **embedded in** or **linked to** another document. For example, you can embed the actual data for a picture into a wordprocessing document, then double-click on the picture to bring up the graphics application used to create the picture, and use that application to edit the picture. With linking, the actual data is stored only in the source file.

This chapter demonstrates how the Clipboard, DDE, and OLE work together to help you integrate information among your applications. It also describes how to use two utilities for managing OLE: the **Object Packager** and the **Registration Info Editor**.

The Clipboard

The **Clipboard** plays an integral role in Windows operations. With the Clipboard, you can easily cut or copy information from a document created in one application, switch to another application, and paste in the information. Together with DDE or OLE, the Clipboard also enables you to link data that you've transferred to its source, or original application, providing your applications can work with DDE or OLE.

The capacity to easily cut and paste information among documents from different applications gives Windows a distinct advantage over DOS. And, when you run a DOS program from within Windows, the Clipboard provides a bridge between Windows and DOS: you can paste text and sometimes graphics from DOS programs into Windows documents, and, under certain conditions, paste text from a Windows document into a DOS application.

Insider's Tip

You can even use the Windows Clipboard to transfer text from one DOS program to another DOS program. The program on the receiving end accepts the text literally, as if it had been entered from the keyboard.

The Clipboard accepts data in a wide variety of formats, so that it can work with almost every Windows application. However, the receiving application may not necessarily understand the information that you try to paste into it. For example, the Notepad will accept text but not graphics.

The common forms of data that the Clipboard can handle are described below in Table 9.1.

TABLE 9.1

Forms of Data that Clipboard Accepts

Clipboard Data Format	Description
Text	Unformatted text. Text is transferred using the standard ANSI character values, which can cause some characters to change appearance (but not ANSI values) when the receiving document uses a different font. To correct the font, just reselect the original font. Text is displayed in the Clipboard Viewer using the font specified in the FONTS.FON= statement in SYSTEM.INI.
OEM text	Unformatted text using the OEM character set (rather than the ANSI character set). OEM text is displayed in the Clipboard Viewer using the font specified in the OEMFONTS.FON= statement in SYSTEM.INI.
RTF text	Formatted text, which is stored using Microsoft's Rich Text Format. RTF text includes special formatting, such as typeface, font size, bold, italic, underline, etc.
Display text	A special text item that provides information about the data on the Clipboard, but does not actually display the data; for example, in Excel, this identifies a region of the spreadsheet.
SYLK data	Tabular data (as from a spreadsheet or database) that uses Microsoft's SYmbolic LinK format.
WK1 data	Tabular data from a spreadsheet that uses the Lotus 1-2-3 WK1 format.
CSV data	Tabular data that uses the Comma Separated Values format.

Clipboard Data Format	Description
DIF data	Tabular data that uses the Data Interchange Format.
BIFF data	Tabular data that uses Microsoft's Binary Interchange File Format. This is the file format normally used by Excel.
Bit Map graphics	A bitmapped graphics image of a specific resolution, composed of many small pixels. To display a bitmapped image in the proper colors, a corresponding color palette must identify the specific colors used to create the image. These images are device-dependent, so they can be displayed only on a particular device, such as a VGA monitor.
Palette	A Windows color palette. Most palettes in Windows contain 256 colors, even if a display can't show that many. The color palette determines the specific colors that are used to create an image and can therefore vary from image to image.
DIB graphics	A bitmapped graphics image saved in the Device Independent Bitmap format. These are 256-color images and are not device-dependent.
TIFF graphics	A bitmapped graphics image that conforms to the Tagged Image File Format. TIFF files often contain their own color (or grayscale) information, so color palettes need not be coordinated when transferring these files between computers.
Picture	A Windows Metafile graphics image. Metafile images are independent of any particular device or resolution because they are stored as GDI graphics instructions, not as bitmaps.
Wave Audio	A digitized sound file compatible with the .wav files used by Window's multimedia extensions.
Owner	A special format available in either a text or a graphics mode. The Owner format relies on the source application to display the data; if the source application is not running, the data cannot be displayed in the Clipboard Viewer.
Native	The source application's native format for data. This is often the binary data format that the application would normally save to a file.

	Clipboard	
• • • • • • • • • • • • • •
TABLE 9.1 *(cont.)*
Forms of Data
that Clipboard
Accepts

	Clipboard Data Format	Description
	Link	A special data format used by applications that support DDE to supply the receiving application with information about how to link the data to its source file.
	ObjectLink	A special data format that an OLE server application uses to provide the client application with the information needed to create a **linked** object.
	OwnerLink	A special data format that an OLE server application uses to provide the client application with the information needed to create an **embedded** object.

The Clipboard can also accept special data formats that are used by a particular application. The application informs the Clipboard how to deal with that type of data, and the Clipboard stores it as raw data bits. To provide the maximum amount of flexibility in what it can handle, the Clipboard will accept data that it knows nothing about, and simply store it in memory until you either save it or paste it to another location.

When you cut or copy some information to the Clipboard, the **source application** determines how to format the data. Occasionally the source application uses a single data format, such as text. More often, the application sends the image to the Clipboard in more than one format—for example text, RTF, and Owner.

The **destination application** determines which of the various formats to use when accepting data that has been pasted into it from the Clipboard. For example, Notepad will accept only the unformatted text version of data supplied as plain text, whereas Word for Windows might use the RTF version, which includes formatting.

The Clipboard Viewer's Display menu lists the data formats used by an application to place information on the Clipboard (Figure 9.1).

The Display menu for Excel, as shown in Figure 9.1 with Excel data in the Clipboard, includes some items that are dimmed. These formats are still available for pasting into an application, but they cannot be viewed. To view any of the formats, just choose them from the menu. Among the various formats that Excel provides to the Clipboard, the receiving application determines which format to accept. Thus Paintbrush could accept only the bitmapped image of the Excel spreadsheet, whereas Write could accept it as unformatted text, bitmapped, picture, or even a complete spreadsheet object.

Some formats, such as Owner, are available only if the source application is still running. Other formats are supplied only if the receiving application

FIGURE 9.1

Display Menu with Excel Data

The Clipboard Viewer's Display menu lists the various formats that the source application (in this case, Excel) used to place its data onto the Clipboard.

requests them, and then the source application must be running to translate the data into the requested format. If you quit Excel, for example, only the formats listed in the Display menu, shown in Figure 9.2, would be available for pasting.

FIGURE 9.2

Display Menu with Excel Data, after Quitting Excel

The formats listed on the Display menu are affected by whether the source application is running.

The exact formats that remain in the Clipboard depend on the data that was selected in Excel before you quit it.

Insider's Tip

You can save a disk image of the Clipboard's contents by using the Save As command on the Clipboard Viewer's File menu. The resulting .CLP file reflects the exact state of the Clipboard when the file was saved, even if it contains a type of data unknown to the Clipboard. You can use this trick to save the contents while the source application is still running, so you won't lose the formats that disappear when you quit the source application.

Dynamic Data Exchange

Dynamic Data Exchange, or **DDE,** allows applications to exchange information dynamically—that is, interactively. DDE is a two-headed beast. One head allows programs to communicate with one another within the operating system— that is, within Windows. The other head provides a standard language for Windows applications to send messages to each other. The two elements combine to form a system for integrating applications that is both powerful and flexible.

Although it was available in Windows 3.0, DDE lacked stability. In 3.1, Microsoft added DDEML, the DDE Management Library, which provides a basic set of programming tools to make DDE work more consistently from application to application. Software developers can use this library to implement DDE rather than create their own implementation from scratch. The library resides in your \SYSTEM subdirectory inside the DDEML.DLL file. If this file is damaged or missing, DDE may not work properly with applications that require it.

Dynamite Product

Currently, standard DDE does not work across a network, although Microsoft has promised this capability for future versions of Windows. To take advantage of DDE, all the applications must be present on your system. To address this shortcoming, a utility from Wonderware, called NetDDE, provides DDE support for a variety of different network operating systems. (See Appendix C for details.)

What DDE Can Do

DDE goes beyond linking data: it allows applications to work together on a wide variety of different tasks. Basically, DDE can let one program take advantage of the services that another program has to offer.

For example, when Windows Setup installs applications onto your system, it uses DDE to operate Program Manager by remote control, in order to create Program Manager groups and icons. In a more sophisticated scenario, DDE could be used to log onto Dow Jones, for example, extract the latest financial data about several companies, transfer this data to your Excel spreadsheet for crunching, then turn this information into a summary table, which is inserted into a memo that is faxed to some people and e-mailed to others.

With a macro language, you could automate this entire process—as long as your Windows applications support DDE. One of the many ways is to send DDE messages using the Word Basic macro language included with Word for Windows. Given the financial scenario described above, these messages would

➡ Run a Windows telecommunication program, log onto the online service, download the financial data, and save it in a data file

➡ Send DDE messages to start the spreadsheet, open the data file with downloaded data, perform calculations on it, and create the summary table

➠ Send DDE messages to select the summary table and paste it into the wordprocessing document

➠ Use DDE to open the fax program, transfer the memo to it, select the users from the dialing directory, and send the faxes

➠ Use DDE to open the e-mail program, transfer the memo to it, look up the e-mail addresses, and send the e-mail

All the applications used to create this macro would have to provide solid support for DDE. In reality, support for DDE in Windows applications ranges from nonexistent, offering static cut-and-paste operations only, to extensive implementation that provides access to most of the functions of the application. Robust DDE support as well as internal macro support in an application offers the most power for users who want to integrate and automate the operation of their applications.

Unfortunately, DDE support is difficult to implement, and implementation itself varies from application to application, so there is no consistency in its usage. You'll have to check an application's documentation to determine exactly what level of DDE support is provided, and how it is implemented in the program.

Danger Zone

On the down side, DDE eats up your system's processor power—and the greater the amount of DDE activity at any given time, the slower your system. You can reduce the amount of DDE activity by using it judiciously; for example, linking to data in a saved file requires less horsepower than linking to data in a program that's running. If you were in Excel, for example, you should use what Excel calls "external references" to link to data in files rather than to data in open worksheets.

How DDE Works

DDE works through the cooperation of two programs, the **client** and the **server**. The client application uses DDE to request information or services, and the server application provides the requested information or services. A Windows application can be designed as a client, a server, or both.

In a typical DDE session, the client sends a request to the server, which responds by either performing a function or sending the requested data. This process is called a **conversation**.

A DDE conversation usually contains three items:

➠ An **application**   Normally, the name of the program acting as the server in this conversation.

➡ A **topic** The general class of data or service that the server application can provide. Often, the topic is one of the server's documents.

➡ An **item** The actual data or service that is provided during the particular DDE conversation.

Here's an example: the client is Word, which requests a table of numbers from an Excel spreadsheet file named BIGMONEY.XLS. Excel is the DDE server, and the DDE conversation breaks down as follows:

➡ The **application** is EXCEL.EXE.

➡ The **topic** is BIGMONEY.XLS.

➡ The **item** is the range of cells that contains the table of numbers.

The DDE conversation can also include other messages, which sometimes go by different names. For example, if an application uses the DDEML library, the application is called the **service**.

Normally, the DDE conversation is carried out, unheard and unseen, between the client and server programs. You only need to select the information in the server, copy it to the Clipboard, and use Paste Link to place the data into the client. However, you would need to understand the semantics of a DDE conversation if you want to use DDE in conjunction with another macro or batch language.

When you link information from a server to a client, you can choose between two types of software links:

➡ **Hot links** Automatically updated in any clients whenever the server data is changed

➡ **Warm links** Changed only if the client specifically requests an update from the server

If you link information between two applications that are both running hot links, the client is updated as soon as the server data is changed; warm links, in contrast, are updated only if the client requests an update. If the server is running but the client document is closed, the client's information will not be updated.

To prevent obsolescence of linked data, whenever you open the client document, a dialog box asks whether you want to update the links in that document. If you respond with an affirmative, both warm and hot links are updated. The server application(s) must be running, however, so the client starts it (or them) up in order to update any links.

Dynamite Product

For techies who want to monitor DDE conversations, check out the DDEWatch utility from TechSmith Corp. DDEWatch helps you learn about DDE and also provides a valuable diagnostic and debugging tool. Another useful programming tool is the Bridge Toolkit from Softbridge, Inc., which lets you use DDE to link Windows and DOS programs.

Object Linking and Embedding

Object Linking and Embedding provides a powerful way to share information among applications. It combines the cut, copy, and paste functions of the Clipboard with the interactive capabilities of DDE. By embedding or linking data into a document with OLE, you can build a document that contains data from a variety of different applications. Such a document is called a **compound document**.

OLE lets you view or edit data in a compound document without having to know what applications created the original data. You can simply double-click on data in a compound document, and the application used to create the data starts automatically, ready for you to edit the data. When you are finished editing, close the application to return to your compound document.

OLE represents a major evolutionary step in the development of computing. No longer are you limited to a single application, which usually includes only a single type of data, such as words or graphics. OLE frees you to create and work with documents that incorporate many kinds of data from various applications. Compound documents can even assume a multimedia dimension, with the incorporation of sound, animation, and digital video.

Uses for OLE

The master plan behind OLE is to allow you to create your own integrated software. Traditional integrated software, such as Microsoft Works, will become obsolete, because you'll be able to combine whatever OLE-supportive software you like, from general purpose to specialized software, to create custom packages. The countless possibilities for combining programs into custom configurations will allow people to personalize their PCs more easily than ever.

OLE will make it easier for organizations to write in-house applications, because they will be able to tap off-the-shelf applications for the key functions of a custom system, then write a much smaller program limited to the software functions unique to their business.

You can put OLE to work in a wide variety of ways, from creating a "smart" clipboard that remembers what applications created the data you have pasted into a document, to building complex, interlinked compound documents, which can form the core of an entire management information system.

OLE lets you stuff vast quantities of information into a tiny OLE package, which can be represented onscreen as an icon or other simple graphic image. These iconic packages can contain documents that in turn contain icons linked to other documents. In this way, OLE allows you to build a hypertext—or more accurately, a hypermedia—information system, which you can navigate by clicking on linked icons.

• •

OLE Terminology

As an emerging standard, OLE has spawned its own vocabulary:

➤ **Object** A self-contained unit of information. An object can encompass a single-cell of a spreadsheet, an entire data file, or a complete application. Objects can usually be edited or played.

➤ **Edit** To edit the data represented by an object, using the server application that created the data.

➤ **Play** To activate the data represented by an object, using the server application. Play entails whatever operation is intrinsic to a program, whether it is to display a graphic image, play an audio file, show an animation, or play a video sequence.

➤ **Package** An iconic or graphical representation of an object. Packages are created by the Object Packager, often as a way to encapsulate data that was created by a non-OLE application.

➤ **Embed** To place both the native and presentation data for an object into an OLE client.

➤ **Link** To place the presentation data for an object and a pointer to the file that contains the object into an OLE client.

➤ **Broken link** What occurs when the link to a source file is moved, deleted, or intentionally broken using the Links dialog box.

➤ **Link maintenance** Use of the Links dialog box to repair broken links, change links, or break links.

➨ **Server** Any Windows application that can create OLE objects for embedding or linking into client documents.

➨ **Client** Any Windows application that can accept, display, and store objects pasted into it by an OLE server application. Only clients can create compound documents.

➨ **Verb** Describes the actions that a server can perform on its data. The most common verbs are edit and play.

➨ **Native data** Information you can edit or play, stored in the server's native data format. Typically, this is the binary data that the application would save in a disk file.

➨ **Presentation data** The information that the client uses strictly to display an object. Presentation data cannot be played or edited.

➨ **Source** The data file in the server application that contains the original object.

➨ **Destination** The document file into which you paste an object. Also called a compound document.

➨ **Registration database** The REG.DAT file, which contains information about all the OLE server applications installed in your system. Windows uses this information to determine how to manipulate data objects for both OLE and drag and drop operations. The RegEdit utility allows you to view and edit the registration database.

. . . .

How OLE Works

Information from a source document can be embedded in or linked to a destination document. The information itself is the object and can encompass almost any type of data, instructions, or software. The application used to create the information is the server, and the program into which the object is pasted is called the client.

To capture an object for embedding or linking, select the information in the source document and use either the Copy or the Cut command in the server application to place the information onto the Clipboard. The Copy command allows data to be linked or embedded, whereas the Cut command only allows you to embed data. To embed the object, use the Paste command in the client application to place the contents of the Clipboard into the destination document; to link it, use the Paste Link or Paste Special command.

Embedding an object places a full copy of the data into the client, along with both its native and presentation data. The native data can be played or edited, whereas the presentation data merely serves as a visual placeholder in the destination document. When you double-click on an embedded object, the server application appears with the object data already loaded and ready to edit or play. If you do edit the object, its original copy (the one in the server's source document) is not updated.

Linking an object inserts a software pointer into the client; the pointer directs the client to the server application and the specific data file that contains the object. The native data is not placed in the destination document. A linked object also includes the presentation data, so that the client document can display a representation of the linked data.

As with embedding, double-clicking on a linked object also brings up the server with the object ready to edit or play; the difference is that any changes made to a linked object will automatically affect all the documents that contain linked copies of that object.

A **package** is a special type of object that can be represented by an icon or almost any other graphic element you choose. A package can contain an OLE object from a server application, data from a non-OLE application in the form of a file, and even DOS command lines.

OLE Clients and OLE Servers

With OLE, the client bears the burden of managing compound documents, whereas the server application maintains the responsibility for editing or playing the embedded or linked object. Because a client application can accept information that it knows nothing about, current OLE client applications will be able to retain compatibility with future OLE servers.

According to software developers, it's fairly straightforward to create OLE server applications, and most applications that support OLE will likely do so as servers. An OLE client application is harder to develop because it has to support the creation of complex compound documents. Therefore, I expect that OLE client programs will be less common than servers.

Insider's Tip

Among the programs bundled with Windows 3.1, Paintbrush and Sound Recorder are server applications, which can only create OLE objects; Write and Cardfile are client applications, which can only accept objects; and the Object Packager is both a server and a client. Examples of other programs that can act as both OLE servers and clients are Word for Windows and Excel.

To make it easier for developers to create applications that work with OLE, Microsoft has developed two special software libraries: OLESVR.DLL for OLE servers, and OLECLI.DLL for OLE clients. These two libraries manage all the DDE conversations between OLE applications, and can start and quit OLE server applications when an object in a compound document needs to be edited or played. These two files are installed in your \SYSTEM subdirectory, and if the files are damaged or missing, OLE may not work properly.

An OLE server can create an OLE object and then edit or play an object when you select it in a client. To create an object from a server, select the information in a source document. Then use either the Copy or the Cut command on the program's Edit menu to capture the object.

If you use Copy, the information is transferred to the Clipboard in the broadest range of formats. A client can almost always use data that has been copied to create an embedded object, and it can often use the copied data to create a link to the source document. If you use Cut, the data is removed from a source document and placed on the Clipboard in a more limited range of formats. Because the data is removed from the source, a client cannot link to it, but it can use the cut data to create an embedded object.

Once you have copied or cut an object from the server and placed it on the Clipboard, you can use the Clipboard Viewer's Display menu to inspect the various data formats that the server has provided for the object. The Clipboard section earlier in the chapter lists the most common data formats. A server usually provides these formats for data objects:

➤ The native format of the data used by the server

➤ The presentation format used by the client to display the object

➤ Other standard formats (such as a bitmap, picture, or text) that the server can work with

➤ The OwnerLink format necesssary for embedding, which identifies the application used to create the object, and the class to which the object belongs

➤ The ObjectLink format necessary for linking, which identifies the class to which the object belongs, and the document that contains the linked object

If the OwnerLink or ObjectLink format isn't in the Viewer, you'll only be able to paste a static copy of the data (that is, neither linked nor embedded) into your destination document. If the OwnerLink format isn't available, you will only be able to embed the object, not link it.

• •

The Client Side of OLE

The real benefits of OLE are realized from clients, which you can use to build a compound document to assemble, organize, and view information created by a diverse assortment of applications. Once you have either copied or cut some information from an OLE server, you can switch to a client and paste an OLE object into a compound document. The nature of what you paste into the destination document depends on what form of the Paste command you select from the client's Edit menu:

➡ **Paste** The client checks the Clipboard data formats that are available for the object and uses the first compatible data format it locates.

➡ **Paste Special** A dialog box appears that lists the data formats available for information on the Clipboard. Depending on the formats listed, you can choose to either embed or link the object, or to paste one of the raw data formats without creating an object.

➡ **Paste Link** If the ObjectLink format is available on the Clipboard, a linked object will be placed in the destination document.

The Paste Command. Use the Paste command when your goal is to embed an object. If the OwnerLink format is available, the Paste command usually embeds the object into the destination document. When an object is embedded, the client stores its raw data, a presentation data format for the object, and additional information, such as the object's printing requirements and the server that created it.

Danger Zone

Because the Paste command uses the first compatible Clipboard format it encounters, the information on the Clipboard is sometimes pasted as data rather than as an object. For example, if your wordprocessor client finds Clipboard data in RTF format, it might paste the information as RTF text data, rather than as an embedded object. You can use the Paste Special command to correct this by selecting a specific Object Format.

Also, if the destination document does not understand the OLE and DDE commands being sent to it from the server, or if it does not understand the necessary formats on the Clipboard, it will place only a static copy, rather than an object, in the destination document.

The Paste Special and Paste Link Commands. Use Paste Special for maximum control over how the information on the Clipboard will be pasted into the destination document. Issuing this command brings up the Paste Special dialog box (Figure 9.3).

• • • • • • • • • • • • • •
FIGURE 9.3
*Paste Special
Dialog Box
with Multiple
Formats*

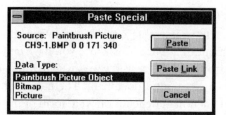

The Paste Special command in OLE clients brings up this dialog box, which lets you control how information is pasted into a destination document.

The Data Types box in the Paste Special dialog box lists the various data formats available for the information currently stored on the Clipboard; the default data format that will be used by the Paste command is highlighted. You can replace the default by selecting an alternate format.

To embed or link the information, select a format that ends with Object, such as Paintbrush Picture Object. Then click the Paste button to create an embedded object, or the Paste Link button, if it's available, to create a linked object.

Some OLE clients provide a Paste Link command directly on the Edit menu, but to use this command, either the OwnerLink or the Link data format must be present in the Clipboard. If only the Link format is available, the information will be inserted as data that uses DDE, not OLE, to maintain its link to the source document.

To create a static copy of the information, select one of the non-Object choices from the Data Type list, such as Bitmap, Picture, or Text. Then click the Paste button to place the unattached copy of the data into your destination document.

Embedded Objects. When you use the Paste or Paste Special command to embed an object—along with all of its native data—the embedded object does not maintain any connection to its server. Therefore any changes you make to an embedded object have no effect on the original data in the server document, and any changes to the server document do not affect the embedded object.

The client receives three types of data from the Clipboard, which together form the embedded OLE object:

➻ The **native data** that is understood only by the server.

➻ **Display data** (such as text or a bitmap) that the client uses to diplay the object on the screen. If the embedded object is a package, the display data can be an icon or other graphic image.

➤ Information contained in the OwnerLink format that identifies the data by its **object class**, such as Paintbrush Picture Object or Excel Worksheet Object.

To activate an embedded object, double-click on it. This causes the client to search the OLE registration database for the associated server. OLE then opens the server (or brings it to the foreground if it is already running), loads the native data contained in the object into the server, and instructs the server to perform its primary verb on the data. The most common OLE verbs are edit and play.

If the server's primary verb is edit, then a modified version of the server appears with the tools for editing the data. Two commands will have been added to the server's File menu:

➤ **Update** Updates the data in the embedded object without quitting the server

➤ **Exit and Return** Updates the data in the embedded object, quits the server, and returns you to the client's compound document

If the server's primary verb is play—as is often the case for sound files, animations, and other multimedia data—then the server plays the data contained in the object. Often the server application does not appear on-screen when the data is played.

Linked Objects. The Paste Link command places a visual representation of the data—not the data itself—into a document. The linked object's actual data remains in the source file. OLE simply places a software pointer in the destination document that provides the path and file name of the source file. The pointer serves as the "link" to the source file, which contains the actual data represented by the linked object.

When you Paste Link an object into a client, two items are transferred from the Clipboard:

➤ The **presentation data** that the client uses to display the object

➤ The **ObjectLink format** that contains the pointer to the source file

After placing these items into the compound document, the client attaches a notice to the source file; this note identifies the file to OLE as containing information linked to a specific compound document. The source data must be in a saved file (so that the client can attach a note to the file); thus, when you create a document, you must first save it before any data it contains can be linked to another document.

An object that is linked to a single source document can appear in many different compound documents. When you edit the source document, the changes are also reflected in all of the linked documents.

Once a linked object is in place, you can edit the information it represents in one of two ways:

➤ Start the server, open the source document, and edit the data as you normally would.

➤ Double-click on the linked object and edit it as if it were an embedded object. Provided the link hasn't been broken, the server automatically starts up (or comes to the foreground if it's already running) with the source file already loaded.

As you edit a linked object, all the other objects that are linked to the same source document are automatically updated. Linked objects in open documents are updated in real time; closed documents are updated the next time you open them.

For example, if you place an object that is linked to a spreadsheet in several compound documents, any changes you make to the spreadsheet— from any of its linked objects— will appear in the source document and in any other documents that contain an object linked to the spreadsheet.

Insider's Tip

To place several copies of the same linked object into different documents, copy the linked object to the Clipboard and simply paste it into the destination documents. You don't have to use Paste Link, because the link to the original source file is copied as part of the object.

Embedding Versus Linking. The biggest decision you face when using OLE is whether to embed or link the object you are pasting into a compound document.

An embedded object is free-standing and contains the full data for the object. A compound document with embedded objects can be copied to another system, and all the information contained in the objects will be included in the document. To transfer a compound document with linked objects to another system, in contrast, you must gather all the source documents that are linked to any of the objects.

With linking, however, you can save disk space and reduce network traffic by avoiding the creation of redundant information. Embedding OLE objects creates duplicate copies of existing information. If you deal with large data files, such as high-resolution graphics, animations, or sound files, replicating them can waste hard-disk space and network resources.

Assume, for example, that a megabyte of color graphics and a 500 kilobyte sound file are embedded in a memo, and that memo is sent to 100 people. You guessed it: the 1.5 megabyte memo has now consumed a whopping 150 megabytes of hard disk space and network load. Had that same memo used linked objects that all pointed to the same source document, the memo could have been distributed at a small fraction of the cost in resources.

Linking, therefore, provides an important technique for network users. Because all the copies of a linked object reflect the information in the source file, distributing documents with linked objects is a good way to provide a large group of people with information that can be automatically updated from time to time.

For example, you could paste a production schedule, some sales goals, and specific sales results into a spreadsheet, and distribute a document that contained objects linked to the spreadsheet. Then, as the schedule, goals, and results changed, you would only have to update the source spreadsheet file to update the recipients of the original document.

However, be forewarned that network support for OLE leaves much to be desired. Because OLE uses DDE to transport its messages, and because DDE does not work across a network, both the OLE client and the server must be running on the same machine in order to work with compound documents. However, OLE does allow the data files used by linked objects to be stored on networks.

Normally, linked objects are updated automatically by the OLE server whenever the source document is changed. However, some objects may be linked manually, which requires the client to request an update, rather than receiving it automatically. Manual links are useful for data that only needs periodic updating. Also, constant updating of automatic links can clog your network and take a toll on your system's performance. Using manual links helps conserve your system and network resources.

To discover whether a link is set to update automatically or manually, you'll need to use the Links dialog box, described in the next section.

Danger Zone

Be careful when creating objects that are linked to source documents that are stored on a network. If the network path changes, if the document is moved or renamed, or if the same servers are not available to everyone, you may encounter broken links.

If the name or path of a source file changes, you'll need to manually update the links for any objects that are linked to it (see the next section on link maintenance). If certain file servers are available only to certain users, you should store any source data files for linked objects on public file servers. If that's not possible, you may need to embed the objects to send to the particular users that back access to the file server.

Link Maintenance. When you use linked objects, you may need to perform some link maintenance tasks. Because a link between an object and its source file is based on the path and file name of the source, if that file is renamed or moved to a different location, a link breaks and the object will not work properly until you update the information about the source file.

To perform this operation and other link maintenance tasks, choose the Links command from the Edit menu, which brings up the Links dialog box (Figure 9.4).

FIGURE 9.4
*Links
Dialog Box*

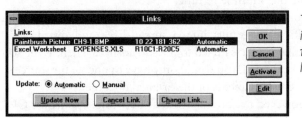

*The Links dialog box
is your control cen-
ter for performing
link maintenance.*

The Links dialog box lets you perform a variety of link maintenance tasks. With the controls in this dialog box you can

➤ Update links for manually linked objects

➤ Switch links from automatic to manual or vice versa

➤ Repair broken links

➤ Break links that you no longer want

➤ Edit or activate the linked object

The Links dialog box lists all the links for any of the objects in the compound document. To work on a particular link, select it from this list.

A linked object can be updated either manually or automatically. When a linked object is set for automatic updating (the default), the graphic representation of the object in the compound document is changed automatically by the server whenever changes are made to the source document.

To change the updating to manual, select a link and click on the Manual button. With a manual link, the image used to represent the linked data is not updated in the compound document unless you manually request an update by selecting a link and clicking the Update Now button. Updating affects only the graphic representation of the object in the compound document. The data itself is stored in the source file and is updated whenever that information is changed. This setting, therefore, is irrelevant if the linked data lacks a graphic representation, as with a linked package for example.

Because linking relies on an exact path and file name, any changes to the name or location of the source file will also break the links of any linked objects. Repairing these broken links is a tedious process: you need to open every compound document that contains a linked object and manually change the information for each source file.

To fix a broken link, open the compound document that contains the linked object and select Links from the Edit menu to bring up the Links dialog box. Then click on the Change Link button, which summons the Change Link dialog box (Figure 9.5).

FIGURE 9.5
*Change Link
Dialog Box*

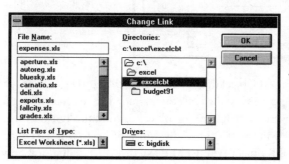

The Change Link dialog box lets you repair a broken link or change an existing link.

The Change Link dialog box, like any Windows browsing dialog box, allows you to search through your volumes and directories for the source file that contains the data for the linked object. When the source file is located, click OK to return to the Links dialog box. The new link information is reported in the dialog box.

You can also change the link so that it points to a different file. The procedure is the same as for repairing a broken link. If you change the link to a completely different source file, you're essentially selecting a new object. This object then appears in your compound document.

If you deliberately break a link, only the presentation data—that is, the graphic representation of the object in the file—remains in the client, as if you had merely used the Clipboard without OLE. To break a link, select the object, choose Links from the Edit menu to access the Links dialog box, then press the Cancel Link button. To break other links, select them while you're in the Links dialog box, and then press the Cancel Link button to break each subsequent link.

To remove the linked object altogether, select it in the client and choose Cut from the Edit menu. This removes both the link and its presentation data from the client and places it on the Clipboard, where you can either ignore it or paste it into another OLE client.

Other OLE Client Commands. In addition to the Paste, Paste Special, Paste Link, and Links commands, OLE clients often include other OLE-related commands in their Edit menus. Because OLE is an evolving standard, these commands are not always consistent from application to application. However, two other common commands are **Insert Object** and **Object**.

The **Insert Object** command brings up a dialog box that lets you choose a server for creating an object to link or embed into a client (Figure 9.6).

FIGURE 9.6
*Insert Object
Dialog Box*

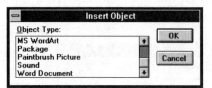

This dialog box provides a quick way to insert an OLE object into a compound document.

The Insert Object dialog box lists all the object classes that can be created by the OLE servers installed on your system. Just select an object type, and a server that can create that type of object automatically starts itself up. (Insider's mini-tip: you can select Package from the list to run the Object Packager.)

An OLE object type will be listed in this dialog box only if the server is properly listed in your OLE registration database. The registration database (which can be viewed with the RegEdit utility) contains the names of both servers and the object types that they can create. Some servers can create more than one type of object; Excel, for example, can create both a Worksheet Object and a Chart Object.

After you create some new data, you can copy or cut the information and return directly to the client to insert the object into your compound document.

Insider's Tip

The Insert Object command provides a shortcut for running the server application independently, so that you don't have to switch to Program Manager. This technique works best for creating new data to place in an object; it's not as convenient if you want to use existing data to create an object.

The **Object** command runs the server associated with the object, so that you can quickly edit or play a linked or embedded object. First select an object. The name of the Object command changes on your Edit menu, depending on what type of object is selected. For example, when no object is selected, the command is listed simply as "Object," and its name is dimmed on the menu (Figure 9.7).

FIGURE 9.7

*Edit Menu
with Dimmed
Object Item*

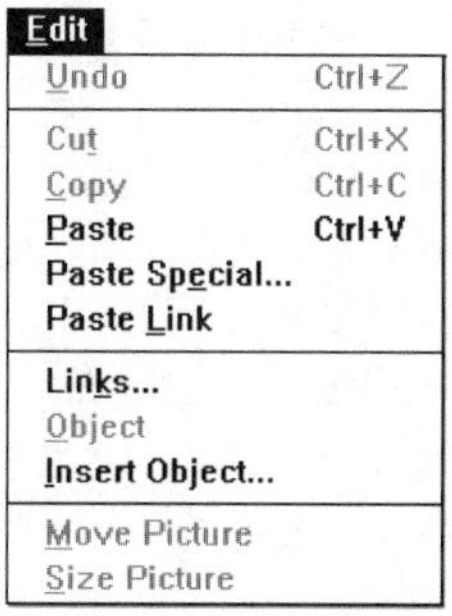

Edit
Undo	Ctrl+Z
Cut	Ctrl+X
Copy	Ctrl+C
Paste	Ctrl+V
Paste Special...	
Paste Link	
Links...	
Object	
Insert Object...	
Move Picture	
Size Picture	

The Object command is dimmed when no objects are selected.

However, if you were to select a graphic object created by Paintbrush, the Object menu item would change to "Edit Paintbrush Picture Object" (Figure 9.8).

FIGURE 9.8

*Edit Menu
with Edit
Paintbrush
Picture Object
Item*

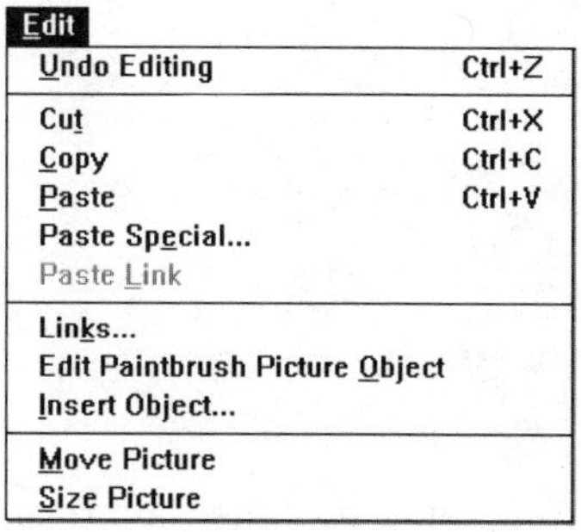

Edit
Undo Editing	Ctrl+Z
Cut	Ctrl+X
Copy	Ctrl+C
Paste	Ctrl+V
Paste Special...	
Paste Link	
Links...	
Edit Paintbrush Picture Object	
Insert Object...	
Move Picture	
Size Picture	

The Object command changes to Edit Paintbrush Picture Object when such an object is selected.

If you select an object for which more than one action is possible, the Object item provides a cascading menu that lists the various actions (that is, the OLE verbs) that can be performed on the object. For example, if you select a Sound object in a compound document, the Object item is labeled "Sound Object" and contains a cascading menu that lists two choices, Play and Edit (Figure 9.9).

FIGURE 9.9

*Edit Menu
with Sound
Object Item
and
Cascading
Menu*

Edit
Undo Editing	Ctrl+Z	
Cut	Ctrl+X	
Copy	Ctrl+C	
Paste	Ctrl+V	
Paste Special...		
Paste Link		
Links...		
Sound Object		**Play**
Insert Object...		**Edit**
Move Picture		
Size Picture		

Because more than one action can be performed on a Sound Object, this menu item provides a cascading menu that lists both the Play and Edit actions.

Insider's Tip

You can use OLE to overcome some of the limitations of Program Manager. For example, in Program Manager, you can't place groups within groups. But with OLE, you can build a compound document that resembles a group and then create a single Program Manager icon that will launch the compound document.

Here's one way to create a compound document that acts like a pseudo-group. First open a compound document in an OLE client, such as Word for Windows. Then open File Manager, hold down Ctrl+Shift (to create links rather than copies), and drag and drop the files that you want into your pseudogroup document. The files are automatically turned into packages by OLE. Figure 9.10 shows a Word for Windows document that contains a number of packaged files placed in a table.

FIGURE 9.10

Word Document with Lots of Packages

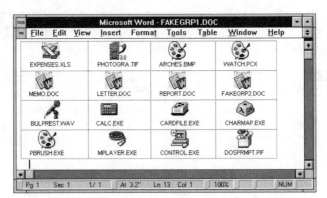

By placing many linked icons in a compound document, you can create a pseudogroup for launching files.

Each of the icons in the compound document represents a link to a file. Double-click on an icon to launch the file together with its application—reminiscent of a group in Program Manager, eh? Now create an icon for your compound document in Program Manager, and—viola!—you have a pseudo-group nested within a real group. Clever OLE hackers will further discover that an icon in a pseudogroup can link them to another pseudogroup, thus extending the strategy into the development of a layered hierarchy.

The Object Packager

The Object Packager is both an OLE client and server program, so that it can create OLE objects and accept them from other servers. Packager can work with a wide variety of data, such as an entire file from almost any program, or even a DOS command line.

The Object Packager is an OLE utility program that lets you encapsulate data from both OLE and non-OLE applications and control the graphic presentation of objects in compound documents. If you package an entire file, the file can be created by either an OLE server or a non-OLE application, but if the package contains only part of a file, the file must be created by an OLE server.

Insider's Tip

When working with non-OLE data, the Packager refers to the file extension information in the WIN.INI file, rather than in the OLE registration database, to determine how to associate that data with particular applications.

The Object Packager allows you to take information and encapsulate it into a package, which is a special type of OLE object represented by whatever icon or graphic image you select. For example, an OLE object that represents a large section of a spreadsheet would normally use presentation data that resembles the entire portion of the spreadsheet. The Object Packager lets you substitute an icon or other graphic image for the presentation data. Thus you can make a packaged object resemble an icon, button, drawing, or whatever other visual you can copy to the Clipboard.

Packages are also automatically used for objects that do not provide presentation data. For example, a sound object is displayed using the Sound Recorder icon, because no graphic representation of the sound file is provided by the Sound Recorder.

You can package non-OLE data, but you can only place a package into an OLE client. Although packages can be embedded only into compound documents, a package can contain a linked object. When such a package is embedded into a document, it behaves as if it were a linked object, with a few exceptions. When you double-click on the package, it loads the source file into the server as with a normally linked object. However, if you select such a package in a document, the Links command will not be available on the client's Edit menu. To do link maintenance on the package, you'll need to edit the package from within the Object Packager.

To edit the package, select it in the compound document; then choose the Package Object item on the client's Edit menu, which reveals two choices:

➥ **Activate Contents** Loads the data contained in the package into the server program and either edits or plays the data, depending on the nature of the data

➥ **Edit Package** Loads the package into the Object Packager

To perform link maintenance, choose the Edit Package choice; the Object Packager appears with the linked object displayed. Choose the Links command from the Packager's Edit menu to access the Links dialog box and perform any necessary link maintenance.

Packaging a File. A package may contain the entire embedded file or only a link to that file. The file can either be a data file or, in some cases, an application program. To create a package that contains an embedded file, start the Packager and make sure the Content window is selected (Figure 9.11).

FIGURE 9.11
Object Packager with Content Window Selected

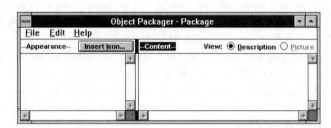

This is how the Object Packager looks when it's empty.

If the Content window is not selected, just click in it or press Tab. Then choose the Import command from the File menu, which summons the Import dialog box. Use this box to browse through your drives and directories to select a file for embedding into the package. When you've located the file you want, click OK to return to the Packager.

The name of the file now appears in the Content window, and the icon of the application associated with that file extension is displayed in the Appearance window (Figure 9.12).

FIGURE 9.12
Packager with Embedded File

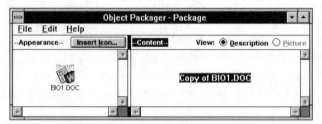

The Object Packager now contains an embedded file.

To change the icon for the embedded file, click on the Insert Icon button in the Appearance window. This brings up the Insert Icon dialog box, which contains the name of the application associated with the file type in the package, along with any icons contained in that application. If more than one icon is displayed in the Current Icon section of the Insert Icon dialog box, you can select one of those other icons. To use an icon not in that application file, click on the Browse button and select another source file for your icons. This process is similar to the way you select an icon in File Manager—you can use program files, DLLs, and .ico files as icon sources.

To make the package resemble something other than an icon, select the Appearance window, switch to a graphics program, copy any type of graphic from that program, switch back to the Packager, and paste the image into the Appearance window.

If you use an icon to represent your package, it will contain a default label that describes what the document contains. The exact label depends on your data. For example, if the package contains a graphic created with Paintbrush, the default will be Paintbrush Picture. To change the label, choose the Label command from the Edit menu; the Label Edit dialog box appears. Enter a new label, then click OK to change labels.

When you paste a graphic other than an icon into the Appearance window, the package will lack a label. If you want one, you'll need to create a title for the image in the graphics program, before you paste it into the Appearance window.

When you're satisfied with the Appearance window, choose Copy Package from the Packager's Edit menu. Then switch to a compound document and issue the Paste command from the client's Edit menu.

Using File Manager to Create Packages. You can use the drag and drop capabilities of File Manager as a shortcut for creating packages that contain embedded or linked files. However, this technique works only with clients that support *all* OLE conventions, so this will exclude some OLE-capable clients.

Insider's Tip

The easiest way to embed a file is to open both File Manager and the compound document. Then select the source file in File Manager and drag it into the window that contains the compound document. When you drop the file icon into the compound document, the package appears at the location of the insertion point.

A similar process is used to create a package that contains a linked file. Open both File Manager and compound document windows and select the source file, but this time hold down Ctrl+Shift while dragging the file icon and dropping it into the compound document.

You can also perform this trick on groups of files. To embed the files, just drag them into the compound document. To link them, hold down Ctrl+Shift while dragging the group of file icons.

Any newly created packages will use the icon associated with the extension of their source file, and the icon label will bear the name of the source file. To change the icon or label, highlight the icon in the document. From the client's Edit menu, choose the Package Object cascading menu; then choose Edit Package to call up the Object Packager.

From the keyboard, select the source file in File Manager. Then press F8 to issue the Copy command. The Copy dialog box appears (Figure 9.13).

••••••••••••••
FIGURE 9.13
File Manager's Copy Dialog Box

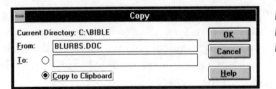

File Manager's Copy dialog box lets you turn files into OLE packages.

Click the Copy to Clipboard button in the dialog box (Alt+C), then click OK (or press Enter). Next start the Object Packager (hint: run PACKAGER.EXE). The Content window should already be selected; if it isn't, press Tab. Choose Paste (Ctrl+V) to embed the file into the package, or Paste Link (Alt,E,L) to link the file to the package.

Switch to the window that contains the compound document and use the Paste command to embed the file into the package, or use the Paste Link command to link the file to the package.

Packaging a Portion of a File. To create a package with only a section of a file, the file must have been created by an OLE server. This technique also lets you package an OLE object, either linked or embedded, that you have already created.

Open the document that contains either the source data or an existing object. Then select the information or object and issue the Copy command. Run the Packager and make sure the Content window is selected. For an embedded object, choose Paste; for a linked object, choose Paste Link. After making adjustments to the appearance of the package, choose Copy Package from the Edit menu.

Next switch to a compound document and issue the Paste command to place the package into that document.

Insider's Tip

Packaging a DOS Command Line. The Packager lets you place a DOS command into a package, so that when you double-click or otherwise activate the package it carries out the command. This technique is useful for starting an application together with a document or for running a batch program.

To package a DOS command, choose Command Line from the Edit menu to bring up a simple dialog box that contains a text box for entering your DOS command line. The command line can include any optional switches or other parameters that the command accepts. Click OK to return to the Packager after you've entered the command. The command now appears in the Content window, but the Appearance window is empty. You can place an icon or any other graphic item into the Appearance window. Then select Copy Package, switch to the compound document, and use Paste to embed the DOS command.

The Registration Database

The **registration database** is fundamental to OLE, although it is also used for other Windows operations, such as drag and drop. The registration database provides Windows with information about every OLE server application that has been installed on your system.

The system registration database is a binary file named REG.DAT, which Setup installs in your main Windows directory. The database contains information about the path and file names of OLE servers, the file name extensions of data files and their associated applications, the class names of OLE objects that the servers can edit, and the OLE verbs and other protocols used by any objects.

Although OLE doesn't rely on the information in your WIN.INI file, information in the database corresponds to information in the [embedding] and [extensions] sections of the WIN.INI, and information in these sections may be altered when new applications are registered in the database.

When you install an OLE-capable application, its setup program usually updates the registration database. If not, you can use the **Registration Info Editor** (or **RegEdit**) utility, REGEDIT.EXE, to add the information to the registration database. The RegEdit program can also be used to view and edit the entries already contained in the database.

Setup installs RegEdit in your system, but doesn't create an icon for it. You may want to create two icons for RegEdit, because it really includes two different programs: a regular version and an advanced version. When you start up RegEdit normally, it begins in **regular mode** (Figure 9.14).

FIGURE 9.14
*RegEdit,
Regular Mode*

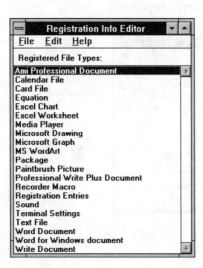

This is how RegEdit looks when it's running in regular mode.

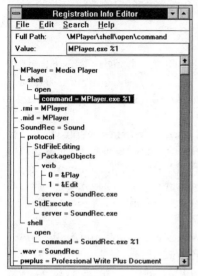

In regular mode, RegEdit presents a single list box, titled Registered File Types, which lists the various data objects that have been registered in the database.

If you run RegEdit with the /V switch, it starts in advanced mode. This looks like an entirely different program, with a hierarchical outline of all the information in the database and a different set of menu commands (Figure 9.15).

You might want to create one icon, titled RegEdit, using the REGEDIT.EXE file name by itself to run the program in regular mode, and a second icon, titled RegEdit Advanced, that starts the program with the REGEDIT.EXE /V command.

Working with RegEdit. Windows applications that can act as OLE servers include a registration file denoted by the .REG file extension. Simply double-click on this file in File Manager to automatically register the application. Another way to add a server to the database is to choose Merge Registration File from the File menu when RegEdit is running and specify the appropriate .REG file.

FIGURE 9.15
RegEdit, Advanced Mode

RegEdit presents a different face when you run it in advanced mode.

To register a new file type for an application that lacks a .REG file, you can either copy an existing registration entry or create a new one.

To copy a registration entry, run RegEdit in standard mode and choose an existing entry from the Registered File Types list in the Registration Info Editor window. Then choose Copy File Type from the Edit menu; the Copy File Type dialog box appears (Figure 9.16).

FIGURE 9.16
Copy File Type Dialog Box

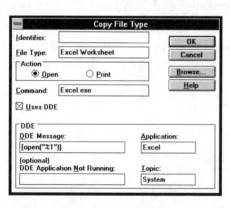

Here's a shortcut to creating a new registration database entry: just copy and modify an existing entry.

You can modify the registration information in the dialog box to suit the new file type.

To add or modify an entry, choose Add File Type or Modify File Type from the Edit menu. Either choice brings up a dialog box that is almost identical to the Copy File Type dialog box in Fig. 9.16.

All three dialog boxes contain these items:

➡ **Identifier** A unique name of up to 63 characters. This cannot be edited in the Modify File Type dialog box.

➡ **File Type** The description used in the Registered File Types list, situated in the Registration Info Editor window, and in File Manager's Associate dialog box.

➡ **Action** The action that can be performed on the file type: either open or print.

➡ **Command** The command that executes an application, along with any switches that need to be sent to the application to perform the action (open or print).

➡ **Uses DDE** Place a check in this box if the application uses DDE messages to open or print files.

➡ **DDE** Enter information here that specifies the DDE messages and DDE topic associated with the action (open or print).

Both the regular and advanced modes of RegEdit include their own help files, which you can consult if you need to find out more about operating the RegEdit utility.

Insider's Tip

If the registration database (that is, the REG.DAT file) becomes damaged or deleted, here's how to reconstruct the original registration database installed by Setup. Quit your Windows session and rename or delete the REG.DAT file, if it still exists. Then restart Windows, run File Manager, and locate the SETUP.REG file in your \SYSTEM subdirectory. Now double-click on this file and RegEdit will rebuild the initial registration database. A dialog box should appear to confirm the success of the operation. Finally double-click on any other .REG files to restore the registration information for other OLE servers installed on your system.

Summary

Windows 3.1 provides three key features that let you share information among applications: the Clipboard, DDE, and OLE. Using the Clipboard, you can copy or cut data from one program and paste it into another. At its basic level, the Clipboard merely serves as a holding area for any information in transit. This cut and paste capability is common to almost all GUIs.

DDE (Dynamic Data Exchange) provides a software mechanism that allows one Windows application to communicate with another. Special software messages actually perform the communications; some of these messages are common to almost all DDE-capable applications, and others are intrinsic to specific applications. Various applications will automatically implement DDE for certain functions, whereas in some instances, you must initiate it yourself by incorporating the DDE messages into a macro or other programming language.

In order to increase the power and accessibility of DDE, Microsoft has developed a specific implementation of it called OLE (Object Linking and Embedding). OLE lets you use the Clipboard to copy information from one application and embed or link it into a compound document, which can contain information created by several applications. OLE server applications provide OLE-compatible data to another application, and OLE client applications can accept the data to create a compound document. When OLE is used to embed data, a copy of the original data is placed in the compound document. When OLE is used to link data, the original data remains with the source file, and only a visual representation of it is placed in the compound document.

Windows provides two utilities to help you work with OLE: the Object Packager and the Registration Info Editor. The Object Packager lets you encapsulate data from both OLE and non-OLE applications for placement in a compound document. The Registration Info Editor lets you inspect and update the registration database, REG.DAT, which contains information about all the OLE server applications installed on your system.

10

Windows Networking and Communications

In computing, as in politics, there is power in numbers. The capabilities of a personal computer can be multiplied when it's connected to other computers through a network or other communications link. And, as in politics, if you make the right connections, you stand to gain access to information that would otherwise be unavailable to you as an individual.

Most offices connect computers through a network to provide electronic mail and facilitate the transfer of computer files, which everyone in the office can share. When connected to a network, you can access information, such as data and programs, available on a network server. Often you can run those programs directly on the server, thus freeing your computer's resources for your own activities. Another major reason for networking computers is to share expensive printing facilities, such as high-speed or color printers. To address the importance of networking, Microsoft has created a special version of Windows 3.1 called Windows for Workgroups.

Even if you have a standalone system, you can dial into a remote network to use its services with remote network access software. In addition, with telecommunications software you can dial another computer to exchange files, or dial into a online service or mainframe host to access large databases and other information sources. In addition, fax hardware and software can turn your system into an intelligent fax machine.

Windows 3.1 provides much better support for both networking and communications than its predecessor, with a more reliable COM driver and improved procedures for installation and administration on a network server. However, network installation can still be a major hassle, and network administrators need to become intimately familiar with the documentation for their specific networks.

This chapter describes how to use the basic Windows 3.1 product with a network, how to install Windows onto a network server, and how to install Windows from the server onto individual workstations. Another section points out special characteristics of the major commercial networks, including Novell's NetWare and Microsoft's LAN Manager. The remainder of the chapter takes a look at remote access software, Windows communications concerns, and fax technologies.

- -

Using Windows on a Network

New in 3.1

Once the network software has been installed on your system, using a network with Windows is fairly straightforward. Windows 3.1 has made real strides since 3.0; now you can easily connect the network drivers and printers, and once your connections have been established, Windows does a fairly good job of reestablishing the connections the next time you run a session.

Before you start your Windows session, you should start the network software. Usually you can install the necessary network drivers using the CONFIG.SYS and AUTOEXEC.BAT files to load the necessary software automatically when your system is first turned on. If the software is not loaded at startup, you'll probably need to run a special batch file from the DOS command prompt that loads the appropriate network software.

Once the network software is loaded, you're often still required to log in as a user on the network. Usually this means you must type your user name and password. Depending on your network configuration, you can log in from Windows using the Network icon in the Control Panel, or from the DOS command prompt. In the latter case, I recommend that you log in or out before you start your Windows session to avert a possible system crash, which can happen when you use the DOS prompt from within Windows on certain networks. If you're unsure about which procedure to use, check with your network adminstrator.

Danger Zone

Some networks allow you to choose a variety of DOS volume letters for establishing network connections, in order to access data or programs located on a particular network server. To avoid confusing Windows, you should always use the same drive letter, even if the network allows you to use different ones.

For example, if you access network information using the N: drive, Windows records N: as part of the path that it will always use to search for that information. If you logged into a different drive letter—even if the same files were also available from that drive letter—Windows might not be able to find them; or worse, if you are running Windows from the server, Windows itself might not be able to start.

Similarly, you should try to address network printers using the same path or port, even if the network allows you a variety of access choices. To change the port or printer path, use the Printers icon in the Control Panel to ensure that Windows updates the information regarding your access to that device.

The Control Panel's Network Icon

On a very simple network, such as one that allows you to share a printer, you'll probably see only one additional drive in File Manager.

If a more complicated network has been properly installed on your system, a Network icon usually appears in the Control Panel. Double-click on this icon to issue the Network dialog box, which varies depending on your choice of network driver. The network controls may allow you to log on and off the network, specify what network connections you want to maintain each time you start Windows, or change your user ID or password.

Figure 10.1 shows the controls associated with the Network icon for the Novell Netware network driver.

• • • • • • • • • • • • • •
FIGURE 10.1
Novell
Netware
Network
Driver
Controls

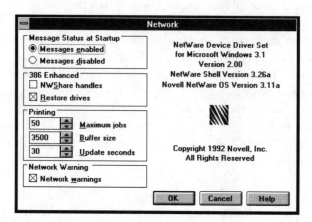

If you're using the Windows Novell Netware driver, you'll see this dialog box when you click on the Network icon in the Control Panel.

In many cases you will need to access this dialog box and supply an appropriate password before you can log onto the network and access network disk drives, printers, and other resources. Once you're connected to the network, you can access applications and data stored on the network server, much as if it were available on your computer's hard disk. The main disadvantage to accessing information over a network is speed; depending on your hardware, it can be considerably slower than retrieving the same information from your own hard disk.

Using Network Printers

A compelling reason for installing a network, especially in a small office, is to share the use of one or more network printers. In this situation, you'll need to know how to switch the connections from your workstation to the various printers, in case one is tied up or you need a printer with a special capability, such as color printing.

To connect to a network printer, you need to access the Network-Printer Connections dialog box, which can be done in one of these ways:

➤ Open the Printers icon in the Control Panel and click on the Connect button to bring up the Connect dialog box. Then click on the Network button.

➤ From Print Manager, choose Network Connections from the Options menu.

➤ If you've already chosen Printer Setup from the Options menu in Print Manager, click the Connect button to access the Connect dialog box, then click the Network button.

Any of these methods summons the Network-Printer Connections dialog box, similar to the one shown in Figure 10.2.

FIGURE 10.2

*Network-
Printer
Connections
Dialog Box*

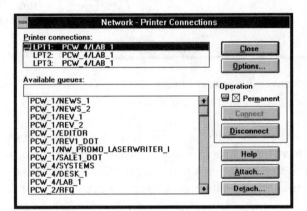

*The Network-
Printer Connec-
tions dialog box
shows you the net-
work printer con-
nections you've
already made and
lets you discon-
nect from them or
connect to new
ones.*

Although the specific options in the Network-Printer Connections dialog box vary by network, most include a section showing your current network connections and another that indicates available print queues.

To connect to a network printer, type the network name or path into the Path box; select the port from the port list; and type a password, if required. An asterisk conceals each character you type in the password box. If a different network printer has already been connected to a port, you'll need to disconnect it by selecting it and clicking on the Disconnect button. Then select the new printer and click on the Connect button. If the new printer isn't automatically added to your list of printers, you may have network problems—see your network administrator. (In fact, see your network administrator if anything described in this chapter doesn't work!)

Many network drivers provide a Browse button in the Network-Printer Connections dialog box, which you can use to point and click your way through the various network volumes attached to your system. Once you've connected to the new network printer, click on the Close button to return to the Connect dialog box; then click OK to return to the printer setup dialog box.

Most network drivers allow you to easily reconnect to a network printer from which you have disconnected without having to repeat the entire connection process. Network drivers that support this option feature a Previous button in the Network Connections dialog box. When you click on this button, you are presented with a list of network printers to which you were previously connected (Figure 10.3).

FIGURE 10.3
*Previous
Network
Connections
Dialog Box*

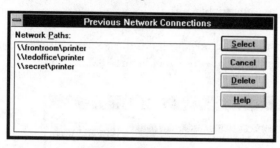

Most network drivers let you easily reestablish a connection to a printer you've used before, although a few require you to repeat the entire connection process.

To reconnect to a printer listed in the Previous Network Connections dialog box, highlight the printer and click on the Select button.

Insider's Tip

If your network driver does not offer a Previous Network Connections option, and you have to frequently reconnect to various network printers, you can create a simple macro using the Recorder utility, described in Chapter 5, to automate your reconnection process.

• •

Using Print Manager with a Network

Most networks provide their own print management services and bypass Windows Print Manager. However, it's often handy to use Print Manager, and you can do so with some network drivers. For example, you can set up Print Manager as a print spooler to offload a print job and return to your document without waiting for the printing to be completed. Print Manager can also provide information about other printers on the network, so you can assess where and when to print.

Print Manager's Option menu provides a Network Connections command, which offers a shortcut to the Network-Printer Connections dialog box. In addition, you can use Print Manager to look at a network printer's queue. Print Manager gives you the ability to view all the files in a network queue, not just your files, and also view other network queues—including ones to which you're not connected.

Usually, when you direct a file to a network printer and then open Print Manager, only the files that you are printing will appear on the network printer. To view the entire queue for your currently selected network printer, choose Selected Net Queue from Print Manager's View menu (Alt,V,S). Print Manager displays a dialog box similar to Figure 10.4. The exact configuration of this dialog box depends on what kind of network driver you're using; some don't even support this option at all. If your network does allow you to view the network queue, you can reissue the Selected Net Queue command from the View menu to update the information about the network queue.

FIGURE 10.4
Selected
Net Queue
Dialog Box

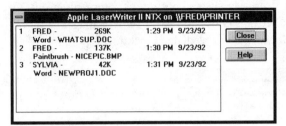

Choose Selected Net Queue from Print Manager's Option menu to view the entire queue for a network printer, not just the files that you've sent to it.

If you're in a hurry to print, first check the entire queue of your selected printer. If there is a wait, use the Other Net Queue command (Alt,V,O) on Print Manager's View menu to check out the lines on the other network printers. This command brings up the Other Net Queue dialog box, shown in Figure 10.5.

FIGURE 10.5
Other Net
Queue
Dialog Box

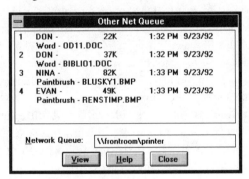

The Other Net Queue command on Print Manager's View menu lets you take a peek at the queues for other network printers to which you're not connected.

This dialog box contains a text box, Network Queue, into which you type the network path of the printer whose queue you want to view. Then click on the View button; Print Manager queries the network and displays the information about the selected queue in the dialog box. Again, the exact contents of this dialog box vary by network driver. To view a different queue, just repeat this process. Keep in mind that looking at another printer's queue doesn't mean that you're connected to it.

The status of any queue is only updated from time to time by the network software. You can force Print Manager to start querying the network and update the status of the print queue by issuing the Refresh command from Print Manager's View menu (F5).

When Print Manager is running as a minimized icon, it suspends the query process in order to keep network traffic to a minimum. When the Print Manager window is open, it sends intermittent queries, which generate additional network traffic for the printer and can slow down your network's printing processes.

If you're on a high-traffic network, and you don't need to be constantly appraised of the status of the network print queue, it would be prudent to turn off Print Manager's continuous query function. To do so, issue the Network Settings command from Print Manager's Option menu. This calls up the Network Options dialog box, shown in Figure 10.6.

FIGURE 10.6
*Network
Options
Dialog Box*

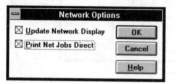

The Network Options dialog box lets you control how Print Manager interacts with a network.

To prevent Print Manager from periodically updating the status of the printer queue, click in the Update Network Display check box to remove the X. Print Manager discontinues its query process until you toggle the X on again.

You can also use the Network Options dialog box to control whether your files will be spooled to Print Manager or sent directly to the network for printing. The latter process usually reduces network traffic and quickens the print time, but Print Manager provides you with queue update information and error messages that may not be available from your network server. The default is to bypass Print Manager. To change the default, remove the X from the Print Net Jobs Direct check box.

Because Print Manager interacts differently with different network drivers, you should test both methods to see which works best for your configuration and network software. To bypass printing with Print Manager, place an X back in the Print Net Jobs Direct check box.

Installing Windows on a Network

New in 3.1

Windows 3.1 has not only improved user operations over a network, it has also significantly simplified and extended the ways for system administrators to install it on a network. In particular, it's now easier to copy the Windows files to a network server; set up networked computers with either a full copy of Windows for each or one shared copy for all; and create an automated custom setup procedure that quickly installs Windows on a group of systems.

You can use the Windows 3.1 installation disks to install Windows on a network server, and then from the server onto individual workstations. Although this can easily be done with a single copy of Windows, Microsoft of course requires that you obtain a special license to run Windows on more than one machine. Contact your Microsoft sales representative for information about such a license.

Windows Setup includes three options for installing Windows onto a network server, or from a server to a workstation:

➤ **SETUP /A** Running Setup with the /A switch invokes Setup's administrative mode. This copies the Windows files onto a network server so the files can be shared among the various users on the network, and allows users to run Setup from the network in order to install Windows on their computers.

➤ **SETUP /H** This runs Setup in a special automated mode that allows you to quickly install Windows on a number of different systems. This mode, also called batch mode setup, works in conjunction with a special system-setting template file called SETUP.SHH.

➤ **SETUP /N** This is Setup's network mode, which configures a PC so that it can run a shared copy of Windows directly from the server. With this option, Setup copies only a few files to each user's Windows directory, and therefore requires less than half a megabyte of space. Each user's Windows directory can be located either on the local hard disk or RAM disk, or on a server.

Before setting up Windows to run on your network, you need to decide where you want to install the program: from the server or from a set of floppy disks. To install from the server, you'll need to use the SETUP /A procedure to load the various Windows files onto the server for transfer to the individual workstations. This choice ensures that each workstation is set up using the same files; it also allows the installation process to run unattended.

Another consideration is whether you want to install a separate copy of Windows on each workstation. This procedure consumes between 8 and 11 megabytes on each computer's hard disk, but speeds up individual Windows performance. Or do you want to configure the system so that users can run Windows from shared files on a server? This requires the SETUP /N option, consumes about 16 megabytes of space on your server disk, and only 300 to 400 kilobytes of hard disk or RAM disk space on each connected computer—but it also slows down performance of Windows on each user's system.

The Windows Setup program allows a considerable amount of customization—you can edit your own SETUP.INF files and automate the setup procedure. See Chapter 16 for details.

Danger Zone

Before running Setup in any of its modes, be sure to disable any TSRs or network messaging systems, such as e-mail or popup programs, because they can cause Setup to fail if a message is sent to your system during the installation process. And of course be sure to build an escape route, by making a complete systemwide backup before installing Windows.

. . . .

Windows Administrative Setup

The Windows Administrative Setup procedure lets you copy all the various Windows files into a directory on a network server. However, it doesn't install a usable copy of Windows; this must be done using one of Setup's installation modes.

To copy the Windows files to a network server, make sure the destination volume or partition on your server contains at least 20 megabytes of free space, and that you have write privileges for that server volume or partition. Then place installation disk 1 into any available floppy disk drive and log onto that drive. Once you're at the command prompt, type

```
SETUP /A
```

and press Enter.

Setup first asks you to type in the path and directory on the server that will contain a copy of the Windows files, for example—N:\NETWIN.

Setup then asks you to type your group name and company name, which it stores in the network directory for use when Windows is installed on individual computers from the server.

Setup then expands the files from the installation disks, renames them as necessary, copies them to the server directory you specify, and marks them as read-only. Individual Windows files must be marked as read-only even if your network server is already set up as a read-only drive. With some networks, you also need to mark the Windows files in this directory as sharable. Refer to your network documentation to see if this is necessary.

Insider's Tip

Here's a shortcut for installing everything onto another server if there's more than one connected to your network: run Setup with the /A switch from your old server directory which already contains copies of your Windows files. Setup again prompts you for the path, directory, company name, and group name for each server to which you copy the Windows files.

Once the Windows files have been copied to a server using Setup's administrative mode, users can log into the directory that contains the files and then run Setup from their computer to install Windows. To set up a full copy of Windows, network users can run Setup without any switches; or, to run a shared copy of Windows from the server, they can run Setup with the /N switch as described in the next section.

By modifying the SETUP.INF file, you can control how Setup configures Windows on each of the computers connected to the network. In addition, you can control what applications and Program Manager groups are installed in each user's system.

You can also create custom PROGMAN.INI files that restrict what actions users can take when running Program Manager. For example, you can remove the Run command from the Program Manager's File menu; you can remove the File menu altogether; and you can prevent users from exiting Windows or from changing any settings or reconfiguring groups. For details, refer to the end of Chapter 2 and to the section on PROGMAN.INI in Chapter 15.

Installing a Shared Copy of Windows

After the Windows files have been copied to a network server, users can install Windows on their own computers. To do this, they can invoke the Setup's Network Installation by running Setup with the /N switch. This copies only the files needed to configure an individual user's system preferences, such as the Windows initialization files and Program Manager group files (that is, files ending in .INI and .GRP, respectively). This lets each user create a customized Windows configuration while still sharing the core Windows files located on the network server.

In such a setup, users can run Windows from two directories: the **network directory**, where the main Windows files are stored, and the **user directory**, which contains the .INI and .GRP files. The user directory should be situated on the user's RAM disk or hard disk, because it requires less than half a megabyte of space and allows faster Windows operations. The user's directory can also be located on a network server as well, but each user should have an individual directory. Setup adds the path of both the shared network directory and the user's individual directory to the path setting in the AUTOEXEC.BAT file on each user's computer.

To install a shared copy of Windows on an individual workstation, first connect to the network drive that contains the shared Windows file and then switch to the directory storing the files. At the DOS prompt, type

```
SETUP /N
```

Setup then prompts you for a path and directory name for placing the .INI, .GRP, and other user files. If a System Setting File (by default, called SETUP.SHH) has been created, as described later in this chapter, it should be specified before the /N switch. For example, to install a shared copy of Windows, you might type

```
SETUP /H:SETUP.SHH /N
```

This command installs the shared copy using the settings specified in the SETUP.SHH file.

If you're setting up Windows to run from a diskless workstation, you should create a TEMP directory for storing temporary files used by programs such as Print Manager. Normally, if you don't create a TEMP directory, the root directory of drive C: is used for storing temporary files. Because a diskless workstation obviously lacks a drive C:, you will need to create a TEMP directory on a RAM disk or on the network server. Creating it on a RAM disk enhances your system's speed but requires that the diskless workstation has enough memory to support it.

To set up TEMP directories on a network server, each user must have an individual TEMP directory. To install a TEMP directory, you'll need to use the AUTOEXEC.BAT file. For example, to specify that the network directory N:\USERTEMP should be used, you would add this line to the AUTOEXEC.BAT file:

```
SET TEMP=N:\USERTEMP
```

Insider's Tip

You can force Setup to always install a shared copy of Windows on a user's computer even if the user tries to specify a different setup option. Add the line

```
NETSETUP=TRUE
```

to the [data] section of the SETUP.INF file, as described in Chapter 16.

. . . .

Running a Shared Copy of Windows

If you're running a shared copy of Windows from a server, remember, syntax counts. The user's individual Windows directory must be listed before the server's Window directory in the user's path statement, located in the AUTOEXEC.BAT file.

Normally, if the user chooses to have Setup make modifications to the AUTOEXEC.BAT file during the installation process, the files are automatically listed in this order. Some networks, however, use special startup procedures that alter a user's directory path when the user logs into the network. If this modification alters the sequence of the user's individual directory and the shared directory, Windows will not run properly. Refer to your network documentation for the correct procedure for resetting the path after the network logon changes the path.

Danger Zone

Some networks are incompatible with the DOS SHARE utility if a user is running a shared copy of Windows from a network server. Because SHARE provides a safety net for the user's local hard disk, you should remove this command only if it's causing problems with the network software.

If you're installing applications on a server that will also be shared across the network, make sure to set the file attributes to read-only by using File Manager; or, if your network offers it, use a specific utility for setting file attributes for network files. Also, if you set up Program Manager groups for these shared applications, you should also set the corresponding .GRP files to read-only.

Windows 3.1 does not support the Execute-Only permissions that you can set for files on some networks. Although these permissions settings will work for DOS applications that are run before you start your Windows sessions, you won't be able to run Execute-Only applications from within Windows.

. . . .

Installing Windows with Automated Setup

The **Automated Setup** option—also called the batch mode setup—makes it easier to set up many networked computers, and provides users a way to run Setup without having to make any system configuration choices. The Automated Setup option works by reading a special **system settings file** that contains the specific information about what hardware devices, printers, and optional Windows components should be installed.

Windows includes a **generic system settings file,** called SETUP.SHH, on installation disk 1, which is copied to the shared Windows server directory when you use the SETUP /A option for installing Windows on the server. You can rename the SETUP.SHH file in order to create several different system settings template files, each of which contains settings for the different workstation configurations you may be using at your site (see Chapter 16).

To run Setup in its special automated mode, run Setup with the /H switch, followed by the path name and file name of the system settings file. For example, if you use the standard SETUP.SHH file name, you would type

```
SETUP /H:SETUP.SHH
```

Insider's Tip

You can use Automated Setup to have Windows run from a shared copy on the server either by using the /N switch or directly from the Windows Setup disks. Using the Setup disks, you would copy your customized SETUP.SHH file to installation disk 1 and run Setup with the /H switch.

. . . .

Troubleshooting Windows Network Installation

Installing Windows on a network can require a fair amount of tweaking and experimentation to resolve problems introduced by memory conflicts or operation in 386 enhanced mode. Networking problems usually result from an incompatibility with a specific network driver or with your hardware.

To resolve network driver problems, make sure you're using the **most recent version of the driver file**. If your network is already installed, be sure to check that you have the latest driver included in Windows 3.1. You may encounter difficulties after Windows 3.1 is installed because the network installation process replaces the Windows 3.1 driver with an older version of its own.

Problems with hardware usually result from **conflicts with memory usage, interrupts, or I/O addresses**. The Microsoft Diagnostic utility described in Chapter 17 can help you analyze and possibly resolve such conflicts.

Danger Zone

You can often prevent potential problems by **adjusting settings related to networks in the** SYSTEM.INI **file**. Normally the network software is installed before you install Windows. However, if you use Windows Setup to install or reconfigure your network *after* Windows is already installed, Setup may not be sure how to modify your Windows initialization files. As a result, Windows Setup may add or leave inappropriate statement lines in your SYSTEM.INI or WIN.INI file because it doesn't know whether they might be needed by whatever other items it presumes may be installed in your system. These leftover statements can sometimes slow down your system, or even cause a crash.

Always back up your .INI files before using Setup to change your network configuration, and compare the settings in your previous .INI files with the new settings. You should also check the SYSTEM.INI file carefully after installing or reconfiguring the network to see if any settings are missing or have been added unnecessarily.

Table 10.1 gives a rundown of the various sections and settings in SYSTEM.INI that affect how Windows interacts with the network.

The behavior of Windows and other applications vis-à-vis the network is sometimes directly affected by **which part of the memory you've loaded** into your network device drivers and other software. You can use the Microsoft Diagnostic utility to determine how device drivers and other memory-resident software is using the computer's memory. Some networks load certain software components into the computer's high memory area. If you suspect this is causing a problem, disable the network's HMA option so that the software loads into conventional memory.

In addition, some memory management utilities, such as EMM386, which is provided with Windows, or third-party memory managers, such as QEMM and 386MAX, can load network software into the computer's upper memory area. Again, try loading the network software or other drivers into the computer's conventional 640K memory.

TABLE 10.1

SYSTEM.INI Section	Network-Related Statements
[boot]	Network.drv=
[standard]	Int28Filter=
	NetHeapSize=
[386Enh]	AllVMsExclusive=
	CachedFileHandles=
	EMMExclude=
	ExcludeHighRegion=
	FileSysChange=
	InDOSPolling=
	Int28Critical=
	NetAsyncFallback=
	NetAsyncTimeout=
	NetDMASize=
	NetHeapSize=
	Network=
	PSPIncrement=
	ReflectDOSInt2A=
	ReservedHighArea=
	TimerCriticalSection=
	TokenRingSearch=
	UniqueDOSPSP=

You can sometimes correct memory conflict problems by adjusting the **EMMExclude= or ReservedHighArea= statements** in the [386Enh] section of SYSTEM.INI, so as to exclude the area of memory used by your network adapter card. In some cases, you will also need to exclude this memory area using the X= switch with EMM386 in your CONFIG.SYS file.

Other memory settings that can cause problems with networks are those related to the **memory buffers**. Some networks work better with larger buffers than Windows usually provides. To increase the DMA (direct memory access) buffer, adjust the NetDMASize= statement in the [386Enh] section of SYSTEM.INI. To increase the data transfer buffer, edit the NetHeapSize= statement in either the [386Enh] or the [Standard] section of SYSTEM.INI.

Danger Zone

Increasing the values of the buffers can rob your other applications of memory, so you may need to first test these settings. For example, the NetHeapSize= statement in the [Standard] section is usually set to a default value of 8, which allocates 8 kilobytes for the buffer. Although some networks require a larger buffer, many will work with only a 4K buffer—in fact some applications require that this value be set to 4K.

Another potential troublespot is the **TimerCriticalSection= statement** in the [386Enh] section. The value of this statement specifies the number of milliseconds that Windows will wait between switching tasks while multitasking. Some networks require this to be set to a value of 10,000 or greater so that a timer interrupt cannot be received by more than one DOS application at a time; but if your network doesn't require setting this value, don't use it—it can slow down your system performance.

Adjusting this setting can also improve the compatibility of DOS applications running on a network. Some DOS programs run afoul of network software unless they are running in exclusive mode. To run a DOS application in exclusive mode, create a PIF for it that is set to exclusive. If the DOS application creates, changes, or deletes files, you will also need to set the value of the FileSysChange= statement to NO in the [386Enh] section to prevent Windows from being notified whenever a file is manipulated.

Installing Windows on Specific Networks

Although Microsoft has improved network compatibility with Windows 3.1, various quirks and potential obstacles must be dealt with before you can successfully set up Windows on many of the networks available today. Here are some of the most common problems you might encounter.

If you're having trouble configuring Windows with your network, see if your network vendor can provide you with any technical documents specific to running that company's network with Windows 3.1. For details about specific network anomalies, also refer to the NETWORKS.WRI file that Setup copies to your main Windows directory during standard installation. Incompatibilities can also be introduced by network interface cards and network transport stacks, so you'll need to contact the manufacturers of these specific products.

Far and away the most common network is **Novell NetWare**. Most other networks—such as 3Com 3+Open, DEC Pathworks, and IBM LAN Server—are based on **Microsoft LAN Manager**.

Novell NetWare. If you select Novell NetWare in Windows Setup, these files are copied into your main Windows directory (which is the shared network directory if you're running a shared copy of Windows):

➤ **IPX.OBJ** NetWare workstation communications driver, dedicated version

➤ **IPXODI.COM** NetWare workstation communications driver, ODI version

➤ **LSL.COM** NetWare workstation link-support layer, ODI version

➤ **NETX.COM** NetWare workstation shell

➤ **TBMI2.COM** NetWare workstation task-switch support for IPX and SPX

In addition, the Windows 3.1 installation disks supply three other files for use with NetWare:

➤ **NETWARE.DRV** The NetWare driver for version 2.10 or higher, or for NetWare 386

➤ **NETWARE.HLP** The NetWare Help file

➤ **NWPOPUP.EXE** A utility that supports popup messages

Setup specifies the NETWARE.DRV file in your SYSTEM.INI file when installing NetWare, and adds the statement

```
LOAD=NWPOPUP
```

to your WIN.INI file, so that the NetWare popup utility will be loaded when you start up Windows. Once this popup utility is installed, incoming messages from the network can be displayed during your Windows session. If you're not receiving network messages, check to make sure this line is included in WIN.INI.

Danger Zone

Windows 3.1 works with NetWare versions as early as 2.10, but you must use version 3.01 or later of the NetWare shell software. The NetWare shell program needs to be replaced with the NETX.COM shell provided with Windows 3.1. This shell is compatible with any verson of MS DOS, and replaces the older shells provided by NetWare, such as Novell's NETX.COM, XMSNETX.COM, or EMSNETX.COM. You'll also need to replace Novell's version of IPXODI.COM and LSL.COM with the version supplied with Windows. If you're using Novell's IPX.COM, you'll need to build a new version using the IPX.OBJ file provided with Windows 3.1.

If you plan to run Windows in standard mode, you'll also need to install the special Task-Switched Buffer Manager for IPX utility (TBMI2.COM) before running Windows. This memory-resident utility can be started from a batch file, which can contain these three lines:

```
TBMI2
WIN
TBMI2 /U
```

The TBMI2.COM utility enables you to run applications using the NetWare IPX and SPS functions. The /U switch makes sure that this utility is unloaded when you exit Windows.

In a default NetWare setup, you may only be able to access 40 files at any given time. For Windows, you'll need to increase the number to at least 60. To do so, set the Files= statement in your CONFIG.SYS file to

```
FILES=60
```

and add the following line to your NetWare SHELL.CFG file:

```
FILE HANDLES=60
```

NetWare does not support the use of the single dot (.) and double dot (..) directory entries that are standard in DOS. This can cause problems when you are trying to delete directories or list files. If you are using NetWare 3.01 or later, the NetWare shell can simulate the single dot and double dot directory entries, provided you add the following line to your SHELL.CFG file:

```
SHOW DOTS=ON
```

However, using this statement may cause incompatibilities with some older versions of NetWare 286 utilities, so you'll have to update them.

If you experience difficulties with a printer connected to a network server, you may need to change some settings in your print job configuration file. To change these settings, run the NetWare PRINTCON utility and change the settings for Auto Endcap and Enable Time-out to NO.

Danger Zone

Make sure you log into NetWare before starting Windows. Never try logging in or out from the DOS prompt running from within Windows. If you need to connect to or disconnect from a NetWare server, use File Manager; and if you need to make or break connections to a network printer, use the Printer section of the Control Panel.

Microsoft LAN Manager. Microsoft LAN Manager, although not as prevalent as Novell NetWare, provides the base technology used by a number of different networks.

LAN Manager uses one of two different sets of drivers: for **version 1** or **version 2.0 Basic** (or networks compatible with one of these versions, as shown in the list below). Windows installs the MSNET.DRV generic network driver and the following networks, all of which use the Microsoft generic network driver:

Banyan Vines 4.0

3Com 3+Share

3Com 3+Open LAN Manager (XMS version only)

IBM PC LAN Program

Microsoft Network

Tiara Computer System's 10Net version 4.1 and later (10Net was formerly sold by DCA)

Ungerman-Bass Net/One

In addition, if Windows Setup detects a network installed in your system but can't identify it, Windows installs this generic network driver. LAN Manager version 1 also requires the LANMAN10.386 virtual device driver to support operation in 386 enhanced mode.

If you're using Microsoft **LAN Manager 2.0 Extended** (or a third-party network compatible with it), these files will be installed:

➠ **LANMAN.DRV** The LAN Manager 2.0 Extended network driver

➠ **LANMAN.HLP** The Help file for LAN Manager 2.0 driver

➠ **NETAPI20.DLL** LAN Manager 2.0 API library

➠ **PMSPL20.DLL** LAN Manager 2.0 printer API library

➠ **WINPOPUP.EXE** LAN Manager network popup utility for standard mode

Windows Communications

Communications applies to many different areas of computing that all concern the exchange of information between two or more computers. Under the broadest interpretation, communications includes everything from networks to telephones. In this book, I restrict use of the term to point-to-point communications over a telephone line—also known as **telecommunications**.

The most common form of communications involves a **modem** and appropriate software, which together with a telephone line enable your computer to call another computer—a personal computer, mainframe, or large information service. I'll also discuss two other forms of communications that use telephone lines: **remote access software**, which lets you dial into a network, and **fax software,** which lets your computer send and receive faxes.

Most communications software works with one of your computer's COM ports, although other types of software—notably fax programs—simulate a printer port or provide their own hardware with a dedicated port. Because the COM port plays the dominant role in communications, it's important to understand how it works with Windows.

• •

COM Ports and Windows

New in 3.1

In Windows 3.0, support for COM ports was problematic, and severely limited both the performance and the range of most communications software. For example, Windows 3.0 used preset addresses for accessing the serial ports in your system, so many users were unable to use the COM3 and COM4 ports when running Windows. In Windows 3.1, however, you can select from among a variety of port addresses and interrupt lines. Windows 3.1 also supports higher communications speeds, up to 57.6K baud.

COM ports are serial communications ports that are either built into your system's motherboard or supplied on add-in cards plugged into the computer's expansion bus. Most computer systems include at least two COM ports, which are assigned the system names COM1 and COM2. DOS versions through 3.2 permitted only two COM ports; DOS 3.3 and above allow a maximum of four COM ports.

Many systems now provide four serial ports, adding COM3 and COM4 as standard options. Windows permits the use of up to nine serial ports (COM1 through COM9); however, if you have more than four ports, you'll need to obtain a special device driver from the manufacturer.

The COM ports in your system are usually accessed through either 9-pin or 25-pin connectors on the back of your system unit. However, some adapter cards, such as modem cards, use the COM port internally on the card and simply provide a standard telephone-jack connector at the back of your system unit. If you're not sure what type of connector is provided, refer to the documentation included with your hardware. You can also use the Microsoft Diagnostics utility to determine the status of the COM ports currently installed in your system, including information about the interrupts and the base I/O addresses they are using.

If you're using a serial mouse with Windows, I recommend that you plug it into the COM1 port and use the other ports for your communications devices. This avoids potential system conflicts and also acknowledges the primary role that the mouse plays with Windows.

DOS sets aside an area in memory called the base I/O address for letting the processor access the COM port. Windows attempts to automatically detect the proper **base I/O addresses** and **interrupt request lines (IRQs)** for the COM ports built into your PC by searching through your system's BIOS chips. However, the BIOS usually only reports the address values for the built-in COM ports, not for those connected by add-in adapter cards. The settings for these additional ports must be configured by hand; you can use the Ports section of the Control Panel, as described in Chapter 4.

Table 10.2 shows the standard interrupts and base I/O addresses used by the various COM ports on an ISA bus system.

TABLE 10.2

ISA Port	Interrupt	Base I/O Address
COM1	4	03F8h
COM2	3	02F8h
COM3	4	03E8h
COM4	3	02E8h

The default interrupts and base I/O addresses shown in Table 10.3 are used for COM ports in MCA bus systems.

TABLE 10.3

MCA Port	Interrupt	Base I/O Address
COM1	4	03F8h
COM2	3	02F8h
COM3	3	3220h
COM4	3	3228h
COM5	3	4220h
COM6	3	4228h
COM7	3	5220h
COM8	3	5228h

Systems with an MCA bus can share interrupt 3 for COM ports 2 through 8. Windows can usually detect whether it is running on a system with an MCA bus, and automatically adjusts the configuration of the COM ports.

By default, and to conserve the number of IRQs used by the COM ports, Windows assigns COM1 and COM3 to use IRQ4, and COM3 and COM4 to share IRQ3. However, many systems do not work well when two devices are used simultaneously with the same IRQ. For example, if IRQ4 is assigned to your COM1 and COM3 ports, you may run into trouble if your serial mouse is connected to COM1 and your modem to COM3. To resolve this, connect your modem to COM2, or change the IRQ value for COM3. Any changes you make to your COM port settings do not take effect until you restart Windows.

Some systems and add-in adapters support a feature called **IRQ sharing.** If your system is based on the AT bus and supports IRQ sharing, you'll need to check the [386Enh] section of your SYSTEM.INI file, to make sure that the COMIrqSharing=TRUE statement is in effect. If your system contains an MCA or EISA bus, IRQ sharing works more smoothly, and you won't need to add this line to your SYSTEM.INI file.

Danger Zone

If your system contains a COM4 port, you'll need to adjust the base I/O value and IRQ value by hand, because the address for COM4 is almost never reported by your computer's BIOS. COM4 is often assigned a base address of 02E8. Unfortunately, this address conflicts with some other adapters, notably the 8514/a display adapter, as well as certain network adapter cards. To resolve this, you'll need to refer to the documentation of your adapters and configure them to use different addresses.

Another potential troublespot concerns the **speed setting** for the port. In Windows 3.1, you can set a port to use speeds as high as 57.6K baud; but to operate at these speeds, you'll need to have a fast processor in your system. As a rule of thumb, you'll need at least a 16 MHz 386 for reliable transmission at 9600 baud; a 25 MHz 386 for 19.2K baud; and a 486 or better for maximum speeds.

Insider's Tip

To fine-tune the performance of your COM ports on a 286, do not load DOS into the upper memory area; reduce the number of TSRs and DOS device drivers in your system; and try adding the following line to your SYSTEM. INI file:

```
FasterModeSwitch=1
```

Another factor that affects the potential speed of serial ports is the **data transfer protocols** you are using, such as Xmodem, Ymodem, and Kermit. These protocols often trade throughput speed for elaborate error-checking schemes. Some are designed to operate at high speeds with a minimal amount of error checking, while others provide more error checking at slower speeds. Generally the Xmodem (and its related Zmodem) protocol works best with Windows at high transmission speeds. The application's software implementation of these protocols varies from program to program, so you may experience a wide discrepancy among different communications applications.

One way to help increase the reliability of high-speed communications is to use a system or adapter card that contains one of the newer **16550 UART chips** for sending and receiving data. The UART (Universal Asynchronous Receiver-Transmitter) chip provides a small data buffer that helps improve high-speed communications. The Windows 3.0 communications driver did not take advantage of this chip, but the new drivers for Windows 3.1 support this buffer and thereby reduce the software overhead needed to access the COM port. To determine whether your serial ports are using the 16550 UART, quit Windows and run the Microsoft Diagnostics utility, as described in Chapter 17.

Running DOS Communications Programs from Within Windows

The 16550 buffer does not apply to DOS applications that are run from within Windows. If you want a DOS program that can otherwise make use of this buffer within a Windows session, you'll need to disable Windows' buffering of the port by editing the [386Enh] section of your SYSTEM.INI file. For example, to allow a DOS application running from within Windows to use the COM2 port buffer, you'd have to disable the Windows' buffering by adding the line

```
COM2Buffer=0
```

Danger Zone

A few of the early 16550 UART chips contained glitches, which could cause COM port problems when either DOS or Windows tried to use the buffer on these chips. In some cases, Windows is able to detect problem chips and disables the buffer to prevent compatiblity problems. In rare cases, though, you may have to disable the buffer manually by editing the SYSTEM. INI file. For example, to disable the buffer feature for COM2, you would type the statement line

```
COM2FIFO=FALSE
```

in the [386Enh] section of SYSTEM.INI.

One other problem can occur when you are using DOS communications software from within Windows: **device contention**. Because Windows is a multitasking operating system, conflicts can occur when two or more applications try to use the same hardware device at the same time. In communications, if two applications try to use one of your COM ports at the same time, you will sometimes get the Device Contention error message.

Only DOS applications can create device contention conflicts—Windows applications must first request permission from Windows before they attempt to use a port. DOS applications, on the other hand, can grab a port without asking permission.

Using the 386 Enhanced section of the Control Panel, you can determine how Windows should deal with these DOS port contentions:

➤ **Always Warn** Tells Windows to always display a dialog box that asks whether a DOS application can take control of a COM port that Windows suspects is in use by another application.

➤ **Never Warn** Tells Windows to always give the DOS application control of the COM port without warning, even if it suspects this port is in use by another application.

➤ **Idle (in sec.)** Lets a DOS application take control of the port without a warning after a specified number of seconds has elapsed. Otherwise, if the specified number of seconds has not elapsed, a dialog box appears asking whether it's OK for the DOS application to assume control of the COM port.

DOS programs are designed to have complete control of your system resources, and can therefore perform at very high speeds—115K baud or higher. Although these programs are capable of running at very high speeds when running *directly* in DOS, the overhead from running within Windows can cause problems and slow them down.

Insider's Tip

In order to minimize the problems you may encounter when running DOS communications programs from within Windows, you should run such programs in full-screen mode; this gives them the priority status of running in the foreground and avoids the software overhead necessary when a DOS application is displayed in a window or in the background. If you do run a DOS program in the background during a data transfer, run it as a minimized icon, rather than within a window.

You should also inspect the .PIF file settings used to run your DOS program; if you're getting errors when your DOS program is running in the background when transferring data, increase the DOS program's execution priority. You can also check the "Lock Application Memory" check box in the

DOS program's .PIF file. If you are using the FastDisk feature to provide 32-bit disk access with a permanent swap file, you may need to disable it so that the entire DOS program remains in memory during the communications session.

· ·

Windows Terminal Programs

A **terminal program** is the most common type of communications software; it essentially turns your computer into a simulation of a dedicated terminal that is used to connect to another computer over a telephone line. In the days before PCs, terminals were dedicated devices—known as **dumb terminals**—which consisted of a monitor, a keyboard, and a modem, and allowed you to log on to a large, host computer.

Personal computers use **terminal software**—also called **terminal emulation software**—to provide a smart terminal that not only emulates a specific type of dedicated terminal but also provides the ability to record your session to a disk file, spool it to a printer, and upload and download files. Terminal programs can be used for exchanging information with another PC; for logging on to a host system, such as CompuServe; or for emulating a special type of terminal required for connecting to a minicomputer or mainframe.

Danger Zone

Windows includes the Terminal applet, a feature-poor terminal utility that provides only a one-way communications link. With Terminal, you can only place a call, not receive one. Terminal is fine for calling up CompuServe or for logging onto one of Microsoft's tech support bulletin boards to download a driver file or utility, but if you want to call up another Windows user, and each of you only has Terminal, you won't be able to make the connection, because Terminal can't answer an incoming call.

Fortunately, almost every commercial terminal package lets you answer a call as well as send one. The DOS terminal program market is dominated by ProComm, which has entered the Windows market with **ProComm for Windows**. Three other popular Windows terminal programs are **DynaComm** (produced by the same folks who created the Windows Terminal applet), **MicroPhone II for Windows**, and **CrossTalk for Windows**. A wide variety of more specialized software provides emulation for specific terminals or other features necessary for specific kinds of connections.

Most comm programs can adequately transfer files from PC to PC over a standard phone line. Most packages also provide a built-in scripting language that allows you to automate log-in procedures and, in effect, provide a dedicated macro language for telecommunications.

For example, MicroPhone II for Windows has a particularly accessible scripting language, which lets you select the script command from a dialog box and merely fill in the options for that command (Figure 10.7).

FIGURE 10.7
Modify Script Dialog Box from MicroPhone II for Windows

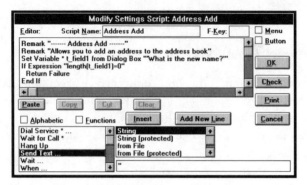

MicroPhone II for Windows provides a powerful yet easy-to-use scripting language that lets you click on a command and fill in the options to create a complex script.

MicroPhone II for Windows and some of the other packages also have a "watch me" feature that records whatever you're doing on the screen and builds a script based on your actions. For example, you can turn this recording feature on, call into an online service, and supply your user name and password; you've just created a script that you can use from this point on to automate your log-in procedure.

When selecting a terminal program, you should also consider what file transfer protocols it supports. For example, CompuServe provides a special QuickB file transfer protocol that can significantly speed up file downloading. Because CompuServe charges you by the minute for download time, using this faster protocol can save you money over the long run. Therefore, if you're a heavy CompuServe user, you should select a package that supports the QuickB protocol.

Insider's Tip

If you have two available serial ports, two modems, two phone lines and a fast system, you can take advantage of the multitasking capabilities of Windows to run two instances of your telecommunications program simultaneously. This would allow you to perform a lengthy download from one port while calling another service from the other port and modem. Although this can double your productivity, it can also double your trouble. Make sure the COM ports are set to different interrupts, and be careful when using high-speed modems, because this can sometimes overburden your system.

Another feature to look for in Windows terminal software is support for dynamic data exchange (DDE). If your Windows terminal program supports DDE, you can create custom scripts that will automatically transfer incoming data into another application. For example, stock quotes could be transferred directly to your spreadsheet; database information from a mainframe could be transferred directly into your Windows database; and information from an online service could be transferred directly into your wordprocessor.

Remote Access Software

Many standalone terminal programs lack the ability to dial into a local area network and fool the network into thinking that your PC is directly connected to it. Some communications programs, such as **Relay Gold**, provide this capability as well as the usual offering of terminal software features. Other programs, such as **Carbon Copy for Windows, Close-Up**, and **PC Anywhere**, are designed specifically with this in mind. These programs are called **remote access software**, to denote their ability to let you hook into a LAN from a remote location. Some LANs support only a specific remote access package. In this case, you'll need to contact your network administrator to determine what program is supported.

You can always set up your own networked PC to provide you with remote access to your own computer at work—and to the network, even if you don't have the package supported by the network. This is called **remote control software**.

For example, you can install a program such as PC Anywhere on your office PC—provided it has a modem—and then use another copy of PC Anywhere to dial into your office PC from your laptop computer. Your laptop becomes a twin of your desktop PC. You can then log into the network from your laptop PC, and as far as the network is concerned, you're in the office using your desktop computer.

Insider's Tip

You can also use remote control software to call up your office computer from home and run applications on your office system in a window while running applications in your home system in another window. You can then cut and paste information between your remote system and your local system by using software that allows you to transfer files easily between computers.

Remote control software is also gaining a split personality, with the ability to remotely access computers running Unix or Macintosh operating systems from DOS or Windows-based systems. For example, Timbuktu from Farallon Systems supports both Macintosh and Windows remote-control capabilities over either a phone line or a direct network connection. Timbuktu lets you bring up a Macintosh desktop in a window on your PC, or bring up a Windows desktop in a window on your Macintosh.

Fax Software

In business, the fax machine has become as ubiquitous as the telephone. Peripheral manufacturers have been quick to acknowledge this trend, and there are literally hundreds of different fax modems available for PCs.

Fax modems fall into two general classes: **send-only**, which allow you to send faxes but not receive them, and **send/receive**, which provide full fax capabilities for your PC. Some fax modems also double as regular modems, providing both communications and fax capabilities.

Fax modems can either be installed directly in your computer or installed on the server; on a server, many users can access them through a local area network. Regardless of how the fax modem itself is connected to your computer, most fax software allows these modems to be configured as if they were a printer, so that you can create a document in any application and "print" it to the fax modem. This allows software that was not designed specifically to work with a fax modem to take advantage of fax capabilities— a logical idea, because most of the documents you fax were created with another kind of program.

Although fax modems work with DOS applications as well, Windows is ideally suited to integrate fax technology with your personal computer because of its WYSIWYG capabilities, which allow you to create and view the document just as it will appear when you fax it.

Sending a fax by computer improves its appearance on the receiving end, because the document is transmitted through the fax modem in its electronic form. On a traditional fax machine, each page is scanned in by an optical scanner, which causes a degradation of the quality of the document before it is ever sent. Some fax modems support high-resolution fax modes that can create stunning results, especially when received on a high-resolution fax machine. Also, pages sent from your computer are never scanned in skewed—another quality edge to the electronic document over its paper counterpart.

Faxed documents that are received on your computer can be viewed in a window and sent to your printer for printing, or stored as a bitmapped image in a disk file. This image can be annotated in a Windows graphics application and then retransmitted to another fax machine.

The only drawback to this procedure is that the bitmapped image of an incoming fax can consume quite a bit of disk space. Luckily, your computer can compensate with two different methods. You can use compression software, such as PKZIP, to compress the image of the fax into a smaller file. This method retains the original document exactly as it was received.

The other method is to use OCR (optical character recognition) software, which is commonly included with Fax Software, to scan the text of the fax and store it as a regular text file. Obviously, this method applies only to incoming text documents, but it lets you reduce a file to a tiny fraction of its original size. It also allows you to edit a text file with a standard wordprocessor and manipulate it with other software—something you can't do with a bitmapped fax file, which stores your text as a graphic image. Because your OCR data is stored as text, you can apply text retrieval software, such as a database or a text-search program like Dragnet, to instantly locate an existing fax by searching for keywords contained in the document.

Dynamite Product

If you only want to send and receive faxes, one of the best applications is **WINFAX PRO** (Yes, it's all caps!), from Delrina Technology, which works with the send and receive capabilities of most fax modems. Like most fax software, WINFAX PRO turns your fax modem into a simulated printer and lets you compose a single fax with pages from a variety of different Windows applications. The program also provides a phonebook capability that lets you search for phone numbers and direct a fax to a single machine or to a number of different recipients.

A handy feature of WINFAX PRO allows you to create custom cover pages, which include your logo, special text, and the ability to merge the names and addresses of the recipients from your phonebook list (Figure 10.8).

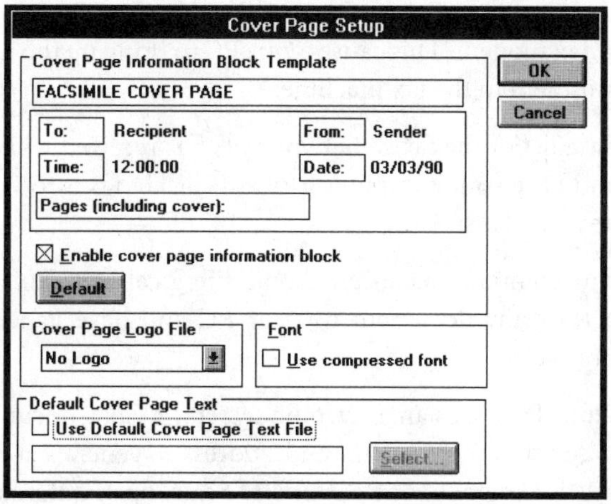

FIGURE 10.8
WINFAX PRO Cover Page

WINFAX PRO lets you create custom cover pages for faxes that merge names from your phone and fax directory.

Cover Page Setup

Cover Page Information Block Template

FACSIMILE COVER PAGE

To:	Recipient	From:	Sender
Time:	12:00:00	Date:	03/03/90
Pages (including cover):			

OK / Cancel

☒ Enable cover page information block

Default

Cover Page Logo File: No Logo

Font: ☐ Use compressed font

Default Cover Page Text
☐ Use Default Cover Page Text File

Select...

WINFAX PRO also provides a variety of options for receiving faxes, so you can view them upon receipt or send them directly to a printer for hard copy. In addition, the program offers DDE capabilities for integrating its fax functions into other applications that support DDE. With WINFAX PRO and a fax modem, you can turn your portable computer into a portable fax machine.

Insider's Tip

A less obvious benefit is providing a worldwide network of printers for your portable computer. One of my favorite tricks while traveling is to fax a document to the nearest fax machine whenever I need a printout from my portable computer. This is handy when you are staying in a hotel, but watch out for the hidden—and sometimes exhorbitant—charges you can incur for *receiving* a fax.

Dynamite Product

A breakthrough Windows product that takes the integration of computers and fax machines several steps further is the **PaperWorks** fax software from Xerox. PaperWorks works in conjunction with most of the popular send/receive fax modems on the market.

PaperWorks turns any fax machine into an extension of your personal computer, allowing you to retrieve, store, and distribute documents without the need to be near your PC. By faxing a special PaperWorks form to your PC, you can send your system instructions that it can use to carry out a variety of tasks. For example, here are a few of the things you can do from a fax machine with PaperWorks:

➤ To retrieve a document from your PC, just fill out a form, send it to your fax modem, have it send you back a form listing the contents of a directory, check off the items you need from that directory, and send that form to your fax modem. This causes your PC to bring up those documents and transmit them to the fax machine.

➤ Request a list of the faxes that your PC has received while you are on the road and have your computer forward certain faxes to your fax machine, or to anyone else's.

➤ Use your computer as an electronic filing cabinet. Fax a news clipping, contract, or any document to your PC and have PaperWorks store an electronic copy.

➤ Make your PC act as an electronic secretary. Fax a document to your PC, have it select certain names and addresses, generate a cover sheet, and refax the document to one person or to a group of different recipients. You can even direct different documents to different people on the list.

In addition, when PaperWorks receives a fax, it automatically straightens the paper and enhances the image to increase readability.

To access information on your PC from a remote fax machine, complete a special form—just place checkmarks in boxes or enter text—and fax it to your PC (Figure 10.9).

FIGURE 10.9
PaperWorks Form

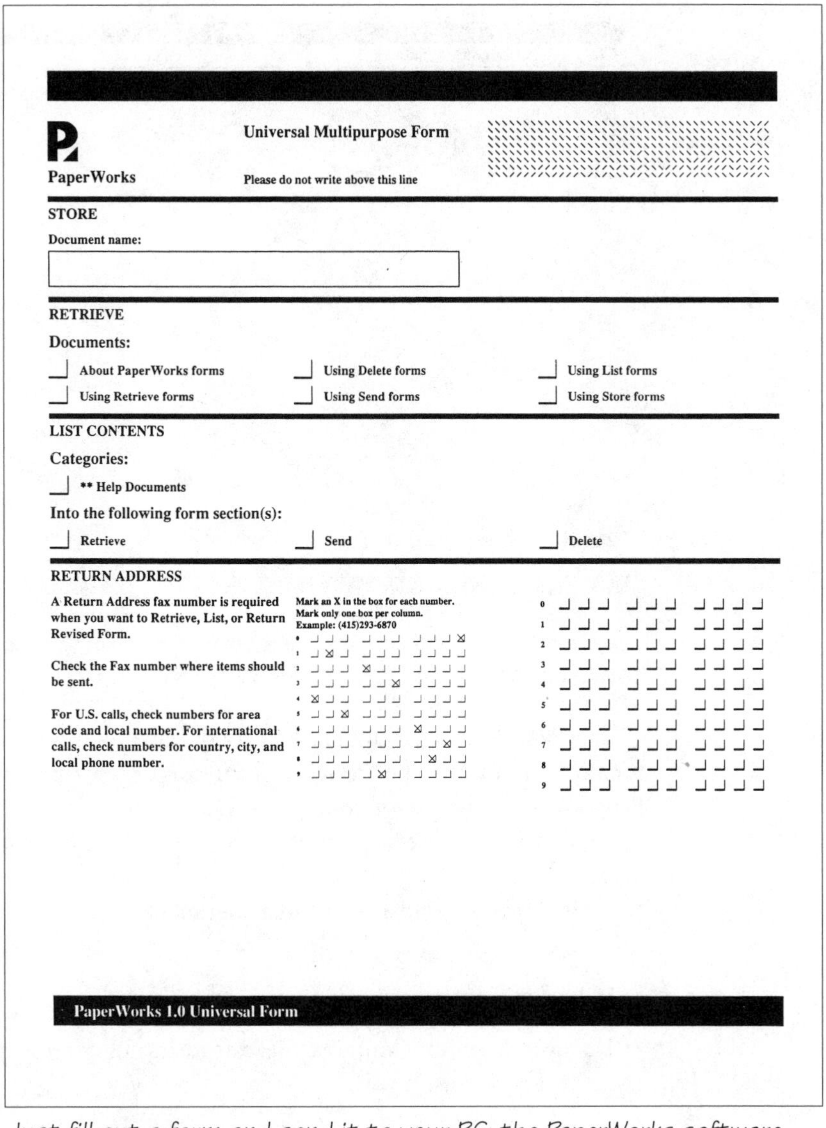

PaperWorks

Universal Multipurpose Form

Please do not write above this line

STORE

Document name:

RETRIEVE

Documents:

- About PaperWorks forms
- Using Delete forms
- Using List forms
- Using Retrieve forms
- Using Send forms
- Using Store forms

LIST CONTENTS

Categories:

- ** Help Documents

Into the following form section(s):

- Retrieve
- Send
- Delete

RETURN ADDRESS

A Return Address fax number is required when you want to Retrieve, List, or Return Revised Form.

Check the Fax number where items should be sent.

For U.S. calls, check numbers for area code and local number. For international calls, check numbers for country, city, and local phone number.

Mark an X in the box for each number.
Mark only one box per column.
Example: (415)293-6870

PaperWorks 1.0 Universal Form

Just fill out a form and send it to your PC; the PaperWorks software reads the form and carries out whatever instructions you specify.

The form you send your computer is interpreted according to the options you've set up with the PaperWorks software, and the actions you've requested are taken.

On the PC side, the PaperWorks program provides its own onscreen desktop (Figure 10.10).

FIGURE 10.10

*PaperWorks
Desktop*

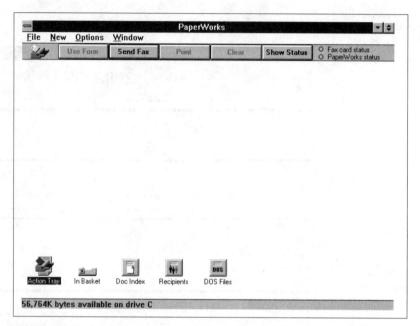

*The PaperWorks desktop is your control center for operating the
sophisticated capabilities of this fax software.*

The PaperWorks desktop packs a good deal of power into a fairly straight-forward interface. The basic concept for organizing information with PaperWorks is the use of containers. The five main containers, represented by the five icons at the bottom of the screen, include these items:

»→ **Action Tray** To send a fax, print a document, or process a form, drag items onto this tray.

»→ **In Basket** Contains your incoming faxes.

»→ **Document Index** Contains the categories for your PaperWorks documents and forms.

»→ **Recipient's Index** This is your address book; it contains the listings of all the individuals and companies to which you've sent faxes.

»→ **DOS File Drawer** Provides access to the files on your computer.

The row of buttons on the top of the desktop contain the most common commands, such as those to send a fax or use a form. Two status lights at the end of the button bar keep you apprised of fax activity.

The PaperWorks interface makes extensive use of Windows drag-and-drop capabilities and provides a simple system for performing complex tasks. For example, you can drag icons that represent individual recipients and drop them into a list box to create a distribution list for a fax you are sending. You also can use the PaperWorks software to generate custom forms that let you retrieve information from remote fax machines. For the security conscious, PaperWorks can generate a custom security code that is printed on the top of each form and prevents unauthorized access to your computer.

PaperWorks provides an unprecedented level of integration between PCs and fax. Although the first release of the software has a few rough edges, PaperWorks is sure to be the inspiration for a whole new class of Windows software that integrates fax technology with your personal computer.

Summary

Windows 3.1 has eradicated many of the problems that plagued Windows 3.0 in the areas of networking and communications. In addition to better compatibility with networks and network software, more options are provided to system administrators for installing and maintaining Windows on a network server. Also, because Microsoft made Windows 3.1 beta software available to network vendors early in the development cycle, third-party packages work better with Windows. Indeed, one result of this open dialog between Microsoft and developers of network software is the improvement to Windows itself, as well as to third-party network software. Despite the increased maturity of Windows and networking, however, installing and maintaining a local area network is still no trivial task.

In the telecommunications arena, Microsoft has greatly enhanced Windows com drivers, which now provide better compatibility and reliability with both the COM ports and communications software. Support for the UART 16550 chip has also been improved, and Windows 3.1 now makes use of the buffer capabilities of this prevalent chip.

In addition to Microsoft's enhancement of the underlying components of Windows communications, third-party developers have advanced the capabilities of applications software. Terminal programs are now more plentiful, and those on the market have been improved. At the same time, groundbreaking applications, such as PaperWorks, have been introduced, making Windows one of the most versatile and advanced platforms for communications software.

· ·

Insider's Tech Support

Q I'm having trouble installing a network.

A: Review the troubleshooting section earlier in this chapter, and read the NETWORK.WRI file that Setup normally copies to your main Windows directory. If this file has not been copied to your system, you can copy it from the Windows installation disks using the Expand utility. Also, see if you can access the network from DOS before Windows has been installed. If not, the problem is with your network or hardware configuration, not with Windows. Because network installation can be a tricky process, you may need to contact your network vendor if you can't solve the problem on your own.

Q: I'm having trouble installing a network using the SETUP/N option.

A: Sometimes Setup's hardware detection routines cause the program to malfunction. Try using the /I switch by typing

```
SETUP /I /N
```

to prevent Setup from performing its hardware detection routines. If you receive the error message "Error Building WIN.COM," you may have a corrupted or missing WIN.CNF or .LGO file. Recopy these files from the installation disks to the server.

Q: When installing a network, I receive the error message "System Error: Cannot read from device NETWORK."

A: This error message can result from using Arcnet or Ethernet adapter cards that have been configured to use the memory address D000. To correct this problem, set the memory address the card uses to D800 and adjust your other network settings accordingly.

Q: Why can't I run Windows with my network?

A: Make sure that you identify the proper network in Windows Setup. Windows includes support for the following networks:

3Com 3+Open and 3+Share

Banyan Vines

DEC PathWorks

IBM OS/2 LAN Server

PC LAN Program

Invisible Network (version 2.21)

LANtastic

LAN Manager

Microsoft Network

Novell Netware

TCS 10Net

If you are using a network other than one of these, you'll need to obtain special drivers from the network manufacturer. Make sure you get the Windows 3.1 version of these drivers.

Q: I can't print to a network printer.

A: Open the Printers icon in the Control Panel, click the Connect button, and then click the Network button. If no network printer connections are listed, click the Browse button and reconnect to your printer. If that doesn't work, try quitting Windows and printing to the network printer from outside Windows. If that doesn't work, there could be a problem with the network printer or with your connection to the network.

If your printer port is redirected to a different network printer within Windows, it must be configured to use an LPT port, not a COM port.

Q: I am using NetWare and although I can connect to a printer, the output is messed up.

A: Open the Printers icon in the Control Panel, click the Network button, and then click the Options button. Remove the check marks from the Enable Banner, Enable Tabs, Enable Timeout, and Form Feed check boxes.

Q: How can I increase the number of people who can run a shared copy of Windows from a network server?

A: You can try decreasing the number of cached file handles allocated by Windows on each user's system and increasing the number of file handles available on the server. Windows normally keeps 14 file handles cached at a time; you can decrease this number to a value as small as 2 by adjusting the CachedFileHandles= statement in the [386Enh] section of SYSTEM.INI. You'll need to experiment to find the right number, but decreasing the number of handles slows down Windows performance on the user's system while increasing network access. To increase the number of file handles available on the server, use your network's configuration or administration software.

Q: I'm having trouble using my COM4 port.

A: Open the Ports icon in the Control Panel and access the Advanced Settings dialog box for COM4. You'll usually need to set the port address and IRQ by hand, because Windows cannot detect these settings automatically.

Q: I upgraded to Windows 3.1 and my communications software no longer works.

A: Several Windows communications programs replaced the Windows 3.0 driver with their own third-party driver to avoid some of the problems with the old Windows driver. Windows Setup does not replace third-party drivers that it doesn't recognize. Therefore you may need to obtain a 3.1-compatible comm driver from your third-party software vendor. Or you may have to replace the third-party driver with the Windows 3.1 comm driver by copying it from the Windows installation disks to the system subdirectory of your main Windows directory and by editing the COMM.DRV= statement in the [Boot] section of your SYSTEM.INI file, so that it reads

```
comm.drv=comm.drv
```

If this doesn't work, you may still be able to use your Windows 3.0 or third-party 3.0 comm driver by adding the following line to the [386Enh] section of SYSTEM.INI:

```
Comdrv30=TRUE
```

Q: I installed a fax modem board and can't start my system, or the system won't recognize the board.

A: You probably have an interrupt conflict with your fax modem board. The presence of an available slot doesn't necessarily indicate an available interrupt to address the hardware. Refer to Chapter 17 for information on how to apply the Microsoft Diagnostics utility to analyze what interrupts are currently in use; a table in that chapter lists the standard PC interrupt assignments. If your system contains only one parallel port, you may be able to use the interrupt normally assigned to LPT2.

Multimedia and Windows

Although the technology is still in swaddling clothes, multimedia has already garnered buzz-word stature. Because multimedia is still an emerging technology, people disagree about what the term actually means. In this book, I define multimedia as a group of different technologies that allow computer users to add graphics and sound capabilities to computer applications.

Graphics can include still images, animations, and video. Sound encompasses recorded sounds, synthesized sounds, and speech.

Traditionally, computers have primarily served as tools for the manipulation of text and numbers. The advent of desktop publishing in the 1980s heralded the use of computers as graphics tools as well. Adding graphics to text allows you to communicate certain information more effectively than text alone, and the incorporation of sound endows computers with yet another important communications medium.

Multimedia will have broad application in almost all phases of computing, from business to entertainment. Business applications will include software for creating presentations, training programs, and multimedia databases. Scientists will use multimedia to create simulations, add voice annotations to their work, and analyze phenomena that include critical sound or movement components.

Educational uses span kindergarten through graduate school; I think multimedia software will someday revolutionize our entire educational system. And multimedia will find a natural fit in the entertainment industry, where it will be used to create interactive movies and TV, virtual reality adventure games, and other, still unimagined, recreational pastimes.

Multimedia is often associated with **interactivity** and **CD ROMs**. Interactivity describes the exchange of information between the user and a program. Such interaction can be as simple as playing and rewinding an animated sequence or answering questions on a history quiz, or as complex as experiencing space flight in a computerized simulation. Numerous studies have shown that interactive presentation of information, using audio and visual elements, is an effective and entertaining method of learning.

CD ROMs play a role because multimedia data, such as sound files or video sequences, take up large amounts of storage space. CD ROMs, which can store more than 500 megabytes on a standard CD disc, provide an inexpensive way to distribute multimedia information.

How Multimedia Works with Windows

Multimedia technology for Windows has suffered from a lack of standards for adding sound, animation, and video. As a result, multimedia software usually worked with only a narrow selection of hardware products, which made integrating different products very difficult. To address this problem, Microsoft developed two related items: standard **multimedia extensions** to Windows and the **MPC** marketing concept.

New in 3.1

The multimedia extensions were originally sold as an add-on to Windows 3.0. With version 3.1, however, these extensions are now included as a standard part of Windows.

The MPC marketing concept was conceived as a way to develop a consistent hardware and software standard for the operation of Windows multimedia software. Thus the MPC logo on a computer system would signify that it could play Windows multimedia software that also bore the MPC logo. This is analogous to VHS in the video world—the VHS trademark on a video recorder means that it can play video tapes that also bear the VHS label.

Windows Multimedia Extensions

The multimedia extensions provide Windows with a variety of features:

» The ability to play standard **digital audio** files from various applications

» The **Sound Recorder** utility for recording, editing, and playing digital audio files

» A software control system called **MCI** that allows the computer to control a variety of multimedia devices

» A standard multimedia data format called **RIFF**

» **Media Player**, a simple utility that lets you control MCI devices and play RIFF files and other multimedia files

» The ability to play standard **MIDI** music files from various applications

» The **MIDI Mapper** Control Panel utility, which lets you remap MIDI instruments so that MIDI files created on a variety of different MIDI hardware are able to play the proper instruments

» The **Drivers** utility in the Control Panel, which lets you easily install and configure multimedia device drivers

» The ability to use a **joystick** in addition to the mouse

The Windows multimedia extensions support a standard for multimedia data files known as the Resource Interchange File Format, or RIFF. RIFF provides Windows applications with a standard way to store and share multimedia data. This means you can save multimedia data from one application in RIFF format and then import it into another Windows application.

RIFF allows you to incorporate the following types of data into a single document:

➤ Bitmapped graphics

➤ Animation

➤ Digital audio

➤ MIDI

In addition, the multimedia extensions include the Media Control Interface, or MCI, which provides Windows applications with a standard method for controlling a wide range of external devices, such as audio CD players, videodisc players, VCRs, MIDI intruments, or anything that includes an MCI-compatible device driver.

One item missing from the Windows 3.1 multimedia palette is support for Audio Video Interleave (AVI), also known as Video for Windows. AVI files contain video data that is coordinated with sound data, so that both tracks play back on a synchronized basis, similar to what you see on television. Apple Computer offers a similar system called QuickTime, which was originally designed for the Macintosh. Both AVI and QuickTime are available as add-on options for Windows.

The Media Player. Windows includes the Media Player utility as a simple tool for controlling any MCI-compatible devices that are installed in your system, and as a way to play any multimedia data files. To install and configure multimedia devices to run with the Media Player, just use the Drivers icon in the Control Panel.

The Media Player first presents a simple application window, reminiscent of the controls on a tape deck, VCR, or CD player (Figure 11.1).

FIGURE 11.1

Media Player

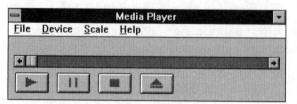

The Media Player lets you control multimedia devices and play multimedia data files.

The Media Player application window contains a scroll bar for scrolling through a multimedia file, and four buttons (from left to right): Play, Pause, Stop, and Eject. The title bar of the window reports what device or file is active, and which of the four buttons has been most recently pressed.

Before you can operate a device or play a file with the Media Player, you need to choose a device from the Device menu. The Device menu lists all the MCI-compatible multimedia devices that are installed in your system. The Media Player can work with two different types of devices:

➡ **Simple** A device that can be started and stopped, but that does not play a computer file; for example, a CD player or VCR.

➡ **Compound** A device that plays a multimedia data file; for example, a sound card or synthesizer. The names of compound devices in the Device menu are followed by an ellipsis (...).

To use a simple device, choose it from the Device menu and then use the Play, Pause, Stop, and Eject buttons to control it. If you quit the Media Player while a simple device is playing, it will continue to play.

To use a compound device to play a media file, choose the device from the Device menu. The first time you choose a compound device, a dialog box appears to let you select the file that you want to play. The next time, you can use the Open command on the File menu to play any other files on the currently selected device.

Insider's Tip

A faster way to play a file is to head directly for the Open command and select a media file. As long as the extension of the file name is recognized by Windows as being associated with a particular device, the Media Player automatically switches to that device. For example, if you select a digital audio file that ends in .WAV, the Media Player automatically switches to the Sound device.

Both simple and compound devices use the scroll bar to provide further control over operating the device or playing the file. When you choose a device or load a file, a numeric scale appears above the scroll bar (Figure 11.2).

FIGURE 11.2
Media Player's Time Scale

The Media Player provides a scale over the scroll bar that displays either the Tracks or Time; this example shows the Time scale.

The scale displays one of two different measurements, Tracks or Time. The Tracks scale applies to simple devices that organize information into tracks. For example, an audio CD player would display the number of tracks on the compact disc. You can move the scroll button to a particular track to start playing that track.

The Time scale works on compound devices and is divided into time intervals that vary according to the length of the media file. You can adjust the position of the scroll button to start playing the file at a particular time.

The Graphics Component of Multimedia

Three main forms of graphics are used in multimedia:

➤ **Still images**

➤ **Animation**

➤ **Video**

Computers use two main forms of still images:

➤ **Bitmap graphics** Composed of a group of small dots called pixels; each pixel is represented by one or more bits in the computer's memory that define its color and intensity. Bitmap graphics are best for images that contain much detail, shading, and subtle color. The resolution of a bit-mapped image is predetermined by the number and layout of the pixels that compose a particular image.

➤ **Vector graphics** Composed of a set of drawing instructions that describe the dimension and shape of every line, circle, arc, or rectangle. Vector graphics are best for line art. The resolution of a vector image is not fixed; the resolution of the output device determines how a vector image will be reproduced.

Because bitmap graphics are stored at a fixed resolution, you can edit the image at that resolution; but if you shrink, stretch, or enlarge the graphic, it may suffer from severe distortion and loss of image quality. Vector graphics, in contrast, can be enlarged, reduced, and otherwise edited without affecting resolution or image quality because the image is redrawn each time it is displayed or output.

Bitmaps require more disk space than vector graphics, because they contain information about each pixel displayed on the screen, whereas vector graphics are stored as commands for creating the actual images. Vector graphics, however, take longer to render because they have to be drawn by the processor, whereas bitmaps are simply loaded directly into memory.

Examples of bitmap graphics are .BMP, .DIB, and .PCX files, which you can edit with Paintbrush, and TIFF files used by desktop publishing software. Examples of vector graphics are Windows metafiles, encapsulated PostScript files, and files created by CAD programs.

Insider's Tip

Although your multimedia application may be designed to import many different graphic formats, most programs run more efficiently if they use the .DIB (device-independent bitmap) format for bitmap images, and the Windows metafile format for vector images.

You can aquire still images for your multimedia application from a variety of sources:

➤ Use a graphics application to create images from scratch. Paint programs are best for creating bitmap images, and draw programs are best for creating vector images.

➤ Purchase computer clip art, and edit or modify it if needed. (Both bitmap and vector clip art are available.)

➤ Scan in bitmap images with a flatbed or hand-held scanner. (Both color and black-and-white scanners are available.)

➤ Take some film (transparencies or negatives) to a photographic processor and have it transferred to a PhotoCD that converts the photos into high-quality color bitmap images stored on a CD ROM.

➤ Use a video digitizer (also called a frame-grabber) to capture an image from a video camera or VCR.

· ·

Animation

Most people asssociate animation with cartoons. With Windows, animation can assume a more businesslike demeanor. Simple animated presentations that let you move items such as images and text items around on the screen, and automatically animate the creation of a chart or bullet list, are fairly easy to assemble.

Danger Zone

For more sophisticated jobs, which include a sound track and cartoonlike sequences, there's software available, but it's complex and can be tedious to use—although not as tedious as doing the job manually. Synchronizing an audio track with the visuals is no easy task, and your efforts may sometimes resemble a poorly dubbed foreign film in which the speech continues long after the lips have stopped moving.

If you plan to use animation in your multimedia endeavors, two types of animation software for Windows are available:

»+ **Presentation software** Horizontal-market products, such as Action or Curtain Call, that are aimed at the broad base of business people, educators, and others who have to make presentations for whatever reason.

»+ **Animation software** Vertical-market packages, such as Animation Works Interactive or MacroMedia Director, that simulate the traditional animation process in software to provide a cartoon artist's or animator's version of desktop publishing. To play this type of animation requires a system with a fast processor, fast disk, fast video, and lots of RAM.

Dynamite Product

In addition, a few products fall on both sides of the fence. Toolbook from Asymetrix, for example, is modeled on Apple's HyperCard program. It can be used by novices in a simple building-block mode, or it can be programmed by advanced users for sophisticated projects. Toolbook provides a variety of ways to incorporate animation into anything from a standard business presentation to an interactive, hypermedia database application. Toolbook programs can be ported to the Macintosh platform as well, and are also available in an OS/2 version.

A similar, though slightly less capable, product is Spinnaker's Plus, which is available in Windows, OS/2, and Macintosh versions.

A number of companies are now selling clip animation libraries. Clip animation allows the computer user to add an artistic, if not altogether original, element to business or other material. Clip animation is usually offered in a format specific to a particular animation product, so check to make sure you get the right file format.

One of the largest libraries of computer animation was developed in the MacroMedia Director format on the Macintosh. In order to allow Windows users to mine this animation motherlode, Microsoft and MacroMedia have codeveloped a utility called the Gaffer, which converts the animation files—together with sound, if any—from the Macintosh version of Director into a format that can be played in Windows using other applications, such as Action! or Toolbook.

· ·

Video

Video has already established itself as a major medium of our times, making it a natural for multimedia. The most prevalent product in consumer electronics is the television, followed by the VCR and the camcorder. Creating your own video is so easy, it's become a major American pastime.

Because the video market is so large, it provides a readily available source of existing video segments and film clips that can be used to create multimedia software titles. Until recently, however, the equipment enabling the computer to use video has been either too expensive or too slow.

Insider's Tip

Recent developments on both the hardware and software fronts promise to change this situation, and video is on its way to becoming a common component of personal computing. In fact, I predict the imminent appearance of a "desktop video" phenomenon, akin to the revolution in desktop publishing—and Windows systems will play an important role.

Like desktop publishers, do-it-yourself video producers will someday be able to concoct anything the video industry can offer, including promotional videos, training demos, sales presentations, and even TV shows.

Two types of video work with personal computers:

➤ **Analog video** The standard video signals used by TVs, VCRs, laserdisc players, and camcorders. Analog video is typically stored on a videotape or videodisc and is the form of video transmitted by a television station or cable company.

➤ **Digital video** A digital form of video that can be stored as a computer file; examples are AVI and QuickTime.

To work with analog video, you'll need a special display adapter card, known as a "video-in-a-window" card. These cards are capable of displaying an analog video image in an onscreen window. The source for the signal can be a laserdisc, VCR, TV, cable converter, camcorder, or other compatible device.

Insider's Tip

Because laserdisc players can easily be controlled by Windows—for example, quite a few models work with the Media Player and other MCI applications—the laserdisc format has become popular with multimedia artists and developers. Laserdisc technology—as compared with videotapes—also provides freedom from jamming, better durability, and fast random access to any location on the disc. Standard videotape can be converted to laserdisc format, providing a bridge between the two formats. By incorporating video from a laser disc into your multimedia system, you can create interactive video training programs, entertainment software, or information kiosks.

Many video-in-a-window cards also provide a frame-grabbing feature that allows you to capture a still image of whatever is displayed in the onscreen video window. Future development of these cards will allow the moving picture to be digitized as a series of video frames. This digitized video can then be stored as digital video on your hard disk and played back on your system, without the need for a video-in-a-window card.

A variety of other devices allow you to output graphics from your computer screen to a standard analog video signal. These video output cards let you create animated presentations and save them onto a videotape, but the image quality of what you save seldom matches the quality of what you see on your computer monitor. And although computers can be outfitted with high-quality gear, the cost is still prohibitive.

When deciding on a video-in-a-window board, determine whether the board captures still frames; check the resolution and pixel depth of the images; and ask if it can double as a video output board. Some boards also include these features:

➺ **Graphic overlay** The ability to overlay a computer image onto a video image; useful for superimposing animation, titles, and special effects.

➺ **Chroma key** Replaces a certain background color in one video source with a second video image. This is how television newscasts insert the weathermap behind the weather reporter, who is really standing in front of a blank blue wall.

➺ **Transition effects** Blends one image into a another to create a smooth transition between two scenes.

Another peripheral you may want to get is a **video switch box,** which lets you choose from among several analog video sources, such as a TV broadcast, camcorder, or VCR.

For the time being, analog video has the edge over digital video, which is barely nascent. Several of the initial schemes, such as AVI and QuickTime, present the digital video images in a low-resolution mode, in order to save storage space. Video data compression schemes, such as MPEG and DVI, have yet to become widely available. Despite these hurdles, digital video promises to become the best solution within the next few years as its associated compression and resolution problems are overcome.

The Sound Component of Multimedia

A primary force in human communications, sound encompasses both speech and music. Sounds can inform, entertain, and provoke great emotion. The ability to use sound with your computer adds an important dimension to its role as a communications tool.

The Windows multimedia extensions allow you to use two forms of sound: **digital audio** and **MIDI**. Digital audio lets you record speech and other natural sounds. MIDI is a format for recording, editing, and playing musical notes on electronic instruments.

Digital Audio

Digital audio software works by turning your hard disk into a virtual tape recorder—the catch is, you usually need a special add-in sound card for connecting a microphone or other sound source to the computer. This card contains the circuitry that can turn analog sound waves into a digital form for use by the computer.

The most popular sound card on the rapidly growing market is the **Sound Blaster** from Creative Labs. Microsoft has also entered the market with a sound card for Windows that features rudimentary voice recognition in addition to sound recording and playback. In another trend, several companies offer so-called multimedia upgrade kits, which combine digital audio, MIDI, and a CD ROM connector on a single card.

In addition, some computer makers offer sound capabilites as a standard component in their systems. For example, Compaq offers a sound recording and playback feature, **Business Audio**, on some of its systems.

Dynamite Product

The high end of the product spectrum includes **hard-disk recording cards**, such as the 56K card from Turtle Beach. Some sound cards can record only brief passages of sound because their recording capacity is limited by the computer's RAM. Hard-disk recording cards allow you to record continuously to your hard disk drive, thus allowing much longer recording times. Hard-disk recording cards also provide the highest recording quality—the 56K card can record stereo sounds at resolutions comparable with audio compact disc recordings.

Digital audio converts natural sound waves into a digital format that can be stored on your hard disk. Because this process requires taking a series of measurements—or "samples"—of the sound, digital audio is sometimes referred to as sampled sound. The frequency of sampling is called the sample rate, and the accuracy with which the samples were taken (either 8- or 16-bit accuracy) determines the overall quality of the sound. High-quality recording (such as an audio compact disc) requires frequent sampling at 16-bit resolution and thus uses a greater amount of storage space than do lower-quality samples.

These are the most common file formats for digital audio files:

➤ **.WAV** The standard format used by the Windows multimedia extensions.

➤ **.VOC** The Sound Blaster format; conversion utilities can translate these files to .WAV if necessary.

The quality of the digital sound depends on the capabilities of your sound board, the quality of the microphone or other sound source, the accuracy of the sample (8- or 16-bit), and the sampling rate at which the sound was digitized. Table 11.1 below shows how storage requirements vary by the type and rate of the sampling.

TABLE 11.1

Sample Type	Sampling Rate	Storage Requirements
8-bit, mono	11.025 kHz	0.6 MB/minute
8-bit, mono	22.05 kHz	1.3 MB/minute
8-bit, stereo	22.05 kHz	2.6 MB/minute
16-bit, mono	44.1 kHz	5.3 MB/minute
16-bit, stereo	44.1 kHz	10.6 MB/minute

As a guideline for evaluating the sounds, 8-bit/mono/11.025 kHz sampling is roughly equivalent to AM radio quality, and is fine for most purposes. The 8-bit/stereo/22.05 kHz sampling is comparable to FM radio quality, and the 16-bit/stereo/44.1 kHz sampling provides outstanding quality, equivalent to an audio compact disc.

Sound Recorder

Sound Recorder is a multimedia utility that comes bundled with Windows. But to make it work, you'll also need to get a Windows-compatible sound card. With this card, Sound Recorder lets you record sounds directly to a file on your hard disk, and then edit and play back the sound files. Sound Recorder works with the standard Windows digitial audio files, denoted by the .WAV extension.

Sound Recorder is an OLE server application, so you can use it to embed or link sound files to compound documents. If you have digital audio files in the .WAV format, Sound Recorder can play them, regardless of what particular sound hardware was used to record the file.

This utility contains five buttons, which provide the controls for recording and playing the sound files (Figure 11.3).

FIGURE 11.3
Sound Recorder

The Sound Recorder is an OLE-compatible utility that lets you record, edit, and play back sound files.

You operate the Sound Recorder buttons much as you would the buttons on an actual tape deck or VCR, with the familiar symbols for Rewind, Fast Forward, Play, and Stop; the button with the small microphone icon denotes Record.

To play a file, open it and click the Play button. As the sound plays, a graphical display of the sound's waveform is displayed in the Sound Recorder window. Press the Stop button to halt the playing, and press Play to resume playing where you left off.

You can also use the scroll bar to move to a certain place in the sound file. Slide the scroll button to move through the sound file. For greater precision, click the scroll arrows to move in .1-second increments; or click in the scroll bar to move in one-second steps.

As you scroll or step through the sound file, the Position box reports your current position in the file, expressed as seconds. The **Length** box reports the total length of the current file in seconds.

The Rewind and Fast Forward buttons operate instantaneously; a single click takes you to the start or end. Keyboard shortcuts in Sound Recorder are shown in Table 11.2.

TABLE 11.2

Keyboard	Sound Recorder Button
End	Fast Forward
Home	Rewind
Right and left arrow keys	Scroll arrows; each keypress moves .1 second through file

Recording. The Record button is dimmed unless you have a sound card and a Windows-compatible device driver for the card.

Sound Recorder can either record a new file or record from the middle or the end of an existing file. To record a new sound file, simply choose New from the File menu and click on Record. When you're finished, press Stop, and then save the new sound file. The length of the recording is affected by the amount of memory your system has available, so you may be cut short if the program runs out of memory.

To start a recording in the middle of a file, scroll to a place in the sound file and press Record. Your new recording records over and erases the remainder of the original file. In audio terms, this is known as an **over-dub**.

Or you can scroll to the end of the file and append your new recording to the original sound file. Note that some sound hardware does not support the ability to over-dub an existing file.

Editing a Sound File. Even if you lack the hardware to record sounds, you can use Sound Recorder to edit and play sound files if you have some type of sound-output hardware. Some add-in cards provide sound output but not recording capabilities.

Insider's Tip

A variety of commercial and shareware products provide Windows-compatible sound drivers for your PC's internal speaker. Although the sound isn't great using the built-in speaker, it's better than nothing, and it's less expensive than purchasing a sound card.

Sound Recorder lets you edit sounds by providing controls in its Edit and Effects menus. After making changes to a sound file, audition it by pressing the Play button. If you're satisfied with the new sound, save the changes. If you aren't happy with the audition, and you haven't yet issued the Save command, you can undo the change you've just made and restore the file to its previous state by choosing the Revert command from the File menu.

The Sound Recorder's Edit menu offers the following commands:

➺ **Insert File** Inserts a second sound file anywhere into the current sound file. The inserted file increases the length of the sound.

➺ **Mix With File** Mixes a second sound file with the current file, blending the sounds in the two files together.

➺ **Delete Before Current Position** Erases from the beginning of the sound file up to the current playing position, as specified in the Position box.

➺ **Delete After Current Position** Erases from the current playing position to the end of the sound file.

To insert the contents of a sound file into the current sound file, scroll to a location in the current file and issue the Insert File command. The Insert File dialog box appears; this is a standard file browsing dialog box. You may insert as many files as you wish, up to the limit of your available memory.

To mix the contents of two files, scroll to a position in the current file. Then choose the Mix With File command to bring up the Mix With File dialog box, from which you can choose a file to blend with the current file.

To delete a portion of the file, scroll to a position in the file and choose the Delete Before Current Position command to zap everything up to that point; or choose Delete After Current Position to erase everything after that point.

Sound Recorder's Effects menu offers several other commands for manipulating your sound files:

➤ **Increase Volume** Increases the volume of the sound by 25 percent

➤ **Decrease Volume** Decreases the volume of the sound by 25 percent

➤ **Increase Speed** Speeds up the playback of the sound by 100 percent

➤ **Decrease Speed** Slows down the playback of the sound by 50 percent

➤ **Add Echo** A simple digital reverb effect that adds an echo to the sound

➤ **Reverse** Reverses the sound so that it plays backward

To use any of these commands, open a file and choose the appropriate command from the Effects menu. The command applies to the entire file. If you want to add an effect to just a portion of a file, you'll have to copy the sound file, chop it up, and apply the effect to one portion at a time.

· ·

Musical Instrument Digital Interface (MIDI)

The **Musical Instrument Digital Interface,** or **MIDI,** standard was jointly established in 1982 by the makers of electronic instruments to create a simple, low-cost way to connect various pieces of equipment, such as synthesizers, keyboards, and computers. MIDI has since blossomed into a multibillion-dollar industry, which is supported by almost all electronic instruments and music software.

MIDI works like a very simple local area network that runs over a serial communications link. The original MIDI standard allows up to 16 different devices to be connected in a daisy-chain configuration with a standard MIDI cable. Once connected, the devices can send and receive MIDI messages that define events, such as what notes were played, how hard they were pressed, and how long they were held down. Electronic keyboards commonly send this information to a synthesizer, which plays the notes accordingly.

If you bring a personal computer into the act, or use a professional MIDI keyboard that includes a special-purpose built-in computer called a sequencer, you can record, save, edit, and play computer MIDI files. In other words, you can manipulate all the MIDI data related to a particular musical composition. Music software for PCs, Macintoshes, and some sequencers supports a common data file format known as the Standard Midi File format; these files often end in the extensions .SMF or .MID.

When you play a MIDI file, the computer sends the messages contained in the file to a MIDI instrument, which converts the messages into the sounds of a specific instrument, pitch, and duration. To acquire MIDI files, you can purchase preprogrammed MIDI music; hire a MIDI music studio; or record your own compositions. Software products range from programs that let you record and edit MIDI compositions, to music education, to applications that transcribe what you play into a professional-appearing musical score.

Hardware support for MIDI includes these major product categories:

➤ **MIDI adapters**

➤ **Synthesizers**

➤ **Samplers**

➤ **Controllers**

A **MIDI adapter** lets you connect your computer to external MIDI devices, such as keyboards, synthesizers, and samplers. Sophisticated MIDI adapters let you connect more than one MIDI network if you need more than 16 MIDI channels. MIDI adapters are supplied either on their own add-in card or as part of a multifunction sound card, such as the Sound Blaster.

Synthesizers use electronics to artificially create the waveforms for sounds, some of which can simulate natural sounds quite realistically. Synthesizers can be located inside your computer on add-in cards, or they can be external units connected via MIDI. External MIDI synthesizers sometimes come as a standalone unit, called a module, which resembles a stereo system component; or they are often included together with a piano-style keyboard.

Samplers play sounds that have been digitally recorded, such as a musical instrument or any other naturally generated sound. Like synthesizers, samplers are available as add-in cards, as external boxes, or combined with a keyboard.

Controllers are devices used to generate MIDI signals. The most common type of MIDI controller is a piano-style keyboard. Often, these keyboards contain fewer than a piano's 88 keys, and some less-expensive models use smaller-than-normal keys. (I suggest avoiding these.) Other types of MIDI controllers include electronic drum pads and a breath controller, which is similar to a reed instrument, such as a clarinet or saxophone.

Your computer can also serve as a MIDI controller with the addition of the right software. If a MIDI instrument is connected to your system, you can use the Media Player to play a MIDI composition. Or you can use some other type of music software to play an onscreen keyboard, program the notes for a song, or otherwise generate MIDI data.

Because MIDI files are much smaller than audio files, playing them places less of a burden on your processor. For example, a 5-minute musical composition could consume as much as 5 megabytes if stored as a digital audio file; the same composition stored as MIDI notes might require only 50 kilobytes.

Danger Zone

Unfortunately, MIDI files only sound as good as the quality of the MIDI devices on which they are played. Also, MIDI files do not always contain data specifying what instruments should be used to play back the music, so sometimes the wrong instrument will play—for example, a trumpet part might mistakenly be played using a drum sound.

How Windows Uses MIDI. Microsoft has developed software guidelines for handling MIDI information in Windows so that software can be designed to work with a variety of MIDI devices in the same way. The Windows MIDI guidelines are based on an emerging MIDI standard, called **General MIDI**, which provides a standard way to configure MIDI sound output devices, such as synthesizers, so that they all play similar sounds when sent the same MIDI data.

Before General MIDI, almost every synthesizer worked with MIDI, but in a slightly different way. Although MIDI defined program codes for up to 128 sounds for each sound bank in a MIDI instrument, these sounds and their arrangements were left undefined. As a result, almost every synthesizer arranged its sounds differently, so that playing a certain note might trigger a tuba on one system, a piano on another, and a gunshot on a third. Musicians had to keep track of what devices played which sounds in response to different MIDI messages; most MIDI files, in fact, would sound right only when played on the same type of synthesizer used to record the sounds.

In order to define a standard configuration for MIDI instruments, several hardware and software companies recently established General MIDI, which is a standardized arrangement for the 128 sounds in a bank of synthesizer sounds. If a synthesizer supports General MIDI, a certain note that is supposed to play a violin always plays a violin sound. The Roland Sound Canvas is an example of a General MIDI synthesizer.

Windows defines two more levels of synthesizer performance in addition to the General MIDI standard:

➡ **General MIDI synthesizers** can simultaneously play up to 16 notes on 15 melodic instruments and up to 8 notes on 8 percussion instruments.

➡ **Base-level synthesizers** can simultaneously play up to 6 notes on 3 different melodic instruments and up to 3 notes on 3 different percussion instruments.

➺ **Extended-level synthesizers** can simultaneously play up to 16 notes on 9 melodic instruments and up to 16 notes on 8 percussion instruments.

In order to allow software developers to create a single MIDI file that could be played on both base-level and extended-level synthesizers, Microsoft developed a method for splitting up the 16 instrument channels allowed by MIDI. According to the Microsoft guidelines—known as the **MPC MIDI file**—base-level synthesizers use channels 13 through 15 as the melodic channels and 16 for the percussive channel; extended-level synthesizers use channels 1 through 9 as the melodic channels and 10 for the percussive channel.

Configuring MIDI for Windows. Windows recognizes two different types of MIDI files, both based on the General MIDI specification. The standard General MIDI file uses all 16 channels and is designed to play on a General MIDI synthesizer. The MPC MIDI file uses channels 13 through 16 to play on base-level synthesizers and channels 1 through 10 to play on extended-level synthesizers.

Insider's Tip

Despite the development of General MIDI, very few MIDI synthesizers and no samplers support General MIDI, and the ones that do tend to be low-end units. If you want to get the full benefit from MIDI, you will need to get a Windows music program that can handle more sophisticated MIDI setups.

Music software for Windows almost always works with MIDI, but support for the General MIDI standard is less common. Also, you should determine if a music application makes use of the standard Windows MIDI setups—the ones used by the MIDI Mapper utility—or provides its own MIDI drivers and MIDI setup procedures.

The Windows Setup program installs MIDI setups for these popular sound boards and synthesizers:

➺ **Extended MIDI** A setup for any extended-level synthesizer that is connected to a Sound Blaster-compatible MIDI port. Use this setup for MPC MIDI files.

➺ **General MIDI** A setup for any General MIDI synthesizer that is connected to a Sound Blaster-compatible MIDI port; use this setup for General MIDI files.

➺ **Ad Lib** A base-level setup for an Ad Lib-compatible sound card.

➺ **Ad Lib General** A General MIDI setup for an Ad Lib-compatible sound card.

➺ **LAPC1** An MPC MIDI file setup for the Roland LAPC1 sound card.

➻ **MT32** An MPC MIDI file setup for the Roland MT32 synthesizer module connected to a Sound Blaster-compatible MIDI port.

➻ **Proteus/1** An extended-level setup for a Proteus/1 synthesizer module connected to a Sound Blaster-compatible MIDI port.

➻ **Proteus General** A General MIDI setup for a Proteus/1 synthesizer module connected to a Sound Blaster-compatible MIDI port.

These setups are contained in the MIDIMAP.CFG file, which Setup places in your \SYSTEM subdirectory. If these setups don't cover your sound card or instrument, you can take one of the following actions:

➻ Obtain a custom-configured MIDIMAP.CFG file from the manufacturer of the card or instrument, if one is available.

➻ Configure your synthesizer's or sampler's sound banks so that they conform to either the General MIDI instrument assignments or to one of the other devices just listed.

➻ Modify an existing setup with MIDI Mapper.

➻ Create a new setup with MIDI Mapper.

Danger Zone

To use any of these setups, your application must also support the MIDI setups created by the MIDI Mapper. The Media Player utility described earlier is such a program, but if your program doesn't use the standard MIDI setups, you'll have to use whatever method is described in its documentation.

A custom MIDIMAP.CFG file for the card or instrument provides the easiest solution. A preconfigured file ensures that the music sounds right when you play it back. Unfortunately, not many vendors offer these preconfigured files yet.

If your vendor is one of the enlightened few, here's how to install the new MIDIMAP.CFG:

1. Rename your original MIDIMAP.CFG to MIDIMAP.BAK (or some other name).

2. Replace your existing file by copying the new MIDIMAP.CFG file to your \SYSTEM subdirectory.

A more difficult approach is to create a custom arrangement of sounds that conforms to the General MIDI standard in one of your synthesizer's sound banks. The method for rearranging the sounds in a bank is intrinsic to each MIDI device, so plan on getting cozy with the device's manual. Not all MIDI devices let you change the sound banks; but if you can, this builds General MIDI right into the device and works best if you plan to use General MIDI on a regular basis. If your MIDI device lets you create a backup of the setup onto a cartridge or floppy disk, be sure to do so.

Insider's Tip

Special MIDI software called a Librarian—or sometimes a Patch Librarian—lets you easily rearrange the sounds in the sound banks of many popular synthesizers. With a MIDI Librarian program, you can simply point-and-click to shuffle your sounds around and thus create a General MIDI sound bank.

If you can't rearrange the sounds in your MIDI device to make them conform to General MIDI, or if you are only a casual General MIDI user and don't want to waste a sound bank on it, you can use the MIDI Mapper utility included with Windows to create a custom MIDI setup (Figure 11.4).

• • • • • • • • • • • • • •
FIGURE 11.4

MIDI Mapper

The MIDI Mapper utility lets you remap the MIDI messages for your instrument so that they match the General MIDI standard.

MIDI Mapper lets you match the various sounds and keys that are used by your instrument to the items needed to support General MIDI. In this way, you can configure just about any brand of synthesizer or sampler to work with Windows programs that support standard MIDI setups. You can either copy one of the existing setups and modify it, or you can start from scratch and specify all the various details about the MIDI device you are mapping.

To access the MIDI Mapper, click on its icon in the Control Panel window; however, this icon only appears if a Windows-compatible MIDI driver has been installed. (MIDI drivers are installed using the Drivers icon in the Control Panel, as described in Chapter 4.)

The process for creating a new MIDI setup is fairly complex, and you should have a good understanding of how MIDI is implemented in your instrument before you undertake the task. Here's a rundown of what you'll need to do:

➤ Create a **key map** for the percussion instruments that matches the keys on a piano-style keyboard to the various drum sounds in the MIDI device.

With some devices, you may also need to create a key map for melodic channels; for example, you may need to adjust the sound to the correct octave range.

➟ Create one **patch map** for the melodic channels and another for the percussion channels. A patch is a particular sound, such as a violin or guitar.

➟ Create a **channel map** for your synthesizer. The MIDI channel assignments differ for base-level, extended-level, and General MIDI synthesizers, as noted earlier.

Key Maps. To create a key map, click on the Key Maps button and then click on the New button to bring up the New MIDI Key Map dialog box. Enter the necessary information in the Name and Description boxes, and click OK. The main dialog box for assigning the key equivalencies appears (Figure 11.5).

FIGURE 11.5
*MIDI
Key Map
Dialog Box*

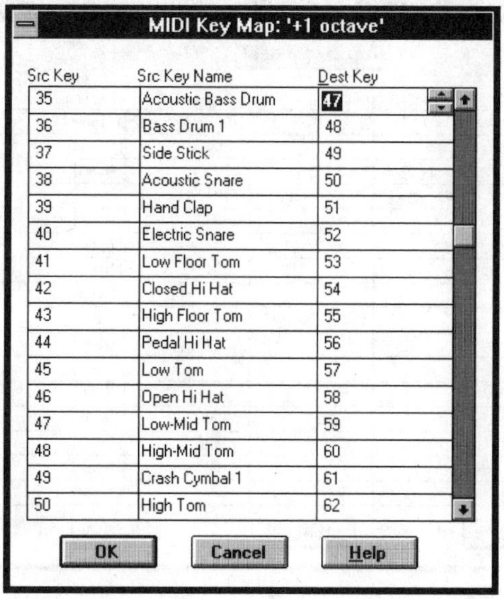

MIDI Key Map: '+1 octave'		
Src Key	Src Key Name	Dest Key
35	Acoustic Bass Drum	47
36	Bass Drum 1	48
37	Side Stick	49
38	Acoustic Snare	50
39	Hand Clap	51
40	Electric Snare	52
41	Low Floor Tom	53
42	Closed Hi Hat	54
43	High Floor Tom	55
44	Pedal Hi Hat	56
45	Low Tom	57
46	Open Hi Hat	58
47	Low-Mid Tom	59
48	High-Mid Tom	60
49	Crash Cymbal 1	61
50	High Tom	62

OK   Cancel   Help

The MIDI Key Map lets you match the keys on a piano-style keyboard to specific sounds in a MIDI instrument.

This MIDI Key Map box lists the source MIDI keys 35 through 81 (these numbers relate to the standard MIDI scheme for numbering the keys on a piano keyboard), along with the percussive sounds for the keys as defined by General MIDI.

You'll need to identify the destination keys that correspond to those sounds in your instrument. You'll also need to enter in the MIDI Key Map dialog box the items shown in Table 11.3.

TABLE 11.3	Item	Description
	Src Key #	The General MIDI key number—you can't change these.
	Src Key Name	The name of the percussion instruments that General MIDI uses for the corresponding source key. Ignore these names if you are adjusting an octave range for a melodic instrument.
	Dest Key #	A synthesizer key you want to match with the General MIDI source key. For percussion instruments, this key generates the appropriate drum sound.

Patch Maps. To create a patch map, click on the Patch Maps button and then click on the New button to bring up the New MIDI Patch Map dialog box (Figure 11.6).

FIGURE 11.6
*New MIDI
Patch Dialog
Box*

MIDI Patch Map: 'MT32'

1 based patches

Src Patch	Src Patch Name	Dest Patch	Volume %	Key Map Name
0	Acoustic Grand Piano	0	100	[None]
1	Bright Acoustic Piano	1	100	[None]
2	Electric Grand Piano	3	100	[None]
3	Honky-tonk Piano	7	100	[None]
4	Rhodes Piano	5	100	[None]
5	Chorused Piano	6	100	[None]
6	Harpsichord	17	100	[None]
7	Clavinet	21	100	[None]
8	Celesta	22	100	[None]
9	Glockenspiel	101	100	[None]
10	Music Box	101	100	[None]
11	Vibraphone	98	100	[None]
12	Marimba	104	100	[None]
13	Xylophone	103	100	[None]
14	Tubular Bells	102	100	[None]
15	Dulcimer	105	100	[None]

OK   Cancel   Help

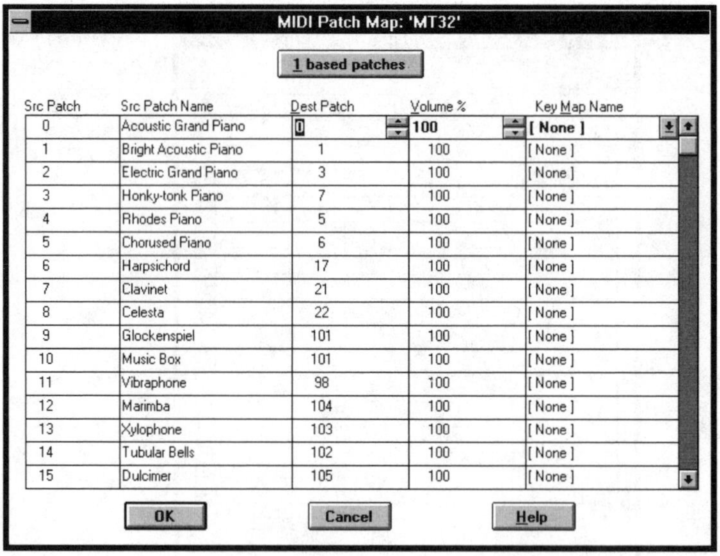

This dialog box lets you match the sounds in your synthesizer to the patch numbers for the sounds defined by General MIDI.

The New MIDI Patch dialog box lists the MIDI patch numbers 0 through 127 and the sounds that are assigned to them by General MIDI. If your synthesizer uses the 1 through 128 numbering scheme, push the "1 based patch #'s" button to reset the numbers. In the MIDI Patch Map dialog box, you'll need to enter the items shown in Table 11.4.

TABLE 11.4

Item	Description
Src Patch #	The General MIDI patch number—you can't change this.
Src Patch Name	The name of the General MIDI sound associated with the corresponding patch number.
Dest Patch #	The patch number of the synthesizer sound that you want to match with the General MIDI source patch. For a General MIDI synthesizer, this is the same as the Src Patch number.
Volume %	The volume at which the synthesizer patch should play, expressed as a percentage of its normal volume.
Key Map Name	The name of the key map you want to use with the patch.

Channel Maps. The channel map matches the MIDI channels in a MIDI file to the actual channels on your synthesizer. Before creating a channel map, you'll need to decide if you are creating a map for a General MIDI file that uses all 16 channels, or for an MPC file that assigns channels 1 through 10 to extended-level synthesizers and channels 13 through 16 to base-level synthesizers.

To create a channel map, click on the Setups button and then click on the New button to bring up the New MIDI Setup dialog box. Complete the information in the Name and Description boxes, then click OK to get to the main MIDI Setup dialog box (Figure 11.7).

		MIDI Setup: 'Proteus/1'		
Src Chan	Dest Chan	Port Name	Patch Map Name	Active
1	1	Creative Labs Sound Bla	Prot/1	☒
2	2	Creative Labs Sound Blaster 1.5	Prot/1	☒
3	3	Creative Labs Sound Blaster 1.5	Prot/1	☒
4	4	Creative Labs Sound Blaster 1.5	Prot/1	☒
5	5	Creative Labs Sound Blaster 1.5	Prot/1	☒
6	6	Creative Labs Sound Blaster 1.5	Prot/1	☒
7	7	Creative Labs Sound Blaster 1.5	Prot/1	☒
8	8	Creative Labs Sound Blaster 1.5	Prot/1	☒
9	9	Creative Labs Sound Blaster 1.5	Prot/1	☒
10	10	Creative Labs Sound Blaster 1.5	Prot/1 Perc	☒
11	11	[None]	[None]	■
12	12	[None]	[None]	■
13	13	[None]	[None]	■
14	14	[None]	[None]	■
15	15	[None]	[None]	■
16	16	[None]	[None]	■

| OK | Cancel | Help |

The MIDI Setup dialog box lets you assign the MIDI channels for synthesizers; designate the MIDI output port; and specify a patch map for each channel.

You'll need to enter the items shown in Table 11.5 in the dialog box .

Item	Description
Src Chan	The MIDI source channels—you can't change these.
Dest Chan	The channel on your synthesizer that you want to match to the source channel.
Port Name	The name of the MIDI output port for the channel. You can assign different channels to different ports if you have more than one sound card or MIDI device.
Patch Map Name	The patch map you want to use with the channel— either melodic or percussive.
Active	Lets you activate or deactive a channel. A check in this box means that the channel is active and will play any sounds sent to it.

Editing Existing Maps. Editing the maps works much like creating a new one. To edit an existing map, follow these steps:

1. Click on the radio button—Setups, Patch Maps, or Key Maps—that corresponds to the kind of map you want to edit. The Setups button lets you select Channel Maps.

2. Select the map in the Name list and click on the Edit button. The Edit dialog box for the map appears.

3. Make your changes and click OK.

A CD ROM Primer

The audio **compact disc,** or **CD,** has made the phonograph record obsolete by becoming the primary medium for selling music and other recorded material.

CD sound is digitally recorded in 16-bit stereo at 44.1 kHz. The information is stored on the disc as a series of microscopic pits on an otherwise polished surface and is covered with a transparent coating. The CD player projects a laser beam that scans the surface of the CD and interprets the pits as binary data. This binary data is digital audio that is converted back to an analog waveform for listening. Because only light touches the surface of the CD, it is less subject to distortion resulting from wear than is a phonograph record.

Each audio CD can store more than 600 megabytes worth of binary data—the equivalent of 100 copies of the *Bible* or more than a quarter-million pages of text. Because CD audio is so popular, the technology has become relatively inexpensive, and CDs can be produced in quantity for less than a dollar per unit. Because of the availability of CD technology, it has become adopted as a data storage medium by the computer industry in a form called **CD ROM**.

The ROM part of CD ROM stands for Read Only Memory, indicating that you cannot write data onto a CD ROM. Although read-write CD technology does exist, it is currently too expensive for most computer users. However, service bureaus are springing up that will produce a single CD ROM from your data as a way to create a demo disc or to back up a hard disk drive.

CD ROM technology allows you to stuff hundreds of megabytes of data onto a format that is far less expensive than a hard disk. Because multimedia data requires so much space, CD ROMs are often the only practical way to distribute multimedia information. A CD ROM is also removable, unlike a hard disk, so you can store many gigabytes of data in a library of only a few CD ROM discs.

CD ROM drives are relatively inexpensive, with many models selling for only a few hundred dollars, and they often include an assortment of bundled starter software. There is a downside to this technology, though: CD ROM drives, especially the older models, are not as fast as hard disks, and in some applications the slow speed can create problems.

Insider's Tip

If you're planning to buy a CD ROM drive, get one of the faster drives. In order to maintain compatibility with the MPC standard (discussed later in this chapter), you'll need a drive with a minimum transfer rate of 150K per second and an average seek rate of 1 second or less. On such a drive, which is still in the slow range, a 300K file will take about 2 seconds to load from the CD ROM drive.

In order to use a CD ROM drive with Windows, you'll need to have a DOS device driver that supports the drive. The most common driver is the Microsoft CD ROM driver, MSCDEX.EXE. This file is not included with Windows, so you will need to obtain it from your drive manufacturer or from Microsoft.

· ·

Other CD ROM Formats

CD ROM XA (CD ROM Extended Architecture) offers a higher-performance standard for CD ROM drives. CD ROM XA, a joint development effort of Sony, Microsoft, and Phillips, allows you to interleave compressed audio together with video and graphics, so you can simultaneously play audio and video.

With CD ROM XA, you can compress audio files and thus store more graphics files on each disc. Compressed audio allows up to 9.5 hours of AM-quality stereo, or as much as 19 hours of monophonic audio, on a single disc.

Some software is marked as requiring CD ROM XA; to use such software you must also have a CD ROM XA-compatible CD ROM drive. You may be able to upgrade your CD ROM drive to CD ROM XA capabilities—check with the manufacturer of your CD ROM drive.

If you're buying a new CD ROM drive, try to get a CD ROM XA drive. Not only will it allow you to use CD ROM XA software, it will also open the door to another important new CD ROM technology: Kodak's **PhotoCD**.

Dynamite Product

PhotoCD is both a process and a product. The process, which will be offered by Kodak's worldwide network of film processors, will convert your 35mm film into high-resolution digitized images and store up to a hundred such images on a CD ROM. For about $20, you will be able to develop a 24-exposure roll into prints and transfer it to a PhotoCD, which can be refilled until it contains a hundred images. PhotoCD technology will transform any camera (even those displosable cardboard models) into a computer accessory that can be used to obtain high-resolution color images.

In order to access the pictures on a PhotoCD, Kodak and Phillips market a special CD player for less than $500, which can play both standard audio CDs though your stereo and PhotoCDs on your television. Computer users can access PhotoCDs on CD ROM XA drives and on other CD ROM drives that are capable of operating in a "multisession" mode. Kodak provides translation utilities that can translate the PhotoCD images into standard bitmapped graphics formats, which are compatible with Windows paint programs.

Computer systems equipped with CD ROM drives will be able to access the images stored on the PhotoCD in standard computer graphics formats. Because of the high quality of the stored images, and the multiplatform support that has emerged for the format, PhotoCD should become the standard format for the distribution of photographic-style color images on computers.

The MPC Standard

The MPC (Multimedia Personal Computer) standard is an attempt by Microsoft, Tandy, and a number of other companies to establish a coordinated brand name for Windows multimedia software titles and the machines that run them.

Through MPC, Microsoft intends to establish software and hardware standards that will encourage the development of multimedia software for Windows. By defining the minimum hardware requirements for playing sounds and displaying graphics, and by defining some fundamental hardware compatibility standards, Microsoft has provided a hardware standard that software developers can target when developing multimedia software.

The MPC logo (Figure 11.8) is administered by the MPC Marketing Council, a subsidiary of the Software Publishers Association (SPA).

FIGURE 11.8
MPC Logo

The MPC logo identifies multimedia software titles and the computer systems that run them.

The MPC brand name appears on these main categories of computer products:

➤ **Complete computer systems** A computer system that bears the MPC logo assures you that it can run MPC software, much as the VHS logo identifies VCRs that can play VHS tapes.

➤ **MPC upgrade kits** Upgrade kits that bear the MPC logo provide the hardware components necessary to transform a standard PC into an MPC machine.

➤ **MPC software** The MPC logo on software titles identifies them as being able to run on MPC-compatible systems.

In order for a computer system to qualify as an MPC-class machine, it must meet the following requirements:

Processor	80386SX, 16 MHz
RAM	2 MB
Storage	30 MB hard drive
	3.5 inch, 1.5 MB floppy disk drive
	CD ROM drive with CD digital audio outputs and transfer rate of 150K per second
Video	VGA, 256 colors

Audio	Digital audio, record, and playback
	Base-level MIDI synthesizer, external MIDI port
	Ability to play CD audio from the CD ROM drive
Input	101-key keyboard
	2-button mouse
	Microphone
	Joystick port
	MIDI port

Danger Zone

These requirements, which were spelled out by the MPC Marketing Council in its Multimedia PC specification version 1.0, represent a bare minimum. A faster processor and more RAM are highly recommended.

The use of the MPC logo on software packages ensures compatibility with MPC-branded hardware. To use the MPC trademark, an application must adhere to specific software guidelines, including the ability to run on MPC-compliant hardware and to take advantage of at least one multimedia element, such as audio.

You can get an MPC machine by purchasing an MPC computer system, or you can upgrade an existing PC. If you are technically competent, have access to an in-house technician, or have a relationship with a dealer who will sell and install an upgrade kit, you may be better off purchasing an MPC upgrade kit. Purchasing an upgrade kit or the individual parts necessary to upgrade can cost less than buying a preconfigured MPC system.

The advantage of the MPC system is that it should work right out of the box. And you'll have the added security of being able to call just one vendor when, or if, you have a problem.

An MPC upgrade kit usually contains two main components:

➥ **A sound card** that provides digital audio, a MIDI synthesizer, and an external MIDI port

➥ **A CD ROM drive**, either internal or external

The sound card may also feature a SCSI connector for connecting the CD ROM. Although including the SCSI connector theoretically provides everything on a single card, it is often not always a fully functional SCSI bus and may allow you to connect only a single SCSI device. Other upgrade kits provide a separate SCSI adapter card, which can usually handle up to seven SCSI devices.

CD ROM drives are offered in either internal or external models. An external CD ROM drive is easier to install, because it hooks up externally through a cable. Internal drives often require special mounting brackets or rails, which differ from system to system and are often not included with the upgrade kits.

Multimedia takes its toll on hardware performance, so buy as powerful a system as you can. Here are some considerations for putting together a multimedia system:

➨ **Processor** Get a fast 386 for playback-only machines. If you plan to create multimedia materials, get at least a 486.

➨ **Memory** You'll need 4 megabytes for playback, 8 megabytes for creating multimedia.

➨ **Storage** Consider getting at least an 80-megabyte drive for playback systems, 200 megabytes or more for creating multimedia.

Summary

Multimedia for Windows is still a work in progress. The new multimedia extensions included in Windows 3.1 enable the program to work with standard formats for using graphics and sound, and to control external multimedia devices.

The Windows Media Player utility lets you play multimedia files, such as sound files and animation, and also lets you control external devices, such as VCRs, laser disc players, and MIDI music synthesizers.

Windows can handle various forms of graphics, including still images, animations, and video. Although video is not a standard part of Windows, third-party add-in cards, called "video-in-a-window" cards, allow you to display analog video in a window on your graphical desktop. Digital video, which allows digital video sequences to be stored on your hard disk, is not ready for "prime time," but promises to become the primary form of computer video.

Windows includes a Sound Recorder utility, which lets you record, edit, and play back digital audio—provided you have the required sound hardware. The sound files you create can be embedded or linked into OLE applications, and can also be assigned to system events, such as Windows startup or exit.

The MIDI Mapper utiltity lets you configure MIDI synthesizers and other MIDI devices to conform with either the General MIDI or MPC MIDI formats that work with Windows.

The MPC logo and MPC marketing council were established to provide a minimum set of standards that identify multimedia software titles and the machines that run them. Although the initial MPC specification is under-powered, it takes an important step toward creating a larger market for multimedia computing.

By enabling you to add graphics and sound to your Windows system, multimedia technology broadens and transforms the computer's role as a communications tool. Multimedia software and hardware products will affect many markets, including business, education, publishing, and entertainment.

Insider's Tech Support

Q: My computer doesn't recognize my CD ROM drive.

A: Here are some things to check:

CD ROM drives require a special device driver; the standard Micro-soft driver is called MSCDEX.EXE. This driver is usually supplied with your CD ROM drive and is not included on the Windows installation disks. To install this driver, add the following line to your CONFIG.SYS file:

```
DEVICE=C:\MSCDEX.EXE.
```

Be sure to specify the full path if the driver file is located inside a directory.

If this driver is already installed, try using the CD ROM drive by logging onto it before starting Windows. Sometimes this solves the problem. If so, you may want to add a line to your AUTOEXEC.BAT file that contains a directory listing of your CD ROM drive to activate it each time you start your system.

Some CD ROM drives also require a Windows device driver, called LANMAN10.DOS, which is supplied on the Windows installation disks. To install this driver, add the line

```
DEVICE=LANMAN10.DOS
```

to the [386Enh] section of your SYSTEM.INI file.

If you have an external drive, make sure the cable is securely at-tached and connected to the right port. Some drives require an external

SCSI terminator. If you need one, check to make sure it is installed. You should also make sure that you have the power turned on to the drive.

Some CD ROM drives require that a disk be in the drive; otherwise, the PC fails to start up correctly. Read the documentation associated with your CD ROM drive to find out whether this is necessary, and if so, which disk to insert. Finally, make sure that you inserted the CD ROM with the label side facing up.

Q: My sound card doesn't work.

A: If the card isn't recognized at all, or if your system freezes up, you may have an interrupt conflict. Use the Microsoft Diagnostic program, or a similar utility, to investigate the status of the interrupts in your system (see Chapter 17).

Also, check the documentation with the card and determine how to set it for one of your unused interrupts. If all your interrupts are already used up, you'll have to remove something else to free one for the sound card.

If the card is recognized by your applications and its own utilities, then it's probably OK. If that's the case, check your various cables, and then check the audio output system. Try plugging headphones directly into the sound output port to see if it is sending out sound.

Q: I'm having trouble with MIDI.

A: Setting up MIDI is no picnic—it can be as much of a hassle as putting together a local area network. The first things to check are all your cables. MIDI devices include three types of connectors: IN, OUT, and THRU.

The OUT and THRU ports are both output ports—the OUT port contains the input mixed with the information created by this device, and the THRU port merely passes the input along, without adding the MIDI messages created by the device. The IN socket is where you plug the output of your computer or the output of another MIDI device.

Also check to see that the MIDI synthesizers and other devices are all set up to send and receive on the channels specified by your software. And make sure you MIDI map is configured properly so that the proper channels are being routed to the correct destinations.

Advanced Windows Techniques

12

Optimizing Windows Resources: Processor, RAM, and Storage

The performance and capabilities of your Windows environment ultimately depend on the selection and configuration of your hardware. The three most important hardware components reside inside your computer's system unit: the processor, memory chips or RAM, and hard disk drive.

These three components work synergistically with Windows to overcome many of the limitations associated with DOS-based computing. For example, if you have a 386 or higher processor, you can extend your physical RAM chips with virtual memory that converts space on your hard disk into what appears to your Windows program as additional RAM. If you have the right kind of hard disk controller card in your 386 or higher system, you can use FastDisk, a new feature in Windows 3.1 that allows Windows to bypass DOS and access your hard disk directly. The FastDisk feature speeds up such operations as the use of virtual memory and the storage and retrieval of files on your hard disk.

In order to make the most of your memory, however, you'll have to learn the fundamentals of PC memory, so that you can use certain parts of it more effectively. Aiding you in this effort are two memory management utilities, HIMEM.SYS and EMM386.EXE, that are included with Windows. Installing and configuring these utilities requires a chapter in itself (see Chapter 13), because to do so you'll need an understanding of the CONFIG.SYS and AUTOEXEC.BAT files, which are part of DOS.

Although Microsoft has added several features to Windows to improve memory management—including virtual memory, FastDisk, SMARTDrive, and swap files—users are still constrained by the 640K limitations of DOS, and can only wrest free of DOS by switching to Windows NT.

By understanding how the three main system components of your computer system—your processor, RAM, and hard disk drive—work together, you can learn how to optimize your computer's hardware to best support the significant demands made on it by Windows.

The Compatibility Myth

Although Windows 3.1 runs on IBM PC and compatible systems, no standard really exists for IBM PC compatibility. Not too surprisingly, almost every PC manufacturer claims that its system really is 100 percent IBM compatible. Indeed, the industry appellation for the IBM market is "the IBM PC-and-compatible market." But profound differences exist among the various systems described as being IBM PC-compatible. Even IBM itself has produced machines that are in many ways incompatible with one another, from the old-style PC, XT, and AT to the newer PS/2 and PS/1 series machines. The only real tie that binds these systems is their ability to run the DOS operating system.

What makes the so-called IBM PC-compatible standard so prevalent is the wide acceptance of DOS applications, along with a cornucopia of third-party accessory hardware designed to work with these systems, such as add-in cards, processors, video displays, and memory. Confusion enters the picture as well, because the term "IBM PC compatible" applies to so many different kinds of hardware, which can and do incorporate an enormous array of different components.

Danger Zone

Windows compounds the hazards introduced by the IBM PC compatibility myth. One of the most sophisticated and complex pieces of software ever to run on the PC, Windows pushes hardware performance to the limit and thereby introduces incompatibilities of its own.

The good news is that most incompatibilities can be easily solved, and once they're out of the way, most Windows applications can share a level of group compatibility that was never possible with DOS. Windows, through its system of device drivers and virtual devices, presents all hardware as similar to your applications; this means that you no longer have to go through the agony of configuring each individual application to run on your hardware setup, as was often the case with DOS.

Because of the wide spectrum of PC-compatible hardware offerings, almost every computer system is configured differently, making it more difficult to identify hardware incompatibilities. In general, however, these hardware items pose most of the compatibility problems:

➼ **ROM BIOS chips** These chips are essentially the personality module of your system, providing it with the ability to run DOS. They vary by manufacturer, such as Phoenix, Compaq, AMI, and IBM.

➼ **Memory configuration** Knowing how much RAM you have isn't enough. You've also got to know whether it's configured as expanded or extended memory.

➼ **Disk drive and controller card** Is it MFM, RLL, IDE, ESDI, or SCSI?

➼ **Bus** Your bus is based on one of these standards: ISA, EISA, or MCA.

Although I'll present ways to avoid many incompatibility and performance pitfalls, I can't promise you all the answers. Some of your problems may be insurmountable—you might even have to purchase a new piece of hardware before you can run Windows. But that seems a small price to pay for the opportunity to select from among so many configuration options offered by so many different manufacturers.

Unlike their DOS counterparts, Windows programs provide a compatibility buffer between your computer's hardware and your Windows applications. So once Windows is properly installed on your system, it should be much easier to run Windows programs and add any peripheral devices.

The Central Processing Unit

The **central processing unit,** or **CPU chip,** is the brain of your computer system. Because the CPU actually runs your programs and operating system, it has the most impact on your system's overall capabilities and performance.

CPU chips are distinguished from other, less powerful chips contained in computers because they can also

➤ Perform arithmetic and logical operations

➤ Decode special instructions

➤ Issue electrical signals that control other chips inside your system

IBM PCs and compatibles presently include one of these five types of CPUs:

➤ **8088** A 16-bit processor with an 8-bit bus. This was the chip found in the original IBM PC.

➤ **8086** A close cousin of the 8088, used in early PCs and PC clones.

➤ **80286** or **286** Introduced in the IBM AT, this chip is the minimum requirement for running Windows 3.1.

➤ **80386** or **386** The first 32-bit processor in the series.

➤ **80486** or **486** This is really just a fast 386 with the addition of a math coprocessor chip.

All of these processors were originally designed by Intel Corporation, although other companies, notably AMD and Cyrix, also produce some of these chips. The Intel family of chips is referred to as the Intel 80X86 family. The X, like the variable in algebraic equations, is a number that changes sequentially to indicate the latest member of the family. Starting with the 286, these chips are commonly referred to by their last three numbers, which is the convention I'll also use.

This series of five CPU chips represents more than ten years of development, which Intel plans to continue for the rest of the 1990s. Intel is already well along in its plans for the next several generations of chips, although the names will change. Each chip in this series retains compatibility with its predecessor while adding new functionality. Thus programs written for the 8086 can still run on a 286, although the 286 adds new features; similarly, programs designed on the 8086 and 286 run on the 386, although the 386 adds capabilities beyond the 286.

The latest member of this series—named the Pentium—is just beginning to rear its head. Unlike the 486, which is really a glorified 386, the Pentium was designed with significant new capabilities that specifically target Windows and other graphical operating systems. Although prices for systems containing the Pentium will be quite high at first, this chip is likely to become a mainstream choice for many Windows users.

The original CPU chips used in the PC—the 8088 and 8086—operated in a special processor mode known as **real mode**. Real mode was limited to addressing only 1 megabyte of memory, and DOS was originally designed to work only in this mode. The limitations of real mode haunt DOS to this day and cause most of the memory management headaches you'll encounter when configuring Windows.

Insider's Tip

Windows 3.0 incorporated a real mode for running Windows on 8088 and 8086 processors; it offered poor performance and more limited capabilities than even standard mode. If you have one of these older systems, you'll have to stick with Windows 3.0. Or maybe you should consider upgrading to GeoWorks.

With the introduction of the 286 chip came **protected mode**, which was designed to protect the memory addresses above 1 megabyte from being corrupted by conflicts that result when several applications try to access that memory at the same time. As a result, when the processor is running in protected mode, it can safely address memory above 1 megabyte, as mentioned earlier. Windows 3.0 offered a special real mode that allowed it to operate using an 8088 or 8086 chip's real mode. Windows 3.1 has done away with real mode; it only runs in the processor's protected mode.

Beginning with the 386 CPU chip, another processor mode was introduced, called **virtual mode**. Virtual mode provides the special ability to create almost any number of self-contained virtual machines that appear to be individual 8086-based systems, each with its own 640K of memory. Windows 386 enhanced mode taps the processor's virtual mode to provide the ability to run multiple DOS sessions, each in its own window.

. . . .

Standard Versus Enhanced Mode

Selection of your computer's CPU is your single most crucial hardware decision. The CPU that you are now using—or the one that you ultimately choose after reading this book—directly affects the performance and functionality of Windows itself and its applications. Other hardware components, such as memory, hard disk controller, and graphics adapter, also play an important role in your Windows performance, but these elements are relatively easy and inexpensive to change. Not so the central processing unit; sometimes it's easier to replace your complete system unit than to change your CPU.

What's the best processor to optimize your Windows operations? In my opinion, you should start with nothing less than a 386. Microsoft maintains that you can run Windows on any computer that has at least a 286, but even Microsoft's chairman, Bill Gates, publicly recommends that Windows be run on a 386 or above. Because there are so many 286-based systems in use, Microsoft has created two different modes for running Windows—standard and 386 enhanced. Standard mode allows Windows to run on a 286; 386 enhanced mode is best if you have a 386 or above.

One of the most important benefits of using Windows in 386 enhanced mode is multitasking: you can work on several Windows and DOS programs at the same time. In standard mode, on the other hand, you can run only one program at a time and must switch from task to task. Also, DOS applications can only be run full screen in standard mode.

However, standard mode does provide better compatibility with some older DOS and Windows applications. For example, DOS programs that use the VCPI memory managment protocol, described later in this chapter, can work best when run in standard mode.

386 enhanced mode offers several other valuable features. You can run a DOS application inside of a Window as part of your graphical desktop. You can cut and paste less than a screenful of information from a DOS application into the Windows Clipboard for later retrieval and pasting into Windows applications. (In standard mode, you can only cut and copy an entire screen.) In 386 enhanced mode, you can create a virtual memory management system that allows you to augment the amount of RAM in your computer with space on your hard disk; although you're not really adding any RAM to your system, the converted space on your hard disk appears like RAM to your Windows environment and its applications.

The Best Processor for Your Needs

How much processor is enough for you? There's no simple answer, but here are some recommendations about processor selection, based on what kinds of applications you plan to use:

286, 8 MHz The original IBM AT is an example of the 286, 8 MHz processor. Windows is unbearably slow on this system; upgrade if possible.

286, 12 MHz Performance is sluggish, even if you have several megabytes of RAM and a reasonably fast hard disk and its controller.

286, 20 MHz In some cases you may get better DOS performance than you would with a 16 MHz 386SX chip, because many older DOS applications were optimized to run on a 286. This is certainly the best type of 286 system for running Windows, but it still won't let you multitask DOS applications or provide other performance benefits of the 386, such as FastDisk.

386SX, 16 MHz The 386SX chip represents a compromise between the 286 and 386 product lines. Unlike its big brother, the 386DX series, the 386SX can handle only a 16-bit bus, such as ISA or 16-bit MCA machines. This is the slowest of the 386SX pack.

386SX, 20 MHz You get an extra performance boost from the 4 MHz increase in speed, but it's still a bit slow.

386SX, 25 MHz This chip is the best of the SX lot and provides a good value in a Windows system.

386DX, 16 MHz The original 386 processor, this unit is no longer being manufactured. Performance is similar to the 16 MHz SX chip.

386DX, 20MHz Systems based on this uncommon chip are slightly faster than those based on the 16 MHz 386 and 20 MHz 286 systems.

386DX, 25 MHz Originally, the mainstream chip in the DX product line. For many business tasks, such as wordprocessing and spreadsheets, this should be considered the entry-level system.

386DX, 33 MHz This chip represents the top of Intel's 386 line and doubles the speed of the 16 MHz entry-level 386 chip. If you use graphics or multimedia applications, such as CorelDraw, PageMaker, or Action, consider this system the bare minimum.

386DX, 40 MHz AMD's CPU one-upmanship brought forth this speedy clone of Intel's 386. A good alternative to a 486 for the budget conscious.

486SX, various speeds When AMD cloned the 386, Intel struck back with the 486SX series. Although SX designates a 16-bit bus in the 386 series, 486SX chips have a full 32-bit bus processor. The 486SX is actually a version of the 486DX that lacks a math coprocessor. Intel is offering clock-doubled 486 chips that plug into the upgrade socket found on most 486SX-based systems.

486DX, 25 MHz The 486 chip essentially combines a 386 processor, a 387 math coprocessor, and 8K worth of on-chip processor RAM cache. For the Windows power or business user, this should be your minimum choice for a mainstream Windows machine. This processor can easily be upgraded with the 486DX2, a clock-doubled chip that boosts performance to 50 MHz.

486DX, 33 MHz An even faster version of the 25 MHz 486DX, this 33 MHz chip actually approaches the capabilities of many workstations and mini-computers. Intel plans to provide a clock-doubled version of this chip that boosts performance to 66 MHz, thus providing an inexpensive way to extend the lifespan of these systems.

486DX, 50 MHz and **66MHz** At the time of this writing, these chips are the fastest available, but Intel has announced plans to produce a clock-doubled version, which would boost the speed of the 50 MHz chip to 100 MHz.

CX486SLC Produced by Cyrix, these chips don't really qualify as a 486 although they offer good performance. These chips are pin compatible with the chip socket for the 386SX chips, which means they have only a 16-bit bus. Also, they do not contain the math coprocessor capabilities and provide only a 1K of on-chip cache.

Insider's Tip

As a general guideline, increasing the speed of the processor improves its ability to perform disk and video access, thereby improving the performance of these important subsystems as well. For example, video accelerator cards work even faster with a fast CPU chip.

My general recommendation is that you buy a 486DX 25MHz system or better if you can afford it. These systems provide good performance at reasonable prices, and most 486 systems can be easily upgraded by replacing their processor chips with faster models.

Although the list of chips just presented was current when this book was written, the field is proliferating rapidly. AMD is introducing its own 486 clone chips, and other companies, such as Chips & Technologies, are working on clone chips of their own. Intel has already announced its successor to the 486 called the Pentium, which seems destined to become the chip you'll want to have if you're a Windows power user.

Processor Cache

Windows uses a variety of complex memory management techniques, which cause your system to access RAM frequently. Normal RAM chips can't keep up with the pace of your Windows environment and its applications, but you can reverse this slowdown by installing or beefing up your **processor RAM cache.**

The processor RAM cache is a special type of RAM—usually found only on high-speed 386 or above systems—that can significantly affect system speed. Basically, your processor uses the processor RAM cache to store information that's being transferred either to or from the normal RAM chips. The processor RAM cache itself contains a special type of high-speed memory that's able to alleviate the time lag between the operations of high-speed CPU chips and the slower system RAM.

The processor RAM cache provides a high-speed holding area that can supply the processor with the data it needs very quickly; at the same time, the processor RAM cache receives information from the slower system RAM. This bifurcation fools the processor into thinking that all your system memory runs at the higher speed of the processor RAM cache, while relying on your lower-cost RAM to run your system memory.

Typically, processor RAM caches range from 8 to 256K in size, with some systems offering the potential for even more. The processor RAM cache serves as a high-speed holding area for the processor; it does not add to the amount of RAM available to your programs.

The location—or existence—of your processor RAM cache depends on what kind of system you're using. In 386-based systems, the processor RAM cache consists of separate chips. These high-speed static RAM chips are either soldered directly onto the motherboard or placed in sockets. This type of cache is known as an **external processor cache**. Some RAM caches provide extra empty sockets for RAM cache expansion. Other PCs lack a RAM cache altogether, and contain only empty sockets for installing normal RAM.

With the 486, Intel placed a small RAM cache directly onto the chip; this is known as an **internal processor cache**. Although the standard 486 chip contains only 8K worth of internal cache, because it is built right into the chip it operates at higher speeds than do caches located on supplementary chips. IBM also produces a special version of the 386 chip, which also contains an internal cache to increase speed; this chip is used in certain models of the PS/2 line of computers, such as the PS/2 Model 57SLC. Other manufacturers are reportedly applying this technique to produce power-boosted 386 chips as well. Even if your 486 or other CPU chip already contains an internal RAM cache, some systems provide sockets on the motherboard for installing a secondary RAM cache for further performance enhancement.

One consideration when purchasing a computer system is whether it features a processor RAM cache. If so, does the motherboard already contain the necessary static RAM chips for the cache, or do you need to purchase them separately? Because of their higher speeds, these static RAM chips cost considerably more than regular RAM chips. Also, not all processor RAM caches work equally well—different manufacturers use different schemes for caching memory—so you may want to test the different systems or refer to published tests to see which systems offer the best performance for Windows. Generally, RAM caches do offer Windows a significant performance boost, and I recommend using a processor cache of at least 64K in size.

Some systems provide for up to 512K of external processor cache. On a 386 system, a 256K cache is noticeably better than a 64K cache, but expanding the cache to 512K doesn't offer as much of a performance boost and may be reaching the point of diminishing returns. On 486 machines, the merits of an external cache are still being debated, and the proper size for an external cache depends on the exact mix of applications you are using. In most cases, the internal 8K cache provides the greatest performance boost and diminishes the need for an external cache.

Upgrading Your Processor

Depending on your pocketbook, there are plenty of ways to upgrade from a 286- to a 386-based system. An **add-in processor card**, for example, places a 386-on-a-board into your 286-based system. The first of these add-in cards to be offered was the Intel Inboard 386/PC; this board (which fits into an 8-bit slot) works with PCs, XTs, and certain clones. It transforms your old computer into a 386-based system, albeit with a 8-bit bus. Any memory you plan to use beyond your computer's base of 640K must be added to the Inboard, because this board cannot properly address additional memory you may already have plugged into another 8-bit slot in your system. Using the Inboard with Windows is a bad idea because it introduces a host of incompatibilities and performance limitations.

Applied Reasoning's PC-Elevator 386 is a higher-powered add-in card that works on the same principle as the Inboard. This system works with PCs, XTs, ATs, and many clones, making it generally more compatible than the Intel Inboard. The PC-Elevator works best with additional memory placed on the board—it can accommodate a whopping 13 megabytes. The PC-Elevator also includes a disk cache and a clever memory-management scheme, which—unlike the Inboard—allows it to use many types of memory add-ins.

AOX, Inc. offers a low-cost 386SX-based **add-in processor module** that plugs directly into the socket used by the 286 chip. Not only does this module bring the street price down to the $200 range, it doesn't require a slot in your system and thus minimizes incompatibilities. Other 386 add-in modules include the SOTA Express, Intel SNAP-IN, and ALL Charge Card. All these cards, however, compromise performance. They often include their own caches to compensate for performance, so the card performs well on a benchmark test; but when you run Windows, the cache becomes flooded and the performance of the system becomes severely impaired.

Insider's Tip

These add-in processor modules make the most sense for people who are more concerned about saving time when upgrading than about saving mo   . For example, if you have to upgrade 50 or 100 computers for a large office, it can be more expedient to plug in a new processor card rather than to replace the motherboard for the entire system. Although vendors are constantly striving to perfect this type of simple processor plug-in module, I've yet to see one that hits the mark.

Some computer systems were designed with processors that can be upgraded. These systems save you from the problems associated with some of the third-party add-in upgrade cards mentioned earlier. These **upgradable systems** typically place the CPU chip on a small circuit board, which plugs into the motherboard. To upgrade the processor, you simply replace the small circuit board.

Applying a different technology, Intel offers 486 system owners a direct chip-replacement method for upgrading their processors. This technology, called **Overdrive**, is the easiest way to upgrade a system. The Overdrive chips are 486 chips that incorporate a clock-doubling process, which allows a chip to run at twice its normal speed. To upgrade your system, just pop out the old 486 and replace it with one that is twice as fast. Some 486 systems contain a special upgrade socket that will accept an overdrive chip without requiring that you remove the original chip.

Another way to upgrade your system is to **replace the entire motherboard;** Hauppage and American Megatrends are both well-known manufacturers of motherboards. Although replacing the motherboard can be more expensive than adding a plug-in processor card, it reduces the possibility of compatibility hassles. Replacement motherboards from no-name companies are offered at surprisingly low prices, with discounters selling 386 boards for well under $500, and 486 motherboards for less than $1,000.

At these prices, some of these motherboards are competitively priced with the plug-in processor modules. If you do buy a new motherboard, make sure it will fit inside the case of your current system and will work with your power supply, disk drive, and other elements. Some motherboard vendors will perform the transplant for you at a nominal additional charge. Although this approach allows you to replace your motherboard, you may still be left with a slow, outdated disk controller, hard disk, display adapter, or power supply.

An enterprising solution—and the one I recommend most often for 286 users—is to simply **upgrade your entire system by selling it** to someone who doesn't need or want Windows. Or take a tax write-off and donate the system to a local school or nonprofit organization. In the long run, it may be cheaper—and a lot less hassle—to replace your system altogether.

· ·

The Math Coprocessor Chip

A **math coprocessor chip**—also called a **floating point unit** or **FPU**—boosts the speed of math calculations in your system. Unless you plan to use applications that require intensive number crunching, such as a spreadsheet or graphics program, you probably won't need to invest in a math coprocessor chip. Whereas a CPU handles all types of instructions, a math coprocessor is specifically designed to handle mathematical computations, which it can perform much more quickly than the CPU.

Intel has designed a family of math coprocessors that directly correspond with its CPU offerings. These coprocessors include the 287, paired with the 286 CPU; and the 387, mated with the 386 CPU. Cyrix also produces Intel-compatible math coprocessors that are offered at a significantly lower price. No corresponding Intel math coprocessor exists for the 486DX chip series, however, because the 486DX essentially includes the math coprocessor function. In essence, the 486DX is a souped-up 386 combined with a 387 math coprocessor, along with 8K of additional on-chip cache.

Math coprocessors accelerate math calculations in number-crunching applications, such as Excel and other spreadsheets, and in graphics programs, which provide specific support for the math coprocessor. Several important Windows graphics packages, such as Arts & Letters and Publisher's Type Foundry, are specifically designed to use the additional math capabilities of the coprocessor. CAD packages also benefit from math coprocessors; in fact, because these programs are so calculation-intensive, they benefit most from the more expensive Weitek coprocessor.

Insider's Tip

If your work requires the use of a math coprocessor, you should consider getting a 486DX. Because it integrates the CPU math coprocessor and the cache on a single chip, it performs mathematical calculations more quickly than does a 386 combined with a 387. With the price difference between a 486 and a 386 getting smaller all the time, there's every reason to opt for a 486 if you often run a number-crunching program.

I recommend against using a 486SX chip, because it is really a 486DX with the math coprocessor part of the chip disabled. Intel sells a 487, which it represents as a way to add the math coprocessor functions lacking in the 486SX. But in truth, the 487 is just a 486DX; when you install it into the so-called 486SX upgrade socket, you're effectively turning off the 486SX. If you bought the 486SX and the 487, then you've been hornswaggled by Intel into buying two redundant processor chips for your system.

Another variety of math coprocessor was developed by Weitek. Weitek's coprocessors are more costly than Intel's, but outperform them. The Weitek chips, however, must be specifically supported by the applications you want to use. Intel's coprocessors also require the specific support of applications, but the Intel chips are far more prevalent and consequently more widely supported than any other. If you are using a Weitek math coprocessor in conjunction with EMM386, be sure to turn on the support for this chip using EMM386's W=ON switch.

The motherboard design also determines whether you can take a math coprocessor on board, because you need an additional socket. Many boards provide this additional socket, usually situated near the CPU socket, and some boards contain sockets for both the Intel and the Weitek coprocessor chips.

Because Windows is a graphical operating system, support for a math coprocessor could help accelerate Windows's own graphics-handling capabilities. Unfortunately, Windows 3.1 does not make use of a math coprocessor; thus adding one to your system will not affect the performance of Windows itself.

The System Bus

The **system bus** provides the electrical highway over which your CPU transmits instructions within your computer's circuitry. You access the system bus through a group of slots, which accept add-in cards for memory, peripherals, and other hardware options.

With IBM PCs and compatibles, CPU data handling and bus structure are characterized by the number of lanes—that is, the number of data groups the computer can transfer to the bus in a single operation. The 8088 is limited to 8 lanes, or 8 bits per transfer; the 286 and 386SX are limited to 16; and the 386DX and 486 provide 32-lane superhighways (Figure 12.1).

In addition to the actual processor bus, PCs contain a **peripheral bus** for accepting add-in cards. The peripheral bus is also called the **I/O bus**, because it's the traffic hub of most input/output activity in your system. Just because your system comes with a 32-bit processor and a 32-bit proces-

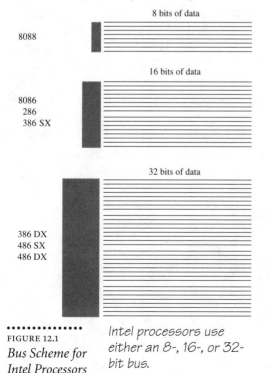

FIGURE 12.1

Bus Scheme for Intel Processors

Intel processors use either an 8-, 16-, or 32-bit bus.

sor bus, don't assume it also includes a 32-bit peripheral bus. Indeed, most 386 systems are shipped with a 16-bit peripheral bus (ISA). These are the various PC peripheral buses:

➡ **8-bit ISA bus** The original peripheral for the PC and XT; not used in today's systems.

➡ **16-bit ISA bus** Introduced with the IBM PC AT, it remains the most prevalent bus in PC systems.

➡ **16-bit MCA bus** The low-end PS/2 bus.

➡ **32-bit MCA bus** The high-end PS/2 bus.

➡ **32-bit EISA bus** The high-end ISA-compatible bus.

The original PC bus is referred to as the ISA, or Industry Standard Architecture, bus—a name that reflects the popularity of this bus among manufacturers of PC compatibles. The EISA (Extended Industry Standard Architecture) bus retains compatibility while extending the capabilities of the ISA bus. MCA, or Micro Channel Architecture, was developed by IBM for the PS/2.

Although both the 8088 and 8086 CPU chips are considered 16-bit processors, the 8088 CPU can only transfer data over the processor bus in groups of 8 bits at a time. Therefore, computers with the 8088 chip, like the original PC and many of its subsequent clones, are restricted to an 8-bit I/O bus.

The first PC series machine to use a 16-bit peripheral bus was the IBM PC AT. The AT introduced a bus that included the original PC bus connector, with the standard 8-bit data path, and a smaller connector at the end of the original PC slot. This smaller connector contained the additional circuitry needed to carry a full 16 bits of data across the bus (Figure 12.2).

FIGURE 12.2
PC and AT Slots

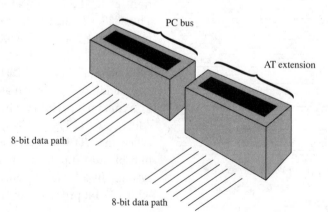

PC bus

AT extension

8-bit data path

8-bit data path

An 8-bit PC slot and a small extension connector, which makes it a 16-bit AT slot.

The 16-bit AT-style bus has become the prevalent one in the industry. Most IBMs and compatibles, add-in cards, and peripherals use the 16-bit AT-style bus, commonly referred to as the ISA bus. Although the ISA bus works with both 8- and 16-bit cards, Windows users should use 16-bit cards whenever possible. This is especially important for disk controller, memory, and video cards, because Windows places heavy demands on these components.

New Bus Architectures: MCA and EISA

Along with the PS/2 series in 1987, IBM launched a new bus architecture: the Micro Channel Architecture, or MCA. MCA was actually a new type of connector for add-in cards and provided both 16-bit and 32-bit implementations. Despite IBM's relatively noble aspiration (extending the AT bus capabilities from 16 to 32 bits while also providing a more advanced bus architecture), the hardware giant also introduced one major drawback: MCA was incompatible with all of IBM's own add-in cards designed for the PC, XT, and AT. MCA, therefore, was also incapable of using any of the thousands of non-IBM add-in cards that worked with the PC- and AT-style buses.

Previously, when the AT and its 16-bit capabilities were launched, compatibility with earlier models had been maintained. Users could still use add-in cards that had been designed to work the 8-bit bus of the PC and XT models and their compatibles. The older 8-bit cards would also work in the 16-bit bus slot of the AT, because the original 8-bit portion of the AT bus maintained the same bus architecture as the PC and XT type of 8-bit slot.

Therefore you could add new memory boards and disk controllers requiring the 16-bit bus capabilities but still use inexpensive 8-bit cards for printers, modems, and other comparatively low-throughput devices. This "backward compatibility" allowed users to upgrade from the PC to the AT and take their boards with them.

The new MCA architecture stymied all these upgrade attempts. Boards developed for the PC or AT bus simply wouldn't function in the MCA bus. Instead, IBM was counting on the development of a new class of MCA add-in cards and MCA-compatible machines, all designed to promote the improved functionality provided by the 32-bit capabilities of the MCA bus.

Such hopes went unfulfilled. Although IBM sold millions of PS/2 systems, the MCA bus didn't garner popularity among third-party developers. And users were dissatisfied because they couldn't use boards designed for their PC and AT bus with MCA machines. As a result, most manufacturers and users continued to use AT-bus machines. In fact, the AT bus, with its 16-bit data path, addresses the capabilities of 286 and 386SX systems perfectly well, because these chips have only 16-bit processor buses.

The advent of the 386DX, 486, and higher-level chips, however, called for 32-bit I/O handling capabilities. With these more powerful chips, the 16-bit AT bus created an I/O bottleneck, which limited system functionality. IBM then offered to license its MCA BUS—with its 32-bit I/O handling capabilities—for a fee that manufacturers found to be unacceptably high relative to their costs for producing the AT-style bus.

Indeed, IBM's announced licensing fees backfired. Led by Compaq, a group of computer manufacturers designed an alternative 32-bit bus, dubbed the EISA, for Extended Industry Standard Architecture. The EISA provided backward compatibility with the 8-bit boards from the original PC, and with the 16-bit boards made for the AT bus.

EISA also broke the ranks with an important technical advance: a new type of add-in card designed specifically for the EISA bus could take advantage of the full 32-bit capabilities of systems based on the 386DX and 486 processors. These EISA-based systems rival 32-bit MCA-based systems as the top performers on the market today.

In counterattack to the EISA assault, IBM set up offensives on two fronts. First, it lowered its MCA license fees and requirements in order to encourage the manufacture of PS/2 clones incorporating the MCA standard, rather than ISA or EISA. On a second front, IBM increased the performance of the MCA bus so that it could rival the new EISA 32-bit specification. IBM also provided add-in card manufacturers with the chip sets they needed to optimize performance of cards for the MCA bus.

As of today, the ISA standard still dominates on the bus battlefield; IBM has retreated and now offers certain PS/2 models with the ISA bus. The MCA bus lags far behind ISA in acceptance, and newcomer EISA remains in the rear ranks, although it is gaining steadily, with the fastest growth rate for all bus types. In price, EISA-based machines far exceed the other two standards, as do their corresponding add-in cards. As the protracted battle continues, however, it seems the EISA bus may someday surpass both ISA and MCA as the prevalent computer bus architecture.

In addition, some systems provide their own proprietary bus for use by memory boards and high-speed video adapters. For example, a system with a 16-bit ISA bus may also include a proprietary 32-bit slot in which you can plug additional RAM; this setup allows your system to access memory directly in 32-bit mode without the bottleneck imposed by a 16-bit bus. The drawback to this type of proprietary type of bus is that you must obtain a special card from your system vendor for adding RAM, high-speed video, or whatever else will work in this special slot.

More recently, in order to establish a standard that could replace some of these proprietary busses, two different standards for so-called local bus implementations were developed, one by VESA and one by Intel. Local busses operate at the speed of the processor and improve performance for add-in hardware, such as display adapter cards and disk drive controllers. The VL-Bus is the VESA standard, and is gaining strong support. If you can afford it, local bus video dramatically speeds Windows' graphics.

Ranking the Busses

The 16-bit ISA bus is the most prevalent PC bus architecture today and offers the widest availability of add-in cards. Because this bus provides a good balance of price and performance, I generally recommend machines with the ISA bus as the best choice for budget-minded Windows users.

The 16- and 32-bit versions of the MCA bus can be found in the various PS/2 models, as well as in an emerging group of MCA clone machines. MCA-based systems are fine for use with Windows, although I strongly recommend limiting yourself to MCA bus types capable of handling 32 bits of data. The downside to the MCA bus is that because of limited availability, add-in cards are often more expensive than their ISA-bus equivalents. Therefore MCA-bus machines are my third choice, after ISA and EISA.

My favorite choice is the 32-bit EISA bus, which offers a good compromise between performance and compatibility. This single bus boosts the flexibility and availability of add-in cards more than any other bus type. Also, for high-performance applications, EISA cards have an edge over their 8- and 16-bit counterparts, although you'll have to pay an additional price to achieve the performance boost.

Another advantage of EISA is that it allows interrupts to be easily shared by more than one peripheral. For example, a single interrupt can be used by two serial ports without causing the internal system conflicts that would result with an ISA bus.

Insider's Tip

An additional consideration on both ISA and EISA bus systems is the speed at which the bus is running. The original ISA bus ran at 8 MHz, and the original EISA specification ran at only 8.5 MHz. Several computer manufacturers now include options that let you increase the bus speed to 10, 12, or even 16 MHz, in order to improve the performance of cards that are designed to operate at these higher bus speeds. However, be alert to compatibility problems that increasing the bus speed can cause.

The Computer's Memory

Memory ranks second only to the CPU as the most important influence on the performance of your system. The memory chips inside your system take one of two forms: RAM or ROM.

ROM chips are basic to internal solid-state memory. These are the read-only memory devices that contain built-in instructions, such as the BIOS (basic input/output system), which controls the basic input/output system of your computer hardware, along with other system functions such as startup routines and diagnostic programs. Most modern BIOS versions (those produced within the past few years) are compatible with Windows, and therefore don't pose any operating problems. ROM chips can be found on your system motherboard and on the add-in adapter cards that control devices such as disk drives and video displays.

Another type of solid-state memory chip is the **processor RAM cache**, discussed earlier in this chapter. Other RAM caches can be found on add-in or peripheral cards, such as disk controllers or video adapters. These dedicated RAM caches are available only for the devices, and cannot be used by your computer as general-purpose memory. Peripheral cards can also include processors, RAMs, and other chips, making them much like small, self-contained computer systems.

In most cases, the term **RAM (random-access memory)** is used to describe the memory chips—whether on your computer's motherboard or on its add-in memory boards—that serve as the main memory available to your system. This system RAM provides your computer its main workspace for storing applications and processing information. For example, when you run an application, it's usually stored on your hard disk and then transferred into the system RAM before you can run it. As you work with the application, the data that you enter or that you recall from a storage device is stored in RAM while you manipulate it.

The RAM chips used in your computer's system memory are known as **dynamic RAM, or DRAM.** This kind of memory is called **volatile memory** because it clears itself of data every time you turn off your computer. Some systems offer static RAM chips, which are nonvolatile, very fast, and retain their information if the power is turned off. At the present time, static RAM chips are much more expensive than DRAM and are therefore relegated to special applications, where the higher price can be justified.

With Windows, RAM works together with hard disk space to provide applications with memory resources. The amount of RAM in your system affects not just the speed of Windows performance but also determines how many applications you can run at one time. Furthermore, when Windows is running in 386 enhanced mode, it can use virtual memory to fool your system into thinking that it has more RAM than it really does.

• •

Random-Access Memory (RAM)

RAM is your most important memory resource. Like all good things in life—friends, wealth, leisure time, and computer games—you can never have too much RAM.

New in 3.1

Windows 3.0 was limited to 16 megabytes of RAM. With Windows 3.1, the 16 megabyte barrier is broken; you can now stuff as much RAM into your system as it will hold. On 286 systems, you can access only 16 megabytes of RAM; and although 386 and higher systems can theoretically access 4 gigabytes of RAM, most systems can accommodate only 64 megabytes, and some components of Windows can work with a maximum of 256 megabytes.

Here's what specific increments of RAM can do for Windows:

➤➤ **1 megabyte** This is the minimum amount of RAM for running Windows—or "crawling" under Windows, which is a more accurate description of your operating speed when you are limited to a single megabyte. In fact, even if you have a 386 processor, if you've only got 1 megabyte of RAM, Windows won't run in 386 enhanced mode.

➤➤ **2 megabytes** The real minimum for running Windows, and a bare one at that. Although 2 megabytes is adequate for running one or two lightweight tasks, you'll soon find yourself experiencing "RAM cram," and your TrueType may not work properly.

➤➤ **4 megabytes** This is what I consider an adequate minimum for running Windows—and it's definitely the minimum requirement for DOS multitasking. Four megabytes puts you in the RAM comfort zone.

➤➤ **8 megabytes** Now you're running laps. You can usually fit this amount of RAM onto a 386 system board or an add-in memory card. Eight megabytes gives you plenty of RAM for your applications. Although it's considered an excessive amount of RAM for DOS usage, even 8 megabytes can be quickly used by Windows.

➤➤ **More than 8 megabytes** Nirvana. If your pocketbook can afford it, you can use as much RAM with Windows as your system can accommodate on most 386 or higher systems. Traditionally, only servers or graphics workstations are configured with more than 8 megabytes, but there's a trend among Windows power users to go for 16.

Adding RAM. It's not only a matter of how much RAM you need, it's where you put it that counts. To add RAM, you can either insert chips into sockets on the motherboard, or you can pop in SIMMs (Single Inline Memory Modules, which are a bunch of chips, welded together in one easy-to-install unit) into SIMM sockets on the motherboard. Another way to add RAM is to plug it into a memory card, which can accept chips, SIPPs (Single Inline Pin Package), or SIMMs. Or you can replace existing chips with higher-density RAM chips.

Plugging In a Memory Card. An add-in card, which plugs into either a proprietary slot or the expansion bus, contains DRAM chips, SIPPs, or SIMMs. Although I recommend that you insert memory directly into the motherboard, sometimes you'll have to use an add-in card because there's no space provided on the motherboard.

When selecting a memory board, choose the kind that uses proprietary slots—they are usually faster than the ones that plug into the peripheral bus, especially if it's an ISA bus. Many 32-bit memory expansion slots provide the same performance level as does RAM that is inserted directly into the motherboard.

Danger Zone

Watch out for these disadvantages of add-in RAM boards: they often take up a slot; they're usually more expensive than chips inserted directly into the motherboard; and, most important, it often takes the computer more time to access cards than to access chips on the motherboard. In fact, a sure way to retard your computer's operating speed is to tack on memory using a 16-bit ISA or 16-bit MCA add-in card; use an 8-bit RAM card, and you can really slow things down.

When the computer reads and writes to RAM located on add-in cards that are on an 8- or 16-bit expansion bus, memory access is limited to the speed of the expansion bus (usually 8 MHz) instead of the speed of the CPU chip. Furthermore, 16-bit ISA and MCA memory cards will force your 386DX or 486 processor to transfer 32-bit memory blocks in two 16-bit transfers, cutting deeper into your system performance.

Installing Higher-Density Chips. You can also increase the total amount of RAM on your system board by replacing existing chips or SIMMs with higher-density RAM chips, which contain more bits per chip. Older systems use 256 kilobit chips, but 1-megabit chips are now the norm. Four-megabit chips are still quite expensive, so it may be more cost-effective to use 1-megabit chips for upgrading RAM.

If you have 256-kilobit chips on your motherboard, you might want to start by replacing them to increase your RAM capacity. For example, by removing the thirty-six 256-kilobit chips (or four 256-kilobyte SIMMs) from the sockets of a 1-megabyte board, and replacing them with the equivalent number of 1-megabit parts, you'll bring the amount of RAM on the system board up to 4 megabytes—a much more satisfactory amount for running Windows.

However, you do need to check the manufacturer's specifications before upgrading the memory in your system, because many system boards address memory idiosyncratically. Part of the price that we pay for freedom of choice in the PC-and-compatible universe is having to deal with system boards made by a wide variety of manufacturers. The number of existing revisions and varieties of system boards extends well into the thousands.

SIMM with 4 megabytes per module are gaining in popularity, but when upgrading your memory with higher-density RAM chips, you may have to expand your memory in multiples of 2 or 4 megabytes, depending on the amount of memory banks available on your motherboard. Table 12.1 shows various scenarios for a typical system that allows eight banks of SIMMs.

TABLE 12.1

Total Megabytes	Number of Banks	Type of SIMMs
1	4	256K
2	8	256K
4	4	1 MB
8	8	1 MB
16	4	4 MB
32	8	4 MB

On many systems, these are the only memory amounts permitted— you can't mix and match different densities of SIMMs within one system. Although some systems permit mixing different densities of chips, restrictions usually apply as to which banks can receive certain densities. These restrictions also apply to some systems that use chips for SIPPs for expansion, so you'll need to investigate your system and determine what kind of chips you need in order to upgrade.

Danger Zone

Adding higher-density RAM chips often involves resetting some jumpers of the DIP switches on the system board. Be sure to follow the exact settings specified by the manufacturer if you change any of these switches or jumpers. Many newer systems automatically detect higher-density memory and can reconfigure your system without your having to flip switches or change jumpers.

Parity Checking and RAM. In theory, it takes eight RAM chips to create one byte of RAM, because there are eight bits to a byte. Although some computers, such as many Macintosh models and a few PC systems, contain eight RAM chips per bank or SIMM, most PCs require nine chips per bank or SIMM, because in these systems nine bits are provided for each byte.

The additional, or ninth, bit—called the **parity bit**—is used for error detection. A crude form of error checking, parity checking uses the ninth bit like a traffic light to warn of a possible error. If any of the eight bits are damaged electrically (by the computer or accidentally changed by some hardware or software failure), the ninth bit changes from red to green, or vice versa (that is, its numerical value changes from odd to even, or vice versa). Parity-bit checking is so primitive, however, that if 2 bits are changed in the same way, the ninth bit doesn't reflect the change (because the two bits balance each other out).

The parity-check error sometimes appears after you start your computer; as part of its startup routine, almost every PC first checks the RAM by a method of writing information to RAM, reading it back, and checking the parity bits to ensure that the data was correctly written and read. If the routine finds a problem in a chip that has failed (usually from a manufacturing defect, old age, or some type of power aberration), you'll see a message that reads something like "Parity check one" if the problem is on your system board, or "Parity check two" if it's on an add-in board.

On IBM PS/2 systems, numerical error codes appear: 110 is the equivalent of "Parity check one" and 111 stands for "Parity check two." If these messages or codes appear after you start your computer, turn off your system and try to solve the problem, either with diagnostic software or by getting your unit serviced.

Another all-too-familiar parity-error message may appear on your screen as a group of numbers that ends with the three digits 201. The digits that precede the 201 are four hexadecimal numbers that suggest exactly where the computer thinks your system contains a failed RAM chip. If you get a parity error message at startup or reboot, fix it without delay so it won't disturb you in the middle of a session.

Parity errors are much more troublesome when they occur during a work session. A parity error can halt your system altogether and force you to restart it; if you fall victim to this disaster, any information in RAM is lost.

Some PC clones allow you to disable parity checking. This prevents a parity error from halting the operation of your system, but it doesn't ensure the integrity of your data. If only one character somewhere off in a stray file is affected, a parity error may not cause you much grief. But the wrong character in a letter to a client could prove embarrassing, and a single incorrect number in a spreadsheet or formula could dramatically alter a financial report.

Windows and RAM. Windows employs various tricks to take advantage of all your available memory. In fact, your total RAM often falls short of what's required by the combined sizes of the application files you've loaded. Windows, and many of its applications, only load part of a program into memory at a time. A spreadsheet program, for example, might load only the data entry portion of the program while you're entering numbers, leaving the graphics portion unloaded until you switch to constructing charts. Or the spreadsheet application might load only a particular section of the data file you're handling, rather than the entire data file. To facilitate this memory conservation process, Windows programming languages are designed to create programs that load only part of themselves into memory at a time.

These software manipulations, however, trade speed for memory swapping. When a program swaps either part of itself or the data that it's handling back and forth between memory and a disk drive, the comparatively slower speed of the disk drive can decelerate the program's performance while the swapping occurs. You'd have far better performance if your system contained enough RAM to store the entire program and the data file. Most programs designed for memory-swapping activity are smart enough to detect an ample supply of RAM, so they auto-load. A few, however, will swap no matter how much memory your system contains.

To understand the chicanery involved in swapping files to and from memory, and the other assorted techniques that Windows employs to make the most of your system resources, you should be familiar with the three basic types of RAM used by PCs: conventional memory, extended memory, and expanded memory. Conventional memory technically refers to the one megabyte of RAM that can be addressed by DOS, but this term is commonly used to designate the user RAM area, which equals the first 640K of this one megabyte. In addition, there's UMA, or upper memory area, and HMA, or high memory area. To make things even more confusing, the UMA is sometimes called UMB, for upper memory blocks. If all this is more than you can fit into your memory, here's a brief rundown of what these terms mean:

➤ **Conventional memory** The first 640K of RAM installed in your machine. To run Windows, you must have a full 640K of conventional memory.

➤ **Extended memory** The RAM in your machine beyond the initial 1 megabyte. You must have some extended memory to run Windows—at least

192K for running in standard mode and at least 1 megabyte for 386 enhanced mode.

➤ **HMA, or high memory area** The first 64K of extended memory.

➤ **UMA, or upper memory area** (also known as **UMB**, upper memory block) The memory between 640K and the 1 megabyte limit of DOS.

➤ **Expanded memory** An older method of increasing RAM based on a technique of using empty memory locations between the end of the 640K conventional memory and 1024K (1 megabyte) of base memory, this area is normally used by ROMs and system software. Windows doesn't use expanded memory, but DOS applications that you run from within Windows may need it.

Figure 12.3 shows how these memory areas are addressed by your system.

FIGURE 12.3

The Layout of Memory Areas

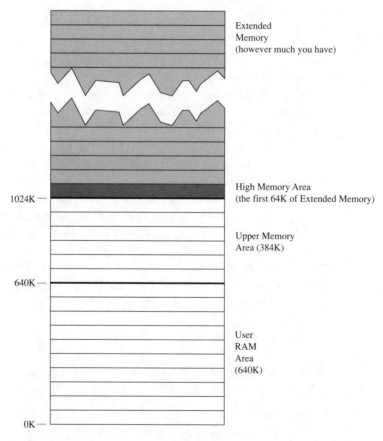

Conventional memory, upper memory, and extended memory are arranged in this fashion so they can be accessed by the system.

Understanding Hexadecimal Memory Addresses

Computer memory locations are often identified by their **hexadecimal number values**—or, in nerd parlance, the hex value. Hexadecimal means 16, and a hex value is a number expressed in base 16, rather than the everyday base 10 or the computer base 2.

In base 10, the decimal system, there are ten digits, 0 through 9. In base 16, there are sixteen digits; 0 through 9 retain the same values as in the decimal system, and the additional six numbers, 10 through 15, are represented by the letters A through F. Sometimes a lowercase h is placed after a hexadecimal value to identify it and avoid confusion with decimal numbers. Table 12.2 compares hexadecimal digits with their corresponding decimal digits.

TABLE 12.2

Hexadecimal	Decimal	Hexadecimal	Decimal
0	0	A	10
1	1	B	11
2	2	C	12
3	3	D	13
4	4	E	14
5	5	F	15
6	6	10	16
7	7	11	17
8	8	FF	255
9	9	100	256

As you may be able to deduce from this list, a single-digit number in hex can be larger than a single-digit number in the decimal system. And the largest double-digit number in hex (FF) is larger than the maximum value of a two-digit number in decimal (99). This allows large numeric values to be expressed with fewer digits.

Also, because computer memory is based on multiples of eight, hex is a more convenient numbering system for programmers than one based on the decimal system. However, as is often the case in computing, what's easier for programmers can cause grief to the average user. To help you get oriented, Table 12.4 shows both hex and decimal values for memory addresses. If you need to convert between the two systems, you can use the scientific mode of the Calculator utility described in Chapter 5.

. . . .

Conventional Memory

It's the Methuselah of RAMs. **Conventional memory** is found in all PC-compatible computers. The original PC contained an 8088 CPU chip, which could address only 1 megabyte of RAM. In other words, it could keep track of a million different 1-byte locations within RAM. This 1-megabyte limit, imposed by the design of the original PC, represents the maximum amount of memory that can be addressed by DOS. In those days, with many systems selling a measly 64K (one-sixteenth of a megabyte) of RAM, a full megabyte seemed like megamemory. That's why it was originally thought that power users would be more than satisifed with 256K RAM (one-quarter of a megabyte).

Most PCs are shipped with the maximum amount of conventional memory, which is limited to 640K. Although DOS can address 1 megabyte at a time, only 640K worth of that megabyte is available for use by applications. Technically, the entire 1 megabyte is conventional memory. However, the remaining 340K is more commonly called upper memory, and is reserved for use by device drivers and other system software.

Why the resulting construction of conventional memory? Because of the design of the 8088 processor, IBM decided to divide the available megabyte of addressable RAM into 16 segments of 64K each. Six of the blocks were set aside for the functions of the ROM chips, which contain low-level instructions for the computer and the computer BIOS, and for the display adapter and ROM extensions, which were used for hard disk controllers and their additional BIOS. That left ten segments of 64K each, or 640K total RAM that could be used by the operating system and by various applications, and their corresponding data. Figure 12.4 depicts the designated segments constituting the megabyte of conventional memory.

Each 64K segment is divided into roughly 4000 subsections, which IBM calls paragraphs, and each paragraph is 16 bytes long. Programmers refer to a specific memory address by first naming the segment and then naming an offset that refers to the beginning paragraph within the segment they're identifying.

As soon as you turn on your computer, conventional memory starts to be devoured by both DOS and the DOS startup files, CONFIG.SYS and AUTOEXEC.BAT. The two startup files, in turn, load drivers, utilities, and applications that consume more of your 640K of conventional memory.

Windows needs at least 256K of free conventional RAM, but I recommend keeping at least 500K free, if you can, in order to provide more memory for the DOS sessions that you start from within Windows. Also,

FIGURE 12.4
Memory Addresses in Upper Memory and Conventional RAM

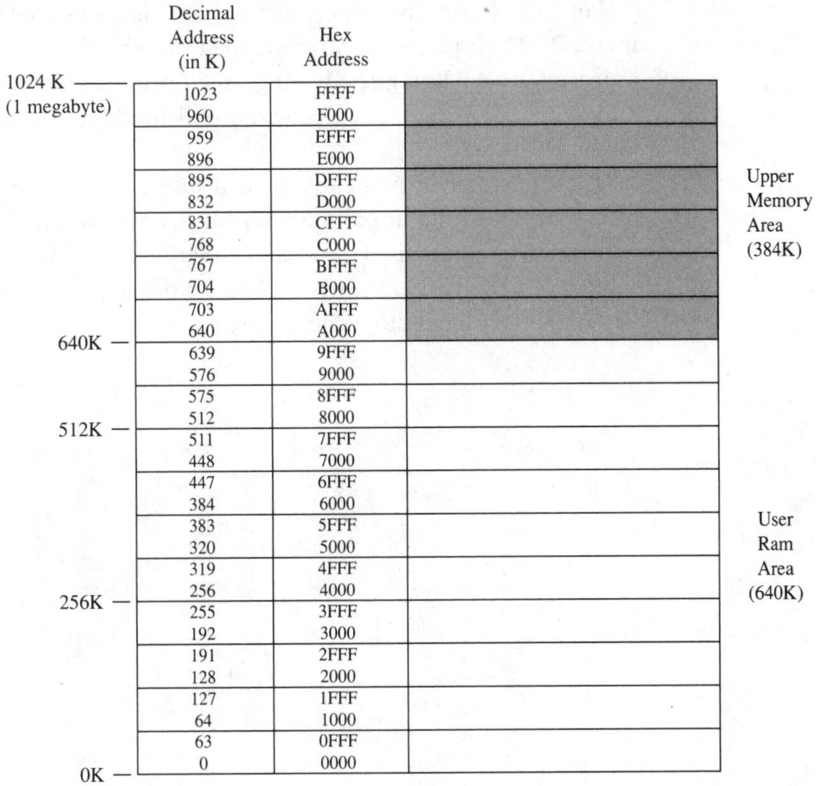

	Decimal Address (in K)	Hex Address		
1024 K — (1 megabyte)	1023	FFFF		
	960	F000		
	959	EFFF		
	896	E000		
	895	DFFF		Upper
	832	D000		Memory
	831	CFFF		Area
	768	C000		(384K)
	767	BFFF		
	704	B000		
	703	AFFF		
	640	A000		
640K —	639	9FFF		
	576	9000		
	575	8FFF		
	512	8000		
512K —	511	7FFF		
	448	7000		
	447	6FFF		
	384	6000		
	383	5FFF		User
	320	5000		Ram
	319	4FFF		Area
	256	4000		(640K)
256K —	255	3FFF		
	192	3000		
	191	2FFF		
	128	2000		
	127	1FFF		
	64	1000		
	63	0FFF		
0K —	0	0000		

The first megabyte of RAM is divided into 16 segments of 64K each. Ten of these segments, or 640K, constitute the user RAM area, or conventional RAM.

even though Windows can run with a comparatively small amount of free conventional RAM, performance can be impaired because less RAM limits the amount of information that can be swapped back and forth from the disk.

Upper Memory Area

The **upper memory area** of your computer refers to the memory addresses from 640K through 1023K. In hex, this range is from A000 through FFFF.

The upper memory area originally did not contain physical RAM. Instead, these addresses were used as reference points that specified ROM and RAM used by adapter cards plugged into the system's expansion bus as well as the ROM chips in the system motherboard that contain the computer's BIOS.

For this reason, the upper memory area is also called the **adapter segment.** ROM chips were later remapped to upper memory area addresses, a process called **ROM shadowing.** This provides DOS with a standard method of accessing the ROMs without its needing to know where they are physically located.

The upper memory area is divided into 24 blocks of 16K each. These blocks are called the **upper memory blocks,** or **UMBs.** Although the acronym UMB is often used interchangeably with UMA, UMBs are actually subunits of the UMA. Figure 12.5 shows the upper memory area and the upper memory blocks that compose it.

FIGURE 12.5

Upper Memory Area

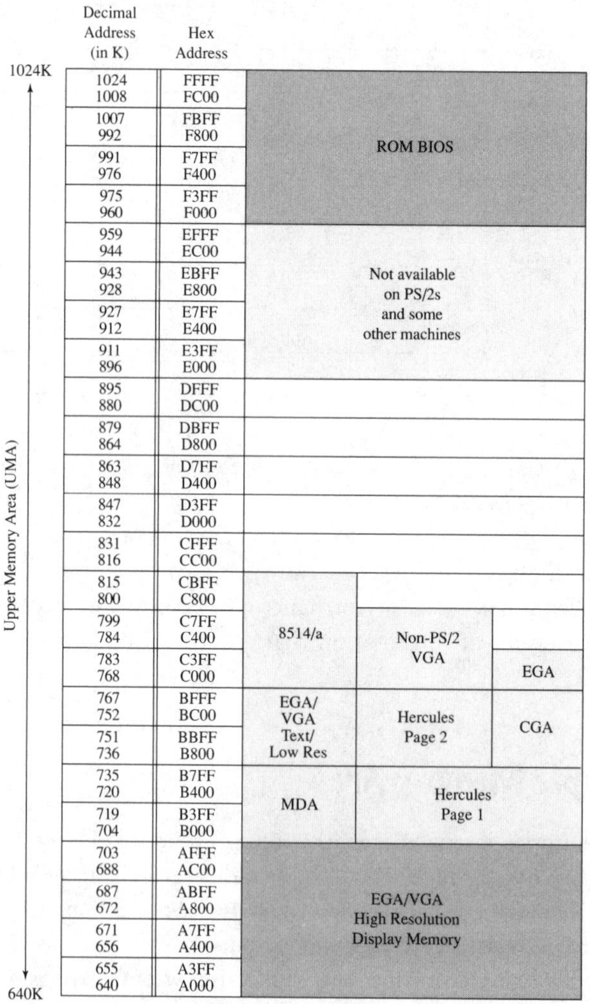

The upper memory area spans the memory addresses between the end of 640K of conventional memory and the 1 megabyte of memory that DOS can address.

Decimal Address (in K)	Hex Address				
1024 / 1008	FFFF / FC00	ROM BIOS			
1007 / 992	FBFF / F800				
991 / 976	F7FF / F400				
975 / 960	F3FF / F000				
959 / 944	EFFF / EC00	Not available on PS/2s and some other machines			
943 / 928	EBFF / E800				
927 / 912	E7FF / E400				
911 / 896	E3FF / E000				
895 / 880	DFFF / DC00				
879 / 864	DBFF / D800				
863 / 848	D7FF / D400				
847 / 832	D3FF / D000				
831 / 816	CFFF / CC00				
815 / 800	CBFF / C800	8514/a			
799 / 784	C7FF / C400		Non-PS/2 VGA		
783 / 768	C3FF / C000			EGA	
767 / 752	BFFF / BC00	EGA/ VGA Text/ Low Res	Hercules Page 2		CGA
751 / 736	BBFF / B800				
735 / 720	B7FF / B400	MDA	Hercules Page 1		
719 / 704	B3FF / B000				
703 / 688	AFFF / AC00	EGA/VGA High Resolution Display Memory			
687 / 672	ABFF / A800				
671 / 656	A7FF / A400				
655 / 640	A3FF / A000				

1024K

640K

Upper Memory Area (UMA)

Figure 12.5 shows some of the common uses for the upper memory area. To determine how your system uses its upper memory area, run the Microsoft Diagnostics Program, described in Chapter 17, or a similar utility that analyzes and maps the memory in your system. You should know how your upper memory area is being used, because both DOS and Windows can exploit the unused memory areas. In addition, system crashes and other failures commonly result when an adapter card and your system software both try to use the same area of upper memory.

To help familiarize you with this critical upper memory area, here's a brief rundown on how some of the common addresses are used.

➤ **A000-AFFF** This 64K section of upper memory is used by the RAM on VGA and EGA display adapter cards. These cards swap information from the RAM they contain into this memory area to make it accessible to your system.

➤ **B000-B7FF** Monochrome display adapter (MDA) cards and Hercules monochrome cards make use of this 32K memory area.

➤ **B800-BFFF** This 32K memory area is used by CGA, EGA, Hercules monochrome, and VGA text cards.

➤ **C000-C7FF** This 32K area is used by non-PS/2 VGA cards as the address space for their ROM chips. Some cards use only 24K of this area, while others consume the entire 32K. This address space is also used by EGA cards and 8514/a adapters.

➤ **C000-CBFF** This 48K area is used by 8514/a adapters.

➤ **CC00-DFFF** This 80K area is often unused, and the address range beginning at D000 is often used by expanded memory managers to begin a 64K page frame.

➤ **E000-EFFF** This 64K memory area is not available on most systems. IBM PS/2s use this address space for an extra ROM BIOS chip.

➤ **F000-FFFF** This 64K address space is used by PCs for the ROM BIOS chips that control the computer's basic I/O functions, such as disk access.

You can use the EMM386 memory manager, described later in this section, or a third-party memory manager to load device drivers and memory-resident software into unused addresses in the upper memory area in order to increase the amount of 640K user RAM available on your system.

When you start Windows, it inspects the upper memory area for additional free space that it can use for further optimizing its own performance. Sometimes Windows inadvertently grabs memory that appears to be free but is actually required by another device. For example, if a video card isn't using a particular area of memory, Windows assumes that area is free; when the video card later tries to use that memory, the screen may look garbled or your system may crash.

By setting parameters in your CONFIG.SYS, SYSTEM.INI, and other files, you can specifically include or exclude Windows or memory managers from using particular areas of upper memory, and thus maximize the use of this memory resource while avoiding potential memory conflicts.

As mentioned earlier, in the original IBM PC design of the early 1980s, the upper memory area did not consist of physical RAM. Most newer systems provide enough physical RAM so that the upper memory area can be composed of actual RAM chips. Such systems include an option to copy the contents of ROM chips into RAM in a process called **RAM shadowing**, which boosts performance because RAM operates more quickly than ROM. Despite this advantage, RAM shadowing sometimes creates compatibility problems. If you're experiencing memory conflicts, first try to see whether temporarily disabling RAM shadowing alleviates the problem.

Expanded Memory

PCs employ two methods of memory expansion: expanded memory and extended memory. Windows itself uses only extended memory, but many DOS applications use expanded memory, and Windows can provide expanded memory to your DOS applications that require it.

In the early days of PCs, a typical user would quickly consume the first 640K of RAM. If more memory was needed for constructing larger spreadsheets, one last frontier was available: upper memory, reserved by IBM but with some portions left unused. Some early programs employed schemes to grab these unused areas of upper memory; unfortunately, each program went about the grab in its own way, so that a system crash was likely to occur when two or more of these programs made a rush for the upper frontiers of memory.

To prevent the conflicts created by an upper-memory free-for-all, **memory managers** were developed. These programs act like software referees, allocating the use of upper memory areas to applications that need the extra RAM.

The first major development to break the 1-megabyte restriction of DOS—spearheaded in 1985 by Lotus Development Corp. in conjunction with Intel—was called expanded memory. Expanded memory employs a scheme called **bank switching**. In bank switching, the computer switches four 16K blocks of RAM—referred to as pages—back and forth from the conventional memory to an area of expanded memory (Figure 12.6). These

four 16K pages form one 64K page frame, and you'll need an expanded
memory manager to keep track of what is being switched.

FIGURE 12.6

*Bank
Switching*

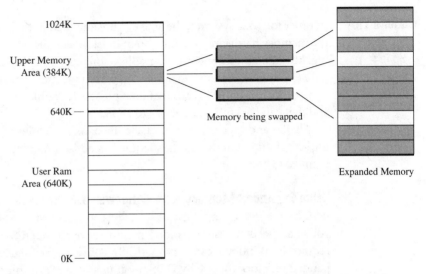

Bank switching swaps several small areas of memory in and out of
RAM as a way of making expanded memory accessible to the CPU.

Lotus and Intel, the developers of bank switching, sought assistance from
Microsoft to develop compatibility with DOS. The three companies together
developed the Lotus/Intel/Microsoft Expanded Memory Specification 3.2,
better known as the LIM EMS 3.2, or simply LIM 3.2. LIM 3.2 was limited to
bank switching a single 64K page frame (composed of four 16K pages) at a
time, and this process took its toll on system performance.

In a typical high-tech leapfrog, AST, then one of the leading suppliers of
add-in memory boards, developed its own enhancement to that standard,
the Enhanced Expanded Memory Specification (EEMS). Later, AST met with
the LIM group to consolidate their schemes into a new standard: the LIM
EMS 4.0, or simply EMS 4.0.

EMS 4.0 sped up the operation of expanded memory using a technique
called **backfilling,** which allows the expanded memory manager to handle
more than just four of the 16K pages of memory. Backfilling works by
rotating groups of 16K pages below the top of the conventional memory area
(usually 640K). By rotating a pool of these backfilled memory pages, a much
larger amount of memory can be swapped between the conventional memory and expanded memory areas.

EMS 4.0 provides for a maximum of 32 megabytes of expanded memory and also includes programming tools. Most DOS applications that use

expanded memory use EMS 4.0, although some older programs still use LIM 3.2. You can check your DOS application to identify which version of EMS it uses.

Insider's Tip

In order for your system to be able to implement all of the EMS 4.0 features, the memory hardware on your system must be capable of EMS bank switching. Most 286 motherboards do not have this capability built in, so you may have to physically remove memory chips from the motherboard and transfer them to an add-on EMS card that does possess the bank-switching capability and that can backfill the memory to DOS.

All 386 and higher machines have the bank switching or "memory paging" capability built in and thus require no add-on memory cards to implement EMS 4.0.

Using Expanded Memory with Windows. Because expanded memory is used by many DOS applications, such as spreadsheets and CAD software, you may need to use expanded memory even though Windows doesn't require it. Windows can automatically convert extended memory to expanded memory for use by DOS programs on a 386 or higher system; this is a function of Windows itself rather than a function of its memory management utilities, such as HIMEM.SYS or EMM386.EXE.

If you do need to run a DOS program when Windows is not running, Microsoft includes a special memory manager called EMM386.EXE, for 386 and higher systems. The EMM386.EXE expanded memory emulator is also supplied with DOS 5, which can use extended memory to emulate expanded memory. If you have a 386 or higher processor in your system, you should configure all of your RAM as extended memory, and use EMM386 to emulate any expanded memory that your DOS applications may require if you want to run them when Windows is not running. In addition, EMM386 lets you load device drivers, TSRs, and other memory-resident programs into the upper memory area.

Danger Zone

Windows cannot supply your applications with expanded memory if you used the NOEMS switch in the CONFIG.SYS file to load EMM386; this switch is sometimes specified when using EMM386 to load TSRs and other memory-resident software into the upper memory area. For more details, see the discussion of EMM386 later in this chapter, and the review of CONFIG.SYS in Chapter 13.

Using Expanded Memory on 286 Systems. To use expanded memory on a 286, you'll need to have an expanded memory board, such as the Intel AboveBoard or the AST RAMPage!, along with an expanded memory manager that works with the respective card. Because this setup involves searching for upper memory blocks to swap out to the expanded memory card, system conflicts can sometimes occur, with subsequent crashes. In that case, you'll need to exclude certain memory areas from use by the expanded memory manager.

A more common problem occurs when your expanded memory manager cannot find a solid block of 64K to use for a page frame. This can easily happen when the various adapter cards in your system each grab their own upper memory area, and in doing so fragment the upper memory. The solution is to relocate the address areas of the adapter cards to create a 64K contiguous page frame.

This is a simple procedure on a PS/2 and other systems that use the MCA bus, and on most computers with an EISA bus, because most systems with these two advanced buses include system utilities that let you easily relocate the memory addresses used by adapter cards. For example, on a PS/2 system, you would boot from the Reference Disk included with the computer, and simply use the Change Configuration option to specify a different address.

With the more common ISA bus machines, however, it's more difficult to relocate the upper memory addresses used by adapter cards; for example, you may have to open the computer's system unit and flip DIP switches or change jumpers. Furthermore, some adapter cards won't let you relocate the address they consume in upper memory, so you will have to play by trial and error.

On 286 systems with more than 1 megabyte installed, you must physically configure the hardware to divide the RAM above 1 megabyte for use as either extended or expanded memory. Usually you can flip a number of DIP switches on the memory card. On 286 machines from AST, for example, all memory is mounted on a FASTRAM card that plugs into the bus. DIP-switch settings allow you to divide the memory for use as conventional, expanded, or extended. Once the hardware configuration has been performed, the appropriate software drivers must also be loaded in the CONFIG.SYS file in order for the memory to be used.

Some 286 systems employ a special hardware device, called a **Memory Management Unit (MMU),** that directly converts all the RAM installed in the system for use as mapped pages by EMS 4.0. Two companies that manufacture MMUs are All Computer Company and SODA Technology.

If your system contains an MMU, you must configure the software memory manager to divide the RAM above 1 megabyte between the extended memory and EMS 4.0. You'll also need to make sure that you load HIMEM.SYS before you load the expanded memory manager into your CONFIG.SYS file. The map of the upper memory area in Figure 12.6 illustrates where you may be able to create a contiguous 64K block of memory for the page frame.

Using Expanded Memory Managers on 386 and Higher Systems. Expanded memory managers that run on 386 or higher systems, such as EMM386, QEMM, and 386MAX, can all be used to place TSRs, device drivers, and other memory-resident software into the upper memory area—but beware, this memory space can get crowded quickly. To view a map depicting actual usage of your system's memory, use the Microsoft Diagnostics program (MSD.EXE) described in Chapter 17. To control how EMM386 uses your system's upper memory, you can apply the special memory option switches when installing EMM386, as described in Chapter 13.

Space conflicts can also occur because Windows reserves a part of the upper memory area to create a special translation buffer, used to translate DOS and network API calls from protected mode into real mode, which is the only mode DOS understands. All too often, there isn't enough free memory for both expanded memory and this translation buffer.

The solution is to relocate the translation buffers to conventional memory, or to remove your expanded memory page frame. The Windows default allocates the space to the page frame first; if there's no room left over, it will try to relocate the buffers to upper memory, or to the 640K conventional memory area. If you are running a large DOS application, however, you may need more conventional memory and run into a space shortage.

To reverse the default order in which Windows allocates the page frame and translation buffers into upper memory, you can change the [386Enh] section of SYSTEM.INI so that the line

```
ReservePageFrame=false
```

is specified. This setting allocates the translation buffers first, and then allocates the page frame memory if space is available. If not, your expanded memory manager may not be able to find a page frame, and your DOS programs won't be able to access the expanded memory they need to run.

You can tweak the placement of translation buffers and expanded memory page frames for 386 enhanced mode by using these other commands in the [386Enh] section of SYSTEM.INI:

➡ EMMExclude=

➡ EMMInclude=

➡ EMMPageFrame=

➡ EMMSize=

➡ IgnoreInstalledEMM=

➡ NoEMMDriver=

➡ ReservedHighArea=

➡ UsableHighArea=

Because Windows attempts to use all the free areas available in upper memory, you probably won't have to use the three commands that instruct it to do just that: EMMInclude=, EMMPageFrame=, and UsableHighArea=. If space is totally unavailable, you can always use the line

```
NoEMMDriver=YES
```

in the [386Enh] section to tell Windows to disable expanded memory altogether and thus drop the search for a 64K page frame in upper memory.

If you're having trouble running Windows in 386 enhanced mode, a hardware adapter may be in conflict for space with the translation buffers. To solve this problem, exclude the memory range E000 through EFFF from being used by either expanded memory or translation table buffers; because no convention applies as to how this area should be used by add-in cards, conflicts can occur and prevent Windows from running in 386 enhanced mode. To exclude this area, add the following line to the [386Enh] section of SYSTEM.INI:

```
EMMExclude=E000-EFFF
```

This line often takes care of the upper memory conflicts that can prevent Windows from running in 386 enhanced mode.

Many of the statement lines in the [386Enh] section of SYSTEM.INI that start with EMM can be used to control placement of translation buffers as well as expanded memory. See Chapter 15 for complete details on how to work with the various statement lines in the SYSTEM.INI file.

If you're running DOS applications in Windows standard mode, you can use expanded memory only if you have an expanded memory card in your system. If you don't have an expanded memory card, you can run these DOS applications only in Windows 386 enhanced mode, which can emulate expanded memory using your extended memory.

Extended Memory

Expanded memory offered a kludgy approach to providing more than 1 megabyte of memory for use by applications. Bank switching segments in and out of the upper memory area consumed much software overhead, vitiated performance, and created conflicts in the upper memory area. But at the time, there was no alternative that could maintain compatibility with the 8088 and 8086.

The advent of the 286 and protected mode allowed your system to directly address many megabytes of memory, which in turn led to the use of extended memory. Extended memory is a linear extension beyond 1 megabyte of continuously addressable memory; no bank switching or other software tricks are needed to access it.

For many years, extended memory had little practical use because the technology that would allow it to work with DOS had not been invented. You could allocate extended memory for use as a disk cache or print spooler, but it could not be used to run DOS applications. Windows 3.0 changed all this with the introduction of Microsoft's newly developed **Extended Memory Specification (XMS)** and **DOS Protected Mode Interface (DPMI)**.

The first 64K of extended memory is called the **high memory area (HMA)**. The HMA is located at the memory address range from 1024K to 1088K. Microsoft has discovered a trick to make the HMA appear to the computer as if it is part of the system's conventional memory. This enables you to load DOS into the HMA, and thus free more of the 640K conventional memory. Other programs, especially network software drivers, can also make use of the HMA; however, only one program can use the HMA, even if it uses only a small portion of it. For details on loading DOS and another program into the HMA, refer to Chapter 13.

Although extended memory actually extends your memory starting at the 1 megabyte limit, for purposes of using Windows, you can envision extended memory as a simple extension to the 640K of conventional memory. In the Windows environment, extended memory plays as important a role as does conventional memory—in fact, you can't run Windows without having at least some extended memory. If you have an add-in memory card that can be configured either way, configure it as extended memory. If your DOS applications need expanded memory, Windows can use the extended memory to emulate expanded memory.

Microsoft's HIMEM.SYS memory manager controls the extended memory on your system using the XMS standard. The HIMEM.SYS utility is an extended memory manager that acts as a referee, controlling the use of your system's extended memory and making sure that Windows, and any applications you are running, don't try to grab the same area of extended memory at the same time—a sure way to crash your system.

Now for a detour back into kludge technology. In order to access extended memory under the DOS real mode operating system, it was necessary to develop utility programs called **DOS extenders,** which were either sold separately or embedded into a specific application. Unfortunately, the various DOS extenders sometimes used conflicting methods for accessing extended memory, which caused system incompatibilities and crashes. This conflict haunted earlier versions of Windows.

Subsequently, two software protocols have been developed to regulate how all applications use extended memory. The first to be introduced was the **Virtual Control Program Interface** (**VCPI**), developed by several companies, including Quarterdeck, Phar Lap, and Rational Systems.

The VCPI protocol allows programs that use DOS extenders on 386 systems to run with 386 expanded memory managers, such as QEMM and 386MAX. Windows 3.0 did not support the VCPI specification, which caused incompatibilities with third-party expanded memory managers that did support the specification.

Windows 3.1 now supports the VCPI protocol, but only when running in standard mode; the VCPI protocol is incompatible with the 386 enhanced mode of Windows 3.1 as well as with most other multitasking operating systems, such as OS/2 and UNIX. This means that DOS-extended programs that use VCPI, such as Paradox 3.5, AutoCAD version 11, and Oracle SQL, cannot run under Windows in 386 enhanced mode.

Insider's Tip

Some DOS programs can use both VCPI-compatible memory and regular memory. When you run a DOS program from Windows 386 enhanced mode, you may receive a warning dialog box whenever the program tries to access VCPI-compatible memory. If the DOS program does not actually require VCPI memory, you may want to turn off this warning message. Just add this line to the [386Enh] section of the SYSTEM.INI file:

```
VCPIWarning=OFF
```

DOS Protected Mode Interface (**DPMI**) was developed as a group effort by Microsoft, Rational Systems, Phar Lap, and several other companies. The DPMI specification provides DOS applications with a standard protocol for switching the processor into protected mode, thereby accessing extended memory. The DPMI standard works with 386 enhanced mode, and most applications that use DOS extenders are being upgraded to support the DPMI standard.

Insider's Tip

When in Windows standard mode you can run DOS applications that use DOS extenders compatible with either protocol, DPMI or VCPI. However, you need to allocate the specific amount of extended memory such applications require by creating a special .PIF file. Program code stored in the extended memory that you allocate in a .PIF file is swapped back and forth to the disk drive when you switch between Windows and the DOS application. Swapping large amounts of code in and out of memory can slow down performance, so be conservative when specifying extended memory in your .PIF file.

• •

Configuring Extended and Expanded Memory

To determine the type and configuration of your system memory, you may need to run a diagnostic program designed for your system. Diagnostic programs are often included with your computer or with your memory manager software, and Windows 3.1 includes the Microsoft Diagnostics program (MSD.EXE,) described in Chapter 17.

Quit Windows before running this program; then, to view your memory configuration, access the Utilities menu or ask MSD to print a report, which will provide detailed information about your system configuration (Figure 12.7).

• • • • • • • • • • • • •
FIGURE 12.7
*MSD
Memory Map*

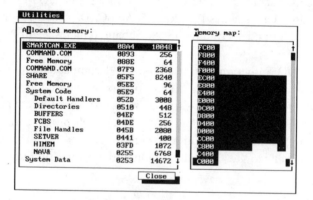

The Microsoft Diagnostics program lets you view your memory configuration on screen, or print a detailed report identifying the kinds of memory in your system and their usage.

If you're using MS DOS 5 or later, its built-in MEM command allows you to see how your computer's memory is being used. If you type **MEM** at the DOS prompt from within Windows, you'll only see the amount of memory available to the DOS virtual machine. To ascertain the total amount of memory available to your system, quit Windows and type **MEM** at the DOS prompt. You'll get a brief report about your system's memory, similar to this one:

```
 655360 bytes total conventional memory
 655360 bytes available to MS-DOS
 582640 largest executable program size
1048576 bytes total EMS memory
1048576 bytes free EMS memory
7733248 bytes total contiguous extended memory
```

```
     0 bytes available contiguous extended memory
1048576 bytes available XMS memory
     MS-DOS resident in High Memory Area
```

For a more detailed report, which tells you how much free memory is available in both the conventional and upper memory area, type

```
MEM /C
```

at the DOS prompt and you'll see a report similar to this one:

```
Conventional Memory :
Name            Size in Decimal          Size in Hex

MSDOS           15296    (14.9K)          3BC0
SETVER            400    ( 0.4K)          190
HIMEM            1072    ( 1.0K)          430
SMARTDRV         2464    ( 2.4K)          9A0
win386           3648    ( 3.6K)          E40
FASTOPEN         5600    ( 5.5K)          15E0
SHARE            8240    ( 8.0K)          2030
COMMAND          2672    ( 2.6K)          A70
SMARTDRV        28304    (27.6K)          6E90
WIN              1584    ( 1.5K)          630
COMMAND          2832    ( 2.8K)          B10
FREE           582832    (569.2K)         8E4B0

Total FREE :    582832    (569.2K)
Total bytes available to programs :      582832   (569.2K)
Largest executable program size :        582608   (569.0K)

1048576 bytes total EMS memory
1048576 bytes free EMS memory

7733248 bytes total contiguous extended memory
      0 bytes available contiguous extended memory
1048576 bytes available XMS memory
      MS-DOS resident in High Memory Area
```

You can use the MEM /P option to display an even more detailed report about memory usage, which will include the order in which items are loaded into memory. This kind of detailed information can help you understand how to optimize your system. For a detailed discussion of how to configure and optimize your system's memory, refer to Chapter 13, which discusses the DOS startup files and the use of third-party memory managers.

Insider's Tip

If you have an expanded memory card that cannot be configured as extended memory, you can still use it if you can configure it as a RAM disk. RAM disks, which are discussed later in this chapter, operate much more quickly than do hard disk drives, and are useful for storing TEMP files.

Hard Disk Storage and Windows

Any graphically oriented operating system, like Windows, consumes your computer's memory resources—both RAM and hard disk—much more quickly than does a character-based system like DOS. With a character-based system, for example, a screen of information has a capacity of 2000 characters, whereas on a Windows screen with a 256-color VGA display, you'll have a full 2,457,600 bits of data per screen.

Data storage also affects memory requirements, and in the Windows environment, data consumes the most storage space. In DOS, not only is the screen display mostly composed of characters, so is the data stored on your hard disk. In Windows, data files more commonly contain graphics in addition to characters. Add multimedia capabilities, and your data storage requirements skyrocket. Animation files can consume 10 to 30 screens of graphics for every second of animation displayed; and sound files can require a megabyte or more for a brief passage of digitized speech or music.

Windows applications can also far exceed the 640K RAM limitation of DOS applications, because they can take advantage of Windows memory-management capabilities. To ensure that only a small portion of an application stays in memory at one time, Windows applications are usually divided into three main segments:

➡ A **moveable code segment**, which is a part of the program that Windows can move around within the computer's memory without disrupting the program

➡ A **discardable code segment**, which Windows can remove from memory and reload from the disk, if necessary

➡ A **swappable code segment**, which Windows can freely swap out to the hard disk as needed

Using this segmentation scheme, Windows assesses your system resources and shuffles various program segments in memory to suit the availability of your system's RAM and hard disk resources. This system minimizes the amount of a Windows application that needs to be loaded into RAM, but also places a larger burden on your hard disk drive.

On top of the added requirements for data storage, applications, and screen displays, consider Windows itself, which includes an entire cadre of software components that must work together to create the environment. All these factors place demands on both your system's RAM and storage devices.

What I said earlier about RAM applies to hard disk storage as well: get as much as you can afford for now, and you'll probably want to save up to buy more later. To give you an idea of how quickly Windows consumes hard disk space, the full Windows installation itself can take more than 10 megabytes of hard disk space, and even a spartan installation requires 5 megabytes of space. Full-fledged Windows applications, such as Word for Windows, PageMaker, or CorelDraw, can consume 5 to 10 megabytes more space each. When you add data and swap files, it becomes apparent why the 20 or 30 megabyte hard disk that was adequate for DOS seems skimpy for Windows.

Insider's Tip

To increase the capacity of your hard disk, consider using compression technology. The Stacker program, for example, automatically compresses and decompresses files going to and from your hard disk and can often double the effective capacity of your disk. Stacker is available in a software-only version and as a combination software-hardware product, which includes a board that plugs into your system to accelerate the compression and decompression process. However, Windows still needs to use uncompressed disk space to store HIMEM.SYS, your DOS startup files, and your permanent swap file.

Buy the fastest hard disk possible, too. The speedier your disk, the faster Windows can manipulate virtual memory and swap files, and the faster the overall performance of your Windows system.

Many types of hard disk drives are found in the loosely affiliated group of computers known as PC compatibles. The determining factor for Windows compatibility is the controller card used to operate the drive, rather than the drive itself. These are the major controller card technologies found in PCs:

➡ **ST506** This was one of the most frequently used controller types for PCs during the early to mid-1980s.

➡ **WD1003** This controller, based on chips produced by Western Digital, replaced the ST506 and remains a major standard.

➡ **ESDI** The Enhanced Small Device Interface standard is a high-speed controller found in many Compaq DeskPro and other high-performance systems.

➸ **IDE** The Integrated Drive Electronics standard places most of the controller circuitry on the drive; this reduces the amount of hardware needed inside the PC. IDE drives often plug directly into the motherboard and are common in portable computers.

➸ **SCSI** The Small Computer System Interface controller provides its own expansion bus, which allows a maximum of seven different SCSI devices to be connected to a single controller card. These devices can include disk drives, tape drives, CD ROM players, and even nonstorage devices, such as scanners.

All of these controllers are compatible with Windows, but the important FastDisk feature of Windows 3.1, described in the next section, will not work with ESDI or SCSI drives without a third-party FastDisk driver.

Optimizing Hard Disk Performance

Because the speed of your hard disk has a significant impact on system performance, Windows provides these three acceleration facilities:

➸ **SMARTDrive** A disk cache utility program

➸ **FastDisk** A system of Windows components that work together to provide 32-bit disk access

➸ **RAMDrive** A memory-resident utility program that allows you to use part of your RAM to simulate a high-speed disk drive

Before discussing these three facilities, I'll describe several actions you should take to improve the performance of your hard disk. First, you should determine how the disk is interleaved. Hard disks usually use one of three interleave ratios:

➸ **3 to 1** The hard disk rotates three times between the reading and writing of each sector on the disk. This is the slowest type of interleave, and was necessary on older IBM XT and AT systems because they were slow to process information coming from the hard disk.

➸ **2 to 1** As computers became faster, the interleave ratio increased to 2 to 1; this meant that disks were read from or written to on every other rotation of the disk.

➸ **1 to 1** Fast 386 and higher systems should be able to use a 1 to 1 interleave ratio. This offers the best performance because it reads and writes to the disk in synch with its rotation, rather than having to skip rotation cycles to compensate for slow processor speed.

PC systems are usually configured by the manufacturer with the correct hard disk interleave for the speed of the processor. Some manufacturers inadvertently slow down disk interleaving: slower-than-necessary interleaving can also result from hard disks that were transferred from a slower to a faster system during an upgrade. If you're unsure whether your hard disk interleave is set properly, you'll need to use a utility program that is able to analyze and change interleave ratios. I recommend Spinrite from Gibson Research, a program that is widely used and known for its reliability.

The next step toward improved performance is to defragment your disk on a regular basis. Because of the way that DOS interacts with your disk drive, a single file is not always written in a contiguous space on your disk. As a result, files are fragmented. After prolonged use of your hard disk—that is, after rewriting and erasing many files—many small file fragments can become scattered on your disk.

Defragmenting your disk regroups all these fragments, allowing them to be read more quickly and creating a larger contiguous free space on your hard disk. Disk defragmenting utilities are easy to obtain; in fact, they are often included as part of utility packages, such as Speed Disk from Norton Utilities and Compress from PC Tools.

Danger Zone

Disk defragmenting utilities must not be run from within Windows. Quit Windows first and run the utility from the DOS prompt.

Another way to keep your hard disk tuned up is to run the DOS CHKDSK utility to search for lost file clusters. These file clusters are created when DOS loses track of a file, which can happen if your machine is shut down before a DOS operation is completed. If CHKDSK notifies you of any lost chains or clusters, you should run the utility by typing

```
CHKDSK /F
```

from the DOS prompt; this converts any lost chains or clusters into disk files that end with the .CHK file extension. Then delete all .CHK files to recover the space they are consuming on your disk. *Warning: Do not run* CHKDSK /F *from within Windows!* Exit Windows first and run this utility from the DOS prompt.

Finally, you can free space by deleting unnecessary files. Good candidates for deletion are temporary files that may have been accidentally left on your system; these files usually end with the .TMP extension. You can also delete backup files, often identified by the .BAK extension. If you're really short on disk space, a number of Windows files can be deleted as well. For a list of the Windows files that are safe to delete, see Chapter 16.

• •

SMARTDrive

Windows provides its own disk cache utility, called SMARTDrive (SMARTDRV.EXE), which can also be used with DOS applications. SMARTDrive and other disk cache programs work on the principle that it's faster for your system to access information from RAM than from your hard disk.

Here's a simplified explanation of how a disk cache works: when files (or disk tracks) are read from the disk, they are stored in the cache. If the currently active program subsequently reaccesses those files or tracks, they are retrieved from RAM rather than from the disk. This process considerably reduces the retrieval time.

Almost all disk caches cache the data that is being read from the disk; some also cache data being written to the disk. In the latter case, your application first writes the data into the cache. Then the cache transfers the data to the disk.

Windows 3.1 includes a new version of SMARTDrive (4.0), which caches both read and write operations, whereas the older version included in Windows 3.0 only cached when reading from the disk. The old version of SMARTDrive only cached drives that used the DOS interrupt 13 method of accessing the drive, which caused incompatibility problems with certain disk drives, such as Bernouli drives, hard cards, and some SCSI drives. Because the new SMARTDrive 4.0 works at the DOS device driver level, it resolves most of these problems.

SMARTDrive can work with many specialized device drivers, such as those used by the Stacker disk compression product. Note that the new SMARTDrive can only use extended memory.

Because SMARTDrive now caches information being written to the disk, a number of safeguards have been incorporated to ensure that SMARTDrive doesn't lose information stored in the cache. The following conditions trigger SMARTDrive to write the information in the cache to the drive:

➠ When your system is idle

➠ When your cache becomes full

➠ When information in the cache becomes more than 5 seconds old

➠ If your system is rebooted by pressing Ctrl+Alt+Del

➠ When a program issues a disk reset function

Despite these precautions, you can sometimes lose data. For example, SMARTDrive can't contend with a power failure, a pulled plug, or a computer that's been inadvertently turned off. Luckily, many Windows applications, such as Word for Windows, save a temporary version of the file you are working on, which allows the program to recover the data the next time you start it.

If you quit Windows and immediately flip your system's off switch, you might lose some data in the write cache. If you want to make sure that all of the cache has been written to disk before you turn off your system (a good idea if you have a large cache), type

```
SMARTDRV /C
```

at the DOS prompt. This forces all the data in the cache to be written to disk. When the disk light stops blinking (sometimes it takes a few seconds), the cache has been written, and it's safe to turn off the system.

It's important not to confuse the SMARTDrive disk cache—which is a software product—with a caching disk controller card—a hardware product. This type of controller card, typified by brands such as DPT and Conan, contains a significant amount of RAM to buffer data retrieved from the hard disk.

These controllers are usually designed for network servers or large database engines, and in those applications they may be worth the extra money. (Many disk controllers, although not considered caching controllers, contain a small RAM cache that buffers only the information being read by the head at that time.) But the high cost of controller cards that contain many megabytes of RAM cache outweigh the performance benefits. With these controllers, the RAM is available only to that card, and not to the system as a whole. Therefore you're usually better off adding more extended RAM to your system and allocating it to SMARTDrive.

Installing and Configuring SMARTDrive. You don't need SMARTDrive to operate Windows, but you'll greatly improve performance if you install it or some other cache software. The size of the disk cache affects SMARTDrive's efficiency. In general, the larger the cache, the less frequently SMARTDrive needs to read information from the disk; and the lower the frequency of this process, the faster your system will perform.

During installation, Setup copies SMARTDRV.EXE to your main Windows directory and adds the SMARTDRV.EXE statement line to your AUTOEXEC.BAT file (see Chapter 13 for details about how to install SMARTDrive with AUTOEXEC.BAT). Although the normal procedure is to start SMARTDrive from the AUTOEXEC.BAT file, if you only use Windows occasionally and therefore don't want SMARTDrive to be used most of the time, you can also start the SMARTDrive by typing **SMARTDRV** at the DOS prompt before starting Windows.

The SMARTDrive statement takes the form

```
<path>SMARTDRV.EXE <drive[+ or -] drive[+ or -] ...> <size
switches> <option switches>
```

The <path> is the directory path where the SMARTDrive file is located (usually your main Windows directory). The <drive[+ or -] drive[+ or -] ...> is a list of the drives that you want SMARTDrive to control. If you don't list any drives, floppy disk drives are cached when they are read but not when they are written; hard disk drives are cached for both reading and writing; and CD-ROM and network drives are not cached at all.

To control the specific caching options, place a plus or minus sign after the drive letter, or list the drive letter by itself. A plus sign (+) will cache the drive for both read and write operations; a minus sign (–) will not cache the drive at all; and a drive letter with no plus or minus sign will cache the drive for reading only.

The <size switches> can be any of the following switches:

```
</E:element size> </B:buffer size> <initial size> <windows size>
```

They should be used in the order listed. The <option switches> can be any of the following switches

```
</C> </L> </Q> </R> </S> </?>
```

Table 12.3 lists the functions of each of the various SMARTDrive switches.

· · · · · · · · · · · · · ·
TABLE 12.3

Switches	Description
/E:<element size>	The number of kilobytes that SMARTDrive moves in and out of the cache at a time—usually related to the sector size of the disk drive. The value of <element size> must be greater than 1, and it must be a power of 2 (2, 4, 8, 16, etc.). The default value is 8192 (an 8K element).
/B:<buffer size>	The number of kilobytes of the read-ahead buffer, which is the amount of additional information that SMARTDrive reads from the hard disk whenever it reads the disk. This gives SMARTDrive access to the next chunk of information before it actually needs it, to speed up the process a little, especially when long,

TABLE 12.3 (cont.)	Switches	Description
		sequential files are being read from disk. The \<buffer size> can be any multiple of the \<element size>. The default value is 16384 (a 16K buffer).
	\<initial size>	The selected size of the cache in kilobytes for SMARTDrive before Windows starts running. If you don't specify a value for \<initial size>, the default value will vary by the amount of extended memory that is installed in your system. (See Table 12.4.)
	\<windows size>	The minimum size in kilobytes you specify for shrinkage of the cache. Windows controls SMARTDrive to trim the cache if it needs more memory. After quitting Windows, SMARTDrive returns to the cache size specified in the \<initial size> value; however, if the \<initial size> is smaller than the \<windows size>, SMARTDrive will be set to the \<windows size> after you quit Windows. The default value will vary by the amount of extended memory that is installed in your system. (See Table 12.4.)
	/C	Forces SMARTDrive to write any information in the cache to the hard disk.
	/L	Loads the SMARTDrive buffers into conventional memory and prevents it from using the upper memory area, even if space is available.
	/Q	Stops SMARTDrive from displaying its startup information.
	/R	Flushes the existing cache and restarts SMARTDrive.
	/S	Tells SMARTDrive to display a status report on your screen, which includes information about the way your drives are being cached and the overall hit rate for the cache.
	/?	Tells SMARTDrive to display a summary of its options.

Table 12.4 lists the default values for \<initial size> and\< windows size>, which vary by the amount of extended memory installed in your system.

• • • • • • • • • • • • • •
TABLE 12.4

Extended Memory	\<initial size\>	\<windows size\>
Less than 1 MB	All extended memory	0
1 MB to 2 MB	1 MB	256K
2 MB to 4 MB	1 MB	512K
4 MB to 6 MB	2 MB	1 MB
6 MB or more	2 MB	2 MB

The bare-bones setup line in your AUTOEXEC.BAT file to load SMART-Drive would be

```
C:\WINDOWS\SMARTDRV
```

which would use the default values listed in Table 12.3 amd 12.4. If the SMARTDrive driver is located in a different directory, adjust the path portion of the installation statement.

If you wanted to override the default choices in order to trim SMART-Drive, you could use the line

```
C:\WINDOWS\SMARTDRV.EXE 512 256
```

The 512 near the end of the line specifies the \<initial size\> of SMARTDrive when you start Windows; the 256 designates the \<windows size\>.

If Windows needs more memory to store active programs and open files, or to perform some other housekeeping tasks, it removes memory from SMARTDrive and reduces the size of the cache to its \<windows size\>; in the example this is 256K, the minimum you should ever use for SMARTDrive. However, I recommend at least 1 megabyte (1024K) as your most effective minimum SMARTDrive cache, and 2 megabytes (2048K) as the minimum for graphics-intensive applications, such as desktop publishing.

If you are using DOS 5 or higher, and SMARTDrive detects that EMM386 is loaded, SMARTDrive will attempt to load itself into upper memory, provided that the upper memory blocks are enabled using either the DOS=UMB or DOS=UMB,HIGH statement line in CONFIG.SYS. You can also load SMARTDrive into upper memory with a third-party memory manager, such as QEMM, by using the third-party utility's loadhigh feature.

Danger Zone

SMARTDrive can cause problems when loaded with Windows 386 enhanced mode if it is loaded into upper memory and if it is using the double-buffering option described later in this section. In such cases, make sure to load SMARTDrive into low memory.

If you run into incompatibilities when using SMARTDrive, you can try one of these tricks: either load the SMARTDrive buffers into the conventional memory area, or disable the caching of a problematic drive. For example, to force SMARTDrive to load its buffers into the 640K of conventional memory, you might use the line

```
C:\WINDOWS\SMARTDRV.EXE /L
```

But remember, this will rob your system of some of its conventional memory.

In other circumstances, you may need to disable caching for certain drives altogether. For example, these drives and applications are incompatible with SMARTDrive: floppy disk drives on the older Compaq DeskPro 386/16; drives compressed with SuperStor; and applications that run from copy-protected floppy disks (or that require you to insert a "key disk" into a floppy disk drive in order to run). In all of these cases, you should disable caching for the particular drives.

For example, to disable caching of your A: and B: floppy drives, but not your C: hard disk drive, you would use the line

```
C:\WINDOWS\SMARTDRV.EXE A- B-
```

This line uses the <drive[+ or −] drive[+ or −] ...> option discussed earlier.

The SMARTDrive Double-Buffer Feature. Certain hard disk controllers use a technique called **bus mastering** that allows them to take control of your computer system's bus while they are transferring data from the hard disk to memory or vice versa. These hard disk controllers can cause problems when Windows is running in 386 enhanced mode, because the virtual memory addresses do not match the actual physical addresses of the memory. To resolve this problem, Microsoft has developed a standard method of working with bus mastering controller cards, called **Virtual DMA Services**.

Most of the new bus mastering hard disk controllers use the Virtual DMA standard, which ensures that the correct memory addresses are accessed; it also provides full compatibility with SMARTDrive. Unfortunately, older bus mastering controller cards do not support the Virtual DMA standard, and this could cause data to be lost or corrupted in your system.

To prevent this problem, the new SMARTDrive included in Windows 3.1 includes a special double-buffering option, which solves incompatibilities that can occur between SMARTDrive and some types of disk controllers as well as with certain utility programs. The double-buffer feature works by creating a second memory buffer that lets your system match virtual addresses to physical addresses. The only drawback is that double-buffering consumes about 2.5K of conventional memory and causes a slight decrease in system performance.

Most disk controllers, including all MFM, RLL, and IDE controllers, as well as many ESDI and SCSI controllers, do not need the double-buffering option. However, if your BIOS is more than three years old, you may need to use the double-buffering option. To play it safe, Setup installs SMARTDrive with the double-buffering option if it can't determine whether you need this feature.

The SMARTDrive double-buffering option is installed using the CONFIG.SYS file (unlike SMARTDrive itself, which is installed in the AUTOEXEC.BAT file or by starting it from the DOS prompt). This statement line takes the form

```
DEVICE=SMARTDRV.EXE /DOUBLE_BUFFER
```

To see whether your system needs the double-buffering feature, type

```
SMARTDRV /S
```

at the DOS prompt. A SMARTDrive status report is displayed similar to this:

```
Microsoft SMARTDrive Disk Cache version 4.0
Copyright 1991,1992 Microsoft Corp.

Room for 256 elements of 8,192 bytes each
There have been 15,362 cache hits
    and 1,376 cache misses

Cache size: 2,097,152 bytes
Cache size while running Windows: 2,097,152 bytes

         Disk Caching Status
drive   read cache   write cache   buffering
 A:       yes           no            no
 B:       yes           no            no
 C:       yes           yes           no
```

The last column in this table, buffering, indicates whether your drives require double-buffering. A hyphen (-) indicates that SMARTDrive is not sure. If every drive in the buffering column reads no, you can remove the double-buffering line from your CONFIG.SYS file.

· ·

Swap Files

RAM and your hard disk cooperate to provide additional resources to Windows through a **swap file.** A swap file is a special file on your hard disk that is used as a temporary storage area for RAM in order to conserve memory and to fool Windows into thinking your system contains more RAM than it really does. Windows uses three types of swap files:

➤ **Application swap file** Used only when running Windows in standard mode, an application swap file serves as a temporary holding space for a DOS application.

➤ **Temporary swap file** Used only when Windows runs in 386 enhanced mode, a temporary swap file increases RAM through the use of virtual memory and is resized by Windows as needed. This is the default type of swap file.

➤ **Permanent swap file** Also used by 386 enhanced mode for creating virtual memory, a permanent swap file is whatever fixed size you determine; it provides faster operation than a temporary swap file. A permanent swap file is required for using FastDisk.

Application Swap Files. In standard mode, Windows uses a special type of swap file for DOS applications, called an **application swap file.** Because standard mode does not offer multitasking of DOS applications, only one program can be active at a time.

Windows creates a separate application swap file for use by each DOS application whenever you start a DOS application in standard mode. When you switch away from an application, Windows moves it from the system's RAM to the application swap file, thus freeing the RAM for other uses. When you return to that DOS application, Windows brings that application swap file back into memory and swaps to disk the DOS application that you are leaving. This procedure leaves as much RAM as possible free for the application you're currently handling. Application swap files are temporary and thus are deleted from the disk when you quit the application.

These temporary application swap files are marked with the DOS "hidden" attribute and start with the characters ~WOA; you can see these files in File Manager only if you have changed your viewing options to display hidden files. Application swap files are created in the directory specified by the swapdisk= parameter in your system.ini file. If no directory is specified in the swapdisk= statement line, the file will be created in whatever directory you designate in the temp statement in your autoexec.bat file; if you use either the temp or the swapdisk= statement, the swap files will be placed in the root directory on the hard disk from which you launched Windows.

Your system speed is directly affected by where Windows places your application. Because application swap files can consume half a megabyte of space or more, the amount of space available on your hard disk may affect the number of DOS applications that you can open at one time. If you do have more than one hard disk, consider reassigning the swap file to the hard disk that is your fastest and also contains the most storage space. And be forewarned, storing application swap files on network drives can slow down your system considerably.

To change the swap file assignment, open SYSTEM.INI with either Notepad or SysEdit and find the section marked

```
[NonWindowsApp]
```

Now change (or create) the SWAPDISK= line so it's followed by the drive letter, a colon, and the path of the directory that you want Windows to use when writing application swap files for DOS applications to disk. For example, to use a directory on drive D called SWAPMEET for storing your application swap files, make this your SWAPDISK= statement:

```
SWAPDISK=D:\SWAPMEET
```

Danger Zone

When you use File Manager or some other technique to inspect the directory containing application swap files, don't delete these files during the Windows session. If you do, you can confuse Windows—which is using the files—and cause a system crash.

If you experience a system crash or power failure for any reason, you may be left with some extraneous application swap files. Be sure to delete them, because they'll needlessly consume disk space. This should be done before you run Windows. (See the section on AUOTEXEC.BAT in Chapter 13 for a technique that you can use to automatically search for and delete unnecessary swap files during system startup.)

Permanent Versus Temporary Swap Files. When running in 386 enhanced mode, Windows doesn't use application swap files for DOS applications. In this mode, Windows employs either a permanent or a temporary swap file to provide virtual memory that is accessible to the entire Windows environment, including the Windows system itself and any applications—Windows or DOS.

When you are using a swap file to create virtual memory, you'll notice that Program Manager or File Manager's About box reports the availability of considerably more memory than what you actually have installed as RAM (Figure 12.8).

The clear benefit of augmenting RAM with virtual memory is that you'll be able to run more programs. On the negative side, virtual memory consumes space on your hard disk, and accessing the hard disk is slower than

• • • • • • • • • • • • • •
FIGURE 12.8

*Program
Manager's
About Box*

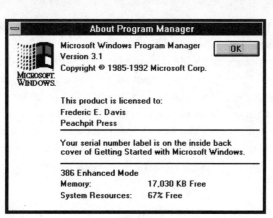

*If virtual memory is
being used, Program
Manager's About box
reports the availability
of more memory than
the amount of RAM you
have installed in your
system.*

accessing physical RAM. But the tradeoff is almost always worth it, because the ability to run a program a bit more slowly with virtual memory is better than not being able to run it all.

Danger Zone

Windows can create permanent swap files—and thus make use of virtual memory—only on hard disks that use 512-byte sectors. If you don't have 512-byte sectors, it's probably because you are using a third-party disk partitioning utility. Rather than forgo the use of permanent swap files and FastDisk, you should consider backing up all your files and reformatting your drive with the standard DOS disk formatting and partitioning utilities to create 512-byte sectors.

A permanent swap file is really two files. The larger of these files is the actual swap file and is named 386PART.PAR—it's marked with the DOS hidden and system attributes and is always located in the root directory of the hard disk. The other part of the permanent swap file is a read-only file named SPART.PAR, located in your main Windows directory. This file contains the details about the size and location of the 386PART.PAR file.

A permanent swap file remains on the hard disk and thus consumes space until you remove it, and it remains the same size until you change it. Permanent swap files speed up your system more than temporary swap files do because they require less software overhead and they contain information in contiguous disk blocks, making it easy for Windows to quickly locate and retrieve data.

In contrast, a temporary swap file is created automatically by Windows each time you start your session in 386 enhanced mode—provided your hard disk contains at least 2 megabytes of free space. Windows first looks for a permanent swap file, and if there isn't one, creates the temporary swap file in your Windows directory. The temporary swap file remains there during your Windows session.

The temporary swap file is a standard DOS file named WIN386.SWP; it's not marked with either the hidden or system attributes; and it changes in size during the session according to Windows's needs. When you quit Windows the temporary swap file is deleted, so it doesn't occupy disk space when you're not using Windows. This is an advantage over the permanent swap file, but temporary swap files are slower because they don't maintain a fixed position on your hard disk, with contiguous disk blocks (Figure 12.9).

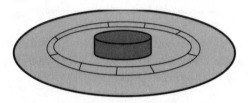

A permanent swap file is contiguous

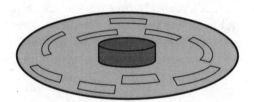

A temporary swap file often has sectors spread all over the disk

Permanent swap files are composed of a fixed section of contiguous disk space, whereas temporary swap files do not contain contiguous disk blocks and are deleted when you quit your Windows session.

To determine which type of swap file Windows is using, start the Control Panel and open the 386 enhanced icon. Then click on the Virtual Memory button to display the Virtual Memory dialog box shown in Figure 12.10.

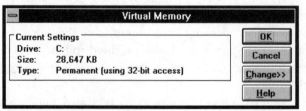

The Virtual Memory dialog box displays the current settings for your swap file.

The Current Setting section of the Virtual Memory dialog box contains three pieces of information:

➤ **Drive** The hard disk drive being used for the swap file.

➤ **Size** The size of your swap file in kilobytes. (Divide by 1024 to determine the number of megabytes.)

➤ **Type** What kind of swap file you are using: Permanent, Temporary, or None. If you are using the FastDisk feature described later in this chapter, the Type entry will read "Permanent (using 32-bit access)."

To change a setting, click on the Change button; the Virtual Memory dialog box expands to reveal the controls for changing the drive, size, and type of your swap file. You may also see a Use 32-Bit Disk Access check box that lets you regulate the FastDisk option (Figure 12.11).

FIGURE 12.11

Expanded Virtual Memory Dialog Box

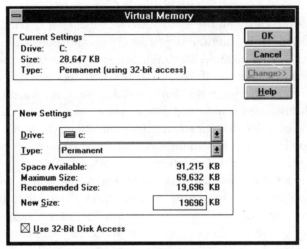

The expanded Virtual Memory dialog box displays the controls for changing the settings for your swap file.

You can further adjust your settings for swap files using a new section that pops up when you enlarge the Virtual Memory dialog box. The New Settings section contains the following items:

➤ **Drive** A drop-down list box that lets you select a drive for storing your swap file (use your fastest drive).

➤ **Type** A drop-down list that lets you select one of these options: Temporary, Permanent, or None.

➤ **Space Available** The amount of free space on the selected drive, in kilobytes.

➤ **Maximum Size** The largest block of contiguous free space on the selected drive.

➹ **Recommended Size** The size that Windows recommends for your swap file.

➹ **New Size** A text box for entering a number that represents how much hard disk space, in kilobytes, you want to devote to your permanent swap file. By default, the New Size box contains the amount of space suggested in the Recommended Size box. To change the size, just select the box and type in your new choice.

Insider's Tip

The Use 32-bit Access check box below the New Settings section indicates whether FastDisk is available on your system. If the box is dimmed, FastDisk is unavailable. Otherwise, you can activate or deactivate FastDisk by checking this box. Remember, FastDisk will run only if you have a permanent swap file.

Before enlarging the Virtual Memory dialog box, Windows scans your hard disk to identify the largest block of contiguous clusters on the disk, which is reported in the Maximum Size entry as the largest possible size for a permanent swap file. If there's a huge discrepancy between the Space Available entry and what you have available for a permanent swap file, you probably have a fragmented disk. Compact your disk by quitting Windows and using a disk defragmentation program. When you restart Windows, your swap file controls should indicate that the maximum permanent size for a swap file has increased significantly.

If more than one hard disk is attached to your system, you can select the Drive drop-down list to have Windows check all your disks before creating a permanent swap file. The Recommended Size entry indicates the number of kilobytes that Windows recommends using for your permanent swap file. I recommend accepting the suggested size (it's easy to change size at any time), but if you want to change it now, type a new number into the New Size box to indicate your preferred size.

Once you've set up your permanent swap file, quit Windows, restart it, and check whether the permanent swap file is active by selecting the About command from the Help menu of either Program Manager or File Manager.

If your permanent swap file was correctly installed, the Free Memory line in the About dialog box will display the total amount of solid-state RAM (conventional 640K plus any extended memory), plus the size of your swap file, minus the combined amount of memory consumed by Windows, your other Windows applications, the underlying DOS, and any device drivers.

Conversely, subtract the amount of memory allocated in your permanent swap file to estimate the amount of free physical RAM that your system can use. For example, if you have 10 megabytes of hard disk space devoted to your permanent swap file, subtract that amount (or 10240 kilobytes) from the amount displayed in the Free Memory line of the About dialog box to get an idea of how much real RAM is left in your system.

Windows makes it easy to switch between using a permanent and a temporary swap file. When you have ample room on your hard disk, go ahead and create a permanent swap file. If your disk becomes too full, you can delete the file and have Windows return to using your temporary file. Of course, your speed decreases when you use a temporary file, so when you've recovered more space on your hard disk, simply reestablish the permanent file.

Danger Zone

Where not to put it: Don't set up a permanent swap file on a network drive or on a RAM disk. If you set it up on a network drive, your system's performance will bog down considerably. If you specify a RAM disk, Windows will replace physical RAM—which is faster and more versatile—with virtual memory, which is definitely slower.

Changing the Default Options for a Swap File. If you do not specify a particular subdirectory, a temporary swap file will be placed in your Windows directory. To change the directory used by Windows to store its temporary swap file, open SYSTEM.INI and scroll through the file until you find the [386Enh] section header. Windows uses this section of SYSTEM.INI for specifying 386 enhanced mode parameters (see Chapter 15).

Continue scrolling down through the [386Enh] section until you find a line that begins with PagingDrive=. (If you don't have a PagingDrive= parameter line, you can add one anywhere below the [386Enh] heading, as long as it precedes the next bracketed heading in the SYSTEM.INI file.) After PagingDrive=, enter the drive letter (followed by a colon) and the directory path where Windows should store the temporary swap file. For example, to save the temporary swap file in the SWAPMEET directory on drive D, edit the line to read

```
PagingDrive=D:\SWAPMEET
```

By default, when Windows starts a 386 enhanced mode session and doesn't find a permanent swap file, it creates a temporary swap file of one megabyte (1024k). If more space is needed, Windows enlarges the swap file—but never beyond the point where less than one-half megabyte of free space remains on the hard disk storing the temporary swap file.

You can adjust the temporary swap file disk space in either of two ways. You can specify a maximum size for the file by using the MaxPagingFileSize parameter in SYSTEM.INI. Or you can use the MinUserDiskSpace= parameter to indicate how much disk space you want left free when Windows creates the temporary swap file.

To alter either of these parameters in the SYSTEM.INI file, follow the technique described in the previous section for changing the PagingDrive= parameter. Look in the SYSTEM.INI file for the [386Enh] subhead. Then find the MaxpagingFileSize= or the MinUserDiskSpace= parameter, depending on which method you've chosen to limit the size of the temporary swap file. After the equals sign of either parameter, enter a number that represents, in kilobytes, the limitation you are setting. For example, to specify a maximum size of 1 megabyte for the file, type

```
MaxPagingFileSize=1024
```

Or, to ensure that Windows always leaves at least 2 megabytes of free space on your hard disk when creating the temporary swap file, type

```
MinUserDiskSpace=2048
```

When you run Windows in 386 enhanced mode, the Windows virtual memory manager uses an advanced technique called **demand paging** to swap 4K pages of memory back and forth to the disk. To implement this scheme, Windows divides all your physical RAM into 4K pages, starting at the beginning of your 640K conventional memory and continuing through your total amount of conventional and extended memory.

The virtual memory manager allocates virtual pages of memory to each application you are running; at any given time, a virtual page can be located either in your physical RAM or on a page that is swapped out to the hard disk. The default settings used by the Windows virtual memory manager are suitable in most cases.

To inspect or change these settings, refer to the following statements that appear in the [386Enh] section of your SYSTEM.INI file:

➤ LocalLoadHigh=

➤ MaxBPs=

➤ MaxPhysPage=

➤ MinUnlockMem=

➤ Paging=

➤ PageOverCommit=

➤ SysVMEMSLimit=

➤ SysVEMSLocked=

➤ SysVMV86Locked=

➤ SysVMXMSLimit=

When determining which pages to swap between RAM and your disk drive, the Windows virtual memory manager uses a Least Recently Used (LRU) replacement method: those pages that have not been accessed for the longest period of time are the first selected for swapping from RAM to the hard disk.

Each page is tagged as being either **Accessed**—a program has referenced it since it was loaded—or **Dirty**—the page has been written to since it was loaded. Accessed pages are swapped first; then Dirty pages. The default settings for the swapping of pages can be changed by editing the entries in the [386Enh] section of SYSTEM.INI.

The following statement lines control the behavior of the LRU replacement method:

➣ LRULowRateMult=

➣ LRURateChngTime=

➣ LRUSweepFreq=

➣ LRUSweepLen=

➣ LRUSweepLowWater=

➣ LRUSweepReset=

· ·

FastDisk

An important new feature of Windows 3.1, FastDisk can speed up system performance by allowing Windows to access the hard disk using 32-bit software rather than the standard 16-bit access provided by DOS. In essence, FastDisk lets Windows bypass the DOS BIOS in order to directly access your hard disk.

FastDisk, which only works when you are running Windows in 386 enhanced mode, also speeds up the system when you are running DOS applications in the background, and allows you to run more DOS applications simultaneously. In addition, the FastDisk feature lets third-party software developers create new disk utilities that allow multitasking of disk maintenance and backup programs.

Not a single software utility, FastDisk is actually a group of four system components that work together to provide 32-bit disk access. These are the four components, which are virtual devices that operate in 386 enhanced mode:

➣ **WDCtrl** The FastDisk virtual device that can take charge of standard Western Digital 1003, IDE, and ST506 hard disk drive controller cards. These AT-style disk controllers account for an estimated 90 percent of existing controller cards. The WDCtrl device is installed only if Setup detects a compatible hard drive controller; if you change your controller card, you may have to reinstall this component.

➤ **Int13** The Int13 virtual device that traps and emulates the standard Int 13h BIOS calls and hands them off to the BlockDev device. The Int13 virtual device is installed only if a FastDisk device, such as WDCtrl, is also installed.

➤ **BlockDev** The virtual device driver that controls the operation of block input/output devices. Setup always installs the BlockDev device in your system because it is used by more than just FastDisk.

➤ **PageFile** The virtual device that handles the Windows virtual memory paging file. PageFile works with BlockDev to support FastDisk device drivers such as WDCtrl. Like BlockDev, Setup always installs the PageFile device.

FastDisk works by intercepting calls to DOS, and bypasses DOS to transmit information directly to the hard disk controller. To carry out the interception, FastDisk watches for calls (such as an Int13h call) that the application would normally make to DOS. FastDisk picks up and processes those calls made to a compatible drive using the speedy 32-bit access; if the calls are for a different drive, such as a floppy disk drive, FastDisk hands them over to DOS.

FastDisk directly manipulates the hard disk drive's controller card, not the drive itself. This feature makes it compatible with a wide range of controllers, because they tend to share common standards—at least, more so than is the case with drives. Microsoft designed FastDisk to operate with the Western Digital 1003-compatible controllers, which includes 90 percent of those in use today.

WD 1003-compatible controllers are found in almost all MFM, RLL, and IDE controller cards; but they are not used with most ESDI and SCSI controllers. For this reason, Microsoft has designed FastDisk with an open architecture, so it can be reproduced by other vendors. Many manufacturers of ESDI and SCSI controllers are already creating their own FastDisk drivers, so you should contact the vendor of your drive or controller about the availability of such a driver. In fact, because FastDisk provides such a performance boost to Windows, you should only purchase hard disks that include controllers with FastDisk support.

The most important benefit of FastDisk is speed: you'll probably notice a marked improvement in how quickly your disk drive carries out instructions. The level of improvement depends, of course, on your BIOS or device driver. As I mentioned earlier in the chapter, BIOS implementations vary in quality, depending on the manufacturer. If your BIOS operates poorly, you'll notice a dramatic improvement when using FastDisk. Other BIOS versions have excellent disk BIOS, so the gain in this area is not as great.

More importantly, because FastDisk handles disk access in the processor's protected mode, rather than in its real mode, it eliminates the need for Windows to switch back into real mode (or virtual 8086 mode) to access DOS and the disk BIOS or drivers. Without FastDisk, your system switches back and forth between real mode and protected mode several times each time the disk is accessed—a real performance drainer. FastDisk cuts down on mode switching by trapping calls made to DOS and handling them in protected mode.

FastDisk also allows you to run more simultaneous DOS applications in 386 enhanced mode. It does this by allowing DOS applications to use virtual memory in much the same way as Windows programs do. Each DOS application is run in its own virtual machine. The characteristics of that virtual machine are determined by its PIF settings. The virtual machine appears to the DOS application as a standalone PC. When you start a DOS program, it requires an entire virtual machine's worth of your physical RAM, leaving much less RAM for Windows. Although plenty of virtual memory remains, Windows has to engage in much more disk swapping to use it. Therefore, there may not be enough physical RAM left to start another DOS application.

FastDisk alleviates this problem by allowing a virtual machine that is still running to be paged out to disk. In this way, a DOS application running in a virtual machine can now use virtual memory in much the same fashion as a Windows application. The next time Windows needs more RAM—typically, when you are starting another DOS application—the system can swap only part of the DOS virtual machine into virtual memory. This FastDisk procedure helps make your Windows system more responsive when running DOS applications because it frees RAM for the work at hand, rather than for storing DOS applications.

FastDisk also accelerates switching from one DOS application to another when you are using Windows to multitask your DOS programs. Instead of having to swap the entire virtual machine out to disk and then have it read by Windows into RAM, with FastDisk, only the amount of memory that the application is actually using needs to be swapped.

FastDisk also provides third-party developers with the opportunity to create new programs that make special use of 32-bit disk access, such as applications capable of handling asynchronous I/O, or utilities that perform disk maintenance in the background. For example, a tape-backup utility could use FastDisk to back up your system in the background. Or a FastDisk utility could be developed for a tape drive to back up your system from inside Windows. Eventually some of the hot disk utilities for Windows may require that your system include a FastDisk-compatible controller card.

Danger Zone

Because FastDisk does pose a few hidden perils, it's not automatically installed in your system when you use Express Setup. In rare cases, when Windows mistakenly thinks that a controller is WD 1003 compatible but it isn't, the WDCtrl device driver can crash the system. To prevent a possible hard disk catastrophe, Microsoft has the WDCtrol device driver perform a series of elaborate tests to make sure that it properly communicates with the hard disk controller card. If FastDisk encounters a problem during any of these tests, it will simply not activate itself—this is the only way you'll know you have a problem, because you won't be otherwise notified. If FastDisk is already loaded and then discovers a problem, an error message is displayed advising you to reboot your system.

Despite these safety checks, a few controllers can still cause problems. These include controllers with only partial WD-1003 compatibility, and fully compatible controllers on some portable computers. On the battery-powered portable systems, the power-management software sometimes turns off the hard disk to conserve power, but does not inform the rest of the system. If a hard disk is being turned on and off while it's being used by the WDCtrl virtual device, Windows loses track of the actual state of the drive, and data can be lost or destroyed on your drive.

For all these reasons, you'll need to activate FastDisk yourself when installing Windows by using the 386 Enhanced icon in the Control Panel. You can view the status of your swap file, change it from a temporary to a permanent one, or change the drive location or size of the swap file by using the 386 enhanced controls in the Control Panel. After starting the Control Panel, open the 386 Enhanced icon, click on the Virtual Memory button, and then click on the Change button to enlarge the Virtual Memory dialog box so that it reveals its full controls, as shown in Figure 12.11.

To turn on FastDisk, first create a permanent swap file and then place a check in the box labeled Use 32-Bit Disk Access. If your controller card works with FastDisk, it will be activated automatically when you start your permanent swap file, which requires that you quit and then restart Windows.

You'll know FastDisk is in operation because the Type section of the Virtual Memory dialog box presents the message "using 32-bit access." If you don't see this message, your controller card is not supported by the standard Windows FastDisk driver.

If you are using third-party disk partitioning software, such as SpeedStor or Disk Manager, you may want to consider repartitioning your hard disk drive using the DOS FDISK utility, because Windows may not install Fast-Disk if it detects third-party disk partitioning software.

Insider's Tip

When you turn on FastDisk, the following two lines are added to the [386enh] section of your SYSTEM.INI file:

```
DEVICE=*INT13
DEVICE=*WDCtrl
```

To turn off FastDisk, you can either use the Control Panel or you can delete these two lines (or have them ignored as comments by placing a semicolon in front of them). You don't need to delete any files because Int13 and WDCtrl virtual devices are built into the WIN386.EXE file.

RAMDrive

In addition to SMARTDrive and swap files, Windows uses one other hybridization of RAM as a storage device: RAMDrive. A special device driver, RAMDRIVE.SYS, sets aside an area of RAM that Windows perceives as a storage volume. File Manager displays whatever amount of memory you've installed for RAMDrive as if it were a physical volume (Figure 12.12).

FIGURE 12.12
RAMDrive Icon

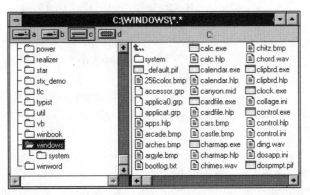

File Manager displays the RAM-Drive icon as drive D: along with the other volume icons at the top of the directory tree window.

RAMDrive represents the typical RAM disk utility. RAM disks are much faster than hard disks—information in your system reads and writes to RAM much faster than to a disk drive. However, because the RAM disk is composed of volatile memory rather than a physical storage device, any information in a RAM disk is lost when your computer shuts down.

The RAMDrive command line has the following form:

```
DEVICE=<path>RAMDRIVE.SYS <disk size> <sector size> <number of
entries> </E or /A>
```

Table 12.5 describes what each of the variables represents.

Options	Description
\<disk size\>	The number of kilobytes of RAM you want to use for the RAM disk. The value of \<disk size\> can be any number between 4 and 32767 (32 megabytes— an excessive amount by any standard). The default value is 64.
\<sector size\>	The number of bytes that you want the RAM disk to allocate to each of its simulated disk sectors. The value of \<sector size\> can be 128, 256, or 512. If you specify a \<sector size\>, you must first specify a \<disk size\>. The default is 512, which works best in most cases.
\<number of entries\>	Represents the maximum number of files and directories allowed in the RAM disk's root directory. The value of \<number of entries\> can be any number from 2 to 1024. The default value is 64; however, if you don't have enough memory to create the RAM disk that you've specified, a limit of 16 will be placed on the \<number of entries\> value. If you specify a \<number of entries\>, you must first specify a \<sector size\> and \<disk size\>.
/A	Uses expanded memory for the RAM disk.
/E	Uses extended memory for the RAM disk.

The /A and the /E switches are optional, but if you don't specify one of them, the RAM disk will be created using your system's precious 640K of conventional memory—a bad idea in most cases. I recommend creating the RAM disk in extended memory if you can, because the RAMDRIVE.SYS provided with Windows works cooperatively with HIMEM.SYS.

When you first install Windows, the Windows Setup program automatically places a copy of the RAMDRIVE.SYS file into your Windows directory, but it doesn't set up RAMDrive—you must do this manually. To install

RAMDrive in your system, open CONFIG.SYS and add the DEVICE= statement for RAMDRIVE.SYS, so that it will be installed at startup. To create a RAMDrive of half a megabyte, for example, enter this statement in CONFIG.SYS:

```
DEVICE=C:\WINDOWS\RAMDRIVE.SYS 512 /E
```

This assumes, of course, that the RAMDrive device driver is still located in the Windows subdirectory. The number at the end of the line indicates that you want the RAM disk to be created with 512K of RAM, and the /E switch specifies that you want the RAM disk to be created in extended memory. If you don't specify a <disk size> parameter, the RAM disk will be set for a default of 64K.

You can also specify additional parameters and switches in the RAMDRIVE.SYS statement. The digit following the number of kilobytes specifies the sector size for your RAM disk. Choose 128, 256, 512, or 1024; these refer to the number of bytes RAMDrive will transfer to and from the RAMDrive virtual disk at a time. If you're storing a number of small files in your RAMDrive, use a smaller sector size for best performance; for larger files, use a large sector size.

Next you need to specify the maximum number of files and directories that can be stored in the RAM disk's root directory, using the <number of entries> parameter. The value of <number of entries> can range from 2 to 1024. If you omit this parameter, the default value is 64.

Once you've set the three size parameters, you can choose from one of two switches: /E indicates that you want RAMDrive to be created in the extended memory, and /A specifies expanded memory. If you omit this switch, Windows assumes that you want to load the RAM disk into conventional memory.

Here's an example of a DEVICE= statement that uses all three parameters and one of the switches:

```
DEVICE=C:\WINDOWS\RAMDRIVE.SYS 256 128 48 /A
```

This statement installs a RAMDrive of 256K with 128 byte sectors; allows only 48 files or subdirectories to be stored in the root directory of the drive; and loads the RAMDrive into expanded memory. Remember, you must position the RAMDrive DEVICE= statement after the line in CONFIG.SYS that loads HIMEM.SYS (or another extended or expanded memory manager, if you are using one).

DOS creates as many RAMDrives as you have RAMDRIVE.SYS driver lines in CONFIG.SYS. It assigns sequential unused drive letters to the additional RAMdrives that you create. These RAMDrives work in either Windows or DOS sessions. When CONFIG.SYS processes one or more DEVICE= statements to set up RAMDrives after you start your computer, a message appears to inform you that the system has created the RAM disks, and also tells you the assigned drive letters.

Insider's Tip

Although RAMDrives are easy to install, I don't recommend using them unless you're loaded with RAM—at least 8 megabytes. In most cases, allocating RAM to SMARTDrive helps Windows more than the addition of RAMDrive.

However, if you do have ample RAM (enough so that SMARTDrive already contains the recommended maximum of 2 megabytes), you can set up a small RAM disk of 256K or 512K to keep temporary files for applications you're currently running. Exercise caution with graphics programs, such as Designer, CorelDraw, or PageMaker, because these applications can create TEMP files greater than 3 megabytes, which require a RAM drive of at least 4 megabytes to store the application's TEMP files. If you have an expanded memory card that cannot be configured as extended memory and you are not running DOS applications in standard mode, by all means devote it for use by RAMDrive.

The 64K Heap Resources

I'm saving the bad news for last. Just when you thought Windows—with virtual memory, FaskDisk, swap files, and SMARTDrive—could provide deliverance from the 640K limitations imposed by DOS, here comes the final holdover and barricade to greater memory usage: the **GDI** and **USER heaps.** These heaps represent two 64K chunks of RAM that can constrain the number of Windows applications that you can run at one time—particularly if you try to use applications containing lots of graphics or interface components. And if you try to run more applications than either of these two heaps can hold, your system can freeze or crash.

The GDI heap is used by the Windows Graphics Device Interface module (GDI.EXE) to store handles and pointers to graphics objects, such as brushes, pens, bit maps, buttons, and other graphic regions that compromise the Windows graphical interface. GDI.EXE also manages certain printing functions. Programs that use complex toolbars or ones that perform many graphics manipulations can consume this 64K space very quickly.

The USER heap is used by the User Interface module (USER.EXE) to store components of the user interface, such as the windows themselves. Thus each time you open a window, you consume more of the USER heap.

The About command (see Figure 12.8) in File Manager or Program Manager contains a report, called System Resources, that lists a percentage representing the lowest amount of free memory available to your GDI and USER heaps. When you first start Windows, your free system resources are reported as somewhere between 75 and 80 percent, depending on how many windows and icons are displayed. Each application you start usually consumes between 5 and 20 percent of your free system resources, and each open window consumes about 2 percent. To see how much of your free system resources an application consumes, check the About box, then open an application and check the percentage in the About box again.

The 64K-heap limitation is imposed by the underlying DOS operating system—you'll have to get Windows NT to escape from this constraint. Even if your system has 16 megabytes of RAM and tens of megabytes of additional virtual memory, you could use only a fraction of it if you ran a number of applications that consumed too much of your GDI and USER heaps space. Windows 3.1 does improve heap space problems somewhat by removing the menu portion of the Windows interface from the USER heap to your main memory and by relieving the USER heap from the responsibility of restoring Program Manager icons.

Danger Zone

Another problem with heaps is created by some programs that fail to clear their resources from the heaps after you quit them. If you've quit all your applications except Program Manager and your free system resources are reported as less than 70 percent, you probably have a dirty application or two hanging around in your heaps. Running these applications several times could place a stranglehold on your ability to run Windows applications; you might even encounter one of those ominous Out of Memory error messages. If this happens, you'll need to quit Windows and then restart it to clear out the GDI and USER heaps.

To keep track of your free system resources, you'll need to get a special utility program, such as the System Resource Monitor, provided in the Windows Resource Kit, or a shareware program, such as WinFSR, available on CompuServe (Figure 12.13).

FIGURE 12.13
System Resource Monitor

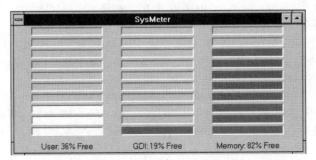

The System Resource Monitor lets you see how much free memory you have left in the USER and GDI heaps.

It's important to keep track of how much free memory you have in both heaps, because Windows may crash if either of these resources becomes depleted. I recommend putting a resource monitoring utility in your Startup group so that you can always keep tabs on your resource levels. Ongoing monitoring of these heaps will help you identify which applications don't remove their resources after quitting. You might want to contact the application's developer to see if an updated, cleaned-up version is available.

Insider's Tip

One way to conserve system resources is to avoid having multiple windows open on your desktop. Minimize any open windows that are not being used to regain some of your GDI and USER resources.

Summary

The performance of your Windows environment and the applications you run within Windows ultimately depend on the quality of your hardware. Key among these components are your processor, your memory, and your hard disk drive. Because of the great variety among these components, Microsoft has attempted to make its program compatible with as many types of hardware elements as possible—but this means you must learn how to tweak your hardware to achieve optimum performance when running Windows.

When selecting a processor, you should consider the types of applications you will be using, and base your decision on whatever performance criteria your system will need to meet. I suggest a fast 386 or a 486 as a minimum for serious Windows users.

Memory consitutes the second most important factor in determining system performance. Internal memory is stored through the use of memory chips, as either RAM or ROM chips. Although it's never possible to have too much RAM, where you place your RAM chips can also have a marked effect on operations. Windows 3.1 operates best with extended memory. Windows can use some of your hard disk to create virtual memory that fools your system into thinking you have extra RAM.

Because Windows makes greater demands on your system's memory resources than DOS does, you'll want to have the fastest hard disk you can afford to accelerate your access to memory. Hard disk drives employ various utilities to speed up performance, such as SMARTDrive—a disk cache program that transfers information from RAM to your hard disk and back. Swap files are another device used to provide a temporary storage area for RAM in order to save memory and make it appear to Windows as if you have more memory than you really do. An added performance booster in Windows 3.1 is the FastDisk feature, which lets Windows bypass the DOS BIOS in order to directly access your hard disk and thereby speed up performance.

Despite all the improvements in memory creation and storage introduced by Windows 3.1, you're still limited when it comes to using applications that include many graphics and interface components. This is because Windows still faces the 64K barrier imposed by the underlying DOS operating system. You'll need to keep track of how much memory these applications are using—at least until the introduction of Windows NT.

Insider's Tech Support

Q: I get an Out of Memory message when I try to run a Windows program.

A: Many types of procedures can free memory on your system, and these are discussed throughout this book. Here are the most important things to try:

➤ Free hard disk space to allow the creation of a larger swap file. If you're using a temporary swap file, try converting it to a permanent swap file. If you're using a permanent swap file, try to make it larger.

➤ Quit any applications you aren't currently using and minimize your other applications.

➤ Check the Clipboard Viewer to see what's on the Clipboard, and either save or discard it.

➤ Change your wallpaper to none.

Q: I get an Out of Memory message when I try to run a DOS program.

A: A variety of techniques are available for freeing memory for use by DOS programs. Several of these involve editing options for the program's .PIF file. (See Chapter 14.)

You can also try to streamline your CONFIG.SYS and AUTOEXEC.BAT files, and remove any TSRs or any other memory-resident programs that aren't absolutely necessary. Also, try loading any device drivers, TSRs, and memory-resident software that you do need into high memory, using the techniques described in Chapter 13. If you are using Windows in 386 enhanced mode and are running DOS applications in a window, maximize them to full screen; this sometimes frees memory for use by another DOS application.

Q: When I run Windows in 386 enhanced mode, I get an error message saying that there is an invalid path for EMM386.

A: You need to tell DOS where EMM386 is located. To do this, use the /Y switch on the statement line in the CONFIG.SYS file that you use to load EMM386. For example, if the EMM386 file is in a directory called \SYSTEM, you would use the line

```
DEVICE=EMM386.EXE /Y=C:\SYSTEM\EMM386.EXE
```

Q: When I run Windows in 386 enhanced mode, I can't access my floppy disk drives.

A: If you are using an external floppy disk drive, its software driver may be incompatible. You'll need to contact the manufacturer to see whether an updated driver is available. If you have an internal floppy disk drive, you can try adding this line to the [386Enh] section of SYSTEM.INI:

```
IRQ9Global=YES
```

Q: Does Stacker work with SMARTDrive?

A: Yes, but SMARTDrive caches the underlying drive used by Stacker and does not cache the stacked volume. To make sure that SMARTDrive only caches the underlying drive, you must load the SMARTDRV.EXE file after the SSWAP.COM driver used by Stacker. You cannot create a permanent swap file on a stacked volume, only on an uncompressed disk area.

Q: My system has trouble reading and writing to the hard disk when I run Windows in 386 enhanced mode.

A: Windows creates a virtual system for handling hard disk interrupt requests (IRQs) when it runs in 386 enhanced mode. This speeds up disk access, but is incompatible with some hard disk drives. To disable this feature, add the following line to the [386Enh] section of your SYSTEM.INI file:

```
VirtualHDIRQ=OFF
```

13

Optimizing DOS for Windows

Although people generally refer to Windows as an operating system, it doesn't really qualify as one on its own. Windows does perform many of the functions of an operating system—especially when it's running in 386 enhanced mode—but it must be combined with DOS in order to meet the technical criteria of a complete operating system. DOS, the venerable PC operating system first introduced in 1981 as a joint effort of Microsoft and IBM, has aged well. It is the most widely used computer operating system in history, and runs on more than 100 million systems in practically every country in the world.

Together, Windows and DOS share great synergy to provide an operating system far more sophisticated than DOS alone. Furthermore, because DOS is part of the operating system, Windows maintains excellent compatibility with DOS programs. DOS is the tie that binds the old world to the new, and DOS together with Windows provides a "best of both worlds" environment that is rapidly becoming the major platform for personal computer software.

However, the partnership between Windows and DOS is not particularly balanced. DOS, like Atlas, must bear the weight of a graphical world on its shoulders—a punishment it was never designed to endure. Although DOS has undergone many overhauls, tuneups, and tweaks over the years, it is still constrained by such problems as a convoluted memory management scheme and a filing system called FAT (for File Allocation Table), which, despite its acronym, only allows for puny file names of eight characters in length.

Performance of Windows is often limited by its DOS dependencies for these crucial operations: loading it into the computer's memory; managing the memory once it is running; maintaining the filing system that keeps track of files and directories on your disks; and communicating with certain hardware and peripherals through DOS device drivers. That's why knowing how to optimize your DOS environment, using the techniques described in this chapter and elsewhere in this book, can often improve the performance of Windows dramatically.

The first part of this chapter explains the symbiotic relationship between DOS and Windows; the different versions of DOS; and how to edit your AUTOEXEC.BAT and CONFIG.SYS files. The second part provides a comprehensive discussion of how special DOS features, such as SMARTDrive and EMM386, work in Windows.

If you're new to DOS, I encourage you to read this chapter. No matter how unappealing it may seem now to learn how to edit your AUTOEXEC.BAT and CONFIG.SYS files, you'll be saving yourself the headaches that could result from compatibility and operational problems. If you plan on running any DOS applications, you should also refer to the next chapter, which explains how DOS multitasking works and how to use the PIF Editor—a utility that lets you tweak the compatibility and performance settings for any DOS programs you want to run during a Windows session.

New DOS-Related Features in Windows 3.1

Windows 3.1 has made solid strides in improving its compatibility with DOS applications. In addition, Microsoft has devised ways of working better with, and sometimes around, the DOS operating system itself. MS-DOS version 5 runs particularly well with Windows 3.1.

Here's a brief rundown of the DOS-related improvements new to 3.1:

➡ Version 4.0 of the SMARTDrive disk cache has been upgraded to the status of an executable file. It is now called SMARTDRV.EXE (formerly SMARTDRV.SYS).

➡ FastDisk—a collection of system drivers, rather than a single utility—lets Windows bypass DOS to speed up disk access in 386 enhanced mode.

➡ The EMM386 expanded memory manager has been upgraded to the status of an executable file and is now called EMM386.EXE. (formerly EMM386.SYS).

➡ A new version of the HIMEM.SYS extended memory manager has been added.

➡ Better support has been included for third-party memory managers, such as QEMM and 386MAX.

➡ The Windows mouse will operate with DOS applications running in a window.

➡ You can select fonts for DOS windows, so that you can run several full DOS screens on a standard VGA display.

➡ A much larger selection of predefined PIFs is provided in the APPS.INF file.

➡ New icons for popular DOS applications are included in the file MORICONS.DLL.

➡ Improved virtual memory features make it more reliable to run multiple DOS applications in the background, and smoother to switch between them.

➡ Addition of a WINSTART.BAT file lets you load special DOS utilities or other items whenever Windows is run in 386 enhanced mode.

➡ Windows now supports DPMI (DOS Protected Mode Interface), and VCPI (Virtual Control Program Interface).

Notice that both SMARTDrive and EMM386 have switched from .sys files to .EXE or executable files. As executable files, they can provide special functions, such as status reports and help information. If you type "**smartdrv**" at a DOS prompt, the following status report appears on your screen:

```
Microsoft SMARTDrive Disk Cache version 4.0
Copyright 1991,1992 Microsoft Corp.

Cache size: 2,097,152 bytes
Cache size while running Windows: 2,097,152 bytes

Disk Caching Status
drive read cache write cache buffering
─────────────────────────────────────────

A: yes no no
B: yes no no
C: yes yes -

For help, type "Smartdrv /?".
```

As indicated by the last line of the status report, you can use the /? switch with SMARTDrive—as well as EMM386.EXE, various utilities in DOS 5, and even Windows itself—to get a quick help screen, which will show you the utility's syntax and switches.

How Windows Works with DOS

In technical jargon, DOS is called a **real mode** operating system. Real mode refers to an operational mode of the Intel x86 processor family that can only directly address 1 megabyte of RAM. But Windows is a multitasking environment that can use many megabytes of RAM to run its own graphic-based programs, or to multitask ordinary DOS applications. How does it do it? Windows uses so many different tricks, workarounds, and downright kludges, its operational flowchart would probably impress Rube Goldberg.

At the risk of oversimplification, here's a glimpse at how Windows overcomes the limitations of DOS. When Windows is first run, the computer starts in real mode as if it were running an ordinary DOS application. But soon after you start it, Windows shifts the computer's processor from real mode into **protected mode**. Protected mode lets the computer directly access the system's extended memory—that is, memory beyond the 1-megabyte limitation imposed by real mode.

When you switch from a Windows to a DOS application in standard mode, Windows saves most of itself to disk, leaving only a stub in the computer's memory. The computer's resources are usurped by the DOS application, which takes complete control of your computer, including the entire screen display. This lets the DOS application overcome many potential conflicts with Windows, but it also explains why you can only run DOS full screen DOS sessions when running Windows in its so-called **standard mode**. When you switch back to Windows, DOS defers to the stub, which Windows uses to pull itself back into memory from disk, and resumes its original position.

If you are running Windows on a 386 or higher processor, Windows runs in **386 enhanced mode** and taps into the processor's **virtual 8086 mode.** The combination of these modes allows Windows to run several DOS applications simultaneously, each in its own individual window on your screen, and with each application fooled into believing that it has control of its own virtual computer. When you run Windows in 386 enhanced mode, it loads itself into a virtual machine so that Windows doesn't have to remove itself, as it does in standard mode. Each DOS session you subsequently start has almost as much memory as you had before you started Windows. The DOS sessions you start under Windows will also inherit the same DOS settings and configuration that were in effect before you started Windows.

* *

Keep Tabs on Your DOS

Before Windows can do its technical tricks, certain system functions must be installed in the computer, and various parameters must be precisely configured. Unwary users often leave these tasks to setup and installation programs, which falsely reassure you that everything will go just fine. In reality, you should always monitor the setup or installation of any program—DOS or Windows—to see how if affects both the DOS and Windows startup files. The Windows initialization files are discussed in Chapter 15, and this chapter reviews the DOS startup files, CONFIG.SYS and AUTOEXEC.BAT.

Sure, the process is tedious, but the consequences of not knowing your way around these files can be dire. For example, if a Windows-compatible high-memory manager (such as HIMEM or QEMM) is not invoked by CONFIG.SYS and set to the proper parameters, Windows will not run. Or, if certain device drivers are not loaded properly, you may not be able to access your network or special storage devices, such as CD ROM drives or SCSI hard disks. Because these two startup files control how DOS is configured, and because DOS is the foundation for running Windows, a thorough understanding of these critical startup files will help you solve, and better yet, prevent, many of the problems that can either obstruct Windows from running or severely impair its performance.

Many installation programs for both Windows and DOS applications automatically modify your startup files so as to incapacitate rather than enhance your system. Installation programs often incorrectly assume that they are the only program you will ever run on your computer, and that you probably have a plain vanilla system that no other installation program has ever touched. Ha! Obviously, this can lead to the wrong configuration for your two DOS startup files, and leave a mess that only a sentient being—not an installation program—can untangle.

To help you understand exactly what transpires in these two files, and resolve any conflicts created by a well-intentioned but not-too-bright installation program, I will step you through a line-by-line examination of CONFIG.SYS and AUTOEXEC.BAT later in this chapter. But first, a few words about the many flavors of DOS.

The Various Versions of DOS

Because it's persisted for a decade, DOS is being used in various different versions. Originally, DOS was a joint development effort of IBM and Microsoft, and each company sold a private-label version of essentially the same product. IBM offered its PC-DOS, which was tweaked to run best on its own hardware, and Microsoft marketed its MS-DOS, which was created as a generic product and sold with most PC clone machines. Because clones subsequently far outsold IBM's own hardware, MS-DOS became the predominant version of DOS. In recognition of the market supremacy of MS-DOS, when I refer to DOS in this book I am referring to MS-DOS, unless I specifically identify the variant, such as PC-DOS or DR-DOS. (DR-DOS is a clone of DOS created by Digital Research, a subsidiary of Netware-creator Novell.)

So, with all these versions of DOS around, which ones work with Windows? The bottom line: Windows 3.1 can run with any version of DOS from 3.1 onward. However, I strongly recommend using Microsoft's DOS version 5.0 or higher, because Windows 3.1 was designed to work best with version 5 of DOS. But in case you need to run a DOS application that is incompatible with DOS 5, or if your company is still standardized on an earlier version, here's a rundown of the different versions of DOS that you can use with Windows:

➡ **DOS version 3.1** The earliest version of DOS that will work with Windows 3.1; the correlating version numbers are purely coincidental.

➡ **DOS version 3.2** The first version to support $3\frac{1}{2}$-inch disks; introduced the XCOPY command.

➺ **DOS version 3.3** A very stable version of DOS that introduced many improvements and is still widely used. It's the only version under 5.0 that I recommend using with Windows.

➺ **DOS version 3.31** A modified version of 3.3 sold by Compaq that added support for hard disk volumes larger than 32 megabytes, the previous limit. Also works with Windows.

➺ **DOS version 4.0** Sometimes referred to as version "four point oh no!" because of its tendency to crash your system without warning. This unstable version of DOS should be avoided.

➺ **DOS version 4.01** A hastily concocted version that fixed the biggest bugs in the disastrous 4.0 version; but, because it robbed more of your system's 640K RAM than did 3.3, very few bothered to upgrade.

➺ **DOS version 5.0** The first version of DOS specifically designed to run with Windows.

➺ **DOS version 6.0** Similar to DOS 5.0 but bundled with more utilities.

You should avoid DOS 3.1 and 3.2 unless your applications only work with them; both these oldies lack several useful system utilities and some enhanced batch file capabilities, and can create incompatibilities with newer DOS applications.

Also note that DOS versions 3.1 through 3.3 include a version of FAT (the File Allocation Table) that only uses 16-bit addresses. This limits the maximum size of a hard disk partition (or volume) to 32 megabytes. DOS version 3.31, a custom version sold by Compaq, was the first to feature a fatter FAT, which supported 32-bit addresses. This enabled a single hard disk partition to break the 32-megabyte barrier and allowed partitions of a gigabyte or more. All the subsequent versions of DOS also allow larger partitions.

MS-DOS 3.3 proved so popular that it's still in widespread use. Although it offers a good, stable version of the DOS operating system, it lacks DOS 5 memory management features and new utilities, such as Undelete. To compensate, many DOS 3.3 followers, who wisely steered clear of DOS 4, have supplemented their operating systems with third-party memory utilities, hard disk management software, and custom hardware drivers. If these enhancements work with Windows (and many of them do), you may not need to upgrade immediately to a newer version of DOS. In fact, in some cases—particularly with older network software—you may still be better off with a customized DOS 3.3 setup than with DOS 5 or 6.

DOS version 4.0 was so unstable and unreliable that users even steered clear of its update, 4.01. In retrospect, many DOS 4 features—such as support for large hard disk partitions, expanded/extended memory management, and a DOS Shell file manager—seem like unfinished prototypes for DOS 5.

For users who want to run DOS applications under Windows, DOS versions 5 and higher offer a vital feature: the ability to load part of the operating system, device drivers, TSRs, and some network software into the memory space above the 640K of conventional RAM. With a major part of DOS and its drivers loaded into either upper memory or high memory, the amount of available conventional RAM increases by at least 37 to 48K, and perhaps even more, depending on your configuration.

Although this amount of RAM increase may seem trivial—especially if you are running a machine with many megabytes—the amount of free memory in the base 640K of conventional RAM affects the number of Windows programs you can run simultaneously and your ability to run a DOS program in a window. With DOS 5, each of the virtual DOS machines launched under Windows may have 600K or more of free memory available—far more than offered in DOS 4, even without running Windows at the same time. DR-DOS version 6, from Digital Research, offers capabilities similar to those of MS-DOS version 5, but DR-DOS may create some extra compatibility problems.

· ·

The DOS Startup Files

Because Windows runs on top of DOS, so to speak, it demands that DOS be configured precisely. Thus you can dramatically improve the performance of Windows operations if you adjust the settings in the DOS startup files, CONFIG.SYS and AUTOEXEC.BAT. You also need to check your files for completeness. If certain statement lines and settings are missing, various problems may occur, including the inability to run Windows. Before I take you line by line through the startup files, here's an overall view of how Windows Setup interacts with your DOS startup files.

Danger Zone

If Windows refuses to run after you install a DOS application, your DOS installation program may have edited (or replaced) the CONFIG.SYS and/or AUTOEXEC.BAT files and thereby inadvertently damaged Windows—by changing a driver or setting an incompatible option, for example. Luckily, many installation programs automatically save the original version of startup files with new extensions, creating names such as CONFIG.001, CONFIG.SAV, or CONFIG.OLD—and of course you made your own backup, just in case. You may need to refer to these original versions to see what the DOS installation program has changed or deleted. In the worst possible case, you may have to reconstruct a new CONFIG.SYS or AUTOEXEC.BAT file by hand and specify the proper information needed by Windows.

Windows Setup and the DOS Startup Files. When you first install Windows, the Windows Setup program presents you with three options for handling DOS startup files. It will

➤ Change the CONFIG.SYS and AUTOEXEC.BAT files for you automatically

➤ Let you view its proposed changes and allow you to make any modifications you consider necessary

➤ Leave these two files alone, which means you'll have to make the necessary inspections and changes at a later time

Although most of the changes proposed by Setup are fine, I recommend that you always exercise the second option: inspect the two files before and after they are modified, whether by Setup or by any other installation program. Note that both of these files are usually located in the root directory of the drive you use to boot your system.

Setup takes these actions to your CONFIG.SYS file:

➤ Looks for any drivers that it deems incompatible with Windows 3.1 and deletes the references to them in CONFIG.SYS.

➤ Installs the HIMEM.SYS extended memory manager by adding a DEVICE= statement to the file if it doesn't already have one.

➤ Adds the SMARTDRV.EXE "double_buffer" control if required (note that SMARTDrive itself is loaded with AUTOEXEC.BAT).

➤ Checks to see if you're using the RAMDRIVE.SYS RAM disk. If so, Setup updates the settings.

➤ Checks for EMM386.EXE, the expanded memory manager, and updates its settings if needed.

➤ Checks for 386MAX (and BlueMAX), and updates the settings if needed.

➤ Checks to see if you have a version 7 or higher .COM or .SYS driver for either the Microsoft or Hewlett-Packard mouse. If you have an older version, it updates you to the new driver and adjusts the settings of the driver.

➤ Checks to see if you are using an EGA display or a Mouse Systems mouse driver, and if so, either adds or adjusts the DEVICE= statement line for EGA.SYS.

Setup searches for and then turns off certain drivers. To change the drivers you want Setup to locate, edit the SETUP.INF file, as described in Chapter 16.

Setup also makes the following changes to your AUTOEXEC.BAT file:

➤ Checks your PATH statement and adds the target directory for the Windows installation if it has not already been specified.

➤ Checks to see if a TEMP directory and variable have been set. If not, it creates the \TEMP subdirectory within your main Windows directory and assigns it the TEMP variable.

➤ Determines whether you should be using SMARTDrive, and if Setup decides you should, checks to see if it has been installed. If not, it adds the SMARTDRV.EXE command line to the file.

Insider's Tip

The SETUP.INF file contains a list of many of the common DOS device drivers, disk caches, antivirus programs, and other utilities known to be incompatible with Setup, Windows 3.1, or both. To view this list, open the file and search for the [incompTSR1], [incompTSR2], [compatibility], [lim], [ramdrive], [diskcache], and [block devices] sections (see Chapter 16).

In addition, the MS-DOS utilities listed in Table 13.1 can also present compatibility problems:

TABLE 13.1

MS-DOS Utiltity	Description
append.com	APPEND utility
assign.com	ASSIGN utility
graphics.com	GRAPHICS utility
join.exe	JOIN utility
print.exe	PRINT utility
subst.exe	SUBST utility

If any of these DOS utilities or the programs listed in SETUP.INF appear in your DOS startup files, it indicates that they are being automatically loaded at startup time. Before you run Setup or Windows, be sure to turn off any of the utilities in the above lists dated before April 1992. Check with the developers of these products to see whether an updated version compatible with Windows 3.1 has been released, or if they know of a specific fix or workaround.

Viewing and Editing Startup Files. It's easy to look at and change the start-up files, but be careful. Although you can edit startup and initialization files with any text editor, I recommend using the Windows Notepad or SysEdit utility from Windows described in Chapter 5, or the DOS 5 Editor utility from MS-DOS version 5.0 and higher. None of these programs will damage the initialization files, because, unlike most full-blown word processors, they will not insert any of their own formatting information into a file or alter the ASCII values of certain characters. Any formatting codes or other non-alphanumeric ASCII characters could corrupt a file and even crash your entire system.

If you haven't installed Windows, or if an attempt at Windows installation has failed, you may need to edit your CONFIG.SYS and AUTOEXEC.BAT files from DOS. Luckily, DOS 5 and DR-DOS 6 are equipped with easy-to-use text editors that can be applied to this task. If you are using DOS 5, just type **EDITOR** from the DOS prompt to run this handy utility (Figure 13.1)

• • • • • • • • • • • • • •
FIGURE 13.1
DOS 5 Editor
with File
Menu Pulled
Down

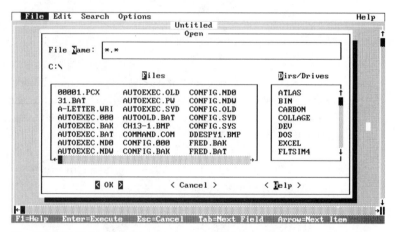

The DOS 5 Editor utility gives you a Windowslike text editor that you can use to view and edit your system files.

Windows users will be glad to know that the DOS 5 Editor works with a mouse and uses the same Alt key menu commands found in many Windows programs. For example, Alt,F,O opens a file, Tab moves you around choices in a dialog box, and Alt,F,X quits the Editor utility.

If you are running an earlier version of DOS, you can struggle with the older EDLIN utility, or you can use any third-party wordprocessor that can save files as pure ASCII text without inserting any of its own formatting codes.

Danger Zone

Be cautious when editing any of these startup files: even the slightest mistake might cause your system to crash, or not start. Always save a version of the file under a different name before making any changes to it. For example, save AUTOEXEC.BAT as AUTOEXEC.BAK before editing it. That way, if you accidently cause an unwanted change, you will have the original, uncorrupted file for comparison or replacement.

It's also a good idea to create a bootable floppy disk (format a disk with the Make System Disk option as described in Chapter 3) and copy the original version of your startup files to this disk before editing them. Then, if worse comes to worst, you can restart your system from the backup disk.

· ·

The CONFIG.SYS and AUTOEXEC.BAT Essentials

The CONFIG.SYS and AUTOEXEC.BAT files contain a number of statement lines that conform to the following general form:

```
<statement name>=<values>  <parameters> <switches>
<statement>
REM comments
```

These statements can represent special keywords that designate values, parameters, and/or special switches; or they can be single statement lines, such as a command on a line in the AUTOEXEC.BAT file. Comments must be preceded by the three letters REM.

The two DOS startup files need to contain certain statements in order for Windows to run properly. The CONFIG.SYS file must include a line specifying a compatible memory manager, and it should contain a Files and Buffers statement.

The Windows default memory manager is HIMEM.SYS; alternatively you can either install this or a third-party product, such as Quarterdeck's QEMM or 386MAX from Qualitas.

If you are using SMARTDrive, you should set the FILES= statement to a value of at least 30 and the BUFFERS= statement to 10. A second number after the BUFFERS= statement lets you specify a secondary buffer. Because SMARTDrive provides its own cache, you don't need a secondary buffer. If you aren't using SMARTDrive, you should increase the number of DOS buffers to 20.

Although you can run Windows without installing a disk cache, Microsoft's SMARTDrive or a third-party cache product greatly enhances performance efficiency. In Windows 3.1, SMARTDrive is loaded from the AUTOEXEC.BAT file, rather than from the CONFIG.SYS file, as was the case with version 3.0. The bare essentials for your AUTOEXEC.BAT consist of two command lines: one to load SMARTDrive and another line to set the PATH variable so that it includes your main Windows directory. To construct a minimal set of startup files for use with Windows, see the next section.

By experimenting with some of the settings—such as those for the size of the SMARTDrive—you can fine-tune the performance of your system as well. The following section highlights those elements of the CONFIG.SYS and AUTOEXEC.BAT files that are relevant to Windows. Remember, however, that before you change any item that is not covered here—that is, any item that relates to DOS or to specific programs or peripherals—you should refer to the appropriate documentation.

Any programs you load from DOS before your Windows session—using either CONFIG.SYS or AUTOEXEC.BAT—reside in your computer's precious 640K conventional RAM area, unless you've taken steps to relocate them. MS-DOS 5 and higher, DR-DOS 6, and most third-party memory management packages, such as QEMM and 386MAX, now allow you to load device drivers and other memory-resident programs into upper memory—that is, the memory region above the conventional 640K of RAM.

Insider's Tip

Be on the lookout for memory-gobblers when editing the CONFIG.SYS and AUTOEXEC.BAT files. Load only your critical device drivers, TSRs, or utilities, such as those that are necessary to access a CD ROM drive or network. All those device drivers, memory-resident programs, and utilities can devour memory and often aren't necessary for your entire system.

For example, there's no need to load a mouse driver if you will be running the mouse only in Windows, not while running DOS programs. Go ahead and disable or remove lines that load unnecessary TSRs or drivers. Then try loading the remaining ones into the upper memory area. Even if you don't load a TSR or utility automatically in your AUTOEXEC.BAT file, you can still run many TSRs and utilities from within a DOS session after you start Windows. This will put the TSRs and utilities under the control of the Windows memory management system, thus relieving the RAM cram that can result when those same TSRs and utilities are loaded by the DOS startup files.

When editing either the CONFIG.SYS or the AUTOEXEC.BAT file, you should use the REM statement liberally to place Remarks, or comments, into these files. REM statements are simple to use: as long as a line starts with the letters REM, DOS ignores the rest of the line. One annoying but harmless exception applies if you are using a DOS version earlier than 4.0 (that is, DOS 3.x). In this case, REM statements in the CONFIG.SYS file generate the error message "Unrecognized Command in CONFIG.SYS." Pay this message little heed; the REM statement will still cause the line to be ignored, and the error message won't do anything to your system. Of course, you might actually have a syntax error in the CONFIG.SYS file, but the chance of this occurring is remote.

You can always check REM statements for comments if you edit the file at a later date. You can also exploit this forced ignorance to temporarily disable lines in either of these files. For example, if your CONFIG.SYS file contains a line like this

```
INSTALL=c:\DOS\fastopen.exe c:=(50,25)
```

and you decide to turn off the Fastopen program to conserve RAM, simply add the letters REM to the beginning of the line:

```
REM INSTALL=c:\DOS\fastopen.exe c:=(50,25)
```

This causes DOS to ignore the line when it reads the file on startup. When you use the REM statement to disable a line, rather than deleting it altogether, you can easily reinstate the line by simply removing the REM statement from the beginning of the line.

. . . .

Inside the CONFIG.SYS File

As its name suggests, the CONFIG.SYS file contains information about your system configuration. DOS expects this file to be located in the root directory of the drive from which you boot, and when it encounters this file, DOS reads it before it reads any other files, including AUTOEXEC.BAT. Although DOS doesn't strictly require this file to run, Windows relies on it to load an extended memory manager and to set several other DOS parameters.

Windows requires that every CONFIG.SYS file include at least four statements: FILES=, BUFFERS=, STACKS=, and DEVICE=, and that these statement lines be followed by the appropriate values. The following example shows a minimal CONFIG.SYS file:

```
FILES=30
BUFFERS=10
STACKS=9,128
DEVICE=C:\HIMEM.SYS
```

If your system has somehow lost its CONFIG.SYS file, try using this bare-bones file to return to Windows, and from there attempt to reconstruct any other necessary statements.

Insider's Tip

If you need to recreate your lost CONFIG.SYS file in order to return to Windows, and you don't have a DOS text editing program for creating the file, try this DOS trick. First type

```
COPY CON CONFIG.SYS
```

at the DOS prompt; then, press Enter. Next type in the example minimal CONFIG.SYS file just given (or a suitable substitute), ending each line with Enter. After the last line, press Ctrl+Z, Enter to copy what you just typed to a newly created CONFIG.SYS file.

The example of a CONFIG.SYS file just given demonstrates the default values valid for most systems using DOS versions 3.3 or higher. This sample file is designed for a single-user system; if you're using a network, you will also need to add any statements necessary to load your network drivers. See your system administrator or read your network documentation to learn what statements need to be in CONFIG.SYS.

The first line in the example contains the FILES statement. FILES tells DOS how many open files the DOS system calls can access at one time; with some qualifications, this is the number of files that can be open at once. The FILES statement can accept any value from 8 to 255. DOS techies take note: even though a DOS program can theoretically have 65,534 files open at one time, that number actually represents the number of file handles (set by DOS system call 67H) the program can address simultaneously, not the true number of open files. DOS is therefore restricted to opening the number of files specified in the FILES statement.

The default value for the maximum number of open files is 8, which is what DOS will use if the CONFIG.SYS file does not contain a FILES statement. However, if the FILES statement value is too small—and 8 *is* too small—Windows might not be able to open enough files in order to run; a FILES value of 30 is almost always a safe bet. Reduce a larger value down to 30 to free additional conventional memory, because DOS reserves a small amount of RAM for each of the files that it can potentially open.

The next line contains the BUFFERS statement, which sets the number of disk buffers DOS will allocate from the 640K of conventional RAM. Each of these buffers requires about 528 bytes of the 640K, so be as conservative as possible in the number of buffers you specify. The acceptable range is from 1 to 99, but you should specify from 10 to 30. If you're using DOS 4 or earlier and SMARTDrive, which provides its own disk buffering system, you should reduce this number to 10 to conserve conventional memory. On the other hand, setting it higher than 20 might improve disk access speed in some systems. With DOS 5 or later, you can set the BUFFERS= value as high as 30 without using extra conventional memory—DOS 5 can place the buffers in the high memory area, provided that DOS is loaded into high memory with the DOS=HIGH statement described later..

The STACKS statement is pure DOS esoterica—it assists your system with the dynamic use of data stacks, and specifies the sizes and number of stack frames that DOS devotes to system hardware interrupts. DOS allocates a stack to each hardware interrupt. The recommended setting of

```
STACKS=9,128
```

instructs DOS to use 9 stack frames that are 128 bytes in size. You probably won't have to worry about changing these values unless you happen to be using DOS 3.2. If you can't upgrade, you should change the statement line to read

```
STACKS=16,192
```

which specifies 16 stack frames, each consisting of 192 bytes of the 640K RAM. This STACKS setting should prevent a hardware interrupt from making DOS 3.2 freeze on you unexpectedly.

Loading HIMEM.SYS and Other DOS Device Drivers. The DEVICE= and DEVICEHIGH= statements in CONFIG.SYS tell DOS what device drivers to load. The DEVICE= statement is the one normally used to load device drivers. However, if you are using DOS 5 or later, you can use the DEVICEHIGH= command, described later in this section, to load certain device drivers into the high memory area (that is, above the first 1 megabyte).

Device drivers can include quite an assortment, from network drivers to memory management systems to DOS extensions that allow you to attach devices such as mice, scanners, and add-in cards. Device driver files usually end with the .SYS or .EXE extension. The example shown earlier illustrates a bare-bones CONFIG.SYS file, loaded with only the HIMEM.SYS driver, which is a memory management system required for running Windows in either standard or 386 enhanced mode. (Refer to Chapter 12 for more details on HIMEM.SYS and how it affects your computer's use of memory.)

The only reason not to load the HIMEM.SYS driver is if you are using an alternative, Windows-compatible, memory management system, such as QEMM386, 386MAX, BlueMAX, or NETROOM. Always make sure your third-party memory manager is compatible with your version of Windows, and follow the manufacturer's guidelines carefully when editing the statements in startup files that relate to these third-party drivers.

Depending on what you need your system to do, you can also include these other DEVICE= statements in your CONFIG.SYS file:

➤ **The SMARTDRV.EXE /double_buffer statement** Adds the double-buffering feature of SMARTDrive to maintain compatibility with certain hard disks.

➤ **RAMDRIVE.SYS, the Windows RAM disk utility** Tricks some of your RAM into acting like a very fast disk drive.

➤ **The MOUSE.SYS version of the Microsoft Mouse driver** Allows you to use a mouse with DOS applications, if you're not using MOUSE.COM or another mouse driver.

➤ **The device driver portion of the dual-purpose SETVER.EXE** Loads the DOS version table into memory.

➤ **EGA.SYS** Helps DOS programs run in standard mode.

➤ **ANSI.SYS** Allows DOS power-users to use the ANSI console device driver with DOS.

➤ **EMM386.EXE, the Microsoft expanded memory manager** Lets you load device drivers, TSRs, or other memory-resident software into upper memory; or enables you to configure extended memory to simulate expanded memory for use by DOS programs run outside of Windows.

During installation, Windows Setup deletes any obsolete versions of the SMARTDrive disk cache (named SMARTDRV.SYS), which any version of DOS prior to 5 or Windows 3.0 placed in your CONFIG.SYS file by using a DEVICE= statement. The Windows 3.1 Setup program replaces these with the new SMARTDRV.EXE statement in the AUTOEXEC.BAT file, and sometimes it may also install SMARTDrive's double-buffer feature by using a statement line such as

```
DEVICE=SMARTDRV.EXE /double_buffer
```

This line lets SMARTDrive work correctly with certain types of hard disk drives. See the AUTOEXEC.BAT section later in this chapter for more details about setting up SMARTDrive.

Setting Up RAMDRIVE.SYS. You can also use the CONFIG.SYS file to install the RAMDRIVE.SYS driver, which creates a RAM disk that can be used with either DOS or Windows. During installation, the Setup program copies this file to the Windows subdirectory on your hard disk, but there is no automatic setup.

The RAMDRIVE.SYS statement takes the form

```
DEVICE=<path>RAMDRIVE.SYS <disk size> <sector size> <number of
entries> </E or /A>
```

The <disk size> is the size in kilobytes that you designate for the RAMdrive. If you don't specify anything, the default RAM disk will be set at only 64K. If you list a second number, it will be interpreted as the <sector size>—this is the sector size, in bytes, that you want your virtual RAM disk to use. RAMDrive employs this sector size to optimize data transfer to and from your hard disk. The <sector size> value should be separated from the <disk size> value by a space, and it must be one of the following four numbers: 128, 256, 512, or 1024. If you're storing a number of small files in your RAMDrive, use a smaller sector size for best performance; for larger files, use a large sector size.

The third number listed after RAMDRIVE.SYS will be interpreted as the <numentries> parameter; this specifies the maximum number of files and directories that can be stored in the RAM disk's root directory. The value of <number of entries> can range from 2 to 1024. If you omit this parameter, the default value is 64. RAM disks are assigned the next available drive letter.

After you have set the values for <disk size>, <sector size>, and <number of entries>, you can set one of two switches that control which type of memory RAMDRIVE.SYS will use to create your RAM disk. These two switches are /E, to create a RAM disk in extended memory; or /A, to create a RAM disk in expanded memory.

If you don't use either switch, Windows will load the RAM disk into your system's 640K of conventional memory by default. But it's not a good idea to create a RAM drive using the precious conventional memory, so you should always use either the /E or the /A switch. Use the /E switch to create the RAM disk in extended memory if you can, because it will run faster; in addition, the HIMEM.SYS and the RAMDRIVE.SYS driver are designed to cooperate when RAMDrive is running in extended memory.

Here's a simple CONFIG.SYS statement that creates a RAMDrive:

```
DEVICE=C:\WINDOWS\RAMDRIVE.SYS 512 /E
```

This statement indicates that RAMDRIVE.SYS is in the \WINDOWS directory on drive C and would create a RAM disk 512K in size, which uses 512 byte sectors for retrieval, permits 64 root directory files and subdirectories, and loads the RAMDrive into extended memory. The 512 refers to the size of the RAM disk; the sector size and number of entries don't need to be specified because they use the default values.

Here's a more complex example that deviates from the various default values:

```
DEVICE=C:\WINDOWS\RAMDRIVE.SYS 256 128 48 /A
```

This statement line tells RAMDRIVE.SYS to create a RAM disk of 256K in size with 128 byte sectors, which would allow only 48 files or subdirectories to be stored in the root directory, and would create the RAM disk using expanded memory.

Danger Zone

You must position the RAMDRIVE.SYS device driver statement *after* the line in your CONFIG.SYS file that loads HIMEM.SYS, or whatever third-party extended or expanded memory manager you use.

Insider's Tip

Each time you restart your computer, RAMDRIVE.SYS creates a new empty RAM disk. If you want to use particular files from your RAM disk, you'll need to recopy them into the RAMDrive each time you use the computer. You can do this automatically by using the COPY command in your AUTOEXEC.BAT file.

Using RAMDrive for Temporary Files. Windows Print Manager, some Windows utility programs, and quite a number of applications, such as PageMaker and ToolBook, create temporary files that are deleted once you exit the program. These temporary files are used to swap information to the disk and conserve RAM. One of the best uses of a RAM disk in Windows is to store these temporary files.

You might want to install RAMDrive if you use a diskless workstation on a network, and if the workstation has plenty of memory. To use RAMDrive for storing your temporary files, you'll need to use the Set command, described later in this chapter, to redirect the temporary files to the RAMDrive volume.

Danger Zone

Watch out for programs that create huge temporary files. Graphics programs can sometimes create multimegabyte temporary files, which require an equally large RAM disk for storage.

To determine the size of the temporary files, use File Manager to inspect the directory where they are stored. If you have trouble finding them, most temporary files begin with the ~ and end with the extension .TMP. If your applications create very large temporary files, and you have less than 6 megabytes of RAM, you would do better to leave that RAM free for use by Windows and let SMARTDrive deal with caching the temporary files.

Setting Up MOUSE.SYS. Windows includes both the MOUSE.SYS device driver and the MOUSE.COM TSR for supporting your mouse with mouse-capable DOS applications. Windows itself doesn't require these drivers, so if you plan to use the mouse only with Windows, don't install these drivers. They can rob your system of some of its limited 640K of conventional RAM.

If you do need to use a DOS mouse driver, I recommend the MOUSE.COM driver that is installed through the AUTOEXEC.BAT file. This version provides more features than the MOUSE.SYS driver. However, if the MOUSE.COM driver causes incompatibilities with your system, you can install the MOUSE.SYS driver with CONFIG.SYS by using the following statement line:

```
DEVICE=C:\WINDOWS\MOUSE.SYS /Y
```

The /Y switch disables the "sprite" cursor, which can cause compatibility problems with certain video drivers.

For non-Microsoft mice, refer to the accompanying documentation for information about the operation of its device driver. Some third-party mouse drivers work like MOUSE.SYS: they are loaded as device drivers in your CONFIG.SYS file. Others, such as MOUSE.COM, are TSRs and are run as program lines by your AUTOEXEC.BAT file, as discussed a little later in this chapter.

Using SETVER.EXE. If you install DOS 5 using its setup program, your CONFIG.SYS file will probably contain a DEVICE= statement line that has loaded the SETVER.EXE program. This program works both as a command and as a device driver. The DOS 5 setup program usually installs the driver automatically with a statement line such as

```
DEVICE=C:\DOS\SETVER.EXE
```

along with a DOS version table, which lists specific programs by the corresponding version of DOS they were designed to run with.

Some DOS programs check this version table, which reports what version the DOS program requires in order to run. Unfortunately, this "false reporting" technique won't solve incompatibility problems if the DOS program you're trying to run is not compatible with DOS 5. (Insider's Mini-tip: you can load SETVER with the DEVICEHIGH= command described later in the chapter.)

To inspect the version table, type **SETVER** at the DOS prompt. Here's what my version table looks like:

```
MSCDEX.EXE 4.00          REDIR40.EXE 4.00
REDIR4.EXE 4.00          DD.EXE 4.01
NET.EXE 4.00             DD.BIN 4.01
NET.COM 3.30             LL3.EXE 4.01
NETWKSTA.EXE 4.00        REDIR.EXE 4.00
DXMA0MOD.SYS 3.30        SSTDRIVE.SYS 4.00
BAN.EXE 4.00             ZDRV.SYS 4.01
BAN.COM 4.00             ZFMT.SYS 4.01
MSREDIR.EXE 4.00         TOPSRDR.EXE 4.00
METRO.EXE 3.31
```

Microsoft includes many of the problem programs in its default version table. If you want to edit this table, either to add programs that are incompatible with DOS 5 or to remove items you don't need, use the SETVER command from the DOS prompt. The SETVER command has the following syntax:

```
SETVER <path> <application> <version> </D> </Q>
```

The <path> is the drive and path location for SETVER.EXE (not for the application) if SETVER.EXE is not in your current path. The <application> is the file name and extension of whatever application you want to run. The <version> is the version of DOS that DOS 5 should emulate for that application. The /D switch is used to delete the item, and the /Q switch is used to suppress SETVER's aggressive warning message (see the Danger Zone at the end of this section).

For example, if a program called OLDAPP.EXE required DOS version 4.01 to run, you would type the following command at the DOS prompt:

```
SETVER OLDAPP.EXE 4.01
```

Conversely, to remove the program from the version table, type

```
SETVER OLDAPP.EXE /D
```

Any changes you make to the version table will not take effect until you restart your computer, so that SETVER can load the new version table.

Danger Zone

Edit the version table with care; with certain programs, you might introduce incompatibilities rather than solve them. That's why SETVER.EXE diplays this disclaimer when you use the SETVER command to edit the table:

```
WARNING—The application you are adding to the MS-DOS version
table may not have been verified by Microsoft on this version
of MS-DOS. Please contact your software vendor for information
on whether this application will operate properly under this
version of MS-DOS. If you execute this application by instruct-
ing MS-DOS to report a different MS-DOS version number, you
may lose or corrupt data, or cause system instabilities. In
that circumstance, Microsoft is not reponsible for any loss
or damage.
```

Setting Up EGA.SYS. EGA.SYS is a special EGA video driver that you will need only if you plan to run DOS applications while you are operating Windows in standard mode. To install the EGA.SYS driver, simply place its name after a DEVICE= statement. For example, the line

```
DEVICE=C:\WINDOWS\EGA.SYS
```

would do the trick, assuming that the EGA.SYS driver was actually located in the Windows subdirectory of your C: drive. You may need to copy the EGA.SYS file over from the original Windows installation disks. If you do, remember to use the Expand utility (described in Chapter 5) to decompress the file as you copy it.

Setting Up Other Device Drivers. If you look, you may see other device driver statements in your CONFIG.SYS file as well; often they've been placed there by the installation program for a hardware device (such as a TIGA video adapter card) or a utility program (such as 386MAX). If you need to add any device driver statements, simply follow the general syntax used in the earlier examples. These take this general form:

```
DEVICE=<drive><path><driver filename><argument>
```

where <argument> represents any options or switches accepted by that particular device driver.

DOS includes several device drivers of its own that are not required by Windows. These are

➤ ANSI.SYS

➤ DISPLAY.SYS

➤ DRIVER.SYS

➤ PRINTER.SYS

➤ COUNTRY.SYS

➤ KEYBOARD.SYS

For information on these device drivers, refer to your DOS documentation. If any of them are unnecessary, disable them by inserting the REM statement at the beginning of their lines. It's a good idea to disable any that you don't need in order to liberate some of that all-important 640K of conventional RAM.

And beware! Don't mess with the two drivers COUNTRY.SYS and KEYBOARD.SYS. Any attempt to load them by CONFIG.SYS may well crash your system. To change the country and keyboard driver settings used in Windows, use only the controls available in the WIN.INI and SYSTEM.INI files described later in this chapter.

The DEVICEHIGH Statement. The DEVICEHIGH statement, which is available only in DOS version 5 and later, is similar to the DEVICE statement just discussed, with one difference: it loads the device drivers into the upper memory area. This frees more of your precious 640K of conventional memory for use by Windows and DOS sessions run from Windows.

The DEVICEHIGH statement takes the form

```
DEVICEHIGH=<path and driver name> <switches>
```

where <path and driver name> is the full path and file name of a DOS device driver you intend to load into high memory, and <switches> identifies any valid parameters or switches to be used with the device driver. Note that the DEVICEHIGH statement will not work unless you have already loaded HIMEM.SYS and EMM386.EXE. A detailed description of how to use the DEVICEHIGH command appears later in this chapter, in the section on memory management.

The DOS Statement. The DOS statement line lets you load DOS into the high memory area in order to free more of your 640K of conventional RAM. However, like the DEVICEHIGH statement just described, the DOS statement works only if you are using DOS version 5 or later. If you are using a later version, and your computer comes with extended memory, the DOS installation program will usually add a line to your CONFIG.SYS file that loads DOS into the high memory area. To see whether this action has occurred, look for this line in your CONFIG.SYS file:

```
DOS=HIGH
```

You can add this line to take advantage of this feature, provided you have the proper version of DOS.

If you have a 386 or higher processor, you can use the EMM386 memory manager, included with Windows, to load TSRs and other memory resident programs into the upper memory area, in conjunction with the DEVICEHIGH statement mentioned above, or with the LOADHIGH statement, which you can use in your AUTOEXEC.BAT file. To designate EMM386 for loading programs and drivers into upper memory, use the UMB option in the DOS statement in CONFIG.SYS, as shown in the following example:

```
DOS=HIGH,UMB
```

The UMB command allows DOS to manage your system's upper memory blocks (UMBs) by maintaining a link between the conventional 640K of

RAM and the upper memory area. The UMB option isn't necessary if you don't plan to use EMM386, or if you're using a third-party memory management utility, such as QEMM or 386MAX. To use EMM386 without loading DOS into high memory, specify **DOS=UMB**. See the discussion of memory management later in this chapter for examples of how to use these various techniques.

Danger Zone

The order in which these statement lines appear in your CONFIG.SYS file can affect how much of your 640K RAM remains free. See the section on memory management later in this chapter for details on how to optimize the order in which devices are listed. If you plan to load both DOS and TSRs into high memory, your CONFIG.SYS file should specify DEVICE=HIMEM.SYS as the first line, followed by the DEVICE=EMM386 statement, and then the DOS=HIGH,UMB line. After these three statement lines, you can use the DEVICEHIGH statement to load other device drivers into high memory.

The SHELL Statement. The SHELL statement starts the execution of the DOS command processor, COMMAND.COM, from the file in the path name, and with any switches that are specified after the file name. One of these switches, /E, sets aside some of the 640K memory area for storage of DOS environment variables. DOS uses these environment variables to store such information as the location of COMMAND.COM, the contents of the current PATH, and the settings for your PROMPT. To see what information DOS is storing in its environment space, type the SET command at the DOS prompt.

You can free some space for Windows by reducing the number associated with the /E switch. This number, which can range from 160 to 32768, sets the amount of RAM reserved for the environment variables.

Here's an example of a typical SHELL statement you might find in your CONFIG.SYS file:

```
SHELL=C:\DOS\COMMAND.COM /P /E:2048
```

In this example, the /P switch tells DOS to keep a second copy of the command processor in memory without returning to the primary command processor. The /E:2048 switch at the end of the line signifies that DOS will reserve 2048 bytes (2K) to store the environment variables. To place the environment on a diet and save some of your coveted 640K of conventional RAM, you could trim the 2048 bytes in the above example down to 512 bytes—the smallest I think it should ever be—by changing the SHELL statement to read

```
SHELL=C:\DOS\COMMAND.COM /P /E:512
```

If you don't use the /E: switch, a default value of 256 is used. For further information about the SHELL statement, refer to your DOS documentation.

The INSTALL Statement. Use the install statement to execute the SHARE.EXE or FASTOPEN.EXE program while DOS is processing the CONFIG.SYS file at startup. The INSTALL statement takes the following form:

```
INSTALL=<drive><path> <SHARE.EXE or FASTOPEN.EXE><parameters>
```

where <parameters> is any appropriate combination of options, switches, or other commands accepted by the install command you specified: either SHARE.EXE or FASTOPEN.EXE.

The FASTOPEN.EXE and SHARE.EXE programs are included with DOS and can be loaded by either AUTOEXEC.BAT or CONFIG.SYS. Loading these utilities with CONFIG.SYS prevents the AUTOEXEC.BAT batch file from trying to rerun them every time the batch file is executed.

FASTOPEN.EXE decreases the time DOS takes to open frequently used files and directories by keeping track of their physical location on the hard disk. Whenever a file is needed, a disk search is unnecessary because DOS retains the file's coordinates.

FASTOPEN works only with hard disks and does not affect the performance of network drives. But unless you are running a massive DOS database program, or some other task that requires the use of many open files outside Windows, I'd advise you not to load FASTOPEN. This utility requires at least 48 bytes of the 640K base RAM for every file or directory that it tracks, and the FASTOPEN.EXE program takes space itself. If you do use FASTOPEN, however, keep the number of files you specify as low as possible. For more information about FASTOPEN.EXE, refer to your DOS manual.

Installing SHARE. SHARE.EXE provides a file sharing and locking function for large hard disks—that is, those with partitions greater than 32 megabytes—and for local area network applications where files are shared between programs and/or users. Some Windows applications, such as Word for Windows 2.0, require that SHARE be installed in order to run more than one instance of themselves.

The SHARE.EXE utility sets up a special file-sharing code that validates all the read/write operations requested by applications. This prevents DOS from accidentally imperiling data and programs by losing track of where to read from or write to. If SHARE discovers that a disk has been changed, or some other unexpected change has taken place, it generates an error message requesting that the proper disk be inserted before it will continue with any pending read/write operations. SHARE employs the FCBS (File Control

Blocks) method of file tracking, but you needn't worry about the FCBS command mentioned later in the chapter; SHARE handles things on its own.

The SHARE.EXE installation statement takes the form

```
INSTALL=<drive><path>SHARE.EXE </F:nnnn> </L:nn>
```

where </F:nnnn> is the file space switch, with nnnn a number that represents the amount of space, in bytes, that DOS should set aside in the precious 640K conventional RAM area for storing the file-sharing data. If you don't include this switch, the default value of 2048 bytes will be used. The </L:nn> switch affects file locking, with nn the number of locks you want used; the default for this value is 20.

A minimal SHARE installation line would be

```
INSTALL=C:\DOS\SHARE.EXE
```

This line uses the default values for the </F:nnnn> and </L:nn> switches.

In the following sample SHARE installation line

```
INSTALL=C:\DOS\SHARE.EXE /F:4096 /L:25
```

the /F:4096 tells DOS to set aside 4096 bytes, or 4K, of RAM for storing the file-sharing codes and related information, and to provide up to 25 file locks.

Danger Zone

If your hard disk contains a partition greater than 32 megabytes, you probably need SHARE in order for your system to operate properly and to prevent DOS from accidentally corrupting files. The SHARE statement is not installed by Windows Setup, so you'll need to add this statement line manually, if it is not already present.

The LASTDRIVE Statement. The LASTDRIVE statement allows you to extend the default limit of five drives—usually in order to access network volumes as if they were DOS drives. DOS provides you with an initial limit of five logical drives, which means that the last drive letter you can assign to a storage device is E: (the fifth letter of the alphabet).

The LASTDRIVE statement lets you set that letter higher—up to Z—for a total of 26 drives. The minimum value of this statement should be the letter that represents the number of actual drives installed in your computer system. Additional drive letters are assigned in alphabetical order to each additional volume that you connect to your system, regardless of whether the volumes are physical drives or drive partitions, RAM disks, or network volumes. However, watch your RAM: DOS consumes 81 bytes of the scant 640K of conventional RAM for each drive letter that is assigned, so you shouldn't reserve more drive letters than you require.

For example, a conservative statement would be

```
LASTDRIVE=F
```

Note that you should omit the colon when specifying the drive letter in this statement.

This would add only one more drive than the DOS default; provide enough letters for two floppy drives (the A: and B: drives); and provide sufficient letters for four other drives. Typically C: is reserved for the hard disk volume from which you boot, so D:, E:, and F: would be available for additional volumes, such as partitions or a RAM disk.

If you still need another volume for a RAM disk (G:) and you also want to access three different network drives (H:, I:, J:), you could reserve the necessary letters by changing the LASTDRIVE statement to

```
LASTDRIVE=J
```

Other CONFIG.SYS Statements. DOS recognizes three other types of statement lines in CONFIG.SYS files that are not related to windows:

➥ BREAK

➥ DRIVPARM

➥ FCBS

BREAK instructs the system whether you want to be able to halt DOS processes—not just programs—by pressing Ctrl+C. DRIVPARM defines the parameters used for block I/O devices such as disk drives. And FCBS specifies the number of FCBs, or File Control Blocks, that can be open simultaneously for use with some older DOS applications. You probably won't need to worry about these three statements. If you want more information about them, refer to your DOS documentation.

· ·

Inside the AUTOEXEC.BAT File

PCs come with very few extras. That's why you need files like CONFIG.SYS, for loading device drivers, and AUTOEXEC.BAT, for setting up your files so that they will be able to run DOS and Windows applications.

AUTOEXEC.BAT is a special DOS batch file, denoted by the requisite .BAT extension, that is executed automatically each time you start your computer, if it's located in your root directory. It consists of a plain text file that contains one or more lines of commands, with optional comments. In DOS, all the commands in a batch file are sequentially executed when you type the name of the file and press Enter.

Batch files can be used for many purposes: to initiate connection sequences to networks; to run a group of DOS applications and their documents together; or to create a selection of menus for DOS programs and command options—virtually anything in DOS that you can program using its COMMAND.COM command processor.

AUTOEXEC.BAT is a standard batch file, so the discussion here also provides information relevant to other batch files. Table 13.2 gives a rundown of the batch file commands that work with DOS (note that the @ and CALL commands are available only in DOS version 3.3 and later):

· · · · · · · · · · · · · ·
TABLE 13.2

Batch Command	Description
:\<label\>	Labels a destination line for a GOTO command. The \<label\> can be any text (case is ignored); the GOTO command will search for a line starting with this text. GOTO always searches from the beginning of the file, so don't use duplicate labels, because only the first one will ever be found.
@\<command\>	Does not display the command specified in \<command\>. Can be used with any DOS or batch file command.
%\<0-9\>	Substitutes whatever you typed at the command line for these variables. The value of \<0-9\> can be any single digit from 0 to 9, allowing the variable to parse any of the first 10 items you typed at the prompt to start the batch file. For example, if you started a batch file by typing "MYBATCH FILE1.DOC FILE2.DOC /P," then the value of %0 is MYBATCH, the value of %1 is FILE1.DOC, %2 is FILE2.DOC, and %3 is /P.
%\<variable\>%	Substitutes the DOS environment variable you specified with the SET command. For example, if you specified "SET FRED=DAVIS," then the batch command %FRED% would be substituted with the string DAVIS.
BREAK ON	Allows the Ctrl+C key combination to halt the execution of the batch file (this is the default).
BREAK OFF	Prevents the Ctrl+C key combination from halting the execution of the batch file.

TABLE 13.2 *(cont.)*

Batch Command	Description
CALL <filespec>	Runs another batch file as if it were a subroutine; <filespec> can be a file name or the path name and file name.
ECHO <ON or OFF>	Determines whether the subsequent lines of a batch file will be displayed. With ECHO ON, the file is displayed (the default); with ECHO OFF, you won't see each line of the file appear on your screen as it's being run.
ECHO <string>	Displays the text contained in <string>.

FOR...IN...DO	Allows you to repeat the execution of a DOS command on a group of files. The syntax for this command is
	
	`FOR %%<variable> IN (<files>) DO <command>`
	`%%<variable>`
	
	An example of how this might be used is
	
	`FOR %%A IN (*.TMP) DO DEL %%A`
	
	This line would delete all the files ending in .TMP, whereas
	
	`FOR %%A IN (*.TMP *.BAK) DO DEL %%A`
	
	would delete both .TMP and .BAK files.

GOTO <label>	Jumps to the line in the batch file that starts with <label>, as described above.

IF <string>	Makes execution of a command contingent on the comparison of two strings. The complete syntax for this command is
	
	`IF [NOT] <string or variable>==<string> <command>`
	
	For example, the line
	
	`IF %1=="HELPME" CALL HELP`
	
	would look at %1 (whatever was entered as the second item); if it is HELPME, it would run the batch file named HELP.BAT. Use the optional NOT to specify that the command should be executed if the two strings do not match.

••••••••••••
TABLE 13.2 *(cont.)*

Batch Command	Description
IF ERRORLEVEL	Makes execution of a command contingent on the ERRORLEVEL variable (also called an exit code or return code). The full syntax for this command is `IF [NOT] ERRORLEVEL <0-255> <command>`

IF EXIST	Makes execution of a command contingent on the existence of a particular file. The full syntax is
	
	`IF [NOT] EXIST <filename> <command>`
	
	Here's how it might be used:
	
	`IF EXIST C:\WINWORD\*.BAK DEL C:\WINWORD\*.BAK`
	
	This line would check the \WINWORD directory for any files ending with .BAK and delete any it finds.

PAUSE <message>	Pauses the execution of a batch file, displays the message "Press any key to continue…," and waits for a keystroke before proceeding.
REM<string>	Lets you add remarks to a file; this line is displayed when the batch file is run unless ECHO OFF is in force, or unless you start the line with @REM.
SHIFT	Shifts the %<0-9> variables down one position. For example, when you use the SHIFT command, the value of %0 is replaced by the value of %1; the value of %2 then replaces %1, and so on.

You can combine these batch commands with any valid DOS commands. A complete discussion of the syntax, usage, and power of batch files is a book in itself, but this list demonstrates their power. Refer to your DOS documentation for a complete description of batch file commands.

Insider's Tip

Batch files can be useful both for starting Windows and for running DOS applications within Windows. For example, you could set up a batch file to do all these operations: load any TSRs needed by a particular application; set any temporary environment variables or options the program needs; and start the program in a mode that works best with Windows.

Batch files can be started with .PIFs, thus creating a powerful combination of DOS configuration tools; see Chapter 14 for more information about PIFs and the PIF Editor. Also, each time you run Windows in 386 enhanced mode, a special batch file, WINSTART.BAT, is started.

The AUTOEXEC.BAT batch file is most often used to set the PATH, install SMARTDrive, create a temporary \TEMP subdirectory, load TSRs and other utilities, install device drivers, and log your computer onto a network. The format of the file is very simple: each command must be on its own line and must end with a return. You can enter comments, which must be preceded by the letters REM.

The general form of the AUTOEXEC.BAT batch file is

```
<command> <argument>
REM comments
```

where <command> is a valid DOS command and <argument> represents any legitimate combination of options, parameters, and switches that COM-MAND.COM will allow for that particular command.

The Very Important PATH. Perhaps the single most important line in your AUTOEXEC.BAT file—at least as far as Windows is concerned—is the PATH statement line. The PATH statement tells DOS which directories to search if it fails to find an item in your current working directory—that is, in the directory currently being accessed by DOS. In DOS terminology, this is called the **command search path**.

PATH can be used either as a DOS command or as a statement with an argument. To use it as a command, simply type PATH at the DOS prompt; and DOS replies by displaying its current command search path. The PATH statement takes the form

```
PATH <drive:><path>;<drive:><path>;<drive:><path>...
```

where the paths are separated by a semicolon (;) and only the first instance of a <drive:> need be listed. For example, the form

```
PATH <drive:><path>;<path>;<path>...
```

would also be acceptable, provided that all the listed paths were on the same drive.

The forms can be mixed—if you have more than one drive, you could use the form

```
PATH <drive:><path>;<path>;<path>...;<drive:><path>;<path>;
<path>...
```

As a minimum requirement for an AUTOEXEC.BAT statement in Windows, you must include a PATH statement that tells DOS where to find your main Windows directory. Without a proper search path, DOS can't run any programs that are not in the current directory. Thus, if you are in the root directory, which is the usual locale for starting your system, you will not be able to run Windows until the PATH is set. Otherwise, if you type WIN at the DOS prompt of the root directory, you'll see this common DOS error message: "Bad command or file name."

A minimalist PATH statement that lets DOS know where to find Windows might be

```
PATH C:\WINDOWS
```

assuming that c:\WINDOWS is the correct drive and directory name for your main Windows directory. This line would meet the minimum requirement for an AUTOEXEC.BAT file for a single-user Windows system, so if you don't have an AUTOEXEC.BAT file, you could try to create a bare-bones one that contained this line.

By default, DOS limits its environment space, which includes the PATH statement, to a maximum length of 127 characters. This cutoff point can create problems when one of your installation programs—either Windows or DOS—automatically updates your AUTOEXEC.BAT file by appending its newly created directory to the PATH statement in the file. If the 127-character limit is exceeded, the PATH statement will be ignored altogether; no path will be set; and DOS will probably not be able to find any of your programs. As a result, you'll get the "Bad command or file name" error message.

To avoid this problem, include a SHELL= statement in your CONFIG.SYS file to increase the environment space. As shown earlier in this chapter, the statement

```
SHELL=C:\COMMAND.COM /P /E:1024
```

when entered in the CONFIG.SYS files, increases the DOS environment space to 1024.

Another way to prevent your PATH from overflowing is to trim any redundant information, such as the redundant drive letters listed when installation programs automatically update your path statement. For example, the path

```
PATH C:\DOS5;C:\DBASE;C:\NORTON;C:\WINDOWS;C:\WINWORD;
C:\EXCEL; C:\BOOKSTUF;C:\LETTERS;C:\WINDEV;C:\ACTOR;C:\CORELDRW
```

could shed redundant drive letters and be reduced to this:

```
PATH C:\DOS5;\DBASE;\NORTON\WINDOWS;\WINWORD;\EXCEL;\BOOKSTUF;
\LETTERS;\WINDEV;\ACTOR;\CORELDRW
```

Setting Up SMARTDrive. SMARTDrive is a disk-caching utility that speeds up disk access by storing frequently accessed data from your disk drives in RAM. As discussed earlier, the new SMARTDrive for Windows 3.1 now loads SMARTDRV.EXE from the AUTOEXEC.BAT file; in Windows 3.0, SMARTDRV.SYS was loaded from CONFIG.SYS.

The SMARTDrive statement offers many options (described fully in Chapter 12). Although the number of options may seem overwhelming, for most purposes you only need to remember these three basic command line parameters for SMARTDrive:

```
<[drive][+ or -]...>
<initial size>
<windows size>
```

These parameters are used in the basic form for the SMARTDrive statement line

```
SMARTDRV.EXE<[drive][+ or -]...> <initial size> <windows size>
```

Here's what these three options do:

<[drive][+ or –]...> — Specifies the letters of the disk drives that you want SMARTDrive to cache. If no drive letter is specified, all physical drives on the system are cached, with two exceptions: floppy drives are cached for reading from the drive only, and CD ROM and network drives are not cached. The optional plus sign (+) enables both read and write caching for a particular drive, whereas the minus sign (–) disables all caching for that drive. If no sign is specified, read caching is turned on and write caching is turned off for that drive.

<initial size> — Specifies in kilobytes the size of SMARTDrive when it starts or when Windows is not running. If you don't specify a value, SMARTDrive will use up to 2 megabytes of extended memory (depending on how much you have available).

<windows size> — Tells Windows to shrink SMARTDrive up to the specified number of kilobytes if additional extended memory is required.

A sample SMARTDrive statement line in your AUTOEXEC.BAT file might look like this:

```
SMARTDRV.EXE 1024 512
```

This line creates a SMARTDrive with 1024K, or 1 megabyte, when it first starts. Because no drive letter is specified, all hard disk drives on the system are cached for both read and write operations, and floppy disk drives are cached for read operations only. If a Windows application runs out of memory with this setting, Windows automatically requests 512K back from SMARTdrive's 1024K cache and holds onto that memory for its own use for the remainder of the session, unless you issue the SMARTDRV/R command. When you quit Windows, SMARTdrive reclaims the 512K and sets the cache size back to 1024K.

If your computer's BIOS is dated earlier than 1990, you may need to use the double-buffering option of SMARTDrive. To set it up, use the line

```
DEVICE=SMARTDRV.EXE /DOUBLE_BUFFER
```

This line should be placed in your CONFIG.SYS file. To determine whether you need this statement, refer to Chapter 12.

The LOADHIGH Command. This command is used to load TSRs and other memory-resident programs into your system's upper memory area for the purpose of freeing RAM in your critical 640K of conventional memory. The LOADHIGH statement takes the following form:

```
LOADHIGH <filename> <parameters>
```

where <filename> is the name of a program you want to load in upper memory (be sure to include the full directory PATH), and <parameters> designates any optional parameters or switches required by the program. As discussed earlier in the chapter, to use the LOADHIGH command you must include the UMB option in your DOS= statement of CONFIG.SYS, and you must also load the EMM386 memory manager. See the discussion of memory management later in this chapter for further details.

Setting Up MOUSE.COM. Windows includes both the MOUSE.SYS and the MOUSE.COM device drivers to support the use of a mouse with mouse-capable DOS applications. If you use your mouse only with Windows applications, you won't need to install either. If you do need a DOS-level mouse driver, the MOUSE.COM driver is preferred because it provides more features. However, if the MOUSE.COM driver causes incompatibilities with your system, you can install the MOUSE.SYS driver with CONFIG.SYS.

To install MOUSE.COM, you can use the following statement line:

```
C:\WINDOWS\MOUSE.COM /Y
```

The /Y switch disables the use of a "sprite" cursor, which can cause compatibility problems with some Windows video drivers. If you are using a mouse other than Microsoft's, you should refer to its documentation about the operation of its device drivers.

The SET Command. The SET can be used for two different actions. When issued as a command from the DOS prompt, or used on a line by itself without arguments, SET displays the current environment settings. In its second role—when used in a statement with the proper arguments—the Set command substitutes one string of characters in the DOS environment variable table for another. To identify the settings for your DOS environment variables—programs sometimes change the settings after startup without telling you—simply start a COMMAND.COM session in Windows and type SET. For example, if you issued the command from a DOS prompt run in Windows, your system might reply with something like this:

```
COMSPEC=C:\DOS\COMMAND.COM
PATH=C:\WINDOWS;C:\DOS;C:\WINWORD;C:\EXCEL;C:\CORELDRW
PROMPT=[$T] $P$G
TEMP=E:\TEMP
windir=C:\WINDOWS
```

which is a list of the information DOS is storing in its environment space.

Insider's Tip

The last line of the sample report issued by the SET command is

```
windir=C:\WINDOWS
```

This is a special environment variable created by Windows that tells you from which directory Windows is running.

The SET command used in a statement line takes the form

```
SET <environment string>=<substitute string>
```

where <environment string> is the string of characters in the environment variable table that you want to replace, and <substitute string> is the replacement.

The SET command is commonly used in conjunction with the TEMP environment variable to set the TEMP directory, a disk area many programs use, much like a scratchpad, to store temporary files created by a program while it is running. During the Windows installation process, Setup creates a subdirectory called \TEMP inside your main Windows directory and places a line in your AUTOEXEC.BAT file similar to this one:

```
SET TEMP=C:\WINDOWS\TEMP
```

This example assumes that your main Windows directory is called \WIN-DOWS and is located on the C: drive.

Here's how to use the SET statement and the TEMP variable together in your AUTOEXEC.BAT file to redirect the temporary files used by Windows applications to any other drive or subdirectory. If you have installed a RAM disk, such as RAMDRIVE.SYS, instruct your system to tell applications to use your RAM disk instead of your hard disk for storage of temporary files. For example, if you set your RAM disk up as drive D:, you would use the line

```
SET TEMP=D:\
```

This example assumes that your RAMDrive is in the D: volume. However, if your hard disk contains multiple partitions that are assigned separate volume letters or network drives, your RAMDrive may be in another volume. To find the location, look in File Manager for the RAM disk volume icon on the icon bar at the top of the directory tree window. Then adjust the line in AUTOEXEC.BAT to reflect the actual drive letter of the RAMDrive.

You can also use the TEMP statement in AUTOEXEC.BAT to redirect the temporary files used by Windows applications to any other drive or sub-directory. In the previous example, I set the path to D:\ to indicate that the temporary files were to be stored in the root directory of the RAMDrive, which was assigned the drive letter D:.

However, you can redirect temporary files to any specific directory on your hard disk by typing a statement line, such as

```
SET TEMP=C:\TEMPFILE
```

This will save the temporary files in a directory called TEMPFILE on your C volume. Make sure that you have created the directory before you assign it to store temporary files. To create such a directory, you can use either File Manager's Create Directory command or the DOS command MKDIR.

If you have more than one hard disk, store your temporary files on your fastest hard disk. But beware: using a network volume for temporary files will considerably slow down your operations and possibly stall certain applications.

Insider's Tip

Many Windows programs use this \TEMP directory as a repository for their temporary files. Unfortunately, if you crash a program or otherwise un-expectedly quit, the temporary files will not be deleted; in fact, they can proliferate to the point where they consume a significant amount of hard disk space. Graphics programs are more likely to proliferate in this way than are other kinds of applications. Check your \TEMP directory to see whether you're garnering a backlog: if you are, you'll see .TMP files with old file creation dates.

It's not a good idea to delete temporary files while Windows is running because you might be using one of the files. Instead, before Windows is started, add a line to your AUTOEXEC.BAT file that will weed the directory. For example, if your \TEMP subdirectory is located in the \WINDOWS directory on your C: drive, you'd add this line:

```
IF EXIST C:\WINDOWS\TEMP\*.TMP DEL C:\WINDOWS\TEMP\*.TMP
```

This line searches for any files in the \TEMP directory that end in .TMP, and zaps them.

The PROMPT Statement. With the PROMPT statement you can format the appearance of the DOS prompt and specify what information it should include. Although you don't need this statement for Windows, I recommend that you set your prompt to include your current path, so that you can identify the directory in which you are working.

The default DOS prompt lists only the drive, followed by a greater-than sign (>), to create the ubiquitous

```
C>
```

If you want to set the prompt so that it will display the current path, type the line

```
PROMPT=$P$G
```

into your AUTOEXEC.BAT file. The next time the batch file is run, your DOS prompt will look like this:

```
C:\WINDOWS
```

assuming that you were logged into the Windows directory. The PROMPT statement accepts as arguments the tokens listed in Table 13.3.

You can combine text and these tokens with almost any other characters or numbers to create a practically limitless variety of prompts. For example, the statement

```
PROMPT You are here: $P$G
```

would create the prompt

```
You are here: C:\WINDOWS
```

• • • • • • • • • • • • •
TABLE 13.3

Type This Token	To Create This Item in Your Prompt
$B	| (the pipe character; ASCII 124)
$D	(the current system date)
$E	Esc (the escape character; ASCII 27)
$G	> (the greater than sign; ASCII 62)
$H	Backspace (ASCII 8; erases a character from the prompt)
$L	< (the less than sign; ASCII 60)
$N	(the current drive letter)
$P	(the current directory path)
$Q	= (the equal sign; ASCII 61)
$T	(the current system time)
$V	(the version number of DOS that is running)
$_	Enter+linefeed (ASCII 13, ASCII 10; advances to next line)
$$	$ (the dollar sign; ASCII 36)

Or you can get really crazy and create all sorts of weird prompts, even multiple-line ones. The PROMPT statement

```
PROMPT $Lo$G $Lo$G$_ $B$_ (___) $P$G
```

would present you with this (inter)face for DOS

```
<o> <o>
    |
(___) C:\WINDOWS
```

This example shows how characters other than text and tokens can be used in the PROMPT statement. It uses tokens, case-sensitive text, spaces, parentheses, the underline character, and the $_ token (twice) to create a three-line prompt.

Insider's Tip

An undocumented feature of Windows 3.1 lets you specify a special DOS prompt that is used in DOS sessions started from within Windows. To use this special feature, you need to choose the SET command to assign a new prompt to the WINPMT environment variable. Then, whenever Windows is run, the prompt specified in the PROMPT statement is exchanged with the one specified in the SET WINPMT= statement.

For example, the following two lines:

```
PROMPT $P$G
SET WINPMT=Windows is Running! $P$G
```

would give you the standard prompt

```
C:\WINDOWS
```

when you were running DOS but not Windows. When you do run Windows and then initiate a DOS session from within Windows, you would see the special Windows prompt:

```
Windows is Running! C:\WINDOWS
```

This provides a handy reminder that you are running DOS from within Windows—which is easy to forget if you're running a full-screen DOS session. If you type the SET command by itself from the DOS prompt within Windows for a report about your current environment, you'll see that the PROMPT and SET WINPMT= statements are reversed. This is because Windows has exchanged one for the other. However, when you quit Windows, the PROMPT and WINPMT variables are returned to their original status, and you'll have your normal DOS prompt back again.

The DATE, TIME, and VER Statements. DATE, TIME, and VER are three innocuous commands you might encounter in your AUTOEXEC.BAT file. DATE and TIME display or set the date and time of your computer's internal clock; VER displays whatever version of DOS you are using. All three commands are usually used on a line by themselves; although both DATE and TIME accept arguments in their statement line, they are rarely set from the AUTOEXEC.BAT file. If either TIME or DATE is placed on a line, the current time or date appears and prompts you for a change. For example, the line

```
TIME
```

causes your AUTOEXEC.BAT file to tell DOS to display

```
Current time is 12:31:44.98a
Enter new time:
```

and then pause until you enter a new time. Or, if you want to accept the time displayed—which is taken from your system clock—press Enter and AUTOEXEC.BAT will continue processing. Similarly, the line DATE causes DOS to display

```
Current date is Tue 02-12-1991
Enter new date (mm-dd-yy):
```

and then pause until you enter a new date or a confirmation of this date (press the Enter key).

The VER command accepts no arguments. For example, the statement line

```
VER
```

causes DOS to display the message

```
MS-DOS Version 5.0
```

or whatever other DOS version you are running.

Other AUTOEXEC.BAT Commands. Batch files, such as an AUTOEXEC.BAT file, can contain a wide variety of DOS commands and statements. The commands and statements discussed earlier include most of what Windows users will need to know, but there are a few other commands that can help you maneuver around your system more easily.

The COPY command, for example, lets you copy some special files into a working directory or a RAM disk when you first start your system. For example, the RAMDRIVE.SYS RAM disk included with Windows creates a new empty RAM disk each time you start your system. If you want to use certain files from your RAM disk, you'll need to recopy them into the RAM drive with a statement in your AUTOEXEC.BAT file, such as

```
COPY C:\WINDOWS\RAMSTUFF\SLOPROG.* D:\
```

This line copies the various files (SLOPROG.EXE, SLOPROG.OVL, SLOPROG.TMP, etc.) associated with the SLOPROG program onto a RAM disk configured as the D: drive.

Another handy command is PAUSE, which suspends the processing of a batch file until another key is pressed—unless you press Control+C, which aborts the batch file and returns you to the DOS prompt. The PAUSE command displays the message "Press any key to continue," and you can add another message that will precede it by using the <comment> option.

The command takes the form

```
PAUSE <comment>
```

where <comment> is the message you want to display when the batch file pauses. If you take the Control+C escape route, DOS responds with the message

```
Terminate batch job (Y/N)?
```

Type Y to get the prompt; if you type N, DOS resumes processing the batch file.

Certain DOS commands, such as APPEND, are known memory hogs, so—if you can get away with it—you may want to disable such lines with REM statements. To help you decide what to disable, here's a description of some other DOS commands found in AUTOEXEC.BAT files:

➤ **CD <path>** Changes directories or displays working directory

➤ **CLS** Clears the screen

➤ **MEM </C or /P or /D>** Displays information about memory usage

➤ **MODE <parameters>** Sets modes and options for various devices

➤ **VERIFY <ON or OFF>** Verifies that files are written to disk properly

These commands are not needed for Windows per se, but some may be used in statements that are necessary for your particular system configuration.

Some commands are not healthy for Windows and should be avoided. Here are some DOS commands that are Windows unfriendly:

➤ **APPEND** Sets a DOS search path for data files

➤ **ASSIGN** Reassigns a drive letter to another drive

➤ **JOIN** Joins a specified disk drive to a path

➤ **SUBST** Substitutes a specified string for a path

Because the APPEND, ASSIGN, JOIN, and SUBST commands alter drive and path information, they may cause Windows to become confused about the actual location of your files.

Putting It All Together

Now that I've reviewed many of the intricacies and ecstasies of editing the CONFIG.SYS and AUTOEXEC.BAT files, it's time to put it all together and create some sample files. You can use these sample CONFIG.SYS and AUTOEXEC.BAT files as a starting place for creating your own.

The following is a simple CONFIG.SYS file:

```
DEVICE=C:\WINDOWS\HIMEM.SYS
FILES=30
BUFFERS=10
STACKS=9,256
```

```
SHELL=C:\DOS\COMMAND.COM /P
INSTALL=C:\DOS\SHARE.EXE
```

This example loads the HIMEM.SYS memory manager; sets the FILES=, BUFFERS=, and STACKS= statements to the recommended settings for use with Windows; specifies the SHELL as COMMAND.COM with the /P switch to load it permanently; and installs SHARE.EXE to prevent file-sharing conflicts.

Here's a somewhat more complex example of a CONFIG.SYS file:

```
DEVICE=C:\WINDOWS\HIMEM.SYS
FILES=30
BUFFERS=10
STACKS=9,256
SHELL=C:\DOS\COMMAND.COM /P /E:1024
INSTALL=C:\DOS\SHARE.EXE /F:4096 /L:25
DEVICE=C:\DOS\SETVER.EXE
DEVICE=C:\WINDOWS\SMARTDRV.EXE /double_buffer
LASTDRIVE=G
```

This example does everything the simple example does and also

➥ Adds the /E:1024 switch to the SHELL statement to increase the DOS environment space to 1024 bytes (1K)

➥ Uses the /F:4096 switch to increase the amount of file space allocated to SHARE.EXE from the default of 2048 (2K) to 4096 (4K), and uses the /L:25 switch to increase the number of file locks from the default of 20 to 25

➥ Loads the DOS version table with SETVER.EXE

➥ Installs the SMARTDrive double-buffer feature

➥ Specifies that the last allowable DOS volume is G, which provides for a maximum of seven volumes

Here's an example of a simple AUTOEXEC.BAT file:

```
C:\WINDOWS\SMARTDRV.EXE
PATH C:\WINDOWS;\DOS;
PROMPT $P$G
WIN
```

This example

➥ Loads the SMARTDrive disk cache with its default settings

➤ Sets the path so that DOS can find files in the \WINDOWS and \DOS directories

➤ Sets the DOS prompt so that it includes the path information

➤ Starts the Windows environment

The last line starts the Windows environment as if you had typed WIN, so this file automatically runs Windows whenever you turn on your system.

Let's say you want to build an escape hatch, so that you can exit before the WIN command. With a slightly more complex script, here's how you could add, among other things, a PAUSE statement to your AUTOEXEC.BAT file:

```
C:\WINDOWS\SMARTDRV.EXE
PROMPT $P$G
SET WINPMT=[Windows] $P$G
PATH C:\WINDOWS;\DOS;
SET TEMP=C:\WINDOWS\TEMP
IF EXIST C:\WINDOWS\TEMP\*.TMP DEL C:\WINDOWS\TEMP\*.TMP
C:\WINDOWS\MOUSE.COM /Y
PAUSE
WIN
```

Here's how this AUTOEXEC.BAT file expands on the first example:

➤ The SET WINPMT= statement changes the DOS prompt in DOS sessions that are run from within Windows, to remind you that Windows is running.

➤ The SET TEMP= statement specifies the directory that should be used to store temporary files.

➤ The IF EXIST command line deletes any leftover temporary files it finds in the \TEMP directory.

➤ The MOUSE.COM version of the Microsoft mouse driver is loaded, so that you can use the mouse with DOS programs.

➤ The PAUSE command stops the execution of the AUTOEXEC.BAT file before starting Windows and displays the message "Press any key to continue" so that you can return to the DOS prompt by pressing Control+C, or start Windows by pressing any other key.

Controlling Memory Management with the DOS Startup Files

CONFIG.SYS and AUTOEXEC.BAT allow you to control how memory is used by your system—in other words, you can use these two files to load and configure the memory management software for your system. More specifically, by knowing how to manage your system's memory, you can

➥ Resolve the conflicts that might arise from competition for the use of your system's upper memory area

➥ Improve the performance of your system by optimizing the use of memory

➥ Free more of the 640K conventional memory area for use by DOS applications

➥ Provide expanded memory to those DOS applications that require it

DOS 5 allows you to load the operating system, memory-resident programs such as TSRs, and DOS device drivers into the upper memory area above the 640K threshold—all without using any third-party memory management utilities. And in conjunction with the HIMEM.SYS and EMM386.EXE memory managers included with Windows 3.1, DOS 5 also lets you use extended memory and expanded memory, and load software above 640K.

Installing and Configuring HIMEM.SYS

Some sort of extended memory manager is essential to running Windows. Microsoft provides the HIMEM.SYS extended memory manager with Windows 3.1.

When running in standard mode, Windows relies on HIMEM.SYS to provide access to extended memory. And even though Windows handles its own memory management while running in 386 enhanced mode, it still depends on HIMEM.SYS to load itself into extended memory. The bottom line is that you can't run Windows without HIMEM.SYS or an equivalent extended memory manager.

The HIMEM.SYS extended memory manager combines the unused portion of your 640K of conventional memory with your system's extended memory to create a pool of memory that can be made available to Windows. Windows

Setup installs the the HIMEM.SYS memory manager into your system by placing a statement line in your CONFIG.SYS file. Because Windows depends on the services of HIMEM.SYS to load itself and its drivers into your system, the line in CONFIG.SYS that loads HIMEM.SYS must come before any other statement lines for other system software—such as SMARTDrive or RAMDrive—that use extended memory. It's usually prudent to load the HIMEM.SYS before any other devices as well.

The HIMEM.SYS statement takes the form

```
DEVICE=<path>HIMEM.SYS <switches>
```

The <path> is the drive and directory path that identifies the location of the HIMEM.SYS file included with Windows (make sure it's not the version installed by DOS). The HIMEM.SYS file should always be on the same drive as your other DOS system files. The <switches> are any of the optional switches listed in Table 13.4. Note that the first two, /HMAMIN and /NUMHANDLES, are used only with standard mode. If you don't include a switch, HIMEM.SYS uses the default values for that option.

TABLE 13.4

Switch	Description
/HMAMIN= <minimum>	Specifies, in kilobytes, the minimum amount of extended memory that an application running in standard mode must request before HIMEM.SYS lets that application use the high memory area. The value of <minimum> can be any number from 0 to 63. The default value, applied if this switch is not used, is 0. When set to 0, HIMEM allots high memory to the first application that requests it, regardless of how much it will use.
/NUMHANDLES= <handles>	Specifies the maximum number of Extended Memory Block (EMB) handles that can be used at once when Windows is running in standard mode. The value can be any number between 1 and 128, but keep in mind that each handle consumes 6 bytes of RAM. The default value is 32.
/A20CONTROL: <ON or OFF>	Tells HIMEM.SYS how it should control the A20 handler, which allows your system to access the high memory area. The default is ON. You need to set this switch to OFF only if the A20 handler was off when HIMEM.SYS was loaded.

• • • • • • • • • • • • • •
TABLE 13.4 *(cont.)*

Switch	Description
/CPUCLOCK:<ON or OFF>	Resolves an incompatibility with some systems in which HIMEM.SYS inadvertently changes the clock speed of your processor. If you encounter this problem, set the switch to ON; this will eliminate the problem but slows down HIMEM.SYS. The default is OFF.
/EISA	Tells HIMEM.SYS that your computer contains an EISA bus with more than 16 megabytes of extended memory (lucky you!). Use this switch in conjunction with the /INT15= switch to reserve any extended memory for device drivers or applications that use the Int 15h/88h BIOS call.
/INT15= <kilobytes>	Specifies the number of kilobytes of extended memory reserved for use by Interrupt 15h. Some DOS applications use Interrupt 15h to access extended memory, rather than using the XMS method applied by HIMEM.SYS. The default value is 0, which turns this feature off. The value (other than 0) can be any number from 64 to 65535. Generally, you should set <kilobytes> to a value that is 64 kilobytes larger than the amount needed by the DOS application.
/SHADOWRAM: <ON or OFF>	Turns the shadow RAM feature on or off. The shadow RAM feature copies the ROM data into RAM, which operates faster, but uses some extended memory. If you have less than 2 megabytes of RAM, HIMEM.SYS tries to turn shadow RAM off and reclaim the extended memory for Windows, but this can slow down your system slightly. You can force HIMEM to keep the shadow RAM option on by setting the switch to ON.
/MACHINE:<code>	Tells HIMEM.SYS the type of computer on which it's running. HIMEM.SYS normally detects the machine type automatically; but if it can't, it uses the IBM AT-compatible default. The value of <code> can be either the <name code> or the <number code> listed in Table 13.5. My preference is to use the name code, even though it takes longer to enter, because it's easier to interpret when you view the file.

Table 13.5 lists the computer <name code> and <number code> values that can be used in conjunction with the /MACHINE: switch.

•••••••••••••••
TABLE 13.5

Computer	<name code>	<number code>
Acer 1100	acer1100	6
AT&T 6300 Plus	att6300plus	5
Bull Micral 60	bullmicral	16
CSS Labs systems	css	12
HP Vectra	fasthp	14
HP Vectra (A and A+)	hpvectra	4
IBM AT compatible (default)	at	1
IBM PC/AT	at1	11
IBM PC/AT (alternative delay)	at2	12
IBM PC/AT (alternative delay)	at3	13
IBM PS/2	ps2	2
IBM 7552 Industrial Computer	ibm7552	15
Philips systems	philips	13
Phoenix Cascade BIOS	ptlcascade	3
Toshiba 1600 & 1200XE	toshiba	7
Tulip SX	tulip	9
Wyse 12.5 Mhz 286	wyse	8
Zenith with ZBIOS	zenith	10

When Windows is running in standard mode, HIMEM.SYS performs the memory management functions for Windows. However, in 386 enhanced mode, Windows assumes the functions of memory management provided by HIMEM.SYS and EMM386. Although Windows does not use the HIMEM.SYS driver when running in 386 enhanced mode, Windows still requires it to gain initial access to your system's extended memory.

The options and switches listed in Tables 13.4 and 13.5 control how HIMEM.SYS works with your memory. These options are set using the CONFIG.SYS file. On the other hand, to control how Windows allocates memory, you need to edit the SYSTEM.INI file, which contains separate sections for standard mode and enhanced 386 mode operation. Refer to Chapter 15 for information on how to control Windows' use of memory by editing the SYSTEM.INI file.

MS DOS 5 includes its own versions of HIMEM.SYS and EMM386.EXE; however, make sure to use the versions of these utilities that come with Windows, not the ones supplied with DOS 5.

· ·

Loading Drivers and Software into Upper Memory

DOS users can tune up their systems by loading device drivers, TSRs, and other memory-resident software into unused memory addresses in the upper memory area. This frees up more of the 640K conventional memory area. To take advantage of this important technique, you will need to use EMM386 or a third-party memory manager, such as QEMM, 386MAX, BlueMAX, or NetRoom. I'll discuss two of these utilities to demonstrate how they work:

➤ **EMM386** Windows includes this memory manager.

➤ **QEMM** This is my personal favorite among the third-party memory managers.

If you are using a different third-party memory management utility, you're on your own, and should use the utility's documentation for guidelines. You can also refer to the general discussion of memory in Chapter 12 if you're new to this complex, and often vexing, topic.

The EMM386.EXE Memory Management Utility. The EMM386.EXE utility program manages the use of your computer's upper memory area—that is, the space above 640K but below the 1-megabyte mark. EMM386.EXE uses the upper memory area for two distinctly different purposes:

➤ To emulate expanded memory for DOS programs when Windows is not running

➤ To load device drivers and TSRs into the upper memory area before Windows is run; this frees space in the 640K user RAM area

As its name implies, EMM386 works only with systems that use a 386 or higher processor. The background information about EMM386 is presented in Chapter 13; this section describes how to install and configure EMM386 using the DOS startup files discussed earlier in this chapter.

Windows and its applications don't use expanded memory; they need extended memory. Many DOS applications, on the other hand, either require or can use expanded memory. Here's how you can provide your DOS applications with expanded memory:

➤ If you have a 386 or higher processor, run Windows in 386 enhanced mode. This automatically creates expanded memory for your DOS programs without using EMM386. To allocate expanded memory to a DOS application, specify the amount needed in the application's .PIF file.

➤ If you have a 386 or high processor, you can use EMM386 to emulate expanded memory when Windows is not running.

➤ If you are running Windows in standard mode—with a 286, 386, or higher processor—you must use an expanded memory card.

Remember that DOS applications launched from *within* Windows can obtain expanded memory from the memory management system provided by Windows in 386 enhanced mode. EMM386.EXE is only necessary if you plan to run expanded memory applications *outside* of Windows or if you wish to take advantage of DOS 5's ability to load software into free UMBs in the upper memory area. Once again, here is the diffference between UMA and UMB: the upper memory area (UMA) is the entire region between 640K and 1024K, whereas an upper memory block (UMB) is a contiguous address range within the upper memory area.

DOS 5 frees space in the critical 640K of conventional memory by automatically loading the operating system kernel above 1 megabyte into the high memory area (HMA) when you install it. The HMA is the first 64K of extended memory, and does not consume any of your upper memory area. To further free space in the 640K conventional memory area, DOS 5 lets you use the upper memory area —which is normally reserved for adapter ROM and the computer's BIOS—to load TSRs, device drivers, and other memory-resident software that would otherwise consume part of the precious 640K of conventional memory.

Installing and Configuring EMM386. To install the EMM386.EXE memory management utility, you need to specify it in your CONFIG.SYS file. To do so, add the line specifying EMM386.EXE directly after the line that specifies HIMEM.SYS. Be sure to disable any other statement lines that install other expanded memory managers, such as QEMM, because only one can be active at a time.

The comand line in CONFIG.SYS that installs EMM386 takes the form

```
DEVICE=<path>EMM386.EXE <ON or OFF or AUTO> <kilobytes>
<switches>
```

The <path> is the drive and path of the EMM386.EXE file, but it can be omitted if it's in the root directory of your boot disk. The <ON or OFF or AUTO> options control the activity of EMM386. ON is the default and runs EMM386 normally; OFF deactivates EMM386; and AUTO places EMM386 in a special automatic mode that turns it on only if a DOS program requests the use of expanded memory.

You can use EMM386 as a DOS command in conjunction with one of these options to change the status of EMM386 after it has started. For example, if you type the command

```
EMM386 OFF
```

at the DOS prompt, it turns EMM386 off, thereby disabling expanded memory. Note that you can't turn EMM386 off if anything has been loaded into upper memory.

The <kilobytes> option specifies how many kilobytes of extended memory you want EMM386 to make available to your DOS applications as expanded memory. You can use any value from 16 to 32768, but EMM386 always rounds the value down to the nearest multiple of 16. If you don't specify a value for the <kilobytes> option, EMM386 uses a default of 256K. Here's an example of an EMM386 statement line in CONFIG.SYS:

```
DEVICE=C:\WINDOWS\EMM386.EXE 512
```

This line tells EMM386 to allocate 512K of extended memory as expanded memory (when you're not running Windows). To allocate 1 megabyte (1024K), for example, as expanded memory, simply change the 512 to 1024.

The <switches> option lets you choose from among a host of special command switches that control how EMM386 uses the memory in your system. By setting these switches, you can specify the location of the 64K EMS page frame and control which addresses EMM386 uses for the 16K EMS pages. Usually you won't have to use these switches, because EMM386 uses default values that work in most cases. The default values are applied if you don't use a switch.

But if you want to do some tweaking, you can use as many of these switches as you need, and in any order—provided they follow the <kilobytes> option (if you have used it). Table 13.6 shows all the switches that EMM386 recognizes.

You can tap into the upper memory area by installing EMM386 with either the RAM or the NOEMS option. When either the RAM or the NOEMS switch is applied, EMM386 searches for any unused UMBs and substitutes the addresses with RAM, allowing DOS to relocate device drivers or TSR programs that would normally consume some of the 640K of conventional

TABLE 13.6

Switches	Description
A=<**alternate registers**>	Designates the number of fast alternate register sets you want EMM386 to use. This can be any number between 0 and 254; the default number is 7. Note that every alternate register set you specify adds about 200 bytes to the amount that EMM386.EXE consumes of your system's memory.
B=<**address**>	Specifies the lowest address that EMM386 should use for bank-switching of 16K pages. The value of <address> can be any memory location in the 1000h–4000h range. The default is never to use an address lower than 4000:0000.
D=<**kilobytes**>	Specifies the number of kilobytes of memory that should be reserved for buffered DMA (direct memory access). This can be any number between 16 and 256. The value should represent the largest DMA transfer you anticipate will occur when EMM386.EXE is running, excluding DMA by the floppy disk drive. The default value is 16.
FRAME= <**address**>	Specifies the base address for the 64K page frame. You can specify any value for <address>, from 8000h to 9000h and from C000h to E000h, but only in increments of 400h. If you don't specify an address, EMM386 uses the first contiguous 64K of upper memory it finds, but never places the page frame below C000:0000. If you use the FRAME= switch, you cannot use the M or /P switch.
H=<**handles**>	Specifies the maximum number of handles that EMM386 can use, which can be any number between 1 and 255; the default is 64.
L=<**minimum kilobytes**>	Sets the minimum number of kilobytes of extended memory that you want to be available in your system after loading EMM386.
M<**address code**>	A number from 1 to 14 that specifies the base address EMM386 should use for the page frame. You should only use the <address code> values between 10 and 14 on systems with 512K of memory. If you use the M switch, you can't use the FRAME= or /P switch. Here

••••••••••••••
TABLE 13.6 *(cont.)*

Switches	Description
M<address code> *(cont.)*	are the <address code> values and their corresponding base memory addresses:

<address code>	Base Address
<1>	C000h
<2>	C400h
<3>	C800h
<4>	CC00h
<5>	D000h
<6>	D400h
<7>	D800h
<8>	DC00h
<9>	E000h
<10>	8000h
<11>	8400h
<12>	8800h
<13>	8C00h
<14>	9000h

Switches	Description
/P<page address>	The address of the page frame. You can specify any memory location from 8000h to 9000h and from C000h to E000h, but only in increments of 400h. Note that you can't use the /P switch with the FRAME= or M switch.
P<number>= <address>	Specifies the segment address for a specific 16K page. The <number> is the number of the 16K page and the <address> is the segment address for that page number. The value for <number> can be any number from 0 to 255. The value for <address> can be any memory location from 8000h to 9C00h and from C000h to EC00h, but only in increments of 400h. Also, the <address> values for page <number> values 0 through 3 must be contiguous memory addresses in order to be compatible with LIM 3.2. You can't use the P switch to specify addresses for pages 0 through 3 if you are also using the /P, FRAME=, or M switch.
X=<address1>- <address2>	Excludes a range of addresses between <address1> and <address2> so that EMM386 won't use any addresses in that range for an EMS page. The values for

	Switches	Description
TABLE 13.6 *(cont.)*	X=<**address1**>- <**address2**> *cont.*	<address1> and <address2> can be any memory locations between A000h and FFFFh, but the values are rounded down to the nearest 4K memory boundary. Note that the range specified in the X= switch takes precedence over the I= switch.
	I=<**address1**>- <**address2**>	Includes a range of addresses between <address1> and <address2> for an EMS page or for RAM. The values for <address1> and <address2> can be any memory locations between A000h and FFFFh, but the values are rounded down to the nearest 4K memory boundary. The range specified in the X= switch takes precedence over the I= switch.
	W=<**ON or OFF**>	Turns support for the Weitek Coprocessor on or off. W=ON turns it on, and W=OFF turns it off. The default is OFF.
	RAM	Lets EMM386 use both expanded memory and the upper memory area. You can only use the RAM switch with DOS version 5.0 or later.
	NOEMS	Lets EMM386 use the upper memory area but not expanded memory in order to make the 64K page frame available for loading TSRs, device drivers, or other software. You can only use the NOEMS switch with DOS 5 or later.

memory. This makes more of your 640K area available for Windows and DOS sessions started from within Windows.

The RAM option allows EMM386 to provide UMB management as well as expanded memory management for DOS programs. NOEMS configures EMM386 for UMB management only and disables the use of expanded memory. If you use the NOEMS option, you will not be able to use expanded memory at all, either with EMM386 or with Windows 386 enhanced mode's built-in expanded memory emulation capabilities.

Insider's Tip

Use the NOEMS switch if you aren't going to be running any DOS programs that require expanded memory. This option makes the 64K EMS page frame available for loading memory-resident software. Here's an example of a device driver line for EMM386:

```
DEVICE=C:\WINDOWS\EMM386.EXE NOEMS
```

The NOEMS switch makes the most upper memory available for device drivers, TSRs, and other memory-resident software.

If you plan to run DOS applications that use expanded memory only from within Windows 386 enhanced mode, you should use the RAM option in a statement such as

```
DEVICE=C:\WINDOWS\EMM386.EXE RAM
```

The RAM parameter allows EMM386 to manage DOS upper memory blocks, and reserves a 64K page frame in upper memory to emulate expanded memory for use by DOS programs.

To enable the UMBs for loading memory-resident software and to provide some expanded memory for DOS programs run outside of Windows, you could use a statement line such as

```
DEVICE=C:\WINDOWS\EMM386.EXE 512 RAM
```

The 512 near the end of this statement tells EMM386 to allocate 512K of memory as expanded memory; because this expanded memory is created in DOS, it is available for DOS applications when you're not running Windows.

Forcing EMM386 to Reclaim More Memory. When either the RAM or the NOEMS option is selected, EMM386.EXE searches for unused UMBs into which it can load device drivers and memory-resident software. Typically, EMM386 takes a timid tack: it will not reclaim all the possible address space in upper memory. Instead, the program only searches the area from C000-DFFF, in order to ensure the greatest degree of compatibility with devices or other software that might also make use of the upper memory area.

Often you can reclaim unused adresses below C800 and above DFFF by using the I= option, which forces EMM386 to include a particular address range. This technique helps locate extra space when you are using EMM386 with the RAM switch, which consumes 64K of your upper memory area for the EMS page frame.

In order to reclaim as much of your upper memory area as possible, you'll need to identify any empty address ranges. To do so, you can use the Microsoft Diagnostics program discussed in Chapter 17, or the MEM /P command from DOS. To get an accurate report from either method, of course, you'll need to quit Windows.

To print a memory usage report using Microsoft Diagnostics, choose the Print Report command from the program's File menu. With the MEM /P method, the report will probably be too long to view in a single screen, so you can redirect the output of the command to a printer connected to the LPT1: port by typing

```
MEM /P > LPT1:
```

at the DOS prompt. You can also redirect the output to a text file. For example, to redirect the MEM /P memory report to a file called MEMORY.TXT, type the command

```
MEM /P > MEMORY.TXT
```

Insider's Tip

For any DOS command that scrolls by too quickly for you to read, or if you want to keep a paper record of it, just redirect the output to a printer port or text file. If you send the output to a laser printer, you may need to manually send a form feed command to the printer to eject the page; this can often be done from the front panel of the printer.

For a headstart in finding free UMBs, try the following hexadecimal address ranges, which are typically overlooked by EMM386, but which may be reclaimed using the I= parameter:

➡ **B000–B7FF** A 32K unused monochrome video area on VGA systems

➡ **E000–EFFF** A 64K area reserved as a shadow RAM area with some BIOS setups, but not available on IBM PS/2 MCA machines

➡ **F000–F7FF** A 32K area not used by some Phoenix BIOS versions

➡ **F200–F2FF** and **F700–F7FF** Two 4K areas not used by some AMI BIOS versions

For example, if you are using a VGA system, you could probably force EMM386 to grab the B000-B7FF address area normally used by a monochome display adapter and thereby recover 32K of memory. To do this, you could use a statement line similar to this one:

```
DEVICE=C:\WINDOWS\EMM386.EXE I=B000-B7FF RAM
```

You can also use more than one I= switch to force EMM386 to include additional areas of upper memory. For example, if you're not using a PS/2, you can recover 64K in the E000–EFFF area; if you're not using a mono-chrome display adapter, you can probably grab 32K in the B000–B7FF area; and if you're using a clone that contains a Phoenix BIOS, you may be able to reclaim an additional 32K in the F000–F7FF area. To recover all three unused upper memory areas, for a total of 128K, you could use a statement line such as

```
DEVICE=C:\WINDOWS\EMM386.EXE I=B000-B7FF I=E000-EFFF I=F000-
F7FF RAM
```

Danger Zone

EMM386 sometimes ignores an address range because there might be an incompatibility. Therefore, if you choose to experiment with the I= parameter, be sure to have a backup boot disk on hand. To create such a disk, format a floppy disk with the Make System Disk option (from the DOS prompt you can format a boot disk by typing **FORMAT A:/S**) and copy your CONFIG.SYS and AUTOEXEC.BAT files onto it. Then, if your system locks up during or after the boot process because of a change you've made, you can reboot from the floppy disk and restore the original CONFIG.SYS values.

Relocating the EMS Page Frame. If you need to use expanded memory with your DOS programs run outside of Windows, EMM386 needs to allocate a contiguous 64K block of the upper memory area to use as an expanded memory page frame. On most systems, EMM386 places the 64K page frame at memory address D000h. Unfortunately, this may truncate the area in upper memory that you can use for loading programs and drivers.

For example, if your system's free memory ranges from C800h to EFFFh, and EMM386—by default—places the page frame at D000h, you will be left with two smaller blocks: one 32K block, from C800h to D000h, and another 64K block, from E000h to EFFFh. What's your solution if you have a TSR larger than 64K that you want to load into a single 96K block?

EMM386 provides several parameters that can be used to relocate the 64K page frame: FRAME=<address>, M<address code>, or /P<page address>. These three parameters, described earlier in this chapter, can all be used to achieve the same effect. In this section, I'll use the FRAME= parameter as the example.

Let's assume your system doesn't use the address range from C800–EFFF. You could relocate the EMS page frame to start at address C800h by typing

```
DEVICE=C:\WINDOWS\EMM386.EXE FRAME=C800 RAM
```

This would place the 64K page frame in the region C800–D7FF and would create a single 96K block of contiguous address space, from D800 to EFFF.

Insider's Tip

Adapter cards plugged into your computer's expansion bus use various address ranges that can fragment free space in the upper memory area. This can prevent EMM386 from finding a contiguous 64K block of upper memory to use as a page frame, or from being able to load a program or driver into upper memory.

To correct this situation, you can often relocate the address ranges used by the adapter cards. Changing the addresses used by an adapter card requires flipping DIP switches on the card, changing jumpers on the card, or running a special utility; check the documentation of your adapter cards to see if the memory addresses they use can be changed, and if so, how.

Loading Drivers and Software into Upper Memory Blocks. Once you've cleared out some contiguous space in your upper memory area, you're ready to load in device drivers, TSRs, and other memory-resident software and thus free the maximum amount of your 640K of conventional memory—the stuff you need for running DOS programs from within Windows.

As mentioned earlier, first you'll need to place the statement DOS=UMB in the CONFIG.SYS file. If possible, you should also try to load DOS into the high memory area with a DOS=HIGH statement. Better yet, you can combine the statements into a single line:

```
DOS=HIGH,UMB
```

To load device drivers into upper memory, change the lines in your CONFIG.SYS file that begin with the DEVICE= command to DEVICEHIGH=. For example, if your MOUSE.SYS driver is installed with the line

```
DEVICE=C:\WINDOWS\MOUSE.SYS /Y
```

you would change it to

```
DEVICEHIGH=C:\WINDOWS\MOUSE.SYS /Y
```

Similarly, to load TSRs and other memory-resident software into upper memory, change the lines that load them in your AUTOEXEC.BAT file by inserting the LOADHIGH command in front of the program name on the appropriate line. (Insider's Mini-tip: LOADHIGH can be abbreviated as LH.) For example, if your AUTOEXEC.BAT file installs the TSR version of the mouse driver, MOUSE.COM, with the line

```
C:\WINDOWS\MOUSE /Y
```

you could change it to

```
LOADHIGH C:\WINDOWS\MOUSE /Y
```

or you could save a few keystrokes and use the abbreviation

```
LH C:\WINDOWS\MOUSE /Y
```

Insider's Tip

You should use the LOADHIGH command in your AUTOEXEC.BAT file only for TSRs and other memory-resident programs that need to be available to *all* of the DOS sessions you start from within Windows. Otherwise, you'll overload your system with TSRs that only one or a few programs need—for these programs, load the TSRs directly within your DOS session after you've started Windows.

Danger Zone

Some device drivers will not work properly when loaded by the DEVICEHIGH= statement in your CONFIG.SYS file. So forsake your initial instincts to load all devices into the upper memory area right off the bat; instead, change the DEVICE= statements to DEVICEHIGH= statements one at a time, and reboot after each change. In this way, if one of the drivers causes a crash, you'll be able to identify which driver should remain in the 640K conventional memory area.

Similarly, not all TSRs and other memory-resident programs can work properly when loaded into upper memory by the LOADHIGH command in AUTOEXEC.BAT. In the worst cases, they can cause your system to crash. If this happens, load the program into conventional memory by removing the LOADHIGH command from the statement. Remember to create a bootable backup disk with your original CONFIG.SYS and AUTOEXEC.BAT files so that you can always restart your system from the floppy disk.

Both the DEVICEHIGH= statement and the LOADHIGH command attempt to load a driver or program into the upper memory area; however, if there's not enough memory, the driver or program will be loaded into conventional memory. DOS does not indicate which memory area it uses during the execution of your AUTOEXEC.BAT file, so to see what's loaded and where, type the MEM /C command from the DOS prompt.

When you use either DEVICEHIGH= or LOADHIGH, DOS grabs the biggest chunk of upper memory first, even if the program will fit into one of the smaller available chunks. For this reason, the order in which you load programs can affect how many will fit into the upper memory area. The general rule is to load the larger programs first, but it may take some experimentation to optimize the loading of programs into upper memory.

To determine the proper loading order of drivers and programs, first run MEM /C to find out how much memory is consumed by each of the device drivers, TSRs, and other memory-resident programs. Then figure how many of these will fit into your upper memory area. Use the DEVICEHIGH= statement to load the largest device drivers with CONFIG.SYS, and use the regular DEVICE= statement to load the smaller drivers. Similarly, use the LOADHIGH command to load the largest TSRs with AUTOEXEC.BAT, and load smaller ones without the LOADHIGH command.

Danger Zone

Some drivers and TSRs inaccurately report how much memory they consume. Whereas some drivers and programs require only the amount of memory they report in MEM /C (the amount the program uses while running), others require as much memory as the actual file size of the program. For example, MEM /C reports that the MOUSE.COM program requires only 16K of memory while running, but the MOUSE.COM file is actually about 57K in size, and requires a full 57K of upper memory to start up.

In this example, everything is loaded into conventional memory, and the CONFIG.SYS and AUTOEXEC.BAT files look like this:

CONFIG.SYS

```
DEVICE=C:\WIN31\HIMEM.SYS
DEVICE=C:\DOS\SETVER.EXER
DOS=HIGH,UMB
FILES=30
BUFFERS=30
STACKS=9,256
DEVICE=C:\DOS\ANSI.SYS
SHELL=C:\COMMAND.COM /P /E:512
DEVICE=C:\WIN31\SMARTDRV.EXE /double_buffer
```

AUTOEXEC.BAT

```
VERIFY OFF
PATH C:\DOS;C:\WINDOWS
PROMPT $P$G
MOUSE /y
MODE COM2:9600,n,8,1
SMARTDRV
```

To inspect the basic details of your memory usage, issue the MEM /C command from the DOS prompt. In this example, the startup files might generate a MEM /C report similar to this:

```
Conventional Memory :
  Name            Size in Decimal              Size in Hex

  MSDOS             67616        ( 66.0K)           10820
  HIMEM              3696        (  3.6K)             E70
  SETVER              400        (  0.4K)             190
  ANSI               4192        (  4.1K)            1060
  SMARTDRV           2464        (  2.4K)             9A0
  COMMAND            4960        (  4.8K)            1360
  MOUSE             16896        ( 16.5K)            4200
  SMARTDRV          28304        ( 27.6K)            6E90
  FREE                 64        (  0.1K)              40
  FREE                160        (  0.2K)              A0
  FREE             526336        (514.0K)           80800
Total  FREE :      526560        (514.2K)

Total bytes available to programs :        526560     (514.2K)
Largest executable program size :          526336     (514.0K)
```

```
7733248 bytes total contiguous extended memory
      0 bytes available contiguous extended memory
5570560 bytes|available XMS memory
        64Kb High Memory Area available
```

The MEM/C report indicates that MS-DOS, SETVER.EXE, ANSI.SYS, SMARTDRV, and MOUSE.COM are all loaded into conventional memory. SMARTDRV is listed twice in the report—the first instance is the double-buffer driver loaded by CONFIG.SYS, and the second instance is the actual SMARTDrive utility that is loaded by AUTOEXEC.BAT.

Because all these items are loaded into conventional memory, only 514K remains free for running DOS programs. Here's how I've modified the example startup files to free a substantial amount of memory:

CONFIG.SYS

```
DEVICE=C:\WIN31\HIMEM.SYS
DEVICE=c:\WIN31\EMM386.EXE I=E000-EFFF I=B000-B7FF NOEMS
DEVICEHIGH=C:\DOS\SETVER.EXE
DOS=HIGH,UMB
FILES=30
BUFFERS=30
STACKS=9,256
DEVICEHIGH=C:\DOS\ANSI.SYS
SHELL=C:\COMMAND.COM255D /P /E:512
DEVICE=C:\WIN31\SMARTDRV.EXE /double_buffer
```

AUTOEXEC.BAT

```
VERIFY OFF
PATH PATH C:\DOS;C:\WINDOWS
PROMPT $P$G
LOADHIGH MOUSE /y
LOADHIGH MODE COM2:9600,n,8,1
SMARTDRV
```

In these examples, I loaded EMM386 to manage the upper memory area and used the I= statement to reclaim the E000–EFFF and B000–B7FF upper memory regions. I also loaded DOS into the HMA region, and used the DEVICEHIGH and LOADHIGH statements to load SETVER.EXE, ANSI.SYS, MOUSE.COM, and MODE into the upper memory blocks. I left the SMART-Drive statements alone—the double-buffer driver needs to remain in conventional memory on my system, and the main SMARTDrive program automatically loads itself into upper memory, if it can.

After making these modifications, I rebooted the system and issued the MEM /C command from DOS, which generated this report:

```
Conventional Memory :
    Name              Size in Decimal            Size in Hex
    MSDOS                15312      ( 15.0K)         3BD0
    HIMEM                 1072      (  1.0K)          430
    EMM386                3232      (  3.2K)          CA0
    SMARTDRV              2464      (  2.4K)          9A0
    COMMAND               2880      (  2.8K)          B40
    FREE                    64      (  0.1K)           40
    FREE                630112      (615.3K)        99D60
Total    FREE :        630176      (615.4K)
Upper Memory :
    Name              Size in Decimal            Size in Hex
    SYSTEM              142928      (139.6K)        22E50
    SMARTDRV            28304       ( 27.6K)         6E90
    SETVER                400       (  0.4K)          190
    ANSI                 4192       (  4.1K)         1060
    MOUSE               16896       ( 16.5K)         4200
    FREE                   32       (  0.0K)           20
    FREE                12624       ( 12.3K)         3150
    FREE               122128       (119.3K)        1DD10
Total    FREE :        134784      (131.6K)

Total bytes available to  programs
   (Conventional+Upper) :                 764960     (747.0K)
Largest executable program size :        629952     (615.2K)
Largest available upper memory block :   122128     (119.3K)

   7733248 bytes total contiguous extended memory
         0 bytes available contiguous extended memory
   5275648 bytes available XMS memory
            MS-DOS resident in High Memory Area
```

As you can see from the new report, the operation was a great success. After I changed the startup files to implement the memory management techniques, the amount of free conventional memory increased by more than 100K, from 514K to 615K. In addition, 131K is still free in the upper memory area, with a large contiguous block of 119K available to accommodate other software or drivers.

Insider's Tip

Although it's a good idea to load most of your drivers and memory-resident programs into upper memory, you may inadvertently decrease your access to the 640K conventional memory area as a result. When Windows runs in 386 enhanced mode, it tries to use part of the upper memory area for the placement of special translation buffers. These translation buffers, each of which is 4K in size, are used to transfer information between Windows, which runs in protected mode, and DOS, which runs in real mode and can therefore only access the first megabyte of memory.

Windows uses two translation buffers (8K) for each virtual DOS machine, and six buffers (24K) if you are running on a network. If Windows can't find enough room in upper memory for these translation buffers, it places them in the 640K conventional memory area, thus robbing this memory space from every DOS session you start from within Windows.

However, because these 4K buffers are relatively small, you may be able to wedge them into some of the unused upper memory areas. For example, I noted earlier in the chapter that some AMI BIOS versions don't use two 4K areas, F200–F2FF and F700–F7FF, which you may want to set aside for the translation buffers. If you selected EMM386 with the NOEMS switch, you can use the X= parameter to specifically exclude these addresses from access by EMM386. For example, the statement line

```
DEVICE=C:\WINDOWS\EMM386.EXE X=F200-F2FF X=F700-F7FF NOEMS
```

would reserve the 4K areas for use by Windows as translation buffers.

Working with QEMM. Quarterdeck's QEMM is my favorite third-party memory management utility. Why should you use QEMM, or some other third-party utility, you may ask yourself, when DOS 5 and Windows already include memory management tools? In fact, if you intend to only run Windows, you may have no need for third-party memory management software. But for users who intend to run DOS applications under Windows, or to run a mix of DOS and Windows, QEMM offers the following improvements over Microsoft's memory management duo, HIMEM.SYS and EMM386.EXE:

➵ You can load more drivers, TSRs, and other memory-resident software above 640K, because QEMM provides access to more than twice as much upper memory. This feature may prove critical in running mixed Windows and DOS configurations in networked environments.

➵ The program includes an OPTIMIZE utility that automatically determines how items should be loaded into upper memory. This means you don't have to use trial and error methods to determine the proper sequence for loading the items, as you do with EMM386.EXE.

➤ With this program, you have the ability to allocate both XMS memory for Windows and EMS memory for DOS applications from a common memory pool. This eliminates the need to maintain different memory configurations for DOS sessions and Windows sessions.

➤ QEMM provides you with greater control over how your system uses memory. QEMM can sort all your RAM according to speed, lets you "borrow" some extra memory from your VGA card, and lets you shadow ROMs in EMS. The memory sorting feature is especially useful if you have 8- or 16-bit memory cards installed in your system. QEMM allows you to use the memory on these slower cards as a disk cache and save the faster memory on the motherboard for running your applications.

Although a complete discussion of QEMM is beyond the scope of this book, here are a few pointers and tricks that may be useful for Windows users of QEMM.

The QEMM installation program automatically places the statement line for QEMM in your CONFIG.SYS file and configures the utility according to your system configuration. If you want, you can also change the default options using an Advanced menu in the installation program.

QEMM makes two small modifications to the SYSTEM.INI file to prevent conflicts with Windows' internal memory management system. If you skip this option during installation, you can have QEMM make the modifications later by running the QWINFIX.COM utility located in your main QEMM directory.

QEMM version 6 and higher automatically removes the DEVICE=HIMEM.SYS and DEVICE=EMM386.EXE statement lines from your CONFIG.SYS files. Earlier versions of QEMM require you to do this manually.

Once QEMM has been installed, you can run the OPTIMIZE program to automatically determine the best loading sequence for drivers and other items. OPTIMIZE reboots your computer several times and edits the CONFIG.SYS and AUTOEXEC.BAT files during its process of squeezing as many items as possible above 640K.

Like EMM386, QEMM lets you specifically include certain areas of upper memory. To include specific memory areas, use the RAM= switch or the INCLUDE= switch, immediately followed by the hexadecimal address range of the memory you want to include.

If you are using QEMM with one of its Stealth options (ST:M or ST:F), even more upper memory will be available as UMBs, into which you can load drivers and software. (QEMM refers to UMBs as "high RAM".) The Stealth Mapping option (ST:M) hides the ROM code for your PC's video card and BIOS and thus creates a contiguous block for the EMS pageframe, from

C000h to FFFEh. Although the Stealth Mapping feature may not work on all PCs, the OPTIMIZE utility can test your system for compatibility before you attempt to use it.

The Stealth Frame option (ST:F) superimposes the EMS page frame over system ROM, without attempting to use other ROM addresses. With Stealth Mapping, up to 225K of upper memory can be made available, as compared with Stealth Frame, which places the limit at about 168K. QEMM includes a system inventory utility, called MANIFEST, that can give you a graphic display of the memory usage on your PC.

Most 386 or better systems provide an option that copies some of the ROM routines into RAM to speed up system performance. On most systems, this shadowing is done inefficiently, wasting as much as 384K of RAM to shadow less than 128K of ROM.

QEMM provides a more sophisticated shadowing feature that lets you use any upper memory address between A000h and FFFFh. On many systems, you can gain up to an additional 384K of extended memory by remapping the shadow RAM area so that it is included in the extended memory pool. To specify smaller address ranges for shadowing the ROMs, you can use QEMM's ROM= switch, which lets you specify a particular hexadecimal address range for shadowing your ROMs.

Here's an example of a QEMM statement line in CONFIG.SYS that specifies a memory address range for shadowing your ROMs:

```
DEVICE=QEMM386.SYS RAM ROM=C000-C7FF ROM=F000-FFFF
```

In this example, QEMM is instructed to shadow the upper memory region used by a VGA video card (C000–C7FFH) and the area used by the ROM BIOS (F000–FFFH). This consumes only 96K of memory for ROM shadowing, compared with the all-or-nothing 384K consumed by the the default method built into many PCs.

If your system uses an add-on memory card plugged into an expansion slot in addition to the RAM installed on the motherboard, the performance of RAM operations will vary, depending on which type of memory is accessed. RAM on the motherboard operates at the full speed of the CPU, whereas the memory card is limited to the speed of the expansion bus. QEMM can arrange the RAM in your system so that the computer accesses the fastest memory first and uses the slowest memory last.

For example, if your system contains 4 megabytes on the motherboard and 2 megabytes on an add-in card, you'll need to use the EMS.COM utility included with QEMM to work this trick. EMS.COM lets you temporarily reserve memory using an EMS "handle," and then later releases the handle and its associated memory.

Here's how you can configure the slower memory on the card as a disk cache and save the faster motherboard memory for applications:

1. Place the SORT=Y switch on the statement line in CONFIG.SYS that installs QEMM; this tells QEMM to sort your memory according to speed.

2. Use a disk cache program that can be loaded from AUTOEXEC.BAT rather than from CONFIG.SYS (examples are SMARTDrive, Hyperdisk, and Super PCKwik).

3. Specify the EMS.COM utility in AUTOEXEC.BAT *before* the statement line that loads your disk cache; EMS.COM temporarily reserves all of the available faster motherboard memory.

4. Tell EMS.COM to reserve the fast block of memory (see example below).

5. Add the statement line that installs the disk cache—it will configure itself using the slower memory on the add-in card.

6. After the disk cache has been loaded, have EMS.COM release the fast memory you have reserved. The faster memory is now available for Windows to use.

In this example there are 5 megabytes of extended memory, but only 3 megabytes of that is situated on the motherboard. The following sample AUTOEXEC.BAT statement lines use SMARTDrive as the disk cache program:

```
C:\QEMM\EMS cfast block1 3096
C:\WINDOWS\SMARTDRIVE
C:\QEMM\EMS free block1
```

The first line tells EMS.COM to create a temporary EMS handle called "Block1" and to reserve 3096K (3 megabytes) of fast RAM on the motherboard. The next line loads SMARTDrive, which then uses the remaining slow memory for the disk cache. The last line tells EMS.COM to release "Block1" and return the 3096K of fast memory to the available memory pool.

Summary

Windows is not an operating system on its own. Windows works in partnership with DOS to provide the complete functions of an operating system. Because Windows is dependent on DOS, your DOS configuration can strongly affect the performance and behavior of Windows.

The DOS environment is configured mainly through the use of its two startup files, CONFIG.SYS and AUTOEXEC.BAT. These files load memory managers, device drivers, and other items that Windows requires in order to run. Although Windows Setup makes the minimum adjustments to these files necessary to run Windows, it doesn't configure DOS in an optimum fashion for your system. To maximize the performance of Windows, you'll need to customize the DOS startup files on your own.

One of the most important areas under your control is your system's memory management. Windows includes two memory management utilities, HIMEM.SYS for managing extended memory and EMM386.EXE for managing expanded memory and your system's upper memory area. By using memory management techniques to load device drivers and other memory-resident software into upper memory and the high memory area, you can free up more of your 640K of conventional RAM to make it available for use by Windows and DOS applications.

Insider's Tech Support

Q: When I install HIMEM.SYS in my CONFIG.SYS, it won't load. The machine displays a message that says "Cannot control A20 request line," and HIMEM aborts. I tried all of the parameters suggested in the Microsoft manual, and it still won't work.

A: The A20 line is a register built into your computer that allows HIMEM.SYS to control the interface between conventional and extended memory. Microsoft offers a series of machine-specific parameters to allow HIMEM to control the A20 line, but they don't always work. The reason is that some 386 machines activate the A20 line and keep it in an active state as soon as you turn the power on. If HIMEM.SYS finds the A20 line already turned on at bootup, it may refuse to load, no matter what parameters you affix to the command line.

You may be able to restore the A20 line to the condition HIMEM.SYS is expecting by using an option in your computer's Setup routine. Run the Setup routine for your machine (usually accessed by pressing the Del key or Ctrl+Esc immediately after the self-check diagnostic routines). Look for an option that says "Enable A20 line." If the option is set to YES, change the setting to NO. This should allow HIMEM.SYS to load correctly from your CONFIG.SYS.

Q: What if I can't figure out what's wrong with my startup files?

A: If you're having trouble figuring out which line is giving you trouble, you may want to revert to a plain vanilla startup file and then add or change only one statement at a time, rebooting your system between changes. This way, if you accidently introduce any fatal errors into either of these files, you will know that it was from your most recent edit change; you can then go right back to your most recent backup of the file.

Q: I'm using QEMM386 as my memory manager and Windows will run in standard mode, but not in enhanced mode.

A: QEMM and Windows may be fighting over control of an upper memory block on your system. Try modifying your QEMM command line to read as follows:

```
DEVICE=QEMM386.SYS RAM X=B000-B7FF
```

You may also experiment with excluding upper memory areas from Windows' control by inserting an EMMEXCLUDE= statement into the [386Enh] section of SYSTEM.INI. For a start, you can try excluding the area from B000 to Cfff. If this solves the problem, you may be able to recover some upper RAM for Windows' use by experimenting with a smaller exclude range.

If the problem persists, you can try excluding the entire upper memory region (EmmExclude=A000–Ffff).

If you're using QEMM's Stealth option, make sure that QWINFIX has placed a "SystemROMBreakPoint=False" statement in the [386Enh] section of SYSTEM.INI. If you're still having trouble starting Windows with Stealth enabled, you may want to try disabling this feature by removing the ST:M or ST:F parameter from the QEMM command line and rerunning the Quarterdeck Optimize program.

Q: How can I get more conventional memory for my DOS application windows?

A: If you are using MS DOS 5, make sure DOS is loading above 640K with the DOS=HIGH statement present in the CONFIG.SYS file. If you add the lines

```
DEVICE=EMM386.EXE RAM
DOS=HIGH,UMB
```

to CONFIG.SYS, this will gain additional memory by allowing Windows to load its sector translation buffers in upper memory.

If you are using QEMM as your memory manager, you may still append the DOS=HIGH,UMB statement to the CONFIG.SYS. Although QEMM includes its own "loadhigh" utilities, adding the UMB parameter informs Windows that sector translation buffers can be loaded above 640K.

A little-known feature of Windows 3.1 allows you to load DOS TSR utilities into separate windows for individual DOS sessions. If you have too many utilities and device drivers to load, so they won't all fit into upper memory at boot time, you may change a parameter in SYSTEM.INI to allow programs to be loaded high, locally, after Windows has been started.

```
[386Enh]
LocalLoadHigh=True
```

With this setting entered into SYSTEM.INI, you can use DOS 5's Loadhigh command or a third-party load high utility to place TSRs into upper memory from a DOS session running within Windows. You can load different programs into upper memory in each DOS session, and Windows will keep track of them.

Q: How can I get Windows 3.1 to work with DR DOS, version 6?

A: Windows 3.1 requires the DR DOS 6 Business Update dated 4/7/92 or later. Previous versions of DR DOS are incompatible with Windows 3.1.

14

Running DOS and DOS Programs from Windows

Windows represents a step up from DOS, but it also lets you run DOS programs. Because most software programs are still written for DOS-based systems, the ability to tap into a vast array of DOS applications gives Windows an advantage over graphical user interfaces (GUIs) that don't work as well with DOS.

Although DOS applications can't take advantage of most Windows features, Windows tries to provide DOS applications with whatever system resources they need, and on a 386 or higher processor, Windows actually enhances the operation of your DOS applications, particularly when it comes to multi-tasking.

DOS programs fall into two main categories:

➺ **Application programs** Full-fledged programs, such as 1-2-3, dBASE, and Flight Simulator. These programs expect to have the full resources of the computer at their disposal while they are running.

➺ **TSRs, popup programs, and other memory-resident software** Designed to load themselves into memory and stay there while other DOS applications are being run. Some of these programs are device drivers for mice, CD-ROM drives, or networks, and are loaded by DOS in the CONFIG.SYS and AUTOEXEC.BAT files before Windows is started. Others are popup programs, such as Sidekick, that lie dormant in memory until you press a special key combination; this causes them to pop up on your screen and provide special functions, such as calculations, note-taking, or screen capture.

Windows can run either type of DOS program, but to do so it needs a special **program information file,** or **PIF**, which spells out how that application can use system resources. Because a PIF is essential for preventing memory conflicts between DOS and Windows, Windows automatically supplies one on its own if you don't. Although many DOS programs work well with these default PIFs, you can often resolve compatibility problems or improve system performance by learning how to create and edit .PIF files.

In standard mode, DOS applications can only be run full screen, not inside a window. Although you can start several DOS applications when running in standard mode, only one of these applications—the one that you're currently working on—can be run at a time. As soon as you switch away from one DOS application, it is deactivated and remains idle until you switch back to it.

Every time you start a DOS application from within Windows in standard mode, Windows creates a special temporary application swap file on your hard disk. When you switch from DOS versions of 1-2-3 to dBASE, for example, Windows removes 1-2-3 from the system's memory and places it in the application swap file as a temporary holding area. Then it transfers dBASE from its swap file into memory. Because each DOS application requires its own swap file, the amount of free space on your hard disk—not how much physical RAM you have—determines how many DOS applications you can run in standard mode. (For more information on swap files, see Chapter 12.)

In 386 enhanced mode, Windows allows several DOS applications to run simultaneously and continue to run when you switch between applications. DOS applications can also run in a window that you can move, resize, and shrink to an icon.

In addition, each time you start a DOS application in 386 enhanced mode, Windows creates a virtual machine in which to run the DOS program. The virtual machine is a simulation of a complete PC, with its own memory, hardware devices, and software configuration. Each of these virtual machines inherits the state that your PC was in when you started Windows, including any device drivers, TSRs, and other memory-resident software that were running when you started Windows. You can also load additional device drivers, TSRs, and other memory-resident software into an individual virtual machine making them available to a single DOS program without affecting the rest of your system.

Running a DOS Command Prompt

The most fundamental DOS program that you can run is COMMAND.COM, the DOS command interpreter that creates the DOS prompt for typing DOS commands or running batch files and programs. All the tips and tricks that apply to running a command prompt session usually apply to other DOS applications as well.

When you first install Windows, Setup creates a Program Manager icon called **MS-DOS Prompt**. This icon runs COMMAND.COM in full-screen mode using the .PIF file DOSPRMPT.PIF. When you start a DOS session from this icon, it takes up the entire screen, whether in standard or 386 enhanced mode.

Insider's Tip

To create a Program Manager icon that starts your DOS session in a window rather than full screen, open the DOSPRMPT.PIF file using the PIF Editor, click on the radio button labeled Windowed in the Display Usage section, and use the Save As command on the File menu to save the PIF under a different name, such as DOSINWIN.PIF. Then create a program item icon for the new .PIF file and give it a different name, such as DOS-in-a-box. You may also want to adjust the PIF for better performance. For more details, see "Using PIFs and the PIF Editor" later in this chapter.

When you run a DOS command prompt session in 386 enhanced mode, Windows places the following message at the top of your screen:

```
* Type EXIT and press Enter to quit this MS-DOS prompt and
return to Windows.
* Press ALT+TAB to switch to Windows or another application.
* Press ALT+ENTER to switch this MS-DOS Prompt between a
window and full screen.
```

As the message indicates, if you're running a full-screen session and want to run the DOS session in a window, just press Alt+Enter, and the session will shrink down into its own window. Similarly, to expand a DOS session running in a window to full-screen mode, press Alt+Enter.

To switch to another application, press Alt+Tab, or use Ctrl+Esc to bring up the Windows Task Manager, which lets you select a different task. To close the window for the session, as indicated by the message on the first line, type Exit at the DOS prompt—the regular method of double-clicking on the Control menu button is inoperative here. To deep-six the nagging first line of this message, add this line to the [386Enh] section of your SYSTEM.INI file:

```
DosPromptExitInstruc=OFF
```

You can run a DOS command prompt from Windows for most standard DOS commands, such as COMPARE, COPY, FIND, MEM, MODE, and XCOPY. But it's not a good idea to use commands that modify information on the disk, such as UNDELETE, because of incompatibilities between how Windows and DOS handle disk access. You should also avoid using these commands: APPEND, ASSIGN, CHKDSK /F, FDISK, JOIN, RECOVER, and SUBST.

Although you can also start a DOS program from a command prompt session, if you do this, the program will use the DOSPRMPT.PIF as its .PIF file (or whatever other PIF you normally use to start a command prompt session) instead of a custom-designed PIF. Although you may be able to get a program to work this way, I strongly recommend running DOS programs from their own custom PIF files.

A DOS command prompt session usually consists of a text screen with 25 lines, each with a maximum of 80 characters. On a standard VGA display, this takes up the entire screen. However, in 386 enhanced mode, you can take advantage of a new Windows 3.1 feature that lets you change the size of the display fonts used by DOS sessions run in a window. To access this feature, click the Control menu for the DOS window and choose Fonts. This brings up the dialog box shown in Figure 14.1.

*Font Selection
Dialog Box*

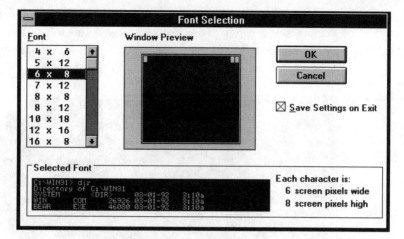

Another reason for running in 386 enhanced mode: you can choose from among 10 different font sizes for the DOS session you run in a window.

The Fonts Selection dialog box provides 10 different fonts, some smaller and some larger than the normal DOS fonts. The smaller fonts reduce your onscreen DOS session so that you can view an entire 80 character x 25 line display in a window that doesn't take up an entire VGA screen. As you click on the various font sizes in the Font section of the dialog box, look at the Window Preview section: a diagram appears showing how much of your screen will be taken over by a DOS session.

The Selected Font section of the dialog box contains a sample of the currently selected font, so that you can judge its legibility for yourself. The smallest size font is 4x6, which creates characters that are 4 pixels wide by 6 pixels high; this font size lets you view almost four DOS sessions on a normal VGA screen, but legibility is minimal. The next two sizes up, 5x12 and 6x8, are the ones I use most often, because they reduce the size of the screen without making the fonts illegible. The largest font sizes are not really suitable for VGA displays; they are intended for high-resolution displays that reduce everything on the screen. With such a display, I find the 12x16 font easiest to read.

Insider's Tip

Although a normal DOS screen is 80 characters wide by 25 lines long, you can use an undocumented feature of Windows to double the number of lines to 50. Open your SYSTEM.INI file and add this line to the [NonWindowsApp] section:

```
ScreenLines=50
```

The new screen length of 50 lines will take effect the next time you start Windows and will apply to both windowed and full-screen DOS sessions. With a standard VGA screen, you can select the 6x8 font to create a 50-line window that will still fit on a VGA display (Figure 14.2).

FIGURE 14.2
*50-Line
Display with
6x8 Font*

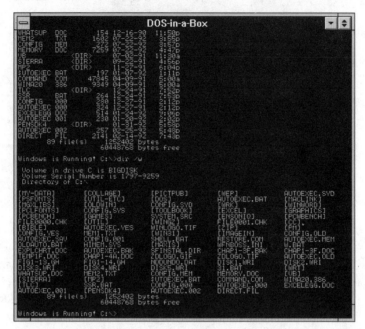

Double your DOS: to view double-sized DOS sessions within the confines of a standard VGA display, just double the number of lines in your DOS session, from 25 to 50, and decrease the size of the fonts used in the DOS window to 6x8.

Most DOS commands and many character-based DOS programs automatically readjust for the increased number of lines per screen. For example, if you issue the DOS directory command by typing either DIR /P or DIR | MORE, the directory list pauses after 50 lines instead of 25. Many DOS character-based applications, such as the DOS 5 Editor, also automatically adjust to the new length. Programs that cannot adjust will just shrink back down to the standard 25-line length.

Reboot in Peace

Most PC users know that if worse comes to worst, they can always resort to the three-fingered panic button, Ctrl+Alt+Del, to reboot their computer and recover from a crash to protect any files that weren't completely written to disk at the time. Windows 3.1 has added a new layer of protection: if you press the Ctrl+Alt+Del key combination, Windows intercedes and offers you various choices, depending on what you are doing at the moment.

If you are running a DOS session, a special message screen appears and offers you three choices:

➤ Press Esc to cancel the reboot request and return to your DOS session. If you were running your DOS session in a window, it will now be running in full-screen mode.

➤ Press Enter to terminate the DOS session and return to Windows. You should probably quit Windows first, however, and restart it, because this method of quitting a DOS session can potentially corrupt your system.

➤ Press Ctrl+Alt+Del again to actually reboot your entire system. Use this option only as a last resort, because it will disrupt your Windows session, and any files that are open may be damaged or lost.

If you press Ctrl+Alt+Del while you are running Windows only, you'll be offered these two choices:

➤ Press any key to return to Windows.

➤ Press Ctrl+Alt+Del again to reboot your system.

Danger Zone

On some systems, using Ctrl+Alt+Del to reboot will not work from within Windows, because Windows takes control of your keyboard in 386 enhanced mode. Instead, your system may hang, and you can only reboot by turning your system off and on again (or by pressing the reset button on your computer, if it has one).

If this happens, try adding the following line to the [386Enh] section of your SYSTEM.INI file:

```
KybdReboot=OFF
```

This will force Windows to quit when you press Ctrl+Alt+Del, return you to DOS, and display a message telling you to press Ctrl+Alt+Del again to actually reboot your system.

Running DOS TSRs and Popup Programs

TSRs and popup programs are often used together with DOS applications. Windows provides several choices for working with TSRs and other memory-resident software. For example, you can load a TSR so that it will be available to all applications; only to Windows; or only to a DOS application run from within Windows. Here's how you would load a TSR for all three situations:

➤ **For all Windows and DOS applications running in Windows** Load the TSR in a DOS startup file before loading Windows. This method consumes the most conventional RAM, but is useful for networks.

➤ **For Windows applications only** Load the TSR by specifying its .EXE file name in the WINSTART.BAT file that is run whenever you start Windows in 386 enhanced mode. This saves the most RAM.

➤ **For a DOS session running within Windows** Load the TSR into a DOS session (a virtual DOS machine) run from 386 enhanced mode. This method only takes RAM from one virtual machine, but you will have to restart the TSR if you want to run it in another DOS window.

Insider's Tip

You can also load some TSRs through the WINSTART.BAT file, which only runs when Windows is started in 386 enhanced mode. However, some TSRs and other memory-resident utilities do not function properly if you start them from WINSTART.BAT. The WINSTART.BAT file is not created automatically by Setup, so you have to create one and place it in your main Windows directory.

A popup program is a special type of TSR or memory-resident program that loads itself into the computer's memory when run but isn't activated until you press a certain key combination, which then pops up the formerly dormant program. These popup programs should be run after you start Windows in order to conserve your system's memory.

You can start a popup program from Windows in several different ways:

➤ Create an icon for it in Program Manager

➤ Start the popup program from its File Manager icon

➤ Use the Run command on the File menu of either Program Manager or File Manager

Any of these methods will run the popup program in a DOS session using the _DEFAULT.PIF file. Windows displays a message that the Windows Pop-up Program Support is in effect and that the popup program is now loaded. This message instructs you to press Ctrl+C after you have finished using the popup to close the window and return to Windows. To use the popup program, press the key combination that normally activates it.

If this doesn't work, you may need to create a custom PIF for the program. This means you'll have to start the program from its PIF, rather than from its program file. The custom PIF startup allows you to resolve conflicts that can arise if the key combination that starts the popup is also reserved by Windows. To resolve the conflict, open the PIF for the popup with the PIF Editor, then select the Reserve Shortcut Keys option that identifies the conflicting key combination.

Insider's Tip

Here's a shortcut for starting specific TSRs or popup programs together with a particular application. You can create a special batch file that will first load any necessary TSRs into a DOS session (a DOS virtual machine) and then start the program in that DOS session. Then run the batch file from its own PIF, which you can refine using the techniques described later in this chapter.

Running DOS Applications

To run a DOS application, Windows needs a .PIF file, which it uses to determine how to allocate system resources for that application. Windows searches for a PIF with the same name as the DOS application but ending with a .PIF instead of an .EXE or a .COM file.

For example, if you want to run the program DOSAPP.EXE, Windows looks for the .PIF file named DOSAPP.PIF. Windows locates the PIF by searching your directories in this sequence: the directory that stores the DOS applications files; the currently active directory; your main Windows directory; the \SYSTEM subdirectory of your main Windows directory; and any directories specified in your PATH statement. If nothing turns up, Windows runs DOSAPP.EXE using the settings contained in the _DEFAULT.PIF file.

Although many DOS programs run without trouble using the settings in the _DEFAULT.PIF file, some programs require a custom PIF, which can be developed in one of three ways:

➤ Have Windows create it for you. This method works only if a PIF profile for the application is contained in the APPS.INF file.

➤ Some DOS applications are supplied with PIFs; or the developer of the application may offer a PIF separately.

➤ Create your own PIF for the application using the PIF Editor, as described later in this chapter.

If you have a choice, use the PIF that's included with your application or provided by the software developer instead of the PIF created by Windows

Setup. Some software makers place the .PIF file on the application disks, so check there first, and copy it to your main Windows directory or to the directory that stores the DOS applications files. If you don't find a .PIF file on the disks, contact the manufacturer. Often the .PIF files can be downloaded from the developer's bulletin board system or from the developer's forum on an online service, such as CompuServe.

To use Windows Setup to create a PIF for a DOS application, double-click Setup's icon in Program Manager, then choose Set Up Applications from the Options menu. This brings up the Setup Applications dialog box, which provides two choices. One option instructs Setup to search through your disk for applications by presenting a dialog box that asks you to specify the drive or path. The second option tells Setup to ask you to select a particular application, by bringing up a dialog box that asks you to enter the path and file name for the program. (See Chapter 4 for more details on this process.) Whichever method you choose, Setup conducts a search for a .PIF file that might already exist for your application. If a file is found, it's used to run the application.

If the search for a corresponding .PIF file runs dry, Windows checks out the APPS.INF file to see if it lists the application. If it does, Setup presents a dialog box that asks if you want to create a PIF using that information.

The APPS.INF file contains different PIFs for some DOS applications that share the same name; sometimes they are two different applications, and other times they are different versions of the same application. If Setup encounters one of these ambiguous situations, it presents another dialog box asking you to identify which PIF should be used.

If no .PIF file can be found or created, Setup uses the _DEFAULT.PIF file as a fallback. Setup creates an icon for whatever PIF it uses for your application and places it in the Applications group in Program Manager. If such a group doesn't exist, Setup creates one. And if the Applications group is full, Setup creates a second group, Applications2.

Insider's Tip

The APPS.INF file contains information for creating PIFs for more than 200 different DOS applications. You can inspect this file to see which applications are included and to determine which PIF settings will be used. You can even edit this file to add new applications or to change the PIF values for the applications it already lists. For details on how to edit and interpret the APPS.INF file, see Chapter 16.

You can also set up a DOS application by creating a program item icon for it in Program Manager. Either use the Program Manager's New command or drag the application's file icon from File Manager into a Program Manager group window. Both methods are described in detail in Chapter 2. In either case, Windows checks the APPS.INF file to see if the application contains a PIF profile in its file. If so, you'll be asked whether you want Windows to create a PIF based on this information.

Let's assume you create a PIF with Windows Setup. The program finds information for the application in the APPS.INF file, and then it selects an appropriate icon for the application from among the icons in either the PROGMAN.EXE or the MORICONS.DLL file.

If you create a PIF with the Program Manager's New command or the drag and drop procedure from File Manager, the program uses the settings found in APPS.INF but it does not specify a custom icon. You'll need to change the icon manually using the program item icon Properties dialog box, as described in Chapter 2. When you minimize a DOS application, it now uses the icon that you have assigned to it, rather than the generic DOS icon that was assigned to all minimized DOS sessions in Windows 3.0.

The Control Menu for DOS Sessions

The Control menu of any DOS session running in a window contains several items that affect your use of the DOS session. To access the menu, click on the menu button or press Alt+spacebar. The Control menu for DOS sessions contains these special commands:

➤ **Edit** Provides controls for copying and pasting information, as well as scrolling the window

➤ **Settings** Provides controls for display options, multitasking, and a special panic button that lets you terminate an application

➤ **Fonts** Brings up the Font Selection dialog box, which was described earlier and shown in Figure 14.1

Edit is a cascading menu item; when you choose it, a submenu pops up revealing four new choices (Figure 14.3).

The four items on the cascading Edit menu are

➤ **Mark** (Alt+spacebar,E,K) Lets you select an area of the screen to be copied

➤ **Copy** (Enter) Transfers the marked area of the screen to the clipboard

➤ **Paste** (Alt+spacebar,E,P) Pastes information on the clipboard at the location of the DOS cursor

➤ **Scroll** (Alt+spacebar,E,L) Lets keyboard users scroll a DOS window with the arrow keys

• • • • • • • • • • • • • •
FIGURE 14.3
*Cascading
Edit Item*

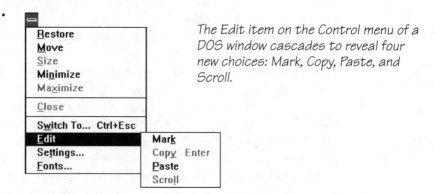

The Edit item on the Control menu of a DOS window cascades to reveal four new choices: Mark, Copy, Paste, and Scroll.

These procedures, which include some of the most awkward keyboard equivalents found in Windows, resolve the discrepancies between the way Windows and DOS handle input from the keyboard and the mouse.

In a DOS window, you can't use the standard Windows keyboard commands to copy and paste information because DOS intercepts your input. Thus, if you were to to press Ctrl+P in a DOS window, DOS would interpret this as the Control-P character, not as the Windows Paste command. To paste something on the Windows clipboard into a DOS Window, you need to choose the Paste command from the cascading Edit item on the Control menu, or type Alt+spacebar,E,P.

In order to use Mark and Paste, you need to know how the Windows Clipboard works with DOS applications. If you are running Windows in standard mode, you can only copy a full screen of text from a DOS application, and you can only paste text into a DOS application. If you are running Windows in 386 enhanced mode, you can copy and paste both text and graphics in a DOS window, but only a few DOS applications let you paste graphics into them from Windows. Whatever your mode, you can only copy—not cut—from a DOS window.

The behavior of the Clipboard is also affected by whether the DOS session is running in full screen or in a window. In full-screen mode, you can copy the DOS screen to the Clipboard by pressing the Print Screen key; this captures the text of the screen, not the graphics.

If you are running your DOS session in a window, press Print Screen to copy the image of the entire screen to the Clipboard as a Windows bitmap (.BMP). Pressing Alt+Print Screen copies the active window to the Clipboard as a bitmap graphic image, even if the window contained only DOS text. To capture the text, use PRINTSCREEN with the DOS session running in full-screen mode, or use the Mark command to first select the text within the window.

To copy part of a DOS window, either text or graphics, you'll need to use the Mark command to select the area you want to copy, and then issue the Copy command to transfer the selected information to the Clipboard. When you select the Mark command, the DOS window shifts into a special Mark mode that lets you use either the mouse or the cursor arrow keys to highlight an area of the DOS window (Figure 14.4).

FIGURE 14.4
Mark Mode with Text Highlighted

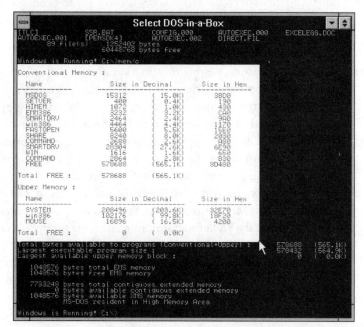

To copy a portion of a DOS window, you need to place the window into a special Mark mode by choosing the Mark command from the cascading Edit item on the window's Control menu.

In Mark mode, the title bar of the DOS window begins with the word Mark. In this mode, only the mouse, cursor arrow keys, Esc, and Enter are recognized—everything else you type is ignored. To select a portion of the window while in Mark mode, simply drag the mouse across the area; or from the keyboard, move the arrow keys to an area and then hold down Shift while moving the arrow keys to select the region. To cancel the Mark mode, press Esc.

Once you have selected an area, press Enter to copy it to the Clipboard and switch from the Mark mode. After copying something from the DOS window, you can use the Clipboard Viewer utility to inspect the contents of the Clipboard. Check the Clipboard Viewer's Display menu to see if your information was captured as text or as a graphics bitmap—some DOS applications display text as graphics, so what you thought you had captured as text may actually have been copied as a graphics image.

To paste information into a DOS window, first copy the information onto the Clipboard and then double-check the contents of the Clipboard by using the Clipboard Viewer. Next, switch to the DOS session window and position the DOS cursor at the desired insertion point. Choose the Paste command from the window's Control menu. If you are running your DOS session in full-screen mode, you can press Ctrl+Esc to switch to Windows Task Manager and thereby reduce the DOS session to an icon on your Windows desktop. If you want, you can then click on the icon to access the DOS session's Control menu to issue the Paste command.

Danger Zone

For various reasons, pasting information into a DOS session doesn't always work. Some applications may not be able to accept graphics; to work around this, you can try pasting the graphics into a Windows graphics program (such as the Paintbrush) and then saving the image as a .BMP, .PCX, or other graphics file. The DOS application may then be able to open that file even though it cannot accept the image directly from the clipboard.

Any text you paste into an application is inserted as a string of characters, just as if they were typed from the keyboard; as a result, any special formatting is ignored. Make sure that the text you are pasting in doesn't contain characters that the DOS program can mistakenly interpret as commands.

Some DOS applications cannot accept information that is pasted using the Windows fast paste method. If you are pasting information into a DOS window and nothing happens, or the information is garbled, your application may not be able to use fast paste. Quit the DOS application, open the PIF that was used to start the application with the PIF Editor, open the Advanced Options dialog box by clicking on the Advanced button, and remove the X from the check box labeled Allow Fast Paste. Then restart the DOS application using that PIF and try again.

Here's something else that could go wrong when you are trying to paste information into a DOS session: Windows may issue an error message reporting that there isn't enough memory to complete the operation. Try minimizing all your other applications; if that doesn't work, you'll have to quit some (or all!) of your other applications and try again.

The Scroll command on the cascading Edit submenu enables mouseless Windows users to handle the scroll bars of a DOS window. Such users need this command because the DOS session normally intercepts cursor arrow keys, which are commonly used by DOS applications for other operations, such as choosing items from DOS menus. When you select the Scroll command by typing Alt+spacebar,E,L, the DOS window switches into a special Scroll mode, and the title bar of the window changes to reflect that mode. You can then use the cursor arrow keys to control the scroll bars and view the contents of the window. Whenever you like, press Esc to leave the Scroll mode.

The Control menu of a DOS session running in 386 enhanced mode also contains the Settings command, which brings up the dialog box shown in Figure 14.5.

••••••••••••••
FIGURE 14.5
*Settings
Dialog Box*

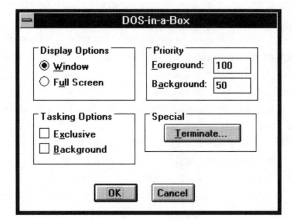

Choose the Settings command on the Control menu of a DOS session to bring up this dialog box.

The title bar displays the title of the DOS session window. The dialog box contains these four sections:

➥ **Display Options** Contains two radio buttons: Window runs the session in a window, and Full Screen runs it in full-screen mode, but it's probably easier to press Alt+Enter to switch between them.

➥ **Tasking Options** Select Exclusive, Background, or both; these settings provide a way to temporarily override the settings in the PIF. These settings are explained later.

➥ **Priority** Lets you set the Foreground Priority and Background Priority for an application. These settings let you temporarily override the equivalent settings in the PIF.

➥ **Special** Contains a single button labeled Terminate. Pressing this button puts an abrupt halt to the execution of your DOS session. This option is equivalent to using Ctrl+Alt+Del and should only be used as a last resort. If you do terminate a DOS session with this panic button, quit Windows and restart your computer to clear up any hidden memory conflicts that can result.

Multitasking with DOS Applications

One clear benefit of running Windows in 386 enhanced mode is the ability to multitask DOS applications. Because DOS applications weren't designed for multitasking, you'll need to decide how you want your system's resources to be devoted to those applications when they are running. You can control whether a DOS application is able to run in the background, how much of the system's resources it should receive, and how the system's resources are shared by Windows and DOS applications. To set these controls, however, you'll have to use resources from different locations. Some of the settings are found in the 386 Enhanced icon on the Control Panel, others are located in the .pif file used to run the DOS application, and still others are available only by editing the system.ini file.

True multitasking can only happen on multiprocessor systems, where several tasks can each run on its own processor. Windows achieves its multitasking effect with a single CPU chip by rapidly switching from task to task. For example, if four applications are running at once, Windows lets one application use the CPU for a number of milliseconds, then it hands control of the CPU to another application for a few more milliseconds, and so on. Because this switching happens so fast, it appears as if all four applications are running simultaneously. The various settings related to multitasking allow you to specify the amount of time that Windows allocates to each task before switching to the next.

The first group of multitasking controls is located in the **386 Enhanced section of the Control Panel** (Figure 14.6).

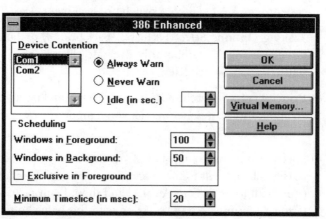

FIGURE 14.6
*Multitasking
Controls in
the Control
Panel*

*The 386
Enhanced sec-
tion of the
Control Panel
contains sev-
eral settings
that allow you
to control
Windows
multitasking.*

The controls in the device contention section instruct Windows what to do if two or more applications try to access one of the COM ports simultaneously. You should normally set this option to Always Warn, but if you want to fiddle with it, see the discussion of device contention in the section on COM ports in Chapter 10.

The Scheduling section of the 386 Enhanced dialog box contains three items:

➤ **Windows in Foreground** The number in this box represents the relative amount of processor time shared by Windows and all of its applications when a Windows application is selected—that is, when the Windows application is in the foreground. This value can be any number from one to 10,000, with the default being 100.

➤ **Windows in Background** This number represents the relative amount of processor time devoted to Windows and all of its applications whenever a DOS session is running in the foreground. This value can be anything from one to 10,000; the default is 50.

➤ **Exclusive in Foreground** If an X is placed in this check box, Windows receives all of the processor's time whenever a Windows application is in the foreground. This prevents any DOS applications from running when a Windows program is selected.

The numbers in the Foreground and Background boxes establish a ratio of Windows-to-DOS processor time during each cycle of the CPU. At the default settings of 100 for the foreground and 50 for the background, for example, Windows receives 100 out of 150, or two-thirds of the processor time. When you switch to a DOS application, and thus place Windows in the background, Windows receives 50 out of 150, or one-third of the total processor time. When you're running more than one DOS application, the relative amount of time devoted to each application is determined by the settings in each application's .PIF file, as described later on.

The **Minimum Timeslice** setting in the Scheduling section specifies the minimum number of milliseconds that an application is allowed to run before Windows transfers control of the processor to another application. The default setting is 20. The smaller the number of milliseconds, the more frequently Windows switches among applications. This makes your multitasking appear to run smoother, but it also drains your system's performance because the time Windows devotes to switching could have been spent running applications. For this reason, don't set this number below 10. If you specify a larger timeslice than the default of 20, you can improve performance, but you'll also introduce a noticeable jerkiness in the your operations.

Another factor that affects multitasking of DOS applications is **FastDisk**, a system of Windows components that bypasses DOS to provide 32-bit access to your hard disk drive (see Chapter 12 for all the details). To see whether FastDisk is in effect, check the virtual memory settings in the 386 Enhanced icon in the Control Panel. If FastDisk is installed, you can run more simultaneous DOS sessions when Windows is run in 386 enhanced mode.

When FastDisk is not running, each DOS program that you start consumes an entire virtual machine's worth of your RAM, which can amount to a megabyte or more, depending on how the memory is configured in the application's .PIF file.

With FastDisk turned on, DOS applications can make use of Windows virtual memory, which usually far exceeds the physical RAM in your system. In addition, your system performs better when running several DOS applications because the physical RAM is free to work on a large task. FastDisk also accelerates switching between DOS programs, because Windows doesn't need to swap the entire DOS virtual machine to disk; instead, FastDisk allows Windows to swap only the required amount of memory needed by the DOS application.

Insider's Tip

Multitasking can all too easily cause your system to run out of memory, even when it seems as if enough should be available for your operations. If Windows displays an Out of Memory message when you try to start another program, here's what you can do to free up some memory:

➥ Minimize any open applications.

➥ If you are running multiple DOS applications, configure some or all of them to run in the foreground only.

➥ If the Clipboard is in use, clear the contents by opening the Clipboard Viewer and using the Delete command on the Edit menu. You can save the contents of the Clipboard to a file before zapping it. Or you can simply copy a single character or word to the Clipboard, and this tidbit will replace the former contents.

➥ Run your DOS applications before running your Windows applications. Windows programs can then configure themselves to run in a limited memory environment, which DOS programs can't do.

➥ Adjust the PIF settings for your DOS programs. Make sure that your memory-related settings don't specify more memory that a program actually needs to run.

➥ Edit the settings in your SYSTEM.INI file—many of these can be used to fine-tune your system's handling of memory.

➤ Remove unnecessary drivers, TSRs, and memory-resident programs from your CONFIG.SYS and AUTOEXEC.BAT files.

➤ Load DOS into the HMA, and load other drivers and programs into upper memory in your CONFIG.SYS and AUTOEXEC.BAT files.

➤ Turn off your desktop wallpaper using the Control Panel.

➤ Increase the size of your permanent swap file (especially useful with FastDisk's 32-bit access).

➤ If worse comes to worst, quit some of your other applications.

Insider's Tip

To improve the performance of your applications in a multitasking environment, you can try these basic techniques:

➤ To speed up your applications, increase the ratio of time devoted to Windows in the foreground or background, depending on where your program is running. These settings are found under the 386 Enhanced icon in the Control Panel.

➤ To speed up a DOS application's performance in the foreground or background, increase either the Foreground Priority or Background Priority value in the application's PIF file. You can also modify this value on the fly by opening the application's Control menu and choosing Settings.

➤ Adjust the PIF settings for your DOS programs. Make sure that the Monitor Ports settings are all unchecked—unless you really do need them.

➤ Make sure the statement line FileSysChange=OFF appears in the [386Enh] section of your SYSTEM.INI file. This line has the side-effect of preventing Windows from updating an open File Manager window automatically, so you'll have to do it manually by pressing F5.

➤ To increase the rate at which Windows refreshes the screen for DOS applications running in a window, adjust the value of the WindowUpdate-Time parameter in the [386Enh] section of the SYSTEM.INI file. The default value is 50, but to accelerate the refresh rate, set a higher value—anywhere from 100 to 200.

Using PIFs and the PIF Editor

Because DOS programs can differ in their individual system requirements, Windows provides the PIF Editor utility, which lets you define custom Program Information Files for individual DOS applications. For instance, one application may require expanded memory or use a serial port. Another application may need extended memory, or require a keystroke combination usually reserved for Windows' internal use.

The PIF Editor lets you set these parameters to provide the DOS application with the resources that it needs, and to avoid conflicts with Windows. The PIF also provides Windows with information about how to manage multiple DOS programs in 386 enhanced mode, and lets you adjust settings that control each program's use of CPU time.

Every time you run a DOS program—which can be an .EXE, .COM, or .BAT file—Windows searches your system for a PIF that has the same name (minus the extension) as the file you are attempting to run. If it doesn't find one, it uses the _DEFAULT.PIF file.

As I mentioned earlier in the chapter, the APPS.INF file—located in the \SYSTEM subdirectory of your main Windows directory—contains PIF profiles for more than 200 DOS programs. You can create PIFs using the information contained in APPS.INF with any of these methods:

➤ Use Windows Setup to install a DOS application.

➤ Drag the file icon for the .EXE or .COM file from File Manager into Program Manager.

➤ Create a new program item icon in Program Manager for an .EXE or .COM file.

With all of these methods, Windows searches the APPS.INF file for the application's file name and, if it finds a match, adds a .PIF file with the same name to your main Windows directory.

If the APPS.INF file doesn't contain the information needed to create a PIF, Windows uses the _DEFAULT.PIF for the program. Although the path of least resistance, these _DEFAULT.PIF file settings were designed for a "worst case" scenario, and may not be optimal for many applications. To obtain the best performance from either the default PIFs or the custom ones, you'll need to learn how to adjust them with the PIF Editor. Also, you may encounter DOS applications for which you will have to create your own PIF as the only way to have them run in Windows.

Danger Zone

Learning to create custom PIFs will let you resolve most of the incompatibilities that DOS programs have with Windows, but there are some exceptions. Some DOS applications may need to run only in full-screen mode; others may need to be run with Windows in standard mode; and a few may be so incompatible that they will not run from Windows at all.

The PIF Editor is located in the Main Group in Windows 3.1; if you upgraded from 3.0, it's located in the Accessories Group. When you open the PIF Editor, it contains default values that are internal to the PIF Editor and Windows. These settings are equivalent to the initial settings in the _DEFAULT.PIF file, but if you change the file, it does not alter these initial PIF Editor settings. You can get context-sensitive help for most of the PIF Editor's options by pressing F1.

When you run PIF Editor, it presents a different opening screen, either standard or 386 enhanced mode, depending on which mode you are running. To select a specific mode, choose either Standard or 386 Enhanced from the PIF Editor's Mode menu. If you run DOS applications in both modes, you don't need to create a separate PIF for each mode; a single .PIF file can contain the settings for both standard and 386 enhanced modes.

Basic Options for 386 Enhanced Mode

In 386 enhanced mode, the PIF Editor presents two screens, each containing various options. First you'll see the basic screen, and then, if you press the Advanced button, an advanced screen. The basic screen is shown in Figure 14.7.

FIGURE 14.7

Basic Screen

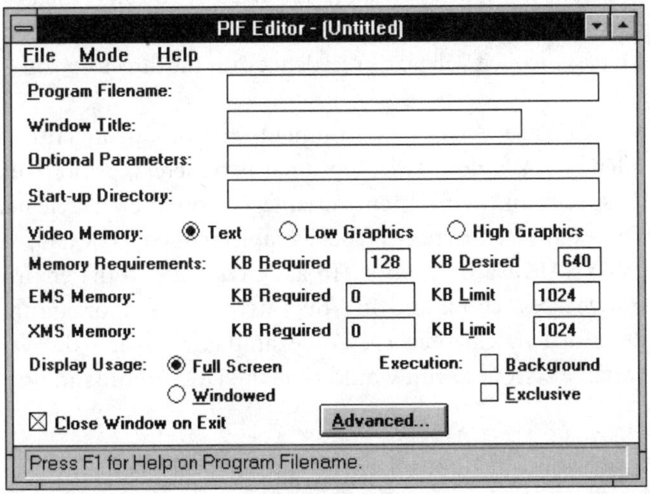

The basic screen is the first of two screens full of options that you can set for .PIF files running in 386 enhanced mode.

The first item in the basic screen is the **Program Filename** box, in which you type the path and file name of the .EXE, .COM, or .BAT file that you use to start the application.

The **Window Title** box contains a space for entering the descriptive title that you want to appear on the title bar of the DOS session when your application is running. This description also appears as the icon label when the application is minimized to an icon. The window title entry is optional; if you leave it blank, the name of the application you are running appears in the title bar. If you create a Program Manager icon for the PIF and specify a title for the Program Manager icon, that title overrides the title in the Window Title box.

The **Optional Parameters** box lets you specify command line parameters as you would enter them from the DOS prompt. For example, to start a wordprocessor with a specific document loaded, you could type the document's path information and file name into the box. You can also use parameters such as special switches or whatever else the application accepts, provided the information in the box does not exceed 62 characters.

If you place only a question mark in this box, Windows pauses and prompts you to type in parameters each time you start the application. Any parameters you specify in this box apply to 386 enhanced mode only. To use these same parameters for the application in standard mode, you'll need to create a separate PIF using the standard mode options described later. If you start the program with the Run command from either Program Manager or File Manager, any switches or other parameters you use will override those specified in this box.

The **Start-Up Directory** box lets you tell Windows which directory should be active when the application is started. If you start the PIF from a program icon in Program Manager and specify a Working Directory for the Program Manager icon, it will take precedence over the directory you specify in this box.

Insider's Tip

You can use a DOS environment variable as an entry in the Program Filename, Window Title, Optional Parameters, or Start-up Directory box. To specify an environment variable, enclose the variable name in (%) signs. For example, to specify the variable named MYNAME, you would enter **%MYNAME%** in the box. To assign a value to the environment variable, use the SET command in your AUTOEXEC.BAT or another batch file, as described in Chapter 13. For example, to assign the value FRED to the variable MYNAME, you would type the DOS command line

```
SET MYNAME=FRED
```

Then the %MYNAME% entry would be replaced by the word FRED.

The **Video Memory** section contains three radio buttons that control the amount of memory that Windows reserves for an application's video display. The three choices are:

➥ **Text** Tells Windows to reserve a small amount of memory, usually between 4 and 16K, for displaying an application in text mode only.

➥ **Low Graphics** Reserves approximately 32K of memory, which is sufficient to display CGA resolution graphics.

➥ **High Graphics** Sets aside a minimum of 128K of memory for displaying DOS applications that use EGA or VGA graphics. Choose this if your application runs in graphics mode. If you select this option and place an X in the Retain Video Memory check box in the advanced screen, Windows will always provide your DOS program with enough video memory. However, this combination of options makes less memory available to your other applications.

Windows uses the Video Memory options to reserve enough memory for the application's initial display. Once the application is running, Windows adjusts the amount of memory reserved for its display. If the program switches from text mode to graphics mode, Windows will give it more memory. (Microsoft recommends that you select High Graphics if you think an application will demand additional video memory after being opened.)

Danger Zone

If you're running an application that switches into a higher resolution display mode, and you haven't reserved sufficient video memory, the application may not be visible on your screen. If this happens, make sure to select High Graphics in conjunction with the Retain Video Memory option in the advanced screen.

The **Memory Requirements** section controls how Windows allots the 640K of conventional memory to the DOS application. The Memory Requirements section lets you set these two values:

➥ **KB Required** Tells Windows how many kilobytes of conventional RAM must be available in order to run the application. If not enough free conventional memory is available, Windows displays a warning message. The default setting is 128, which is fine for most programs.

If you set this value to –1, Windows will start the application using the total amount of available conventional memory. Because this setting forces any Windows applications that are running to purge themselves of any unnecessary program code stored in conventional memory, it can sometimes provide your DOS application with more conventional memory.

➡️ **KB Desired** Sets the upper limit for the amount of conventional memory that Windows will allocate to the application. The default value is 640K, which is the maximum amount of conventional memory. If your application can run with less memory, set this value to that smaller number to reserve more memory for your other applications and accelerate the loading of your program. If you set this value to −1, it instructs Windows to give the application as much conventional memory as it can, up to the limit of 640K.

The **EMS Memory** section lets you control how much expanded memory Windows should create for use by the DOS application. This section contains two entries:

➡️ **KB Required** Tells Windows how many kilobytes of expanded memory are required to run the DOS applications. The default value of 0 specifies that the application does not require expanded memory. This number does not limit the amount of expanded memory available to the application. Windows provides it with at least as much as is specified here, and up to the amount specified in the KB Limit box. If Windows cannot supply what's specified in this box, it displays a warning message saying there is not enough expanded memory to run the application.

➡️ **KB Limit** Specifies the maximum number of kilobytes of expanded memory that Windows should allocate to the application. Windows does not automatically create the amount of expanded memory specified in this box—the application must first request it. The default setting is 1024, which provides the application with up to 1 megabyte of expanded memory.

If you set this value to −1, Windows provides the program with as much expanded memory as it requests. Use this option with care, because some applications may request most of your system's memory, even if they don't require it, and this can slow down Windows operation as well as prevent you from running other applications.

The **XMS Memory** section lets you control how much extended memory Windows provides to the DOS application. The XMS Memory section works similarly to the EMS Memory section and contains these two settings:

➡️ **KB Required** Specifies how many kilobytes of extended memory must be free in order to run the DOS program. Because very few DOS programs can use extended memory, you can usually use the default setting of 0, which indicates that the program does not need extended memory to run.

➤ **KB Limit** Identifies the maximum number of kilobytes of extended memory that Windows provides to the application. The default setting is 1024, which lets Windows give the application up to 1 megabyte of extended memory.

If you set this value to –1, Windows lets the application use as much extended memory as it wants. Again, use this with care, because it's possible that the application will request all of your system memory, thus impairing performance and your ability to run other applications.

In general, it's a good strategy to leave the KB Required and KB Limit boxes set at the Windows defaults of 0 and 1024. Most of the time, you will want to reserve memory for other applications. The KB Limit box can be changed if a program hogs memory resources unnecessarily, or does not get enough memory of a given type. A setting of –1 in any box tells Windows to reserve or allocate *all* available memory as extended or expanded.

(Note that in Windows 3.0, the EMS and XMS Memory options are found on the advanced options screen rather than on the basic screen as in 3.1.)

The Display Usage section tells Windows to start the application in either full-screen mode or in a window. The windowed option generally consumes more memory and can slow down performance, but makes it more convenient to view your DOS sessions as part of your graphical desktop. Whatever setting you choose, while a DOS application is running in 386 enhanced mode, you can toggle back and forth between a full screen and a windowed display by pressing Alt+Enter.

Insider's Tip

Some DOS programs are incompatible with Windows when run in a window. If you are having trouble running a DOS program in a window, try running it in full-screen mode.

The **Execution** section lets you control how the application runs. If you place an X in the **Background** check box, you allow the application to keep running when you switch to another window. If the Background box is left unchecked, Windows freezes the program when you switch away. If you place an X in the **Exclusive** check box, all other DOS applications are suspended while you're working on this application, regardless of the Background options settings for the other applications.

If you really want the DOS application to receive all of the system's resources, set the application to run in full-screen mode as well. When you run a DOS application in a window, even if the Exclusive option is checked, Windows uses some of the system's resources for displaying the window and for running other Windows applications.

If you place an X in the **Close Window on Exit** check box, the application's window is closed automatically when you quit the application. This is also the default setting. (To quit a DOS command prompt session, you will still need to type Exit, however, even if this box is checked.) Remove the X if you want the window to remain on the screen after you quit the DOS application.

Insider's Tip

This option is handy if you're running a program that directs its output to the screen after it is finished running such as a batch file or utility. When you quit an application, the title bar of the window changes to "inactive." When you are ready to close the window, double-click on the Control menu button or choose Close from the Control menu.

Advanced Options for 386 Enhanced Mode

To view the PIF Editor's advanced screen, click on the Advanced button in the basic screen. You are presented with the Advanced Options dialog box shown in Figure 14.8.

FIGURE 14.8
*Advanced
Options
Dialog Box*

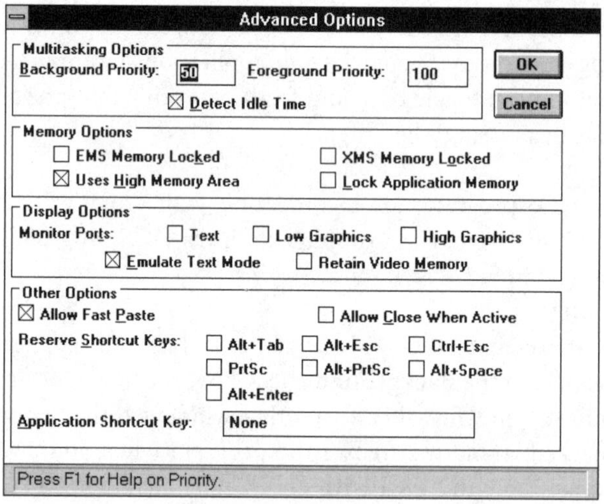

This dialog box provides additional PIF Editor parameters for 386 enhanced mode.

The Advanced Options dialog box contains four sections: Multitasking Options, Memory Options, Display Options, and Other Options. When you have finished adjusting these settings, click OK to return to the PIF Editor's basic screen.

Multitasking Options. The Multitasking Options section contains the settings for Background Priority, Foreground Priority, and Detect Idle Time.

The **Background Priority** box lets you specify a relative number that tells Windows how much processor time it should allot to the DOS application when it runs in the background. This setting applies only if the Background check box is selected in the Execution section of the basic PIF Editor screen. Otherwise this setting is ignored. The default value is 50, but you can enter any number from 0 to 10,000.

The **Foreground Priority** box lets you specify a relative number that tells Windows how much processor time to give the DOS application when it is run in the foreground—that is, when it is the active application. The default value is 100, but you can type any number from 0 to 10,000. You can give the application all the processing time it needs by setting this number to its maximum value of 10,000. This prevents any background applications from running unless your DOS application is idle, as for example when it's waiting for input. This is the best way to give the application priority, because it allows other applications to run when the program is idle.

The numbers you enter in the Foreground and Background priorities boxes affect only the allocation of processor time Windows reserves to the sum total of all your DOS applications, foreground and background. Here's a sample setup, assuming you're running three DOS applications:

	Foreground Value	Background Value
Application A	100	0
Application B	100	50
Application C	100	50
Subtotal*	100	100

Total processor time: 200 (100 for the foreground application and 50 for each of the two background applications)

*The subtotal is 100 because only one of the applications can run in the foreground at any given time.

In this example, Application A in the foreground receives 50 percent of the CPU processor time (its Foreground Priority value of 100 divided by the total of 200), whereas Applications B and C running in the background each receive 25 percent (their Background Priority values of 50 divided by the total of 200).

If you switched tasks to place Application B in the foreground, the total priority would equal 150: 100 for Application B, 50 for Application C, and nothing for Application A, because it hasn't been set to run in the background. Application B would now receive two-thirds of the total processor time devoted to DOS applications (its Foreground value of 100 divided by the total of 150), with the other third of the time going to Application C.

These priority settings values in the PIF Editor represent only the percentage of the DOS time slice each program will receive, not a percentage of total processor time, which is controlled by your adjustments to the Windows in Background and Windows in Foreground settings in the 386 Enhanced section of the Control Panel, as decribed earlier. Sometimes Windows will override your choices, particularly if you've created a piggy PIF; in this case, Windows may not feel that it is getting enough priority to run efficiently, and it may temporarily alter the Windows in Background and Windows in Foreground settings.

When a DOS program is running, you can temporarily override the multitasking options that were set in the program's PIF. If your program is running in a window or minimized as an icon, just select the Settings item on the DOS session's Control menu to bring up the dialog box with the multitasking settings shown earlier in Figure 14.8.

The **Detect Idle Time** check box instructs Windows to monitor an application and reclaim CPU time when the program is waiting for user input or some other event. For instance, if a spreadsheet recalculation has been completed, and the program is now idle, Windows will reclaim part of the spreadsheet's allotted CPU share and give it to other programs until the spreadsheet becomes "busy" again.

Danger Zone

If a DOS application seems to be running slower than a snail on Valium, remove the X from the Detect Idle Time check box. What's happening is that Windows is interfering with your DOS program while it's conducting some operation that Windows can't detect.

Memory Options. If you want to fine-tune memory management for each of your DOS applications, you should become familiar with the Memory Options section, which contains these four check boxes:

➤ **EMS Memory Locked** When checked, this option prevents the DOS application's expanded memory (EMS) from being swapped from memory onto the hard disk. This usually improves the program's performance, but it bogs down the rest of your system and eats a certain amount of your physical RAM. The default is off (no X in the box).

➤ **XMS Memory Locked** Works like the above item, except that this option prevents the application's extended memory (XMS) from being swapped from RAM onto the hard disk. Sometimes this improves performance of the program, but usually at the expense of everything else. The default is off.

➺ **Lock Application Memory** Works like the previous two items, except that this option prevents the conventional memory the program is using from being swapped from RAM onto the hard disk. In other words, this is yet another option that improves performance of the program at the expense of everything else. The default is off.

➺ **Uses High Memory Area** When checked, this option lets the DOS application use the computer's HMA (high memory area—that is, the first 64K of extended memory). Your system has only one HMA—if it's empty when you start Windows, each DOS session will have its own virtual HMA within its virtual machine. However, if the HMA contains DOS or a network driver, for example, none of the virtual machines, and hence none of your DOS programs, will have access to it. An X in this box is the default setting. I recommend using the default unless you want to prevent a program from using the HMA.

Ordinarily, Windows dynamically assigns and reallocates expanded and extended memory. Clicking the EMS Memory Locked or XMS Memory Locked box prevents Windows from repositioning this memory. If you have difficulty with a program when you switch away and return to it, you may solve the problem by selecting Lock Application Memory. Programs like Xerox Ventura Publisher for DOS and 4DOS gain an extra 64K when you select the Uses High Memory Area option.

Display Options. The Display Options section contains a Monitor Ports section as well as two check boxes for individual options: Emulate Text Mode and Retain Video Memory.

Some applications write directly to hardware input and output ports in order to gain display speed. These three check boxes in the **Monitor Ports** section let you instruct Windows to pay special attention to the way an application handles its interaction with the computer's video display system:

➺ Monitor Text

➺ Monitor Low Graphics

➺ Monitor High Graphics

When checked, any one of these options tells Windows to monitor the display system when the application is running in the mode indicated by the option. For example, to have Windows monitor the program whenever it is in high-resolution graphics mode, place an X in the Monitor High Graphics check box. The default setting for all of these items is off. Unless you are having specific problems with an application, it's best to leave these options unselected.

Danger Zone

The Monitor Ports section can cause trouble. Some high-resolution graphics applications will not let you switch back to Windows unless Monitor High Graphics is turned off. In general, when one of the monitor options is turned on the application's performance is impaired, and Windows may update the display sluggishly.

The only reason to turn on any of these items is when you get an empty screen or one full of garbage when you switch to a DOS application. Try selecting one of the Monitor Ports settings to see if it alleviates the problem, and if not, turn it back off.

The **Emulate Text Mode** option increases the speed at which many applications display text. The default setting is on, and in general you should leave it checked unless you are having trouble running a program, especially if the onscreen text is garbled or if the cursor has run amok. In that case, try removing the X from this check box.

The **Retain Video Memory** option prevents Windows from letting another application use the program's display memory. When this item is off (the default), Windows manages your video memory for better efficiency. The only time to use this option is if you switch away from a DOS application, do something that uses up too much of your available memory, and then switch back to your DOS program and kick it into a higher-resolution graphics mode. In this rare case, Windows may not be able to get the memory it needs to display the high-resolution graphics, and your display can distort, go blank, or even disappear. You can probably recover the application by freeing some memory or quitting some other applications.

When the Retain Video Memory option is checked, along with the corresponding Text, Low Graphics, or High Graphics option in the Video Memory section of the basic screen, Windows always allocates enough video memory for the application to be properly displayed. Whereas the Video Memory item provides the application with its initial needs, the Retain Video Memory option ensures that Windows doesn't give any of the video memory to other applications. This combination prevents Windows from managing your video memory, so that it can be shared by all the running applications.

Other Options. The Other Options section at the bottom of the Advanced Options dialog box contains a hodgepodge of leftover options. The first two items in the section are both check boxes:

➺ **Allow Fast Paste** Keep this box checked (the default) unless your application is having trouble when you paste things in from the Clipboard.

➺ **Allow Close When Active** When checked, this option lets you terminate a DOS session without having to quit the application or type Exit at the DOS prompt; you can also quit Windows while DOS sessions are still running.

Danger Zone

The Allow Close When Active option can corrupt files your DOS application is using if it's applied while a DOS application is still running. Never use this option for any application that opens files while it is running.

Most of the remaining options assign shortcut keys to DOS applications you plan to run under Windows. The **Reserve Shortcut Keys** area contains seven check boxes, one for each of the seven primary reserved key combinations that affect DOS sessions running in Windows:

➺ **Alt+Tab** Fast task switcher

➺ **Alt+Esc** Rotates through tasks in the order you started them

➺ **Ctrl+Esc** Brings up the Task Manager

➺ **PrtSc** Copies the entire screen to the Clipboard

➺ **Alt+PrtSc** Copies the active window

➺ **Alt+Space** Accesses the Control menu

➺ **Alt+Enter** Switches between full screen and window

The default setting is to leave all of these boxes unchecked. If you check a box, that key combination is reserved for use by the DOS application; any other function it might have had in Windows is disabled while the application is active.

The Application Shortcut Key lets you assign a special key combination to the application so that the program immediately pops up in the foreground, where you can work on it. By assigning unique key combinations to your various applications, you can quickly switch between different programs.

Each key combination must include either the Alt or Ctrl key. Shortcut keys are based on three- or four-key combinations, such as Ctrl+Alt+<the key you select>, Ctrl+Shift+<the key you select>, or Ctrl+Alt+Shift+<the key you select>, where <the key you select> cannot include backspace, spacebar, Enter, Esc, Tab, or Print Screen. When you run a program using the Application Shortcut Key, that key combination cannot be used for other tasks within Windows or for any other application.

To cancel a shortcut key definition, select the **Application Shortcut Key** option and press Shift+Backspace. This changes the setting to None. To restore the shortcut key to its previous value, just press backspace.

Insider's Tip

You can also assign shortcut keys for applications that were started using Program Manager icons (see Chapter 2). These keys let you launch an application that is not running, but shortcut keys assigned in the PIF Editor let you switch to the application only if it is already running. The shortcut keys you assign in Program Manager take precedence over the ones in the PIF.

Standard Mode Options for the PIF Editor

The PIF Editor lets you create a single .PIF file that contains the settings for running a DOS program in both standard and 386 enhanced modes. When you start the PIF Editor, it determines what mode you are running and displays the appropriate settings.

To switch modes, make your choice from the Mode menu, but be prepared to be jolted by the appearance of this overly strident warning message (Figure 14.9).

FIGURE 14.9
*Mode Change
Warning Box*

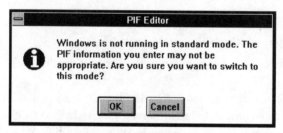

When you use the Mode menu to switch the PIF Editor between its 386 enhanced and standard mode options, it overreacts with this dialog box.

Although this dialog box makes it seem as if you're about to irreversibly mutate the human gene pool, ignore it.

If you start Windows in standard mode, or use the Mode menu to choose the standard mode settings, the PIF Editor diplays the options shown in Figure 14.10.

The standard mode settings fit within one window and share four similar settings with those for 386 enhanced mode:

➠ Program Filename

➠ Window Title

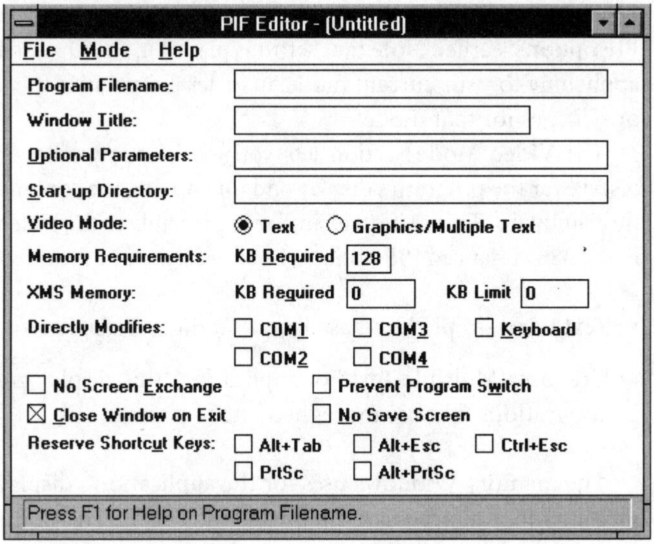

••••••••••••••
FIGURE 14.10
PIF Editor
Standard
Mode Options

These PIF Editor options allow you to control how a DOS application will run under Windows standard mode.

➺ Start-up Directory

➺ Close Window on Exit

Any value you enter for these four settings remains the same in both modes.

These next four items also appear in both the standard and 386 enhanced PIF Editor options, but their values are not shared:

➺ Optional Parameters

➺ Memory Requirements

➺ XMS Memory

➺ Reserve Shortcut Keys

Any values for these items must be set separately for each mode.

The first four items in the standard mode options screen of the PIF Editor operate just as they do in 386 enhanced mode:

➺ **Program Filename** The .EXE, .COM, or .BAT file that starts the application.

➺ **Window Title** The descriptive name that appears in the title bar of the application's window, or under its minimized icon.

➺ **Optional Parameters** Any command line parameters that the application accepts. If you put only a question mark (?) in the box, Windows will prompt you for options whenever the program is run.

➺ **Start-up Directory** The directory that should be active when the application is started.

For further details about these items, see the section on 386 enhanced mode PIF options, earlier. Note that settings placed in the Optional Parameters box apply only to your current mode, in order to optimize the use of parameters or switches for that mode.

The **Video Mode** section lets you tell Windows how much memory to reserve for the program's display and for copying the contents of the display to the Clipboard. This section is similar in principle to the Video Memory section in the 386 enhanced PIF options, but it is limited to these two settings:

➦ **Text** For a simple text-based application that displays only one screen

➦ **Graphics/Multiple Text** For applications that display graphics, or for text applications that use more than one text screen

The memory Windows uses for the application's display comes from the total memory allocated to the program. The Text setting requires the least memory and thus provides more for the program. If you're not certain which setting to use, choose Graphics/Multiple Text; this ensures that the program receives enough video memory to display itself.

The **Memory Requirements** section contains a single item, **KB Required**. This is similar to the corresponding setting in the 386 enhanced PIF options, although the value is not shared between the two modes. The number in the box represents how many kilobytes of conventional memory must be free for the application to run. The KB Required setting doesn't limit the amount of memory Windows gives to the application, but it will not run the application unless a specified minimum amount is available.

The **XMS Memory** section works the same way as in the 386 enhanced PIF options, but again, the values are not shared between modes. The two items in this section are

➦ **KB Required** The number of kilobytes of extended memory that must be free for the application to run. This setting should usually be left at 0, because any other value slows down switching to and from the program.

➦ **KB Limit** The maximum amount of extended memory that Windows will let the application use. If you type in 0, the application will not get any extended memory. If you type in −1, Windows gives the application as much extended memory as it requests.

The **Directly Modifies** section lets you tell Windows if the DOS application uses a COM port or needs to directly access the keyboard. Check the appropriate one of these five check boxes:

➤ **COM1** If the application uses COM1.

➤ **COM2** If the application uses COM2.

➤ **COM3** If the application uses COM3.

➤ **COM4** If the application uses COM4.

➤ **Keyboard** If the application needs to directly access the keyboard. When checked, the keyboard is recognized only by this application and not by Windows.

The **No Screen Exchange** check box, when checked, disables the use of the Print Screen key and the related Alt+Print Screen key combination. This effectively disables use of the Clipboard. The only reason to check this box is to conserve the small amount of memory that Windows steals from the application to capture its text screen.

The **Prevent Program Switch** check box, when checked, prevents Windows from switching away from the program until you quit it. This prevents Windows from using memory for program switching, and thus provides the application with a tad more memory. Microsoft also recommends checking this box if you're using a Microsoft Basic application that uses one of the COM ports.

The **Close Window on Exit** setting works like its counterpart in the 386 enhanced PIF options, and its value is shared by both modes. The default value for this setting is checked, which closes the DOS session as soon as you quit the application. If unchecked, the output of your DOS session remains on the screen after you quit the program. When you quit a text-based DOS program, a message comes up telling you to press any key to return to Windows. Although graphics-based programs do not display this message, you can also press any key to return to Windows.

The **No Save Screen** setting, when checked, lets you force Windows to discard the screen information for your program whenever you switch away from it; this lets Windows reclaim the memory used by the screen. The default for this setting is not checked; use this option only if your DOS application has the rare capability of saving its own screen information.

The **Reserve Shortcut Keys** section works much like the similar section in the 386 enhanced PIF options, but its values are not shared by both modes. With the standard mode PIF options, you can reserve the Alt+Tab, Alt+Esc, Ctrl+Esc, Print Screen, and Alt+Print Screen keys for use by the DOS application. (The Alt+Enter and Alt+spacebar combinations are only pertinent to 386 enhanced mode.) The default value for all of the shortcut key check boxes is not checked; checking a key combination causes it to be unrecognized by Windows and passes it directly to the DOS application.

• •

Modifying the _DEFAULT.PIF File

Windows will use the settings contained in the special _DEFAULT.PIF file. The underline character that starts the name of this file identifies it to Windows and ensures that it is always listed first in any alphabetical list of file names, such as those found in dialog boxes or in File Manager.

The initial settings contained in the _DEFAULT.PIF file match those that appear automatically when you start the PIF Editor without any associated .PIF file. To change these settings, simply edit your _DEFAULT.PIF file.

Insider's Tip

To return to the original _DEFAULT.PIF, you can back it up, or simply start the PIF Editor without an associated .PIF file and then save those settings in a file named _DEFAULT.PIF.

Because the settings in _DEFAULT.PIF were designed for a "worst case" scenario, you should update them to best match your system setup and the DOS programs that you run. Tables 14.1, 14.2, and 14.3 offer some suggestions.

• • • • • • • • • • • • • •
TABLE 14.1

386 Enhanced Mode: Basic Options

Options	Default Settings	Notes
Program Filename	_DEFAULT.BAT	Although this entry contains _DEFAULT.BAT, Windows substitutes the name of whatever .EXE, .COM, or .BAT file you are executing.
Window Title	Empty	If you leave this empty, Windows uses the name of the .EXE, .COM, or .BAT file as the title.
Optional Parameters	Empty	Leave this empty, or place a ? in the box if you always want to be prompted for parameters. If you pass any parameters to the .PIF when you run the file, they will override the instructions in this box.
Start-Up Directory	Empty	Leave this entry empty; instead, use the Working Directory setting in Program Manager.

Options	Default Settings	Notes
Video Memory: Text	Selected	To save memory, leave this selected.
Video Memory: Low Graphics	Not selected	
Video Memory: High Graphics	Not selected	
Memory Requirements: KB Required	128	This default value is fine for most situations.
Memory Requirements: KB Desired	640	Change to −1 so that the application receives only the memory it needs.
EMS Memory: KB Required	0	
EMS Memory: KB Limit	1024	Change to 0, and then create custom PIFs for DOS applications that use expanded memory.
XMS Memory: KB Required	0	
XMS Memory: KB Limit	1024	Change to 0, and then create custom PIFs for DOS applications that use extended memory.
Display Usage: Full Screen	Selected	If you frequently use programs that do not work if run in a window, leave this selected.
Display Usage: Windowed	Not selected	Select this if you want DOS applications to start in a window by default.
Execution: Background	Not checked	Leave this option off.
Execution: Exclusive	Not checked	Leave this option off.
Close Window on Exit	Checked	Leave this checked unless you usually want to view the result of an application after it has quit.

Options	Default Settings	Notes
Background Priority	50	Leave at 50, unless you want lots of background activity and don't mind the resulting loss in foreground performance; for a higher setting, try 100–200.
Foreground Priority	100	Set to 10,000 to make the application in the foreground as responsive as possible.
Detect Idle Time	Checked	
EMS Memory Locked	Not checked	
XMS Memory Locked	Not checked	
Use High Memory Area	Checked	
Lock Application Memory	Not checked	
Monitor Ports: Text, Low Graphics, High Graphics	None checked	Make sure that all of these are not checked; create a custom PIF for any DOS applications that need one of these settings to be checked.
Emulate Text Mode	Checked	
Retain Video Memory	Not checked	
Allow Fast Paste	Checked	
Allow Close When Active	Not checked	
Reserve Shortcut Keys	None checked	
Application Shortcut Key	None	

Options	Default Settings	Notes
Program Filename	_DEFAULT.BAT	This setting is shared with the 386 enhanced mode PIF options.
Window Title	Empty	This setting is shared with the 386 enhanced mode PIF options.

Options	Default Settings	Notes
Optional Parameters	Empty	Leave blank, or use a ? to be prompted for parameters.
Start-Up Directory	Empty	This setting is shared with the 386 enhanced mode PIF options.
Video Mode: Text	Selected	
Video Mode: Graphics/Multiple Text	Not selected	
Memory Requirements: KB Required	128	
XMS Memory: KB Required	0	Leave at 0 and create custom PIFs for DOS applications that use extended memory.
XMS Memory: KB Limit	0	
Directly Modifies: COM1, COM2, COM3, COM4	None checked	
Directly Modifies: Keyboard	Not checked	
No Screen Exchange	Not checked	
Prevent Program Switch	Not checked	
Close Window on Exit	Checked	This setting is shared with the 386 enhanced mode PIF options.
No Save Screen	Not checked	
Reserve Shortcut Keys	None checked	

Creating Program Manager Icons for PIFs

If you use Program Manager, I recommend that you create a Program Manager icon that runs the .PIF file rather than the .EXE or .COM file; in this way, you can create separate icons for each PIF if a DOS program has more than one. It also ensures that the program will be run from the custom PIF rather than from the _DEFAULT.PIF file.

To create an icon for a PIF in Program Manager,

1. Select the group in which you want to locate the PIF's icon.

2. Choose the New command from the File menu and select the Program Item radio button if it's not already selected. The Properties dialog box appears.

3. Type a descriptive title for the PIF's icon in the Description box.

4. Use the Browse button to place the path and file name for the PIF in the Command Line box.

5. Click on the Change Icon button and ignore the dialog box informing you that there is no icon for the file.

6. Select an icon for your application—use the Browse button to choose icons from another file, such as MORICONS.DLL.

There are two ways to specify what directory will be active when you start a DOS application from its PIF. You can specify a Working Directory for the icon in Program Manager, or you can specify a Start-Up Directory in the PIF Editor. If you use both methods, the Working Directory will take precedence over the Start-Up Directory. Both programs also let you specify a shortcut key combination, and the Program Manager combination again takes precedence over the .PIF file. Also, the Program Manager shortcut key actually runs the program, whereas the .PIF file shortcut key merely switches to the program if it's already running.

Insider's Tip   You may want to create more than one custom PIF for a DOS application. For example, you might want to specify different amounts of memory, different startup directories, different display options, or whatever. If you decide to create more than one PIF for an application, be sure to start the application from its .PIF rather than from its .EXE, .COM, or .BAT file.

Working with DOS Batch Files

A DOS batch file, identified by its .BAT file extension, is a special type of program that is composed of a series of DOS commands. A batch file is a plain text file; each line is executed as if you had typed it at the command prompt. DOS also includes some special batch commands that endow batch files with the ability to perform a few limited programming functions. DOS batch file commands are discussed in the section on AUTOEXEC.BAT in Chapter 13.

If you like to write macros, you'll be able to use batch files to their best advantage. And if you're the type who thinks macros are for biotics, you can still automate many repetitive DOS maneuvers by creating a simple batch file, which lists just a few commands.

It's often handy to start a DOS program from a .BAT file in order to preload whatever TSRs or drivers you use with the program, or so that you can adjust some DOS environment variables before you run the program. Because Windows recognizes both .PIF and .BAT files as programs, you can

➣ Run batch files from a PIF. This lets you create a custom PIF that runs the batch file itself, and whatever else is run from the batch file.

➣ Run PIFs from a batch file. This lets you run the batch file from one PIF, and then specify another PIF from within the batch file; in this way, you can switch to the settings stored in the new PIF.

.PIF files offer a great deal of flexibility for starting and configuring DOS programs when they are used together with batch files. With batch files you can set environment variables, change hardware options, load drivers, install TSRs, change the path, and employ a host of other DOS-driven configuration options. You can use the PIF to set other characteristics of the virtual machine, such as memory configuration and multitasking behaviour. By exercising both techniques, you can create an almost unlimited number of custom-configured virtual PCs, each one designed specifically for the application you intend to run on it. The only price you pay for each custom PC is your sweat—it takes a lot of PIF tweaking and batch brewing to get everything set up just right.

There is one idiosyncracy in the way a batch file works under Windows: when Windows runs a batch file, it first loads a temporary copy of COMMAND.COM, the DOS command processor, to process the batch file. When COMMAND.COM quits, so does your window—instantly—if your .PIF file has a check in the Close Window on Exit box (the default). In some cases, you may want to view the result of the batch file, or keep the DOS prompt for further duty. To do this, just remove the X from the Close Window on Exit check box in the PIF that was used to start the batch file.

If the batch file was started from _DEFAULT.PIF or DOSPRMPT.PIF or another PIF, use the PAUSE command at the end of your batch file. DOS will display the message "Press any key to continue" before obliterating the window.

To return to the DOS prompt after a batch file is run, use the DOS environment variable COMSPEC. The COMSPEC variable is created by DOS and indicates the directory location of your COMMAND.COM file. If you used the SET command to view your environment variables, for example, you might find a line such as

```
COMSPEC=C:\DOS\COMMAND.COM
```

If you use the COMSPEC variable as the last line of the batch file, the batch file will run COMAND.COM when it quits, keeping the command prompt on the screen so that the window won't close after running a batch file, even if the Close Window on Exit box is checked.

To use the COMSPEC variable in a batch file, you need to enclose it in percent signs (%) so that DOS will recognize it as a variable. For example, here's a little batch file that displays the environment setting and the status of your memory, and then returns you to the DOS prompt:

```
SET
MEM
%COMSPEC%
```

When the file is run from within Windows, a copy of COMMAND.COM is loaded to run the SET and MEM commands. The SET command displays the environment settings, and the MEM command displays a brief summary of memory availability. Then the %COMSPEC% line runs another copy of COM-MAND.COM to replace the one that ran the batch file, and presents you with a DOS command prompt after the batch file is finished running.

Insider's Tip

Batch files, by default, are recognized as programs by Windows and are therefore executed when you activate them from within Windows. However, you may want to prevent batch files from running without a custom PIF, because they behave more predictably when run from a PIF. To do that, you'll need to edit the [windows] section of your WIN.INI file. Find the line

```
Programs=com exe bat pif
```

and remove the "bat" entry. Windows will no longer recognize batch files as programs, and their File Manager icons will revert from application icons to generic icons. The batch file can now only be run from a PIF. You may also want to associate the .BAT file extension with a text editor, such as Notepad, by using File Manager's Associate command. This upgrades the generic icon to a document icon, which, when double-clicked, loads your batch file directly into the Notepad for viewing or editing.

Summary

DOS programs represent the largest category of software for personal computers. Because Windows runs on top of DOS, it provides good compatibility with the vast majority of DOS applications. You can run a DOS prompt session, standalone programs, and popup programs from within Windows. In standard mode, these programs must all be run full screen. In 386 enhanced mode, you can choose to run these programs full screen or in a self-contained window on your desktop.

When you run DOS sessions or applications in a window, you can set a wide variety of options, such as memory configuration and fonts. Windows' 386 enhanced mode also lets you multitask DOS applications, so that they can run simultaneously with your Windows applications.

You can use the Windows Clipboard to cut and paste text, and sometimes graphics, among both DOS and Windows programs.

In order to configure and fine-tune your DOS programs, Windows provides the PIF Editor utility, which lets you specify how programs will run in both standard and 386 enhanced mode. DOS programs cannot run without a PIF, and if you don't specify a particular PIF, Windows uses the default PIF settings.

Creating a proper PIF can mean the difference between a DOS program working and not working with Windows. Fine-tuning PIFs can affect the performance and behavior of your DOS programs, and allows you to manage their multitasking capabilities when run under Windows. You can combine the use of PIFs and batch files to add further power and flexibility in configuring DOS sessions and programs.

Insider's Tech Support

Q: When I try to start a program by double-clicking on it in File Manager, I get a File Not Found message, even though everything is there, and I have a .PIF file set up for it.

A: Inspect the directory in which the program resides for multiple PIFs. For instance, WordPerfect 5.1 installs itself with a default PIF called WP.PIF, which specifies the program location as C:\WP51. If you've installed WordPerfect in a different path and/or created a second PIF, File Manager still attempts to start WordPerfect using the default values for WP.PIF. Check all .PIF files in the directory in the PIF Editor to make certain they contain correct drive and path information to the program; delete extraneous .pif files.

Q: When I run my DOS program in a small window, I can't access my floppy drives.

A: Try making the following change to the [386enh] section of system.ini:

```
[386enh]
IRQ9Global=YES
```

If this doesn't solve the problem, try disabling the Monitor Ports option and set Video Memory to Text instead of High Graphics in the Advanced options for the application's .pif file.

Q: I can't switch away from a DOS application back to Windows or another program.

A: Check to see that Retain Video Memory is enabled in the application's PIF. If Windows is running in standard mode, check to see whether Directly Modifies or Prevent Program Switch has been enabled in the PIF settings. If they have, disable these options.

Q: When I run my DOS program in a window, the mouse doesn't work.

A: To use a mouse in a windowed DOS application, you must load a Windows 3.1-aware mouse driver before starting Windows. During installation, Windows searches for an old mouse driver in the autoexec.bat and config.sys. If one is found, Windows replaces it with a newer version. However, if no mouse driver was present in the original config.sys, the setup program does not copy the new files into the Windows directory. You have to do this yourself by expanding the appropriate file from the Windows installation disks.

You may also need to add the following statement to the [NonWindowsApps] section of system.ini:

```
[NonWindowsApps]
MouseInDosBox=1
```

Q: When I try to run Lotus 1-2-3, release 3.1, under Windows, I get a "DOS16M" error message, and the program won't start.

A: Try locking 1-2-3's use of conventional, extended, and expanded memory usage by selecting the Lock Memory option in the Memory Options section of the Advanced Options dialog box for the PIF.

Q: I'm low on memory and get an Out of Memory message when I try to run my DOS applications.

A: Try loading the "problem" application first in a full-screen window; you may then be able to load your other programs. Clearing the Retain Video Memory and Lock Application Memory options from the PIFs of other programs will also release memory to the system.

Q: When I open more than one DOS application under Windows, performance gets unacceptably sludgy.

A: If you don't need a DOS program to be continuously active, deselect the Runs in Background box in the Control menu's settings. (Or permanently deselect this option in the application's PIF.) You can also choose the Exclusive option in the Control menu or in the PIF settings, to give an application the full attention of Windows when it runs in the foreground.

If you need to run DOS applications in the background, try experimenting with the Detect Idle Time option in their PIFs. With some applications, turning this option on allows Windows to recover unused CPU time.

Inside the Windows Initialization Files

Most computer systems, including the PC, contain files that are read when the computer is first started. Called "boot files" in computer slang, these are formally known as either "initialization files" or "startup files." Without these files, you wouldn't be able to configure your software to work in tandem with your particular kind of hardware.

In fact, without these files, you wouldn't be able to run any kind of application software whatsoever.

Since the advent of the IBM Personal Computer and DOS in 1981, two startup files—CONFIG.SYS and AUTOEXEC.BAT—have played a crucial role. Essentially, these files provide ways to describe your system configuration, load device drivers, and set various other options so that your computer system can run with your particular hardware and software configuration.

To make these two startup files easy to edit, they are stored in DOS as generic text files. Chapter 13 contains detailed instructions on how to edit the CONFIG.SYS and AUTOEXEC.BAT files to ensure that DOS is correctly configured for running Windows. Windows also edits the CONFIG.SYS and AUTOEXEC.BAT files; in fact, Windows Setup usually automatically alters these files during installation to set and load special DOS options and DOS drivers.

Because Windows settings requirements far surpass what can be achieved using either of these two DOS startup files, Windows adds its own collection of initialization files, identified by the extension .INI. Windows reads these files each time it is started and retains key pieces of information it reads from these files into memory during your Windows session, automatically updating the disk files if the settings are changed.

Two of these Windows initialization files—**WIN.INI** and **SYSTEM.INI**—are crucial to starting the Windows environment. The WIN.INI file contains the settings that let you customize your Windows environment for such items as printers, fonts, ports, and the color scheme on your screen. The SYSTEM.INI file contains settings that control hardware configuration, device drivers, memory management, and virtual machines. Like DOS, Windows stores its initialization files as plain text files to make editing easy.

Danger Zone

Although you can edit startup and initialization files with any text editor, it's safest to use the Windows Notepad or the SysEdit utility. A full-blown wordprocessor might damage the initialization files by inserting its own formatting information into a file or altering the ASCII values of certain characters—actions that could corrupt a file and possibly crash your entire system.

Many Windows programs also include their own initialization files, which are read on startup. For example, Program Manager and File Manager, which are themselves Windows applications, use **PROGMAN.INI** and **WINFILE.INI**, respectively, to store their various settings. In addition, the Control Panel uses **CONTROL.INI** to store settings for printer information, multimedia drivers, desktop color schemes, desktop patterns, and screen saver options.

DOSAPP.INI contains a list of all the DOS applications you have run from within Windows.

The same is true for some third-party applications. Excel, for example, uses EXCEL.INI, and Adobe Type Manager has ATM.INI. The documentation that came with your Windows applications should describe any corresponding initialization files.

Some applications act a bit like a virus: they add their own information to the WIN.INI file (or to some other preexisting .INI file). Because .INI files can't exceed 64K, however, and because the WIN.INI file tends to be the largest of the initialization files, Microsoft recommends that developers create application-specific .INI files, rather than append information to the WIN.INI file. Although many developers have taken this advice, quite a few still append the information to WIN.INI, including Microsoft—witness the Write, Cardfile, and Paintbrush applets. These are the application .INI files created by programs included with Windows:

➻ **CLOCK.INI** Created by the Clock utility

➻ **MPLAYER.INI** Created by the Media Player

➻ **MSD.INI** Created by the Microsoft Diagnostics utility

➻ **SOL.INI** Created by the Solitaire game

➻ **WINMINE.INI** Created by the Minesweeper game

Editing .INI Files

The general structure of all .INI files is similar, and so are the techniques for editing them. All the settings for the main Windows environment and shell initialization files are discussed in this chapter. For information about application-specific .INI files, contact the application vendor.

To edit the two Windows environment initialization files, WIN.INI and SYSTEM.INI, together with the two DOS startup files, CONFIG.SYS and AUTOEXEC.BAT, discussed in Chapter 13, just use SysEdit. The SysEdit file-editing utility is described in Chapter 5. SysEdit opens all four files simultaneously, thus ensuring that the four files you open are the ones in active use by Windows. This feature is handy when you have multiple copies or versions of these files and can't recall which file Windows is actually using.

To make changes to only one of these startup files, or to edit another one, such as PROGMAN.INI, use the Notepad utility, also discussed in Chapter 5.

Be careful when editing any of these startup files; even the slightest error can cause Windows to behave strangely or even crash. Save a version of the file under a different name before you start making changes. For example, save WIN.INI with a name such as WININI.BAK before editing it. That way, your original (and uncorrupted) file will be available if you inadvertently damage the edited version.

The two Windows environment initialization files—WIN.INI and SYSTEM.INI—are read every time Windows is started, and can be automatically updated during your session. Shell or application initialization files, such as WINFILE.INI or CLOCK.INI, are read by the appropriate application only when it is run. You should leave these initialization files in the directories in which they were originally placed by the application's installation program—usually the Windows subdirectory, but sometimes the application's own subdirectory.

All Windows initialization files (denoted by the .INI file name suffix) are text files, organized in this fashion:

➼ Each file contains one or more sections.

➼ Each section begins with the section name enclosed in brackets, such as [386Enh].

➼ The bracketed section name is followed by statements detailing the settings values for that section.

Although these initialization files are plain ASCII text files, formatting must be precise. Here's the generic structure of a section in an initialization file:

```
[SectionName]
SettingName=<value>
;comments
```

Windows requires that the left bracket of the SectionName be in the leftmost column of the document. The SettingName is the specific name of a particular setting or option. The SettingName can contain any combination of letters, from a through z, and any combination of digits, from 0 through 9. However, every entry must be followed by an equal sign (=) with no space between the setting name and the equal sign. The order of the sections and of the settings within a section has no significance.

The <value> immediately follows the equal sign. For the value (which defines the information required to specify a certain setting or option) you can designate a number, a series of numbers, a word, an alphanumeric string, or a text string enclosed in quotes. Many of the settings in initialization files have a **boolean value**, which is used to turn the setting on or off, and can contain several synonymous values, as shown in Table 15.1.

Boolean True	Boolean False
true	false
on	off
yes	no
1	0

For example, Spooler=YES is the same as Spooler=ON.

Initialization files can also contain comments; each line of comments must begin with a semicolon in the leftmost column.

When you first install Windows, Setup creates the SYSTEM.INI, WIN.INI, and CONTROL.INI files based on the template files SYSTEM.SRC, WIN.SRC., and CONTROL.SRC, respectively. These .SRC files remain on your installation disks, where you can refer to them in order to determine the original state of these files. The other .INI files are created by the applications that use them, but sometimes an .INI file will not be created by an application unless you change one of its default settings. If a statement or section is not listed in an .INI file, the default value for that setting is used.

Editing the WIN.INI File

WIN.INI, along with SYSTEM.INI, is one of the two initialization files that Windows reads each time it launches the environment. Certain sections of these files are held in memory, where they are accessed during your Windows session. For example, your system refers to the [Extensions] section of the WIN.INI file each time you open a document that has been associated with a particular application.

Many settings in the WIN.INI file can also be edited graphically by using the Control Panel, which is discussed in Chapter 4. The Control Panel allows you to set the following options: Color, Fonts, Ports, Mouse, Desktop, Printers, International, Keyboard, Date/Time, Sound, and—if you have them—Network and 386 Enhanced. Setting the options graphically by using the various icons in the Control Panel actually changes the corresponding lines in your WIN.INI and SYSTEM.INI files.

Most changes invoked with the Control Panel take effect as soon as you click OK. Three exceptions occur, however: Date/Time, Networks, and 386 Enhanced, which all relate to settings found in the SYSTEM.INI file. These settings do not take effect until you restart Windows.

In addition, WIN.INI contains sections that cannot be accessed through the Control Panel. For example, entries in the [Extensions] section are edited using the Associate command in File Manager. Some entries, furthermore, can only be modified by editing the file directly.

Insider's Tip

If you need to update a large number of items in the .INI files on several different systems, it's easier to just cut and paste the affected sections of the file than to use the Control Panel on each machine to change the settings by hand. Understanding how to edit the text entries also allows you to design your own utility programs that automatically modify the settings.

Organization of the WIN.INI File

WIN.INI files normally contain all of the following sections—usually, but not always, in this order:

[Windows] The settings in this section affect your entire Windows environment and include keyboard speed, mouse settings, and the width of window borders. This section relates to the mouse icon, keyboard icon, and sound icon in the Control Panel.

[Desktop] Corresponds to the desktop icon in the Control Panel and contains the settings for the screen background, positioning of windows, and spacing of icons.

[Extensions] Contains the list of file extensions and their corresponding applications. Extensions is not affected by the Control Panel. You can add entries to this list by using the Associate command in the File Manager.

[Intl] Corresponds to the international icon in the Control Panel; contains the settings for country, language, number formats, and currency formats.

[Ports] Contains the settings for all the I/O ports. Some of these ports can be set with the port icon from the Control Panel.

[Fonts] Relates to the Font icon in the Control Panel. This section lists the screen fonts that can be used by Windows.

[**FontSubstitutes**] Lists font names that will be substituted with a different font when printed.

[**TrueType**] Contains settings specific to the use of TrueType fonts.

[**MCI Extensions**] Lists file extensions for multimedia files and the device driver that can be used to play that type of file.

[**Network**] Contains settings used by network drivers and the information about your previous network connections.

[**Embedding**] Only used by applications developed for Windows version 3.0; lists objects that can be used with OLE and specifies the program used to create them and their file format. Windows 3.1 applications use the OLE registration database instead.

[**Windows Help**] Contains the settings used by the Windows Help system.

[**Sound**] Lists system events and their corresponding sound files.

[**PrinterPorts**] Contains the active and inactive printers that you have set up for use with Windows.

[**Devices**] Only used by applications developed for Windows version 2.x. These programs must check the [devices] section to identify what printers can be used. Applications for Windows 3 and higher refer instead to the [PrinterPorts] section.

[**Programs**] Lists directory paths that Windows will search to locate applications that are not identified by the PATH statement in your AUTOEXEC.BAT file.

[**Colors**] Relates to the Colors icon in the Control Panel and contains the settings that control the color of the desktop and its related elements.

Although the WIN.INI file uses this as the default sequence, you can organize the sections in any order. Within each section, the settings can also be arranged in any order. In addition, other Windows applications may add their own sections or other information to the WIN.INI file. Consult the documentation supplied with your applications to determine what effect, if any, it has on WIN.INI as well as on other Windows initialization and startup files. Also check to see if the program features a deinstall feature that neatly removes all of its additions and modifications to your system files. Although this feature is uncommon, it's something Windows users should vociferously demand.

. . . .

The [Windows] Section of WIN.INI

The first section in WIN.INI, the [Windows] section, contains information about a variety of settings that need to be determined when you first start your Windows session. These settings include statements that determine what applications, if any, will be loaded or run when you start Windows; your keyboard and mouse settings; and some printer options. This is the default [Windows] section that Setup creates for a new installation of Windows 3.1:

```
[Windows]
load=
run=
Beep=yes
Spooler=yes
NullPort=None
device=
BorderWidth=3
CursorBlinkRate=530
DoubleClickSpeed=452
Programs=com exe bat pif
Documents=
DeviceNotSelectedTimeout=15
TransmissionRetryTimeout=45
KeyboardDelay=2
KeyboardSpeed=31
ScreenSaveActive=0
ScreenSaveTimeOut=120
```

Optional items, such as SwapMouseButtons, that can occur in the [Windows] section but that are not initially listed, are set to their default values, as described later in the chapter.

Load. The first statement in a typical WIN.INI file is the Load statement, which takes the form

```
Load=<file name(s)>
```

where <file name(s)> is the name of one or more applications that should be loaded—that is, run as icons—when you start your Windows session. To load the applications along with specific documents, you can list one or more document file names, but only if that document is associated with an application—that is, if its extension is listed in the [Extensions] section of the WIN.INI file. If you list more than one file, whether an application or a document, each one should include the full path name (if it is not in the active directory) and be separated from every other file name by a space. For example, the line

```
LOAD=WINFILE.EXE GOFORIT.REC C:\AUDREY\FEEDME.TXT
```

would first load the WINFILE program—that is, File Manager; then it would initiate the macro utility Recorder, along with the script GOFORIT.REC; finally it would start Notepad together with the document FEEDME.TXT located in the directory c:\audrey. All three would appear as minimized icons.

The Windows default setting contains no specification for loading a file. The Load statement was provided to force the startup of a third-party shell. Although this statement works if you are using Program Manager (and is the only way to create startup files with Windows 3.0), Windows 3.1 adds a new feature to Program Manager that lets you create a group called StartUp. By using a valid Program Manager icon in the StartUp group, you can load all the applications—and related documents, if any—represented by the icons in the StartUp group. Using the Load command is the equivalent of placing an icon in the StartUp group and setting it to MinimizeOnUse in the icon's Properties dialog box. They will also run as minimized icons whenever you start Windows.

Run. This statement is usually found as the second item in the [Windows] section, directly following Load. It is similar to the Load statement, but Run differs because it instructs Windows to place the application and associated document, if any, in an open window rather than as a minimized icon on the desktop. The Run statement takes the form

```
Run=<file name(s)>
```

where <file name(s)> designates the applications or associated documents that you want opened into application windows when you start your Windows session. For example,

```
Run=WINFILE.EXE
```

runs File Manager in an open application window when you launch Windows.

Using the Run statement is similar to placing an icon in Program Manager's StartUp group. The default value for the Run statement is to leave it blank.

Beep. This setting determines whether Windows will sound a warning beep to alert you to a special condition, such as a printer error, or to an action you are taking that is not permitted or available. The beep statement takes the form

```
Beep=<YES or NO>
```

where the word yes or no is specified. The default setting is

```
Beep=YES
```

to signify that a warning beep should be sounded. This function is usually controlled by the Sound icon in the Control Panel, and the value can be changed by checking or unchecking the Enable System Sounds check box in the Sound dialog box (Figure 15.1).

• • • • • • • • • • • • • •
FIGURE 15.1
*Sound
Dialog Box*

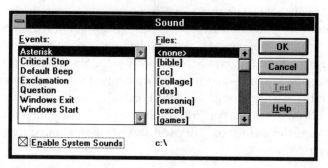

The Beep= statement corresponds to the Enable System Sounds check box.

An X in the check box sets the beep to YES; an empty box sets it to NO.

Spooler. The Spooler statement tells Windows whether to use Print Manager to handle output sent to the printer. The statement takes the form

```
Spooler=<YES or NO>
```

The default setting is

```
Spooler=YES
```

signifying that Print Manager will be used to handle all output jobs. If you change this value to NO, Windows bypasses Print Manager and sends the output directly to the printer. To change this value, alter the status of the UsePrint Manager check box, using the Printers icon in the Control Panel (Figure 15.2).

••••••••••••••
FIGURE 15.2
*Print
Manager
Section of
Printers
Dialog Box*

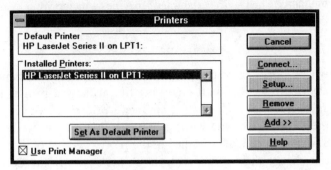

The Spooler= statement corresponds to the Use Print Manager check box in the Printers dialog box.

NullPort. This statement is used to specify the name that Windows uses for a null port. The null port is the designation for an output device that is not currently connected to any active port, such as LPT1:. The name of the null port appears in various printer dialog boxes to show a device that is installed. Specifically, the null port name indicates that a device driver, although present, is not connected to a specific output port. This statement takes the form

```
NullPort=<name>
```

where <name> is the name you designate to appear in Printer dialog boxes. The default value is

```
NullPort=None
```

which causes the word None to appear as the null port in Printer dialog boxes. Changing this value in this line to

```
NullPort=Ice
```

changes the null port name to Ice, as shown in Figure 15.3.

••••••••••••••
FIGURE 15.3
*Printers
Dialog Box
with Ice as
Null Port
Name*

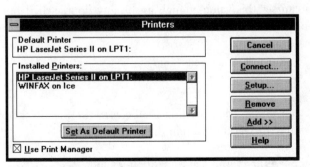

Change the null port setting to alter the listing in the Printers dialog box.

You can't set the null port name using the Control Panel. To change the default value of None, you must edit the NullPort statement.

Device=. The Device= statement specifies which printer Windows uses as its default selection. The statement takes the form

```
Device=<printer name>, <printer driver>, <port>
```

where <printer name> is the name of any device name listed in the [Devices] section of the WIN.INI file, usually a printer but sometimes another device such as a fax modem; <printer driver> is the file name of the device driver you wish to use with that output device; and <port> is any valid port name specified in the [Ports] section of the WIN.INI file. You can change these values with the Printers icon in the Control Panel. The default for any of these values is determined by whatever you specified in the Printers dialog setup box during or after Windows installation.

If you want to designate an output device in this statement, be sure to specify its exact port and driver. Here's how you might set up this statement:

```
Device=HP LaserJet Series II, HPPCL, LPT1:
```

This specifies that the default printer is an HP LaserJet II using the HPPCL printer driver that is connected to the main printer port, LPT1:.

BorderWidth. This statement lets you specify the thickness of the borders that Windows places around the resizable windows in the display. The BorderWidth statement takes the form

```
BorderWidth=<number>
```

where <number> is a number from 1 to 49 that represents your designated pixel width. Windows initially sets a default value of 3, which works well. If you narrow your border to 1, unless you have the dexterity of an oral surgeon, you'll find it difficult to grab the edge of the window with the mouse.

To catch hold of the border more easily, increase the width to 5. Although you can set this value as high as 49, any double-digit border seems ludicrously large. In fact, a border 49 pixels wide produces an area greater than most windows.

To adjust the statement

```
BorderWidth=5
```

you can either edit this line in the WIN.INI file or change the value by accessing the Desktop icon in the Control Panel.

KeyboardSpeed and KeyBoardDelay. The KeyboardSpeed statement is used to set the interval between automatic repetitions of any key you choose to press. To adjust this setting graphically, access the Keyboard icon in the Control Panel. You can drag the Repeat Rate scroll bar in the Keyboard dialog box to adjust the key repeat rate in a quick-and-dirty fashion (Figure 15.4).

FIGURE 15.4
Repeat Rate Scroll Bar in the Keyboard Dialog Box

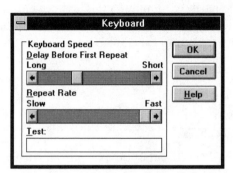

The KeyboardSpeed= statement corresponds to the Repeat Rate scroll bar in the Keyboard dialog box.

Editing the KeyboardSpeed statement in the WIN.INI file gives you a more precise way to adjust this speed. The KeyboardSpeed statement assumes the form

```
KeyboardSpeed=<rate>
```

where <rate> quantifies the amount of time between repetitions. The value of <rate> can be any number from 0 through 31—the higher the value, the faster the key repeats. For example, the default setting of

```
KeyBoardSpeed=31
```

signifies that a key will repeat itself at the fastest rate. Note that this feature does not work with all models of keyboards.

The KeyboardDelay statement specifies how many milliseconds elapse before the key starts to repeat after you press it. The KeyBoardDelay statement takes the form

```
KeyBoardDelay=<0-3>
```

where 0 provides approximately $\frac{1}{4}$-second delay; 1 provides $\frac{1}{2}$-second delay; 2 provides 1-second delay; and 3 provides a delay of $1\frac{1}{2}$ seconds. The default is 2, indicating that about a second elapses before the key begins to repeat. This statement can be set graphically using the Delay Before First Repeat scroll bar in the Keyboard section of the Control Panel shown in Figure 15.4.

CursorBlinkRate. This statement specifies how many milliseconds you want to elapse between each blink of the cursor. The statement takes the form:

```
CursorBlinkRate=<milliseconds>
```

where milliseconds designates the interval between blinks of the cursor. The default setting is

```
CursorBlinkRate=530
```

which obviously designates 530 milliseconds between blinks. You can adjust this setting graphically with the Cursor Blink Rate scroll bar found in the Desktop section of the Control Panel (Figure 15.5).

• • • • • • • • • • • • •
FIGURE 15.5

Cursor Rate Scroll Bar from the Desktop

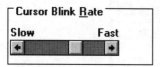

The CursorBlinkRate statement can be adjusted less precisely using the CursorBlinkRate scroll bar in the Desktop section of the Control Panel.

Using the Control Panel to adjust this rate provides direct visual feedback, because the cursor blink rate varies as you change the corresponding settings. The scroll bar provides access to values that range from 200 through 1200 milliseconds. A more precise way, however, is to designate the value in the CursorBlinkRate statement.

DoubleClickSpeed, DoubleClickWidth, and DoubleClickHeight.

The DoubleClickSpeed statement lets you define the number of milliseconds you wish to set as the maximum interval between two clicks of the mouse button that Windows will interpret as a double-click, as opposed to two separate clicks. This statement takes the form

```
DoubleClickSpeed=<milliseconds>
```

where <milliseconds> specifies the maximum amount of time desired between two consecutive clicks that will constitute a double-click. The default setting of

```
DoubleClickSpeed=452
```

sets the maximum double-click interval at 452 milliseconds. Decreasing this value decreases the amount of time in which you can click twice to create a double-click. A higher value lets you double-click at a more leisurely pace. To change this setting graphically, access the Mouse icon in the Control Panel (Figure 15.6).

Although you cannot set as precise a value, the graphical setting gives you immediate feedback; the Test button darkens when you click it twice within the valid double-click interval.

The DoubleClickWidth and DoubleClickHeight statements let you define an area on the screen within which two clicks of the mouse will count as a double-click, rather than as two single clicks. The statements take the form:

•••••••••••••
FIGURE 15.6
*Double Click
Speed Setting
in the Mouse
Dialog Box*

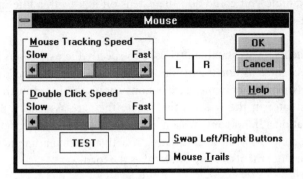

*The
DoubleClickSpeed
setting can be
graphically adjusted
using the Mouse
section of the
Control Panel.*

```
DoubleClickWidth=<pixels>
DoubleClickHeight=<pixels>
```

The default for the <pixels> in both of these statements is 4, signifying that an area 4 pixels wide by 4 pixels high defines the boundaries within which two clicks count as a double-click. This setting works fine for a mouse, but if you're using Windows for Pen Computing, or some other stylus-based pointer, you may want to increase your double-clicking area to something like

```
DoubleClickWidth=32
DoubleClickHeight=32
```

Note that Windows only accepts an even number; odd numbers are rounded to the nearest even number. These settings do not relate to any items in the Control Panel and can only be altered by editing these statement lines.

Programs. This statement specifies those file extensions that Windows associates with files that can be run as applications. The statement takes the form

```
Programs=<extensions>
```

Each extension name must contain three characters, must be separated from another extension name by a space, and should not include the periods that normally precede extensions. For example, the default value for this statement

```
Programs=com exe bat pif
```

specifies that files ending in .com, .exe, and .bat can be run as programs—the normal DOS convention. In addition, it indicates that files ending with the .pif extension can also be run as applications—a feature unique to Windows. To change these values, you must edit this line in the win.ini file.

For example you could add the extension scr to this line in order to run screen-saver files as programs.

Documents. This statement is used to specify file extensions that Windows will recognize as document files (rather than as programs or unassociated files). Normally, document extensions should be listed in the [Extensions] section later in the win.ini file, where they are associated with particular applications. If, for some reason, you want Windows to recognize a file-type as a document, without associating it with a particular application, you can use the Documents statement. It takes the form

```
Documents=<extensions>
```

where <extensions> is one or more three-character file extensions, separated by spaces, and without the preceding periods. For example,

```
Documents=dat
```

indicates that files with the extension .dat are to be recognized as documents (and have the appropriate document-style icon in File Manager), although they are not associated with a particular application. The default value for this statement is to leave it blank.

DeviceNotSelectedTimeout and TransmissionRetryTimeout. The Device-NotSelected Timeout statement is used to set the number of seconds that Windows will wait for a device to be activated, or turned on, before it attempts to send output to that device. If Windows receives no response from the device after the designated number of seconds, it halts its attempt to send output and then usually displays an error message to that effect. Sometimes, however, Windows jumps the gun and displays an error message as soon as it senses that a device is inactive. The DeviceNotSelectedTimeout statement takes the form

```
DeviceNotSelectedTimeout=<seconds>
```

where <seconds> is the number of seconds Windows will wait for an output device to be activated. The default value is 15 seconds. To double that amount, you would change the value to

```
DeviceNotSelectedTimeout=30
```

Note that this statement applies only to the system default value. To assign an individual output device its own DeviceNotSelectedTimeout value, designate that value in the [PrinterPorts] section later in the win.ini file. You can also change this value for a specific printer by accessing the

Printers icon in the Control Panel and pressing the Connect button. Figure 15.7 depicts a section of the Printers dialog box in which you can change that item.

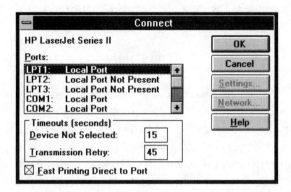

Any changes made through the Control Panel affect only the value for the selected printer in the [PrinterPorts] section; the default value listed in the DeviceNotSelectedTimeout statement here remains the same and can only be changed by editing this statement line.

The TransmissionRetryTimeout statement specifies the time Windows will wait between its attempts to transmit to an output device, as opposed to the time it will wait for the device to be activated as in the previous statement. The TransmissionRetryTimeout statement takes the form

```
TransmissionRetryTimeout=<seconds>
```

where <seconds> specifies the number of seconds Windows will wait before it retries a transmission. If Windows cannot initiate a successful transmission within this time limit, it responds with an alert box stating that the printer is not responding. The default value for this statement is 45 seconds, unless you have specified a PostScript printer, in which case the default is set to 90 seconds.

As with the DeviceNotSelectedTimeout statement, the Transmission-RetryTimeout statement assigns the default value used by Windows for this setting. You can assign any individual output device its own Transmission-RetryTimeout value, as specified in the [PrinterPorts] section of the WIN.INI file. You can also change this value for a specific printer using the Printers icon in the Control Panel. Figure 15.7 shows the area in the Printers dialog box where you can change this value.

Changes you make using the Control Panel affect only the values in the [PrinterPorts] section and do not affect the default value listed in the Trans-missionRetryTimeout statement. To change the default value, you must edit this statement line.

MouseSpeed, MouseThreshold1, and MouseThreshold2. These three statements control the tracking speed of the mouse. The master control switch for this trio is MouseSpeed, which controls the relationship between mouse and pointer movements, subject to the values set with MouseThreshold1 and MouseThreshold2. The three statements take the form

```
MouseSpeed=<0 or 1 or 2>
MouseThreshold1=<pixels>
MouseThreshold2=<pixels>
```

where the <0 or 1 or 2> serves as a switch that controls how the other two statements are interpreted. The <pixels> value represents the number of pixels that the mouse must move between the mouse's hardware interrupts in order to trigger a condition set by the <switch>. Windows monitors the number of pixels that the pointer has traveled across the screen between each of its hardware interrupts in order to measure the speed of your mouse movements. Windows sets one of two acceleration speeds you specify in the MouseThreshold 1 and 2 statements, based on the number of pixels the pointer moves between the two interrupts.

The MouseSpeed <0 or 1 or 2> variable can be set to only 0, 1, or 2. At 0, the mouse acceleration feature used in mouse tracking is turned off. At 1, Windows accelerates the pointer to twice its normal speed if you're moving the mouse faster than the value set in MouseThreshold1; Windows does this by doubling the number of pixels that the pointer moves for every actual pixel of mouse movement. At 2, the pointer is accelerated to twice its normal speed when the movement of the mouse exceeds the value of MouseThreshold1, or four times the normal speed if you move the mouse faster than the speed set in MouseThreshold2.

The Windows default settings are

```
MouseSpeed=1
MouseThreshold1=5
MouseThreshold2=10
```

This sets the MouseSpeed switch to 1. In other words, Windows speeds the pointer to twice its normal pace if it determines that you are moving the mouse farther than 5 pixels between interrupts. If the switch is set to 1, however, the quadruple-speed tracking option is turned off. Changing the lines to read

```
MouseSpeed=2
MouseThreshold1=5
MouseThreshold2=10
```

sets the switch to 2 and activates the quadruple-speed tracking option. This setting doubles the speed of the pointer while it moves in the 5-to-9 pixel-per-interrupt range, and accelerates the speed four-fold if the mouse movement exceeds 10 pixels per interrupt. With two thresholds available, you can create a ballistic tracking effect, so that the pointer moves faster the faster you move the mouse. This technique takes some practice, but it can be very helpful, especially with large-screen and high-resolution monitors, because it makes moving the pointer across the screen much faster.

The MouseSpeed, MouseThreshold1, and MouseThreshold2 statements offer precise control over the two ballistic speed-up trigger points. You can also change these settings—although much more crudely—by accessing the Mouse icon in the Control Panel and adjusting the Mouse Tracking Speed scroll bar (Figure 15.8).

• • • • • • • • • • • • • •
FIGURE 15.8
Mouse
Tracking
Speed Section
of Control
Panel

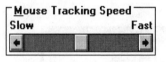

Adjusting the Mouse Tracking Speed scroll bar is a graphic but crude method of making changes to the MouseSpeed and MouseThreshold settings.

MouseTrails and SwapMouseButtons. The MouseTrails statement lets you specify how many pointers trail behind the actual pointer when the Mouse Trails feature is activated. The Mouse Trails feature is designed for laptop computers that use an LCD display, because the pointer often disappears when you move the mouse quickly. In order to use MouseTrails, you must also be using a display driver that supports this feature. (The EGA ,VGA, and SuperVGA drivers included in Windows 3.1 all support Mouse Trails.)

The MouseTrails statement takes the form

```
MouseTrails=<number of pointers>
```

The <number of pointers> can be any number between 1 and 7, depending on how many trailing pointers you desire. For example, the line

```
MouseTrails=4
```

leaves a trail of four pointers behind a moving, and perhaps vanishing, cursor. To turn this feature off, either remove the statement line altogether, or set the value of <number of pointers> to be blank or a negative number between –1 and –7.

If the MouseTrails option has never been used, this line does not appear. If the option has been turned on by placing an X in the MouseTrails check box (see Figure 15.8), then the value of <number of pointers> is set to 7. If it is subsequently turned off, the value is set to –7.

The SwapMouseButtons statement lets you reverse the left and right mouse buttons. The statement takes the form

```
SwapMouseButtons=<YES or NO>
```

The default value is NO; if you change it to YES, the left and right buttons exchange their functions, so that the right button becomes the primary mouse button. This statement corresponds to the Swap Left/Right Buttons check box in the Mouse dialog box shown in Figure 15.6.

NetWarn. This statement is a simple on-off switch that controls whether Windows will display a warning message (Figure 15.9) when it senses an error in your system's ability to run on a particular network. This usually occurs when the network you've selected is not running, or when you are attempting to run your system on a network for which it is not configured.

• • • • • • • • • • • • • •
FIGURE 15.9
*Network
Warning
Dialog Box*

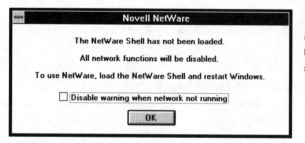

*The NetWarn state-
ment determines
whether or not you
see this dialog box.*

The NetWarn statement takes the form

```
NetWarn=<0 or 1>
```

where <0 or 1> is either 0 for off, or 1 for on. The default value is

```
NetWarn=1
```

This tells Windows to display the warning message if it encounters a problem when it tries to connect with the network. If this value is set to 0, then Windows does not display the warning message. If you are using a network, leave NetWarn set to 1 so that you will be alerted that Windows will not provide any network services during that session. Then if you see the network warning message, you'll know that you have to restart Windows to gain access to the network.

The NetWarn switch can also be set by accessing the Network icon in the Control Panel (Figure 15.10).

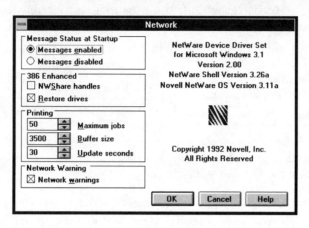

You can change
the value of the
NetWarn state-
ment using the
Network Warnings
check box in the
Network section of
the Control Panel.

DosPrint. The DosPrint statement lets you control whether Windows will use DOS interrupts when printing. The statement takes the form

```
DosPrint=<YES or NO>
```

The default value is NO, which tells Windows to direct printer output to the printer port without going through DOS. This is also the fastest way for Windows to print. If you change the value to YES, Windows redirects printer output to the standard DOS interrupts, which lets DOS handle the printer port and thereby improves compatibility, but at the expense of speed. The DosPrint statement corresponds to the Fast Printing Direct to Port check box in the Connect dialog box, which you reach through the Printers dialog box.

ScreenSaveActive and ScreenSaveTimeOut. The ScreenSaveActive and ScreenSaveTimeOut statements tell Windows whether and when to use its screen saver. In order to set other conditions applying to Windows's built-in screen saver with the Desktop controls of the Control Panel, see the [ScreenSaver] section of the CONTROL.INI file described later in this chapter.

The ScreenSaveActive statement is a simple on/off switch that instructs Windows whether to use the built-in screen saver. The statement takes the form

```
ScreenSaveActive=<0 or 1>
```

where <0 or 1> is either 1 (for on) or 0 (for off). Therefore, the statement line

```
ScreenSaveActive=1
```

denotes that the Windows built-in screen saver is on, and it will turn itself on after the number of seconds specified in the ScreenSaveTimeOut statement has elapsed. The default value for this statement is 0, which means that the screen saver is turned off; this condition corresponds to the selection "(None)" in the Name list box of the Screen Saver section, located on the Desktop controls in the Control Panel (Figure 15.11).

FIGURE 15.11

Screen Saver
Dialog Box in
Control Panel

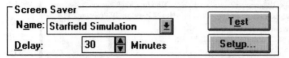

The Screen Saver section of the desktop section of the Control Panel provides graphical equivalents for the ScreenSaveActive and ScreenSaveTimeOut statements.

The ScreenSaveTimeOut statement tells Windows when to activate the built-in screen saver whenever your screen saver option is turned on. The statement takes the form

```
ScreenSaveTimeOut=<seconds>
```

where <seconds> specifies the number of seconds of inactivity that must elapse before the screen saver is activated. For example, the line

```
ScreenSaveTimeOut=120
```

would activate the built-in screen saver after 120 seconds (two minutes) have elapsed with no user activity (such as hitting a key or moving the mouse). The default value for this setting is to leave it blank. The ScreenSaveTimeOut statement can be adjusted graphically by accessing the Desktop section of the Control Panel and using the Delay scroll box (see Figure 15.11).

Settings related to the actual screen savers are stored in the [Screen Saver] section of the CONTROL.INI file; see the section on CONTROL.INI later in this chapter for further details.

MenuDropAlignment and MenuShowDelay. The MenuDrop Alignment statement lets you control how menus are aligned with the menu title. The statement takes the form

```
MenuDropAlignment=<0 or 1>
```

The default value is 0, which causes menus to open aligned to the left margin of the menu title. If you change the value to 1, menus will be aligned along the right margin of the menu title, as depicted in Figure 15.12. With menus aligned to the right, it may be more natural for lefthanded Windows users to choose items from the menu. The only way to adjust this entry is to edit this statement line.

FIGURE 15.12
Right-Aligned Menus

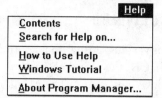

You can realign your menus to the right margin of the menu title by using the MenuDropAlignment statement.

The MenuShowDelay statement lets you specify the time period that Windows will wait before it displays a cascading menu. The statement takes the form

```
MenuShowDelay=<milliseconds>
```

The default value is 400 for 286 computers, which provides a 400-millisecond delay to compensate for the slow speed at which Windows runs on such systems. For 386 and higher processors, the default value is 0. This statement can only be changed by editing it directly.

CoolSwitch. The CoolSwitch statement lets you turn Windows' fast Alt+Tab switching option on or off. The statement takes the form

```
CoolSwitch=<0 or 1>
```

The default value is 1, which turns this feature on. This statement corresponds to the Fast "Alt+Tab" Switching check box in the Desktop section of the Control Panel. When this feature is turned on, pressing Alt+Tab displays a special dialog box that contains the icon and name of each application that is running at that time (Figure 15.13).

FIGURE 15.13
Fast Switch Dialog Box

Whether this special dialog box appears depends on the setting of the CoolSwitch statement.

If the CoolSwitch statement is set to 0, pressing Alt+Tab brings up the actual window of the application with each press of Alt+Tab, rather than this special dialog box.

DefaultQueueSize. This statement indicates how many messages a Windows application can hold in its message queue. This statement is not related to the printer queue. The default value is 8. The statement is sometimes adjusted by specific applications, and you will probably never need to edit it by hand.

. . . .

The [Desktop] Section of WIN.INI

This section of WIN.INI contains various settings that control the appearance of the screen background—that is, the Windows desktop, as well as the onscreen positioning of windows and icons. The [Desktop] section can contain these statements:

➠ Pattern

➠ Wallpaper

➠ TileWallpaper

➠ WallpaperOriginX

➠ WallpaperOriginY

➠ GridGranularity

➠ IconSpacing

➠ IconVerticalSpacing

➠ IconTitleWrap

➠ IconTitleFaceName

➠ IconTitleSize

➠ IconTitleStyle

All the statements in the [Desktop] section of WIN.INI relate to the appearance of icons, background patterns, and wallpaper on your Windows desktop. When Setup creates a WIN.INI file during a new installation of Windows, it also creates the small [Desktop] section shown below:

```
[Desktop]
Pattern=(None)
Wallpaper=(None)
GridGranularity=0
```

Other statement lines are added automatically when you modify items using the Control Panel, but some will need to be added manually. Any items not listed in the [Desktop] section are set to their default values.

Many of these settings can be adjusted using the Desktop section of the Control Panel, but the statements in this section do not contain settings for all the desktop-related controls. The remaining desktop-related settings not found in the WIN.INI file are in the CONTROL.INI file, described later in this chapter.

Pattern. This statement lets you specify the pattern that Windows uses for the screen background. Eight decimal numbers are listed in the pattern statement, each representing 1 byte in binary arithmetic. Each of these bytes defines one row of a grid 8 pixels wide by 8 pixels high. Thus each decimal number in the statement represents a byte's worth of 0s and 1s, and each byte represents a row of 8 pixels. Each byte can range from 0 (00000000) to 255 (11111111).

The pattern statement takes the form

```
Pattern=<byte1 byte2 byte3 byte4 byte5 byte6 byte7 byte8>
```

where <byte1 ... byte8> represents the sequence of 8-bit bytes (byte1 is the top row and byte8 the bottom row) that defines the 8x8 pixel grid. For example, the following statement line

```
Pattern=20 12 200 121 158 19 48 40
```

generates this 8x8 pixel grid:

```
0 0 0 1 0 1 0 0
0 0 0 0 1 1 0 0
1 1 0 0 1 0 0 0
0 1 1 1 1 0 0 1
1 0 0 1 1 1 1 0
0 0 0 1 0 0 1 0
0 0 1 1 0 0 0 0
0 0 1 0 1 0 0 0
```

This grid in turn creates the Spinner pattern provided with Windows. Windows interprets all the 0s to be the background color and all the 1s to be the foreground color. The Background color is defined in the Background setting of the [Colors] section of the WIN.INI file (as described later in this chapter), and the foreground color is specified by the WindowText setting of the [Colors] section.

The default setting for the Pattern statement is

```
Pattern=(None)
```

which denotes that no pattern has been selected. The Pattern section of the Desktop controls in the Control Panel (Figure 15.14) allows you to change these settings.

••••••••••••••
FIGURE 15.14

*Pattern
Section of the
Desktop
Controls in
the Control
Panel*

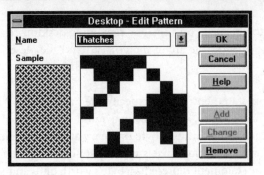

*The Pattern section of the
Desktop controls in the
Control Panel provides a
graphical way to edit the
pattern statement.*

The easiest way to alter the number values in the <byte1 ... byte8> part of the Pattern statement is by editing the 8x8 pixel pattern grid in the Edit Pattern dialog box. This statement specifies only the currently active pattern. The statements that define the pattern supplied with Windows as well as any new patterns you have created are stored in the [Patterns] section of the CONTROL.INI file, described later in the chapter.

Wallpaper. This statement tells Windows what graphic image, if any, to use as your screen background—that is, the Windows desktop. The Wallpaper covers any background pattern (as specified in the Pattern statement) that is beneath it. Any Windows bitmap file will serve as a Wallpaper; to create or edit such a file, just use the Windows Paintbrush utility. The Wallpaper statement takes the form

```
Wallpaper=<file name>
```

where <file name> identifies the graphics file you want to use. For example, the statement line

```
Wallpaper=PARTY.BMP
```

tells Windows to use the PARTY.BMP file as the wallpaper. The graphics file specified in this statement must be a Windows bitmap file (usually denoted by the extension .BMP) or a Run Length Encoded bitmap file, denoted by the extension .RLE. If the file is not in the main Windows directory or in the Windows System directory, you must include the full path name of the file. The default setting for this statement is

```
Wallpaper=(None)
```

which means that no Wallpaper is to be displayed on the desktop.

The Wallpaper statement corresponds to the File list box in the Wallpaper section of the Desktop controls in the Control Panel (Figure 15.15).

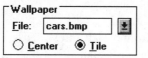

The Wallpaper section of the Desktop controls in the Control Panel lets you graphically adjust the wallpaper statement.

The File list box in the Wallpaper section of the Control Panel only lists the .BMP files found in your main Windows directory. To specify a file that is not in the list box, you will need to use the Wallpaper statement in WIN.INI, as just discussed.

TileWallpaper. This statement presents a simple on-off switch that tells Windows whether to center a single instance of the Wallpaper graphics file on the screen or to arrange as many instances of the file image as will fit on the screen into a tiled grid. The statement takes the following form

```
TileWallpaper=<0 or 1>
```

where <0 or 1> is either 1 (on) or 0 (off). When the switch is off, the screen contains a single centered image; when the switch is on, the wallpaper image repeats itself in a tiled arrangement to fill the screen. The default setting for this statement is

```
TileWallpaper=0
```

which centers a single .BMP image on the desktop.

This statement corresponds to the two radio buttons, Tile and Center, that appear in the Wallpaper section of the Desktop controls (see Figure 15.15).

WallpaperOriginX and WallpaperOriginY. These statements tell Windows at which horizontal and vertical points it should start tiling or centering the wallpaper images onto your screen. In this way, you can adjust the positioning of the images in a tiled arrangement of wallpaper or change the location of a centered image that is smaller than the full screen. The WallpaperOriginX statement takes the form

```
WallpaperOriginX=<x-coordinate>
```

where <x-coordinate> represents the number of pixels from the left, along the horizontal x-axis and starting from 0, to place the first tile of the wallpaper.

The WallpaperOriginY statement is similar and takes the form

```
WallpaperOriginY=<y-coordinate>
```

where <y-coordinate> represents the number of pixels from the top, along the vertical y-axis, to place the first tile of the wallpaper. For example, the statements:

```
WallpaperOriginX=10
WallpaperOriginY=12
```

would start the first tile 10 pixels from the left and 12 pixels from the top of the screen. The default is not to list these two statements at all which is equivalent to X,Y values of 0,0. With the default values a centered image appears at the center of the screen, and tiling starts in the upper left corner. Because there is no corresponding way to set these statements from the Control Panel, you'll need to add the appropriate statements to the WIN.INI file yourself.

GridGranularity. This statement controls an imaginary grid that Windows uses to align icons, windows, and other onscreen elements. The GridGranularity statement takes the form

```
GridGranularity=<number>
```

where <number> ranges from 0 to 49. When the value of <number> is set to 0, which is the default, the grid is turned off. When the value is set between 1 and 49, the grid is activated so that onscreen objects will snap into place along the imaginary grid. What's happening is that the centers of the objects are forced to coincide with the cross points of the grid.

Each 1-unit increment in the value of <number> increases the distance of the gridlines by an additional 8 pixels. For example, the statement line

```
GridGranularity=2
```

places the gridlines 16 pixels apart. This number should be kept low; at the maximum value of 49, your gridlines would be 392 pixels apart, making your onscreen operations unwieldy. Settings of more than 4 or 5 should be used only with high-resolution monitors, where pixel distances are smaller.

The easiest way to change this setting is to use the Granularity box in the Sizing Grid section of the Desktop controls (Figure 15.16)

Sizing Grid Section of the Desktop Controls

Sizing Grid	
Granularity:	0 ▲▼
Border Width:	5 ▲▼

The Sizing Grid section of the Desktop controls lets you graphically adjust the GridGranularity statement.

IconSpacing and IconVerticalSpacing. The IconSpacing statement tells Windows how far to distance icons from each other horizontally. The statement takes the form

```
IconSpacing=<pixels>
```

where <pixels> ranges from 32 to 512 and represents the number of pixels, from midpoint to midpoint, between icons. Windows will not accept a value less than 32; if you attempt to specify a lower number, Windows reverts back to 32. This decision is based on sheer graphical sense: even a value of 32 makes for crowded icons. The default value is

```
IconSpacing=77
```

This places icons 77 pixels apart—a nice, comfortable distance if you're using a 640x480 VGA display. If your icon names are really long, or if you like plenty of elbow room, you can set this number to 100, but anything more places too much distance between them.

The Spacing scroll box in the Icons section of the Desktop controls provides the easiest way to change this setting (Figure 15.17) .

FIGURE 15.17
*Icons Section
of the Desktop
Controls*

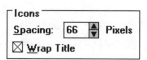

*The Icons section of the Desktop controls
in the Control Panel lets you graphically
adjust the IconSpacing statement.*

The IconVerticalSpacing statement lets you tell Windows how far apart vertically to space icons. The statement takes the form

```
IconVerticalSpacing=<pixels>
```

Windows calculates the default value for this statement based on the font you are using for the icon's title and the display driver. Increasing the number provides more vertical space between your rows of icons. There is no graphical method for adjusting this statement; to do so, you must edit it directly.

IconTitleWrap, IconTitleFaceName, IconTitleSize, and IconTitleStyle. A simple on-off switch, the IconTitleWrap statement tells Windows whether to wrap long icon titles onto more than one line. The statement takes the form

```
IconTitleWrap=<0 or 1>
```

where <0 or 1> is either 1 (on) or 0 (off). The default setting is

```
IconTitleWrap=1
```

which tells Windows to wrap long icon titles onto more than one line and to increase the vertical spacing of icons to accommodate multiline titles. This setting corresponds to the Wrap Title check box in the Icons section of the Desktop controls (see Figure 15.17).

The IconTitleFaceName statement lets you choose the font used to display icon titles in Program Manager. The statement takes the form:

```
IconTitleFaceName=<font>
```

where <font> is the name of a font (not the font file) listed in the [Fonts] section of WIN.INI. The default font is MS Sans Serif, which is used if this statement line is not present.

There are no graphical controls for this statement; you must add this line to the file yourself. For example, to use the Small Fonts typeface, you would add the line

```
IconTitleFaceName=Small Fonts
```

The IconTitleSize statement specifies the point size of the font designated in the IconTitleFaceName statement. The statement takes the form

```
IconTitleSize=<point size>
```

The default value for <point size> is 8, which means that an 8-point font is used for icon titles. There is no graphical control for this setting, so you must add the statement by hand.

The IconTitleStyle statement specifies the type style of the font specified in the IconTitleFaceName statement. The statement takes the form

```
IconTitleStyle=<0 or 1>
```

If this value equals 0, the title is normal; if the value is set to 1, the title is displayed in a bold typeface. There is no graphical control for this setting, so you must add the statement by hand.

Insider's Tip

Customizing Your Desktop with the Icon Settings. You can use the various icon settings in the [Desktop] section of WIN.INI to customize the configuration of your Program Manager groups. One of the most common complaints about Program Manager is that it is not very efficient at presenting the icons, and not many icons can be viewed at one time on a standard VGA display. You can remedy this situation and squeeze more icons onto your screen using the following method.

To obtain a greater population density of icons, trim the horizontal and vertical spacing, and then reduce the size of the font used for the icon titles. For example, I use these values for my icon settings:

```
IconSpacing=65
IconVerticalSpacing=58
IconTitleFaceName=Small Fonts
IconTitleSize=6
```

These settings bring the icons quite a bit closer together, as shown in Figures 15.18 and 15.19.

FIGURE 15.18
*Normal Icon
Layout*

Here's how the icons are normally positioned by Windows.

FIGURE 15.19
*Condensed
Icon Layout*

Here's how densely packed the icons appear using the settings in the example.

If your icon titles are lengthy, set the IconTitleWrap to 1 to activate tile-wrapping. If you keep your icon titles short, you can set the IconTitleWrap to 0 to turn off tile-wrapping; this lets you pack the icons even closer.

One word of caution: the font that you specify in the IconTitleFaceName statement is also used for other Windows elements, such as the display of print jobs in Print Manager. Some fonts, like the Small Fonts used in the preceding example, look fine in Program Manager but can be illegible in Print Manager.

· ·

The [Extensions] Section of WIN.INI

This section identifies which document files correspond to what applications. It's this section that allows you to automatically start an application when you open a particular document.

Documents and file types are paired by associating a file extension (such as .TXT, .WRI, or .BMP) with a particular application. For example, Windows normally associates files containing the extension .WRI with the application WRITE.EXE. So if you open a document with the file name LETTER.WRI, Windows starts the WRITE.EXE application (Windows Write) and automatically loads the LETTER.WRI file. For details about associations between documents and applications, see Chapters 2 and 3.

The [Extensions] section contains only one type of statement line, which always takes the form

```
<extension>=<DOS command-line>
```

where <extension> is a valid DOS file name extension of one to three characters, without the preceding period; and <command-line> is a valid DOS command line that starts with the complete file name of an executable application—that is, it must contain the .EXE or .COM extension.

Each statement line specifies a file extension and a command line that is invoked whenever you open a file with that extension. The <command-line> can contain any special parameters the application needs, such as the document file name, which is usually included. The caret (^) is used when the original document file name is needed as part of the command line. When Windows looks up a file extension, it replaces the caret with the document's file name (without the extension).

Although any valid DOS command line can be used, including any parameters the application accepts, most statement lines in the [Extensions] section list only the application name and the document's file name extension. For example, the statement line

```
.TXT=NOTEPAD.EXE ^.TXT
```

specifies that files with the extension .TXT will be opened when you launch the NOTEPAD.EXE application.

Often an application is associated with more than one file extension. For example, the NOTEPAD.EXE application is usually associated with files containing the extension .INI or .TXT. However, each extension can only be associated with one application. Windows uses only the first application if you list more than one for a given file extension.

When you install Windows, Windows Setup places this list of associations in your WIN.INI file:

```
[Extensions]
cal=calendar.exe ^.cal
crd=cardfile.exe ^.crd
trm=terminal.exe ^.trm
txt=notepad.exe ^.txt
ini=notepad.exe ^.ini
pcx=pbrush.exe ^.pcx
bmp=pbrush.exe ^.bmp
wri=write.exe ^.wri
rec=recorder.exe ^.rec
hlp=winhelp.exe ^.hlp
```

When you install a new Windows application, its installation program usually automatically adds its associated file extensions to the [Extensions] section of WIN.INI. If you install Excel, for example, these extension statements are automatically added:

```
xls=excel.exe ^.xls
xlc=excel.exe ^.xlc
xlw=excel.exe ^.xlw
xlm=excel.exe ^.xlm
xlt=excel.exe ^.xlt
xla=excel.exe ^.xla
```

Some Windows applications also work with a list of "registered" file extensions. These kinds of applications register their file types with Windows by updating the information in the registration database. The names of these registered file types appear in the File Type scroll box of the Associate With section of the Associate dialog box, situated in File Manager (Figure 15.20).

••••••••••••••
FIGURE 15.20
Associate
Dialog Box in
File Manager

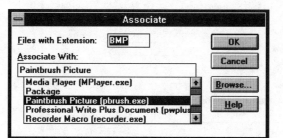

The Associate dialog box in File Manager provides a graphical way to edit the [Extensions] section.

To access this dialog box, choose Associate from the File menu in File Manager (see Chapter 3).

The list of registered file types in the registration database can be edited with the RegEdit utility, which is discussed in Chapter 9. If either you or another application makes changes to the registration database, Windows updates the related entries in the [Extensions] section. If any file types are listed differently in the [Extensions] section than they are in the registration database, the database listing takes precedence.

Because thousands of file name extensions can be created, developers try to select original extension names for their applications. However, sometimes two different applications inadvertently use the same file extension for a file type. In this case, you'd have to edit the associations manually either in the [Extension] section, in the registration database, or in both. If this doesn't work, you may have to use another method to get your application launched with its corresponding document. One way is to drag the document icon in File Manager on top of the application icon that you want to launch together with the document. You can also use this technique to open a document in an application that it's not associated with.

• •

The [Intl] Section of WIN.INI

Here you'll find statements that tell Windows what formats to use when it displays dates, times, currency, measures, and other variables for different countries. The default values correspond with the settings for the United States; you can change the default, of course, to match the settings for whatever country you select.

The [Intl] section contains the statement lines that correspond to the setting found by clicking on the International icon in the Control Panel (Figure 15.21).

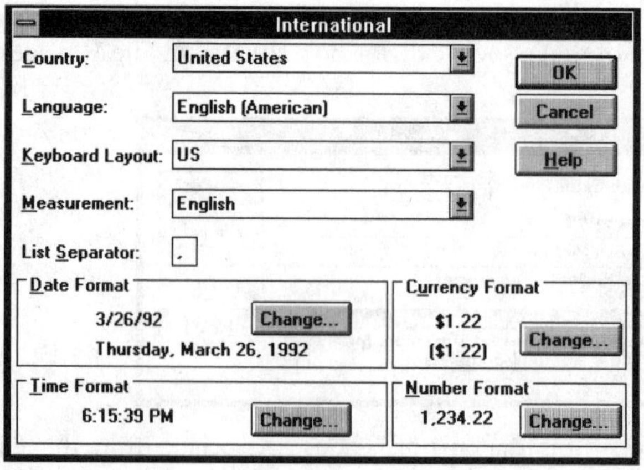

• • • • • • • • • • • • • •
FIGURE 15.21
*International
Dialog Box in
the Control
Panel*

*This dialog box lets
you display the
date, time, and
other variables for
whatever country
you select.*

Clicking on the International icon allows you to select preassigned settings for these countries:

Australia	France	South Korea
Austria	Germany	Spain
Belgium (Dutch)	Iceland	Sweden
Belgium (French)	Italy	Switzerland (French)
Brazil	Mexico	Switzerland (German)
Canada (English)	Netherlands	Switzerland (Italian)
Canada (French)	New Zealand	Taiwan
Denmark	Norway	United Kingdom
Finland	Portugal	United States

Each of these entries contains all the various settings, based on standard conventions, related to that country. If more than one language is spoken in a country, such as Canada or Switzerland, there is more than one setting profile. The specific settings associated with each country can be found in the [Country] section of the CONTROL.INI file, described later in this chapter.

To alter, add to, or otherwise customize the settings, just change the information in the following statement lines, either by altering their values graphically with the Control Panel or by editing the statement lines in this section. The various entries in this section start with either the letter i—to indicate that the corresponding value is an integer, or whole number—or the letter s—to indicate that the value is a string, or a combination of letters, numbers, or symbols.

sCountry. Select this statement to use one of the standard settings packages that Windows provides for the countries in the preceding list. The statement takes the form

```
sCountry=<country name>
```

where <country name> is any country on the list. The default setting is

```
sCountry=United States
```

This specifies that Windows should use the standard settings for the United States. This statement line corresponds to the Country setting of the International dialog box in the Control Panel (see Figure 15.21).

iCountry. This statement is used to identify the country. In all cases except Canada, which has 2 as its iCountry value, the iCountry value is the country's international telephone code. The iCountry statement takes the form

```
iCountry=<country-code>
```

where the <country-code> is equal to the country's international telephone code, except with Canada, which is 2.

The default value for this statement is

```
iCountry=1
```

which sets the <country-code> to 1, the number for the United States.

sLanguage. This statement serves as a reference to inform Windows and certain Windows applications, such as spell checkers, which language to use. The statement takes the form

```
sLanguage=<language-code>
```

where <language-code> contains a three-letter code used as an abbreviation for a language supported by Windows. The acceptable language codes are shown in Table 15.2.

TABLE 15.2

Code	Language
dan	Danish
nld	Dutch
eng	International English
fin	Finnish
fra	French
frc	French Canadian
deu	German
isl	Icelandic
ita	Italian
nor	Norwegian
ptg	Portuguese
esp	Spanish, Castilian
esn	Spanish, modern
sve	Swedish
enu	U.S. English

The default setting is

```
sLanguage=enu
```

which designates U.S. English as the official language of Windows. This statement corresponds to the Language setting in the International dialog box shown in Figure 15.21.

iMeasure. This statement instructs Windows whether to use the metric or the English system of measurement. The statement takes the form

```
iMeasure=<0 or 1>
```

where <0 or 1> is either 0 for metric, or 1 for English. The default is

```
iMeasure=1
```

which specifies the English measurement system. This statement corresponds to the Measurement setting of the International dialog box shown in Figure 15.21.

sList. This statement designates which character Windows should use to separate items in a list. This character, a comma in the U.S., is sometimes called the **list separator**. The sList statement takes the form

```
sList=<separator>
```

where <separator> is any single character designated as a list separator. The default statement line is

```
sList=,
```

which specifies that a comma (,) should be used as the list separator. This statement corresponds to the List Separator setting in the International dialog box shown in Figure 15.21.

iCurrDigits. This statement tells Windows how many digits to place to the right of the decimal separator in currency values. It takes the form

```
iCurrDigits=<0-9>
```

where <0-9> ranges from 0 to 9. The default value is

```
iCurrDigits=2
```

This is the U.S. standard, which places two digits after the decimal point. This statement line corresponds to the Decimal Digits setting of the International–Currency Formats dialog box in the International section of the Control Panel (Figure 15.22).

International - Currency Format	
Symbol Placement:	$1
Negative:	[$123.22]
Symbol:	$
Decimal Digits:	2

OK

Cancel

Help

This dialog box lets you specify how many digits to place after the decimal when displaying currency.

iCurrency. This statement controls how Windows displays monetary amounts. The statement takes the form

```
iCurrency=<0-3>
```

where <0-3> is either 0, 1, 2, or 3. The value of <0-3> is matched to the currency format shown in Table 15.3.

Value of <0-3>	Currency Format
0	$1
1	1$
2	$ 1
3	1 $

In this table, the dollar sign ($)—which is the Windows default setting—designates the currency symbol. If a different currency symbol is specified in the sCurrency statement line (described next), that symbol will be used in the same way as shown in the table. The iCurrency statement corresponds to the Symbol Placement section of the International—Currency Formats dialog box (see Figure 15.22).

sCurrency. This statement tells Windows what symbol to use for displaying monetary amounts of local currency. The statement takes the form

```
sCurrency=<symbol>
```

where <symbol> is any alphanumeric string of up to four characters long. The default statement line is

```
sCurrency=$
```

which specifies the dollar sign ($) as the currency symbol. This statement line corresponds to the Symbol section of the International–Currency Formats dialog box (see Figure 15.22).

iNegCurr. This statement tells Windows how to format negative numbers for local currency. The iNegCurr statement takes the form

```
iNegCurr=<0-10>
```

where <0-10> is any one of the 11 numbers from 0 through 10. The value of <0-10> sets the format for diplaying negative currency amounts according to Table 15.4.

Value of <0–7>	Currency Format
0	($1)
1	–$1
2	$–1
3	$1–
4	(1$)
5	–1$
6	1–$
7	1$–
8	–1 $
9	–$ 1
10	1$–

The dollar sign ($) is used here as the currency symbol; a different currency symbol can be specified in the sCurrency statement line as just described. The default setting is

```
iNegCurr=0
```

which places parentheses around negative currency amounts. This statement corresponds to the Negative setting in the International–Currency Formats dialog box (see Figure 15.22).

iDigits. This statement tells Windows how many digits to place to the right of the decimal separator (or decimal point) when displaying numbers. It takes the form

```
iDigits=<0-9>
```

where <0–9> can be any of the 10 numbers from 0 through 9. The default setting is

```
iDigits=2
```

which tells Windows to place two digits after the decimal separator when displaying a number. This statement corresponds to the Decimal Digits setting of the International–Number Format dialog box in the Control Panel (Figure 15.23).

FIGURE 15.23
International–
Number
Format
Dialog Box

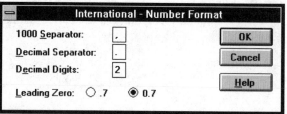

This dialog box lets you specify how many digits to place after the decimal when displaying numbers.

iLzero. This statement tells Windows whether to place a 0 in front of decimal numbers less than 1. The statement takes the form

```
iLzero=<0 or 1>
```

where <0 or 1> can be either 0 or 1. If the value is 0, a leading 0 is not displayed; if the value is 1, a leading 0 is displayed. The default setting is

```
iLzero=1
```

which specifies that a leading 0 is used, so that decimal numbers are displayed like this:

```
0.1
```

Although this example uses a decimal point (.), Windows uses whatever separator is specified in the sDecimal setting discussed next. The iLzero statement corresponds to the Leading Zeros settings in the International–Number Format dialog box in the Control Panel (see Figure 15.23).

sDecimal. This statement tells Windows what punctuation mark or other character should be used to separate the two parts of a decimal number—that is, to separate the integer from the fractional part. In the United States, a period (.) separates the two parts—it's commonly called the **decimal point**. The statement takes the form

```
sDecimal=<separator>
```

where <separator> is the punctuation mark or other character selected as the decimal separator. The default setting is

```
sDecimal=.
```

This specifies that the period is to be used as the separator. This statement corresponds to the Decimal Separator of the International–Number Format dialog box, shown in Figure 15.23.

sThousand. This statement tells Windows what punctuation mark or other character should be used to separate thousands in a number containing more than three digits. For example, in the United States a comma separates millions from thousands from hundreds—it's called the **thousands separator**. The statement takes the form

```
sThousand=<separator>
```

where <separator> is the punctuation mark or other character designated as the thousands separator. The default setting is

```
sThousand=,
```

which specifies that the comma should be used as the thousands separator. This statement corresponds to the 1000 Separator setting in the International–Number Format dialog box shown in Figure 15.23.

iTime. This statement tells Windows whether it should use the 12-hour time format, which repeats the 12-hour cycle twice a day, or the 24-hour military-style format, which identifies time as part of the 24-hour cycle. The iTime statement takes the form

```
iTime=<0 or 1>
```

where <0 or 1> can be either 0 or 1. If the value of <0 or 1> is 0, then a 12-hour clock format is used. If the value of <0 or 1> is 1, a 24-hour time format is installed. The default statement line is

```
iTime=0
```

which specifies that Windows will display the time according to a 12-hour clock format. This statement corresponds to the 12 Hour and 24 Hour radio button settings in the International–Time Format dialog box, which is part of the International controls in the Control Panel (Figure 15.24).

••••••••••••••
FIGURE 15.24

*International–
Time Format
Dialog Box*

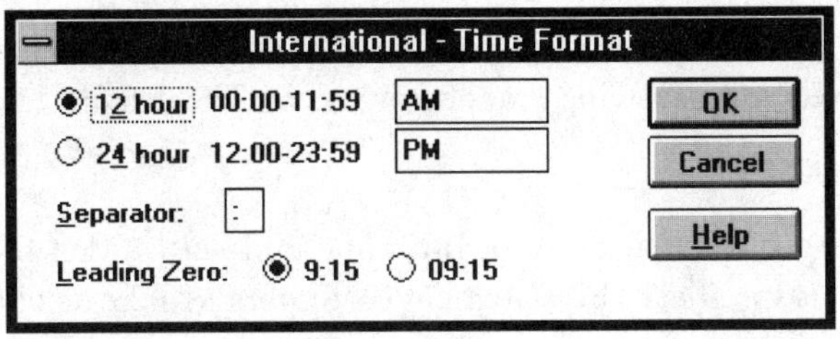

*This dialog box lets
you specify how Win-
dows formats the
time display.*

The settings in this dialog box and the corresponding statements in WIN.INI only control the way Windows formats the time; they do not affect the way time is actually set. To set the time, use the Time/Date controls in the Control Panel.

iTLZero. This statement tells Windows whether to insert a leading 0 in front of a single-digit time notation. For example, it controls whether 8 A.M. is displayed as 8:00 or 08:00. The iTLZero statement takes the form

```
iTLZero=<0 or 1>
```

where <0 or 1> is either 0 or 1. If the value of <0 or 1> is 0, then a leading 0 is not used when Windows displays the time. If the value of <0 or 1> is 1, then Windows inserts the 0. The default statement line is

```
iTLZero=0
```

which specifies that a leading 0 is not used. This statement corresponds to the Leading Zero setting in the International–Time Format dialog box shown in Figure 15.24.

sTime. This statement tells Windows what punctuation mark or character to use as a separator between the hours, minutes, and seconds when displaying time. The sTime statement takes the form

```
sTime=<separator>
```

where <separator> is any punctuation mark or other character you designate as the separator. The default statement line is

```
sTime=:
```

which specifies that the colon (:) is used as the separator. This statement corresponds to the Separator setting in the International–Time Format dialog box shown in Figure 15.24.

s1159. This statement tells Windows what characters to place after the time before noon (right up to 11:59) if Windows is using the 12-hour clock format. The s1159 statement takes the form

```
s1159=<morning suffix>
```

where <morning suffix> is any character string up to 8 characters long that you select for displaying times before noon. The default statement line is

```
s1159=AM
```

which specifies that times before noon end with AM if the 12-hour clock format is specified. This statement corresponds to the text box that is part of the 12-Hour radio button setting in the International–Time Format dialog box shown in Figure 15.24.

s2359. This statement tells Windows what characters to place following the time after noon if Windows is using the 12-hour clock format, or following all times if Windows is using the 24-hour clock format. The s2359 statement takes the form

```
s2359=<time suffix>
```

where <time suffix> is any character string up to 8 characters long that you designate for Windows to display after all the times with a 24-hour clock, or after all the times past noon with a 12-hour clock. The default statement line is

```
s2359=PM
```

which specifies that times past noon end with PM if the 12-hour clock format is specified in the iTime setting, and that all times end with PM if the 24-hour clock format is specified. This statement corresponds to the text box that is part of the 24 Hour radio button setting in the International–Time Format dialog box shown in Figure 15.24.

sLongDate. This statement tells Windows how to format the long version of the date. Special date-picture codes are used to specify those elements you want Windows to display in the date. The sLongDate statement takes the form

```
sLongDate=<date-picture>
```

where <date-picture> is a combination of special codes that provide Windows with specific instructions about how to format the date (Table 15.5).

TABLE 15.5

<date-picture> Code	Date Element	Format
d	Day	1-31
dd	Day	01-31
ddd	Day	Mon-Sun
dddd	Day	Monday-Sunday
M	Month	1-12
MM	Month	01-12
MMM	Month	Jan-Dec
MMMM	Month	January-December
yy	Year	00-99
yyyy	Year	1900-2040

The default statement line is

```
sLongDate=dddd, MMMM dd, yyyy
```

which specifies the date picture that Windows should use to format the long version of the date. By default, Windows displays a date like this:

```
Wednesday, June 17, 1992
```

This statement corresponds to the settings in the Long Date Format section of the International–Date Format dialog box (Figure 15.25).

FIGURE 15.25
*International–
Date Format
Dialog Box*

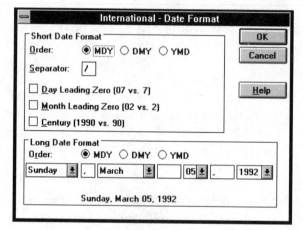

*This dialog box lets
you specify how
Windows formats
the date display.*

Windows will not accept certain <date-picture> combinations. To make sure you have a valid <date-picture>, use the Control Panel settings to change the sLongDate statement line.

sShortDate. This statement tells Windows how to display the short version of a date, such as 6/17/92. The sShortDate statement takes the form

```
sShortDate=<date-picture>
```

where <date-picture> is a combination of the date-picture codes listed in the sLongDate section just described. The default statement line is

```
sShortDate=M/d/yy
```

which specifies which date picture Windows uses to display the short version of the date. By default, Windows displays a date like this:

```
6/17/92
```

This statement corresponds to the various settings in the Short Date Format section of the International–Date Format dialog box, shown in Figure 15.25.

As with the sLongDate statement, Windows will not accept certain <date-picture> combinations for the sShortDate. To make sure you have a valid <date-picture>, use the Control Panel settings to change the sShortDate statement line.

sDate. The sDate statement specifies the character used to separate the parts of a date. The statement takes the form

```
sDate=<separator>
```

The default value for the separator is /.

iDate. The iDate statement is an old WIN.INI statement line used in Windows 2.0 for setting date formats. The iDate statement is not used by Windows 3.0 or later, so if you encounter this relic, you may want to remove it altogether.

· ·

The [Ports] Section of WIN.INI

This section tells Windows what communications and printer ports are available and how they are configured. The [Ports] section can also be used to redirect Windows output from an actual port to a file.

The Ports icon contains only the settings for communications ports. The statements in the [Ports] section correspond to two areas of the Control Panel: the Ports icon and the Printers icon. The statement lines that specify COM ports correspond to the Ports icon in the Control Panel (Figure 15.26), whereas all the statement lines (both communications- and printer-related) correspond to settings found in the Ports section of the Connections dialog box, which is located in the Printers section of the Control Panel (Figure 15.27).

· · · · · · · · · · · · · ·
FIGURE 15.26
Ports Icon
Dialog Box

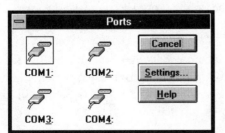

This dialog box lets you access communications ports.

Because Windows has redundant controls for communications ports, you can use the Control Panel to access the COM port settings in two ways:

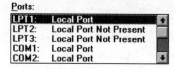

FIGURE 15.27

*Ports Section
of the
Connections
Dialog Box*

This dialog box lets you access both
communications and printer ports.

separately, in the Ports icon; or together with the other ports settings in the
[Ports] section of the Connections dialog box, which you access by pressing
the Connect button in the main Printers dialog box. Either way, you are
guided to the Settings dialog box shown in Figure 15.28, which demonstrates
the use of the COM1 port.

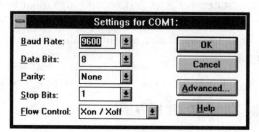

FIGURE 15.28

*Settings for
COM1
Dialog Box*

You can access this dialog
box either through the
Ports icon or through the
[Ports] section of the Connections dialog box.

All the statement lines in the [Ports] section follow the same basic form,
whether the statement specifies a communications port, a printer port, or an
output file. Windows regards all the various types of ports, even nonexistent
ones that are redirected to output files, as essentially the same: they are all
output ports.

Danger Zone

Because Windows restricts you to 10 ports, make sure your [Ports] section
doesn't contain more than 10 statement lines—any lines beyond the tenth
one will be ignored.

The statement lines in the [Ports] section take the form

```
<portname>[:]=[parameters]
```

where a <portname> and equals sign (=) are required for each statement
line; an optional colon (:) is needed for most statements; and an optional set
of parameters is necessary only for COM ports. Setup will create this default
[Ports] section in a new installation:

```
[Ports]
LPT1:=
LPT2:=
LPT3:=
```

```
COM1:=9600,n,8,1,x
COM2:=9600,n,8,1,x
COM3:=9600,n,8,1,x
COM4:=9600,n,8,1,x
EPT:=
FILE:=
LPT1.DOS=
LPT2.DOS=
```

The <portname> variable can be the name of any valid DOS output port, or the name of a file for directing output. The items shown in Table 15.6 can be used as a value for the <portname> variable:

<portname>	Description
COM1:	Serial communcations port
COM2:	Serial communcations port
COM3:	Serial communcations port
COM4:	Serial communcations port
LPT1:	Parallel printer port
LPT2:	Parallel printer port
LPT3:	Parallel printer port
LPT1.DOS	Use DOS to access parallel printer port
LPT2.DOS	Use DOS to access parallel printer port
LPT3.DOS	Use DOS to access parallel printer port
LPT4.DOS	Use DOS to access parallel printer port
EPT:	Special IBM printer port
FILE:	Have Windows prompt you for a file name at output time
<file name>.PRN	An output file that will be listed as a Printer choice

Specifying the Parameters for COM Ports. If a statement line specifies as the <portname> a COM port—that is, a serial communications port—then you'll need a group of parameters to instruct Windows on how to communicate with that port. The statement line for COM ports takes the form

```
COM<1-4>:=<speed>,<parity>,<word-length>,<stop-bits>[,p or ,x]
```

where <1–4> is any number from 1 to 4 that indicates which of the four COM ports (COM1 through COM4) you want to specify. The <speed> variable (also called the baud rate) is your selected speed in bps (bits per second). The <parity> variable can be one of these three letters: *e* for even parity, *o* for odd parity, or *n* for no parity. The <word-length> is the length of the data word, in bits, that is being used. The <stop-bits> specifies the number of stop bits for communications, and the optional [,p or ,x] parameter, when present, tells Windows what type of handshaking to use. If the ,p option is specified, Windows will use hardware handshaking; if the ,x option is specified, Windows will implement x-on/x-off handshaking.

The statement line

```
COM1:=9600,n,8,1,x
```

specifies that the COM1 port will run at a speed of 9600 bps, with no parity, a word-length of 8 bits, 1 stop bit, and x-on/x-off handshaking.

Sending Output to a File. Rather than send output to a physical port, Windows can turn a file into a virtual output port, then redirect any output sent to that port to a file. Here's how to direct output to a file. Use the <file name>.PRN option. If you specify a file name that ends with the .PRN extension, and follow the file name with an equal sign (=), then Windows lists the file as a printer in any print-related dialog boxes. Remember, if you specify an output file, do not place a colon at the end of the file name.

Here's an example of a statement line using the <file name>.PRN option

```
PRINTOUT.PRN=
```

This will list the file PRINTOUT.PRN as a virtual printer in print-related dialog boxes (Figure 15.29) and redirect output to the file.

••••••••••••••
FIGURE 15.29
Connect Dialog Box with File Appearing as Printer

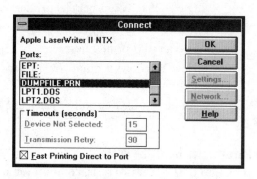

You can make a file appear as a printer in dialog boxes by using the <file name>.PRN option.

To remind you of this trick, the WIN.INI file includes these three lines of comments in the [Ports] section:

```
; A line with [filename].PRN followed by an equal sign causes
; [filename] to appear in the Control Panel's Printer Configuration dialog
; box. A printer connected to [filename] directs its output into this file.
```

In the interest of keeping the WIN.INI file as lean as possible, you can delete these comment lines.

If, on the other hand, you don't wish to specify a particular file, you can have Windows ask you for a file name each time output is sent to the port. To do so, use FILE: as the <portname>. The statement line

```
FILE:=
```

tells Windows to prompt you for a file name rather than directing output to a specific file.

Accessing a Parallel Port Through DOS. Windows normally prints directly to parallel ports and thus bypasses the normal DOS method of accessing the port. This maneuver speeds the printing process but can introduce incompabilities when you are using a print-sharing device or printing to a network printer. To resolve incompatibilities, Windows lets you redirect ouptut headed for the parallel port to DOS. DOS, rather than Windows, then has control of the use of the port. To use this maneuver, specify one of the following four special port names:

```
LPT1.DOS=
LPT2.DOS=
LPT3.DOS=
LPT4.DOS=
```

If one or more of these choices is listed in the [Ports] section, you will be able to select it as a printer port rather than the standard LPT port. If you are printing to a network printer, you can include the path name of the printer to the right of the = sign. In Windows 3.0, a similar entry used the OS/2 extension instead, as in LPT1.OS2, which was run when you operated Windows inside a DOS compatibility box from OS/2 1.x. In Windows 3.1, any file extension will redirect output to DOS because DOS recognizes LPT as a reserved word that identifies a parallel printer port. The extension .DOS is used by convention rather than as a requirement.

. . . .

The [Fonts] Section of WIN.INI

This section tells Windows what screen font files to load into memory during its startup process. The [Fonts] section of WIN.INI corresponds to the controls associated with the Fonts icon in the Control Panel (Figure 15.30).

To preview a font, click on its name in the Fonts dialog box shown in Figure 15.30; a sample font is displayed. To preview another, just click on its name.

• • • • • • • • • • • • •
FIGURE 15.30
Fonts
Dialog Box

```
┌─────────────────────────────────────────────────┐
│ ═      TrueType                                   │
│ ┌─TrueType Options──────────────┐  ┌──────────┐  │
│ │ ☒ Enable TrueType Fonts       │  │    OK    │  │
│ │ ☐ Show Only TrueType Fonts in │  ├──────────┤  │
│ │   Applications                │  │  Cancel  │  │
│ └───────────────────────────────┘  ├──────────┤  │
│                                     │   Help   │  │
│                                     └──────────┘  │
└─────────────────────────────────────────────────┘
```

*The Fonts dialog box in the Control Panel identifies the screen fonts
that are listed in the [Fonts] section of WIN.INI.*

Insider's Tip

Because these fonts are loaded into memory, you may want to prune unwanted fonts from this list if you find yourself short on memory.

Each of the statement lines in the [Fonts] section is the font name for the
specific font file that contains the actual font resources. These statement lines
all take the basic form

```
<font name>=<file name>
```

where <font name> is the descriptive name of a font as it will be displayed in
dialog boxes (such as the one shown in Figure 15.30) and in other locations
within Windows. The <file name> value is any valid DOS file name of an
existing file containing the appropriate font resources. You should keep these
files in the System directory of your primary Windows directory; if you can't,
be sure to include the full path name of the fonts in the <file name>.

By convention, rather than by requirement, the <font name> often contains helpful information about the nature of the font. For example, the
statement line

```
Courier 10,12,15 (VGA res)=COURE.FON
```

lets you know that the COURE.FON file contains Courier screen fonts at 10, 12,
and 15 point sizes, applied in VGA resolution.

The statement line

```
Times New Roman (TrueType)=times.fot
```

tells you that the TIMES.FOT file contains a scalable font called Times New
Roman. The "(TrueType)" part of the font name identifies this as a TrueType
font, which works at all resolutions with the screen and with most printers.
TrueType fonts files come in pairs: one with an .FOT extension and one with
a .TTF extension. Only the file with the .FOT extension needs to be listed for
TrueType fonts in the [Fonts] section.

Another example is the statement

```
MS Sans Serif 8,10,12,14,18,24 (VGA res)=SSERIFE.FON
```

This lets you know that MS Sans Serif is a VGA screen font that is supplied in the following point sizes: 8, 10, 12, 14, 18, and 24. The SSERIFE.FON file contains the actual screen font, and is not paired with another file. For more information about fonts, refer to Chapter 7.

The [TrueType] Section of WIN.INI

No, this isn't the section that lists the TrueType fonts—instead, this section tells Windows whether TrueType is turned on or off, and, if it is turned on, whether TrueType should be used exclusively. Because TrueType was not included in any version of Windows before 3.1, the [TrueType] section does not appear in the earlier WIN.INI files.

Two of the statement lines that can appear in the [TrueType] section correspond to the two check boxes found in the TrueType dialog box, shown in Figure 15.30. To access this dialog box, open the Fonts icon in the Control Panel and press the TrueType button. The check box labeled Use TrueType corresponds to the TTEnable statement, and the check box labeled TrueType Only corresponds to TTOnly. Both these statements are simple on-off switches and take the form

```
TTEnable=<0 or 1>
TTOnly=<0 or 1>
```

where <0 or 1> represents the switch status; 0 signifies off, and 1 means on. If TTEnable is set to 0, TrueType is turned off; if TTEnable is set to 1, TrueType is turned on. If TTOnly is set to 1, the TTOnly switch is set to on and TrueType fonts are used exclusively—provided, of course, that the TTEnable switch is also activated. Therefore, the statement line

```
TTEnable=0
```

signifies that TrueType is turned off and will not be used, whereas the statement lines

```
TTEnable=1
TTOnly=1
```

indicate that Truetype is turned on and is used exclusively.

Two other items can appear in the [TrueType] section: TTIfCollisions and OutlineThreshold, which can only be added by editing WIN.INI directly. The TTIfCollisions statement is a simple on-off switch that tells Windows which font to use if it encounters two with the same name, and one of them is a TrueType font. When set to 1, the switch is on and TrueType fonts prevail.

When set to 0, the switch is off and the TrueType font yields to the other font with the same name. The statement takes the form

```
TTIfCollisions=<0 or 1>
```

The default value is 1, which means the TrueType font is used in case of name conflicts.

The OutlineThreshold statement lets you set a threshold above which Windows will render TrueType fonts as outlines instead of bitmaps. Normally, Windows creates bitmaps of the TrueType fonts at resolutions lower than the threshold specified in this statement as a way of speeding performance—at the expense of memory. The statement takes the form

```
OutlineThreshold=<pels per em>
```

where <pels per em> refers to the number of dots per em (the width of the letter "m" in that font) that represents the threshold for creating bitmaps. The default value for this statement is

```
OutlineThreshold=256
```

If your memory situation is tight, lower this value. Higher values consume memory, and in no case should the value of <pels per em> exceed 300, because this can cause problems with the behavior of TrueType and potentially prevent characters from printing.

The [FontSubstitutes] Section of WIN.INI

The [FontSubstitutes] section was introduced in Windows 3.1. The statements in this section tell Windows to replace any listed font with your desired substitute. You can use this statement, for example, to substitute TrueType fonts for older, nonscalable fonts, or for other similar fonts that are not installed on your system.

The statement lines in the [FontSubstitutes] section take the form

```
<font name>=<replacement font>
```

where <font name> is the name of the original font and <replacement font> is the name of your desired substitution. The <replacement font> must be listed in the [Fonts] section, discussed earlier in this chapter. For example, this statement line

```
TmsRmn=MS Serif
```

tells Windows to replace the TmsRmn with the MS Serif font.

Setup will create this default [FontSubstitutes] section for a new Windows installation:

```
[FontSubstitutes]
Helv=MS Sans Serif
Tms Rmn=MS Serif
Times=Times New Roman
Helvetica=Arial
```

These statement lines specify replacements for fonts used in Windows 3.0, but missing from 3.1, that are still used by some older Windows programs.

. . . .

The [PrinterPorts] Section of WIN.INI

This section contains information about printers and their device drivers. The statement lines in this section identify which active and inactive printers can be used with each particular device driver. Other parameters identify the port to which the device is connected, and what timeout value, if different from the default, should be used with that port. The [PrinterPorts] section corresponds to controls associated with the Printers icon in the Control Panel.

Statement lines in the [PrinterPorts] section follow the format

```
<printer name>=<driver>,<port>,<DeviceNotSelectedTimeout>,
<TransmissionRetryTimeout>
```

where <printer name> is the name of the printer as it will appear in dialog boxes and other places in Windows. The <driver> is the file name of the driver that corresponds to the named printer. Windows printer driver files usually end with the file extension .DRV, but this extension should not be included when you list the driver's name in <printer-driver name>. Also, check the System subdirectory of your main Windows directory to make sure that any printer driver file you list is actually in your system.

The <port> is the name of a serial or parallel port that is connected to the type of printer you are specifying. If no printer is currently connected, the value of the <port name> is whatever you specified in the NullPort statement of the [Windows] section, earlier in this chapter. The <DeviceNotSelectedTimeout> is the number of seconds, from 0 to 999, that specifies how long the Windows Print Manager will wait for a printer to be connected or turned on. The <TransmissionRetryTimeout> is the number of seconds, from 0 to 999, that Windows will wait between attempting transmissions to that port. If the <DeviceNotSelectedTimeout> and <TransmissionRetryTimeout> values are not specified, Windows uses the default timeout settings for that port listed in the [Windows] section, earlier in this chapter.

This example of a [PrinterPorts] statement line

```
HP LaserJet Series II=HPPCL,LPT1:,15,45
```

reports these conditions:

➤ There is a printer named HP LaserJet Series II.

➤ The printer is using the printer-driver file named HPPCL.DRV.

➤ The printer is attached to the LPT1: parallel port.

➤ Print Manager will wait 15 seconds for the printer to be turned on.

➤ Windows will wait 45 seconds between attempts to transmit data to that port.

If the printer driver specified in a statement line can run on more than one port (which is connected to a compatible printer), those ports, along with their timeouts, can be listed after the parameters for the first port, as in this example:

```
HP LaserJet Series II=HPPCL,LPT1:,15,45,LPT2:,15,45
```

This line repeats the <port>,<DeviceNotSelectedTimeout>, and <TransmissionRetryTimeout> information for the second HP LaserJet connected to LPT2:. Note that only one device driver can be specified per statement line. There is no default value for this statement because it depends on your particular system configuration.

. . . .

The [Devices] Section of WIN.INI

This section is used to name the active printers for old applications from Windows version 2. Although it's rare to find an old version 2 program, and even rarer to find ones that won't crash your system, WIN.INI files can include this section as a precaution.

The settings in the [Devices] section must match those listed in the [PrinterPorts] section discussed earlier, except that no timeout values should be listed. The proper [Device] statement for the same printer shown in the first example in the [PrinterPorts] section would be

```
HP LaserJet Series II=HPPCL,LPT1:
```

If you need to change any values in the [Devices] section, make sure that it remains consistent with the information listed in the [PrinterPorts] section—otherwise you may not be able to print from the old application.

• •

The [Colors] Section of WIN.INI

This section tells Windows what colors to use for the various components of its interface: buttons, menus, scroll bars, and other elements. The [Colors] section corresponds to the controls you can access through the Color icon in the Control Panel (Figure 15.31).

FIGURE 15.31
*Color
Dialog Box*

This dialog box lets you select the active color scheme that is set with the statement lines in the [Colors] section.

The statements in the [Colors] section take this form:

```
<interface component>=<red> <green> <blue>
```

The <interface component> specifies the component of the Windows interface, and the <red>, <green>, and <blue> variables are integers from 0 to 255 that specify the color intensities of red, green, and blue, respectively. A value of 0 represents the minimum color intensity (none); a value of 255 represents the maximum intensity possible for any selected color. As artists and anyone who is familiar with color theory know, if all three values are set to 0, the resulting color is black; when all three are set to 255, white is the resulting color.

Windows uses a 24-bit color scheme, which allocates 8 bits of data, equivalent to 256 different shades, to each of the three primary colors. By varying these numbers for each primary color, millions of different colors can be created. However, most displays cannot show 24-bit color; in fact, most computer displays are limited to 16 or 256 colors. If your display cannot show true 24-bit color, Windows will try to match whatever color you specify to its closest approximation.

Table 15.7 lists the components of the Windows interface.

TABLE 15.7

<component name>	Description
ActiveBorder	Border of the active window
ActiveTitle	Title bar of the active window
AppWorkspace	Workspace inside an application window
Background	The screen background; i.e. the desktop
ButtonFace	The top face of buttons
ButtonShadow	The shadows of buttons
ButtonText	The text on all buttons
GrayText	Any text that is dimmed
Hilight	Background of any highlighted text
HilightText	Highlighted text
InactiveBorder	Border of any inactive windows
InactiveTitle	Title bar of any inactive windows
InactiveTitleText	Text in the title bar of an inactive window
Menu	Background color of all menus
MenuText	Text of all menus
Scrollbar	Scroll bars of all windows
TitleText	Text on the title bar of a window
Window	A window's workspace
WindowFrame	The frame around a window
WindowText	Text in any window

This example of a statement line in the [Colors] section

```
WindowText=0 0 0
```

tells Windows that all the text in a window should be black. In Windows 3.0, you could only change the ButtonFace, ButtonShadow, ButtonText, GrayText, Hilight, and HilightText by editing the [Colors] section by hand. In Windows 3.1, however, you can change all these values using the Control Panel. The InactiveTitleText setting was introduced in Windows 3.1.

. . . .

The [Embedding] Section of WIN.INI

This section provides information to Windows 3.0 applications about what objects can be embedded using OLE (Object Linking and Embedding). It's designed to provide backward compatibility with Windows 3.0 applications. Windows 3.1 does not refer to this section; instead, it uses the information in the OLE registration database, which you can view and edit with the Regedit utility. For further details about OLE, the registration database, and Regedit, see Chapter 9.

The statement lines in the [Embedding] section follow this format:

```
<OLE object>=<description1>, <description2>, <program file>,
<file format>
```

The <OLE object> is the name of an object created by an OLE server; <description1> is the descriptive name of the OLE server object; and <description2> is a descriptive name of the object—equivalent to the description that appears in the list of registered file types in the OLE registration database. The <program file> is the file name of the application that can be used to edit the object, which is usually the program that created it. The <file format> is the format of the file that contains the object. Often this entry is "picture," which denotes that the file is in the Windows metafile file format.

. . . .

The [Sounds] Section of WIN.INI

This section lists the Windows events that trigger a sound, along with the corresponding sound. The [Sounds] section corresponds to the Sound icon in the Control Panel (Figure 15.32).

FIGURE 15.32

Sound Icon in the Control Panel

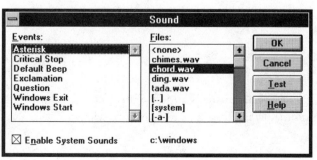

The Sound icon in the Control Panel provides a graphical way to edit the statements in the [Sounds] section.

The statements in the [Sounds] section follow this format:

```
<system event>=<sound file>, <event description>
```

The <system event> is the name internal to Windows for that particular event. The <sound file> is the name of any Windows sound file; these files are identified by the extension .WAV. The <event description> is the name of the system event as it appears in the Control Panel.

When Setup installs a new copy of Windows, it creates the following [Sounds] section:

```
[Sounds]
SystemDefault=ding.wav, Default Beep
SystemExclamation=chord.wav, Exclamation
SystemStart=tada.wav, Windows Start
SystemExit=chimes.wav, Windows Exit
SystemHand=chord.wav, Critical Stop
SystemQuestion=chord.wav, Question
SystemAsterisk=chord.wav, Asterisk
```

If you assign sounds to other events, corresponding statement lines are added. For example, the following line is added if you assign the chimes sound to the Program Launch item:

```
StartProgram=chimes.wav, Program Launch
```

. . . .

The [MCI Extensions] Section of WIN.INI

This section lists the extensions of multimedia files, together with the Media Control Interface (MCI) driver that can play these kinds of files. This statement takes the form

```
<file extension>=<MCI device>
```

The default entries for this section are

```
wav=waveaudio
mid=sequencer
rmi=sequencer
```

Other entries are usually added to this section by the installation programs of multimedia applications or hardware devices.

The [Programs] Section of WIN.INI

This section lists the directory paths that Windows will search to find an application associated with a data file you are trying to open. This happens only if Windows is unable to find the application in the current directory or in the other directories specified by the PATH statement in your AUTOEXEC.BAT file.

Whenever you open a data file and Windows is unable to locate the application, you are presented with a dialog box asking you to enter the path for the application associated with that data file (Figure 15.33).

FIGURE 15.33

Program Not Found Dialog Box

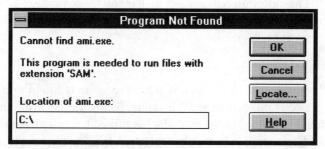

If Windows can't find an application for a document file you are trying to open, it presents this dialog box requesting the path where the application can be found.

When you respond to this dialog box, Windows updates the information in the [Programs] section. The statements in this section follow this format:

```
<program file>=<drive:><directory path><program file>
```

There is no default value for this statement—it's only created when Windows can't find an application needed to open a document file. An example statement line is

```
AMI.EXE=C:\PROGRAMS\AMI\AMI.EXE
```

The [Network] Section of WIN.INI

This section contains statement lines that define your previous network connections and other network-related settings. The Drive statement lists the network server connections that Windows should restore each time it starts.

This statement corresponds to the Network Connections command on File Manager's Disk menu and takes the form

```
Drive=<network server path>
```

The Port statement specifies the network printer to which Windows should connect each time it is started. The statement takes the form

```
Port=<network printer path>
```

This statement can be edited graphically using either the Printers icon in the Control Panel or the Network Connections command on Print Manager's Options menu. Neither the Drive nor the Port statement has a default value—they reflect specific settings you choose for your network.

The InRestoreNetConnect statement tells Windows whether it should reestablish your previous Windows connection to the network servers. The statement takes the form

```
InRestoreNetConnect=<0 or 1>
```

If the value is 1, the default, Windows reconnects you to your servers; if it's 0, you won't be reconnected. This statement works only with networks that are based on LAN Manager or MS-Net. To edit this statement graphically, use the Networks icon in the Control Panel. In some cases the Control Panel does not provide controls for reconnecting to your network server, but you can still edit this statement by hand and enable reconnection.

• •

The [Windows Help] Section of WIN.INI

This section contains the settings that tell Windows where to position the Help window and dialog boxes on your screen, and contains statements that let you choose the color of the text hot-spots that display macros or popup windows when you click them.

These statements in the [Windows Help] section control the positioning of the Help window and the dialog boxes:

```
M_WindowPosition=[<x coordinate>,<y coordinate>,<pixels
 wide>,<pixels high>,<0 or 1>]
H_WindowPosition=[<x coordinate>,<y coordinate>,<pixels
 wide>,<pixels high>,0]
A_WindowPosition=[<x coordinate>,<y coordinate>,<pixels
 wide>,<pixels high>,0]
C_WindowPosition=[<x coordinate>,<y coordinate>,<pixels
 wide>,<pixels high>,0]
```

These four statements control the position of the corresponding items:

➤ **M_WindowPosition** The main Help window

➤ **H_WindowPosition** The History dialog box

➤ **A_WindowPosition** The Annotate dialog box

➤ **C_WindowPosition** The Copy dialog box

The <x coordinate> value specifies the x coordinate of the upper-left corner of the item on the screen. The <y coordinate> value specifies the y coordinate of the upper-left corner. The <pixels wide> and <pixels high> values specify the default width and height of each item in pixels. The <0 or 1> switch specifies whether the main Help window should be maximized to fit the entire screen. When it is set to 1, the main Help window is maximized; when it is set to 0, the window is displayed at the height and width specified by <pixels wide> and <pixels high>.

The statement lines for the dialog boxes always use the 0 switch for this setting, because they cannot be maximized. An example of this statement line is

```
M_WindowPosition=[188,28,427,401,0]
```

which identifies the location and size of the main Help window. These statement lines are automatically updated by the Windows Help program whenever you move or resize the Help window or one of the three dialog boxes.

The [Windows Help] section can also contain statements that allow you to specify custom colors for the text hot-spots, which respond like buttons when you click on them. These statements take the form

```
JumpColor=<red><green><blue>
PopupColor=<red><green><blue>
MacroColor=<red><green><blue>
IFJumpColor=<red><green><blue>
IFPopupColor=<red><green><blue>
```

These five statements control the color of these text hot-buttons:

➤ **JumpColor** Text that takes you to a new page of Help

➤ **PopupColor** Text that exposes a popup panel, such as those used to display glossary definitions

➤ **MacroColor** Text that runs a Help macro

➤ **IFJumpColor** Text that takes you to a new page of Help in a different Help file

➥ **IFPopupColor** Text that exposes a popup panel located in a different Help file

The <red>, <green>, and <blue> values are integers from 0 to 255 that represent the color intensities of those colors. A value of 0 specifies the minimum color intensity, and a value of 255 represents the maximum intensity. For example, the statement line

```
JumpColor=000 000 000
```

specifies black as the color of the text that represents a hot button that takes you to a different Help page. The only way to change these values is to edit the WIN.INI file.

• •

The [Compatibility] Section of WIN.INI

This section provides special parameters to Windows 3.1 that allow it to retain compatibility with certain applications designed for Windows 3.0. The statements in this section follow this format:

```
<3.0 program>=<parameters>
```

where <3.0 program> is the name of the .EXE file without the extension of the incompatible 3.0 program, and <parameters> is the special code that tells Windows 3.1 how to maintain compatibility with the 3.0 application. Individual numbers in the <parameters> serve as switches that cause Windows 3.1 to behave as if it were version 3.0, but only for the application specified by <3.0 program>.

Danger Zone

The entries in this section are installed by Windows Setup or are provided by the developer of the incompatible application. If you're having compatibility problems with a Windows 3.0 program, contact the manufacturer to see if there is a statement line you can add to this section to alleviate the problem. Be extremely careful with the statements in this section—they're hacker witchcraft, and incorrect parameters can crash your system.

• •

Other Sections of WIN.INI

Most of the sections mentioned up to this point are commonly found in WIN.INI files. However, specific applications have the potential to create many other sections as well. Some Windows applications, such as Program Manager and the Clock utility, create their own .INI files: PROGMAN.INI and CLOCK.INI.

Some Windows programs do not require any initialization file; the .EXE file does it all. However, many applications that do require initialization information simply add their own section to WIN.INI rather than create an individual .INI file. Other applications do both: they add a section to WIN.INI *and* create their own initialization files.

Microsoft recommends that applications use their own initialization files to avoid cluttering the WIN.INI file and causing it to exceed its memory allotment. In Windows 3.1, for example, the Clock utility creates and uses its own CLOCK.INI initialization file, whereas in Windows 3.0 this utility added its own [clock] section to the WIN.INI file. An advantage to the new approach is that it frees memory in the WIN.INI file and it also frees Windows from reading it into memory every time it reads WIN.INI. However, Microsoft ignores its own recommendation; many of the Windows applets and utilities add their own sections to WIN.INI.

If an application does create a section in WIN.INI, however, the application may not work if the section is missing. The application may also encounter operating problems if any information that it writes in other sections, such as [extensions], [ports], and [fonts], is missing. You should be aware of this potential problem if you are upgrading Windows versions or peforming some other operation that might create a new WIN.INI file and abandon the old one or overwrite settings in your existing file.

Insider's Tip

Sections added to WIN.INI by other applications can often be cut from an old WIN.INI file and then pasted into a new WIN.INI using the Windows Clipboard. However, be sure to check whether the application has modified any other sections (for example, [Extensions], [Fonts], [Embedding]); if it has made changes, note them, and then make the same changes to the sections of the new file using the methods outlined in this chapter.

The content and syntax of statement lines that applications add to WIN.INI can vary widely, although most follow the standards described earlier. However, consult an applications manual (or, if that proves unproductive, contact the manufacturer) to determine the purpose and exact syntax of the statement lines that other applications add to WIN.INI.

Editing the SYSTEM.INI File

The SYSTEM.INI file, along with the WIN.INI file, is one of the two primary initialization files used by Windows. Most of the information in SYSTEM.INI describes your hardware configuration to Windows.

The SYSTEM.INI file is created by Windows Setup when Windows is first installed, and contains settings related to the hardware information specified in Setup during the installation process. Unlike the WIN.INI file, many of the statements in SYSTEM.INI do not have graphical controls for editing from the Control Panel. Some of the statement lines can be changed using Windows Setup, but most must be added manually, according to the guidelines described here. Changes you make to the SYSTEM.INI file do not take effect until Windows is restarted.

Many of the statement lines described in this chapter do not normally appear in the SYSTEM.INI file; you'll only need them for special circumstances. By understanding more about the various settings available in SYSTEM.INI, however, you can fine-tune your system to enhance your Windows performance and improve the way your applications run under your system.

In format, the SYSTEM.INI file is similar to the WIN.INI file. Both are structured as sections, each of which contains a collection of statement lines. The syntax of the statement lines is also similar and follows the form that is common to all Windows initialization files:

```
<setting name>=<value>
```

Finally, as noted at the beginning of this chapter, the SYSTEM.INI file is a plain text file, and is therefore sensitive to any formatting commands added by a wordprocessing program. It's important when you edit this file to use a nondisruptive text editor, such as SysEdit or the Notepad.

Table 15.8 lists the sections contained in the SYSTEM.INI file.

· · · · · · · · · · · · · ·
TABLE 15.8

Section	Description
[boot]	Lists program modules and device drivers that Windows loads during startup
[boot.description]	Lists the device drivers controlled by the Windows Setup program
[keyboard]	Contains settings related to the keyboard
[386Enh]	Lists special parameters used when Windows is run in 386 enhanced mode
[standard]	Lists special parameters used when Windows is run in standard mode
[NonWindowsApp]	Lists special parameters for running DOS programs
[MCI]	Contains a list of drivers that are compatible with the Media Control Interface (MCI)
[drivers]	Contains aliases for driver files listed in the [boot] section and parameters used by those drivers

Danger Zone

Use special caution when editing any entries in the [boot],[keyboard], and [386Enh] sections of the SYSTEM.INI file, because if any of the information in these sections is either deleted or changed improperly, Windows may not run them correctly. It's always a good idea to back up your SYSTEM.INI file before editing it.

Many of the device driver files, font files, and other files you can specify in statement lines in SYSTEM.INI are stored on your Windows installation disks. Windows Setup only copies the files it needs during installation, so if you plan to use others later, you'll need to copy them from the installation disks. These files will need to be decompressed before they can be used by Windows.

If you change any settings in SYSTEM.INI by using the Windows Setup program, Setup prompts you for installation disks if it needs a device driver or other file; and Setup automatically decompresses the file when copying it to your System directory. If you change any settings by hand, and need to retrieve a file from the installation disk, remember that you must first decompress the file from the installation disk by using the EXPAND.EXE utility described in Chapter 5.

. . . .

The [Boot] Section of SYSTEM.INI

The first section of the SYSTEM.INI file is the [boot] section, which tells Windows what program modules and device drivers to load each time you start a Windows session. Unlike some of the other sections in SYSTEM.INI, where many of the statement lines are optional, all the settings in the [boot] section are required for Windows to run properly. Many of the settings in the [boot] section have no default values; their values are based on your computer's specific hardware configuration and are specified by Windows Setup during installation, according to the hardware options you chose during the installation process.

The [boot] section contains these statements:

```
shell=                      286grabber=
display.drv=                mouse.drv=
system.drv=                 keyboard.drv=
comm.drv=                   sound.drv=
network.drv=                language.dll=
oemfonts.fon=               Taskman.exe=
fonts.fon=                  Drivers=
fixedfon.fon=               CachedFileHandles=
386grabber=
```

The Shell Statement. This statement tells Windows what program to run when Windows is first started. Usually this statement specifies a Windows shell program, such as Program Manager or File Manager, or a third-party shell, but you can specify any Windows program. Whatever program you designate will run during your entire Windows session; quitting that program will also quit Windows and end the session.

The statement takes the form

```
shell=<file name>
```

where <file name> is the name of the program you want to use as your Windows shell.

Windows provides two shells that you can specify with this statement: PROGMAN.EXE and WINFILE.EXE. The default for this statement is

```
shell=progman.exe
```

which specifies PROGMAN.EXE, Program Manager, as the shell. If this statement is left blank, Program Manager is used as the shell.

Insider's Tip

Windows power users who run many different programs and files may want to specify File Manager, rather than Program Manager, as the primary shell. To make the File Manager program, WINFILE.EXE, your primary shell, simply change this line to read

```
shell=winfile.exe
```

This triggers Windows to start with File Manager rather than Program Manager; with the shell set to WINFILE.EXE, quitting File Manager also quits Windows.

The Display.drv Statement. This statement tells Windows what to use as its main display driver. Windows supplies a fair number of display drivers, which have been updated in Windows 3.1. If you are using a video card that is not listed here, you may need to obtain a special driver from the manufacturer of your display adapter card.

Be careful when you change this setting; if you specify an invalid or incompatible driver, your Windows screen may be garbled or blank. To correct this problem, you'll need to rerun Setup from DOS or edit the SYSTEM.INI file in DOS by specifying the proper driver or reverting to the back-up copy of the file, which—of course—you made before editing it. The statement takes the form

```
display.drv=<file name>
```

where <file name> identifies the display driver that Windows will use.

A sample statement line

```
display.drv=VGA.DRV
```

specifies that the standard VGA driver file, VGA.DRV, will be used as the Windows display driver.

Table 15.9 lists the display drivers (compressed, of course) that Windows 3.1 supplies on the installation disks.

Display Driver	File Description
vga.drv	VGA with color display
vgamono.drv	VGA with monochrome display
supervga.drv	Super VGA 800x600*
v7vga.drv	Video Seven 256 colors—640x480, 720x512, 800x600, 1024x768**
tiga.drv	TIGA
8514.drv	8514/a
plasma.drv	Compaq Portable Plasma
ega.drv	EGA
egahibw.drv	EGA black and white (286 only)
egamono.drv	EGA monochrome (286 only)
hercules.drv	Hercules monochrome
olibw.drv	Olivetti/AT&T monochrome or PVC display
xga.drv	XGA display

*When using the SuperVGA driver, the WIN.INI file must contain a [Displays] section that sets a value for the VGA mode parameter. See Chapter 8 for a discussion of displays and display drivers.

**When using the Video Seven driver supplied with Windows 3.1, you should add a section called [Kernel] to the end of the SYSTEM.INI file (if it doesn't already exist), and add a statement line that specifies the resolution mode that you want the Video Seven driver to operate in. The statement takes the form

```
display.drv=<resolution>
```

where <resolution> is one of the following possible video resolutions:

```
640x480
720x512
800x600
1024x768
```

A sample section and statement line would be:

```
[kernel]
display.drv=800x600
```

which would put the Video Seven driver into a mode capable of displaying 800x600 pixels. Also, in order for the Windows version 3.1 Video Seven driver to work properly you must

➥ copy the file V7VDD.386 to your System directory if it isn't already there

➥ delete the line "v7device=" from the [386enh] section, if present

➥ add the line "display=v7vdd.386" to the [386enh] section

The System.drv Statement. This statement tells Windows which computer system device driver to use. The statement takes the form

```
system.drv=<file name>
```

where <file name> identifies the computer system driver. The default statement line is

```
system.drv=SYSTEM.DRV
```

which specifies the standard SYSTEM.DRV driver that works with most IBM-compatible PCs. Windows also provides a special system driver, HPSYSTEM.DRV, that is required for all Hewlett-Packard PCs. Some computer systems provide their own system driver; in that case, consult the manufacturer's documentation for operating instructions.

The Comm.drv Statement. This statement tells Windows which serial communications port driver to use. The statement takes the form

```
comm.drv=<file name>
```

where <file name> is the name of the serial communications driver. The default statement line is

```
comm.drv=COMM.DRV
```

which specifies that the COMM.DRV device driver should be used.

The COMM.DRV driver is the only communications driver provided on the Windows installation disks. Some hardware devices that use serial communications ports provide their own communications drivers; if you are using a third-party driver, consult the manufacturer for specific details.

The Network.drv Statement. This statement tells Windows what network driver to use if a network is installed. For more information about networks and Windows, refer to Chapter 10. The statement takes the form

```
network.drv=<file name>
```

where <file name> is the network driver you want Windows to use.

Table 15.10 lists the network drivers that Windows 3.1 supplies on its installation disks.

TABLE 15.10

Network Driver	Description
msnet.drv	Generic network driver; works with 3Com 3+Open LAN Manager (XNS only), 3Com 3+Share, Banyan Vines 4.0, LAN Manager Basic, Microsoft Network, IBM PC LAN Program
lanman.drv	LAN Manager 2.0 Extended (or 100% compatible)
netware.drv	Novell Netware 2.10 or higher, Novell Netware 386
pcsa.drv	DEC Pathworks network driver

The Oemfonts.fon Statement. This statement tells Windows what font file contains the OEM character set. Different OEM character sets are required, depending on the language selected and the kind of display driver Windows is using. The statement takes the form

```
oemfonts.fon=<file name>
```

where <file name> identifies which font file to use as the OEM font. There is no default for this font, because the choice depends on what video driver Windows is using.

Table 15.11 lists the OEM fonts that Windows 3.1 provides on the installation disks.

TABLE 15.11

OEM Font File	Description
egaoem.fon	EGA (640x350) Terminal Font (USA/Europe)
cgaoem.fon	CGA (640x200) Terminal Font (USA/Europe)
8514oem.fon	8514/a (1024x768) Terminal Font (USA/Europe)
vgaoem.fon	VGA (640x480) Terminal Font (USA/Europe)

The Fonts.fon Statement. This statement tells Windows what proportionately spaced system font file to use. Your selected font is displayed in menu choices, dialog boxes, and other places throughout the Windows environment. The statement takes the form:

```
fonts.fon=<file name>
```

where <file name> identifies the font file selected as the main system font. There is no default system font, because the font used depends on what video driver Windows is using. Be careful not to specify an invalid choice, or Windows may not be able to start up.

Table 15.12 lists the system fonts that Windows 3.1 provides on the installation disks.

Font File	Description
egasys.fon	EGA (640x350) resolution System Font
vgasys.fon	VGA (640x480) resolution System Font
8514sys.fon	8514/a (1024x768) resolution System Font

Insider's Tip

If you are using a high-resolution display mode, such as SuperVGA at 1024x768, you should specify the 8514sys.fon; this makes the system font larger and easier to read on high pixel-resolution monitors that shrink the size of images on the screen.

The Fixedfon.fon Statement. This statement tells Windows what fixed (that is, nonproportional) font to use as the system font for Windows 2.x programs. It's included only to provide compatibility with these old programs. The statement takes the form

```
fixedfon.fon=<file name>
```

where <file name> identifies the font file to use as the system font for Windows 2.x programs. There is no default fixedfon.fon font; again, the choice depends on what video driver Windows is using.

Table 15.13 lists the fixed fonts that Windows 3.1 provides on the installation disks.

TABLE 15.13

Fixed Font File	Description
egafix.fon	EGA (640x350) resolution, AT&T (640x400) resolution
vgafix.fon	VGA (640x480) resolution
8514fix.fon	8514/a (1024x768) resolution

The 386grabber Statement. This statement tells Windows which display grabber to use when you are running Windows in 386 enhanced mode. The grabber is a special type of device driver for "grabbing" the image of a DOS application so that it can be displayed in Windows. The statement takes the form

```
386grabber=<file name>
```

where <file name> is the name of the grabber file. There is no default grabber file, because it is related to the kind of video display driver Windows is using.

Table 15.14 lists the 386grabber files that Windows provides.

•••••••••••••
TABLE 15.14

Grabber File Name	Description
VGA.3GR	Standard VGA
VGA30.3GR	VGA grabber for Windows 3.0 display drivers
V7VGA.3GR	Video 7/Headland VGA
VGADIB.3GR	8514/a monochrome
EGA.3GR	EGA
HERC.3GR	Hercules
PLASMA.3GR	Compaq Plasma, Olivetti/AT&T Monochrome or PVC Display

A typical 386grabber statement is

```
386grabber=vga.3gr
```

which tells Windows to use the VGA grabber to display DOS applications.

The 286grabber Statement. This statement tells Windows which display grabber to use to display DOS applications when Windows is running in either real mode or standard mode. The statement takes the form

```
286grabber=<file name>
```

where <file name> identifies the grabber file. There is no default 286grabber file, because it is related to what type of video display driver Windows is using.

Table 15.15 lists the 286grabbers that Windows provides.

•••••••••••••
TABLE 15.15

Grabber File Name	Description
VGACOLOR.2GR	Standard VGA, color display
VGAMONO.2GR	Standard VGA, monochrome display
CGA.2GR	CGA
EGACOLOR.2GR	EGA, color display
EGAMONO.2GR	EGA, monochrome display

Grabber File Name	Description
HERCULES.2GR	Hercules
OLIGRAB.2GR	Olivetti/AT&T PVC display

••••••••••••••
TABLE 15.15 (cont.)

The Mouse.drv Statement. The mouse.drv statement tells Windows which mouse driver to use. The statement takes the form

```
mouse.drv=<file name>
```

where <file name> is the name of the mouse driver.

Table 15.16 lists the mouse drivers that Windows 3.1 provides, in a compressed format, on the installation disks.

••••••••••••••
TABLE 15.16

Driver File Name	Description (As It Appears in Setup)
MOUSE.DRV	Microsoft or IBM PS/2
NOMOUSE.DRV	No mouse or other pointing device
HPMOUSE.DRV	HP Mouse (HP-HIL)
KBDMOUSE.DRV	Olivetti/AT&T Keyboard Mouse
LMOUSE.DRV	Logitech
MSC3BC2.DRV	Mouse Systems 3 button serial mouse on COM2:
MSCMOUSE.DRV	Mouse Systems

You can use any of these device drivers if the appropriate driver file is located in your Windows System directory. If you specify a supplemental or third-party driver, be sure to copy it to the System directory.

The Keyboard.drv Statement. This statement tells Windows which keyboard driver to use. The keyboard driver controls the way that Windows interacts with the computer to receive information from the keyboard. For information about specific keyboards and keyboard layouts, refer to the [keyboard] section of SYSTEM.INI, described later in this chapter. The statement takes the form

```
keyboard.drv=<file name>
```

where <file name> identifies the keyboard driver. The default statement line is

```
keyboard.drv=KEYBOARD.DRV
```

which specifies that the standard KEYBOARD.DRV device driver should be used. Windows 3.1 also provides the KBDHP.DRV driver for Hewlett-Packard computers and the KBDMOUSE.DRV driver for the Olivetti/AT&T keyboard-mouse combination.

The Sound.drv Statement. This statement tells Windows which sound driver to use. The statement takes the form

```
sound.drv=<file name>
```

where <file name> is the name of the sound driver. The default for this statement is to leave the line blank.

To use the multimedia sound driver, change the statement to read

```
sound.drv=MMSOUND.DRV
```

which specifies that the MMSOUND.DRV device driver should be used.

The Language.dll Statement. This statement tells Windows what Dynamic Link Library (DLL) should be used for Windows language-specific functions—except for American English (the USA setting), which is built into Windows. The statement takes the form

```
language.dll=<DLL name>
```

where <DLL name> is the Dynamic Link Library that contains the language-specific information needed to run Windows in a language other than American English.

Table 15.17 lists the language DLLs that are supplied with Windows.

· · · · · · · · · · · · · ·
TABLE 15.17

<DLL name>	Language
langsca.dll	Danish, Finnish, Icelandic, Norwegian, Swedish
langdut.dll	Dutch
langeng.dll	English (Great Britain), French Canadian, Italian, Portuguese
langfrn.dll	French
langger.dll	German
langspa.dll	Spanish

If no language DLL is specified in this statement, the built-in USA values are used.

The Taskman.exe Statement. This statement tells Windows what program to run when you press Ctrl+Esc or double-click in an empty area of the Windows desktop. The statement takes the form

```
Taskman.exe=<filename>
```

where <filename> is the program you want to run. The default is TASK-MAN.EXE, which is the Task Manager program. You can specify another task-switching program here, or any program that you want to appear instead of Task Manager. If the setting is blank or missing, the TASKMAN.EXE program is used.

The Drivers Statement. This statement identifies the name or alias of an installable driver that Windows should load. Installable drivers are Dynamic Link Libraries (DLLs) that serve the same function as a device driver. The statement takes the form

```
drivers=<file or alias>
```

where <file or alias> can be the actual file name of the DLL or its alias. If the DLL requires special switches or other parameters, you must give it an alias, and list the alias—along with the parameters—in the [Drivers] section that appears later in the SYSTEM.INI file. There is no default for this statement, because these statement lines are usually installed by setup programs for third-party software or hardware products. Setup installs one Drivers statement

```
drivers=MMSYSTEM.DLL
```

which loads the multimedia system driver for Windows.

The CachedFileHandles Statement. This statement tells Windows how many program and Dynamic Link Library files can remain open at any given time. The statement takes the form

```
CachedFileHandles=<number of handles>
```

where <number of handles> is a number from 2 to 12 representing the total number of files that can be open at once. The default value, 12, lets Windows keep the maximum number files open in order to ensure the best performance. Some networks limit the number of open files in order to prevent problems.

The [Boot.description] Section of SYSTEM.INI

This section identifies the settings for those devices that can be altered by using the Windows Setup utility. The statements in the boot description follow the form

```
<setting>=<name>
```

where setting is the statement parameter accepted by SYSTEM.INI and <name> is the name of that setting as it appears in Windows Setup.

Here is an example of a [Boot.description] section:

```
network.drv=No Network Installed
language.dll=English (American)
system.drv=MS-DOS System
codepage=437
display.drv=VGA
keyboard.typ=Enhanced 101 or 102 key US and Non US keyboards
mouse.drv=Microsoft or IBM PS/2
```

This sample section would cause the <name> values it specifies to be displayed as your current settings by the Windows Setup program.

Danger Zone

If you change the values in this file, Windows Setup will not be able to update your drivers unless you also change the corresponding setting names in SETUP.INF.

The [Keyboard] Section of SYSTEM.INI

This section tells Windows your type of keyboard, what character set to use with the keyboard, and your type of layout. The only item not covered here is a description of what keyboard device driver to use, because that setting is controlled by the keyboard.drv= statement line in the [Boot] section of SYSTEM.INI, as described earlier in this chapter. Windows requires most of the statement lines in this section and will not run correctly if improper values are given for any of these settings.

The [keyboard] section contains the following statement lines:

```
type=
subtype=
keyboard.dll=
oemansi.bin=
```

The Type Statement. This statement tells the Windows keyboard driver what type of keyboard the computer is using, and takes the form

```
type=<1-4>
```

where <1–4> is one of the numbers 1 to 4 that identifies the keyboard type according to the values shown in Table 15.18.

Value of <1–4>	Keyboard Type
1	IBM PC or XT compatible (83 keys)
2	Olivetti 102-key ICO
3	IBM AT compatible (84 or 86 keys)
4	Enhanced keyboard (101 or 102 keys)

If this <1–4> value is left blank, or if the type= statement line is missing altogether, the keyboard driver selects a default value, depending on what driver is in use. For example, if Windows is using the KEYBOARD.DRV driver, the driver will check the BIOS ROMs to determine the computer's keyboard type.

The Subtype Statement. This statement tells the keyboard device driver about certain keyboards, listed in the Type statement just discussed, with the same key layout but different special features. The statement takes the form

```
subtype=<type number>
```

where <type number> is a number, usually from 1 to 4, that identifies the subtype of the keyboard. The value of <type number> depends on what keyboard driver Windows is using. If the standard KEYBOARD.DRV driver is being used, then the subtype values shown in Table 15.19 apply:

Type=	Subtype=	Keyboard Type
1	2	Olivetti M24 83-key or AT&T 6300 type 301 83-key
1	4	AT&T type 302, sometimes used on the 6300 Plus
2	1	Olivetti 102-key ICO used on M24 systems

The Oemansi.bin Statement. This statement tells Windows which OEM/ANSI code-page file contains the translation table for character sets used on non-U.S. keyboards. The statement takes the form

```
oemansi.bin=<code-page file name>
```

where <code-page file name> is the name of the file that contains the code-page translation table. If the <code-page file name> is left blank, the standard U.S. OEM character set, code-page 437, is used.

The OEM/ANSI code-page translation table files included with Windows 3.1 are listed in Table 15.20.

TABLE 15.20

Translation Table	<code-page file name>	Language
863	xlat863.bin	French Canadian
861	xlat861.bin	Icelandic
865	xlat865.bin	Norwegian and Danish
850	xlat850.bin	International
860	xlat860.bin	Portuguese

The code-page translation table listed in the oemansi.bin statement should match the font specified in the oemfonts.fon statement discussed earlier in this section.

The Keyboard.dll Statement. This statement tells Windows which Dynamic Link Library (DLL) file contains the information about the layout of your keyboard. If you have one of the following keyboards

IBM XT

IBM PC/AT

IBM enhanced

AT&T type 301 or 302

Olivetti 83-key

then you do not need to include this line. All other keyboards, including those for U.S. keyboards not listed here, require this statement line specifying the approprite DLL. The statement takes the form

```
keyboard.dll=<DLL file name>
```

where <DLL file name> is the name of the DLL file that contains the keyboard layout information.

The DLL files provided with Windows 3.1 are listed in Table 15.21.

TABLE 15.21

<DLL file name>	Layout	<DLL file name>	Layout
kbdbe.dll	Belgian	kbdit.dll	Italian
kbduk.dll	British	kbdla.dll	Latin American
kbdfc.dll	Canadian multilingual	kbdno.dll	Norwegian
		kbdpo.dll	Portuguese
kbdda.dll	Danish	kbdsp.dll	Spanish
kbdne.dll	Dutch	kbdsw.dll	Swedish
kbdfi.dll	Finnish	kbdsf.dll	Swiss French
kbdfr.dll	French	kbdsg.dll	Swiss German
kbdca.dll	French Canadian	kbdus.dll	U.S.
		kbddv.dll	U.S.-Dvorak
kbdgr.dll	German	kbdusx.dll	U.S.-International
kbdic.dll	Icelandic		

Insider's Tip

You can specify the KBDDV.DLL in the keyboard.dll statement to change your U.S. keyboard layout to a Dvorak layout, which ergonomic studies have shown to be faster for typing than the standard QWERTY keyboard layout, as discussed in Chapter 8.

The [386Enh] Section of SYSTEM.INI

This important section gives Windows information on running in 386 enhanced mode. If you are using a 286-based system, you do not need this section. If you do have a 386 or higher chip, you should be using 386 enhanced mode as your main Windows mode, and should pay special attention to the items in this section.

During the installation process, Windows Setup places only a small number of the myriad possible statement lines in this section. Some of the other statements can be added or changed using the 386 Enhanced controls found in the Control Panel (Figure 15.34). To learn more about adusting the settings in the 386 Enhanced section of the Control Panel, refer to Chapter 4, which covers this topic in detail.

••••••••••••••
FIGURE 15.34
*386 Enhanced
Controls*

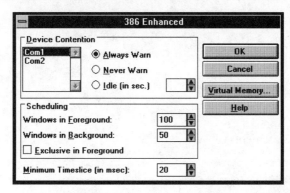

*The 386 Enhanced
section of the Control
Panel allows you to add
or adjust settings
affecting the perfor-
mance of your system.*

The [386Enh] section contains a greater variety of statements than does any other section in the Windows initialization files. The [386Enh] settings allow you to fine-tune the performance of Windows' 386 enhanced mode operation, and to resolve incompatibilities and other problems that might result from running DOS applications or from using certain hardware configurations. Most of these statements are optional and have to be set by hand, using the methods described here. Note that some of the statements accept logical switches, such as <yes or no>, <on or off>, and <true or false>. The examples in this book employ whichever of the logical expressions is used by Windows, or the most descriptive expression for understanding the setting.

The [386Enh] section can contain any of these statement lines:

Device Statements

```
Device=                      Keyboard=
Display=                     Mouse=
Ebios=                       Network=
```

I/O Port Statements

```
COM1AutoAssign=              COMdrv30=
COM2AutoAssign=              COM1FIFO=
COM3AutoAssign=              COM2FIFO=
COM4AutoAssign=              COM3FIFO=
COM1Base=                    COM4FIF0=
COM2Base=                    COM1Irq=
COM3Base=                    COM2Irq=
COM4Base=                    COM3Irq=
COMBoostTime=                COM4Irq=
COM1Buffer=                  COMIrqSharing
COM2Buffer=                  COM1Protocol=
COM3Buffer=                  COM2Protocol=
COM4Buffer=                  COM3Protocol=
```

I/O Port Statements *(cont.)*

```
COM4Protocol=                    MaxCOMPort=
LPT1AutoAssign=                  NoWaitNetIO=
LPT2AutoAssign=                  OverlappedIO=
LPT3AutoAssign=                  SGrabLPT=
LPT4AutoAssign=
```

Display Statements

```
AutoRestoreScreen=               MessageBackColor=
BkGrndNotifyAtPFault=            MessageTextColor=
CGA40WOA.FON=                    ScrollFrequency=
CGA80WOA.FON=                    UseROMFont=
CGANoSnow=                       VGAMonoText=
DualDisplay=                     VideoBackgroundMsg=
EGA40WOA.FON=                    VideoSuspendDisable=
EGA80WOA.FON=
```

Keyboard Statements

```
AltKeyDelay=                     KeyPasteDelay=
AltPasteDelay=                   KeyPasteSkipCount=
KeyBoostTime=                    KeyPasteTimeout=
KeyBufferDelay=                  KybdPasswd=
KeyIdleDelay=                    KybdReboot=
KeyPasteCRSkipCount=             TranslateScans=
```

Swap File Statements

```
32BitDiskAccess=                 PageBuffers=
MaxPagingFileSize=               PagingFile=
MinUserDiskSpace=                PermSwapDOSDrive=
Paging=                          PermSwapSizeK=
PagingDrive=
```

DMA Statements

```
DMABufferIn1MB=                  HardDiskDMABuffer=
DMABufferSize=                   MaxDMAPGAddress=
EISADMA=                         MCADMA=
```

Network Statements

```
NetAsynchFallback=               NetHeapSize=
NetAsynchTimeout=                TokenRingSearch=
NetDMASize=
```

Interrupt Handling Statements

```
InDOSPolling=                    NMIReboot=
INT28Critical=                   ReflectDosInt2A=
IRQ9Global=                      TimerCriticalSection=
MouseSoftInit=                   VirtualHDIrq=
```

Memory Handling Statements

```
A20EnableCount=                  PerformBackfill=
AllEMSLocked=                    ReservedHighArea=
AllXMSLocked=                    ReservePageFrame
EMMExclude=                      ReserveVideoROM=
EMMInclude=                      ROMScanThreshold=
EMMPageFrame=                    SystemROMBreakPoint=
EMMSize=                         SysVMEMSLimit=
IgnoreInstalledEMM=              SysVMEMSLocked=
LRULowRateMult=                  SysVMEMSRequired=
LRURateChngTime=                 SysVMV86Locked=
LRUSweepFreq=                    SysVMXMSLimit=
LRUSweepLen=                     SysVMXMSRequired=
LRUSweepLowWater=                UseableHighArea=
LRUSweepReset=                   VCPIWarning=
MapPhysAddress=                  WindowKBRequired=
MaxBPS=                          WindowMemSize=
MaxPhysPage=                     XlatBufferSize=
NoEMMDriver=                     XMSUMBInitCalls=
PageOverCommit=
```

Virtual Machine and Multitasking Statements

```
AllVMsExclusive=                 MinUnlockMem=
DOSPromptExitInstruc=            PerVMFILES=
FileSysChange=                   PSPIncrement=
Global=                          UniqueDOSPSP=
IdleVMWakeUpTime=                WindowUpdateTime=
Local=                           WinExclusive=
LocalLoadHigh=                   WinTimeSlice=
LocalReboot=                     WOAFont=
MinTimeSlice=
```

Other 386 Enhanced Statements

```
SyncTime=                        UseInstFile=
TrapTimerPorts=
```

Windows Setup usually only includes a list of device= statements, a local= statement, a FileSysChange= statement, and some font file statements when setting up an 386 enhanced file. A typical [386Enh] section might look like this:

```
[386Enh]
display=*vddvga
keyboard=*vkd
mouse=*vmd
network=*vnetbios, *dosnet
ebios=*ebios
device=*vpicd
device=*vtd
device=*reboot
device=*vdmad
device=*vsd
device=*v86mmgr
device=*pageswap
device=*dosmgr
device=*vmpoll
device=*wshell
device=*BLOCKDEV
device=*PAGEFILE
device=*vfd
device=*parity
device=*biosxlat
device=*vcd
device=*vmcpd
device=*combuff
device=*cdpscsi
local=CON
FileSysChange=off
CGA40WOA.FON=CGA40WOA.FON
CGA80WOA.FON=CGA80WOA.FON
EGA40WOA.FON=EGA40WOA.FON
EGA80WOA.FON=EGA80WOA.FON
```

This bare-bones [386Enh] section uses only a fraction of the possible statement lines. Other statements depend on your particular hardware configuration. One such set of statements, and the most important, are the device= statements; they are absolutely necessary for operating Windows in 386 enhanced mode. After the various device statements, the many other

[386Enh] statements are presented in alphabetical order (rather than in the topical groupings just listed) to make it easier to locate a specific statement.

The Virtual Device Statements. When Windows is running in 386 enhanced mode, you can create several virtual machines, each capable of running different programs as if it were an individual computer with its own system resources. Running several programs at once on multiple virtual machines would normally cause a conflict whenever two or more programs tried to access the physical hardware at the same time. To avoid these conflicts, Windows prevents each of the virtual machines from accessing the hardware directly. Instead, Windows provides the virtual machines with virtual devices that, using software, simulate the actual hardware. Windows then arbitrates the requests for use of the virtual devices and shares the physical hardware resources among the various virtual machines.

The device= statements tell Windows what virtual device drivers to use; the particular driver used depends on the hardware configuration you specified in Windows Setup, either during the Windows installation process or by running Setup after installation.

The Device Statement. This statement tells Windows which virtual devices to use when it runs in 386 enhanced mode. Windows recognizes two types of virtual devices: those that are part of the WIN386.EXE program file itself, and those that are contained in a separate virtual device driver file. The first kind is specified by an asterisk (*) immediately before the name of the virtual device itself. The drivers that are not part of the WIN386.EXE file can be specified by the name of the file that contains the virtual device driver; most of these files end with the extension .386.

These virtual device drivers are part of the Windows 3.1 version of WIN386.EXE:

*biosxlat	*pageswap	*vkd
*blockdev	*parity	*vmcpd
*cdpscsi	*reboot	*vmd
*combuff	*t4s0enha	*vmpoll
*dosmgr	*v86mmgr	*vnetbios
*dosnet	*vcd	*vpicd
*ebios	*vddvga	*vsd
*egahires	*vfd	*vtd
*int13	*vdmad	*wdctrl
*olibw	*vga	*wshell
*pagefile	*vipx	

The virtual device drivers listed in Table 15.22 are supplied as separate files on the Windows 3.1 installation disks.

TABLE 15.22

Virtual Device Driver	Description
BANINST.386	Banyan Vines 4.0 instancing device
DECNB.386	DEC Pathworks network driver
DECNET.386	DEC Pathworks network driver
LANMAN10.386	LAN Manager version 1.0 network driver
HPEBIOS.386	EBIOS for Hewlett-Packard machines
LVMD.386	Logitech mouse device
MSCVMD.386	Mouse Systems mouse device
V7VDD.386	Video Seven display device
VADLIBD.386	DMA device for Adlib
VDD8514.386	8514/a display device
VDDCGA.386	CGA display device
VDDCT441.386	82C441 VGA display device
VDDEGA.386	EGA display device
VDDHERC.386	Hercules monochrome display device
VDDTIGA.386	TIGA display device
VDDVGA30.386	VGA (version 3.0) display device
VDDXGA.386	XGA display device
VIPX.386	Novell NetWare IPX driver
VNETWARE.386	NetWare network driver
VPOWERD.386	Advanced Power Management device
VSBD.386	SoundBlaster device
VTDAPI.386	MultiMedia timer device
WIN386.PS2	PS/2 driver

New in 3.1

The BPVKD.386 and VPICDA.386 drivers that were separate files in Windows 3.0 have been replaced by the *vkd and *vpicd devices drivers that are built into WIN386.EXE in Windows 3.1. In addition, the *vhd hard disk driver in Windows 3.0 has been replaced by the *blockdev device driver in version 3.1. The old *vhd driver used the DOS BIOS to access the hard disk, whereas the new *blockdev driver supports the use of FastDisk to bypass DOS and access the hard disk directly; this can enhance the speed of Windows dramatically when used with a permanent swap file.

Insider's Tip

If FastDisk is installed, the lines

```
device=*int13
device=*wdctrl
```

provide the *blockdev driver the ability to use FastDisk with Western Digital-compatible controller cards. To turn off FastDisk, remove these two lines, but do not remove the line that installs *blockdev. Refer to Chapter 12 for more information about Windows and hard disks.

The device statement takes the form

```
device=<*devicename or file name>
```

where <*devicename or file name> is either the virtual device driver name (provided it is part of the WIN386.EXE file) or the file name of a virtual device driver. The device statement permits five synonyms for device=:

```
display=, ebios=, keyboard=, mouse=, and network=
```

The Display Statement. This statement, which is a synonym of the device statement, tells Windows what display driver to use when running in 386 enhanced mode. The statement takes the form

```
display=<*devicename or file name>
```

where <*devicename or file name> is either the virtual display driver name (preceded by an asterisk) or the file name of a virtual display driver. For example, if you are using a standard VGA display adapter, this statement line would be

```
display=*vddvga
```

which specifies the VGA virtual display device that is built-in into WIN386.EXE.

The Ebios Statement. This statement, another synonym of the device statement, tells Windows what extended BIOS device driver to use when running in 386-enhanced mode. The statement takes the form

```
ebios=<*devicename or file name>
```

where <*devicename or file name> is either the virtual device driver name or the file name of a virtual device driver. The standard setting is

```
ebios=*ebios
```

which applies to all machines except Hewlett-Packard 386 systems; these require that the separate HP extended BIOS device be specified as

```
ebios=HPEBIOS.386
```

The Keyboard Statement. This statement, which is a synonym of the device statement, tells Windows what virtual keyboard driver to use. The statement takes the form

```
keyboard=<*devicename or file name>
```

where <*devicename or file name> is either the virtual keyboard driver name or the file name of a virtual keyboard driver. The standard virtual keyboard driver that is built into WIN386.EXE is installed using the following statement line:

```
keyboard=*vkd
```

The Mouse Statement. This statement, a synonym of the device statement, tells Windows what virtual mouse driver to use. The statement takes the form

```
mouse=<*devicename or file name>
```

where <*devicename or file name> is either the virtual mouse driver name or the file name of a mouse driver. There is no default for this statement, because it depends on what mouse you are using. If you are using a Microsoft or compatible mouse, the following statement line

```
mouse=*vmd
```

installs the virtual mouse driver for the Microsoft mouse.

The Network Statement. This statement, another synonym of the device statement, tells Windows what virtual network drivers to use. The statement takes the form

```
network=<*devicename or file name>,<*devicename or file
name>[,...]
```

where <*devicename or file name> is a virtual network driver name or the file name of a network driver. More than one device is typically listed in this line. For example,

```
network=*vnetbios,*dosnet
```

would be used for LAN Manager 2.0 and

```
network=*vnetbios,vnetware.386,vipx.386
```

would be used for Novell Netware 2.10. Refer to Chapter 10 for more information about Windows and networks.

The 32BitDiskAccess Statement. This statement lets you turn the FastDisk feature on or off. The statement takes the form

```
32BitDiskAccess=<On or Off>
```

There is no default for this statement, because it depends on whether your system has a Western Digital hard disk controller that works with FastDisk's 32-bit access. If Setup does not determine whether you have the Western Digital controller, this statement line is not placed in your SYSTEM.INI file and the "32-Bit Disk Access" check box does not appear in the Virtual Memory dialog box (found in the Control Panel's 386 Enhanced section). If Setup does determine that your system contains a Western Digital controller card, this statement is added to the SYSTEM.INI file, but it is set to off. It's up to you to turn on the control yourself, as described in Chapter 12.

The A20EnableCount Statement. This statement specifies how HIMEM.SYS uses the A20 handler to access your system's extended memory. The statement takes the form

```
A20EnableCount=<initial count>
```

where the <initial count> is a number that specifies the A20 enable count that the extended memory manager uses at startup. If you are using HIMEM.SYS, the default value will be calculated by Windows when it starts up.

The AllEMSLocked Statement. This statement provides an on-off switch that lets you lock the contents of expanded memory used by DOS applications to prevent it from being swapped to disk. The value of this statement overrides the EMS Memory Locked settings in a DOS program's .PIF file. The statement takes the form

```
AllEMSLocked=<ON or OFF>
```

The default value is off, which allows expanded memory to be swapped to disk. You'll probably need to change this setting to on only if you use a disk cache program other than SMARTDrive or another TSR that uses expanded memory.

The AllVMsExclusive Statement. This statement can be used to override the settings in .PIF files and force all DOS applications to run in exclusive full-screen mode. The statement takes the form:

```
AllVMsExclusive=<ON or OFF>
```

where <ON or OFF> is a switch that turns this feature on or off. The default setting—which is in effect if this statement is omitted—is OFF. However, if you are running a DOS session that uses network drivers, TSRs, or other memory-resident programs that are incompatible with DOS, you may want to add the line

```
AllVMsExclusive=ON
```

to force all DOS sessions to run in full-screen exclusive mode; this is the most stable way to run DOS and may prevent crashes caused by DOS software that is incompatible with Windows. When this setting is in effect, you will not be able to toggle between full-screen and windowed DOS sessions with Alt+Enter.

The AllXMSLocked Statement. This statement provides an on-off switch that lets you lock extended memory to prevent it from being swapped out to disk. The value of this statement overrides the XMS Memory Locked settings in any .pif files. This statement takes the form

```
AllXMSLocked=ON or OFF
```

The default setting is OFF.

The AltKeyDelay Statement. This statement tells Windows how long to wait for another keyboard interrupt to be processed after the Alt key has been pressed. The statement takes the form

```
AltKeyDelay=<seconds>
```

where <seconds> is the time period you want Windows to wait after the Alt key has been pressed before processing another keyboard interrupt. The default value is .005 seconds. If an application you are running has trouble recognizing the Alt key, try setting this value to a longer time period.

The AltPasteDelay Statement. This statement tells Windows how long to wait before pasting any characters after the Alt key has been pasted. The statement takes the form

```
AltPasteDelay=<seconds>
```

where <seconds> is the time period you want Windows to wait. The default value is .025 seconds. If an application has trouble recognizing the Alt key, try setting this value to a longer time period.

The AutoRestoreScreen Statement. This statement determines whether Windows or a DOS application has the responsibility for restoring the screen of a DOS application after you switch to it. The statement takes the form

```
AutoRestoreScreen=<ON or OFF>
```

The default value is ON, which tells Windows to take responsibility for restoring the DOS screen. This is usually the fastest method, but consumes additional memory. To save memory at the expense of speed, set this value to OFF, provided your DOS application is capable of restoring its screen if Windows sends it a program call telling it to update its display. This statement works only with VGA displays.

The BkGndNotifyAtPFault Statement. This statement controls how Windows handles the updating of the screen when switching among applications. The statement takes the form

```
BkGndNotifyAtPFault=<ON or OFF>
```

When this value is set to OFF, Windows notifies a DOS application to prevent it from attempting to use the display whenever you switch between applications. This prevents one application from corrupting another's display. The default setting is ON for VGA displays and OFF for 8514 displays. You may need to set this to OFF for other non-VGA displays, such as TIGA, to accommodate the display hardware.

The CGA40WOA.FON and CGA80WOA.FON Statements. The CGA40WOA.FON statement tells Windows what font to use for DOS applications that use 40 columns and 25 or fewer lines in their display. The statement takes the form

```
CGA40WOA.FON=<file name>
```

where <file name> is the name of the font file. The standard value for this statement line is

```
CGA40WOA.FON=CGA40WOA.FON
```

The CGA80WOA.FON statement tells Windows what font to use for DOS applications that use 80 columns and 25 or fewer lines in their display. The statement takes the form

```
CGA80WOA.FON=<file name>
```

where <file name> is the name of the font file. The standard value for this statement line is

```
CGA80WOA.FON=CGA80WOA.FON
```

The CGANoSnow Statement. This statement tells Windows to use a special software routine that helps eliminate the display static, or snow, that appears on some IBM CGA displays. The statement takes the form

```
CGANoSnow=<YES or NO>
```

where <YES or NO> is a switch that turns this feature on if set to YES. The default value, which operates when the statement line is not present, is NO.

The COM1AutoAssign, COM2AutoAssign, COM3AutoAssign, and COM4AutoAssign Statements. These four statements control how Windows allocates the use of the four COM ports when two or more applications, one of which is a DOS application, request to use one of the ports at the same time. The statements take the form

```
COM1AutoAssign=<-1 or 0 or 1-999>
COM2AutoAssign=<-1 or 0 or 1-999>
COM3AutoAssign=<-1 or 0 or 1-999>
COM4AutoAssign=<-1 or 0 or 1-999>
```

where <-1 or 0 or 1–999> can have a value of –1, 0, or any number between 1 and 999. If the value is set to –1, Windows displays a dialog box that lets you select which application can use the contested port. A value of 0 allows any application to use the port at any time; this can lead to conflict if two applications try to access the port simultaneously. If the value is a number from 1 to 999, Windows waits that many seconds after one application uses the port before allowing another one to access it. The default value for this statement, which applies if the statement is missing, is 2.

This statement corresponds to the Device Contention section of the 386 Enhanced controls in the Control Panel (Figure 15.35).

FIGURE 15.35
*Device
Contention
Section*

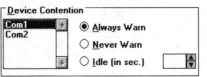

This section of the 386 Enhanced controls in the Control Panel lets you resolve conflicts arising from access to ports.

A value of –1 corresponds to the Always Warn radio button; a value of 0 is equivalent to selecting the Never Warn radio button; and a number from 1 to 999 corresponds to selecting the Idle radio button and entering the number in the Idle text box.

The COM1Base, COM2Base, COM3Base, and COM4Base Statements. These four statements identify to Windows the appropriate base port for your particular serial communications adapter. The statements take the form

```
COM1Base=<base port>
COM2Base=<base port>
COM3Base=<base port>
COM4Base=<base port>
```

where <base port> is the location of the base, or first, port of your serial communications adapter. The default values are

```
COM1Base=3F8h
COM2Base=2F8h
COM3Base=2E8h
COM4Base=2E0h
```

These values are correct for most systems, and are the default values for Windows.

If you need to change these values, check either the documentation for your adapter card or the system documentation, if the COM ports are built into the motherboard. You can ascertain the current values by using the Microsoft Diagnostics utility, described in Chapter 17.

The COMBoostTime Statement. This statement tells Windows how long to let a DOS virtual machine process a COM port interrupt. The statement takes the form

```
COMBoostTime=<milliseconds>
```

where <milliseconds> is the length of time that you want Windows to allow for COM interrupt processing by virtual machines. The default for this statement is

```
COMBoostTime=2
```

which specifies 2 milliseconds. If a DOS communications program is not diplaying all the characters you type on the keyboard, this setting might need to be increased.

The COM1Buffer, COM2Buffer, COM3Buffer, and COM4Buffer Statements. These four statements tell Windows what size buffer to set for each of the four COM ports that can be used by DOS. The statements take the form

```
COM1Buffer=<number of characters>
COM2Buffer=<number of characters>
COM3Buffer=<number of characters>
COM4Buffer=<number of characters>
```

where <number of characters> is the size of the buffer measured in number of characters. The default value for these settings is 128. If you are losing transmitted characters when you use a communications program, especially at high baud rates, try setting this value higher. Start with 256, then increase slowly until the correct setting is found. Be forewarned, though, that increasing the buffer size can slow down the effective communications rate at which the port can operate, so don't set it higher unless necessary.

Before you increase the buffer size, check the COM1Protocol, COM2Protocol, COM3Protocol, and COM4Protocol statements described later in this chapter to make sure that the X-ON/X-OFF flow control is set properly. Often it is this setting, rather than the buffer size, that causes loss of characters during high-speed communications.

The COMdrv30 Statement. This statement is included to provide compatibility with COM drivers designed for Windows 3.0. The statement takes the form

```
COMdrv30=<ON or OFF>
```

The default setting is OFF, which instructs Windows to use the 3.1 version of the COM driver to access COM ports. Set this value to ON if you are using a 3.0 version of the COM driver; this will provide compatibility with an older application.

The COM1FIFO, COM2FIFO, COM3FIFO, and COM4FIFO Statements. These statements tell Windows whether or not to use the FIFO buffer of a 16550 UART chip that controls a serial port. This statement is ignored if the COM port does not use a 16550 UART chip. The statements take the form

```
COM1FIFO=<ON or OFF>
COM2FIFO=<ON or OFF>
COM3FIFO=<ON or OFF>
COM4FIFO=<ON or OFF>
```

where the <ON or OFF> setting controls the status of the corresponding COM port. The default setting is ON for all four ports; the only reason this should be off is if you're having compatibility problems with your COM port. Although these statements appear in the [386Enh] section, Windows uses these settings in both standard and 386 enhanced modes.

The COM1Irq, COM2Irq, COM3Irq, and COM4Irq Statements. These four statements tell Windows which interrupt line to use for each of the four COM ports. The statements take the form:

```
COM1Irq=<interrupt>
COM2Irq=<interrupt>
COM3Irq=<interrupt>
COM4Irq=<interrupt>
```

where <interrupt> is the number of the interrupt line. You can also set the value of <number> to -1 in order to disable the port in case of an interrupt conflict between ports or with another hardware device. The default settings for ISA and EISA systems are

```
COM1Irq=4
COM2Irq=3
COM3Irq=4
COM4Irq=3
```

The default settings for MCA-based systems are

```
COM1Irq=4
COM2Irq=3
COM3Irq=3
COM4Irq=3
```

The COMIrqSharingStatement. This statement tells Windows whether or not COM IRQs (interrupt requests) can be shared among the ports (or by other hardware devices). The statement takes the form

```
COMIrqSharing=<YES or NO>
```

where a <YES or NO> value of YES allows COM IRQs to be shared, and a value of NO does not. The default for this setting varies by type of machine. If your system contains a Micro Channel or EISA bus, then the default is YES; for all other systems, the default is NO.

The COM1Protocol, COM2Protocol, COM3Protocol, and COM4Protocol Statements. These four statements tell Windows whether to use the X-ON/X-OFF protocol for communications by virtual machines. The statements take the form

```
COM1Protocol=<XOFF or leave blank>
COM2Protocol=<XOFF or leave blank>
COM3Protocol=<XOFF or leave blank>
COM4Protocol=<XOFF or leave blank>
```

where you can either set the value of <XOFF or leave blank> to XOFF, or simply leave it blank. If you set the value to XOFF, Windows stops sending characters to the specified port of a virtual machine as soon as that machine sends the XOFF character, and transmission resumes as soon as any other character is sent after the XOFF. If the statement is absent, left blank, or contains anything other than XOFF, Windows ignores the XOFF character. This value is relevant only to text transfers; for binary transfers, it should be left blank, because it could inadvertently halt them.

Insider's Tip

If you are losing characters in DOS transmission of text while running in 386 enhanced mode, set this value to XOFF. If that doesn't work, increase the value of COM1Buffer, COM2Buffer, COM3Buffer, or COM4Buffer (depending on which port is giving you trouble).

The DMABufferIn1MB Statement. This statement tells Windows where to place the DMA (direct memory access) buffer in the system's memory. The statement takes the form

```
DMABufferIn1MB=<YES or NO>
```

with the default value being NO. If you set this value to YES, Windows places the DMA buffer in the first megabyte of conventional memory (above 640K in high memory, if possible) in order to provide compatibility with 8-bit bus-master adapter cards.

The DMABufferSize Statement. This statement tells Windows how much memory to reserve for a DMA buffer. If possible, Windows places this buffer above the 640K conventional RAM area. The statement takes the form

```
DMABufferSize=<kilobytes>
```

where <kilobytes> is the size of the buffer in kilobytes. The default is

```
DMABufferSize=16
```

which provides a 16K buffer.

The DOSPromptExitInstruc Statement. This statement lets you decide whether you want Windows to display the message about how to exit the DOS prompt whenever you start a DOS prompt session. The statement takes the form

```
DOSPromptExitInstruc=<ON or OFF>
```

The default, which is used if this statement line is not present, is ON. If you're tired of seeing the message every time you start a DOS prompt session, add the statement line and set the value to OFF.

The DualDisplay Statement. This statement tells Windows whether to save a special memory location for a second video display adapter. If you use this statement, you will also need to use the I=8700-87FF switch with the device line in CONFIG.SYS that installs EMM386.EXE. In most cases, Windows uses the memory between B000:0000 and B7FF:000F as general system memory when it is running in 386 enhanced mode. However, if it detects a second adapter card, it leaves that memory area open for that adapter's use. The statement takes the form

```
DualDisplay=<YES or NO>
```

with YES indicating that Windows should reserve that memory space for the second display adapter. The default value is NO. If the value of the statement is NO, the memory from B000:0000 to B7FF:000F will still be available for EGA adapter cards but not for most VGA cards, which use portions of this memory address space. See Chapters 8 and 12 for further details about display adapters and memory.

The EGA40WOA.FON and EGA80WOA.FON Statements. The EGA40WOA.FON statement designates the font Windows should use for DOS applications with 40 columns and more than 25 lines in their display. The statement takes the form

```
EGA40WOA.FON=<file name>
```

where <file name> is the name of the font file. The standard value for this statement line is

```
EGA40WOA.FON=EGA40WOA.FON
```

The EGA80WOA.FON statement tells Windows what font to use for DOS applications with 80 columns and more than 25 lines in their display. The statement takes the form

```
EGA80WOA.FON=<file name>
```

where <file name> is the name of the font file. The standard value for this statement line is

```
EGA80WOA.FON=EGA80WOA.FON
```

The EISADMA Statement. This statement tells Windows how to manage direct memory access (DMA) with computers equipped with an EISA bus. Unless your system contains an EISA bus, Windows ignores this line. The statement takes the form

```
EISADMA=<OFF or channel,size-code>
```

where if <OFF or channel,size-code> is set to OFF, Windows treats the system as if it contained a regular ISA bus. Or you can turn this feature on by listing the channel number and a size-code that specifies the default transfer size for data travelling across the EISA bus. If your EISA machine has trouble running Windows in 386 enhanced mode, try setting this value to OFF.

If you want, you can specify the transfer size-code for one or more bus channels. The acceptable size-code values are shown in Table 15.23.

••••••••••••••
TABLE 15.23

Size-code	Default Bus Transfer Size
8	8-bit
16b	16-bit specified in bytes
16w	16-bit specified in words
32	32-bit

The default settings for the EISADMA statements (that will be used only if Windows detects an EISA bus) is

```
EISADMA=0,8
EISADMA=1,8
EISADMA=2,8
EISADMA=3,8
EISADMA=5,16w
EISADMA=6,16w
EISADMA=7,16w
```

The EMMExclude Statement. This statement tells Windows not to scan a specific range of memory when searching for unused memory address space to use for expanded memory. This prevents Windows from using a memory area that, although empty, is needed by another application or device, unless that memory area is included in the EMMInclude (described next). The statement takes the form

```
EMMExclude=<paragraph address-paragraph address>
```

where <paragraph address-paragraph address> is the beginning memory paragraph address (rounded down in 16K increments to the beginning of the paragraph) followed by a hyphen and the ending paragraph address (rounded up in 16K increments to the end of the paragraph). The memory addresses specified must fall between the addresses A000 and EFFF. For example, the statement line

```
EMMExclude=C800-CFFF
```

would prevent Windows from scanning the memory addresses from C800:0000 through CFFF:000F. You can use more than one EMMExclude statement line to specify multiple memory areas that you don't want Windows to scan.

The EMMInclude Statement. This statement forces Windows to scan a specific range of memory when searching for unused memory address space. This statement takes priority over the EMMExclude statement (just discussed) when both statements specify the same, or overlapping, memory addresses. The statement takes the form

```
EMMInclude=<paragraph address-paragraph address>
```

where <paragraph address-paragraph address> is the beginning memory paragraph address (rounded down in 16K increments to the beginning of the paragraph) followed by a hyphen and the ending paragraph address (rounded up in 16K increments to the end of the paragraph). The memory addresses specified, as with the previous statement, must fall between the addresses A000 and EFFF. You can use more than one EMMInclude statement if you want Windows to scan multiple memory areas.

The EMMPageFrame Statement. This statement tells Windows at what memory address the expanded memory 64K page frame should start. You can use this statement to improve the efficiency of memory usage if you can identify a specific unused area of RAM or ROM. The statement takes the form

```
EMMPageFrame=<paragraph address>
```

where <paragraph address> is the memory location where you want the 64K page frame to begin. For example, the statement line

```
EMMPageFrame=C400
```

would tell Windows to begin the page frame at the memory address C400:0000.

The EMMSize Statement. This statement tells the Windows expanded memory manager how much expanded memory to make available to the system when Windows is running in 386 enhanced mode. The statement takes the form

```
EMMSize=<kilobytes>
```

where <kilobytes> is the number of bytes worth of expanded memory that you want Windows to allocate for use by the system. The default statement is

```
EMMSize=65,536
```

which specifies the maximum 64K (65536 bytes) as the amount of expanded memory. If this value is set to zero, no expanded memory will be available, but the expanded memory manager will still be loaded. To prevent the expanded memory manager from being loaded, use the NoEMMDriver statement discussed later in this section.

Insider's Tip

Specify a value lower than 64K if you run a DOS application that uses all of the expanded memory available. If you are unable to create any new virtual machines, this type of problem may be occurring.

The FileSysChange Statement. This statement tells Windows whether it should inform File Manager if a DOS application creates, renames, or deletes a file. Windows always informs File Manager when Windows programs perform these operations on a file, regardless of this setting. The statement takes the form

```
FileSysChange=<ON or OFF>
```

If the value of this setting is ON, Windows informs File Manager any time a DOS program creates, renames, or deletes a file—but it also noticeably slows down the performance of your system. If the value of the statement is set to OFF, the file activities of DOS programs are not reported to File Manager, although a DOS virtual machine will still be able to run in exclusive mode, even if it creates, renames, or deletes files.

Windows default is to add the line

```
FileSysChange=OFF
```

to your SYSTEM.INI file in order to accelerate performance, even though File Manager will be oblivious, as a result, to the file activities of DOS programs. To force File Manager to update a window, press F5. If this line is not present in the file, or if the value of the statement line is left blank, Windows takes the precaution of turning this function on.

The Global Statement. This statement tells Windows which of the DOS devices specified to be loaded into DOS by the system's CONFIG.SYS file need to be shared globally with all the applications and virtual machines running in the system. Usually, Windows assumes that all the devices are to be globally shared throughout the system.

However, sometimes a virtual device driver specifies that a certain DOS device be kept local to a DOS virtual machine. An example is the *vmd virtual mouse driver, which makes the DOS device MS$MOUSE local rather than global, because Windows provides its own mouse support. The statement takes the form

```
Global=<DEVICE NAME>
```

where <DEVICE NAME> is the name of the DOS device. Unlike most of the statement lines in Windows initialization files, which can be entered as either upper case or lower case, the <DEVICE NAME> must be entered exactly as it is named. For example, ms$mouse will not be accepted as equivalent to MS$MOUSE. Most DOS device names use all capital letters; in those cases, you will need to enter the <DEVICE NAME> in capitals as well.

The HardDiskDMABuffer Statement. This statement tells Windows how much memory to set aside for the DMA (direct memory access) buffer. The statement takes the form

```
HardDiskDMABuffer=<kilobytes>
```

where <kilobytes> is the size of the DMA buffer. The default value depends on your system configuration. If you are using SMARTDrive, and the double-buffering feature is installed in your CONFIG.SYS file, the DMA buffer is set automatically. If the double-buffering feature is not installed, the default is set to 0 for ISA systems and to 64 for MCA systems or EISA systems that use DMA Channel 3. Changing the default values can improve performance if you're using DMA but not SMARTDrive.

The IdleVMWakeUpTime Statement. This statement tells Windows to generate periodic timer interrupts that serve as a wake-up call to otherwise dormant virtual machines. The statement takes the form

```
IdleVMWakeUpTime=<seconds>
```

The value of <seconds> must be a power of 2; otherwise, the number is rounded down to the nearest power of 2. Normally, if a virtual machine does not use timer interrupts, Windows does not send such interrupts to the machine when it is inactive. Setting this value instructs Windows to send timer interrupts to the virtual machine even when it is idle.

The IgnoreInstalledEMM Statement. This statement tells Windows whether to disable any EMMs (expanded memory managers) that it doesn't recognize before starting up in 386 enhanced mode. The statement takes the form

```
IgnoreInstalledEMM=<YES or NO>
```

The default value is NO, which instructs Windows to disable any unknown EMMs before starting in 386 enhanced mode and to replace them with the Windows EMMs.

Danger Zone

If this value is set to YES, Windows will start without disabling any alien EMMs. The disadvantage is that Windows can crash if it encounters any TSR or other memory-resident software that was using the alien EMM before Windows was run. Therefore, set the value to YES only if you are certain that no software is using the alien EMM, or if you know that the EMM will remain inactive during the Windows session, allowing Windows to use its own EMM. In addition, because this statement affects only EMM software that addresses actual expanded memory hardware, it will not work with expanded memory emulators.

The InDOSPolling Statement. This statement can be used to overcome certain incompatibilities between Windows and memory-resident software, such as TSRs and DOS device drivers that use the InDOS flag. The statement takes the form

```
InDOSPolling=<YES or NO>
```

If the value is set to YES, Windows will not allow any other DOS applications to be run if the memory-resident software has set the InDOS flag. Setting the value to YES, however, slows down your system's performance. The default is NO and should be used unless you are running memory-resident software that uses the INT21 interrupt hook for accessing the system.

The INT28Critical Statement. This statement can help Windows overcome certain incompatibilities with memory-resident software, such as network device drivers that rely on the INT28h. The statement takes the form

```
INT28Critical=<YES or NO>
```

If the value of <YES or NO> is YES, then Windows provides memory-resident software with special access to the INT28h interrupt, which is used by some Windows network virtual device drivers for internal task switching.

Insider's Tip

Use of the INT28h interrupt by these virtual device drivers can sometimes cause conflicts with simultaneous access by network software, so the default value is YES, to prevent potential network incompatibilities. But, if you are not using a network driver or other memory-resident software that needs access to the INT28h interrupt, set this statement to NO to accelerate Windows' task-switching capabilities.

The IRQ9Global Statement. This statement helps overcome incompatibilities with some floppy disk drive controllers. The statement takes the form

```
IRQ9Global=<YES or NO>
```

The default setting for this statement is NO. If you set the value to YES, Windows converts local IRQ9 masks to global masks.

Try setting this value to YES if your system crashes whenever it attempts to access a floppy disk drive or if you want to force Windows to read the floppy disk drive on startup.

The KeyBoostTime Statement. This statement can be used to increase the responsiveness of the keyboard if it slows down when several background applications are being run. The statement takes the form

```
KeyBoostTime=<seconds>
```

where <seconds> is the length of time, in seconds, for the priority status that Windows confers when it receives a keystroke. The default setting is

```
KeyBoostTime=.001
```

which indicates that Windows will let an application receive increased priority for 1 millisecond after each keystroke. To increase the foreground application's response to keyboard input, increase the value of <seconds>.

The KeyBufferDelay Statement. This statement can be used to adjust the amount of time that Windows waits before it transfers keyboard input to an application after the keyboard buffer is full. The statement takes the form

```
KeyBufferDelay=<seconds>
```

The default setting is .2 seconds, but you may need to set this value higher for some applications if they appear unable to accept all the keystrokes in the buffer.

The KeyIdleDelay Statement. This statement can be used to specify how long Windows ignores idle calls after passing a keystroke to a virtual machine. The statement takes the form

```
KeyIdleDelay=<seconds>
```

The default value is .5 seconds, but you might be able to accelerate keyboard input by setting this value to 0. Some applications, however, actually slow down if this value is 0, so you will have to discover the optimum setting by trial and error.

The KeyPasteCRSkipCount and KeyPastSkipCount Statements. These statements let you slow down the speed at which Windows pastes text from the Clipboard into the system's keyboard buffer. When Windows pastes text into a DOS application, it pastes the data to the keyboard buffer in the system's BIOS. If you lose characters that are being pasted into a DOS application, you may need to increase these two values.

The KeyPasteCRSkipCount statement tells Windows how many times it should report that the keyboard buffer is empty after it pastes a carriage return and before it pastes another character. Windows reports the empty status when the DOS application generates an INT16 call to read the status of the buffer. The statement takes the form

```
KeyPasteCRSkipCount=<number>
```

where <number> is the number of times that Windows should generate the empty status. The default value is 10; increasing this value can help remedy lost characters or slow screen updating during pasting.

The KeyPasteSkipCount statement takes the form

```
KeyPasteSkipCount=<number>
```

where <number> indicates how many times Windows should report that the keyboard buffer is empty before pasting another character. The default setting is 2; again, increasing this value can help prevent characters from being lost when text is pasted into a DOS application from the Windows Clipboard during fast paste operations.

The KeyPasteDelay Statement. This statement can be used to adjust the amount of time that Windows waits before pasting a character into the system after a key has been pressed. The statement takes the form

```
KeyPasteDelay=<seconds>
```

The default setting is .003 seconds, but you may need to set this value higher because some applications require more than .003 seconds to recognize a keystroke as a particular character.

The KeyPasteTimeout Statement. This statement tells Windows how much time to allot an application to make its calls to the BIOS for reading keyboard input before Windows changes from the fast paste mode, which uses the INT16h interrupt, to the slow paste mode, which employs INT9h. The statement takes the form

```
KeyPasteTimeout=<seconds>
```

The default value is 1 second.

The KybdPasswd Statement. This statement is an on-off switch that affects only PS/2 systems with an 8042 keyboard controller, which features password protection. The statement takes the form:

```
KybdPasswd=<ON or OFF>
```

The default setting is ON for PS/2s and OFF for everything else. When set to ON with a PS/2 system, Windows' Virtual Keyboard Device (*vkd) supports the keyboard's password protection feature.

The KybdReboot Statement. This statement tells Windows whether it should reboot your system by sending the machine a Ctrl+Alt+Del command. The statement takes the form

```
KybdReboot=<ON or OFF>
```

The default for this setting is ON, which allows Windows to reboot your system while it is running. This can cause some systems to crash instead; if this happens, change the setting to OFF. Thereafter, when you press Ctrl+Alt+Del, Windows will not pass the command on to the system—instead, it will quit and cause DOS to display a message instructing you to press Ctrl+Alt+Del a second time to actually reboot the system.

The Local Statement. This statement tells Windows which of the DOS devices specified to be loaded into DOS by the system's CONFIG.SYS file should be considered as local to each virtual machine the system is running. If a device driver is set to local, Windows uses a separate copy of the driver for each virtual machine, and each of the machines keeps different statement information about the device driver. The statement takes the form

```
Local=<DEVICE NAME>
```

where <DEVICE NAME> must be entered exactly as it is named, because the statement is sensitive to the use of upper-case and lower-case letters.

The default statement line is

```
Local=CON
```

which tells Windows that the CON device, the DOS console, should be local, and therefore prevents Windows from filling the input buffer with incoming data from several virtual machines.

Danger Zone

Be warned that most other devices will not work properly if they are defined as local devices in this statement line.

The LocalLoadHigh Statement. This statement controls how Windows allocates the upper memory blocks (UMBs). This statement takes effect only if you are using MS-DOS 5 or later. The statement takes the form

```
LocalLoadHigh=<ON or OFF>
```

The default setting is OFF, which tells Windows that it should feel free to use the entire upper memory area and not worry about leaving any UMBs available for DOS virtual machines.

Insider's Tip

Set this to ON if you want Windows to keep some of the upper memory area free and thus provide UMBs to virtual machines. Each virtual machine then acquires its own free UMBs, which allows you to load a TSR or other memory-resident program into the upper memory area in an individual virtual machine. This allows you to customize each individual DOS session with a unique upper memory configuration.

The LocalReboot Statement. This statement controls whether pressing Ctrl+Alt+Del terminates an application or reboots your entire system. The statement takes the form

```
LocalReboot=<ON or OFF>
```

The default setting is ON, which lets you quit an application by pressing Ctrl+Alt+Del without quitting Windows. You should quit an application this way only if it has crashed, because using this technique can corrupt your Windows environment. Once you've terminated the application this way, it's a good idea to save any work in progress and restart Windows. If you set this statement to OFF, pressing Ctrl+Alt+Del terminates the application and Windows, and then reboots your system.

The LPT1AutoAssign, LPT2AutoAssign, LPT3AutoAssign, and LPT4AutoAssign Statements. These four statements are relics from Windows 3.0. If you upgraded to 3.1, you may find them in your SYSTEM.INI. If you find them, feel free to delete them.

The LRULowRateMult, LRURateChngTime, LRUSweepFreq, LRUSweepLen, LRUSweepLowWater, and LRUSweepReset Statements. These statements control how the Windows' virtual memory manager pages memory from RAM to the hard disk. When determining which pages to swap between RAM and your disk drive, the virtual memory manager uses a least recently used (LRU) replacement method: those pages that have not been accessed for the longest period of time are the first to be swapped from RAM to the hard disk.

Each page of memory is tagged as Accessed (which indicates that a program has referenced it since it was loaded) or Dirty (one that has been written to since it was loaded). Accessed pages are swapped first, followed by Dirty pages.

Table 15.24 summarizes how these statement lines control the behavior of the LRU replacement method.

Statement	Description
LRULowRateMult=<number>	<number> is multiplied by the value of <milliseconds> specified in the LRUSweepFreq statement, in order to determine the low paging rate sweep frequency. The default value for <number> is 10, but you can specify any number between 1 and 65535.
LRURateChngTime=<milliseconds>	<milliseconds> is the number of milliseconds that the virtual memory manager remains at its high rate without paging before it switches to the low rate, and the length of time it then stays at the low rate without paging before turning off the LRU Sweep. The default is 10000.
LRUSweepFreq=<milliseconds>	<milliseconds> is the number of milliseconds that elapse between sweep passes. The value of <milliseconds> in this statement is also used as the high paging rate sweep frequency.
LRUSweepLen=<length in pages>	<length in pages> is the number of memory pages that are swept in each pass. The value of this statement is usually automatically set to a value equal to the LRUSweepReset divided by the LRUSweepFreq; otherwise, it defaults to 1024.
LRUSweepLowWater=<number>	<number> is the number of free pages below which the LRU sweeper should be turned on. The default value is 24.

TABLE 15.24 *(cont.)*

Statement	Description
LRUSweepReset=<milliseconds>	<milliseconds> is the number of milliseconds before an ACC bit (identifying the page as accessed) is reset. The default is 500, and the value must be at least 100.

The MapPhysAddress Statement. This statement tells the Windows memory manager what address range to initially allocate for storing physical page-table entries and linear memory address space. You may need this statement if you are using a DOS device driver, such as certain RAM disk software that only works with a contiguous block of memory. The statement takes the form

```
MapPhysAddress=<range>
```

where <range> is the address range of memory, in megabytes, that you want Windows to allocate for linear address space or page-table entries that need to remain in a fixed physical location in memory.

The MaxBPS Statement. This statement sets the maximum number of break points that the virtual memory manager can use. The statement takes the form

```
MaxBPS=<number>
```

where <number> is the maximum number of break points. The default value is 200, but you may need to increase this when using certain third-party virtual device drivers.

The MaxCOMPort Statement. This statement tells Windows how many COM ports to allow when you are running in 386 enhanced mode. The statement takes the form

```
MaxCOMPort=<number>
```

The default is 4; you can change this if you have more than four COM ports installed in your system. Windows permits a maximum of nine COM ports; hence the maximum value is 9.

The MaxDMAPGAddress Statement. This statement is provided for the benefit of hard disk drives that use direct memory access (DMA); it sets the upper limit in the system's physical memory that Windows will use for DMA. The statement takes the form

```
MaxDMAPGAddress=<hex address>
```

where <hex address> is the maximum physical page address that should be used for hard disk DMA. The default value is 0FFF for ISA and MCA systems, and 0FFFFF for EISA systems.

The MaxPagingFileSize Statement. This statement tells Windows the maximum size for a temporary swap file. These files are discussed at length in Chapter 12. The statement takes the form

```
MaxPagingFileSize=<kilobytes>
```

where <kilobytes> is the maximum size that Windows can use for a temporary swap file. The default value is half of all your available hard disk space. This statement has no effect on permanent swap files and is ignored if you are using one.

The MaxPhysPage Statement. This statement informs the virtual memory manager about how much memory you have in your system. The statement takes the form

```
MaxPhysPage=<hex page number>
```

where <hex page number> identifies the maximum physical page of RAM in your system. The default value is determined by the virtual memory manager during Windows startup.

Insider's Tip

If you are using hardware devices that cannot recognize all of the physical RAM in your system, or if the virtual memory manager fails to recognize all of your RAM, you may need to add this statement line, which specifies the page number that identifies the total capacity of the RAM installed in your system. You probably won't need to use this statement unless you have more than 16 megabytes of physical RAM.

The MCADMA Statement. This statement turns support for Micro Channel DMA on or off. The statement takes the form

```
MCADMA=<ON or OFF>
```

The default is ON for MCA systems and OFF for all others. If you have an MCA-based system that does not use DMA, turn this setting to OFF.

The MesssageBackColor and MessageTextColor Statements. These statements specify the background and text colors of text-based message screens that appear in Windows, such as the one that warns you if you press Ctrl+Alt+Del. The statements take the form

```
MessageBackColor=<VGA color code>
MesssageTextColor=<VGA color code>
```

The default value for MessageBackColor is 1, which sets the background to blue; the default for MessageTextColor is F, which sets the text to white. You can specify any of the colors supported by the color VGA attribute code, as long as they can be displayed by your adapter card.

The MinTimeSlice Statement. Windows creates the effect of multitasking by rapidly switching from task to task among the various virtual machines that are running at one time. The switching is so rapid that it appears as if all the virtual machines are actually running simultaneously.

The MinTimeSlice statement tells Windows the minimum amount of time it should allow a virtual machine to run before the next virtual machine can assume the system's resources. The statement takes the form

```
MinTimeSlice=<milliseconds>
```

where <milliseconds> is a number between 1 and 10000 that represents the minimum number of milliseconds each machine is allotted to run. The default for this statement is

```
MinTimeSlice=20
```

which allots a minimum of 20 milliseconds to each virtual machine. Changing to a smaller number, such as 10, makes the multitasking appear smoother, but can slow down system performance, because Windows must switch tasks twice as often. Conversely, a larger number improves system performance slightly, but makes the multitasking appear jerky as Windows suspends other tasks longer than normal. This statement corresponds to the Minimum Timeslice section of the 386 Enhanced controls in the Control Panel (Figure 15.36).

• • • • • • • • • • • • • • •
FIGURE 15.36
*Minimum
Timeslice
Section*

Minimum Timeslice (in msec):

This section of the 386 Enhanced controls in the Control Panel lets you specify the minimum amount of time Windows allows each virtual machine to run.

The MinUnlockMem Statement. This statement tells Windows how much memory must be available for use for a virtual machine to continue to operate if more than one virtual machine is running. The statement takes the form

```
MinUnlockMem=<kilobytes>
```

The default value is 40, which means that 40K must remain unlocked for a virtual machine to resume operating.

The MinUserDiskSpace Statement. This statement tells Windows how much hard disk space to leave free when creating a temporary swap file. For details on how to set up temporary swap files, refer to Chapter 12. The statement takes the form

```
MinUserDiskSpace=<kilobytes>
```

where <kilobytes> is the minimum amount of disk space size that Windows should leave free on your hard disk. The default is 2000, which leaves only 2 megabytes free on your hard disk, and should be decreased a little to let your temporary swap file gain a little more space to use for virtual memory. Or, you could increase the value if you plan to perform another operation (such as sorting a large database) that requires a large amount of disk space. This statement has no effect on permanent swap files, and is ignored if you are using one.

The MouseSoftInit Statement. This statement tells Windows whether to convert the interrupt INT 33h function 0 hard initialization calls, which interfere with mouse operations, into function 33 soft initialization calls, which do not reset the mouse hardware. The statement takes the form

```
MouseSoftInit=<YES or NO>
```

If the value is set to YES, which is the default, you will be able to use a mouse with DOS applications that are running in a window. Set this value to NO only if the mouse is triggering some interference, such as a distorted cursor or garbage on the screen. When this value is set to NO, you can't use your mouse with DOS applications that are running in a window.

The NetAsynchFallback and the NetAsynchTimeout Statements. The NetAsynchFallback statement tells Windows to attempt to save NetBIOS requests that are in danger of failing. Whenever a DOS application running in a virtual machine issues an asynchronous NetBIOS request, Windows tries to allocate it space in the global network buffer for incoming data. If not enough space is available, Windows usually fails the NetBIOS request. The statement takes the form

```
NetAsynchFallback=<YES or NO>
```

The default value for this setting is NO. However, if this value is set to YES, Windows attempts to rescue an imperiled NetBIOS request by reserving a special buffer in local memory and stopping any other virtual machines from running until the data is received and the timeout period expires.

The NetAsynchTimeout statement defines the timeout period for Windows when it enters a critical section of the system in order to save an imperiled NetBIOS request. This statement is used only when the NetAsynchFallback statement just described is active. The statement takes the form

```
NetAsynchTimeout=<seconds>
```

where <seconds> is a decimal number that specifies the timeout value. The default value for this statement is 5.0 seconds.

The NetDMASize Statement. This statement specifies the size of the DMA buffer for NetBIOS transport software; it is only active if a network is installed and running. The statement takes the form

```
NetDMASize=<kilobytes>
```

where <kilobytes> specifies the size of the DMA buffer. If a larger buffer size has been specified in the DMABufferSize statement discussed earlier in this section, that value overrides the value specified in the NetDMASize. The default value for this statement is 32 for computers equipped with a Micro Channel bus and 0 for all other systems.

The NetHeapSize Statement. This statement tells Windows what size buffers to create in the conventional 640K memory area for transferring data over a network. The statement takes the form

```
NetHeapSize=<kilobytes>
```

where <kilobytes> is the size of the buffer, rounded to the nearest 4K increment. The default value for this statement is

```
NetHeapSize=12
```

which creates 12K buffers for network data transfer.

The NMIReboot Statement. This statement tells Windows to reboot the system if it receives a nonmaskable interrupt. The statement takes the form

```
NMIReboot=<YES or NO>
```

The default value is NO, which prevents Windows from rebooting when it encounters an interrupt that cannot be properly masked.

The NoEMMDriver Statement. This statement tells Windows whether to install its expanded memory driver. The statement takes the form

```
NoEMMDriver=<YES or NO>
```

If the value of the statement is YES, Windows does not load its EMM driver when it starts in 386 enhanced mode. As mentioned earlier in this section, using the NoEMMDriver prevents the EMM driver from being loaded, whereas setting the EMMSize to 0 loads the driver but does not allocate any memory to it. The default sets the value to NO, so that Windows is free to load its EMM driver when starting in 386 enhanced mode.

The NoWaitNetIO Statement. This statement tells Windows whether it should convert synchronous net BIOS commands into asynchronous commands. The statement takes the form

```
NoWaitNetIO=<ON or OFF>
```

The default is ON, which tells Windows to make the conversion in order to improve system performance. If you're experiencing network incompatibility problems, try turning this setting off, although your system may slow down if you're running several applications.

The OverlappedIO Statement. This statement controls whether several virtual machines are allowed to read and write to a disk drive simultaneously. The statement takes the form

```
OverlappedIO=<ON or OFF>
```

The default setting is ON, which allows virtual machines to make read and write requests before the first request has been completed. If the InDOSPolling statement is set to ON, the default for OverlappedIO is OFF. When this statement is set to OFF, virtual machines cannot request that information be read or written until all previous requests have been completed.

The PageBuffers Statement. This statement lets you adjust the number of 4K page buffers used by FastDisk for its 32-bit disk access. The statement takes the form

```
PageBuffers=<number>
```

The default is 4, but you can specify any number between 0 and 32. Increasing this number can improve Windows performance at the expense of memory. This setting is ignored if you are not using FastDisk.

The PageOverCommit Statement. This statement controls the amount of virtual memory linear memory address space that Windows' internal virtual memory manager will create for the system. The statement takes the form

```
PageOverCommit=<multiplier>
```

The amount of linear memory address space that the virtual memory manager will create is calculated by taking the amount of actual RAM you have and rounding it to the nearest 4 megabytes, then multiplying that amount of memory by <multiplier>. The default value is 4, but you can enter any number between 1 and 20.

For example, if you have 2 megabytes of RAM installed in your system and use the default value, the virtual memory manager rounds your 2 megabytes to 4, and multiplies it by 4, to provide your system with a combination of physical RAM and virtual memory that totals 16 megabytes.

Insider's Tip

You can increase this value to provide more virtual memory, but at the expense of slowing down your system. If you have plenty of free space on your hard disk, try using a mulitplier from 5 to 8 to increase your virtual memory.

The Paging, PagingDrive, and PagingFile Statements. These three statements control your temporary swap file; refer to Chapter 12 for more information about temporary swap files.

The Paging statement tells Windows whether to use demand paging to create a temporary swap file to provide your system with virtual memory. The statement takes the form

```
Paging=<YES or NO>
```

The default is to set the value to YES in order to allow demand paging. Use NO only if you need to free some hard disk space that would otherwise be used for a temporary swap file.

The PagingDrive statement tells Windows what drive to use for storing your temporary swap file. The statement takes the form

```
PagingDrive=PermSwapDOSDrive=<drive letter>
```

where <drive letter> is the drive letter (not followed by a colon) that you want to use for a temporary swap file. Windows disregards this statement if a permanent swap file is being used. Note that you cannot specify a particular directory using this statement; to specify the directory for your temporary swap file, you need to use the PagingFile statement. If you don't specify a drive, or if you specify an invalid drive, Windows attempts to place the temporary swap file on the drive containing your SYSTEM.INI file. If the drive is full, Windows will not create a temporary swap file.

The PagingFile statement lets you specify a path and file name for your temporary swap file. The statement takes the form

```
PagingFile=<path><filename>
```

The default value for this statement is

```
PagingFile=WINDOWS\WIN386.SWP
```

assuming that your main Windows directory is named WINDOWS. If you're using a temporary swap file, the file specified in this statement line is created each time you start Windows and then deleted when you quit.

The PerformBackfill Statement. This statement tells Windows whether it should provide a full 640K of conventional memory on a system that actually has less than 640K of conventional RAM. The statement takes the form

```
PerformBackfill=<ON or OFF>
```

The default is ON, which tells Windows to automatically fill in memory to bring it up to 640K if less than that amount is available.

Danger Zone

If you change this to OFF, it will prevent Windows from performing this function and potentially limit the amount of memory available to your system.

The PermSwapDOSDrive and PermSwapSizeK Statements. These two statements control the placement and size of your permanent swap file. These settings are ignored if you are not using a permanent swap file. The PermSwapDOSDrive and PermSwapSizeK statements correspond to the Drive and New Size boxes, respectively, located in the Virtual Memory dialog box, which is accessible through the 386 Enhanced icon in the Control Panel. Refer to Chapter 12 for more information about swap files.

The PermSwapDOSDrive statement specifies on which disk drive your permanent file is located. The permanent swap file is always named 386PART.PAR and is always located in the root directory of the specified drive. The statement takes the form

```
PermSwapDOSDrive=<drive letter>
```

where <drive letter> designates the drive (without the customary colon) in which you want to place your permanent swap file.

The PermSwapSizeK statement specifies whatever size, in kilobytes, you designate for your permanent swap file. Because this area must be a contiguous region on your hard disk, you should use the Control Panel to determine the largest available contiguous space on your drive. The statement takes the form:

```
PermSwapSizeK=<kilobytes>
```

where <kilobytes> is whatever number of kilobytes (without commas separating the thousands) you allocate to the swap file.

The PerVMFILES Statement. This statement tells Windows the number of private file handles it should allocate to each virtual machine. The statement takes the form

```
PerVMFILES=<number>
```

where <number> is a number between 0 and 255 that represents the number of private file handles to allocate to each virtual machine. The default value is 10, which gives each virtual machine 10 private file handles.

Insider's Tip

A file handle is required for every open file, and DOS permits a maximum of 255 handles. You can increase this number if a DOS application running on a virtual machine needs more than 10 file handles. In such cases you may see an error message suggesting that your increase the FILES= value in CONFIG.SYS. Instead, try increasing teh value of PerVMFILES. However, you cannot exceed a total of 255 file handles, including the handles specified in the FILES= statement of CONFIG.SYS. If the total number of handles specified both here and in CONFIG.SYS does exceed 255, the PerVMFILES value is rounded down until the total equals 255. If you set this value to 0, virtual machines are prevented from containing any private file handles. If you have installed SHARE, then that utility handles the allocation of file handles, and this statement line is disregarded.

The PSPIncrement and UniqueDOSPSP Statements. The PSPIncrement statement tells Windows how much memory, in 16-byte increments, it should reserve in each virtual DOS machine if the UniqueDOSPSP statement is set to YES. The PSPIncrement statement takes the form

```
PSPIncrement=<number>
```

where <number> is the number from 2 to 64 that represents how many 16-byte increments to reserve. The default setting is

```
PSPIncrement=2
```

which reserves 32 bytes for each virtual machine. You may need to experiment to find the optimum setting for your system, which depends on your memory configuration and the applications you have running.

The UniqueDOSPSP statement tells Windows whether to start every application at a unique memory address, known as the program starting point (PSP). The statement takes the form:

```
UniqueDOSPSP=<YES or NO>
```

The default value is NO unless you are running a network based on LAN Manager or the older Microsoft Network, in which case the default is YES.

Some networks use the PSP to identify the different applications that are using it. If you are using a network with the PSP as an identifier and the statement value is set to NO, it might cause one program to crash when you quit another program, because the network confuses their PSPs. To prevent this from happening, set the UniqueDOSPSP value to YES so that Windows is forced to start every application at a unique PSP. One drawback with this setting is that less conventional memory is available for DOS applications. Also, you will need to set the PSPIncrement statement described earlier in this section.

When the statement is set to YES, Windows reserves a unique amount of memory (the amount specified in PSPIncrement) below the application. For example, if the first application is loaded at the PSP address M, the second would be loaded at the address M plus the value of the PSPIncrement; the third would be loaded at the address M plus two times the value of PSPIncrement; and so on. This technique helps ensure that different virtual machines all start at different PSP addresses.

The ReflectDosInt2A Statement. This statement tells Windows whether it should absorb or reflect any INT2A interrupts that it receives. If Windows absorbs these signals, it runs more efficiently. However, if you are running any memory-resident software that needs to detect INT2A interrupts, Windows will have to be set to reflect the interrupts back to DOS. The statement takes the form

```
ReflectDosInt2A=<YES or NO>
```

When set to YES, Windows reflects INT2A interrupts back to DOS; when set to NO, Windows absorbs these interrupts.

The ReservedHighArea Statement. This statement tells Windows not to scan a particular memory range between A000 and EFFF for unused address space. The scanning sometimes interferes with certain adapters, so specifying the address range that the adapters use can often alleviate these incompatibilities. The statement takes the form

```
ReservedHighArea=<hex address-hex address>
```

where <hex address-hex address> specifies two hex addresses of the paragraphs of memory separated by a hyphen. If the hex adresseses you specify do not fall on a 4K paragraph boundary, the first address is rounded down and the second address is rounded up to a multiple of 4K. For example, the statement line:

```
ReservedHighArea=D100-D3FF
```

prevents Windows from scanning the first 12K of memory starting at D100. You can reserve more than one area by using additional statement lines.

The ReservePageFrame Statement. This statement instructs Windows what to do when it cannot find memory space for DOS transfer buffers in the high memory area between 640K and 1 megabyte, other than memory space already reserved for an EMS page frame. The statement takes the form

```
ReservePageFrame=<YES or NO>
```

If the value of this statement is YES, which is the default, Windows leaves the EMS page frame space alone, but at the expense of the 640K conventional memory area.

Insider's Tip

If you are sure you won't be running DOS applications that use expanded memory, you should set the ReservePageFrame value to NO to provide more of the precious 640K of conventional memory to your DOS applications.

The ReserveVideoROM Statement. This statement tells Windows whether the video ROM occupies memory pages C6 and C7. The statement takes the form

```
ReserveVideoROM=<ON or OFF>
```

The default is OFF, which lets Windows use its automatic detection scheme to see if the video ROM is using these pages. If the text font is distorted when you start a DOS application, try setting this statement to ON.

ROMScanThreshold Statement. This statement is used to set a parameter that helps Windows—whenever it encounters an area that lacks the standard ROM header information—to determine if a memory address in the upper memory area is ROM or RAM. The statement takes the form

```
ROMScanThreshold=<number>
```

where <number> identifies the number of memory value changes that Windows needs to make the proper ROM-or-RAM determination. If Windows senses more value changes than specified in this entry, it is interpreted as ROM; if fewer changes are detected, Windows decides that it is usable RAM. The default value for this statement is 20. The only other setting you might need to use is 0, which would force Windows to treat all unrecognizable memory locations in upper memory as ROM.

The ScrollFrequency Statement. This statement tells Windows when to update the screen display based on the number of lines scrolled in a DOS window. The statement takes the form

```
ScrollFrequency=<number of lines>
```

The default value is 2, which means that the screen is updated every two lines.

The SGrabLPT Statement. This statement tells Windows to redirect all printer interrupts on a specified parallel port to the system virtual machine (the Windows screen) rather than to the current virtual machine (the DOS session). The statement takes the form

```
SGrabLPT=<port number>
```

where <port number> is a number from 1 to 4 that specifies which LPT port printer interrupts should be redirected to the system virtual machine. The default value is none. Each LPT port you want to specify for interrupt redirection requires its own statement line.

The SyncTime Statement. This statement tells Windows whether it should periodically synchronize its own time with the computer's CMOS clock. The statement takes the form

```
SyncTime=<YES or NO>
```

The default is YES, which tells Windows to keep track of the computer's clock. If this value is set to NO, Windows can usually keep track of the correct time, unless the TrapTimerPorts is set to OFF, in which case the Windows clock may be faster or slower than the computer's.

The SystemROMBreakPoint Statement. This statement tells Windows whether to use the address space between F000:0000 and 1 megabyte for a system break point. This address space is usually devoted to ROM. The statement takes the form

```
SystemROMBreakPoint=<ON or OFF>
```

If the value is set to ON, Windows searches the address space between F000:0000 and 1 megabyte for a special instruction used as a system break point. The default is ON if Windows is started when the processor is operating in real mode, and OFF if Windows is started when the processor is operating in virtual mode. If this memory area is used for anything other than ROM, or if you are using a third-party memory manager such as QEMM or 386MAX, set the value to OFF.

The SysVMEMSLimit Statement. This statement tells Windows how many kilobytes of expanded memory it can use to provide DOS applications with expanded memory. The statement takes the form

```
SysVMEMSLimit=<0 or -1 or kilobytes>
```

where <0 or −1 or kilobytes> is either the number of kilobytes of expanded memory Windows can use or the switches 0 or −1. The default is

```
SysVMEMSLimit=2048
```

which lets Windows use 2 megabytes of expanded memory. If you set this value to 0, Windows is not able to use any expanded memory; if you set the value to −1, Windows is able to use all of the available expanded memory that it wants.

The SysVMEMSLocked Statement. This statement tells Windows whether it may swap its expanded memory to the hard disk. The statement takes the form

```
SysVMEMSLocked=<YES or NO>
```

The default value is NO, which allows Windows to swap expanded memory to the hard disk. If the value is set to YES, Windows locks in expanded memory and does not swap it to disk. This can speed the performance of a DOS application that uses expanded memory, but slows down the performance of the rest of the system.

The SysVMEMSRequired Statement. This statement indicates how many kilobytes of expanded memory must be free in order to start Windows. The statement takes the form

```
SysVMEMSRequired=<kilobytes>
```

where <kilobytes> is the number of kilobytes of expanded memory that must be free in order to run Windows. The default value is 0, which should be selected if none of the DOS applications you plan to run from within Windows uses expanded memory.

The SysVMV86Locked Statement. This statement tells Windows whether virtual-mode memory that it uses in the system virtual machine should be locked in memory or whether it can be swapped out to disk. The statement takes the form

```
SysVMV86Locked=<YES or NO>
```

The default value is NO, and because Windows manages memory on its own, you will probably never need to change this setting.

The SysVMXMSLimit Statement. This statement tells the Windows extended memory manager how much memory to allocate to DOS device drivers, TSRs, and other memory-resident software that is loaded into the system virtual machine in which Windows itself runs. If you used WINSTART.BAT to load programs, they are loaded into the system virtual machine. The statement takes the form

```
SysVMXMSLimit=<-1 or kilobytes>
```

where <kilobytes> is either the number of kilobytes or the switch –1. The default value is 2048, which sets a maximum of 2 megabytes. If you set this value to –1, the extended memory manager gives DOS device drivers, TSRs, and other memory-resident software all the available extended memory they request.

The SysVMXMSRequired Statement. This statement tells Windows how much extended memory the XMS driver must reserve in order for Windows to run. The statement takes the form

```
SysVMXMSRequired=<kilobytes>
```

where <kilobytes> is the number of kilobytes of extended memory required to start Windows. The default value is 0, which is appropriate as long as no drivers or memory-resident programs are loaded into the system virtual machine by the WINSTART.BAT program. Otherwise, set the value to the minimum number of kilobytes that will satisfy the needs of whatever drivers or memory-resident programs are loaded into the system virtual machine.

The TimerCriticalSection Statement. This statement tells Windows to enter a critical section whenever it senses any timer interrupt codes, and it also specifies the timeout period for the critical section. The statement takes the form

```
TimerCriticalSection=<milliseconds>
```

where <milliseconds> is the number of milliseconds for the duration of the timeout period. The default value is 0, which disables this feature.

Danger Zone

If you set the value to any number greater than 0, only one virtual machine at a time is able to receive timer interrupts. Use this statement only when it's required by your network driver or other memory-resident software, because it can slow down system performance dramatically, to the point where your system can even appear to stop altogether for a few moments.

The TokenRingSearch Statement. This statement tells Windows whether to search for a token ring network adapter card on machines with an ISA (that is, an AT-style) bus. The statement takes the form

```
TokenRingSearch=<YES or NO>
```

The default value is YES, but it's safer to set it to NO if you are not using a token ring network with an ISA bus machine, because the search can sometimes cause problems with another adapter card in your system.

The TranslateScans Statement. This statement tells Windows whether to translate keyboard scan codes into standard IBM keyboard scan codes. The statement takes the form

```
TranslateScans=<YES or NO>
```

The default value for this statement is NO. Set the statement to YES only if you have a keyboard that generates nonstandard scan codes.

The TrapTimerPorts Statement. This statement tells Windows whether it should trap any read and write operations that applications attempt to make to the system timer ports. The statement takes the form

```
TrapTimerPorts=<YES or NO>
```

The default is YES, which means that Windows traps reads and writes to the timer and prevents applications from accessing the timer directly. If you set this statement to NO, applications can directly access the timer ports, and those programs that frequently read or write to the timer run faster.

Insider's Tip

When the statement is set to NO, Windows may not be able to accurately keep track of the system time. You can still have your NO and correct time, too, if you set SyncTime to YES; this tells Windows to access the computer's CMOS clock from time to time, thus keeping Windows informed of the correct time.

The UseableHighArea Statement. This statement specifies a range of memory that Windows will treat as unused address space without first checking to see what that area contains, forcing Windows to use that address space. The statement takes the form

```
UseableHighArea=<hex address-hex address>
```

where <hex address-hex address> specifies two hex addresses of memory separated by a hyphen. The addresses must be between A000 and EFFF. If the hex addresses you specify do not fall on a 4K paragraph boundary, the first address is rounded down and the second address is rounded up to a multiple of 4K.

For example, the statement line

```
UseableHighArea=D100-D3FF
```

forces Windows to use the 12K of memory starting at D100. You can force Windows to use more than one memory area by using additional statement lines. The memory range you specify in the UseableHighArea statement takes precedence over the range specified in the ReservedHighArea, if the ranges overlap.

The UseInstFile Statement. This statement tells Windows whether to check the INSTANCE.386 file for certain data structures within DOS that need to be local rather than global. The UseInstFile statement is provided only for compatibility with the old Windows 2.x program, which rarely works with Windows 3.1, and you will probably never need to use it. If you do, the statement takes the form

```
UseInstFile=<YES or NO>
```

The default is NO, but if you set the value to YES, Windows searches the INSTANCE.386 file.

The UseROMFont Statement. This statement tells Windows whether to use the soft font, stored in the video ROM, to display text messages when a DOS application is running in full-screen mode as well as text that appears when you switch from a DOS application. The statement takes the form

```
UseROMFont=<YES or NO>
```

The default is YES, but you should set this statement to NO if random dots and shapes appear on your screen, if the message font differs from the font used in the DOS application, or if you are using the VGASwap option with 386Max or Bluemax..

The VCPIWarning Statement. This statement tells Windows whether to display a warning message if a DOS application attempts to use the Virtual Control Program Interface (VCPI). The statement takes the form

```
VCPIWarning=<ON or OFF>
```

The default is ON, but you can set it to OFF if you are using a program that does a VCPI call but will still run without VCPI support from Windows.

The VGAMonoText Statement. This statement tells Windows to ignore the VGA memory address space usually used for monochrome adapters. This address space is the area from B000 through B7FF. The statement takes the form

```
VGAMonoText=<YES or NO>
```

The default is YES, which prevents Windows from using this memory address range. You can set this value to NO to free up this memory range for use by Windows if you're sure of two conditions: first, that no applications are using the VGA monochrome display mode, and second, that no other hardware device is using the B000-B7FF address range.

The VideoBackgroundMsg Statement. This statement tells Windows whether to display a warning message if a background DOS application is suspended, or if Windows can't update the DOS application's display properly because the system is running out of video memory. The statement takes the form

```
VideoBackgroundMsg=<YES or NO>
```

The default is YES, but you can set it to NO if you don't want to get the warning message.

The VideoSuspendDisable Statement. This statement tells Windows whether or not it should stop a DOS application that is running in the background if its display becomes corrupted. The statement applies only to VGA displays, and takes the form

```
VideoSuspendDisable=<ON or OFF>
```

The default is OFF, which means that the DOS application is suspended and Windows displays a warning message, provided that the VideoBackgroundMsg statement is set to YES. If you set VideoSuspendDisable to ON, the application continues to run.

The VirtualHDIrq Statement. This statement tells Windows whether it may terminate interrupts from the hard disk and bypass the ROM routine that usually handles hard disk interrupts. The statement takes the form

```
VirtualHDIrq=<ON or OFF>
```

The default value for this statement is ON for ISA systems and OFF for all others.

You may need to set this statement to OFF to allow your hard disk controller to handle interrupts properly—this is one of the most frequent causes of Windows compatibility problems. Troublesome software products that can be helped include older versions of SuperPC-KWIK, Borland's Reflex, and some computer games. Problem hardware includes the PLUS Hardcard 80II, some RAM disk cards, and some ESDI hard disk controller cards. However, if you do set it to OFF, performance is hampered because the ROM routines take longer to process the interrupts.

The WindowKBRequired Statement. This statement indicates how much of the 640K of conventional memory must be free in order to run Windows. The statement takes the form

```
WindowKBRequired=<kilobytes>
```

The default is 256, which specifies that Windows will not run unless at least 256K of conventional RAM is available. You can set this number higher if you need more memory for Windows.

The WindowMemSize Statement. This statement tells Windows how much of the 640K conventional memory it can use for itself when running. The statement takes the form

```
WindowMemSize=<-1 or kilobytes>
```

where the value of <–1 or kilobytes> can be either the number of kilobytes or the switch –1. The default value is to use the switch –1, which tells Windows that it can use an unlimited amount of the 640K.

If Windows lacks enough conventional memory to run in 386 enhanced mode, or if you're getting insufficient-memory messages trying to run a DOS program on a 2 megabyte system, try setting this value to slightly less than 640.

The WindowUpdateTime Statement. This statement tells Windows the amount of time it can take between screen updates for a DOS application that is running in a window. The statement takes the form

```
WindowUpdateTime=<milliseconds>
```

where <milliseconds> is the number of milliseconds between screen updates. The default for this value is 50. If you set the value to a higher number, you may gain some system performance at the expense of screen updating. If you set the value lower, your DOS application may display graphics more smoothly, but you will slow down the performance of the system as a whole.

The WinExclusive Statement. This statement tells Windows whether it will receive all of the systems's processing time when a Windows application is running in the foreground. The statement takes the form

```
WinExclusive=<YES or NO>
```

The default setting is NO, which permits other DOS programs to run when a Windows application is in the foreground. If you set this value to YES, all DOS applications in the background are halted whenever a Windows application is in the foreground. This setting corresponds to the Exclusive in Foreground setting in the Scheduling section of the 386 Enhanced controls in the Control Panel (Figure 15.37).

FIGURE 15.37
Scheduling Section of the 386 Enhanced Controls

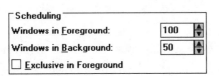

The Scheduling section lets you specify whether Windows receives all of the system's processing time when a Windows application is in the foreground.

The WinTimeSlice Statement. This statement tells Windows what priority to give DOS and Windows applications, depending on what is running in the foreground and background. The numbers for foreground and background scheduling determine how much time to apportion to each application, based on the MinTimeSlice setting described earlier in this section. The statement takes the form

```
WinTimeSlice=<number,number>
```

where <number,number> is two numbers from 1 to 10000 that signify the relative priorities for various applications. The first number of <number,number> determines the relative amount of CPU time that Windows devotes to Windows applications running in the foreground relative to all DOS programs running in the background. The second number of <number,number> indicates the relative amount of CPU time given to Windows applications running in the background if a DOS program is running in the foreground. For example, the Windows default of

```
WinTimeSlice=100,50
```

allows an application to use twice as much time in the foreground as in the background.

Scheduling of applications is also affected by settings in the .PIF file of DOS applications. Setting the scheduling options is most relevant to running DOS applications in Windows; for a full technical understanding of these options settings, refer to the discussion of the PIF Editor in Chapter 14. The WinTimeSlice statement corresponds to the Windows in Foreground and Windows in Background settings in the Scheduling section of the 386 Enhanced controls in the Control Panel (see Figure 15.37).

The WOAFont Statement. This statement tells Windows which font files to use for DOS applications. The statement takes the form

```
WOAFont=<filename>
```

where <filename> is the name of the font file. The default is DOSAPP.FON, which is the U.S. character set. The multilingual font file, APP850.FON, provides support for multilingual character sets. The fonts specified in this statement can be used by Windows applications when a DOS application is running. To make them permanently available to Windows, install them as screen fonts using the Fonts icon in the Control Panel. The value of this statement is affected if you use Setup to change either the display or the Codepage setting.

The XlatBufferSize Statement. This statement determines the size of the conventional memory buffer used by Windows to translate DOS protected mode calls into virtual 386 enhanced mode calls. The statement takes the form

```
XlatBufferSize=<kilobytes>
```

The value of <kilobytes> must be a multiple of 4. The default is 8, which sets aside an 8K translation buffer.

Insider's Tip

You can use a higher number to provide a larger translation buffer, which can increase the performance of Windows applications that read and write large amounts of data, such as database programs and some graphics applications. If you increase this value, however, you take conventional memory away from DOS applications. Also, networks that use named pipes may require that this value be reduced to 4.

The XMSUMBInitCalls Statement. This statement tells Windows whether it should call the XMS driver's upper memory block management routines. This statement takes the form

```
XMSUMBInitCalls=<ON or OFF>
```

The default is ON, but if you're using a third-party extended memory manager, its installation program may have set this value to OFF.

. . . .

The [Standard] Section of SYSTEM.INI

This section is used only when Windows is run in standard mode and can contain the following statement lines:

```
FasterModeSwitch=
Int28Filter=
MouseSyncTime=
NetHeapSize=
PadCodeSegments=
Stacks=
StacksSize=
```

The FasterModeSwitch Statement. This statement, which is used only for 286-based computers, tells Windows whether it should use a fast method of switching between protected and real mode. The statement takes the form

```
FasterModeSwitch=<0 or 1>
```

The default is 0, which tells Windows not to use the fast switching method. You can set this value to 1 in order to speed Windows performance on a 286-based system. But you'll have to keep this statement set to 0 for some older IBM AT systems and clones containing a BIOS that is incompatible with the fast switching mode.

The Int28Filter Statement. This statement tells Windows what percentage of INT28h interrupts calls, generated during periods of system inactivity, were passed on to memory-resident software, which was running from DOS before the Windows session was started. The statement takes the form

```
Int28Filter=<number>
```

where <number> is a number that represents the amount of INT28h interrupts you want Windows to filter out. In this statement, Windows filters out every nth interrupt, where n is the value of <number>. Setting this value to 0 filters out all INT28h interrupts. The default value is 10.

Danger Zone

If the value is set higher, you can improve the performance of Windows, but you may cause malfunctions in some network drivers and other memory-resident software that use this interrupt. Setting the value too low could slow down the system and possibly interfere with the communications ports.

The MouseSyncTime Statement. This statement tells Windows how many milliseconds can elapse between databytes issuing from the mouse before

Windows determines that a particular data packet is complete. This statement is relevant only to IBM PS/2 systems that are running Windows in standard mode. The statement takes the form

```
MouseSyncTime=<milliseconds>
```

The default is 500, but you can increase this value if your mouse is not responding properly.

The NetHeapSize Statement. This statement tells Windows what size buffers to create in the conventional 640K memory area; these buffers are used to transfer data over a network when Windows is running in standard mode. The statement takes the form

```
NetHeapSize=<kilobytes>
```

where <kilobytes> is the size of the buffer, rounded to the nearest 4K increment. The default value for this statement is

```
NetHeapSize=8
```

which creates 8K buffers for network data transfers. Some networks require a larger buffer, but increasing the buffer size consumes some of the precious 640K of conventional memory needed for applications. If you are not running a network, this statement has no effect, and does not use any memory.

The PadCodeSegments Statement. This statement tells Windows whether to pad code segments with additional single bytes of memory. You'll need this padding with some 286 processors; otherwise, the last instruction in the code segment is located too close to the memory segment limit to be able to engage in 80286 C2 stepping. The statement takes the form

```
PadCodeSegments=<0 or 1>
```

where <0 or 1> is a simple on-off switch. If the value is set to 0, the default, no padding occurs. If the value is set to 1, code segments are padded with an extra 16 bytes of memory. Normally the default setting works well, but if your system crashes in standard mode, it may contain an 80286 CPU chip that requires you set this value to 1.

The Stacks and StackSize Statements. These statements determine the number and size of the interrupt reflector stacks used by DOSX.EXE, which is the DOS extender used by Windows standard mode. The Stacks statement takes the form

```
Stacks=<number>
```

where <number> is the number of interrupt reflector stacks used by DOSX.EXE to translate BIOS between the processor's real and protected modes. The default value is 12, but you can specify any number between 8 and 64.

Insider's Tip

If you get an error message stating "Standard Mode: Stack Overflow," you may be able to alleviate the problem by increasing this value.

The StacksSize statement takes the form

```
StacksSize=<bytes>
```

The default is 384, which means that each interrupt reflector stack specified in the Stacks statement is 384 bytes in size.

• •

The [NonWindowsApp] Section of SYSTEM.INI

This section contains statement lines that are related to DOS applications. The [NonWindowsApp] section can contain the following statements:

```
CommandEnvSize=
DisablePositionSave=
FontChangeEnable=
GlobalHeapSize=
LocalTSRs=
MouseInDOSBox=
NetAsynchSwitching=
ScreenLines=
SwapDisk=
```

The CommandEnvSize Statement. This statement tells Windows what size to make the DOS environment variable space when you're running COM-MAND.COM, the DOS command prompt program. The statement takes the form

```
CommandEnvSize=<bytes>
```

The value of <bytes> must be 0, which disables this statement, or a number between 160 and 32678. The default is the value of the /E: parameter that you specify in the SHELL= statement in your CONFIG.SYS file, as described in Chapter 13. If you specify a value that results in a smaller environment than you set using the /E: parameter, this statement is disabled and you are provided with the larger environment space.

Also, if you specified a different environment space in the .PIF file that you use to start COMMAND.COM (such as the DOSPRMPT.PIF file), the PIF setting takes precedence. Because running a batch file also runs COMMAND.COM, this statement affects the environment size available to your batch file as well.

The DisablePositionSave Statement. This statement tells Windows whether it should save the position of the window and display the fonts used by a DOS session in the DOSAPP.INI file. Each time you use a DOS application, Windows checks the DOSAPP.INI file to determine where to place the DOS application window. When you quit a DOS application, its current state is saved in the DOSAPP.INI file, so that Windows can reopen it using that information the next time you run the program.

The statement takes the form

```
DisablePositionSave=<YES or NO>
```

The default is NO, which means that Windows saves the position and font information for all your DOS applications in the DOSAPP.INI file when you quit an application. If you set the value to YES, the information is not saved, provided that the Save Settings on Exit check box is also unchecked in the Fonts dialog box, which is accessible through the Control menu of your DOS session (Figure 15. 38).

FIGURE 15.38

*A DOS
Session's
Fonts
Dialog Box*

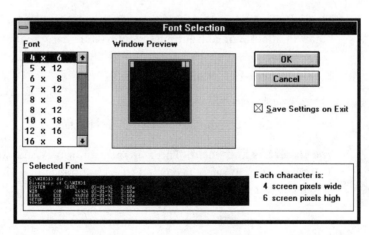

The Fonts dialog box lets you select the screen font for a DOS session.

If you set the DisablePositionSave statement to YES, and thus remove the check from the [Save Settings on Exit] check box, your DOS applications will always open using the position and fonts listed in the DOSAPP.INI file. The DOSAPP.INI file maintains the screen arrangements for your DOS applications, automatically restoring the settings the next time you use the applications.

The DOSAPP.INI file contains a single section labeled [DOS Applications]. The statement lines in the file contain the name of a DOS application or PIF, followed by a string of numbers. The last four numbers of this string use a system of pixel coordinates to indicate the location of the DOS window. These coordinates reference the upper-left corner of your display as 0,0. The first two numbers are the X and Y coordinates of the upper-left corner of the window, and the last two numbers represent the X and Y coordinates of the lower-right corner.

The FontChangeEnable Statement. This statement tells Windows whether you should be able to change the fonts used to display DOS applications in a window using the Fonts dialog box shown in Figure 15.38. The statement takes the form

```
FontChangeEnable=<YES or NO>
```

The default is YES if you're using a display grabber file compatible with Windows 3.1, and 0 if you're using a Windows 3.0 grabber. In the latter case, you can try to change this setting to 1. This will let you change the fonts of your DOS applications, but it can also cause incompatibilities on some systems that might affect the size and position of the cursor or cause loss of characters on the screen. Refer to Chapter 8 for more information on display grabber files.

TheGlobalHeapSize Statement. This statement tells Windows how big a buffer to allocate in conventional memory for sharing information among DOS applications. The statement applies only to DOS applications started in Windows standard mode and takes the form

```
GlobalHeapSize=<kilobytes>
```

where <kilobytes> is the size of the buffer. The default is 0.

The LocalTSRs Statement. This statement informs Windows about which TSR programs can safely be copied to each instance of a virtual DOS machine that you run. The statement takes the form

```
LocalTSRs=<TSR name,TSR name,...>
```

where <TSR name,TSR name,...> is a list of the TSRs that are safe to copy to a virtual machine. When Windows starts up, it notes what TSRs are already running, and if any of them are listed in this statement, Windows copies them to every virtual machine that you start. The default is

```
LocalTSRs=dosedit,pced,ced
```

Danger Zone Many TSRs are incompatible with this method and should not be listed in this statement. Only list TSRs that you know are compatible with Windows.

The MouseInDOSBox Statement. This statement tells Windows whether it should support the use of a mouse with a DOS application that runs in a window. The statement takes the form

```
MouseInDosBox=<YES or NO>
```

The default is YES if a DOS mouse driver (such as MOUSE.COM or MOUSE.SYS) is loaded, and NO if it isn't or if you are using a Windows 3.0 display grabber. With a 3.0 display grabber, set this value to YES to see if you can use the mouse in a DOS window; however, this trick doesn't always work.

Some users prefer the old Windows 3.0 system: mark text in a DOS application for copying by simply dragging with the mouse. If you're willing to forgo the use of the mouse by the DOS application running in a window, change this setting to NO, and you can easily regress to the Windows 3.0 mouse behavior.

The NetAsynchSwitching Statement. This statement tells Windows whether you can switch to another application after the application you are using has made an asynchronous NetBIOS call and you are running Windows in either standard or real mode. The statement takes the form

```
NetAsynchSwitching=<0 or 1>
```

The default value of 0 tells Windows not to let you switch to another application. You should set this value to 1 only if you are certain that none of your applications will receive NetBIOS calls while you have switched away from them; otherwise, you can crash your system.

The ScreenLines Statement. This statement tells Windows how many lines of text to display on the screen when you are running a DOS application. The statement takes the form

```
ScreenLines=<number>
```

The default setting is 25, which corresponds to a standard 25-line video display. However, if a DOS application specifies a special screen mode, it takes precedence over the value of this statement.

The SwapDisk Statement. This statement directs Windows to the disk drive and directory path for swapping DOS applications if it is running in either standard or real mode. The statement takes the form

```
SwapDisk=<pathname>
```

where <pathname> is the designated drive and directory path for swapping DOS applications. The default is the path listed by the TEMP variable in DOS. If no TEMP path is set, then the main Windows directory is the default path.

. . . .

The [Drivers] Section of SYSTEM.INI

The [Drivers] section contains a list of aliases that are assigned to installable driver files, along with any parameters that those drivers require for proper operation. Installable drivers are Dynamic Link Libraries (DLLs) that serve the same function as device drivers. The [Drivers] section can contain one or more statement lines that follow the format

```
<alias>=<driver file name><parameters>
```

where <alias> is the alias name of an installable device driver listed in a Drivers= statement in the [Boot] section of the SYSTEM.INI file; the <driver file name> is the name of the device driver file; and <parameters> is an optional item that includes any switches or parameters that the driver needs to configure itself for your system. The default statements added by Windows Setup are

```
midimapper=midimap.drv
timer=timer.drv
```

You can define multiple aliases for your drivers by separate statement lines in this section. These statement lines are usually added by installation programs or by the Drivers option in the Control Panel.

. . . .

The [MCI] Section of SYSTEM.INI

The [MCI] section contains a list of the device drivers that Windows, in conjunction with the Media Control Interface (MCI), can use to play multimedia files. The [MCI] section can contain one or more statement lines that follow the format

```
<file type>=<driver file name>
```

where <file type> indicates the type of media file, and <driver file name> is the MCI device driver that can play the file type. Windows Setup adds these default driver statements:

```
CDAudio=mcicda.drv
Sequencer=mciseq.drv
WaveAudio=mciwave.drv
```

The <file type> statements correspond to the statements in the [MCI Extensions] section of WIN.INI. This section specifies what file extensions are associated with each <file type>. Entries are usually added to this section by the installation programs of multimedia applications or hardware devices, or by the Drivers option in the Control Panel.

The PROGMAN.INI File

PROGMAN.INI is the initialization file used by Program Manager for storing settings, information about groups, and the status of any restrictions that can limit its features. To store this information, a PROGMAN.INI file can contain the following three sections:

➺ [**Settings**] Contains settings for such items as position of its window, whether it should automatically arrange icons, and the name of the startup group

➺ [**Groups**] Tells Program Manager what groups to load, where to find the .GRP files that represent the groups, and in what order the groups should be loaded

➺ [**Restrictions**] An optional section that can let system administrators block access to certain Program Manager features

The [Settings] Section of PROGMAN.INI

The [Settings] section is present in all PROGMAN.INI files, and contains the user settings that Program Manager uses to configure itself when it starts up. A sample [Settings] section might look like this:

```
[Settings]
Window=2 3 642 415 1
SaveSettings=1
MinOnRun=0
AutoArrange=1
Startup=
```

The Window statement determines the position of the application window and takes the form

```
Window=<x coordinate>,<y coordinate>,<pixels wide>,<pixels high>,
<0 or 1>
```

The <x coordinate> value specifies the x coordinate of the upper-left corner of the window and the <y coordinate> value specifies the y coordinate of the upper-left corner. The <pixels wide> and <pixels high> values specify the default width and height of the window in pixels. The <0 or 1> switch specifies whether the window should be maximized to fit the entire screen; when set to 1, the main window is maximized, and when set to 0, the window is displayed at its default size.

The SaveSettings section is a simple on-off switch that tells Program Manager whether to save its current settings when you quit. The statement takes the form

```
SaveSettings=<0 or 1>
```

where 1, the default, indicates that the settings should be saved, and 0 indicates that they should not be saved. This statement corresponds to the check that can appear next to the Save Settings On Exit item on Program Manager's Options menu. A value of 1 is equivalent to a check, and a 0 is equivalent to an unchecked option.

The MinOnRun statement corresponds to the Minimize On Use item on Program Manager's Options menu. The statement takes the form

```
MinOnRun=<0 or 1>
```

The default value is 0, which means that Program Manager is not minimized whenever another application is run. If you change this setting to 1, Program Manager is shrunk down to an icon whenever you run another application. A value of 0 is equivalent to an unchecked Minimize On Use item, and a value of 1 is equivalent to a check mark.

The AutoArrange statement corresponds to the AutoArrange item on Program Manager's Options menu. The statement takes the form

```
AutoArrange=<0 or 1>
```

The default is 0, which means that Program Manager does not automatically arrange the icons if you change the size of a group window. When the setting is 1, the icons are automatically arranged. A value of 0 corresponds to an unchecked AutoArrange item, and a value of 1 indicates that the item will be checked.

The Startup statement identifies the name of the group that Program Manager uses as your startup group—any items in this group are run whenever you start Program Manager. The statement takes the form

```
Startup=<group name>
```

The default value for this entry is Startup, which is the name Program Manager uses if the value is left blank.

• •

The [Groups] Section of PROGMAN.INI

The PROGMAN.INI file always contains a section named [Groups], which includes information about what .GRP files to use and the order in which the groups should be loaded. Here's an example of a [Groups] section:

```
[Groups]
Group1=C:\WINDOWS\MAIN.GRP
Group2=C:\WINDOWS\ACCESSOR.GRP
Group3=C:\WINDOWS\GAMES.GRP
Group4=C:\WINDOWS\STARTUP.GRP
Group5=C:\WINDOWS\APPLICAT.GRP
Group6=C:\WINDOWS\VB.GRP
Group8=C:\WINDOWS\WORDFORW.GRP
Group10=C:\WINDOWS\EXCEL.GRP
Group14=C:\WINDOWS\DATA.GRP
Group9=C:\WINDOWS\MOTLEY.GRP
Group12=C:\WINDOWS\MICROSOF.GRP
Group13=C:\WINDOWS\MUSIC.GRP
Group15=C:\WINDOWS\WINDOWSR.GRP
Order=13 6 11 3 5 14 8 4 9 2 1 15 12 10
```

The Group statement identifies the file name and location of each .GRP file and assigns it a group number. The .GRP file contains the information about the icons in each group. The statement takes the form

```
Group<group number>=<drive><path><file name>
```

The <group number> values are assigned in consecutive order, so if you delete a group, a number may be missing from the sequence.The statement lines that define the groups need not be in any particular order, but you should include the full and correct path information for each group.

The Order statement specifies the order in which Program Manager loads the various groups. The statement takes the form

```
Order=<list of group numbers>
```

where the <list of group numbers> is a list of the group numbers assigned in the Group statement, separated by spaces.

· ·

The [Restrictions] Section of PROGMAN.INI

Insider's Tip

The [Restrictions] section is optional and provides you with the ability to restrict some Program Manager features. This capability was designed mostly for use by system administrators who want to prevent users from changing their Program Manager groups, quitting the Program Manager, or running any other programs.

To use these features, you need to create a section called [Restrictions] (if it doesn't already exist); Setup does not create this section by default. The [Restrictions] section can contain a maximum of five restrictive statements:

```
NoRun=
NoClose=
NoSaveSettings=
NoFileMenu=
EditLevel=
```

The NoRun statement lets you disable the Run Command on the File menu. The statement takes the form

```
NoRun=<0 or 1>
```

If the value is set to 1, the Run command on the File menu cannot be used. The Run command is dimmed, and the user will only find it easy to run programs from icons in a group. This restriction acts as a deterrent, however, not as a total blockade: a determined user can still run programs from File Manager, macro languages, and through other methods. The default is 0, which is the same as leaving this value blank.

The NoClose statement lets you disable the Exit Windows command on the File menu. The statement takes the form

```
NoClose=<0 or 1>
```

If the value is set to 1, the Exit Windows command on the File menu cannot be used, nor can any of the other standard methods, such as issuing the keyboard shortcut Alt+F4. The Exit Windows command on the File menu is then dimmed, as is the Close command on the Control menu. The default is 0, which is the same as leaving this value blank.

The NoSaveSettings statement lets you disable the Exit Windows command on the File menu. The statement takes the form

```
NoSaveSettings=<0 or 1>
```

If the value is set to 1, the Save Settings on Exit command on the Options menu cannot be used and appears dimmed on the menu. Any changes made to the arrangement of windows and icons will not be saved. The status of this statement line overrides the SaveSettings= statement in the [Settings] section described earlier. The default is 0, which is the same as leaving this value blank.

The NoFileMenu command completely removes the File menu from Program Manager. The statement takes the form

```
NoFileMenu=<0 or 1>
```

If the value is set to 1, the File menu is not available, nor are any of its commands. However, unless you've also set NoClose=1, you can still quit by using Close on the Control menu or by pressing Alt+F4. The default is 0, which is the same as leaving this value blank.

The EditLevel statement limits what the user can do to icons and groups. The statement takes the form

```
EditLevel=<0-4>.
```

where the number specified in <0-4> sets the restrictions based on the values listed in Table 15.25.

TABLE 15.25

EditLevel Statement	What a User Cannot Do
EditLevel=0	No restrictions. This is the default.
EditLevel=1	The user cannot create, delete, or rename any groups. If a group is selected, the New, Move, Copy, and Delete commands on the File menu are not available.
EditLevel=2	Sets all the restrictions specified in EditLevel=1 and prevents the user from creating or deleting program items. The New, Move, Copy, and Delete commands on the File menu are not available, even if a group or an icon is selected.
EditLevel=3	Sets all the restrictions in EditLevel=2 and prevents the user from changing anything in the Command Line box in the Properties dialog box for an icon.
EditLevel=4	This most restrictive level sets all restrictions in EditLevel=3 and prevents the user from altering any program item information. At this level, none of the items in the Properties dialog box for any icon can be changed, and all the items are dimmed.

Use of EditLevel=4, when combined with the NoRun=1 and NoClose=1 statements, prevents users from running any applications other than those used in Program Manager. To prevent users from running any other applications, you'll also have to restrict usage to some of the items normally found in Program Manager itself. File Manager, for instance, allows users to run applications, and some applications contain their own Run menus or use macro languages capable of launching other applications.

Insider's Tip

To remove any of the restrictions, either set its value to 0 or remove the statement line from the PROGMAN.INI file.

. . . .

The WINFILE.INI File

File Manager stores its settings in the WINFILE.INI file. This file always always contains a section named [Settings]; you can set the values for all of the items in the [Settings] section by using the various menu commands in File Manager.

The WINFILE.INI file can also contain a section named [AddOns], which alerts File Manager to supplementary commands that can be installed onto its menus through the use of Dynamic Link Libraries (DLLs). Here is a sample [Settings] section:

```
[Settings]
Window=9,13,586,443, , ,1
dir1=368,0,574,370,-1,-1,1,30,201,1814,0,C:\WINDOWS\SYSTEM\*.*
dir2=0,0,368,370,-1,-1,1,30,201,1814,155,C:\*.*
Face=Small Fonts
Size=7
LowerCase=1
FaceWeight=400
ConfirmDelete=0
ConfirmSubDel=0
ConfirmReplace=1
ConfirmMouse=0
ConfirmFormat=1
```

Table 15.26 gives the meaning of each of the statements in the [Settings] section.

TABLE 15.26

Statement	Description
Window= <x>,<y>,<wide>, <high>,,,<0 or 1>	The <x> value specifies the x coordinate of the upper-left corner of the window, and the <y> value specifies the y coordinate of the upper-left corner. The <wide> and <high> values specify the default width and height of the window in pixels. The <0 or 1> switch specifies whether the window should be maximized; if it is set to 1, the window is maximized.
dir<window number>= <parameters><selected path>	The <window number> is 1 for the first open window, 2 for the second, and so on for each of the open volume windows. <parameters> are values internal to File Manager that let it know what to display in the volume window, and <selected path> specifies the drive and directory that is displayed in the window.
Face=<font name>	The <font name> is the name of the screen font to be used for directory and file icons and other onscreen information. The default value is Face=Small Fonts. This statement corresponds to the Font scroll box in the Fonts dialog box, accessible through File Manager's Options menu.
Size=<font size>	The <font size> is the point size for the font that is specified in the Face= statement. The default value is 8. This statement corresponds to the Size scroll box in the Fonts dialog box, accessible through File Manager's Options menu.
LowerCase=<0 or 1 or 4 or 5>	This statement is used to control font size and whether the font will be displayed in an italic style. When this value is set to 1, the default, the file and directory names appear in lowercase; when it is set to 0, they appear in uppercase. If the value is set to 4, the font is in uppercase italic, and if set to 5, lowercase italic. This statement corresponds to the Lower Case check box

•••••••••••••
TABLE 15.26 (*cont.*)

Statement	Description
	and the Font Style scroll box in the Fonts dialog box, which can be accessed through File Manager's Options menu.
FaceWeight=\<number>	The \<number> determines whether the font is normal or boldface. For example, when used with the Small Fonts font, a value of 400 is normal, and a value of 700 is boldface.
ConfirmDelete=\<0 or 1>	When this value is set to 1, the default, you are prompted to confirm the deletion of a file. This statement corresponds to the File Delete check box in the Confirmation dialog box, accessible through File Manager's Options menu.
ConfirmSubDel=\<0 or 1>	When this value is set to 1, the default, you are prompted to confirm the deletion of a directory. This statement corresponds to the Directory Delete check box in the Confirmation dialog box, accessible through File Manager's Options menu.
ConfirmReplace=\<0 or 1>	When this value is set to 1, the default, you are prompted to confirm the replacement of a file. This statement corresponds to the File Replace check box in the Confirmation dialog box, accessible through File Manager's Options menu.
ConfirmMouse=\<0 or 1>	When this value is set to 1, the default, you are prompted to confirm the actions you undertake with your mouse, such as drag-and-drop maneuvers. This statement corresponds to the Mouse Action check box in the Confirmation dialog box, accessible through File Manager's Options menu.
ConfirmFormat=\<0 or 1>	When this value is set to 1, the default, you are prompted to confirm the formatting of a disk. This statement corresponds to the Disk Commands check box in the Confirmation dialog box, accessible through File Manager's Options menu.

The [AddOns] section is optional, and appears only if you have installed a File Manager add-on utility that provides a new command or function. For example, the following sample [AddOns] section installs the FileSize add-on:

```
[AddOns]
File Size Extension=C:\WINDOWS\FILESIZE.DLL
```

This add-on to File Manager is contained in a new Info menu added to the FILESIZE.DLL (Figure 15.39), which lets you obtain the file size for a selected item (Figure 15.40).

• • • • • • • • • • • • •
FIGURE 15.39
Info Menu

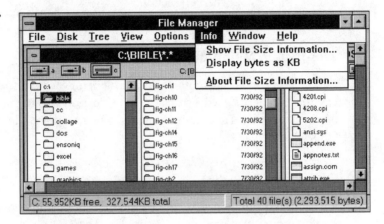

This Info menu was added to File Manager by the FILESIZE.DLL.

• • • • • • • • • • • • •
FIGURE 15.40
*Info Dialog
Box*

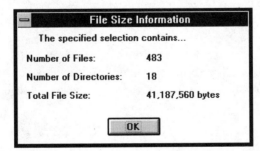

The Info menu provides file size information about items in File Manager.

• •

The CONTROL.INI File

The CONTROL.INI file is used by the Control Panel to store information about color schemes, desktop patterns, multimedia items, screen savers, the version of Windows you are using, and the kinds of printer drivers installed in your system.

The [Current] Section of CONTROL.INI

This section specifies your current color scheme and corresponds to the Colors icon in the Control Panel. A sample section would be

```
[Current]
color schemes=Monochrome
```

This section lists only a single entry, which must be one of the color schemes listed in the [Color Schemes] section.

The [Color Schemes] Section of CONTROL.INI

This section contains definitions of the colors for each element of the interface that can be assigned a special color; it corresponds to the Color icon in the Control Panel. The section can contain one or more statement lines that follow this format:

```
<scheme name>=<color values>
```

where <scheme name> is the name of the color scheme, and <color values> is a list of hex numbers that identify the color of each interface component. A sample entry would be

```
Monochrome=C0C0C0,FFFFFF,FFFFFF,0,FFFFFF,0,0,C0C0C0,FFFFFF,
C0C0C0,C0C0C0,0,808080,C0C0C0,808080,0,808080,0,FFFFFF,0,FFFFFF
```

Insider's Tip

To create a new statement line, use the Color icon in the Control Panel. Once you've created some new schemes, you can cut and paste the schemes into another CONTROL.INI file and thereby transfer the schemes to another system.

The [Custom Colors] Section of CONTROL.INI

This section specifies the custom colors you have created in the color palette section of the Color controls in the Control Panel. A sample section would be

```
[Custom Colors]
ColorA=E6CB99
ColorB=97BFE8
ColorC=FFFFFF
ColorD=FFFFFF
```

```
ColorE=FFFFFF
ColorF=FFFFFF
ColorG=FFFFFF
ColorH=FFFFFF
ColorI=F0D68E
ColorJ=A6D9B0
ColorK=FFFFFF
ColorL=FFFFFF
ColorM=FFFFFF
ColorN=FFFFFF
ColorO=FFFFFF
ColorP=FFFFFF
```

If you've created some new custom colors, you can cut and paste the section or just the relevant statements into another CONTROL.INI file to transfer the new colors to another system.

The [Patterns] Section of CONTROL.INI

The table containing all of your saved patterns—both the default patterns and any you have designed with the bit editor or otherwise added on your own—is saved in the [Patterns] section of the CONTROL.INI file. For example, here is a section of CONTROL.INI that lists the bitmap codes for a baker's dozen desktop patterns:

```
[Patterns]
(None)=(None)
Boxes=127 65 65 65 65 65 127 0
Paisley=2 7 7 2 32 80 80 32
Weave=136 84 34 69 136 21 34 81
Waffle=0 0 0 0 128 128 128 240
Tulip=0 0 84 124 124 56 146 124
Spinner=20 12 200 121 158 19 48 40
Scottie=64 192 200 120 120 72 0 0
Critters=0 80 114 32 0 5 39 2
50% Gray=170 85 170 85 170 85 170 85
Quilt=130 68 40 17 40 68 130 1
Diamonds=32 80 136 80 32 0 0 0
Thatches=248 116 34 71 143 23 34 113
Pattern=224 128 142 136 234 10 14 0
```

To add new patterns to this list, you create them with the bit editor provided in the Control Panel (see Chapter 4) and they will appear in the list.

If you want to transfer any new patterns to another system, you can access the CONTROL.INI file and paste the relevant statement lines into the file.

The statement takes the form

```
<pattern name>=<byte1 byte2 byte3 byte4 byte5 byte6 byte7 byte8>
```

where <byte1...byte8> represents a sequence of 8-bit bytes (byte1 is the top row and byte8 the bottom row) that defines an 8x8 pixel grid. Each of the eight decimal numbers in <byte1...byte8> represents one byte in binary arithmetic. Each of these bytes defines one row of a grid 8 pixels wide by 8 pixels high. Thus each decimal number in the statement represents a byte's worth of 0s and 1s, and each byte represents a row of 8 pixels. Each byte can range from 0 (00000000) to 255 (11111111). For example, the numbers

```
20 12 200 121 158 19 48 40
```

would generate this 8x8 pixel grid:

```
0 0 0 1 0 1 0 0
0 0 0 0 1 1 0 0
1 1 0 0 1 0 0 0
0 1 1 1 1 0 0 1
1 0 0 1 1 1 1 0
0 0 0 1 0 0 1 0
0 0 1 1 0 0 0 0
0 0 1 0 1 0 0 0
```

which in turn creates the Spinner pattern provided with Windows.

Windows interprets all the 0s to be the background color and all the 1s to be the foreground color. The Background color is defined in the Background setting of the [Colors] section of the WIN.INI file, and the foreground color is specified by the WindowText setting of the [Colors] section. To create a new pattern, use the Desktop icon in the Control Panel. Once you've created some new patterns, you can cut and paste them into another CONTROL.INI file to transfer the patterns to another system.

The actual pattern that Windows is currently using is defined by the Pattern= statement in the [Desktop] section of WIN.INI, discussed ealier in the chapter.

. . . .

The [Screen Saver] Section of CONTROL.INI

This section varies according to what screen saver you have installed. The section named [ScreenSaver] contains a line that includes the encoded password. Here's an example of the screen saver password section:

```
[ScreenSaver]
Password=l{A;
```

The screen saver itself has its own section. Here's the section for the Starfield Simulation:

```
[Screen Saver.Stars]
Density=144
WarpSpeed=5
PWProtected=0
```

The PWProtected statement determines whether this particular screen saver requires the password specified in the Password= statement. If the value is 0, a password is not required; if the value is 1, the password is needed to clear off the screen saver.

Sections for screen savers can vary widely, depending on what customization options are offered. For example, here are the sample sections for the Mystify and Marquee screen savers:

```
[Screen Saver.Mystify]
Clear Screen=1
PWProtected=0
Active1=1
WalkRandom1=0
Lines1=10
StartColor1=0 0 0
EndColor1=0 255 0
Active2=1
WalkRandom2=0
Lines2=6
StartColor2=176 55 8
EndColor2=255 0 255

[Screen Saver.Marquee]
PWProtected=0
Font=Lucida Handwriting
Size=22
Text=Where is Fred?
TextColor=0 128 128
BackgroundColor=0 0 0
Mode=1
Speed=9
CharSet=0
Attributes=00111
```

In addition to the information contained in the CONTROL.INI file, two statements in the [Windows] section of the WIN.INI file are used to set the values for your screen saver:

➥ ScreenSaveTimeOut=

➥ ScreenSaveActive=

See the section on WIN.INI earlier in this chapter for details on these two statements.

The [Installed] Section of CONTROL.INI

This section specifies the version of Windows that is running and lists all the printer drivers that have been installed in your system (even if they are not currently active). A sample section would be

```
[installed]
3.1=yes
HPPCL.DRV=yes
UNIDRV.DLL=yes
FINSTALL.DLL=yes
FINSTALL.HLP=yes
UNIDRV.HLP=yes
PSCRIPT.DRV=yes
PSCRIPT.HLP=yes
TESTPS.TXT=yes
EPSON24.DRV=yes
```

The [MMCPL], [Userinstallable.drivers], and [Drivers.Desc] Sections of CONTROL.INI

These three sections relate to the multimedia components installed in your system:

➥ **[MMCPL]** Contains statements that install multimedia items in the Control Panel

➥ **[Userinstallable.drivers]** Contains statements that define the installable drivers used for multimedia

➥ **[Drivers.Desc]** Lists the descriptions of the drivers that appear in the Drivers option in the control panel

Here are examples of these three sections:

```
[MMCPL]
NumApps=12
X=130
Y=262
W=448
H=191
```

The NumApps= statement lists the number of icons that are in the Control Panel; the X= and Y= statements define the position of the Control Panel on your screen; and the W= and H= statements define the width and height of the Control Panel in pixels.

```
[Userinstallable.drivers]
LastTime=11451
Wave=speaker.drv

[drivers.desc]
midimapper=MIDI Mapper
timer=Timer
Wave=Sound Driver for PC-Speaker
mciseq.drv=[MCI] MIDI Sequencer
mciwave.drv=[MCI] Sound
midimap.drv=MIDI Mapper
timer.drv=Timer
speaker.drv=Sound Driver for PC-Speaker
```

Insider's Tip

You can prevent the Control Panel from loading specific icons by creating a new section called [DON'T LOAD] and listing the icons equated with TRUE. For example, the statement International=True would prevent the International icon from appearing in the Control Panel.

Other .INI Files

In addition to WIN.INI, SYSTEM.INI, PROGMAN.INI, WINFILE.INI, and CONTROL.INI, both Windows and the applications provided with Windows can create a number of other .INI files, such as the following:

➥ **DOSAPPS.INI** Created by Windows; contains the position of DOS applications the last time they were run, and the particular font size that was

used. See the section on the DisablePositionSave statement in the SYS-
TEM.INI file earlier in this chapter for details.

➤ **CLOCK.INI** Created by the Clock utility, described in Chapter 5; stores the
position and state of the clock and its fonts.

➤ **MPLAYER.INI** Created by the Media Player utility, described in Chapter 11.

➤ **PENWIN.INI** Created if you are using Windows for Pens.

➤ **SOL.INI** Created by the Solitaire game.

➤ **WINMINE.INI** Created by the MineSweeper game.

In addition, the DOS program MSD.EXE, the Microsoft Diagnostics, creates
the file MSD.INI, which is described in Chapter 17.

Other applications also create their own .INI files. Although most of the
files follow the same format as the .INI files described in this chapter, you may
need to obtain documentation from the program's developer in order to
fathom the meaning of all the .INI settings used by a particular application.

16

Inside the Windows Installation Process

Like the stagehands assembling props and scenery before the opening act of a play, the Windows Setup program works silently to get your program in place before the opening curtain is lifted to reveal the set. A sophisticated application, Windows Setup works in two acts: it starts installing Windows while it is a DOS program. Then, halfway through the installation process, Setup converts into a Windows program. Like the acts in a play, the two halves of Windows Setup are joined together—into one executable file, in this case.

Chapter 4 discussed how to direct the play—Windows Setup itself—so that you can install or change device drivers, for example. But for a behind-the-screens look at how the Setup program actually installs Windows, and an examination of the various installation information files used in the process, you'll have to follow the rest of the script presented in this chapter.

First, the Windows installation process introduces the following major players—the information files:

➤ **SETUP.INF** The primary Setup reference file for running in either DOS or Windows mode. During installation, Setup refers to the SETUP.INF file to obtain details about how to install Windows on your particular hardware configuration; what Windows files to install based on your configuration; and how to create the program groups for Program Manager.

➤ **SETUP.SHH** Contains the information normally specified by the user during installation, such as details about hardware and what files to install. This file becomes your template for automatically installing any other files, if you use it together with Setup's batch mode (SETUP /H). Network administrators who have to install Windows on many similar machines will appreciate this feature.

➤ **CONTROL.INF** The Control Panel uses this file to determine the correct settings and files for installing printers and the values for creating international settings. You can edit this file to inform the Control Panel about custom printer drivers or to alter the international settings.

➤ **APPS.INF** Contains the information that Windows uses to create .PIF files for DOS applications. You can edit this file to create or customize the PIF profiles for the DOS applications used in your business; Windows will refer to them when creating program item icons for the DOS applications.

To know the information in these files is to know how Setup works. More specifically, you'll understand how drivers, fonts, programs, and other items are configured to work with your system through the installation process. You'll be able to interpret your various .INF files. And you'll have more opportunities to customize (or mess up!) your Windows operations.

System administrators and value-added resellers (VARs) who learn how to modify these information files can custom-tailor the installation process to match their hardware and software. As a system administrator, you'll be able to determine what drivers Setup and the Control Panel will recognize, for example. You'll also be able to write special installation scripts that will make it a snap to install Windows on groups of systems by changing entries in the information files to adjust for hardware options available during installation.

Danger Zone

Although you can edit .INF files with any text editor, make sure that you save the files as plain ASCII text. Some wordprocessors can damage the initialization files, because they can insert their own formatting information into a file or alter the ASCII values of certain characters. (Initialization files cannot contain any characters with ASCII values above 127.)

The Notepad utility edits most system files well, because it doesn't change the ASCII values or add formatting codes, but it won't work with either the SETUP.INF or the APPS.INF file, both of which exceed the puny 54K limit that Notepad can handle. You can use the Write utility, but be sure to save your files using the "Text Files" option. If you have MS-DOS 5.0 or later, you can also use the MS-DOS Editor program to edit these files safely. And, of course, always back up any .INF files before you edit them.

The Windows Installation Process

Setup provides two different installation options: **Express Setup** and **Custom Setup**. Express Setup attempts to determine your hardware and software configuration; ensures that your hard disk contains enough free space, and if not, suggests ways to trim the size of the Windows installation; and then installs Windows based on its best guesses, pausing only to ask you for a few details, such as your name and the name of your printer.

The Custom Setup option lets you monitor and thereby exercise more control over the installation process. With Custom Setup, you can inspect and verify the specific details of your hardware configuration, such as the monitor, mouse, keyboard, network, and printer. The entries in the [**display**], [**keyboard.types**], [**pointing.device**], and [**machine**] sections of SETUP.INF list the hardware from which you can make your selection, and you can add items to this list by editing the hardware-related entries in SETUP.INF and the printer entries in CONTROL.INF. In addition, you can be more selective about which Windows components are loaded onto your hard disk; monitor the changes that Setup makes to your CONFIG.SYS and AUTOEXEC.BAT files; and specify your virtual memory settings.

Danger Zone

Regardless of which option you use, you should turn off any DOS TSRs or other memory-resident software that may be loaded into your system by DOS, because they can sometimes interfere with the installation process—

unless, of course, a utility is required to connect or preconfigure a device, such as a disk drive or monitor.

The entries in the [**incompTSR1**] and [**incompTSR2**] sections of SETUP.INF provide a list of problematic memory-resident software. The programs listed in [incompTSR1] can cause trouble with Setup but may work with Windows; those listed in [incompTSR2] should be avoided when using either Setup or Windows. The entries in the [block devices] section identify incompatible block devices. Also, be sure to log off any networks to speed up your installation—unless, of course, you are installing Windows from a network server. You should also read the SETUP.TXT file for information about other incompatibilities and problems that can arise during Setup. The SETUP.TXT file is located on installation disk 1; Setup copies this file to the main Windows directory during installtion.

When you run the Setup program from DOS to install Windows, you can use any of the optional switches described in Table 16.1.

TABLE 16.1

Switch	Description
/A	Starts Setup in Administrative mode. This mode does not install a usable copy of Windows; instead, it expands and copies all the files on the installation disks to a network server and sets the Read-Only attribute for all of these files (see Chapter 10).
/B	Instructs Setup to install Windows for a system with a monochrome display.
/C	Prevents Setup from searching for TSRs before installation.
/I	Forces Setup to ignore automatic detection of your hardware configuration.
/N	Tells Setup to install a shared copy of Windows onto your system from a network server, after the files have been copied to the server using the /A switch (see Chapter 10).
/T	Forces Setup to search the drive for software that may be incompatible with it or Windows.
/H:<path><file name>	Runs Setup in batch mode to automatically install Windows using the settings file specified in <file name>, a file based on the SETUP.SHH

TABLE 16.1 *(cont.)*

Switch	Description
/H:<path><file name> *(cont.)*	template. You should include the drive and directory path in <path> if the settings file named in <file name> is not in the same drive or directory as the installation files.
/O:<path><file name>	<path> lets you specify the path where the SETUP.INF file is located; <file name> lets you specify a setup file that has a name other than SETUP.INF.
/S:<path><file name>	<path> lets you specify the path for both SETUP.INF and the Windows installation disks; <file name> lets you specify a setup file that has a name other than SETUP.INF.

Chapter 10 contains a more detailed discussion of how to install Windows in a networked environment, but here's a brief rundown of how you can combine the various Setup options. The SETUP /A option lets you copy the Windows files onto a network server. Individual users can then set up their machines to run a shared copy of Windows by using the SETUP /N option; they can also set up their machines to install an individual copy of Windows using SETUP without the /N switch.

To let users install a shared copy of Windows, add the line

```
NetSetup=TRUE
```

to the [**data**] section of SETUP.INF. This overrides any other options the user might try to use with Setup.

The /H option lets you or a user install Windows automatically according to a predefined set of options, which are contained in a system settings file (derived from SETUP.SHH). If you place this file on the Windows installation disks, a user can install Windows from the disks by placing disk 1 in a floppy disk drive and typing

```
SETUP /H:SETUP.SHH
```

Or users can be set up to automatically install an individual copy of Windows using the system settings file from a network drive. For example, if you copy the installation files to the \INSTALL directory on the network drive N:, a user can type

```
SETUP /H:N:\INSTALL\SETUP.SHH
```

If you want users to automatically install a shared copy of Windows using the system settings file, they could type

```
SETUP /H:N:\INSTALL\SETUP.SHH /N
```

You can also create several different system settings files, one for each different system configuration. For example, you could create a VGA settings file and name it VGASETUP.SHH; an XGA settings file called XGASETUP.SHH; or a PS/2 settings file called PS2SETUP.SHH. In this way, someone with a PS/2 system could then set up an individual copy of Windows by typing

```
SETUP /H:N:\INSTALL\PS2SETUP.SHH
```

or a shared copy by typing

```
SETUP /H:N:\INSTALL\PS2SETUP.SHH /N
```

Later in this chapter, I'll discuss the details for creating custom settings files based on the SETUP.SHH template.

Besides fiddling around with the settings files, you can customize the Windows installation process using these techniques:

➤ Copy other programs or data files not normally installed by Setup by adding instructions to the [**win.copy**] and [**win.copy.win386**] sections of SETUP.INF that control what is copied to a system during a full standalone installation, or to the sections in [**win.copy.net**] and [**win.copy.net.win386**] that determine what is copied to a system during a network installation (SETUP /N).

➤ Tell Setup to create or modify Program Manager groups by editing the [**new.groups**] and [**progman.groups**] sections of SETUP.INF.

➤ Install custom PIFs for DOS programs by editing the APPS.INF file.

➤ Tell Setup to delete or rename specific files by adding entries to the [**DelFile**] and [**RenFiles**] sections of SETUP.INF

➤ Tell Setup to remove drivers from a user's CONFIG.SYS file by listing the offending drivers in the [**compatability**] section of SETUP.INF.

➤ Modify the Windows environment settings by editing the WIN.SRC and SYSTEM.SRC files that Setup uses as templates to create the WIN.INI and SYSTEM.INI files.

By combining these various techniques, you can play a significant role in determining how Windows is installed and configured.

Running the DOS Portion of Setup

When you run Setup from DOS to install Windows, you are actually running the DOS portion of Setup, which is a separate program from the Windows portion, although it's part of the same executable file. The DOS portion of Setup begins by displaying the initial Setup welcome screen while it checks your system to determine the processor type, the availability of free memory, and whether optional switches have been specified.

Here are some other tasks Setup conducts at first: it makes sure it can read the SETUP.INF file and that this file is not corrupted; and it identifies your DOS version, which must be 3.10 or later. If there's a problem, Setup brings up a dialog box identifying it and returns you to DOS.

If there are no initial problems, Setup searches your path for any previous versions of Windows. If nothing is found, the search continues on all your hard disks. However, if Setup does find a similar version of Windows 3.1 already installed on your system, it switches to maintenance mode to let you update your system drivers. Figure 16.1 depicts the initial screen of Setup's maintenance mode.

FIGURE 16.1

Setup's Maintenance Mode

```
 Windows Setup
 ─────────────

    If your computer or network appears on the Hardware Compatibility List
    with an asterisk next to it, press F1 before continuing.

    System Information
        Computer:           MS-DOS System
        Display:            VGA
        Mouse:              Microsoft, or IBM PS/2
        Keyboard:           Enhanced 101 or 102 key US and Non US keyboards
        Keyboard Layout:    US
        Language:           English (American)
        Codepage:           English (437)
        Network:            No Network Installed

    Complete Changes:   Accept the configuration shown above.

    To change a system setting, press the UP or DOWN ARROW key to
    move the highlight to the setting you want to change. Then press
    ENTER to see alternatives for that item. When you have finished
    changing your settings, select the "Complete Changes" option
    to quit Setup.

  ENTER=Continue  F1=Help  F3=Exit
```

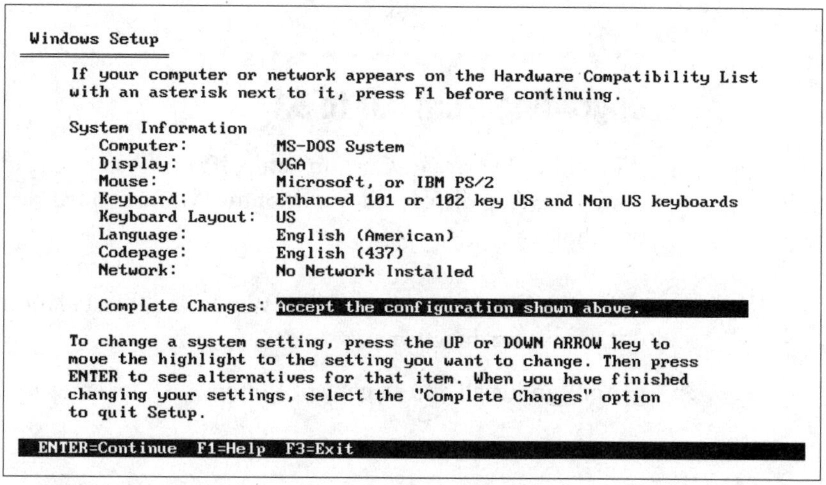

If Setup discovers an already installed copy of Windows 3.1, it starts in maintenance mode and displays this screen.

If Setup does not find the same version of Windows 3.1 installed, it checks to make sure that at least 376K of conventional memory is available. If this much memory is not free, Setup quits and sends you back to DOS; if the memory is available, installation proceeds, and Setup starts up in installation mode rather than maintenance mode. Figure 16.2 depicts the initial screen of Setup's installation mode, which lets you choose between Express and Custom Setup.

FIGURE 16.2
*Setup's
Installation
Mode*

```
Windows Setup
─────────────────

    Welcome to Setup.

    The Setup program for Windows 3.1 prepares Windows
    to run on your computer.

        • To learn more about Windows Setup before continuing, press F1.

        • To set up Windows now, press ENTER.

        • To quit Setup without installing Windows, press F3.




    ENTER=Continue   F3=Exit   F1=Help
```

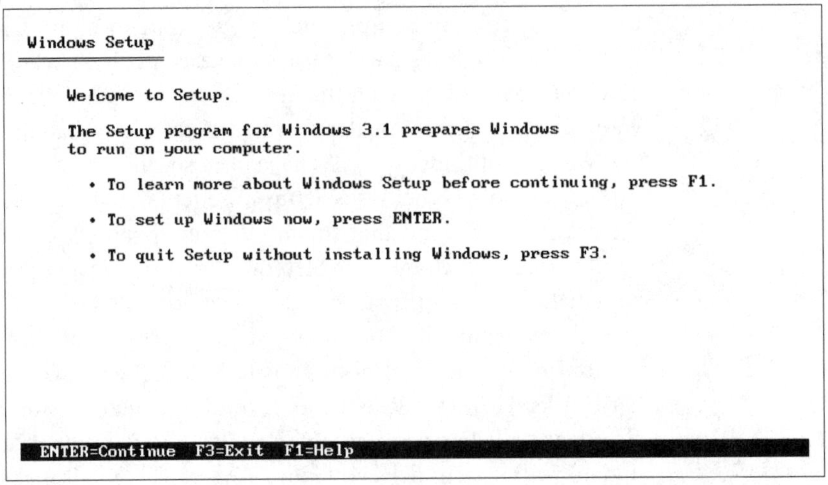

If Setup doesn't find Windows 3.1 in your system, it starts in installation mode and displays this initial screen.

• •

Upgrading from 3.0 to 3.1

With either Express or Custom Setup, if your system already contains Windows 3.0, Setup displays the name of the Windows 3.0 directory and presents two choices:

➤ You can upgrade your previous Windows 3.0 installation and place 3.1 in the existing directory.

➤ You can install a fresh copy of Windows 3.1 by entering a different directory.

If you decide to install a fresh copy of Windows 3.1, Setup will install 3.1 as if it were the first time Windows has been installed on your system.

If you choose to have Setup upgrade, it will

➤ Copy the files listed in the [win.copy] section onto systems with a 286 processor; or it will copy the files listed in the [win.copy.386] for systems with a 386 or higher processor.

➤ Copy the files listed in the [win.copy.net] section for 286 systems, or in the [win.copy.net.386] section for 386 and higher systems if the system is being installed to work with a network.

➤ Copy the files listed in the [update.files] section of SETUP.INF to all systems being updated from 3.0 to 3.1.

➤ Copy the optional Windows components in the [win.apps], [win.games], [win.scrs], [win.bmps], and [win.readme] sections; Express Setup copies all of these components, and Custom Setup lets you trim the list to save disk space.

➤ Delete files listed in the [DelFiles] section of SETUP.INF.

➤ Rename files listed in the [RenFiles] section of SETUP.INF.

➤ Replace various entries in WIN.INI and SYSTEM.INI, according to whatever entries are in the [ini.upd.31] section of SETUP.INF.

➤ Redefine the Program Manager groups, according to the entries in the [new.groups] section of SETUP.INF.

➤ Delete the old WINVER.EXE version identification utility and replace it with the 3.1 version.

Danger Zone

When upgrading, Setup assumes that you will be using the currently installed hardware devices, and it will update any drivers for these devices if it recognizes your driver. If Setup doesn't recognize your device driver, it won't install it, and you will have to run Setup again, after installation, to install the new version of the driver. Because of this behavior, Setup can leave a driver in place that is not compatible with 3.1. If you use the SETUP /I option to start Setup, it will force Setup to display the hardware configuration screen so that you can override Setup's default choices for hardware drivers. You'll then be able to select the various elements of your system, such as system type, display, and mouse driver (Figure 16.3). If you need more details about the options in this screen, press F1 during Setup, or refer to the detailed discussion of the hardware configuration screen in Chapter 4.

After Setup has finished upgrading, it displays the closing screen, which asks if you want to restart Windows or return to DOS. If you install Windows from a network, returning to DOS is your only option.

FIGURE 16.3

Setup's
Hardware
Configuration
Screen

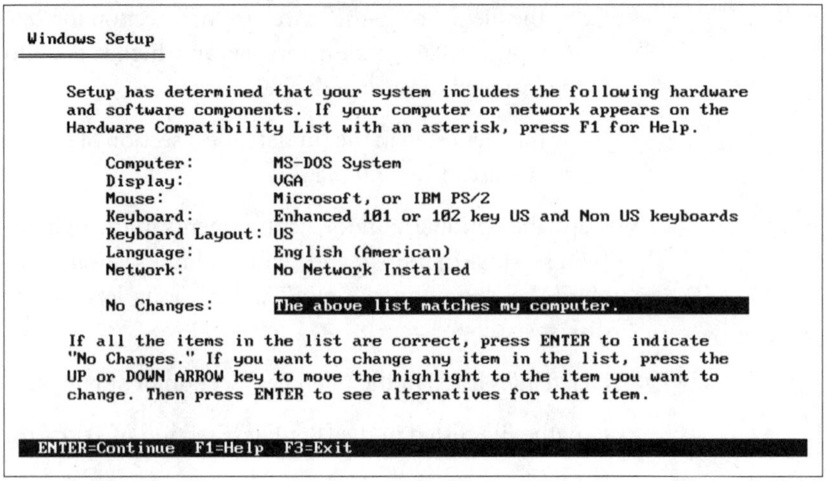

```
Windows Setup
─────────────

    Setup has determined that your system includes the following hardware
    and software components. If your computer or network appears on the
    Hardware Compatibility List with an asterisk, press F1 for Help.

        Computer:         MS-DOS System
        Display:          VGA
        Mouse:            Microsoft, or IBM PS/2
        Keyboard:         Enhanced 101 or 102 key US and Non US keyboards
        Keyboard Layout:  US
        Language:         English (American)
        Network:          No Network Installed

        No Changes:      The above list matches my computer.

    If all the items in the list are correct, press ENTER to indicate
    "No Changes." If you want to change any item in the list, press the
    UP or DOWN ARROW key to move the highlight to the item you want to
    change. Then press ENTER to see alternatives for that item.


    ENTER=Continue   F1=Help   F3=Exit
```

If you use the /I switch to run Setup, it displays this screen so that
you can identify your hardware manually.

Installing a Fresh Copy of 3.1

If you are installing Windows 3.1 on a system that contains no previous
version of Windows, Setup will operate differently, depending on whether
you've selected Express or Custom Setup. With the Express option, Setup
creates the default directory listed in the DEFDIR= entry in SETUP.INF—this
is usually C:\WINDOWS—and moves right on to rest of the installation
procedures.

For Custom Setup, a prompt suggests a directory for installing Windows
(the directory listed in the DEFDIR= statement), and you have the opportunity to change the directory name. After you specify a directory for installing
Windows, Setup determines whether it's a valid choice—the path must point
to an existing drive, and you can't place Windows in the same directory that
contains the source files Setup is using to install Windows from a network
server. If you specify an invalid path, a dialog box instructs you to enter a
different directory path for installing Windows.

If you didn't use the /I switch to start Setup, it performs its special
hardware auto-detection routines. With Custom Setup, you are given an
opportunity to OK the system configuration settings; with Express, this is
not an option. When the hardware identification is completed, Setup inspects your system for incompatible TSRs and drivers that are listed in the
[incompTSR1], [incompTSR2], and [block devices] sections of SETUP.INF. It
may either try to remove these items on its own or display a dialog box

advising that you must remove any incompatible drivers or TSRs and restart your system before running Setup again.

Next, Setup copies the files needed to start Windows and assemble a preliminary SYSTEM.INI file to use when it switches to the Windows portion of Setup. To create the file, Setup renames the SYSTEM.SRC source file to SYSTEM.INI and makes the following modifications to the new SYSTEM.INI file, in order to specify the hardware configuration.

➤ Changes the shell= entry in the [boot] section to SHELL=SETUP to make the Windows portion of Setup your temporary Windows shell.

➤ Supplies the hardware drivers for these entries in the [boot] section: system.drv=, display.drv=, keyboard.drv=, mouse.drv=, fonts.fon=, oemfonts.fon=, fixedfon.fon=, language.dll=, sound.drv=, comm.drv=, and network.drv=.

➤ Adds the name of the appropriate video grabber files to the 286grabber= and 386grabber= entries in the [boot] section.

➤ Adds these entries to the [keyboard] section: keyboard.dll=, oemansi.bin=, type=, and subtype=. For most installations, only the type= entry is assigned an actual value.

➤ Adds the descriptive names of the hardware drivers to the entries in the [boot.description] section.

➤ For systems with 386 and higher processors, places entries in the [386Enh] section to specify the virtual device drivers such as the virtual display device, EBIOS, and any other settings, such as EMMExclude= values, required by certain machines.

After modifying the SYSTEM.INI file to list the specific drivers that the system will use, Setup copies the related driver and system font files to the Windows \SYSTEM subdirectory. Setup also temporarily changes the name of the [Fonts] section in WIN.INI to [wt4gpi8s56bz]—the Windows portion of Setup changes the name of this section back to [Fonts] later in the installation process.

Setup's next job is to create the WIN.COM file that is used to actually run Windows and then place the new WIN.COM file in the main Windows directory. When you type **WIN** at the DOS prompt to start Windows, you are running the WIN.COM program, which is not Windows itself, but rather the program that loads the various Windows components into your system.

WIN.COM is created by combining the WIN.CNF file with the correct logo code and logo data files from the Windows installation disks. For example, if you are using a standard VGA driver, the WIN.CNF file is combined with the VGALOGO.LGO logo display code and VGALOGO.RLE graphic file to create WIN.COM.

Insider's Tip

The action carried out by Setup to create WIN.COM is the equivalent of the DOS command

```
COPY WIN.CNF+VGALOGO.LGO+VGALOGO.RLE WIN.COM
```

This command combines the three files by literally attaching them to one another. The three source files remain in your \SYSTEM subdirectory, and you can use the COPY command from DOS to rebuild the WIN.COM file by hand.

One reason to rebuild the WIN.COM file would be to replace the VGALOGO.RLE file with a different .RLE graphics file in order to customize your startup screen. Of course, you could also edit the entries in the [display] section of SETUP.INF to specify a different .RLE file if you wanted Setup to create WIN.COM using a different startup screen. Note that the .RLE graphics file is a run-length encoded file format, which compresses the graphics file so that it takes up less disk space.

As one of its final acts, the DOS part of Setup builds a command line to start the Windows portion of Setup. The command line begins with the name of the program that will be run first, which is identified in the **startup**= statement line located in the [**data**] section of SETUP.INF; this is usually WIN.COM, the Windows loader.

Next, Setup reads the default command line from the **execcmd**= entry in the [**winexec**] section of SETUP.INF; for example, here is the default statement line:

```
execcmd = " krnl286.exe /b /q:"
```

Using the default values, the command line would thus far combine values of the startup= and execcmd= statements to form

```
WIN.COM KRNL286.EXE /B /Q:
```

Finally, the DOS portion of Setup actually runs Windows using the command line it has built. If HIMEM.SYS has already been loaded by your CONFIG.SYS file, Windows starts using HIMEM.SYS as its memory manager. If HIMEM.SYS is not already loaded, then XMSMMGR.EXE is used as a temporary extended memory manager. If Setup fails at this point, your system may lack the required amount of extended memory.

Setup starts Windows by running WIN.COM, the Windows loader, which in turn loads the other files needed to run Windows. Once Windows takes over, it looks at the SHELL= statement line in SYSTEM.INI, sees that SETUP.EXE is listed as the shell, and runs the Windows portion of Setup to complete the installation. When this has been successfully completed, the Windows Setup screen appears (Figure 16.4).

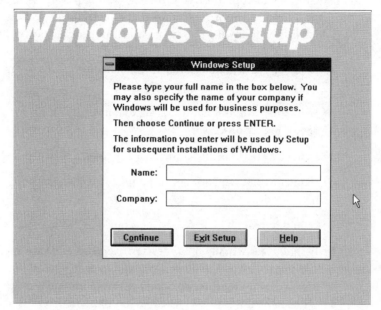

When the Windows portion of Setup first starts, it displays this screen.

If you don't get this far, your system is having trouble running Windows—check your hardware configuration choices, make sure that you've turned off any unneccessary or incompatible drivers, and try again.

The Windows Portion of Setup

This part of the Setup program reads SETUP.INF and searches the file for the [**blowaway**] section. It then discards everything in the file that follows this section, in order to free as much system memory as possible, because the remainder of the file is used only by the DOS portion of Setup that is already finished. As the comment line in the SETUP.INF file aptly remarks, the [blowaway] section is "Used by the windows half to shrink the memory needed to hold this pig."

Setup then checks the shell= statement in the [Boot] section of SYSTEM.INI to see whether it is listed as the shell program. If it isn't listed, Setup assumes that Windows is already installed and that you are running Setup in order to tinker with your system, whether to change drivers, set up applications, or perform other maintenance tasks. If Setup is listed as the shell program (a temporary condition created by the DOS portion of Setup), it assumes you are installing a new copy of Windows and proceeds with the installation.

In order to copy the Windows files and applications to your hard disk, Setup now uses information from the "copy files" sections of SETUP.INF, which list the following files to be copied, depending on your system:

➤ [**win.copy**] For a full, standalone installation on a system that contains a 286 processor

➤ [**win.copy.win386**] For a full, standalone installation for a system with a 386 or higher processor

➤ [**win.copy.net**] For installing on a 286 from a network drive

➤ [**win.copy.net.win386**] For installing on a 386 or higher processor from a network drive

➤ [**win.devices**] DOS device drivers copied to 286 systems

➤ [**win.devices.win386**] DOS device drivers copied to 386 and higher systems

If you're running Custom Setup, at this point you'll see the Add/Remove Files dialog box, which asks whether you want Setup to install everything, or just essential components. The dialog box displays the total amount of disk space required for each option and lets you further customize each choice. The items listed in the Add/Remove Files dialog box relate to the files listed in the following sections of SETUP.INF:

➤ [**win.apps**] Application files

➤ [**win.games**] Games

➤ [**win.scrs**] Screen savers

➤ [**win.bmps**] Wallpaper, sound, and MIDI files

➤ [**win.readme**] Readme files

After copying the appropriate files onto your system, Setup installs the remaining virtual device drivers and fonts by

➤ Copying the virtual device drivers for the display, mouse, and network.

➤ Copying the TrueType and other screen fonts to your \SYSTEM subdirectory; Setup matches the screen fonts to the display driver you are using.

➤ Updating the sections of the WIN.INI and SYSTEM.INI files to reflect the installation of the device drivers and fonts that it has copied to your system.

Next, Setup changes the value of the **shell**= statement in the [boot] section of SYSTEM.INI from SETUP.EXE (Setup) to PROGMAN.EXE (Program Manager). As noted earlier, the DOS portion of Setup temporarily makes Setup the shell so that the Windows portion of Setup will start in installation mode rather than maintenance mode; changing it to Program Manager (or anything other than Setup) forces Setup to start in maintenance mode the next time you run it.

Setup then runs Program Manager and uses DDE commands to operate it by remote control, prompting it to first create any groups specified in the [progman.groups] section, and then to install the program items for each group as specified in the [group<number>] sections of SETUP.INF.

Setup then reads your AUTOEXEC.BAT and CONFIG.SYS files, and presents a dialog box asking if you want it to

➤ Make any changes for you automatically

➤ Propose changes and let you review them before making them

➤ Not make any changes

If you let Setup make the changes, it takes the following actions on your AUTOEXEC.BAT file:

➤ Adds the name of the directory in which you are installing Windows to your PATH statement, and creates the statement if it's not present.

➤ Creates a directory named \TEMP inside your main Windows directory, and sets the TEMP variable to reflect that directory.

➤ Checks to see if SMARTDRV.EXE is specified, and if not, adds a line to install it, provided you have at least 512K of extended memory available. If Setup finds that SMARTDRV.EXE is specified, it adjusts the settings to reflect your system configuration.

Here's the technical rundown on what Setup either adds to or changes in your computer's CONFIG.SYS file:

➤ Checks to see if you have a DEVICE= statement that loads HIMEM.SYS. If not, it adds one. You may want to override this choice if you are using a third-party high memory manager, such as QEMM or 386MAX. If it encounters 386MAX, Setup may attempt to adjust the parameters.

➻ Sets your STACKS= statement to STACKS=9,256.

➻ Sets your FILES= statement to 30, if it's set lower.

➻ Checks to see if you have a DEVICE= statement specifying the SMART-Drive double-buffer option, which it adds if Setup determines you need it, according to guidelines in SETUP.INF. Note that SMARTDRV.EXE itself is installed using AUTOEXEC.BAT.

➻ Looks for the DEVICE= statement for RAMDRIVE.SYS and updates this line if necessary.

➻ Checks for a DEVICE= statement that specifies the EMM386.EXE expanded memory manager and updates this line if necessary. If you are using an EGA display or a Mouse Systems mouse, Setup adds a DEVICE= statement that installs EGA.SYS.

➻ Updates your mouse driver for use with DOS if you are using a Microsoft or Hewlett-Packard mouse.

➻ Searches for a list of drivers known to be incompatible with Windows that are listed in the [compatibility] section of the SETUP.INF file. If it encounters any of these drivers, it disables their statement lines.

Note that Setup preserves the LOADHIGH= statements in your AUTOEXEC.BAT file and the DEVICEHIGH= statements in your CONFIG.SYS file to control your computer's use of its upper memory area.

Danger Zone

If you are running DOS 4.0 or 5.0 and have a disk partition larger than 32 megabytes, be sure that Microsoft's SHARE.EXE DOS utility is in your root directory (or other directory included in your PATH statement), and that your AUTOEXEC.BAT file contains the statement to load SHARE; Setup does not add this line. Without SHARE, Windows can lose track of what program is writing to what file; resulting system errors can lead to loss of data, termination of an application, or even a system crash. For more information on editing AUTOEXEC.BAT and CONFIG.SYS, including details on SHARE, refer to Chapter 13.

You have a last chance, of course, to review the changes that Custom Setup makes to your CONFIG.SYS and AUTOEXEC.BAT files. A dialog box pops up to ask whether you wish the proposed changes to be made automatically or if you want to review and edit them. Setup will take the requested action and also save previous versions automatically in backup files. If you've selected Express Setup, your changes will be made automatically.

The final step in the installation of your Windows files takes place when Setup renames WINVER to WINVER.EXE.

Once you've installed Windows, you can run a tutorial to practice using your mouse—if you have one—and to get accustomed to the elements in your window, such as scroll bars. The tutorial program is identified in the tutor= statement in the [data] section of SETUP.INF. The default tutorial program is WINTUTOR.EXE, but you can substitute a different program, if you want.

Setup's last message asks whether you want to restart your computer, reboot Windows (not an option if you're on a network, however), or return to DOS.

· ·

Troubleshooting Installation

Sometimes you can make it all the way through the installation process, but still can't run Windows, or can run only in standard mode, even though you have a 386 or higher system. The most common problems that prevent Windows from running properly after installation are

➡ A conflict with your upper memory

➡ A problem with how Windows processes hard disk interrupts

To determine if there is an upper memory area conflict, start Windows by typing

```
WIN /D:X
```

This special method of starting Windows prevents it from searching the upper memory area for available memory (usually in the memory address from A000–FFFF). If you're able to run Windows in 386 enhanced mode using this switch but only in standard mode otherwise, you probably have an upper memory conflict. Refer to Chapter 12, which explains the use of the upper memory memory, and Chapter 17, which explains how to use the Microsoft Diagnostics utility. Once you locate the area causing the conflict, you should add an EMMExclude statement to your SYSTEM.INI file and exclude only the region causing the conflict rather than use the /D: switch to start Windows.

To determine whether the problem is caused by the way Windows handles hard disk interrupts, start it using the special diagnostic switch

```
WIN /D:V
```

If this successfully starts Windows in 386 enhanced mode, you'll need to add the following line to your SYSTEM.INI file:

```
VirtualHDirq=FALSE
```

Customizing Setup

Every Setup operation follows the instructions in SETUP.INF, so to make any changes in Setup's behavior, you only need to play with this file. By editing the SETUP.INF and CONTROL.INF files, you can play God on a network: you have complete control over the choices users will be granted when they install Windows, and you can determine what Windows components and other files they will be able to install as well. In addition, you can use the SETUP.SHH file to automate the installation process and predetermine the choices that would usually require input from the user.

To carry out these fiats, you'll need to be aware of some of the strategies for editing the SETUP.INF and CONTROL.INF files, discussed later in the chapter. Then I'll describe how to create automated scripts by editing the SETUP.SHH template file. Finally I'll give a blow-by-blow account of all the major settings and options related to installation in the SETUP.INF file, and I'll do the same for the CONTROL.INF file, which contains the list of printers that can be installed, as well as the values for the various international settings.

Insider's Tip

Editing the values in SETUP.INF lets you control what Program Manager groups will be installed and what applications each group will contain. You can specify either the standard programs and utilities that come with Windows or any other programs—both Windows and DOS varieties—that you may want Setup to install for users during their Windows installation. You can also edit SETUP.INF and CONTROL.INF to add the drivers and adjust the settings for hardware devices or options that are not normally available; or you can remove items from the files to limit the choices to specific hardware devices.

Removing Items from Setup

To remove one or more of the printers that appear in both Setup and the Control Panel, delete the statement line for that printer from the [**io.device**] section of CONTROL.INF. For example, delete the line

```
7:pscript.DRV,"IBM Personal Pageprinter","DEVICESPECIFIC"
```

to remove the choice for the IBM Personal Pageprinter. Because Microsoft tries to support as many printers as possible, the list of printer choices is daunting. I recommend that you remove everything except what you are using, so that users have less room for making errors.

To remove any of the other hardware devices that appear as choices in Setup, delete the relevant entries from the [**display**], [**pointing.device**], [**network**], [**keyboard.types**], [**system**], and [**machine**] sections in SETUP.INF. Removing an entry for hardware from SETUP.INF or CONTROL.INF affects not only the initial installation process but any subsequent use of Setup or the Control Panel to change hardware afterward.

To trim the size of an installation in a user's system, you can prevent optional Windows components from being installed by removing their entries from the following sections of SETUP.INF:

➽ [**win.apps**] Lists the standard bundled applications, utilities, and their associated help files.

➽ [**win.dependents**] Lists the other files, such as DLLs, needed by some of the bundled applications.

➽ [**win.games**] Lists the two bundled games, Solitaire and Minesweeper, and their help files.

➽ [**win.scrs**] Lists the Windows screen saver files.

➽ [**win.bmps**] Lists the wallpaper, sound, and MIDI files included with Windows; can be easily deleted.

At the end of the line that lists each program, along with its components, is the size, in bytes, that it consumes on your disk. For example, here's a line from the [win.bmps] section:

```
3:canyon.mid, "Canyon MIDI Song", 33883
```

This line tells Setup to install the Canyon MIDI Song, which requires about 33K of space. In addition, each section ends with a line that identifies how much space all the entries in that section consume. For example, the [win.bmps] section ends with the line

```
diskspace=272609
```

which reports that all your wallpaper, sound, and MIDI files—after they've been decompressed—consume more than 270K of disk space. Setup uses this number in its Add/Remove Windows Components dialog box, so if you remove items from this section, you can subtract the equivalent number of bytes for each item removed in this dialog box.

· ·

Installing Custom Items

You can add your own components to Windows by inserting them into any of the sections listed earlier. Later in this chapter, I'll describe the exact syntax for adding items. But first, why would you want to add items?

Let's say you want to add a custom wallpaper file that contains the logo for your company, and that logo is in a file called OURLOGO.BMP, which contains 16473 bytes. To do this, you could add your .BMP file to the list of items in the [win.bmps] with this line:

```
3:OURLOGO.BMP, "Our Company Logo", 16473
```

and then place the OURLOGO.BMP file on installation disk 3—if you can find room for it or make room by deleting some other files. Or, if you have already copied the Windows installation files to a network server with the SETUP /A option, you could put the OURLOGO.BMP file in the installation directory; the "3:" at the beginning of the line will be ignored.

If you have trouble finding room for additional files, you can create another installation disk specifically for this purpose. Number the disk 8 or 9, or use a single letter from A to Y. (0 is reserved by Setup; 1 through 7 are reserved for the standard Windows installation disks; and Z is reserved for the Hewlett-Packard DeskJet driver disk.) Let's say you create a disk X, which you identify to Setup by listing it in the [disks] section of SETUP.INF with a line such as

```
X =. ,"The Special Disk with Our Company's Stuff on It",DISKX
```

The period specifies that Setup should look for the disk on the same drive from which Windows was installed. Write anything you like in the description section, indicated by the quotes. The entry at the end of the line (DISKX) identifies the volume name of the disk.

Now add the corporate-logo wallpaper file to your new disk. First copy the OURLOGO.BMP to the new diskette, and add this line to the [disks] section of SETUP.INF:

```
X:OURLOGO.BMP "Our Company Logo", 16473
```

Then add the 16473 bytes to the number specified in the **diskspace**= statement line at the end of the [win.bmps] section. From now on, when Setup installs your Windows program, it will pause when it starts to copy the items in the [win.bmps] section to ask that you insert "The Special Disk with Our Company's Stuff on It" into the appropriate disk drive. Place the disk into the drive and click OK, which causes Setup to verify the name of the disk as DISKX. If it's incorrect, Setup requests that you insert the correct disk.

This is the best procedure for adding components such as wallpaper, sounds, or a MIDI file. For simple Windows applications, you can add lines that copy the program and help files to the [**win.apps**] section; if any of the applications require DLLs or special data files, you can list them in the [win.dependents] section, then create program item icons for the added applications. If they are DOS applications, create a PIF for them, and add a line that copies the .PIF files as well.

To install an application that requires new entries in one of your .INI files, you can specify the entries in the [**ini.upd.31**] section. For example, to specify installation of the program SCHEDULE.EXE, which uses a data file with the extension .PIM, you might want to add an entry to the [Extensions] section of the WIN.INI file that would associate the program with its data files. To do so, you would add the line

```
WIN.INI, Extensions, ,"pim=schedule.exe ^.pim"
```

to the [ini.upd.31] section of SETUP.INF. (For an explanation of the exact syntax for entries in [ini.upd.31], refer to the section on SETUP.INF later in this chapter.)

You can also instruct Setup to install items that vary by the type of processor or network configuration. Simply create a new section and add a statement line that specifies the new section name to one or more of these sections:

➤► [**win.copy**] To install the items on 286 standalone machines

➤► [**win.copy.win386**] To install the items on 386 or higher standalone machines

➤► [**win.copy.net**] To install the items on 286 networked machines

➤► [**win.copy.net.win386**] To install the items on 386 or higher networked machines

Thus, to install the SCHEDULE.EXE program and its help file SCHED-ULE.HLP—located on my mythical DISKX installation disk—on standalone systems, you would add the line

```
#more.apps, 0:
```

to both the [win.copy] and [win.copy.win386] sections. This tells Setup to copy all the files listed in the section [more.apps] to the main Windows directory of both 286 and 386 or higher systems. Next you would create a new [more.apps] section, which would look like this:

```
[more.apps]
X:SCHEDULE.EXE, "The Appointment Book Program"
X:SCHEDULE.HLP, "The Appointment Book Help File"
```

You can also install other items, such as fonts and device drivers. To add TrueType fonts, add the appropriate entry to the [ttfonts] section in SETUP.INF. To copy drivers or other files, you can add a new entry to one or more of the [win.copy] sections and then list the files to copy in that new section.

Customizing Program Manager Installations

Any changes you make to Windows programs or utilities must also be updated in the corresponding SETUP.INF sections that tell Program Manager what groups to create and what icons to place in the groups. For example, if you add two new applications, UTILITY.EXE and REPORT.EXE, and want to install icons for these two programs in a new group named Utilities, here's what you would do. First, create the new group by adding its statement line to these two sections:

➥ [**progman.groups**] used by Setup for new Windows installations

➥ [**new.groups**] used by Setup when users are upgrading

This statement line creates the new Utilities group:

```
group9=Utilities
```

Don't name your group any number from 1 to 8, because Windows also uses these numbers.

Next, create a new section called [group9] that tells Setup what to install into the Utilities group, such as the following:

```
[group9]
"Big Utility", UTILITY.EXE
"Report Generator", REPORT.EXE
```

Setup then creates the program item icons Big Utility and Report Generator for the two programs. If the applications are not located in the main Windows directory, be sure to include the path information. For example, if the two programs in the previous example were located in a directory called \UTILS on the C: drive, the section would look like this:

```
[group9]
"Big Utility",C:\UTILS\UTILITY.EXE
"Report Generator", C:\UTILS\REPORT.EXE
```

Using the SETUP.SHH File To Automate Setup

A template file containing system settings, called SETUP.SHH, comes with each copy of Windows. By using this template, which you can copy or modify, you can create a custom system settings file. When you use Setup/A, Windows copies the SETUP.SHH file from installation disk 1 to the shared Windows directory. Table 16.2 summarizes the system settings file sections.

Section	Description
[sysinfo]	Specifies whether the System Configuration screen appears during Setup. Specify **showsysinfo=YES** to display the screen or **showsysinfo=NO** if you don't want to display it—this is the default.
[configuration]	Identifies the devices on the user's system. If you leave this blank, the detected device or default device is used. If you are updating Windows, Setup uses the devices that are already installed. To force the update and override an installed device, you need to precede the value of your **machine=**, **display=**, **mouse=**, and **device=** statement lines with an exclamation point (!); for example mouse=!lmouse. Any **keyboard=**, **language=**, or **kblayout=** values you specify automatically override the installed device. If you specify a network that has specific version requirements, you need to specify the version code; for example, the [novell.versions] section in SETUP.INF lists 00032100 as the version code for NetWare ver. 3.21; you would enter this as network=novell/00032100.
[windir]	Tells Setup where to place the Windows files. If Windows is already installed, Setup updates the specified directory. If you don't specify a directory or if you specify an invalid one, Setup presents a dialog box asking the user to specify the directory in which to set up Windows.
[userinfo]	Specifies the user and company name. The first line, which is required unless you're setting up a shared copy (SETUP/N), specifies the user name; the second line, which is optional, specifies the company name. Both items can use up to 30 characters and must be

·············
TABLE 16.2 *(cont.)*

Section	Description
[userinfo] *(cont.)*	enclosed in quotation marks if they include any blank spaces; for example "Fred Davis." If you leave this blank, a dialog box appears during Setup to ask the user for his or her name.
[dontinstall]	Specifies components that should not be installed. If this section is not present or is empty, all Windows components are installed. You can specify **readmes**, **accessories**, **games**, **screensavers**, and **bitmaps** not to install the corresponding components.
[options]	Specifies various Setup options. Use **setupapps** to let users set up applications; use **autosetupapps** to automatically set up any applications; use **tutorial** to run the Windows tutorial after Setup. If you don't need any of these options, omit this section.
[printers]	Specifies what printers need to be set up. To install a printer, specify its name and a port by using one of the descriptive strings found in the [io.device] section of the CONTROL.INF file. Enclose the printer name in quotation marks if it contains blank spaces (for example "HP LaserJet III") and specify the port using one of the values found in the [ports] section of WIN.INI. The printer name and the port must be separated by a comma. You can omit this section if you don't want to install any printers during Setup.
[endinstall]	Specifies whether Setup modifies the CONFIG.SYS and AUTOEXEC.BAT files, and whether the system is rebooted after Windows is installed. Specify **configfiles=modify** to make all changes in these files for the user; **configfiles=save** to save proposed changes to these files in backup files; and **endopt=exit**, **endopt=restart**, or **endopt=reboot** to take the corresponding actions after Setup is completed.

Here is how you might set up a system settings file that installs Windows on a PC-compatible computer with the following characteristics:

➺ The System Information screen is not displayed for confirmation.

➤ Hardware choices are predetermined as PC compatible; Super VGA display; Logitech mouse; Novell Netware network version 3.26; and 101-key U.S. keyboard.

➤ The Windows files are placed in the c:\WINDOWS directory.

➤ The user information is presupplied.

➤ No README files, games, or bitmaps (such as wallpapers and MIDI files) are installed.

➤ Setup automatically sets up any applications it finds on the C:\ volume.

➤ An HP LaserJet IIID printer is installed on LPT1.

➤ The CONFIG.SYS and AUTOEXEC.BAT files are modified by Setup.

➤ After Windows is set up, Windows is restarted.

```
[sysinfo]
showsysinfo=NO

[configuration]
machine=ibm_compatible
display=svga
mouse=lmouse
network=novel/00032600
keyboard=t4s0enha
language=enu
kblayout=nodll

[windir]
c:\windows

[userinfo]
"Frederic E. Davis"
"Peachpit Press"
```

```
[dontinstall]
readmes
games
bitmaps

[options]
autosetupapps

[printers]
"HP LaserJet IIID",LPT1:

[endinstall]
configfiles=modify
endopt=restart
```

Inside the SETUP.INF File

The SETUP.INF file guides Setup through the Windows installation process. The SETUP.INF file is written in plain ASCII text and is located on disk 1of the installation disks. Unlike most of the other files on these disks, SETUP.INF has not been compressed, so you can inspect it before installation with a text editor, such as the MS-DOS Editor. Or you can display one screen at a time from DOS by typing

```
TYPE SETUP.INF | MORE
```

Insider's Tip

If you read the file prior to installation, you can see what DOS device drivers, TSRs, and other memory-resident software Microsoft has identified as being hostile to Setup. These incompatible items are listed in the [incompTSR1] and [incompTSR2] sections of SETUP.INF. The SETUP.INF file also contains comments about its contents.

Because SETUP.INF is a plain text file, you can edit it as you would any text file to customize the installation process. Syntax in this file mirrors that in the WIN.INI and SYSTEM.INI files: sections are identified by a description enclosed in square brackets, followed by one or more statement lines. The SETUP.INF file can also contain comments that are preceded by a semicolon, and can be on the same line as the statements or on their own line. The sections in SETUP.INF follow this format:

```
[section name]
setting = value          ; this is a comment
; this is another comment
```

The sections can appear in any order, except that all the sections before or after the [blowaway] section must remain in the same position relative to this section. These are the sections in SETUP.INF, listed in roughly the order of their appearance:

➤➤ **Installation instruction sections** Provide Setup with general installation instructions, such as the name of the help file, the disks that it can use, messages to display during installation, and any programs that should be run after Setup is finished.

[**setup**] Identifies the Help file for Setup to use

[**run**] Lets you list any programs you want run after Setup is finished

[**dialog**] Specifies the text to display in dialog boxes during installation

[**data**] Specifies the amount of disk space that must be free, and provides Setup with other data

[**winexec**] Tells the DOS portion of Setup what files it needs to start Setup in Windows mode

[**disks**] Identifies the disks that Setup can request

[**oemdisks**] Identifies additional disks that Setup can request

[**user**] Identifies the location of the temporary SETUP.INI file that contains user information

[**windows**] Specifies the minimum files that Setup should copy to the main Windows directory

[**windows.system**] Specifies the minimum files that Setup should copy to the \SYSTEM subdirectory

[**windows.system.386**] Specifies the minimum files required for 386 machines

[**bluemax**] and [**386max**] Specifies additional files required for these two memory managers

[**shell**] Specifies the shell program that Setup should list in the SYSTEM.INI file; usually this is PROGMAN.EXE

➡ **Display driver sections** Identify the display drivers, grabbers, and grabber font files.

[**display**] Lists the display drivers

[<display>] Lists additional files required by specific displays

[<display>.3gr] Lists font files required for specific 386 grabbers

➡ **Keyboard and code page sections** Identify the keyboard drivers and international code pages.

[**keyboard.drivers**] Lists the keyboard names and their driver files

[**keyboard.types**] Lists keyboard types used by Setup

[**keyboard.tables**] Lists international layouts

[**codepages**] Lists international code pages

➡ **Mouse driver sections** Identify mouse drivers.

[**pointing.device**] Lists the Windows mouse drivers

[**dos.mouse.driver**] Lists the DOS mouse drivers

[**lmouse**] Lists the Logitech MS-DOS mouse drivers

➡ **Network sections** Identify network support files and changes that Setup should make to the .INI files for each network.

[**network**] Lists network files and changes to .INI files required for certain networks

[<network name>.**versions**] Lists specific versions of networks

[<specific network name>] Lists further changes to .INI files required for specific networks

➡ **System screen fonts sections** Identify the system screen fonts.

[**sysfonts**] Lists system font files

[**fixedfonts**] Lists fixed-pitch font files

[**oemfonts**] Lists OEM system font files

➡ **Copy-files sections** Tell Setup what files to copy, delete, or rename during installation.

[**win.copy**] Lists files to copy for 286 systems

[**win.copy.net**] Lists files to copy for networked systems

[**win.copy.net.win386**] Lists files to copy for 386 and higher networked systems

[**win.copy.win386**] Lists files to copy for 386 and higher systems

[**DelFiles**] Lists files to delete if upgrading

[**RenFiles**] Lists files to rename if upgrading

[**net**] Lists files to copy for networked systems

[**win.devices.win386**] Lists files to copy for 386 and higher systems

[**win.other**] Lists other files to copy

[**win.shell**] Lists shell files to copy

[**win.apps**] Lists applications and utilities to copy

[**win.dependents**] Lists DLLs and other files to copy

[**win.games**] Lists games to copy

[**win.scrs**] Lists screen savers to copy

[**win.bmps**] Lists wallpaper, sounds, and MIDI files to copy

[**win.readme**] Lists README files to copy

➽ **Program Manager sections** Contain instructions about what Program Manager groups to create, what program item icons they should contain, and the properties for the icons.

[**new.groups**] Specifies which Program Manager groups to modify if upgrading

[**progman.groups**] Lists Program Manager groups to create

[**group**<number>] Specifies properties for items in program groups

➽ **Fonts sections** Identify the raster and vector screen fonts and the True-Type typefaces to install.

[**fonts**] Lists vector and raster screen font files to install

[**ttfonts**] Lists TrueType font files to install

➽ **Incompatibility sections** List incompatible TSRs and block devices, and tell Setup which drivers should be removed from CONFIG.SYS.

[**compatibility**] Lists incompatible drivers to remove from CONFIG.SYS

[**incompTSR1**] Lists TSRs and drivers that are incompatible with Setup

[**incompTSR2**] Lists TSRs and drivers that are incompatible with Windows

[**block_devices**] Lists block devices that are incompatible with Windows

➽ **Miscellaneous sections** Identify multimedia drivers and installable drivers that should be updated, and tells Setup how to temporarily set the path of the .INI files during installation.

[**installable.drivers**] Lists multimedia drivers to install

[**translate**] Lists file name translation information for OEM disks created for Windows 3.0

[**update.files**] Lists installable drivers that need updating

[**ini.upd.patches**] Lists .INI file modifications that may be required if upgrading

➽ **Blowaway section** Marks the end of the installation portion used by Setup's DOS mode and the beginning of the configuration portion of the file used by Setup's Windows mode.

[**blowaway**] Marks the end of the installation sections and beginning of the configuration sections

➡ **Configuration sections** Tell Setup how to update .INI files, and identify system names, extended BIOS names, and Language DLL names.

[**ini.upd.31**] Lists updates to .INI file needed when upgrading to Windows 3.1

[**system**] Lists system short names used by Setup

[**machine**] Lists system names for specific computers

[**special_adapter**] Lists special data required for EtherLink MC network adapter cards

[**ebios**] Lists extended BIOS names

[**language**] Lists language DLL names

Insider's Tip

The SETUP.INF file contains extensive comments that describe the syntax of most of the entries in the various sections. You may want to print a copy of the file to keep on hand as a reference. If you do, I suggest using a fixed-space (that is, nonproportional) font, such as Courier, and a small point size, say 8 points; this formatting will help make it easier for you to interpret the entries and comments included in the file.

Inside the CONTROL.INF File

If you want to install custom printer drivers or set up international settings you'll need to modify the settings in this file. During installation, Setup places the CONTROL.INF file in your system subdirectory; the file itself contains these three sections:

➡ [**io.device**] Specifies the printers that Windows supports

➡ [**io.dependent**] Defines additional files required for some printer drivers

➡ [**country**] Specifies international formats

The first two sections allow you to install a printer driver during Setup other than the one that's supplied with Windows. As for fonts, your printer driver may be able to use the fonts installed with Windows, or you may have to install additional font files in the various fonts sections of SETUP.INF.

The [io. device] section lists all the printers supported by Windows 3.1 and is used by the Control Panel to install printer support. Each entry in this section follows this format:

```
<file name>, "<description>", "<scaling string>", "<scaling string>"
```

where the <file name> is the file name and extension, with the installation disk number; the <description> is the string that WIN.INI uses and that is displayed in the Control Panel; and <scaling string> includes one or two strings that indicate the scaling for the device.

Here's an example of a driver with more than one entry in [io.device], to specify settings that correspond to different printers

```
6:HPPCL.DRV, 6:unidrv.dll,"HP LaserJet IID", "DEVICESPECIFIC"
```

The Control Panel checks the [io.dependent] section to see whether the printer driver requires other files—such as font files, soft fonts installers, or help files—that should be copied to the \SYSTEM subdirectory. Each entry in this section follows this form:

```
<driver filename>=<disk number>:<file name>, <disk number>:
<file name>, ...
```

where the <driver file name> is the name of the printer driver file; the <disk number> represents the number of the installation disk that contains the additional file; and the <file name> is the name of the additional file that is copied. Here are a couple of examples:

```
pscript.drv = 7:pscript.hlp, 7:testps.txt
hppcl.drv = 7:finstall.dll, 7:finstall.hlp, 7:unidrv.hlp
```

The [country] section is used by the Control Panel for international formats, but the following examples show why Microsoft recommends that you make changes using the Country icon in the Control Panel.

```
"France", "33!1!3!2!1!1!0!2!8!1!!!F! !,!/!:!;!dd/MM/yyyy!dddd d MMMM yyyy!FRA"
"Germany", "49!1!3!2!1!1!0!2!8!1!!!DM!.!,!.!:!;!dd.MM.yyyy!dddd, d. MMMM yyyy!DEU"
```

. . . .

Inside the APPS.INF File

To install custom DOS applications for running with Windows, you'll need to modify the APPS.INF file, which contains information for creating a PIF and assigning an icon. During installation, Setup places the APPS.INF file in the system subdirectory. Windows Setup refers to this file when you use its

Set Up Applications feature, and File Manager refers to this file when you drag a DOS application's file icon into Program Manager to create an icon for the DOS application.

Here's what the main sections in the APPS.INF file contain:

[dialog] Specifies the text that Setup displays for the PIF in the Setup Applications dialog box

[base_PIFs] Specifies a batch file that Setup uses to create _DEFAULT.PIF, and specifies settings for the MS-DOS Prompt icon that runs COMMAND.COM

[enha_dosprompt] Specifies memory requirements for COMMAND.COM when the MS-DOS Prompt icon is run from 386 enhanced mode

[dontfind] Lists Windows applications (mostly from Windows itself and from the Windows Software Development Kit) that Setup should ignore in order to avoid setting up duplicate icons

[pif] Contains the PIF settings for DOS applications

In addition to these main sections, the APPS.INF file contains numerous other sections that provide specific PIF settings used by more than one application. PIF profiles for certain applications refer to these other sections in order to avoid having to repeat the settings for each application's PIF profile.

The most important section is the [pif] section, which contains the actual PIF information for the applications. Each entry in the [pif] section follows this format:

```
<program file>= <pif name>, <window title>, <startup directory>,
<close window flag>, <icon file>, <icon number>, <standard pif
section>, <386 pif section>, <ambiguous names>, <optimized pifs>
```

These entries are defined in Table 16.3.

You can edit these values to create your own custom PIF profiles, but you must keep the list of programs in the [pif] section in precise alphabetical order. Before you edit the APPS.INF file, make sure that you're well versed in the art of PIF tweaking. Like the SETUP.INF file, the APPS.INF file contains an extensive number of comments that can inform you about the techniques for editing the file.

Entry	Description
<program file>	The file name and extension of the program.
<pif name>	The name for the .PIF file, minus the .PIF extension.
<window title>	The text, enclosed in quotes, that the program displays in its title bar.
<startup directory>	The directory to make active when the program is started.
<close window flag>	Specifies whether the application window will be closed when the program is quit. Use the **cwe** flag if you want the window to be closed; omit the flag if you want the window to remain open.
<icon file>	The file that contains the icon for the program. The default file is PROGMAN.EXE, but many PIFs use icons in the MORICONS.DLL file.
<icon number>	The number of the icon to extract from <icon file> (the position of the icon in the file); the default is 0.
<standard pif section>	The section that contains the PIF settings to use for standard mode; the default is [std_dflt].
<386 pif section>	The section that contains the PIF settings to use for 386 enhanced mode; the default is [enha_dflt].
<ambiguous names>	Specifies the section that lists programs with identical file names.
<optimized pifs>	Specifies sections that contain additional PIF settings.

17

Diagnosing Your System with MSD and Dr. Watson

Windows 3.1 includes two important trouble-shooting tools: the Microsoft Diagnostics (MSD) and Dr. Watson. These tools can be incredibly useful in helping you prevent crashes and analyzing what went wrong when there is a crash, but there's barely any documentation for them included in the Windows package. Maybe Microsoft wants to deny the need for such tools.

Windows ... trouble? You better believe it! (Otherwise I wouldn't have spent two years writing this book!)

Microsoft Diagnostics is a DOS utility that helps you determine the details of your hardware configuration and lets you inspect how your system's memory is being used. Learning how to make the most of Microsoft Diagnostics requires a solid understanding of memory management, DOS, and your .INI files—information covered in some of the preceding chapters. The Dr. Watson program is a diagnostic tool that takes a snapshot of your system whenever it crashes and provides you with information that can help you identify the culprit and thus avoid a repeat performance.

Neither of these utilities will benefit the faint of heart; only if you've mastered the rest of this book are you ready to get a doctorate in diagnostics. If you're not prepared to delve into the mysteries of memory management and DOS, you can use the following rudimentary diagnostic routines; they are built into Windows, and can be activated by using special parameters on startup. The optional switches are described in Table 17.1.

TABLE 17.1

Switch	Description
/B	Creates the BOOTLOG.TXT file, a plain text file that records whatever system messages Windows generates during its startup process. If Windows fails to start, use the BOOTLOG.TXT file to try to identify whether a basic Windows component failed during startup.
/D:F	Turns off the FastDisk 32-bit disk access feature. This switch is equivalent to using the 32BitDiskAccess=OFF statement in the [386Enh] section of your SYSTEM.INI file.
/D:S	Tells Windows not to use the ROM address space between F000 and FFFF for a break point. This switch is equivalent to using the SystemROMBreakPoint=NO statement in the [386Enh] section of your SYSTEM.INI file.
/D:V	Tells Windows to let the ROM BIOS routines handle interrupts from the hard disk controller, rather than using its own faster but less compatible method. This switch is equivalent to using the VirtualHDIRQ=FALSE statement in the [386Enh] section of your SYSTEM.INI file.
/D:X	Tells Windows not to scan any of the upper memory area to find unused space. This switch is equivalent to using the EMMExclude=A000–FFFF statement in the [386Enh] section of your SYSTEM.INI file.

To use any of these switches, simply place them after the WIN command that you use to start Windows. For example, to create a BOOTLOG.TXT file, type

```
WIN /B
```

to start Windows.

If Windows fails during startup, substitute one of the /D switches, using each one in turn to get the system to work. If either the /D:F, /D:S, or /D:V switch does the trick, simply add the statement line corresponding to the proper switch (listed in Table 17.1) to SYSTEM.INI.

Insider's Tip

If the /D:X switch lets Windows start, you have an upper memory conflict. Rather than exclude the entire upper memory area from being used by Windows, use the guidelines discussed in Chapter 12 to see whether the system will run when you exclude only a portion of this area. If none of the /D switches work, try using the /B switch to create a BOOTLOG.TXT file; then examine the contents of the file to see if you can identify the problem component.

Another place you can search to diagnose startup failure is the BOOTLOG.TXT file itself. One kind of statement in this file contains a pair of lines that indicates an attempt to load a driver and then reports whether the driver was loaded successfully. For example, the lines

```
LoadStart = system.drv
LoadSuccess = system.drv
```

relate to the SYSTEM.DRV file. This is the main system driver that tells Windows how to work with your computer's hardware. The LoadStart line indicates an attempt to load the driver, and the LoadSuccess line indicates that it was loaded successfully. If you don't see a complete pair, that file may have been corrupted and you may need to copy a fresh version from your installation disks.

The other type of statement in BOOTLOG.TXT works pretty much the same way. For example, in the statement lines

```
INIT=Mouse
STATUS=Mouse driver installed
INITDONE=Mouse
```

the INIT statement marks an attempt to load the driver, the STATUS line reports the status of the driver, and the INITDONE line tells you that the driver was successfully loaded and initialized for use by Windows. Although these kinds of statements don't always include a STATUS statement, if both an INIT line and an INITDONE line are missing, you may well have a problem with that particular component, and you may need to either copy a new file from the installation disks or reinstall Windows using Setup.

Microsoft Diagnostics

Microsoft Diagnostics—new to Windows 3.1—is one of the most important new utilities in Windows 3.1, even though it runs in DOS. Originally created for Microsoft's own technical support staff, the company has wisely decided to provide the program to all users as part of Windows 3.1. This utility tracks down many technical details, such as the specifics of your hardware, software drivers, and the way your system uses memory. If you take the time to find out what this program can do, you'll be tempted to go ahead and actually learn how to use it. The gain will be worth the effort, because you'll be able to resolve potential hardware, memory, and interrupt conflicts, which can impair the performance of your system or prevent it from running altogether.

Windows Setup copies the Microsoft Diagnostics program, MSD.EXE, to your main Windows directory during installation. The Microsoft Diagnostics (MSD) utility offers 13 large, onscreen buttons that let you know what's going on with the following parts of your system:

➥ **Computer** Provides details about your processor, ROM BIOS, and other system hardware

➥ **Memory** Provides a map of your upper memory area between 640K and 1 megabyte, and reports other details about your memory configuration

➥ **Video** Provides information about your display adapter card

➥ **Network** Attempts to identify the network you are using, if any

➥ **OS Version** Provides details about your version of DOS

➥ **Mouse** Provides details about your mouse configuration

➥ **Other Adapters** Reports whether you have a Game Adapter

➥ **Disk Drives** Identifies the characteristics of the disk drives attached to your system

➥ **LPT Ports** Reports the status of LPT1:, LPT2:, and LPT3

➤ **COM Ports** Reports the status of COM1:, COM2:, COM3:, and COM4

➤ **IRQ Status** Displays information about how your hardware interrupts are being used

➤ **TSR Programs** Displays information about memory allocated to TSRs

➤ **Device Drivers** Displays information about device drivers that are installed in your system

In addition, the menus in the MSD File and Utilities offer several options:

➤ **Find File** Lets you search for a file and display its contents

➤ **Print Report** Lets you create a custom report about your system configuration

➤ **Display the contents** Shows the contents of your AUTOEXEC.BAT, CONFIG.SYS, SYSTEM.INI, and WIN.INI files

➤ **Memory Block Display** Displays an onscreen map of how your memory is allocated

➤ **Memory Browser** Searches for keywords in the ROM area and displays an onscreen map of ROM

➤ **Insert Command** Automatically adds common commands to your system files

➤ **Test Printer** Checks your current printer connection

➤ **Help** A spurious helper which only brings up an About box that lists the version number of MSD and copyright information

Because it's a DOS program, you can start the MSD utility either before you start Windows or from within a Windows session. For the most accurate reporting of your system configuration, you should run it before you start Windows, because Windows can affect its ability to correctly detect certain system characteristics.

The advantage to having this program run from DOS is that you can troubleshoot important system difficulties that prevent you from installing or running Windows. Sometimes it's convenient to run MSD from within Windows, so that you get a status report about the configuration of the virtual machine from which you were running MSD. Of course, the information reported by the virtual machine does not accurately reflect your actual hardware configuration—only the simulated hardware that Windows has created for the virtual machine.

To run the MSD utility, simply type **MSD** at the DOS prompt. Or you can also use a number of optional switches, as described in Table 17.2.

TABLE 17.2

Switch	Description
/B	Runs MSD in black-and-white mode for monochrome monitors, LCD displays, and other monitors that cannot display MSD in color.
/I	Prevents MSD from performing its initial hardware detection routines. You'll need to use this only if MSD does not start properly; this is similar to the /I option available with Setup.
/F \<**file name**\>	Prepares a complete MSD report and writes it to the specified file after prompting you for information, such as your name, address, phone number, and comments, which it includes in the report file.
/P \<**file name**\>	Prepares a complete MSD report and writes it to the specified file without prompting you for any information.
/S \<**file name**\>	Prepares a brief summary MSD report, and writes it to the specified file. You can use this option without specifying a file name; the report will be displayed on the screen.

If you select the detailed report options, you'll get a lengthy report—usually more than 10 pages—which provides a hard-copy reference about your system configuration. I recommend that you generate such a report, print it out, and keep it handy as a reference in case you run into a snag later on. It's especially useful for determining what interrupts are available for new hardware options you may be installing. It also prints a map of your upper memory, so that you can figure out how to load TSRs and device drivers into it and thus provide more free space in the critical 640K of conventional memory.

MSD provides character-based pulldown menus and onscreen buttons that support the use of a mouse. If you do use a mouse with MSD, you'll need to supply a DOS-level mouse driver, such as MOUSE.SYS or MOUSE.COM. If you run MSD in its normal mode by typing **MSD** at the DOS prompt, the initial screen depicted in Figure 17.1 makes a brief entry.

FIGURE 17.1

*MSD Initial
Screen*

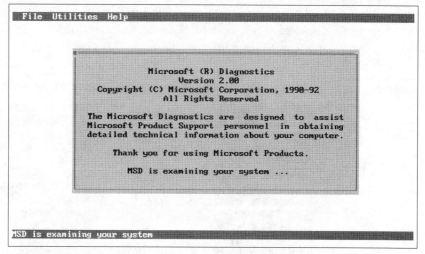

```
 File  Utilities  Help

                    Microsoft (R) Diagnostics
                         Version 2.00
              Copyright (C) Microsoft Corporation, 1990-92
                       All Rights Reserved

           The Microsoft Diagnostics are  designed  to  assist
           Microsoft Product Support  personnel  in  obtaining
           detailed technical information about your computer.

                Thank you for using Microsoft Products.

                    MSD is examining your system ...

 MSD is examining your system
```

FIGURE 17.1

*MSD Initial
Screen*

*MSD displays this screen while it probes your system hardware to
determine its configuration.*

If MSD freezes on this screen or crashes, you're in for a manual workout.
Evidently, the techniques used to probe your hardware are incompatible with
something in your system, such as your BIOS or a TSR. Your (poor) alternative is to start MSD with the /I switch, which doesn't report any of your
hardware details, so you'll need to select them one by one. Because any item
could have locked up or crashed your screen, you'll need to track down the
culprit by the time-tested trial and error method.

If you run MSD from within Windows, it displays the warning message
depicted in Figure 17.2.

FIGURE 17.2

*MSD
Warning
Screen*

```
                 You are running Microsoft Windows.

     MSD can only report information specified by its associated
     Windows Program Information File (.PIF).  Therefore information
     presented may be less accurate or complete than if MSD is run
     outside of Windows.  For more accurate information please exit
     Windows and run MSD from the MS-DOS prompt.

     Some areas may be affected while MSD is run under Windows:
     Memory values and types will reflect what Windows provides by
     itself, and through the associated .PIF file; IRQ values may
     be reported differently; and the visual memory map in Memory,
     Memory Block Display, and Memory Browser may show different
     results.  Other areas that may be affected include Video,
     OS Version, Mouse, Disk Drives, and COM Ports.

            Choose OK to continue or Cancel to quit MSD.

                      OK          Cancel
```

*The main MSD screen displays this warning message whenever you run
it from within Windows.*

After the startup screen has run (and the warning message has been displayed if you ran MSD from Windows), the main MSD screen then appears, as shown in Figure 17.3.

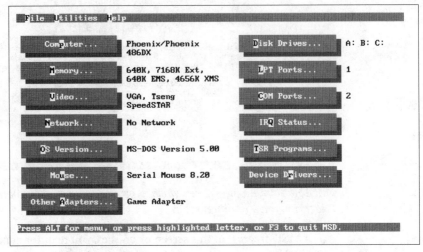

The main MSD screen displays a summary of the information that MSD has gleaned from your system configuration.

This screen contains three menus—Files, Utilities, and Help (spurious)—and 13 buttons. To review the summary information shown to the right of most of the large rectangular buttons, click on the button or on the highlighted letter in the button name.

• •

The Computer Section

Computer, the first large button in the upper-left portion of the screen, lists the variety of your system's ROM, followed by the name of the BIOS manufacturer—often this is the same. Underneath this information you'll see the processor type contained in your computer. If you press the Computer button or type **p**, you'll see the computer information section, depicted in Figure 17.4.

The following items are listed on the computer information screen:

➺ **Computer Name** The name of your computer: either the name of the manufacturer or the BIOS creator. For an IBM or Compaq, MSD will probably report the manufacturer name; for a clone, it will probably report the BIOS vendor.

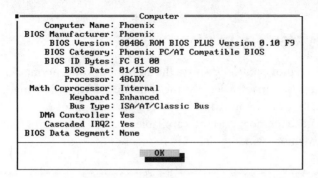

```
============================ Computer ============================
           Computer Name: Phoenix
        BIOS Manufacturer: Phoenix
            BIOS Version: 80486 ROM BIOS PLUS Version 0.10 F9
           BIOS Category: Phoenix PC/AT Compatible BIOS
           BIOS ID Bytes: FC 81 00
               BIOS Date: 01/15/88
               Processor: 486DX
         Math Coprocessor: Internal
                Keyboard: Enhanced
                Bus Type: ISA/AT/Classic Bus
          DMA Controller: Yes
            Cascaded IRQ2: Yes
        BIOS Data Segment: None

                        OK
```

▸▸ **BIOS Manufacturer** The company that created the ROM BIOS chips in your computer, such as Phoenix, AMI, etc.

▸▸ **BIOS Version** The software version of the ROM BIOS chip, as identified by the BIOS manufacturer.

▸▸ **BIOS Category** The generic description of your ROM BIOS. This identifies whether your system is an AT-compatible machine.

▸▸ **BIOS ID Bytes** A hexadecimal number that identifies the ROM BIOS.

▸▸ **BIOS Date** The date contained in the ROM BIOS chips, which is often earlier than the actual date of the ROM BIOS version.

▸▸ **Processor** The CPU chip contained in your system.

▸▸ **Math Coprocessor** Identifies whether you have a math coprocessor that MSD can recognize installed. If you have a 486DX chip, this entry specifies Internal, to reflect the built-in math coprocessor contained in the CPU chip.

▸▸ **Keyboard** Reports your type of keyboard; the most common is Enhanced.

▸▸ **Bus Type** Identifies whether you have an ISA, EISA, or MCA bus.

▸▸ **DMA Controller** YES indicates that your hard disk supports direct memory access (DMA); NO indicates that it does not.

▸▸ **Cascaded IRQ2** YES indicates your system supports the cascaded IRQ2 feature that allows several devices to share the IRQ2 interrupt by using IRQ8 through IRQ15. NO indicates that your system does not support this feature.

▸▸ **BIOS Data Segment** Indicates whether or not MSD detects a data segment in the ROM BIOS.

• •

The Memory Section

The Memory button displays the amount of conventional RAM installed in your system, followed by the amount of extended memory you have installed; on the next line, you see the amounts of expanded memory and extended memory currently available, if any. Click on this button to bring up the Memory window, depicted in Figure 17.5.

• • • • • • • • • • • • • • •

FIGURE 17.5

Memory Window

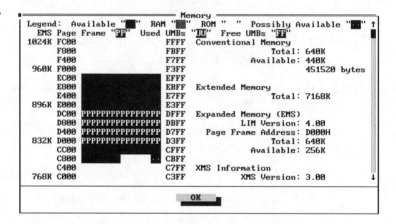

The Memory window displays a visual map of your upper memory area, the memory addresses between 640K and 1024K. This map is crudely constructed from various text characters; although it's a little on the homely side, it gets the job done. The entire map doesn't fit on a standard VGA display; to view it all, you will need to scroll the window.

The map is divided into 24 rows, each identified by a hexadecimal address range. For example, the top row of the map contains the address range FC00 through FFFF. Each of these 16K rows is divided into 1K increments, represented by a block the size of a single character. Each character block identifies the status of that particular 1K area of memory.

A legend describing the contents of each character block and what it means is located at the top of the memory window. For example, a solid black block indicates that that area is available for use by your system. Any blocks containing the letter P are part of the EMS page frame. Blocks containing the letter U are upper memory blocks currently in use. And any blocks containing the letter F are free upper memory blocks available for loading device drivers, TSRs, or other memory-resident software. As noted, each letter represents a 1K memory area, so four consecutive Fs would indicate a 4K free upper memory block.

A summary of your current memory configuration appears to the right of the memory map. The first section reports on your conventional memory, indicating the total number of kilobytes installed in your system (usually 640K); below this information, you'll see the amount of available conventional memory, measured in kilobytes and bytes.

After the Conventional Memory section, the information varies, depending on what types of memory you are currently using. You might see any of the following sections, depending on what kind of memory MSD detects in your system:

➤ **Extended Memory** Reports the total amount of extended memory installed in your system.

➤ **MS-DOS Upper Memory Blocks** Reports the total amount of memory used by your UMBs, the total amount of memory in your free UMBs, and the largest free block available.

➤ **Expanded Memory** Reports the details about your expanded memory. The first line reports the version of LIM-compatible memory you are using (usually either 3.2 or 4.0). The next line identifies the beginning hexadecimal address of the expanded memory page frame. The next two lines report the total amount of expanded memory installed and the amount of free expanded memory available to your DOS applications.

➤ **XMS Information** Reports details about your extended memory manager and its use of extended memory. The first line reports the XMS version, which identifies the type of XMS memory available rather than the version number of your extended memory driver. The driver version is contained on the next line. Other items in this section include the status of your A20 address line, a report on whether your high memory area is currently being used, and information about the total amount of available extended memory and the largest free block within that amount.

➤ **VCPI Information** Reports whether MSD detects the Virtual Control Program Interface (VCPI), and if so, what version is in use and how much memory is allocated to it.

➤ **DPMI Information** Reports whether MSD detects the DOS Protected Mode Interface (DPMI), and if so, what version of DPMI is in use.

The memory map and memory configuration information can help you determine how best to configure your upper memory area. For details about how to manage your upper memory, see the section on EMM386 in Chapter 13.

The Video Section

The Video button lists the current display type manufacturer and model of
your video card. When you click on this button, the Video information
window appears (Figure 17.6).

FIGURE 17.6

*Video
Information
Window*

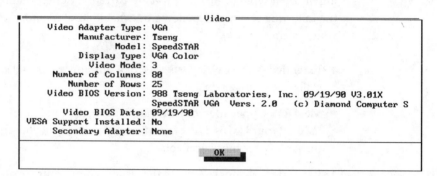

```
═══════════════════════════ Video ═══════════════
    Video Adapter Type: VGA
           Manufacturer: Tseng
                  Model: SpeedSTAR
           Display Type: VGA Color
             Video Mode: 3
      Number of Columns: 80
         Number of Rows: 25
    Video BIOS Version: 988 Tseng Laboratories, Inc. 09/19/90 V3.01X
                         SpeedSTAR VGA  Vers. 2.0   (c) Diamond Computer S
        Video BIOS Date: 09/19/90
  VESA Support Installed: No
      Secondary Adapter: None

                              ▐  OK  ▌
```

The Video information window contains the following information:

➤ **Video Adapter Type** Reports what kind of video adapter is installed in
your system, such as VGA, XGA, EGA, etc.

➤ **Manufacturer** Identifies the manufacturer of the video adapter card, as
reported by the card's ROMs. This may not be the name of the vendor
who sold you the card.

➤ **Model** Reports the name of the model as contained in the card's ROM.

➤ **Display Type** Reports what kind of display you are using, such as VGA
color.

➤ **Video Mode** Reports the number of the video mode in which the adapter
card is currently running.

➤ **Number of Columns** Reports the character width of the screen in the
current mode of your display card. This is usually 80, but some cards
provide special modes that let you obtain more columns across the width
of your screen.

➤ **Number of Rows** The number of lines of text that can be displayed in the
current video mode of the card. This is usually 25, but again many cards
use special modes that can increase this number.

➤ **Video BIOS version** The version of the BIOS ROM on your display
adapter card.

➺ **Video BIOS date** The date of the version of the ROM chips on your display adapter card.

➺ **VESA Support Installed** YES means the adapter card conforms to the Video Electronic Standards Association (VESA) specifications; NO means the card doesn't conform to the standard.

➺ **Secondary Adapter** Reports whether a second display adapter card is detected in your system.

The Network Section

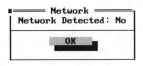

FIGURE 17.7
Network Information Window

The Network button displays the name that is detected by MSD. If no network is present, the words No Network appear. When you click on the button, the Network information window appears (Figure 17.7). This window contains the name of your network or simply states that no network is detected.

The OS Version Section

The OS Version button spells out the name of the current version of DOS you are using. When you click on this button, the OS Version information window appears (Figure 17.8).

FIGURE 17.8
OS Version Information Window

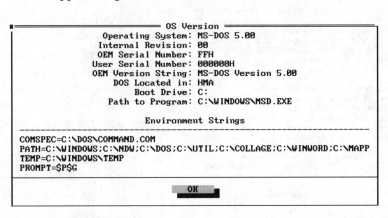

The OS Version information window contains the following items:

➺ **Operating System** Reports the version of DOS you are currently running.

➣ **Internal Revision** Specifies the revision number of DOS that is running. Sometimes a revision makes such minor modifications to DOS that a new version number is not justified.

➣ **OEM Serial Number** A two-digit hexadecimal number identifying the brand of DOS. The number FF specifies Microsoft's own version for MS-DOS 5.0.

➣ **User Serial Number** A hexadecimal number identifying the serial number of the individual copy of DOS you are using. If this number is all 0s, your version of DOS was not serialized.

➣ **OEM Version String** The full name of the DOS product you are running—for example, "MS-DOS, Version 5.0."

➣ **DOS Located in** Reports whether DOS is located in the HMA (high memory area) or the conventional 640K of RAM.

➣ **Boot Drive** Reports the volume letter from which DOS was booted.

➣ **Path to Program** Reports the drive letter and directory path of the MSD program currently running.

➣ **Environment Strings** Lists the DOS environment variables that are currently set. This same information is available by typing **SET** at the DOS prompt.

The Mouse Section

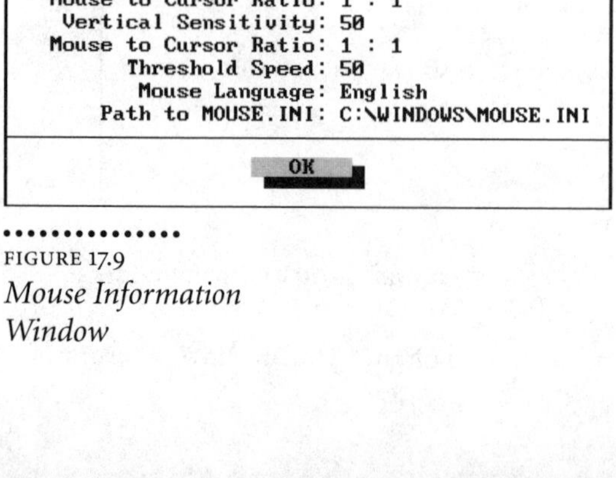

```
════════════════ Mouse ═════════════════
         Mouse Hardware: Serial Mouse
    Driver Manufacturer: Microsoft
        DOS Driver Type: Serial Mouse
        Driver File Type: .COM File
     DOS Driver Version: 8.20
             Mouse IRQ: 4
        Mouse COM Port: COM1:
 Mouse COM Port Address: 03F8H
 Number of Mouse Buttons: 2
  Horizontal Sensitivity: 50
   Mouse to Cursor Ratio: 1 : 1
     Vertical Sensitivity: 50
   Mouse to Cursor Ratio: 1 : 1
         Threshold Speed: 50
         Mouse Language: English
      Path to MOUSE.INI: C:\WINDOWS\MOUSE.INI

              ┌──────────┐
              │    OK    │
              └──────────┘
```

FIGURE 17.9

Mouse Information Window

The Mouse button identifies your mouse hardware and the version number of the DOS mouse driver, if one is in use. Clicking on the Mouse button brings up the Mouse information window, shown in Figure 17.9.

The Mouse information window contains the following information:

➣ **Mouse Hardware** The manufacturer or brand of mouse you are using, such as Microsoft, Logitech, etc.

➣ **Driver Manufacturer** The creator of the DOS software driver currently installed, if any.

➤ **DOS Driver Type** Reports whether the driver supports a serial mouse, bus mouse, or other type of mouse.

➤ **Driver File Type** Reports whether a .com file or .sys file is being used for the mouse driver.

➤ **DOS Driver Version** The version number of the DOS mouse driver.

➤ **Mouse IRQ** The hardware interrupt being used by the mouse. If the mouse is plugged into a COM port, this is the IRQ used by that COM port.

➤ **Mouse COM Port** The name of the COM port, such as COM1:, to which the mouse is connected.

➤ **Mouse COM Port Address** The base I/O address of the COM port the mouse is using.

➤ **Number of Mouse Buttons** The number of buttons supported by the DOS mouse driver; not necessarily the actual number of buttons on your mouse.

➤ **Horizontal Sensitivity** The number of points per inch of horizontal resolution supported by the DOS mouse driver; not necessarily the actual resolution of your mouse.

➤ **Mouse to Cursor Ratio** The ratio of horizontal mouse movement to the horizontal movement of the cursor; usually 1:1, unless a ballistic or accelerated driver is in effect.

➤ **Vertical Sensitivity** The number of points per inch of vertical resolution supported by the DOS mouse driver; not necessarily the actual resolution of your mouse.

➤ **Mouse to Cursor Ratio** The ratio of vertical mouse movement to the vertical movement of the cursor; usually 1:1, unless a ballistic or accelerated driver is in effect.

➤ **Threshold Speed** The speed that the mouse must exceed for ballistic tracking—if active—to take effect.

➤ **Mouse Language** No, the mouse doesn't talk; this is the language of the DOS mouse driver that is installed.

➤ **Path to MOUSE.INI** The drive and directory location of the MOUSE.INI used by the Microsoft mouse driver.

The Other Adapters Section

```
■══ Other Adapters ══
   Game Adapter: Detected
 Joystick A - X: 0
            Y: 0
     Button 1: On
     Button 2: On
 Joystick B - X: 0
            Y: 0
     Button 1: On
     Button 2: On

        ┌──────┐
        │  OK  │
        └──────┘
```

FIGURE 17.10
*Other Adapters
Information Window*

This section displays information about a game adapter, such as a joystick, only if you have one. If a game adapter is not detected, nothing appears next to the button. Click on the Other Adapters button to display the Other Adapters window, shown in Figure 17.10.

This window simply reports that a game adapter was not detected if one is not connected to your system. If you do have a game adapter, such as a joystick, connected to your system, this window contains such information as the number of buttons on the joystick and the x and y coordinates that represent the position of the joystick or other adapter.

The Disk Drives Section

This section contains information about the disk drives currently accessible to your system. The Disk Drives button lists the drive letters of the disk drives detected by MSD. When you click on the Disk Drives button, the Disk Drives information window appears (Figure 17.11).

FIGURE 17.11
*Disk Drives
Information
Window*

```
■════════════ Disk Drives ═══════════
 Drive  Type                      Free Space  Total Size
 ─────  ────                      ──────────  ──────────
  A:    Floppy Drive, 5.25" 1.2M
        80 Cylinders, 2 Heads
        512 Bytes/Sector, 15 Sectors/Track
  B:    Floppy Drive, 3.5" 1.44M
        80 Cylinders, 2 Heads
        512 Bytes/Sector, 18 Sectors/Track
  C:    Fixed Disk, CMOS Type 42       43M        201M
        986 Cylinders, 12 Heads
        512 Bytes/Sector, 35 Sectors/Track
 SHARE Installed
 LASTDRIVE=E:

              ┌──────┐
              │  OK  │
              └──────┘
```

The Disk Drives information window contains a table with the following four headings:

➤ **Drive** The drive letter of the disk drive.

➤ **Type** For floppy disk drives, this reports the size of the disk drive media, such as 5$\frac{1}{4}$- or 3$\frac{1}{2}$-inch, and the capacity of the drive, such as 1.2 MB or

4.4 MB, as well as the number of cylinders used by the floppy disk drive. For a hard disk, this reports that it is a fixed disk and identifies the type of the drive as reported by the system's CMOS settings, the number of cylinders on the drive, the number of heads, the number of bytes per sector, and the number of sectors per track.

➤ **Free Space** The amount of free space on a hard disk drive. This information is not reported for floppy disk drives.

➤ **Total Size** The total capacity of your hard disk. This information is not reported for floppy disk drives.

Other information related to your disk drives may be reported by DOS below the information about the drives, such as whether SHARE is installed, and the setting for the LASTDRIVE parameter.

The LPT Ports Section

This section details the status of the LPT1, LPT2, and LPT3 ports installed in your system. The LPT Ports button displays a number from 1 to 3 that indicates how many LPT ports MSD detects in your system. When you click on the LPT Ports button, you see the LPT Ports information window (Figure 17.12).

FIGURE 17.12
*LPT Ports
Information
Window*

Port	Port Address	On Line	Paper Out	I/O Error	Time Out	Busy	ACK
LPT1:	0378H	No	No	Yes	No	No	No
LPT2:	–	–	–	–	–	–	–
LPT3:	–	–	–	–	–	–	–

LPT Ports

OK

The LPT Ports information window displays a table that contains the following eight items, which indicate the status of your parallel ports. Status information is reported only for physical ports that MSD detects.

➤ **Port** Lists LPT1, LPT2, and LPT.

➤ **Port Address** The base I/O address of the LPT port.

➤ **On Line** Reports whether the printer attached to that port is turned on.

➤ **Paper Out** Reports whether a Paper Out message is being received from the printer.

➣ **I/O Error** Reports whether a communications problem is detected. If the printer is not turned on or connected, this will report YES.

➣ **Time Out** Reports whether the printer is sending a timeout signal to the computer.

➣ **Busy** Reports whether the printer is sending a busy signal to the computer.

➣ **ACK** Reports whether the printer is sending an acknowledge signal to the computer.

The COM Ports Section

This section reports the status of your serial ports, up to a total of four ports. The COM Ports button lists a number from 1 to 4, which indicates how many COM ports MSD detects in your system. When you click on the COM Ports button, the COM Ports information window appears (Figure 17.13).

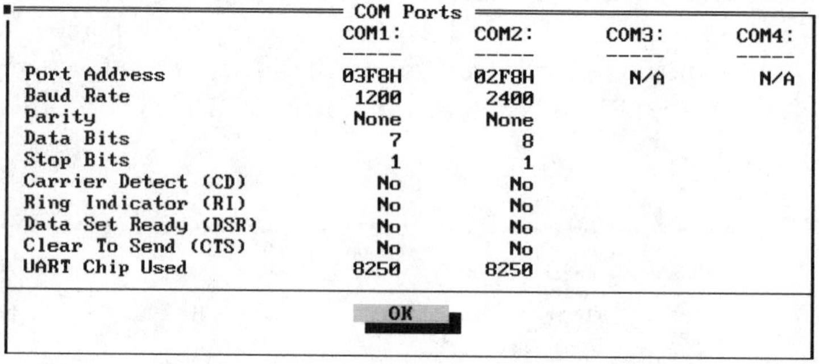

FIGURE 17.13
*COM Ports
Information
Window*

```
═════════════════════ COM Ports ═════════════════════
                        COM1:     COM2:    COM3:    COM4:
                        ─────     ─────    ─────    ─────
Port Address            03F8H     02F8H     N/A      N/A
Baud Rate                1200      2400
Parity                   None      None
Data Bits                   7         8
Stop Bits                   1         1
Carrier Detect (CD)        No        No
Ring Indicator (RI)        No        No
Data Set Ready (DSR)       No        No
Clear To Send (CTS)        No        No
UART Chip Used           8250      8250
                     ┌─────────┐
                     │   OK    │
                     └─────────┘
```

The COM Ports information window reports the current status of your COM ports. This window contains four columns, one containing the status information for each COM port that is detected. If a COM port is not detected, the column contains N/A. Here is what's reported for each COM port:

➣ **Port Address** The base I/O address of the COM port

➣ **Baud Rate** The number of characters per second that the port is currently set to transmit and receive

➣ **Parity** The current status of the parity setting

➣ **Data Bits** The number of bits required to complete one character of information

➤ **Stop Bits** The number of bits that signifies the end of a character

➤ **Carrier Detect** Indicates whether a signal is being received at that COM port

➤ **Ring Indicator** Indicates whether the ring indicator signal is being received

➤ **Data Set Ready** Indicates whether the data set ready signal is being received

➤ **Clear To Send** Indicates whether the clear to send signal is being received

➤ **UART Chip Used** The model number of the serial communications chip used by the COM port

• •

The IRQ Status Section

This section displays information about the current status of your system's hardware interrupts. Click on the IRQ Status button to display the IRQ Status information window (Figure 17.14).

FIGURE 17.14

IRQ Status Information Window

```
========================= IRQ Status =========================
 IRQ    Address     Description        Detected             Handled By
 ---    --------    -----------        --------             ----------
  0     19BE:04B7   Timer Click        Yes                  SNAP.EXE
  1     8CD7:16E8   Keyboard           Yes                  Block Device
  2     06DA:0057   Second 8259A       Yes                  Default Handlers
  3     06DA:006F   COM2: COM4:        COM2:                Default Handlers
  4     13BC:02CD   COM1: COM3:        COM1: Serial Mouse   SNAP.EXE
  5     06DA:009F   LPT2:              No                   Default Handlers
  6     06DA:00B7   Floppy Disk        Yes                  Default Handlers
  7     0070:06F4   LPT1:              Yes                  System Area
  8     06DA:0052   Real-Time Clock    Yes                  Default Handlers
  9     F000:D322   Redirected IRQ2    Yes                  BIOS
 10     06DA:00CF   (Reserved)                              Default Handlers
 11     06DA:00E7   (Reserved)                              Default Handlers
 12     06DA:00FF   (Reserved)                              Default Handlers
 13     F000:D313   Math Coprocessor   Yes                  BIOS
 14     06DA:0117   Fixed Disk         Yes                  Default Handlers
 15     F000:FF53   (Reserved)                              BIOS

                            [ OK ]
```

The IRQ Status information window displays a table with these five columns:

➤ **IRQ** Lists the numbers 0 through 15, in sequence, representing the 16 hardware interrupts available in PC systems.

➤ **Address** Lists the hexadecimal memory address used by the hardware interrupt.

➻ **Description** The standard description of the devices using the interrupt. Any entries marked "(Reserved)" cannot be used or assigned by any other hardware.

➻ **Detected** Reports whether the interrupt is being used, and if the interrupt is shared, which device is using it. Entries marked NO can be reassigned to another hardware device if you need another interrupt.

➻ **Handled by** The system software or other program currently using the interrupt.

The TSR Programs Section

This section displays information about the memory control blocks that have been allocated to TSRs or other memory-resident programs. When you press the TSR Programs button, the TSR Programs information window appears (Figure 17.15).

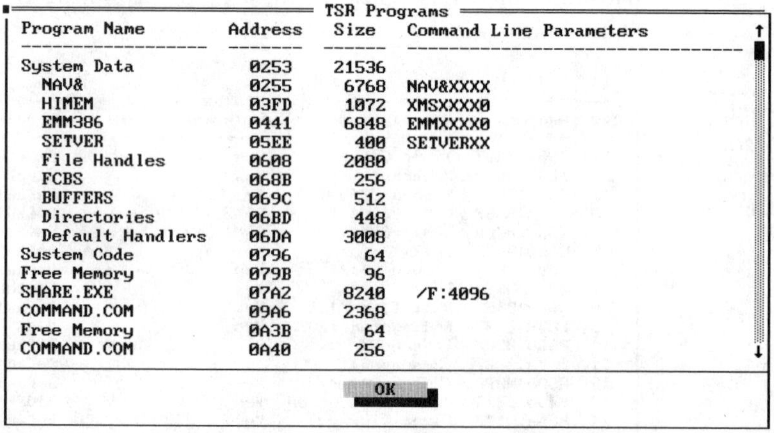

FIGURE 17.15
*TSR
Programs
Information
Window*

```
╒══════════════════════════ TSR Programs ══════════════════════╕
│ Program Name        Address   Size   Command Line Parameters   ↑│
│ ─────────────────   ───────   ─────  ─────────────────────────  ▓│
│ System Data          0253     21536                             │
│   NAV&               0255      6768  NAV&XXXX                    │
│   HIMEM              03FD      1072  XMSXXXX0                    │
│   EMM386             0441      6848  EMMXXXX0                    │
│   SETVER             05EE       400  SETVERXX                    │
│   File Handles       0608      2080                             │
│   FCBS               068B       256                             │
│   BUFFERS            069C       512                             │
│   Directories        06BD       448                             │
│   Default Handlers   06DA      3008                             │
│ System Code          0796        64                             │
│ Free Memory          079B        96                             │
│ SHARE.EXE            07A2      8240  /F:4096                     │
│ COMMAND.COM          09A6      2368                             │
│ Free Memory          0A3B        64                             │
│ COMMAND.COM          0A40       256                            ↓│
├───────────────────────────────────────────────────────────────┤
│                          [  OK  ]                              │
╘═══════════════════════════════════════════════════════════════╛
```

This window usually contains more than one screenful of information, so you'll need to scroll through it. The TSR Programs section contains a table with these four entries:

➻ **Program Name** The name of the TSR or other program currently loaded into memory. The entry "Free Memory" indicates unused memory areas.

➻ **Address** The starting hexadecimal memory address of the program.

➻ **Size** The size of the program in bytes.

➠ **Command Line Parameters** Any command line parameters used to start the program that are retained in memory along with the program.

• •

The Device Drivers Section

This section displays information about installable device drivers that MSD detects in your system. Some of these device drivers are part of DOS, such as the COM ports, the LPT ports, and the CON, AUX, and PRN devices. Others are installed from files, such as HIMEM.SYS and EMM386.EXE. Click on the Device Drivers button to display the Device Drivers information window, as shown in Figure 17.16.

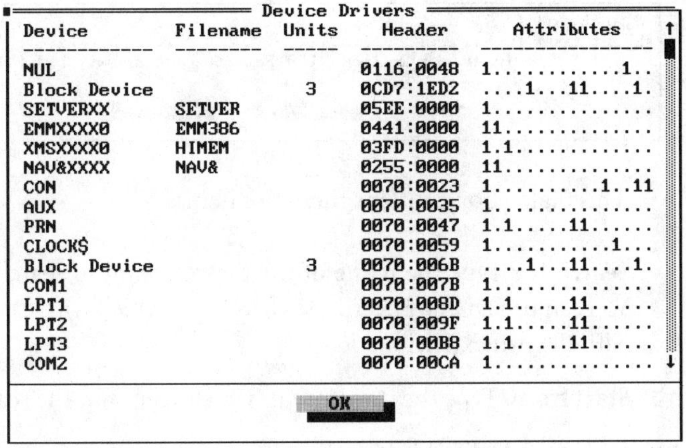

• • • • • • • • • • • • • • •
FIGURE 17.16
*Device
Drivers
Information
Window*

```
 ═══════════════════ Device Drivers ═══════════════════
  Device      Filename  Units   Header      Attributes      ↑
  ──────────  ────────  ─────   ────────  ─────────────────
  NUL                           0116:0048  1............1..
  Block Device          3       0CD7:1ED2  ....1...11....1.
  SETVERXX    SETVER            05EE:0000  1...............
  EMMXXXX0    EMM386            0441:0000  11..............
  XMSXXXX0    HIMEM             03FD:0000  1.1.............
  NAV&XXXX    NAV&              0255:0000  11..............
  CON                           0070:0023  1..........1..11
  AUX                           0070:0035  1...............
  PRN                           0070:0047  1.1.....11......
  CLOCK$                        0070:0059  1............1..
  Block Device          3       0070:006B  ....1...11....1.
  COM1                          0070:007B  1...............
  LPT1                          0070:008D  1.1.....11......
  LPT2                          0070:009F  1.1.....11......
  LPT3                          0070:00B8  1.1.....11......
  COM2                          0070:00CA  1............... ↓

                     ▓  OK  ▓
```

The Device Drivers information window contains a table with these five items:

➠ **Device** The name of the device as it is known to DOS.

➠ **Filename** The file name used to install the device driver, if it is not built into DOS.

➠ **Units** The number of units required by the device; usually applies only to block devices.

➠ **Header** The hexadecimal address that identifies the device driver header.

➠ **Attributes** The bit flags that identify the device. A 1 indicates that the bit is turned on.

The File Menu

File Menu

This menu contains commands that let you locate and view the contents of a file, print a report about your system configuration, or view the AUTOEXEC.BAT, CONFIG.SYS, SYSTEM.INI, and WIN.INI files (Figure 17.17).

To access the File menu, click on it with the mouse—as you would in Windows—or press Alt+F and the highlighted menu item. Click on the first item in the File menu, Find File, to bring up the Find File dialog box, shown in Figure 17.18.

FIGURE 17.18

Find File
Dialog Box

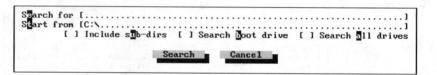

This dialog box contains these five items:

➤ **Search for** Type the name of the file you want to search for on this line. You can use DOS wildcards, such as *.INI, which will search for all the files with the .INI extension.

➤ **Start from** Type the directory in which you want the search to begin.

➤ **Include sub-dirs** Place an X in this check box to search the subdirectories located within the directory you specified in the Start from line.

➤ **Search boot drive** Place an X in this check box to search only the drive from which DOS was booted.

➤ **Search all drives** Place an X in this check box to search all the drives connected to your system.

When you've filled in the search criteria, click on the Search button at the bottom of the box; a list box appears with all the files that meet those search criteria. Highlight the files you want to view and then click on the Display File button. This brings up a simple text box listing the contents of the file. You will only be able to view, not edit, the file.

Click on Print Report to bring up the Report dialog box, shown in Figure 17.19.

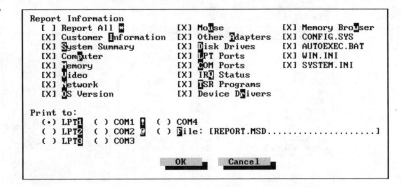

FIGURE 17.19

*Report
Dialog Box*

The Report Information section of this box lets you select the items you want to include in the report. Place an X in the check box for each item you want to include, or place an X in the Report All box for a complete report. The Print To section of this dialog box lets you choose an LPT port, a COM port, or a file to receive the generated report. To send the report to a file, the default file name is REPORT.MSD, but you can type any file name in this box. When you click OK, you are presented with the Customer Information dialog box, which lets you type in your name, address, and other information, if you desire; if not, simply click OK to generate the report.

The next four items on the File menu are AUTOEXEC.BAT, CONFIG.SYS, SYSTEM.INI, and WIN.INI. Select one of the items to view—not edit—the corresponding file.

The last item on the File menu is the Exit command, which lets you quit MSD. The keyboard equivalent is F3.

The Utilities Menu

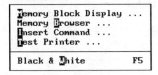

FIGURE 17.20

Utilities Menu

This menu contains commands that let you view additional details about your memory configuration. It also includes a command that lets you insert lines into your system files; conduct a quick test of your printer; and change the MSD onscreen display to black and white, for your monochrome monitor (Figure 17.20).

The first item on the Utilities menu, Memory Block Display, displays a map of all the memory in your system (Figure 17.21).

The Memory Block Map dialog box contains an allocated memory section that lists the programs and device drivers currently loaded into memory, along with the starting memory address and length in bytes of each item. When you highlight an entry in this list, the

• • • • • • • • • • • • •
FIGURE 17.21

Memory
Block Map

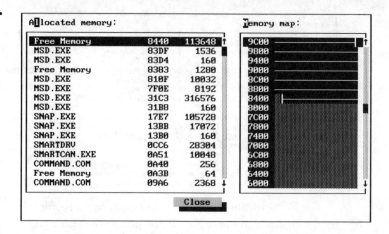

• • • • • • • • • • • • •
FIGURE 17.22

Memory
Browser
Dialog Box

memory map provides a visual display of the location of the program in memory.

The Memory Browser command lets you search for specific key words in the ROM areas of your system and also provides a display of your memory map. When you choose this command, the Memory Browser dialog box appears (Figure 17.22).

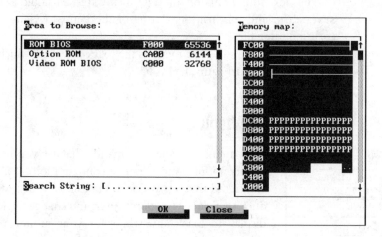

The Area to Browse section lists the various ROM areas identified by MSD, along with their starting memory addresses and their lengths in bytes. When you select an item in this section, the Memory Map display indicates the area in memory occupied by that ROM.

A text line labeled Search String appears below the Area to Browse section. Type a text string in this space and click OK. If the text string is found in the

ROM, a dialog box appears indicating the memory address containing the text string. If the text is not found, a Search Text Not Found message appears.

Choose Insert Command to display the Insert Command dialog box. This dialog box lets you insert frequently used commands into your system files. The dialog box lists the command to be inserted, the section in the file where the command will be inserted, and the file name where the command will be placed. This dialog box lists frequently used statement lines that you may want to add to your SYSTEM.INI, WIN.INI, CONFIG.SYS, and AUTOEXEC.BAT files. Highlight the command you want to insert and click OK; this brings up a dialog box that lets you edit or adjust the command (Figure 17.23).

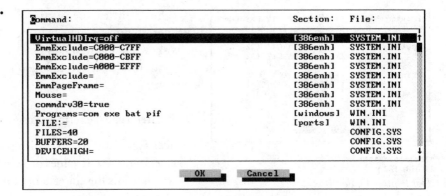

•••••••••••••
FIGURE 17.23
*Command
Edit Dialog
Box*

Click OK after editing the command. Another dialog box appears asking what action to take, such as adding the line to the file or replacing an existing line with the new line. Choose the desired action and click OK to complete the insertion.

Danger Zone

This method of editing your system files may not place the statement line in the proper sequence. For example, the line that loads HIMEM.SYS must appear in your CONFIG.SYS file before any other commands that make use of memory management features. Always inspect the file after inserting a command using this method to ensure that the statement was added in the proper place.

The commands listed in the Insert Command dialog box are derived from statement lines in the MSD.INI file. You can add your own commands to this file so that they will automatically appear in the dialog box by opening the MSD.INI file using a text editor and adding the command to the [Command] section of the file. The statement lines in this section follow the format

```
<command>,<section>,<filename>
```

For example, here's a statement line in MSD.INI that would add the 32BitDiskAccess=OFF to the [386Enh] section of a SYSTEM.INI file:

```
32BitDiskAccess=OFF,[386Enh],SYSTEM.INI
```

If you're adding a statement line in MSD.INI for a command that needs to be placed in your CONFIG.SYS or AUTOEXEC.BAT file, the line must include a blank space where the <section> item appears, and it must also include the commas. For example, this line would add a command to your CONFIG.SYS file:

```
DOS=HIGH,,CONFIG.SYS
```

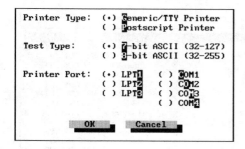

FIGURE 17.24
Test Printer Dialog Box

The Utilities menu also includes a Test Printer command, which brings up the dialog box shown in Figure 17.24

The Test Printer dialog box offers these options:

➤ **Printer Type** Generic or PostScript

➤ **Test Type** 7-bit ASCII, which prints the characters with ASCII values of 32 to 127; or 8-bit, which prints the characters with ASCII values of 32 to 255

➤ **Printer Port** The LPT or COM port that is connected to whatever printer you want to test

After you've made your selections, press OK to initiate the test. If nothing prints, or you get an error message, you've got a problem with your printer or printer connection. (Check the cable!)

Dr. Watson

Dr. Watson is modeled after the literary character of the same name; both versions—the famous detective's assistant and the diagnostic utility—are designed to track down culprits, albeit the computer version was developed to identify the cause of system crashes.

Dr. Watson seems a fitting response to the dreaded "Unrecoverable Application Error" message, which used to appear in Windows 3.0—a less stable (read "more buggy") version than Windows 3.1. This same message reared up whether your application or Windows itself crashed; the problem was, you never knew what had crashed. Dr. Watson makes it easier to track down the real culprit, and also provides some details about the condition of your Windows environment when it crashed.

Setup copies Dr. Watson into your main Windows directory during installation, but it doesn't create a program item icon for it; to do so, you'll need to drag its icon from File Manager into Program Manager. Because Dr. Watson needs to be running in order to do its detective work, you should place its program item icon in the StartUp group. Dr. Watson always starts as a minimized icon. If you double-click on the Dr. Watson icon (or open it in some other way) when Windows is running smoothly, you are presented with the simple dialog box shown in Figure 17.25, which indicates that no faults were detected.

FIGURE 17.25

Dr. Watson OK Dialog Box

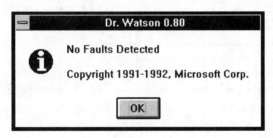

Open Dr. Watson when everything's hunky-dory, and you'll get the message that no faults were detected.

Dr. Watson keeps a log file—DRWATSON.LOG—which is a plain text file created when you first run this utility. It is updated every time you run the Good Doctor. If you place Dr. Watson in your StartUp group, the DRWAT-SON.LOG file keeps a record of all the start and stop times of your Windows sessions (provided that Program Manager is your primary shell). Here's a sample section of a DRWATSON.LOG file:

```
Start Dr. Watson 1.0—Wed Sep 16 10:34:13 1992
Stop Dr. Watson 1.0—Thu Sep 17 01:26:08 1992

Start Dr. Watson 1.0—Thu Sep 17 10:14:02 1992

Start Dr. Watson 1.0—Fri Sep 18 09:30:37 1992
Stop Dr. Watson 1.0—Fri Sep 18 11:47:42 1992
```

The start and stop times of Dr. Watson (and your Windows sessions) are listed in paired lines, which are separated by a blank line. Note that the second Start line is not followed by a stop time—this indicates that Windows was halted without quitting your shell (such as turning off your system without exiting Windows).

If a program (or Windows) crashes while you are running Dr. Watson, the utility takes a snapshot of various system parameters and other data, and presents you with the dialog box shown in Figure 17.26. This dialog box requests that you type in a description of what was happening at the time.

••••••••••••••
FIGURE 17.26
*Dr. Watson
Crash Dialog
Box*

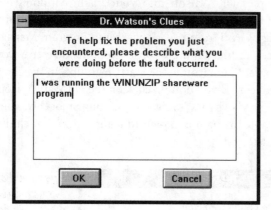

When Dr. Watson detects a crash, it presents you with this dialog box so that you can describe what you were doing when the crash occurred.

The system snapshot information, and the description you entered, if any, are recorded in the DRWATSON.LOG file. The technical gobbledygook that follows is an example of a single Dr. Watson log report that occurred when I was running the shareware file-decompression utility WINUNZIP.EXE. Note the asterisks that precede the entry in the log file.

```
*****************************************************************************
Dr. Watson 1.0 Failure Report—Fri Sep 18 14:40:20 1992
WINUNZIP had a 'Unknown' fault at WINUNZIP 3:13a4
$tag$WINUNZIP$Unknown$WINUNZIP 3:13a4$pop ds$Fri Sep 18 14:40:20 1992
$param$, Last param error was: Invalid handle passed to KERNEL 1:0276: 0x0000

CPU Registers (regs)
ax=060c bx=e998 cx=060c dx=e998 si=1bc8 di=0111
ip=13a4 sp=eaaa bp=eaac O- D- I+ S+ Z- A- P- C-
cs = 127f 806affc0:153f Code Ex/R
ss = 082f 806eb000:fb9f Data R/W
ds = 082f 806eb000:fb9f Data R/W
es = 082f 806eb000:fb9f Data R/W

CPU 32 bit Registers (32bit)
eax = 0000060c ebx = 0000e998 ecx = 0000060c edx = 0000e998
esi = 00001bc8 edi = 00000111 ebp = 0000eaac esp = 8001ea9a
fs = 0000     0:0000 Null Ptr
gs = 0000     0:0000 Null Ptr
eflag = 00000002
```

System Info (info)
Windows version 3.10
Retail build
Windows Build 3.1.00
Username Frederic E. Davis
Organization Peachpit Press
System Free Space 31412768
Stack base 55320, top 60290, lowest 57900, size 4970
System resources: USER: 90% free, seg 076f GDI: 85% free, seg 05c7
LargestFree 30363648, MaxPagesAvail 7413, MaxPagesLockable 1827
TotalLinear 7900, TotalUnlockedPages 1834, FreePages 1459
TotalPages 2031, FreeLinearSpace 7433, SwapFilePages 6806
Page Size 4096
3 tasks executing.
WinFlags -
 80386 or 80386 SX
 Enhanced mode
 Protect mode

Stack Dump (stack)
Stack Frame 0 is WINUNZIP 3:13a4   ss:bp 082f:eaac
127f:139a 0e   push   cs
127f:139b e8 fef3   call   near 1291
127f:139e 83 c4 06   add   sp, 06
127f:13a1 8d 66 fe   lea   sp, [bp+fe]
(WINUNZIP:3:13a4)
127f:13a4 1f   pop   ds
127f:13a5 5d   pop   bp
127f:13a6 4d   dec   bp
127f:13a7 cb   retf

System Tasks (tasks)
Task DRWATSON, Handle 131f, Flags 0001, Info 26832 06-17-92 3:10
 FileName C:\WIN31\DRWATSON.EXE
Task PROGMAN, Handle 05ff, Flags 0001, Info 113936 06-17-92 3:10
 FileName C:\WIN31\PROGMAN.EXE
Task WINUNZIP, Handle 083f, Flags 0001, Info 80896 08-31-92 15:13
 FileName C:\WIN31\WINUNZIP.EXE

1> I was running the WINUNZIP shareware program

Attempting to continue execution at user request, Fri Sep 18 14:40:22 1992

The technical details in this log entry will enable the technical support staff at Microsoft to decipher the cause of the crash (or so one would hope). In fact, when you call Microsoft's technical support, you may be asked to send in your DRWATSON.LOG file.

However, you can identify a few things yourself by looking at the file. The second line of the entry tells you what Dr. Watson thinks caused the problem—in this case, WINUNZIP.EXE. If Windows caused the crash, you'll see the component that was the culprit listed in this line. For example, if GDI.EXE is listed, this means your Windows graphics kernel crashed. If a DOS application running from within Windows caused the crash, either WINOLDAP.MOD (if you're in standard mode) or WINOA386.MOD (for 386 enhanced mode) is identified.

Further down in the entry, the System Info section identifies you and your version of Windows. The System Tasks section lists what other programs were running—in this case, the culprit-program WINUNZIP.EXE, Dr. Watson, and Program Manager. Note that the path is included, along with the file name. This line appears toward the end of the log entry:

```
1> I was running the WINUNZIP shareware program
```

which is what I typed in the Dr. Watson dialog box. The last line of the entry indicates that I opted to continue running Windows.

Because each entry can run to an even greater length than the one listed above, the DRWATSON.LOG file can grow to gargantuan dimensions. If it grows too large, Dr. Watson may protest by issuing a warning dialog box. You may want to check its file size periodically; if it's getting unwieldy, you can delete it (after backing it up, if you want to save it).

What's on the Windows Installation Disks

The Windows installation disks contain the files that Setup uses to install Windows 3.1 or to upgrade from Windows 3.0 to version 3.1. Whether you purchase a version with the seven 5¼-inch 1.2-megabyte floppy disks or one with the six 3½-inch 1.44-megabyte floppy disks, each disk bears the same volume name, ranging from WIN31DISK1 through WIN31DISK6 or WIN31DISK7, depending on the number of disks in your version. If you need to reconstruct a damaged disk, use these volume names and be sure to copy the corresponding disk identification file (DISK1, DISK2, etc.) described in Table A.1.

For users with older systems, Microsoft also offers Windows in both 720K $3\frac{1}{2}$-inch and 360K $5\frac{1}{4}$-inch disk formats. To obtain one of these special formats, however, you need to first purchase Windows 3.1 and then place a special order with Microsoft.

Most of the files on the installation disks are compressed and can be identified by their file extensions, which always end with the underline character. For example, the SETUP.HLP file is compressed on the disk and therefore named SETUP.HL_. Some of the files on the installation disks are not compressed and can be identified by their complete extensions, such as SETUP.EXE.

Setup decompresses files automatically as it copies them to your system. If you copy any compressed files by hand, you'll need to use the EXPAND.EXE utility described in Chapter 5. Table A.1 indicates the compressed and expanded size of all the files.

Trimming the Windows Installation Size

Windows 3.1 installation consumes from 8 to 9 megabytes of hard disk space, depending on your system configuration and options. In addition, your swap file can easily absorb another 5 to 20 megabytes of disk space, depending on your mode of operation (standard or 386 enhanced), the number of applications you run, and the amount of your free space.

If you're short on hard disk space, you can trim the size of the installation using one of several different strategies. The easiest way is to remove components you don't absolutely need by **using Setup and the Control Panel from within Windows**. Here's the procedure:

1. Run Setup from within Windows and choose the Add/Remove Windows Components command from the Options menu. The resulting dialog box lets you select from the various applets, utilities, games, screen savers, wallpaper, sound files, and readme files that are optional for running Windows. The dialog box interactively reports the amount of space you will save.

2. Open the Fonts icon in the Control Panel. Select the fonts you don't use, make sure an X is placed in the Delete Font File from Disk check box, and click on the Remove button.

3. Open the Drivers icon in the Control Panel. Select any unnecessary device drivers and click on the Remove button. Then use File Manager to remove the related .DRV files from your \SYSTEM directory.

4. Open the Printers icon in the Control Panel. Select any printers you don't need and click on the Remove button. Then use File Manager to remove the related .DRV or other files from your \SYSTEM directory. In addition to .DRV files, some printers also include .DLL, font installer, and help files that can be removed. (See Chapter 7 for details about printer drivers and related files.)

For details about using Setup and the Control Panel, see Chapter 4.

This method lets you easily restore any components at a later time and also prevents you from accidently removing a component that Windows requires to run. Using this method to strip everything nonessential, you can reduce the size of Windows to a tad under 6 megabytes.

Also, be sure to eliminate any leftover temporary files—these waste space on your hard disk. If you quit Windows first, it's safe to remove any files in your \TEMP directory, including files that start with ~WOA or ~GRB, or the WIN386.SWP temporary swap file.

To trim Windows down even further, you'll need to consider **major surgery**. You can cut the following files, which are optional items and cannot be removed by Setup or the Control Panel:

AUTOEXEC.WIN	MSD.INI
BOOTLOG.TXT	RAMDRIVE.SYS
CLIPBRD.EXE	SETUP.HLP
CONFIG.WIN	SETUP.TXT
CONTROL.HLP	SYSEDIT.EXE
MORICONS.DLL	WRITE.EXE
MOUSE.INI	WRITE.HLP
MSD.EXE	

If you're willing to forgo Print Manager, the Task Manager (the utility that pops up when you press Ctrl+Esc), the Help system, and EMM386's memory management services, you can delete these files:

PRINTMAN.EXE	WINHELP.EXE
TASKMAN.EXE	EMM386.EXE

If you don't need to run Windows in standard mode, you can remove these files:

DOSX.EXE	WINOLDAP.MOD
DSWAP.EXE	WSWAP.EXE
KRNL286.EXE	Any files that end with the extension .2GR

If you don't need to run Windows in 386 enhanced mode, you can remove these files:

CGA40WOA.FON	WIN386.EXE
CGA80WOA.FON	WIN386.PS2
EGA40WOA.FON	WINOA386.MOD
EGA80WOA.FON	Any files that end with the extension .3GR or .386
CPWIN386.CPL	
DOSAPP.FON	

If you don't need to run DOS applications from within Windows, you can remove these files:

APPS.INF	MOUSE.SYS
CGA40WOA.FON	MOUSE.COM
CGA80WOA.FON	PIFEDIT.EXE
EGA40WOA.FON	WINOLDAP.MOD
EGA80WOA.FON	WINOA386.MOD
DOSAPP.FON	Any files that end with the extensions .2GR, .3GR, or .PIF
DSWAP.EXE	

To create the smallest Windows configuration possible, **amputate everything except the files necessary for standard mode**. In this way, you can run Windows applications, access both Program Manager and File Manager, and use only 2.5 megabytes of space. To run DOS applications, simply quit Windows.

If you only need to run a single Windows application, you can strip away Program Manager and File Manager as well. Just remove their files—PROG-

MAN.EXE and WINFILE.EXE—and then specify the Windows application as the shell program using the SHELL= statement in the WIN.INI file.

The Windows Files

Table A.1 describes the contents of all the Windows files, along with their disk location, their target directory, and their compressed and decompressed file sizes. File sizes are given in bytes.

TABLE A.1
Contents of Windows Installation Disks

File Name (after expansion)	1.2 MB Disks	1.44 MB Disks	Size on Disk	Expanded Size	Target Directory	Description
256COLOR.BMP	4	3	4312	5078	Windows	256-color wallpaper
386MAX.VXD	2	2	20237	35167	\SYSTEM	386MAX virtual device
4029l730.WPD	6	6	1105	2941	\SYSTEM	PostScript description file for IBM LaserPrinter 4029 equipped with 17 fonts
4029l930.WPD	7	6	1741	5411	\SYSTEM	PostScript description file for IBM LaserPrinter 4029 equipped with 39 fonts
8514.DRV	1	1	50425	92032	\SYSTEM	8514/a display driver
8514FIX.FON	2	2	3646	10976	\SYSTEM	8514/a monospaced system font—1024x768 resolution
8514OEM.FON	2	2	4237	12288	\SYSTEM	8514/a terminal font—1024x768 resolution
8514SYS.FON	2	1	3633	9280	\SYSTEM	8514/a system font—1024x768 resolution
APP850.FON	1	1	16663	36672	\SYSTEM	DOS session font for 386 enhanced mode—International code page 850
APPS.HLP	3	3	11491	15930	Windows	Help file with information about compatibility problems with third-party applications
APPS.INF	6	4	16889	57475	\SYSTEM	Information file containing PIF profiles for many popular DOS applications
ARCADE.BMP	6	4	375	630	Windows	Arcade wallpaper
ARCHES.BMP	4	4	3137	10358	Windows	Arches wallpaper
ARGYLE.BMP	3	3	245	630	Windows	Argyle wallpaper
ARIAL.FOT	6	5	427	1306	\SYSTEM	Font resource file for ARIAL.TTF
ARIAL.TTF	6	5	52532	65692	\SYSTEM	Arial TrueType font file
ARIALB.FON	6	5	10358	22144	\SYSTEM	Arial screen font 8,10 (EGA resolution)

ARIALBD.FOT	6	5	427	1308	\SYSTEM	Font resource file for ARIALBD.TTF
ARIALBD.TTF	6	5	51841	66080	\SYSTEM	Arial Bold TrueType font file
ARIALBI.FOT	6	5	436	1322	\SYSTEM	Font resource file for ARIALBI.TTF
ARIALBI.TTF	6	5	57729	71880	\SYSTEM	Arial Bold Italic TrueType font file
ARIALI.FOT	6	5	429	1312	\SYSTEM	Font resource file for ARIALI.TTF
ARIALI.TTF	6	5	47643	61656	\SYSTEM	Arial Italic TrueType font file
BANINST.386	2	2	992	4861	\SYSTEM	Banyan VINES 4.0 instancing virtual device driver
BLUEMAX.VXD	2	2	20270	35189	\SYSTEM	BlueMAX virtual device driver
CALC.EXE	5	3	27999	43072	Windows	Calculator application file
CALC.HLP	5	3	12989	18076	Windows	Calculator Help file
CALENDAR.EXE	4	3	37995	59824	Windows	Calendar application file
CALENDAR.HLP	5	3	13794	20656	Windows	Calendar Help file
CANON10E.DRV	7	6	2652	6000	\SYSTEM	Canon Bubble-Jet BJ-10e printer driver
CANON130.DRV	7	6	2931	7536	\SYSTEM	Canon Bubble-Jet BJ-130e printer driver
CANON330.DRV	7	6	5694	20064	\SYSTEM	Canon Bubble-Jet BJ-300/330 printer driver
CANYON.MID	5	3	17632	33883	Windows	Canyon MIDI music file
CAN_ADF.EXE	7	6	36591	69232	\SYSTEM	Soft Font installer utility for LBPIII.DRV and LBPII.DRV
CARDFILE.EXE	4	3	48673	93184	Windows	Cardfile application file
CARDFILE.HLP	4	4	18523	24810	Windows	Cardfile Help file
CARS.BMP	3	4	332	630	Windows	Cars wallpaper
CASTLE.BMP	6	4	544	778	Windows	Castle wallpaper
CGA.2GR	2	2	1768	2106	\SYSTEM	CGA display grabber for standard mode
CGA40850.FON	2	2	3729	6352	\SYSTEM	DOS session font for 386 enhanced mode—International code page 850, 40-column CGA resolution
CGA40WOA.FON	2	2	3563	6336	\SYSTEM	DOS session font for 386 enhanced mode—USA code page 437, 40-column CGA resolution

File Name (after expansion)	1.2 MB Disks	1.44 MB Disks	Size on Disk	Expanded Size	Target Directory	Description
CGA80850.FON	2	2	3049	4320	\SYSTEM	DOS session font for 386 enhanced mode—International code page 850, 80-column CGA resolution
CGA80WOA.FON	2	2	3039	4304	\SYSTEM	DOS session font for 386 enhanced mode—USA code page 437, 80-column CGA resolution
CGALOGO.LGO	3	2	902	896	\SYSTEM	Startup logo code—CGA resolution
CGALOGO.RLE	3	2	3815	11878	\SYSTEM	Startup logo artwork, run-length encoded bitmap—CGA resolution
CHARMAP.EXE	3	3	12015	22016	Windows	Character Map application file
CHARMAP.HLP	4	4	4689	10797	Windows	Character Map Help file
CHIMES.WAV	4	3	10591	15920	Windows	Chimes sound
CHITZ.BMP						
CHORD.WAV	3	3	11235	24982	Windows	Chord sound
CIT24US.DRV	7	6	8493	30912	\SYSTEM	Citizen 24-pin printer driver
CIT9US.DRV	7	6	6979	24800	\SYSTEM	Citizen 9-pin printer driver
CITOH.DRV	7	6	2422	4720	\SYSTEM	C-Itoh 8510 or AT&T 470/475 printer driver
CLIPBRD.EXE	4	5	11384	18512	Windows	Clipboard Viewer application file
CLIPBRD.HLP	6	4	7668	13071	Windows	Clipboard Viewer Help file
CLOCK.EXE	4	3	10140	16416	Windows	Windows Clock application file
COMM.DRV	2	1	7157	9280	\SYSTEM	Communications driver
COMMDLG.DLL	4	4	50924	89232	\SYSTEM	Common Dialogs Dynamic Link Library (used by applications to provide ready-made dialog boxes)
CONTROL.EXE	4	5	10270	15872	Windows	Control Panel application file

CONTROL.HLP	3	2	95210	121672	Windows	Control Panel Help file
CONTROL.INF	6	5	20993	20993*	\SYSTEM	Information file used by the Control Panel and for printer installation (*not compressed)
CONTROL.SRC	6	5	1278	3609	Not copied	Source file used to create the CONTROL.INI file
COUR.FOT	6	5	428	1318	\SYSTEM	Font resource file for COUR.TTF
COUR.TTF	6	5	53733	72356	\SYSTEM	Courier New TrueType font file
COURB.FON	6	5	8118	21856	\SYSTEM	Courier screen font 10,12,15 (EGA resolution)
COURBD.FOT	6	5	430	1320	\SYSTEM	Font resource file for COURBD.TTF
COURBD.TTF	6	5	56871	78564	\SYSTEM	Courier New Bold TrueType font file
COURBI.FOT	6	6	437	1334	\SYSTEM	Font resource file for COURBI.TTF
COURBI.TTF	6	5	64330	84436	\SYSTEM	Courier New Bold Italic TrueType font file
COURE.FON	6	5	8612	23408	\SYSTEM	Courier screen font 10,12,15 (VGA resolution)
COURF.FON	6	5	11021	31712	\SYSTEM	Courier screen font 10,12,15 (8514/a resolution)
COURI.FOT	6	5	435	1324	\SYSTEM	Font resource file for COURI.TTF
COURI.TTF	6	5	60757	80588	\SYSTEM	Courier New Italic TrueType font file
CPWIN386.CPL	1	1	48841	104816	\SYSTEM	Control Panel extension for 386 enhanced mode icon
DDEML.DLL	5	4	22366	36864	\SYSTEM	DDE Management dynamic link library
DEC1150.WPD	7	6	1875	6006	\SYSTEM	PostScript description file for Digital DEClaser 1150
DEC2150.WPD	7	6	1835	5900	\SYSTEM	PostScript description file for Digital DEClaser 2150
DEC2250.WPD	7	6	1972	6434	\SYSTEM	PostScript description file for Digital DEClaser 2250
DEC3250.WPD	7	6	2012	6580	\SYSTEM	PostScript description file for Digital DEClaser 3250
DECCOLOR.WPD	7	6	1308	4271	\SYSTEM	PostScript description file for Digital ColorMate PS
DECLPS20.WPD	7	6	1533	4944	\SYSTEM	PostScript description file for Digital LPS Print Server
DECNB.386	2	2	4860	9375	\SYSTEM	DEC Pathworks virtual NetBios device
DECNET.386	2	2	5817	14058	\SYSTEM	DEC Pathworks virtual network device
DICONIX.DRV	7	6	2201	4256	\SYSTEM	Kodak Diconix printer driver

File Name (after expansion)	1.2 MB Disks	1.44 MB Disks	Size on Disk	Expanded Size	Target Directory	Description
DING.WAV	5	5	6011	11598	Windows	Ding sound
DISK1	1	1	8*		Not copied	A reference file used by Setup to determine the disk's name; the file contains the text string "DISK1" (*not compressed)
DISK2	2	2	8*		Not copied	A reference file used by Setup to determine the disk's name; the file contains the text string "DISK2" (*not compressed)
DISK3	3	3	8*		Not copied	A reference file used by Setup to determine the disk's name; the file contains the text string "DISK3" (*not compressed)
DISK4	4	4	8*		Not copied	A reference file used by Setup to determine the disk's name; the file contains the text string "DISK4" (*not compressed)
DISK5	5	5	8*		Not copied	A reference file used by Setup to determine the disk's name; the file contains the text string "DISK5" (*not compressed)
DISK6	6	6	8*		Not copied	A reference file used by Setup to determine the disk's name; the file contains the text string "DISK6" (*not compressed)
DISK7	7	7	8*		Not copied	A reference file used by Setup to determine the disk's name; the file contains the text string "DISK7" (*not compressed)
DM309.DRV	7	6	3225	6688	\SYSTEM	Olivetti DM 309 printer driver
DMCOLOR.DLL	7	6	14744	18480	\SYSTEM	Color printing Dynamic Link Library; used by the universal printer driver
DOSAPP.FON	3	2	16721	36656	\SYSTEM	DOS session font for 386 enhanced mode—USA code page 437
DOSX.EXE	2	2	27426	32682	\SYSTEM	MS-DOS extender used to run Windows in standard mode
DRIVERS.CPL	5	4	21385	41440	\SYSTEM	Control Panel extension for the Drivers icon

DRWATSON.EXE	4	4	18559	26864	Windows	Dr. Watson diagnostic utility program
DSWAP.EXE	5	4	18810	27474	\SYSTEM	DOS task-switcher for Windows standard mode
EGA.3GR	1	1	9460	14336	\SYSTEM	EGA display grabber for 386 enhanced mode
EGA.DRV	2	1	43319	71552	\SYSTEM	EGA display driver
EGA.SYS	2	2	4190	5039	\SYSTEM	DOS-level EGA driver
EGA40850.FON	2	2	4058	8384	\SYSTEM	DOS session font for 386 enhanced mode—International code page 850, 40-column EGA resolution
EGA40WOA.FON	2	2	3933	8368	\SYSTEM	DOS session font for 386 enhanced mode—USA code page 437, 40-column EGA resolution
EGA80850.FON	2	2	3243	5328	\SYSTEM	DOS session font for 386 enhanced mode—International code page 850, 80-column EGA resolution
EGA80WOA.FON	2	2	3259	5312	\SYSTEM	DOS session font for 386 enhanced mode—USA code page 437, 80-column EGA resolution
EGACOLOR.2GR	2	1	2729	3260	\SYSTEM	EGA color display grabber for standard mode
EGAFIX.FON	1	1	2534	4240	\SYSTEM	EGA monospaced system font—640x350 or AT&T 640x400 resolution
EGAHIBW.DRV	2	2	26886	45264	\SYSTEM	EGA black-and-white display driver
EGALOGO.LGO	2	1	1073	1136	\SYSTEM	Startup logo code—EGA resolution, color
EGALOGO.RLE	2	1	5125	17082	\SYSTEM	Startup logo artwork, run-length-encoded bitmap—EGA resolution, color
EGAMONO.2GR	2	2	2563	3030	\SYSTEM	EGA monochrome display grabber for standard mode
EGAMONO.DRV	2	2	26941	45328	\SYSTEM	EGA monochrome display driver
EGAMONO.LGO	2	2	1073	1104	\SYSTEM	Startup logo code—EGA resolution, monochrome
EGAMONO.RLE	3	2	4619	15966	\SYSTEM	Startup logo artwork, run-length-encoded bitmap—EGA resolution, monochrome
EGAOEM.FON	2	1	3027	4176	\SYSTEM	EGA terminal font—(640x350) or AT&T (640x400) resolution

TABLE A.1 (cont.)
Contents of Windows Installation Disks

File Name (after expansion)	1.2 MB Disks	1.44 MB Disks	Size on Disk	Expanded Size	Target Directory	Description
EGASYS.FON	2	1	2879	5264	\SYSTEM	EGA system font—(640x350) or AT&T (640x400) resolution
EGYPT.BMP	5	3	225	630	Windows	Egypt wallpaper
EMM386.EXE	4	4	52996	110174	\SYSTEM	EMM386 expanded memory manager
EPL75523.WPD	7	6	1554	4714	\SYSTEM	PostScript description file for Epson EPL-7500
EPSON24.DRV	7	6	5158	14960	\SYSTEM	Epson 24-pin printer driver
EPSON9.DRV	7	6	6872	22192	\SYSTEM	Epson 9-pin printer driver
ESCP2.DRV	7	6	4488	7904	\SYSTEM	Epson ESCP2 dot matrix printer driver
EXECJET.DRV	7	6	5979	20240	\SYSTEM	IBM ExecJet printer driver
EXPAND.EXE	3	3	15285	15285*	Windows	DOS file expansion utility (*not compressed)
FINSTALL.DLL	7	6	110030	200368	\SYSTEM	Soft Font installer Dynamic Link Library for HPPCL5/A printer driver
FINSTALL.HLP	7	6	15386	19202	\SYSTEM	Soft Font installer Help file for HPPCL5/A printer driver
FLOCK.BMP	3	3	468	1630	Windows	Flock wallpaper
FUJI24.DRV	7	6	5907	17088	\SYSTEM	Fujitsu 24-pin printer driver
FUJI9.DRV	7	6	3478	8576	\SYSTEM	Fujitsu 9-pin printer driver
GDI.EXE	1	1	167674	220480	\SYSTEM	Graphics Device Interface core component; the Windows graphics engine that draws all images and data on the screen and often on other output devices, such as printers
GENDRV.DLL	7	6	49648	99328	\SYSTEM	Generic printer driver Dynamic Link Library
GLOSSARY.HLP	3	3	37606	46570	Windows	Windows Help glossary file
HERC.3GR	2	2	5988	9216	\SYSTEM	Hercules monochrome display grabber for 386 enhanced mode

HERC850.FON	2	2	3524	8880	\SYSTEM	DOS session font for 386 enhanced mode—International code page 850, Hercules monochrome resolution
HERCLOGO.LGO	2	2	1019	1008	\SYSTEM	Startup logo code—Hercules monochrome
HERCLOGO.RLE	2	1	4690	15808	\SYSTEM	Startup logo artwork, run-length-encoded bitmap—Hercules monochrome format
HERCULES.2GR	2	1	1809	2155	\SYSTEM	Hercules monochrome display grabber for standard mode
HERCULES.DRV	2	3	27462	47296	\SYSTEM	Hercules display driver
HERCWOA.FON	2	2	3509	8864	\SYSTEM	DOS session font for 386 enhanced mode—USA code page 437
HERMES_1.WPD	6	6	781	1937	\SYSTEM	PostScript description file for Hermes H 606 PS equipped with 13 fonts
HERMES_2.WPD	6	6	1424	4411	\SYSTEM	Windows PostScript description file for Hermes H 606 PS equipped with 35 fonts
HIMEM.SYS	4	5	9384	13824	Windows	HIMEM extended memory manager
HONEY.BMP	4	4	345	854	Windows	Honey wallpaper
HPDSKJET.DRV	7	6	23308	61856	\SYSTEM	HP DeskJet Series printer driver
HPEBIOS.386	3	1	2108	9348	\SYSTEM	386 enhanced mode EBIOS virtual device for Hewlett-Packard computers
HPELI523.WPD	6	6	1592	4899	\SYSTEM	PostScript description file for HP LaserJet IIISi with PostScript
HPIID522.WPD	6	6	1556	4799	\SYSTEM	PostScript description file for HP LaserJet IID with PostScript
HPIII522.WPD	6	6	1540	4725	\SYSTEM	PostScript description file for HP LaserJet III with PostScript
HPIIP522.WPD	6	6	1547	4762	\SYSTEM	PostScript description file for HP LaserJet IIP with PostScript
HPMOUSE.DRV	2	2	2540	4896	\SYSTEM	HP HIL mouse driver
HPPCL.DRV	7	6	54150	153120	\SYSTEM	HP LaserJet II Series printer driver
HPPCL5A.DRV	7	6	185016	428736	\SYSTEM	HP LaserJet III Series printer driver
HPPCL5A.HLP	7	6	17386	21805	\SYSTEM	Help file for HP LaserJet III Series printer driver
HPPCL5OP.HLP	7	6	8013	13195	\SYSTEM	Help file for HP LaserJet III Series printer driver

Contents of Windows Installation Disks

File Name (after expansion)	1.2 MB Disks	1.44 MB Disks	Size on Disk	Expanded Size	Target Directory	Description
HPPLOT.DRV	6	6	34950	66680	\SYSTEM	HP Plotter printer driver
HPSYSTEM.DRV	2	2	2108	2832	\SYSTEM	Device driver for HP Vectra computers
HP_3D522.WPD	6	6	1642	4988	\SYSTEM	PostScript description file for HP LaserJet IIID with PostScript
HP_3P522.WPD	7	6	1566	4784	\SYSTEM	PostScript description file for HP LaserJet IIIP with PostScript
IBM17521.WPD	6	6	1034	2695	\SYSTEM	PostScript description file for IBM 4019 equipped with 17 fonts
IBM39521.WPD	7	6	1675	5165	\SYSTEM	Windows PostScript description file for IBM 4019 equipped with 39 fonts
IBM4019.DRV	7	6	30069	68368	\SYSTEM	IBM Laser Printer 4019 printer driver
IBM5204.DRV	7	6	4797	16304	\SYSTEM	IBM Quickwriter 5204 printer driver
IBMCOLOR.DRV	7	6	12699	21424	\SYSTEM	IBM Color printer driver
IPXODI.COM	3	2	13552	20903	\SYSTEM	Novell NetWare workstation communications driver (ODI model)
KBDBE.DLL	2	2	2049	2449	\SYSTEM	Belgian keyboard layout DLL
KBDCA.DLL	2	2	2127	2673	\SYSTEM	French-Canadian keyboard layout DLL
KBDDA.DLL	2	2	2032	2364	\SYSTEM	Danish keyboard layout DLL
KBDDV.DLL	3	2	1000	1332	\SYSTEM	US-Dvorak keyboard layout DLL
KBDFC.DLL	2	2	2272	2769	\SYSTEM	Canadian multilingual keyboard layout DLL
KBDFI.DLL	2	2	2079	2404	\SYSTEM	Finnish keyboard layout DLL
KBDFR.DLL	2	2	1928	2353	\SYSTEM	French keyboard layout DLL

KBDGR.DLL	2		1976	2481	\SYSTEM	German keyboard layout DLL
KBDHP.DRV	1		6835	8480	\SYSTEM	Keyboard driver for Hewlett-Packard computers
KBDIC.DLL	2		1412	1724	\SYSTEM	Icelandic keyboard layout DLL
KBDIT.DLL	2		1806	2146	\SYSTEM	Italian keyboard layout DLL
KBDLA.DLL	2		2091	2465	\SYSTEM	Latin-American keyboard layout DLL
KBDMOUSE.DRV	3		1078	1408	\SYSTEM	Olivetti/AT&T keyboard mouse driver
KBDNE.DLL	2		2029	2358	\SYSTEM	Dutch keyboard layout DLL
KBDNO.DLL	2		2059	2402	\SYSTEM	Norwegian keyboard layout DLL
KBDPO.DLL	2		1982	2352	\SYSTEM	Portuguese keyboard layout DLL
KBDSF.DLL	2		2002	2489	\SYSTEM	Swiss-French keyboard layout DLL
KBDSG.DLL	2		1374	1653	\SYSTEM	Swiss-German keyboard layout DLL
KBDSP.DLL	3		2074	2401	\SYSTEM	Spanish keyboard layout DLL
KBDSW.DLL	2		2070	2374	\SYSTEM	Swedish keyboard layout DLL
KBDUK.DLL	2		1153	1428	\SYSTEM	British keyboard layout DLL
KBDUS.DLL	3		996	1300	\SYSTEM	US keyboard layout DLL
KBDUSX.DLL	2		1329	1641	\SYSTEM	US-International keyboard layout DLL
KEYBOARD.DRV	2		6115	7568	\SYSTEM	Keyboard driver
KRNL286.EXE	2		55774	71682	\SYSTEM	Standard mode kernal program; controls the allocation of system resources, memory management, and loading of applications for standard mode operation
KRNL386.EXE	2		59399	77375	\SYSTEM	386 enhanced mode kernal program; controls the allocation of system resources, memory management, and loading of applications for 386 enhanced mode operation
L2002308&.WPD	7	6	749	1863	\SYSTEM	PostScript description file for Linotronic 200/230 typesetter
L330_528&.WPD	7	6	859	2335	\SYSTEM	Windows PostScript description file for Linotronic 330 typesetter

File Name (after expansion)	1.2 MB Disks	1.44 MB Disks	Size on Disk	Expanded Size	Target Directory	Description
L530_528.WPD	7	6	858	2335	\SYSTEM	Windows PostScript description file for Linotronic 530 typesetter
L630_528.WPD	7	6	859	2335	\SYSTEM	Windows PostScript description file for Linotronic 630 typesetter
LANGDUT.DLL	2	2	1425	3072	\SYSTEM	Dutch language driver
LANGENG.DLL	2	2	1430	3072	\SYSTEM	General International language driver
LANGFRN.DLL	3	2	1457	3072	\SYSTEM	French language driver
LANGGER.DLL	2	2	1425	3072	\SYSTEM	German language driver
LANGSCA.DLL	2	2	1429	3072	\SYSTEM	Finnish, Icelandic, Norwegian, and Swedish language driver
LANGSPA.DLL	2	2	1494	3072	\SYSTEM	Spanish language driver
LANMAN.DRV	2	2	26011	63488	\SYSTEM	Microsoft LAN Manager 2.0 network driver
LANMAN.HLP	3	2	14000	31724	\SYSTEM	Help file for Microsoft LAN Manager 2.0 network driver
LANMAN10.386	2	2	1550	8786	\SYSTEM	Microsoft LAN Manager 1.x virtual device
LBPII.DRV	7	6	26846	65968	\SYSTEM	Canon LBP-8 II printer driver
LBPIII.DRV	7	6	36482	89504	\SYSTEM	Canon LBPIII printer driver
LEAVES.BMP	6	4	4616	15118	Windows	Leaves wallpaper LMOUSE.COM
LMOUSE.DRV	2	2	7898	12928	\SYSTEM	Logitech mouse driver
LSL.COM	2	2	6278	7662	\SYSTEM	Novell NetWare workstation link support layer (ODI model)
LVMD.386	2	2	4018	9688	\SYSTEM	Logitech virtual mouse device

LZEXPAND.DLL	1	2	6551	9936	\SYSTEM	File expansion Dynamic Link Library; used by the Control Panel to install drivers and fonts from compressed files on installation disks; provides a Windows equivalent to EXPAND.EXE for programs (and clever programmers!) that know how to use this DLL
MAIN.CPL	5	4	89396	148560	\SYSTEM	Main Control Panel extension
MARBLE.BMP	4	4	7666	27646	Windows	Marble wallpaper
MCICDA.DRV	5	4	8368	13824	\SYSTEM	MCI driver for playing audio compact discs from a CD-ROM drive
MCISEQ.DRV	5	4	16359	25264	\SYSTEM	MCI driver for playing files on MIDI devices
MCIWAVE.DRV	6	4	17133	28160	\SYSTEM	MCI driver for playing waveform audio
MIDIMAP.CFG	6	4	7333	34522	\SYSTEM	Information file for the MIDI Mapper Control Panel extension
MIDIMAP.DRV	4	4	34150	52784	\SYSTEM	Control Panel extension for the MIDI Mapper icon
MMSOUND.DRV	2	1	2829	3440	\SYSTEM	Multimedia sound driver
MMSYSTEM.DLL	5	4	35478	61648	\SYSTEM	Multimedia system Dynamic Link Library
MMTASK.TSK	6	5	777	1104	\SYSTEM	Multimedia background task application file
MONOUMB2.386	4	4	1017	46161	\SYSTEM	Upper memory block utility for 386 enhanced mode
MORICONS.DLL	4	3	40447	118864	\SYSTEM	A Dynamic Link Library filled with various icons for DOS applications
MOUSE.COM	4	4	31328	56408	\SYSTEM	DOS-level device driver for Microsoft Mouse
MOUSE.DRV	2	2	8000	10672	\SYSTEM	Microsoft Mouse driver
MOUSE.SYS	5	4	30733	55160	Windows	DOS-level device driver for Microsoft Mouse
MOUSEHP.COM	4	4	20729	34061	Windows	DOS-level device driver for HP HIL mouse
MOUSEHP.SYS	5	4	20642	33909	Windows	DOS-level device driver for HP HIL mouse
MPLAYER.EXE	5	3	21454	33312	Windows	Media Player application file
MPLAYER.HLP	3	3	7872	12825	Windows	Media Player Help file

TABLE A.1 (cont.)
Contents of Windows Installation Disks

File Name (after expansion)	1.2 MB Disks	1.44 MB Disks	Size on Disk	Expanded Size	Target Directory	Description
MPU401.DRV	4	4	5265	7056	\SYSTEM	MIDI device driver for MPU401-compatible MIDI interface cards
MSADLIB.DRV	3	3	10495	22064	\SYSTEM	MIDI device driver for Adlib-compatible MIDI cards
MSC3BC2.DRV	3	2	2823	4832	\SYSTEM	Device driver for 3-button Mouse Systems mice connected to COM2
MSCMOUSE.DRV	2	2	2901	4960	\SYSTEM	Mouse Systems Serial or Bus mouse driver
MSCVMD.386	2	1	3275	9327	\SYSTEM	Mouse Systems virtual mouse device
MSD.EXE	5	4	155538	155538*	Windows	Microsoft Diagnostics utility (*not compressed)
MSD.INI	6	5	350	620	Windows	Microsoft Diagnostics utility initialization file
MSNET.DRV	2	1	4619	7072	\SYSTEM	Generic network driver
MT_TI101.WPD	7	6	1392	4383	\SYSTEM	PostScript description file for Microtek TrueLaser
N209052.WPD	7	6	1465	4444	\SYSTEM	PostScript description file for NEC Silentwriter2090
N2290520.WPD	7	6	1373	4328	\SYSTEM	PostScript description file for NEC Silentwriter2290
N2990523.WPD	7	6	1499	4544	\SYSTEM	PostScript description file for NEC Silentwriter2990
N890X505.WPD	7	6	1415	4462	\SYSTEM	PostScript description file for NEC Silentwriter LC890XL
N890_470.WPD	7	6	1414	4462	\SYSTEM	PostScript description file for NEC Silentwriter LC890
NCM40519.WPD	7	6	687	2069	\SYSTEM	PostScript description file for NEC Colormate PS/40
NCM80519.WPD	7	6	1248	4103	\SYSTEM	PostScript description file for NEC Colormate PS/80
NEC24PIN.DRV	6	6	10791	29552	\SYSTEM	NEC 24-pin printer driver
NETAPI20.DLL	2	2	60374	113520	\SYSTEM	Microsoft LAN Manager API Dynamic Link Library
NETWARE.DRV	2	2	59787	125712	\SYSTEM	Novell NetWare network driver
NETWARE.HLP	3	2	18204	34348	\SYSTEM	Help file for Novell NetWare network driver

NETWORKS.WRI	3	3	26489	62336	Windows	Readme file with technical information about networks
NETX.COM	3	2	38642	52459	\SYSTEM	Novell NetWare workstation shell
NOMOUSE.DRV	2	2	315	416	\SYSTEM	Device driver for No Mouse
NOTEPAD.EXE	3	3	20018	32736	Windows	Notepad application file
NOTEPAD.HLP	4	4	8334	13894	Windows	Notepad Help file
NWPOPUP.EXE	3	2	1577	2992	\SYSTEM	Novell NetWare message popup utility
O5241503.WPD	7	6	1496	4521	\SYSTEM	PostScript description file for OceColor G5241 PS
O5242503.WPD	7	6	1476	4447	\SYSTEM	PostScript description file for OceColor G5242 PS
OKI24.DRV	7	6	5720	20784	\SYSTEM	Okidata 24-pin printer driver
OKI9.DRV	7	6	4129	11072	\SYSTEM	Okidata 9-pin printer driver
OKI9IBM.DRV	7	6	3769	10736	\SYSTEM	Okidata 9-Pin IBM Model printer driver
OL840518.WPD	7	6	1575	4759	\SYSTEM	PostScript description file for Oki OL840/PS
OLECLI.DLL	4	5	45422	83456	\SYSTEM	Dynamic Link Library for OLE client applications
OLESVR.DLL	5	4	14552	24064	\SYSTEM	Dynamic Link Library for OLE server applications
OLIBW.DRV	2	2	27824	47744	\SYSTEM	Olivetti/AT&T PVC display driver
OLIGRAB.2GR	2	1	2618	3714	\SYSTEM	Olivetti/AT&T PVC display grabber for standard mode
OLIVETI1.WPD	7	6	784	1937	\SYSTEM	PostScript description file for Olivetti PG 306 PS equipped with 13 fonts
OLIVETI2.WPD	7	6	1428	4411	\SYSTEM	PostScript description file for Olivetti PG 306 PS equipped with 35 fonts
P4455514.WPD	7	6	1619	5134	\SYSTEM	PostScript description file for Panasonic KX-P4455
PACKAGER.EXE	4	3	40667	76480	Windows	Packager application file
PACKAGER.HLP	3	3	16647	21156	Windows	Packager Help file
PAINTJET.DRV	7	6	2903	5520	\SYSTEM	HP PaintJet printer driver
PANSON24.DRV	7	6	4405	14592	\SYSTEM	Panasonic 24-pin printer driver
PANSON9.DRV	7	6	4789	16352	\SYSTEM	Panasonic 9-pin printer driver

TABLE A.1 (cont.)
Contents of Windows Installation Disks

File Name (after expansion)	1.2 MB Disks	1.44 MB Disks	Size on Disk	Expanded Size	Target Directory	Description
PBRUSH.DLL	4	3	4904	6766	\SYSTEM	Paintbrush Dynamic Link Library
PBRUSH.EXE	5	3	102781	183168	Windows	Paintbrush application file
PBRUSH.HLP	4	3	31527	40269	Windows	Paintbrush Help file
PCSA.DRV	2	2	6177	9168	\SYSTEM	DEC Pathworks network driver
PG306.DRV	7	6	18336	43392	\SYSTEM	PG 306 printer driver
PHIIPX.WPD	7	6	1219	3984	\SYSTEM	PostScript description file for Phaser II PX
PIFEDIT.EXE	5	5	25970	55168	Windows	PIF Editor application file
PIFEDIT.HLP	5	3	27098	33270	Windows	PIF Editor Help file
PLASMA.3GR	2	2	6405	9728	\SYSTEM	Compaq Portable plasma display grabber for 386 enhanced mode
PLASMA.DRV	2	2	27311	47216	\SYSTEM	Compaq Portable plasma display driver
PMSPL20.DLL	2	1	22506	43328	\SYSTEM	Microsoft LAN Manager Printer API Dynamic Link Library
POWER.DRV	3	2	9461	14736	\SYSTEM	Advanced Power Management device driver
POWER.HLP	2	2	7763	13100	\SYSTEM	Help file for Advanced Power Management Power device driver
PRINTERS.WRI	3	3	15312	41984	Windows	Readme file with technical information about printers
PRINTMAN.EXE	4	4	27709	43248	Windows	Print Manager application file
PRINTMAN.HLP	4	3	32765	40879	Windows	Print Manager Help file
PROGMAN.EXE	4	4	56919	115312	Windows	Program Manager application file
PROGMAN.HLP	5	5	23516	30911	Windows	Program Manager Help file
PROPRINT.DRV	7	6	3576	8288	\SYSTEM	IBM Proprinter series printer driver

PROPRN24.DRV	7	6	3539	8032	\SYSTEM	IBM Proprinter series 24-pin printer driver
PRTUPD.INF	6	6	15855	15855*	Not copied	Information file for printer driver updates; used only if upgrading to Windows 3.1 (*not compressed)
PS1.DRV	7	6	3768	11872	\SYSTEM	IBM PS/1 printer driver
PSCRIPT.DRV	7	6	135968	311760	\SYSTEM	Generic Postscript printer driver
PSCRIPT.HLP	7	6	32727	43793	\SYSTEM	Help file for generic Postscript printer driver
Q2200510.WPD	7	6	1621	5182	\SYSTEM	PostScript description file for QMS-PS 2200
Q820_517.WPD	7	6	1520	4942	\SYSTEM	PostScript description file for QMS-PS 820
QWIII.DRV	7	6	4709	14832	\SYSTEM	IBM QuietWriter III printer driver
RAMDRIVE.SYS	5	4	3765	5873	Windows	RAMDrive RAM disk utility
README.WRI	3	3	32717	92928	Windows	The main Windows Readme file
RECORDER.DLL	3	3	7779	10414	\SYSTEM	Recorder Dynamic Link Library
RECORDER.EXE	3	3	24091	39152	Windows	Recorder application file
RECORDER.HLP	3	4	12440	18200	Windows	Recorder Help file
REDBRICK.BMP	3	4	459	630	Windows	Redbrick wallpaper
REGEDIT.EXE	3	4	20050	32336	Windows	Registration Editor application file
REGEDIT.HLP	6	4	16339	22681	Windows	Registration Editor Help file
REGEDITV.HLP	5	5	10677	15731	Windows	Registration Editor Advanced-mode Help file
RIVETS.BMP	4	4	159	630	Windows	Rivets wallpaper
ROMAN.FON	6	5	6356	13312	\SYSTEM	Roman screen font (all resolutions)
SCRIPT.FON	6	5	5502	12288	\SYSTEM	Script screen font (all resolutions)
SCRNSAVE.SCR	4	3	2626	5328	Windows	Default screen saver
SEIKO_04.WPD	7	6	1385	4612	\SYSTEM	PostScript description file for Seiko ColorPoint PS Model 04
SEIKO_14.WPD	7	6	1472	4789	\SYSTEM	PostScript description file for Seiko ColorPoint PS Model 14
SERIFB.FON	6	5	18777	45536	\SYSTEM	MS Serif screen font 8,10,12,14,18,24 (EGA resolution)
SERIFE.FON	6	5	21454	57936	\SYSTEM	MS Serif screen font 8,10,12,14,18,24 (VGA resolution)

TABLE A.1 (cont.)
Contents of Windows Installation Disks

File Name (after expansion)	1.2 MB Disks	1.44 MB Disks	Size on Disk	Expanded Size	Target Directory	Description
SERIFF.FON	5	5	27241	81728	\SYSTEM	MS Serif screen font 8,10,12,14,18,24 (8514/a resolution)
SETUP.EXE	1	1	422080	422080*	Windows	Windows Setup application file (*not compressed)
SETUP.HLP	1	1	33683	41453	Windows	Windows Setup Help file
SETUP.INF	1	1	59167	59167*	\SYSTEM	Windows Setup information file (*not compressed)
SETUP.INI	3	3	92	92*	Not copied	Initialization file for Setup (*not compressed)
SETUP.REG	6	5	1364	3508	\SYSTEM	Registration Database template file
SETUP.SHH	1	1	6525	6525*	Network directory	Automated Setup template file (*not compressed)
SETUP.TXT	1	1	41724	41724*	Windows	Readme file with information about installing Windows (*not compressed)
SF4019.EXE	7	6	33831	58800	\SYSTEM	Soft Font installer utility for IBM Laser Printer 4019
SFINST.EXE	7	6	35394	67360	\SYSTEM	Soft Font installer utiltiy for PG 306 Printer
SHELL.DLL	5	4	25821	41600	\SYSTEM	Windows Shell Dynamic Link Library
SL.DLL	2	2	9547	15600	\SYSTEM	Advanced Power Management SL DLL
SL.HLP	2	2	9094	15841	\SYSTEM	Help file for Advanced Power Management SL DLL
SMALLB.FON	6	5	10928	22016	\SYSTEM	Small screen font (EGA resolution)
SMALLE.FON	6	5	12501	26112	\SYSTEM	Small screen font (VGA resolution)
SMALLF.FON	6	5	10489	21504	\SYSTEM	Small screen font (8514/a resolution)
SMARTDRV.EXE	5	4	17324	43609	Windows	SMARTDrive disk caching utility
SND.CPL	6	4	4986	8192	\SYSTEM	Control Panel extension for Sound icon
SNDBLST.DRV	3	3	10122	13808	\SYSTEM	Device driver for SoundBlaster cards with version 1.5 DSP

SNDBLST2.DRV	3	3	10445	14464	\SYSTEM	Device driver for SoundBlaster cards with version 2.0 DSP
SOL.EXE	4	3	62451	180688	Windows	Solitare game application file
SOL.HLP	5	3	8208	13753	Windows	Solitare game Help file
SOUNDREC.EXE	4	3	31764	51241	Windows	Sound Recorder application file
SOUNDREC.HLP	3	3	10058	17730	Windows	Sound Recorder Help file
SQUARES.BMP	6	4	163	630	Windows	Squares wallpaper
SSERIFB.FON	6	5	18968	50608	\SYSTEM	MS Sans Serif screen font 8,10,12,14,18,24 (EGA resolution)
SSERIFE.FON	5	5	21643	64544	\SYSTEM	MS Sans Serif screen font 8,10,12,14,18,24 (VGA resolution)
SSERIFF.FON	5	5	27627	89680	\SYSTEM	MS San Serif screen font 8,10,12,14,18,24 (8514/a resolution)
SSFLYWIN.SCR	3	3	9705	16160	Windows	Flying Windows screen saver
SSMARQUE.SCR	4	3	9635	16896	Windows	Marquee screen saver
SSMYST.SCR	4	3	11282	19456	Windows	Mystify screen saver
SSSTARS.SCR	4	4	9444	17536	Windows	Stars screen saver
SUPERVGA.DRV	2	2	44303	73504	\SYSTEM	Super VGA display driver—800x600 resolution, 16 colors
SYMBOL.FOT	6	6	428	1308	\SYSTEM	Font resource file for SYMBOL.TTF
SYMBOL.TTF	6	6	50450	64516	\SYSTEM	Symbol TrueType font file
SYMBOLB.FON	6	5	19890	48352	\SYSTEM	Symbol screen font 8,10,12,14,18,24 (EGA resolution)
SYMBOLE.FON	6	5	21296	56336	\SYSTEM	Symbol screen font 8,10,12,14,18,24 (VGA resolution)
SYMBOLF.FON	3	5	27198	80912	\SYSTEM	Symbol screen font 8,10,12,14,18,24 (8514/a resolution)
SYSEDIT.EXE	5	5	10761	18896	\SYSTEM	SysEdit application file
SYSINI.WRI	3	3	16616	52864	Windows	Readme file with technical details about the SYSTEM.INI file
SYSTEM.DRV	2	1	1780	2304	\SYSTEM	System driver; manages the system timer, and system disks, and provides access to OEM system hooks
SYSTEM.SRC	2	1	642	1009	Not copied	Source file used by Setup to create the SYSTEM.INI file
TADA.WAV	4	3	23658	27804	Windows	TADA sound file
TARTAN.BMP	4	4	4498	32886	Windows	Tartan wallpaper

TABLE A.1 *(cont.)*
Contents of Windows Installation Disks

File Name (after expansion)	1.2 MB Disks	1.44 MB Disks	Size on Disk	Expanded Size	Target Directory	Description
TASKMAN.EXE	6	5	2230	3744	Windows	Task Manager application file
TBMI2.COM	3	2	6616	17999	\SYSTEM	Novell Netware workstation task-switching support for IPX/SPX
TERMINAL.EXE	4	4	84383	148160	Windows	Terminal application file
TERMINAL.HLP	4	3	25674	36279	Windows	Terminal Help file
TESTPS.TXT	7	6	1242	2640	\SYSTEM	Text file for testing PostScript printers
THATCH.BMP	4	3	210	598	Windows	Thatch wallpaper
THINKJET.DRV	7	6	2305	4720	\SYSTEM	HP ThinkJet (2225 C-D) printer driver
TI850.DRV	7	6	2156	4352	\SYSTEM	TI 850/855 printer driver
TIGA.DRV	2	1	38829	74352	\SYSTEM	TIGA display driver
TIGAWIN.RLM	2	2	23493	42658	\SYSTEM	TIGA firmware code for Windows
TIM17521.WPD	7	6	1048	2686	\SYSTEM	PostScript description file for TI microLaser PS17
TIM35521.WPD	7	6	1577	4688	\SYSTEM	PostScript description file for TI microLaser PS35
TIMER.DRV	3	3	3166	4192	\SYSTEM	Multimedia timer driver TIMES.FOT
TIMES.TTF	6	5	69074	83260	\SYSTEM	Times New Roman TrueType font file
TIMESB.FON	6	5	10361	21088	\SYSTEM	Times New Roman screen font 8,10 (EGA resolution)
TIMESBD.FOT	6	5	437	1328	\SYSTEM	Font resource file for TIMESBD.TTF
TIMESBD.TTF	6	5	63489	79804	\SYSTEM	Times New Roman Bold TrueType font file
TIMESBI.FOT	6	5	445	1342	\SYSTEM	Font resource file for TIMESBI.TTF
TIMESBI.TTF	6	5	60539	76452	\SYSTEM	Times New Roman Bold Italic TrueType font file
TIMESI.FOT	6	5	439	1332	\SYSTEM	Font resource file for TIMESI.TTF

TIMESI.TTF	6	5	61880	78172	\SYSTEM	Times New Roman Italic TrueType font file
TKPHZR21.WPD	7	6	1510	5175	\SYSTEM	PostScript description file for Phaser II PX I
TKPHZR31.WPD	7	6	1613	5422	\SYSTEM	PostScript description file for Phaser III PX I
TOOLHELP.DLL	5	5	10372	14128	\SYSTEM	Windows Tool Helper Dynamic Link Library
TOSHIBA.DRV	7	6	3320	8000	\SYSTEM	Toshiba p351/1351 driver
TRIUMPH1.WPD	7	6	785	1937	\SYSTEM	PostScript description file for Triumph Adler SDR 7706 PS equipped with 13 fonts
TRIUMPH2.WPD	7	6	1428	4411	\SYSTEM	Windows PostScript description file for Triumph Adler SDR 7706 PS equipped with 35 fonts
TTY.DRV	7	6	16675	30496	\SYSTEM	Generic/Text only printer driver
TTY.HLP	7	6	8859	14666	\SYSTEM	Help file for Generic/Text only printer driver
U9415470.WPD	7	6	1345	4320	\SYSTEM	PostScript description file for Unisys AP9415
UNIDRV.DLL	7	6	72378	119008	\SYSTEM	Universal printer driver Dynamic Link Library
UNIDRV.HLP	7	6	23219	31429	\SYSTEM	Help file for Universal printer driver
USER.EXE	3	2	195465	263984	\SYSTEM	User-interface core component; creates and maintains the appearance of windows, icons, and other onscreen interface items; manages input sources, such as the keyboard and mouse; and sends the input to the appropriate application
V7VDD.386	2	1	19315	40385	\SYSTEM	Video Seven virtual display device
V7VGA.3GR	2	2	8690	13824	\SYSTEM	Video Seven display grabber for 386 enhanced mode
V7VGA.DRV	2	2	47671	99296	\SYSTEM	Video Seven display driver—256 colors
VADLIBD.386	3	3	1952	5542	\SYSTEM	Virtual DMA device for Adlib sound cards
VDD8514.386	2	1	27808	46161	\SYSTEM	8514/a virtual display device
VDDCGA.386	2	2	8906	15227	\SYSTEM	CGA virtual display device
VDDCT441.386	1	1	18366	40007	\SYSTEM	82C441 VGA virtual display device
VDDEGA.386	2	1	19421	40584	\SYSTEM	EGA virtual display device

File Name (after expansion)	1.2 MB Disks	1.44 MB Disks	Size on Disk	Expanded Size	Target Directory	Description
VDDHERC.386	2	2	7023	10426	\SYSTEM	Hercules monochrome virtual display device
VDDTIGA.386	1	1	27647	41997	\SYSTEM	TIGA virtual display device
VDDVGA30.386	1	1	19651	40945	\SYSTEM	VGA virtual display device; provides compatibility with older display drivers created for Windows 3.0
VDDXGA.386	2	1	20367	40906	\SYSTEM	XGA virtual display device
VER.DLL	2	2	6307	9008	\SYSTEM	Dynamic Link Library for the Version utility and for file installation
VGA.3GR	1	1	11256	16384	\SYSTEM	VGA display grabber for 386 enhanced mode
VGA.DRV	3	2	43952	73200	\SYSTEM	VGA display driver
VGA30.3GR	3	2	9803	14848	\SYSTEM	VGA display grabber for 386 enhanced mode—provides compatibility with older display drivers designed for Windows 3.0
VGA850.FON	2	2	3264	5232	\SYSTEM	VGA terminal font—640x480 resolution, International code page 850
VGA860.FON	2	2	3237	5184	\SYSTEM	VGA terminal font—640x480 resolution, Portuguese code page 860
VGA861.FON	2	2	3260	5184	\SYSTEM	VGA terminal font—640x480 resolution, Icelandic code page 861
VGA863.FON	3	2	3266	5200	\SYSTEM	VGA terminal font—640x480 resolution, French-Canadian code page 863
VGA865.FON	3	2	3261	5184	\SYSTEM	VGA terminal font—640x480 resolution, Norwegian/Danish code page 865

File			Size	Size	Location	Description
VGACOLOR.2GR	2	2	3658	4484	\SYSTEM	VGA standard mode display component
VGADIB.3GR	2	2	10382	15360	\SYSTEM	DIB display grabber for 386 enhanced mode—8514/a, VGA Monochrome
VGAFIX.FON	2	2	2715	5360	\SYSTEM	VGA monospaced system font—640x480 resolution
VGALOGO.LGO	2	2	1245	1280	\SYSTEM	Startup logo code—VGA resolution
VGALOGO.RLE	3	2	9204	26778	\SYSTEM	Startup logo artwork, run-length-encoded bitmap—VGA resolution
VGAMONO.2GR	2	2	3644	4472	\SYSTEM	VGA monochrome display grabber for standard mode
VGAMONO.DRV	2	2	26679	45024	\SYSTEM	VGA monochrome display driver
VGAOEM.FON	2	2	3219	5168	\SYSTEM	VGA terminal font—640x480 resolution
VGASYS.FON	2	1	3111	7280	\SYSTEM	VGA system font—640x480 resolution
VIPX.386	2	2	8864	19197	\SYSTEM	Novell NetWare IXP virtual device
VNETWARE.386	2	2	3903	10102	\SYSTEM	Novell NetWare API virtual device
VPOWERD.386	3	2	2224	9426	\SYSTEM	Advanced Power Management virtual device
VSBD.386	3	3	2463	5650	\SYSTEM	SoundBlaster virtual device
VTDAPI.386	3	3	1824	5245	\SYSTEM	Multimedia timer virtual device
VTDAPI.386	3	3	1824	5245	\SYSTEM	Multimedia timer virtual device WIN.CNF
WIN.SRC	1	1	1666	2251	Not copied	Source file used by Setup to create the WIN.INI file
WIN386.EXE	5	4	284215	544789	\SYSTEM	Windows 386 enhanced mode core component
WIN386.PS2	6	5	418	852	\SYSTEM	PS/2 BIOS data for 386 enhanced mode
WIN87EM.DLL	4	4	8973	12800	\SYSTEM	80x87 math coprocessor emulation library
WIN.COM	*	*	*	varies	Windows	The Windows loader program that runs when you type WIN at the DOS prompt; it loads items such as WIN386.EXE, KRNL386.EXE, USER.EXE, and GDI.EXE, which comprise Windows. WIN.COM is created by Setup using components that differ, according to your system configuration (*not included on installation disks)

TABLE A.1 *(cont.)*
Contents of Windows Installation Disks

File Name (after expansion)	1.2 MB Disks	1.44 MB Disks	Size on Disk	Expanded Size	Target Directory	Description
WINDOWS.LOD	3	2	878	1988	\SYSTEM	386MAX/BlueMax loadable module
WINFILE.EXE	4	3	89663	146864	Windows	File Manager application file
WINFILE.HLP	3	4	56961	76855	Windows	File Manager Help file
WINGDING.FOT	6	6	430	1314	\SYSTEM	Font resource file for WINGDING.TTF
WINGDING.TTF	6	6	52533	70608	\SYSTEM	WingDing TrueType font file
WINHELP.EXE	1	1	163861	256192	Windows	Windows Help application file
WINHELP.HLP	3	3	20313	26960	Windows	Help file for the Windows Help program
WININI.WRI	3	3	9556	31104	Windows	Readme file with technical details about the WIN.INI file
WINLOGO.BMP	4	4	12211	38518	Windows	Windows Logo wallpaper
WINMINE.EXE	4	3	13634	27776	Windows	MineSweeper game application file
WINMINE.HLP	4	4	7098	12754	Windows	MineSweeper game Help file
WINOA386.MOD	4	4	30564	49104	\SYSTEM	DOS session support for 386 enhanced mode
WINOLDAP.MOD	5	5	16879	31232	\SYSTEM	DOS support for standard mode
WINPOPUP.EXE	2	2	15453	27344	\SYSTEM	LAN Manager network popup utility
WINPOPUP.HLP	3	2	1289	2476	\SYSTEM	Help file for LAN Manager network popup utility
WINTUTOR.DAT	4	3	51813	57356	Windows	Windows Tutorial data file
WINTUTOR.EXE	3	3	66632	124416	Windows	Windows Tutorial application file
WINVER	5	5	1820	3904	Windows	Version utility; renamed WINVER.EXE during installation
WRITE.EXE	3	3	154980	244976	Windows	Write application file
WRITE.HLP	4	3	29556	36971	Windows	Write Help file
WSWAP.EXE	5	5	11757	16302	\SYSTEM	Windows task-switcher for standard mode

XGA.DRV	1		139776	55181	\SYSTEM	XGA display driver
XLAT850.BIN	1	2	407	440	\SYSTEM	International (code page 850) support file
XLAT860.BIN	2	2	407	412	\SYSTEM	Portuguese (860) code page support file
XLAT861.BIN	2	2	407	415	\SYSTEM	Icelandic (861) code page support file
XLAT863.BIN	1	2	407	415	\SYSTEM	French-Canadian (863) code page support file
XLAT865.BIN	3	2	407	410	\SYSTEM	Norwegian and Danish (865) code page support file
XMSMMGR.EXE	1	1	14144*	14144	Temporary	Temporary extended memory manager utility used by Windows Setup (*not compressed)
ZIGZAG.BMP	3	4	630	210	Windows	Zigzag wallpaper

*Note: In addition, Windows can create other files as needed. For example, Setup creates .PIF files for many DOS programs; and several applets create their own .INI files if you change their default options.

B

Hacker Tools and Hints

This appendix is a repository for technical information that would primarily interest advanced Windows users. Although the term "hacker" often connotes a programmer with insidious intentions, I favor its original meaning, which is used to admiringly describe a technically proficient computerist who isn't a professional programmer. If you're a Windows power user, some items in this appendix may prove of interest. If you're just an average user, then you'll probably be glad I didn't clutter the main part of the book with this stuff.

Two main sections—Hacker Tools and Hacker Hints—incorporate the miscellany of information in this appendix. Hacker Tools rounds up my favorite technical utilities, which I didn't have a chance to mention previously. Hacker Hints is an assortment of technical tips that I considered too esoteric for the main text. Finally, a table at the end of the appendix lists common file extensions and the types of files they usually represent.

Hacker Tools

This section briefly describes several utility programs, many of which help you to see the internal operations of Windows. Other applications described here don't fall into any particular category, except that they are useful to anyone who is interested in eking more power out of Windows and Windows programs. The following descriptions are rough—to do them justice would take far more pages than my publisher will allow. For further details, use the information in Appendix C to contact the vendors directly.

Whitewater Resource Toolkit

**Dynamite
Product**

The Whitewater Resource Toolkit by Symantec lets you edit Windows resources—items that Windows stores as separate programming objects, including dialog boxes, cursors, and menus. With a resource editor such as the Whitewater Toolkit, you can easily alter these resources without affecting the internal operations of Windows. Some programs, however, can be affected when you change their resources, so you should always make a copy of the application file before applying this utility. The Whitewater Toolkit lets you edit these Windows resources:

ſ Bitmaps

ſ Cursors

ſ Dialog boxes

ſ Icons

ſ Keyboard accelerators (shortcut keys)

➳ Menus

➳ Strings

The Whitewater Toolkit can edit resources in the following file formats:

➳ **.EXE** Executable files

➳ **.DLL** Dynamic Link Libraries

➳ **.RES** Resource files

➳ **.BMP** Bitmap files

➳ **.CUR** Cursor files

You can modify resources to customize your applications; for example, you can change the names of items on menus or add information to dialog boxes. You can also be creative. As an illustration, Figure B.1 compares a "normal" dialog box with a humorously modified one.

FIGURE B.1

Modifying Resources on a Dr. Watson Dialog Box

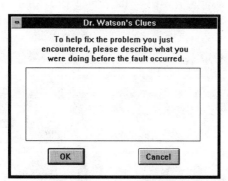

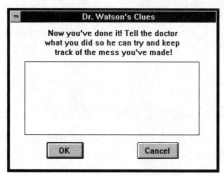

A dialog box from Dr. Watson, compared with the same box after some comedian has applied the Whitewater Resource Toolkit to it.

Visual Basic

**Dynamite
Product**

Most commercial software developers use some flavor of the C programming language, which offers the most sophisticated and well-supported programming environment for PCs. If you don't know C but want to start Windows programming, Microsoft's Visual Basic provides a more accessible alternative. Although BASIC, the programming language used in Visual Basic, is scorned by some programmers, Visual Basic uses the best version of BASIC ever written; it allows you to create sophisticated Windows programs that can incorporate DDE, DLLs, OLE, MCI, and capabilities for Windows for Pens. In addition, the program works with standard Windows resources, so you can use third-party resource editors such as the Whitewater Resource Toolkit.

Visual Basic lets you interactively test your program as you evolve it and then create an executable standalone version of the program. Because it's actually a Windows program, Visual Basic provides an attractive and approachable workbench for crafting your program (Figure B.2).

FIGURE B.2

Visual Basic

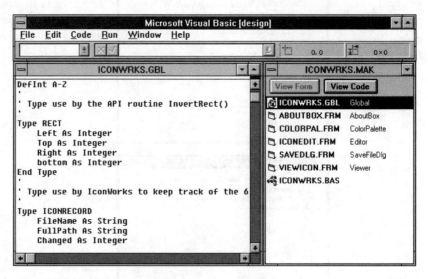

Visual Basic offers an accessible, interactive programming environment for creating your own Windows programs and utilities.

Learning Visual Basic will also give you a headstart in understanding Microsoft's future universal macro language for Windows, which is based on Visual Basic.

Spy and DDESpy

In technical parlance, Windows is a message-based environment. Users can send messages, of course, by mouse and by keyboard actions, but the system can also initiate messages, and DDE conversations can occur as well. When debugging a program or writing a DDE script, you'll find it useful to apply a utility that lets you inspect the various Windows messages. The most common of these is the Spy utility (Figure B.3), which Microsoft includes with its **Windows Software Development Kit** (SDK).

FIGURE B.3

The Spy Utility

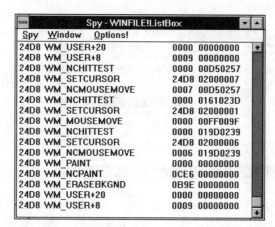

The Spy utility lets you intercept Windows messages.

With Spy, you can either view the messages onscreen, save the output to a file, or do both. Spy lets you monitor these types of Windows messages:

➣ Clipboard

➣ DDE

➣ Initialization

➣ Input

➣ Mouse

➣ System

➣ Window

➣ Non client

In addition, you can use Spy to inspect the properties of a window, such as its class, parent, style, size, and position. In order to run the Spy utility, the

HOOK.DLL file must be copied to your \SYSTEM subdirectory. The HOOK.DLL file can also be found in the Windows SDK.

Although the Spy utility tracks DDE messages as one of its message types, the Windows SDK also includes the specialized DDE Spy utility (Figure B.4), which provides added features for tracking DDE messages, such as the ability to hone in on a special type of message.

FIGURE B.4

The DDESpy Utility

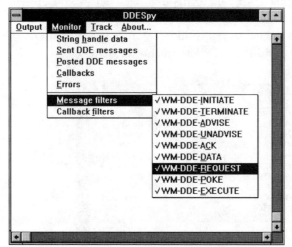

DDESpy lets you monitor the DDE conversations between Windows applications.

At the time of writing, you can only obtain Spy and DDESpy with the Windows SDK; but try contacting Microsoft—the company may have changed its policy by the time you read this.

HeapWalker

The HeapWalker is another utility that Microsoft includes with the Windows SDK. HeapWalker lets you inspect the memory that DOS allocates to Windows as well as view Windows' global heap and its contents.

The HeapWalker display contains information about each item in the heap, including its name, owner, type, total size, and the size of both its discardable and nondiscardable memory segments (Figure B.5).

You can use HeapWalker to inspect the heap, to eliminate discardable objects, and to sort objects by address, object size, or other criteria. If the object in the heap is a graphic item, such as a cursor, you can view its bitmap to identify it. HeapWalker is handy for determining what applications are gobbling up your heap memory, which is the most limited memory resource within Windows.

FIGURE B.5

The HeapWalker Utility

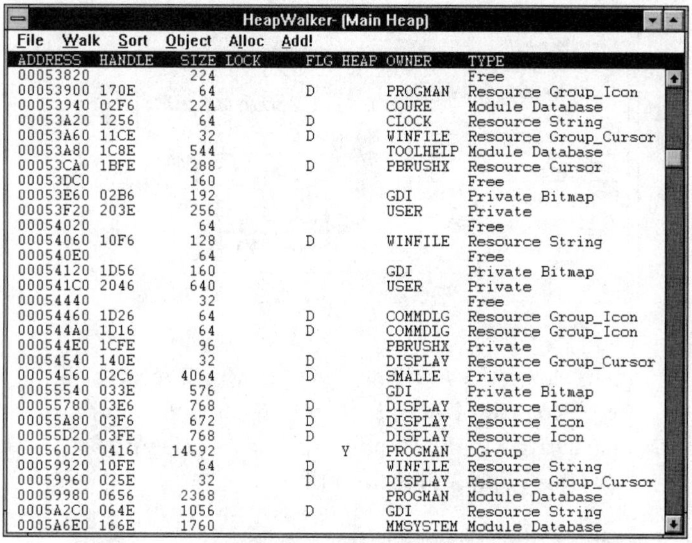

```
                          HeapWalker- [Main Heap]
 File   Walk   Sort   Object   Alloc   Add!
 ADDRESS   HANDLE   SIZE LOCK      FLG HEAP OWNER    TYPE
 00053820           224                            Free
 00053900  170E      64        D        PROGMAN    Resource Group_Icon
 00053940  02F6     224                 COURE      Module Database
 00053A20  1256      64        D        CLOCK      Resource String
 00053A60  11CE      32        D        WINFILE    Resource Group_Cursor
 00053A80  1C8E     544                 TOOLHELP   Module Database
 00053CA0  1BFE     288        D        PBRUSHX    Resource Cursor
 00053DC0           160                            Free
 00053E60  02B6     192                 GDI        Private Bitmap
 00053F20  203E     256                 USER       Private
 00054020            64                            Free
 00054060  10F6     128        D        WINFILE    Resource String
 000540E0            64                            Free
 00054120  1D56     160                 GDI        Private Bitmap
 000541C0  2046     640                 USER       Private
 00054440            32                            Free
 00054460  1D26      64        D        COMMDLG    Resource Group_Icon
 000544A0  1D16      64        D        COMMDLG    Resource Group_Icon
 000544E0  1CFE      96                 PBRUSHX    Private
 00054540  140E      32        D        DISPLAY    Resource Group_Cursor
 00054560  02C6    4064        D        SMALLE     Private
 00055540  033E     576                 GDI        Private Bitmap
 00055780  03E6     768        D        DISPLAY    Resource Icon
 00055A80  03F6     672        D        DISPLAY    Resource Icon
 00055D20  03FE     768        D        DISPLAY    Resource Icon
 00056020  0416   14592             Y   PROGMAN    DGroup
 00059920  10FE      64        D        WINFILE    Resource String
 00059960  025E      32        D        DISPLAY    Resource Group_Cursor
 00059980  0656    2368                 PROGMAN    Module Database
 0005A2C0  064E    1056        D        GDI        Resource String
 0005A6E0  166E    1760                 MMSYSTEM   Module Database
```

HeapWalker lets you view details about how Windows components are using memory.

As noted at the end of Chapter 12, some Windows applications misbehave by not cleaning up after themselves and thus do not release portions of the heap after using them. HeapWalker can help you identify the guilty applications.

SmartDrive Monitor

The SmartDrive Monitor utility, or SmartMon, lets you monitor the activity of the SmartDRIVE disk cache utility included with Windows. By monitoring the cache, you can determine the best settings for SmartDRIVE. Unfortunately, SmartMon itself is available only as part of the Microsoft's Windows Resource Kit.

SmartMon provides a visual display of cache activity and efficiency; it also allows you to easily change the cache mode for each drive as well as adjust some SmartDrive parameters (Figure B.6).

SmartMon's Cache Memory controls display the cache size set for DOS and Windows operations. The Commit button lets you force SmartDRIVE to write back its cache, and the Reset button forces SmartDRIVE to write back the cache and then discard its contents. The Drive Controls section enables you to select any drive on your system, then view and set its cache mode. The Cache Hit Rate chart displays a histogram, which represents the cache hit rate. Below this chart, you'll see a display of the average cache hit rate.

FIGURE B.6

*The
SmartDrive
Monitor
Utility*

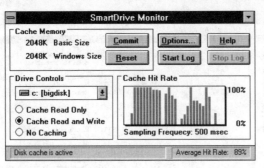

*SmartMon lets you view
SmartDRIVE's disk cache
activity and efficiency
and adjust some of
SmartDRIVE's settings.*

SmartMon lets you create a log file, which records all the cache activities to the file for your later inspection. Clicking the Options button brings up the SmartDrive Monitor Options dialog box (Figure B.7), which lets you adjust the various options for this utility.

FIGURE B.7

*SmartDrive
Monitor
Options
Dialog Box*

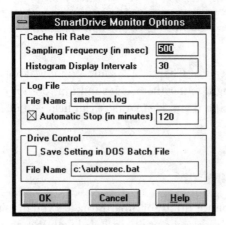

*You can use this dialog box to adjust the sampling frequency of
SmartMon, specify the log file and its duration, and indicate whether
you want SmartMon to save your changes to your DOS startup file
automatically.*

Other Utilities

In addition to the utilities just listed, a few other software programs can also come in handy for hacking your software. For further details, contact the vendors listed in Appendix C.

➤ **Toolbook** from Asymetrix is a multimedia-savvy authoring system similar to HyperCard on the Macintosh. You can use Toolbook to create hypertext databases, educational software, and presentations, all with a minimum of actual programming.

➤ **Easy Boot** from Clear Software lets you create 15 different CONFIG.SYS and AUTOEXEC.BAT boot configurations and switch among them easily. This utility provides a great way for creating separate boot sequences for Windows, DOS, and Desqview.

➤ **Encrypt-It** from MaeDae Enterprises is a DES-level encryption program that can be used to keep your private data safely encoded with a password.

➤ **Bridge Tool Kit** from Softbridge lets you integrate DOS programs into Windows at a much higher level than is possible with Windows alone. With Bridge Tool Kit, you can send messages to and from DOS applications with support for DDE and NetBIOS.

➤ **TextPert Developer's Toolkit** from CTA, Inc., allows you to add OCR capabilities to whatever Windows program you are developing. To do this, TextPert provides a Windows-compatible OCR subsystem that can be called by your program.

➤ **DataLIB** from Dattel Communications Systems provides a pre-constructed program module that lets you add data import/export capabilities to whatever Windows program you are developing. DataLIB reads and writes most spreadsheet, database, and ASCII file formats.

➤ **HALO Image File Format Library** from Media Cybernetics is a DLL that offers whatever program you are developing calls for reading and writing a large number of different graphic file formats.

Hacker Hints

Danger Zone

This section contains a true miscellany of tips, tricks, and techniques that are intended primarily for advanced Windows users. Some of these items apply only in rare circumstances; others, such as the hierarchical Program Manager scheme, are just goofy or cool. I make no guarantee that these tips will work with your system, although they work for me and some of my more courageous (or foolhardy) friends. In other words: WARNING! DANGER! CAUTION! KIDS, DON'T TRY THIS AT HOME! By the way, if you'd like to share any of your own hacks, write to me in care of Peachpit Press, and I'll be happy to consider them for the next edition of this book.

. . . .

Saving Multiple Windows Configurations

If you plan to run Windows in multiple-screen resolutions, such as 640x480x256 and 1024x720x16, it's faster to store multiple configurations of the Windows initialization files in your Windows directory than to rerun the Setup procedure each time you make a change. You can also use this technique to quickly set up alternate Windows configurations with third-party file managers, custom colors for the desktop, and similar variations.

To save a Windows configuration, copy WIN.INI to a file named WIN1.INI and SYSTEM.INI to a file named SYS1.INI. If you plan to use different desktop patterns or colors, copy the file named CONTROL.INI to CON1.INI. The same scheme for renaming .INI files applies if you want to save the current state of any other programs that rely on .INIs. Now make any intended changes to Windows by running the Setup program or the Control Panel, or installing a third-party file manager. When you've developed a new configuration, copy the new .INI files to WIN2.INI, SYS2.INI, CON2.INI, and so on for any other .INIs. This process can be repeated any number of times using names such as WIN3.INI, WIN4.INI, and so on for the other configurations.

You can then choose which Windows configuration to run by constructing a simple DOS batch file that presents a menu listing the different configuration options. Here's an example: first create a text file named WINMENU.TXT, which contains various choices that a batch file can use to create a menu. The WINMENU.TXT file might look like this:

```
Select a Configuration Number and Press Enter:

1. 640x480 Screen Resolution, 256 colors
2. 800x600 Screen Resolution, 16 colors
3. 1024x768 Screen Resolution, 16 colors
4. 640x480 Screen Resolution with Norton Desktop
```

The next step is to create a batch file for each of the numbered choices in the WINMENU.TXT file. The batch files will be named 1.BAT, 2.BAT, 3.BAT, and so on. The menu works this way: when you type the number 1 and press enter, DOS runs the 1.BAT file. Here's an example of how the 1.BAT file might look:

```
COPY WIN1.INI WIN.INI
COPY SYS1.INI SYSTEM.INI
COPY CON1.INI CONTROL.INI
WIN
```

Similarly, the 2.BAT file could contain these lines:

```
COPY WIN2.INI WIN.INI
COPY SYS2.INI SYSTEM.INI
COPY CON2.INI CONTROL.INI
WIN
```

And so forth for the rest of the menu choices.

You can then create a batch file named WINMENU.BAT that would contain only the following two lines:

```
CD\WINDOWS
TYPE WINMENU.TXT
```

The first line changes to your Windows directory (assuming the file is located there). The second line displays the menu in the WINMENU.TXT file on the screen and returns to DOS. When you enter the menu number and press the Enter key, DOS executes the appropriate .BAT file and replaces the various .INI files before starting Windows.

Tracking Down Wasteful and Empty Files

If your Windows software has ever crashed, or if your machine was rebooted or turned off before you gracefully exited Windows, some dead temporary files may be wasting space on your hard disk. Also, you should weed out any empty files languishing in your system that were left by sloppy programs. Unfortunately, tracking down these deadweights with File Manager can take a lot of time if you've got a big disk with many files. Here's a quick DOS batch file trick that will target all your potentially wasteful files and prepare a report of the files that you can view, print, or save.

```
@ECHO OFF
CD \
DIR /S|FIND" 0 " > EMPTY.TXT
DIR /S|FIND"~" > TEMPS.TXT
DIR /S|FIND".TMP" > TEMPS.TXT
```

This batch file should be run before you start your Windows session so that it doesn't list valid temporary files used by Windows. After running the batch file, you can use any text editor to view the list and then prune useless files accordingly.

The batch file works by logging into your root directory and then requesting a directory listing of all the files on the drive. The directory listings are fed to the FIND function by the pipe (|); FIND first looks for files that contain a zero surrounded by a space on either side—usually an indication of an empty (0 byte) file—and saves what it finds to a text file name EMPTY.TXT. The process is then repeated twice more to search for common indications used to designate temporary files—once to search for files containing a tilde (~) and once for files with the extension .TMP. The results of the last two directory searches are saved in a file called TEMPS.TXT. (Insider's mini-tip: You can use this same technique to search for any files on your disk.)

How To Get Rid of Your Unwanted Windows Programs

Installing Windows programs is far easier than getting rid of one. Most programs include an installation utility that automates the task of placing the program on your hard disk, along with any related files. Setup programs can edit your DOS startup files and .INI files as well. Although a few programs, such as Norton Desktop, provide a standard deinstallation utility, most Windows programs do not, and this can create a problem if you need to eliminate a program.

Sometimes, you'll need to remove a program and all its traces because it interferes with the operation of another program. Simply removing the application file, however, won't usually resolve the problem. You probably need to remove lines or change settings in your CONFIG.SYS, AUTOEXEC.BAT, WIN.INI, and SYSTEM.INI files, and you may need to remove DLLs, fonts, and other components of the application as well.

To remove an application, you first need to know what it did to your system during its installation. Although a couple of shareware utilities can help, the easiest way to keep track of this process is to use the DOS batch file language to create two small utilities. The first, called BEFORE.BAT, takes a snapshot of your system files and saves them in text files with the extension .BEF. Run BEFORE.BAT immediately prior to installing a Windows program. The second utility—AFTER.BAT—takes a snapshot of your system files after the installation and uses the DOS File Compare command to compare the .BEF files with the corresponding .AFT files. Run AFTER.BAT immediately after installing a program. The AFTER.BAT program prepares a simple text file report noting the changes made by the installation of the application.

To create this pair of utility programs, use the Notepad or a similar text editor. Then create a directory named UNINSTAL. This directory will serve as a repository for the two .BAT files, their associated .PIF files, the .BEF and .AFT files they create, and the .TXT text file reports generated by the utilities. These batch files assume that your main Windows directory is named WINDOWS and is located on drive C:. If your directory name or drive location is different, you'll need to modify the batch files accordingly. Also, if you install programs on a different drive, such as D: drive or network volumes, you'll need to add additional lines to the batch files that replicate the searching of directories for those other drives.

The BEFORE.BAT utility should be entered as shown below:

```
@ECHO OFF
ECHO Now recording your current configuration into .BEF files.
ECHO Copying Startup and Initialization Files...
COPY C:\CONFIG.SYS CONFIG.BEF
COPY C:\AUTOEXEC.BAT AUTOEXEC.BEF
COPY C:\WINDOWS\WIN.INI WIN.BEF
COPY C:\WINDOWS\SYSTEM.INI SYSTEM.BEF
ECHO Recording Information About Directories and Files...
TREE C:\ /a  TREE.BEF
DIR C:\*.* /a-d /b /l  ROOT.BEF
DIR C:\WINDOWS\*.* /a /b /l  WINDIR.BEF
DIR C:\WINDOWS\SYSTEM\*.* /a /b /l  SYSDIR.BEF
ECHO --- DONE! ---
```

After you save the BEFORE.BAT file, create a PIF for it, similar to the one shown in Figure B.8.

FIGURE B.8

*PIF settings
for BEFORE.PIF*

Now you should create the AFTER.BAT batch program. This one is a little trickier, because it's longer and uses a DOS variable, in this case, %1. The value of this variable is the name (up to eight characters) of the application you are installing. Supply this name when you run the .PIF file that starts this batch file. Here's the procedure.

First enter the AFTER.BAT file as shown below.

```
@ECHO OFF
ECHO Now searching for changes caused by installing %1
ECHO Changes will be reported in the file C:\UNINSTAL\%1.txt
ECHO. >> %1
ECHO These changes were made to your configuration >> %1
ECHO by the installation proceedure for %1 >> %1
ECHO. >> %1
ECHO Checking Changes to DOS Startup Files...
ECHO--Modifications made to CONFIG.SYS-->> %1
FC CONFIG.BEF C:\CONFIG.SYS >> %1
ECHO--Modifications made to AUTOEXEC.BAT-->> %1
FC AUTOEXEC.BEF C:\AUTOEXEC.BAT > %1
ECHO Checking Changes to .INI Files...
ECHO--Modifications made to WIN.INI-->> %1
FC WIN.BEF C:\WINDOWS\WIN.INI > %1
ECHO--Modifications made to SYSTEM.INI-->> %1
FC SYSTEM.BEF C:\WINDOWS\SYSTEM.INI >> %1
ECHO Checking for New Directories or Files...
ECHO--Changes made to the directory tree of C:-->> %1
TREE C:\ /a > TREE.AFT
FC TREE.BEF TREE.AFT >> %1
ECHO--New files added to the root directory C:\-->> %1
DIR c:\*.* /a-d /b /l > ROOT.AFT
FC ROOT.BEF ROOT.AFT >> %1
ECHO--New files added to C:\WINDOWS-->> %1
DIR C:\WINDOWS\*.* /a /b /l  WINDIR.AFT
FC WINDIR.BEF WINDIR.AFT >> %1
ECHO--New files added to C:\WINDOWS\SYSTEM-->> %1
DIR C:\WINDOWS\SYSTEM\*.* /a /b /l  SYSDIR.AFT
FC SYSDIR.BEF SYSDIR.AFT >> %1
FIND /v "Comparing files" %1  %1.TXT
DEL *.BEF
DEL *.AFT
DEL %1
ECHO --- DONE! ---
```

Now create a PIF for the AFTER.BAT utility, using the settings shown in Figure B.9.

```
┌─────────────────────────────────────────────────────────────┐
│ ─        PIF Editor - AFTER.PIF            ▼ ▲ │
│ File   Mode   Help                                           │
│                                                              │
│ Program Filename:      C:\UNINSTAL\AFTER.BAT                 │
│ Window Title:          Analyzing Changes                     │
│ Optional Parameters:   ?                                     │
│ Start-up Directory:    C:\UNINSTAL                           │
│                                                              │
│ Video Memory:    ● Text   ○ Low Graphics   ○ High Graphics  │
│ Memory Requirements:  KB Required  128   KB Desired   640    │
│ EMS Memory:           KB Required  0     KB Limit    1024    │
│ XMS Memory:           KB Required  0     KB Limit    1024    │
│ Display Usage: ○ Full Screen       Execution: ☐ Background  │
│                ● Windowed                     ☐ Exclusive    │
│ ☐ Close Window on Exit        [ Advanced... ]               │
│                                                              │
│ Press F1 for Help on Window Title.                           │
└─────────────────────────────────────────────────────────────┘
```

Place a question mark in the Optional Parameters text box. The question mark causes a dialog box to appear when you run the PIF and prompts you for the parameters. In this case, you'll enter the name of the application you are installing. This name will be used as the %1 variable. The text file report that records the changes made during the installation process will bear this name as well. Finish up by creating program icons for the BEFORE.PIF and AFTER.PIF files so that you can easily run them right before and right after installing an application.

Note that in the example PIF settings, I removed the X from the Close Window on Exit check box. This leaves the DOS window open after the batch file has run, so that you can verify the progress and completion of the job. If you don't care about seeing this, leave the X in the check box, and the DOS window will automatically disappear after the batch file has run.

Speeding Up PostScript Printing

When working with documents that use PostScript soft fonts, you can configure Windows to download the fonts "as needed" from a Windows application, or you can download the fonts to the printer before starting Windows. If you take the latter approach, you'll save quite a deal of printing time.

Each Windows output device includes a corresponding section in WIN.INI. The font list under each printer section controls how soft fonts are treated for that device. A font name listing with a .PFM extension makes the font available on menus in each individual Windows application. A font name listing with a .PFB extension causes Windows to download the font to the printer each time it is called in a print job. If no .PFB font listing appears, Windows assumes that the font is already resident in the printer and skips the download procedure.

For example, the following section in WIN.INI tells Windows to download Caslon Roman and Franklin Gothic from your hard disk every time you print:

```
[Postscript, LPT1]
sfdir=c:\psfonts
softfonts=2
softfont1=c:\psfonts\pfm\cfr_____.pfm,c:\psfonts\cfr_____.pfb
softfont2=c:\psfonts\pfm\frh_____.pfm,c:\psfonts\frh_____.pfb
```

To speed up your Windows PostScript printing, you should disable Windows font downloading and then download each soft font from DOS in advance. To disable Windows font downloading, just remove the .PFB listings from the printer section in WIN.INI, as follows:

```
[Postscript, LPT1]
sfdir=c:\psfonts
softfonts=2
softfont1=c:\psfonts\pfm\cfr_____.pfm
softfont2=c:\psfonts\pfm\frh_____.pfm
```

Windows now assumes that Caslon and Franklin Gothic are resident printer fonts. To print them, use the download utility supplied by the appropriate soft font vendor before starting Windows.

For Adobe Type Library fonts, the font downloader for parallel printers is PCSEND.EXE and for serial printers it is PSDOWN. The following sample batch file predownloads Caslon Roman and Franklin Gothic to a printer on LPT1:

```
PCSEND -1 -v c:\psfonts\cfr_____.pfb
PCSEND -1 -v c:\psfonts\frquad.pfm
```

For a printer with a serial interface, run Adobe's PSDOWN program (or another third-party equivalent). Starting PSDOWN brings up a menu-driven interface. Choose the fonts you wish to pre-download from the menu and press D. (If you're downloading to the printer's hard disk, press M first, followed by D.)

With Windows' on-the-fly font downloading disabled, your document print speed will be greatly enhanced. The soft fonts remain resident in the printer until you switch off the power.

Running Lotus 1-2-3 Version 3.1 in a Window

Lotus 1-2-3 version 3.1 only runs in a full-screen window. Attempts to switch to a small window in 386 enhanced mode result in this error message: "You cannot run this application in a window or in the background. You can display it in a window, but it will be suspended until you run it full screen."

Actually, you can make this version of 1-2-3 run in a small window by configuring it for a CGA rather than a VGA screen display. To do this, run the 1-2-3 Install program and select CGA for your primary display; this may cause 1-2-3 to come up in a small window by default. (Edit the .PIF file to start 1-2-3 with the -c option in order to disable the graphics startup screen.)

If you select VGA for your primary display of 1-2-3 and CGA for the secondary display, you can start 1-2-3 full-screen under Windows and then switch to the CGA driver. To do this, choose 1-2-3's Worksheet/Display option and select the secondary display driver. When 1-2-3 has been switched to CGA resolution, press Alt+Enter under Windows to shift it to a small window.

Liberating 8K of RAM with QEMM

You can gain about 8K of conventional memory for each DOS program run under Windows with QEMM by retaining the DOS=UMB parameter in your CONFIG.SYS file. Although DOS=UMB does not affect QEMM's special loadhigh utilities, it does cause Windows to load its translation buffers into upper memory, instead of into conventional memory, which results in memory gains similar to those described in Chapter 13.

Using the Upper Memory of Individual DOS Sessions

Here's how to conserve memory if you need to use different TSRs for separate DOS sessions running under Windows. Load the TSRs above 640K locally in each individual session, instead of placing them in your AUTOEXEC.BAT file. To enable this feature, make the following change to SYSTEM.INI:

```
[386enh] LocalLoadHigh=True
```

Your CONFIG.SYS file must contain the statement

```
Device=EMM386.SYS RAM DOS=UMB
```

or a third-party EMS manager, such as QEMM, 386MAX, or NETROOM.

Once you open a DOS session under Windows, you can place programs into upper memory with MS-DOS 5's Loadhigh statement or with the loader utilities from various third-party packages. Windows keeps track of what's loaded high in each individual DOS session, allowing you to reuse your available upper memory blocks many times in separate sessions.

Loading TSRs into Individual DOS Sessions

Normally, any device drivers and TSRs that are preloaded into memory before starting Windows are shared globally in any DOS session opened under Windows. In some cases, though, this may not work to your benefit.

For instance, ANSI.SYS allows you to create custom screen color settings and to remap specific keyboard combinations. By default, ANSI screen customization of one DOS session under Windows bleeds through to any subsequently opened DOS session. You can force Windows to load a separate instance of a shared device driver or TSR into each individual DOS session by adding the name of the program to the "LocalTSRs" list in the [NonWindowsApp] section of SYSTEM.INI. By default, two command-line editors, dosedit and ced, are configured this way. To add ANSI.SYS to the list of instanced drivers, simply append it to the end of the list:

```
[NonWindowsApp] localtsrs=dosedit,ced,ANSI.SYS
```

This allows you to define separate foreground/background color combinations for each DOS session and to remap individual keyboard functions in each DOS session without bleeds to other DOS sessions.

Using FastDisk with QEMM

As discussed in Chapter 12, FastDisk is a 32-bit Windows program that provides a faster way of accessing your hard disk in 386 enhanced mode when you use a permanent swapfile to provide virtual memory. To confirm that faster disk writes are indeed enabled on your system, click on the 386 icon in Control Panel, select Virtual Memory, and examine the information displayed for your swapfile. If you are using a temporary swapfile, click on the Change button and select Permanent. Windows gives you the option to restart automatically with the new settings. Then open the 386 icon in

Control Panel and select Virtual again. The message in the window under Type should say "Permanent (Using 32 bit access)."

Using QEMM as your memory manager with the Stealth feature turned on may prevent you from being able to use FastDisk. If this is the case, the message in the Type box reads "Permanent (Using BIOS)." Here's how to continue using QEMM as your memory manager and enable FastDisk as well:

1. Remove the parameter ST:M from the line in your Config.Sys that loads QEMM386.SYS; *or* retain the ST:M feature and add the following parameter to the QEMM386 command line:

```
XST=F000
```

2. Open the SYSTEM.INI file in a text editor and add the following statements in the [386 Enhanced] section:

```
Device=*wdctrl
Device=*int13
Device=*blockdev
32bitDiskAccess=On
```

3. Restart Windows and establish a permanent swapfile, as shown earlier.

• •

Using the LZEXPAND.DLL

Windows 3.1 includes a special DLL named LZEXPAND.DLL that decompresses files compressed with Microsoft's COMPRESS.EXE utility, such as the files on the Windows installation disks. (The COMPRESS.EXE utility is included with the Windows SDK.) Setup and the Control Panel use the LZEXPAND.DLL, which is located in the Windows \SYSTEM subdirectory.

If you know how to use DLLs in your own programs, you can take advantage of this handy DLL to automatically decompress files—or even portions of files—from within your own utility programs. The DLL can also copy mixed groups of compressed and uncompressed files and intelligently decompress only the compressed files.

The following functions are supported by the LZEXPAND.DLL:

➡ **CopyLZFile** Copies the source file to a destination file and decompresses only if the source file is compressed. For use with multiple files.

➡ **GetExpandedName** Gets the original name of the compressed file (works only if the source file was compressed with the /R switch).

➠ **LZClose** Closes a file that was opened with LZOpenFile.

➠ **LZCopy** Copies a source file to a destination file and decompresses it only if compressed. For use with single files.

➠ **LZDone** Designates the end of a multiple-file operation initiated with LZStart.

➠ **LZInit** Prepares the DLL for decompressing files.

➠ **LZOpenFile** Opens a file. If compressed, returns a special handle; if not compressed, returns a standard DOS file handle.

➠ **LZRead** Reads a specific number of bytes (while decompressing them, if necessary) to allow operations on specific sections of a file located with LZSeek.

➠ **LZSeek** Positions a software pointer within the decompressed image of a compressed file so that LZRead can then decompress only a specific portion of the file.

➠ **LZStart** Signals the beginning of a multiple-file copy process that uses CopyLZFile, and allocates the memory necessary for that process.

For example, to decompress a single file, you can use LZOpenFile to open the source file and the destination file, and then copy the source (while decompressing it, if necessary) by calling the LZCopy function and passing the file handles returned by LZOpenFile. To finish the job, call LZClose to close all the files and free up any memory that was used by the process.

Decompressing a group of files works similarly. You start by using LZOpenFile to open the source file and destination file. Then you need to call LZStart to allocate memory for the job. Next, use CopyLZFile to copy the source files to the destination files. To finish the job, call LZDone to release the memory allocated by LZStart, and then call LZClose to close the files.

If you really want to hack into a compressed file, you can use the LZSeek and LZRead functions to decompress only part of a file.

· ·

Creating a Hierarchical Program Manager

You can actually use a clever hack to configure Windows to nest a series of program groups inside of one another. Just run subsidiary copies of Program Manager from inside the first copy that Windows uses as its shell. The subsidiary copies of Program Manager, when launched, pop up one or more groups inside of the primary group in your original Program Manager.

To perform this trick, you must give the subsidiary Program Manager a different name and change the name of the .INI file that the nested Program Manager can use to keep track of the subsidiary application groups. Otherwise, the nested Program Managers will confuse one another and may crash your system.

For example, let's say you want to make another copy of PROGMAN.EXE called PROGMAN2.EXE. You'll also want to alter PROGMAN2.EXE to use a file called PROGMAN2.INI to track its application icons and groups. To do this, you'll need to use the DOS Debug program.

1. Copy PROGMAN.EXE to a file named PROGMAN2.FIL (This file will be renamed later to PROGRMAN2.EXE, after it's been modified with Debug.)

2. From the DOS prompt, type

   ```
   DEBUG PROGMAN2.FIL -
   ```

   Debug returns a hyphen (-) prompt.

3. Type the following at the (-) prompt:

   ```
   -S 0000 ffff "N.INI"
   ```

   This searches your second Program Manager for the relevant text to modify.

   ```
   269B:C8B0
   ```

   Debug returns a single address that contains the text string.

4. Type the letter **d** followed by the segment offset (the four alphanumeric characters that follow the colon in the last line).

   ```
   -d c8b0 269B:C8B0 4E 2E 49 4E 49 08 53 65-74 74 69 6E 67 73 00
   00  N.INI.Settings.. 269B:C8C0 00 00 00 00 00 00 00 00-00 00
   00 00 00 00 00 00  ...............
   ```

5. Now use the Debug E[nter] command to change the hex number 4E (ASCII "N") to hex 32 (ASCII "2")

   ```
   -e c8b0 269B:C8B0 4E.  (Type in "32" and press ENTER)
   269B:C8B0 4E.3
   ```

6. Type **d** followed by the four-digit alphanumeric segment offset again, to confirm that the change has been made.

   ```
   -d c8b0 269B:C8B0 31 2E 49 4E 49 08 53 65-74 74 69 6E 67 73 00
   00 2.INI.Settings.. 269B:C8C0 00 00 00 00 00 00 00 00-00 00 00
   00 00 00 00 00
   ```

7. Save the change by entering **W** (write) at the hyphen prompt.

```
-w
```

Debug responds:

```
writing 1BD10 bytes
```

8. Use the Q (Quit) command to exit Debug and return to DOS.

9. Rename PROGMAN2.FIL back to PROGRAM2.EXE, so it can be launched from within Windows.

You now have a copy of the Program Manager (PROGRAM2.EXE) that uses a file called PROGRAM2.INI to store icon information.

With Windows 3.1, one additional step is necessary. You must rename your original PROGMAN.EXE to some other name (for instance PR.EXE). Otherwise, the second Program Manager you've created will become confused later. To do this, go into the SYSTEM.INI settings and modify the Shell= statement in the [Boot] section to reflect the name change, as shown in this line:

```
Shell=PR.EXE
```

To make use of your second Program Manager, start Windows and select the primary program group for placing your nested group. Tell Program Manager to add a new program icon to the group by choosing New from the File menu and Program Item from the next menu. On the Description line, enter a name for the new group. For the command line, enter PROG-MAN2.EXE. You can also use the Change Icon command to give PROG-MAN2.EXE a group icon instead of the Program Manager icon.

The second Program Manager now appears in your primary group with your selected description and icon. When you click on this icon, a second Program Manager opens. You can now set up one or more groups full of icons under this second Program Manager, and they will pop up promptly whenever you open PROGMAN2.EXE from the primary group.

Common File Extensions

Table B.1 represents only a small sample of the many file extensions used on Windows systems, but it does cover all the extensions used by the basic Windows 3.1 product. Remember that extensions are used by convention only—sometimes two different types of files use the same extension, and sometimes people don't save data files with the proper extension.

Extension	Description
386	Virtual device driver files for 386 enhanced mode
$$$	DOS redirection files; created by the DOS pipe character (I) when it redirects output
1ST	ASCII text files used for Readme files, such as README.1ST
2GR	DOS session display grabber files for standard mode
3GR	DOS session display grabber files for 386 enhanced mode
ACT	Actor source code files
AMG	Actor system image files
ANS	ANSII text files
ASC	ASCII text files
BAK	Widely used for backup files
BAS	BASIC language source code files
BAT	DOS batch files; can be edited with Notepad or any text editor
BIN	Widely used for binary files; often contains data and programming code used by applications
BMP	Generic Windows bitmap graphics files; can be edited with Paintbrush
C	C language source code files
CAL	SuperCalc spreadsheet files
CAL	Windows Calendar data files
CFG	Used for configuration files by various applications
CGM	Graphics files that conform to the Computer Graphics Metafile format
CHK	CHKDSK recovered data files; created by using the /F option with the DOS CHKDSK command
CLS	Actor class library files
CMD	dBASE command files
CMP	Microsoft Word compare files
CNF	Used by various applications for configuration files
CNV	Word for Windows conversion files
COB	COBOL language source code files
COM	DOS program files; also used by TSRs and DOS device drivers
CPL	Control Panel module files
CRD	Windows Cardfile data files

• • • • • • • • • • • • • •
TABLE B.1 *(cont.)*
*A Sampling of
File Extensions
Used on
Windows
Systems*

Extension	Description
CSV	Data files that conform to the Comma Separated Values format
CUR	Windows cursor files
DAT	Used by various applications for data files
DB	Paradox table data files
DBF	dBASE data files
DBT	dBASE text data files
DEF	Windows system definition files
DEV	DOS device driver files
DIB	Device independent bitmap files
DIF	Data files that conform to the Data Interchange Format
DLL	Dynamic Link Library files; contain program code that can be used by various Windows applications
DOC	Used for document files by many different wordprocessing programs
DOT	Microsoft Word document template files
DRV	Device driver files
DRW	Micrografx Designer picture files
DXF	Graphics files that conform to AutoCAD format 2
ECA	hDC action editor files
EPS	Encapsulated PostScript files
ERR	Used for error log files by various applications
EXE	Executable program files for DOS and Windows applications
F#	Paradox form files
FLI	Animator animation files
FLT	Word for Windows filter files
FMT	dBASE screen format files
FNT	Font files
FON	Windows GDI-loadable font files
FOT	TrueType font resource files
FRM	dBASE report form files
FRM	Visual Basic form files
GIF	CompuServe-format graphic files
GRP	Program Manager group files
GUI	Guide document files

Extension	Description

Extension	Description
HGL	Graphics files that conform to HP Graphics Language format
HLP	Used by many applications (both DOS and Windows) for Help files
ICO	Windows icon files; can be used with Program Manager and other applications
IMG	Scanned image files
INF	Information files; usually plain text files used by Setup, Control Panel, and other installation utilities
INI	Initialization files; used by Windows and many applications
LBL	dBASE label files
LEX	Used by various programs for dictionary or thesaurus files
LGO	Windows startup-logo code files
LOD	Loadable modules used by Windows; load files used by applications and copy-protection schemes
MAK	Visual Basic "make" files
MCW	Document files formatted for Microsoft Word for the Macintosh
ME	Used by various applications for READ.ME files
MEM	dBASE memory files
MID	MIDI music files
MOD	Windows system module files
MSP	Bitmapped graphics files created by Microsoft Paint; can be used with Windows Paintbrush
NET	Network configuration files
NIL	Norton Desktop icon files
NSS	Norton Desktop screen saver files
OBJ	Object code files
OLD	Used by various applications for backup file
OV#	Used by various DOS applications for program overlay files
OVD	Paradox overlay files
OVL	Used by various DOS applications for program overlay files
OVR	Used by various DOS applications for program overlay files
PAL	Color palette files
PAS	Pascal language source code file
PCC	PC Paintbrush cutout picture files

Extension	Description
PCX	PC Paintbrush bitmap graphics files; also works with Windows Paintbrush
PFM	Printer font metric files
PGM	Used by various DOS applications for program overlay files
PIC	Used by various applications for graphics files
PIF	Program Information File; use with PIF Editor
PIX	Used by various applications for graphics files
PLT	AutoCAD plot file
PM3	PageMaker files (version 3)
PM4	PageMaker files (version 4)
PRG	dBASE; procedure files
PRS	Norton Desktop viewer files
PS2	PS/2 system drivers
PUB	PageMaker publication files
PX	Paradox primary index files
R#	Paradox report format files
REC	Windows Recorder macro files
REG	OLE registration database files
RES	Windows resource file that contains code resources used by programming languages
RLE	Bitmap graphics files that conform to the Run Length Encoded file format
RLM	TIGA firmware code files
RMI	Multimedia data files; can be used with Media Player
RTF	Files that conform to Microsoft's Rich Text File format
SAM	AMI Pro document files
SC	Screen files used by online tutorials for various DOS applications
SCR	Windows screen-saver files
SET	Paradox settings files
SET	Norton Desktop desk set files
SHH	Setup automated settings files
SLK	Files that conform to Microsoft's Symbolic Link format (SYLK)
SOM	Paradox sort information files

Extension	Description
SRC	Source files; usually a plain text file used by Setup to create a settings or .INI file
SYM	Symbolic debugging definitions for Windows programs
SYS	DOS device driver files; DOS system files
TBK	ToolBook book files
TIF	Graphic files that conform to the TIFF format
TMP	Temporary files
TRM	Windows Terminal settings files
TSK	Background task application files
TTF	TrueType font files
TX8	DOS text files
TXT	Generic text files
VAL	Paradox validity check files
WAV	Digital audio files
WCM	Microsoft Works communications files
WDB	Microsoft Works database files
WIN	Used by Windows to denote backup files; for example, AUTOEXEC.WIN
WK1	Lotus 1-2-3 spreadsheet files (version 2)
WK3	Lotus 1-2-3 spreadsheet files (version 3)
WKS	Lotus 1-2-3 spreadsheet files (version 1)
WKS	Microsoft Works spreadsheet files
WMF	Graphics files that conform to the Windows Metafile format
WPD	Windows PostScript description files
WPG	DrawPerfect picture files
WPS	Microsoft Works wordprocessing files
WRI	Windows Write document files
XLA	Excel add-in files
XLC	Microsoft Excel chart files
XLM	Excel macro files
XLS	Microsoft Excel spreadsheet files
XLT	Excel template files
XLW	Excel workspace files
ZIP	Files that have been compressed by PKZIP

Windows
Address Book

Abacist Software Co.
5580 LaJolla Boulevard, #340
La Jolla, California 92037
Phone: 619/488-3929, 800/729-3597
Fax: 619/483-9713
HotWin

Abacus
5370-52nd Street SE
Grand Rapids, Michigan 49512
Phone: 616/698-0330, 800/451-4319
Fax: 616/698-0325
Utility software: Becker Tools, Virus Secure,
NoMouse

Ace Software Corporation
1740 Technology Drive, Suite 680
San Jose, California 95110
Phone: 408/451-0100
Fax: 408/437-1018
The AceFile Database program is a top-flight con-
tender in the personal database category

Adobe Systems, Inc.
1585 Charleston Road, P.O. Box 7900
Mountain View, California 94039-7900
Phone: 415/961-4400, 800/383-FONTS
Fax: 415/961-3769
The creator of PostScript also sells first-rate graph-
ics software and collections of typefaces. Major
products: Adobe Illustrator, Adobe Streamline,
Adobe Type Library, Adobe Type Manager

Affinity Microsystems
1050 Walnut Street, Suite 425
Boulder, Colorado 80302
Phone: 303/442-4840, 800/367-6771
Fax: 303/442-4999
Tempo, a sophisticated macro utility

AimTech Corporation
20 Trafalgar Square
Nashua, New Hampshire 03063
Phone: 603/883-0220, 800/289-2884
Fax: 603/883-5582
Multimedia software and utilities: IconAuthor,
IconAnimate, RezSolution

Aldus Corporation
411 First Avenue South, Suite 200
Seattle, Washington 98104
Phone: 206/622-5500, 800/333-2538
Fax: 206/888-3665
Leading vendor of desktop publishing and graph-
ics software. Noteworthy products: PageMaker,
PhotoStyler, Freehand, IntelliDraw

Altech Software
5964 La Place Court
Carlsbad, California 92008
Phone: 619/438-6883, 800/748-5657
Fax: 619/438-6898
Desktop publishing utilities: Publisher's
Powerpack, AllType Typeface Converter

Approach Software Corp.
311 Penobscot Drive
Redwood City, California 94063
Phone: 800/APPROACH
Approach database software

Aristosoft
6920 Koll Center Parkway, Suite 209
Pleasanton, California 94566
Phone: 800/338-2629, 800/426-8288
Fax: 510/426-6703
Utilities: Wired for Sound, More Windows

Artisoft
691 East River Road
Tuscon, Arizona 85704
Phone: 602/293-4000, 800/TINYRAM
Fax: 602/293-8065
Local area networks

ARTIST Graphics
2675 Patton Road
St. Paul, Minnesota 55113
Phone: 612/631-7800, 800/627-8478
Fax: 612/631-7802
The WinSprint family of display adapter cards and Windows accelerators

Ashlar Incorporated
1290 Oakmead Parkway
Sunnyvale, California 94086
Phone: 408/746-3900
Fax: 408/746-0749
Ashlar Vellum

AST
16215 Alton Parkway
Irvine, California 92713
Phone: 800/876-4278
Fax: 714/727-8845
Computer systems

Astral Development Corporation
Londonberry Square, Suite 112
Londonberry, New Hampshire 03053
Phone: 603/432-6800
Fax: 603/434-6904
Picture Publisher

Asymetrix Corporation
110-110th Avenue NE, Suite 717
Bellevue, Washington 98004
Phone: 206/637-1500, 800/624-8999
Fax: 206/455-3071
Toolbook, a HyperCard-like program for Windows

Atech
5964 La Place Court, Suite 100
Carlsbad, California 92008
Phone: 619/438-6883, 800/786-3668
Fax: 619/438-6898
Typography software: AllType, AllFonts, FastFonts

ATI Technologies
3761 Victoria Park Avenue
Scarborough, Ontario, Canada M1W 3S2
Phone: 416/756-0718
Fax: 416/756-0720
Display adapter cards and Windows accelerators: VGAWonder, Ultra, Graphics Vantage

Attachmate Corporation
13231 SE 36th Street
Bellevue, Washington 98006
Phone: 206/644-4010, 800/426-6283
Fax: 206/747-9924
EXTRA! PC-to-mainframe software

Attitash Software, Inc.
20 Trafalgar Square
Nashua, New Hampshire 03063
Phone: 603/882-4809, 800/736-4198
Fax: 603/882-4936
Utility software: AttiTools, DragNet

Autodesk, Inc.
2320 Marinship Way
Sausalito, California 94965
Phone: 800/223-3601
Fax: 415/491-8308
The world's premier CAD software company also develops multimedia and graphics products.
Notable products: AutoCAD, Animator, Multimedia Explorer

Automated Design System
375 Northridge Road, Suite 270
Atlanta, Georgia 30350
Phone: 404/394-2552, 800/366-2552
Fax: 404/394-2191
Windows Workstation is an excellent example of
network and management utilities for the end
user

Banyan Systems Inc.
120 Flanders Road
Westboro, Massachusetts 01581
Phone: 508/898-1000
Fax: 508/898-3604
Banyan Vines network operating system

Bear Rock Technologies
6069 Enterprise Drive
Diamond Springs, California 95619
Phone: 916/622-4640, 800/232-7625
Fax: 916/622-4775
Bear Rock Labeler for making all types of labels,
including name tags, envelopes, and bar codes

Bell Atlantic
1310 N. Court House Road
Arlington, Virginia 22201
Phone: 215/768-5683, 800/688-4469
Fax: 215/341-9242
Thinx data analysis software

Berkeley Systems
2095 Rose St.
Berkeley, California 94709
Phone: 510/540-5535, 800/877-5535
Fax: 510/540-5115
After Dark, Flying Toasters, Star Trek, and other
screen-saver madness

Bit Software, Inc.
47987 Fremont Boulevard
Fremont, California 94538
Phone: 510/490-2928
Fax: 510/490-9490
Bitfax

Bitstream, Inc.
215 First Street
Cambridge, Massachusetts 02142
Phone: 617/497-6222, 800/522-FONT,
800/873-2480
Fax: 617/868-4732
Desktop publishing utilities and typeface collec-
tions: FaceLift, MakeUp, TrueType Font Packs

Blue Sky Software Corporation
7486 La Jolla Boulevard, Suite 3
La Jolla, California 92037
Phone: 619/459-6365, 800-677-4WIN
Fax: 619/459-6366
Programming utilities: RoboHELP, BugMAN,
QuickMENU, Magic Fields, WindowsMAKER

Blyth Software, Inc.
1065 E. Hillsdale Blvd., Suite 320
Foster City, California 94404
Phone: 415/571-0222, 800/843-8615
Fax: 415/571-1132
Omnis cross-platform database development sys-
tem for Windows and Macintosh; a powerful pro-
gram that you either love or hate

Borland International, Inc.
1800 Green Hills Road
Scotts Valley, California 95066
Phone: 408/438-5300, 800/331-0877
Fax: 408/438-9119
One of the industry's giants, Borland develops
productivity software and programming tools:
Borland C++, ObjectVision, Turbo Pascal, Para-
dox, Quattro, dBASE

Caere Corporation
100 Cooper Court
Los Gatos, California 95030
Phone: 408/395-7000, 800/535-7226
Fax: 408/354-2743
OCR software and hardware: OmniPage, Typist

CalComp Digitizer Products Group
14555 N. 82nd Avenue
Scottsdale, Arizona 85260
Phone: 800/458-5888
Fax: 602-948-5508
Graphics tablets: DrawingBoard, DrawingPad

Calera Recognition Systems, Inc.
475 Potrero Avenue
Sunnyvale, California 94086
Phone: 408/720-0999, 800/544-7051
Fax: 408/720-1330
OCR software and hardware: WordScan,
TopScan

Caseworks
One Dunwoody Park, Suite 130
Atlanta, Georgia 30338
Phone: 404/399-6236, 800/635-1577
Fax: 404/399-9516
CASE:W code generator

Central Point Software
15220 NW Greenbrier Parkway
Beaverton, Oregon 97006
Phone: 503/690-8088
Fax: 503/690-8083
Utilities: Central Point Backup, PC Tools

Chinon America, Inc.
615 Hawaii Avenue
Torrance, California 90503
Phone: 213/533-0274, 800/441-0222
Fax: 213/533-1727
Color scanners

Claris Corporation
5201 Patrick Henry Dr., Box 58168
Santa Clara, California 95052-8618
Phone: 408/987-7000
Apple's software subsidiary is now generating
Windows products: Hollywood, FileMaker

Clear Software Inc.
385 Elliot Street
Newton, Massachusetts 02164
Phone: 617/965-6755, 800/338-1759
Easy Boot

The Cobb Group, Inc.
9420 Bunsen Parkway, Suite 300
Louisville, Kentucky 40220
Phone: 502/491-1900, 800/223-8720
Fax: 502/491-4200
Newsletters

CODA Music Software
1401 E. 79th Street
Bloomington, Minnesota 55425
Phone: 612/854-1288, 800/843-2066
Fax: 612/854-4631
Finale music transcription and score publishing
software

Colorgraphic Communications
5388 New Peachtree Road
Atlanta, Georgia 30341
Phone: 404/455-3921
Fax: 404/458-0616
Super Dual VGA lets you run two monitors on
one PC

The Complete PC
1983 Concourse Drive
San Jose, California 95131
Phone: 408/434-0145
Fax: 408/434-1048
The Complete Fax, The Complete Answering
Machine

CompuAdd Express
12306 Technology Boulevard
Austin, Texas 78727
Phone: 512/219-1800, 800/925-7811
Fax: 512/219-2890
Computer systems

Computer Associates International, Inc.
One Computer Associates Plaza
Islandia, New York 11788-7000
Phone: 800/531-5236
Fax: 408/432-0614
A top-seller of mainframe software has entered the Windows market by acquiring outside products: CA-Compete!, CA-Cricket Graph, CA-Cricket Presents, ACCPAC Simply Accounting, Realizer, SuperProject, dBFast

Computer Support Corporation
15926 Midway Road
Dallas, Texas 75244-9982
Phone: 214/661-8960
Fax: 214/661-5429
The Arts & Letters family of graphics and desktop publishing software

CompuThink, Inc.
15127 NE 24th, Suite 344
Redmond, Washington 98052
Phone: 206/881-7354
Fax: 206/883-1452
Publishes Jesse Berst's Windows Watcher Newsletter, mandatory reading for Windows software developers; it's as if Berst stationed a spy in Microsoft's corporate backyard

Connect, Inc.
10161 Bubb Road
Cupertino, California 95014
Phone: 408/973-0110, 800/262-2638
Fax: 408/973-0497
Governet, PC.MacNet for Windows

Consumers Software Ltd.
106-314 East Holly Street
Bellingham, Washington 98225
Phone: 800/663-8935
Fax: 604/682-1378
The Network Courier

Corel Systems Corporation
1600 Carling Avenue
Ottawa, Ontario, Canada K1Z 8R7
Phone: 613/728-8200, 800/836-DRAW
Fax: 613/728-9790
CorelDRAW, considered by many to be the best drawing package for the PC

CTA, Inc.
25 Science Park, Suite 310
New Haven, Connecticut 06511
Phone: 203/786-5828, 800/252-1442
Fax: 203/786-5833
TexPert Developer's ToolKit lets you add OCR capabilities to programs under development

Custom Applications, Inc.
900 Technology Park Drive, Building 8
Billerica, Massachusetts 01821
Phone: 508/667-8585, 800/873-4367
Fax: 508/667-8821
Freedom of Press (provides disk-based PostScript compatibility)

Datacopy Corporation
535 Oakmead Parkway
Sunnyvale, California 94086
Phone: 408/522-3826
Fax: 408/522-3800
PC Image

Datastorm Technologies, Inc.
P.O. Box 1471
Columbia, Missouri 65205
Phone: 314/443-3282, 800/326-4999
ProComm telecommunications software

Data Translation
100 Locke Drive
Marlboro, Massachusetts 01752-1192
Phone: 508/481-3700
Global Lab Image

Dattel Communication Systems
3508 Market Street, Suite 415
Philadelphia, Pennsylvania 19104
Phone: 215/564-5577
Fax: 215/243-3705
Programming utilities: DataLIB, ZipLIB

Da Vinci Systems
P.O. Box 17449
Raleigh, North Carolina 27619
Phone: 800/328-4624, 800-DAVINCI
Fax: 919/787-3550
DaVinci eMAIL

Dell Computer Corp.
9505 Arboretum Boulevard
Austin, Texas 78759
Phone: 800/424-1366
Computer systems

DeLorme Mapping Systems
Lower Main St., P.O. Box 298
Freeport, Maine 04032
Phone: 207/865-4171
Fax: 207/865-9628
Mapping software; the U.S. Atlas and Gazetteer incorporates a complete collection of U.S. street maps on a single CD-ROM

Delrina Technology, Inc.
6830 Via Del Oro, Suite 240
San Jose, California 95119
Phone: 408/363-2345, 800/268-6082
Fax: 408/363-2340
WinFax, PerForm

Desktop Computing, Inc.
2635 North First Street, Suite 203
San Jose, California 95134
Phone: 415/323-5535
Fax: 415/323-4434
Desktop Draw, Desktop Studio, Hummingbird

Diamond Computer Systems, Inc.
532 Mercury Drive
Sunnyvale, California 94086
Phone: 408/736-2000
Fax: 408/730-5750
Display adapter cards

Digital Communications Associates
1000 Alderman Drive
Alpharetta, Georgia 30202
Phone: 404/442-4000, 800/241-IRMA
Fax: 404/442-4399
Communications software: Crosstalk, IRMA

Digital Equipment Corporation
10 Tara Boulevard, 4/D6
Nashua, New Hampshire 03062
Phone: 603/884-0614
Fax: 603/884-5284
With minicomputer sales cooling, DEC is turning to PCs and Windows software for new revenues. Products include complete PC systems and software, such as DECWrite for Windows and the PathWorks network system

Digitalk, Inc.
9841 Airport Blvd.
Los Angeles, California 90045
Phone: 213/645-1082, 800/922-8255
Fax: 213/645-1306
Smalltalk/V

Dr. T's Music Software, Inc.
100 Crescent Road #18
Needham, Massachusetts 02194
Phone: 617/455-1454
Fax: 617/455-1460
MIDI performance and educational software:
X-or, Composer Quest

Dvorak International
Box 128
Brandon, Vermont 85733
Phone: 802/247-6747
Supports use of the Dvorak-keyboard layout

Easel Corporation
25 Corporate Drive
Burlington, Massachusetts 01803
Phone: 617/221-2100
Fax: 617/221-3099
The EASEL application development system

Eicon Technology Corporation
2196-32nd Avenue
Montreal, Quebec
Canada H8T 3H7
Phone: 514/631-2592
Fax: 514/631-3092
The Access family of terminal-emulation software

Electronic Music Company
15922 Strathern Street, #3
Van Nuys, California 91406
Phone: 818/780-2248
Fax: 818/709-7376
EM Arranger

ElseWare Corporation
3201 Fremont Avenue North
Seattle, Washington 98103-8866
Phone: 206/547-9623
Fax: 206/632-7255
DataShaper database report generator

Emerald City Software
1040 Marsh Road, Suite 110
Menlo Park, California 94025
Phone: 415/324-8080, 800/323-0417
Fax: 415/324-0316
Lasertalk

Emerald Systems Corporation
12230 World Trade Drive
San Diego, California 92128
Phone: 619/673-2161, 800/767-2587
Fax: 619/673-2288
Back-up products: Xpress Librarian, EmQ, Tape
Backup Server, System EmSave

Epson America, Inc.
20770 Madrona Avenue
Torrance, California 90503
Phone: 310/782-0770, 800/922-8911
Fax: 310/782-5179
One of the world's largest electronics companies,
offers a complete line of PCs and printers

Everex Systems Inc.
48431 Milmont Drive
Fremont, California 94538
Phone: 510/683-2100
Fax: 510/651-0728
Computer systems and peripherals

Finalsoft Corporation
3900 NW 79th Avenue
Miami, Florida 33166
Phone: 800/232-8228
Fax: 305/477-0680
FinalSoft Executive

First Byte
19840 Pioneer Avenue
Torrance, California 90503
Phone: 310/793-0610, 800/523-2983
Fax: 310/793-0611
*Adds synthesized speech capabilities to Windows
with Monologue and ProVoice*

Flashpoint Development
P.O. Box 270492
Houston, Texas 77277
Phone: 713/726-1892
Utilities: WinNAV, WIZiper, ZIPX

FORMTEK, Inc.
661 Anderson Drive
Foster Plaza VII
Pittsburgh, Pennsylvania 15220
Phone: 412/937-4900, 800/FORMTEK
Fax: 412/937-4946
*Engineering document management:
REDLINEPC, VIEWPC*

FormWorx Corporation
Reservoir Place, 1601 Trapelo Road
Waltham, Massachusetts 02154
Phone: 617/890-4499, 800/992-0085
Fax: 617/890-4496
Form Publisher

Fractal Design Corporation
335 Spreckels Drive, Suite F
Aptos, California 95003
Phone: 408/688-5300
Fax: 408/688-8836
*Fractal Design Painter is one of the best paint pro-
grams for artists*

FTG Data Systems
8381 Katella Avenue
Stanton, California 90680
Phone: 714/995-3900, 800/962-3900
Fax: 714/995-3989
Light pens

Future Soft Engineering, Inc.
1001 S. Dairy Ashford, Suite 203
Houston, Texas 77077
Phone: 713/496-9400
Fax: 713/496-1090
*The DynaComm family of telecommunications
programs*

Future Tech Systems, Inc.
824 East Main Street
Auburn, Washington 98002
Phone: 206/939-7552
Fax: 206/735-6763
Envision

Gateway 2000
610 Gateway Drive
North Sioux City, South Dakota 57049-2000
Phone: 605/232-2000, 800/523-2000
Fax: 605/232-2023
Computer systems

Genoa Systems Corporation
75 E. Trimble Road
San Jose, California 95131
Phone: 408/432-9090
Fax: 408/434-0997
Display adapter cards

Geovision, Inc.
5680 Peachtree Parkway
Norcross, Georgia 30092
Phone: 404/448-8224
Fax: 404/447-4525
Mapping tools: Tiger Tools, Windows/On the World, StatMap

Gold Disk, Inc.
P.O. Box 789, Streetsville
Mississauga, Ontario
Canada L5M 2C2
Phone: 416/602-4000, 800/465-3375
Fax: 416/602-4001
Graphics and multimedia software: Animation Works Interactive, Professional Draw, and ScreenCraze

Gupta Technologies, Inc.
1040 Marsh Road
Menlo Park, California 94025
Phone: 415/321-9500, 800/876-3267
Fax: 415/321-5471
SQLWindows, Quest

Halcyon Software
1590 La Pradera Drive
Campbell, California 95008
Phone: 408/378-9898
Fax: 408/378-9935
Graphics utilities: DoDot, DoView, DoSnap, DoThumbnail, DoConvert

Hauppauge Computer Works, Inc.
91 Cabot Court
Hauppauge, New York 11788-3706
Phone: 516/434-1600
Fax: 516/434-3198
Peripherals and motherboards; Win/TV provides a TV tuner on a video card with frame-grabbing capabilities

hDC Computer Corporation
6742-185th Avenue NE
Redmond, Washington 98052
Phone: 206/885-5550, 800/321-4606
Fax: 206/881-9770
Utilities: Power Launcher, hDC FileApps, hDC FirstApps, hDC Windows Express, hDC Card Designer, hDC Icon Designer, hDC Windows Color

Headland Technology, Inc.
46221 Landing Parkway
Fremont, California 94538
Phone: 415/623-7587, 800/238-0101
Fax: 415/656-0397
Video display cards, including the Video Seven series; windows accelerators

Heizer Software
P.O. Box 232019
Pleasant Hill, California 94523
Phone: 510/943-7667, 800/888-7667
Fax: 510/943-6882
Utilities and educational software: Earthquake Preparedness, HandTalk, Convert-it

Hercules Computer Technology, Inc.
3839 Spinnaker Ct.
Fremont, California 94538
Phone: 800/532-0600, 510/623-6030
Fax: 510/623-1112
Display adapter cards, including the Graphics Station series

Hewlett-Packard
974 East Arquez Avenue
Sunnyvale, California 95086
Phone: 800/554-1305, 800/752-0900
Fax: 408/720-3560
One of the world's top computer manufacturers; produces Vectra computer systems, LaserJet printers, ScanJet scanners, DeskJet printers, NewWave graphic desktop

Houston Instrument
8500 Cameron Road
Austin, Texas 78753
Phone: 512/835-0900, 800/444-3425
Fax: 512/835-1916
HI Image Maker, pen plotters, digitizing tablets

HSC Software
1661 Lincoln Boulevard, Suite 101
Santa Monica, California 90404
Phone: 310/393-8441
Fax: 310/392-6015
Multimedia software: Santa Fe Media Manager, Audio Tracks, InterActive, QuickShow!

IBM (International Business Machines)
I can never keep track of all the various addresses and phone numbers for Big Blue—its phone book is massive, and the company is being dramatically reorganized—so you're on your own with this one

ICOM Simulations, Inc.
648 South Wheeling Road
Wheeling, Illinois 60090
Phone: 708/520-4440, 800/877-4266
Fax: 708/459-7456
Graphics and utilities software: Intermission, Writepaint, Squeegee

Iconix Software Engineering, Inc.
2800-28th Street, Suite 320
Santa Monica, California 90405
Phone: 213/458-0092
Fax: 213/396-3454
FreeFlow

IEV International, Inc.
3030 S. Main Street, Suite 300
Salt Lake City, Utah 84115
Phone: 801/466-9093, 800/438-6161
Fax: 801/466-5921
Video hardware and utilities: Revolution video editing, ProMotion, SimulScan, Image Access, ProFile, VIP-8800

Image-In, Inc.
406 E. 79th Street
Minneapolis, Minnesota 55420
Phone: 612/888-3633, 800/345-3540
Fax: 612/888-3665
Graphics software: Full Pack, Plus, Read, Vect, Panorama, Scan and Paint

IMARA Research Corporation
111 Peter Street, Suite 804
Toronto, Ontario
Canada M5V 2H1
Phone: 416/516-4422
Fax: 416/516-4429
Document management software: Imara, CabNET

Individual Software
5870 Stoneridge Drive, Suite 1
Pleasanton, California 94588-9900
Phone: 510/734-6767, 800/822-3522
Fax: 510/734-8337
Training software for Windows applications

Information Builders, Inc.
1250 Broadway
New York, New York 10001
Phone: 212/736-4433, 800/969-INFO
Fax: 212/629-3612
Database software: Focus, Level5 Object

Informix Software, Inc.
4100 Bohannon Drive
Menlo Park, California 94025
Phone: 415/926-6300, 800/438-7627
Fax: 913/599-8429
Wingz

Inner Media, Inc.
60 Plain Road
Hollis, New Hampshire 03049
Phone: 603/465-3216, 800/962-2949
Fax: 603/465-7195
Collage screen-capture utility

Inset Systems, Inc.
71 Commerce Drive
Brookfield, Connecticut 06804-3405
Phone: 203/740-2400, 800/374-6738
Fax: 203/775-5634
*HiJaak screen capture and format conversion
utility*

Intel Corporation
5200 N.E. Elam Young Parkway
Hillsboro, Oregon 97124
Phone: 800/538-3373
Fax: 800/458-6231
*CPU chips and PC hardware: OverDrive accelera-
tor chips, Intel Above Board Memory Cards,
IntelInboard 386/PC, Intel Math coprocessors,
iRMX , MULTIBUS II PC/AT Subsystem,
SatisFAXtion*

IntelliCorp., Inc.
1975 El Camino Real West
Mountain View, California 94040-2216
Phone: 415/965-5500
Fax: 415/965-5647
KAPPA-PC, KEE

International Data Sciences, Inc
7 Wellington Road
Lincoln, Rhode Island 02917
Phone: 401/333-6200
800/IDS-DATA
Fax: 401/333-3584
Range Rider network monitoring software

Iris Associates
One Technology Park
Westford, Massachusetts 01886
Phone: 508/692-2800
Fax: 508/692-7365
IRIS 3-for-3

Jenson-Jones, Inc.
328 Newman Springs Road
Redbank, New Jersey 07701
Phone: 800/289-1548
Fax: 908/530-9827
Commence

JetForm Corporation
P.O. Box 606
163 Pioneer Drive
Leominster, Massachusetts 01453
Phone: 613/594-3026
800/267-9976
Fax: 613/594-8886
JetForm

Kensington Microware, Inc.
2855 Campus Drive
San Mateo, California 94403
Phone: 415/572-2700, 800/535-4242
Fax: 415/572-9675
Computer accessories: Expert Mouse

Knowledge Garden, Inc.
12-8 Technology Drive
Setauket, New York 11733
Phone: 516/246-5400
Fax: 516/246-5452
KnowledgePro

Kraft Systems
450 West California Avenue
Vista, California 92083
Phone: 619/724-7146
Fax: 619/941-1770
Kraft Mouse, Kraft Trackball

Kyocera Electronics, Inc.
100 Randolph Road
Somerset, New Jersey 08875
Phone: 800/232-6797
Printers, scanners, and other peripherals

LaserMaster Corporation
6900 Shady Oak Road
Eden Prarie, Minnesota 55344
Phone: 612/944-9330, 800/767-8004
Fax: 612/944-9519
WinPrinter, WinJet

LaserTools Corporation
1250-45th Street, Suite 100
Emeryville, California 94608
Phone: 510/420-8777, 800/767-8004
Fax: 510/420-1150
*Printing utilities: Fonts-on-the-Fly, PrintCash,
Printer Control Panel*

Logitech
6505 Kaiser Drive
Fremont, California 94555
Phone: 415/795-8500
Fax: 415/792-8100
*Input devices: MouseMan, TrackMan, Photo-
Man, ScanMan*

Lotus Development Corp.
55 Cambridge Parkway
Cambridge, Massachusetts 02142
Phone: 800/343-5414
Lotus 1-2-3, Ami Pro, Notes

Macromedia, Inc.
600 Townsend Street, Suite 310
San Francisco, California 94103
Phone: 415/442-0200
Fax: 415/595-3077
*Multimedia software: Authorware Professional,
Action!, Director*

MaeDae Enterprises
5430 Murr Road
Peyton, Colorado 80831
Phone: 719/683-3860
Utility software: Encrypt-It, Mortgage Designer

Mag Innovision
4392 Corporate Center Drive
Los Alamitos, California 90720
Phone: 714/827-3998, 800/827-3998
Fax: 714/827-5522
Video displays

Magni Systems Inc.
9500 SW Gemini Drive
Beaverton, Oregon 97005
Phone: 503/626-8400, 800/624-6465
Fax: 503/626-6225
*Multimedia video hardware: VGA Producer
series of NTSC video display cards*

MapInfo Corporation
200 Broadway
Troy, New York 12180
Phone: 518/274-8673, 800-FAST-MAP
Fax: 518/274-0510
MapInfo

Matesys Corp. N.A.
900 Larkspur Landing Circle, Suite 175
Larkspur, California 94939
Phone: 415/925-2900, 800/777-0545
Fax: 415/925-2909
ObjectView, ObjectScript/Object Script Pro, SIM-PLE Win

Mathematica, Inc.
402 S. Kentucky Avenue, Suite 210
Lakeland, Florida 33801
Phone: 813/682-1128
Fax: 813/686-5969
The Tempra series of graphics software

Matrox Electronic Systems, Ltd.
1055 St. Regis Boulevard
Dorval, Quebec
Canada H9P 2T4
Phone: 514/685-2630, 800/361-4903
Fax: 514/685-2853
M-WIN 1280

Maxis
2 Theater Square, Suite 230
Orinda, California 94563
Phone: 510/254-9700, 800/336-2947
Fax: 510/263-3736
Entertainment software: SimCity, SimEarth, RoboSport

Media Cybernetics, Inc.
848 Georgia Avenue
Silver Springs, Maryland 20910
Phone: 301/495-3305, 800/992-4256
Fax: 301/495-5964
The HALO series of graphics software

Media Vision Inc.
47221 Fremont Boulevard
Fremont, California 94538
Phone: 510/770-8600, 800/845-5870
Fax: 510/770-9592
Multimedia hardware: Pro AudioSpectrum series of sound cards

Meta Software Corporation
125 Cambridge Park Drive
Cambridge, Massachusetts 02140
Phone: 617/576-6920, 800/227-4106
Fax: 617/661-2008
MetaDesign, Design/IDEF, Design/OA Development System

Meta Systems, Ltd.
315 East Eisenhower Parkway, Suite 200
Ann Arbor, Michigan 48108
Phone: 313/663-6027
Fax: 313/663-6119
Structured Architect Workbench

Metz Software
P.O. Box 6699
Bellevue, Washington 98008-0699
Phone: 206/641-4525, 800/447-1712
Fax: 206/644-6026
Utilities: Task Manager, File F/X, Metz Lock

Microcom
500 River Ridge Drive
Norwood, Massachusetts 02062-5028
Phone: 617/551-1000, 800/822-8224
Fax: 617/551-1968
Communications and utility software: RELAY
Gold, Carbon Copy, Virex

Micrografx, Inc.
1303 Arapaho
Richardson, Texas 75081-2444
Phone: 214/234-1769, 800/733-3729
Fax: 214/234-2410
One of the oldest Windows software companies
and a top producer of graphics software: Picture
Publisher, Charisma, Micrografx Designer,
Micrografx ClipArt, Micrografx Draw Plus,
Micrografx Mirrors, Micrografx Xport

Micron Technology, Inc.
2805 East Columbia Road
Boise, Idaho 83706
Phone: 208/368-3800, 800/642-7661
Fax: 208/368-4431
Ascend

MicroQuill, Inc.
4900-25th Avenue NE #206
Seattle, Washington 98105
Phone: 206/525-8218, 800/441-7822
Fax: 206/525-8309
Programming utilities: DeMystifiers, The
Segmentor

Microsoft Corporation
One Microsoft Way
Redmond, Washington 98052-6399
Phone: 206/882-8080, 800/426-9400
Tech support for Windows: 206/637-7098
Product support BBS: 206/637-9009
Fax: 206/93MSFAX
Creator of Windows and a wide spectrum of soft-
ware: Excel, Word, Powerpoint, Project, Mail,
Office, Money, Publisher, OnLine, Visual Basic,
C++, Entertainment Pack, FoxPro, Access, Works,
Mouse, BallPoint

Microspeed, Inc.
44000 Old Warm Springs Blvd.
Fremont, California 94538
Phone: 415/490-1403, 800/232-7888
Fax: 415/490-1665
Mice, trackballs

Microtek
680 Knox Street
Torrance, California 90502
Phone: 310/321-2121, 800/654-4160
Fax: 310/538-1193
Scanners

Micro Tempus Corporation
800 South Street
Waltham, Massachusetts 02154
Phone: 617/899-4046
Fax: 617/899-2604
Micro-to-host software: Enterprise Router,
TEMPUS-LINK, TEMPUS-SHARE,
TEMPUS-TALK, TEMPUS-TRANSFER

Midisoft Corporation
P.O. Box 1000
Bellevue, Washington 98009
Phone: 206/881-7176, 800/PRO-MIDI
Fax: 206/883-1368
Music software: Midisoft DLL, Midisoft Studio,
Music Mentor

Mitsubishi Electronics America, Inc.
5665 Plaza Drive
Cypress, California 90630
Phone: 800/843-2515
Video monitors, printers, scanners

Moniterm Corporation
5740 Green Circle Drive
Minnetonka, Minnesota 55343
Phone: 612/935-4151, 800/933-5740
Fax: 612/933-5701
Video monitors

Moon Valley Software
706 East Bell Road, Suite 112
Phoenix, Arizona 85022
Phone: 602/375-9502, 800/473-5509
Fax: 602/993-4950
Utilities: D'Compress, IconTamer, Icon Do-It

Mouse Systems, Inc.
47505 Seabridge Drive
Fremont, California 94538
Phone: 510/656-1117, 800/RU-MOUSE
Fax: 510/656-4409
Input devices: Little Mouse, NewMouse, New-
Point, OmniMouse, PageBrush, PenMate, PC
Mouse, PC Trackball, White Mouse

Mustek, Inc.
15225 Alton Parkway
Irvine, California 92720
Phone: 714/833-7740, 800/366-4620
Fax: 714/833-7813
Scanners and scanning software

National Instruments
6504 Bridge Point Parkway
Austin, Texas 78730-5039
Phone: 512/794-0100, 800/433-3488
Fax: 512/794-8411
Data acquisition and laboratory control hardware
and software

NEC Information Systems, Inc.
1414 Massachusetts Avenue
Boxboro, Massachusetts 01719
Phone: 508/264-8000
Computer systems, video monitors, display adapt-
ers, printers, CD-ROM drives

Netlogic, Inc.
915 Broadway, 17th Floor
New York, New York 10010
Phone: 212/533-9090, 800/638-0048
Fax: 212/533-9524
Programming utilities: DDEX, Cezanne

Network Dimensions, Inc.
5339 Prospect Road, Suite 122
San Jose, California 95129
Phone: 408/446-9598
Fax: 408/255-4576
GrafNet Plus, GrafVUE

Network General Corporation
4200 Bohannon Drive
Menlo Park, California 94025
Phone: 415/688-2700
Sniffer Network Analyzer

Neuron Data, Inc.
156 University Avenue
Palo Alto, California 94301
Phone: 800/876-4900
Fax: 415/321-3728
Nexpert Object

New Media Graphics Corp.
780 Boston Road
Billerica, Massachusetts 01821
Phone: 508/663-0666, 800/288-2207
Fax: 508/663-6678
Display adapter cards and graphics hardware:
Super TV Tuner, SuperVideoWindows, Super
Motion Compression

NewQuest Technologies Inc.
2550 South Decker Lake Boulevard
Salt Lake City, Utah 84119
Phone: 801/975-9992, 800/877-1814
Fax: 801/975-9995
Ascend

North Coast Software, Inc.
P.O. Box 343
Barrington, New Hampshire 03825
Phone: 603/332-9363
Fax: 603/335-0042
Graphics software: ANIMaxx, Conversion Artist,
ImageExpress

Norton-Lambert Corp.
P.O. Box 4085
Santa Barbara, California 93140
Phone: 805/964-6767
Fax: 805/683-5679
Close-Up remote access software

Novell, Inc.
122 East 1700 South
Provo, Utah 84606
Phone: 801/379-5900, 800/453-1267
Fax: 801/747-4366
NetWare, DR-DOS

Number Nine Computer Corporation
725 Concord Avenue
Cambridge, Massachusetts 02138
Phone: 617/492-0999
Fax: 617/864-9329
Video display cards

OCR Systems
1800 Byberry Road, Suite 1405
Huntington Valley, Pennsylvania 19006
Phone: 215/938-7460, 800/233-4627
Fax: 215/938-7465
ReadRight, FormRight

Off The WALL Software
7680 Cottonwood Lane
Pleasanton, California 94588-4322
Phone: 510/484-4129
Utilities: Accesses, Archives

Okidata Printers
532 Fellowship Road
Mt. Laurel, New Jersey 08054-3499
Phone: 609/235-2600
Printers

Olduvai Corporation
7520 Red Road, #A
South Miami, Florida 33143
Phone: 305/665-4665, 800/822-0772
Fax: 305/665-0671
READ-IT!, O.C.R.

Optronics Technology
P.O. Box 3239
Ashland, Oregon 97520
Phone: 503/488-5040
Desktop Stereo is an FM stereo receiver on a card

Orchid Technology
45365 Northport Loop, West
Fremont, California 94538
Phone: 510/683-0300, 800/7ORCHID
Fax: 510/490-9312
Motherboards, display adapter cards; the latter category includes the ProDesigner series and the Fahrenheit series

OWL International, Inc.
2800-156th Avenue SE
Bellevue, Washington 98007
Phone: 206/747-3202, 800/344-9737
Fax: 206/641-9367
Guide

Pacific Data Products, Inc.
9125 Rehco Road
San Diego, California 92024
Phone: 619/597-4632
Fax: 619/552-0889
Fonts and printing utilities: Pacific Page, 25-in-One

PageAhead Software Corp.
2125 Western Avenue, Suite 300
Seattle, Washington 98121
Phone: 206/441-0340
PageAhead

Panacea, Inc.
24 Orchard View Drive
Londonderry, New Hampshire 03053
Phone: 800/729-7920
Fax: 603/434-2461
WinSpeed display accelerator software

Paradise/Western Digital Imaging
800 E. Middlefield Road
Mountain View, California 94043
Phone: 415/960-3360, 800/356-5787
Paradise series of display adapter cards

ParcPlace Systems
999 E. Arques Avenue
Sunnyvale, California 94086-4593
Phone: 408/481-9090
Fax: 408/481-9095
Objectworks/Smalltalk

Passport Designs, Inc.
100 Stone Pine Road
Half Moon Bay, California 94019
Phone: 415/726-0280
Fax: 415/726-2254
Music software: Master Track, Trax, Encore, MusicTime

PC Brand
405 Science Drive
Moorpark, California 93021
Phone: 805/378-6069
Fax: 805/529-8408
Computer systems

PC-Kwik Corporation
15100 S.W. Koll Parkway, Suite L
Beaverton, Oregon 97006
Phone: 503/644-5644, 800/395-5945
Fax: 503/646-8267
Utilities: Super PC-Kwik Disk Accelerator, WinMaster, Power Pack

Peachtree Software
1505 Pavilion Place
Norcross, Virginia 30093
Phone: 404/564-5700, 800/247-3224
Fax: 404/564-5888
Peachtree Accounting, Peachtree Client Write-Up

PeopleSoft, Inc.
1331 N. California Blvd., 4th Floor
Walnut Creek, California 94596-4502
Phone: 510/946-9460, 800/947-7753
Fax: 510/946-9461
PeopleSoft HRMS

Personal Library Software, Inc.
2400 Research Boulevard, Suite 350
Rockville, Maryland 20850
Phone: 301/990-1155
Fax: 301/963-9738
Personal Librarian

Pinnacle Publishing, Inc.
18000-72nd Avenue S., Suite 217
Kent, Washington 98032-1035
Phone: 206/941-2300, 800/231-1293
Fax: 206/251-5075
Chartbuilder, Graphics Server

Pioneer Software
5540 Centerview Drive, Suite 324
Raleigh, North Carolina 27606
Phone: 919/859-2220, 800/876-3101
Fax: 919/859-9334
Q+E database software

Pixelworks, Inc.
7 Park Avenue
Hudson, New Hampshire 03051
Phone: 603/880-1322, 800/247-2476
Fax: 603/880-6558
Ultra Clipper Graphics

Polaris Software
17150 Via del Campo, Suite 307
San Diego, California 92127
Phone: 619/674-6500, 800-PACKRAT
Fax: 619/674-7315
Polaris PackRat, PackRat for Networks

Prisma Software Corporation
2301 Clay Street
Cedar Falls, Iowa 50613
Phone: 800/373-0241
Fax: 319/266-2522
YourWay

ProHance Technologies, Inc.
1307 S. Mary Avenue, Suite 104
Sunnyvale, California 94087
Phone: 408/746-0950
Fax: 408/746-0741
PowerMouse, PowerTrack, ProMouse

Promised Land Technologies, Inc.
900 Chapel Street, Suite 300
New Haven, Connecticut 06510
Phone: 203/562-7335, 800/243-1806
Fax: 203/624-0655
*Braincel; add neural network capabilities to your
spreadsheet*

Publishing Technologies, Inc.
7719 Wood Hollow Drive, Suite 260
Austin, Texas 78713
Phone: 512/346-2835, 800/782-8324
Fax: 512/338-9718
*PubTech BatchWorks, PubTech File Organizer,
PubTech MultiTrack*

Qualitas, Inc.
7101 Wisconsin Avenue, Suite 1386
Bethesda, Maryland 20814
Phone: 301/907-6700, 800/733-1377
Fax: 301/907-0905
386MAX, BlueMAX

Quarterdeck Office Systems
150 Pico Boulevard
Santa Monica, California 90405
Phone: 213/392-9851
Quarterdeck Expanded Memory Manager
(QEMM)

Questar Corporation
P.O. Box 59, Route 202
New Hope, Pennsylvania 18938
Phone: 614/294-8306
QRMS-II

Quintar Company
370 Amapola Avenue, Suite 106
Torrance, California 90501
Phone: 213/320-5700, 800/223-5231
Fax: 213/618-1282
Q-Print

Radius, Inc.
1710 Fortune Drive
San Jose, California 95131-1744
Phone: 408/434-1010, 800/227-2795
Fax: 408/434-0127
Display adapter cards, video monitors; Multi-
View, PrecisionColor, Pivot, Two Page Display

Raima Corporation
3245-146th Place SE
Bellevue, Washington 98007
Phone: 206/747-5570
Fax: 206/747-1991
db-Vista, Raima Data Manager

Rainbow Technologies, Inc.
9292 Jeronimo Road
Irvine, California 92718
Phone: 714/454-2100, 800/852-8569
Fax: 714/454-8557
Software Sentinel

Rasterops Corp.
2500 Walsh Avenue
Santa Clara, California 95051
Phone: 408/562-4200, 800/468-7600
Fax: 408/562-4065
Display adapter cards, video monitors, color
printers

Ray Dream Inc.
1804 N. Shoreline Boulevard, Suite 240
Mountain View, California 94043
Phone: 800/846-0111
Fax: 415/960-1198
Graphics and rendering software: JAG

Reach Software Corporation
330 Potrero Avenue
Sunnyvale, California 94086
Phone: 408/733-8685, 800/MAILFLO
Fax: 408/778-6256
Electronic mail: MailMAN, WorkMAN

Redlake Corporation IPG
718 University Avenue, Suite 100
Los Gatos, California 95030
Phone: 408/770-6464, 800/543-6563
Fax: 408/778-6526
Desktop video products: PC2TV, SPECTRUM-
NTSC+

Reference Software International
330 Townsend Street
San Francisco, California 94107
Phone: 415/541-0222, 800/872-9933
Fax: 415/541-0509
Grammatik Windows

Retrix
2644-30th Street
Santa Monica, California 90405
Phone: 213/399-2200
Fax: 213/458-2685
5010 Network Management Center

RIX SoftWorks, Inc.
18023 Sky Park Circle, Suite J
Irvine, California 92714
Phone: 714/476-8266, 800/345-9059
Fax: 714/476-8486
WinRIX image processing software

Roland Digital Group
1961 McGaw Avenue
Irvine, California 92714
Phone: 714/975-0560
Fax: 714/975-0569
*Pen plotters, graphics tablets, desktop signmaker,
desktop engraver*

RoseSoft, Inc.
P.O. Box 70337
Bellevue, Washington 98007
Phone: 206/562-0225
Fax: 206/562-9846
ProKey macro utility

Samsung Information Systems America
3655 North First Street
San Jose, California 95134
Phone: 408/434-5482, 800/446-0262
Fax: 408/434-5653
Computer systems and peripherals

Saros Corporation
10900 8th Street NE, 700 Plaza Center
Bellevue, Washington 98004
Phone: 206/646-1066, 800/82-SAROS
Fax: 206/462-0879
Mezzanine, Saros FileShare

Scientific Software Tools, Inc.
30 E. Swedesford Road
Malvern, Pennsylvania 19355
Phone: 215/889-1630
Fax: 215/889-1630
DriverLINX data acquisition driver

Seagull Scientific Systems, Inc.
15127 NE 24th, Suite 333
Redmond, Washington 98052
Phone: 206/451-8966, 800/758-2001
Fax: 206/451-8982
Bar Tender bar code software

Seiko Instruments, Inc.
1130 Ringwood Court
San Jose, California 95131
Phone: 408/922-5950, 800/825-9711
Fax: 408/922-5840
Printers, monitors, and other peripherals

Sigma Designs
46501 Landing Parkway
Fremont, California 94538
Phone: 510/770-0100
Fax: 510/770-0110
Video monitors, display adapter cards

SmartApps Inc.
213 Elm Street
Santa Cruz, California 95060
Phone: 408/459-0856
Fax: 408/425-1709
Shades

Softac Corporation
23 Sunset Road
Winchester, Massachusetts 01890
Phone: 800/433-0486
Fax: 617/721-2590
K.U.I. keyboard utility

Softbridge, Inc.
125 Cambridge Park Drive
Cambridge, Massachusetts 02140
Phone: 617/576-2257, 800/955-9190
Fax: 617/864-7747
Bridge Batch, Bridge Toolkit, Automated Test Facility

SoftView, Inc.
1721 Pacific Avenue, Suite 100
Oxnard, California 93033
Phone: 805/385-5000, 800/622-6829
Fax: 805/385/5001
Accounting software

Software Products International
10240 Sorrento Valley Road
San Diego, California 92121
Phone: 619/450-1526, 800/937-4774
Fax: 619/450-1921
Access SQL

Software Publishing Corporation
3165 Kifer Road
Santa Clara, California 95051
Phone: 408/986-8000
Professional Write, Superbase, Harvard Graphics, InfoAlliance

Software Ventures Corporation
2907 Claremont Avenue
Berkeley, California 94705
Phone: 510/644-3232
Fax: 510/848-0885
MicroPhone Pro for Windows

Software Workshop, Inc.
75 South Mountain Way
Orem, Utah 84058
Phone: 801/224-6865, 800/762-9550
Fax: 801/224-8121
Utilities: Icon Pak, DelGuard, The Button Cube

Spectragraphics
9590 SW Gemini Drive
Beaverton, Oregon 97005
Phone: 503/641-2200, 800/800-9599
Fax: 503/643-8642
Squeegee series of graphics adapters

Spectral Synthesis, Inc.
19501-144th Avenue NE, Suite 1000A
Woodinville, Washington 98072
Phone: 206/487-2931
Fax: 206/487-3431
Digital audio hardware and software: StudioTracks, AudioScape, AudioVision

Spinnaker Software
201 Broadway
Cambridge, Massachusetts 02139
Phone: 617/494-1200, 800/323-8088
Fax: 617/494-1219
Spinnaker PLUS, Personal Access

SPSS, Inc.
444 North Michigan Avenue
Chicago, Illinois 60611
Phone: 312/329-3300, 800/543-6609
Fax: 312/329-3668
SPSS for Windows

Stac Electronics
5993 Avenida Encinas
Carlsbad, California 92008
Phone: 619/431-7474, 800/522-7822
Stacker disk compression products

STB Systems, Inc.
1651 North Glenville, Suite 210
Richardson, Texas 75081
Phone: 214/234-8750, 800/234-4334
Fax: 214/234-1306
Display adapter cards and Windows accelerators: Power Graph, Wind/X

The Stirling Group
172 Old Mill Drive
Schaumburg, Illinois 60193
Phone: 708/307-9197, 800/374-4353
Fax: 708/307-9340
The SHIELD series of programming tools

StylusTech, Inc.
P.O. Box 9171
Cambridge, Massachusetts 02139
Phone: 617/277-7007
Fax: 617/277-8907
InputMaster programming tools for pen-based
application development

Summagraphics Corporation
8500 Cameron Road
Austin, Texas 78753
Phone: 512/8835-0900, 800/444-3425
Fax: 512/835-1916
Graphics tablets and input devices:
SummaSketch, SummaDraw, SummaScribe,
MicroGrid, SummaGrid

Symantec Corporation
10201 Torre Avenue
Cupertino, California 95014-2132
Phone: 408/253-9600
Fax: 408/253-4092
Top software producer: Norton Desktop, Norton
Backup, JustWrite, On Target, Zortec languages,
Whitewater Resource Toolkit, Actor, Q&A, Time
Line, Game Pack

Symbologic Corporation
15379 NE 90th Street
Redmond, Washington 98052
Phone: 206/881-3938, 800/448-9292
Fax: 206/881-7198
Symbologic Adept

SYSTAT, Inc.
1800 Sherman Avenue
Evanston, Illinois 60201-3793
Phone: 708/864-5670
Fax: 708/492-3567
SYSTAT for Windows

Tandy Corporation
1800 One Tandy Center
Fort Worth, Texas 76102
Phone: 817/390-3011
Fax: 817/878-6508
Computer systems

Technical Aesthetics Operations
501 West 5th Street, P.O. Box 1254
Rolla, Missouri 65401
Phone: 800/264-1121
Fax: 314/364-5631
The Editizer desktop video editing system

TechSoft Systems Inc.
1375 Kemper Meadow Drive, Suite 11
Cincinnati, Ohio 45240-1650
Phone: 513/825-8386, 800/825-8386
Fax: 513/825-9726
deskMinder

Tektronix, Inc.
MS 631583, P.O. Box 10000
Wilsonville, Oregon 97070
Phone: 503/682-7377, 800/835-6100
Fax: 503/682-3408
Printers

Telware, Inc.
300 Roundhill Drive
Rockaway, New Jersey 07866
Phone: 201/586-8885
M.Y.O.B. accounting system

Teradata
5400 Alla Road
Los Angeles, California 90066
Phone: 213/827-8777
Fax: 213/822-0703
Teradata Excel Interface

T/Maker Company
1390 Villa Street
Mountain View, California 94041
Phone: 415/962-0195
Fax: 415/962-0201
ClickArt series of clip art, FaxMania

Tool Technology Publishing
1125 A Street, Suite 107
San Rafael, California 94901
Phone: 415/459-3700
Fax: 415/459-1079
WinTools, WinDesk

Traveling Software
18702 North Creek Parkway
Bothwell, Washington 98011
Phone: 206/483-8088, 800/343-8080
Fax: 206/487-1284
*Utilities for portable computing: WinConnect,
LapLink*

Tri-Data Systems, Inc.
3279 Scott Blvd.
Santa Clara, California 95054
Phone: 408/727-3270, 800/TRI-DATA
Fax: 408/980-6565
WIN 3270 for Netway

Trident Microsystems, Inc.
321 Soquel Way
Sunnyvale, California 94086
Phone: 408/738-0905, 800/348-8808
Impact III

Triton Technologies, Inc.
200 Middlesex Turnpike
Iselin, New Jersey 08830
Phone: 908/855-9440, 800/322-9440
Fax: 908/855-9608
CO/Session series of communications software

Truevision, Inc.
7340 Shadeland Station
Indianapolis, Indiana 46256
Phone: 317/841-0332, 800/344-TRUE
Fax: 317/576-7700
Display adapter cards

Turtle Beach Systems
P.O. Box 5074
York, Pennsylvania 17405
Phone: 717/843-6916
Fax: 717/854-8391
Music software and hardware: MultiSound, Wave

U-Lead Systems, Inc.
970 West 190th Street, Suite 520
Torrance, California 90502
Phone: 310/523-9393, 800/858-5323 x600
Fax: 310/523-9399
Graphics software: ImagePals

Ventura Software Inc.
15175 Innovation Drive
San Diego, California 92128
Phone: 800/822-8221
Fax: 619/673-7777
Ventura Database Publisher

Video Seven/Headland Technology
46221 Landing Parkway
Fremont, California 94538
Phone: 510/623-7857, 800/238-0101
Display adapter cards

ViewSonic
20480 E. Business Parkway
Walnut, California 91789
Phone: 714/869-7976, 800/888-8583
Fax: 714/869-7958
Video monitors

Virtual Reality Laboratories, Inc.
2341 Ganador Court
San Luis Obispo, California 93401
Phone: 805/545-8515
Fax: 805/545-8515
Distant Suns

The Voyager Company
1351 Pacific Coast Highway
Santa Monica, California 90401
Phone: 213/451-1383
Fax: 213/394-2156
Multimedia software: Amanda Stories

Voyetra Technologies
333 Fifth Avenue
Pelham, New York 10803
Phone: 914/738-4500, 800/233-9377
Fax: 914/738-6946
Music software: M/PC, MusiClips, AudioView,
PatchView, MIDI Toolkit, MIDI Express

Wall Data Incorporated
17769 NE 78th Place
Redmond, Washington 98052
Phone: 206/883-4777, 800/48R-UMBA
Fax: 206/885-9250
Rumba, Rumba Mailbox, Rumba Software Devel-
opment Kit

Wang Laboratories, Inc.
One Industrial Avenue, MS 019-32A
Lowell, Massachusetts 01851
Phone: 508/459-5000, 800/522-9264
Fax: 508/452-0896
Image Wizard, Open/Image Windows, SeaView

WaveTek Corporation
9045 Balboa Avenue
San Diego, California 92123
Phone: 619/279-2200, 800/874-4835
Fax: 619/565-9558
WaveForm DSP, WaveTest

Weitek, Inc.
1060 E. Arques Avenue
Sunnyvale, California 94086
Phone: 900/845-0150
Fax: 415/863-2686
Math coprocessors and Windows accelerators;
Weitek Power for Windows

Wholesale Ergonomic Products
2635 Cleveland Ave. #5
Santa Rosa, California 95403
Phone: 707/544-3020
Compu-Rest arm support keyboard and mouse
support

Willow Peripherals
190 Willow Avenue
Bronx, New York 10454
Phone: 718/402-9500, 800/4441585
Fax: 718/402-9603
Multimedia video hardware: VGA-TV series

Wilson WindowWare
2701 California Avenue SW, Suite 212
Seattle, Washington 98116
Phone: 800/762-8383
Fax: 206/935-7129
Utilities: Command Post, WinBatch, WinCheck,
WinEdit, Address Manager, Reminder

Windowcraft Corporation
6 New England Executive Park
Burlington, Massachusetts 01803
Phone: 617/272-0999, 800/828-2268
Fax: 617/273-0749
Windowcraft

Windows User Group Network (WUGNET)
P.O. Box 1967
Media, Pennsylvania 19063
Phone: 215/565-1861
Fax: 215/565-7106
User group publications and services

Wolfram Research, Inc.
100 Trade Center Drive
Champaign, Illinois 61820-7237
Phone: 217/398-0700, 800/441-MATH
Fax: 217/398-0747
Mathematica for Windows

Wonderware
16 Technology, Suite 154
Irvine, California 92718
Phone: 714/727-3200
Fax: 714/727-3270
Programming tools: NetDDE, DDE I/O Servers,
InTouch

WordPerfect Corporation
1555 North Technology Way
Orem, Utah 84057-2399
Phone: 801/255-5000, 800/451-5151
Fax: 801/222-5077
WordPerfect for Windows

WordStar International, Inc.
201 Alameda del Prado
Novato, California 94949
Phone: 415/382-8000, 800/523-3520
Fax: 415/382-4952
Wordstar, Correct Grammar, Correct Letters, Cor-
rect Quotes, Correct Writing, American Heritage
Dictionary

Wyse Technology
3471 North First Street
San Jose, California 95134-1803
Phone: 408/433-1000, 800/GET-WYSE
Video monitors

Xerox Corporation/XSoft
3400 Hillview Avenue
Palo Alto, California 94303
Phone: 415/424-0111
Fax: 800/HAVEFAX
PaperWorks, Rooms for Windows

Xerox Imaging Systems, Inc.
535 Oakmead Parkway
Sunnyvale, California 94086
Phone: 800/821-2898
DISCOVER Freedom

Xing Technology Corporation
P.O. Box 950
Arroyo Grande, California 93420
Phone: 805/473-0145
Fax: 805/473-0147
Graphics software: VT-Express JPEG Accelerator,
VT-Compress JPEG Compression, VT-Motion
MPEG Software

Zenith
1501 Feehanville Drive
Mount Prospect, Illinois 60056
Phone: 800/553-0331, 800/842-9000
Fax: 708/699-3989
Video monitors

Zenith Data Systems/Groupe Bull
Phone: 800/472-9234
Fax: 800/472-7211
Computer systems: Z-Note, Z-Station

Zenographics Inc.
4 Executive Circle
Irvine, California 92714
Phone: 714/851-6352, 800/366-7494
Fax: 714/851-1314
Graphics software and utilities: ImPort for Win-
dows, Pixie, SuperPrint

Zeos International Inc.
530-5th Avenue NW
St. Paul, Minnesota 55112
Phone: 612/633-6131, 800/423-5891
Fax: 612/633-1325
Computer systems

Z-Nix Company, Inc.
211 Erie Street
Pomona, California 91768
Phone: 714/629-8050
Mice

ZSoft Corporation
450 Franklin Road, Suite 100
Marietta, Georgia 30067
Phone: 404/428-0008, 800/444-4780
Fax: 404/427-1150
Graphics software: Publishers Paintbrush, Pub-
lishers Type Foundry, SoftType, PhotoFinish,
UltraFAX

3-D Visions
2780 Skypark Drive
Torrance, California 90505
Phone: 310/325-1339, 800/729-4723
Fax: 310/325-1505
Stanford Graphics

Index

Bold numbers indicate where key terms are defined.

More from Peachpit Press. . .

101 Windows Tips and Tricks
Jesse Berst and Scott Dunn
Compiled by the editors of *Windows Watcher* newsletter, this power-packed, user-friendly survival guide gives you tips and tricks to make Windows faster, easier, and more fun. *(216 pages)*

Desktop Publishing Secrets
Robert Eckhardt, Bob Weibel, Ted Nace
This is a compilation of hundreds of the best desktop publishing tips from five years of *Publish* magazine. It covers all the major graphics and layout programs on the PC and Macintosh platforms, and valuable tips on publishing as a business. *(550 pages)*

Dr. Daniel's Windows Diet
Daniel Will-Harris
Put Windows on a high-performance diet! This little book offers simple solutions to a universal problem—Windows can be slow. This set of easy-to-follow prescriptions, each boiled down to five steps or less, covers the essentials of making Windows work faster— from autoexec.bat to virtual memory. It helps you work faster, too, with keyboard short-cuts, file tips and more. *(96 pages)*

Jargon
Robin Williams
Finally! A book that explains over 1200 of the most useful computer terms in a way that readers can understand. This straight-forward guide not only defines computer-related terms but also explains how and why they are used. Covers both the Macintosh and PC worlds. *(688 pages)*

The Little OS/2 Book, 2.1 Edition
Kay Yarborough Nelson
This book provides a simple introduction to the basics of IBM's OS/2 operating system. It discusses pop-up menus, objects and folders, drag and drop features, using dialog windows and switching between Windows and DOS. *(160 pages)*

The Little PC Book
Larry Magid
Friendly advice on the basic concepts of operating a computer in non-technical, bite-size pieces. *The Little PC Book* is a painless way to become PC literate, without being buried in details. Rather than covering a wide range of non-essential information, this book helps make a novice more comfortable with his or her computer. *(376 pages)*

The Little Windows Book, 3.1 Edition
Kay Yarborough Nelson
This second edition of Peachpit's popular book explains the subtle and not-so-subtle changes in version 3.1 as it gives the essentials of getting started with Windows. Additionally, each chapter includes a handy summary chart of keyboard shortcuts and quick tips. *(144 pages)*

The Little WordPerfect for Windows Book
Kay Yarborough Nelson
This book gives you the basic skills you need in order to create simple documents and helps you become familiar with Word-Perfect's new Windows interface. *(200 pages)*

Mastering Corel Draw 3
Chris Dickman

Like its earlier versions, this terrific tutorial book is studded with tips and undocumented features, and covers topics such as service bureau output and default customizing. Includes two disks that contain utilities and 26 commercial-grade TrueType fonts. *(600 pages)*

The PC is not a typewriter
Robin Williams

PC users can now learn trade secrets from author Robin Williams, whose best-selling *The Mac is not a typewriter* introduced tens of thousands of Mac users to the secrets of creating beautiful type. In less than 100 pages, the book explains why Typing 101 rules such as "two spaces between sentences" don't apply when using a keyboard. Covers punctuation, leading, special characters, kerning, fonts, justification, and more. *(96 pages)*

The QuarkXPress Book, Windows Edition
David Blatner and Bob Weibel

The Mac version of this book has been a bestseller for two years—so useful that Quark's own support staff uses it. It tells you everything you need to know about QuarkXPress—importing and modifying graphics, creating large documents, printing, and much more. *(542 pages)*

Windows 3.1 Font Book
David Angell and Brent Heslop

This book is the first hands-on font guide for Windows users. It explains managing, choosing, and using fonts to enhance all kinds of documents, with instructions for working with TrueType and PostScript fonts. It also contains suggestions for building a font library, with a list of font vendors and over 100 font samples. *(216 pages)*

Word for Windows Essentials
Geoffrey Mandel

This book is a handy reference to Word for Windows 2.0, loaded with useful tips and tricks. It explains both basic and advanced features, and you'll learn how to customize your program and use the math and graphics features. Now you can master this popular and sophisticated program! *(232 pages)*

WordPerfect: Desktop Publishing in Style, 2nd Edition
Daniel Will-Harris

This popular guide (over 90,000 in print) to producing documents with WordPerfect 5.0 or 5.1 opens with a simple tutorial and proceeds through 20 sample documents, each complete with keystroke instructions. Humorous, informative, and fun to read, this book is invaluable to people who desktop publish using WordPerfect. *(672 pages)*

WordPerfect for Windows with Style
Daniel Will-Harris

This generously illustrated handbook gives step-by-step instructions for creating good-looking business documents using WordPerfect for Windows. The book shows a variety of documents and provides the exact commands, codes, and keystrokes used to create each one. Includes valuable insights into styles, graphics, fonts, tables, macros, clip art, printers, and utilities. Daniel Will-Harris combines technical accuracy, detailed and easy-to-understand explanations, and a sense of just plain fun. *(528 pages)*

Order Form

to order, call:
(800) 283-9444 or (510) 548-4393 or (510) 548-5991 (fax)

#	Title	Price	Total
	101 Windows Tips & Tricks	12.95	
	Desktop Publishing Secrets	27.95	
	Dr. Daniel's Windows Diet	8.95	
	Jargon	22.00	
	The Little OS/2 Book, 2.1 Edition	13.00	
	The Little PC Book	17.95	
	The Little Windows Book, 3.1 Edition	12.95	
	The Little WordPerfect for Windows Book	12.95	
	Mastering Corel Draw 3 (with 2 disks)	38.00	
	The PC is not a typewriter	9.95	
	The QuarkXPress Book, Windows Edition	28.00	
	Windows 3.1 Bible	28.00	
	Windows 3.1 Font Book	12.95	
	Word for Windows Essentials	14.00	
	WordPerfect: Desktop Publishing in Style, 2nd Edition	23.95	
	WordPerfect for Windows with Style	24.95	
	Other:		

SHIPPING:	First Item	Each Additional	Subtotal	
UPS Ground	$ 4	$ 1	8.25% Tax (CA only)	
UPS Blue	$ 8	$ 2	Shipping	
Canada	$ 6	$ 4	**TOTAL**	
Overseas	$14	$14		

Name	
Company	
Address	
City	State Zip
Phone	Fax
❑ Check enclosed ❑ Visa ❑ MasterCard	
Company purchase order #	
Credit card # Expiration Date	

Peachpit Press, Inc. • 2414 Sixth Street • Berkeley, CA • 94710
Your satisfaction is guaranteed or your money will be cheerfully refunded!